W9-CTW-391

DRAMA

CRITICISM

Guide to Gale Literary Criticism Series

When you need to review criticism of literary works, these are the Gale series to use:

If the author's death date is:	You should turn to:
After Dec. 31, 1959 (or author is still living)	*CONTEMPORARY LITERARY CRITICISM* for example: Jorge Luis Borges, Anthony Burgess, William Faulkner, Mary Gordon, Ernest Hemingway, Iris Murdoch
1900 through 1959	*TWENTIETH-CENTURY LITERARY CRITICISM* for example: Willa Cather, F. Scott Fitzgerald, Henry James, Mark Twain, Virginia Woolf
1800 through 1899	*NINETEENTH-CENTURY LITERATURE CRITICISM* for example: Fyodor Dostoevsky, Nathaniel Hawthorne, George Sand, William Wordsworth
1400 through 1799	*LITERATURE CRITICISM FROM 1400 TO 1800 (excluding Shakespeare)* for example: Anne Bradstreet, Daniel Defoe, Alexander Pope, François Rabelais, Jonathan Swift, Phillis Wheatley
	SHAKESPEAREAN CRITICISM Shakespeare's plays and poetry
Antiquity through 1399	*CLASSICAL AND MEDIEVAL LITERATURE CRITICISM* for example: Dante, Homer, Plato, Sophocles, Vergil, the Beowulf Poet

---

Gale also publishes related criticism series:

CHILDREN'S LITERATURE REVIEW

This series covers authors of all eras who have written for the preschool through high school audience.

SHORT STORY CRITICISM

This series covers the major short fiction writers of all nationalities and periods of literary history.

POETRY CRITICISM

This series covers poets of all nationalities and periods of literary history.

DRAMA CRITICISM

This series covers dramatists of all nationalities and periods of literary history.

ISSN 1056-4349

Criticism of the Most Significant and Widely Studied Dramatic Works from All the World's Literatures

VOLUME 3

Lawrence J. Trudeau, Editor

Judith Galens, Michael W. Jones, Zoran Minderović
Associate Editors

The paper used in this publication meets the minimum requirements of American National Standard for Information Sciences—Permanence Paper for Printed Library Materials, ANSI Z39.48-1984. ™

835 Penobscot Building
Detroit, MI 48226-4094

ISBN 0-8103-7959-7
ISSN 1056-4349

Printed in the United States of America

Published simultaneously in the United Kingdom
by Gale Research International Limited
(An affiliated company of Gale Research Inc.)

10 9 8 7 6 5 4 3 2 1

Contents

Preface vii
Acknowledgments ix

Bertolt Brecht 1
Author Commentary 3
Overviews and General Studies 9
Galileo 38
Mother Courage 60
The Caucasian Chalk Circle 75

Pedro Calderón de la Barca 87
Overviews and General Studies 89
The Constant Prince 110
Life Is A Dream 117
The Devotion of the Cross 127
The Doctor of His Honor 136

John Dryden 144
Author Commentary 146
Overviews and General Studies 151
All for Love 193

Athol Fugard 220
Author Commentary 222
Overviews and General Studies 227
The Blood Knot 239
The Island and *Sizwe Bansi Is Dead* 246
"Master Harold" . . . and the boys 256

Langston Hughes 265
Overviews and General Studies 268
Mule Bone 278
Mulatto 280
Soul Gone Home 285
Black Nativity 287
Tambourines to Glory 290

Thomas Kyd 293

The Spanish Tragedy 296

Menander 339

Overviews and General Studies 341

The Girl from Samos 368

The Dour Man 380

Joe Orton 389

Author Commentary 390

Overviews and General Studies 392

Entertaining Mr. Sloan 403

Loot 410

What the Butler Saw 419

Jean-Paul Sartre 429

Author Commentary 431

Overviews and General Studies 435

No Exit 456

Ntozake Shange 467

Author Commentary 469

Overviews and General Studies 473

For Colored Girls . . . 479

Spell #7 490

Literary Criticism Series Cumulative Author Index 497

Drama Criticism Cumulative Nationality Index 565

Drama Criticism Cumulative Title Index 567

Preface

Drama Criticism (*DC*) is principally intended for beginning students of literature and theater as well as the average playgoer. The series is therefore designed to introduce readers to the most frequently studied playwrights of all time periods and nationalities and to present discerning commentary on dramatic works of enduring popular appeal. Furthermore, *DC* seeks to acquaint students with the uses and functions of criticism itself. Selected from a diverse body of commentary, the essays in *DC* offer insights into the authors and their works but do not require that the reader possess a wide background in literary studies. Where appropriate, reviews of important productions of the plays discussed are also included to give students a heightened awareness of drama as a dynamic art form, one that many claim is fully realized only in performance.

DC was created in response to suggestions by the staffs of high school, college, and public libraries. These librarians observed a need for a series that assembles critical commentary on the world's most renowned dramatists in the same manner as Gale's *Short Story Criticism* (*SSC*) and *Poetry Criticism* (*PC*), which present material on writers of short fiction and poetry. Although playwrights are covered in such Gale literary criticism series as *Contemporary Literary Criticism* (*CLC*), *Twentieth-Century Literary Criticism* (*TCLC*), *Nineteenth-Century Literature Criticism* (*NCLC*), *Literature Criticism from 1400 to 1800* (*LC*), and *Classical and Medieval Literature Criticism* (*CMLC*), *Drama Criticism* directs more concentrated attention on individual dramatists than is possible in the broader, survey-oriented entries in these Gale series. Commentary on the works of William Shakespeare may be found in *Shakespearean Criticism* (*SC*).

Scope of the Series

By collecting and organizing commentary on dramatists, *DC* assists students in their efforts to gain insight into literature, achieve better understanding of the texts, and formulate ideas for papers and assignments. A variety of interpretations and assessments is offered, allowing students to pursue their own interests and promoting awareness that literature is dynamic and responsive to many different opinions.

Each volume of *DC* presents:

- 10-12 author entries
- authors and works representing a wide range of nationalities and time periods
- a diversity of viewpoints and critical opinions.

Organization of an Author Entry

Each author entry consists of some or all of the following elements, depending on the scope and complexity of the criticism:

- The **author heading** consists of the playwright's most commonly used name, followed by birth and death dates. If an author consistently wrote under a pseudonym, the pseudonym is listed in the author heading and the real name given on the first line of the introduction. Also located at the beginning of the introduction are any name variations under which the dramatist wrote, including transliterated forms of the names of authors whose languages use nonroman alphabets.

- A **portrait** of the author is included when available. Most entries also feature illustrations of people, places, and events pertinent to a study of the playwright and his or her works. When appropriate, photographs of the plays in performance are also presented.

- The **biographical and critical introduction** contains background information that familiarizes the reader with the author and the critical debates surrounding his or her works.

- The list of **principal works** is divided into two sections, each of which is organized chronologically by date of first performance. If this has not been conclusively determined, the composition or publication date is used. The first section of the principal works list contains the author's dramatic pieces. The second section provides information on the author's major works in other genres.

- Whenever available, **author commentary** is provided. This section consists of essays or interviews in which the dramatist discusses his or her own work or the art of playwriting in general.
- Essays offering **overviews and general studies of the dramatist's entire literary career** give the student broad perspectives on the writer's artistic development, themes and concerns that recur in several of his or her works, the author's place in literary history, and other wide-ranging topics.
- **Criticism of individual plays** offers the reader in-depth discussions of a select number of the author's most important works. In some cases, the criticism is divided into two sections, each arranged chronologically. When a significant performance of a play can be identified (typically, the premiere of a twentieth-century work), the first section of criticism will feature **production reviews** of this staging. Most entries include sections devoted to **critical commentary** that assesses the literary merit of the selected plays. When necessary, essays are carefully excerpted to focus on the work under consideration; often, however, essays and reviews are reprinted in their entirety.
- As an additional aid to students, the critical essays and excerpts are prefaced by **explanatory annotations.** These notes provide several types of useful information, including the critic's reputation and approach to literary studies as well as the scope and significance of the criticism that follows.
- A complete **bibliographic citation,** designed to help the interested reader locate the original essay or book, follows each piece of criticism.
- The **further reading** list at the end of each entry comprises additional studies of the dramatist. It is divided into sections that will help students quickly locate the specific information they need.

Other Features

- A **cumulative author index** lists all the authors who have appeared in *DC,* and Gale's other Literature Criticism Series, as well as cross-references to related titles published by Gale, including *Contemporary Authors* and *Dictionary of Literary Biography.* A complete listing of the series included appears at the beginning of the index.
- A **cumulative nationality index** includes each author featured in *DC* by nationality, followed by the number of the *DC* volume in which the author appears.
- A **cumulative title index** lists in alphabetical order the individual plays discussed in the criticism contained in *DC.* Each title is followed by the author's name and the corresponding volume and page number(s) where commentary on the work may be located. Translations and variant titles are cross-referenced to the title of the play in its original language so that all references to the work are combined in one listing.

A Note to the Reader

When writing papers, students who quote directly from any volume in the Literary Criticism Series may use the following general formats to footnote reprinted criticism. The first example pertains to material drawn from periodicals, the second to materials reprinted from books.

[1]Susan Sontag, "Going to the Theater, Etc.," *Partisan Review* XXXI, No. 3 (Summer 1964), 389-94; excerpted and reprinted in *Drama Criticism,* Vol. 1, ed. Lawrence J. Trudeau (Detroit: Gale Research, 1991), pp. 17-20.

[2]Eugene M. Waith, *The Herculean Hero in Marlowe, Chapman, Shakespeare and Dryden* (Chatto & Windus, 1962); excerpted and reprinted in *Drama Criticism,* Vol. 1, ed. Lawrence J. Trudeau (Detroit: Gale Research, 1991), pp. 237-247.

Suggestions are Welcome

Readers who wish to suggest authors to appear in future volumes of *DC,* or who have other suggestions, are cordially invited to contact the editor.

Acknowledgments

The editors wish to thank the copyright holders of the excerpted criticism included in this volume, the permissions managers of many book and magazine publishing companies for assisting us in securing reprint rights, and Anthony Bogucki for assistance with copyright research. We are also grateful to the staffs of the Detroit Public Library, the University of Detroit Library, Wayne State University Purdy/Kresge Library Complex, and the University of Michigan Libraries for making their resources available to us. Following is a list of the copyright holders who have granted us permission to reprint material in this volume of *DC*. Every effort has been made to trace copyright, but if omissions have been made, please let us know.

COPYRIGHTED EXCERPTS IN *DC*, VOLUME 3, WERE REPRINTED FROM THE FOLLOWING PERIODICALS:

Black American Literature Forum, v. 13, Winter, 1979 for an interview with Ntozake Shange by Henry Blackwell; v. 15, Summer, 1981 for "Colored Girls: Textbook for the Eighties" by Sandra Hollin Flowers. Copyright © 1979, 1981 Indiana State University. Both reprinted by permission of Indiana State University and the respective authors.—***CLA Journal,*** v. XI, June, 1968. Copyright, 1968 by The College Language Association. Used by permission of The College Language Association.—***Commonweal,*** v. LXXXVIII, April 19, 1968. Copyright © 1968 Commonweal Publishing Co., Inc. Reprinted by permission of Commonweal Foundation.—***Comparative Drama,*** v. 17, Summer, 1983. Copyright © 1983, by the Editors of Comparative Drama. Reprinted by permission of the publisher.—***Daily News,*** New York, March 25, 1966; April 7, 1978. © 1966, 1978 New York News Inc. Both used with permission.—***Drama,*** London, n. 151, Spring, 1984.—***The Drama Review,*** v. 15, Fall, 1970 for "The Theatre of Sartre" by Lucien Goldmann, translated by Sandy MacDonald. Copyright © 1970, *The Drama Review.* Translation copyright © 1970, Sandy MacDonald. Reprinted by permission of The MIT Press, Cambridge, MA and the translator./ v. 26, Winter, 1982. Copyright © New York University and the Massachusetts Institute of Technology. Reprinted by permission of The MIT Press, Cambridge, MA.—***Educational Theatre Journal,*** v. 29, May, 1977. © 1977 University College Theatre Association of the American Theatre Association. Reprinted by permission of the publisher.—***The Germanic Review,*** v. XLI, January, 1966 for " 'The Life of Galileo': The Focus of Ambiguity in the Villain Hero" by Charles R. Lyons. Copyright 1966 by Helen Dwight Reid Educational Foundation. Reprinted by permission of the author.—***Greece & Rome,*** v. XXII, October, 1975. © Oxford University Press 1975. Reprinted by permission of the publisher.—***The Hudson Review,*** v. XXXIV, Winter, 1981-82. Copyright © 1981 by The Hudson Review, Inc. Reprinted by permission of the publisher.—***Journal of Commonwealth Literature,*** v. XII, April, 1978 for "Athol Fugard's 'Poor Theatre' " by Patrick O'Sheel. Copyright by the author. Reprinted by permission of Hans Zell Publishers, an imprint of Bowker-Saur Ltd.—***The Journal of English and Germanic Philology,*** v. LXIV, January, 1965, for "Kyd's 'Spanish Tragedy': The Play Explains Itself" by Ejner J. Jensen. © 1965 by the Board of Trustees of the University of Illinois. Reprinted by permission of the publisher and the author.—***The Journal of Ethnic Studies,*** v. 6, Spring, 1978. Copyright © 1978 by *The Journal of Ethnic Studies.* Reprinted by permission of the publisher.—***Mirabella,*** March, 1991 for "Just Folks" by Randall Short. Reprinted by permission of the author.—***Modern Drama,*** v. XIV, September, 1971; v. XXIV, December, 1981; v. XXX, December, 1987. Copyright 1971, 1981, 1987 *Modern Drama,* University of Toronto. All reprinted by permission of the publisher.—***The Nation,*** New York, v. 198, March 30, 1964; v. 206, April 8, 1968. Copyright 1964, 1968 *The Nation* magazine/The Nation Company, Inc. Both reprinted by permission of the publisher./ v. 196, January 5, 1963. Copyright 1963, renewed 1991 *The Nation* magazine/The Nation Company, Inc. Reprinted by permission of the publisher.—***The New Republic,*** v. 186, June 23, 1982. © 1982 The New Republic, Inc. Reprinted by permission of *The New Republic.*—***New York*** Magazine, v. 14, September 7, 1981; v. 15, May 17, 1982. Copyright © 1993 K-III Magazine Corporation. All rights reserved. Both reprinted by the permission of *New York* Magazine.—***New York Herald Tribune,*** March 25, 1966. © 1966, *The Washington Post.* Reprinted with permission of the publisher.—***New York Post,*** April 14, 1967; April 6, 1978; June 5, 1979. © 1967, 1978, 1979, *New York Post.* All reprinted by permission of the publisher.—***The New York Times,*** March 25, 1966; April 14, 1967; March 19, 1968; March 31, 1968; March 7, 1969; May 5, 1970; November 14, 1974; November 25, 1974; April 6, 1978; June 4, 1979; December 30, 1980; May 21, 1981; May 5, 1982; February 10, 1991. Copyright © 1966, 1967, 1968, 1969, 1970, 1974, 1978, 1979, 1980, 1981, 1982, 1991 by The New York Times Company. All reprinted by permission of the publisher./ October 25, 1935. Copyright 1935, renewed 1963 by The New York Times Company. Reprinted by permission of the publisher./ December 12, 1961; October 27, 1963; November 4, 1963. Copyright © 1961, renewed 1989; © 1963, renewed 1991 by The New York Times Company. All reprinted by permission of the publisher.—***New York World-Telegram & The Sun,*** October 13, 1965 for " 'Entertaining Mr. Sloane' Opens" by Norman Nadel. Copyright 1965, New

York World-Telegram Corporation. Reprinted by permission of the author.—***The New Yorker,*** v. LVII, July 6, 1981 for "Reënter Mr. Sloane" by Edith Oliver. © 1981 by the author. Reprinted by permission of the publisher./ v. XL, March 14, 1964. © 1964, renewed 1992 by The New Yorker Magazine, Inc. Reprinted by permission of the publisher.—***Newsweek,*** v. LXXV, May 18, 1970; v. LXXXVII, June 14, 1976. Copyright 1970, 1976, by Newsweek, Inc. All rights reserved. Both reprinted by permission of the publisher.—***The Paris Review,*** v. 31, Summer, 1989. © 1989 The Paris Review, Inc. Reprinted by permission of the publisher.—***Philosophy and Literature,*** v. 8, October, 1984. Copyright © 1984 by the University of Michigan—Dearborn. Reprinted by permission of the publisher.—***Plays and Players,*** v. 11, August, 1964. © 1964 Plusloop. Reprinted with permission of the publisher.—***Renaissance Drama,*** v. VIII, 1965. Copyright © 1965 by Northwestern University Press. All rights reserved. Reprinted by permission of the publisher.—***Studies in American Drama, 1945-Present,*** v. 4, 1989. Copyright 1989 by Philip C. Kolin and Colby H. Kullman. All rights reserved. Reprinted by permission of the publisher.—***Studies in Philology,*** v. LXV, October, 1968; v. LXVII, April, 1970. © 1968, 1970 by The University of North Carolina Press. Both reprinted by permission of the publisher.—***The Sunday Times,*** May 17, 1970. Copyright © 1970 by The New York Times Company. Reprinted by permission of the publisher.—***The Theatre Annual,*** v. XX, 1963. © Western Reserve University Press, 1963. Renewed 1992 by The University of Akron. Reprinted by permission of the publisher, John Falconieri, Owner and Editor, Wallace Sterling, Executive Editor.—***Theatre Journal,*** v. 34, December, 1982. © 1982, University and College Theatre Association of the American Theatre Association. Reprinted by permission of the publisher.—***Themes in Drama,*** v. 10, 1988 for "Joe Orton's Jacobean Assimilations in 'What the Butler Saw' " by William Hutchings. © Cambridge University Press 1988. Reprinted with the permission of Cambridge University Press and the author./ v. 9, 1987. © Cambridge University Press 1987. Reprinted with the permission of Cambridge University Press.—***Thoth,*** v. 16, Spring, 1976.—***Time,*** New York, v. 83, March 13, 1964. Copyright 1964 Time Warner Inc. All rights reserved. Reprinted by permission from *Time.*—***The Times,*** London, May 7, 1964; June 8, 1992. © Times Newspaper Limited 1964, 1992. Both reproduced from *The Times,* London by permission.—***The USF Language Quarterly,*** v. XV, Winter, 1976. Reprinted by permission of the publisher.—***The Wall Street Journal,*** September 21, 1976 for a review of "For Colored Girls Who Have Considered Suicide/When the Rainbow is Enuf" by Edwin Wilson. © Dow Jones & Company, Inc. 1976. All rights reserved. Reprinted by permission of the author.—***World Journal Tribune,*** April 14, 1967. © 1967, *The Washington Post.* Reprinted by permission of the publisher.

COPYRIGHTED EXCERPTS IN *DC,* VOLUME 3, WERE REPRINTED FROM THE FOLLOWING BOOKS:

Abbott, Anthony S. From ***The Vital Lie: Reality and Illusion in Modern Drama.*** The University of Alabama Press, 1989. Copyright © 1989 by The University of Alabama Press. All rights reserved. Reprinted by permission of the publisher.—Abramson, Doris E. From ***Negro Playwrights in the American Theatre: 1925-1959.*** Columbia, 1969. Copyright © 1967, 1969 Columbia University Press. Used by permission of the publisher, Columbia University Press.—Barthes, Roland. From ***Critical Essays.*** Translated by Richard Howard. Northwestern University Press, 1972. Copyright © 1972 Northwestern University Press. All rights reserved. Reprinted by permission of the publisher.—Bentley, Eric. From ***Theatre of War: Comments on 32 Occasions.*** The Viking Press, 1962. Copyright © 1960, 1965, 1966, 1968, 1969, 1970, 1972 by Eric Bentley. All rights reserved. Used by permission of Grove Press, Inc.—Bowers, Fredson. From ***Elizabethan Revenge Tragedy, 1587-1642.*** Princeton University Press, 1940. Copyright 1940, renewed 1968, Princeton University Press. Reprinted by permission of the publisher.—Brecht, Bertolt. From ***Brecht on Theatre: The Development of an Aesthetic.*** Edited and translated by John Willett. Hill and Wang, 1964. Translation and notes © 1964 by John Willett. Reprinted by permission of Hill and Wang, a division of Farrar, Straus and Giroux, Inc.—Brecht, Bertolt. From "Observations on 'Mother Courage'," translated by Herman Salinger, in ***The Creative Vision: Modern European Writers on Their Art.*** Edited by Haskell M. Block and Herman Salinger. Grove Press, 1960. Copyright © 1960 by Grove Press, Inc. From *Gesammelte Werke.* © Suhrkamp Verlag Frankfurt am Main 1967. Reprinted by permission of Suhrkamp Verlag and the Literary Estate of Herman Salinger.—Brecht, Bertolt. From ***Seven Plays.*** By Bertolt Brecht, edited by Eric Bentley. Grove Press, 1961. Copyright © 1961 by Eric Bentley. All rights reserved.—Bull, John, and Frances Gray. From "Joe Orton," in ***Essays on Contemporary British Drama.*** Edited by Hedwig Bock and Albert Wertheim. Max Huebner, 1981. © Max Huebner Verlag München. Reprinted by permission of the publisher.—Champigny, Robert. From ***Sartre and Drama.*** French Literature Publications, 1982. Copyright 1982 French Literature Publications Company. Reprinted by permission of Summa Publications, P. O. Box 20725, Birmingham, AL 35216.—Charney, Maurice. From ***Joe Orton.*** Macmillan, 1984. Copyright © 1984 Maurice Charney. All rights reserved. Reprinted by permission of Macmillan Ltd.—Curtius, E. R. From ***Essays on European Literature.*** Translated by Michael Kowal. Princeton University Press, 1973. Copyright © 1973 by Princeton University Press. Reprinted by permission of the publisher.—Gaskell, Ronald. From ***Drama and Reality: The European Theatre Since Isben.*** Routledge & Kegan Paul, 1972. © Ronald Gaskell 1972. Reprinted by permission of the publisher.—Geis, Deborah R. From "Distraught Laughter: Monologue in Ntozake Shange's Theatre Pieces," in ***Feminine Focus: The New Women Playwrights.*** Edited by Enoch Brater. Oxford University Press, 1989. Copyright © 1989 by Oxford University Press, Inc. All rights reserved. Reprinted by permission of the publisher.—Goldberg, Sander M. From ***The Making of Menander's Comedy.*** University of California Press, 1980. © Sander M. Goldberg 1980. Reprinted by permission of the publisher.—Hagstrum, Jean

PHOTOGRAPHS AND ILLUSTRATIONS APPEARING IN *DC*, VOLUME 3, WERE RECEIVED FROM THE FOLLOWING SOURCES:

Ullstein Bilderdienst: **pp. 1, 19, 35;** Lilly Library, Indiana University: **p. 11;** © Martha Swope: **p. 44;** Courtesy of the Spanish Embassy: **p. 95;** Goethe House: **pp. 102, 109, 121;** French Cultural Services: **pp. 131, 451;** Photograph by Gerry Goodstein: **p. 228;** © David Sim/Observer: **p. 240;** © Brain Astbury: **p. 247;** Photograph by William L. Smith: **p. 253;** © 1982 Martha Swope: **p. 258;** Courtesy of the Yale Collection of American Literature, Beinecke Rare Book and Manuscript Library, Yale University: **p. 265;** The Bettmann Archive: **p. 288;** Photograph by Alix Jeffry: **p. 371;** Associated Newspaper Group Ltd.: **p. 389;** Photograph by John Haynes: **p. 407;** Romano Cagnoni-Report London: **p. 414;** Photograph by William Leftwich: **p. 429;** Lipnitski-Viollet: **p. 436;** Photograph by Harcourt: **pp. 442, 458;** Agence de Presse Bernand/Archives Photob.: **p. 464;** Photograph by Val Wilmer: **p. 467;** Photograph by Sy Friedman: **p. 472;** © 1993 Martha Swope: **p. 492.**

Bertolt Brecht

1898-1956

INTRODUCTION

Full name Eugen Bertolt Friedrich Brecht; also wrote under the pseudonym Bertold Eugen.

A controversial innovator of modern theatrical techniques, Brecht is regarded as one of the most important writers of the twentieth century. Brecht was an advocate of Marxism and sought to arouse the social conscience of his audience by addressing political and humanistic concerns in his plays. Intending to motivate spectators to action by disturbing them intellectually, Brecht introduced his concepts of "epic theater" and "alienation effects"—the best known features of his dramatic theory—in stagings of his plays. Epic drama, which Brecht also designated "Theater for Learning," interrupts the narrative with dance, soliloquies, songs, subtitles, and choral readings, among other conventions, to reduce tension in the play and undermine its sense of reality; alienation effects—for example, an actor commenting on the play itself during performance—seek to create viewer detachment and promote objective questioning of the subject matter. The resulting estrangement, according to Brecht's theory, will make the drama appeal "less to the feeling than to the spectator's reason," causing a theatergoer to view critically the ideas and situations presented in the play.

Brecht was born in the Bavarian town of Augsburg, where his family lived the middle-class existence he would later reject in favor of the Marxist ideal of a proletarian society. He began studying medicine at Ludwig Maximilian University in Munich, and when World War I broke out he served in a military hospital; his exposure to human suffering there solidified his lifelong commitment to pacifism. Brecht joined Germany's Independent Social Democratic party in 1919 and completely abandoned his studies at the University in 1921, when he began writing drama criticism for a Socialist periodical. *Baal,* the earliest written of Brecht's plays, was published the following year, and shortly thereafter his *Trommeln in der Nacht* (*Drums in the Night*) became the first of his works to be staged. In 1924 the dramatist moved to Berlin, where he became acquainted with such noted producer/directors as Max Reinhardt, Leopold Jessner, and Erwin Piscator. Brecht became *Dramaturg* (playreader and adapter) at the Deutsches Theater and for the next several years staged productions of his own works—including his *Im Dickicht der Städte*: *Der Kampf zweier Manner in der Reisenstadt Chicago* (*In the Jungle of Cities*) and *Mann ist Mann* (*A Man's a Man*)—while also studying Karl Marx's *Das Kapital.* Brecht began collaborating with composer Kurt Weill, and by the end of the decade, *Die Dreigroschenoper* (*The Threepenny Opera*)—Brecht's Marxist adaptation of John Gay's *Beggar's Opera* featuring an acclaimed score by Weill—had earned both men widespread popular recognition.

In the early 1930s Brecht completed a series of *Lehrstücke,* or didactic plays; largely vehicles for his Marxist views, these writings prompted his self-imposed exile from fascist Germany in 1933. The dramatist resided temporarily in Denmark, Sweden, and Finland before settling in the United States in 1941, where he lived for the remainder of the Second World War. While in exile Brecht completed what are considered his finest plays: *Mutter Courage und ihre Kinder* (*Mother Courage and Her Children*), *Leben des Galileo* (*Galileo*), and *Der kaukasische Kreidekreis* (*The Caucasian Chalk Circle*). He returned to Europe in 1947, settling in Zurich, Switzerland, before accepting a Communist Party offer of a theater and acting company of his own in East Berlin. He spent the last years of his life working with this company, known as the Berliner Ensemble, implementing the production theories that he elucidated in essays and treatises composed during this time—most notably his *Kleines Organon für das Theatre* (*Little Organum for the Theatre*). Brecht died in 1956.

Critics suggest that the innovative production techniques for which Brecht is so well known were most effectively employed in his later works. Although a strong proponent of didacticism, or instruction, as the primary purpose of drama, Brecht demonstrated in his later plays an increasing awareness of drama's need to entertain in order to convey ideas effectively. Critics note that Brecht's mature works correspondingly stress the human dilemma in social or political conflicts rather than the conflicts themselves, highlighting the dramatist's widening sympathy for the plight of humanity. While Brecht continued to employ alienation effects in the speech and actions of his players, his characterizations became more complex and human. For instance, *Mother Courage,* subtitled "A Chronicle of the Thirty Years' War," does not present the story of major historical figures or battles, but rather the experiences of a poor canteen woman who loses everything in her attempt to exploit the war for profit. Through his depiction of Mother Courage, Brecht condemns commerce, especially capitalism, as the root of war. However, his multifaceted portrayal of his heroine, with whom many have sympathized, has resulted in interpretations of the play as a tragedy depicting the destruction of virtue in a corrupt world, and not a political statement, as Brecht had intended, warning that "if you sup with the devil, you need a long spoon."

Galileo, another chronicle play, recounts the life of the seventeenth-century scientist who, under threat of physical torture by Catholic church authorities, recanted his confirmation of Copernicus's findings regarding the earth's orbit around the sun. In the first version of the play, written in 1938, Galileo's retraction is presented as a heroic ploy to avoid persecution and thus surreptitiously complete the writing of his *Discorsi,* a work which featured the results of his experiments and meditations on physics. A later version of Brecht's play, written in English with the actor Charles Laughton around the time of the bombing of Hiroshima, explicitly portrays the scientist as a sensuous individual with a voracious appetite for intellectual and physical gratification. When Galileo disavows his scientific discoveries in this rendition, the act is presented as one of cowardice; he furtively completes the manuscript of his *Discorsi,* not to serve humankind, but to indulge an insatiable intellectual need. Most critics agree that this later version of *Galileo* was intended to caution scientists against alienating themselves from society, and to remind them of their responsibility for the future of humanity. However, Brecht's depiction of Galileo, considered one of the most complex characterizations in modern theater, has led many critics to sympathize with the scientist's plight. As Eric Bentley has written: "What makes this Galileo a fascinating figure is that his goodness and badness, strength and weakness, have the same source: a big appetite and a Wildean disposition to give way to it. His appetite for knowledge is of a piece with his appetite for food, and so the same quality can appear, in different circumstances, as magnificent or as mean."

The Caucasian Chalk Circle presents in the figure of Azdak what many commentators consider Brecht's finest character portrayal. A parable play based on the Chinese drama *The Circle of Chalk,* this work relates the story of an infant abandoned by his mother and rescued by a maid, who cares for the child through various wartime ordeals. When the child's mother later returns to claim him, the case is brought before Azdak, who as a judge has accepted bribes and shown little regard for justice. He orders a circle drawn on the floor and places the child in the middle, announcing that he will award the boy to whomever wins the subsequent tug-of-war using the child rather than a rope. The maid, however, demonstrates a genuine fear of harming the child, moving Azdak to rule in her favor. The play, according to its prologue and epilogue, was intended to address a contemporary issue that had arisen between two Soviet communes over the ownership of a tract of land. Critics, however, have focused on Brecht's portrayal of Azdak. Ronald Gray has described Azdak as "the most fascinating character in the play, insulting and generous, preposterous and humble, ignorant and wise, blasphemous and pious." As such, Azdak embodies dialectical contrasts typical of the dramatist's mature works, which emphasize the problematic relationship of the individual to society. Presenting what critics regard as a characteristic Brechtian struggle between good and evil, *The Caucasian Chalk Circle* demonstrates its author's optimistic Marxist faith in positive change through political action and in the "temptation of goodness" through which human nature transcends a corrupt world.

Robert Brustein has indicated the difficulty of assessing Brecht's achievement, noting that the dramatist was "an extremely divided artist, whose works, for all their ideological intentions, remain peculiarly enticing and elusive." Critics continue to analyze the relationship between Brecht's artistry and his declared didactic aims. Many commentators contend that the vivid characterizations of the later plays detract from the dramatist's innovative efforts to "alienate" the audience; others maintain that Brecht's increasingly complex character portrayals are consistent with his progressive concern for what Bentley has termed "the dialectics of living." Accordingly, if Brecht's early work was designed to shock and instruct, his mature plays offer a rich and varied view of existence wherein, as Bentley suggests, his primary aim was neither to entertain nor to teach but to awaken.

PRINCIPAL WORKS

PLAYS

Baal 1922
[*Baal,* 1964]
Trommeln in der Nacht 1922
[*Drums in the Night,* 1966]
Im Dickicht der Städte: Der Kampf zweier Männer in der Riesenstadt Chicago 1923
[*In the Jungle of Cities,* 1957]
Mann ist Mann: Die Verwandlung des Packers Galy Gay in den Militärbaracken von Kilkoa im Jahre 1925, Lustspiel 1926
[*A Man's a Man,* 1957]

Aufstieg und Fall der Stadt Mahagonny: Oper in drei Akten 1927
[*The Rise and Fall of the City of Mahagonny,* 1959]
Die Dreigroschenoper 1928 [adapter, with Kurt Weill; from the play *The Beggar's Opera* by John Gay]
[*The Threepenny Opera,* 1949]
Die Maßnahme: Lehrstück 1930
[*The Measures Taken,* 1956]
Die Mutter 1931
[*The Mother,* 1956]
Die heilige Johanna der Schlachthöfe 1932
[*St. Joan of the Stockyards,* 1956]
Furcht und Elend des dritten Reiches 1938
[*Fear and Misery in the Third Reich,* 1942]
Leben des Galilei 1938
[*Galileo,* 1947]
Mutter Courage und ihre Kinder: Eine Chronik aus dem Dreißigjährigen Krieg 1941
[*Mother Courage and Her Children,* 1949]
Der gute Mensch von Setzuan 1943
[*The Good Woman of Setzuan,* 1948]
Herr Puntila und sein Knecht Matti: Nach Erzählungen der Hella Wuolijoki 1948
[*Mr. Puntila and his Hired Man Matti,* 1954]
Der kaukasische Kreidekreis 1948
[*The Caucasian Chalk Circle,* 1948]

OTHER MAJOR WORKS

Die Hauspostille (poetry) 1927
[*A Manual of Piety,* 1966]
Dreigroschenroman (novel) 1934
[*A Penny for the Poor,* 1937; also published as *Threepenny Novel,* 1956]
Fünf Schwierigkeiten beim Schreiben der Wahrheit (essays) 1934
[*Writing the Truth: Five Difficulties,* 1948]
Selected Poems (poetry) 1947
Kalendergeschichten (short stories and poetry) 1948
[*Tales from the Calendar,* 1961]
Kleines Organon für das Theatre (treatise) 1949
[*A Little Organum for the Theatre,* 1951]

AUTHOR COMMENTARY

Theatre for Pleasure or Theatre for Learning? (1936)

[*In the following essay, written around 1936, Brecht offers a definition and analysis of epic theatre.*]

When anyone spoke of modern theatre a few years ago, he mentioned the Moscow, the New York, or the Berlin theatre. He may also have spoken of a particular production of Jouvet's in Paris, of Cochran's in London, or the Habima performance of *The Dybbuk,* which, in fact, belonged to Russian theatre, since it was directed by Vakhtangov; but, by and large, there were only three capitals as far as modern theatre was concerned.

The Russian, the American, and the German theatres were very different from one another, but they were alike in being modern, i.e., in introducing technical and artistic innovations. In a certain sense they even developed stylistic similarities, probably because technique is international (not only the technique directly required for the stage, but also that which exerts an influence on it, the film, for example) and because the cities in question were great progressive cities in great industrial countries. Most recently, the Berlin theatre seemed to have taken the lead among the most advanced capitalist countries. For a time, what was common to modern theatre found there its strongest and, for the moment, its most mature expression.

The last phase of the Berlin theatre, which as I said only revealed in its purest form the direction in which modern theatre was developing, was the so-called epic theatre. What was known as the "*Zeitstück*"—the play dealing with current problems—or the Piscator theatre, or the didactic play, all belong to epic theatre.

EPIC THEATRE

The expression "epic theatre" seemed self-contradictory to many people, since according to the teachings of Aristotle the epic and the dramatic forms of presenting a story were considered basically different from one another. The difference between the two forms was by no means merely seen in the fact that one was performed by living people while the other made use of a book—epic works like those of Homer and the Minnesingers of the Middle Ages were likewise theatrical performances, and dramas like Goethe's *Faust* or Byron's *Manfred* admittedly achieved their greatest effect as books. Aristotle's teachings themselves distinguished the dramatic from the epic form as a difference in construction, whose laws were dealt with under two different branches of aesthetics. This construction depended on the different way in which the works were presented to the public, either on the stage or through a book, but nevertheless, apart from that, "the dramatic" could also be found in the epic works and "the epic" in dramatic works. The bourgeois novel in the last century considerably developed "the dramatic," which meant the strong centralization of plot and an organic interdependence of the separate parts. "The dramatic" is characterized by a certain passion in the tone of the exposition and a working out of the collision of forces. The epic writer, Döblin, gave an excellent characterization when he said that the epic, in contrast to the dramatic, could practically be cut up with a scissors into single pieces, each of which could stand alone.

I do not intend to discuss here in what way the contrasts between the epic and the dramatic, long regarded as irreconcilable, lost their rigidity; let it suffice to point out that technical achievements alone enabled the stage to incorporate narrative elements into dramatic presentations. The potentialities of projection, the film, the greater facility in changing sets through machinery, completed the equipment of the stage and did so at a moment when the most important human events could no longer be so simply portrayed as through personification of the moving forces or through subordinating the characters to invisible, metaphysical powers.

To make the events understandable, the environment of human activity had to be given great and "significant" value.

Of course this environment had been shown in plays before, not, however, as an independent element but only from the viewpoint of the main figure of the drama. It rose out of the hero's reaction to it. It was seen as a storm may be "seen" if you observe on the sea a ship spreading its sails and the sails bellying. But in the epic theatre it was now to appear as an independent element.

The stage began to narrate. The narrator no longer vanished with the fourth wall. Not only did the background make its own comment on stage happenings through large screens which evoked other events occurring at the same time in other places, documenting or contradicting statements by characters through phrases projected onto a screen, lending tangible, concrete statistics to abstract discussions, providing facts and figures for happenings which were plastic but unclear in their meaning; the actors no longer threw themselves completely into their roles but maintained a certain distance from the character performed by them, even distinctly inviting criticism.

Nothing permitted the audience any more to lose itself through simple identification, uncritically (and without any practical consequences), in the experiences of the characters on the stage. The presentation exposed the subject matter and the happenings to a process of alienation. Alienation was required to make things understood. When things are "self-evident," understanding is simply dispensed with.

The "natural" had to be given an element of the conspicuous. Only in this way could the laws of cause and effect become plain. Characters had to behave as they did behave, and, at the same time, they had to be capable of behaving otherwise.

These were great changes.

The spectator in the dramatic theatre says: Yes, I have felt that too.—That's how I am.—That is only natural.—That will always be so.—This person's suffering shocks me because he has no way out.—This is great art: everything in it is self-evident.—I weep with the weeping, I laugh with the laughing.

The spectator in the epic theatre says: I wouldn't have thought that.—People shouldn't do things like that.—That's extremely odd, almost unbelievable.—This has to stop.—This person's suffering shocks me, because there might be a way out for him.—This is great art: nothing in it is self-evident.—I laugh over the weeping, I weep over the laughing.

Didactic Theatre

The stage began to instruct.

Oil, inflation, war, social struggles, the family, religion, wheat, the meat-packing industry became subjects for theatrical portrayal. Choruses informed the audience about facts it did not know. Films displayed events from all over the world. Projections provided statistical data. As the "background" came to the fore, the actions of the characters became exposed to criticism. Wrong and right actions were exhibited. People were shown who knew what they were doing, and other people were shown who did not know. The theatre became a matter for philosophers—for that sort of philosopher, to be sure, who wanted not only to explain the world but also to change it. For this reason, the theatre philosophized; for this reason, it instructed. And what became of entertainment? Were the audiences put back in school, treated as illiterates? Were they to pass examinations? Be given marks?

It is the general opinion that a very decided difference exists between learning and being entertained. The former may be useful, but only the latter is pleasant. Thus we have to defend the epic theatre against a suspicion that it must be an extremely unpleasant, a joyless, indeed a wearing business.

Well, we can actually only say that the contrast between learning and being entertained does not necessarily exist by nature, it has not always existed, and it need not always exist.

Undoubtedly, the kind of learning we did in school, in training for a profession or the like, is a laborious business. But consider under what circumstances and for what purpose it is done.

It is, in fact, a purchase. Knowledge is simply a commodity. It is acquired for the purpose of being resold. All those who have grown too old for school have to pursue knowledge secretly, so to speak, because anybody who admits he still has to study depreciates himself as one who knows too little. Apart from that, the utility of learning is very much limited by factors over which the student has no control. There is unemployment, against which no knowledge protects. There is the division of labor, which makes comprehensive knowledge unnecessary and impossible. Often, those who study make the effort only when they see that no other effort offers a possibility of getting ahead. There is not much knowledge that procures power, but there is much knowledge which is only procured through power.

Learning means something very different to different strata of socicty. There are strata of people who cannot conceive of any improvement in conditions; conditions seem good enough to them. Whatever may happen to petroleum, they make a profit out of it. And they feel, after all, that they are getting rather old. They can scarcely expect many more years of life. So why continue to learn? They have already spoken their last word! But there are also strata of people who have not yet "had their turn," who are discontented with the way things are, who have an immense practical interest in learning, who want orientation badly, who know they are lost without learning—these are the best and most ambitious learners. Such differences also exist among nations and peoples. Thus the lust for learning is dependent on various things; in short, there is such a thing as thrilling learning, joyous and militant learning.

If learning could not be delightful, then the theatre, by its very structure, would not be in a position to instruct.

Theatre remains theatre, even when it is didactic theatre, and insofar as it is good theatre, it will entertain.

Theatre and Science

But what has science to do with art? We know very well that science can be diverting, but not everything that diverts belongs to the theatre.

I have often been told when I pointed out the inestimable services that modern science, properly utilized, can render to art, especially to the theatre, that art and science were two valuable but completely different fields of human activity. This is a dreadful platitude, of course, and the best thing to do is admit at once that it is quite right, like most platitudes. Art and science operate in very different ways—agreed. Still, I must admit—bad as this may sound—that I cannot manage as an artist without making use of certain sciences. This may make many people seriously doubt my artistic ability. They are accustomed to regarding poets as unique, almost unnatural beings who, with truly godlike infallibility, perceive things that others can only perceive through the greatest efforts and hard work. Naturally, it is unpleasant to have to admit not being one of those so endowed. But it must be admitted. It must also be denied that these admitted scientific efforts have anything to do with some pardonable avocation indulged in the evening after work is done. Everyone knows that Goethe also went in for natural science, Schiller for history, presumably—this is the charitable assumption—as a sort of hobby. I would not simply accuse these two of having needed the science for their poetic labors, nor would I use them to excuse myself, but I must say I need the sciences. And I must even admit that I regard suspiciously all sorts of people who I know do not keep abreast of science, who, in other words, sing as the birds sing, or as they imagine the birds sing. This does not mean that I would reject a nice poem about the taste of a flounder or the pleasure of a boating party just because the author had not studied gastronomy or navigation. But I think that unless every resource is employed toward understanding the great, complicated events in the world of man, they cannot be seen adequately for what they are.

Let us assume that we want to portray great passions or events which influence the fates of peoples. Such a passion today might be the drive for power. Supposing that a poet "felt" this drive and wanted to show someone striving for power—how could he absorb into his own experience the extremely complicated mechanism within which the struggle for power today takes place? If his hero is a political man, what are the workings of politics; if he is a business man, what are the workings of business? And then there are poets who are much less passionately interested in any individual's drive for power than in business affairs and politics as such! How are they to acquire the necessary knowledge? They will scarcely find out enough by going around and keeping their eyes open, although that is at least better than rolling their eyes in a fine frenzy! The establishment of a newspaper like *Der Völkische Beobachter* or a business like Standard Oil is a rather complicated matter, and these things are not simply absorbed through the pores. Psychology is an important field for the dramatist. It is supposed that while an ordinary person may not be in a position to discover, without special instruction, what makes a man commit murder, certainly a writer ought to have the "inner resources" to be able to give a picture of a murderer's mental state. The assumption is that you only need look into yourself in such a case; after all, there is such a thing as imagination. . . . For a number of reasons I can no longer abandon myself in this amiable hope of managing so comfortably. I cannot find in myself alone all the motives which, as we learn from newspapers and scientific reports, are discovered in human beings. No more than any judge passing sentence am I able to imagine adequately, unaided, the mental state of a murderer. Modern psychology, from psychoanalysis to behaviorism, provides me with insights which help me to form a quite different judgment of the case, especially when I take into consideration the findings of sociology, and do not ignore economics or history. You may say: this is getting complicated. I must answer, it *is* complicated. Perhaps I can talk you into agreeing with me that a lot of literature is extremely primitive; yet you will ask in grave concern: Wouldn't such an evening in the theatre be a pretty alarming business? The answer to that is: No.

Whatever knowledge may be contained in a literary work, it must be completely converted into literature. In its transmuted form, it gives the same type of satisfaction as any literary work. And although it does not provide that satisfaction found in science as such, a certain inclination to penetrate more deeply into the nature of things, a desire to make the world controllable, are necessary to ensure enjoyment of literary works generated by this era of great discoveries and inventions.

Is the Epic Theatre Perhaps a "Moral Institution"?

According to Friedrich Schiller, the theatre should be a moral institution. When Schiller posed this demand, it scarcely occurred to him that by moralizing from the stage he might drive the audience out of the theatre. In his day the audience had no objection to moralizing. Only later on did Friedrich Nietzsche abuse him as the moral trumpeter of Säckingen. To Nietzsche a concern with morality seemed a dismal affair; to Schiller it seemed completely gratifying. He knew of nothing more entertaining and satisfying than to propagate ideals. The bourgeoisie was just establishing the concept of the nation. To furnish your house, show off your new hat, present your bills for payment is highly gratifying. But to speak of the decay of your house, to have to sell your old hat, and pay the bills yourself is a truly dismal affair, and that was how Friedrich Nietzsche saw it a century later. He had nothing good to say of morality, nor, consequently, of the other Friedrich.

Many people also attacked the epic theatre, claiming it was too moralistic. Yet moral utterances were secondary in the epic theatre. Its intention was less to moralize than to study. And it did study, but then came the rub: the moral of the story. Naturally, we cannot claim that we began making studies just because studying was so much fun and not for any concrete reason, or that the results of our studies then took us completely by surprise. Undoubtedly there were painful discrepancies in the world around us, conditions that were hard to bear, conditions of a kind hard to bear not only for moral reasons. Hunger, cold, and hardship are not only burdensome for moral reasons. And the purpose of our investigation was not merely to arouse moral misgivings about certain conditions (although such misgivings might easily be felt, if not by every member of the audience; such misgivings, for example, were seldom felt by those who profited by the conditions in question). The purpose of our investigation was to reveal the means by which those onerous conditions could be done away with. We were not speaking on behalf of morality but on behalf of the wronged. These are really two different things, for moral allusions are often used in telling the wronged that they must put up with their situation. For such moralists, people exist for morality, not morality for people.

Nevertheless it can be deduced from these remarks to what extent and in what sense the epic theater is a moral institution.

CAN EPIC THEATRE BE PERFORMED ANYWHERE?

From the standpoint of style, the epic theatre is nothing especially new. In its character of show, of demonstration, and its emphasis on the artistic, it is related to the ancient Asian theatre. The medieval mystery play, and also the classical Spanish and Jesuit theatres, showed an instructive tendency.

Those theatre forms corresponded to certain tendencies of their time and disappeared with them. The modern epic theatre is also linked to definite tendencies. It can by no means be performed anywhere. Few of the great nations today are inclined to discuss their problems in the theatre. London, Paris, Tokyo, and Rome maintain their theatres for quite different purposes. Only in a few places, and not for long, have circumstances been favorable to an epic, instructive theatre. In Berlin, fascism put a violent stop to the development of such a theatre.

Besides a certain technical standard, it presupposes a powerful social movement which has an interest in the free discussion of vital problems, the better to solve them, and which can defend this interest against all opposing tendencies.

The epic theatre is the broadest and most far-reaching experiment in great modern theatre, and it has to overcome all the enormous difficulties that all vital forces in the area of politics, philosophy, science, and art have to overcome. (pp. 149-57)

Bertolt Brecht, "Theatre for Pleasure or Theatre for Learning?" translated by Edith Anderson, in The Creative Vision: Modern European Writers on Their Art, *edited by Haskell M. Block and Herman Salinger, Grove Press, Inc., 1960, pp. 149-57.*

Short Description of a New Technique of Acting which Produces an Alienation Effect (1933-47)

[*In the following essay, written sometime in the period 1933-47, Brecht defines the alienation effect and describes methods used to achieve it.*]

What follows represents an attempt to describe a technique of acting which was applied in certain theatres with a view to taking the incidents portrayed and alienating them from the spectator. The aim of this technique, known as the alienation effect, was to make the spectator adopt an attitude of inquiry and criticism in his approach to the incident. The means were artistic.

The first condition for the A-effect's application to this end is that stage and auditorium must be purged of everything 'magical' and that no 'hypnotic tensions' should be set up. This ruled out any attempt to make the stage convey the flavour of a particular place (a room at evening, a road in the autumn), or to create atmosphere by relaxing the tempo of the conversation. The audience was not 'worked up' by a display of temperament or 'swept away' by acting with tautened muscles; in short, no attempt was made to put it in a trance and give it the illusion of watching an ordinary unrehearsed event. As will be seen presently, the audience's tendency to plunge into such illusions has to be checked by specific artistic means.

The first condition for the achievement of the A-effect is that the actor must invest what he has to show with a definite gest of showing. It is of course necessary to drop the assumption that there is a fourth wall cutting the audience off from the stage and the consequent illusion that the stage action is taking place in reality and without an audience. That being so, it is possible for the actor in principle to address the audience direct.

It is well known that contact between audience and stage is normally made on the basis of empathy. Conventional actors devote their efforts so exclusively to bringing about this psychological operation that they may be said to see it as the principal aim of their art. Our introductory remarks will already have made it clear that the technique which produces an A-effect is the exact opposite of that which aims at empathy. The actor applying it is bound not to try to bring about the empathy operation.

Yet in his efforts to reproduce particular characters and show their behaviour he need not renounce the means of empathy entirely. He uses these means just as any normal person with no particular acting talent would use them if he wanted to portray someone else, i.e. show how he behaves. This showing of other people's behaviour happens time and again in ordinary life (witnesses of an accident demonstrating to newcomers how the victim behaved, a facetious person imitating a friend's walk, etc.), without those involved making the least effort to subject their spectators to an illusion. At the same time they do feel their way into their characters' skins with a view to acquiring their characteristics.

As has already been said, the actor too will make use of this psychological operation. But whereas the usual practice in acting is to execute it during the actual performance, in the hope of stimulating the spectator into a similar operation, he will achieve it only at an earlier stage, at some time during rehearsals.

To safeguard against an unduly 'impulsive', frictionless and uncritical creation of characters and incidents, more reading rehearsals can be held than usual. The actor should refrain from living himself into the part prematurely in any way, and should go on functioning as long as possible as a reader (which does not mean a reader-aloud). An important step is memorizing one's first impressions.

When reading his part the actor's attitude should be one of a man who is astounded and contradicts. Not only the occurrence of the incidents, as he reads about them, but the conduct of the man he is playing, as he experiences it, must be weighed up by him and their peculiarities understood; none can be taken as given, as something that 'was bound to turn out that way', that was 'only to be expected from a character like that'. Before memorizing the words he must memorize what he felt astounded at and where he felt impelled to contradict. For these are dynamic forces that he must preserve in creating his performance.

When he appears on the stage, besides what he actually is doing he will at all essential points discover, specify, imply what he is not doing; that is to say he will act in such a way that the alternative emerges as clearly as possible, that his acting allows the other possibilities to be inferred and only represents one out of the possible variants. He will say for instance 'You'll pay for that', and not say 'I forgive you'. He detests his children; it is not the case that he loves them. He moves down stage left and not up stage right. Whatever he doesn't do must be contained and conserved in what he does. In this way every sentence and every gesture signifies a decision; the character remains under observation and is tested. The technical term for this procedure is 'fixing the "not . . . but" '.

The actor does not allow himself to become completely transformed on the stage into the character he is portraying. He is not Lear, Harpagon, Schweik; he shows them. He reproduces their remarks as authentically as he can; he puts forward their way of behaving to the best of his abilities and knowledge of men; but he never tries to persuade himself (and thereby others) that this amounts to a complete transformation. Actors will know what it means if I say that a typical kind of acting without this complete transformation takes place when a producer or colleague shows one how to play a particular passage. It is not his own part, so he is not completely transformed; he underlines the technical aspect and retains the attitude of someone just making suggestions.

Once the idea of total transformation is abandoned the actor speaks his part not as if he were improvising it himself but like a quotation. At the same time he obviously has to render all the quotation's overtones, the remark's full human and concrete shape; similarly the gesture he makes must have the full substance of a human gesture even though it now represents a copy.

Given this absence of total transformation in the acting there are three aids which may help to alienate the actions and remarks of the characters being portrayed:

1. Transposition into the third person.
2. Transposition into the past.
3. Speaking the stage directions out loud.

Using the third person and the past tense allows the actor to adopt the right attitude of detachment. In addition he will look for stage directions and remarks that comment on his lines, and speak them aloud at rehearsal ('He stood up and exclaimed angrily, not having eaten: . . . ', or 'He had never been told so before, and didn't know if it was true or not', or 'He smiled, and said with forced nonchalance: . . . '). Speaking the stage directions out loud in the third person results in a clash between two tones of voice, alienating the second of them, the text proper. This style of acting is further alienated by taking place on the stage after having already been outlined and announced in words. Transposing it into the past gives the speaker a standpoint from which he can look back at his sentence. The sentence too is thereby alienated without the speaker adopting an unreal point of view; unlike the spectator, he has read the play right through and is better placed to judge the sentence in accordance with the ending, with its consequences, than the former, who knows less and is more of a stranger to the sentence.

This composite process leads to an alienation of the text in the rehearsals which generally persists in the performance too. The directness of the relationship with the audience allows and indeed forces the actual speech delivery to be varied in accordance with the greater or smaller significance attaching to the sentences. Take the case of witnesses addressing a court. The underlinings, the characters' insistence on their remarks, must be developed as a piece of effective virtuosity. If the actor turns to the audience it must be a whole-hearted turn rather than the asides and soliloquizing technique of the old-fashioned theatre. To get the full A-effect from the poetic medium the actor should start at rehearsal by paraphrasing the verse's content in vulgar prose, possibly accompanying this by the gestures designed for the verse. A daring and beautiful handling of verbal media will alienate the text. (Prose can be alienated by translation into the actor's native dialect.)

Gesture will be dealt with below, but it can at once be said that everything to do with the emotions has to be externalized; that is to say, it must be developed into a gesture. The actor has to find a sensibly perceptible outward expression for his character's emotions, preferably some action that gives away what is going on inside him. The emotion in question must be brought out, must lose all its restrictions so that it can be treated on a big scale. Special elegance, power and grace of gesture bring about the A-effect.

A masterly use of gesture can be seen in Chinese acting. The Chinese actor achieves the A-effect by being seen to observe his own movements.

Whatever the actor offers in the way of gesture, verse structure, etc., must be finished and bear the hallmarks of something rehearsed and rounded-off. The impression to be given is one of ease, which is at the same time one of difficulties overcome. The actor must make it possible for the audience to take his own art, his mastery of technique, lightly too. He puts an incident before the spectator with perfection and as he thinks it really happened or might have happened. He does not conceal the fact that he has rehearsed it, any more than an acrobat conceals his training, and he emphasizes that it is his own (actor's) account, view, version of the incident.

Because he doesn't identify himself with him he can pick

a definite attitude to adopt towards the character whom he portrays, can show what he thinks of him and invite the spectator, who is likewise not asked to identify himself, to criticize the character portrayed.

The attitude which he adopts is a socially critical one. In his exposition of the incidents and in his characterization of the person he tries to bring out those features which come within society's sphere. In this way his performance becomes a discussion (about social conditions) with the audience he is addressing. He prompts the spectator to justify or abolish these conditions according to what class he belongs to.

The object of the A-effect is to alienate the social gest underlying every incident. By social gest is meant the mimetic and gestural expression of the social relationship prevailing between people of a given period.

It helps to formulate the incident for society, and to put it across in such a way that society is given the key, if titles are thought up for the scenes. These titles must have a historical quality.

This brings us to a crucial technical device: historicization.

The actor must play the incidents as historical ones. Historical incidents are unique, transitory incidents associated with particular periods. The conduct of the persons involved in them is not fixed and 'universally human'; it includes elements that have been or may be overtaken by the course of history, and is subject to criticism from the immediately following period's point of view. The conduct of those born before us is alienated from us by an incessant evolution.

It is up to the actor to treat present-day events and modes of behaviour with the same detachment as the historian adopts with regard to those of the past. He must alienate these characters and incidents from us.

Characters and incidents from ordinary life, from our immediate surroundings, being familiar, strike us as more or less natural. Alienating them helps to make them seem remarkable to us. Science has carefully developed a technique of getting irritated with the everyday, 'self-evident', universally accepted occurrence, and there is no reason why this infinitely useful attitude should not be taken over by art. It is an attitude which arose in science as a result of the growth in human productive powers. In art the same motive applies.

As for the emotions, the experimental use of the A-effect in the epic theatre's German productions indicated that this way of acting too can stimulate them, though possibly a different class of emotion is involved from those of the orthodox theatre. A critical attitude on the audience's part is a thoroughly artistic one. Nor does the actual practice of the A-effect seem anything like so unnatural as its description. Of course it is a way of acting that has nothing to do with stylization as commonly practised. The main advantage of the epic theatre with its A-effect, intended purely to show the world in such a way that it becomes manageable, is precisely its quality of being natural and earthly, its humour and its renunciation of all the mystical elements that have stuck to the orthodox theatre from the old days. (pp. 136-40)

Bertolt Brecht, in his Brecht on Theatre: The Development of an Aesthetic, *edited and translated by John Willett, Hill and Wang, 1964, 294 p.*

Observations on *Mother Courage* (1950-52)

[*In the essay below, originally written between 1950 and 1952, Brecht comments on the title character in* Mother Courage.]

I

MOTHER COURAGE PRESENTED IN TWO WAYS

In the usual manner of stage presentation, which produces a feeling of identification with the principal character, the spectator of ***Mother Courage*** (according to the testimony of many) comes to enjoy a peculiar pleasure: a triumph over the indestructibility of a vital person who has been visited by the tribulations and injuries of war. The active participation of Mother Courage in the war is not taken seriously; it is a means of support, possibly the only one. Apart from this motive of participation—indeed, in spite of it—the effect is similar to that in the case of *The Good Soldier Schweik,* where—of course, in a comic sphere—the spectator triumphs with Schweik over the plans for his sacrifice by the major belligerent Powers. The similar effect in the case of Mother Courage is, however, of far less social value because her very participation, as indirectly as it may be presented, is not deliberated. In actuality, this effect is even quite negative. Mother Courage appears principally as a mother and, like Niobe, she is unable to protect her children from the doom of war. Her trade as a dealer and the manner in which she practices it, give her at most something "realistically not ideal," without, however, taking from the war anything of its character of doom. It is, of course, here too, purely negative, but in the end she survives it, even though marred. In the face of this, Helene Weigel, employing a technique which prevented complete empathy, treated the dealer's occupation not as a merely natural, but as an historical one, that is to say, as belonging to an historical and *past* epoch, and the war as the best time for business. Here, too, trade was to be taken for granted as a means of support, but a dirty one after all, from which Mother Courage drank death. The trader-mother became a great living contradiction and it was this that defaced and deformed her, to the point of making her unrecognizable. In the scene on the battlefield, which is generally omitted in the usual manner of presentation, she was really a hyena; she brought out the shirts only because she saw the hate of her daughter and feared the use of force, and, cursing, she flung herself like a tiger upon the soldier with the cloak. After the maiming of her daughter, she damned the war with a sincerity just as deep as that with which she praised it in the scene immediately following. Thus, she gave expression to opposites in all their abruptness and irreconcilability. The rebellion of her daughter against her (at the rescue of the city of Halle) stunned her completely and taught her nothing. The tragedy of Mother Courage and of her life, deeply felt by the audience, consisted in the fact that here a terrible contradiction existed which destroyed a human being, a contradiction which could be resolved, but only by society itself and in long, terrible struggles. And the moral superiority of this type of presentation consisted in its showing man—even the most vigorous type of man—as destructible!

II

NOTES TO MOTHER COURAGE

The first performance of ***Mother Courage and Her Children*** in Zürich during the Hitler war, with the extraordinary Therese Giehse in the title role, made it possible—in spite of the anti-Fascist and pacifist attitude of the Zürich theatre audience, consisting mainly of German émigrés—for the bourgeois press to speak of a "Niobe tragedy" and of the mother-animal's tremendously moving energy of life. Warned by this, the playwright made a few changes for the Berlin performance.

In the Peasants' Wars, the greatest misfortune of German history—from a sociological standpoint—the Reformation had its canine teeth pulled. There remained: business and cynicism. Mother Courage—let this be said by way of help to the theatrical performance—together with her friends and guests and nearly everybody else, recognizes the purely mercantile character of the war: that is exactly what attracts her. She believes in the war to the end. It does not even dawn on her that you must have a large pair of shears in order to get your own cut from a war. The spectators at catastrophes expect without justification that those concerned and hardest hit are going to learn from the experience. As long as the masses are the *object* of politics, they can look upon what happens to them not as an experiment but only as a destiny; they learn as little from the catastrophe as the guinea pig in an experiment learns about biology. It is not the business of the playwright to endow Mother Courage with final insight—she does have some insight toward the middle of the play, at the end of Scene Six, and then she loses it again; his concern is, to make the spectator see.

III

DRAMATIC FORM AND EFFECT

The chronicle play, ***Mother Courage and Her Children***—the term "chronicle play" correspondds, as a literary type, approximately to the term "History" in the Elizabethan drama—naturally does not represent any attempt to convince anyone at all about anything at all through the exposition of naked facts. Facts very rarely allow themselves to be taken by surprise in a condition of nakedness, and they would seduce only a very few. It is of course necessary for chronicle plays to have a factual content, that is, to be realistic. Even the division, "objectivizing theatre opposed to psychologizing theatre," does not really help us along, since one can also devise theatre that would be objectivizing and psychologizing, by taking chiefly psychological "material" as the principal object of artistic presentation and at the same time striving for objectivity. So far as the present play is concerned, I do not believe that it leaves the spectator in a state of objectivity (that is, of dispassionately balancing "for" and "against"). On the contrary, I believe—or let us say, I hope—that the play makes him critical. (pp. 158-61)

Bertolt Brecht, "Observations on 'Mother Courage'," translated by Herman Salinger, in The Creative Vision: Modern European Writers on Their Art, *edited by Haskell M. Block and Herman Salinger, Grove Press, Inc., 1960, pp. 158-61.*

OVERVIEWS AND GENERAL STUDIES

Raymond Williams (essay date 1961)

[*Williams was an English educator and critic. His literary theory is informed by his socialist ideology and his belief that a reader's perception of literature is directly related to cultural attitudes which are subject to change over the course of time. Williams is best known for the study* Modern Tragedy *(1958), which asserts that modern tragedy derives from the inadequacies of social systems rather than weaknesses of character (as in classical tragedy); and for* Drama from Ibsen to Brecht *(1968), a study which utilizes his definition of tragedy to explain the development of modern drama. Here, Williams examines Brecht's career as playwright, concluding that his principal achievement was "that he took the powerful analytic techniques of expressionism and succeeded in reintegrating them with the main body of humanist drama."*]

It quite often happens that a writer's reputation reaches us before we have any close knowledge of his work. It was so with Ibsen in England, in the 1890s; it has been so, with Brecht, in the 1950s. Ideas can travel faster than the literature from which they are derived. In the case of Brecht, two kinds of ideas were associated with him before we knew his plays with any adequacy: first, the idea of an epic theatre, centred not on identification but on alienation; second, that he was a communist, a Marxist intellectual, deeply involved in current political controversy and therefore open to straight political reactions. As we get to know Brecht better, we do not find either of these ideas irrelevant; each is very close to his essential achievement. But at best, with the frame ready-made, we read the achievement backwards; at worst we cut down the picture to fit the frame. Most of us have still to gain a full knowledge of Brecht's work. . . . But it seems that we may now have just enough [translated] work to begin a critical estimate: one which grows out of what seem to be the major plays rather than out of the reputation.

The movement against naturalism in the theatre was never merely technical. At its most mature, naturalism effectively embodied all that was best in the general middle-class view of life: respect for individuals and family relationships, a general humanitarianism, a preoccupation with individual conscience. This view was taken to breaking-point in Ibsen, at that historical period (of fundamental importance to modern culture) when the best men trained to this view of life were beginning radically to question its adequacy. One main line of this reaction was to break the domestic frame, to confront man again with God and with certain absolute human demands. This line has led to the best of our own verse drama. The second main reaction was to confront man with his real society, to widen the scope of moral questions from personal to social behaviour.

Ibsen stands at the head of both these reactions, but each, obviously, had to develop beyond him. His major achievement, though he looked penetratingly in every direction from the deadlock that preoccupied him, was the dramatic realisation of men faced by a false society, which could not remain external but which in its consequences broke in on the family and on the most secret individual life. Much interesting modern drama has simply repeated this pattern: the calling to make life, the debt and complication that drag back and destroy. Only a few have searched beyond this, towards the sources of the destructive element. One source has been identified as the inevitable collapse of humanism: man's pride, detached from God, taking its fall. A second source, mapped by the new psychology, was identified as a permanent destructive element in man: the roots of guilt and hate. Between them, these sources have supplied much of our best twentieth-century work.

Brecht looked in a different direction. He saw the destructive forces as parts of a false social consciousness, which had perverted moral thinking and erected many kinds of specious defence and disguise. So deep was this perversion that sympathy was the last thing wanted. We must be shocked into seeing the real situation, with no temptation to draw back because it would expose someone with whom we had identified ourselves. Only the shock would do, in the first instance: it was not a case of refining the argument, but of throwing us back on reality and breaking its terms.

In his early plays, in the 1920s, this impulse to shock, at any level, is very clear. At this stage, very similar to some English drama in the 1950s, there is a raw chaotic resentment, a hurt so deep that it requires new hurting, a sense of outrage which demands that people be outraged. So deep is this that it is very often expressed in crude physical imagery; it is a revulsion from spit and excrement which demands the exposure of both; a revulsion from false loving which leads straight to the whore. Many writers have used this simple exposure of dirt, this conscious turning to whores and criminals, as a way of expressing the tragic collapse of virtue. In Joyce, Mayakowsky, Brecht, the same patterns of attraction and disgust are clear. And for some time, in Brecht, there was nothing more. In ***The Threepenny Opera,*** the criminals and whores are offered as a portrait of respectable bourgeois society—not exactly a representation which that society will wish to acknowledge. And indeed there can be no acknowledgement. There is quite enough disgust, quite enough sense that life and society are immoral, to support successive generations of middle-class playgoers in their *enjoyment* of such plays: the crooks and whores are the licensed types of the society, and can be warmed to because they live out the reality without pretence. All such work reveals itself, finally, as a protection of conventional morality: there is no real shock, because these are a special class, with no relation to ourselves. It is profoundly discouraging to see so much contemporary English drama and fiction still tramping this same road: the consciously outrageous that nobody even pretends to be outraged by, but simply settles back to enjoy. Brecht, when this happened to his ***Threepenny Opera,*** was driven into a new creative effort. He thought he had turned the trick in the play's production, but he had been caught in his own paradox: the more people sat back and watched this kind of action, the less they identified themselves with its characters, the safer their ordinary view of life was. When the ***Threepenny Opera*** was published, Brecht wrote:

> It is a sort of summary of what the spectator in the theatre wishes to see of life. Since, however, he sees at the same time certain things that he does not wish to see and thus sees his wishes not only fulfilled but also criticised . . . he is, in theory, able to give the theatre a new function . . . Complex seeing must be practised . . . Thinking *about* the flow of the play is more important than thinking from *within* the flow of the play.

He certainly considered that he had written the play in such a way that this complex seeing was enforced: in his "epic style" and in distancing effects that pushed the spectator into "the attitude of one who smokes at ease and watches". But he was still himself confused, himself not distanced, and moreover

> today the theatre exerts an absolute primacy over dramatic writing . . . The moment it gets hold of a play, the theatre immediately starts transforming it—except those passages which are not in direct contradiction to the theatre—so that it no longer in any way remains a foreign body.

The realisation of this fact drove Brecht, as it has again and again driven dramatists in this century, into a frontal attack on existing theatrical traditions and methods, and into the development of his own previously scattered amendments. It led him also to another characteristic conclusion:

> Since the theatre itself is resisting the transformation of its function, it is a good thing if those dramas whose purpose is not only to be produced in the theatre but also to change the theatre are read by the spectator himself—out of sheer mistrust of the present-day theatre . . . In drama too we should introduce footnotes and the practice of thumbing through and checking up.

He even wrote of elements of his epic style—such as the boards describing coming scenes—as a start towards the "literarisation of the theatre . . . to establish contact with other institutions of intellectual activity".

Yet the conception of the ***Threepenny Opera*** was against him; it fitted too easily, in spite of his efforts, into "what the spectator wishes to see". It is not a matter of technical immaturity; in method the play is often brilliant. It is really that too much of himself was still contained within

Cover for Brecht's first published play.

what had become a conventionally dissident pattern of feeling: that faced with an immoral society you can display immorality as a kind of truth. People buy and sell each other, in the ***Threepenny Opera,*** with cold hearts and with only occasional covering sentiments. But yes *of course,* the audience comments; that's life. Never "that shouldn't be life"; never even "that needn't be life"; but the old cold-hearted muck about the warm-hearted crooks and whores who at least are *honest,* who have seen through this nonsense about society and all that earnest moralising. Brecht thought he had seen through these things himself—the society was false and the moralising hypocritical—but he already realised that at this point you have really seen nothing, because what you have seen is what the society wants you to see: "eats first, morals after". Brecht thinks he is detaching himself from this by calling it bourgeois morality, but in the ***Threepenny Opera*** this is so external, so casual and incidental, that it is in effect an indulgence. The displacement of feelings about modern commercial society on to a group of pseudo-eighteenth century robbers and whores is as good as an escape clause. Nobody leaves the theatre saying "I am like that"; he leaves saying "they are like that", the people on the stage and no doubt a good many others too, but not us. To a dramatist who wanted to teach new ideas, the inevitable reception of the ***Threepenny Opera*** was a challenge to new methods.

At the end of the 1920s Brecht turned consciously to a didactic theatre and to Marxism. ***St. Joan of the Stockyards*** is an exciting exploration towards the manner of his late plays, but a more characteristic result of his new emphasis was ***The Measures Taken,*** a bare exposition of revolutionary morality which seems to me wholly devoid of any kind of interest. Escaping the cynical paradoxes of the ***Threepenny Opera,*** Brecht had also left behind the idea of "complex seeing" which was his most original dramatic contribution. Temporarily, for the sake of discipline and simplicity, his unique insight into the contradictions of morality was set aside, for a willed conclusion. The same is true, really, of his more substantial version of Gorki's *Mother,* which is genuinely dramatic and yet which he had later to revise to get the necessary complexity of interpretation. Slowly, and now through the tensions of exile, he was working towards dramatic methods which could do justice to his vision, and then suddenly, in two or three extraordinary years at the end of the 1930s, he broke through to his ***Good Woman of Setzuan,*** his ***Mother Courage,*** and his ***Galileo.*** If we add to these the later ***Caucasian Chalk Circle,*** we are at the heart of Brecht's important drama.

The Good Woman of Setzuan is a brilliant matching of Brecht's essential moral complexity with a dramatic method which can genuinely embody it. The moral framework is explicit, as it was in Strindberg's *Dreamplay,* in the traditional device of the gods visiting earth to find a good person. But the action which this initiates is clearer in Brecht than in Strindberg, because the central perception is more precise. In his early plays Brecht had been attracted to morally ambiguous characters, whom he could use to point a cynical paradox about conventional morality. In ***The Good Woman of Setzuan*** these feelings have developed and clarified. He can now invite us to look at what happens to a good person in a bad society, not through argument, but through a dramatic demonstration. Shen Te is linked to some of his earlier characters in that she is first presented as the conventional kind-hearted prostitute, but this is almost incidental and certainly does not count in the main action. Brecht can show, through her, without ambiguity, the ways in which goodness is exploited, by gods and men alike, if it remains on a purely individual basis. If it is always a sin against life to allow oneself to be destroyed by cruelty or indifference or greed, then goodness is trapped in an intolerable dilemma: the real split in consciousness which a purely individual morality, seriously lived through, inevitably leads to. Goodness turns into its opposite, and then back again, and then both co-exist, for the dilemma is beyond individual solution. And this is conveyed with simplicity and power in Shen Te's transformation of herself into her tough male cousin, Shui Ta, who is first a disguise and then in effect takes on an independent existence. Brecht is always impressive, in his mature plays, in the discovery of ways of enacting genuine alternatives: not so much, as in traditional drama, through the embodiment of alternatives in opposing characters, but by their embodiment in one person, who lives through this way and then that and invites us to draw our conclusions. This is "complex seeing" integrated in depth with the dramatic form, and it is carried right through in that there is no imposed resolution—the tension is there to the end, and we are formally invited to consider it. The ordinary reactions with which we cover this tension are carefully put into the mouths of other characters, so that we can discover their inadequacy while the tension is still there to see. The methods of expressionist drama, normally used to manifest this breaking tension within a single consciousness, are used by Brecht with power and skill, but have acquired a new clarity, a genuine absence of the hysteria characteristic of ordinary expressionism, by the use of controlling and distancing elements which spring from the desire to examine rather than to expose. Brecht is as far as possible, in this play, from the method of special pleading which insists on the spectator or reader seeing the world through the action and tensions of a single mind. This ordinary expressionist emphasis has been transformed by deliberate generalisation, and by the appeal to impersonal judgment. ***The Good Woman of Setzuan,*** if not Brecht's greatest play, is a profoundly original development of dramatic form in its most important sense.

In certain ways, the ***Caucasian Chalk Circle*** belongs with ***The Good Woman of Setzuan,*** in dramatic method, but it is a very much less successful play. The framework of the Soviet collective farm dispute is arbitrary and distracting; the issue it raises is not followed through. In the main action, two stories—of Azdac and of Grusha—are again quite arbitrarily related. The dramatic image in the title is effective, and is given Brecht's characteristic twist: the woman who fails the test wins because she is more concerned with life than with property and therefore cannot compete. This genuinely dramatises a revolutionary morality, putting life and growth before precedent and formal title. But the simplicity and dramatic point of the Grusha story are blunted by the quite different conception of Azdac, who is a survival (interesting in that it shows the element of persistence in Brecht) from the earlier vision of anarchic paradox. Azdac's caricature of justice is like Macheath's caricature of free enterprise: each reminds us of negative elements of the original by living out an even more preposterous negative. Like all good caricature, Azdac is enjoyable, but it is then only arbitrarily, by a kind of reckless coincidence, that he is in the end dramatically identified with the positive morality of the story of Grusha. Brecht's vitality and brilliance, clear in this play as in nearly everything he wrote, are not dramatic virtues that we can accept unanalysed. He is often very like Shaw in this: that he becomes more exciting—more consciously vital and brilliant—as he becomes more confused. About experimental drama, people are often afraid to say this, restricting themselves, because of uneasiness, to comment on the techniques as such. But we shall always fall short of true judgement if we suppose that these isolable qualities are the whole terms of value; we have to look at what the wit is for, what the engaging roughness is for, and in the case of ***The Caucasian Chalk Circle*** I think we shall discover that in effect they distract both audience and author from a central confusion of experience.

The first great merit of ***Mother Courage*** is that it brings back into drama a kind of action which on the whole has been abandoned to the novel. To call this action Shakespearean is not to put the praise too high: history and people come alive on the stage, leaping past the isolated, virtually static action that we have got used to in modern theatre, yet replacing it not by a simple pell-mell but by an action that continually multiplies rooted detail, in an active history of events and persons, controlled from a centre of moral concern which is not the earlier desire to demonstrate but the mature commitment to "complex seeing". What is important about this play is that the drama simultaneously occurs and is seen; it is not an action assumed and then argued. Such an achievement ought not to be rare—it is what all the textbooks prescribe—but it is in fact only rarely (Synge's *Playboy of the Western World* is another good example) that it is unmistakeably there.

Criticism of the play has usually got off on the wrong track by starting with the question whether Mother Courage, as a person, is meant to be admired or despised. But the point is not what we feel about her hard, lively opportunism; it is what we see, in the action, of where this leads. By enacting a genuine consequence, Brecht raises his old paradox to a new level, both dramatically and intellectually. It is not "take the case of this woman", but "see the case of these people, in movement". What else can be done, here, where blind power is loose, but to submit, to chisel, to try to stay safe? And by doing these things, here—submitting and pretending to virtue, or submitting and cheating round the back—a family is destroyed. The question is then not "what should they have done?" but "what are they doing, what have they done?" All Brecht's dramatic skill is deployed to lead us to this critical realism; it is not an abstract morality, with force and pressure temporarily set aside, but an active process which is simultaneously moral and dramatic. The terrible drumming of the dumb girl, at the end, is not a solution, or an isolated heroic gesture; it is part of the urgency of the whole conception, calling the city to attend to what is happening:

> You'll sleep forever when you're dead
> But if you're not, then look alive.

The play is written, throughout, to present this urgency without identification. The contradictions in the characters—that they are sometimes hard, sometimes generous, and so on—are real, but they exist not only at the level of personal qualities; they exist also at the level of the play as a whole. Much of the speech is the play speaking, drawing strength from its characters but also moving beyond them, as here:

> CHAPLAIN. . . . Mother Courage, I see how you got your name.
>
> MOTHER COURAGE. Poorer people need courage. They're lost, that's why.
>
> That they even get up in the morning is something—in *their* plight. Or that they plough a field, in wartime. Or that they have an Emperor and a Pope, what courage *that* takes, when you can lose your life by it. The poor! They hang each other one by one, they slaughter each other in the lump, so if they want to look each other in the face once in a while—well, it takes courage, that's all.

The control here, in so complex a piece of dramatic writing, is remarkable. The direct comment comes through, and indicates the main concern of the whole work, but at the same time the word-play on "courage" follows with exactly the right amount of emphasis: we need this woman if we are to look ourselves in the face; the drama, with this character at its centre, is a way of looking.

Galileo is an achievement of a quite different kind. It is a play of the crisis of consciousness, as opposed to the dramatisation of conflicting instincts, conflicting illusions and momentary perceptions, in ***Mother Courage***—a play that had rightly to reach crisis with the frantic drumming of one who cannot speak. Galileo is conscious, and to that extent he is a free man, in ways that the pressed and driven cannot be expected to be. In abstraction, the choice presented to him looks the same: accept our terms or be destroyed. But in detail, the choice is quite different. Because he is conscious, not only can he foresee consequence, but also, inevitably, he represents more than himself, embodies in his person reason and liberation.

Once again, criticism of the play has got off to a wrong start, with the question "Is Galileo to be admired or despised?" Brecht is not asking this question. He is asking what happens to consciousness when it is caught in the apparent deadlock between the terms of individual and social morality. Galileo's submission can be rationalised, and perhaps justified, at the individual level, as a way of gaining time to go on with his scientific work. But the point this misses is what the scientific work is for. If it is for common human understanding of the world, the betrayal is fundamental. It is by detaching his individual scientific work from the general human purposes which it ought to serve that Galileo has failed. It is not, in the end, what we think of him as a man, but what we think of this result. In the detail of its writing, and in the force of its presentation of Galileo himself, the play brings this issue to real consciousness: not as a "problem", but as a matter of real pressures. It has often been said, by Western critics, that Brecht's Marxism was a handicap or at best an irrelevance. Yet surely here, at least, it is the intellectual quality of a new way of looking at the world that lays the foundations for the play's greatness. We are used to the issues of martyrdom, or of the individual in conflict with his society, but we are not used to this radically different way of looking at the matter:

> GALILEO. Could we deny ourselves to the crowd and still remain scientists? The movements of the stars have become clearer; but to the mass of the people the movements of their masters are still incalculable . . . With time you may discover all that is to be discovered, and your progress will only be a progression away from mankind. The gulf between you and them can one day become so great that your cry of jubilation over some new achievement may be answered by a universal cry of horror.

It is true that, trained to a different consciousness, we struggle to reduce the play to a different meaning, or, more honestly, argue that this conclusion is only there in one speech, and not in the play as a whole. But I think this is a simple misreading, starting from the fact that we come to the story of Galileo with our own powerful fixed image of the liberal martyr, and then cannot see what is actually being presented. Certainly the text itself is explicit: it is not only Galileo but the play that speaks. Thus Galileo's first great speech presents the terms of the subsequent moral action:

> The most solemn truths are being tapped on the shoulder; what was never doubted is now in doubt. And because of that a great wind has arisen, lifting even the gold-embroidered coat-tails of princes and prelates, so that the fat legs and the thin legs underneath are seen; legs like our legs . . . I predict that in our lifetimes astronomy will be talked about in the market-places. Even the sons of fishwives will go to school.

And then this is followed in the next scene, that of the presentation of the telescope, by this speech of the Curator of the Great Arsenal of Venice:

> Once again a page of fame in the great book of the arts is embellished with Venetian characters. A scholar of world repute here presents to you, and you alone, a highly saleable cylinder to manufacture and put on the market in any way you please. And has it occurred to you that in wartime by means of this instrument we shall be able to distinguish the build and number of an enemy's ships a full two hours earlier than he can decry ours . . . ?

The contrast is hardly too subtle to be seen; if we miss it, it is because we are resolutely interested in something else. Our ordinary reception of the play is an ironic illustration of the power of particular patterns of consciousness, through which we can see one action and make it another. This is typically true in the theatre, where as Brecht observed, this play can 'without much adjustment of the contemporary theatrical style, be presented as a piece of historical "ham" with a star part'. But the play, as written, is firm. Galileo, committed to a universal view of science, is trapped from the beginning by another kind of consciousness: the imperatives of a different loyalty, to the particular ruling group that maintains him, to produce for the market and for war. It is not that as an individual he is a hypocrite; it is that under these real pressures he embodies both a true consciousness and a false consciousness—the fact of their coexistence is what Brecht invites us to see. The movement of the play is from the ironic, apparently safe acceptance of false consciousness (what you say to get by, in an imperfect world) to the point where false consciousness becomes false action and is not irony but tragedy and waste. In the end Brecht is showing us not an individual and his history but a structure of feeling and its consequences: this is the central strength of his mature drama.

In the history of drama, Brecht's achievement will perhaps be seen as this: that he took the powerful analytic techniques of expressionism and succeeded in reintegrating them with the main body of humanist drama. Naturalism and expressionism had in common the fact that they were ordinarily static: the unfolding of a character or group of characters; the exposition of a state of mind. Brecht took from expressionism the techniques of exposition, but broke out from its ordinary deadlock by a sense of human history and movement which had been absent from drama for many generations. The great power of Ibsen and Strindberg sprang from the depth of their exposure to the deadlock. More generally, the power of naturalism had been in its commitment to the detail of human experience; the power of expressionism in its commitment to certain basic patterns. The other developments we have seen in drama (especially in our own verse drama) were essentially refinements of these achievements: in particular the development of a dramatic language in which both detail and pattern were more specifically alive. Brecht, in his mature work, and especially in ***Mother Courage*** and ***Galileo,*** at least partly broke the deadlock: this was not the end of the action, for history was moving through it, adding a new dimension. In practical terms, the sense of history became active through the rediscovery of techniques of dramatic movement: the action is not single in space and time, and certainly not 'permanent and timeless'; it is, rather, complex in actual development, and, through the distancing that invites critical appraisal, complex and dynamic in actual reference. Struggling always with his own fixed consciousness, Brecht could only begin this transformation. But the idea and the practice of his 'epic theatre' were at once a recovery of very early elements in the humanist drama of the Renaissance (where this capacity for action seemed at its full creative power), and a remaking of these elements in terms of a modern consciousness. Continually limited by his own weaknesses—both his constant opportunism, which too often comes through as dramatic cheating, and his vestigial jeering and coarseness, the real dregs of his time and ours—he struggled towards a transformation and in part achieved it. Instead of trying to convert his work to the complacencies of our fashionable despair, or more easily to the grossness of our defensive cynicism, which at times he readily nourishes, we should try to see what it means to drama when in recovering a sense of history and of the future a writer recovers the means of an action both complex and dynamic. In most modern drama, the best conclusion is that that is how it was. Only an occasional major play goes further, with the specific excitement of recognition that this is how it is. Brecht, at his best, reaches out to and touches the necessary next stage: that this is how it is, for this reason, but the action is continually being replayed, and it could be otherwise. And this happens, not in separate stages of seeing and reflection, but in the complex seeing of a single dramatic experience. (pp. 153-62)

Raymond Williams, "The Achievement of Brecht," in Critical Quarterly, *Vol. 3, No. 2, Summer, 1961, pp. 153-62.*

Robert Brustein (essay date 1963)

[*An American drama critic and the artistic director of the American Repertory Theatre Company, Brustein is well-known for his insistence upon excellence and innovation in the theater. As drama critic for the* New Republic, *he attacked what he considered the debased standards of commercial acting, directing, and playwriting in America. While serving as the dean of Yale University's School of Drama from 1966 to 1979, he continued to develop innovative and controversial dramatic techniques; under his direction, Yale gained a reputation as one of the leading drama schools in the nation. In the following essay, an abridged version of a chapter later appearing in his acclaimed study* The Theatre of Revolt *(1964), Brustein examines Brecht's thought and temperament as elucidated in his works, maintaining that the playwright's dramas and other writings reflect his social rebellion against the "injustice of bourgeois society" and his existential revolt against "the disorder of the universe and the chaos in the human soul."*]

Of all the great modern dramatists, Bertolt Brecht is the most enigmatic—at once direct and hidden, at once simple and complex. The bulk of his work is designed to be an impersonal and schematic contribution to Marxist mythmaking. Yet, despite his unambiguous commitment to the Communist cause throughout most of his career, Brecht is an extremely divided artist, whose works, for all their ideological intentions, remain peculiarly enticing and elusive. This reminds us of another Marxist dramatist, Bernard Shaw, and, superficially, Shaw would seem to be Brecht's closest companion in the theatre of revolt. Both support a "non-Aristotelian" theatre, characterized not by cathartic emotional effects but by preachment, protest, and persuasion. Both are absorbed with the materialistic motives behind human ideals. Outwardly both are social rebels, attempting the salvation of mankind through a change in the external environment. And both involuntarily overcome the narrow utilitarian limitations they impose on their art. Still, for all their surface similarities, Brecht is even further removed from Shaw, temperamentally, than Strindberg is from Ibsen. For whereas Shaw's revolt is modified by the geniality of his character and the meliorism of his social philosophy, Brecht's is intensified by his savage indignation and his harrowing vision of life. Shaw is a suppressed poet who rarely breaks the skin of the unconscious; and, though he calls himself a Puritan, he cannot bring himself to contemplate evil in the soul of man. But Brecht is a lyrical, dramatic, and satiric poet of fierce intensity; and few Calvinist theologians have been more fascinated than he with the brutal, the satanic, and the irrational aspects of human nature.

Brecht's obsession with the darker side of man stems from his struggles with his own character, and so does his relationship to ideology. For while Shaw's Fabianism is the extension of his cheerful, rationalistic personality, Brecht's Communism is a discipline imposed, by a mighty effort of will, on a Self which is essentially morbid, sensual, and anarchical. Beginning his career as an existential rebel, abnormally preoccupied with crime, blind instinctualism, and decay, Brecht becomes a social revolutionary only after he has investigated all the blind alleys of his early nihilism. The Communist ideology helps him to objectify his feelings and rationalize his art, and it encourages him to attribute an external cause to the cruelty, greed, and lust that he finds in life; but it is never fully adequate to Brecht's metaphysical *Angst.* Brecht may try to convince us that man's aggressive instincts are an outgrowth of the capitalist system, but he never seems wholly convinced himself, especially when his own aggressive instincts are so difficult to control. Even at his most scientifically objective, Brecht continues to introduce a subjective note; even at his most social and political, he remains an essentially moral and religious poet. And though he supports a political orthodoxy which promises social order and benevolence through revolutionary change, he never quite suppresses his sense of the fixed malevolence of nature as reflected in the voracious appetites of man. Brecht's revolt, therefore, is double-layered. On the surface, it is directed against the hypocrisy, avarice, and injustice of bourgeois society; in the depths, against the disorder of the universe and the chaos in the human soul. Brecht's social revolt is objective, active, remedial, realistic; his existential revolt is subjective, passive, irremediable, and romantic. The conflict between these two modes of rebellion is the dialectic of Brecht's plays; and the conflict is not fully resolved until the very end of his career.

The existential aspect of Brecht's revolt, while present in most of his writings, can be most clearly detected in his early work—the poems and plays which precede ***The Threepenny Opera.*** Here Brecht reveals affinities with two other German dramatists, separated in time but not in temperament, George Büchner and Frank Wedekind. Together with the plays of these two dramatists, Brecht's early plays comprise what we might call a German Neo-Romantic movement—a tradition defined by its opposition to the lofty moral postures and Messianic stances of the early German Romantics. Negative and ironic, scrupulously anti-heroic, anti-individualist, and anti-idealist, Brecht developed out of this tradition a determinedly low opinion of human nature, fastening on the criminal or abnormal side of life, and charting these subterranean avenues in searing, distended images. And it is out of this tradition that Brecht investigates the underside of life, exploiting—like his two mentors—the popular entertainments, culture, and expressions of the lower classes: proverbs, vernacular poetry, idiomatic speech, the variety theatre, the circus, the cabaret, and the streetsinger's ballad, the *Moritat.*

Despite the studied indifference with which Brecht affects to examine life in this period, however, he cannot disguise his sense of horror at it. To adapt Joyce's phrase about Stephen Dedalus' Jesuit conditioning, he has the cursed Calvinist strain in him, injected the wrong way. Like Büchner, whose disgust and hatred are clear enough, Brecht exposes, through his exaggerated view of human nature, a strain of disappointed Romanticism. For the Neo-Romantic, apparently agonized by the failure of Romantic ideals of unlimited human freedom, is inclined to see man as wholly determined by external and internal forces, his aspiration mocked by animal instincts and physical decay. Images of rot, stench, and decomposition pervade this drama; characters deteriorate under a peeling shell of flesh. Under the spell of this Augustinian vision. Büchner perceives the "horrible fatalism of all history," a horror which Brecht introduces into all his early drama, where man is merely an excremental object of no value, a "creature eating on a latrine."

The typical development of the Neo-Romantic drama, then, follows the progress of human deterioration—the gradual stripping away of morals, ideals, individualization, and civilized veneer until the human being is revealed in all his naked cruelty or insignificance—accompanied by sex nausea, hatred of the flesh, and ill-disguised sado-masochistic feelings. The masterpiece of the genre is Büchner's *Wozzeck*—at once the most typical and the most original of Neo-Romantic plays—and one which exercised a powerful influence on all of Brecht's early writings.

To Büchner, society is merely another form of nature; and in the state of nature, man is simply another one of the beasts. Much the same inflamed vision of man in nature burns through Wedekind's *Erdgeist* where—this time with the author's energetic approval—domestic animals are transformed into wild beasts, degenerating under the influence of Lulu, an amoral spirit of the earth; it permeates the film, *The Blue Angel,* where a highly respectable teacher is totally dehumanized through a sordid relationship with a cabaret singer; and it accounts for the lurid horrors and ghastly rot in so much expressionist painting.

German Neo-Romanticism culminates in the early work of Brecht, where it takes the form of extreme antipathy to the social and natural world. As Herbert Ihering observed of Brecht when the poet was only twenty-four, "Brecht is impregnated with the horror of this age in his nerves, in his blood. . . . Brecht physically feels the chaos and putrid decay of the times." Much of this physical revulsion pervades Brecht's early poems, collected in his volume ***Hauspostille*** (***The Domestic Breviary,*** 1927), where he deals obsessively with such Neo-Romantic themes as the meaninglessness of individualism, the inescapable isolation of the natural man, and the vileness of the natural functions, besides displaying a typically Germanic interest in decay and death. And in his moving autobiographical poem, **"Concerning Poor B.B.,"** Brecht openly reveals his conviction that human beings (and he includes himself) are "strangely stinking animals," while proceeding to describe the beauties of nature in these elegiac images: "Towards morning the fir trees piss in the gray light / And their vermin, the birds, begin to cheep."

This obsession with man and nature in a state of putrefaction is also central to Brecht's early drama, where he deals with lower forms of humanity, deteriorating in a terrible environment. In ***Baal,*** for example, Brecht follows the career of a ruthless, bisexual poet, who satisfies his instincts without conscience, and finally dies in swinish degradation, amidst offal and urine, declaring that the world is merely "the excrement of God." In ***Drums in the Night,*** he dramatizes the anarchy and isolation of the central character, a returning soldier named Kragler, who rejects the heroic demands of the Spartakus revolution in order to follow the safest and most comfortable way: "I am a swine, and the swine go home." Brecht's ***In the Jungle of Cities*** illustrates the disorder of the universe and the gratuitous cruelty of mankind, also concluding with the passive acceptance of evil. And in ***Man is Man,*** he demonstrates the insignificance of the individual by showing how the meek, Wozzeck-like water carrier, Galy Gay, is transformed into a "human fighting machine" by three brutal soldiers—meanwhile illustrating the violence of human instinct in the martinet sergeant, Bloody Five, who can discipline his sexual appetite only by castrating himself.

Much of this savagery and cynicism is deliberately designed to shock; and John Willett has ably described how Brecht was eager to outrage the maddening complacence of the Weimar bourgeoisie. Nevertheless, Brecht's mordant attitudes are deeply rooted in his own nature—so deeply, in fact, that he feared this *Bitterkeit* would affect his creative powers. In **"Concerning Poor B.B.,"** he writes: "In the earthquakes to come it is to be hoped / I shan't allow bitterness to quench my cigar's glow." Like Strindberg, whom he so much resembles in this period, Brecht tries to deal with his own desperation by turning it into art: Baal, Kragler, Garga, Shlink, Bloody Five, Galy Gay, almost all his early characters are aspects of himself, projected into semi-autobiographical form. These characters can be roughly divided into two main types: the active and the passive, those who create violence and those who seek to avoid it—but whether victimizers or victims, almost all of Brecht's characters seem repelled by their own instincts, and seek to achieve a state of calm beyond the turmoil of the appetitive life. Brecht, who is remembered as an incorrigible womanizer, almost invariably associates some dire penalty with the indulgence of the appetites; for him, physical satisfaction leads directly to catastrophe—which may explain why Bloody Five in ***Man is Man,*** and, later, Lauffer in ***The Tutor,*** resort to such desperate expedients as self-castration in order to control themselves. Not only sex, but passions of any uncontrolled kind seem to be a source of anxiety to Brecht: anger, outrage, panic, revenge, violence, all are vital elements of his work, and all stand condemned. Brecht is probably trying to master these emotions in himself, for his work exposes his desire for absolute submission, a state of being in which he can conquer his unbridled feelings, and, instead of engaging himself with the external world, merge with it. Brecht's favorite symbol for this passionless state is the condition of the child in its mother's womb. In **"Concerning Poor B.B.,"** he speaks of how "My mother carried me to town while in her womb I lay," and he refers repeatedly to the pleasant passivity of this kind of pre-natal transportation. What Brecht really desires is the Buddhist Nirvana—but his own physical needs and his rebellious spirit continually press him back into material life. Brecht's unremitting attempts to control his rebellious instincts by surrendering to a discipline outside himself are to issue, later, in his submission to the Communist orthodoxy, and, still later, in his aspiration towards Oriental impassivity, where one becomes a vessel of the universe—acquiescent, will-less, and obedient. But whatever form it finds, Brecht's desire for impersonality and control reflects his need to escape from the pulls of the flesh.

At this point in his career, Brecht openly reveals his existential horror of life and loathing of the instincts. As for personality, how can one believe in that when Copernicus has shown "that Man is not in the middle of the universe"? Though Brecht shares Nietzsche's assumption that Copernicus banished the gods from the heavens, he sings not the *Uebermensch* but the *Untermensch,* the man without possibilities. And his concentration on the more insuperable human limitations, the source of his quarrel with existence, leads him to attack not only the God of the Christians but the God of the Romantics as well: "The good god," as he puts it in ***Baal,*** "who so distinguished himself by joining the urinary passage with the sex organ"—in short, the God of Nature. Choking on the same bone that stuck in the throat of Strindberg, Brecht cannot swallow the fact that man is born *inter faeces et urinas;* and his pronounced excrementalism makes him fiercely antagonistic to all Romantic aspiration. In this stage of his career, and probably throughout it, Brecht cannot convince himself that this "strangely stinking animal" is capable of heroism, morality, freedom, or anything more than the cynical pursuit of his own advantage and survival. In short, he leaves open no avenues of idealism; his is a negative assault of thundering aggressiveness. Yet, for all his scorn of Romanticism in its more positive forms, his own Romantic temperament can still be glimpsed in his subjective poetic attack, in his ferocious bitterness and disillusionment, and, especially, in his unremitting rebellion against the straitened conditions of modern existence.

Brecht's existentialism is best seen in ***In the Jungle of Cities,*** his third play, completed when he was barely twenty-five. Extremely puzzling and sometimes incoherent, this work is often hastily dismissed as an obscure experiment; but for all its difficulty, it is clearly a major achievement of a poet-genius, which batters at the nerves even when it is baffling the mind. Here Brecht is at his most frenzied and diabolical, displaying that "prodigious and rational disordering of all the senses" which Rimbaud held to be the special attainment of the visionary and seer. Rimbaud's influence, in fact, is unmistakable throughout the play. ***In the Jungle of Cities*** consists of eleven scenes, some extremely brief, essentially disconnected, but held together by a single sustained action. Characters act upon each other with no apparent cause-and-effect motivation, as in a dream. Its atmosphere is that of a feverish hallucination.

The general location of the play is Chicago, during the period from 1912 to 1915. The action moves from the business section to the slums to Chinatown to the shores of Lake Michigan. Yet, all the settings are mythical; Brecht's Chicago, for example, is a seaport, and his seedy Chinese bars and hotels seem to have come out of Anna May Wong movies or Charlie Chan novels. The central image of the play, if we discount the numerous jungle images, is a metaphor from the world of sport: "The inexplicable boxing match between two men." And the eleven scenes of the play represent the ten rounds of the combat, with an extra scene devoted to the victor, after the other combatant has been "knocked out."

The motives of this seemingly gratuitous conflict have been the subject of some speculation, especially by Martin Esslin and Eric Bentley, who have detected homosexual and sado-masochistic elements in the relationship between the two antagonists. These are undoubtedly there. But more important than the psychological aspects of the work are the philosophical ones—the conflict between the central characters is less physical than metaphysical. The theme of ***In the Jungle of Cities*** is the impossibility of establishing permanent contact between human beings—not only sexual contact, but social, verbal, and spiritual contact, too.

The opening scene, which takes place in a rental library,

initiates the conflict—between the fifty-one-year-old Malayan merchant, Shlink, and the young librarian, George Garga. Under the pretense of buying a book, Shlink offers money to Garga for his opinion of a mystery story. But though Garga is willing to give his opinions freely—or to sell Shlink the opinions of "Mr. J. V. Jensen and Mr. Arthur Rimbaud"—he absolutely refuses to make his own intelligence an object of barter. Actually, Shlink's offer has been carefully calculated to lead to combat. Garga is penniless, and his family is starving; but he has somehow preserved his Romantic insistence on personal freedom. Like Brecht, who moved from "the black forests" to "the concrete cities," Garga has come to Chicago from the spacious prairies; his love of freedom is intimately associated with his natural origins. To sell an opinion is to become a bought thing; and thus, as Shlink continually raises his offer, Garga becomes increasingly incensed and humiliated.

Since Brecht already assumes the total determination of modern city life by economic necessity, Garga's romantic idealism is his Achilles heel—and Shlink proceeds to goad and prod it. Though he recognizes the vulnerability of the Romantic idealist in the city jungle, Garga stubbornly refuses to be a "prostitute." And Shlink, cheered to have found a real "fighting man," begins the match by "rocking the ring." First, he arranges to have Garga's girlfriend, Jane Larry, turned into a prostitute by another of his henchmen. And then he has Garga fired: "Your economic security! Watch the boxing ring! It's shaking!" Forced into action against his will, Garga begins quoting from Rimbaud, rips off his clothes, and runs into the streets, still begging for his freedom. He is prepared to sacrifice everything to defend his personal independence. And the fight is on.

For in order to recover his freedom, Garga must destroy his opponent—a turn which Shlink, who desires to be destroyed, had shrewdly foreseen. "When I heard of your habits," he tells Garga, "I thought: a good fighter"—for Shlink knows that Garga is a man without limits, a Romantic who will go all the way to keep his self inviolate. To aid in his own destruction, and to equalize the odds, Shlink becomes Garga's thrall: "From today on, Mr. Garga, I place my fate in your hands. . . . From today on, I am your creature. . . . My feelings will be dedicated to you alone, and you will be evil." Garga plays on this advantage to plot Shlink's downfall, first haphazardly, then more cunningly.

Schlink's desire for pain, and ultimately for annihilation, are the result of a "disease" which he contracted during his youth on the Yangtze junks, where the rule of life was torture, and man's skin grew so thick that only the most violent probes could pierce it. Garga has been hired to be his executioner, "to stuff a bit of disgust or decay in my mouth so I'd have the taste of death on my tongue." For only through torture, disgust, and death will Shlink be able to feel.

The tenth scene (the last round of the match) takes place in an abandoned railroad tent where Garga, like Judas, spends three last weeks with his sacrificial victim. Here Shlink expresses his love for Garga, and filled with the darkest despair, explains the symptoms of his "disease," the dreadful loneliness he had suffered for forty years. Now at the end, he has fallen victim to "the black mania of this planet—the mania for contact," to be reached "through enmity," the Romantic form of love. But even this final will-to-life has failed:

> The endless isolation of man makes even enmity an unattainable goal. Even with the animals it is impossible to come to an understanding. . . . I have watched animals. Love—warmth from bodily proximity—is our only grace in the darkness. But the union of the organs is the only union and it can never bridge the gap of speech. Still, they come together to beget new beings who can stand at their side in their inconsolable isolation. And the generations look coldly into each other's eyes. . . . The jungle! That's where mankind comes from. Hairy, with the teeth of an ape, good beasts who knew how to live, everything was so easy, they simply tore each other to bits.

In the jungle of cities, man's hide has accumulated so many layers of defensive skin that even the contact between clawing, ferocious beasts is no longer achievable: "Yes, so terrible is the isolation that there isn't even a fight."

Garga, however, averts his face from this nihilistic abyss. Having lost interest in Shlink's "metaphysical action," he has determined to escape with his "naked life." For him, survival has become the *summum bonum*—"a naked life is better than any other life."

The course of the combat has taught him that the end of such struggles is always the same: "It is not important to be the stronger one, but to be the living one." Idealism, heroism, individualism, freedom, significant combat—all are "words, on a planet which is not even in the middle." And leaving the ring, he carries his "raw flesh into the icy rains," as Shlink—kayoed—falls to the floor. For Shlink, it only remains to finish himself; and he commits hari-kari, the howl of the lynch mob in his ears, after a burst of surrealist prose. As for Garga, he survives. In the last scene, he has sold Shlink's business—along with his own father and sister—and with the proceeds, is preparing to enter the jungle of New York. He has repudiated his combative need for personal opinions; his passion is spent; he will fight no more.

The philosophical conclusions of this work are much too bleak to sustain an artist for long—there is nothing in the suicidal nihilism of Shlink to inspire the process of creation—and so it is not surprising that, a few years later, in 1927 or 1928, Brecht begins to take instruction at the Marxist Worker's College in Berlin. Brecht's decision is clearly foreshadowed in the development of Garga. For like his semi-autobiographical hero, Brecht has repudiated the quest for identity and the need for personal opinions; like Garga, he is pursuing, though somewhat less cynically, the path of his own survival. If subjective individualism leads to chaos, then the subjective consciousness must be expunged; if personal rebellion leads to madness, then one must learn to conform. For him, the way out of existential despair lies along the ideological path of Communism:

"Not madness," as Brecht characterizes it in ***Die Mutter,*** "but the end of madness . . . not chaos but order." ***In The Jungle of Cities*** powerfully suggests the madness Brecht perceives in Nature and the chaos he senses in the universe; and it is certainly true, as Martin Esslin observes, that Communism "dissolved the nightmare of absurdity" for the dramatist, and "dispelled the oppressive feeling that life was ruled by vast and impersonal forces." On the other hand, the play also suggests that the anarchy he describes is projected from inside, and the aggressions of his central characters are a crucial element of his own nature. His attraction to Communism, therefore, can also be ascribed to the fact that it offers a system of regimentation, a form of rational control over his frightening individualism and terrifying subjectivity. Brecht's desire for passivity, in short, stems from his fear of activity. And his rage for order is really an extension of his desire to drift with the tide, for Communism represents a tide with a meaningful direction. As Lion Feuchtwanger has observed in a fictionalized biography of the author, Brecht "really suffered from his personality. He wanted to escape from it, he wanted to be only one atom among many," later adding the interesting reflection that he was "singularly deficient in social instincts." For such a one, Communism could be the ideal creed, because it couples anti-social rebellion with the promise of true community—and more important, because it encourages the escape from personality, offering the most impersonal and selfless discipline since primitive Christianity.

I am suggesting that Brecht responded as eagerly to the Communist discipline as to the Communist dogma; there is something almost religious about his attachment to his new creed. Like most new converts, his fanaticism begins to exceed that of the orthodox; using "science" and "reason" as ritualistic passwords, he turns to ideology as if it were theology, and enters politics as if he were joining a monastic order. Brecht's monkishness is expressed not only in the new simplicity of his poetry, which grows more functional and clipped, but in almost every aspect of his behavior. He begins to wear a simple worker's uniform as if it were a monk's habit; he crops his hair short; his surroundings become more stark and austere; and his private life more ascetic. Most important, he begins to urge the complete extinction of the personality, accompanied by total obedience to a higher order.

As Esslin has noted, the word *Einverständnis* (acquiescence or consent) begins to run like a *leit-motif* through his work, especially through those five *Lehrstücke* he writes in quick succession from 1928 to 1930. A few of these plays, in fact, are wholly concerned with teaching acquiescence to a rebellious individual, climaxing at the moment when the central figure renounces his personal feelings, denounces his insubordination, and accepts the death sentence imposed by his judges. In ***The Measures Taken,*** for example, a sympathetic Young Comrade, having permitted his hatred of injustice to jeopardize the mission of his fellow agitators, is taught the dangers of individual rebellion and instinctual reactions, and consents to his own liquidation. It has been observed that the rigid orthodoxy of such a play is probably more of an embarrassment than a service to the Communist cause; and under pressure from the Party, Brecht withdrew ***The Measures Taken*** from performance, commenting that nobody could learn anything from it except the actor who plays the Young Comrade. On the other hand, one begins to suspect that Brecht wrote such works less for the enlightenment of other ideologues than as a self-disciplinary measure. The Young Comrade is probably himself; the subjective, instinctual, and individual qualities he is trying to punish are his own. Even in the act of celebrating impersonality and obedience Brecht is likely to betray his personal conflicts, inadvertently remaining the hero of his own work. In their harsh, incantatory quality, Brecht's agit-prop plays seem like the *Aves* of a novitiate, paying penance for a recurrent sin. But his subjective anarchy is never quite subdued, and his probationary period never really comes to an end.

Brecht's Communism, then, is less a substitute for his early Neo-Romanticism than a layer superimposed on top of it—his rational ideology emerges as the dialectical counterpart of his irrationalism and despair. Brecht's new commitment permits him to function as an artist, but his political solutions are fashioned for essentially metaphysical problems. To be sure, Brecht's assumptions are now more hopeful and optimistic. Where he once identified evil with fate and assumed it to be fixed, he now identifies it with bourgeois society and assumes it to be changeable. "According to the ancients," he writes in his notes to an adaptation of Sophocles' *Antigone* (1948), "man is powerless before the workings of fate. In the adaptation of Bertolt Brecht, man's fate is in the hands of man himself." His despairing belief in Darwinist science (behaviorism and determinism) has been replaced by an affirmative belief in Marxist science (class war and revolution)—his despondent feelings about the future of the individual have given way to more cheerful feelings about the future of the collective. Whatever his expectations of the future, however, Brecht continues to focus on the bleaker aspects of present-day reality. While he refuses to reach tragic conclusions, he is still primarily occupied with tragic conditions. Human deterioration may now be attributed to the social system, but rot still catches his eye, even if it is now called by the name of Capitalism. As for the natural environment, Brecht now believes that "science is able to change nature to an extent that makes the world appear almost habitable" (the "almost" is good); but he still finds man victimized by the external world—still lost in the emptiness of the Copernican universe.

Brecht's characters, however, are also victimized now by a cruel society. As we might expect, his Marxist orientation puts social-economic concerns at the center of his art. The rebel against the chaos of nature has turned a rebel against the social system. And while his existential revolt found its literary roots in a German Neo-Romantic tradition, his social revolt is influenced by a more international group of writers—I refer not only to the Communist dialecticians but also to pre- and post-Marxist dramatists in a Jonsonian tradition: Ben Jonson, William Wycherly, John Gay, Henri Becque, Henrik Ibsen, and (to a lesser degree) Bernard Shaw.

Even here, however, we can see that Brecht has not so

much changed his old assumptions as assimilated them within a new intellectual structure. For between the Neo-Romantic dramatist and the Jonsonian satirist there is one important point of agreement—that Man (to use a Renaissance adage) is a Wolf to Man. If nature is a jungle to Büchner, Wedekind, and the early Brecht, then to Jonson, Becque, and the later Brecht, it is society which harbors the wild beasts—the buzzard, the crow, the raven, the fly, and the fox, all picking each other's bones in an orgy of greed and acquisitiveness. These authors generally resemble Marx in their *negative* critique of society. For if they are silent about the perfectability of man, the class struggle, and the classless society, they all visualize a world dominated by economic determinism, where the true God of man is Plutus, the God of Gold.

Brecht, himself, seems to be more responsive to the critical than to the Utopian side of Marx—at least, in his plays. Interpreting life as dominated by the search for food and the lust for money (he wanted money and food to replace sex and power as the central subjects of the drama), he also conceives of man as an aggressive beast of prey who grows fat by battening on the flesh of his victims. "What keeps a man alive," asks Peachum, in a song from ***The Threepenny Opera,*** "he lives on others—by grinding, sweating, defeating, beating, cheating, eating some other man." And in ***The Rise and Fall of the City of Mahagonny,*** the hero, Jimmy Mahoney, is forced to learn that the only capital crime is the lack of money. Brecht's inexhaustible gallery of thieves, swindlers, soldiers, whores, brothel madams, gangsters, landowners, Nazis, and businessmen form the population of a human bestiary, concealing behind their charming smiles the razor teeth of the shark.

On the other hand, Brecht's Communist orientation does make him ambivalent about which human faculty creates evil—for here the views of his double inheritance are in conflict. The characters of Neo-Romantic drama—Büchner's Wozzeck, Wedekind's Lulu, Strindberg's Laura—are usually driven by the unconscious, while those of satiric drama—Jonson's Volpone, Gay's Macheath, Becque's M. Tessier—generally follow the path of their rational self-interest, impervious to all drives besides greed and lust. Brecht's early characters, as we have seen, are clearly at the mercy of anarchical impulses, but his later characters seem to alternate between emotional chaos and rational control, intermittently dominated by and dominating the instinctual pulls of their natures. Many critics, and most notably Esslin, have commented on the omnipresent Brechtian conflict between reason and instinct as personified in split characters. But, in a sense, all of Brecht's later characters are split, vacillating between reason and instinct as dizzily as classical heroes vacillate between love and duty. These conflicts suggest some of the contradictions inherent in Brecht's double revolt. As a Marxist, Brecht is convinced that society is based on rational self-interest, and believes that a more unselfish use of reason will bring about a more perfect man and a more benevolent world. As an existential rebel, however, he is more dubious about the power of human reason; and his own vestigial anarchism forces him to deal with the wildness of the instincts and the irrationality of life—in short, with *im*perfectability.

Brecht in 1927.

Consider his ambivalent treatment of his central conflict. On the social-objective level of his plays, Brecht is drawing a clear-cut moral: Man's instincts are healthy, compassionate, kindly, and courteous, but in a competitive society, he must suppress these natural feelings, exercising selfish reason in order to survive. The emotional Anna of ***The Seven Deadly Sins,*** for example, can build her *kleine haus' im Louisiana* only by squelching her impuslive decency and charity (identified with Christian "sins"), and following the practical advice of her rational sister. Since unselfishness comes naturally and instinctually, selfishness is an extremely difficult discipline. "Terrible is the temptation to goodness," notes The Storyteller in ***The Caucasian Chalk Circle,*** while Brecht, in a poem, observing the swollen veins of a Japanese demon, reflects: "What a strain it is to be evil." Nevertheless, the nature of the system demands that man suppress his brotherly feelings, and realistically look after himself. "For when feet are bare and bellies empty," goes a verse in "The Invigorating Effect of Money," "Love of virtue always turns to greed." Or as Peachum puts it: "We would be good, not coarse and crude / It's just that circumstance won't have it so." Man is good, the system bad; ergo, conform to the system, or change the world.

This is the Marxist Brecht speaking—but the Calvinist Brecht is much less sanguine about the healthiness of human instinct. For though Brecht may insist that man must eat before he can become a moral being, he cannot always disguise the fact that the process of ingestion fills him with a little disgust. *Das Fressen,* one of the most important activities in Brechtian drama, invariably seems singularly unappealing on the stage. Galileo's wolfish appetite, as Brecht tells us in ***The Little Organon,*** is the key to his moral flabbiness; and Jacob Schmidt of ***Mahagonny,*** so gluttonous that he wants to devour himself, destroys himself by stuffing his stomach with three whole calves. Not only *das Fressen* is accompanied by a hint of nausea, but *die Liebe* as well—more often than not, Brecht's lovers are merely lechers and whores. Objectively, Brecht may associate instinct with virtue; subjectively, he identifies it with appetites—and appetites, generally, of a debased kind. A fetid, hot-house sensuality runs through most of Brecht's work. And instead of positive Marxist heroes, amoral, appetitive types like Baal continue to dominate his plays, still seen through the hideous focus of the excremental vision. In short, Brecht still seems unconsciously convinced that man is a creature eating on a latrine. And just as often as instinct issues in economic bankruptcy, it issues in spiritual bankruptcy—decay and death. In ***Mahagonny,*** for example, Jimmy Mahoney opens the city to total license after a typhoon. His motto (like that of Rabelais' Abbey of Thélème) becomes *Du Darfst* (Do What Thou Wilt). And after abandoning himself to the greedy consumption of food, sex, sport, and whiskey, Mahoney discovers that his appetites have led to ruin. Politically, Brecht can condemn unbridled instinct as an anti-social trait; psychologically, it probably represents his own unredeemable flaw, the main constituent of his continuingly anarchical nature.

Brecht's ambivalence accounts for the dialectical power and texture of his work. Through the clash of opposites, his *Widersprüchsgeist* (contradictory spirit), as he liked to call it, is able to find its complicated expression. Unable to resolve his contradictions, Brecht fails to create unambiguous political ideology, a lapse for which he is curiously chided by Herbert Luethy ("Never has Brecht been able to indicate by even the simplest poetic image or symbol what the world for which he is agitating should really look like"). Yet, his failure to be a Utopian ideologist is his triumph as a dramatic poet; like all the great rebel dramatists, he draws his power from the clash of thesis and antithesis, always skirting a fake harmonious synthesis. Whether Brecht is examining the conflict of reason and instinct, vice and virtue, cowardice and heroism, adaptation and revolt, science and religion, Marxism and Neo-Romanticism, he almost invariably concentrates on the opposition rather than the resolution of his terms; and he even suggests that life is good because it is unresolved:

Humanity! Two souls abide
Within thy breast!
Do not set either one aside:
To live with both is best!
Be torn apart with constant care!
Be two in one! Be here, be there!
Hold the low one, hold the high one—
Hold the straight one, hold the sly one—
Hold the pair!

Even here, the content of the statement is being dissolved by its tone—the passage is a burlesque of Goethe's *Faust.* Brecht seems constitutionally incapable of creating a positive idea without somehow undermining it. Making parody a crucial element of his art, he finds his function in ridiculing the positive ideas of others—and himself; playing on incongruities, he invariably hedges his own commitment with a mocking, derisory, deflating irony.

Now irony, of course, is the literary device not of the political ideologue but of the free artist. And Brecht's derisive tone may explain why he has never been wholly accepted in Communist countries—and for that matter, in the democracies either. He is very rarely able to make those warm affirmations so beloved by the manipulators of culture on both sides of the iron curtain. Just as he mocks the sentimentality, humanitarianism, and idealism of the liberal West, so is he curiously reluctant to celebrate the "brighter side" of Communism, to create a "positive hero," or even to follow his own declared intention to depict man "as he might become." Brecht is more comfortable as a sceptic. "Scepticism moves mountains," he declares, and "Of all things certain the most certain is doubt." For Brecht, wariness and mistrust are scientific attitudes, essential to an impartial examination of the world. But they are also the qualities of a Socratic temperament, suspicious from the very beginning:

I gather some fellows around me towards evening:
We address each other as "gentlemen."
They put their feet up on my table
And say: things will improve. And I don't ask when.

("Concerning Poor B.B.")

How Brecht manages to maintain his scepticism, detachment, and irony while declaring his unquestioning allegiance to the Communist cause is one of the most skillful accomplishments of dramatic literature. But it is the achievement of a man who is split in half.

Few plays demonstrate so well how the split is transformed into the delicate equilibrium of art as ***The Threepenny Opera,*** that inspired collaboration between Brecht and the composer Kurt Weill. Along with Brecht's theory of the *Verfremdungseffekt,* this work is too well known to need discussion here; but one may note how at the end, with Macheath's sudden pardon by the Queen, the whole play, including its apparent ideological tendency, is inverted, the world is suddenly seen from the underside, and even Brecht's positive affirmations seem to come out backward. And one finally comes away from ***The Threepenny Opera*** unbalanced by contrasts, dislocated by contradictions, foundering in the shifting perspective—secure only in the author's unrelenting revolt as transmitted through his negative, ironic tone.

Much the same doubleness of vision and unity of tone can be found in ***Mother Courage,*** Brecht's masterpiece and, without doubt, one of the finest works of the modern theatre. Completed in 1939, when World War II is just beginning and Brecht is in exile in Scandinavia, ***Mother Courage*** ostensibly deals with the Thirty Years War, that seventeenth-century feast of death, fire, and pestilence. But its real subject is all wars, as seen from the perspective of one who loathes military heroism. This play, according to Bentley, can be partly construed as a reply to Schiller's *Wallenstein,* but it is also a reply to all works which glorify heroism or eulogize national ideals. Brecht has finally made the passive side of his nature the source of a positive position: that of a belligerent pacifism. He observes the exploits of war, like those of peace, from the underside, examining what Edmund Wilson has called "the self-assertive sounds" which man "utters when he is fighting and swallowing others." To achieve his satire on the morality of the military life, Brecht concentrates not on the battles but on the commonplace activities of day-to-day living, as performed by the war's orphans, truants, and subordinates. In the background of ***Mother Courage*** pass the victories, defeats, reversals, sieges, assaults, retreats, and advances which form the substance of history. In the foreground, the private lives of the noncombatants provide a non-heroic contrast. The external course of the conflict is narrated, like newspaper headlines, in the legends preceding each scene, but it interests Brecht only insofar as it influences local commerce: "General Tilley's victory at Leipzig," the title informs us, "costs Mother Courage four shirts."

For the real struggle is over money, food, and clothing. Brecht, still examining the relationship between capitalism and crime, is now applying his Marxist perceptions to the crimes of history itself. If the businessman is identified with the gangster in ***The Threepenny Opera,*** then he is identified with the warmaker in ***Mother Courage.*** Property is not only theft, but murder, rape, and pillage; war may be the extension of diplomacy but it is also an extension of free enterprise. Locked in endless combat, the Protestant Swedes and the Catholic Germans are told they are fighting for religious ideals, but like the Swedish King Gustavus, whose zeal was so great that he not only liberated Poland from the Germans but offered to liberate Germany as well, the crusading warlords usually make "quite a profit on the deal." Religious piety, jingo patriotism, bourgeois respectability, all are merely synonyms for greed, acquisition, and self-advancement. And since war is "just the same as trading," the morality which justifies it must be considered an evil sanction.

Seen from this perspective, heroism looks like a ghastly skeleton, rattling its bones in the wind; and in ***Mother Courage,*** heroic actions invariably stem either from stupidity, insanity, brutality, or simple human error. The spokesman for Brecht's anti-heroic point of view is Anna Fierling, the canteen woman known more familiarly as Mother Courage. Like so many of Brecht's rascally characters, this salty, cunning, self-serving woman has much in common with Falstaff; and like Falstaff, she functions as a satirical commentator and comic deflator. To her, the only quality worthy of respect is cowardice; and she commands respect herself because of her consistency—she invariably chooses the most selfish, ignominious, and profitable course. Even her nickname is ironic: her "courageous" breach of the lines during the bombardment at Riga was made to keep some loaves from going moldy. As the supreme advocate of adaptation and acquiescence, Courage is extremely cynical about the motives of others. She attributes the death of General Tilley, for example, to the fact that he got lost in a fog and strayed to the front by mistake. She is probably right. Brecht, in other words, gives us a Falstaff without a Hal or Hotspur. Courage's unhesitating assumption about the baseness of human motives belongs to the author; and it is not modified by any contrasting ideal.

Yet, Brecht's all-embracing cynicism implies an ideal, for he is rebelling against a reality he despises. **"The Song of the Great Capitulation"**—possibly the most moving lyric in the entire Brechtian canon—reveals the history behind Brecht's cynical attitudes. For here Mother Courage, trying to discourage an indignant soldier from endangering his safety, sings of the degeneration of her own rage against injustice. Beginning as a romantic individualist—"All or nothing. Anyway never take second best. I am the master of my fate. I'll take no orders from no one"—she eventually becomes the cautious compromiser, marching in time with the band: "You must get in with people. If you scratch my back, I'll scratch yours. Don't stick your neck out!" It is the story of how George Garga is eventually forced to repudiate his belief in freedom. And it may very well be the story of how Brecht abandons his early Romantic idealism under the pressure of internal passions and external constraints:

> Our plans are big, our hopes colossal.
> We hitch our wagon to a star.
> (Where there's a will, there's a way. You can't
> hold a good man down).
> "We can lift mountains," says the apostle.
> And yet: how heavy one cigar!

Lifting that cigar has become the whole ambition of Brecht's heroine: her sole purpose is to keep herself and her family safe and alive. In the fulfillment of this difficult and ultimately fruitless task, she employs ruthlessness, charm, bribery, guile, and simple horse sense, always true to her coward's creed that discretion is the better part of valor.

Mother Courage's bitter hostility to heroism has made her, paradoxically, a heroic figure to audiences—an image of the "little people," beleaguered by forces beyond their control, yet resiliently continuing to make their way. There is no question that Mother Courage—like Falstaff, who was meant to be a Vice figure (Sloth and Vanity) but who somehow transcended his morality play role—got away from the author. And like the rejection of Falstaff, the pathos of Courage does begin to take on larger dimensions. Nevertheless, one must also realize that Brecht *does* realize his conscious intentions with the character, and that the tragedy he unintentionally created co-exists with the morality play he designed. The responses evoked by Brecht's heroine are a good deal more complicated than those evoked, say, by the pathetic Nora Clitheroe, the heroine of another anti-war play, O'Casey's *Plough and the Stars;* Courage is not just a passive sufferer, playing on the sentiment of the audience, but also an active source of suffering. She may be a victim of the war, but she is also an instrument of the war, and the embodiment of its evils. Brecht's revolt, in short, remains double. Like Macheath, Mother Courage is both the agent of the author's rebellion and the thing rebelled against. Her determination to play it safe makes her the enemy of hypocrisy, but it also makes her cold and grasping. And though her singleminded devotion to survival is sympathetic in relation to her three children, it becomes mere aggrandizement in relation to her fourth child—the wagon. Thus, Mother Courage is no Noibe, all tears, but the author of her own destruction. One of those lower-class capitalists whom Brecht was always creating, she is, as the Chaplain tells her, a "hyena of the battlefield," and those who live by the war must die by it.

Mother Courage haggles while her children die—this is the spine of the play. For while Courage is pursuing commercial advantage, her family is sacrificed, one by one, to the war. Eric Bentley has already commented on the tripartite structure of the work where, at the end of three discrete sections, another child is laid on the war's altar. The offspring of three different fathers, Finnish Eilif, Swiss Cheese, and German Kattrin are an international brigade of victims. But it is not a supernatural agent which strikes the children down; it is the cruel hand of man, abetted by their own self-destroying instincts. In **"The Song of the Wise and the Good,"** Caesar's bravery is identified with Eilif 's heroism, Socrates' honesty with Swiss Cheese's incorruptibility, St. Martin's unselfishness with Kattrin's kindness, and Solomon's wisdom with Courage's shrewdness. The dominant qualities of both the great and the common lay them low; virtue doesn't pay: "God's Ten Commandments" have not "done us any good."

Brecht, however, cannot refrain from giving an ironic twist to his already ironic statement—for the "virtues" he describes are all, with the exception of Kattrin's kindness, highly dubious qualities. Eilif 's bravery, for example, is, at best, impulsive foolishness. While the Sergeant is cunningly distracting Courage's attention by bargaining with her over a belt, Eilif is off with the Recruiting Officer, pressed into war by his lust for glory. Eilif 's song, **"The Fishwife and the Soldier,"** predicts the outcome of such rashness, for it tells how a headstrong son is killed by his own bravery, despite all his mother's cautious warnings. Impulsiveness leads to death: "The lad is swept out by the tide: / He floats with the ice to the sea." Eilif soon drifts with the tide of death because he ignored his mother's advice to drift with the tide of life. Having "played the hero in God's own war" by slaughtering a number of innocent peasants who wished only to protect their cattle (here bravery turns into sadistic brutality), Eilif repeats this heroic exploit during an interlude of peace—and is led off to be shot. Like Chaplin's Verdoux, he discovers that virtues in wartime are considered crimes in peacetime, and that law and morality shift their ground to accommodate a nation's needs.

Swiss Cheese, the "honest child," is another victim of a dubious virtue. As paymaster of a Protestant regiment, he is entrusted with the cashbox; and when he is captured by the Catholics, he refuses to surrender it up. This kind of honesty, as Courage observes, is sheer stupidity: Swiss Cheese is too simpleminded to provide for his own safety. Here, however, Courage is in a position to save her child through the exercise of her Solomon-like wisdom: "They're not wolves," she observes of his Catholic captors, "they're human and after money. God is merciful and men are bribable." Her analysis of motive is perfectly accurate, but it is precisely because of her excessive shrewdness that the device does not work. Forced to pawn her wagon to obtain sufficient bribe money, Courage is anxious to reserve enough for her own security. But the Catholics are in a hurry, and her prolonged bargaining is climaxed by the terrible realization, "I believe—I haggled too long." Swiss Cheese, the significance of his name finally clear, is carried in on a stretcher riddled by eleven bullets—to be thrown on a garbage heap because his mother is afraid to claim the body.

Kattrin is Courage's only truly virtuous child, the soul of kindness and the most positive figure in the play. It is a characteristic of Brecht's attitude towards positive values that she is a mute; but through her expressive gestures and responses, the cruelty and horror of the war are most eloquently told. Even her dumbness is related to these terrors—"a soldier stuck something in her mouth when she was little." Because of her muteness, her serenity, and her love of children, Kattrin sometimes achieves allegorical stature—she is much like Aristophanes' Peace, blinded, gagged, raped, and buried by war. But Brecht's war is endless; and, unlike Aristophanes' mute figure, Kattrin is led to enjoy no hymeneal banquet at the end. Instead of being pulled out of the pit, she is hurled into one: the war buries Kattrin for all time. Courtesans like the camp follower, Yvette, may thrive on conflict, for Yvette accepts the whore's barrenness, so much like that of the war. But Kattrin is *Kindernkarr,* children-crazy, and it is her consuming love for these fruits of Peace that finally destroys her.

Once again, the death occurs because the mother is haggling. Having successfully resisted the temptation to leave Kattrin behind and find a secure berth with her lover, the Cook, Courage is, nevertheless, still looking after her profits: she has left Kattrin with the wagon while she buys stocks cheap from the frightened townspeople. While she is gone, the Catholics capture a farmhouse, preparing for an ambush of the town. The farmers, afraid for their family in the town, appeal to God to save their four grandchildren. But, to their horror, their prayers for once are answered. Moved by the mention of children in danger, Kattrin has climbed to the roof of the farmhouse, where she begins to beat her drum. At last, Peace has found a tongue, rhythmically commenting on its ancient invincile enemy. To smother the sounds of this alarum, the soldiers and peasants try to create their own noises—peaceful ones, they begin to chop wood. Yet, Kattrin's drumming mounts in intensity, and in desperation. When a lieutenant offers to spare her mother if she descends from the roof, Kattrin drums more heatedly; when he backs his promise with his word of honor, she drums most furiously of all. The smashing of the wagon, the knifing of a sympathetic peasant, the threat to her own life—nothing stops this desperate tattoo. She is finally shot off the roof by a hail of musketry; but the town is saved.

The episode is simple, startling, magnificent, with a mounting emotional crescendo created primarily through the use of drumbeats. But the catharsis it accomplishes, so rare in Brecht's drama, is followed, almost immediately, by grim, cooling irony. Kattrin's sacrifice has really been in vain. The town is saved, but the sound which signifies this is the explosion of a cannon. The war will continue for another twelve years; and after this war is finished, three hundred more years of killing will follow.

Brought on stage for the *threnos,* Courage witnesses the utter desolation of her hopes. The fault, again, has partially been hers ("If you hadn't gone off to get your cut," says an old peasant, "maybe it wouldn't have happened"), but she is too dazed now to know it. Thinking that Kattrin is only asleep, she sings her a lullaby; even the lullaby concerns the need for clothing and food. Her sustaining illusion is that Eilif may still be alive. Without this illusion, only nothingness confronts her—the inconsolable blankness of life, induced by a malignant universe, inhuman men, and her own flawed nature. We are out of the world of Falstaffian comedy and into the desolate world of *King Lear;* but unlike Lear, Brecht's heroine is denied even the release of death. When the armies move by, singing her song about the certainty of the seasons and the certainty of man's mortality—the coming of the springtime of life before the winter of death—she cries to them: "Hey, take me with you"—and straps herself to the wagon. She is pulling it alone now, but it is no longer very heavy: supplies and passengers have all been destroyed. Courage and the wagon merge—both bruised and battered by war, both somehow still durable. Courage has dragged it over half of Europe, learning nothing. She will drag it a good deal further before she stops, animated only by that basic life instinct: the need to survive. The smallness and the greatness of this woman are clear at the end, as they are clear throughout this monumental work, where Brecht so angrily takes away from the human race—and gives it back so much.

Mother Courage is the culminating work of Brecht's career, but it is hardly the end of it. During the war and after, in exile and back in East Berlin, Brecht continues to create a profusion of plays—including at least one masterpiece, ***The Caucasian Chalk Circle.*** But after ***Mother Courage,*** Brecht's savage indignation begins to leave him, his rebellion progressively cools. Even as his plays become more openly Communistic in subject matter, his approach grows more sweet and even-tempered. Virtuous, maternal women like Kattrin—Shen Te, Simone Machard, Grusha—move in to the center of the action, while his secondary characters develop deeper dimensions, and more complex motivations than simple greed and lust. Instead of castigating humanity, Brecht is beginning to celebrate it; instead of illustrating his themes through ironic comparisons, he is beginning to employ moral allegories and parables. Brecht's later approach to character and his use of less exaggerated comparisons suggest how he is losing his need to rebel against reality; as further proof, Nature has returned to his work—no longer hostile and ugly, but calm, serene, and even beautiful. Less sardonic, more relaxed, Brecht grows more lyrical and carefree; in fact, if Brecht's first period is Büchnerian, and his second Jonsonian, then his third is clearly Shakespearean—some of his plays have an atmosphere akin to Shakespeare's romantic comedies. Even Brecht's theory is loosening up from the rigid didacticism of his early days. In that latter-day Poetics, ***The Little Organon For the Theatre*** (1948), Brecht finally permits himself to speak of "entertainment" in the drama, an element he used to scorn as hypnotic and culinary; and he even expresses the ideological heresy that "the easiest form of existence is in art."

"A contemplative attitude," notes Ronald Gray, "is thus yoked with the revolutionary one that Brecht still maintained." And this contemplative attitude, we should add, is the final development of Brecht's existential revolt. While Brecht has remained a Marxist, he has finally transcended his Neo-Romantic horror at life. Brecht's contemplative interests are underlined by his increasing interest in Oriental forms, characters, and subject matter—a large proportion of his poems and plays are now inspired by the East. It is true that Brecht is attracted to the Noh play, the Chinese drama, and the Kabuki theatre because of their alienation techniques; and like Yeats, he uses conventions like masks, mime, dance, and gesture in order to restore that naiveté and simplicity that the over-sophisticated Western theatre has lost. Still, Brecht has a very special philosophical affinity with the drama of the Orient, for it is a drama of submission, in which the characters recognize a universal intelligence and try to merge with it, freeing themselves of worldly desire.

As proof, Brecht's interest in the Oriental drama is accompanied, during this last period, by an interest in the Eastern religious thinkers: Confucius, Buddha, Lao-Tse, the philosophers of obedience through the annihilation of the physical self. It is probable that, with the advance of age, Brecht had finally subdued his troublesome passions. No longer harried by appetite, he gives himself up to that drifting and merging which he desired all his life. Like Strindberg, in short, Brecht works his way through, after a career of fierce rebellion, to a position of resignation; at last, he achieves that security and serenity he associates with the mother's womb. In a late poem, **"Buddha's Parable of the Burning House,"** Brecht returns to that recurrent water image of passive suspension. Buddha has preached the doctrine of the wheel of desire, and advised "That we shed all craving and thus / Undesiring enter the nothingness that he called Nirvana"; and a student, trying to understand the doctrine, has compared Nirvana with floating in water, wondering whether the sensation is pleasing or "*kalt, leer, und bedeutunglos*" (cold, empty, and meaningless). Buddha replies with his famous parable of those who, while their house was burning, wondered what the weather was like outside; and Brecht, at the end of the poem, applies this lesson to those who would resist Communist revolution, wondering whether it was good. Brecht's desire for revolt is still satisfied by his identification with Communism; but his desire for peace is now expressed through images of Oriental calm. Brecht, therefore, comes to terms with life only by continuing to reject it—by drifting with a political tide, he overcomes his spiritual horror and nausea. And this is the only synthesis of Brecht's double revolt. Only by merging with evil did he feel he could still function for good; only by embracing the destroyers could he still join the ranks of the creators. The chicanery and compromises Brecht accepted for the sake of the survival of himself and his art are not always very attractive. And no modern playwright better exemplifies the dwindling possibilities of revolt in an age of totalitarianism, war, and the mass state. But if Brecht sometimes sacrificed his personal integrity to a collective falsehood, then this was in order that his individualism could still be secretly expressed. His drama remains the final measurement of this achievement—acts of bitterness which did not quench his cigar but rather kept it aglow. (pp. 29-54)

Robert Brustein, "Brecht against Brecht," in Partisan Review, *Vol. XXX, No. 1, Spring, 1963, pp. 29-54.*

J. L. Styan (essay date 1981)

[*Styan is an English educator and critic who has written several studies of the theater, including the three-volume* Modern Drama in Theory and Practice *(1981). In the following excerpt from that work, he surveys Brecht's career and major plays, tracing the development of his dramaturgy and judging him "the outstanding example in modern times of a theatre artist who believed it necessary for every area of stagecraft to undergo a regular, radical rethinking."*]

Bertolt Brecht (1898–1956) entered the German theatre as one of a number of young playwrights at a time when stage production was in a whirl of experiment: realism was crumbling and new approaches were being put to the test. . . . [Brecht] acknowledged a special debt to Piscator and his idea of epic theatre; the two men worked together at the Volksbühne over the period 1919 to 1930, and Brecht had a hand in the famous production of *The Good Soldier Schweik.* Yet Brecht was also one of Reinhardt's assistants in his Deutsches Theater complex for a time, and was able to watch rehearsals for the great seasons of 1924–5 and 1925–6. In these years Reinhardt experimented with acting as role-playing, having the players mingle with the spectators as he had done for *Danton's Death* in 1916 and 1921. This was also the time when Reinhardt was trying out Pirandellian non-illusory devices, with actors stepping out of the play in *Six Characters in Search of an Author,* or improvising the action in Goldoni's *The Servant of Two Masters* as if they were a *commedia dell'arte* troupe. In addition to these great influences on Brecht's work, there were other powerful interests—in the energetic, scatalogical Wedekind, and in the recently rediscovered Büchner, a young revolutionary like Brecht himself, whose techniques in *Woyzeck* supplied exciting precedents for his early writing. And during this same period the young Brecht was avidly educating himself in every form of ritual playwriting he could find in Greek and Elizabethan drama.

Like others before him, Brecht would rebel not only against the ponderous style of German realism, but also against Reinhardt's baroque manner and the fever of the new expressionists. The expressionist hero had been messianic, a man of incredible vision, a poet—but at his worst a pompous ass. Brecht's disillusionment moved him to prick the expressionist idealism by substituting the *Gummimensch,* the 'rubber man', as an anti-hero. Such a one is a Kragler, the returning solder of ***Trommeln in der Nacht*** (*Drums in the Night,* 1922), who decides that the better part of valour is to make do with the pregnant girl who was unfaithful to him. As both a stage director and a playwright, Brecht was always watching his own and other experiments, borrowing and rejecting, modifying theory with practice, changing his ideas as each new production was conceived and tested. And during his career, Brecht never ceased to return to the past, particularly to the plays of Shakespeare and the eighteenth century, for material which seemed adaptable to his method and suitable for his themes. His many attempts to apply a didactic; and often political, ideology to the stage consequently resulted in a major new aesthetic for the theatre, one which has since proved eminently acceptable to the sceptical spirit of our time. What follows is a summary of Brecht's general approach to drama, although in fact he evolved it over many years.

Brecht's work embodied Piscator's way of epic theatre. Although Brecht inclined towards the more closed, 'parable' play which focused on a moral dilemma, his was still a narrative form, telling a story by the use of illustrative scenes, choruses and commentators, songs and dances, projected titles and summaries, and making use of much of the mechanical apparatus Piscator held dear. Brecht's special contribution was to envisage a particular role for the actor in all this, using him to help destroy conventional illusion. It was the actor's task to put himself 'at a distance' from the character he was portraying and the situation he was involved with, in order to arouse a thinking, enquiring response in the spectator.

Brecht's essay **'The Street Scene'** provides the basic explanation of this approach. We are to imagine a traffic accident involving a driver and a pedestrian, together with a bystander on a street corner who witnessed what happened. When he tries to explain the accident to others afterwards, the bystander re-enacts what the driver and the pedestrian did so that they can judge for themselves. This kind of performance can be good theatre without having to be the traditional artistic 'event'. The demonstrator is not asked to give a perfect imitation of those who were involved in the accident, nor is he required to cast a spell over his listeners. He is merely reporting the incident, and no illusion of reality is necessary. Thus epic theatre is at bottom non-illusory. It does not disguise the fact that it is only a piece of theatre. Performance will make it clear that lines have been learned, action rehearsed, stage equipment made ready.

Feelings and emotions may well be part of the experience for the audience, but the actor is not asked to convey them himself. Instead, just as in 'the street scene', the activity will have a social purpose—perhaps to show who is guilty, or how to avoid such an accident in the future. The purpose served must justify the effort made. Brecht's epic theatre, like Piscator's, aimed therefore at a political examination of society and its working elements, like the class structure or the economic system. Brecht would produce *'Lehrstücke'* or 'teaching plays', and 'insofar as they are good theatre, they will amuse': he cited with approval Schiller's dictum that there was no reason why a concern for morality should not be thoroughly enjoyable. Brecht's was to be a didactic theatre for the scientific age, and he saw drama as a critique of life, a critique which he increasingly embodied in the structure of his plays.

The actor was to make clear to his audience his *'Gestus'* or demonstrable social attitude, his basic disposition. He would derive his 'character' from the actions of the person he portrayed, not, as is usual in drama, the actions from the character, which procedure 'shields actions from criticism'. And if the actor was to do his work objectively, he would speak with a certain reserve or distance, or repeat an action slowly, or stop to explain to the audience what he was doing. By this behaviour the actor would create the desirable *'Verfremdungseffekt',* the 'alienation effect' of epic theatre. In a play which is distanced in this way, a transition in the action from presentation to commentary, and vice versa, is characteristic and constant.

So it was that acting as 'impersonation', even the purpose of acting as 'imitation' in Aristotle's sense, was supplanted by acting that was 'gestic' and 'epic'. Epic acting is acting that is intended to be entirely natural, and Roland Barthes has pointed out that 'the verisimilitude of [epic] acting has its meaning in the objective meaning of the *play,* and not, as in "naturalist" dramaturgy, in the truth inherent in the actor' (*Tulane Drama Review,* 37)—the actor's reference point was always to be the meaning of the play. Brecht's method was therefore diametrically opposed to that of Stanislavsky and the drama of realistic illusion. Brecht's stage was to be stripped of its theatrical magic, and the audience refused the state of emotional, empathetic trance, a degrading condition he associated with what he called the 'Aristotelian' theatre.

The idea of distancing lay at the very centre of Brecht's theory, although it grew in importance only gradually, until it was seen as essential for the inducement of a proper critical attitude in the spectator. As early as 1920, he wrote a note that 'humour is a sense of distance' (*Distanzgefühl*). He then made use of the Marxist term *'Entfremdung'* or 'alienation', and sometimes *'Fremdheit'* or 'strangeness', but after a visit to Moscow in 1935, when he saw a performance of Mei Lan-fang's Chinese company, he virtually coined the word *'Verfremdung'* to identify the quality he recognized more clearly. Brecht saw that the symbolic Chinese theatre never pretended there was no audience, and in his essay 'Alienation Effects in Chinese Acting' he compared this kind of theatre with 'the acrobat who will glance at us for approval'. The Chinese actor conveyed passion without having to be passionate himself, and he was at all times in control, as in a ritualistic performance.

As the theory developed, Brecht argued that all theatre artists, from the writer to the lighting engineer, should work together to induce the distancing effect and make the performance truly objective. This idea, however, had nothing to do with the old Wagnerian unity of the arts. In epic theatre each artist was to make a *separate* contribution.

1. *The actor,* as we have seen, would 'show' rather than imitate, and Brecht advocated a number of rehearsal devices to encourage this: the actor would speak in the third person, or in the past tense, or even speak the stage directions (as in, 'He stood up and, since he had nothing to eat, said angrily . . . ') Gesture would consciously indicate his inner feeling, as if the actor were visibly observing his own movements. Direct address to the audience would be complete, unlike the traditionally hasty aside.

2. *The designer* of the set, following Piscator, would dispense with illusion and symbolism, and build according to the actor's needs. There would be no suggestion of a 'fourth wall', and, except for props, the stage would be bare, merely an open space on which to tell a story. Set changes would be made in full view of the audience, and if there had to be a curtain, it would simply be strung on a string across the stage. In this way stage and audience would be joined, not separated, and speaking directly to the house would be encouraged.

3. *The playwright* would structure his play episodically, preceding each scene with a written title, which would remain in position until replaced by another one, and offer an 'historical' account of the action of the scene. 'Historicization' was another of Brecht's concepts that was closely related to distancing—encouraging an awareness that an event had happened as if in the past, making the present look strange.

4. *The director* would arrange the blocking or grouping of the actors on the stage, not merely to achieve some formal beauty of good composition, but essentially to clarify the structure of human relationships in the play.

5. *The lighting designer* would abandon the idea of hiding the sources of light to achieve a mysterious effect that would draw the audience into the action. Instead, his apparatus would be perfectly visible, so that the spectator would be conscious he was in a theatre. The stage itself would be lit with a plain white light so that the actor would seem to be in the same world as the audience.

6. *The composer* of the music should express his idea of the play's theme independently, and so provide a separate comment on the action, which might often be in conflict with the activity of the characters. Unlike opera, in which aria and recitative are continuous, and music is used to reinforce the text, an epic production would have music and song which was in counterpoint with the action on the stage. At one time, Paul Dessau inserted tacks into the hammers of his piano to make it sound like another speaking voice.

Certain of Brecht's earlier plays mark out his rapid development as an epic playwright. His first, ***Baal*** (1918), was a play of extraordinary maturity. It was written when Brecht was a medical student at Munich, and planned as a riposte to Hanns Johst's expressionistic idealism in *Der Einsame* (*The Lonely One,* 1917). Johst's play on the life of the playwright Christian Dietrich Grabbe had irritated Brecht with its exalted tone, its precious language and its cliché image of human suffering. ***Baal*** was also a play expressing moral indignation, but its central character, ironically named after the fertility god, was designed to be an obscenely anti-social and selfish hedonist, as a way of having him resist the demands of an anti-social world—an interesting forerunner of the characters Puntila and Azdak. The play was clearly conceived to shock and repel, yet it might be said to be lyrical in its arrangement of poetic interludes, and even in its callous, colloquial dialogue.

Baal opens with a mock expressionistic 'Chorale of the Great Baal', which is followed by twenty-two expressionistic scenes and ballads telling the hero's story. He is a ruthless cynic, drunken and sensual, and he spends much of his time in bar-rooms singing to a guitar. He seduces a series of women, one of whom, Johanna, becomes pregnant and kills herself when Baal turns her away. He also has a homosexual lover in his friend Ekart, whom he later murders in jealousy. Declaring the world to be 'the excrement of God', Baal finally dies in a filthy hovel in the Black Forest, ignored by the foresters who live there. Brecht loads his lines with the bestial imagery of feeding, sex and evacuating, and his poet without a conscience meets a fitting end in a dirty world.

Baal was first produced in Leipzig in 1923, and received a major production in Vienna in 1926 with Oscar Homolka in the title role. Needless to say, the play made no sense to its first audiences and was totally misunderstood. We can see now that Brecht was using his monstrous portrait of Baal to suggest ironically the larger one of modern man living a life of self-interest. Peter Ferran has suggested that in this treatment already lay the later Brechtian concept of a character's *Gestus,* and as a symbolic figure Brecht's Baal was as romantic in his way as Johst's Grabbe. Five years later, ***The Threepenny Opera*** would be equally misunderstood, but with more profitable results for its author.

Brecht's gifts as a writer of dramatic verse and prose showed themselves strongly in ***Baal.*** The telegraphic style of expressionistic drama, made up of punctuated 'poetic' utterances, was radically changed. Brecht wrote in a realistic mixture of dialect and slang, with every line composed with its delivery in mind, capturing in tone and rhythm the exact quality of vitality intended in the speaker. Brecht's sense of the stage emerged particularly in his growing ability to write *gestische Sprache,* 'gestic language', which made the lines physically actable and conveyed the basic posture and attitude of the speaker as well.

In Brecht's second play, ***Trommeln in der Nacht*** (***Drums in the Night,*** 1922), the epic theatre's use of placards and signs begins to appear; for the Munich production which won him the Kleist prize, slogans were posted in the auditorium. But the first play to embody epic characteristics with any rigour was ***Mann ist Mann*** (***A Man's a Man***), an anti-war comedy first produced in Darmstadt and Düsseldorf in 1926. It was revised for production at the Berlin Volksbühne in 1928 and at the Berlin Staatstheater in 1931, where it was directed by Brecht himself with Peter Lorre and Brecht's wife Helene Weigel in the chief parts.

A Man's a Man is a frankly didactic play full of the tricks of the circus, the cabaret and the music hall, devices which dispelled the last traces of expressionistic idealism and soul-suffering. Set in British imperial India, its ballads are cheeky parodies of Kipling, and its central character, the good-natured dock labourer Galy Gay is, in Eric Bentley's view, an elephantine mixture of Falstaff and Chaplin. It is Galy Gay who, by a series of misadventures, is persuaded to impersonate a missing machine-gunner at roll call, and who, in the course of the play's eleven scenes, is transformed into a 'human fighting machine'. With the new name of Jeriah Jip, he becomes the perfect soldier who single-handedly destroys a fortress in Tibet:

> A man's a man, says Mr Bertolt Brecht
> And that is hardly more than you'd expect.
>
> But Mr Bertolt Brecht goes on to show
> That you can change a man from top to toe.
> (translated Gerhard Nellhaus)

Galy Gay's counterpart is Sergeant Bloody Five, a Kipling caricature, the 'Tiger of Kilkoa', the 'Human Typhoon', who acquired his name by shooting five Hindu prisoners without a qualm. A typical sergeant when the sun shines, Bloody Five is consumed by lust when it rains; furious at his own lack of self-control, he castrates himself with a pistol. In these two characters we see Brecht's early propensity to split his creations into two, as he does with Shen Te and Shui Ta in ***The Good Woman of Setzuan.***

A Man's a Man was received with mixed and uncertain reviews, and was criticized for its lack of well-made suspense and its failure to supply a character, even Galy Gay, with whom the audience could sympathize. The play's vision of a man as a cipher, both weak and cruel, and forced to conform to the requirements of society, was obscured. The point was made in John Hancock's production in New York in 1962, when everyone in the play wore a white mask except Galy Gay, who nevertheless little by little acquired one of his own before the last scene. ***A Man's a Man*** was Brecht's first play to extend the idea of a character by the use of a mask; others later were ***Die Massnahme*** (***The Measures Taken***), ***Die Rondköpfe und die Spitzköpfe*** (***Roundheads and Peakheads***), ***The Good Woman of Setzuan*** and ***The Caucasian Chalk Circle.***

The play which brought Brecht world-wide attention, and which possibly exemplifies his early epic manner best, was ***Die Dreigroschenoper*** (***The Threepenny Opera,*** 1928). Inspired by Nigel Playfair's success with John Gay's *The Beggar's Opera* at the Lyric Theatre, Hammersmith, 1920–3, Brecht asked Elisabeth Hauptmann to translate the text into German, and he had found another English play for epic adaptation, having previously treated Marlowe's *Edward II* in 1924. He changed Gay's eighteenth-century scene to one of late nineteenth-century Soho in London, and with Caspar Neher as designer and Kurt Weill as composer, the new play ran for 400 performances at the Theater am Schiffbauerdamm in Berlin. It was subsequently made into a film in parallel German and French versions by G. W. Pabst in 1931, although Brecht fought a legal battle to have it suppressed because he considered the film too light weight. This film nevertheless remains our best film record of the early epic style. ***The Threepenny Opera*** was also produced at the Kamerny Theatre, Moscow in 1930, at the Théâtre Montparnasse, Paris in 1930 and at the Empire Theatre, New York in 1933, but London, the source of the play's original inspiration, did not see it until 1956, when it was produced at the Royal Court Theatre by Sam Wanamaker.

Where Gay had particular political targets for his delight-

Kurt Weill, who composed the score for Brecht's popular Threepenny Opera.

ful burlesque opera, Brecht attacked capitalism generally. There is war in the underworld of London when the thief Macheath and Peachum the receiver fall out. Peachum is 'The Beggar's Friend', supplying thieves with disguises as beggars—the Moscow production introduced the amusing idea of having normal men and women enter Peachum's shop on one side, only to emerge on the other as human derelicts. Macheath marries Peachum's daughter Polly, setting up the wedding in style with stolen furniture. But Peachum is angry, and betrays Macheath to the police. The law then appears in the person of Chief of Police 'Tiger' Brown (Gay's Lockit). Lucy, Brown's daughter, helps Macheath to escape, but he is again arrested when he is found frequenting his favourite brothel, and this time his neck is put in the noose. For a satirical conclusion, Macheath is given a pardon by the Queen, together with a handsome pension. In Pabst's film, he becomes a bank president.

The characters in Brecht's play are criminals as a kind of self-defence. Crime is seen to be a capitalistic enterprise, and Peachum and Macheath have all the bourgeois virtues. Peachum sees poverty as a way of making money, and Macheath is a businessman who does not want his business disrupted, like Mother Courage in a later play. The satire lies in reproducing these attitudes in a criminal setting, and the image of corruption is complete when Macheath is given his royal pardon. However, audiences found it aesthetically satisfying to recognize an allegory which embraced both higher and lower classes, and merely to equate capitalists with gangsters did not have the caustic effect Brecht wanted. As a result, the play was popular with fashionable middle-class audiences everywhere.

In spite of this, there are many important technical advances in ***The Threepenny Opera.*** The curtain appeared to be nothing but a dirty sheet drawn on a string across the stage. A fair-ground organ stood at the back of the stage, with a jazz band on the steps in front of it. Coloured lights lit up when the music played. Free use was made of titles and drawings projected on screens in red satin frames on either side of the organ, and mock-religious signs were pinned on Peachum's walls, such as, 'It is more blessed to give than to receive' and 'Give and it shall be given unto you'. By these means, the audience was persuaded to practise Brecht's notion of 'complex seeing'. And just as Gay made fun of the tradition of Italian opera, so the nineteen songs in ***The Threepenny Opera,*** based more on François Villon than on John Gay, were carefully planned to counter Wagnerian principles of music-drama: Brecht asked that setting, story and music should be 'mingled without mixing', each element making its own statement. In the production Brecht also developed the technique of having the actor speak against the music, and in his notes he insisted that the actor must not only sing, but 'show a man singing'. His experience in this play encouraged him in the composition of the operatic ***Happy End*** (the original title, 1929), which failed, and of ***Aufstieg und Fall der Stadt Mahagonny*** (***Rise and Fall of the City of Mahagonny,*** 1930), which enjoyed a *succès de scandale,* with riots, whistling and applause descending on the performance in every German city where it was played. These plays also cemented the collaboration between Brecht and Kurt Weill, and prepared the way for the total integration of theatrical elements in the mature masterpieces which followed. (pp. 139-49)

. . . . .

From the time Brecht left Hitler's Germany in 1933 until his return to East Berlin in 1948—fifteen years of exile which he spent in Switzerland, Denmark, Sweden, Finland, the United States, again Switzerland and finally Austria—this essentially pragmatic playwright was without a regular company to try out his plays. Yet these were the years of his masterpieces, ***Leben des Galilei*** (***Life of Galileo,*** written 1938–9), ***Mutter Courage und ihre Kinder*** (***Mother Courage and Her Children,*** written 1939), ***Der gute Mensch von Sezuan*** (***The Good Woman of Setzuan,*** written 1938–40) and ***Der Kaukasische Kreidekreis*** (***The Caucasian Chalk Circle,*** written 1943–5). The years 1941–7 in America, where 'The Method' was in the ascendancy and where epic theatre and its strange ways were meaningless, were largely lost to him. So he thought of his plays as *'Versuche',* 'attempts' or 'experiments', and restlessly he picked at his plays, wrote and rewrote them, knowing they were untried and hence unfinished. And he also resorted to the extensive writing of dramatic theory. No other playwright of this century has written so much about his work, and so his exile was not without a legacy.

Never was there a better opportunity to raise the issue of judging intentions by results, although in the last twenty years of his life, his theories grew increasingly tentative and open-ended.

Brecht's most important statement of theory during these years was the ***Kleines Organon für das Theater*** (***A Short Organum for the Theatre***), written near Zürich in Switzerland in 1948 and published in Potsdam in 1949. To this essay should be added a number of appendices which Brecht left after his death. Taken together, these statements may be taken as Brecht's mature aesthetic of the theatre. They constituted a final modification of the epic idea, and embraced the developing concept of what he called *'dialektisches Theater'*, 'dialectical theatre'.

Brecht reaffirmed his earlier idea of social purpose, the commitment of a theatre 'fit for the scientific age'. The ***Kleines Organon*** again attacked popular contemporary drama as 'a branch of the narcotics business', but the difference now was that the attack did not conflict with a revised notion of the theatre as entertainment. The 'critical attitude' and the 'solution of problems' were taken to be pleasurable. Otherwise the former complaint was heard again that current theatre induced a state of emotional trance, a form of sleep. What was needed was a theatre which would release impulses to transform 'the particular historical field of human relations' with which a play might be dealing.

To ensure that significant social impulses were visible in the characters and their actions, a special kind of acting was needed, one based on the alienation effect. Here Brecht returned comfortably to the acting and production technique he had spent his life focusing upon. His final definition was reduced to:

> A representation that alienates is one which allows us to recognize its subject, but at the same time makes it seem unfamiliar (translated John Willett).

The actor's movement, gesture and speech must be 'matter-of-fact', so that he would not wholly assume the character he was playing, and so that the audience would not easily empathize with him. The action would be performed as if it were an experiment, a demonstration, and on stage the difference between the actor and the character he was playing would be readily apparent. Today we should say that Brecht's actor was 'role-playing'.

Brecht's actor would have a viewpoint of his own, a social attitude, which would affect his posture, voice and facial expression. This was the former idea of *'Gestus'*. It was the 'story' of the play, what happened between people, that would provide the material for the audience to 'discuss, criticize, alter'. So, too, the structure of a play would be episodic, like a chronicle, to give the audience the chance to interpose its judgment. Indeed, all the theatre arts would work in their different ways to tell the story, but they would relate to one another in 'mutual alienation'.

So Brecht felt less need to write didactic 'teaching plays'. At the same time he began to drop his use of the term 'epic', and at the end identified as 'dialectical' the kind of process by which he planned a scene to induce the critical attitude. This development went along with his recognition of his own inability to bring about a completely distancing effect, and the discrepancy between theory and practice seems most glaring in the last plays. He riddled them with techniques of alienation, and yet in 1940 he admitted that German productions acted in the alienated manner had resulted in strong emotional responses. It seems that the spectator soon adjusts his perception to the new techniques, and is liable to find sympathy for a character even when it is not intended. Nevertheless, Brecht's great contribution to modern drama lay in his constant insight into the incongruities and contradictions of human motive, and his ironic approach to the material of his plays could produce an acute sense of ambivalence in his audience. Irony and ambivalence remained to the end the source of vitality in his drama.

When he returned to East Berlin, Brecht reunited many of the actors who had been dispersed by the war, and in 1949 he founded the Berliner Ensemble. This company, run by Helene Weigel (1900-72), found a home in Brecht's pre-war Theater am Schiffbauerdamm, which became the company's own in 1954. According to an eyewitness, George Devine, it also found a dedicated audience, one which gave the productions 'an air of religious ritual'. It remains a question, however, whether Brecht ever found the audience of workers, either in Berlin or elsewhere, that he was working for, but at least the creation of the Berliner Ensemble finally gave him the chance to try out his theories using his own actors and his own stage and an audience he knew. It was the achievement of this company in the short time before Brecht's death in 1956 that has provided a unique example of epic theatre in performance.

In these excellent new circumstances, Brecht tested his scenes again and again in rehearsal, trying a variety of alternative ways, rewriting as the rehearsal, trying a variety of alternative ways, rewriting as the rehearsal progressed, arranging the actors so that the stage composition told the story, taking as many as nine months to put a play together. The disposition and movement of a scene's characters over the acting space generally provided the key to the point of the action, and at any significant moment would almost suggest a moral tableau in the manner of a Victorian domestic melodrama. It became important to find a way of keeping as careful a record of rehearsal decisions as possible.

The details of some of Brecht's productions have consequently been kept in what he called a *'Modellbuch'*, a stage record that was far more than the usual prompt book or even a Reinhardt *Regiebuch.* It not only contained the patterns of movement and the positions of the actors as evolved by the director in rehearsal, but it also filed hundreds of photographs of each scene in performance, together with a detailed commentary explaining the principles behind the action. These *Modellbücher* reflected Brecht's scrupulous attention to detail and his concern for the exact word and gesture needed to achieve the effect he wanted. When challenged with the criticism that these records might limit the work of other directors who wished to produce the same plays, he retorted that any director would naturally wish to begin where his predecessor had left off. Brecht was here, of course, indicating his own way of working.

Unfortunately perhaps, Brecht set such a standard, and followed so idiosyncratic a path, that subsequent directors could not readily take his advice and begin where he left off. Yet their inability or unwillingness to carry out all that Brecht's idea of epic theatre demanded may have been fortunate in another way. Those directors all over the world who tried to follow him in the 1960s were compelled to accommodate the epic method to the demands of their separate audiences and their own native traditions, and this resulted in a rather more versatile treatment of Brecht's plays in the contemporary theatre than the existence of a *Modellbuch* would suggest. Purists in the Brechtian camp may groan, but the more various treatment of the masterpieces may have proved that they can survive all manner of handling as other great plays have before them.

Galileo was the most rewritten of Brecht's plays. With three versions completed over seventeen years, the revisions themselves tell the story of his development towards a dialectical drama. A first version was written in Denmark in 1938-9, and had a successful production by German refugee actors directed by Leonard Steckel in the Zürich Schauspielhaus in 1943, when the author was in America. A second version was written in English in an extraordinary collaboration with the actor Charles Laughton between 1944 and 1947. The only language the two men had in common was that of the stage itself, and a brilliantly stageworthy dialogue, as well as some radical changes in the scenes, emerged from their mutual attempt to communicate with each other by miming and demonstration. They did not hesitate to manipulate historical fact to emphasize Galileo's social betrayal, and made class differences between characters more pointed. In 1947 this version was given twelve performances in the Coronet Theatre, Beverly Hills, Los Angeles and twelve in the Maxine Elliott Theatre, New York, with Joseph Losey directing and Hanns Eisler composing the music. But the style was unfamiliar, and the notices were bad. The shape of the play was considered to be 'rambling and episodic', and lacking in any emotional peaks. Even Laughton's performance, popular as he was as a screen actor, was found to be baffling. The apparatus of alienation remained a mystery, and its challenges dismissed. A third version of ***Galileo,*** which drew upon both of the others for a final text, was begun in 1953, and had a production in Cologne in 1955 and in East Berlin in 1956.

The object of Brecht's dramaturgy in this play, and the source of the spectator's unease, is a duality in the central character. The play was written against the growing terror of atomic warfare, and Brecht was anxious that Galileo should not be the idealized scholar and scientist of history, the 'stargazer' remote from reality, but an ordinary man with earth-bound responsibilities. Indeed, Brecht chose this subject because in spite of Galileo's scientific discoveries it was hard to ignore the fact of his apparently shameful recantation when he was threatened with torture and death by the Inquisition. While it remains ambiguous whether this recantation was an act of cowardice or one of cunning, since Galileo's survival enabled him to carry on his work and smuggle a copy of the *Discorsi* out of the country, Brecht was at pains to stress that to recant was to rob science of its social importance, and permit the Church to reassert its primitive power over the people of that age. This he emphasized in revision: in the first version Galileo was shown to be carrying on his work in secret, but in the two later revisions he was represented as more and more unscrupulous, anti-social and even criminal.

The scenes in ***Galileo*** are therefore planned to secure ambivalent, dialectical, responses from the audience. Galileo is at once the great scientist, and the thief who steals the concept of the telescope from Holland. He goes to Florence to make some money 'to fill his belly', and yet while he is there he courageously defies the plague in order to continue his studies. More than this, every detail of characterization is introduced to fill out the character of Galileo as a complete human being. He is the sensualist whom we first see stripped to the waist as he enjoys his wash in cool water; it gives him pleasure to have his back rubbed. He enjoys drinking his milk, as well as his wine. As an old man he is still the glutton who greedily consumes a goose, that greasiest of birds. He shows up badly as a teacher, and when his work is interruped by a student, he betrays his irritation. As a father, be behaves unfeelingly towards his daughter Virginia and prevents her marrying, so that we see her later as a bitter old maid, happy to spy on her father for the Inquisition. When he recants in scene 13, as Galileo Laughton showed his degradation by assuming an infantile grin which indicated, in Brecht's description of the performance, 'a self-release of the lowest order'. Just as the recantation itself is not allowed to be a simple matter for praise or blame, so in such ways Galileo's contradictory personality is managed in every detail to inhibit the audience's facile reaction to him. Yet, for all the vivid realism of the action, Brecht required that the scenes should also appear like historical paintings, an effect assisted by the use of titles suspended behind the stage to lend the play the appearance of being a history lesson.

Mother Courage also had an early production by the German actors in exile in Zürich in 1941, when Brecht was in Finland. This play was to be his first production in Berlin after the war in 1949, with Erich Engel co-directing at the Deutsches Theater. The ***Courage-Modell,*** 1949 was published in Dresden in 1952. Not only are the changes between the Zürich and Berlin productions illuminating, but the details of the final production are richly documented. This play, therefore, offers a special insight into the nature of mature epic theatre.

The settings for both productions were based on Teo Otto's Zürich design. This consisted of a permanent set of canvas screens lashed to wooden posts, with simple suggestions of location, like a farmhouse or the Commander's tent, introduced as necessary. Behind it all was a large white cloth, something less than a skycloth and certainly no cyclorama. The stage was virtually bare, and lit by a cold white light, with no modifications for night or day. Placards dropped from the flies, each indicating the change of scene from country to country, and captions were projected on to the screens. Four musicians sat in a box beside the stage, and in the Berlin production Paul Dessau's songs were introduced by a painted musical symbol like a drum or a trumpet lowered from the flies to indicate to the audience that the songs did not spring from the action. Orchestral music of a threatening character was used to accompany a quiet scene as an ironic commentary on the action.

The play was to represent war, said Brecht, as a 'business idyll'. War was a matter of business not only for the leaders, but also for Mother Courage herself. She needs the hostilities to continue for her own survival, while at the same time she fears what the soldiery can do to her family. Brecht wrote,

> With her eldest son she is afraid of his bravery, but counts on his cleverness. With the second she is afraid of his stupidity, but counts on his honesty. With her daughter she is afraid of her pity, but counts on her dumbness. Only her fears prove to be justified (translated John Willett and Ralph Manheim).

Eilif, the eldest, robs peasants and achieves a short-lived fame with his Commander, while Courage sells a capon in time of famine and makes money. When it is necessary to change sides from Lutheran to Catholic, the honesty of Swiss Cheese makes a prisoner of him, and Courage's bargaining over his ransom costs him his life. As for daughter Kattrin, she dies because she takes pity on other people's children. At the end of the play, the old woman is still following the army for a living. As Brecht said, she has learned nothing.

The Zürich production, directed by Leopold Lindtberg, presented the play as a lesson in pacificism, with war simply a natural catastrophe and Courage (played by Therese Giehse) its innocent victim. It was a success for the wrong reason. The critics found it a 'Niobe tragedy', with Courage a tragic figure of a woman who loses her children one by one, and they failed to see the play as an epic conflict designed to show Courage as both victim and villain. Brecht therefore inserted a number of new details chosen to alienate the character more obviously. In the revised version, she is distracted by the sale of a belt buckle at the same time as Eilif is being recruited into the army (scene 1). When the Chaplain wants the shirts she has for sale in order to make bandages for the wounded, she fights to keep them (scene 5). As the war proceeds, she is shown to be doing well, with rings on her fingers and a chain of silver talers round her neck (scene 7). Courage is both mother and businesswoman, but in situation after situation, the two roles prove to be incompatible and survival comes first. To make the scenes true to his idea of reality, Brecht created a split character, an anti-heroine, an inhuman woman who wants the war to go on, but at the same time a natural mother who tries to protect her young. The wagon from which she conducts business throughout the play becomes a symbol of the dichotomy. It is essential for trade, and it is seen, like her life, always rolling on. And yet, like one of Piscator's treadmills, it cannot go anywhere when placed on the revolve of the Deutsches Theater, just as Courage cannot change her nature. It is this criss-crossing of motives in the play that makes it an excellent example of epic theatre. In *The Impossible Theater*, the American director Herbert Blau found that the genius of the play was that Courage had been corrupted by the same social forces that produced the war in the first place; she has capitulated, and 'the capitulation is the chief source of the drama's alienating effect'.

Nevertheless, even the more explicit treatment in Berlin did not solve the problem of controlling the audience's response. The Marxist critic Max Schroeder counted it a success for exactly the same reason as before in Zürich, believing Courage to be 'a humanist saint from the tribe of Niobe and the *mater dolorosa*'. An audience perceives what it chooses to perceive, and certainly in a case of total ambiguity. So the audience chose to see ***Mother Courage*** as a story about themselves, the common victims of war, doubtlessly recognizing in the dilemmas of the play its own recent condition in war-torn Berlin. At the end, when Courage is finally reduced to pulling the wagon alone, her tenacity cannot be judged simply as an act of a predator and a villain. Ernest Bornemann, writing in *Encore* in July 1958, summed up the issue of Brecht's success or failure generally:

> Every play that was successful with his audience succeeded for the wrong reasons: only those passages that did not conform to his theories, that were unextruded remnants of conventional theatre, really moved his audience, while those passages on which he had worked hardest and which most lucidly demonstrated his theories of the epic stage pleased no one except his fellow-artists.

However, Bornemann was not dismissing Brecht's achievement: when he also found that 'Every device which he had contrived to destroy the "magic" of theatre became magin in his hands', he pointed to the ultimate paradox.

In Berlin, Helene Weigel played the title part in a colder manner than Giehse had in Zürich. According to Eric Bentley in his record of a visit to the Berliner Ensemble, in *In Search of Theater,* Weigel was 'cool, relaxed and ironical', standing outside the role and acting with 'great precision of movement and intonation'. But she also introduced a great deal of realistic detail into her performance, although this realism in effect served only to make her more pathetic. In scene 9, where she is forced to beg in the Fichtelgebirge mountains in bitter weather, her tones grew dull and lifeless, like those of the poor whom Weigel had seen on the streets of Berlin. In scene 12, she hesitated as she was paying the peasants for Kattrin's funeral, and took back one of the coins she had given, accentuating the gesture by the click of her bag. As she harnessed herself to the wagon and began to drag it for the last time round the stage, the song from scene 1 was heard again, and no amount of military music could undercut the pathos of the moment. This production, although directed by Brecht himself, taught no lesson about war that was not already known; if anything, it demonstrated that at bottom human nature was frighteningly contradictory and unpredictable, an awesome mystery.

Brecht wrote most of ***The Good Woman of Setzuan*** in Finland, and in 1943 this 'parable play' also received a first production in Zurich, with Leonard Steckell directing. After the war it was performed in Frankfurt and Rostock, but it was not taken up by the Berliner Ensemble until after Brecht had died. In Britain it was produced at the Royal Court Theatre in 1956, with Peggy Ashcroft in the title part. The play is given a brief mention here because it takes to an extreme the dialectical device of the split character, as seen in Galileo and Courage. In 1933 Brecht and Kurt Weill had written a ballet for Weill's wife Lotte Lenya, ***Die Sieben Todsünden der Kleinburger*** (***Anna Anna***), known in English as both ***The Seven Deadly Sins*** and ***Anna-Anna.*** In this, two sisters are both named Anna, the emotional Anna expressing herself by dancing, and the rational Anna by singing. Reason and instinct are here two aspects of the same personality, but represented on the stage simultaneously. A related idea is present in ***Herr Puntila und sein Knecht Matti*** (***Mr. Puntila and His Man Matti***), written in Finland at about the same time as ***The Good Woman of Setzuan:*** Puntila is generous when he is drunk, but mean when he is sober. These plays all extend the ambiguity of character by representing it visibly on the stage.

In ***The Good Woman of Setzuan,*** three gods descend from above looking for signs of goodness in human beings. They find them in a prostitute, Shen Te, when she shelters them, and they reward her with money to open a tobacco shop. With her new-found prosperity, she is immediately besieged by poor relations and every other beggar, so that in self-defence she has to assume the person of her ruthless male cousin Shui Ta, in order to drive the parasites away. That is the beginning of a series of *Doppelgänger,* 'doubles', situations. The message here is that it is impossible for a good person to survive in the world without being corrupted. Hence, the world should be changed. Conflicts in the human personality have been transformed into moral dilemmas in the last plays, and in ***The Good Woman of Setzuan,*** the representation of two contrasting attitudes to life in what appear to be two different persons when in fact they are one, made the dilemma transparent to audiences. At the same time, this device was adopted at the cost of a certain simplification of character, and only Azdak in ***The Caucasian Chalk Circle*** could match Galileo and Courage in depth and complexity.

The Caucasian Chalk Circle was written in America, the last play Brecht wrote in exile. It was given its first production in English at Carleton College, Minnesota in 1948, and had its first Berlin production in 1954. This play has proved to be Brecht's most popular since ***The Threepenny Opera,*** and it is easy to see why this is so. The play was another parable, and Brecht gave it a semi-political frame, in which two collectives in Soviet Georgia dispute the ownership of a piece of land. The purpose of this frame was to historicize the core of the tale and make it a play-within-a-play; it also provided a reason for retelling the ancient Chinese legend of the chalk circle. However, it is possible to ignore or forget this prologue entirely, so that the inner play seems to be presented as a romantic folk-story, complete with story-teller. Its subject, the contest between the common people and their rulers, is told in terms of the love shown towards a child, and it has exactly the attractions of a folk-tale or a simple melodrama. The central character, the peasant girl Grusha, has the immediate appeal of a pathetic victim of injustice, since her maternal instinct leads her into one difficulty after another. The more she does the right thing, the more she must make personal sacrifices—even to the point of taking a husband to give the child a father and losing her own fiancé in the process. Brecht could not have conceived a more moving story.

The Berlin production was loaded with all the epic elements. A ballad-singer, using Paul Dessau's simple score, not only provided the narrative link between the many scenes of the play, but also pleasantly distanced the action by singing of it in the past. Five musicians sat on the stage with the singer, but otherwise the stage was virtually bare in the usual way. The Governor, his Wife and the Prince, with the palace officials, wore grotesque masks, clearly isolating them as villains. Probably to reduce the pathos, Grusha was played by a plain actress with thick legs and seemed less glamorous. Azdak, the wise old rogue who becomes the judge after the revolution, was a Rabelaisian character who delighted the audience by choosing Grusha over the Governor's Wife as the one to keep the child. No one noticed that Brecht had ironically reversed the decision in the original, which was that the true mother should win. He made his point that ties of blood do not always count, and the audience had the total satisfaction of seeing poetic justice done. ***The Caucasian Chalk Circle*** is therefore hardly the best example of the effective workings of epic theatre practice, but it is a clear-cut comedy of ideas.

The production of Brecht's plays in Britain and America has been notably weak and insipid. The strong tradition of naturalistic playing doubtless contributed to the anaemic productions done in English since the war, since the acting, by epic standards, has generally lacked the sharp definition of continental performance. When Jerome Robbins chose to direct ***Mother Courage*** on Broadway in 1963, restraint characterized the production. He even dispensed with the obligatory revolve, so that Courage's endless and agonizing passage across the stage with her wagon was politely reduced by Anne Bancroft to an occasional push or pull that seemed of little account in her momentous journey across Europe. When the actor in a play by Brecht misses the point of his character, he falls back upon the sort of conventional type-playing that Brecht spent his life trying to eliminate. The result might be called 'debilitated epic'.

Is it yet possible to judge what Brecht's theatrical reforms may have achieved? Prolific and dedicated as a playwright, a director and a philosopher of theatre, he is the outstanding example in modern times of a theatre artist who believed it necessary for every area of stagecraft to undergo a regular radical rethinking. At all times restlessly creative himself, but often working under the most difficult circumstances, he insisted that the vitality of drama depended upon constant testing, discussion and revision, a neverending process. He was the complete man of the theatre, and he has attracted by his vision every director who ever found the business of mounting a play a truly imaginative challenge in dramatic communication. His theories of a logical theatre, and his pursuit of multifarious devices for distancing the stage and manipulating his audience, have moved modern drama towards a new kind of comedy, dry and intelligent, but not necessarily without compassion, and often powerful as theatre. (pp. 150-64)

J. L. Styan, "Epic Theatre in Germany: Early Brecht" and "Epic Theatre in Germany: Later Brecht," in his Modern Drama in Theory and Practice: Expressionism and Epic Theatre, Vol. 3, *Cambridge University Press, 1981, pp. 139-49, 150-64.*

Anthony S. Abbott (essay date 1989)

[*Abbott is an American educator and critic. In the excerpt below, he assesses Brecht's artistic method, focusing on the dramatist's presentation of reality in his works.*]

Drama proceeds by dualities. Drama is conflict. The conflict between reality and illusion . . . tends to take the form of a kind of Hegelian triad: thesis, antithesis, synthesis, with an attempt to break through to a deeper reality in the synthesis thwarted by the inexplicable and final reality of death itself. Failing to find a new breakthrough, the hero may retreat to a world of dreams, drugs, or drunkenness, an escape from the unbearable nature of reality without purpose. But there is usually that sense of the glimpsed vision, the moment of release or insight that precedes either death or the failure to sustain the vision.

In Brecht we have all kinds of dualities: instinct versus reason, the individual versus society, the dramatic theater versus epic theater, capitalism versus Marxism. Nearly all Brecht's major protagonists are forced to struggle with dualities in their own natures, so much so that the concept of the split character may be the key to understanding Brecht. But Brecht, like Pirandello, . . . does not treat the dualities in Hegelian fashion. There is not in either Pirandello or Brecht the sense of conflict (thesis versus antithesis) leading to synthesis. Pirandello is too much of a relativist, too subjective in his view of the human situation, to be a Hegelian. Brecht rejects the Hegelian idea of progress for different reasons, reasons that are ably described by Austin Quigley in his new study *The Modern Stage and Other Worlds.* Quigley notes, "For Korsch and Brecht, the dialectical progress of human society is no longer a Hegelian dialectic leading inevitably toward a pre-conceived social and spiritual synthesis, but a mode of social interaction that leads us to examine the need for, and possibility of, intervention in domains neither fully understood nor in their final form." Brecht rejects both the concept of transcendence and the idea that change is a movement toward a necessarily better or more permanent mode of social interaction. Synthesis implies an end to contradiction. At the end of a Brecht play contradictions are seldom resolved, but the audience is invited to choose a course of action that would be appropriate for that particular situation at that particular time in history. I find it interesting that Martin Esslin uses the title *Brecht: A Choice of Evils* for the English edition of his influential book on the playwright to underline the theme of choice in Brecht. His central characters must always make difficult, almost excruciating choices, and those choices are, by necessity, a choice of evils. We as audience must learn, through our participation in the action of the plays, how to choose the lesser of two evils. Both Pirandello and Brecht hope to humanize us with their plays. They both remind us frequently that we are in the theater so that we cannot escape from the reality of the *human* issues into the make-believe of the story. We may best understand reality and illusion in Brecht through the motif of choice. To explain what I mean I would like to begin with a fairly late play, ***The Good Woman of Setzuan*** (1943), and then go back and examine the playwright's overall development in light of my thesis.

Three gods arrive in the city of Setzuan. Atheists are saying, "The world must be changed because no one can *be* good and *stay* good." The gods hope to refute the atheists by finding at least one good person, but thus far not only have they failed to turn up a good person, they have not even found a place to spend the night. Finally, Wang, the water seller, persuades Shen Te, the play's title character, to take them in. Pleased that they have found a good person, even though she is a prostitute, the gods reward her with enough money to set up a tobacco shop. The results are disastrous. An almost indescribable family of eight takes advantages of her, she falls in love with an unemployed pilot who needs money, and the gift of the gods turns into a curse. How can Shen Te be good and stay good? Her role as "the Angel of the Slums" is driving her out of business, and her love affair runs directly counter to the dictates of reason and good sense. Her lover, Yang Sun, is really a scoundrel.

So Shen Te "invents" a cousin, the shrewd and practical Shui Ta, who drives off the spongers, finds out the truth about Yang Sun, the pilot, and parlays Shen Te's small nest egg into a thriving business, even employing the erstwhile lover as a foreman, thus bringing out his true character. But there is one problem even the astute Shui Ta cannot solve: Shen Te is pregnant. He can hide it for a time under the cover of his own increasing weight as a successful entrepreneur, but sooner or later the truth will come out, and it does—in the form of a concluding trial in which the three gods act as judges. Accused of murdering Shen Te, Shui Ta asks that the court be cleared, takes off his mask, and makes this confession:

> Your injunction
> To be good and yet to live
> Was a thunderbolt:
> It has torn me in two . . .
> When we extend our hand to a beggar, he tears
> it off for us
> And so
> Since not to eat is to die
> Who can long refuse to be bad . . .
> I truly wished to be the Angel of the Slums
> But washed by a foster-mother in the water of
> the gutter
> I developed a sharp eye
> The time came when pity was a thorn in my side
> And later, when kind words turned to ashes in
> my mouth.

It is the archetypal Brechtian situation. The gods are useless. "We never meddle in economics," they say at the beginning and go off on a pink cloud at the end, a classic deus in machina that reverses the traditional happy ending, leaving poor Shen Te-Shui Ta as split as ever and with no advice except to try and be as good as she can. "Help!" screams Shen Te. "Help," asks the audience. If ever there was a Brecht play that works the way he wanted it to, it is this one. The audience is given no help. They must take their brains home after the play and figure it out. As Brecht wrote, "Epic theatre turns the spectator into an observer, but arouses his capacity for action, forces him to make decisions. . . ."

What kind of questions does the audience ask itself? This is important. We do not ask ourselves the kinds of questions about reality and illusion that we might after viewing a Pirandello play. We do not ask whether or not Shen Te is more "real" than Shui Ta, though we might. We do not ask whether Shen Te represents illusion and Shui Ta reality, though we could. We do not ask these questions, because the performance of the play has convinced us of the innate reality of the split character. Both Shen Te and Shui Ta are real. If she invents him, it is only that she is calling forth an aspect of herself that she needs in order to survive. We accept the device as a symbol and the play as a parable. What Brecht makes us ask is quite a different question: Does reality have to be that way? And, is there something we can do about it? The answer to the first question is "no" and to the second "yes."

Human beings, according to Brecht's Marxist view, develop the traits, values, and institutions necessary to be successful in the economic system within which they live. Competitiveness, resourcefulness, avarice, shrewdness, practicality are all qualities that enable one to survive in a capitalistic system. Man is an adaptable animal. In Brecht's famous table of contrasts between dramatic and epic theater, man is described under epic theater as "alterable and able to alter." Brecht believes both in fate and in freedom. Within the framework of a capitalistic system, Shui Ta will inevitably succeed and Shen Te will inevitably fail. But the system itself is not inevitable, and if the system can be altered, so can human beings. In Brecht's universe extreme heroism, goodness, and unselfishness of the sort exhibited by Shen Te or Grusha are, in part, marks of an aberration in the social and economic system. In a good society these traits would not be necessary. "Unhappy is the land that has no heroes," says Andrea to Galileo after his leader's capitulation to the Inquisition. "No, Andrea," answers Galileo. "Unhappy is the land that needs a hero." It is a point Brecht makes frequently.

From this look at ***The Good Woman of Setzuan*** we may derive some working generalizations that seem, at least on the surface, consistent with the views Brecht put forward during the early thirties when he did most of his writing on epic theater. There is no such thing as the innate nature of man. Man is not by nature good or evil, heroic or nonheroic. Man is a "process," and the nature of that process is determined by social conditions. "Social being determines thought" is one of Brecht's favorite terms. There are two sides to man—the feeling or instinctual side (Shen Te) and the rational, practical side (Shui Ta). Feelings, instincts are dangerous because they lead people to commit irrational acts or acts inconsistent with their welfare. The difference between Brecht's theory and his practice as a playwright is most emphatic at this point. In Brecht's theory the instinctual or feeling side is viewed negatively. Brecht's reactions to productions of his plays are like Chekhov's responses to Stanislavsky. Audiences were moved to tears by ***Mother Courage,*** so Brecht rewrote the play to make her less sympathetic. Chekhov insisted that his plays were comedies. Both playwrights insisted that they wrote plays with the intention of making their audiences see their lives in order to change them. It takes rationally, objectivity to make changes. The real purpose of the celebrated *Verfremdungseffekte* (principle of alienation) is to keep the audience rationally involved, thinking, throughout the production. Brecht did not want a cathartic, emotional release that would send the audience out of the theater saying, "Wasn't that a powerful experience?" Rather, the audience should leave asking, "What can be done?"

The premise of Brechtian theater then is that reality can be changed, and that people who go to the theater can do something in the process of change. While the characters in the plays seem to be victims of their circumstances, we do not have to be victims of ours. Brecht leaves us with the same paradox that Marx does: he is both an environmental determinist (social and economic conditions determine behavior) and a revolutionist (workers, cast off your chains). The two seem contradictory. How are we expected to change the world if our ideas are simply the outgrowth of conditions we have no control over. Paradox upon paradox. Brecht's plays are more humanly moving than he meant them to be. Why? Because from the very beginning of his career his rationalism is a kind of protection against his own natural instincts, which he saw both as decadent and practically debilitating.

The process really begins during the First World War when Brecht, as an eighteen-year-old medical orderly, was called up to the front:

> I was mobilized in the war and placed in a hospital, I dressed wounds, applied iodine, gave enemas, performed blood transfusions. If the doctor ordered me: "Amputate a leg, Brecht!" I would answer: "Yes, Your Excellency!" and cut off the leg. If I was told: "Make a trepanning!" I opened the man's skull and tinkered with his brains. I saw how they patched people up in order to ship them back to the front as soon as possible.

Martin Esslin's analysis of this passage [in his *Brecht: A Choice of Evils,* 1984] is illuminating:

> . . . even Brecht's ostentatious display of defiant toughness in later life, the disgusted rejection of anything even remotely smacking of high-minded sentiment, whether religious or patriotic, can be seen as the reaction of a basically tender mind, shaken to its core by the sheer horror of existence in a world where such suffering was allowed to happen. The blatant cynicism of his public *persona* in later life is all too obviously the mask of one whose faith has been shattered and who has decided to meet the world on its own inhuman terms.

I could not improve on Esslin's statement. Brecht goes in two directions. Distrusting the gentler emotions, he sees that pity, compassion, feelings about what happens to soldiers in war or workers in peacetime are useless. They accomplish nothing and only open the self to further victimizing by the state. One alternative is personal rebellion, the pose of the decadent artist—the Baal, Kruger, Garga figures in the early plays—a self-indulgent sensationalism, an exploration of the world of the senses for its own sake, a total giving in to instincts.

Brecht at first rejects all social solidarity. The title character of ***Baal*** (1918) destroys his women and turns mindlessly on the composer, Ekart, his best friend, because Ekart leaves him for a waitress. At the end of ***In the Swamp*** (1923), Shlink announces to his opponent, Garga, "the union of organs is the only union, and it can never bridge the gap of speech. . . . If you stuff a ship with human bodies till it bursts, there will still be such loneliness in it that one and all will freeze." The world of the early plays as well as Brecht's personal pose during the time he wrote them—that of the bohemian artist—is obviously a defense against his horror at the world he lived in. But it was a dead end, quite literally. All the early heroes—Baal, Kragler in ***Drums in the Night*** (1922), Shlink, and Garga—are essentially self-destructive.

By 1926, he has made the turn in the other direction. He has read Marx's *Das Kapital,* he has developed around him a group of friends and collaborators—Kurt Weill, Elisabeth Hauptmann, and Erwin Piscator being the best known—and he has begun to shape, under Piscator's influence, the fundamental ideas of the epic theater. As early as 1927, he writes, "It is understood that the radical transformation of the theatre can't be the result of some artistic whim. It has simply to correspond to the whole radical transformation of the mentality of our time."

Plays like ***A Man's a Man*** (1926) and ***The Threepenny Opera*** (1928) illustrate the change. Here Brecht is able to experiment more fully with the development of social themes, the use of music for educative purposes, and the juxtaposition of bawdy comedy with political and sociological commentary in order to shock audiences into new perceptions. If in ***A Man's a Man*** the gentle porter, Galy Gay, can be transformed before our very eyes into the fiery soldier, Jeremiah Jip, what then can society as a whole do to any man? "One man is just like all the others," says Polly Baker. "A man's a man." With Peachum and Macheath in ***The Threepenny Opera,*** Brecht presents subtle yet acerbic criticism of the modern bourgeois. Frederic Ewen [in his *Bartolt Brecht: His Life, His Art, and His Times,* 1967] points out perceptively that there are two, overlapping Brechts in this play:

> There is the sky-storming nihilist, laureate of the asphalt jungle; and there is theinitiate into Marxism, who was attempting to parallel the lesser duplicities and betrayals, the thievery of the netherworld with the more seemingly respectable but crasscr and more thoroughgoing iniquities and corruption of the upper world.

By 1930, the Marxist had won the day; in this year Brecht finished his most overtly economic and political play, ***Saint Joan of the Stockyards.*** Inspired in part both by Shaw's *Saint Joan* and *Major Barbara,* which Brecht admired, the play shows how capitalist power in the mammoth figure of Pierpont Mauler can utilize religious figures like Joan for its own ends. Mauler works on a basic premise: if you can't beat them canonize them; a dead saint is better than a live protester. Joan, who has been converted to Marxism in the course of her struggles to help the workers, cries out:

> Therefore, anyone down here who says there is a God
> When none can be seen
> A God who can be invisible and yet help them,
> Should have his head knocked on the pavement
> until he croaks. . . .
> And the ones that tell them they may be raised in spirit
> And still be stuck in the mud, they should have their heads
> Knocked on the pavement.

No one wants to hear this, and so the black strawhats, the packers, and the stockbrokers all combine to sing a magnificent closing chorale in order to drown her out. It may well be that Joan dies as much of discouragement as of pneumonia. The play closes with a kind of anthem which is both a brilliant parody of the ending of Goethe's *Faust* and an illuminating comment on the future of the Brechtian hero:

> Humanity! Two souls abide
> Within thy breast!
> Do not set either one aside:
> Be torn apart with constant care!
> Be two in one! Be here, be there!
> Hold the low one, hold the high one—
> Hold the straight one, hold the sly one—
> Hold the pair!

Here is Brechtian irony at its finest, and it is but a step from this speech to the position we find ourselves in the three great plays Brecht wrote first between 1938 and 1940—***Mother Courage and Her Children, Galileo,*** and ***The Good Woman of Setzuan.*** In these plays we see the Brechtian dualities in their clearest and most mature form. Having rejected instinct, whether in its early anarchistic-nihilistic form or in its later self-sacrificial form embodied in the heroic Joan Dark (Jeanne d'Arc), Brecht explores in the later plays the development of the rational, pragmatic side as a survival mechanism. Before we look closely at these plays, however, we must look somewhat more generally at one of the central problems with which they deal—human nature.

In ***Saint Joan of the Stockyards*** the cynical Mauler explains to Joan that he would like to help the poor but that human nature is evil and help would not really do any good. "Mankind's not ripe for what you have in mind," he says. "Before the world can change, humanity must change its nature" (a blunt version of the conservative argument paraded so much in the eighties). We know that Brecht as a Marxist would not agree with this position. We know in fact that Mauler uses the argument to defend the status quo. "Don't give the poor money, they'll just abuse it." Brecht's position is that before human nature

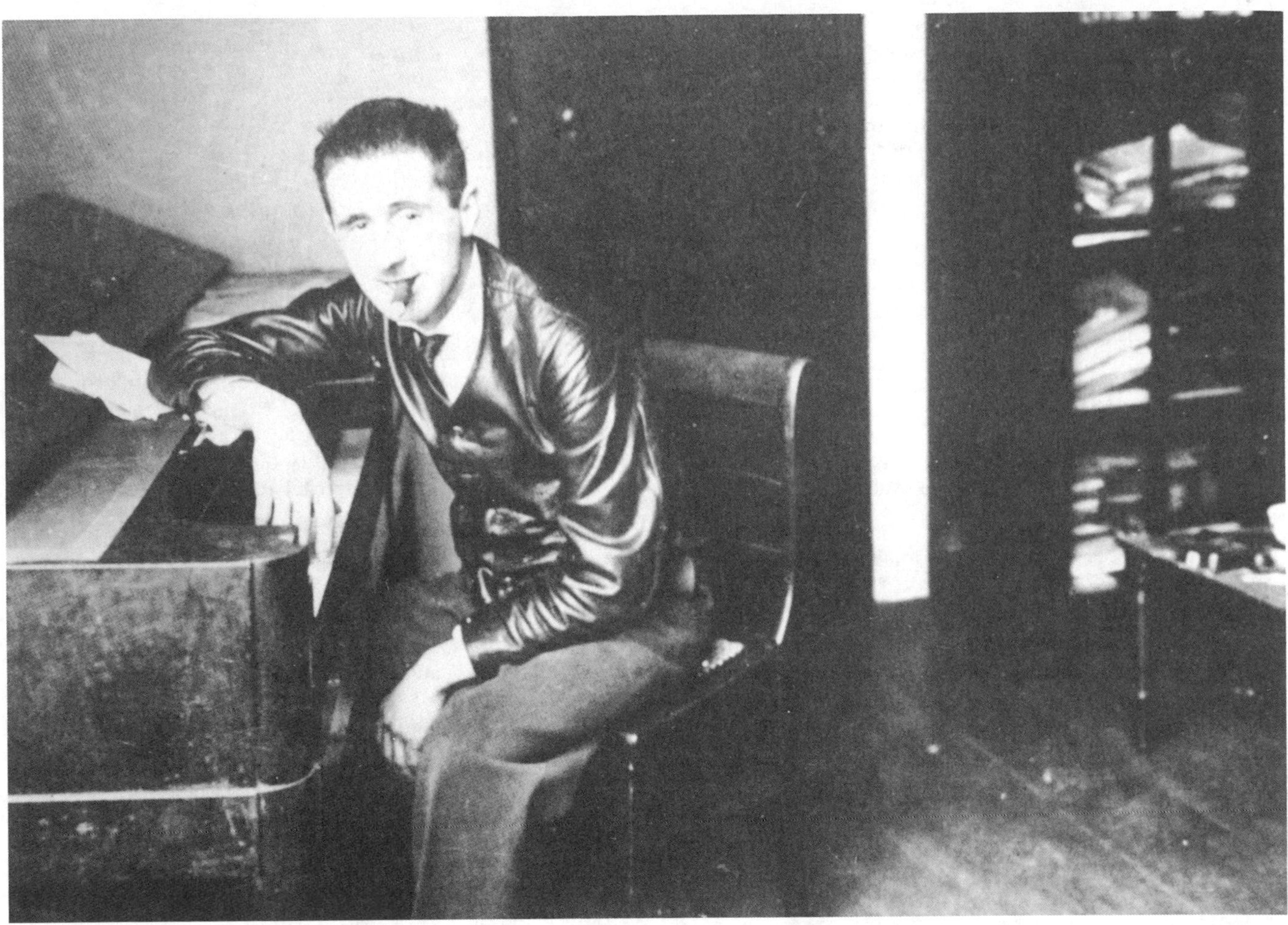

Brecht in 1931.

can change, the world must change. Man is, we remember, "alterable and able to alter." If the soldiers can make Galy Gay into Jeremiah Jip, cannot a good environment perform the reverse process? Yes, we argue theoretically. The trouble is that plays don't change the world. Do we ever in Brecht or in any other major playwright see the world actually changed by someone? "The world is out of joint," says Hamlet. "O cursed spite / that ever I was born to set it right." The heroes [of modern drama] are not much different from Hamlet in this regard. They all want to change the world and almost always at the moment of climax find that the world cannot be changed—so they leave it, transcend, adopt their own philosophy, and die, or they go into exile, literally or symbolically. It is the movement we have been watching: that from illusion to reality to ideal or dream. Even Pirandello, who has . . . rejected the Hegelian pattern, dramatizes this sort of action.

But Brecht won't have that. Except in ***The Caucasian Chalk Circle,*** which we will examine at the end of this [essay], the world is not changed. Nor do the heroes make the leap we have been discussing. Instead, they *adapt!* They want to live. "Better a live dog than a dead lion," is Galileo's motto. Thus, we *appear* to have almost a reverse of the paradigm that has guided us thus far. Brecht's heroes go from dreams and ideals to reality to illusion, if we define illusion as a kind of necessary game or role that allows one to survive, a kind of putting on of the mask instead of taking it off. We must, therefore, examine the pattern and ask how Brecht wanted his audiences to respond to such adaptations.

We begin with Anna Fierling, known as Mother Courage. As a young woman she was full of dreams; she believed she was special. "With my looks and my talent and my love of the Higher Things," she sings in the **"Song of the Great Capitulation,"**

> Our plans are big, our hopes colossal.
> We hitch our wagon to a star. . . .
> "We can lift mountains," says the apostle.
> And yet how heavy one cigar!

She has three children—Eilif, brave and foolhardy; Swiss Cheese, the honest one; Kattrin, good and loving. How can she support them except to adapt and conform? There's a war on: the only way to make a living is to adapt to the values of wartime—cunning, avarice, business acumen. How else is she to save her children? This is the central irony of the play—that Mother Courage is involved in a business deal each time one of her children is killed.

The pattern is devastatingly obvious. Eilif is drafted by the recruiting officer while she is selling the sergeant a belt; Swiss Cheese is executed while she is debating whether to pay the ransom; Kattrin is shot while her mother is in the town of Halle buying up stocks "because the shopkeepers are running away and selling cheap." But is she wrong? What would happen to the children if she didn't do this? **"The Song of the Great Souls of This Earth"** makes it clear that none of the children could survive alone. Solomon (Mother Courage), Julius Caesar (Eilif), Socrates (Swiss Cheese), and Saint Martin (Kattrin) represent the virtues of wisdom, bravery, honesty, and unselfishness. Mother Courage argues, "for the virtues are dangerous in this world, you're better off without." In Brecht's play there is no reward for virtue; on the other hand, vice doesn't help much either.

Brecht's notes on the play, written largely for his classic 1949 production in Berlin, suggest an answer to Mother Courage's problem:

> What is a performance of ***Mother Courage and Her Children*** primarily meant to show?
>
> That in wartime big business is not conducted by small people. That war is a continuation of business by other means, making the human virtues fatal even to those who exercise them. That no sacrifice is too great for the struggle against war.

The last sentence is telling. Mother Courage's sacrifices do *nothing* to stop war. She lives and acts as if the condition of war is both natural and inevitable. Brecht wants the play to illustrate the fact that "Courage has learned nothing from the disasters that befall her." He goes on, "But even if Courage learns nothing else at least the audience can, in my view, learn something from observing her." Paradoxically, what audiences seem to have learned from seeing the play was not what the playwright wanted them to learn. Audiences, again and again, have seen Courage as the symbol of the common person, battered by the forces of war and big business, who gets up from near-death to keep going. But to Brecht she was an antihero, and it is worthwhile to note that the revisions the playwright made both in this play and in his other masterpiece, ***Galileo,*** attest to his desire to make his heroes less sympathetic rather than more.

Galileo is one of Brecht's great creations. Like Mother Courage, he has so much energy, so much pure vitality, that he tends to appeal to audiences for what Brecht would argue are the wrong reasons. "He has more enjoyment in him than any man I ever saw," says the Pope. "He loves eating and drinking and thinking. To excess." Perhaps this is the key to his character. Instinct versus reason again. For Galileo, even the thinking process has become instinctual. He gorges himself on it. For this we love him more than we would a cool, rational type. But Galileo himself knows better. The two scenes critical for an understanding of his character are the seventh and the thirteenth—the dialogue with the Little Monk and the revelation scene when Andrea comes to visit at the end.

"I take it the intent of science is to ease human existence," says Galileo to Andrea. In other words, Galileo's role in a rational universe is not to indulge in thinking bouts but to use reason to improve the lot of humanity (Marx again). Galileo explains this point to the Little Monk in the earlier scene: "virtues are not exclusive to misery. If your parents were prosperous and happy, they might develop the virtues of happiness and prosperity. Today the virtues of exhaustion are caused by the exhausted land." The Little Monk's parents need God (illusion) because they have nothing else. God gives their lives meaning. "How could they take it," cries the Little Monk, "were I to tell them that they are on a lump of stone ceaselessly spinning in empty space, circling around a second-rate star?"

Galileo understands that the purpose personified in God must be internalized. People must learn to think for themselves, to use the instruments of reason and scientific technology to help themselves. The central issue of the play becomes the moral responsibility of the scientific community. This is the point that Galileo stresses to Andrea:

> As a scientist I had an almost unique opportunity. In my day astronomy emerged into the market place. At that particular time, had one man put up a fight, it could have had repercussions. I have come to believe that I was never in real danger; for some years I was as strong as the authorities, and I surrendered my knowledge to the powers that be to use it, no *abuse* it, as it suits their ends. I have betrayed my profession.

It is important to understand that this emphasis was not in the original (1938) German version but was added by the playwright in collaboration with Charles Laughton for the 1947 English version Brecht and Laughton prepared together in California. The new emphasis, Brecht pointed out, was made necessary by Hiroshima. Brecht's explanation of the change is instructive:

> The "atomic age" made its debut in Hiroshima in the middle of our work. Overnight the biography of the founder of modern physics had to be read differently. . . . In the first version of the piece, the last scene was different. Galileo had written his *Discorsi* in the greatest secrecy. When his favorite pupil Andrea visits him, he arranges to have the book smuggled abroad across the frontier. His recantation offered him the possibility of creating a crucial work. He was wise. In the California version Galileo interrupts the pupil's encomium and proves to him that the recantation was a crime, and not to be balanced by the work, no matter how important. *Should it interest anyone, this too is the opinion of the playwright* [Brecht's emphasis].

Galileo was Brecht's favorite play. He never tired of tinkering with it, and at the time of his death he was preparing another version of it for production by the Berliner Ensemble. In this version Galileo's self-criticism, while in substance the same as the Laughton version, is even more severe. The playwright's fascination with the play surely stems in part from the parallels between the creature and his creator. Galileo is Brecht's portrait of the artist as an old chameleon. It certainly raises questions about Brecht's personal life-style and his relations to both East and West. Did Brecht, like Galileo, tell the authorities what they wanted to hear so he could get on with his work? Did

Brecht, also like Galileo, feel he had betrayed humanity by not speaking out more forcefully? "Better stained than empty," cries Galileo, but the playwright himself seems to undercut that position.

We are now back to ***The Good Woman of Setzuan,*** and the question here is: Does Shen Te, in creating the cousin, Shui Ta, commit the same crimes as Mother Courage and Galileo? Is she one more antihero who chooses adaptation first and humanity second? The issue reminds me of the perennial argument about ethics. If you use an evil means to a good end, does the means itself destroy the end for which you are working? If a person says, for example, "I wish to do good in this world and help my fellow man, but I cannot do any good without real power," does his use of evil means to gain power thereby destroy his potential for doing good? This is the question Shaw raises with the character of Undershaft in *Major Barbara.* To consider Brecht's position, we must examine both the Shen Te / Shui Ta character and the Grusha / Azdak figures in ***The Caucasian Chalk Circle,*** completed in 1945 and the last of Brecht's major plays.

Shen Te and Grusha are variants of the same character (Kattrin in ***Mother Courage*** and Joan Dark are others). Both are young women, gentle and motherly. Both love easily and naturally; both take risks to help other, Shen Te in putting up the gods, Grusha in caring for the child.

Both are moral in an "immoral" kind of way. Both pause and consider for a long time before committing the acts that start their plays. "Terrible is the seductive power of goodness," exclaims Grusha when she finally takes the child. Shen Te might have said the same. The way the world is, Brecht implies, being good will inevitably get you into trouble. It may kill you, as it does Joan Dark and Kattrin. But Shen Te and Grusha have protectors: Shen Te has Shui Ta, and Grusha has Azdak. And there is a difference between the two. The Shen Te / Shui Ta relationship will not change the world. The Grusha / Azdak relationship might. It is not so much that Shen Te's ends are defeated by Shui Ta's means, because Shui Ta exists to help Shen Te; the issue is that nothing happens during the course of the play to make the world any different. It is exactly the same at the end of the play as it was in the beginning. So is the world of ***Mother Courage*** and, to some extent, the world of ***Galileo.*** But at the end of ***The Caucasian Chalk Circle*** the world is, at least momentarily, different:

> And after that evening Azdak disappeared and was not seen again.
> The people of Grusinia did not forget him but long remembered
> The period of his judging as a brief golden age
> Almost an age of justice.
> But you who have listened to the story of the Chalk Circle
> Take note what men of old concluded:
> That what there is shall go to those who are good for it
> Thus, the children to the motherly, that they prosper
> The carts to good drivers, that they are driven well
> And the valley to the waterers, that it bring forth fruit.

There is at the end of this play an unusual environment of festivity. The traditional images of comedy—marriage, the feast, the dance—are observed. The usurpers are cast out, the blocking characters defeated, Grusha and Simon married. *All the couples dance off.* Of course, we know that Brecht, the practical theater man, gave ***The Caucasian Chalk Circle*** a happy ending because the thought he could more readily get it produced in the United States; but it would be pure cynicism to think of the ending as crafted for that purpose alone.

Finally it's a matter of *being* versus *doing.* There seem to be two fundamentally different ways of viewing the world. Some view it primarily in terms of being (with its concomitant sides of experience and perception—"being" as experiencing, "being" as seeing). Others view it primarily in terms of action. Brecht is one of the latter. It is not so much a question of who Azdak is, but of what he does. Azdak is a good judge. He awards the child to Grusha, as Eric Bentley reminds us [in his *Brecht Commentaries,* 1981], because of what she has done. She deserves the child *because* she has been a good mother, just as the valley of the prologue will be awarded to the fruit growers because they have proved themselves better for the valley.

Thus, the term "epic theater" *is* appropriate for Brecht's work. As audiences we are placed in front of actions and asked, as a result of the choices characters make, to evaluate their decisions and to try to discover how the world might be changed so that those decisions might have been different. Quigley asserts, correctly I think, in *The Modern Stage and Other Worlds* that Brecht is asking his audience to "participate in an inquiry" rather than "assent to preexisting values." Epic theater invites us to participate in an inquiry, and that is, finally, why it is so difficult to discuss Brecht in terms of the reality-illusion conflict. The pattern in the action of Brecht's plays really redefines the conflict by eliminating the Hegelian synthesis, by subordinating the idea of being to that of action, and by asserting that reality—the tough, tangible stuff of life—is what there is. It is an illusion to believe in some inner being, some "real" self that transcends this life. For Brecht those high ideals of the Ibsenian and Chekhovian heroes are the real illusions. We must face reality squarely, but facing it does not mean *adapting* to it. For reality is "alterable and able to alter." The function of the hero in Brecht is not to separate himself from the impurities of the world, to keep inviolate some illusionary sanctuary of the self. The function of the hero is to immerse himself in reality, as Azdak does, as Galileo does, and to use his creative powers to remake the world so that the sacrifices of the gentler figures will not be necessary. Ronald Hayman, one of Brecht's recent biographers [*Brecht: A Biography,* 1983], reminds us that his first play, ***The Bible,*** written when the playwright was fifteen, deals with the question of whether an innocent girl should be sacrificed to save her native city. Brecht's interest in the necessary sacrifice of the good person to save the community was literally lifelong. And that life's work is a reminder to us as human beings that the sacrifice will continue as long as we permit it. In a good society such sacrifices would not be called for. (pp. 87-99)

Anthony S. Abbott, "Bertolt Brecht," in his The Vital Lie: Reality and Illusion in Modern Drama, *The University of Alabama Press, 1989, pp. 87-99.*

GALILEO

PRODUCTION REVIEWS

Richard Watts, Jr. (review date 14 April 1967)

[*In the following review of John Hirsch's production of* Galileo, *Watts enthusiastically summarizes various issues and ideas in the play, concluding that "all of Brecht's talent as a shrewd theatrical showman" was in evidence in this "imaginative staging."*]

Galileo is very likely Bertolt Brecht's best play, and the Lincoln Center Repertory Company rose to the occasion by giving it a fine production at the Vivian Beaumont Theater last night. With Anthony Quayle portraying the title role brilliantly, the drama about the great astronomer and physicist who recanted his scientific faith under pressure justified all the admiration dedicated Brechtians have for the celebrated but decidedly controversial German playwright.

It may be largely because Brecht himself was a man who was capable of yielding unheroically to various pressures exerted on him that he was able to understand and appreciate someone like Galileo who had powerful and extreme convictions, wanted to fight for them, but succumbed readily to the physical threat of punishment by the Inquisition. The play paints its detailed portrait of the scientist with all the warts visible, concealing none of the weaknesses and equivocations, but it is at the same time a compassionate depiction of a self-tormented man.

It is a paradoxical aspect of Brecht that he is at his dramatic best when he is going against his proclaimed esthetic theories. An advocate of emotional detachment who scorned the idea of involving his audiences in the personal fate of his characters, he is most effective in the moments when he falls back on emotions. The beaten and humiliated Galileo, no hero like Sir Thomas More, but a man lacking the courage to stand up for his beliefs to the death, he is nonetheless a deeply touching figure in the awareness of his humble surrender.

Although these frank emotions can run deep. ***Galileo*** is essentially an intellectual play, and a bitterly sad one, not because of the fate of its central character but through its implications. The scientist believes that his recantation is more than a temporary setback for physical progress. To him it represents the end of the opportunity for science to bring happiness to mankind; it will thereafter be at the mercy of forces that will bend it to their own purposes. The world, he believes, is made darker because of a failure of integrity.

While the play is thus both a character study and a contemplation of ideas, it is also filled with action. It is remarkable how interesting its account of a scientist and his loyal assistants at their experiments can be, but there is more to it than that. The populace, aroused to rebellion by sensing how their universe has been changed, riot vividly, the Pope, the cardinals, a Medici boy prince and the doge of Venice are colorfully presented, a ballad singer and his family introduce the many scenes with their songs, and all of Brecht's talent as a shrewd theatrical showman is in evidence in John Hirsch's imaginative staging.

Mr. Quayle is splendid in showing both the weak humanity and the intellectual stature of Galileo and there are a number of excellent performances, notably George Voskovec's tolerant Pope Urban, Shepperd Strudwick's coldly ominous Cardinal Inquisitor, and the loyal henchmen of the scientist, Stephen Joyce, Robert Symonds and John Carpenter, if I read my program correctly. The Lincoln Center Repertory Company has finally come up with a richly stimulating evening.

Richard Watts, Jr., "Recantation of a Scientist," in New York Post, *April 14, 1967.*

Walter Kerr (review date 14 April 1967)

[*Kerr is a Pulitzer Prize-winning drama critic, essayist, and playwright. In the following review of John Hirsch's production of* Galileo, *Kerr contends that the staging was weakened by "Hollywooditis" manifested in its incorporation of stock melodramatic features and its awkward colloquial phrasing that sacrificed "a good bit of* [Galileo's] *natural intellectual interest." Kerr adds, however, that "the material [was] interesting, the mounting colorful, and the performing (in general) respectable."*]

While Galileo is waiting to be picked up by the Inquisition, in the new mounting of Bertolt Brecht's historical lecture-cum-pageant at the Vivian Beaumont, a friendly industrialist who has made a fortune in iron claps the badgered scientist on the shoulder and lets him know he still has friends. Anthony Quayle, the Galileo of the occasion, is grateful, but with reservations. "I don't know why he's got to be so friendly in public," he frets. "His voice carries."

The very best thing about John Hirsch's staging of the piece is that its voice does carry. More than anything that has yet been done at the Beaumont, the production walks the stage unafraid, confident that it will be listened to, conscious of its vocal and visual authority.

The key is set instantly by Mr. Quayle's playful, but very precise, treatment of a lad who is fascinated by science but pretty certain that the earth he's standing on is dutifully standing still. With a sharp clap of laughter and a wonderfully generous patience, Mr. Quayle turns the sun around for the boy simply by spinning a chair, then spears an apple with a knife to show him that knives—like people—don't necessarily fall off a sphere when the sphere is spun around.

With an alert mind, attentive eyes, and a kindly care for

the sound of words, Mr. Quayle establishes the classroom tone that is going to mark the whole occasion, but establishes it with geniality as well as with precision. From his other principal players, Mr. Hirsch has got much the same insistence on minding thought, sound and energy.

Visually, the production is not only handsome but open in its use of the available forward spaces of the Beaumont stage. The vast mottled floor is crossed and recrossed endlessly, by masked-ball fantastics with griffin's heads for faces, by salmon-colored cardinals, hurried cowled monks, Venetian doges riding sedanchairs ablaze with gilded lions.

Lackey's climb twin scaffolds that spiral to the top of the auditorium, lighted candelabra in hand, to suggest the fires that are being lighted by the force of one man's mind. An edgy Pope, determined not to "set himself against the mathematical tables" but succumbing to the conservative pressures around him nonetheless, attires himself in a great gold jewel-encrusted cape and stalks into the upstage darkness, turning his back on light.

Robin Wagner's settings are fluid and functional. James Hart Stearns's costumes are judiciously monochromatic until the forceful thrust of a primary color is called for—at which point the spectrum lets rip.

There is very little production for production's sake—when the stage moves, it is escorting the play. The play, as it happens, can use the discreet help it gets. Brecht's ***Galileo*** occupies a curious and somewhat awkward middle-ground between the world of "epic" theater and the much more mundane world of commonplace historical melodrama. There are, in the experimental Brecht manner, brief and sometimes ironic sung introductions to the evening's thirteen scenes, accompanied by train-station announcements of the content that is to come.

On the other—and rather feebly conventional—hand, there are the standard domestic crises and foreseeable sentimental stage effect of anybody else's accounting of The Scientist at Home or The Scientist at Bay. At the very moment that Galileo is defying the Inquisition by resuming his study of sun-spots, his daughter bursts into the laboratory freshly pallid from the loss of a lover. "I must know the truth!" the scientist thunders, ignoring her.

While friends and co-workers wait in horror for the sound of a bell that will say Galileo has recanted, we are offered standard suspense that cannot work as suspense. The bell doesn't ring at the promised time. Those waiting are ecstatic. As they sound their most triumphant note, the bell of course rings. But the scene is plain cardboard because we have seen its familiar mechanics coming; we could give the backstage cue for the bell with our own ready hand.

And the language, adapted by Charles Laughton, belongs for the most part to the "Bring me something to discover" school. Perfectly able actors struggle to find human and fresh inflections for "Yes, a new age has dawned, a great age," "Why, those are stars, countless stars!" and "Galileo, you're setting out on a fearful road." There's some Hollywooditis in all of this, and the play sacrifices a good bit of its natural intellectual interest in its determination to make certain that the Common Man—nay, the babe in arms—will understand.

Fortunately, the calculated repetitions and the scientific and ecclesiastical baby-talk are made tolerable by the fact that the material is interesting, the mounting colorful, and the performing (in general) respectable. Although the supers on the fringes still seem unable to put foot on the Beaumort stage without announcing that they are acting, there are controlled and clearly spoken vignettes from John Carpenter as a loyal industrialist. Aline MacMahon as a housekeeper who shudders every time she hears scientists laugh. Frank Bayer as a monk with a passion for physics. Philip Bosco in a brief appearance as a man who learns to believe his own eyes, and from George Voskovec. Ted van Griethuysen, and Shepperd Strudwick as an assortment of stubborn and / or grieving clerics.

On the whole, better than average work for the house.

Walter Kerr, "Lincoln Repertory's 'Galileo'," in The New York Times, *April 14, 1967, p. 31.*

Herbert Kupferberg (review date 14 April 1967)

[*In the following review of John Hirsch's production of* Galileo, *Kupferberg comments favorably on Anthony Quayle's portrayal of Galileo, the performances of the supporting cast, and Hirsch's stagecraft.*]

To the accomplishments of Galileo Galilei, the early seventeenth century astronomer and physicist, must now be added one more small miracle—he has given the Lincoln Center Repertory company its closest approximation so far to a stimulating theatrical evening.

Of course, everything is relative, as another more recent scientist observed, and last night's production at the Vivian Beaumont Theater in Lincoln Center must be viewed against the background of the totally dispirited undertakings which have preceded it during the past two seasons. ***Galileo*** itself represents Bertolt Brecht at his most didactic and pointed, and the Beaumont production is such as to miss some of the opportunities for dramatic tension in the struggles between reason and faith, and, even more important, between science and conscience.

But at least Brecht's play is a play of ideas, and in Anthony Quayle it has an actor who is able to express them with clarity and conviction.

It does take Quayle quite a while to grow into the part. Brecht's Galileo is a sensual, gluttonous sort of fellow, and Quayle's bluff and hearty figure, rolling with a kind of sailor's gait, doesn't seem like much of a scientist at first—not even the kind of scientist who can casually remark: "All I've done is write a book about the mechanics of the universe. What they do or don't do with it is no concern of mine."

But by the time Quayle progressed to the old and weary man who has made his peace with the Inquisition only to be secretly appalled by the horrors his science has let loose, he summons up a sense of torment and tragedy that points up the human predicament of our own day no less than Galileo's.

Brecht's play, which was first presented here twenty years ago in a production with the late Charles Laughton (who also did the translation), is very much a modern sermon. But that doesn't prevent it from employing a wide range of theatrical tricks and pageantry. Richly costumed princes and prelates, courtesans with bulging bosoms, cripples and beggars, clerks and artisans, all crowd the stage of the Beaumont.

The company as a whole seems to be operating on a more consistent level than in the past productions. One or two of Galileo's intimates make little impression, but Philip Bosco plays one of his supporters among the nobility sturdily, Ronald Weyand and Earl Montgomery turn two pedants into incisive caricatures, and Ronald Bishop contributes a memorable scene as a corpulent and pompous churchman.

Some of the most engaging moments come from the ballads that link the scenes together. The technique seems a bit dated and artificial, but the songs (by Hanns Eisler updated by Stanley Silverman) have quality, and they are set forth resolutely by a vocal trio that includes an utterly delightful large-eyed little boy named Robert Puelo. As a matter of fact, two other youngsters. Donnie Melvin as a pupil of Galileo, and Charles Abruzzo as a Medici child-prince, also make a fine impression. Help may be on the way for the Lincoln Center company.

But it will still need somebody to do something about its crowd scenes. Director John Hirsch handles individual confrontations skilfully, such as the episode in which a Cardinal suddenly turns a jesting conversation with Galileo into a scarcely veiled warning of the perils ahead for a scientist who insists on proclaiming that the earth revolves about the sun. He also shows a touch of imagination in using projections of the night sky and the sun as backgrounds while Galileo argues astronomy with his friends, although one feels that an opportunity for greater use of the device was missed.

But crowds are what really throw Hirsch, just as they have thrown every director who has worked with the company. People rush on and off with frantic aimlessness, and for one hectic moment in the last-act one almost imagined oneself back in the disastrous *Danton's Death* of two years ago. Fortunately, it is Quayle who has the last word.

Herbert Kupferberg, "'Galileo' Proves Stimulating Fare," in World Journal Tribune, *April 14, 1967.*

CRITICAL COMMENTARY

Günter Rohrmoser (essay date 1958)

[In the following excerpt from an essay originally published in German in 1958, Rohrmoser examines Brecht's revisions of Galileo, *focusing on the dramatist's treatment of such themes as truth, integrity, social progress, and the relations between an individual and society.]*

There are three versions of ***Galileo.*** Brecht wrote the first in 1938-39 in Denmark; it was published by Suhrkamp as a theater script and performed in Zurich in 1943. The second, American version was written in 1945-46 during the translation of the play into English which Brecht undertook with Charles Laughton, who played Galileo in 1947 at Beverly Hills, California, and in 1948 at New York. Finally the third version, which is based upon the English one, was written during Brecht's rehearsals on the stage of the *Schiffbauerdamm Theater* in Berlin. The essential difference between the individual versions is the ending, which is concerned with judging the figure of Galileo, his submission to the Inquisition, and answer to the question about the beginning of modern times and a new age.

The 1938 version shows Galileo as an old man who outsmarts the Inquisition and, simulating blindness, completes his work and has the results smuggled out of the country by one of his pupils. Thus the cunning of reason triumphs also in the ethic of the scientist's political action, it is as far ahead of its century as his knowledge is, and causes a light to dawn in the darkness of his age. "I insist that this is a new age. If it looks like a blood-stained old hag, then that's what a new age looks like. The burst of light takes place in the deepest darkness." In the version of 1947 the last sentence, among others, has been deleted, just as in general the judgment upon Galileo has become harsher. Now he practices science like a vice, secretly and without any obligation to humanity. Galileo retracts his doctrines out of cowardice, and his contributions to the progress of science do not outweigh his failure to human society. Because of Galileo's failure in succumbing to sensual temptation, the new age, which emerges as a real possibility on the horizon of history, is no different from the dark ages of the past. Modern science, in itself an instrument of progress, transforms itself into a force for oppression in the hands of the rulers to whom Galileo has delivered himself.

There is no possible doubt that Brecht altered his view of Galileo and the historical importance of his scientific discoveries under the influence of the atomic bomb, which was developed and first dropped on Hiroshima during the creation of ***Galileo.*** Brecht could not ignore the fact that the atomic bomb with its fateful possibilities was a product of the science founded by Galileo at the beginning of the scientific age. In 1938-39 German physicists succeeded in splitting the uranium atom; in 1945 the atomic age began to exhibit its destructive possibilities; and in 1945 Galileo answers the question, "Do you no longer believe that a new age has begun?" this way: "Quite. Be careful when you pass through Germany with the truth in your pocket."

In Brecht's notes to his ***Galileo*** of 1938 we read:

> In the midst of the fast-growing darkness over a feverish world, surrounded by bloody deeds and no less bloody thoughts, by increasing barbarism which seems to be leading irresistibly to perhaps the greatest and most terrible war of all time, it is difficult to maintain an attitude proper for people on the threshold of a new and happy age. Does not everything indicate that night is coming, and nothing that a new age is beginning? Therefore should we not maintain an attitude proper for people heading into the night?

> Do I not already lie in bed thinking of the morning that has gone by in order not to think of the one coming? Is this not why I occupy myself with that epoch, the golden age of the arts and sciences of 300 years ago? I hope not.

These remarks are extraordinarily illuminating for Brecht's relationship to the hero of the play, as well as for the immediacy of the problem to which we owe its creation. It is true even in the earliest version that the perspective in which Bertolt Brecht views an event of the past is oriented to the present and its oppressive problems. But Brecht is by no means concerned with opposing to the night of barbarism threatening his own present a picture of an age in which, like the morning after a long night, an epoch of renewal and hope for mankind begins. For Brecht continues in his notes: "The symbols of morning and night are misleading. The fortunate ages do not come like the morning after a good night's sleep." Here Brecht is not only attacking the oversimplification of an image of history which separates epochs from one another like day and night, light and darkness, good and evil: rather he is questioning the total relevance to history of an analogy based upon a process of nature. What fascinates Brecht primarily in the historical problem of the beginning of a new age is the abstract aspect of a situation still concealing within itself all possibilities, and the courageous feeling of a man who has complete trust in the situation because he has not yet tested its strength against reality.

> Beloved is the sense of beginning, the pioneer situation, thrilling the effect of the beginner's attitude, beloved the feeling of happiness of those who oil a new machine before it is to demonstrate its power, those who fill in a blank spot on an old map, those who dig the foundation of a new house, their house. The researcher who makes a discovery that changes everything knows this feeling—as well as the speaker who prepares a speech that will create a new situation.

It is clear that with these formulations Brecht is seeking a newly grounded ethos. It is to correspond to the spirit which animates the children of a scientific age, who in an almost sporting manner lay hold of the possibilities science and technology open up to them. This ethic is uninterested in the inner man and is directed completely toward the area where things can be made and manufactured. The satisfaction which this ethic supplies is the purely functional joy of being able to do well and easily what is possible. It is the ethic of the artist transferred to the area of technical manufacture and social practice. Technology and art have in common that they are both abstracted from a purpose determined by their content. They can be measured against this purpose, and indeed it is the reason for their existence.

It is self-evident that Marxist doctrine does not permit such a late bourgeois philosophy of *l'art pour l'art.* It insists that all forms of human activity—including technological and artistic activity—be subordinate to the Marxist's highest concern, the goal of the classless society. We owe Brecht's most exciting achievements to his inability to kill the artist in himself for the sake of blind obedience to the party line, and to his skill in extracting artistically the greatest use from the tension which resulted from it.

Galileo's life embraces a twofold responsibility: first to the work to be achieved, and then to the society to which this work is committed and which it seeks to serve. Can the two requirements be reconciled or do they stand in an irreconcilable contradiction to each other? If it is characteristic of a new age that society as a whole begins to move and the unquestioned oneness of the individual with its institutions begins to dissolve, then such a society offers Brecht an excellent model on which to demonstrate his basic propositions.

The shortest answer to the question of whether a new age has begun, which Brecht formulated in the Berlin text of 1955, is the one that causes the most torment and tension. It is all the more difficult to understand, as Galileo expounded shortly before the passing of judgment in his case:

> As a scientist I had an almost unique opportunity. In my day astronomy emerged in the market place. At that particular time, had one man put up a fight, it would have had wide repercussions. If only I had resisted! If only the scientists could have developed something like the Hippocratic oath of the physicians, a vow to use their knowledge for the welfare of humanity alone. As it now stands, the best one can hope for is a race of inventive dwarfs who can be hired for anything.

But how does this obviously changing interpretation in the several versions relate to the artistic and dramatic structure of the work? If it were possible to interpret the play as a revue-like, "epic" chronicle striving for colorful details, our final judgment on Galileo's life would indeed be a matter of indifference. For then the structure of the play would pursue the theatrical goal of reproducing his biography as such. The same would be true if the play were concerned with the interpretive dramatization of a complex character. Both possibilities are rejected. In turning to history Brecht is concerned in substance with the basic historical and human problem of his own age, which he is certainly correct in calling a scientific one. Galileo does not interest him as a character, but as a case, although the individual vital substance of the hero is not sacrificed to an abstract scheme to the same extent as in the plays of a Marxist cast, the didactic plays. Galileo is "shown" in the concrete detail of his daily, even intimate life, because it is just exactly here that the characteristics clearly appear which explain his behavior in the great trans-personal, historically important decisions of his life. The importance the individual physiognomy of Galileo, who cannot be reduced to a social type, acquires for the answer to the question about the beginning of a new age (from a Marxist standpoint quite questionable in its estimate of the role of the great individual for the course of history) forbids us to interpret ***Galileo*** as a drama of modern science. From this standpoint Galileo would even be morally coresponsible for the terrors of the modern atomic age.

The arrangement and execution of the play permit us to interpret Galileo's behavior in recanting under pressure from the Inquisition in the sense of a rational cunning, which accommodates itself to the powerful only formally and seemingly, in order to be able to undermine their authority more effectively. For the fact that Galileo does not fear death under all circumstances, indeed is ready to face it if the execution of his experiments requires it, is proved by his attitude during the plague: he passionately continues his experiments despite constant mortal danger. He had proved repeatedly that he only judged the forces and powers of the world functionally, insofar as they were advantageous or detrimental to his researches. Decisive however is the way in which Brecht has Galileo's inner make-up determined by a hedonistic view of life and an obsessive joy in experimentation and discovery.

The new method is made possible by Galileo's driving interest in "alienating" the world, his childish joy in removing things from their familiar, traditional explanations in an act of amazed wonder and seeing them, as though for the first time, untouched and fresh from the moment of creation. The demand Brecht made of the theater in his ***Little Organon***—namely, that the communication of the moral must give pleasure and that theater entertainment must instruct us about the methods in which the children of a scientific age acquire their sustenance—has, according to Brecht, entered history in the person of Galileo as a new possibility for the human being was realized by him. Teaching a new science in a new way, he practices a new human attitude in a world which he sees in a new way, a world which turns out to be both needful and capable of change.

Thus in the very first scene of the drama we read:

> On our continent a rumor has appeared: There are new continents. And since the time that our ships have been traveling to them, people have been saying all over the laughing continents: The much-feared ocean is a little pond. And a great desire to investigate the causes of all things has arisen—why the stone falls when one drops it, and how it rises when one throws it up. Every day something is found. Even men a hundred years old have boys shout into their ears what new things have been discovered. . . . Because where faith has been for a thousand years there is doubt now. . . . The most honored truths are being tapped on the shoulder; that which was never doubted is being doubted now.

Brecht's extraordinary closeness to the position which he expresses in these sentences is immediately clear. To this extent the life of Galileo is a key to the interpretation of the total phenomenon Bertolt Brecht.

The responsibility for future, unforeseeable possibilities with which Galileo is burdened is not only historically an anachronism, but also disguises, perhaps consciously, the problem of the play. The suspense, the dramatic substance lives on the open dialectic with which the question of the beginning of a new age is put. From Brecht's humane, even radically anthropological position the question of a new age is identical with the possibility of developing a new type of human existence and establishing it in the face of the resistant tradition. Time and man stand in a dialectical union which cannot be dissolved one-sidedly in a moralistic way. If Galileo had resisted the Inquisition and had been prepared to stand up for truth with the sacrifice of his life, then he would have been able to aid progress as well as reaction. The solution to this question is dependent upon another: namely whether—and how far—the new method and attitude to things already represented an element of general social practice. If it does, then Galileo's insistence could have meant *its* final victory. If, on the other hand, the new truth had not yet entered the general consciousness, then one would have to see a meaningful action in Galileo's self-preservation. There can be no abstract yardstick here, unless one were to judge *post eventum,* which would be nothing other than making the outcome of an historical experiment the basis for its moral justification. Only the atomic bomb motivates internally the judgment which Galileo makes over himself. The suspense increasing from scene to scene is not immanent in the course of the play, but is the result of the contrast between the possibilities apparent in the described events and the actual outcome which contradicts the expectations that were called forth. The scene showing the effect of his step among his pupils allows us to recognize the method according to which the whole play is constructed. The audience knows that what Galileo does will be decisive for the fate of truth in the historical world. Truth itself is not in question, but rather the possibility of its establishing itself in the historical process. Galileo—like no one else in previous history—seems to have the chance of bringing about a turning point of epoch-making importance. By letting tense expectation, triumphant exultation, deep depression, and shocked despair among the pupils follow directly upon one another, Brecht succeeds in transforming the drama of the historical decision into a perceptible scenic movement. The "basic gestus" articulates with dialectical and most extreme intensity the meaning of this event which determines the coming centuries. No talk of epic theater ought to obscure our eye for the mastery with which Brecht forms the dialectic of thought. "Unhappy is the land that breeds no hero!" "Unhappy is the land that needs a hero!" Set up this way, the problem no longer permits of a moral solution.

Galileo cannot fulfill the historical heroic role in which his pupils would like to see him, because he is unable to transcend, and hopelessly falls victim to, the law of human frailty. He could have overcome the limitation of action forced upon him by social determinants with the sacrifice of his life. His pupils call him "winebibber" and "glutton" and fail to recognize that without the joy in good food Galileo would never have possessed the weakness of pursuing the vice of his thirst for knowledge so intemperately. That one person can at the same time discover and suppress the truth, this contradiction is grounded in the structure of a newly beginning epoch which must first establish itself against the traditions. Its knowledge does not correpond to its ability. The church, which here represents all authority but is by no means polemically presented, takes this inability into account.

One problem remains remarkably unclear in Brecht's play: the relationship of the truth of Christianity to the church which is supposed to represent truth in the scientific age, or its relationship to the truth of these sciences and especially to their instrinsic claim upon men not directly concerned in the work of science and its discoveries. The question is not one of the truth of revelation, but of the conformity of revelation to the Aristotelian view of the world and the need to secure the authority of the papal throne through this view. The historical Galileo probably used his Biblical faith in creation in his fight against the presumptions of a formal tradition; Brecht makes no use of it, because for him the refutation of Aristotelian astronomy involves a denial of the Biblical faith in creation. "The heavens, it appears, are empty. People are laughing with delight because of this." For Brecht, the change in the comprehension of truth itself comes with the new method and its application, represents the newly discovered possibility of changing the sociological, historical world by means of revolutionary intervention. Since Brecht views the process from the end, backwards—from the atomic bomb, from the transformation of liberation into destruction—the reasons with which the representatives of the Church opposed the teachers of the new truth become more valid for him. The formula that the Church defended its order only for the sake of its sovereignty is too simple; instead history has taught that the Church hierarchy could be of the opinion, and not only out of self-interest, that it must protect men from the terrible possibilities to which they would be exposed on the new path. His undogmatic position permits Brecht to show masterfully a picture of the situation in which it is obvious how even the Church, in itself the force for the preservation of the old, acquires an interest in the new and cannot escape the force of the changing course of history.

A runaway monk—who, after Galileo abjures the truth, returns to the bosom of the Church—belongs to Galileo's most intimate pupils, and a cardinal favorable to the new sciences ascends the papal throne. Brecht, the epic narrator of the plot, who judges by hindsight, lets us know that at no time was Galileo's life in serious danger; bold, decisive behavior would have saved him from the torture.

What has Brecht achieved dramaturgically with this device? The event acquires the depth of tragedy in its perspective backward. Galileo's failure is based upon a false assumption; he could have avoided his renunciation of truth. If Galileo had been right, the catastrophe for which humanity was to pay with infinite suffering would not have seemed unavoidable. Brecht does not make an argument for a tragic view of history out of his insight into the objective senselessness of the situation. When he calls the attention of the audience to the fact that the tragic process taking place before its eyes would have taken another course if Galileo had been conscious of the strength of his position, he calls upon the audience to apply this consideration to the historical situation of the present. Whether or not this hope is based upon a false assumption is a matter of indifference for the effect of the play. Through the magic of the theater, the artful interplay of varying interpretations and perspectives changes the laborious profundity of speculation upon the philosophy of history into the cheerful surface of scenic and balladesque events. It is a triumph of Brecht's sovereign mastery of his means, that he does not need to interrupt the immediacy of the stage action with extraneous elements in order to make the didactic meaning transparent. The commentary has been absorbed into the text, and only the dynamic tension between the scenes produces the drama and its meaning. It would overstep the limits of our discussion if we attempted to show in detail how Brecht integrates the interpretation into the events so that the course of events becomes a commentary to what is happening. The pleasurable representation of thinking makes thinking itself a pleasure. The thesis to be demonstrated depends, to be sure, upon the premise that stupidity is the archenemy of mankind. But thinking does not take place in a vacuum that is withdrawn from history and its vicissitudes.

The abandonment of the traditional division into acts, the substitution of a loose succession of scenes which seems to be based only upon chronological order corresponds to the necessity of bringing together all the evidence which enables the audience to pass judgment on the case. The various and surprising points of view serve as an exercise in the dialectical way of looking at things which for its part determines the arrangement and construction of the scenes.

The artistic method which Brecht follows in ***Galileo*** does not develop suspense out of what is represented, but rather out of the relationship in which the mode of representation stands to the factual events. Traditional drama tends to concentrate on elements advancing the action; Brecht, however, assumes the "epic" narrative attitude of a painter of mores concerned with completeness of material. But the completeness is that of a prosecuting attorney who makes his plea for a just verdict. The oversimplified idea which people have of the founder of a new epoch and of the epoch itself is destroyed by new arguments stressing the complexity of the matter, and the members of the audience, called as witnesses, are driven to a reconsideration of the case, even seduced into it by the force of scenic suggestion.

While traditional drama developed its specifically dramatic quality out of the suspense of the process of actively and passively overcoming a given contradiction, Brecht's dramaturgy proves how impossible it is to stop the dialectic of the whole process by a one-sided solution that transcends history. It is not consistent with Marxist doctrine that Brecht permits his Galileo to be an individual, a "hero," and accords to him such a decisive role for the course of history. Rather, the part played by Marxist theory in Galileo's life is limited to the extent to which it calls attention to the truth of contradiction and its dialectical force in moving history. In the rest of Brecht's late plays, written primarily during his exile, he deals as a rule with truth as it is or ought to be, in similes disguised as parables. The playwright communicates morality didactically or narratively in such a form that the comprehended truth can intervene effectively in the world. The theme of ***Galileo*** is the process of discovering truth.

The dramatic weakness of the late plays such as ***The Caucasian Chalk Circle*** and ***The Good Woman of Setzuan*** is connected with their problematic relationship to Marxist doctrine. They are plays of great theatrical effectiveness, but are dramatic only in a derived sense. The exemplary function they serve in displaying the role that cunning and

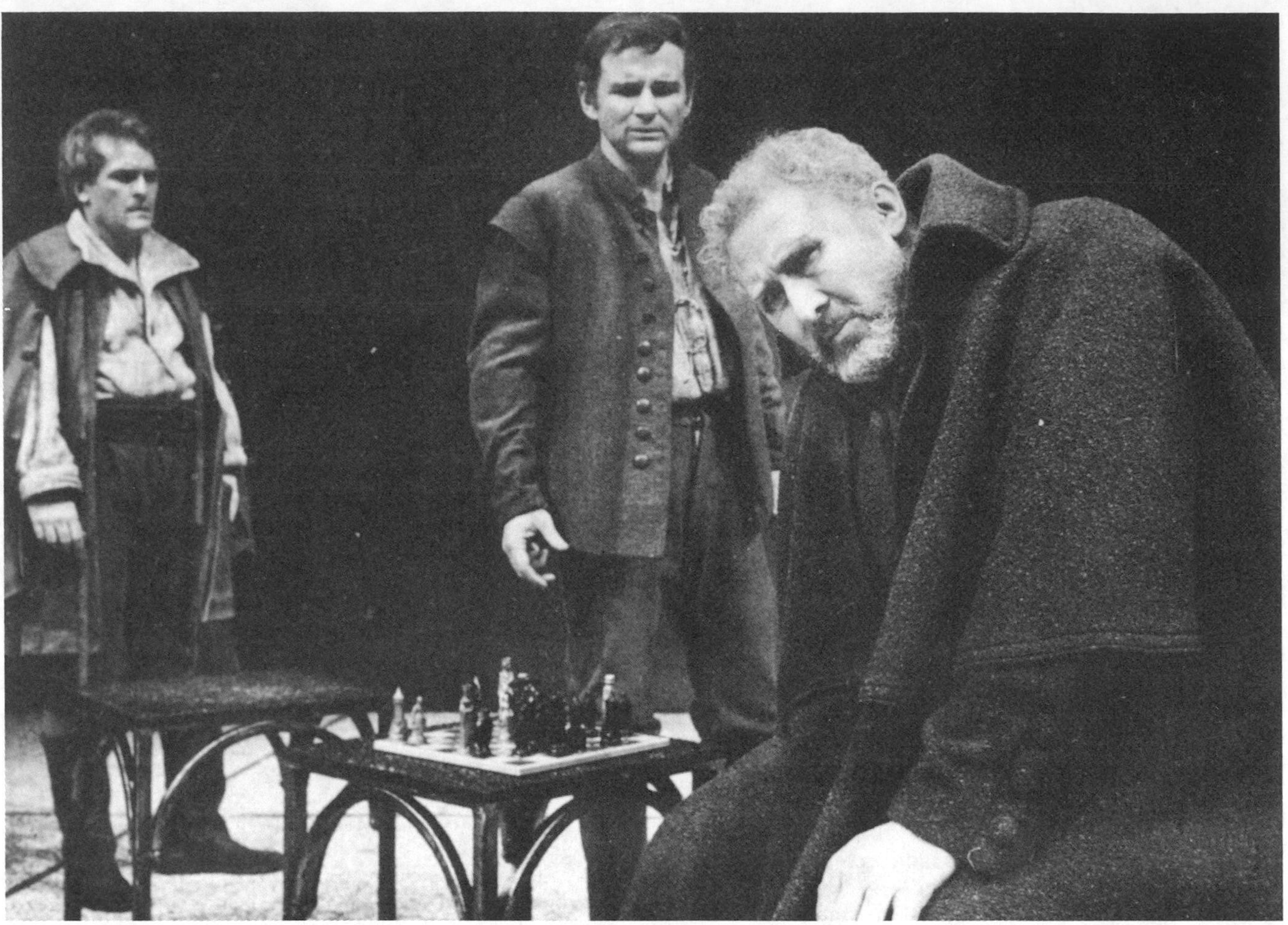

Anthony Quayle, foreground, in John Hirsch's 1967 production of Galileo.

goodness play in the historical process stands only in a loose relation to the conditions of the concrete social and historical situation in which the events, which have been turned into a paradigm, transpire. The parabolic content consists in the transtemporal, transhistorical meaning which the application of the doctrine to any and all historical situations of man permits. The trial forming the center of the stage action in ***The Caucasian Chalk Circle*** has no contemporary referent, indeed avoids any and transfers the event into the legendary past. ***The Good Woman of Setzuan,*** finally, demonstrates the impossibility of being good and staying alive at the same time so impressively that one is tempted to look for the failing in the structure of the world itself. It is not a question of changing the world but of adapting to the world as it is. No process is set in motion, but rather a condition is revealed. The revelation of the truth masked in the parable takes place in sententiously pointed remarks which are directed straight at the audience, and justification in the dramatic action itself remains accidental and not very convincing. The question of how the possibilities of mankind relate basically to the necessities of history is not even put. But it is given in the life of Galileo. Indeed, one can characterize the real message of the play by saying that history is basically open in its outcome and that its course is exposed to so many surprises that the activity of man is needed if the destiny of mankind is to be achieved.

Galileo's failure illustrates a fundamental failing of the Marxist historical dialectic. The materialistic view of history is in principle incapable of producing an ethic of political action. In it situations are not foreseen in which the spontaneous intervention of the individual is required in order to give to the movement of history a direction toward the human *telos.* Galileo does not betray materialism, but betrays rather his humane and social intention just because he is a consistent materialist. This is the source of the ambiguous light in which he appears in the play. It can be understood both as an accusation and as a defense. The autobiographical substance as well as the unsettled question of the extent of the individual's importance for the outcome of historical processes contribute to this ambiguity. The contradiction to the official doctrine in which Brecht finds himself in this question (it is most closely connected with the moral heritage of his late-bourgeois origins) to be sure contributes to the aesthetic quality, but on the other hand makes it almost impossible to determine the specific character of the work. It is not a tragedy, because the final result of the historical experiment still lies in the future. It cannot be interpreted as history, either, because of its forceful contemporary reference. It cannot be counted among the parable plays, because the figure of Galileo and his fate are inseparably bound to concrete history. We cannot speak at all of a "didactic play" because the "example" has a character of inimitable uniqueness which is not transferable or even applicable. In a peculiar manner the life of Galileo unites all these characteristics so that they are metamorphosed into a new form of drama. The diverging aspects are unified by the double function of the dialectic: as artistic play and as a method of overcoming the world historically.

The inconclusiveness of historical experiments transforms the dialectic into a kind of artistry; and the fate that hangs over all events calls the artist back into history, in order to use the dialectic desperately, but not without hope, in the fight for the final achievement of a free society planned for human beings and their needs. The epic elements of Brecht's theater serve to regain the original drama of a man who refuses to accept passively an uncomprehended fate. He tries to withstand it by thinking and acting. Like a second Oedipus the human being himself discovers the solution to the riddle with which the sphinx of history challenges him.

Brecht's drama communicates something of the cheerful and courageous attitude of the Enlightenment which, aware of the regressive character of one-sided progress, holds undeviatingly to progress itself and its necessity. Brecht's theater is no longer a moralistic place, but a school and courtroom in which things are accounted for: what has been gained and lost is remembered and, above all, new steps forward are practiced. Progress consists not in progress, but in progressing. This is why the Galileo of the third version is right in answering affirmatively the question about the beginning of a new age. His sensuality was not the cause of his failure—it was only a part of it—but rather a lack of knowledge concerning the importance of the demand made by the unique moment. He risked his life during the plague and endangered what he had gained by submitting to the Inquisition when history was waiting only for a sign from him.

Brecht's drama is a question which becomes a demand. Who will make up for what has been let slip? Or is it already too late? The question might be asked of Brecht whether the truth to which he refers possesses enough authority to justify the sacrifice of a human being for it. This question seems to be the inevitable result of the play and of pursuing its problems. (pp. 117-26)

Günter Rohrmoser, "Brecht's 'Galileo'," translated by J. F. Sammons, in Brecht: A Collection of Critical Essays, *edited by Peter Demetz, Prentice-Hall, Inc., 1962, pp. 117-26.*

Charles R. Lyons (essay date 1966)

[In the following essay, Lyons argues that Galileo is an ambiguous character whose recantation is an ironic and tragic result of the same "hunger for life" that prompted his scientific discoveries.]

Brecht intended Galileo to be a consummate villain, and he would, in all probability have agreed with Harold Hobson's critical assertion "[in *The Sunday Times,* 19 June 1960]: "As in one view humanity is saved by the grace and death of Christ, so in Brecht's, by the life and disgrace of Galileo, humanity is damned." Brecht himself considered his Galileo to be a hero-villain in the tradition of Shakespeare's evil protagonists: "He [Galileo] should be presented as a phenomenon, rather like Richard III, whereby the audience's emotional acceptance is gained through the vitality of this alien manifestation." Brecht's phrase, "the vitality of this alien manifestation," is a concise and perceptive definition of the spectator's emotional reaction to Shakespeare's villain, but while Shakespeare's characterization is complex, Richard III is more purely evil and less ambiguous than Brecht's Galileo. Despite the magnitude of Galileo's sin, the literal condemnation of his evil in Brecht's polemic is complicated by the fact that his insatiable appetite for life is both the source of his genius and his essential human weakness. Brecht's image of Galileo's appetite is ambiguous. In the metaphoric structure of the play, Galileo's appetite is the motive for his acquisition of scientific knowledge; in a sense, he consumes truth for the pleasure of its consumption. But his appetite for the pleasures of life, both intellectual and sensual, makes him unable to sacrifice himself to demonstrate the integrity of the truth he seeks. The tension between Galileo's hunger for life and his hunger for truth results in a tragic paradox, and Brecht's firm declaration that ***The Life of Galileo*** does not contain a tragic action does not alter the implicit tragedy of his conception of the recantation.

The work of the New Criticism has defined ambiguity as a primary value in poetry; and the encounter with the verbal puzzle or the ethical contradiction is now seen as a most profound and meaningful experience between poem and reader. Discussing a "clear case of the Freudian use of opposites" in Hopkins' *The Windhover, to Christ Our Lord,* William Empson states [in his *Seven Types of Ambiguity,* 1955]:

> . . . two things thought of as incompatible, but desired intensely by different systems of judgments, are spoken of simultaneously by words applying to both; both desires are thus given a transient and exhausting satisfaction, and the two systems of judgment are forced into open conflict before the reader. Such a process, one might imagine, could pierce to regions that underlie the whole structure of our thought; could tap the energies of the very depths of the mind.

Empson's own teacher, I. A. Richards [in his *Principles of Literary Criticism,* 1925], has defined tragedy, " . . . perhaps the most general, all-accepting, all-ordering experience known," as the accommodation of opposites: Hence the supreme ambiguity. Richards writes: "What clearer instance of the 'balance or reconciliation of opposite and discordant qualities' can be found than Tragedy. Pity, the impulse to approach, and Terror, the impulse to retreat, are brought in Tragedy to a reconciliation which they find nowhere else, . . . Their union in an ordered single response is the *catharsis* by which Tragedy is recognized, whether Aristotle meant anything of this kind or not." In the "Preface to the Second Edition" of *Seven Types of Ambiguity,* Empson quotes extensively from James Smith's strongly negative review of the first edition of his study of ambiguity. Smith does not find Empson's application of ambiguity relevant to the criticism of drama, and he claims that "The first business of the student of drama, so far as he is concerned with ambiguity, is historical; he records that situations are treacherous, that men are consciously or unconsciously hypocritical, to such or such a degree." Bertolt Brecht's critical theories concerning the function of the theatre make it seem likely that Brecht, the critic, would agree with the critical response of James Smith. In fact, the primary function of the epic theater seems to be to serve as an arena for demonstrations which will invoke not only an ethical judgment but an ethical action. The ***Short Organum for the Theatre*** insists that dramatic action exists to demonstrate the weakness and injustice of human society which, by rational processes, can be clarified and relieved: "The 'historical conditions' must of course not be imagined . . . as mysterious Powers (in the background); on the contrary, they are created and maintained by men (and will in due course be altered by them). It is the actions taking place before us that allow us to see what they are."

Brecht's attitude towards dramatic action and his strong reaction against the interpretations of his own poetry in terms of depth psychology put Brecht the critic in direct opposition to the kind of criticism practiced by people like Empson and Richards, in which the suspension of the ambiguities is considered to be more valuable than the production of a clear ethical judgment. The exploration of ambiguity in a work of art assumes the presence of both conscious and subconscious processes working in the creative experience. But Brecht's own aesthetic is suspicious of the influence of images from the subconscious. He desired a supremely conscious art, one directed by ethical judgment which also generated an ethical judgment in the conscious attention of the spectator. He wrote: "The subconscious is not at all responsive to guidance; it has as it were a bad memory." Martin Esslin [in his *Brecht: The Man and His Work,* 1961] discusses this suspicious attitude towards the influence of the subconscious: "But if a poet like T. S. Eliot wisely acknowledges the mystery behind his own poetic activity, and therefore declines to explain what he *intended* his poetry to mean, Brecht obstinately refused to acknowledge that there was more in what he wrote than the rationally calculated effects he had wanted to achieve. This attitude, which sprang from Brecht's highly complex personality, had very curious results. As he refused even to consider the presence of subconscious emotional factors in his poetry, he could not and did not control it, so that the subconscious elements are, if anything, *more* clearly visible in Brecht's work than in that of poets who understand, and are therefore able to conceal, their subconscious impulses."

As Esslin discusses the matter, Brecht the poet could not create without ambiguity; and while Brecht the critic and theoretician may have demanded explicit clarity, Brecht the functioning poet and playwright produced ambiguous poems. Even ***Die Maßnahme,*** the most didactic of the *Lehrstücke,* maintains a double perspective in spite of the clear intention of the poet. In the ethical structure of this explicit play, the sacrifice of The Young Comrade is seen as an action which is necessary, and logically determined, for the achievement of an ultimate good.

And yet, in the dialectic conflict between the immediately compassionate act and the maintenance of a distant ideal, the vital humanity of The Young Comrade who cannot reconcile the present act and the ultimate end questions the ethic which demands their separation. Significantly, it is not The Young Comrade himself who questions that ethic; it is the tension between the demands of a specific sense of compassion and an absolute ideal within the play itself which qualifies the acceptance of the comrades' execution of their fellow worker. Martin Esslin writes: ***Die Maßnahme*** is " . . . a devastating revelation of the tragic dilemma facing the adherents of a creed that demands the subordination of all human feeling to a dry and abstract ideal." In his discussion of the tension in Brecht's work as the result of a conflict between reason and instinct in the poet himself, Martin Esslin sees Brecht's motive of the split personality as an expression of this conflict. In an interesting and perceptive critical essay ["Brecht's Split Characters and His Sense of the Tragic," in *Brecht: A Collection of Critical Essays,* edited by Peter Demetz, 1962], Walter H. Sokel develops Esslin's point in his consideration of the theme of split personality as a means of clarifying "his deep-seated though oft-denied sense of the tragic." Sokel finds this motive working directly in ***A Man's a Man,*** the ballet ***Seven Deadly Sins, The Good Woman of Setzuan,*** and ***Puntila.*** He notes: "Indirectly schizoid behavior forms an essential aspect of ***Mother Courage*** and an important one in ***Galileo.***" In ***Galileo,*** as in ***Mother Courage,*** the split is not actually dramatized but instead it exists in the tension between Galileo the altruistic scientist who holds the vision of a world freed from limitation by science and Galileo the human being whose sensual appetites demand satisfaction.

While Brecht the polemicist considered ***Galileo*** in terms of a clear, literal meaning, Brecht the poet responded to the human action in the building of a complex verbal structure. It is the potential meaning in the complexity of the verbal structure, as an extension of the literal meaning, to which people like Empson and Richards refer in their use of "ambiguity." Allen Tate [in his *On the Limits of Poetry,* 1948] states " . . . we may begin with the literal statement and by stages develop the complications of metaphor: at every stage we may pause to state the meaning so far apprehended, and, at every stage the meaning will be coherent." In ***Galileo,*** that "coherent meaning" includes a realization that Galileo's human appetite includes an insatiable desire for knowledge and, as well, that his recantation, which denies the validity of that very knowledge, is motivated by his desire to avoid pain and continue to satisfy his appetites, both intellectual and sensuous. Galileo the scientist is subject to the demands of Galileo the human being. Galileo's guilt, consequently, is not the clear matter of Brecht's polemic. His character is ambiguous, and this essay intends to explore that ambiguity.

As I noted above, Brecht claimed that the audience's acceptance of Galileo is gained "through the vitality of this alien manifestation"; and the much discussed process of alienation is related to Brecht's desire that his audience be free enough from emotional involvement to make the ethical judgment that Galileo is a villain. However, the image of Galileo as a human being is so strong that such a detachment seems impossible. The very complexity of the character and the play denies that detachment. Consider the following passage from Ernst Kris' essay on "Aesthetic Ambiguity" [in his *Psychoanalytic Explorations in Art,* 1952] in relation to Brecht's ***Galileo***.

> The response is not aesthetic at all unless is comprises a shift in *psychic distance,* that is fluctuation in the degree of involvement in action. . . . The aesthetic illusion requires, as was emphasized by Kant, a detachment from the workings of the practical reason. In the drama and novel failure to attain such detachment is manifested in that extreme of identification with the characters which focuses interest and attention solely on 'how it all comes out.' In poetry, the Kantian emphasis on detachment can be expressed by Coleridge's formula of 'willing suspension of disbelief.' More generally, when distance is minimal, the reaction to works of art is pragmatic rather than aesthetic. Art is transformed to pin-up and propaganda, magic and ritual, and becomes an important determinant of belief and action. The ambiguities with which interpretation must deal are disjunctive and additive: meanings are selected and abstracted in the service of practical ends.

It is the argument of this essay that the nature of Brecht's play, in Kris' terms, is aesthetic rather than pragmatic—that the spectator responds to the figure of Galileo not only as a "phenomenon" of human evil but also as a human being who shares, with him, the weakness of being human.

In the original version of this play, which was written in 1938 and 1939, while Brecht was in exile in Denmark, Galileo is condemned as a coward in his act of recantation. However, as Gunter Rohrmoser notes ["Brecht's ***Galileo,***" translated by J. F. Sammons, in *Brecht: A Collection of Critical Essays,* edited by Peter Demetz, 1962], in the first version there is greater emphasis upon Galileo's cleverness as he outsmarts the Inquisition and, under the guise of blindness, completes his work and smuggles it out of the country by a pupil. "Thus the cunning of reason triumphs also in the ethic of the scientist's political action, it is as far ahead of its century as his knowledge is, and causes light to dawn in the darkness of his age." However, there is evidence which would suggest that Brecht composed ***Galileo*** with the knowledge that the Nazis were exploiting the science of physics to produce the terrible atom bomb; and while Brecht and Charles Laughton were working on the English translation and revision of the play, the version this essay studies, America exploded the atomic bomb in Hiroshima. Certainly this event related to Brecht's conception of the action and its meaning, and the sin of Galileo's recantation assumed gigantic proportions in the poet's mind.

> The 'atomic' age made its debut at Hiroshima in the middle of our work. Overnight the biography of the founder of the new system of physics read differently . . . Galileo's crime can be regarded as the 'original sin' of modern nature sciences. From the new astronomy, which deeply interested a new class—the bourgeoisie—since it gave an impetus to the revolutionary social current of the time, he made a sharply defined special science which—admittedly through its very 'purity,' i.e., its indifference to modes of production—was able to develop comparatively undisturbed. The atom bomb is, both as a technical and as a social phenomenon, the classical end product of his contribution to science and his failure to society.

Certainly Brecht's clearly defined purpose in the second version of ***Galileo*** is to demonstrate the scientist's sin as an historic explanation for the subjugation of science to authority. And this play existed in the playwright's mind, obviously, as a demonstration made in the terrifying context of the ultimate result of that subjugation: the already realized mass-killing of the atomic explosions in Japan and the potential annihilation ahead. This definition of Galileo's action is accomplished through the celebration of both the scientist and his discovery as the potential source of the birth of a new age, an age free from the dogmatic veneration of Rome as the focal point of the Ptolemaic universe—from the dogmatic veneration of any absolute—and through the acutely critical presentation of his failure to realize that birth.

The actual presence of the astronomical model, a construction of the Ptolemaic conception of the earth-centered universe, functions symbolically and realistically in the first scene of ***Galileo.*** This archaic conception is described in metaphors which oppose freedom:

> Those metal bands represent crystal globes, eight of them. . . . Like huge soap bubbles one inside the other and the stars are supposed to be tacked on them. Spin the band with the sun on it. . . . You see the fixed ball in the middle? . . . That's the earth. For two thousand years man has chosen to believe that the sun and all the host of stars revolve about him. Well. The Pope, the Cardinals, the princes, the scholars, captains, merchants, housewives, have pictured themselves squatting in the middle of an affair like that.

Andrea completes the image in his question: "Locked up inside? . . . It's like a cage." The suggestion that the Ptolemaic schematic is maintained to nourish and sustain the ego of authority is answered in the weak and senile Old Cardinal's use of the same image in a desperate attempt to affirm his own value:

> I won't have it! I won't have it! I won't be a nobody on an inconsequential star briefly twirling hither and thither. I tread the earth, and the earth is firm beneath my feet, and there is no motion to the earth, and the earth is the center of all things, and I am the center of the earth, and the eye of the creator is upon me. About me revolve, affixed to their crystal shells, the lesser lights of the stars and the great light of the sun, created to give light upon me that God might see

> me—Man, God's greatest effort, the center of creation.

In the ethical structure of ***Galileo,*** the scientist's relative truth is opposed to the absolute dogma of the church, a dogma which, significantly, is not maintained by Christian conviction but rather by the power of the capitalistic aristocracy which would collapse if dogma lost its authority. The conflict of the Copernican concept of the universe and the Christian concept of a creating God provides, in essence, only a minor aspect of the conflict of ***Galileo.*** However, it does exist at certain points; for example: after being shown the stars of Jupiter, Sagredo asks Galileo insistently, "Where is God then. . . . God? Where is God?" Galileo answers: "(*angrily*): Not there! Any more than he'd be here—if creatures of the moon came down to look for Him!" Sagredo cries: "Where is God in your system of the universe?"; and Galileo's answer is significant: "Within ourselves. Or—nowhere." Even the Little Monk, in an attempt to convince Galileo and himself, does not argue from theology but from psychology, believing that the Christian conception gives meaning to his parents' otherwise pointless existence. The intellectual assumptions of Brecht's ***Galileo*** deny the existence of God; consequently, since the conflict which produced the play exists apart from a theological motive, Brecht assumes that Galileo is opposed, not from a theological motive, but from a political one. This opposition is defined in Brecht's use of Ludovico to represent Galileo's real enemy—the moneyed aristocracy. Galileo's real confrontation with the opposition comes when Ludovico forces him to decide between a commitment to scientific freedom and the compromise of silence which he has maintained for eight years. Galileo's conflict with the authorities of the church is one level removed from the essential conflict. Barberini's rationality could accommodate Galileo's truth within the church, but—as Pope Urban VIII—he is subject to the pressures of the aristocracy. And Ludovico's family will sanction the marriage between him and Galileo's daughter only if Galileo continues to be silent. Under the promise of freedom, which the scientist anticipates in the papal reign of Barberini, Galileo commits himself to the integrity of science. Ludovico is well aware of the concentration of real power and his assessment is valid in the dialectic of the play: " . . . the new Pope, whoever he turns out to be, will respect the convictions held by the solid families of the country. . . . If we Marsilis were to countenance teaching frowned on by the church, it would unsettle the peasants." When Ludovico leaves, Galileo, Andrea, and Federzoni continue the definition of the real adversary: "To hell with all Marsilis, Villanis, Orsinis, Canes, Nuccolis, Soldanieris. . . . who ordered the earth to stand still because their castles might be shaken loose if it revolves . . . and who only kiss the Pope's feet as long as he uses them to trample on the people." There is sufficient internal evidence within the text of the play to demonstrate that the conflict is not a theological one. Brecht's own foreword states that he considered Galileo's opposition to be the aristocracy, neither Christian doctrine nor the Church; and, in order to clarify this conflict in contemporary terms, Brecht's foreword instructs that "The casting of the church dignitaries must be done particularly realistically. No kind of caricature of the Church is intended. . . . In this play the Church represents chiefly Authority; as types the dignitaries of the church should resemble our present-day bankers and senators." In ***Galileo*** the theological conflict is always secondary to the political; and Rome opposes Galileo, not because he has banished God from the heavens, but because his banishment of man from the center of the universe threatens the hierarchy of the church and the aristocracy which supports it. This social and economic disintegration which the church and aristocracy fear is demonstrated in the ballad and anarchic revel of Scene ix. After describing the obedient scheme of the sun revolving around the earth and the cardinals around the Pope is a hierarchic organization extending to the revolution of the lowly domestic animals around the servants, in the Great Chain of Being, the ballad singer continues:

> Up stood the learned Galileo
> Glanced briefly at the sun
> And said: 'Almighty God was wrong.
> In Genesis, Chapter One!'
> Now that was rash, my friends, it is no matter small
> For heresy will spread today like foul diseases.
> Change Holy Writ, forsooth? What will be left at all?
> Why: each of us would say and do just what he pleases!
> Good people, what will come to pass
> If Galileo's teachings spread?
> No altar boy will serve the mass
> No servant girl will make the bed.
> Now that is grave, my friends, it is no matter small:
> For independent spirit spreads like foul diseases!
> (Yet life is sweet and man is weak and after all—
> How nice it is, for a little change, to do just as one pleases!)

The licentious freedom of the pantomime celebrates that promised anarchy.

Perhaps the strongest statement within the play in the judgment of Galileo's recantation rests in the brilliant contrapuntal structure of Scene xii, in which his assistants and his daughter await the results of the trial in the garden of the Florentine Ambassador in Rome. Andrea, Federzoni, and the Little Monk reveal their anxiety in their increasingly strong affirmation of their faith in the master's integrity as the moment of trial approaches. Against the counterpoint of Virginia's Latin prayers, prayers made in her acute fear that her father will not recant, they vehemently deny the statement of the informer who claims that at five o'clock the big bell of Saint Marcus will be rung to announce the recantation. Andrea affirms the truth of Galileo's discovery in a shouted declaration which, ironically, has the sound of a new liturgy: "The moon is an earth because the light of the moon is not her own. Jupiter is a fixed star, and four moons turn around Jupiter, therefore we are not shut in by crystal shells. The sun is the pivot of our world, therefore the earth is not the center. The earth moves, spinning about the sun. And he showed us. You can't make a man unsee what he has seen." Federzoni announces, "Five o'clock is one minute," and Virginia's frenzied prayers intensify. The assistants stand, hands covering their ears, as the moment comes and goes in silence; their tension breaks into joy. Against Virginia's grief and the irony of reality, the assistants express their response to the acute significance of Galileo's gesture. The magnificent integrity, with its potentially infinite meaning to a new age, counteracts their grief at the master's pain or death; and they celebrate his gesture. Federzoni cries: "June 22, 1633: dawn of the age of reason. I wouldn't have wanted to go on living if he had recanted." The Little Monk confesses the agony of suspense and condemns his "little faith" in an association of Galileo with Christ. In the meaningful images of darkness and light, Federzoni sees the recantation, which he no longer fears, as a return to irrationality and ignorance from the promise of reason and truth: "It would have turned our morning to night." And the potential strength of Galileo is defined as Andrea declares in painful irony: "It would have been as if the mountain had turned to water." This celebration is played against Virginia's despair; and at its peak, the bell begins to toll. The counterpoint reverses its rhythm, and the assistants stand in despair against the rejoicing of Virginia. The mountain had turned to water. Galileo enters, and he confronts his assistants, transformed, "almost unrecognizable." In hysterical despair, the center of his idealism dissolved, Andrea cries: "He saved his big gut." To Galileo he says, "Unhappy is the land that breeds no hero"; and Galileo says simply, "Unhappy is the land that needs a hero."

Brecht's attempt to define Galileo's sin explicitly is seen in the obvious structural relationship of Scenes i and xiii. In the first scene, the middleaged Galileo enchants Andrea, the young son of his housekeeper and Galileo's student, with his description of the birth of a new age in which man will break out of the Ptolemaic cage: "There was a group of masons arguing. They had to raise a block of granite. It was hot. To help matters, one of them wanted to try a new arrangement of ropes. After five minutes discussion, out went a method which had been employed for a thousand years. The millenium of faith is ended, said I, this is the millenium of doubt. And we are pulling out of that contraption." Galileo's enthusiasm for the birth of a new age predicts that science will be the possession of the common people, and the arbitrary hierarchy will disintegrate: ". . . in our time astronomy will become the gossip of the market place and the sons of fishwives will pack the schools. . . . By that time . . . they will be learning that the earth rolls round the sun, and that their mothers, the captains, the scholars, the princes and the Pope are rolling with it."

In Scene xiii the birth of the new age is also discussed by Andrea and Galileo; but now it is a discussion between an old Galileo and an adult Andrea, a confrontation of the disillusioned student and the master who betrayed his ideal by selling his science to the authorities. The implicit tension in this confrontation belies Brechtian objectivity. In his dedication to the search for knowledge, Galileo kindled a scientific idealism in his young pupil and fellow scientist. Against the standard of this idealism, a faith in the freedom of knowledge which he had inculcated, Galileo's realistic action, the compromise of his recantation, was unacceptable—a betrayal of the very freedom from dogma which his discoveries promised. In the apparent simplicity of this confrontation, a sophisticated complexity is working. When Galileo presents Andrea with the completed *Discorsi* and suggests how the mask of the faithful Christian has allowed him to complete his work, the younger man sees the value of Galileo's realism: "With the crowd at the street corners we said: 'He will die, he will never surrender.' You came back: 'I surrendered but I am alive.' We cried: 'Your hands are stained!' You say: 'Better stained than empty.' . . . You gained time to write a book that only you could write. Had you burned at the stake in a blaze of glory they would have won." Then Galileo, again assuming the role of teacher, attempts to counter Andrea's realism with a rekindling of the idealism he has maintained:

> The practice of science would seem to call for valor. She trades in knowledge, which is the product of doubt. And this new art of doubt has enchanted the public. The plight of the multitude is old as the rocks, and is believed to be as basic as the rocks. . . . But now they have learned to doubt. . . . As a scientist I had almost an unique opportunity. In my day astronomy emerged into the marketplace. At that particular time, had one man put up a fight, it could have had wide repercussions.

Instead, the new age, which began in the ships venturing freely from the coasts and which could have been confirmed as the "dawn of the age of reason" at the moment when Galileo refused to recant, has been transformed into the image of a "whore, spattered with blood." Rohrmoser notes a significant revision from the original text to the reworked version by Brecht and Laughton. He quotes the earlier text: " 'I insist that this is a new age. If it looks like a blood-stained old hag, then that's what a new age looks like. The burst of light takes place in the deepest darkness.' " The later text, in the context of the Hiroshima explosion, reads more ambiguously: "—This age of ours turned out to be a whore, spattered with blood. Maybe, new ages look like blood-spattered whores." Brecht's later plays contain a controlled language which is in strong contrast to the richly textured imagery of the early plays and poems. The conscious deliberation of this image is, consequently, very significant. As Rohrmoser's essay on Galileo suggests, and Brecht's introductory remarks confirm, the concept of the new age is a primary concern of the play. And it is vital that Galileo, who sees his own sin with such intense clarity, conceives of the new age in the image of the "blood-spattered whore"—sold and exploited. Implicit in Galileo's image is the idea that Galileo himself has sold the age, which was in his hands, which, purchased and consumed, has become the bloody whore.

The Life of Galileo is not the clear and simple defamation of Galileo's act which the isolation of these images and actions would suggest—and which, according to his own descriptions of the play, Brecht intended it to be. However, what the play loses in the explication of thesis it gains in an increasing profundity in its ambiguity—an ambiguity which sees the action in a complex of perspectives.

This ambiguity is focused in the implicitly schizoid structure of its hero. Brecht uses the structural device of the split personality more obviously in a minor character than in the character of Galileo, but he uses it to define the action of compromise which anticipates Galileo's recantation. One of the most dynamic scenes of the play is that in which Barberini, being clothed in the robes of the church, moves from the identity of the Cardinal, sympathetic to science, to the identity of the Pope, opposed to the threat which science presents to dogma and papal security. This transformation is clarified in the stage directions:

> *During the scene the* POPE *is being robed for the conclave he is about to attend: at the beginning of the scene he is plainly Barberini, but as the scene proceeds he is more and more obscured by the grandiose vestments.*

The little scene begins with Barberini's insistent negation of the Cardinal Inquisitor's demands that Galileo be forced to recant, but the Inquisitor's pervasive arguments and the restlessness of the Papal Court, expressed in the noise of shuffling feet, break down Barberini's scientific considerations as he assumes the identity of Pope Urban VIII. As Cardinal Barberini, he can insure that Galileo will neither be executed nor tortured; as Pope Urban VIII, he cannot insure that Galileo will not be threatened.

This transformation relates to another meaningful use of the symbol of the dual personality, integrity and compromise. At the ball at the residence of Bellarmin in Rome, the two Cardinals, Bellarmin and Barberini, charge Galileo, in the guise of friendship, to abandon his teachings. Barberini is sympathetic—already torn between his belief in science and his obligation to the Holy Church. Ironically, the Cardinals approach in masks: Barberini as a dove, Bellarmin as a lamb. The masks are lowered as they discuss and debate with Galileo; but, resuming the guise of social amenity, Barberini comments: "Let us replace our masks, Ballarmin. Poor Galileo hasn't got one." However, in the development of the play, Galileo assumes his mask; and he uses it in much the manner of Barberini's mask of the dove and the mask of identity as Pope Urban VIII.

While Gunter Rohrmoser responds to the complexities of Brecht's ***Galileo,*** he insists upon rejecting the idea that the play is concerned "with the interpretative dramatization of a complex character." He continues: "In turning to history Brecht is concerned in substance with the basic historical and human problem of his own age. . . . Galileo does not interest him as a character, but as a case, although the individual vital substance of the hero is not sacrificed to an abstract scheme to the same extent as in the plays of a Marxist cast, the didactic plays." From his Marxist perspective, surely Brecht saw Galileo's betrayal of science as an historical action which issues in the real and the potential horrors of the atomic age. However, in Brecht's poetic imitation of this action, Galileo's failure becomes not exceptional but, on the contrary, essentially human; and, as the focal point of a complex of opposing motives, Galileo embodies human failure. To consume life, with all the pleasures that consumption entails, becomes a stronger motive than to maintain an abstract ideal—if forced to make a choice. And, in the central ambiguity, that ideal is generated in the very appetite for life which demands its sacrifice. The ambiguity extends to another level: while we resond to Andrea's argument that Galileo's cunning has allowed him to complete his work and make an historic gesture even more significant than his sacrifice would have been, we know that the Schweikian acquiescence which assured the continuation of his work did not derive from an abstract dedication to continue performing the birth of a new age. The suggestion of the recantation as a Schweikian trick is present in both of Brecht's major versions of ***The Life of Galileo,*** but it is not as strong an image in the second. And, it is important to realize that Galileo's continued work is accomplished itself in a compulsive joy of discovery and affirmation of hypothesis, not purely in the altruism of scientific contribution. Galileo does not plot to smuggle the *Discorsi* out of Italy; it is mere chance that Andrea comes. Surely Brecht enjoyed this final irony. While Galileo again assumes the role of idealist to convince Andrea that his master was wrong and is guilty of the separation of science and humanity, he himself—divorced from humanity in his false identity—continues his work, because of his appetite, whether or not it will be realized in application. Brecht creates his Galileo as a man with an incessant hunger for life; Cardinal Barberini, become Pope Urban VIII, declares: "He has more enjoyment in him than any man I ever saw. He loves eating and drinking and thinking. To excess. He indulges in thinking-bouts! He cannot say no to an old wine or a new thought." Brecht's Galileo has an insatiable appetite for knowledge which is only one aspect of a total appetite for life itself, an indulgence in pleasure as well as an attempt to free mankind from the prison of misconceptions in which they are bound. His work is both altruistic and essentially selfish at the same time. He is committed both to the salvation of mankind and his own indulgence in life; and when put to a decision between mankind and life, the division cannot be made—hence the tragic course.

Brecht continually associates Galileo's hunger for food with his hunger for knowledge. Considering the possibility of attaching himself to the Florentine Court of the Medici in order to give himself time for research, Galileo tells the Curator that he is dissatisfied with his position in Venice, but that his primary source of discontent is his lack of scientific achievement: "My discontent, Priuli, is for the most part with myself. I am forty-six years of age and have achieved nothing which satisfies me." His justification to Sagredo and Virginia for the move to Florence, and the compromises a court appointment will bring, is made in other terms: "Your father, my dear, is going to take his share of the pleasures in life in exchange for all his hardwork, and about time too. I have no patience, Sagredo, with a man who doesn't use his brains to fill his belly."

The contrast of relationships between Galileo and Andrea in Scenes i and xiii has already been discussed, primarily however, to clarify Brecht's explicit structuring of the conflict. The scenes also relate to the play's ambiguity. Essentially Galileo's schizoid personality is divided into Galileo the scientist and visionary of a new age and Galileo the glutton who satisfies his appetite for food, wine, and ideas in the same indulgence. In order to satisfy his appetite for knowledge, to gain time both for research and physical pleasure, he trades his intellectual freedom. And, at the crucial moment, to avoid pain—again an indulgence in pleasure—he submits to authority, trading the freedom of scientific truth. The specific relationship of these indulgences Brecht saw clearly and identified, not only in the play, but in his commentary on epic acting in **"A Short Organum."** Discussing the first scene of ***Galileo,*** he says:

> To play this, surely you have got to know that we shall be ending with the man of seventy-eight having his supper, just after he said good-bye forever to the same pupil. He is then more terribly altered than this passage of time could possibly have brought about. He wolfs his food with unrestrained greed, no other idea in his head; he has rid himself of his educational mission in shameful circumstances, as though it were a burden: he, who once drank his morning milk without a care, greedy to teach the boy. But does he really drink it without care? Isn't the pleasure of drinking and washing one with the pleasure he takes in the new ideas? Don't forget: he thinks out of self-indulgence. . . . [sic]

The primary ambiguity of ***The Life of Galileo*** finds its source in the fact that Galileo's indulgence in life's pleasure generates the appetite for knowledge and hence the knowledge itself, and simultaneously, generates the human weakness which makes him unable to say no to the threat of pain. His submission to appetite is both his strength and his weakness.

I. A. Richards considers tragedy to be "the balance or reconciliation of opposite and discordant qualities," and in ***Galileo*** we have that balance in this specific ambiguity. Galileo cannot separate the appetite for knowledge, and, consequently, the ideal of scientific freedom, from the appetite for life itself; both are the same. In Brecht's polemic, Galileo should have subordinated one appetite to the other: Galileo the scientist should have triumphed over Galileo the human being, and the ideal of scientific freedom should have been maintained. However, in the schizoid structure of ***The Good Woman of Setzuan,*** Shen Te cannot maintain the division of herself into the compassionate Shen Te and the efficient realist Shui-Ta; neither can she accommodate the unification of the schizoid personality at the conclusion of the action. Galileo himself cannot subordinate one aspect of himself to the other; and ***Galileo*** ends, as ***The Good Woman of Setzuan*** ends, with the human personality in conflict with itself.

Brecht himself writes that the appetite for physical pleasure motivated Galileo's capitulation to deceit in the telescope fraud and he claims that this deception leads to Galileo's excitement of discovery, an excitement that brings a satisfaction which is the same as that of physical indulgence. The satisfaction of appetite trains Galileo in the process of compromise: ". . . his charlatanry . . . shows how determined this man is to take the easy course, and to apply his reason in a base as well as a noble manner. A more significant test awaits him; and does not every capitulation bring the next one nearer?"

Galileo is forced to choose between his indulgence in life's pleasures and the retreat from pain and the maintenance of an abstract ideal. The tragic ambiguity remains in the fact that this ideal is meaningful to Galileo only when it relates to his own personal satisfaction; his tragic course in inevitable in the terms in which Brecht has drawn his character.

The sense of tragedy in ***The Life of Galileo*** grows out of this paradox. Reconsider I. A. Richards' definition of tragedy in its application to Galileo: "Pity, the impulse to approach, and Terror, the impulse to retreat, are brought in tragedy to a reconciliation which they find nowhere else, . . . Their union is an ordered response in the *catharsis* by which Tragedy is recognized. . . ." Galileo suffers acutely from the knowledge that his act of cowardice is the antecedent of terrifying destructive force. The intensity of Galileo's sensuousness, the equation of his indulgence in scientific experimentation and his indulgence in the gratification of physical pleasures, relate him to Brecht's celebration of sensuality, the grotesque Baal. However, Baal cannot comprehend an ethical concept, and Galileo is acutely aware of his ethical responsibility. Galileo experiences "THE COMPREHENSION OF THE SINGLE MAN AND THE WHOLE." However, unlike The Young Comrade in ***Die Maßnahme,*** he is unable to perform the act of "cold acquiescence." The Young Comrade agrees to his own sacrifice with the knowledge that his death is a necessary process in the revolutionizing of the world. Galileo is unable to sacrifice his humanity, but with The Young Comrade he shares an understanding that the birth of a new age is dependent upon his acquiescence and this knowledge engenders in Galileo his painful guilt.

In scene xiii, Brechtian alienation occurs when the spectators are made aware that Galileo refers to the terrors of the atom bomb when he discusses the gap between science and humanity which his act of cowardice has rendered: "Should you then, in time, discover all there is to be discovered, your progress must then become a progress away from the bulk of humanity. The gulf might even grow so wide that the sound of your cheering at some new achievement would be echoed by a universal howl of horror." This juxtaposition of the historic Galileo and our contemporary knowledge functions to alienate; however, this awareness magnifies Galileo's grief and guilt, especially guilt, to an incomprehensible extreme. Consequently, as spectators, we retreat, in Richards' terms, in terror for a criminal who could really bear no greater guilt. He placed science in the hands of those who used it, in secret, to produce the most extensive destructive force the world has ever seen. However, at the same time as we retreat from the horror of Galileo's action, we pity him as an acute sufferer, the bearer of an immense and destructive guilt. And we recognize that his failure is an essential human failure: a weakness which produced his knowledge and sacrificed it to its source. In this ambiguity, these "opposite and discordant qualities" are suspended in a single response.

The tragic nature of ***The Life of Galileo*** defeats, to a considerable degree, the explication of its didactic motive. The spectator cannot withdraw from Galileo's action and state: "He should have been willing to sacrifice himself to pain, certainly, even death because he fully recognized the ultimate consequence of his acquiescence to the demands of authority. He should have realized that the strength of his position would have insured his safety." However, the perceptive spectator cannot make this judgment, because for Galileo to deny life would be for him to deny the source of scientific truth; and the Galileo trained in the denial of life could not have been the Galileo whose affirmation of life brought forth his discoveries. (pp. 57-71)

> *Charles R. Lyons, " 'The Life of Galileo': The Focus of Ambiguity in the Villain Hero," in* The Germanic Review, *Vol. XLI, No. 1, January, 1966, pp. 57-71.*

Eric Bentley (essay date 1966)

[*Bentley is considered one of the most erudite and innovative critics of the modern theater. He is credited with introducing Bertolt Brecht, Luigi Pirandello, and other European playwrights to America through his studies, translations, and stage adaptations of their plays. In his critical works, Bentley concentrates on the playwright and the dramatic text rather than on production aspects of the play. Bentley's finest work,* The Life of Drama *(1964), is a comprehensive study of the development of dramatic form, specifically examining aspects of melodrama, farce, comedy, tragedy, and tragicomedy. His most recent critical works include anthologies of reviews written during his years as drama critic (1952-56) for the* New Republic, *and a collection of his essays on Brecht—*The Brecht Commentaries: 1943-80 *(1981). In the following excerpt, originally published in 1966, Bentley explores the historical validity of Brecht's characterization of Galileo through a comparison of the 1938 and 1947 versions of the play. Bentley focuses on contemporary events—including the construction and subsequent employment of the atom bomb—that altered the dramatist's conception of the character.*]

Brecht was all wrong about the seventeenth century in general and about Galileo Galilei in particular. His main assumption is that the new cosmology gave man only a peripheral importance, where the old cosmology had given him a central one. In actual fact, this argument is not found in the works or conversation of Galileo, or of his friends, or of his enemies, or of anyone in his time. Discussing the point in his *Great Chain of Being,* the historian Arthur O. Lovejoy observes that the center was not held to be the place of honor anyway: prestige was out beyond the periphery, where God lived.

So much for the universe. As for the new scientific attitude, for Brecht it apparently is summed up in the pebble which his Galileo likes to drop from one hand to the other to remind himself that pebbles do not fly but fall. In short, the scientist notices, in a down-to-earth way, what actually goes on: he accepts the evidence of his senses. In this he is contrasted with the theologian, who uses imagination and reasoning. Which is all very well except that the little parable of the pebble does not characterize the stage to which physical science was brought by Galileo. It does cover his initial use of the telescope. That was a matter of looking through lenses and believing his own eyes. However, no startling conclusions could be reached, and above all nothing could be proved, without doing a great deal more. What happened to physics in the seventeenth century is that it became mathematical. This meant that it became not more concrete but just the opposite. After all, the evidence of one's senses is that the sun goes round the earth. That the earth should go round the sun is directly counter to that evidence. The average man today accepts the latter idea on pure faith. So far as he knows, it could be wholly untrue. For the demonstration lies in the realm of the abstract and the abstruse.

Brecht is no nearer to the kind of truth that interests a biographer than he is to the kind that interests a historian of science. A good deal is known about the historical Galileo Galilei. For example, he had a mistress who bore him three children. The most human document of his biography is his correspondence with one of the daughters. The love between these two may well have been the greatest love of his life, as it certainly was of hers. But Brecht is interested in none of this, nor can it be retorted that the details of Galileo's professional life preoccupied him. Much is known of the trial of Galileo, and the material has the highest human and dramatic quality, on which various biographers have capitalized. But Brecht passes by the trial "scenes" too. Even the character of his Galileo seems only in part to have been suggested by the personality of the great scientist. The historical Galileo was a proud, even a vain, man. This makes him the villain of Arthur Koestler's book *The Sleepwalkers,* and, to be sure, it contributes to the villainous element in Brecht's Galileo, though Brecht is less concerned than Koestler to nag him, and more concerned to show that there are social reasons why excessive self-reliance fails to get results. Yet Galileo's self-reliance *would* have got results—as Brecht tells the story—but for a quality which has to be invented for him: cowardice. The axis of Brecht's story is passivity-activity, cowardice-courage, slyness-boldness. To make his story into a play, Brecht exploited whatever ready-made material came to hand, but must himself take full responsibility for the final product.

Would Brecht have admitted this, or would he have claimed that he was writing history? If I may be permitted to draw on my memory of Brecht's conversation on the point, I'd say he had a variable attitude. Sometimes he talked as if he had indeed taken everything from the historical record; other times (and this is true in the printed notes too) he would admit to changes but maintain that they didn't distort history; at other times still, he would talk as if he had an entirely free hand (as when in 1945-1956 he changed Galileo's big speech in his last scene).

Whatever Brecht thought he was doing, what good playwrights always do was perceived by Aristotle and confirmed by Lessing. When Aristotle observed that tragedy was more philosophical than history, he was noting that drama has a different logic from that of fact. History can be (or appear to be) chaotic and meaningless; drama cannot. Truth may be stranger than fiction; by the same token, it is not as orderly. Or as Pirandello saw the matter: the truth doesn't have to be plausible but fiction does. The facts of Jeanne d'Arc's life, as the historical record supplies them, did not seem to Bernard Shaw to have either plausibility or interest, for the historical Jeanne was the victim of the machinations of a vulgar politician (the historical Cauchon). The story becomes plausible and interesting by the replacement of this Cauchon with an invented one who can oppose Jeanne on principle. Now the antagonists of Brecht's Galileo would be inconceivable had Shaw not created Warwick, Cauchon, and the Inquisitor, and, equally, Brecht's Barberini and Inquisitor could not get into his play except by replacing the Barberini and the Inquisitor of history. The historical Barberini seems to have made himself a personal enemy of Galileo, and the Inquisitor (Firenzuola) seems to have intrigued most mercilessly against him, but Brecht follows Shaw in having his protagonist's foes proceed solely from the logic of their situation. In this way the central situations of both ***Saint Joan*** and ***Galileo*** take on form and meaning. It is a paradox. The historical truth, rejected for its implausibility, has the air of an artifact, whereas the artifact, the play, has an air of truth. The villains of history seemed too melodramatic to both authors. The truth offended their sense of truth, and out of the less dramatic they made the more dramatic.

If what playwrights are after is fiction, why do they purport to offer us history plays at all? People who ask this question generally have in mind the whole expanse of human history and see it all as available to the playwright, yet a glance at history plays that have had success of any sort will reveal that they are not about the great figures of history taken indiscriminately but only about those few, like Julius Caesar, Joan of Arc, and Napoleon, whose names have become bywords. Another paradox: only when a figure has become *legendary* is he or she a fit subject for a *history* play.

Are such figures as Shakespeare's *Henry IV* or Strindberg's *Eric XIV* exceptions? Not really. Within Britain, at least, the kings were legends: certainly Henry V was, as a great deal of ballad lore attests, and *Henry IV* is a preparation for *Henry V.* Something similar is true of Strindberg's histories: Swedish history was suitable for plays insofar as it was the folklore of nationalism. Because the historical dramatist is concerned with the bits of history that have stuck in people's imagination, he may well find himself handling bits of pseudo history that are the very *product* of people's imagination. Is it likely that William Tell actually shot an apple off his son's head? What is certain is that Schiller would never have written a play about him had that story not existed.

Again, why do playwrights purport to put history on stage? Is it because the events of a history at least *seem* more real, since many spectators will assume that such a play *is* all true? After all, very much of our "knowledge" of the past is based on fiction. Has not Churchill himself claimed to learn English history from Shakespeare? Was Shakespeare's distortion of the Anglo-French quarrel just Providence's way of preparing Churchill for the Battle of Britain? So should we be prepared to see a modern, Marxist playwright distorting history in order to prepare young Communists for some future Battle of Russia? The proposition is not as remote as it may sound from Bertolt Brecht's ***Galileo.*** The question is whether the factual distortions have to be accepted at face value. It seems to me that even for spectators who know that a history play is bad history, such a play might still seem to have some sort of special relevancy, a more urgent truth.

Writing on Schiller's *Don Carlos,* George Lukacs has suggested that, while playwrights and novelists depart from the *facts* of history, they still present the larger *forces* of history. But the forces of what period in history, that of the ostensible action, or that of the playwright? To me it seems that the claim of the chronicle play to be close to history is valid only if it is contemporary history that is in question. *Don Carlos* belongs to the eighteenth century, not the sixteenth; Shakespeare's histories belong to the sixteenth century, not the fifteenth. Now obviously there is a departure from the contemporary facts. It is not even possible to be close to these facts, since nothing factually contemporary is there at all. What is it that the historical dramatist finds in the earlier period? In Brecht's terminology, it is an alienation of the subject. The familiar subject is placed in a strange setting, so that one can sit back and look and be amazed. What kind of strangeness? It is a matter of what strangeness will throw the subject into highest relief, and of what strangeness a particular writer's gift can re-create. But the strangeness is, anyhow, *only* a setting, and within the setting there must be a situation, a grouping of events, an Action, which provide a little model of what the playwright believes is going on in the present. Dramatists may spend decades looking for such settings and such Actions, or hoping to stumble on them.

Sometimes a sudden irruption of the past into the present will call the dramatist's attention to the new relevance of some old event. The canonization of Jeanne d'Arc in 1920 was such an irruption. It prompted the writing of a play which seemed to be about the age which burned Joan yet which was actually about the age that canonized her though it would burn her if she returned. Like ***Saint Joan*** and all other good history plays, ***Galileo*** is about the playwright's own time.

Like many of Brecht's works, it exists in a number of different drafts, but it is unusual among them in taking two broadly different forms. There are two ***Galileo*** plays here, both of which exist in their entirety, the version of 1938, and the version of 1947. Partial analogies to the changes exist in other Brecht plays. For Brecht, it was no unique thing that he should create a winning rogue and then later decide he must make the audience dislike him. The revisions of both ***Mother Courage*** and ***Puntila*** show this. But in Galileo the change was more radical.

Brecht became interested in the historical Galileo at a time when he was preoccupied with friends and comrades who remained in Germany and somehow managed to continue to work. Prominent in his thoughts was the underground political worker plotting to subvert the Hitler regime. He himself was not a "worker," he was a poet, but a poet in love with the idea of science, a poet who believed that his own philosophy was scientific. It is easy to understand how Galileo came to mind! And to think of Galileo is to think of a single anecdote (incidentally not found before 1757):

> The moment he [Galileo] was set at liberty, he looked up to the sky and down to the ground,

> and, stamping with his foot, in a contemplative mood, said, *Eppur si muove;* that is, still it moves, meaning the earth.

His study was the universe, and its laws are what they are, irrespective of ecclesiastical pronouncement. "Still it moves!" And Galileo can now write a new, epoch-making work, and smuggle it out of the country with these words:

> Take care when you travel through Germany with the truth under your coat!

This sentence puts in a nutshell the most striking analogy between the first version of Brecht's ***Galileo*** and the present, the present being the 1930s, in which, indeed, truth in Germany had to be hidden under coats. It was the time when Wilhelm Reich had copies of his writings on the orgasm bound and inscribed to look like prayer books and in that form mailed from abroad to Germany. It was the time when Brecht himself wrote the essay **"Five Difficulties in Writing the Truth."** The fifth of these difficulties, and the one which Brecht gave most attention to, was the need of "cunning in disseminating the truth." Although Galileo is not included in the essay's list of heroes who showed such cunning, the whole passage is quite close to the thought and frame of mind reflected in the first version of the Galileo play. Even the special perspective which caused Brecht's friend Walter Benjamin to say its hero was not Galileo but the people is found in sentences like: "Propaganda for thinking, in whatever field, is useful to the cause of the oppressed." The early version of ***Galileo*** is nothing if not propaganda for thinking.

The later version of ***Galileo*** is also about the playwright's own time, but this was now, not the thirties, but the middle forties. Brecht has himself recorded what the motive force of the new ***Galileo*** was:

> The atomic age made its debut at Hiroshima in the middle of our work. Overnight the biography of the founder of the new system of physics read differently.

To a historian it would seem bizarre to suggest that he should reverse a judgment he had made on something in the seventeenth century on account of something which had just happened in the twentieth. To a dramatist, however, the question would mainly be whether a subject which had suggested itself because it resembled something in the twentieth century would still be usable when asked to resembled something quite different in the twentieth century.

In the thirties, as I have been saying, what presumably commended the subject of Galileo to Brecht was the analogy between the seventeenth-century scientist's underground activities and those of twentieth-century left-wingers in Hitler Germany. But that is not all that Brecht, even in the early version, made of the *exemplum.* The abjuration was defined as an act of cowardice, and the act of cowardice was then deplored for a precise reason, namely, that more than certain notions about astronomy were at stake. At stake was the liberty to advance these and any other notions.

> ANDREA. . . . many on all sides followed you with their eyes and ears, believing that you stood, not only for a particular view of the movement of the stars, but even more for the liberty of teaching—in all fields. Not then for any particular thoughts, but for the right to think at all.

> GALILEO. . . . a member of the scientific community cannot logically just point to his possible merits as a researcher if he has neglected to honor his profession as such and to defend it against coercion of every kind. But this is a business of some scope. For science demands that facts not be subordinated to opinions but that opinions be subordinated to facts. It is not in a position to limit these propositions and apply them to "some opinions" and "such and such" facts. To be certain that these propositions can always and without limitation be acted on, science must do battle to ensure that they are respected in all fields.

After Hiroshima, Brecht deleted these speeches, in order to substitute another idea. The point was no longer to demand from the authorities liberty to teach all things but to demand from the scientists themselves a sense of social responsibility, a sense of identification with the destiny, not of other scientists only, but of people at large. The point was now to dissent from those who see scientific advance as "an end in itself," thus playing into the hands of those who happen to be in power, and to advance the alternate, utilitarian conception of science:

> GALILEO. . . . I take it that the intent of science is to ease human existence. If you give way to coercion, science can be crippled, and your new machines may simply suggest new drudgeries. Should you, then, in time, discover all there is to be discovered, your progress must become a progress away from the bulk of humanity. The gulf might even grow so wide that the sound of your cheering at some new achievement would be echoed by a universal howl of horror.

In this respect, ***Galileo*** I is a "liberal" defense of freedom against tyranny, while ***Galileo*** II is a Marxist defense of a social conception of science against the "liberal" view that truth is an end in itself.

If this philosophic change is large enough, it is accompanied by an even larger change in the dramatic action. In ***Galileo*** I, a balance is struck between two opposing motifs. On the one hand, Galileo is admired for his slyness and cunning, while on the other being condemned for his cowardice. The admiration is never entirely swallowed up in the disapproval. On the contrary, we give Galileo a good mark for conceding his own weakness. Then, too, Brecht brings about a partial rehabilitation of his hero in two distinct ways: first, by stressing the admirable cunning of the underground worker who can write a new masterpiece under these conditions and arrange to smuggle it out to freer lands; second, by defining his hero's lapse as a limited one, thus:

> ANDREA. . . . it is as if a very high tower which had been thought indestructible should fall to the ground. The noise of its collapse was far louder than the din of the builders and the machines had been during the whole period of its construction. And the pillar of dust which the

> collapse occasioned rose higher than the tower had ever done. But possibly it turns out, when the dust clears, that, while twelve top floors have fallen, thirty floors below are still standing. Is that what you mean? There is this to be said for it: the things that are wrong in this science of ours are out in the open. . . . The difficulty may be the greater; but the necessity has also become greater.

Indeed there is something good about the new book's having a disgraced author. It must now make its way on its own, and not by authority; which will be a gain for science and the scientific community. And dramatically it means a lot that ***Galileo*** I ends with the emphasis on the renewal of friendship between Galileo and Andrea. The old scientist is after all able to hand his work on, as to a son.

Revising the play after Hiroshima, Brecht decided to condemn Galileo far more strongly, and in fact not only to render an unqualified verdict of guilty, but also to picture a shipwrecked, a totally corrupted human being. The sense of the earlier text is: "I should not have let my fear of death make me overlook the fact that I had something more to defend than a theory in pure astronomy." The sense of the later text is: "To be a coward in those circumstances entailed something worse than cowardice itself, namely, treachery." In the early text, Brecht alludes to the Church's belief that Galileo risked damnation for squandering the gift of intellect. In the later text, it is clear that Galileo sees himself as already in hell for having *actually* squandered (betrayed) the gift of intellect, so what we see in the penultimate scene of the later text is a portrait of a "collaborator," a renegade. And Brecht's Notes stress that Galileo should register a malign, misanthropic contempt for Federzoni, as well as shouting in sheer self-hatred to Andrea:

> Welcome to the gutter, dear colleague in science and brother in treason: I sold out, you are a buyer. . . . Blessed be our bargaining, whitewashing, deathfearing community!

Which version is better? There can be no doubt that many improvements were made throughout the play by which the later version benefited, but as far as this penultimate scene is concerned, it is not clear that, in making it more ambitious, Brecht also improved it. To show the foulness of Galileo's crime he has to try to plumb deeper depths. The question is whether this befouled, denatured Galileo can be believed to be the same man we have seen up to then. The impression is, rather, of someone Brecht arbitrarily declares bad at this stage in order to make a point. Which would be of a piece with Communist Party treatment of the betrayal theme generally. One moment a Tito is a Jesus, and the next a Judas. There is, perhaps, an intrusion of unfelt C. P. clichés about traitors and renegades in the later ***Galileo.*** One cannot find, within the boundaries of the play itself, a full justification for the virulence of the final condemnation.

If the crime of Galileo, in the earlier text, being less cataclysmic in its results and less anguished in its style, at first seems less dramatic, it is actually rendered *more* dramatic by the tragicomic relationship in which it stands to Galileo's Schweykian cunning. Personally I find the ambiguity of the earlier ending more human and more richly dramatic as well as more Brechtian and more consistent with the rest of the play.

Sidelights are provided by performances of the play, and their background. It seems to me that even Ernst Busch, the Galileo of the Berlin Ensemble production, could not make real the image of a corrupted Galileo. Busch was very much the Old Communist. He never seemed the sinner in hell but, rather, the Party member who had strayed and was now practicing self-criticism. Charles Laughton would seem a likelier casting. Brecht said Laughton felt guilty for having stayed in Hollywood during World War II instead of returning to fight for Britain, and this sense of guilt, he said, was what would come in useful in ***Galileo.*** Laughton did indeed have subtly personal ways of making guilt seem real that would have delighted Stanislavski himself. When he made his entrance after the abjuration, he seemed, as Brecht said, a little boy who had wet his pants, but, in the last scene, when Brecht wanted the audience to reject Galileo in horror, Laughton made sure they accepted him in pity—while loving him at the same time for the way he outwitted the Inquisition. In other words, the actor put something of ***Galileo*** I back into ***Galileo*** II. Perhaps it is hard not to. The *action* (Galileo smuggling his new book out) is apt, in a theatre, to speak louder than mere *words* of denunciation, but then again the way in which Laughton "stood out" from his part was not exactly what the Brechtian theory bargains for. It was through an actorish narcissism that he kept aloof; and that limited his power to communicate the content of the play. It also

Charles Laughton in Galileo.

made the sinister and self-defeating pride of the scientist dwindle into a movie-star's showy and nervous vanity. Laughton had a unique equipment for this role. It is unlikely that anyone again will combine as he did every appearance of intellectual brilliance with every appearance of physical self-indulgence, yet actorish vanity allowed him to let the brilliance slide over into drawing-room-comedy smartness. Narcissism prevented him from even trying to enter those somewhat Dostoevskian depths into which Brecht invites the actor of the final scene, version two.

Brecht added a detail in the later text which could help a great deal to define that "tragedy of pride" which is certainly a part of this drama. Galileo is offered the chance to escape the Inquisition if he will accept the patronage of the industrialist Vanni, yet he is not an astute enough politician to see the wisdom of such acceptance, and prefers to believe not only in the authorities themselves but in his own ability to go it alone. Laughton, by seeming not to take in what Vanni was saying, threw this little scene away. The effect was not of arrogant overconfidence, merely of lack of rapport or maybe, again, trivial vanity.

It was also through Charles Laughton that the notion was first spread around that ***Galileo*** not only touches on the atom bomb but is essentially concerned with it. Here is Brecht himself in this vein:

> Galileo's crime can be regarded as the original sin of modern physical science. . . . The atom bomb, both as a technical and as a social phenomenon, is the classical end product of his contribution to science and his failure to society.

But such a meaning does not emerge from the story as told either by historians or by Brecht. Had those who wished to stop Galileo and scientific advance had their way, there would be no atom bomb today. Contrariwise, if we accept the Brechtian premise that Galileo could have changed history by making an opposite decision, then he would have changed history by joining hands with Vanni the industrialist, and the atom bomb might have been invented a little earlier—say, by Wernher von Braun.

In East Berlin today Heinar Kipphardt's play about J. Robert Oppenheimer begins in the setting left on stage from Brecht's ***Galileo,*** and the newer play "shows what society exacts from its individuals, what it needs from them," as Brecht said his ***Galileo*** did. However, one is struck by the extreme difference between the two main dramatic situations—that in which it is Reaction that suppresses discovery, and that in which it was inhumane to push *for* science and the *making* of a discovery.

One American production of Brecht's ***Galileo,*** at my suggestion, posted up the following words for the audience to read after the abjuration scene:

> I was not in a policy-making position at Los Alamos. I would have done anything that I was asked to do.
>
> —J. Robert Oppenheimer

I now think there is too much sensationalism in this idea, for Galileo has not offered to do "anything" he might be "asked to do" at all, and dramatically it makes a big difference that he is not being asked to do something but being asked not to do something. He is being asked not to pursue his researches. Then he goes and pursues them anyway, muttering, "*Eppur si muove.*"

The story to which the Oppenheimer dossier leads, when interpreted by a Marxist, is told, not in Brecht's ***Galileo,*** but in Haakon Chevalier's novel *The Man Who Would Be God.* Here the faith the protagonist stands for is obviously Marxism. He betrays it and his best friend (who is also his best Comrade) in order to become the man who can make Reaction a present of the atom bomb. The ending resembles ***Galileo*** II to the extent that both protagonists are shown as burnt-out ruins of their former selves; but Chevalier's man does not practice self-criticism.

Chevalier makes it clear he thinks the Action of his story describes a curve like that of Greek tragedy; and this curve may suggest, too, the Action of Brecht's play. The rhythm of both novel and play, we might at first think, is: from battle to defeat, loyalty to betrayal, commitment to alienation. But of course Galileo's writing of religious tracts for a cardinal in no way resembles Oppenheimer's devising of a monstrous weapon. For one thing, while it is quite credible that devising a monstrous weapon would give a man delusions of satanic grandeur, thus corrupting him, Galileo's obligation to turn out a little conformist journalism is merely a boring chore.

It is true that ***Galileo*** II touches on, or almost touches on, many of the problems which were created or augmented by the atomic bomb. Still, even ***Galileo*** II is not based on Oppenheimer folklore but on Galileo folklore; and a preoccupation with the similarities, by blinding critics to the enormous differences, disables judgment and is, in my view, a disservice to Brecht the dramatist. It prevents the Action as a whole from being perceived. If we begin by assuming that the play is about the atomic scientists, we shall end by complaining that Brecht doesn't get to the point till very near the end.

If ***Galileo*** is not "all about the atom bomb" is it a tragedy of pride? One might begin to answer this question with the observation that no tragedy of pride would end in its hero's lacking, not only pride, but even self-respect. At the end, supremely, the true hero reveals his true heroism, and if lack of self-respect has been in question, as in Conrad's *Lord Jim,* then what he will do with his self-respect at the end is precisely to regain it. ***Galileo*** (I or II) is more of a tragedy of *lack* of pride; but that, to be sure, is no tragedy at all. Brecht himself, speaking of his play in terms of a commitment abandoned and betrayed, indicates that he has nothing against writers like Copernicus who never made a commitment. Copernicus simply left his book for men to make what they would of it after his death. Galileo embarked on a campaign to change the world, then quit. Brecht shows the trend of his own thinking about the play by the use of words like "opportunism," "collaboration," "betrayal." To these one must add the equally Brechtian term: "capitulation." To begin full of fighting spirit, to end capitulating ignominiously: this is the rhythm of life as Brecht so often depicted it and so deeply felt it. In ***Mother Courage*** the "great" capitulation—Courage's own—is over before the first curtain rises. We find it only in certain speeches and a retrospective song. In ***Galileo,*** on the other hand, it is the hinge of the whole Action. The play is a tragicomedy of heroic combat followed by unheroic capitulation, and the ending of the later version is of the harrowing sort common in tragicomedy when it achieves greatness: no noble contrition, no belated rebellion even, but savage, misanthropic self-hatred. This Galileo is the victim of his own curse upon Mucius:

> He who does not know the truth is merely an idiot. But he who knows it and calls it a lie is a criminal.

Received "into the ranks of the faithful" he is exiled from the ranks of mankind, *and that by his own decree.*

That the horror of ***Galileo*** II, Scene Thirteen, did not fully emerge in the 1947 production Brecht was inclined to blame on Laughton. It was one of the few passages, he says, which the actor had difficulties with. He did not seem to grasp the playwright's plea that a condemnation of the opportunist must be inherent in the condemnation of those who accept the fruits of the opportunism. Not using the squint-eyed, worried grin he had worn in the abjuration scene, Laughton here robbed the opening of the big speech on science of its superciliousness:

> It did not entirely emerge [says Brecht] that you are on the lowest rung of the ladder of teaching when you deride the ignorant and that it is a hateful light which a man emits just to have his own light shine. . . .

Laughton failed to make his audiences feel that "that man sits in a hell worse than Dante's where the gift of intellect has been gambled away."

But could not Laughton be partly excused for not playing what Brecht calls the low point of the action on the grounds that this low point is hardly reached in the writing? When we ask this we are asking a question not only about the dialogue of the penultimate scene but also about the scene that sets it up: the abjuration scene. This scene represents an extreme instance of Brechtian method. Brecht well knew that the obvious way to write the scene is to confront Galileo with his enemies. Some playwrights would make you sit there three hours for the sole pleasure of seeing this happen at the end.* Brecht's reason for doing otherwise is clear: the people he wishes to confront Galileo with are—his friends. In the theatre, Scene Twelve is a truly marvelous scene, with its off-stage action, its two groups waiting on stage (the friends and the daughter), its climactic, anticlimactic entrance of Galileo Galilei, the collapse of Andrea, and the laconic, meaning-packed summing up of Galileo's retort to him: "Unhappy is the land that *needs* heroes!" This line has a partly new meaning in ***Galileo*** II, being now far more ironical, yet it contains a direct, unironic truth still, expressing, as Brecht says, the scientist's wish to deprive Nature of her privilege of making life tragic and heroism necessary. Yet the scene is perhaps a shade *too* oblique. One senses the presence of an intention which is not entirely achieved: to avoid the hackneyed, overprepared climax of conventional drama in the big, long trial scene by bringing down the hero with a flick of the wrist. The abjuration is there before one is ready for it. Our man collapses without a fight. Something is gained. There is a special interest in collapse being so prompt, so sudden, so actionless, after all the overconfidence that had gone before. The Brechtian avoidance of psychology does pay off here in shock, but I wonder if it doesn't force the playwright to omit something we need, at once for continuity of narrative and later for our understanding of Galileo's descent into hatred of himself and contempt for others?

To condemn Galileo for his abjuration, one must believe, first, that he had a real alternative and, second, that this alternative was worth all the trouble. Thirdly, his enemies must be as convincing in their way as he is in his, or the whole conflict lacks magnitude. Now, to take the last point first, the enemy figures in ***Galileo,*** though done with adroitness, are markedly less impressive than those they are roughly modeled on—the enemies in ***Saint Joan.*** As to Galileo's alternative, the trouble is not that we may feel asked to believe that the *historical* Galileo had such an alternative, the trouble is that, unless we can see all history and society in these terms of progressives and reactionaries, we shall not respond as Brecht would like us to. Faced with this kind of objection, Brecht used to say that *all* plays require agreement with the author's philosophy. But do they? Don't they require, rather, only a suspension of disbelief, a temporary willingness to see things through the playwright's spectacles? And is that the issue here? Could not the terms of this conflict be objected to on the grounds of the very philosophy Brecht did accept, Marxism? It seems to me that a Marxist should object that the dialectic of history and society is here excessively attenuated, and that the result is a melodramatic black and white. The fact that this story cannot be thought of as actually taking place in the seventeenth century does become a dramatic defect *by being called attention to.* In this it resembles the story of Mother Courage, who is condemned for what she did, though what she ought to have done instead (namely, help to destroy the system) was not in the seventeenth-century cards. There is something absurd in condemning her, and there is something absurd in asking Galileo Galilei to strike a blow for the philosophy of Bertolt Brecht. If Cardinal and Inquisitor are abstract and simplistic, so is the play's rendering of the alternative to them, as shown in the character of Federzoni, the idealized worker. *Federzoni is made of wood,* and so, even more obviously, are various smaller characters, introduced to make points, like Mucius the Renegade and Vanni the Business Man. Before Galileo is arrested, Brecht offers him through Vanni the alternative of working for the rising bourgeoisie. The point is made, but only by being mentioned, as it might be mentioned in an essay. It does not register as drama, because Vanni exercises no pull on Galileo; and this is because he is a mere mouthpiece.

These weaknesses would be cruelly displayed by any director who labored under the misapprehension that this was a Shaw play. ***Galileo*** can suffer by being compared to ***Saint Joan*** in that Shaw puts much more thought into drama and finds much more drama in thought. ***Saint Joan,*** on the other hand, might suffer a little by comparison with ***Galileo*** if what one was after was not thinking but poetry—whether the poetry of the word or the poetry of stagecraft.

"The hero is the people." Walter Benjamin's hyperbole applies, not to the prosaically imposed "vulgar" Marxism of the Federzoni figure, but to the impact of Galileo's life upon the commonalty, a topic to which two whole scenes are devoted (Nine and Fourteen). The people are the hero in that the final interest is not in Galileo himself but in what he did, and what he failed to do, *for* the people. And here an objection on historical grounds—to the effect that the seventeenth-century populace did not react in this way, or that Galileo wrote in Italian instead of Latin, not to reach the people, who couldn't read, but to reach the middle class—cannot be upheld, because the poet has created a vision that transcends literal reportage. Scene Nine usually goes over better with an audience than any other scene in the play. Cynics may say that is because it is a creation of the director and composer. The design remains Brecht's own. The little scene gives us an image that resembles the image of Azdak in ***The Caucasian Chalk Circle.*** In each case, the common folk, in their long night of slavery, are given a brief glimpse of a possible dawn, and Brecht is able to convey this, not discursively, but in direct, poetic-dramatic vision.

And, of course, it is a matter, not just of a scene, but of the whole play. As we work our way back from the last scene, through the scene of abjuration, to the long preparation for the abjuration scene, we can discern the curve of the whole Action. One might find the key to this Action in the phrase "The New Age." It is a favorite Brechtian topic, and Brecht explains in the notes to this very play of ***Galileo*** that the phrase "The New Age" brought to his mind the Workers' Movement as of the beginning of the twentieth century:

> . . . no other line from a song so powerfully inspired the workers as the line, "Now a new age is dawning": old and young marched to it. . . .

This is the theme that is sounded in the very first scene of ***Galileo,*** and again I wish to make a somewhat more than parenthetic allusion to Charles Laughton, since here Laughton the adapter conspired with Laughton the actor to evade an important issue. The actor found the speech about the New Age far too long, so the adapter cut most of it out, and had the remainder rebuked by an Andrea who says, "You're off again, Mr. Galilei." But it was Mr. Brecht who was off again, and a really long speech is needed here, a veritable paean to the idea of a New Age, or we cannot grasp the importance of the conception or the sentiment in the main design. The paean is a poem, though in prose. It creates a sense of that Enchantment, which will later, as the very climax of the Action, turn to Disenchantment (ambiguously in one version, unequivocally in the other). In ***The Caucasian Chalk Circle,*** we learn how much too early the carpet weavers tried to establish a people's regime, and for how short a time Azdak's people's regime can eke out its fluky existence. In ***Galileo*** the point is that the coming of such a regime is actually postponed by the protagonist's principal act. And though we cannot take this as history (of the seventeenth century) we can certainly make sense of it as politics (of the twentieth century).

It has become customary to cut the last scene (Fourteen), but this is because directors insist on believing that Galileo is the hero. If the people are the hero, the last scene is a needed conclusion and a needed correction of Scene Nine. The people will not emerge into the dawn in the sudden ecstasy of Carnival. The journey out of night is long and slow, all the slower because of Galileo's abjuration and all analogous capitulations. At the end, the play abuts upon the Marxist realization that the people must learn not to rely on the Great Men of the bourgeoisie for their salvation: they will have to save themselves. But discreetly enough, this is not spelled out. Brecht speaks here through image and action. The smuggling out of the new book has a somewhat different meaning in ***Galileo*** II. It is less of a triumph for Galileo, but it does take up the theme of *eppur si muove* and partially redeem it from the cynicism which, especially in this version, it must carry. The earth continues to revolve, and even the bad man can continue to contribute good science. Or, on a more literal plane: though a social setback is recorded, science marches ahead—in which contrast, that between a rotten society and a flourishing science, we again glimpse the twentieth century.

A further comment is perhaps needed on the protagonist of Brecht's play. What does this Galileo—not the Galileo of the historians—finally amount to? The topic can be approached through the following passage from Isaac Deutscher's life of Trotsky:

> He [Brecht] had been in some sympathy with Trotskyism and was shaken by the purges; but he could not bring himself to break with Stalinism. He surrendered to it with a load of doubt on his mind, as the capitulators in Russia had done; and he expressed artistically his and their predicament in ***Galileo Galilei.*** It was through the prism of the Bolshevik experience that he saw Galileo going down on his knees before the Inquisition and doing this from an "historic necessity," because of the people's political and spiritual immaturity. The Galileo of his drama is Zinoviev or Bukharin or Rakovsky dressed up in historical costume. He is haunted by the "fruitless" martyrdom of Giordano Bruno; that terrible example causes him to surrender to the Inquisition, just as Trotsky's fate caused so many Communists to surrender to Stalin. And Brecht's famous duologue: "Happy is the country that produces such a hero" and "Unhappy is the people that needs such a hero" epitomizes clearly enough the problem of Trotsky and Stalinist Russia rather than Galileo's quandary in Renaissance Italy. (Brecht wrote the original version of ***Galileo Galilei*** in 1937-8, at the height of the Great Purges.)

Unless Mr. Deutscher has his hands on some version of ***Galileo*** not known by anyone else to exist he can't read straight. ***Galileo*** II *cannot* be taken the way he proposes, since the capitulation, there, is denounced as loudly as he could wish. If we assume, as perhaps we must, it is ***Galileo*** I he is talking about, then how could he take the Church (Stalinism) as something Galileo "could not bring himself to break with," in view of the fact that this Galileo cheats and outwits the Church triumphantly? Or maybe Mr. Deutscher never got to the penultimate scene? Brecht's Galileo is not haunted by the martyrdom of Bruno, either, and if Bruno is Trotsky, then Trotsky hardly comes within the purview of the play at all. Does Mr. Deutscher take "Happy is the country that produces such a hero" to be about Trotsky? If so, inaccuracy has again tripped him up, as the line actually reads: "Unhappy is the land that has no heroes!" and the reference is to Galileo's failure to be heroic.

But Mr. Deutscher's incursion into dramatic criticism raises the question whether he claims to describe Brecht's conscious thoughts or things that crept in in the author's despite? If the former, then the Deutscher thesis is highly implausible. Brecht may have been troubled by inner doubts, but on the whole he must be said to have given his approval to the Moscow trials, much in the spirit of his close friend Feuchtwanger, whose ardently Stalinist book *Moscow 1937* is mentioned by Mr. Deutscher. Besides, the abjuration in ***Galileo*** I is in part a means to an end, which is to go on writing subversive things. Though reprehensible, it is also a neat trick, and no occasion for Slavic breast-beating. That Brecht, in that period, would knowingly have depicted Stalin simply as the enemy is improbable in the extreme.

Yet it may well be true that not only the Nazi but the Bolshevik experience found their way into the play, especially into its later version, which Mr. Deutscher doesn't seem to have read. The Bolshevik idea of self-criticism, going to all possible lengths of self-denunciation and a demand for punishment, undoubtedly exerted considerable sway over Brecht. In 1944-1945, he is using it in ***The Caucasian Chalk Circle,*** in a passage so "Russian" that Western audiences have trouble following the argument. If we are now guessing at unconscious motives, instead of just noting the provable ones, we might by all means guess that the self-denunciation of the new version of ***Galileo,*** written in 1945 or so, was put there to correct and place in proper perspective the famous self-denunciation before the Inquisition around which the story is built. The abjuration is a spurious piece of self-denunciation. It cries out, Brecht might well have felt, for a real one, and the real one, by all means, suggests the world of Zinoviev, Bukharin, and Rakovsky. However, if this interpretation is valid, Brecht's unconscious made, surely, the same identification as his conscious mind, namely with Stalin, not with his enemies, who are felt to be guilty as charged.

But wasn't the Nazi experience far more important to the play than the Bolshevik one? The real complaint against Galileo is that he did not rise up like Georgi Dimitrov at the Reichstag trial in Leipzig and denounce his judges. The real complaint is against German physicists who announced that there was such a thing as Aryan physics as distinct from Jewish physics. The real complaint is against the conspiracy of silence in which most German scholars and writers took part in those years. Brecht's poetry of the thirties reverts again and again to this subject.

> *Aber man wird nicht sagen: Die Zeiten waren finster*
> *Sondern: Warum haben ihre Dichter geschwiegen?*
>
> (But men won't say: The times were dark,
> but: Why were their poets silent?)

And Brecht's personal relation to this subject? He was by no means silent, but he knew how to take care of himself. He did not volunteer in Spain. He did not go to Moscow to risk his neck at the headquarters of Revolution. And undoubtedly such guilt as was felt (if any was) by Charles Laughton at not taking part in the Battle of Britain was felt by Brecht a thousand times over at not taking more than a literary part in any of the battles of his lifetime. This guilt, one can readily believe, is concentrated in the protagonist in whose footsteps some people think Brecht trod when before the Un-American Activities Committee he cried, "No, no, no, no, no, never," at the question, "Have you ever made application to join the Communist Party?"

"The sick inmost being of a poet," Jean Paul has it, "betrays itself nowhere more than in his hero, whom he never fails to stain with the secret weaknesses of his own nature." Brecht felt in himself a natural affinity with the shirker and the quitter. In that respect, the late play ***Galileo*** looks all the way back to the earliest plays, and especially to ***Drums in the Night.*** A whole row of Brecht protagonists belongs to this species in one way or another (Baal, Galy Gay, Macheath, Mother Courage, Schweyk, Azdak . . . and what gives these figures dramatic tension is that their natural passivity has either to be redeemed by the addition of some other quality (as with Schweyk's intuitive shrewdness and humanity) or worked up into something much worse that can be roundly denounced. This working up took Brecht a little time, as we know from the revisions of ***Mother Courage*** and ***Puntila.*** It was a quarter of a century before Brecht made it clear that Kragler, of ***Drums in the Night,*** was to be utterly rejected, and the wholehearted rejection of Galileo's "crime" took Brecht nearly ten years to make—ten years and two atom bombs. Brecht, one might put it, was a moralist on second thought, and, however moralist-critics may judge him as a man, they can hardly deny that this "contradiction" in him was dramatically dynamic and productive.

Galileo is a self-portrait in respect of incarnating the main contradiction of Brecht's own personality. That can hardly fail to have interest for students of his work, but it can hardly be the main point of ***Galileo*** if we judge ***Galileo*** to be a good play, since good plays are not, in the first or last instance, personal outpourings. A writer writes himself, but a playwright has written a play only when he has written more than, or other than, himself. Even should his material stem from himself, the test is whether he can get it outside himself and make it not-himself. He has to let himself be strewn about like dragon's teeth so that other men may spring up, armed. In ***Galileo,*** a contradiction that had once merely been Brecht's own, merely a character trait, is translated into action, into an Action, and this action, reciprocally, attaches itself to someone who is neither Bertolt Brecht nor the Galileo Galilei of history. Though he bear the latter's name, he is a *creation* of the former, and surely a very notable one. It is not just that Brecht's Galileo is contradictory. Such a contradiction would count for comparatively little if the *man* who is contradictory were not both deeply, complexly human and—great. Nor is greatness, in plays, taken on trust or proved by citation of the evidence. Rather, it must be there as a visible halo, and felt as an actual charisma. As the man speaks, moves, or merely stands there, his greatness must, for his audience in the theatre, be beyond cavil. In this play, Brecht proves himself to be, with Shaw, one of the very few modern playwrights who can compel belief in the greatness of their great ones.

It would be a pity if we were so busy arguing the *Problematik* of science and authority that we overlooked an achievement of this sort. After all, playwrights should be allowed their limitations in the stratosphere of science and philosophy, since their main job is down on earth, giving life to characters. The role which, however, misleadingly, goes by the name of Galileo Galilei is not only notable in itself, and functions well in the Action, as I have tried to show, it also solves a very real problem posed by Brecht's subject. Our world is no longer in the center of the universe, *ergo* man has lost his central importance in the scheme of things. If this proposition is not of the seventeenth century, it is very much of the twentieth, and it had always been important to Bertolt Brecht. He places it at the heart of Garga's nihilism in ***In the Swamp*** (***Jungle of Cities***), and of Uriah Shelley's in one of the versions of ***A Man's a Man.*** Man is absolutely nothing, is Uriah's premise and conclusion. And yet Galileo Galilei, who (allegedly) made this discovery, is something? Is this in fact the ultimate contradiction about him? He is assigned his share in worthlessness and nihilism (if nothingness is divisible), particularly in the later text, but the main point is in the contrast between this discovery of nothingness and the somethingness, the greatness, of the discoverer. God, as Brecht's Galileo puts it, will be found, from now on, "in ourselves or nowhere." Man will be great, not by the role assigned to him by Another, nor yet by his position in space, but by his own inherent qualities. If ***Galileo*** II verges on being merely a repudiation of its protagonist, then, as I have already intimated, it carries Brecht's vision of things less completely than ***Galileo*** I. But even in ***Galileo*** I the "crime" must be taken very seriously, because it is an abdication of what he alone among the characters has to offer (human greatness) and if human greatness were wiped from the record, then the "discovery" that "man is nothing" would be the truth.

Or are the sterling but more modest merits of Andrea and Federzoni sufficient to justify existence? In the terms imposed by the play, it is not clear that they are. That these two men disapprove of the abjuration tells us nothing to the purpose. They were never put to such a test, nor could they be since, not possessing greatness, they could never have had as much to lose as Galileo had. "The people are the hero." I have conceded that there is much truth in Benjamin's dictum, but the thought in the play is dialectical, many-sided, ironic, and the individual greatness of the protagonist is essential to the scheme. In the final crisis he is an antihero, and that is bad (or, in the first version, partly bad). What I am stressing, as a final point, is that he is also a hero: the hero as great man; human greatness being what offsets the Copernican blow to human narcissism.

> It was . . . a time which called for giants and produced giants—giants in power of thought, passion, and character, in universality and learning. The men who founded the modern rule of the bourgeoisie had anything but bourgeois limitations. On the contrary the adventurous character of the time inspired them to a greater or less degree. . . . But what is especially characteristic of them is that they almost all pursue their lives and activities in the midst of the contemporary movements, in the practical struggle; they take sides and join in the fight. . . . Hence the fullness and force of character that makes them complete men.

I don't know if this passage from Engels' *Dialectics of Nature* suggested the theme of Galileo Galilei to Brecht. It *is* cited in the Berlin Ensemble program of his play. Reading it, one reflects that, of course, Galileo, according to Brecht, was one who at a crucial moment was disloyal to his "side" in "the fight." That can hardly be unimportant. The character will stand, as Brecht intended, as an exemplar of a certain kind of weakness. But will it not stand, even more impressively, as the exemplar of human greatness, a proof that greatness is possible to humankind? For that matter, would the weakness be even interesting if it were not that of a great (which is to say: in many ways, a strong) man? (pp. 146-64)

Eric Bentley, "Galileo," in his Theatre of War: Comments on 32 Occasions, *The Viking Press, 1972, pp. 146-64.*

MOTHER COURAGE

PRODUCTION REVIEWS

Clive Barnes (review date 6 April 1978)

[*A British-born American drama and dance critic, Barnes has been called the "first, second, and third most powerful critic in New York." He insists, however, that criticism of the arts is a public service, and therefore the function of a reviewer is to advise and inform audiences rather than determine a production's success or failure. In the following review, Barnes praises Alan Schneider's production of* Mother Courage *as an interesting departure from the traditional staging techniques developed by Brecht and his Berliner Ensemble.*]

[The Acting Company's] New York season opened last night—I saw it at a preview—with its new staging of Bertolt Brecht's ***Mother Courage and her Children.*** It is a valuable production, not simply on its own account, but more because it is the first English-speaking Brecht production to make an attempt to escape from the Brecht formula, laid down specifically, in presence and also in print, by Brecht's own Berliner Ensemble. The production may have faded in memory, but the notes are there, from Weigel's "silent scream" onwards.

Schneider, who is directing this version, has sensibly decided to eschew precedent. He, and his marvelous designer Ming Cho Lee, maintain the proprieties of the Brechtian theatrical world. There are indeed alienating screens, acting as subtitles for a scene still uncovered, and the style is certainly brash enough.

What is interesting about Schneider's production is that it is not a staple reproduction of the classic production by the Berliner Ensemble. He takes this woman—Mother Courage—a survivor through a war we can hardly envisage, a creature like a cockroach, dedicated to survival—and makes her live. Or at least survive.

This is unquestionably one of the great plays of our time simply because it touches our mythic guilt. Courage's attitudes, self-seeking, self-prompting, self-sacrificing, happen to be our own.

Ming Cho Lee's setting is classic but inevitable, and works as perfectly and effectively as a nightmare. It has to be a dream image of someone else's eternity, and it is. Jeanne Button's costumes are also helpful.

Schneider's staging seems almost intent on being different. It takes as little as possible from the Berliner Ensemble, which is an odd choice, but a respectful one. At first it plays very slowly indeed—imagine playing without using any of the Brecht formulas—but Schneider is a good director, so careful with the commonplaces of details, that eventually he pulls it off.

But the main role itself offers difficulties. Mother Courage is not the world's easiest part. You usually have to have an Anne Bancroft or an Eileen Heckart. Schneider has no such star pleasures. He has Mary Lou Rosato, who has been with the Acting Company since its beginning, and tries magnificently. But not magnificently enough.

Miss Rosato plays Mother Courage as if she were auditioning for a Norman Lear late-night soap-opera on television. She is very good but she is very wrong.

David Schramm as the Cook has a certain power, even authenticity, but also lacks, in the final issue, credibility. ***Mother Courage*** has always been a tricky play. Here, it only emerges in its tricks.

Yet there genuinely are moments of revelation—watch for Frances Conroy as the mute Kattrin—for this is the actual play, more than any other, of our century. But from this production you would not always know it. The messages were muted, the connections seemed oddly disjointed.

Clive Barnes, " *'Courage' Needs Mothering,*" *in* New York Post, *April 6, 1978.*

Mel Gussow (review date 6 April 1978)

[*In the following excerpt, Gussow maintains that director Alan Schneider staged an "astringent"* Mother Courage, *which lost some of the play's humor, but captured its "caustic sense of irreconcilability."*]

Mother Courage is a war monger. She does not actively promote war, but the battlefield is her natural habitat and, from the back of her canteen wagon, she sells to soldiers during wartime. Finally, when peace momentarily "breaks out" after decades of strife, she quickly tries to conduct a clearance sale.

She is the ultimate entrepreneur, as Brecht described her, "a merchant-mother," with the two halves of her character irretrievably bound together. She sells in order to stay alive and to keep her children alive, but because war is endemic to her existence, the children die. They are victims of maternal negligence.

Mother Courage is far from the indomitable martyr of the common misconception. Her survival—stooped and bowed, she harnesses herself as cart horse—is not so much heroic as tragic. Along the road, she has sacrificed her humanity as well as her family. How do you play a character whom the author conceived of as a "great living contradiction?" For one thing, you do it through irony, guarding against empathy and underscoring the incongruities.

In his production of ***Mother Courage and Her Children*** for the Acting Company, which opened a three-week season of repertory last night at the American Place Theater, Alan Schneider seems fully aware of the complexities and the pitfalls of this masterwork. Using Ralph Manheim's translation, he has staged an astringent ***Mother Courage,*** which loses some of the play's humor, but captures its caustic sense of irreconcilability.

This Mother Courage (Mary Lou Rosato) is a sparrow hawk marked by her acerbity and cynicism. Angry at her son, she slaps him hard across the head, the sound reverberating as if a board had crashed to the floor. Her mute daughter is not simply shy, but also pathologically removed from society. When her mother brings her food, she burrows her head into the bowl like a starved stray.

The stage is filled with cheats and scoundrels, pursuing self interest out of fear that the war will end and ruin business—although, for Brecht, peace is only another name for war. Chief among the opportunists is Mother Courage. She is cheap and tight-fisted, an expert at pragmatic bargaining.

Grasping for a foothold in an acquisitive, self-destructive civilization, Miss Rosato's Mother Courage almost courts capitulation. When her gentle younger son, Swiss Cheese, is killed, she is shocked to her boots. Wordlessly and tearlessly communicating her torment, the actress—her eyes lifted toward the sky—offers a vivid approximation of Helene Weigel's famous silent scream. This is not a titanic performance, but it is mordant and resolute. To her credit, Miss Rosato does not overwhelm the play. Clearly, ***Mother Courage*** has been chosen not only for its dramatic merits, but also as an ensemble piece.

Kevin Conroy gives a visceral performance as Courage's argumentative older son, and Jeffrey Hayenga has a quiet sincerity as the impressionable Swiss Cheese. Frances Conroy is convincingly wounded as the mute daughter. Patricia Hodges is effective as the prostitute Yvette, although Barbara Harris's lovely portrayal of the role is the most ineradicable memory of Jerome Robbins's 1963 Broadway production.

Ming Cho Lee's set—an almost barren plane surmounted

by Mother Courage's rustic wagon—is stark. Paul Dessau's score complements the sardonic quality of the script. In many ways, this is a more authentically Brechtian production than usual. In it we also see at least a tinge of Beckett: Mother Courage's journey as an unrelenting ordeal, a circuit without an end.

Mel Gussow, "'Mother Courage' By Acting Company," in The New York Times, *April 6, 1978, p. C17.*

Douglas Watt (review date 7 April 1978)

[*In the following review of Alan Schneider's staging of* Mother Courage, *written in the form of a letter to the title character, Watt comments favorably on elements of stagecraft—particularly designer Ming Cho Lee's sets and musical director Albert Hague's score—but finds the production flawed by Mary Lou Rosato's performance in the title role.*]

Dear Mother Courage:

If you'll just stop hauling that damn wagon 'round and 'round and stand still for a minute, I'd like to tell you what they're doing to your image at the American Place Theater. That's where the Acting Company settled in on Wednesday for a couple of weeks of repertory, leading off with your epic story ***Mother Courage and Her Children.***

People's images are very important nowadays, even if they have nothing at all to do with their real natures, and I'm sure Bert Brecht never thought of you—Anna Fierling, by right—as a stand-up comic. But that's the way an actress named Mary Lou Rosato is playing you. Sort of, anyway.

Coming on in most of the 12 scenes (divided by an intermission) with a cocky air belying the fact that, as a kind of peregrinating sutler, she's been shlepping goods all over the map of Europe during the 30 Years War, she delivers her dialogue like so many snappy one-liners, and with an occasional wolfish grin making her resemble a cross between Margaret Hamilton and the late Ed Begley. Not that Miss Rosato is any slouch as a performer: but that quick intelligence would be better applied to comedy than to you, you tough old bird.

I think you'd be pleased with the way things look. Designer Ming Cho Lee has enclosed the action in dull gray walls and on a mostly bare stage across which soiled drawstring curtains are used to separate the scenes and, by means of projected legends, describe each one in advance. Jeanne Button's costumes enhance the desired impression of a wearisome, meaningless, endless religious war during which your children are killed, one by one, along with half the Germans, but which threatens your trade only when peace breaks out momentarily.

The single other remaining member of John Houseman's original Juilliard graduating class, origin of the touring Acting Company six years ago, is David Schramm, who is quite good as the Cook and who, you might be interested to know, is also playing King Lear in the repertory. I think Frances Conroy overdoes the wacky side of your mute daughter Kattrin, but it must have been terribly confusing being a Finn during those years.

Kevin Conroy has swagger as your foolishly brave son Elif, and Jeffrey Hayenga is appropriately vague as your dopey son Swiss Cheese, though I'll never know why Brecht had you say you called him that because he pulled a wagon so well, a hole in the head I could understand. Anderson Matthews is the sorry sight he is meant to be as the vacillating Chaplain. As for that baggage Yvette, the diseased camp follower, Patricia Hodges certainly picks things up for a few minutes when she makes an imperious reappearance as a widowed countess.

Alan Schneider has staged everything knowingly, and musical director Albert Hague has seen to it that Paul Dessau's songs, most of which sound wrong in English, are set forth strongly and clearly. David F. Segal's lighting is just right, too.

But Mother—if I may address you so—I know the fortitude and stoicism that keeps you going, a tiny spark in a deranged world, just like a woman I remember who ran a candy store up in the Bronx. Miss Rosato doesn't show it: she just shows a feisty quality, with even that silent scream of yours ending in a muffled croak. And without it, you and Bert's epic story about you just aren't there.

Sorry to interrupt you this way. I'll shove along now. You, too; ha, ha.

Respectfully,
Douglas Watt

Douglas Watt, "An Open Letter to Mother Courage," in Daily News, *New York, April 7, 1978.*

CRITICAL COMMENTARY

Roland Barthes (essay date 1955)

[*Barthes was among the most influential and revolutionary writers in modern critical thought. His importance derives from a dominant method of critical analysis which reflects his insight that language—or any other medium of communication: painting, fashion, advertising—is a "system of signs," the artificial construction of a particular society at a given time. The aim of Barthes's criticism is to expose the "myths" of a specific sign system, revealing their origins in custom and convention. The value of Barthes's method, however, is not centered on the strictly intellectual pleasures of perceiving symbolic abstractions at work, but rather on the insight that what seems to be fundamental—the norms of middle-class society, the techniques of conveying "reality" in realistic fiction—are in fact accidental and artificial, supported only by the internal structure of a closed system. In the following excerpt from an essay originally published in 1955, Barthes affirms the need for spectators to maintain an emotional distance from* Mother Courage *in order to understand the play's moral didacticism.*]

Brecht's ***Mutter Courage*** is not for those who, at close range or out of earshot, get rich on war; it would be grotesque, explaining to *them* war's mercantile character! No, it is to those who suffer from wars without profiting by them that ***Mutter Courage*** is addressed, and that is the primary reason for its greatness: ***Mutter Courage*** is an entirely popular work, for it is a work whose profound intention can be understood only by the people.

This theater starts from a double vision: of the social evil, and of its remedies. In the case of ***Mutter Courage,*** the point is to show those who believe in the fatality of war, like Mother Courage, that war is precisely a human phenomenon, not a fatality, and that by attacking its mercantile causes its military consequences can finally be abolished. That is the idea, and this is how Brecht unites his crucial intention to a true theater, so that the proposition's evidence results not from sermon or argument but from the theatrical act itself: Brecht sets before us the whole sweep of the Thirty Years' War; caught up in this implacable duration, everything is corrupted (objects, faces, affections), is destroyed (Mother Courage's children, killed one after the next); Mother Courage, a sutler whose trade and life are the wretched fruits of the war, is so much inside the war that she does not see it (merely a glimmer at the end of the first part): she is blind, she submits without understanding; for her, the war is an indisputable fatality.

For her, but no longer for us: because we *see* Mother Courage blind, we *see* what she does not see. Mother Courage is for us a ductile substance: she sees nothing, but we see through her; we understand, in the grip of this dramatic evidence which is the most immediate kind of persuasion, that Mother Courage blind is the victim of what she does not see, which is a remediable evil. This theater creates a decisive split within us: we are at once Mother Courage and we are those who explain her; we participate in the blinding of Mother Courage and we *see* this same blinding; we are passive actors mired in war's fatality and free spectators led to the demystification of this fatality.

For Brecht, the stage narrates, the audience judges; the stage is epic, the audience tragic. This is the very definition of a great popular theater. Take Guignol or Punch, for instance, a theater which has risen out of an ancestral mythology: here too the audience *knows* what the actor does not know; and upon seeing him act so harmfully and so stupidly, the audience is amazed, disturbed, indignant, shouts out the truth, offers the solution: one step more and the spectator will see that the suffering and ignorant actor is himself, will know that when he is plunged into one of those countless Thirty Years' Wars which every age imposes upon him in one form or another, he is in it exactly like Mother Courage, stupidly suffering and unaware of her own power to bring her miseries to an end.

It is therefore crucial that this theater never completely implicate the audience in the spectacle: if the spectator does not keep that slight distance necessary in order to see himself suffering and mystified, all is lost: the spectator must partly identify himself with Mother Courage, and espouse her blindness only to withdraw from it in time and to judge it. The whole of Brecht's dramaturgy is subject to a necessity of *distance,* and the essence of the theater is staked on the perpetuation of this distance: it is not the success of any particular dramatic style which is in question, it is the spectator's consciousness and hence his capacity to make history. Brecht pitilessly excludes as uncivic the dramatic solutions which involve the audience in the spectacle, and by heartfelt pity or knowing winks favors a shameless complicity between history's victim and his new witnesses. Brecht consequently rejects romanticism, rhetoric, naturalism, truculence, estheticism, opera, all the styles of *viscosity* or participation which would lead the spectator to identify himself completely with Mother Courage, to be lost in her, to let himself be swept into her blindness or her futility.

The problem of participation—the delight of our theater estheticians, always ecstatic when they can postulate a diffuse religiosity of the spectacle—is here altogether reconceived; nor have we seen the last of the beneficial consequences of this new principle, which is perhaps a very old principle, moreover, since it rests on the ancestral status of the civic theater, in which the stage is always the object of a tribunal which is in the audience (as it was for the Greek tragedians). We now understand why our traditional dramaturgies are radically false: they congeal the spectator, they are dramaturgies of abdication. Brecht's, on the contrary, possesses a maieutic power; it represents and brings to judgment, it is at once overwhelming and isolating: everything combines to impress without inundating us; it is a theater of solidarity, not of contagion. (pp. 33-5)

Roland Barthes, "Mother Courage Blind," in his Critical Essays, *translated by Richard Howard, Northwestern University Press, 1972, pp. 33-6.*

Herbert Blau (essay date 1957)

[*Blau is an American educator, stage director, and critic who has written extensively on the theater. The director of the first American production of* Mother Courage, *he describes in the following excerpt the effects of Brecht's techniques of alienation on the play's audiences.*]

The conventions of ***Mother Courage*** are not entirely new; others have written very intelligently about the Epic theater of Brecht, where it comes from, and what it purports to do. What it does is another thing; that is contingent on the given production, and the production on the particular audience, and both in part on the special, inescapable rhythm of the play. A distinctively European drama, ***Mother Courage*** has had an astonishing success abroad. It should be of value to record (conceding the limitations of director as critic and critic as director) what Americans—those who did it and those who watched it—felt and thought about the play. By doing so, not only may we learn through the theater something about the incalculable differences between Americans and Europeans, but also something about the ubiquitous art of the theater in one of its important modern forms.

In the beginning there was the idea of "alienation." For Brecht, alienation is a theory of art, a method of acting, and a type of production. The notion itself is alienating and to the unprepared sensibility—actor, director, or audience—somewhat intimidating. No wonder, then, that of all the plays done by our company, this was the first to arouse the kind of controversy which has long become foreign to the American theater, certainly the "tributary" theater: self-consciously contentious and widely variant reviews, letters of protest, public discussions and the like. We have bored audiences before; we have no doubt put some to sleep. But we have never *driven* anybody out of the theater, as we did occasionally with this play. What relationship is there between the idea of alienation, the subject of the play, and what actually occurred on stage that led to such active extremes of approval or antagonism? What are the real sources of alienation in the play and what does the reaction imply?

Brecht is a polemicist, not a strict logician. His dialectic approaches a rhetoric; Aristotle is his scapegoat. In spurning what he considers the emotional and intellectual vices of conventional western theater, he has *verbally* discarded some of its most affective qualities and he has presumed to revivify the modern drama by being undramatic: no suspense, no spurious tensions, no indulgent pathos, no chiaroscuros of mood, no continuity of plot. In reading ***Mother Courage*** for the first time, the company—most of whom had not been in a Brecht play before—felt that Brecht had done precisely what they had been told he would do. They were alienated; they were also bored. The play was static. Only one scene was really moving, that in which the Dumb Daughter Catherine beats her drum on the roof to warn the citizens of Halle of an attack. This engaged them; this was what they wanted from the play. For the rest, it was a lot of talk.

But every play has to be discovered, and the discovery of this play was, embarrassingly, a measure of our private inadequacies and cultural prejudices. One ordinarily produces a play he knows and likes; here we were producing a play which, now, we thought we knew, and when we disliked it, disliked it for the wrong reasons. What we soon realized about the play, particularly as it went on its feet, was that its activity is manifold and unceasing: where it seemed to stand still, there were countless detailed bits of implicit business; where it appeared to be verbose, there were various stratas of relevant irony, disguised and overt. In Scene 6, for instance, Mother Courage, the Chaplain, the Regimental Clerk, and the Dumb Daughter are spending a rainy afternoon in a canteen tent, engaged in conversations on war, the two women taking inventory. The stage, which previously had been rather bare, is now full of sausages, linens, cheeses, belts, buckles, boots, tins, baskets, and shirts, all the innumerable paraphernalia of Mother Courage's enterprise. For Mother Courage, times are good. But the pre-scene projection announces that the great Commander Tilly has fallen in battle. There is funeral music. The scene opens reflectively. And though nothing "dramatic" happens until late in the long scene, the predominant impression, arising out of the talk, is one of abundance, of a steady throb of counting, checking, sorting, tallying, collecting money for drinks—the business of the actors and the business of war forming a single ritualistic image, the business of business, giving point and substance to the conscious ironies of Mother Courage and the ingenuous ones of the Chaplain.

Or take the opening scene, where Mother Courage and her children, travelling with their wagon, are stopped by a Recruiting Officer and a Sergeant, who are interested in her sons. She identifies herself and, when asked how she got her nickname, explains that she drove through the bombardment of Riga like a madwoman to save some loaves of bread she had in her cart. Her action was not heroic, as some who gave her the name thought (and as some who came to the play thought when they read the title in our advertising; one woman even called for tickets to *Mothers Courageous*). Mother Courage is a pragmatist not a martyr. But the irony is sharper and partially directed against herself. Not only does she discredit the romantic interpretation of her deed, she discredits the deed itself: what a fool, her tone implies, to risk one's life for a few moldy loaves of bread. Business comes first, *except* where it threatens survival. The same attitude prevails in the following scene when, immediately after a surprise reunion, she boxes her son's ear for having too bravely outwitted some enemy peasants. Better always to surrender than to die.

Set in the framework of great events, the mundane career of Mother Courage is alienated, then, in the various senses that Brecht intends: estranged, put at a distance, made famous (or infamous), historified. Our critical faculties are trained on that part of history which history slights. Tilly wins a battle at Lutzen; Mother Courage loses four shirts. And in the hectic little scene which juxtaposes these two important events, so much happens so quickly that one can hardly keep up with it: onstage some soldiers, taking respite from looting, are having a drink at Mother Courage's canteen. Catherine is distraught, running up and down on the periphery. Offstage, a fire is ravaging a peasant's farm. There are cries; wounded people are brought on. The Chaplain runs in, calling for linen. Mother Courage, keeping an eye on the soldiers, one of whom has already stolen a fur coat in the town, tries to protect her goods. She has given all her linen before, she says; she explains to the Chaplain that things are getting worse—taxes, duties, bribes to pay. Furious at her mother's apparent inhumanity, Catherine grabs a stick and rushes at her. Mother Courage shouts her down, but the Chaplain pulls her bodily from the wagon and takes out some shirts which he rips for bandages. There is a cry offstage—a baby is trapped by the fire. Torn between her daughter and her shirts, Mother Courage watches as Catherine dashes off to save the child. Catherine reappears with the baby. Mother Courage, relieved, stalks across the stage to chastize her and tries to take the baby away. Catherine snarls and hugs it fiercely. Meanwhile the soldier with the coat is trying to make off with a bottle of brandy. Mother Courage sees him and, instead of taking back the liquor, snatches the fur coat in exchange, even in the midst of the tumult managing to pull off a deal. The victory music, which had been playing all during the scene, mounts as Catherine joyfully raises the baby over her head.

I have recounted the activity of the scene because so much of it is missed in the reading and because—though it took us hours to work it out—all of it, and a good deal of incidental business that I have left out, happens in approximately one minute.

Thus the initial impression of alienation was mitigated for the actors by the necessity of having to *act* the play. It imposed its will and ways upon them. They could not worry about what they resented when the drama gave them so much to think about and *do.* Gradually they began to realize what Brecht means when he compares Epic theater to the painting of Brueghel. The canvas is large, diffuse, apparently undramatic. But every element has its unique energy. One looks closer and recognizes that nothing is ever still. The sensation of diversity disappears in the apprehended unity of a common vitality. Degraded and demoralized by the black marketry of war, the people of the play express their consciously rationalized submission with a remarkable vigor. What we have is the caustically robust power of ineffectuality. The stones begin to talk, as one of the projections declares, even before the mute daughter provides the climactic irony of the play with the drum that the war puts into her hands.

In structure, the idea of alienation becomes the fact of interruption. The narrative action—and ***Mother Courage*** is subtitled a Chronicle of the Thirty Years' War—is repeatedly intruded upon by ballads, slides, banners, insignia, dance, march music, and blackouts. The purpose of such interruptions any student of Brecht knows well: Epic theater is scientific and tactical; its aim is social criticism. Having rejected the obfuscating "magic" of the theater of illusion, it has enlisted very archaic conventions and types of entertainment to create the rational and rhetorical magic of the contemporary tribunal. Brecht pretends to be nothing but didactic; but he knows, like Shaw, that didacticism can and must be pleasurable, "from this, of course," he writes in his ***A Little Organum for the Theater,*** "morality can only be the gainer. . . . To demand more of the theater or to interpret its function more broadly is to put too low a value on the end proper to it."

Nevertheless, in developing "the special means of pleasure, the proper entertainment, for our own age," Brecht places his production facilities in the same relation to the theater that the audio-visual center has to modern education, except that where the tape recorder and the camera have become devices for avoiding the issues of education, the resources of technology have become for Brecht a way of delineating and intensifying the issues of politics and society. A banner with slightly wrenched black (Germanic) letters drops from the flies announcing the place of action: Sweden, Saxony, Bavaria, Saxony, Poland. Why? Because war, like the snow settling over Joyce's Ireland, is general and undifferentiated; it looks the same everywhere. It is the source of confusion in the most classical sense of that word. You *need* to be told where you are. You also need to be reminded you are in the theater, especially when you are most engrossed in what you see. This is disturbing. But objective truth—and that is what Brecht seeks to display—*is* disturbing, more so when Brecht floods it with white, searching, surgical light. How shocked we were at our first dress rehearsal, though we should have known, that our costumes looked like costumes (and should) and how embarrassed when the minutest fault in performance or staging was exaggerated in the glare. (I must admit that, though we never put gelatins in front of our lamps, we have progressively lowered readings on our dimmers which were originally at maximum, so that now the light is naturally softer and more merciful—this a concession to our own irritated senses, as well as to the uneasiness of the audience.)

But the structure of ***Mother Courage*** is more than a matter of interruptions, ironies, and incongruities. What we finally realized about it none of our research on Brecht's techniques had made clear and would have been impossible to ascertain without performance. It is related to the peculiar rhythm of Brecht's dramatic perception, that rhythm which is always present and never completely manifest, and which makes of every theatrical event an important differential in the recurrent variable of the art. It is that part of a play which is unformulable and which we may know, so to speak, only through the bones. Those closest to it are the actors who, even when they are detached or alienated from their roles, become the instruments of its motion. This is what Stark Young meant, I suppose, when he spoke of the art of acting as the body of the theater, and Francis Fergusson when he describes the "histrionic sensibility" as the taproot of dramatic form. Alienation and detachment, the sundry stoppages in the action, are qualities in the special rhythm of ***Mother Courage,*** and the actor knows it even when he cannot speak about it, and most particularly when he is annoyed, as Brecht presumably wants him to be. The director is the instrument of provocation; in a Brecht play he is as much gadfly as counselor.

What both actors and director began to sense as rehearsals moved forward was that somehow the diffuse, omnibus, verbal, novelistic character of the play became more and more active, visual, empathic, concentrated, and dramatic toward the end. A play, like a poem, should not mean, but be; but there was meaning for us in the graduated contrast. In the beginning we had the characteristic rhythm and action of apathy and the materialistic urgency of survival by bargaining. As in a dramatist like Chekov, so apparently different from Brecht, we have continual self-justification and transference of blame by the characters through commentary on public affairs and motives in Brecht, commentary beyond their scope as people. The songs, with their discreetly sardonic music by Paul Dessau, reflect something of this tendency; even the Mother Courage ballad suggests with its insistent base the long, tedious way into the war. There is a sustained relationship with the audience; Mother Courage talks through the proscenium and there are frequent interruptions in the narrative. One desires very much to participate in the action, but Brecht makes one stand off and observe it. Later in the play, however, the characters, who have carried a heavy burden as symbols and concepts, become more strictly people, and we are made more fully aware of their human relationships with each other, which should have been obvious enough before except that we were distracted by a host of other factors.

Now we pick up events and values by reflexive reference. Back in Scene 3, Yvette, the prostitute, had sung her Song of Fraternization, prompted by memories of her unfaithful lover, Peter Piper. Much later, in Scene 8, the Cook is revealed to be the culprit. The son Eilif reappears, to be exe-

Helene Weigel as Mother Courage.

cuted for a deed for which he had been previously honored. His armor is new and burnished, he dies rich. The Chaplain puts on his robe again and sings the Song of Hours, which suggests the idealistic theological student he must have been. In Scene 12, Mother Courage sings a lullaby to her dead daughter, the only song we did *ohne Verfremdung,* without alienation, although Brecht immediately cuts off the developing pathos by reintroducing the pipes and drums of a regiment on the march, as well as a choral reprise of the Mother Courage ballad. And Courage, who learns *nothing* from her suffering, makes the last "deal" of the play, paying a peasant to bury her daughter, and struggles off, bent as she is, to follow the war, which has not, according to the projected narrative, reached its end.

One realizes finally that the play of person on person has not been minimized in the earlier part of the drama, simply that it has been so forcibly brought to our attention. There was much else to say and demonstrate, and it is not until we have accepted through action, gesture, speeches, music, and all the technical elements the unrelenting presence and localized quality of the abstract war that Brecht lets us indulge in the easier and more rapid dramatic emotions. Hence the preference for the latter part of the play; most of us are still prone to recognize as dramatic mainly that which is fast-paced and violent. But drama exists at the calm peripheries of history as much as at its excited middle. In an age of speed many of us have forgotten that there is an infinite variety of dramatic action, that thought can be felt, paraphrasing Eliot, as strongly as the odor of a rose, that there is a pleasure and a tension that can only be described as dramatic in the ineluctable movement of dialectic, and that even the absolute qualities of music can acquire, in context, when one is listening and alert to analogies, the concrete force of a form which is not its own. (pp. 1-6)

[We] are prone to say that a play is not a play until it is staged; but this too is a qualitative matter. There are plays whose life is apparent in manuscript or at least largely discernible. But one sees very little of a Brecht play on the printed page. Despite all the anxiety that enshrouds opening nights, the sense of chance that is the peculiar delight and horror of the theater, there is something predictable about most plays. This was much less true about ***Mother Courage;*** however vain it might have been, we felt like Ahab's Pequod plunging into the blind Atlantic. There was no way of foretelling what to expect, because ***Mother Courage,*** aside from the jarring quality of its subject and the incongruity of its music, both of which made it even more threatening than ***The Threepenny Opera*** or ***The Good Woman of Setzuan,*** demanded a peculiar engagement of drama, actor, and audience that we as a company had not experienced before. The ground rules had to be written as we went along.

Now that one can read them a little better, they appear, despite the heresies of Brecht, to be the same old ones: the urgency of the special vision will be redeemed in form, and the theater will find the means of its mimicry. Unorthodox, severe, and fragmentary as it might be, the dramatic rhythm of ***Mother Courage*** is unavoidable because,

The Song of *Mother Courage*

Here's Mother Courage and her wagon!
Hey, Captain, let them come and buy!
Beer by the keg! Wine by the flagon!
Let your men drink before they die!
Sabres and swords are hard to swallow:
First you must give them beer to drink.
Then they can face what is to follow—
But let 'em swim before they sink!
Christians, awake! The winter's gone!
The snows depart. The dead sleep on.
And though you may not long survive,
Get out of bed and look alive!

Your men will march till they are dead, sir,
But cannot fight unless they eat.
The blood they spill for you is red, sir,
What fires that blood is my red meat.
For meat and soup and jam and jelly
In this old cart of mine are found:
So fill the hole up in your belly
Before you fill one underground!
Christians, awake! The winter's gone!
The snows depart. The dead sleep on.
And though you may not long survive,
Get out of bed and look alive!

So cheer up, boys, the rose is fading!
When victory comes you may be dead!
A war is just the same as trading:
But not with cheese—with steel and lead!
Christians, awake! The winter's gone!
The snows depart. The dead sleep on.
And though you may not long survive,
Get out of bed and look alive!

Up hill, down dale, past dome and steeple,
My wagon always moves ahead.
The war can care for all its people
So long as there is steel and lead.
Though steel and lead are stout supporters,
A war needs human beings too.
Report today to your headquarters!
If it's to last, this war needs you!
Christians, awake! The winter's gone!
The snows depart. The dead sleep on.
And though you may not long survive,
Get out of bed and look alive!

Dangers, surprises, devastations—
The war takes hold and will not quit.
But though it last three generations,
We shall get nothing out of it.
Starvation, filth, and cold enslave us.
The army robs us of our pay.
Only a miracle can save us
And miracles have had their day.
Christians, awake! The winter's gone!
The snows depart. The dead sleep on.
And though you may not long survive,
Get out of bed and look alive!

Bertolt Brecht, in his Seven Plays by Bertolt Brecht, *edited by Eric Bentley, Grove Press, 1961.*

though Brecht may not see as much of life as we would prefer, what he prefers to see he sees shrewdly and what he says he documents. And though the conventional dramatic experience is one which leads us through a series of events whose end is accompanied by emotional appeasement of some sort, a suspension of hostilities, the intention of Mother Courage *is* to alienate you. Whether you like it or not, you have been reached. (p. 10)

Herbert Blau, "Brecht's 'Mother Courage': The Rite of War and the Rhythm of Epic," in Educational Theatre Journal, *Vol. IX, No. 1, March, 1957, pp. 1-10.*

Ronald Speirs (essay date 1987)

[*In the following excerpt, Speirs analyzes thematic, stylistic, and performance-related aspects of* Mother Courage, *focusing especially on Brecht's characterization of his eponymous heroine.*]

Written on the eve of the Second World War, while Brecht was living in exile in Scandinavia, ***Mother Courage and her Children*** was intended as a reminder that it is not possible to play with fire without getting burnt. The place of its composition fed into the play in a number of ways. The need to give such warning was borne in on Brecht by his perception that the Scandinavians were prepared to collaborate with Hitler's preparations for war in the expectation of profit and in the mistaken belief that they would not be among Hitler's victims. The moral of the play—that 'you need a big pair of scissors to make a cut from a war'—had particular relevance to Germany's less powerful Northern neighbours, as did its setting in the Thirty Years War (1618-1648), a war in which Scandinavian countries (particularly Sweden) were embroiled and which cost Europe dearly in both life and property.

Scandinavian history also supplied one of the models for the play's protagonist, in the person of Lotta Svärd, a Swedish cantinière celebrated in popular imagination for her loyal, motherly care towards the soldiers of the regiment in which her beloved had once served. What is most significant about the influence of the Scandinavian background on the play, however, is its contradictory character, arising from the mixture of historical memories it supplied. Although Brecht's Mother Courage is a much less romantically seen figure than the Lotta Svärd in Johan Runeberg's ballad, she retains enough of Lotta's positive qualities for the play to make a more complicated statement about war than the straightforward indictment of the link between profiteering and warmongering on which many of Brecht's statements about the play concentrate.

In comparison with Brecht's preference for relatively direct didacticism in the plays of the early 1930s, in ***Saint Joan of the Stockyards,*** say, or ***The Mother,*** where the central characters undergo a (more or less exemplary) learning process that makes explicit the lessons to be learned by the audience, ***Mother Courage*** approaches its educative task in a new, rather more oblique way. As such, it is the best known of a group of plays, written between the late 1930s and the mid-1940s, which are now regarded as Brecht's classic works. In these plays he drew together elements of his work that had previously tended to operate separately, with the result that the realistic sketches of contemporary life in ***Fear and Misery of the Third Reich,*** for example, were weakened dramatically by the lack of an overall structure, while the parabolic cohesiveness of ***Saint Joan*** or ***Round Heads and Pointed Heads*** was achieved at the cost of realism in situation and character. At the same time Brecht now placed a new trust in the complexity of the spectator's theatrical experience as the source of his enlightenment. Thus, although Mother Courage frequently makes acute observations about the way war affects people like herself, she remains incorrigible to the end in her attachment to the war. Brecht's intention was not, of course, to make a pessimistic statement about man's inability to learn from experience (although a number of commentators have regarded this as the real, if unintended, truth expressed by the play), but to enable the spectator to gain the kind of historical conspectus of her situation that Courage, caught up in the thick of things, cannot sustain. One of his principal means of doing this was to expose the contradictions in Mother Courage's experiences, another was to incorporate these contradictions in patterns of irony.

Mother Courage is a dialectically conceived figure. In other words, both she and the situations she finds herself in are systematically built on contradiction. Earning her living as a 'sutler' or camp-follower who provisions the soldiery, Mother Courage occupies a contradictory class position. Her 'crime' in seeking out the war in order to profit from it ('I can't wait till the war is good enough to come to Bamberg') is that of the capitalist class (at that time a rising class, according to the Marxist interpretation of history). On the other hand, as a small trader—and businesses do not come much smaller than hers—she is also one of the common people who simply have to survive as best they can in the social and economic system of their times. This class ambiguity underlies the most obvious contradiction in her life, that between her trade and her role as mother. As Brecht put it, 'The trader-mother became a great, living contradiction.' She embodies, as it were, the class-struggle in her own person, for whenever she acts as a 'capitalist', seizing some opportunity for profit, she invariably damages her interest as a member of the exploited classes, or, more particularly, as the mother of children who belong to that group. The fate of the family illustrates the fundamental contradiction of war—that it 'renders human virtues deadly, even for those who possess them,' and shows this in turn to be the outcome of the harsh logic of class-society, by virtue of which the productivity of ordinary people is turned into a force that operates against their own interests.

Courage's ambiguous social position enabled Brecht to give her the function of articulating many of his own criticisms of war and especially of the class-interests he saw underlying it. Because her own involvement in the war is purely mercenary she is well-placed to perceive the material interests behind all high-sounding justifications for war:

> To go by what the big shots say, they're waging war for almighty God and in the name of every-

> thing that's good and lovely. But look closer, they ain't so silly, they're waging it for what they can get. Else little folk like me wouldn't be in it at all.

On the other hand, her willingness to tell the unvarnished truth is motivated by the fact that, although she has her wagon, she and her family belong to the mass of ordinary folk whose lives are ruined by the politics of the powerful: 'The best thing for us is when politics get bogged down solid.'

That men are indeed mostly motivated by concern for their own material and physical well-being is confirmed again and again in the course of the play. Religion is regarded by all ranks as an irrelevance or an embarrassment, 'piety' is used to justify cruelty, but scorned as soon as it represents an obstacle to enjoying the spoils of war. Even as the great Field Marshall Tilly is being carried to his grave with full military pomp, his soldiers are interested only in using the opportunity to enjoy a rest, a smoke and a brandy. Mother Courage's challenge to the official version of the war is supported by the voice of the playwright, who, in the texts introducing each scene, counterpoints the major events that are represented in history books with the minor events that are in fact of much greater significance in the lives of ordinary folk: 'Tilly's victory at Leipzig costs Mother Courage four officers' shirts.'

With her wit, perceptiveness and ability to bamboozle figures of authority, Mother Courage is cast in the mould of Jaroslav Hasek's 'Good Soldier Schwejk'. To the extent that she presents, in an appealing manner, a critical view of war that Brecht himself endorsed, the playwright is still using direct rhetorical methods to shape the opinions of the audience. However, Mother Courage is far from being an unambiguously positive heroine, and irony plays a large part in making this plain. The audience is encouraged to criticise the war with Mother Courage, but also to develop a critical view of her attitudes and behaviour. In fact, Mother Courage's very perceptiveness contributes importantly to the ironic presentation of her fate.

An ironic tone is established as soon as the play begins, for the first thing with which the audience is confronted is a projected text (a modern descendent of the 'naive' Shakespearean device of simply announcing the place and time of the action), telling them that a recruiting campaign is going on and that 'A son of the sutler Anna Fierling, known under the name of Mother Courage, gets mislaid.' Apart from the flat, dead-pan tone, the irony emerges in the odd way of describing the loss of a son as if he were some object, like a walking stick. This verbal hint is then picked up by a whole series of images in the scene that follows which put human beings on the same level as animals and objects of use, for example: 'Takes a war to get proper nominal rolls and inventories—shoes in bundles and corn in bags, and man and beast properly numbered and carted off, 'cause it stands to reason: no order, no war.' Here the irony is laid on so thickly that the corporal's eulogy of wartime order takes on the quality of verbal farce, an effect heightened by the fact that, as he recites it, he is freezing in the April wind, an eloquent example of the miserable reality of war for the men on the ground.

When first introduced into this context, Mother Courage appears to be a master of irony rather than its object. The corporal and recruiting officer are determined to recruit her sons, but it seems at first that Mother Courage is so much more alert and in control of each situation that the recruiters are as likely to fail here as they have elsewhere. Yet by the end of the scene, despite her quick-witted handling of the situation (she knows what the recruiters are up to, and seeks to deflect them by a whole series of tactical ploys), she has become the victim of irony, when one of her own initial tactics rebounds on her. Early in the confrontation she tries to distract the 'gentlemen officers' by offering to sell them a pistol or buckle. When the threat to her sons seems to be past, and Courage has climbed eagerly back on to the wagon, the Recruiting Officer in turn distracts *her,* simply by suggesting that the corporal should take a look at the buckle after all. After only the briefest hesitation (and at great risk to the psychological plausibility of the scene) Mother Courage climbs down again and allows herself to be drawn into conversation on one side of the wagon while on the other the officer signs up her son, Eilif, who is all too eager to exchange the harness of a cart-horse for the uniform of a soldier. Whereas Mother Courage came on to the stage seated, on the wagon, with her daughter Kattrin by her side, she has to continue her journey on foot, with the wagon being pulled by Kattrin and her remaining brother.

Not only is this opening scene structured ironically, it also serves as the starting point of a longer ironic curve that stretches from the first to the last scene, holding together a loose sequence of incidents which are not bound into the traditional dramatic structure of action and counteraction between protagonist and antagonist. Just as Baal's ubiquitous, but hidden antagonist was Death, Mother Courage's is the war. Like him, she will eventually be defeated. To make us expect this outcome from the outset, Brecht builds into his play very familiar ironic structures such as the association of pride with a fall, insight with blindness, greatness with a tragic flaw or error. That Anna Fierling has a greater stature than most people is indicated by her by-name; that she is both wise and stupid, insightful and blind is evident from the events leading up to the loss of Eilif; that she is proud is evident from her response to the corporal's sarcastic remark that hers is 'a nice family': 'Aye, me cart and me have seen the whole world.' Subsequent scenes pick up these motifs so that events are perceived as parts of a coherent whole. Courage's moments of insight, for example, are juxtaposed with examples of blindness: immediately after a scene where Courage curses the war because of the harm it has done to her daughter, she is seen, once more astride a well-loaded wagon, pulled by the bandaged Kattrin, singing the praises of the war.

It is part of Brecht's irony to give to Mother Courage herself the function of announcing the bleak pattern to be completed by the action, when, in the opening scene, she pretends to foretell the future. By requiring first the recruiters and then her own children to draw black crosses from a helmet she hopes to frighten and distract the soldiers, and to intimidate Eilif, whose boldness she fears will draw him into soldiering. Yet what she foretells comes about. By the end of the opening scene she has already lost

Eilif to the army. By the end of the play her own actions will have (directly or indirectly) brought upon her children the very fate which, by pretending to predict it, she had intended to prevent.

In one sense, the pattern completed by the action is a moral one: Mother Courage's hubris in believing that *she* can bring *her* family safely through the war, regardless of whatever else it may destroy, is 'punished' by the loss, one by one, of all her children. The moral thus exemplified is announced, not at the end of the play, but at the end of the first scene: 'Like the war to nourish you? / Have to feed it something too.' This moral pattern is reinforced by the fates of other characters: the whore Yvette, initially an attractive girl, enjoys material success when she becomes the mistress of an old colonel, but pays for this by the loss of her physical attractiveness and human warmth. Eilif is at first rewarded for his cunning and cruelty, but a similar 'brave' action, done during an *apparent* cessation of hostilities, leads to his execution.

Yet the play as a whole does not encourage a morally smug response. Courage's other son, Swiss Cheese, is also executed, but he is a gentle, rather stupid soul whose only fault is excessive honesty and a sense of duty. Kattrin, kindly and so fond of children that she ultimately lays down her life to save the children of Halle, repeatedly and innocently falls victim to the barbarity of soldiers. The fates of Swiss Cheese and Kattrin *can* be drawn into the moral pattern of guilt and punishment by seeing them as victims of their mother's guilt, for she haggles so long over the sale of her wagon that she fails to save Swiss Cheese from execution, while Kattrin receives the mutilating injury that destroys any possibility of marriage and children of her own while away doing a business errand for her mother. But the moral case against Mother Courage also reveals an objective crux in her life. Certainly, the harm done to her children is associated with her business dealings. These business dealings, however, are the means by which she attempts to fulfil a mother's obligation to provide for her family. Mother Courage haggles long over the price of the wagon because she knows that, if the sale produces no more than the bribe needed to save Swiss Cheese, she and her children will be left destitute in the midst of war. Equally, she depends on Kattrin's contribution to the business that feeds the pair of them. That Mother Courage is not at bottom uncaring, or malicious towards her family is evident throughout, from her willingness to defend them with a knife from the recruiters in the opening scene, from her grief for the dead Swiss Cheese, from her refusal, even when near starvation, to abandon Kattrin in order to follow the cook to Utrecht. Ironically, this decision does not save Kattrin, because the girl's frustrated desire for children (frustrated by the mutilations she has received while in the care of her own mother) makes her prepared to sacrifice her life in an attempt to save the city of Halle.

Taking together all these elements—the heroine's great personal qualities and her blindness, her pride and her fall, her guilt and her suffering, the subjective errors and the objective coercion—it is evident that the ironic organisation of the whole serves not only to illuminate events intellectually, but also to cast Courage's life in the mould of tragedy. Repeatedly, she is made the object of a complex mix of emotions, not only of anger and outrage but also of fear and pity—as she sits by Kattrin's side waiting to hear if Swiss Cheese will be reprieved, or even as she strides along, singing the praises of war, seemingly oblivious of Kattrin's bandaged face, an emblem of past and probably future suffering. Courage is no monster but a fallible human being, whose failings are both part of her humanity and fostered by circumstances. She is tempted to live in a way that destroys herself and her family because the world she inhabits is so organised that the natural urge to provide for oneself is forced into destructive and ultimately self-destructive channels.

Tragedy, as the form forced on life by historical contingency, was not something that Brecht in practice entirely excluded from his Epic Theatre—provided that it stimulated a determination to eradicate the causes of suffering. On the other hand, it was a chancy experiment which could backfire if the painful experiences the audience is made to share were divorced in its reception of the play from a clear insight into the objective historical conditions that seduced to blindness, maimed lives and produced pain. Here Brecht relied heavily on the double function of irony, as a generator both of insight and pathos, to create a form of tragedy that not only faced up to the painful complexity of man's historically conditioned existence but also sought to offer something more than a mere counsel of despair.

After experimenting with the *Antigone* adaptation in Chur and with ***Mr Puntila*** in Zürich, the production of ***Mother Courage*** that opened at the Deutsches Theater in East Berlin in January 1949 was Brecht's greatest opportunity so far to put into practice his ideas about production and acting and to discover whether both plays and ideas would stand up to the demands of actual theatrical performance. In the event, the enormous success of this production (which led to the establishment of the Berliner Ensemble) and of the variants he developed over a number of years with different casts and in different theatres, proved that his writing and his theatrical ideas were eminently practicable and effective. ***Mother Courage*** became one of the foremost models of powerful, living theatre in the post-war period.

This outcome was achieved because Brecht's theatrical practice was a good deal more flexible than some of his theoretical statements, particularly those made at the beginning of the 1930s, had suggested it would be. Brecht's theatre 'worked' largely because of his unremitting insistence that the full sensuous resources of the medium (or media) of theatre should be employed to put flesh on to the skeleton of the *Fabel.* In practice Brecht did not direct his plays so as to produce intellectual *rather than* emotional theatre. His notes on his *Theaterarbeit* (theatre work) naturally tend to stress the point that was being made by this arrangement or that detail because it was this emphasis on the argumentative, demonstrative function of theatre that gave his work its peculiar character in relation to other available forms of theatre. However it is quite clear, both from his own record of work and from the actual effect of his productions on audiences, that the result was not dry didacticism. In fact, if anything, his problem was that his productions packed so much emotional punch that, despite all his intensive intellectual input, audiences and critics left the theatre deeply affected but not necessarily in agreement about what it was they were supposed to have learned from the experience. The following account of his staging will both describe the ways he used the resources of the theatre to persuade the audience to take a particular view of Mother Courage's experiences, and attempt to explain why the actual effect of the play in performance diverged from what he intended.

The design of Mother Courage's covered wagon, something 'half-way between a military vehicle and a general store,' was taken over by Brecht from Teo Otto's designs for the first production of the play in Zürich in 1943, as was much of the blocking of the scenes, which naturally was closely bound up with the position and functions of the wagon. The wagon is on stage in ten out of the twelve scenes of the play (the exceptions are Scene 2, played in a Captain's tent and kitchen, and Scene 4, played in front of an officer's tent). It is used to convey 'narratorial' information of a materialist nature that is intended to explain (in accordance with the Marxist tenet that consciousness is determined by the material conditions of life) the behaviour of the characters, particularly that of Mother Courage. When the wagon first trundles on to the stage at the beginning of the Thirty Years War its new awning and a freshly-painted sign correspond to Courage's keen spirit of enterprise as she pursues a new opportunity for profit. When the wagon leaves the stage (twelve years later) its tattered and battered state not only reflects the disappointment of her material ambitions but also suggests her spiritual reduction to a state of bare, desperate determination to struggle on. When, in between, the wagon is hung with a wide variety of goods, we are invited to see the connection between the fact that she is 'now at the peak of her business career' and her cynical, devil-may-care defence of war (in words that echo and parody Clausewitz's definition of war as politics conducted by other means): 'But what is war but private trading / That deals in blood instead of boots.' As she sings the wagon is pulled by Kattrin, her disfigured face swathed in bandages.

The wagon is thus a powerful device for tracing a coherent development in the various episodes that befall Courage and her family over a long period of time. It also creates the impression of a unity of place, for, although the locations of the play constantly change as the family follows the armies up and down Europe for twelve years, the scene of the action is almost invariably the space around the wagon. This scenic focus is one of Brecht's most effective means of subverting the 'official' view of history, since it insists that the measure of history is its effects on the limited domestic sphere on which the lives of common people are centred. At the same time as it asserts the little man's right to concern himself primarily with the banal business of everyday life, however, this scenic arrangement implies criticism of such political apathy by showing the recurrent disruption of the domestic sphere by events decided elsewhere. By constantly showing life in the perspective of people who are the passive 'objects of history', the play implicitly raises the question of why they do not make themselves into the active 'subjects of history'. However, in order to perceive this, particularly in relation to a historical period in which the common man's scope for political action was virtually non-existent, the spectator would already need to have the political awareness the play seeks to develop. Indeed, Brecht was criticised in Communist circles because of the alleged absence from the play of the 'idea of the revolutionary critical transformation of the world.'

Above all, the wagon gives concrete, visual expression to the 'great living contradiction' Courage embodies as businesswoman and mother. It is at one and the same time a place of refuge and relaxation, a territory to be defended, the price she pays for Swiss Cheese's life, and a source of sustenance for the family. It is also used to clarify the 'gestic' (that is, relational) substance of events. Thus, although the wagon is a means of sustaining the *whole* family, when it first appears it is being pulled by her two sons, while Courage and her daughter ride on top. Relations within the family are thereby shown also to be relations of exploitation—which partly explains why Eilif is so keen to seek his fortune as a soldier. In the opening scene the wagon halts near the front of the stage, somewhat off-centre, so as to mark off distinctly family from soldiers, the intended prey from the hunters. The soldiers then try a variety of ploys to invade the family 'territory'. When they eventually succeed in separating the mother and one member of her family, by tempting each of them with the prospect of personal gain, the wagon ironically provides the means of driving a wedge between mother and children. The family 'fortress' has thus been transformed into—or revealed to be—a trap.

There is a multitude of such examples of the wagon being used to show, in a manner that is theatrically forceful but not forced, what Marxist analysis defines as the power of the material conditions of life to alienate man from his own humanity. When Mother Courage is shown in the final scene, old, bent double, pulling the heavy wagon alone, on the seemingly endlessly revolving stage (Brecht deliberately made her walk-off last much longer than the audience is at first prepared for), the wagon is used to make the point to great pathetic effect. Yet it also makes points comically, as in the scene where it supports one end of a washing line, the other end of which is tethered to a cannon. Here the domestication even of war is both a tribute to man's tenacious ability to get on with the business of living by adapting to whatever situation he finds himself in, and (seen retrospectively, in the light of the family's destruction) a symptom of the deadly habituation which allows untenable conditions to be sustained. From these few examples alone, it should be apparent that, at its best, Brecht's art of theatre consisted of creating scenes that were both intellectually *and* emotionally telling, and that these effects were clearly designed to reinforce each other.

In order to create the most favourable conditions for the intensive exploitation of major stage properties, such as Mother Courage's wagon, Brecht favoured an otherwise uncluttered stage and even, white lighting—'As much of it as our equipment permitted'. The effect of the concentration produced by surrounding a central object with empty space is naturally the greater, the larger the stage. At the Deutsches Theater in 1949 Brecht had the advantage of working on a vast stage, the depth of which was further emphasised by the use of a semi-circular backdrop or 'cyclorama'. The grey tones of the set, combined with the huge empty space, naturally had a powerfully suggestive effect on audiences in bomb-flattened Berlin in 1949. At the other end of the scale, great attention was paid to matters of detail. Helene Weigel used a handful of carefully selected properties in a variety of ways to help tell the story of Courage, her children and her wagon. In her lapel she wore a large metal spoon, badge of her dual functions as mother and victualler. To focus attention on the importance of business dealings in Courage's life, Weigel found a purse with a particularly loud click. Even when paying for Kattrin's funeral, Weigel-Courage counted out a sum of money and then, seemingly absent-mindedly, put one of the coins back in the purse. A chain of silver coins worn around the character's neck simultaneously connoted vanity, enslavement and, possibly, the thirty silver pieces paid to Judas for his treachery.

The acting of Helene Weigel, was by common consent, one of the main reasons for the 'unforgettable' quality of the Berlin production of *Courage.* According to the account [in *Die neue Zeitung,* 15 January 1949] by Friedrich Luft (nowadays Berlin's senior theatre critic), Weigel's performance was epic in the manner prescribed by Brecht:

> An acting *tour de force* which she achieved without any apparent effort (. . .) Standing, as it were, intelligently *beside* her role, she presented the fate of this woman caught up in the war, without losing her own identity in that of the character. In her playing she made an example of the character, with a mimetic persuasiveness that seemed to be the most natural thing in the world. How she did all this is something that needs to be studied more closely and analysed on the basis of repeated observation. There is an expressive force at work here which was new and frequently took one's breath away.

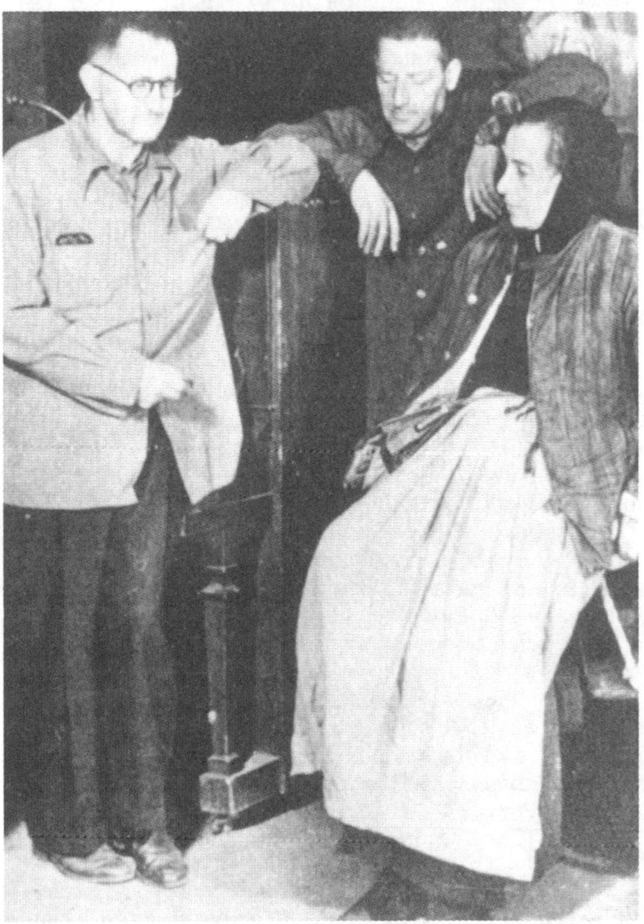

Brecht, composer Paul Dessau, and actress Helene Weigel—Brecht's second wife—during rehearsals for the Berliner Ensemble's production of Mother Courage *in 1949.*

Weigel's acting technique was reportedly [according to Wolfgang Harich in *Tägliche Rundschav,* 14 January 1949] 'restrained, unpathetic, direct, employing only a minimum of mimic devices'. But several reviewers also make equally clear that her technique of 'underplaying' the role, far from precluding emotion or preventing the illusion that the character was 'real', actually enhanced the persuasive power of her interpretation, as in this remark [by Harich]: 'Weigel's Courage was felt to be deeply moving in her moments of pain.' Another critic [in an unsigned review in *Der Sonntag,* 16 January 1949]. summed up his experience thus: 'At last a great actress showed once more that perfect, un-learnable correspondence between word and mimic expression, between sound and gesture, between a way of walking and a way of looking. One simply has to dig out that very hackneyed epithet "inspired" to say anything more about the experience.' This impression was shared by Brecht's old friend from Augsburg days, Otto Müllereisert, who wrote [in a review in *Die Welt,* 15 January 1949], 'the spectator shares the heroine's joy and pain during the action as if they were his own and feels a close bond between the character and himself.'

Such responses were the rule rather than the exception. They confirm, as a fact of theatrical life, that spectators readily adapt to whatever acting or presentational conventions are employed. Willingly suspending their disbelief, they then concentrate on the human content of the performance. If one considers the imaginative capacity of children to enter the world of Punch and Judy, it is hardly surprising that Weigel's fundamentally realistic acting (she spoke the part with a dialect colouring) had a powerfully illusionistic effect, with the result that most critics commented on the persuasiveness and emotional impact of the central characters, and not, as Friedrich Luft did, on the actors' maintenance of critical distance between themselves and the part they were playing.

In theory Brecht did not want the mimetic persuasiveness of any performance to be so powerful as to make the spectator feel that the actor 'was' the character rather than its presenter. Yet this is precisely how Weigel's Courage affected the writer Anna Seghers. Brecht himself, far from regarding it as an 'annihilating verdict' on her acting, was quite clearly proud to be able to note in his journal that mothers watching a procession pointed out Weigel to their children, saying, 'Look, there is Mother Courage'.

Despite his theoretical opposition to the organic conception of dramatic character, Brecht in fact built up any given role as an individual with a particular set of qualities—albeit contradictory ones—who is seen to develop from experience to experience. When, for example, he makes Courage refuse to allow her expensive shirts to be torn up for bandages, he argues that her increased hardness is motivated by her loss of Swiss Cheese. Particularly when working in the realistic mode of a play like ***Courage,*** it seems that Brecht's work was informed less by abstract preconceptions than by the *Bretterinstinkt* (theatrical instinct) which, as a young man, he took to be the prerequisite for creating convincing theatre in any given mode.

Courage's refusal to hand over the officers' shirts voluntarily is one of a number of changes introduced by Brecht in the hope of eliciting a more critical response to the heroine than that evinced by those commentators on Leopold Lindtberg's Zürich production of 1943, who had been struck more by the 'universal mother' aspect of the figure and by the fated, unfree quality of her 'animal-like', instinctively led life, than by her sociological significance as an embodiment of entrepreneurial self-interest. Although the version of the text played in Zürich already contained many of the details which, in Brecht's view, argued for a critical appraisal of Courage's conduct, he decided to increase the elements on the negative side of the balance for the Berlin production. However, there is no reason to suppose that the intended effect was the one actually achieved. Seen in relation to the loss of Swiss Cheese and the constant struggle to make a living, Courage's refusal to hand over the shirts for bandages makes her a more credible figure than in the earlier version. And it is precisely because the increased plausibility arises from seeing her as a person moulded—or deformed—by objective social circumstance, that the change does not oblige the spectator to take a simply condemnatory view of her behaviour.

Related to this question of the limiting or conditioning influence on behaviour of social and material factors, there is a further problem concerning the relation of theory to practice in Brecht's theatre. In order to intuit the reasons for Mother Courage's refusal to hand out the shirts it is necessary for the spectator to enter her situation by an act of identification or empathy—the very Aristotelian form of response to theatrical events against which Brecht directed so much venom. Nor is this an isolated exception to an otherwise firmly established principle in his theatrical practice. On the contrary, his directing, with its entirely conventional reliance on the suggestive power of this gesture or that expression consistently exploits the empathetic ability of the audience (which in any case is the necessary condition of communication within the, broadly speaking, realistic theatrical tradition of the West, lacking as it does the elaborately and explicitly codified set of symbolic conventions on which much oriental theatre is based).

Rather than think of Brecht's work as dispensing with the spectator's empathy, it is better to think of it as an attempt to manipulate the identificatory process and to steer it in particular directions. Thus the scene where Mother Courage is shown, triumphantly singing, immediately (in theatrical time) after she has cursed the war, presupposes the working of empathy at a number of levels. Empathy in the technical sense is involved in interpreting Mother Courage's expressions of feelings, just as intuition is required to relate these feelings to her present material success. The shock-effect of the scene depends, further, on the spectator's having identified—in the sense of sympathised—with Courage in the previous scene. Nor does this identification with Courage simply cease when, with the bandaged Kattrin by her side, she marches along singing the praise of war and trading. Her admittedly only too evident faults do nothing to make her less affecting as a human being, for how many spectators could honestly deny ever having been blinded by a sense of immediate personal well-being to the cost of that well-being to others, or could pretend never to have had profound experiences or insights that later faded? The educative shock-effect of the scene thus depends on the spectator's continuing, disturbing, identification with Mother Courage, and simultaneously with the point of view of those pulling the wagon while she walks freely. In other words, empathy, in a variety of forms, was a central element in Brecht's strategy of using the theatre to provoke insight and, as he hoped, action based on that insight.

Those spectators who felt intensely affected by Weigel's realistic playing of Courage, or by Angelika Hurwicz's presentation of Kattrin's complex mix of feelings as she desperately tries to drum the citizens of Halle awake, were not responding in an aberrant manner nor to aberrant realisations of Brecht's intentions. They were responding to the convincing sense of life (for want of a better term) that informed the play and the production. This powerful illusion that the characters and incidents were taken from life permitted Brecht unusual latitude in deploying various forms of stylisation, both in the writing and in the production of his plays, in order to urge a particular view of events on the spectator. On a verbal level, he peppered the dialogue with unusual, witty formulations that etch themselves in the memory. For example, he would produce surprise effects by using a noun with a verb that is usually used with its antonym: 'Don't tell me peace has broken out, just after I laid in new stock'. The army chaplain uses slang when talking about the most solemn subject, Christ's passion: 'Cases of people getting clobbered like this are by no means unknown in the history of religion'.

On a visual level the general plausibility of the central figures and their dilemmas permitted Brecht to underline his social or moral satire by physical or behavioural caricature: the captain who exploits Eilif 's 'boldness' is a drunken sot whose praise for the 'pious warrior' carries a suggestion of homosexuality. When the initially attractive whore, Yvette, achieves social advancement, the ugliness of her body and manner emphasise the price she has paid for success, as does the figure of the doddering, impotent Colonel, whose mistress she now is. In Berlin both the cook and the chaplain were played [according to an unsigned review in *Die Welt,* 15 January 1949] as 'caricatures after the manner of Callot'.

However, such stylisation remained peripheral to the overall effect of (tragic) realism produced by the play. Whereas most playwrights would have been delighted to make such an impact, to have gone so far down the road of realism created problems for Brecht. His ideal was 'combative realism', that is to produce convincing images of life that would nevertheless give rise to specific, predictable responses from the spectator. But the two elements in this conception proved very difficult to marry. Whenever he attempted to retain tight control over character and situation, through strong stylisation or by moving in the direction of allegory, the indefinable feel of life tended to suffer (this difficulty arose particularly with ***The Good Person of Szechwan***). On the other hand when, as in ***Mother Courage,*** he gave freer rein to his natural feel for life, the realism of the figures provoked a variety of interpretations and evaluations much as life itself does.

Even after Brecht had changed the text, had shared the direction of the first Berlin production, and had put Helene Weigel in the leading role, he found that many commentators still did not get the intended 'message', but interpreted it in more or less the same ways as those who had seen Therese Giehse playing Courage in Zürich under Lindtberg's direction. Some saw in the Brecht production a hymn to the common man (or woman), indestructable despite all that history could throw at him. Others saw in it a pessimistic picture of man's inherent weakness and proneness to evil. A (communist) variant of this response was to attack the play for its decadence and defeatism. While one commentator declared that it was not a propagandist contribution to the class struggle, another acknowledged that the playwright's intention was didactic, but claimed that the audience was likely to ignore this and simply relish the richness of his characters.

There is no need to assume obtuseness or malevolence on the part of the commentators to account for such evaluations of the play. They are explicable, rather, as responses to features of the text and its performance which made it very difficult for Brecht to achieve the effects he declaredly intended. One source of difficulty is the complex conception of Mother Courage's situation. Mother Courage is not simply a nasty businesswoman who also happens to have some children. Nor is she simply a good mother gone to the bad because of personal failings. She is an energetic, capable human being who, in the attempt to provide for her family and herself by following the rules of survival current in her society, experiences the conflict inherent in that society between human productivity on the one hand, and the social exploitation of productivity on the other. The destruction of Courage and her family by these deep-seated contradictions in class-society reveals more than she can possibly comprehend. It is difficult even for the reader—and more so for the theatrical spectator—to hold a steady focus on Courage, for she embodies *all* the features observed by critics: she is an example of the ordinary man's will and capacity to survive, a destructive and self-destructive obsessive, a cynical collaborator and a deeply-suffering, well-intentioned victim of the machinations of the powerful. Because she is all of these things, it requires what Brecht himself aptly defined as the difficult art of 'complex seeing' to grasp the complementary relations between the contradictory facets of her conduct.

A further source of difficulty for Brecht's didactic enterprise is his use of allusion, usually with the intention of underlining the peculiarity of what his play shows by calling to mind a familiar model that both resembles and contrasts with some aspect of the play. Thus, the chaplain sings the 'Song of the Hours', concerning Christ's Passion, during the scene in which Swiss Cheese is executed. By analogy, this puts Mother Courage in the situation of the Mother of Sorrows. But, as she then has to deny that Swiss Cheese is her son in order to save her own skin, she is also put in the situation of Peter denying Christ (a motif that appears repeatedly, obsessively even, throughout Brecht's oeuvre). As her business dealings are partly responsible for Swiss Cheese's death—her bitter reward for betraying him is the chain of silver coins she earns with the sale of the wagon—she is also in the situation of Judas. I take it that the intention of these allusions is to 'de-mythologize' the Biblical story, by re-interpreting the relation of model and reality. Whereas Christ's Passion and the roles in it of Judas and Mary are commonly taken to express a general, symbolic truth about the 'eternal' martyrdom and suffering of goodness in a world corrupted by evil, Brecht's concretisation of the model was presumably intended to be read as saying that the recurrence throughout history of the martyrdom of the 'Son of Man' arises from man's own failure to construct a form of society in which men would be free of the material pressures that produce their guilt and their suffering: at bottom, suffering is all a matter of the production and distribution of wealth.

However, although the relation of event to model *can* be understood like this, the reverse is more likely to be the case, particularly because of the relative power exercised by words and visual, physical images in stage performance. What the spectator sees, and inevitably identifies with, is a mother's suffering, culminating in Weigel's famous silent scream. This sense of suffering is intensified, rather than undermined, by the spectator's simultaneous awareness of her guilt (of which, as he knows, she is also aware), and by seeing her forced to perform the charade of denying their kinship.

The effect of this scene is multiplied throughout the play. Although full of historical inaccuracies and anachronisms, ***Mother Courage*** conjures up the seventeenth century setting of the action by numerous allusions to the religious and literary concerns of the baroque period. In the self-understanding of the times, the religious war had made Christ's martyrdom a contemporary reality, giving renewed life to the *topoi* of the transience of earthly existence, the vanity of man's efforts to control life, the fickleness of Fortuna (whose rolling ball or wheel is hinted at in the rise and fall of Courage's business, and possibly even in the turning of the stage and of the wheels on her wagon).

If Brecht's hope was to make the audience relate this baroque ideology to the historically specific base of early capitalist society, he was taking a very dangerous gamble, particularly in presenting the play to an audience that had just lived through the Second World War. Heinrich Kilger's 'Crown of Thorns' design of the lettering in the names of the various locations, the heavily emphasised circularity of Courage's career (the play opens with the wagon being pulled onto and around an empty stage, and closes with it being pulled around and off an empty stage), the seasonal progression from the beginning of spring to the depths of winter, the transformation of Courage from a cheerful, energetic woman in her middle years into a broken, bent and desperate old woman, the dramatic rhythm whereby the frequency and intensity of scenes of suffering increase as the 'epic' chronicle unfolds; the cumulative effect of all this was virtually bound to ensure that the play was received and remembered above all as a tragedy of the suffering of ordinary people across the centuries, while the indictment of petit-bourgeois collaboration could not be expected to play more than a subsidiary role. *If* this is to be accounted a failure, measured against Brecht's didactic intentions, it is surely of less importance than the undoubted achievement of Brecht, the theatrical practitioner, in keeping his audience's attention concentrated on a complex and painful subject. (pp. 91-115)

Ronald Speirs, in his Bertolt Brecht, *St. Martin's Press, 1987, 190 p.*

THE CAUCASIAN CHALK CIRCLE

PRODUCTION REVIEWS

Douglas Watt (review date 25 March 1966)

[*In the following review of Jules Irving's staging of* The Caucasian Chalk Circle, *Watt summarizes the plot and highlights central themes of the play, asserting that "possibly because of the nature of the work, which demands no stellar performances, the [Lincoln Repertory] company [came] off better than it has on earlier occasions." Watt praises the production's costuming and stagecraft and maintains that "Robert Symonds [was] especially good in the only role with any real meat, that of Azdak."*]

In ***The Caucasian Chalk Circle,*** which was given its New York premiere last evening at the Vivian Beaumont, the familiar Brecht apparatus—vaudeville-like scenes, each announced in advance and strewn with tinny little songs—is employed to full effect.

This is the fourth and final production of the season, the first under the new administration, by the Repertory Theatre of Lincoln Center and it is by all odds the best. The company has shot the works with some excellent scenery, costumes and masks designed by James Hart Stearns, and Jules Irving has directed his players with considerable skill on a turn-table stage with apron.

Brecht wrote his play in California in 1945, when the war in Europe had ended and when he had already espoused the Communist cause. It opens with a poster-art prologue that takes place in a Caucasian valley just after the war. A band of goat breeders and another of fruit growers are contending for the land, but not for long. "The Soviet people shall be the home of reason," observes one character and, lo and behold, the fruit growers acquire it, with little opposition, because they will irrigate and improve the land. Poor Brecht.

As entertainment, the play proper, is then staged for the comrades. Adapted from an ancient Chinese fable, it relates events that occurred in the same area in the year 1200.

During a political upheaval the rich governor of the area is beheaded and his wife, making her escape, leaves behind their infant son. A palace kitchen maid harbors it, carries it up a mountain, across a glacier and down the other side, and eventually decides to make it her own. A kind of younger Mother Courage, she.

When caught years later, she is brought to trial before a drunken, venal yet intelligent poacher who finally decides to settle the case by having a chalk circle drawn on the floor, the child placed in it and the two women, the rightful mother and the maid, placed on either side. Each grasps one of the boy's hands and the judge decrees that the one who succeeds in pulling the boy her way shall be declared the winner.

He's fooling, though. For when the peasant girl loses in two tries, it is not because of weakness but because she cannot bear having the child pulled apart. So the judge awards her custody and then skips town.

The purpose of all this elementary stuff is to provide the audience with a nice candy which Brecht has loaded with his convictions about the menace of vested interests, corruption in high places, the monstrous inhumanity of the professional soldier, the incompetence of the clergy, the persecution of the poor and other matters.

It's a long play, running close to three hours, and even with all the low-down comedy (the courtroom business in the final act is like a series of burlesque sketches), it lags frequently. Moreover, Brecht's particular kind of theatre, though it abounds in philosophy, in necessarily lacking in any stimulating play of ideas.

Possibly because of the nature of the work, which demands no stellar performances, the company comes off better than it has on earlier occasions.

Robert Symonds is especially good in the only role with any real meat, that of Azdak, the village scrivener turned judge. Elizabeth Huddle is appealing as Grusha, the kitchen maid, and there is good comic work turned in by Michael Granger as Grusha's henpecked brother, Glenn Mazen as a chap who pretends mortal illness until the end of the draft and Ray Fry as a bibulous monk. Brock Peters is fine as the Storyteller and the combo (accordion, balalaika, guitar and percussion) plays Morton Subotnick's thin score animatedly.

In providing us with so able a rendering of a much-discussed play and one that has been presented in numerous other cities here and abroad, The Lincoln Rep has honorably discharged a probable obligation to theatre-goers.

Douglas Watt, "Brecht's 'Caucasian Chalk Circle' in Fine Lincoln Rep Production," in Daily News, *New York, March 25, 1966.*

Walter Kerr (review date 25 March 1966)

[In the following review, Kerr offers an unfavorable assessment of Jules Irving's staging of The Caucasian Chalk Circle, *arguing that in this production " 'epic theater' [became] simply hasty, cluttered, and then much too often interrupted theater, not a masterly survey of a vast human and political landscape but a log-ridden river moving erratically when it moves at all."*]

Here is what I want to know. Why don't the men who admire Brecht most discover more in him when they put him on the stage?

In general, I remain a heathen where the methods of Bertolt Brecht are concerned, and it is only fair that you should know that. But I must say I feel a profound urge to defend both the man and the methods from the assaults of the converted.

Surely the auspices should be right for a decent showcasing of Brecht at Lincoln Center. The Blau-Irving management, which has now offered us ***The Caucasian Chalk Circle,*** is well known for its forthright admiration of the inventor of "epic theater." Mr. Blau has written extensively about the special revelations the Brechtian style is intended to offer us in the playhouse, and Mr. Irving has gone to the enormous trouble of moving houses and thrones, mobs and assorted masks, in order to place the present three-hour fable on the stage. He has, in fact, quite literally moved Chinese mountains, sweeping them past us on painted landscapes with a curtness that seems to mean business. The English text, furthermore, has been provided by Eric Bentley, whose scholarship has been untiring in a so far unrewarded cause.

Yet the experience at the Vivian Beaumont is heavy, attenuated, ultimately and unmistakably wearisome, and not merely because the acting company is without invention, variety, or command. The evening is defeating precisely where it should be most revealing, stumbling grossly over its own feet at the very moments the technique begins to tantalize us.

A few examples. Brecht adapted his conceit from a traditional Chinese play in which two women claim a child before a puzzled judge. The real mother, a governor's wife with jewels sparkling to the tips of her five-inch-long fingernails, has indifferently abandoned the baby during an uprising. A palace kitchen-maid has rescued it, really wanting to be rid of it but unable to rise above her own emotional simplicity. The kitchen-maid, hurrying across the ravaged countryside with her hastily bundled burden, comes to a time when she must sing The Song of the Rotted Bridge. A narrator clad in goatskin and karakulwool cap, and accompanied by a twanging of carefully unsweetened instruments, tells us so.

The girl stands poised above the bridge, a fearful ladder of disintegrating slats, swaying as she clutches a slender lifeline thousands of feet high over a gorge. The naivete of the situation is deliberate, the cliff-hanging calculated to remind us of ancient theatrical trickery at the same time that it detaches us from its foolish suspense. Two things are set at odds here: the familiar picture with its overtones of mere thrill, and the fact that the girl freezes on the precipice to detain us with formal song. The theater turns inside out: we see it through the other side of the mirror, understanding it instead of submitting to it.

But the meeting is botched both ways as Mr. Irving manages it. There is no sharp stylistic cut-off to frame our vision in a crisp, crystalline, fiercely angular new way. The universe does not, for the moment, go into deep shock. And when the song is blurred through, the old, shaky, next-to-absurd realism of watching a heroine navigate a presumably threatening gorge is done with the clumsy and undesigned earnestness of an Eliza surviving the ice again.

We are given neither formal nor illusory satisfaction, much less the clear contest between the two that might have brilliantly silhouetted both. Again, the kitchen-maid's brother, who has temporarily given her shelter, looks toward the skies to say that when the snow melts she must go. Without pause, he announces that the snow on the roof is at last melting, and something odd and attractive should happen in and to the playhouse—time should turn in on itself as our senses dissolve, and perhaps delight, in our awareness of what it means to be in a theater where such things can happen. At the Beaumont nothing at all happens. The actor simply speaks the second line, and we wonder—if we are still attending that closely—whether we have heard the first or the second line wrong.

The masks worn by the uprooted parties in a revolution are striking grotesques as James Heart Stearns has designed them: chalkcliff noses and trailing wisps of scarlet beard flow above and about the costumes that are like so many walking Persian rugs. There are fountains of feathers and mountains of fur, but behind them there are no identities, no pointed meanings rising in toward a focus. Voices gasp and growl—the players frequently sound as though they were wearing their whiskers on the inside of their throats—but they are nearly all interchangeable, supers hired to carry banners bearing painted winged animals for the night. "Epic theater" becomes simply hasty, cluttered, and then much too often interrupted theater, not a masterly survey of a vast human and political landscape but a log-ridden river moving erratically when it moves at all.

We watch, and we listen, and we wonder what Brecht really wanted. We catch a glimmer when Brock Peters is singing some of his storyteller's verses, standing still and facing us. We hear an echo in Elizabeth Huddle's unsentimental decision that the baby will simply have to accept her as a mother, though the folk-and-peasant images are generally sentimentalized throughout. Robert Symonds' carefree judge, wrapped in red robes on the spur of the moment, amuses us briefly as he investigates the suit for divorce of an octogenerian couple (they just don't like each other, never have). But the balance of the ironies are red-nosed and thumping as they are presented, pretty much the obvious comic balloons sent up by the essentially humorless, and the texture of the performance as a whole is uninflected enough to suggest that the director has never heard it from the front of the house.

The stage promises mystery: a rocky plateau for musicians here, a corrugated-iron curtain there, a way of putting a play together that is circuitous with secrets. The secrets are kept, the mystery of Brecht—in the American professional theater-still stands.

Walter Kerr, " 'The Caucasian Chalk Circle': Kerr's Review," in New York Herald Tribune, *March 25, 1966.*

Stanley Kauffmann (review date 25 March 1966)

[*Kauffmann is one of America's best-known contemporary film and theater critics, contributing reviews to several magazines. In the following review, he praises Jules Irving's staging of* The Caucasian Chalk Circle, *commenting on elements of stagecraft and the performance of the cast.*]

A doubly pleasant occasion. One of the best of of Bertolt Brecht's plays has at last reached New York (22 years after it was written). In presenting it, the Lincoln Center Repertory Theater has given us its best production to date, and a good production by any standards.

The Caucasian Chalk Circle, which opened last night at the Vivian Beaumont, seems a kind of busman's holiday for Brecht. It is a diversion from his activist political plays into the arena of theatrical high jinks, with plentiful opportunities for pageantry, music, horseplay and sheer heart-tugging.

It is a big, conscious, melodramatic *show,* complete with infant waif, estranged lovers, Eliza-effects like an escape across a rickety bridge, and a happy ending without the deliberate fakery of Macheath's rescue in ***The Threepenny Opera.*** Yet it is all founded on a view of life as a pitched social battle between the rulers and the ruled, and it has a utilitarian purpose.

The body of the three-hour play follows a prologue about collective farmers in a Caucasian village in the Soviet Union at the end of the Second World War. Two groups of farmers lay claim to a valley. The dispute is in fact settled quickly, but (the utilitarian point) to drive home the idea, a play is performed before the reconciled groups: to prove that anything—a valley or a baby—belongs morally to the person or persons who will do best by it.

The play-within-the-play is set in the very same locality seven hundred years earlier. In one of the wars of princes, a governor's infant is abandoned, and is rescued by a kitchen maid named Grusha, who takes him with her on her various risky journeyings, all of which are interesting and some of which are funny.

At the end of the war, the child is found by soldiers and re-claimed by the governor's widow. Grusha, who has reared him for several years, wants to keep him. The case comes to trial.

That trial is held before a judge named Azdak, but before the play proceeds, we backtrack to learn how this wily, good-hearted scoundrel—out of Shakespeare and Rabelais—became a judge in the first place. In the trial itself, Azdak uses a version of Solomon's old device: He determines which of the contesting women is willing to harm the child by pulling it out of a chalk circle.

Jules Irving has directed—the third director whose work has been seen with this company and, on the basis of this season, the one with the most truly theatrical gifts. This is a circus-like show and is played as such, yet the broad character touches and the bitter flavors are well used. Movement swirls; the riotous colors of peasants like Breughel's are splashed in; the interplay among the narrator (the Storyteller), the on-stage musicians and the action is well balanced. And for the first time, we feel that the physical resources of this theater—revolving stages and so on—are dominated by the director, instead of dominating him.

The costumes are gorgeous when need be (some of the actors wear resplendent Persian rugs like gowns) and are fine peasant stuff otherwise. All the upper-class characters and their attendants wear masks, slightly outsize and grotesque. These and the costumes are by James Hart Stearns, and all are excellent.

Mr. Stearns' settings suggest a continuity between the ancient and modern Caucasus in their rough textures, but is it literal-minded to ask about corrugated iron roofs in A.D. 1200?

The prime performance is by Robert Symonds as Azdak. Which is as it ought to be, because Azdak is a dream-part, sly, pragmatic, brusquely idealistic, and loaded with punch-lines. Some believe that the part is a Brecht self-portrait: an ironic realist whose principles come second only to his peasant's instinct for survival. Mr. Symonds—wiry, slippery, sharp—is first-class.

Elizabeth Huddle plays Grusha adequately, although she has not quite enough voice for her songs. Her chief asset is that her sturdy, snub-nosed, rose-cheeked effect is very likable. Brock Peters, the Storyteller, conducts himself with the dignity of a veteran village ballad-singer.

Ray Fry, whose Sir Jasper Fidget was the best thing in *The Country Wife,* has a cameo comic turn as a besotted monk. In the enormous cast, many of whom double and triple, one can note the valuable addition to the company of Earl Montgomery and Murvyn Vye, the good work of Michael Granger in a couple of parts and Edward Winter's decently dignified soldier-fiance of Grusha.

Eric Bentley's translation is, happily, the standard one for this play, as it is for so much of Brecht.

Richard Nelson's lighting is purposely stagy but sometimes, I think, distractingly so. Morton Subotnick's music is flavorless, the least rewarding aspect of the production.

And hands should be mentioned. This is a play in which a disguised nobleman is recognized by his soft white hands. Most of the peasants in this cast—ancient and modern—have nobleman's hands. Boris Tumarin, supposedly a grizzled dairy farmer, uses his very white hands like a ladies' hairdresser.

Perhaps the Lincoln Center company looks best, so far, in this play because it requires neither the high style of Wycherley nor the high acting virtuosity of the Büchner and Sartre plays that preceded it. But, even if it is for negative reasons, the result is positive. This production of ***The Caucasian Chalk Circle*** achieves much of what Brecht presumably intended: a good show, firmly based on an undeceived view of the world, but nonetheless a charming, thoroughly theatrical show.

Stanley Kauffmann, "At Last, 'The Caucasian Chalk Circle'," in The New York Times, *March 25, 1966, p. 35.*

CRITICAL COMMENTARY

Ronald Gray (essay date 1961)

[*Gray is an English educator and critic who specializes in German literature. In the following excerpt from a discussion of Brecht's later plays, Gray focuses on Brecht's portrayal of Azdak and Grusha in* The Caucasian Chalk Circle. *Gray concludes that "the virtue of Grusha is both convincingly stated and brought into question, the amoralism of Azdak is made to look both repugnant and curiously attractive, and yet in the final moments a fusion of Grusha's human demands and Azdak's inhuman unpredictability brings about a sense of at least temporary fulfillment."*]

It is as well to say at the outset that the Communistic message which [***The Caucasian Chalk Circle***] seems to convey is only loosely connected with the main plot. This is the story of a young Georgian girl, Grusha, who saves the infant child of a tyrannical governor during an insurrection, who brings up the boy until the day when his real mother disputes possession of him before the "good, bad judge" Azdak, and who finally, through the unorthodox wisdom of the judge, is allowed to retain the child because she alone has shown a true motherly nature. It scarcely follows from this that (as the epilogue suggests) the Soviet authorities are entitled to deprive industrious dairy-farming peasants of their land in order to hand it over to others who will make use of it for viniculture. And the prologue, in which this contemporary problem is outlined (the play itself being performed as a means of persuading the reluctant dairy-farmers to yield), is remarkable for the prim diction of the Soviet officials, the conventional picture it gives of shrewd, but good-hearted peasants, and the "socialist realism" of its style and presentation.

All this is in contrast to the non-naturalistic, many-sided, lyrical, humorous, Rabelaisian, socially conscious elements of the "play within the play." The girl Grusha is not in the least conventionally drawn, though she too is shrewd and good-hearted. We do not sit back in uncomfortable or smug contentment telling ourselves that this is what sturdy peasants are really like, as we are invited to do in the prologue. She shows considerable courage in crossing a rickety bridge over a mountain chasm while being pursued by insurrectionist soldiers; she combines this with artfulness, a ready wit, blunt honesty, stubborn insistence, and an unshakable moral probity. When she is married for convenience sake to a dying man who will be at least a nominal father for the child she has saved, and when the man, a skrimshanker, rises from his "deathbed" on hearing that the war is over, she continues to pay him a wifely respect, shows no resentment or self-pity. When, later, her lover Simon to whom she is betrothed returns from the war, she allows him to suspect her of infidelity rather than betray the child to its enemies. Courage, perseverance, motherliness, dutifulness, self-sacrifice she shows time and again. Yet because of her equanimity and lack of self-regard, these qualities have no false ring. And this is due also in part to the deliberately non-naturalistic language she speaks. Brecht makes no attempt to reproduce peasant speech faithfully: Grusha's is sprinkled with proverbs and dialect forms, but it also includes direct translations of English idiom; when she sings a lullaby to the child it is at once a song that vividly recalls ancient German folk-art and at the same time has a modern ring. Subtly and continuously through the language Brecht persuades us not quite to believe in Grusha, to accept her as a creation of art, and to look beyond her to a reality which in part we re-create ourselves. The formality of his presentation reaches its climax in the scene, concluding the first part of Grusha's adventures, where Simon returns and speaks with her across a river that separates them. The lovers address each other at first in an exchange of proverbs which is both humorous and characteristic of their peasant origins. It is also, however, quite impersonal, a drawing on common tradition, and it is only by reflexion that the deep personal relationship between them is felt. In the climactic moment of the scene, in fact, neither speaks, and it is left to the narrator to reveal what each "thought, but did not say." Thus they confront each other in formal attitudes which are never realistically portrayed but are at the same time deeply moving, and it is by a similar estrangement that Brecht succeeds in making the outstanding human qualities of Grusha credible and acceptable.

The scenes of Grusha's escape, adventures, marriage, and rejection by Simon, forming about half the play, make a loosely-strung narrative in the fashion of "epic" theatre. While there is a certain thread connecting them, however—they do not stand "each for themselves," as Brecht suggested earlier that "epic" scenes should do—the interest is sustained not so much by the thin plot as by the detailed interactions of the characters and by the beauty of the portrayal. Since ***Baal,*** Brecht had scarcely made any use in his plays of the natural scene. In ***The Caucasian Chalk Circle,*** as in ***Puntila*** and ***The Good Woman*** and in his later poetry, the world of nature returns. The scene by the river itself, indicated on the stage merely by two ground-rows of reeds, evokes by its bareness, coupled with the lyrical song of the narrator preceding it, an awareness of loveliness. The icicles above Grusha's hut, as she waits in isolation for the winter to pass, become moving tokens of spring as they melt, and the musical notes of a xylophone offstage, recording the falling drops of water, add excitement by their rising intensity. There is time for contemplation and for exhilaration in these austerely presented moments; the spectator is not whirled along as he was by the action of earlier plays, and not encouraged to indulge in ecstatic Nature-worship, but rather to recognise with pleasure the delight that is to be had from Nature, off the stage. There is both detachment and attachment.

The settings also, in this part of the play, evoke an astringent delight. The descending white back-cloth has already been mentioned. There is also the scene of Grusha's wedding, contrived to give a Breughelesque harmony of brown, oatmeal, sepia, has an occasional splash of red: peasant colours in a peasant setting, crowded, earthy, vulgarly frank, but shaped into a frame of unity that is comic, sympathetic, and has a lop-sided symmetry of its own. There is the strange effect of the empty stage after the insurrection has passed by, with the voice of the narrator emerging from one side to comment on the silence and thereby, oddly enough, to intensify it. Meanwhile, from time to time, the prose speech breaks into verse such as that in which Grusha affirms her love at Simon's first departure:

> Simon Chachava, I will wait for you.
> Go in good heart to the battle, soldier,
> The bloody battle, the bitter battle
> From which not all come back:
> When you come back, I will be there.
> I will wait for you under the green elm
> I will wait for you under the bare elm
> I will wait till the last man comes back
> And longer.
> When you come back from the battle
> No boots will stand by the door
> The pillow by mine will be empty
> And my mouth unkissed.
> When you come back, when you come back
> You can say it is all as it was.

It comes as a shock to go on from this moving language and these scenes to the following series which forgets Grusha entirely in order to introduce the story of the judge Azdak. From Azdak's first speech, the spectator is hit by a forceful language which English can barely reproduce: "Schnaub nicht, du bist kein Gaul. Und es hilft dir nicht bei der Polizei, wenn du läufst, wie ein Rotz im April. Steh, sag ich. . . . Setz dich nieder und futtre, da ist ein Stück Käse. Lang nichts gefressen? Warum bist du gerannt, du Arschloch?" The crudity of this, the rough vigour, the cynicism and humour and the underlying sympathy introduce the character of Azdak himself, which stands in strange contrast to Grusha's. Azdak is a thief, a time-server, a coward, who by a lucky accident is raised during the insurrection to a position of authority. As a judge he is corrupt, licentious, contemptuous of law and order, a lickspittle. His life is spent, unlike Grusha's, not in rebellious opposition to society's moral standards, but in careful adaptation to them, going along with the tide, and keeping an eye on the main chance. But such an account does less than justice to this unpredictable rogue. In the first scene, finding that the poor man he thought he was sheltering is in fact the Grand Duke, fleeing from the insurrection, he still does not hand him over to the police, although whether from sheer contempt for the police, as he says, or contempt for the Duke, or from an inscrutable sympathy such as Ernst Busch implies when he plays him, is never clear. Promptly, he rushes into town to denounce himself, believing that the soldiery will welcome the news of his treachery—some strange conscientiousness is at work in him. Yet on discovering them to be indifferent to the rights and wrongs of the insurrection, he willingly allows them to clothe him in judicial robes, and goes off on his rampaging procession through the countryside, delivering sentences that completely reverse accepted standards of justice. He accepts bribes, but (though he keeps the money) only as an indication of the wealth of the litigants, which stands in his eyes in inverse proportion to their rights. He makes an award in favour of a poor woman who has been helped by a bandit, on the grounds that only a miracle could explain how a leg of pork came to fly through a poor woman's window: those who accuse the bandit of stealing the pork and throwing it through the window are condemned for godlessness and disbelief in miracles. When a buxom young woman accuses a farm-hand of rape, he considers her luxurious gait and the shape of her buttocks and finds her guilty of assault and battery with a dangerous weapon, after which he goes off with her to "examine the scene of the crime." And when order is re-established he falls over himself with dutiful promises that Grusha, whom he has not yet met, shall be beheaded as soon as she is found.

Azdak is a standing affront, and at the same time a standing reminder of the questionable values on which society is based. He has one principle, that the rights of the poor are disregarded and that this situation must be reversed. Apart from that, he proceeds *ad hoc.* If a buxom girl is likely to commit rape he offers her the opportunity. On the other hand, if he foresees danger in maintaining his one principle, he gives way immediately: "I'm not doing any one the favour of showing human greatness." Yet all this is not mere self-gratification or concern for his own skin. There is nothing that can properly be called a self in Azdak, nothing consistent or foreseeable in his actions: he acts on impulse. He sets no store by his actions, any more than Grusha does by hers, and it is this that helps to make him the most fascinating character in the play, insulting and generous, preposterous and humble, ignorant and wise, blasphemous and pious. In his Villonesque song to the poor woman he addresses her as though she were the Virgin Mary and begs mercy for such damned creatures as himself—a strange translation from religious into human terms which still has an atmosphere of genuine devoutness. In the scene where he is buffeted in his false robes by the soldiery, the production of the Berliner Ensemble is deliberately styled to recall another buffeting. And in the comment of the narrator there is a further suggestion of a wider scope: "And so he broke the laws, as he broke bread, that it might feed them." The suggestion need not be taken too far. Yet there is in Azdak, the scandal, the gnome, the cynical good-liver, something immensely disturbing and provocative as well as attractive. He denies all the virtues, mocks at repentance and charity, ridicules courage, and, strangely enough, he gets our sympathy in the process. For he is plainly being himself to the top of his bent, lusting and helping the poor, crawling in abject fear and at the same time inviting the soldiers to recognise their own doglike obedience, answering every prompting with instinctive recklessness. If we give him our sympathy, as we cannot help doing, in a way, so long as he dominates the stage, he sets all Grusha's virtuousness at naught. This is Baal, returned to the scene in a new guise, and all Baal's fascination pours out from him.

In the final scene of all, the two sides are confronted with one another, the disruptive, ambiguous underminer and the calm, shrewd, motherly girl who would rather die than forego her humanity. Azdak is called to try the case in which the real mother of Grusha's "child," the wife of the former governor of the province, claims possession of her son. By a fortunate turn of events, the same Grand Duke whose life Azdak saved earlier on has now returned to power, and thus Azdak's servile promise to the governor's wife no longer has any hold over him, if indeed he ever meant to keep it. Azdak proceeds, however, as usual, accepting bribes from the wealthier party, while abusing Simon and Grusha who have nothing to offer him, and it is this which brings on the first serious opposition he has had to encounter. Grusha declares that she has no respect for a judge such as he is, "no more than I have for a thief and a murderer that does what he likes." Her moral protest is a straightforward indictment of his libertinism (which is no mere show), and none the worse for that; in fact she has all, or nearly all, our sympathy. Yet the end will have already been guessed. After the "trial of the chalk circle" in which each woman is to pull at the child from different sides, and Grusha fails to pull for fear of hurting the boy, Azdak ceremonially declares that Grusha is the true mother since she alone has shown true motherly feelings. This is not, however, a sentimental ending awarding victory to justice against the run of the odds. Rather, it is the fusion of two conceptions of justice. Azdak's instinctive prompting on this occasion (he is, after all, in safety now, with the governor's wife in political disgrace) is to award Grusha the custody of the child. But this instinctive prompting is a part of his elemental originality, his closeness to the roots of his nature, and his complete detachment from them. His decision has gathered the weight and incontrovertibility of a natural phenomenon, and despite his mockery of the virtues here is one virtue in Grusha that he respects without thought of argument.

Thus the two sides come together. Like Nietzsche, Azdak demands opposition such as he gets from Grusha, and thrives on it. Like Nature itself, he is ambiguous and amoral and requires the rebelliousness of humanity to bring out his qualities to the full. Then, however, when he meets with opposition, he reveals an unexpected generosity (as Nietzsche never did). He is like Baal, it is true. But Baal was never opposed, lived his life in pure self-fulfilment, and died only to the tune of contempt from others. Azdak is Baal, and all that lies behind Baal, brought into relationship with human beings, and this relationship and conflict serve to make ***The Caucasian Chalk Circle*** far greater in scope than its predecessor. The virtue of Grusha is both convincingly stated and brought into question, the amoralism of Azdak is made to look both repugnant and curiously attractive, and yet in the final moments a fusion of Grusha's human demands and Azdak's inhuman unpredictability brings about a sense of at least temporary fulfilment. As the narrator has it, the period of Azdak's life as a judge could be looked back upon as "a brief Golden Age almost of justice." It was not *the* Golden Age, and it was not a time of complete justice. Both Azdak and Grusha have been too "estranged" for us to be able to accept them as models or heroes. But while steering clear of absolutes Brecht creates here an ending which is satisfying on a purely human plane. Despite the riotous exaggeration of a great part of the play, from which he never recants for an instant, the conclusion is moderately and accurately stated. (pp. 105-13)

Ronald Gray, in his Bertolt Brecht, *Grove Press, Inc., 1961, 120 p.*

Ronald Gaskell (essay date 1972)

[*In the following excerpt, Gaskell evaluates Brecht's use of techniques that alienate the audience, arguing that* The Caucasian Chalk Circle *is essentially realistic and that its strengths lie in "the permanent core of truth in the play, the integrity of Brecht's vision, and the energy with which that vision animates his whole dramatic form."*]

Brecht takes every opportunity to stress the simplest needs and sensations of the body (hunger, cold, sexuality, fatigue) and the resistance of the physical world. For the life of man, as Brecht sees it, is social, that is, economic; and the basis of economics is biology. ***The Threepenny Opera*** announces the priorities that will govern all his later work: 'eats first, morals after'. Not because morals are a luxury, but because our freedom to lead a decent life varies with the strength of economic pressures which we have to meet in order to live at all.

This realism of Brecht's, though it gives his plays their bedrock of conviction, would be nothing without his delight in the humour and resilience of men. Like Synge he has a grasp not just of the world of the peasant—what we can touch and smell and taste—but of emotions uncorrupted by sentiment or habit. Unlike Synge, he sees the life of action as essentially political; for the world, in Brecht's view, must be changed before men can lead lives worthy of a human being.

This is the clue to that belief in narrative which runs through all his experiments in the theatre. A strong narrative line on the stage makes the point that man belongs inescapably to history. By showing events as they happen it lets us see that they might have happened otherwise if men had acted differently; and in doing this, reminds us that men can always change their world. At the same time, as in Shakespeare, the episodic structure of narrative, since it leaves the dramatist free to turn from the general's tent to the cook's, admits ironic juxtapositions that expose the significance of events.

To illuminate social change is harder in drama than in the novel; harder still, with the immensely complicated societies of industrial Europe, if we are looking for more than documentary or the crudest caricature. (Brecht's work offers examples of both.) What is needed, clearly, is some kind of simplification: a dramatic form that can isolate the essential without reducing it to the abstract. The historical past—***Galileo, Mother Courage***—points to one possibility. Another, which Brecht discovered with ***The Threepenny Opera*** and went on to explore more fully in his parable plays, ***The Good Person of Setzuan*** and ***The Caucasian Chalk Circle,*** is to design a world too different from our own to be mistakable for a mere cartoon of it. Both kinds of play, the historical and the parable, can readily be structured as narrative. The parable, however, brings two further advantages.

First, it allows a more imaginative use of the resources of drama as an art of the theatre—heightened speech, expressive gesture, grouping, costume, music, light—to define the theme of the play. The action of ***The Caucasian Chalk Circle*** could have been given a specific historical context; indeed, Brecht's earlier version of the parable, his short story **"The Augsburg Chalk Circle"**, was set, like ***Mother Courage,*** in the Europe of the Thirty Years' War. But a setting of that kind would have precluded, if nothing else, the sharply stylized characters of the play he wrote.

Second, the poetic form of the play, the imaginative logic of its design, sets ***The Caucasian Chalk Circle*** more decisively away from the world of the twentieth century than distance in time or space alone could do. Brecht, therefore, can go further in surprising us by parallels between our own way of life and the world we see before us on the stage; a vaguely feudal, wholly invented world—with rising prices, war contracts, army service and draft dodging, taxes going up to pay for the war, and a military ready to obey anyone in power. And to do this is to jolt us, as Brecht intended, into looking freshly at a society which, because we happen to live in it, we take, with all its built-in values, as the norm.

Partly for these reasons ***The Caucasian Chalk Circle*** seems a finer achievement than ***Mother Courage.*** But the strength of ***The Caucasian Chalk Circle,*** as of any work of art, is not its topical relevance. It is the permanent core of truth in the play, the integrity of Brecht's vision, and the energy with which that vision animates his whole dramatic form.

The text is divided into sections forming a prologue and five acts. In production the five acts fall into two parts, with fifteen or sixteen scenes in the first part (Grusha's flight to the mountains with the child) and seven or eight in the second (the career of Azdak). No doubt the stories of Grusha and Azdak could have been presented together rather than consecutively, the action being laid out as a pattern of relationships developing from beginning to end. Nothing, however, would have been further from Brecht's purpose, since development encourages in the audience that emotional absorption in the play which he sought to avoid. With rare exceptions he plans the action of a play loosely, arranging it as narrative rather than plot, breaking it down into scenes of a few minutes, and preventing the scenes from gliding into each other. The episodes, he writes in ***A Short Organum for the Theatre,*** must be 'knotted together in such a way that the knots are easily noticed'. A spectator can then enjoy the play critically, judging the action as it proceeds.

The dangers of this method are apparent. It rejects suspense, reduces the possibilities of conflict, and lays the stage open to an aimless dawdle of events. Of ***Mother Courage*** it might be said, as Eric Bentley has said of *Tristan and Isolde,* that it seems too long however much you cut it.

One would not say this of ***The Caucasian Chalk Circle.*** There are weak places, certainly: the scene between Grusha and the two elegant ladies, and the first and third of Azdak's cases as a judge. In each of these the tempo sags, so that the next scene has to start completely cold. What saves the play is its initial momentum (the early scenes are excellent) and the vigorous personalities of Grusha and Azdak. Just over half-way through Brecht launches his second story, contrasting with the mood of the first, and the final episode brings the two stories together in a trial scene of twenty minutes. The trial is Brecht's favourite dramatic situation, since it challenges the audience to assessment and decision. At the same time, as he well knew, it provides that clash of opposites that is the simplest and most primitive source of excitement in the theatre.

More significant than particular episodes is the way that Brecht presents them. The device of a singer/story-teller, with a small chorus of musicians, sets the action in the mode of narrative from the beginning. It meets the problem of knotting the episodes so that the knots are visible. It allows the Chorus to direct our attention, as well as to guide our sympathies, and the Singer to interpret the reasons that prompt Grusha to act. Her emotions are thus held quietly at a distance so that we can evaluate without surrendering to them.

Our impression of Grusha is built up chiefly from her acts. She watches over the child through the evening and the night, tucking it in with a coat for warmth. When they are far enough from the city for safety, she leaves it at a farm where there seems to be plenty of milk, and runs back only when she finds the Ironshirts outside. At the broken bridge, where she carries the child over the glacier, she has the presence of mind to beg the merchants to throw their stick into the abyss in case the Ironshirts should catch the rope with it and follow. Throughout the play, since Brecht has an unsentimental respect for the body, her affection for the child comes through as a real relationship. Her reaction when the old man demands more than they can afford for milk is characteristic: 'Michael, did you hear that? Three piasters! We can't afford it! (*She goes back, sits down again, and gives the child her breast.*) Suck. Think of the three piasters. There's nothing there, but you *think* you're drinking, and that's something.'

The purpose of the episodes in which she appears is not, however, to throw light on Grusha's personality. Of her interests, tastes and habits we learn nothing. The reason for this is primarily that ***The Chalk Circle*** is a parable. What matters, therefore, is the story and the point it illustrates: that 'what there is shall go to those who are good for it'. But in none of his plays had Brecht much time for individual psychology of the kind we meet in Ibsen or Chekhov. This is true even of the mature plays (1938-45), which have a humanity one would hardly have expected from the Brecht of the early thirties. ***Galileo,*** it might be said, presents a remarkable individual: the sensuality of the man, his hunger for knowledge, his humour, tolerance and capacity for wonder, invigorate the clumsy didacti-

The Theater am Schiffbauerdamm, home of Brecht's Berliner Ensemble.

cism of the play. Yet his weakness in submitting to the Church springs, as Brecht presents it, from an appetite for life that had been the source of his achievements in science. Brecht, in other words, is not investigating character for its own sake. The hero of the play, he agreed with Walter Benjamin, is the people.

Is the people the hero of ***The Chalk Circle***? The rising of the carpet weavers, the only democratic movement in the action, is kept offstage, partly so as not to distract attention from the parable, partly perhaps because it would disrupt the tone of comedy in which the politics of Grusinia are treated. But in its narrative line and panoramic treatment the play could hardly be more remote from the bourgeois theatre's assumption of the primacy of the individual. Apart from beggars, soldiers, servants, wedding guests, there are more than fifty characters, and the closing tableau is a general dance. Neither Azdak nor Grusha, except with the child, has a strong relationship with anyone, while both are intimately involved with a changing society. To be sure, each half of the play takes most of its life from a single character, but the prominence given them is essential to Brecht's theme. Azdak, for example, does more than expose the chicanery of the law; his resource and bluntness, like the pungency of his speech, make right action seem not only sympathetic (as in Grusha's story) but exhilarating.

The closeness of Azdak's speech to gesture gives it special force in the theatre. The syntax is aggressively idiomatic, the phrasing terse, the diction concrete. There is a comparable, though less colloquial, energy in the speech of Grusha, the peasants, and the Ironshirts. Both Simon and Azdak take readily to proverbs, and many of Azdak's phrases have the pith of proverbs in the making. Nothing could express a more decided contempt for the abstract. Brecht is a materialist, the body is real for him, and his grasp of this reality is the source of the play's characteristic humour, as when Ludovica sways across the stage to pick up the public prosecutor's knife ('Think you can run around with a behind like that and get away with it in court?').

Brecht's preference for the concrete finds expression again in metaphor. In none of his plays after ***Drums in the Night*** is there a consistent pattern of imagery of the kind we recognize in a play by Shakespeare or Lorca. Instead, as in his non-dramatic poetry, he uses images in isolation to make a point cleanly and succinctly. In ***The Chalk Circle*** the images are simple, in keeping with the simple morality of the play:

> Someone must help!
> For the little tree needs water
> The lamb loses its way when the shepherd is asleep
> And its cry is unheard.

'In a good play,' wrote Synge, 'every speech should be as fully flavoured as a nut or apple.' But in a good play vividness of speech is not there for its own sake. The directness of Grusha and Azdak exposes the canting rhetoric of politics and the law—'Let the people decide', 'In the foreground stands the human tragedy of a mother', etc. It creates, moreover, a strong sense of the reality not only of the physical but of the moral world. For Brecht's use of imagery of birds and animals, of trees, clouds and streams to define human experience in metaphor and proverb, does more than renew our sense of the continuity between the world and the human body. It extends this continuity to our emotional life. To be good, though difficult, seems natural, and man has no need to live on several planes at once. He can, and should, lead a single life: physical, emotional and moral. In the vigour and coarseness of Azdak's speech, as in the forthright candour of Grusha's, this is made plain.

The use of verse, as of imagery, is strictly functional. Like Lorca, Brecht had discovered by working in the theatre that verse can be more telling when used sparingly. Songs, however, are important in his plays, and most of them also include some dialogue in verse. In ***The Chalk Circle*** the recitative of Singer and Chorus is marked off by irregular syncopated rhythms, deriving partly from the Lutheran Bible (in the use of repetition and parallel phrases), partly from Waley's translation of the Japanese Noh plays. A similar metric is used for three short monologues, the most effective of which is Grusha's at her parting with Simon. Here, in contrast with the surrounding prose, the rhythm creates a pause for feeling in the midst of violence and confusion. The situation is traditional and the writing, appropriately, has the simplicity of folk song:

> I shall be waiting for you under the green elm
> I shall be waiting for you under the bare elm
> I shall wait until the last soldier has returned
> And longer.
>
> When you come back from the battle
> No boots will stand at my door
> The pillow beside mine will be empty
> And my mouth will be unkissed.
>
> When you return, when you return
> You will be able to say: It is just as it was.

The Singer and Chorus are given verse throughout to separate them clearly from the action. In the first part of the play the Singer tells the story, frames and compresses the episodes, and elicits for us the unspoken thoughts of Grusha. The writing is therefore based on speech rhythms, occasionally steadying to bring a scene to its close:

> And she rose and bent down and, sighing, took the child
> And carried it away.
> As if it was stolen goods she picked it up.
> As if she was a thief she crept away.

In the second part, Singer and Chorus come together to acclaim the pragmatic morality of Azdak in strongly percussive rhythms tightened by rhyme and alliteration. These four choruses, with their iterated, emphatic rhyming on Azdak's name, lose more in translation than any other part of the play:

> *Als die grossen Feuer brannten*
> *Und in Blut die Städte standen*
> *Aus der Tiefe krochen Spinn und Kakerlak.*
> *Vor dem Schlosstor stand ein Schlächter*
> *Am Altar ein Gottverächter*
> *Und es sass im Rock des Richters der Azdak.*

In performance the excitement of the verse is heightened by music. Brecht had a working knowledge of music himself (he sang his early songs and ballads to his own guitar accompaniment), and his collaborations with Weill, Eisler and Dessau were close and fruitful. Dessau's score for ***The Chalk Circle,*** like the music for most of Brecht's other plays, is designed not to evoke atmosphere but to support the text by decisive rhythms or to comment, often sardonically, by tonal colouring. None of the lyrics has the swagger of the rice profiteer's song in ***The Measures Taken*** or the energy of the work song for Shui Ta's tobacco factory in ***The Good Person of Setzuan.*** But Grusha's singing to the child makes clearer the imaginative quality of her affection for him, and by generalizing their relationship reminds us that we are watching a parable, not just a story. Azdak's songs are less successful, since they have no real focus and no traditional situation to supply him with effective images. Like Grusha's, however, they vary the dramatic tempo, allow us for a moment to relax our attention to the narrative, and enforce a certain detachment.

How far this detachment is maintained throughout can be determined only partly by the text. Clearly the use of singer and chorus, of masks (in the Berliner Ensemble's production) for the inhuman rulers of the city, and of verse at various points, sets the action at a distance. Equally clearly we respond to Grusha and enjoy the effrontery of Azdak. That some degree of involvement is intended seems plain from Brecht's directions—a red sky for the city in flames, dimmed lighting for the evening and night through which Grusha watches over the child. And as always in his best work, Brecht has a superb sense of the visual element in the theatre. A detail early in the play is typical: when the groom answers Grusha's frightened enquiry, 'What have they done with the Governor?' not with a sentence but a gesture—'Fffft'. The disorder in the city when Azdak arrives to confess his guilt in letting the Grand-Duke escape is epitomized in the body swinging from the rafters, and for the last half hour of the action the satire on legal justice is driven home by the presence of Azdak, dirty, ragged and half-drunk, in the judge's robes.

The production of a play is shaped by the text, which has been shaped by convictions held so deeply that the writer may scarcely be aware of them. Thus Brecht's invention and treatment of his material, no less than the narrative mode and speech of the play, have their origin in a vision firmly objective and realistic. Yet ***The Chalk Circle*** includes a surprising degree of artifice: stylized characters, the formality of Simon's speeches to Grusha, the use of singer and chorus. Since Brecht's aim is not naturalistic illusion, such devices can be accommodated without strain. The arrival of a dust-covered rider to reinstate Azdak as judge in the final scene is scarcely more plausible than the arrival of the mounted messenger who brings a pardon for Macheath at the end of ***The Threepenny Opera.*** That we accept it gladly should remind us that realism has little to do with naturalism, for the scene that the rider interrupts, the beating up of Azdak by the Ironshirts, is one of the most grimly convincing in the play in the sharp contradiction it reveals between men as they are and as we like to think they are.

Brecht, for all his hostility to illusion, is as realistic as Synge or Chekhov, and his vision takes fuller account of the interdependence of men. It is a harder, less humane vision than theirs, but in his mature work neither narrow nor dogmatic. Chekhov, in a letter of November 1892 to Suvorin, suggests that the writers whom we value have one characteristic in common: they have a definite aim and call upon us to go with them. This is certainly true of Brecht, though it would cover even his weakest plays. More relevant to ***The Chalk Circle*** are the words that Chekhov added: 'The best of them are realists and depict life as it is, but because every line they write is permeated, as with a juice, by a consciousness of an aim, you feel, in addition to life as it is, also life as it should be, and it is that that delights you.' (pp. 139-46)

Ronald Gaskell, "Brecht: 'The Caucasian Chalk Circle'," in his Drama and Reality: The European Theatre Since Ibsen, *Routledge & Kegan Paul, 1972, pp. 139-46.*

FURTHER READING

AUTHOR COMMENTARY

Brecht, Bertolt. "On *The Caucasian Chalk Circle,*" translated by Hugo Schmidt and Jerome Clegg. *The Drama Review* 12, No. 1 (Fall 1967): 88-100.

Comments on themes and performance-related issues of *The Caucasian Chalk Circle.*

Hayman, Ronald. "A Last Interview with Brecht." *The London Magazine* 3, No. 11 (November 1956): 47-52.

Interview in which Brecht relates some of his thoughts concerning theater and politics, and comments on the works of such dramatists as William Shakespeare, Jean-Paul Sartre, and Henrik Ibsen.

OVERVIEWS AND GENERAL STUDIES

Adler, Henry. "Bertolt Brecht's Theatre." *The Twentieth Century* 160, No. 954 (August 1956): 114-23.

Reflections on Brecht's ideology and dramatic technique, occasioned by Adler's visit to the Berliner Ensemble for a rehearsal of *Galileo.* Adler concludes that "what Brecht has done is to cast a clear light in the prevalent fog in the theatre, to give a hard core of thought to emotional sogginess, to relate the theatre to life by widening the scope of the drama."

Benjamin, Walter. "What is Epic Theater?" In his *Illuminations,* edited by Hannah Arendt, translated by Harry Zohn, pp. 147-54. New York: Schocken Books, 1969.

Delineates the distinguishing features and aims of the Brechtian epic theater.

Bentley, Eric. *The Brecht Commentaries: 1943-1980.* New York: Grove Press, 1981, 320 p.

Collection of Bentley's essays on Brecht.

Chiari, J. "Brecht." In *Landmarks of Contemporary Drama,* pp. 161-83. London: Herbert Jenkins, 1965.

Examines Brecht's epic theater in theory and in practice. Chiari maintains that "in genius, the human heart must needs have its say, and Brecht was a genius; so his great characters generally walk out of the classroom where they are sometimes supposed to stay, on to the road of living and suffering, and they struggle with the problems which confront them, in a concrete and singular way which makes them and their author, memorable."

Dickson, Keith A. *Towards Utopia: A Study of Brecht.* Oxford: Clarendon Press, 1978, 332 p.

Analyzes Brecht's thought and technique, attempting to demonstrate his "belief in the perfectibility of human society, of which the classless Utopia is an attainable, though by no means inevitable, goal."

Dort, Bernard. "Epic Form in Brecht's Theatre," translated by Christopher Ostergren. *Yale/Theatre* 1, No. 2 (Summer 1968): 24-33.

Assesses the originality of Brechtian drama by analyzing Brecht's approach to the text, stage directions, and the relationship between the play and the audience.

Esslin, Martin. *Brecht: A Choice of Evils: A Critical Study of the Man, His Work, and His Opinions.* London: Eyre & Spottiswoode, 1959, 305 p.

Examines Brecht's life, political philosophy, and artistic theories, elucidating the themes and style of his writings. This work also includes a descriptive list of Brecht's works and a bibliography of secondary sources.

Ewen, Frederic. *Bertolt Brecht: His Life, His Art, and His Times.* New York: Citadel Press, 1967, 573 p.

Critical biography.

Fuegi, John. *The Essential Brecht.* Los Angeles: Hennessey & Ingalls, 1972, 343 p.

Studies Brecht's productions of his major dramas.

———. *Chaos, According to Plan.* Cambridge: Cambridge University Press, 1987, 223 p.

Examines Brecht's work as director, seeking to provide "a sense of how Brecht dealt with real problems in real theatres."

Gray, Ronald. "Brecht and Tragedy." *The Cambridge Quarterly* VIII, No. 3 (1979): 236-49.

Discusses various historical and philosophical reasons for Brecht's rejection of tragedy. Gray maintains that the characters in the dramatist's plays are largely "adapters" who "avoid tragedy or Fate because they are cunning enough to smell the traps, or able to turn adverse conditions to their own advantage."

Hecht, Werner. "The Development of Brecht's Theory of the Epic Theatre, 1918-1933." *The Tulane Drama Review* 6, No. 1 (September 1961): 40-97.

Traces the evolution of Brecht's views on drama and the theater.

Hoffmann, Charles W. "Brecht's Humor: Laughter While the Shark Bites." *The Germanic Review* XXXVIII, No. 2 (March 1963): 157-66.

Compares the humor of Brecht's later plays with that of his early works, highlighting the evolution of the dramatist's thought.

Jenkinson, David. "*Verfremdung* and the Critique of the Bourgeoisie: The Myth of Brecht's Theory of an 'Unemotional' Theatre." In *Patterns of Change: German Drama and the European Tradition,* edited by Dorothy James and others, pp. 269-83. New York: Peter Lang, 1990.

Contends that the emotional impact of Brecht's plays was not, as many critics suggest, unintended by the dramatist. Analyzing Brecht's works and artistic method, Jenkinson maintains that "his conception of the relationship between thought and feeling needs to be understood if we are properly to grasp the vision of bourgeois social practice and mentality that is at the heart of . . . his greatest plays."

Leiter, Samuel L. "Bertolt Brecht, 1898-1956." In his *From Stanislavsky to Barrault: Representative Directors of the European Stage,* pp. 151-83. New York: Greenwood Press, 1991.

Overview of Brecht's career followed by a discussion of the dramatist's conception of the theater and directing as well as his production methods. Leiter writes: "Taken as a whole, Brecht's theatrical career displays a decided unity, a continual give-and-take between his frequently revised and sometimes contradictory theoretical conceptions and their practical enactment in writing and directing."

Lyons, Charles R. *Bertolt Brecht: The Despair and the Polemic.* Carbondale: Southern Illinois University Press, 1968, 165 p.

Analyzes a sequence of Brecht's major plays, beginning with *Baal* and concluding with *The Caucasian Chalk Circle.* Lyons maintains that the unity of these works—all explorations of an individual's "struggle to attain a sense of consistent and meaningful identity"—demonstrate the integrity of the dramatist's vision.

Marx, Robert. "The Operatic Brecht." *The American Scholar* 44, No. 2 (Spring 1975): 283-90.

Discusses Brecht's contributions to opera. Marx asserts that "no modern playwright had a better sense of the power of music in the theater, and few ever used music more shrewdly or effectively than Brecht."

McLean, Sammy. "Sexuality and Incest in the Plays of Bertolt Brecht." In *Psychoanalytic Approaches to Literature and Film,* edited by Maurice Charney and Joseph Reppen, pp. 192-212. London: Associated University Presses, 1987.

Analyzes "inner psychological themes" of several of Brecht's major plays. McLean argues that in these works the dramatist's "interest in the psychosexual factors of human character and object relationships . . . develops from a concern with sexually deviant (as culturally defined) male personality to a concern with a heterosexual female personality."

Merchant, W. Moelwyn. "The Irony of Bertolt Brecht." In *Man in the Modern Theatre,* edited by Nathan A. Scott, Jr., pp. 58-75. Richmond, Va.: John Knox Press, 1965.

Explores an ironic "holding in tension of profound social commitment . . . with an equally aloof detachment and emotional uninvolvement" in Brecht's plays.

Mews, Siegfried, and Knust, Herbert, eds. *Essays on Brecht: Theater and Politics.* Chapel Hill: University of North Carolina Press, 1974, 238 p.

Includes essays on Brecht by Siegfried Mews, John Fuegi, and others.

Milnes, Humphrey. "The Concept of Man in Bertolt Brecht." *University of Toronto Quarterly* XXXII, No. 3 (April 1963): 217-28.

Examines Brecht's concern with human nature in his works, contending that "however dark the background, there is throughout Brecht a tacit recognition of man's potential goodness."

Nägele, Rainer. "Brecht's Theater of Cruelty." In his *Reading After Freud: Essays on Goethe, Hölderlin, Habermas, Nietzsche, Brecht, Celan, and Freud,* pp. 111-34. New York: Columbia University Press, 1987.

Examines cruelty in Brecht's early *Lehrstücke* (teaching plays or learning plays), maintaining that in these works "violence is not merely 'content,' but form, an inseparable linking of the aesthetic with the pedagogical elements."

Politzer, Heinz. "How Epic is Bertolt Brecht's Epic Theater?" In *Modern Drama: Essays in Criticism,* edited by Travis Bogard and William I. Oliver, pp. 54-72. Oxford: Oxford University Press, 1965.

Analyzes Brecht's dramas in relation to his theory of epic theater, seeking to reconcile Brecht's political ideology with the popularity of his plays among Western audiences.

Ruland, Richard. "The American Plays of Bertolt Brecht." *American Quarterly* XV, No. 3 (Fall 1963): 371-89.

Discusses the significance of the American settings in many of Brecht's early plays. Ruland writes: "As [Brecht's] concern with evil focused itself on capitalism . . . , he came more and more to narrow and simplify his image of America into a symbol for the violence and greed of the commercial classes."

Russell, Charles. "Literature, Politics, and the Critical Spirit: Brecht." In his *Poets, Prophets, and Revolutionaries: The Literary Avant-Garde from Rimbaud through Postmodernism,* pp. 206-35. New York: Oxford University Press, 1985.

Examines Brecht in the context of surrealism and other contemporary avant-garde movements. Russell notes that the dramatist's plays "adopted the main tendency of avant-garde art of the first half-century—critical distance—and joined it with a faith in historical change."

Ryan, Lawrence. "Bertolt Brecht: A Marxist Dramatist?" In *Aspects of Drama and the Theatre,* pp. 71-111. Sydney: Sydney University Press, 1965.

Investigates the relationship between Brecht's political philosophy and his artistic technique.

Weales, Gerald. "Brecht and the Drama of Ideas." In *Ideas*

in the Drama, edited by John Gassner, pp. 125-54. New York: Columbia University Press, 1964.

Explores the relationship between individual and society in several of Brecht's plays, concluding that through his dialogue and characterizations Brecht suggests that the individual "can only survive in our world by accepting that he is not an individual."

GALILEO

Berckman, Edward M. "Brecht's *Galileo* and the Openness of History." *Modernist Studies* I, No. 2 (1974): 41-50.

Identifies aspects of Brecht's dramas that emphasize humanity's ability to effect social change and comments on their implementation in *Galileo.* Berckman maintains that "the emphasis on human possibility in Brecht's theatre is based on his view of history as open and the world as alterable."

Cohen, M. A. "History and Moral in Brecht's *The Life of Galileo.*" *Contemporary Literature* 11, No. 1 (Winter 1970): 80-97.

Analyzes the "crucial manipulations of accepted fact" in Brecht's version of the life of *Galileo,* attempting to elucidate the dramatist's didactic aim.

Homan, Sidney. "Brecht, *Galileo:* 'And Yet It Moves!' " In his *The Audience as Actor and Character: The Modern Theater of Beckett, Brecht, Genet, Ionesco, Pinter, Stoppard, and Williams,* pp. 78-105. London: Associated University Presses, 1989.

Recounts Homan's experiences and techniques in staging Brecht's *Galileo.* Homan asserts: "Having staged the play, having watched that audience with the bifocal vision of director and scholar, I think that Brecht *does* demand of anyone staging his work that they offer the audience a collaborative role more graphic, more self-conscious, and at times perhaps even more threatening or challenging than do the playwrights of his despised illusionist theater."

Sorensen, Otto M. "Brecht's *Galileo:* Its Development from Ideational into Ideological Theater." *Modern Drama* XI, No. 4 (February 1969): 410-22.

Finds the later version of Brecht's *Galileo* inferior to the earlier one, contending that "with his political sharpening of the issues . . . the author eventually came up with a hodgepodge of ideas which left his message and central character most unconvincing."

MOTHER COURAGE AND HER CHILDREN

Jones, David Richard. "Bertolt Brecht and *Couragemodell* 1949: Meaning in Detail." In his *Great Directors at Work: Stanislavsky, Brecht, Kazan, Brook,* pp. 78-137. Berkeley: University of California Press, 1986.

Explores Brecht's modelbook, or illustrated and annotated text, for *Mother Courage,* discussing such staging issues as "ground arrangements" and dialogue delivery.

Speidel, E. "The Mute Person's Voice: Mutter Courage and her Daughter." *German Life & Letters* XXIII, No. 4 (July 1970): 332-39.

Examines the function of mute characters in drama by focusing on Kattrin's means of expression and the relation of her actions to the dialogue of *Mother Courage.*

THE CAUCASIAN CHALK CIRCLE

Marinello, Leone J. "The Christian Side of Brecht? An Examination of *The Caucasian Chalk Circle.*" *Drama Critique* IV, No. 2 (May 1961): 77-86.

Argues that *The Caucasian Chalk Circle* presents "Brecht's moral values [as] . . . fundamentally Christian in nature."

Steer, W. A. J. "The Thematic Unity of Brecht's *Der Kaukasische Kreidekreis.*" *German Life and Letters* XXI, No. 1 (October 1967): 1-10.

Examines "the conflict between moral values and self-interest" in *The Caucasian Chalk Circle.*

Additional coverage of Brecht's life and career is contained in the following sources published by Gale Research: *Contemporary Authors,* Vols. 104, 133; *Dictionary of Literary Biography,* Vol. 56; *Twentieth-Century Literary Criticism,* Vols. 1, 6, 13, 35; *World Literature Criticism, 1500 to the Present,* Vol. 1.

Pedro Calderón de la Barca

1600-1681

INTRODUCTION

Full name Pedro Calderón de la Barca Henao de la Barrera y Riaño.

Calderón was one of the chief dramatists of Spain's Golden Age, a period marked by great artistic, cultural, and spiritual achievements. During his tenure as a playwright to the royal courts of Philip IV and Charles II of Spain, he composed over one hundred and twenty dramas, treating such issues as honor, patriotism, and conjugal fidelity with wit, candor, and insight. Calderón is acknowledged as the perfecter of the *comedia,* a three-act play in verse which critics rank in importance with Greek classical and Elizabethan dramatic forms. His most celebrated *comedias, El príncipe constante* (*The Constant Prince*), *El médico de su honra* (*The Doctor of His Honor*), *La devoción de la cruz* (*The Devotion of the Cross*), and *La vida es sueño* (*Life is a Dream*), have captured scholars' attention for their vivid characterization and astute commentary on ethical questions. In addition to the fifty *comedias,* Calderón wrote over seventy *autos sacramentales,* one-act religious dramas commemorating the Roman Catholic feast of Corpus Christi.

Born in Madrid in 1600 into a prosperous family with connections to the royal court, Calderón was educated at the Colegio Imperial, a Jesuit school, and later attended the Universities of Alcalá and Salamanca. He received a degree in canon law in 1620 but also studied theology, logic, and scholastic philosophy; the influence of these disciplines is evident in his employment of argumentation and reasoning in his dramas. His literary career began shortly thereafter when he entered a poetry contest held to celebrate the beatification of Saint Isidore, patron saint of Madrid. As a result of his participation in this contest, he received the recognition of court dramatist Lope de Vega, the master of the form of the *comedia.* Influenced by Lope, Calderón composed his first *comedia, Amor, honor y poder* (*Love, Honor, and Power*), which was first performed in 1623. His reputation as a skilled dramatist was firmly established by 1634, when he composed *El nuevo palacio del retiro* (*The New Palace of the Retiro*) at Philip IV's command to write a play for the opening of the royal theater. The following year, Calderón premiered *Life is a Dream* and *El mayor encanto, amor* (*Love the Greatest Enchantment*) at the royal theater, greatly impressing the Spanish court. When Lope died shortly thereafter, Calderón replaced him as court dramatist. Following the deaths of two brothers, a mistress, and an illegitimate son, Calderón decided to enter the religious life and was ordained a Roman Catholic priest in 1651. For the remainder of his life he served as a private chaplain to the Spanish monarchs, writing *comedias* for the court and *autos* for the municipality of Madrid. He died in Madrid in 1681.

Although Calderón employed the *comedia*'s tripartite structure of explanation, complication, and resolution as established by Lope, he reshaped and developed it in a variety of ways, leading scholars such as Henryk Ziomek to assert that Calderón's plays represent "the most systematic development of Spanish drama during the Golden Age." Among his most notable innovations was his incorporation of the techniques of gongorism and conceptism. The former term, derived from a leading seventeenth-century Spanish poet, Luis de Góngora y Argóte, refers to the ornamentation of a work through exaggerated use of mythological allusions, rhetorical devices, and figures of speech such as neologisms, archaisms, and hyperboles. Conceptism, closely related to gongorism, indicates the use of extended and sometimes far-fetched metaphors to present complex ideas. Scholars agree that Calderón, educated in Scholastic thought and viewing his dramas as intellectual investigations, brilliantly fused the verbal elaboration of gongorism with the sophisticated logic of conceptism in his efforts to expose false beliefs and establish truths. At the same time, he brought greater realism to the *comedia* by creating more fully developed and more psychologically complex characters to illustrate his ideas.

Writing during a time of great change, when his country was witnessing the decline of its political and economic power, Calderón focused his rationalist perspective on numerous aspects of Spanish culture. A number of his dramas explore problems associated with the code of honor that required Spanish men to seek fame through heroic exploits and obliged women to preserve family honor through docility, modesty, and prudence. His *comedias capa y espada,* or cloak-and-sword dramas, illustrate the impossibility of enforcing the code of chastity by presenting clandestine love affairs that foil the most vigilant of guardians, while his "honor dramas" examine the code's sanguinary extremes, which justified the murder of women if even suspected of infidelity. In *The Doctor of His Honor,* for example, in which a husband suspects his wife and has her bled to death, Calderón creates a compelling portrait of the innocent wife's suffering as well as that of her spouse.

Religion and history figure prominently in many Calderonian *comedias.* Regarded by most scholars as the finest Spanish play on religion and chivalry, *The Constant Prince* is based on Portuguese Prince Fernando's fifteenth-century expedition to Tangier. The drama's plot stems from Fernando's decision to suffer degradation, torture, and death rather than surrender the Christian city of Ceuta to the Moslems. Calderón provides an interesting twist in the play's final scene, in which Fernando's ghost leads the Portuguese army to defeat the "infidels," thus achieving victory for himself, Spain, and the church. The superiority of faith over egocentrism is treated in *El mágico prodigioso* (*The Wonder-Working Magician*). Organized around the Faustian theme of a wizard who enters into a compact with the devil, the drama relates the legend of fourth-century Saint Cyprian of Antioch, who sells his soul to Satan in order to win the love of Justina, a young girl renowned for her virtue; ultimately, Cyprian is redeemed through faith. Likewise, *The Devotion of the Cross,* an exploration of humanity's fall and its redemption through Jesus' death, expounds the doctrine that faith alone is necessary for salvation. There are also numerous Calderonian dramas based on the lives of notable historical and biblical personages. The most famous, *La hija del aire* (*The Daughter of the Air*), dramatizes the life of Semiramis (c. 800 B.C.), an Assyrian queen known for her beauty, wisdom, seductive charm, and spectacular military conquests. Other subjects include Alexander the Great (356-323 B.C.), Jewish patriot Judas Maccabaeus (c. 160 B.C.), and biblical figures such as King Solomon, the Queen of Sheba, and Absalom. Scholars believe that by illustrating imperial myths and episodes from the Bible and ancient history, Calderón sought to evoke a glorious past in an age of religious and socio-economic decline in Spain.

Calderón's philosophical drama *Life is a Dream* stands, in most critics' opinion, as the greatest Spanish play of all time. Based on an ancient Indian story, the drama explores the mysterious nature of reality. The main plot of Calderón's version focuses on the Polish king Basilio who has read in the stars that his newly born son Segismundo is destined to be a tyrant. Accepting the prediction as true, he confines his son to a mountain tower, forbidding him any human contact except with his jailer and tutor, Clotaldo. Twenty years later Basilio, concerned about the succession to his throne, decides to see whether predestination or free will is the stronger force. Segismundo, who has grown into a mixture of man and beast, is drugged and brought to court asleep: if he can control his passions, the king judges, he is fit to reign; if not, he will be returned to his prison and told that his palace experience was only a dream. Upon awakening in court, Segismundo is told of his royal heritage. Unable to control his rage, he kills Clotaldo and assaults Rosaura, a young girl who has come to court to accuse the Duke of Muscovy of compromising her honor. Drugged again and returned to his cell, Segismundo awakens and ponders whether it is his palace experience or his solitary confinement that is illusory. When Basilio selects the Duke of Muscovy, a foreigner, as his successor, the Polish army rebels and sets Segismundo free. Though he reproves his father for his cruelty, Segismundo exacts no retribution. He does, however, force the Duke to marry Rosaura, who is revealed as Clotaldo's daughter, and takes the visiting Princess Estrella as his wife. While the play appears to end happily, Segismundo is haunted by the fear that he may awaken to discover that life, as he now knows it, is only a dream. Critics have lauded *Life is a Dream,* with its lyrical power and vibrant images, as a masterful blending of two plots—that depicting Segismundo's trial and the one concerning Rosaura's honor—into a unified dramatic whole. Praising Calderón's philosophical investigation of reality and human destiny, scholars have also pointed to the play's political overtones, viewing Segismundo as a regenerative king whose wisdom issues from knowledge of his own failures and from contact with people. As Alan K. G. Paterson has written, "*La vida es sueño* is a succession of spectacular breakthroughs into new perceptions of consciousness and states of being . . . [leading] us forward through its charms into subtler mysteries of human enlightenment and human dereliction."

Critics also admire Calderón's *autos sacramentales.* Calderón employed elaborate symbols and allegories to present subjects from scripture, legends, history, and mythology. The *auto El gran teatro del mundo* (*The Great Theater of the World*) is a "metaplay"—a play about a play—in which God Himself presents a drama upon the stage of the universe. The play's actors, Beauty, Poverty, Discretion, and Wealth, are allegorical characters exemplifying the theological precept that repentance must precede salvation. The sanctity of the Eucharist is the theme of another Calderonian *auto, La cena del rey Baltasar* (*Belshazzar's Feast*). Based on the biblical narrative of the idolatrous King Belshazzar who is slain after desecrating holy vessels during a banquet, the *auto* applies a New Testament understanding to the Old Testament story, interpreting Belshazzar's death as symbolic punishment for unworthily partaking of the Eucharist. Calderón also combined mythology with Christian theology in several *autos. El divino Orfeo* (*The Divine Orpheus*), which is derived from the popular Greek myth in which Orpheus attempts to rescue his wife Eurydicé from the underworld, illustrates Saint Paul's teaching that there is strength in weakness, since God is always victorious over evil. Critics not only esteem Calderón's *autos* for their sophisticated theological content, but also for their form. Departing from the rigid structure established by his predecessors Tirso de Molina and José de Valdivieso, Calderón refined the genre by embellishing the sacramental pieces with music, dance, and prosodic chant.

Building upon the favorable criticism of the Calderonian *comedia* by nineteenth-century German and American commentators such as August Wilhelm Schlegel, Johann Wolfgang von Goethe, James Russell Lowell, and Henry Wadsworth Longfellow, twentieth-century scholars have focused much attention on the genre's imagery and structure. E. M. Wilson revitalized interest in Spanish Golden Age drama as a whole through a study of the imagery of the four elements (earth, wind, fire, water) in *Life is a Dream, The Constant Prince,* and several other *comedias* and *autos.* Some scholars, notably William Whitby and Bruce W. Wardropper, have investigated the *comedias* as poetry rich in symbolism, and others, like Barbara Mujica, have analyzed them as existentialist works similar to the French dramas of Jean-Paul Sartre and Albert Camus. A. A. Parker, W. J. Entwistle, and Albert E. Sloman have scrutinized the dramas' allegorical aspects, finding a strong tie between a Calderonian play's meaning and its structure. Critics continue to praise Calderón's insightful characterizations and penetrating discussion of philosophical and theological issues. In addition, commentators observe, Calderón's works remain effective in performance, as evidenced by recent productions of *The Constant Prince* and *Life is a Dream.* Sloman expressed a widely held opinion when he called Calderón "a meticulous and subtle craftsman, whose stagecraft at its best was impeccable," adding that he was "a poetic dramatist of deep human significance."

PRINCIPAL WORKS

PLAYS

Amor, honor y poder (*Love, Honor, and Power*) 1623
Casa con dos puertas, mala es de quardar (*A House with Two Doors is Difficult to Guard*) 1629
La dama duende (*The Phantom Lady*) 1629
El príncipe constante (*The Constant Prince*) 1629
La banda y la flor (*The Scarf and the Flower*) 1631
La vida es sueño (*Life is a Dream*) 1631-32
La devoción de la cruz (*The Devotion of the Cross*) 1633
Los Cabellos de Absalón (*Absalom's Hair*) 1634
La cena del rey Baltasar (*Belshazzar's Feast*) 1634
La gran Cenobia (*The Great Zenobia*) 1634
El mayor monstruo del mundo (*No Monster Like Jealousy*) 1634
El nuevo palacio del retiro (*The New Palace of the Retiro*) 1634
El purgatorio de San Patricio (*The Purgatory of Saint Patrick*) 1634
El gran teatro del mundo (*The Great Theater of the World*) 1635?
El mayor encanto, amor (*Love the Greatest Enchantment*) 1635
El médico de su honra (*The Doctor of His Honor*) 1635
A secreto agravio, secreto venganza (*A Secret Vengeance for a Secret Insult*) 1635
Las cadenas del demonio (*The Devil's Chains*) 1635-36
Las tres justicias en una (*Three Judgments at a Blow*) 1636-37
El mágico prodigioso (*The Wonder-Working Magician*) 1637
La niña de Gomez Arias (*The Daughter of Gomez Arias*) 1637-39
El alcade de Zalamea (*The Mayor of Zalamea)* 1640-44
El pintor de su deshonra (*The Painter of His Own Dishonor*) 1648-50
Guárdate del agua mensa (*Beware of Still Water*) 1649
La hija del aire, Partes I y II (*The Daughter of the Air, Parts I & II*) 1653
No hay más fortuna que Diós (*There is No Other Fortune than God*) 1653?
Eco y Narciso (*Echo and Narcissus*) 1661
El gran príncipe de Fez (*The Great Prince of Fez*) 1668
La estatua de Prometeo (*The Statue of Prometheus*) 1669
Tu prójimo como a ti (*Thy Neighbor as Thyself*) 1674?
**Six Dramas of Calderón* 1853
Obras completas de Calderón de la Barca. 2 Vols. 1945, 1956
†*Four Plays* 1961

*Includes *Beware of Still Water; Gil Perez, the Gallician; Keep Your Own Secret; The Mayor of Zalamea; The Painter of His Own Dishonor; Three Judgments at a Blow.*

†Includes *The Devotion of the Cross, The Mayor of Zalamea, The Phantom Lady, A Secret Vengeance for a Secret Insult.*

OVERVIEWS AND GENERAL STUDIES

August Wilhelm Schlegel (lecture date 1808)

[*Schlegel was a German critic, translator, and poet. With his younger brother, Friedrich, he founded the periodical* Das Athenäum *(1798-1800), which was influential in the establishment and development of the German Romantic movement. He is perhaps best known for his translation of Shakespeare's works into German and for his* Über dramatische Kunst und Literatur *(1809-11;* Lectures on Dramatic Art and Literature, *1815). In the following excerpt taken from a lecture delivered in 1808, Schlegel acknowledges Calderón's prominence in the history of Spanish literature, extolling him as "the last summit in romantic poetry."*]

If a feeling of religion, a loyal heroism, honour, and love, be the foundation of romantic poetry, it could not fail to attain to its highest development in Spain, where its birth and growth were cherished by the most friendly auspices. The fancy of the Spaniards, like their active powers, was bold and venturesome; no mental adventure seemed too hazardous for it to essay. The popular predilection for surpassing marvels had already shown itself in its chivalrous romaunts. And so they wished also to see the wonderful on the stage; when, therefore, their poets, standing on the lofty eminence of a highly polished state of art and society, gave it the requisite form, breathed into it a musical soul, and refined its beautiful hues and fragrance from all corporeal grossness, there arose, from the very contrast of the matter and the form, an irresistible fascination. Amid the harmony of the most varied metre, the elegance of fanciful allusions, and that splendour of imagery and simile which no other language than their own could hope to furnish, combined with inventions ever new, and almost always pre-eminently ingenious, the spectators perceived in imagination a faint refulgence of the former greatness of their nation which had measured the whole world with its victories. The most distant zones were called upon to contribute, for the gratification of the mother country, the treasures of fancy as well as of nature, and on the dominions of this poetry, as on that of Charles V., the sun may truly be said never to set.

Even those plays of Calderon which, cast in modern manners, descend the most to the tone of common life, still fascinate us by a sort of fanciful magic, and cannot be considered in the same light with the ordinary run of comedies. Of those of Shakspeare, [we see] that they are always composed of two dissimilar elements: the comic, which, in so far as comic imitation requires the observance of local conditions, is true to English manners; and the romantic, which, as the native soil was not sufficiently poetical for it, is invariably transplanted to a foreign scene. In Spain, on the other hand, the national costume of that day still admitted of an ideal exhibition. This would not indeed have been possible, had Calderon introduced us into the interior of domestic life, where want and habit generally reduce all things to every-day narrowness. His comedies, like those of the ancients, end with marriages; but how different is all that precedes! With them the most immoral means are set in motion for the gratification of sensual passions and selfish views, human beings with their mental powers stand opposed to each other as mere physical beings, endeavouring to spy out and to expose their mutual weaknesses. Calderon, it is true, also represents to us his principal characters of both sexes carried away by the first ebullitions of youth, and in its unwavering pursuit of the honours and pleasures of life; but the aim after which they strive, and in the prosecution of which every thing else kicks the beam, is never in their minds confounded with any other good. Honour, love, and jealousy, are uniformly the motives out of which, by their dangerous but noble conflict, the plot arises, and is not purposely complicated by knavish trickery and deception. Honour is always an ideal principle; for it rests . . . on that higher morality which consecrates principles without regard to consequences. It may sink down to a mere conventional observance of social opinions or prejudices, to a mere instrument of vanity, but even when so disfigured we may still recognize in it some faint feature of a sublime idea. I know no apter symbol of tender sensibility of honour as portrayed by Calderon, than the fable of the ermine, which is said to prize so highly the whiteness of its fur, that rather than stain it in flight, it at once yields itself up to the hunters and death. This sense of honour is equally powerful in the female characters; it rules over love, which is only allowed a place beside it, but not above it. According to the sentiments of Calderon's dramas, the honour of woman consists in loving only one man of pure and spotless honour, and loving him with perfect purity, free from all ambiguous homage which encroaches too closely on the severe dignity of woman. Love requires inviolable secrecy till a lawful union permits it to be publicly declared. This secrecy secures it from the poisonous intermixture of vanity, which might plume itself with pretensions or boasts of a confessed preference; it gives it the appearance of a vow, which from its mystery is the more sacredly observed. This morality does not, it is true, condemn cunning and dissimulation if employed in the cause of love, and in so far as the rights of honour may be said to be infringed; but nevertheless the most delicate consideration is observed in the conflict with other duties,—with the obligations, for instance, of friendship. Moreover, a power of jealousy, always alive and often breaking out into fearful violence,—not, like that of the East, a jealousy of possession,—but one watchful of the slightest emotions of the heart and its most imperceptible demonstrations serves to ennoble love, as this feeling, whenever it is not absolutely exclusive, ceases to be itself. The perplexity to which the mental conflict of all these motives gives rise, frequently ends in nothing, and in such cases the catastrophe is truly comic; sometimes, however, it takes a tragic turn, and then honour becomes a hostile destiny for all who cannot satisfy its requisitions without sacrificing either their happiness or their innocence.

These are the dramas of a higher kind, which by foreigners are called Pieces of Intrigue, but by Spaniards, from the dress in which they are acted, Comedies of Cloak and Sword (*Comedias de Capa y Espada*). They have commonly no other burlesque part than that of the merry valet, known by the name of the *Gracioso.* This valet serves chiefly to parody the ideal motives from which his master acts, and this he frequently does with much wit and grace. Seldom is he with his artifices employed as an efficient lever in establishing the intrigue, in which we rather admire the wit of accident than of contrivance. Other pieces are called *Comedias de figuron;* all the figures, with one exception, are usually the same as those in the former class, and this one is always drawn in caricature, and occupies a prominent place in the composition. To many of Calderon's dramas we cannot refuse the name of pieces of character, although we cannot look for very delicate characterization from the poets of a nation in which vehemence of passion and exaltation of fancy neither leave sufficient leisure nor sufficient coolness for prying observation.

Another class of his pieces is called by Calderon himself festal dramas (*fiestas*). They were destined for representation at court on solemn occasions; and though they require the theatrical pomp of frequent change of decoration and visible wonders, and though music also is often introduced into them, still we may call them poetical operas, that is, dramas which, by the mere splendour of poetry, perform what in the opera can only be attained by the machinery, the music, and the dancing. Here the poet gives himself wholly up to the boldest flights of fancy, and his creations hardly seem to touch the earth.

The mind of Calderon, however, is most distinctly expressed in the pieces on religious subjects. Love he paints merely in its most general features; he but speaks her technical poetical language. Religion is his peculiar love, the heart of his heart. For religion alone he excites the most overpowering emotions, which penetrate into the inmost recesses of the soul. He did not wish, it would seem, to do the same for mere worldly events. However turbid they may be in themselves to him, such is the religious medium through which he views them, they are all cleared up and perfectly bright. Blessed man! he had escaped from the wild labyrinths of doubt into the stronghold of belief; from thence, with undisturbed tranquillity of soul, he beheld and portrayed the storms of the world; to him human life was no longer a dark riddle. Even his tears reflect the image of heaven, like dew-drops on a flower in the sun. His poetry, whatever its apparent object, is a never-ending hymn of joy on the majesty of the creation; he celebrates the productions of nature and human art with an astonishment always joyful and always new, as if he saw them for the first time in an unworn festal splendour. It is the first awaking of Adam, and an eloquence withal, a skill of expression, and a thorough insight into the most mysterious affinities of nature, such as high mental culture and mature contemplation can alone bestow. When he compares the most remote objects, the greatest and the smallest, stars and flowers, the sense of all his metaphors is the mutual attraction subsisting between created things by virtue of their common origin, and this delightful harmony and unity of the world again is merely a refulgence of the eternal all-embracing love.

[Calderón's] poetry, whatever its apparent object, is a never-ending hymn of joy on the majesty of the creation; he celebrates the productions of nature and human art with an astonishment always joyful and always new, as if he saw them for the first time in an unworn festal splendour.

—August Wilhelm Schlegel

Calderon was still flourishing at the time when other countries of Europe began to manifest a strong inclination for that mannerism of taste in the arts, and those prosaic views in literature, which in the eighteenth century obtained such universal dominion. He is consequently to be considered as the last summit of romantic poetry. All its magnificence is lavished in his writings, as in fireworks the most brilliant and rarest combinations of colours, the most dazzling of fiery showers and circles are usually reserved for the last explosion.

The Spanish theatre continued for nearly a century after Calderon to be cultivated in the same spirit. All, however, that was produced in that period is but an echo of previous productions, and nothing new and truly peculiar appeared such as deserves to be named after Calderon. (pp. 500-04)

August Wilhelm Schlegel, "Lecture XXIX," in his A Course of Lectures on Dramatic Art and Literature, *edited by Rev. A. J. W. Morrison, translated by John Black, revised edition, 1846. Reprint by AMS Press, Inc., 1973, pp. 488-505.*

E. R. Curtius (essay date 1934)

[*Curtius was a prominent German philologist, educator, essayist, and critic. An authority in the area of Romance languages and literatures, he is best known for his monumental* Europäische Literatur und lateinisches Mittelalter (1948; European Literature and the Latin Middle Ages, *1953), a fundamental work in which he demonstrates the unity of Western European literature on the basis of historical and linguistic continuity from classical antiquity to modern times. In the following excerpt from a 1934 essay reprinted in his* Kritische Essays zur europäischen Literatur (1950; Essays on European Literature, *1973), Curtius discusses the unique characteristics of Calderon's dramas in the context of Spanish literature and culture.*]

From the earliest periods of its history, Spain has always gone its own way. It never shared the common destinies of Europe—except for a brief moment: during the era of Philip II; but at that time it ruled these destinies instead of enduring them. The great historical memories of Spain: the Gothic kings, the sway of the Moors, the Reconquista, then the founding of an overseas empire, finally the colorful decline and fall—all this is joined together in a national history which shows different destinies and different accents from those of the rest of Europe. Spain takes little or no part in the great movements with which the modern era begins: the Reformation, the Renaissance, Humanism and the classical attitude toward art. It has different obligations and a different ambition. Out of Castile and Aragon it forges the unified dynastic state; it breaks the last remnants of Moorish domination and in the latter half of the sixteenth century still has to carry on tenacious struggles with the Moriscos. It discovers and conquers the new world, it engenders in asceticism and mysticism the prototypes of Catholic orthodoxy, which then radiate out to all of Europe—and it creates a grandiose literature that springs from its native soil and its own genius in simply inexhaustible abundance. The art of this Spanish Golden Age is little concerned with the classical models of Antiquity or with Aristotle's alleged system of rules. It has no intercourse at all with the spirit of rationalism in France. In aesthetics as in philosophical outlook, it draws upon the boundless wealth of a tradition that never broke with the Middle Ages. Monarchy and the Catholic faith are the pillars that support this world. It is permeated by the powers of magic and miracle. Whereas the heroes of the French stage fight out psychological conflicts, Calderón's spiritual plays revolve around the mystery of the Holy Sacrament. European Classicism finds edification in a stoic Roman world and erects an image of Antiquity that stands in immediate and unreconciled juxtaposition with the Christian state religions. In Calderón's world Rome and Greece are never models for ethical or human attitudes: they are always a mere decorative background, in quite the same sense as Semiramis's Babylon, Phocas's Byzantium, Sigismund's Poland. To the Spaniard's eye, world history is a single vast picture-book in which all the pages are equally important: an "Archive of the Ages," in which the nations of all periods and places have recorded their memoirs: the Goths as well as the Arabs, the Dutch as well as the Peruvians. The Atridae are no more eminent, no more interesting than the kings of Nineveh or the "Landgraves of Asia." History is a great procession of marvelous figures. The demigods of Greek mythology stand beside the crowned martyrs of Christianity. They all form part of the great chronicle of the miraculous. They are all actors on the great stage of the world. The world as a stage on which divine powers direct the destinies—this ancient idea, which can be traced back to Plato: in Calderón's dramatic survey of the world it has been realized as never before or since. And, in addition, all these human destinies are now interwoven with the orbits of the stars, with the poisons and the healing powers of Nature, with the movement of the eleven celestial spheres. Magic and cosmic forces rule in this world; diabolical witchcraft flares up—and yet in the last analysis everything is governed by ordinance of divine grace and wisdom.

That is Calderón's world. And we now understand why this world [can be a guidepost, pointing to the] timeless Middle Ages. . . . The term Middle Ages is not to be understood literally here. It does not denote a unique period of history, but a spiritual realm in which the Catholic-Christian view of the world prevails. In this sense the Middle Ages is the creation of Christian philosophy, not, to be sure, of scholasticism, but of the Church fathers. From them comes Christian history's image of the world, which takes shape in accordance with the cardinal facts of the Creation, the Fall, the Redemption, and the Last Judgment. This image was decomposed by the new paganism of the Renaissance, by the systems of Rationalism, by the mechanistic view of nature, and by the spirit of the Enlightenment. But these forces could not be operative in Calderón's Spain. There, the mediaeval Christian image of the world still held undisputed sway in an era which, from the European perspective, is called Baroque and which is separated by scarcely three generations from the year in which Goethe was born. It is this image of the world, however, that supports the magnificent structure of ideas that is Calderón's metaphysical theater.

This theater is just as remote from that of Shakespeare as from that of French and German Classicism. It cannot be measured by any of these standards. In spite of profound differences in structure, the English, French, and German theaters are connected with each other by a common conception of man. The human being is the pivot of this theater. He rises to his greatest majesty in the person of the tragic hero. This hero bears individual traits. He is a "character," a unique person. And his character is his destiny—indeed, character is the only form in which destiny becomes at all comprehensible and effective. The more exclusively the dramatic action is determined by the characters of the heroes, the higher we tend to value it. Neoclassical aesthetics demands the greatest degree of inwardness. The spokesmen for this aesthetics have always reproached Calderón with not knowing how to depict characters. This reproach misses the essence of the Calderonian drama. Naturally, Calderón shows familiarity with psychological conflicts too. But with him they never become the pivotal points of the drama, because his drama is not centered in man; on the contrary, man always acts as defined by cosmic and religious ties. It is the movement of the constellations and, on a higher plane, the mysterious reciprocity between divine mercy and human freedom that determine his destiny. Calderón's stage, at least in his *autos sacramentales,* is theocentric. Allegorical figures: the world, wisdom, death, vanity, idolatry, light, the four elements . . . and many others, appear as intermediaries between God and Mankind. Accordingly, Calderón's people are not characters independent in themselves, but types. Such types are the wise man, the soldier, the droll servant, the king, the beggar, the peasant . . . and many others. Under ever-new names they come together for the intricate play of the most diverse and colorful plot. The essential element of this theater is rapid flow of action combined with surprising changes of situation. It satisfies the people's delight in spectacle no less than the thinker's need for profundity. These dramatic situations are not resolved psychologically; they exist for their own sake, they symbolize the infinite nature of cosmic relations. They are alive with symbolic significance. (pp. 157-61)

In Calderón's theater we again and again encounter the figure of the royal personage who has grown up and been kept in solitude, either in the wilderness, in a grotto, or in a dungeon, far from the world. Such figures are Prince Sigismund in ***La vida es sueño,*** the sons of the king in the Phocas drama, Semiramis herself, but also mythological figures like Narcissus and heroic ones like Achilles. All these figures are then torn from their dream existence, their cave, their prison by a reversal of fortune. At the moment of their awakening to the world their souls are subject to the most awful tensions. This "awakening to the world," as I term it, is one of the typical situations of Calderón's theater. How rich is the symbolism of this situation! It is already hinted at in Plato's allegory of the cave, and to conceive of the body as the prison of the mind is likewise a Platonic myth. But this cave-existence, this prison-tower represents at the same time the preexistence of souls before birth, which is exhibited in Calderón's ***Gran Teatro del Mundo***. . . . And, finally, Prince Sigismund's awakening to the world, his liberation from the tower, his failure in this trial, is only the allegorical vesture for the destiny of the human soul through preexistence, birth, the Fall, and redemption. Calderón himself hinted at this allegory by writing a sequel to ***La vida es sueño,*** a sacramental play with the same title that transposes the action of the first drama to the theological plane. (pp. 161-62)

The exact counterpart of this palingenesis we now find in ***Semiramis.*** The ancient historians impressed Semiramis on the memory of the millennia as the founder of the Assyrian Empire, the constructor of Babylon, and the creator of one of the seven wonders of the world: the hanging gardens. She was said to have been the daughter of a fish-goddess, nursed by doves after she had been exposed, found by shepherds. As the consort of the governor of Syria she undertakes a sudden offensive which alters the fortunes of the land. King Ninos snatches her away from her husband and makes her his queen. She bears him a son: Ninyas. Ninos dies. Semiramis now rules for forty-two years and conquers one country after the other. Finally she resigns the throne to Ninyas and dies. For Antiquity Semiramis is a superhuman woman, as titanic in her greed for power as in her voluptuousness, which assured her a place in Dante's *Inferno.* Calderón omitted the latter trait. He emphasizes her pride and her craving for power. He loves such heroic women, as is also shown by his ***Zenobia.*** The second quality that may have attracted Calderón to this material was its aura of the miraculous and the astonishing. By this I mean the essence of all that the Romans called *prodigium* and the Middle Ages *mirabilia.* The feeding by the doves fits in here, but so does the miraculous construction of the hanging gardens, and so does an anecdotal element . . . : the impending danger of war is announced to the queen while her hair is being done and she rushes from her dressing table into battle. Finally Calderón, like many others, made this material more significant through the rule of fate, which man struggles against in vain. (pp. 162-63)

There are only two poets of the Christian world: Dante and Calderón. They alone have mirrored the entire Christian world with its hierarchical gradations of classes and spheres. Also, they alone wrote for the entire Christian world. Nevertheless, within this common province they represent the most extreme antitheses. Dante forged in language of metallic strength a mathematical and strictly circumscribed work which grew to perfect form and which carries the stamp of his person from the first to the hundredth canto. Calderón's work is as limitless as the web of an immense tapestry that has neither beginning nor end, and which the eye, proceeding from figure to figure, from ornament to ornament, has to take in piece by piece. The person of the poet is nowhere to be seen. What we see is only the immense spectacle of the theater of the world. Dante is the methodical calculator and the implacable judge. He possesses the ordering will and the realism of eternal Rome, from which he traced his descent. His solitary work remains a standard outside of and above time. Calderón writes for the people and the Church, for kings and lords, for soldiers and scholars. In the magic mirror of his two hundred plays he catches all the variegated activity of the world and interweaves it with the symbols of the superterrestrial. (pp. 167-68)

E. R. Curtius, "George, Hofmannsthal, and Calderón," in his Essays on European Literature, *translated by Michael Kowal, Princeton University Press, 1973, pp. 142-68.*

Shelley on Calderón in a letter dated 21 September 1819:

Some of [Calderón's philosophical dramas] certainly deserve to be ranked among the grandest and most perfect productions of the human mind. He excels all modern dramatists with the exception of Shakespeare, whom he resembles, however, in the depth of thought and subtlety of imagination of his writings, and in the one rare power of interweaving delicate and powerful comic traits with the most tragic situations, without diminishing their interest. I rank him far above Beaumont and Fletcher.

Percy Bysshe Shelley, as quoted by Salvador de Madariage, in his Shelley and Calderon and Other Essays on English and Spanish Poetry, *Constable and Co., Ltd., 1920.*

A. A. Parker (essay date 1962)

[*A Scottish Hispanist, Parker has written several works on Spain's Golden Age, including* The Allegorical Drama of Calderón: An Introduction to the "Auto Sacramentales" *(1943). In the following essay, he refutes the notion that Spain has produced no real tragedies. Upon examination of plot structure and characterization in Calderón's works, Parker concludes that the playwright's dramas reveal "an original, significant, and valid conception of tragedy," in which a character's moral guilt is always linked to his downfall.*]

It is generally considered that Spain has made no significant and original contribution to tragic drama. The belief is in fact prevalent that the Spanish drama possesses no real tragedies. This is often explicitly stated in general histories of the European theatre. In particular studies of Tragedy it is explicitly stated, for instance, in Herbert Muller's *The Spirit of Tragedy* [1956], where there are separate sections on the tragedy of the Greeks, of the Elizabethans, of the French and of modern times, and where the Spanish drama is dismissed in eighteen lines, among which we find this statement: "For Spain remained orthodox, Catholic, hierarchical; and Spain wrote no tragedy. Its greatest dramatist, Calderón, presented some nominally tragic actions but always arrived at a pious or patriotic conclusion, resounding with devotion to God, king or country." Sometimes the existence of Spanish tragedies is acknowledged and not discussed, but generally these particular studies of Tragedy leave the non-existence of Spanish examples to be inferred, because in modern works of this kind Spanish dramatists are not included.

Hispanists have done little to dispel this belief because many of them share it themselves. Sometimes an incapacity to write tragedies is ascribed by Spaniards to their own temperament—to an alleged innate contempt for pity, for example. But as regards the seventeenth century the explanation is usually looked for in the religious spirit of the times. Vossler [in his *Lope de Vega und sein Zeitalter,* 1932], for example, holds that Lope and his audiences were never grieved or troubled by the problem of suffering; for them it was not a problem, but a given fact of experience that implied purification and redemption: for Lope the only worthwhile and heroic attitude on the stage was not to be cowed and broken by suffering or injustice but to react bravely against them. What Vossler implied can be found more explicitly stated elsewhere [e.g. in Clifford Leech, *Shakespeare's Tragedies and Other Studies in Seventeenth-Century Drama,* 1950]:

> We should not look for tragedy in the drama of seventeenth-century Spain, for always there the spirit of religion burned brightly; Calderón and

> Lope de Vega might show evil in their plays, but it was an evil which attended on divine forgiveness or on an acceptable retribution; they might show suffering, but with them indeed it was the suffering of purgatorial fire.

With this background of prevalent opinion it is not perhaps surprising that the student of the Spanish drama will look in vain for any full and detailed study of the theory of tragedy as exemplified in the practice of the great dramatists of the Golden Age. In fact, until the appearance of Dr. Raymond MacCurdy's book on Rojas Zorrilla [*Francisco de Rojas Zorrilla and the Tragedy,* 1958], he would have looked in vain for any modern monograph dealing specifically with tragedy in the work of any one dramatist. Rojas is, of course, the one exception allowed by the histories of Spanish literature to the general statement that Golden Age drama is weak in tragedy. Dr. MacCurdy concedes the general statement, maintaining that "the pressures of [the] age conspired against the writing of tragedy", and he seeks to justify the belief that Rojas is the only striking exception in that he "had the most powerful tragic mood of his age." But his book scarcely shakes my own belief that Rojas is not a significant tragedian. Certainly his plays are full of horrors and violence, but except where he is handling an accepted tragic story his heightened tragic situations seem to me to be *ad hoc* ones, devised for stage effect in order to produce novelty and surprise; they do not correspond to any deep awareness of the tragedy of human existence. It is not to Rojas we should go in search of an answer to the charge that the Golden Age made no significant contribution to tragic drama. My purpose is to suggest that in the drama of Calderón it is possible to detect an original, significant and valid conception of tragedy which has hitherto been overlooked.

The omission of the Golden Age drama from modern studies on Tragedy, where not explicable by ignorance, seems to be due to the fact that the most commonly accepted theories of tragic drama evolved since the Romantic period, however much they may differ in detail, have in common one general assumption with which Spanish tragedies refuse to comply. This is a dissatisfaction with the classical insistence that the tragic hero must to some extent be responsible for bringing about the events that engulf him and others in disaster; and, more especially, a dissatisfaction with linking the suffering of tragedy with any degree of moral guilt. Thus it is maintained that Destiny or Fate is a deeper conception of tragedy than the responsibility of the tragic hero for his own actions. If he cannot blame fate, if he cannot blame anything but himself, then his final fall merely vindicates the principle of poetic justice, which mechanically turns everything into white or black. By putting the individual in the wrong the dramatist puts the universe in the right, and thus shirks the central problem of the tragedy of life. Mankind is thus not helpless in the face of an implacable Fate; if, for instance, King Lear had only had the sense to be saner he would not have been defeated. The form of tragedy which stresses human responsibility thus proclaims not human weakness but human power, since it turns the world into a place where virtue, foresight and wisdom may guide men and shield them from the worst. By this process of interpretation, it is held, tragedy is not so much explained as explained away; by declining to a morality tragedy, it is alleged, is "ameliorated". For it is an obvious fact of experience that the helplessness of man in face of the hostility of life—the hostility of a universe which he cannot control—is more deeply tragic than a moral foolishness which he is able to control if he wishes. It is more tragic when a man is the victim of life than when he is the victim of his own unforced imprudence. As against this explaining away or amelioration of tragedy is set the sense of mystery as an essential of true tragedy; mystery associated with something wrong in the universe, an inexplicable failure in the general justice of things. The function of tragedy, according to this view, is to raise the question whether human life has any value in the ultimate scheme of things, whether, in fact, there *is* any such scheme of things. The greatest quality of a tragic poet, it is thus held, is his power to make us feel the presence of problems which we cannot solve.

Another modern conception of tragedy [see U. Ellis-Fermor, *The Frontiers of Drama,* 1945], and one that has found wide acceptance, makes it reside in a conflict between two different views of human experience: the awareness of evil and pain on the one hand, and the apprehension of an immanent goodness in life; the conflict, that is to say, between a chaotic universe and a "patterned" one. Tragedy will be great in proportion to its success in maintaining an equilibrium between these two conflicting readings of the universe, an equilibrium that consists in leaving the conflict unresolved. The equilibrium can be upset by tilting either end of the scale: by accepting the totality of evil and seeing the universe as a malevolent mechanism, or by accepting the belief that good does or can triumph over evil, whether the triumph be by social and economic reforms or by the religious conviction that the tribulations of the seen world are overcome in the truer reality of the unseen world. Religion, it is thus generally claimed, is incompatible with tragic drama, which must show a balance or uncertainty that consists in seeing two worlds of being and in finding it impossible wholly to accept either.

There is clearly a close affinity between these two theories of tragedy. What they have in common is the shift away from the conception of good and evil as moral actions which can be strictly distinguished and confidently identified according to a clear-cut code. On the face of it, these theories do seem to exclude the Spanish drama from the sphere of tragedy. For its tone is so strongly coloured by the very large number of specifically religious plays that the religious spirit is felt to be the implicit framework of all the rest. Because the Spanish dramatists are Christians they cannot be true tragedians, since they are thereby compelled to differentiate sharply between good and evil and to come down unequivocally on the side of what they hold, on religious or social grounds, to be the good. Calderón in particular, being the Catholic dramatist *par excellence,* can never be poised in uncertainty between two worlds of being, one good and one bad; nor can he fail to stress the moral responsibility of his characters. In his drama, therefore, *ipso facto* removed from the sphere of tragedy?

The Compañía Lope de Vega performs the auto, Belshazzar's Feast, *1954.*

It is against the background of this theory that I present some examples of Calderón's handling of tragic themes. All dramatic theory is, or should be, a deduction from dramatic practice, and it will be my purpose to show that if Calderón's practice as a tragedian is taken into account instead of being ignored, the theory that I have sketched will be seen to be not only incomplete but singularly unsubtle. I do not, however, condemn all the assumptions behind this theory. We may, I think, accept in principle the fact that any clear-cut presentation of good and evil—all white and all black—in which good unequivocally triumphs, punishing evil by a mechanical poetic justice, will not make for a good tragedy. There must be a problem, a questioning and sense of unease, not a straightforward solution to a conflict that constitutes no problem. But, none the less, I hope to demonstrate that uncertainty between these two worlds of being is not the only possible equilibrium of tragedy, and that Calderón does in fact show an equilibrium between two worlds of being whereby, though the dramatist (as a Catholic and a scholastic theologian) knows that goodness is the positive law of Being, and evil its negation and not a positive counterpart, he none the less leaves us poised between the two.

Menéndez Pelayo thought that only six of Calderón's plays deserved to be called tragedies. Dr. MacCurdy rightly adds ***La hija del aire*** to this number (a play which in my opinion has strong claims to be considered Calderón's supreme masterpiece), but since he excludes the four honour plays, only three tragedies remain. With these—***La niña de Gómez Arias, El mayor monstruo del mundo*** and ***La hija del aire***—I am not going to deal because their status as tragedies is not called in question. Instead I wish to point to what I claim to be a profound and original conception of tragedy which, if the claim is acceptable, will considerably increase the number of Calderonian tragedies, though it is no part of my present purpose to decide exactly how many of his plays should come into this category.

One for which I do claim this title is ***La devoción de la cruz.*** It did not appear in Menéndez Pelayo's list of six because it is, to a considerable extent, a religious play. The young protagonist, Eusebio, meets with a tragic death; but he is miraculously restored to life in order that he may confess his sins and receive absolution from a priest before dying. This in itself extravagant incident has, of course, a symbolical meaning—it is the concrete representation on the stage of the fact that Eusebio's soul is saved through repentance; and spiritual salvation despite human catastrophe is what Calderón wishes to emphasize at the end in his particular case. The play does not end in the human tragedy to which the incidents of the plot lead, but in a spiritual triumph that is dramatically irrelevant: it is therefore no tragedy at all. This interpretation, if correct, would offer cogent proof of one aspect of the dramatic theory outlined above: the equilibrium proper to tragedy is lost, because the powers of good come to rescue human beings from the tentacles and suffering of fatality.

I have, however, argued elsewhere that this interpretation is the wrong one because it does not take into account, as one always must in Calderón, the structure of the plot. The whole plot is admirably constructed along an unbroken chain of cause and effect, whereby the final catastrophe that overwhelms Eusebio is seen to be the result of something that happened before he was born—the result of the cruel self-centredness and warped sense of honour of his father, Curcio. In this way, Curcio and not Eusebio is seen to be the real centre, because he is the primary agent, of the tragedy, despite the fact that he does not die while the latter does. His tragedy is the ruin in which he engulfs his family and the social disgrace he brings upon himself by creating a real dishonour in the attempt to avoid an unreal dishonour that was in the first place only the imaginary fruit of his obsessive egotism. There is, however, one important point about this play which I did not bring into my discussion of it because it was not relevant to the context of my particular argument on that occasion, but it is relevant here for my different purpose of elucidating a typically Calderonian conception of tragedy. We do not have here the equilibrium between good and evil which has been considered essential for tragedy; and we certainly have an implicit insistence on moral responsibility which so many theorists hold to be inimical to tragedy. But where is the moral responsibility for Eusebio's death to be fixed? On Eusebio? Yes and no. Yes, because he commits the crimes; no, because the fact that he was placed in the circumstances that made him commit them was the responsibility of another. Is the responsibility, then, to be fixed on Curcio? Again yes and no. Yes, because he was responsible for an act that in time produced the circumstances of Eusebio's crimes; no, because he did not himself commit these crimes, nor did he wittingly lead Eusebio to commit them. There is here both a conception of moral responsibility and a tragic equilibrium for which the modern theorists of tragedy have made no provision. I am going to suggest that Calderón's tragic equilibrium and his conception of moral responsibility are more subtle than those the modern theorists put forward; for Calderón leaves us suspended, not between two worlds of being, but between sin and guilt: the sin is there—in Eusebio's crimes—but where is the guilt to be placed?

Already at what must have been a point very near the start of his dramatic career Calderón was aware, as most modern theorists of drama are not, that good and evil cannot be differentiated by a simple division into right and wrong and exemplified by a straightforward conception of poetic justice. Eusebio is both guilty and not guilty; while Curcio must share the guilt for crimes that he has not himself committed. If a situation such as this is indeed part of our human predicament (and who can deny it?), is it not something deeply tragic?

This conception of diffused responsibility, of the impossibility of confining the guilt of wrongdoing to any one individual, lies at the heart of the Calderonian sense of tragedy. If Segismundo [in ***Life is a Dream***] had been killed in the vain attempt to recover his freedom while Basilio had been forced to see him die before his eyes as the price of retaining his throne, the Curcio-Eusebio situation would have been exactly paralleled. The crime of sedition and recourse to violence would have been clear, but where would the guilt have been placed?

The development and clarification of this sense of tragedy is best exemplified by ***Las tres justicias en una,*** a splendid play that does not deserve the neglect into which it has fallen since Fitzgerald translated it. Less passionate and melodramatic than ***La devoción de la cruz,*** more measured and restrained, it is on that account a work of greater maturity which might tentatively be assigned to the period 1635-40.

The tragedy centres in a young man, Don Lope de Urrea *hijo,* whose impetuous character leads him into a disorderly and criminal life, which is punished at the end by the legal sentence of death. At the beginning of the play he appears as a criminal; slowly the circumstances surrounding his actions are disclosed until the complete revelation coincides at the end with his death. He himself attributes his disorderly impulses to an antagonism he feels towards his father (Don Lope de Urrea *padre*), whose cold and unloving character has not only brought an unhappiness to his wife Doña Blanca, which the son cannot bear to witness, but has created an atmosphere of strained hostility between father and son for which the latter seeks an outlet in anarchical behaviour, and which culminates in the son's striking the father in public. This personal dishonour impels Don Lope *padre* to denounce his son to the law. This strained family situation follows from its being an unnatural home in more senses than one. Unknown to himself and to Don Lope *padre* the young man is in fact not the son of either of his reputed parents. In him, as external causes of his tragedy, two strands converge. Doña Blanca is responsible for the one: made miserable by her unhappy marriage, she had set her hopes on having a child who would create a band of affection between her husband and herself. Frustrated in this hope, but clinging to it, she had deceived her husband by successfully passing off her sister's baby as her own. In this she aimed not only at her own good but at that of mother and child, for the latter was the offspring of dishonour—the fruit of a promise of marriage which the father, Don Mendo, had not fulfilled. This fourth character thus represents the second strand in the tragedy and is directly involved, by reason of his position as the King's Chief Justice, in the tragic fate of someone he does not know until the end to be his son. There thus unfolds a pattern of responsibility in which Don Lope, the reputed father, also has his share: his lack of affection is what drove his wife to deceive him in the hope of winning it. But his coldness is not genuine: at heart he is fond in his own way of his wife and of the boy he thinks to be his son, but he has been brought up and hardened in the belief that it is unmanly and undignified for a husband and father to demonstrate outwardly any tenderness or affection, sternness and discipline being the hallmark of the man of honour. Ultimately the responsibility goes further back to Doña Blanca's parents, who had forced her as a girl against her will into a marriage with a man, very much her senior, for whom she could feel no natural affection.

The tragedy therefore flows from a pattern of interwoven human relationships, each one of which violates in an understandable way the natural norm. Each of the three characters in the strained family relationship is the victim of circumstances over which he has no control, yet each aggravates the situation by his own actions, which though wrong *per se* are in no case wholly evil. Again we have a clear sin—the criminal rebelliousness of the son that leads to his execution—but again we ask, where is the guilt? Who is responsible for the fact that he incurs the sentence of death? He himself? Yes and no. He commits the crimes, but he was not responsible for placing himself in the circumstances that made him commit them. If he had been born in wedlock and brought up as the son of his rightful parents he would not have been placed under the particular family strains against which he reacted by rebellion and violence. Is then the responsibility to be fixed on Don Lope *padre,* or Doña Blanca, or Don Mendo? In each single case the answer is again yes and no. Yes, because each of these three was responsible for an act or acts that in time produced the circumstances of the young man's crimes or produced in him the impulse to disorderly behaviour; no, because none of these three wittingly led him to commit these crimes. Justice falls on the young man who is both guilty and not guilty, while the law must of necessity leave unpunished three other people who must share the guilt for crimes they never committed.

In ***Las tres justicias en una*** the greatest sinner is at the same time the most sinned against, in that others, before he was born, had begun to dig his grave and had unwittingly handed him the spade with which to complete it. Casuistry is not poetic drama. The just legal retribution that follows the deliberate choice of evil is exemplary; it may be lamentable but it is not tragic in any deep sense. On the other hand, without suffering, whether retributive on the theological plane or consequential on the social plane, guilt by itself is also not tragic on the stage. Calderón's dramatic vision of the nature of moral evil is, I submit, a tragic and not a casuistical one: all men dig each other's graves as well as their own, for since all human acts engender others in an unbreakable chain of cause and effect, the lesser evil that one man does can combine with that of others to engender a major evil. Calderón's dramatic world is one in which individual responsibility clashes with the fatality of the causal nexus of events.

This being so, the problem of evil takes on, as it were, a new dimension. As an illustration of how Calderón developed this in his mature drama I take ***El pintor de su deshonra,*** so marvellous a play in its transformation of ideas into symbols, and of symbols into both action and imagery, that to dissect the structure of the plot is to present only the driest of dry bones. It must, I think, be assigned to the decade preceding 1650, in which year it was first printed. Being an example of Calderón's maturity it has in large measure all the difficulties inherent in his fully developed technique: the action is stylized, the structure taut and compressed.

The plot deals, once more, with an unhappy marriage. Serafina had secretly pledged her hand to her lover Álvaro, but he is believed to have been drowned at sea; she therefore does not resist the marriage her father has arranged with Don Juan Roca, a man much older than herself. But Álvaro has not been drowned, and he returns to upbraid her with her infidelity and to pursue her relentlessly. Grief-stricken, she resists the man she loves in order to remain faithful to the man she does not love, but Álvaro abducts her and keeps her in hiding; yet still she remains faithful to her husband. The latter sets out in search of his lost wife and eventually tracks her down; without waiting for an explanation and believing her guilty, he kills her and Álvaro.

The catastrophe—the murder of the innocent Serafina—is due to the uncontrolled passion of love in Álvaro and to the impetuous passion of jealousy in Don Juan. These are individual motives arising from the clash of their individual circumstances brought about by the unfortunate marriage which brings suffering to both men as well as to the woman; but the two men are not in this respect the victims of fate since the marriage was itself the direct result of imprudence on the part of each. Don Juan is a painter, and in the first scene of the play it is emphasized that he had wasted his youth and early manhood by allowing himself to become absorbed in study and in his art to the neglect of his social responsibilities. Though urged by all his friends to think of marriage, it was not until well advanced into middle age that he heeded the fact that the preservation of his entailed fortune required an heir. He is therefore guilty of the imprudence not only of neglecting his social responsibilities but of marrying a woman very many years his junior, an imprudence for which her father also shares the responsibility. Álvaro, for his part, had been guilty of keeping secret his courtship of Serafina and her acceptance of his hand: had he not done so she could have resisted the marriage, or at least the fact of her attachment would have warned Don Juan that she could not give him her heart.

The events leading from the marriage to the catastrophe are linked together by a chain of cause and effect forged by all the remaining characters in the play, excluding the servants. By reconstructing this chain backwards from the catastrophe we find that the sequence of events is as follows. Journeying with his bride to his home after his wedding, Don Juan visits the father of Álvaro, his friend Don Luis, whose vanity it is to be effusive in his hospitality. He importunes Don Juan to lodge in his house despite the latter's clearly expressed wish not to do so. The Prince of Ursino, who is a friend of Don Luis, also arrives, and the latter insists on offering hospitality to him and all his retinue, insisting at the same time that Don Juan should remain, although the latter is, naturally, now more anxious than ever to leave. The result of this effusive and ostentatious hospitality is that the Prince meets Serafina, with whom he is immediately captivated. He, however, is already secretly courting Porcia, the daughter of Don Luis, who has accepted his suit. He continues this secret courtship although his heart is now elsewhere, and he is thus guilty of deception towards the women he professes to love. She, to facilitate their secret courtship, arranges for him to meet her at a country house belonging to her father, to which in the meantime Álvaro has secretly taken the captive Serafina. Porcia is anxious that Álvaro should not see the Prince, and Álvaro is anxious that Porcia should not see Serafina; the two (Porcia and Álvaro) therefore return together to the city. Their eagerness to hide their respective secrets leaves the Prince and Serafina together in the house where they meet for the second time. Though he makes no attempt to take advantage of her tragic situation, the meeting so inflames the love he feels for her that he resolves, now that he knows her hiding place, to commission an artist to paint her portrait which he wishes to possess since he cannot possess her. The Prince does not know that this artist is her husband. The commission to paint the portrait brings Don Juan face to face with Álvaro and Serafina and the murder follows.

The purpose of this strikingly contrived plot is to implicate every single major character, directly or indirectly, in the catastrophe. If at the beginning Don Luis had not been so vain and demonstrative about his hospitality, to the inconvenience of his household and of his guests, the outraged husband would not have been led at the end to the hiding place of his abducted wife. In the first link of this chain of causality Don Luis does not act evilly, but he acts reprehensibly none the less, since he thinks primarily of himself and is motivated by the vanity of appearing a generous man. The actions of the Prince and Porcia that link the beginning of the chain with the end are also reprehensible, since they involve secrecy and deception: each indulges in secrecy because each is concerned only with his or her private world. Their secrecy parallels that of Álvaro and Serafina when they pledged their love to each other. If all four characters had been open instead of self-centered the tragedy would not have happened. Again we have an example, and a still more subtle one, of the equilibrium between sin and guilt. This is no dramatic world of clear-cut black and white ruled by an automatic poetic justice disposing of all problems.

This linking of dramatic causality with some degree of moral guilt in all the major characters of the play constitutes the centre of Calderón's conception of tragedy. The individual human being must base his judgement and actions on "I and my circumstances"; yet an individual's circumstances are never his own: they are the tangled net of human relationships cast wide in time, a net in which all men are caught up by the inescapable fact that, though individuals, they are cast in a collective mould. The dramatic originality that flows from this sense of human solidarity is to have extended the traditional conception of tragedy as a catastrophe resulting from a flaw in the character of the individual hero or from an error in his judgement. The flaw is not his alone, there is a flaw in each and every character; each single error trickles down and combines with all the others to form the river that floods the tragic stage of life. No single man has the right to protest in indignation against the unjust suffering that is the lot of humanity, since all men in solidarity together make life what it is. In the Calderonian drama individuals are caught in the net of collective circumstances, in which they cannot know all the facts because they cannot see beyond their individually restricted range of vision. The fact that every single human action is a stone cast into the water of social life, producing ripples that eddy out into unforeseeable consequences, makes it the inescapable duty of each man to look outwards towards other men, and not inwards towards himself. Self-centredness, the self-assertive construction of a private world of one's own, is, for Calderón, the root of moral evil. In his drama, the individual cannot see beyond his restricted range of vision; yet with the confidence born of self-centredness he deludes himself into the belief that his vision is complete and aims at what seems a clear goal, only to blunder into something unforeseen.

Don Juan Roca is an example of this. There are three symbols in the action of the play and in the imagery of the verse—fire, sea and painting. Fire and the sea together represent the self-centred passion of love and its corollary the self-centred passion of jealousy; painting represents the self-centred activity of the imagination. Only the third of these is important for my present purposes. The general significance of the symbol should be obvious from the title: it is not just that Don Juan is commissioned to paint the portrait of his wife when she is in the possession of another man, it is also that his dishonour is imaginary only. When the symbol appears in the first scene, Don Luis praises Don Juan's skill as a painter in these terms:

pues es tanta la destreza
con que las líneas formáis,
que parece que le dais
ser a la naturaleza.

The phrase is very odd: one would expect "dar ser al lienzo" or "dar vida a lo inanimado". The departure from the expected image points to a special significance; "dar ser" is to create: Don Juan "creates nature", i.e. he imagines reality, he does not see it—which is why in this particular context his painting is blamed for his shutting his eyes to the responsibilities of life. At the beginning of Act II the symbol appears in the action: Don Juan is painting Serafina's portrait but gives up in despair when he cannot capture her likeness. A second odd metaphor makes the symbol explicit: instead of saying that his brush cannot follow his eyes, he says they cannot follow his imagination, although the model is before him:

Deste arte la obligación
(mírame ahora, y no te rías)
es sacar las simetrias,
que medida, proporción
y correspondencia son
de la facción; y aunque ha sido
mi estudio, he reconocido
que no puedo, desvelado,
haberlas yo imaginado
como haberlas tú tenido.
Luego si en su perfección
la imaginación exceden,
mal hoy los pinceles pueden
seguir la imaginación.

On the first occasion his painting is what prevented him from marrying; on the second occasion he is married, but he can no longer paint. The point is beautifully made: his painting was a substitute for reality, now that he has faced up to reality by marrying, his marriage is unreal because it is to a woman who does not love him. Because it is, so to speak, a figment of his imagination he is unable to paint his wife's portrait. He can, however, paint his dishonour by imagining it. From the evidence presented to his limited and self-centred vision he imagines her to be guilty and punishes her, without asking for the explanation that would complete his vision of the circumstances. He thus creates a non-existent dishonour ("dando ser a la naturaleza").

Here Calderón uses the device of not letting the tragic hero meet with death as a means to deepen the sense of tragedy by imbuing it with a bitter irony. All the major characters in the play, who all in their various ways have been responsible for bringing the tragedy to pass, are assembled together at the end as the murder is committed. Don Juan turns to them, asking for the death he presumes they will think he deserves. But all of them, deprived by the murder of hearing Serafina assert her innocence, believe in her guilt and exonerate Don Juan because in their eyes he has acted as a man of honour. He therefore paints his own dishonour not only in his own imagination but in that of everybody else. By refraining from punishing him with death Calderón is neither upholding vengeance as morally legitimate nor departing from the principle of poetic justice: he is accentuating the tragic tone of the play, for the act of vengeance, which in Don Juan's eyes and those of everybody else restores his honour and gives him the right to continue living, is in fact what creates the dishonour he will carry with him to the grave—the dishonour which, together with the ruin of his marriage and the consequent frustration of his purpose in marrying, constitutes his "punishment".

In short, the good that Don Juan sought to achieve by the evil act of murder is an imaginary good only. Many other examples could be given to show that in the Calderonian drama all moral evil lies in the divorce of the imagination from reality, in that tragic capacity of men to go counter to truth by distorting, through their self-centred and limited vision, something that is unworthy of their human nature into a worthy good for themselves. This, of course, is the traditional Christian conception of moral evil; yet Christianity, we have often been naïvely told, is incompatible with a tragic sense of life.

Because Calderón is a Christian dramatist the effect his tragedies have on the readers and auditors who can respond to the subtleties of his art is not that sense of exaltation which those modern theorists of tragedy who repudiate the principle of poetic justice must hold to be the function of tragic drama to excite—an exaltation that flows from our admiration for the energy and resolution of the heroes of tragedy, which even Macbeth in his crimes can show. Since, it is held, they possess these qualities, they can be overthrown but not overcome: they are cast in a heroic mould, not in that of cowards, and so, by showing splendour even in death, they triumph in defeat. The exaltation of triumph in defeat is reserved in the Spanish drama for Christian martyrs. The human world, as Calderón presents it, is not one to arouse in us any exaltation; his view of the human predicament is not a heroic but a sad one. It is the predicament of man individualized from all other men yet in intimate solidarity with them, caught in circumstances that are the responsibility of all, whose ramifications the individual cannot see, prisoner as he is of the partial perspectives of a limited time and space, yet both the sufferer of acts that come in from outside the partial perspectives and the agent of acts that have their repercussions beyond them. From the recognition of the human predicament as consisting in the solidarity of all men in this inextricable intermingling of their actions, and therefore in their solidarity in wrongdoing, flows that sense of sadness which is the hallmark of the most typical Calderonian tragedy, and with this sadness a sense of compassion—not only pity for the wrongdoer because, although he is guilty, he is so to a large extent because others, both before him and with him, are guilty too, but also "co-suffering"—the realization that the solidarity in wrongdoing of each one of us with the whole of humanity makes us sharers in the afflictions of human life.

If, as I would contend, this expansion of the Aristotelian catharsis is clearly grounded in the facts of experience, and as such adds to our understanding of life, then the Spanish drama of the Golden Age, through Calderón, has a contribution to make to the theory of tragedy and to tragic drama which should no longer be so consistently ignored.

It should scarcely be necessary to point out in conclusion how misguided is the contention that Spanish honour plays cannot be "true" tragedies—as misguided as the, until recently, exclusive preoccupation of critics with the formalism of the code of honour. The existence of this formalization can obscure the fact, certainly as far as Calderón's honour plays are concerned, that the situations they portray are essentially human. What, one may ask, would any man do if, like Don Juan Roca, he were to find his abducted wife in the arms of another? It would need no acquaintance with or training in Spanish seventeenth-century *pundonor* to feel, under the stress of emotion, the instinctive urge to violence. Why then say that the violence committed in these circumstances is "in response to external imperatives"? To proceed from this to the conclusion that the experience of such a husband, since it "results in the death of others than himself", may be "painful" but is not "truly tragic" [MacCurdy], is to fall far short of the comprehension that Calderón possesses of the pain of human experience. Even more misguided is this contention about these Spanish plays [as Leech states]:

> Honour led to plays with violent endings, but these are rarely tragedies proper, because they are concerned more frequently with pointing a moral, the moral that at all costs honour is sacred, than with showing the individual at odds with fate.

Need one, in the light of ***El pintor de su deshonra,*** insist how childish this is? The Calderonian tragic hero, caught in the tangled net of interrelated human actions and imprisoned in his own limited vision, is not at odds with fate in the ordinary sense of the term—he is the victim of something more profound and more tragic, the victim of the sad irony of human life itself, in which each man is compelled to construct, and act upon, his own individuality in a world where the human individual, *qua* individual, cannot exist. (pp. 222-37)

A. A. Parker, "Towards a Definition of Calderonian Tragedy," in Bulletin of Hispanic Studies, *Vol. XXXIX, No. 4, October, 1962, pp. 222-37.*

Everett W. Hesse (essay date 1967)

[Hesse is an American educator and a recognized Hi-

spanist. In the excerpt below, he surveys Calderón's dramatic oeuvre.]

Calderón's dramatic art belongs to the period known as the high baroque; it is characterized by balance and contrast in regard to imagery, linguistic style, plot structure and character portrayal. His imagery is rich in its profusion and at times profound in the range of meaning it suggests. (p. 37)

I Imagery

Calderón's poetic images are largely visual. They are drawn from the cosmos, mythology, the court, nature, light and the animal world. From nature the poet borrows images of landscapes—wild, barren, rugged—to underline the unchecked passions of man. He depicts cataclysmic manifestations of nature on the rampage to portend a fatal event. From astronomy Calderón takes images to describe the beauty of woman and the majesty of kingship. He employs images of light to represent reason, human life, love and truth. From mythology he selects figures, characters and fabled animals to express universal truths, emotional imbalance and the hybrid nature of man. From the animal kingdom he chooses the horse to convey the meanings of fate and pride, and the eagle to connote the Hapsburg lineage of royalty. By a combination of images involving animals and nature he is able to epitomize the idea of chaos in the emotional, mental, moral and political state of man. To show more vividly man's emotional disturbance, the dramatist resorts to the unusual: hybrid animals, monsters, desolate or densely covered landscapes and often extraordinary displays of nature such as eclipses and the eruptions of volcanos.

The concept of the four elements of fire, air, earth and water which played so basic a role in the classical understanding of the universe had been integrated into the scholastic system. The notion held by the ancients that the harmony of the four elements separated order from chaos reached the status of a belief. Calderón found the idea useful to explain natural law. He also dramatized the conflict of the elements to show man's imperfection and his dependence upon the equilibrium of the elements for his salvation. To express motion or violent action, Calderón may refer to any one of the four elements in terms of the others. Thus to underscore the speed of a ship he calls it a "bird of the sea," or a "horse of the sea."

II Linguistic Style

Calderón's linguistic style is highly formalized and is punctuated by many rhetorical flourishes and stylized devices which follow the classical poetic tradition.

Simile and Metaphor. Simile and metaphor are high on his list. To stress the speed of a horse Calderón likens it to the hippogriff, the fabled animal whose wings are indicative of its ability to hurl itself through space at a rapid rate. Usually the dramatist is not content to employ one comparison at a time; he is fond of the repetition and accumulation of comparisons.

Play on Words. A play on words (*equívoco*) was thought by the eighteenth-century critics to be an example of bad taste, but modern critics now consider such an embellishment as an admired feature of baroque expression. A special kind of ingenious play on words designated as a paronomasia involves vocables that sound almost alike but have different meanings:

> (¡Que un *hombre* con tanta *hambre!*)
> To think that a man with so much hunger!
> (***Life is a Dream***)

Calderón was also fond of playing with names; one recalls an untranslatable play on words from ***The Wonder-Working Magician*** (***El mágico prodigioso***):

> (. . . llega Livia,
> al *na,* y sé, Livia, *liviana.*)

The chiaroscuro. Another aspect of Calderón's baroque style is the *chiaroscuro* or light and shadow effect:

> Is not that dim light some expiring breath, some pale star which, in tremulous flickerings, in pulsating ardors and throbbing rays, makes more obscure the dark room with doubtful light?
> (***Life is a Dream***)

> ¿No es breve luz aquella
> caduca exhalación, pálida estrella,
> que en trémulos desmayos,
> pulsando ardores y latiendo rayos,
> hace más tenebrosa
> la oscura habitación con luz dudosa?)
> (***La vida es sueño***)

Oxymoron. An oxymoron is a figure of speech in which an adjective implies the contrary of the noun that it modifies. Calderón was fond of violent contrasts to heighten the impact upon his reader:

> being a living skeleton,
> being an animated corpse.
> (***Life is a Dream***)

> (siendo un esqueleto vivo,
> siendo un animado muerto.)
> (***La vida es sueño.***)

Catachresis. A catachresis is a rhetorical device and figure of speech in which a word is applied to an object outside the word's usual range of meaning. Thus the combination of terms often turns out to be an overstrained metaphor bordering on distortion. For example, a male character, greeting a female relative in formal court-terms, refers to the salvo of trumpets and the chattering of birds in a kind of cross reference:

> some, feathered trumpets,
> others, birds of metal.
> (***Life is a Dream***)

> (¡unos, clarines de pluma,
> y otras, aves de metal!)
> (***La vida es sueño***)

Chiasmus. Defined as a balancing of the members of the ends against those of the middle, the chiasmus is a common stylistic feature of Calderón's art. In ***Life is a Dream,*** the protagonist refers to himself as follows:

> I am a man among beasts,
> and a beast among men.
> (soy un hombre de las fieras

y una fiera de los hombres.)

Parody. Parody is often found in Calderón's art. When a male character in ***Life is a Dream*** first meets one of the female characters, he parodies the words, "*bien*" (good) and "*parabién*" (good wishes or congratulations):

Although it is good to receive your good wishes
for the good which I have received, the only
good that I can admit is having seen you today;
and so I am grateful to you for the good wishes,
a good which I really don't deserve.

(Aunque el parabién es bien
darme el bien que conquisto,
de sólo haberos hoy visto
os admito el parabién;
y así, del llegarme a ver
con el bien que no merezco,
el parabién agradezco.)

Dialectics and Casuistry. Dialectics and casuistry are hallmarks of Calderón's art. The syllogism is one of the most common forms of reasoning he employs, and closely allied to it is reasoning by analogy and from example. Sometimes the debate takes the form of a pseudo-disputation by the use of rhetorical questions. To give even greater emphasis to dialectics, Calderón propels a dramatic conflict by means of the antithesis of two words or ideas. Concatenation or accumulation of arguments is another favorite device.

Dialectics and casuistry are used for persuasion in matters religious, philosophical, moral, ethical and erotic. They reveal the mental anguish of a character, and justify his course of conduct. Sometimes they create comic effect and at other times they heighten the lyrical impression. They are characterized by such features as the stylization of formulae, stereotyped terminology, and antithesis and parallel structure in the pro and con of the debate.

At first glance Calderón's *racionalismo* (rationalism) seems to possess the quality of a never-ending search for new truth, but a closer scrutiny reveals that there is always a truth in his mind which is fixed and complete for all eternity. The dialectical method is in no way investigatory; it is an Aristotelian device which in Calderón's theater draws the consequences from truths already acknowledged through the teachings of the Church, rather than through seeking new truths. The convolutions of controlled arguments do no more than simulate the search for truth; their real value lies in the dramatic conflict they depict and the emotional impact they produce on the audience and reader.

Accumulation of ideas. This is little more than rhetorical embellishment, designed for greater emotional impact through parallel use of certain parts of speech. In the following example, Calderón masses nouns, verbs and possessive adjectives:

mi seguridad te pido,
mis temores desvanezco,
mis quietudes facilito,
mis deseos aseguro,
mis contentos solicito,
mis recelos acobardo,
mis esperanzas animo.

(***Jealousy, the Greatest Monster***)

III Plot Structure

Calderón develops the action of a play by means of a single or a double plot. A single action moves forward as a linear progression implemented by parallels and contrasts in the manipulation of theme, characters and imagery. Where there is a double plot, the two actions alternate and are progressively knotted until they fuse. The fusion may take place in Act Two or Act Three. The plots are sometimes linked thematically as in ***Absalom's Hair*** (***Los cabellos de Absalón***), where the rape of Tamar (lust of the flesh) is associated with the rape of the state (lust for power).

The opening scene of a play plunges the reader or spectator *in medias res* to capture immediate audience interest. Sometimes a young lady may stumble or pretend to stumble in order to win a gentleman's attention. Sometimes a character has a problem in dire need of a solution. Background information of what happened before the play opened is given in a flashback (*relación*). The flashback may occur anywhere to provide the audience with the information it needs in order to understand the play, but it is usually found early in Act One. It is almost always introduced by some form of the verb *escuchar* (to listen) or *oír* (to hear).

Regardless of whether or not the plot is single or double, it is developed piecemeal, segment by segment, somewhat as a rosebud unfolds gradually into a beautiful flower. The author relates the characters to each other and ultimately effects the confrontation of protagonist and antagonist. The intensity of the action rises within each act to a crisis; acts usually end on a climactic note. In the last act, crisis precipitates the major climax and the resolution takes place immediately, or in what little action, denoted as the falling action, is left. At the points of climax and resolution, all of the important characters are on the stage and all the needed explanations are given for complete audience comprehension.

Conflict is generally depicted on at least two levels: as an exterior clash between two opposing forces (antagonist versus protagonist) and as a disruption experienced within the mind of one or more of the leading characters. The internal struggle brought about by forces outside or inside a character is often the major reality that gives a play its significance. A common device to create audience suspense is the interruption of a character who is about to reveal important information.

IV Characterization

Ever since Aristotle declared that character should be subordinate to action there has been confusion in the minds of critics and theorists of drama. In the case of Calderón, the Aristotelian generalization may be true for his mediocre plays. But in his masterworks character determines the plot, since the situations that will arise develop from character and spring logically from it. Indeed, Calderón has provided a number of excellent character portrayals. One thinks, for example, of Segismundo in ***Life is a Dream*** (***La vida es sueño***), of old Pedro Crespo in ***The Mayor of Zalamea*** (***El alcalde de Zalamea***), of Eusebio in ***The Devo-***

tion to the Cross* (*La devoción de la cruz*)**, or of Semíramis in ***Daughter of the Air* (*La hija del aire*)**. In addition, he has left some excellent portraits of minor characters, in such low-life figures as La Chispa and Rebolledo in ***The Mayor of Zalamea. Both major and minor characters in his outstanding plays are persons of flesh and blood endowed with all the major emotions of the seventeenth-century Spaniard. Sometimes, however, Calderón presents his best creations, like Segismundo, larger than life, so to speak, so that the prince becomes a symbol of mankind. Semíramis, like Lady Macbeth, may be viewed as a symbol of evil. Of Calderón's female characters, however, very few are depicted in any great detail. The mother is almost entirely absent from his plays—as in all Golden Age *comedias*—unless she has some unusually important dramatic function. One outstanding mother, though thoroughly denigrated in the play, is the Empress Semíramis.

The characters are usually well orchestrated; that is, they are not all alike. One or more characters may be more sharply defined than the rest whose figures are enveloped in a misty haze. This technique is sometimes called the "law of subordination."

Some characters in the Calderonian repertory remain the same throughout the play; that is, they are unbending in their attitude and point of view. The Captain in ***The Mayor of Zalamea*** will never change for the better, and is in opposition to the ideals of Pedro Crespo as well as to the social conventions of the period. The unbending quality of his attitude provides the intensifying conflict of the play. Many of the characters of Calderón's drama suffer from an excessive pride which is left unchecked and brings about their downfall. As for Segismundo of ***Life is a Dream,*** he is in conflict with all those he meets, although during the course of the drama, his character evinces a change and by the final curtain he has undergone a basic transformation. Cipriano in ***The Wonder-Working Magician* (*El mágico prodigioso*)** likewise changes, moving from evil to good.

German production of The Mayor of Zalamea, *1961.*

Most plays contain a number of stock characters. The *gracioso* or clown is usually a servant. He is garrulous and is addicted to eating and drinking. He was considered so important for comic relief by the writers of the Golden Age *comedia* that he was included even in religious and serious plays. Servants were often used as confidants of their masters to eavesdrop on important conversations and relay messages to advance the action. The father, esquire or some older person served as the guardian of the heroine. Sometimes it was the girl's brother who was assigned the custody of her honor.

Professor Oppenheimer [in his "The Baroque Impasse in the Calderonian Drama," *PMLA* LXV, 1950] sees Calderonian characters in revolt against the stringent social patterns in their attempt to achieve self-realization. Under the influence of Humanism they act out of emotional needs and desires in such a way as to break normal behavior patterns and seem out of step with the logical development of the plot. Oppenheimer concludes that the characters ultimately realize their human limitations and resolve their difficulties in an "illusory harmonious synthesis of discordant elements: this is Baroque."

V Thematic Cluster

One of the reasons why there have been so many interpretations of any one of Calderón's plays is that the dramatist may deal with a variety of themes all related in varying degrees to the main theme of the work. In the welter of thematic confusion, the reader may have difficulty in determining which is the principal theme and which are the subordinate ones. In the dramas on jealousy, for example, other themes related to it such as love, hate, envy, infidelity, truth and death also play important roles. The effect of multiple themes is to endow the play with a greater degree of reality and naturalness, thus mirroring life itself. Moreover, the multiplicity of themes produces the bewilderment, doubt and confusion found in life which Calderón dramatizes throughout his repertory.

VI Techniques

The Soliloquy. The soliloquy is the vehicle par excellence to portray the changing manifestations of a character's mental struggle often expressed through finespun reasoning. A pattern may be established whereby an individual reviews his predicament and weighs the consequences of alternative paths of action before reaching a decision. In many cases the soliloquy serves to convey a plausible explanation of an action, or of an attitude of which the real, though often unconscious, motive is of such a nature that one would consciously disavow it. Sometimes Calderón employs argumentation in the form of the soliloquy as a substitute for action. That is, the soliloquy may reveal character just as action may.

The Flashback (*relación*). Closely akin to the soliloquy is the long-winded speech designed to impart information to the audience regarding events which took place prior to the opening of the play. This type of exposition usually occurs near the beginning of the first act. At times there may be exposition toward the middle or end of the third act to clear up doubts and complete the recounting of a previously interrupted narration. A variation is the pause in the action so that a character may bring his colleagues up to date on what has happened. The pause also gives the audience (or reader) time to review the situation before another sequence of events is unfolded. The tendency of all this protracted speech is to delay the culmination of the action; this interruption in the flow of events helps to increase the suspense, but it may result in producing boredom in the modern reader.

Meters. All of Calderón's plays, like those of his contemporaries, were written in verse. He follows Lope de Vega generally in regard to the use of meters: *romance* and *redondilla* for dialogue, narration and exposition; *silva* and *décima* for serious actions often involving characters of the higher echelons of society; *silva* for dialogue of a more lyric tone; *soneto* for soliloquy; *décima* or *octava* for special effects and *quintilla* for narration in palace scenes.

Often Calderón changes a meter within a scene to indicate a change in mood. The same meter may spill over into another scene, or continue for several scenes. The same spillover technique in the use of meters may occur in the same act even when there are primary and secondary actions.

Dialogue. Even though the dialogue is cast in verse, it does not seem unnatural. In a play like ***The Mayor of Zalamea*** where the action has a strong ring of realism, the conversation is likewise realistic, from the chatter of the picaresque characters to the arguments between the mayor and the gouty old general. To stress haste or emotional upset, Calderón favors sticomythic (or dovetailed) dialogue in which one character in staccato-like fashion completes in a few words what another has started to say.

Anecdotal Material. Occasionally Calderón relies on anecdotal material to emphasize a point. In ***Life is a Dream,*** on finding that Segismundo is so wretched and a fellow companion in misery, Rosaura relates briefly an anecdote the point of which is applicable to her own situation. It is the story of a man who was so poor that he felt sorry for himself until he found another eating what he threw away.

Asides. An aside is a device used to reveal the true feelings of a character, usually surprise or fear. Editors are likely to set it apart from the rest of the text by enclosing it in parentheses. The word "*aparte*" (aside) is sometimes indicated outside the lines or part-lines of the text that are to be read as an aside. When almost an entire speech is interrupted by asides in every line, the effect is to increase the suspense and sharpen the emotional intensity of the passage.

Recapitulation. Recapitulation is a summary of the various words, usually nouns, employed as parts of a comparison. The recapitulation may summarize the words in an inverse order or in the same order in which they were first presented. In ***Life is a Dream,*** the protagonist Segismundo cannot understand why he has been deprived of his freedom. He compares himself to a bird, a beast, a fish and a stream, all of which have no soul but more freedom. Then he sums up the comparison in reverse order, asking what law can deny to men the cherished privilege God has given to a stream, a fish, a beast and a bird.

VII Fusion of the Arts

A fusion of music, painting and scenic effects permeates Calderón's lavish court spectacle, ***Love the Greatest Enchanter*** (***El mayor encanto, amor***), performed in 1635 on three stages by three different companies of players in the formal gardens of the Buen Retiro palace.

Baroque sensibility assimilated the sphere of the natural world and man's world of the arts. In a tract on painting written in 1677, Calderón admitted he had always felt a natural inclination toward painting which he defined as an

An excerpt from *The Wonder-Working Magician:* the Spirit in response to Cyprian's question, "Who are you?"

Since thou desirest, I will then unveil
Myself to thee;—for in myself I am
A world of happiness and misery;
This I have lost, and that I must lament
For ever. In my attributes I stood
So high and so heroically great,
In lineage so supreme, and with a genius
Which penetrated with a glance the world
Beneath my feet, that was by my high merit.
A King—whom I may call the King of kings,
Because all others tremble in their pride
Before the terrors of his countenance—
In his high palace roofed with brightest gems
Of living light—call them the stars of heaven—
Named me his counsellor. But the high praise
Stung me with pride and envy, and I rose
In mighty competition, to ascend
His seat, and place my foot triumphantly
Upon his subject thrones. Chastised, I know
The depth to which ambition falls: too mad
Was the attempt, and yet more mad were now
Repentance of the irrevocable deed;
Therefore I close this ruin with the glory
Of not to be subdued, before the shame
Of reconciling me with him who reigns
By coward cession. Nor was I alone,
Nor am I now, nor shall I be alone;
And there was hope, and there may still be hope,
For many suffrages among his vassals
Hailed me their lord and king, and many still
Are mine, and many more shall be.
Thus vanquished, though in fact victorious,
I left his seat of empire.

Calderón, as quoted by James Fitzmaurice-Kelly, in his A History of Spanish Literature, *D. Appleton and Co., 1921.*

imitation of God's handiwork and emulation of nature. He believed that all the arts had their origin in God and were designed to serve the Creator's purposes.

That Calderón borrowed metaphors and conceits from painting can be seen in his descriptions of court ceremonies, festivities and the formal gardens. One can find examples in such plays as ***The House with Two Doors*** (***Casa con dos puertas***), ***The Sash and the Flower*** (***La banda y la flor***), and ***Beware of Smooth Water*** (***Guárdate del agua mansa***).

Calderón's art is a synthesis of many facets of his learning: mythology, rhetoric, logic, philosophy, theology and law, all neatly integrated into the various plays of his repertory.

E. R. Curtius [in his *European Literature and the Latin Middle Ages,* 1953] has given us a succinct and adequate evaluation of Calderón's style:

> The mannered ornamental style of a Calderón was understood and enjoyed by the Madrid public, always eager for a good show. His recondite images and comparisons were borne on the stream of a ringing rhetoric which delighted the ears even of the common man. To the *conceptos,* with their plays on words and ideas, the common man was receptive too. The imagery of writing and the book was for the most part, as we have seen, a private domain for educated, if not for erudite, circles. Calderón makes it popular once again; at the same time he represents its final apogee in Western poetry.

(pp. 37-47)

Everett W. Hesse, in his Calderón de la Barca, *Twayne Publishers, Inc., 1967, 192 p.*

James E. Maraniss (essay date 1978)

[*In the following excerpt, Maraniss notes Calderón's reliance on the conventions of the* comedia *honor plays, as developed by seventeenth-century dramatist Lope de Vega. While admitting that Calderón is a "remaker and rearranger" of Lope, he also acknowledges Calderón's contributions to the genre, which stand in some ways as "antithetical to Lope's theater."*]

Calderón's theater is the sober celebration of order triumphant—a celebration of the order of the universe; of the state; of the family; of the human personality; and, not the least, of language and thought. His plays are conceived in the spirit of demonstration; they show the value and the vulnerability of the powers of restraint, discipline, and renunciation; and they solemnize, with a grim logic, the will and ingenuity necessary to keep life's chaotic impulses under control. Plays of this type, which include some of European literature's greatest dramatic works, would hardly have survived their own time if they did not in some ways transcend their didactic propositions with a personal vision of life as it is lived and dreamed and acted; yet they are still essentially demonstrations, and the actions they set forth result less from a direct observation of life than from the application of thought and feeling to a preexisting literary world, the world of the *comedia.* In reading Calderón one must keep the *comedia* of Lope de Vega in mind as a subtext, as a set of conventions and possibilities, of actions and implicit meanings, from which Calderón borrows and refashions verse forms, images, themes, characters, and even entire plots. Calderón is a remaker and rearranger as much as he is an inventor, yet his plays are unique and unmistakable; they have been made out of the *comedia,* but made to serve a new end: to serve order as an end in itself.

Anyone seeking to learn about Spanish life during the Golden Age should look at the plays of Lope de Vega. Lope "imitates" life, his own as often as not, and his imitations have in turn affected the actions and self-conceptions of his audience to such a degree that most modern notions of what "real life" was like for Lope and his contemporaries derive in some way from an intuitive response to Lope's plays themselves. But no matter how faithful the *comedia* of Lope may be to the life of the time, it is still a self-sufficient poetic world of action and movement—a created world. Calderón's world is a creation upon a creation, and for this reason alone it is a criticism both of Lope's created world and, at a greater distance, of Spanish life. Lope's genius is such that no subsequent playwright, not even the great craftsman Calderón, could improve upon Lope's initial creation. What Calderón does is bring his own sense of order and logic, his own peculiar obsessions, to Lope's literary world; and in so doing he transforms it into something quite different from, and in some ways antithetical to, Lope's theater. Although Calderón's theater is closer to Lope's *comedia* than to anything else, it is also cut off, unique, alone in a way that the theater of no other Spanish playwright is. Calderón's method of borrowing, because it serves his thought, results in plays that are distinct from his models.

To the hotly flowing theatrical language of Lope de Vega, Calderón brings coldly passionate discipline; his verses always scan, his grammar never fails, his images, no matter how extravagant, never get out of control. His best passages are triumphs of thought and schematization:

> de la pena mía
> no sé la naturaleza:
> que entonces fuera tristeza
> lo que hoy es melancolía.
> Sole sé que sé sentir;
> lo que sé sentir no sé;
> que ilusión del alma fue.

Yet this language, for all its coherence, can be violent, in the sense that its logical abstractness and total control inhibit lyric consummation and repose. His mind is always more subtle than his senses, and it enables him to lead his characters out of difficult situations; but still the irrational intrudes, and Calderón's logic can fence it in but cannot disarm it. His plots, so carefully and tightly worked out, envelop more ambiguities than do the loose precursors from which they are molded. Critics still argue over the essential meaning of some of Calderón's most limpidly syllogistic plays. It is not surprising that the last word about an elusive ironist such as Lope should never be written; but Calderón, who seems so straight-forward in his none-too-subtle logic, should not have caused as much controversy as he has. That he has done so indicates that there is more in his plays than can be perfectly controlled, no matter how persistent the effort. It may not be possible to establish exactly what that "more" is. It could be the ghostly presence of the playwright's repressed emotions; or his resigned awareness that order and control demand a high, sometimes terrible, price; or inevitable resistance to the outside control inherent in life itself; or the expression of a contradiction in the seventeenth-century Spanish consciousness. All of these are plausible hypotheses and merit consideration.

It could be argued that Calderón's raw material, the *comedia* of Lope, does not offer the best opportunity for elaborating serious problems. Lope's plays have a way of skirting problems or subsuming them in lyricism; mostly, they deal uncritically (or rather, on many sympathetically conceived levels) with received values: national myths, heroism, affective religion, popular cultural motifs. Américo Castro has asserted [in the Introduction to his *Hacia Cervantes*], convincingly, that in Spain, by the seventeenth century, the Inquisition had done its work so well that the avoidance of critical thought had become the common practice. Cervantes, an uncommon writer by any standard, is not a *comedia* playwright for reasons that include an inability to accept the whole body of received dogmas and transcendent values associated with the ascendancy of the caste of *cristianos viejos* [old Christians]. Nevertheless, Calderón's reshaping of the *comedia* does bring out, and seek solutions to, some problems, albeit not in a way that could be termed a systematic criticism of Spanish national values as they are embodied in the *comedia;* rather he heightens some of the *comedia*'s inherent contradictions. His obsession with the problem of order leads him to create a world on stage that alters and undercuts some of the *comedia*'s vital presuppositions and raises new problems that are more personal, less social, and, because of their logical abstractness, more susceptible to logical analysis.

The *comedia* survives because of its adequacy in representing certain ways of being and acting that are interesting in themselves and are made more so through the contributions of several great dramatic poets. It is the theater of celebration, not of analysis. Like the Hollywood movie industry, it has fed the escapist aspirations of a mass audience. For every Hollywood cliché (the happy ending, the gangster who gets his just reward, the noble sacrifice) one could find an analogous convention in the *comedia,* just as predictable and just as circumscribed by the narrow limits of public tolerance and taste. Both Hollywood and the *comedia* have produced a great deal of trash and ephemera, and both at times have received the second-best efforts of some excellent writers who write down to their audience with some flippancy and cynicism. Yet the *comedia* playwrights and the Hollywood screenwriters and directors succeed in giving an entire culture a picture of its real or imagined life in precise and poetic images that, however unsophisticated they may be in their subject matter, are sometimes of great aesthetic power.

An ordinary Hollywood Western, in many ways comparable to an ordinary *comedia* "honor play," might be built upon a plot that goes something like this: a villain, or group of villains (outlaws or Indians), commits an atrocity upon a good, innocent man's wife or family; the innocent man sets out in search of the malefactors; eventually he catches up with them, punishes them, and the moral balance is regained. During the course of the film, the protagonist will have a series of adventures in which he will show courage, resourcefulness, determination, self-reliance, and other traits highly regarded by the American public; the adventures are set in a mythic past and are given concreteness through specific actions: taming a horse, shooting the rapids, following a trail. Some of these events occur in two very good, but very different, movies: *The Searchers* (John Ford, 1956) and *Rancho Notorious* (Fritz Lang, 1951). The films use similar character types, they are set in the same historical period, and their plots have much in common; yet in their depictions of human experience these films do not resemble each other. Ford, through his visual composition, selection of events, timing, and direction of actors, underlines the ceremonial bonds that bind men to a common enterprise; he celebrates American values. Lang, a Central European with preoccupations of his own, uses fatalistic camera angles to communicate determinism; and he directs scenes (such as the one in which Marlene Dietrich is a dance-hall girl riding on a drunken cowboy's back in a saloon race) so that they emphasize power relationships among men. When Ford's hero avenges himself, he is wise enough to see the futility of vengeance; Lang's hero becomes corrupted in the search for justice.

A history of the Hollywood Western that presumes to encompass the works of both Ford and Lang should make a distinction between the general characteristics of the genre, which appear in the works of both directors, and the personal stylistic traits that make their works unique. Such a distinction must be based upon a study of their means of expression, which are visual: camera angles, movements, pictorial compositions. From this study the critic might deduce each director's attitude toward the values implicit in the Western as well as each director's idea of significant human action. It is not possible to distinguish a Ford Western from a Lang Western without looking beyond what is on the surface, beyond the general characteristics common to all Hollywood Westerns. Likewise, a historian of the *comedia* must see beyond the obvious similarities between an honor play by Lope and one by Calderón to find the personal stylistic traits of each, which in turn carry visions of life that can be independent of the meanings implicitly conveyed by the honor play as a generic entity. The honor play is the common property of a whole society; at the same time, each particular play by Lope or by Calderón is an individual perception and re-creation of the world and cannot be treated simply as a manifestation of the society, although it certainly is that, too.

Américo Castro, in his discussions of the social basis of the Spanish honor drama, is careful to point out that social conditions cannot be said to have caused the appearance of such works as *Peribáñez* or ***El alcalde de Zalamea;*** they can only be said to have made these plays possible. Historical criticism, especially of the kind and quality practiced by Castro, can be especially helpful in forcing the distinction between the general and the unique. If one accepts (and there is no good reason not to) Castro's contention that in the Spain of Calderón's time direct critical treatment of society's obsession with honor was, because of its caste basis, scarcely possible in an art dependent upon acceptance by a mass audience, he can more easily focus attention upon aspects of Calderón's plays not directly connected with the honor plot. The honor plot is there, but what happens within the honor plot and the ends to which Calderón bends the plot are of greater interest than the plot itself. Preoccupation with honor, however strange it may seem now, is certainly taken for granted as a fact of life by the *comedia* playwrights. This intuition of Castro's can be backed up sufficiently to convince the skeptical, if not the hostile (whose writings will be given some attention herein).

Castro, in his later writings, has come to reject his own earlier studies of honor as a static idea and to view it as a historical process, an activity. It should be apparent that in the *comedia,* too, honor is an activity; it informs a series of stage actions that, as Castro has argued, seem to be analogous to certain historical actions. Viewed in the abstract, independent of the particular handling of a given playwright, the honor activity, which is probably the single most common and characteristic feature of all seventeenth-century Spanish plays, has an outline that to the modern reader is as fearsome as it is predictable. In the honor plays, the honor activity involves a response to a threat to the protagonist's reputation, brought about by the real or suspected infidelity of his wife, daughter, sister, or other female relative, which provokes a terrible effort to keep the "dishonor" secret, usually through the elimination of the offending parties. There are other types of plays in the *comedia* that have plots dealing with the protection of honor and reputation: the so-called cape-and-sword play, in which honor is preserved not through vengeance but through marriage, and the peasant honor drama, in which a peasant-hero assumes the role of a man of honor to protect a reputation threatened by a nobleman's misbehavior. A sense of personal honor informs the motives of all *comedia* characters (with the occasional but not automatic exception of the *graciosos*). In historical plays, such as Lope's *Pedro Carbonero* or Calderón's ***El príncipe constante,*** the national honor of Spain and the honor of Catholicism, both as an institution and as a set of beliefs, are upheld and affirmed. There are plays such as Calderón's ***La vida es sueño,*** in which the honor plot serves as a subplot, almost as a key to understanding the main plot. Calderón even includes the honor action in some of his *autos sacramentales;* in the *auto* titled ***El pintor de su deshonra,*** God himself is the dishonored party.

The plot of a *comedia* honor play, like the plot of a Hollywood Western, can be understood in terms of social values in action. Castro, taking as his point of departure a recognition of the strangeness of such plays as *Peribáñez*—in which a peasant acts to defend his honor in a way usually associated with the class values of the nobility—has come to regard the honor values not as ones of class but as ones of caste. According to Castro, Lope's Peribáñez and Calderón's Pedro Crespo are the idealized incarnations of the pure caste of *cristianos viejos,* untainted by Moorish or Jewish blood. "Limpio linaje" is a character's proof of title in the *comedia;* and this concept can be expressly stated, as it is by Pedro Crespo [in ***El alcalde de Zalamea***]:

> Dime, por tu vida, ¿o hay alguien
> que no sepa que yo soy,
> si bien de limpio linaje,
> hombre llano?

Where it is not expressly stated, it is implied in the working out of the honor plot, where so much of what a character is depends upon what others think he is. As Spanish society through the Inquisition sacrificed a part of its own body to eliminate the source of racial and ideological impurity, so the heroes of the honor plays carry out their purges against the sources of their dishonor:

> En esa misma sociedad en donde las personas—solas, quietas en cuanto crear objetos materiales o mentales—se enfrentaban con el monstruo de la opinión, en ese ambiente, urgía mostrarse "hombre," mantener hombría frente a la mujer amada como presa codiciable, cuyo amor puede tornarse nube frágil y huidiza. Toda faceta humana expuesta a las ráfagas de la opinión, se volvió tema dramático capaz de encandilar el ánimo y la fantasía del público de los corrales.
> [Américo Castro, *De la edad conflictiva*]

It is not difficult to accept that it is this analogy between honor and caste that moves Lope de Vega to use the honor plot so often. Honor plays are crowd pleasers, as Lope himself says in his ironic apologia, *Arte nuevo:*

> Los casos de la honra son mejores
> porque mueven con fuerza a toda gente
> (Matters of honor are the best,
> for they move everyone, and strongly)

One may deplore the taste of Lope's audience, just as one may deplore the taste of an American movie audience. One may regard the social values enacted in an honor play as brutal and unreflective, responsible for an inhuman ritual of sacrifice in the service of an immoral social code (the consequences of this social code for Spanish civilization are now well known, and Castro has devoted his life's work to an attempt at alleviating the consequences through understanding and self-analysis of the most generous and encompassing kind). One might regret some of the obvious limitations of the honor plot, most of all its inability to convey a truly tragic sense of life, an inability due largely to the playwrights' insufficient provision for a realization by the sacrificer (the husband, and the man of honor) that he himself has been partly responsible for the existence of the sacrificed—that is, there is a lack of "tragic realization." Almost all recent critics and scholars who have dealt with the *comedia* have expressed various degrees of shock and dismay at the implied values of the honor play and at the state of the society from which they come. Often, especially in the case of recent Calderonian critics in England, some sort of critical attempt, usually unconvincing, is made to force a separation between the playwright and the honor ideology, even to the extent of maintaining that the playwright is consciously condemning that ideology.

Impossible as it may be to divorce the meanings of the generic honor plot from the concrete meanings of individual plays, we need not reduce our reaction to those plays to an appalled rejection of the honor values or assume that *comedia* writers, whose works are so admirable in other respects, must also doubt those values. Lope uses the honor plot, as Ford and Lang use the Western plot, as a frame (one sure to be a popular success) to enable him to present certain states of being and acting that are closer to his expressive purpose and poetic sensibility than are the honor values. Lope is an erotic poet, a writer who seems to take nothing seriously, except for art and love in all its forms. In his honor plays, of whatever kind, Lope elaborates the poetry of spontaneous affection, of passion and loss, of jealousy, deceit, grace and courtship, love of country, of God, unifying Platonic love, impersonally beautiful sexual aggression—almost any amorous state or love-caused way of behaving imaginable—and he always does so with a multi-leveled ironic delicacy and poetic grace. Eros is the great uniter in Lope's plays; it erases contradictions and links enemies. In *Peribáñez,* the Comendador's love for Casilda complements and even assists the perfect union of man and wife; the Comendador dies for love as beautifully as Peribáñez and Casilda live for it.

In the theater of Calderón, honor plots similar to those found in Lope's plays are used toward different ends: to enact conflicts between the forces of disruption and a desire for control. In such a context Eros becomes a problem in itself and is no longer available as a means of nullifying or transcending other problems. The amorous actions and situations that Calderón's plays might share with the *comedias* of Lope acquire a darker meaning; love appears as an impure thought or an attempted rape, as an evil woman or a melancholy distraction, as an illusion, as a source of sadness, deceit, and, most of all, disorder. Calderón's lovers triumph through a renunciation of their love (Segismundo renounces Rosaura, Cipriano and Justina find union only in martyrdom); and when they are united in marriage, as in ***La dama duende,*** the marriage comes as a truce. Eros in Calderón has a quickness and glitter, a flashy surface, as in the love chorus of ***El mágico prodigioso:***

> UNA VOZ. ¿Cuál es la gloria mayor
> de esta vida?
>
> CORO. Amor, amor.
>
> UNA VOZ. No hay sujeto en quien no imprima
> el fuego de amor su llama,
> pues vive más donde ama
> el hombre, que a donde anima.
> Amor solamente estima
> cuanto tener vida sabe
> el tronco, la flor y el ave;
> luego es la gloria mayor
> de esta vida . . .
>
> CORO: Amor, amor.

This chorus is led by the Devil, to tempt Justina away from the true path of renunciation and martyrdom. Such a scene might occur in a play by Lope; but the chorus would more probably be a chorus of shepherds, and the mood would be authentically celebrative. In ***El mágico prodigioso,*** the scene has an undertone of futility and danger. The titles of Calderón's plays alone tell what he thinks of pleasure: ***No hay más fortuna que Dios, La vida es sueño, Las cadenas del demonio.*** Calderón states explicitly, and demonstrates (by using the forms of the *comedia,* which are most typically, at least with Lope, an incarnation of the most transcendental values in the most human of actions) the gulf between this world and the next, the futility of earthly action, and the advisability of cleaving unto the eternal. In those plays in which a strictly terrestrial plane of action inhibits any explicit contrast between the rewards of this world and those of the next (the honor plays and the cape-and-sword plays), Calderón creates a feeling of melancholy hopelessness and self-negating theatricality. Even as Calderón demonstrates, with the greatest sympathy, the need to maintain order by protecting the ideal of honor, he shows that the process, because of the terrible price and the need for dissimulation and trickery it entails, is a difficult and pathetic, if not a tragic, one.

A conflict between rash impulse and controlling reaction characterizes all of Calderón's plays, giving them a fundamental duality of action that sets them apart from Lope's unifying dramas of love. Calderón's dualities can be formulated in sharp intellectual terms: love versus honor, freedom versus restraint, earthly pleasure versus divine glory, personal interest versus national interest, belief in life versus belief in afterlife, rebellion versus containment. These dualities, which Lope transcends or avoids, are the problems of Calderón's theater; it is in the treatment of these issues that he shows his intellect and his strange passion, which is, as Calderón himself might describe it, both icy and inflamed.

Calderón's intellect must be taken for what it is in order to be appreciated rightly. His contemporaries fittingly designated him the "Monstruo del Ingenio," a title that both sets him apart from Lope, the "Monstruo de la Naturaleza," and gives him the proper credit for his great gifts—his cleverness, the lucidity of his writing, his powers of association and contrast, his ability to pull off *coups de théâtre.* These qualities do not necessarily make an original thinker, much less a "philosophic" one. It was the German romantics—Goethe, Schlegel, and Tieck, the last two of whom translated Calderón into German—who elevated Calderón to the position of great philosopher, of a writer who not only posed life's important questions in his plays but went on to solve them. For this, the Schlegels thought Calderón superior to Shakespeare. Perhaps the Germans' admiration and overestimation of Calderón could be attributed to their joy in "discovering" a literature of which they had previously been unaware and which seemed to offer so much when compared to the classicism that was their immediate heritage. Perhaps they were attracted to Calderón's almost Germanic penchant for metaphysical abstraction and grand conception. The Schlegels most certainly liked Calderón's spiritualism and his Catholicism. But surely they were wrong about his originality; his answers are not new, they are old, and his theater forces a reimposition of medieval values upon a world that had already passed them by. This forced reimposition has its stylistic parallel in Calderón's schematization of Lope's freely flowing forms.

One can admire Calderón's mind without concluding that

it is deeper than Lope's heart; it is not. Nor is Calderón's theater more mature than Lope's in its means of expressing human life in action, rather Calderón's fancy is bred not in the heart but in the head. Some of Calderón's early admirers among the romantics saw the difference soon enough; and as the nineteenth century advanced, Calderón's reputation declined. Shelley stated his disillusionment in his *Defence of Poetry:*

> Calderón . . . has attempted to fulfill some of the high conditions of dramatic representation neglected by Shakespeare; such as the establishing a relation between the drama and religion, and the accommodation of them to music and dancing; but he omits the observation of conditions still more important, and more is lost than gained by the substitution of the rigidly defined and ever-repeated idealisms of a distorted superstition for the living impersonations of the truth of human passion.

This criticism, an overreaction to a previous overestimation, was soon taken up in England by the essayist and critic G. H. Lewes, who [in his *Spanish Drama: Lope de Vega and Calderón*] subverted Calderón's reputation as a thinker in the English-speaking world, although it has been revived recently. In Spain it was taken up by Menéndez Pelayo [in his *Calderón y su teatro*], who could not forgive what he saw to be the immorality and tediousness of the honor plot and who scornfully dismissed Calderón's metaphysical reasonings as "ergotismo." These attacks are not wholly deserved, and those who made them were perhaps seeking more from literature than one can reasonably expect to be given. It is idle to hold Calderón to a philosophical standard to which he does not aspire, nor should he be held responsible for the limitations of the honor plot. His metaphysical reasonings, as constrained as they may be by their orthodox axioms, can only reasonably be asked to meet a purely dramatic standard, which they do: in Calderón's theater ratiocination can be a kind of action, with its own dramatic meaning and merit. No doubt Calderón's reasonings are meant to be convincing intellectually as well as dramatically, but the modern reader finds it difficult to share the belief that might make them so.

The ideological and moral positions that are axiomatic in Calderón's theater, though they can be illustrated and made vivid and compelling, cannot be proved; they are matters of faith. Lope de Vega may or may not have cared deeply about the subtleties of Catholic thought, the need to maintain honor, the greatness of the Spanish realm—principles that Castro has described as being, to the seventeenth-century Spaniard, "impossibles de analizar a fondo, y mucho menos de derrocar" [Impossible to analyze in depth, let alone overthrow]. Lope takes these principles for granted and does not present them in his theater as problematic. But to Calderón they need defence, and he defends them in a manner that can justly be called reactionary; that is, he upholds the authority of husband, church, and state as necessary for the maintenance of the order that is his obsession. His desire to defend these principles affects his presentation of the threat to them. Because Calderón takes both the threat and the need for a defense so seriously, he has suffered the scorn and neglect of those who consider themselves progressive thinkers. Castro himself has been guilty of taking this attitude.

Fundamental to Calderón's theater is the idea that freedom can be defined in the vocabulary of restraint. This idea depends upon the belief that man is rational and capable of making reasonable choices. The choices made and celebrated in Calderón's theater, although they are free and logical within their setting, always lead to an affirmation of the orthodox values in which Calderón believes, even though they may not be values with which the modern reader can agree. In Calderón's theater it is rational to overcome one's animal instincts, to sacrifice earthly happiness to achieve salvation, to subordinate one's self-interest to the interests of church and state. Calderón is straightforward in his presentation of choices; in ***La vida es sueño***, the prince must recognize and renounce his natural instincts in order to embrace his function as a leader of the state, as a restorer of the old regime that he himself has threatened. In Calderón's *autos sacramentales,* the allegorical figures who symbolize humanity make logical choices in favor of salvation; those who choose wrongly are damned. Calderón's liking for allegory is related to his ability to see all human beings as sharing certain circumstances that are essentially the same; one may find the kinds of choices and opportunities for renunciation most characteristic of the *autos* even in those plays that seem most similar, in their general outlines, to the *comedias* of Lope de Vega.

Calderón's affirmation of the act of choice usually makes his dramatic vision something other than a tragic one, no matter how melancholy his plays might be in their overall effect. The concept of freedom of choice appears in its clearest form in the *autos sacramentales,* sometimes even as an independent allegorical character such as ***Libre Albedrío;*** in the "metaphysical" plays, such as ***El príncipe constante*** and ***La vida es sueño,*** it is discussed openly and acted upon (Segismundo chooses restraint, Fernando chooses martyrdom); and in the honor plays it is implied. In Calderón's plays a correct choice brings peace, even salvation. Earthly appetites, and the strong emotions they arouse, are presented as a kind of limitation to Calderón's characters' efforts to achieve self-fulfillment. But these limitations can be overcome through acts of will; and Calderón constructs his plays to emphasize the will, which, no matter how powerful the obstacles to its functioning, always functions and always succeeds. The will triumphs with the aid of an explicit or implied heavenly intervention or sanction; and it can secure a heavenly reward compared with which most earthly glories are insignificant, although there are some earthly institutions, such as the Church, the family, and the state, that are elevated to the position of divinely protected gifts in themselves. Calderón's firm belief in these rewards keeps him (except, perhaps, in ***El príncipe constante***) from being a real tragedian. Writers of tragedy show nothing like Calderón's faith in the power of will to overcome limitation. The Oedipus of Sophocles' drama, a strong and highly principled character, cannot escape the limitation inherent in his fate; in the tragedies of Racine and Shakespeare man's will is not represented as omnipotent, but rather as something like a fault of character for which man must pay a catastrophic price, even if he achieves his ends. Writers of tragedy underline limitation as a fact of life by writing plays in which the human will, as dramatized in actions plausibly possible in human terms, is kept distinct from the finally mysterious and adverse workings of the universe. No such distinction is made by Calderón. In Calderón's theater the correct courses of action are available to the characters; the plays are arranged to relate means to ends, and one must always assume that the ends justify the means. One might feel after reading one of Calderón's plays that no ends could justify the means invoked, but care must be taken to separate this impression from the play's own testimony, which is marshaled in such a way as to demonstrate the correct course of action. There are ambiguities, however, and the plays by Calderón that offer the most ambiguity are the honor plays, in which the means taken to maintain honor are so self-destructive that one finds it hard to believe that Calderón could retain faith in them, although there can be no doubt about his acceptance of the ends, which represent none other than the stability, however tenuous, that repression of the passions insures.

A theatrical, confused, quickened, and dreamlike life is to be found in all of Calderón's plays, not just those, such as ***La vida es sueño,*** that explicitly bring home the message that life is an illusion. The honor plays (whose plots, in the hands of other *comedia* playwrights, are elaborated with a relaxed certainty and comparatively little exaggeration) are charged with contradictions and self-defeating paradoxes, poetically heightened and violent to a degree that makes them seem to undermine the bases of all action. Calderón's brilliant linguistic associations can destroy or distort one's sense of reality. There is little that is lifelike in his characters' speech; its effect is to promote the belief that life itself is not lifelike, that reality must be sought elsewhere, in another world. This cannot be explained away by demonstrating that Calderón's theater is "theatrical" because it is built upon literature rather than upon life (though this is true), nor is it enough to say that all art is illusion built upon illusion. Calderón's theater enacts a kind of illusory life because Calderón himself assumes, and in this he is not alone among baroque writers, that life itself is an illusion. Beneath the glittering panoply of theatrical effects can be perceived the heart of an ascetic. To say that life is a dream is to say that all the world is a stage, an assertion that Shakespeare reserved for the melancholy stoic, Jacques.

Angela visits Manuel in a German production of The Phantom Lady.

Calderón's despair about this world does not extend to the next; his theater enhances the glory of God. His devaluation of earthly life assists the spectator's vital and logical apprehension of the rewards of the life of the spirit. Calderón argues for the spiritual life with all his logic; he illustrates his theological points with the resources available to him as a playwright, and he reduces the pursuit of pleasure, through theatrical distortion, so that it appears meaningless. For all the grimness of his solutions to the problems of honor and statecraft, they are meant to be seen as preferable to the alternative, anarchy.

Still, one might ask, is not all this a betrayal of the *comedia?* Is not the *comedia*'s chief glory its heightening of the grace and meaning of human action and love? Is not the theater that Lope created a theater of light irony and spontaneity that, no matter how disorganized, redeems itself and the life it enacts through lyric affirmation? To these objections one might respond that the plays of Lope and Calderón's have less in common than is generally supposed and that one's inevitable liking for Lope need not prohibit an admiration for Calderón, though he is difficult to love. Calderón is no lyricist, nor is he an ironist. His justice is stern; he finds division where Lope finds unity; he does not indulge his enemies; he does not believe in the redeeming power of love. But his very disbelief in erotic and lyrical unification and reconciliation, which makes him so different from Lope, gives his plays a certain kind of intensity not found in those by Lope. Where conflicts can be seen but not resolved, they drive on to inevitable conclusions with all their excitement and contradictions intact. Many of Calderón's plays are expressive of those states of mind that most acutely need lyric resolution but cannot find it; hence, those states of mind lead to actions that for all their (relative) rightness cannot remain pure. At the end of ***El médico de su honra,*** an audience (at least, a seventeenth-century audience) might have felt the need for Gutierre to kill his wife to protect his honor and integrity; still, the cost as shown by Calderón himself is very high. At the end of ***El alcalde de Zalamea,*** Calderón seems to assert that Crespo is dignified and ingenious, but perhaps also that he is too crafty; in ***La dama duende*** the heroine gets married, but she is still volatile and possibly dangerous. If Calderón's were a lyric drama it might find ways to give a real sense of renewal or restoration, but it is not and does not. (pp. 1-16)

[Calderón's plays] have much in common. All partake of the outward apparatus of the *comedia:* reliance upon poetry to supply background; use of different verse forms for different, strongly typed situations; conventional endings; and conventional plots, usually having something to do with honor. ***El médico de su honra*** has a pure *comedia* honor plot; in ***El alcalde de Zalamea*** there is a rural honor plot of the *Peribáñez* type; ***La dama duende*** has a *comedia* cape-and-sword honor plot; ***El príncipe constante*** deals with national and religious honor; ***La vida es sueño*** has a *comedia* honor plot as a subplot. These plots alone show the extent to which Calderón's theater is built upon previous literature. . . .

But Calderón's plays differ from one another, too, most importantly in what Kenneth Burke would call their "circumferences," or backgrounds. The circumference of the *autos* includes both the world and the superworld; in the "metaphysical" plays it comprises an imaginary kingdom of the mind; in the historico-religious plays it is a mythic past; and in the cape-and-sword plays and the honor plays, it is the restricted world of seventeenth-century society. In general it may be said that the smaller the circumference, the more pessimistic and contradictory the play. In the plays with backgrounds that are social and contemporary, it is more difficult for Calderón's characters to find ways out of their complicated predicaments; and, whether Calderón sees it that way or not, the conflicts that are successfully, if fancifully, resolved in the *autos* must, in the honor plays, be faced from within, and in their resolution there is a distortion of the world. (p. 17)

James E. Maraniss, in his On Calderón, *University of Missouri Press, 1978, 129 p.*

THE CONSTANT PRINCE

CRITICAL COMMENTARY

E. M. Wilson and William J. Entwistle (essay date 1939)

[*Wilson was an English educator, translator, editor, and prolific writer on Spanish literature; Entwistle was an English scholar and linguist admired for his examination of foreign influences on English literature. The following essay offers the two men's interpretations of* The Constant Prince. *In Part I Wilson reads the drama as a Christian play in which Prince Fernando suffers martyrdom for his religious convictions; in Part II Entwistle views it as a great symbolic drama in which Calderón explores the conflict between "eternal and abstract values."*]

I

El Principe Constante is the story of a saint. What is the point of the play? It is, I think, that the man who follows out his beliefs sincerely to the end is superior to his fellows. Every character in this play has good feelings—even the Moorish King is only vilainous when he is thwarted—but Fernando rises above all of them. He is measured successively against the other figures; none of them come up to him.

Fernando is introduced to us as the Christian soldier. In the first act he is more the soldier than the Christian; he is a gentleman. The first to set foot on African shore, he captures the bravest of the Moors and sets him free—as Don Rodrigo de Narváez is said to have done—and he does not surrender to the Moors until further resistance would have been useless; then he has the officer's satisfaction of surrendering to the King himself. We meet a chivalrous man of action, whose battle-cry is 'Avis y Cristo'. His catholicism is obvious; he is a crusader and not frightened by auguries like his brother—he is prepared to die for the true faith. He is a soldier who may develop into a saint, but he is above all a soldier.

When he is taken prisoner the Moorish King says that he cannot consider releasing Fernando except in exchange for Ceuta. On hearing this Fernando shows that however much of a hero he may be, he is only human after all. Saying farewell to Enrique he says:

> Enrique, preso quedo,
> ni al mal, ni a la fortuna tengo miedo.
> Dirásle a nuestro hermano
> que haga aquí como Príncipe cristiano
> en la desdicha mía.
>
> I.xix

A brave beginning. But how is the Christian Prince to act? In the light of later scenes we know that his duty would be to keep Fernando a prisoner and to save Ceuta for Christianity. But might not this request also mean that the Christian Prince should sacrifice one of his possessions in ransom for a Prince of the Blood? So at least Enrique seems to understand him, for he replies:

> ¿Pués quién de sus grandezas desconfía?
>
> I.xix

King Duarte will not be afraid of making this generous exchange. Thereupon Fernando repeats his request:

> Esto te encargo y digo
> que haga como cristiano.
>
> I.xix

He is still not quite explicit, but the first meaning seems to be uppermost now. Finally he says to his brother:

> Dirásle al rey . . . mas no le digas nada,
> si con grande silencio el miedo vano
> estas lágrimas lleva ál rey mi hermano.
>
> I.xix

Has self-interest repressed altruism, or altruism self-interest? We cannot say. But these lines seem senseless unless they convey that Fernando both wishes to be free, and feels that it would be unworthy to be free at such a price (the loss of weaker souls to Mahomet) at the same time. The Fernando of the later acts would have given no uncertain answer to his brother. And though we may take the later Fernando to be speaking here, he has been misunderstood by Enrique; though he must have seen that he was being misunderstood, he does not undeceive him. Fernando has shown human frailty, and this makes his later saintliness all the more convincing.

This moral uncertainty of Fernando's is continued into the second act. Enrique enters with the Portuguese embassy, dressed in black. Fernando, not knowing that Duarte is dead, takes the mourning to be a sign of his own captivity.

> ¡Ay, don Juan, cierta es mi muerte!
>
> II.vi

he exclaims. Now, however, he is a different man; it has only been a momentary shock. He is able to rise superior to his last meeting, going on to say:

> No llores: que si es decirme
> que es mi esclavitud eterna,
> eso es lo que más deseo;
> albricias pedir pudieras
> y en vez de dolor y luto,
> vestir galas y hacer fiestas.
>
> II.vii

This was all that was necessary for him to become a saint. When it appears that the Portuguese were willing to sacrifice Ceuta for him—and in no other way, except by another expensive military expedition, could he have hoped to become free—he utterly refuses to have anything to do with it. Now he is indeed the Constant Prince. Henceforth he will be remarkable for his fortitude and humility, not for the more showy virtues of chivalry and courage.

The foil to Fernando in the first act is, as I have already hinted, Enrique, the historical Prince Henry the Navigator. Enrique comes ashore bravely, but trips up as he lands (I.vii). We take this as an omen, and so does Enrique; it foretells the failure of the expedition and shows that Enrique is not his brother's equal. Fernando is right, though, when he reproves Enrique for his superstition in paying attention to it as an omen; this is not Christian, and though neither know it, through the failure of the expedition, Fernando will finally triumph. The omen is both true and not true, and it has dramatic value either way. Enrique fights bravely in the battle, but he never outshines Fernando; he merely has better luck.

Later Enrique returns with the embassy: King Alfonso will exchange Ceuta for Fernando, and it is Enrique who bears the message (II.vii). Again the weak prince contrasts with the strong prince, for Fernando could not have brought such a message. And when he hears Fernando's determination to stay on he can only exclaim: '¡Qué desdicha!' '¡Qué desventura!' '¡Qué llanto!' But at last he promises to return with an armed force which shall free Fernando.

We must now consider Fernando in relation to the Moorish characters. The absence of rancour towards the Moors in this play is very notable. Here there is no brutal husband who tortures his wife, no cruel king who takes away his subjects' property and orders them to be flogged when they protest; the element of caricature that can be found in Lope and in Cervantes is absent. The King of Fez is not wantonly cruel; Muley and Fénix are sympathetic. The Moorish court is first and foremost a court; it might be the scene of a *comedia palaciega.* Calderón does not make his adversaries into ridiculous monsters of iniquity; avoiding crudity he shows them as worthy human beings, often moved by generous impulses.

> Pues no es el vencedor más estimado
> de aquello en que el vencido es reputado.

We may consider the play as the story of the conflict of two wills: Fernando's against that of the King of Fez. Both are actuated by high motives; Fernando wishes to save a Christian town, the King to add to his domains. In Calderón's day the act of conquest was considered noble, and the King's desire a justifiable one. He acts strictly within the law and shows no signs of having a particularly cruel nature. While the negotiations respecting Fernando's release are proceeding, the King presses Fernando to see a tiger fight, an offer which Fernando greatly appreciates:

> Señor,
> gustos por puntos inventas
> para agradarme: si así
> a tus esclavos festejas,
> no echarán menos la patria.
>
> II.v

Words that are indeed ironical in the light of future events. The King replies:

> Cautivos de tales prendas,
> que honran el dueño, es razón
> servirlos de esta manera.

No, the King has a due sense of his obligations and he strives to fulfil them. When he hears of the death of King Duarte he shows at least conventional grief.

At last there arrives the moment when the two men are driven into opposition. Fernando refuses to resign Ceuta and delivers himself up to life-long slavery. The King is able to attack him for his ingratitude:

> Desagradecido, ingrato
> a las glorias y grandezas
> de mi reino . . .
>
> II.vii

and goes on to show that he is piqued in his kingship:

> si en mi reino gobiernas
> más que en el tuyo. . . .

Then he proceeds to assert his ownership of Fernando (who obediently kneels at his feet before the Portuguese envoys) and appeals to law:

> Siendo esclavo tú, no puedes
> tener títulos ni rentas.
> Hoy Ceuta está en mi poder;
> si cautivo te confiesas,
> si me confiesas por dueño,
> ¿por qué no me das a Ceuta?

Whereupon comes Fernando's famous answer:

> Porque es de Dios y no es mía.

But the King is not satisfied and continues to appeal to man's abstract principles:

¿No es precepto de obediencia,
obedecer al señor?
Pues yo te mando con ella,
que la entregues.

Fernando appeals to the law of God:

En lo justo
dice el cielo, que obedezca
el esclavo a su señor;
porque si el señor dijera
a su esclavo, que pecara,
obligación no tuviera
de obedecerle; porque
quien peca mandado, peca.

After this the King can only do what a tyrant would have done at first, threaten him. Fernando has forced him to become a cruel tyrant, when he was in no way vindictive by nature. From now on he can, and does, always claim, with reason, that he is not cruel to Fernando; the prince is cruel to himself. The Moorish King cannot be expected to understand the workings of a Christian conscience directed *ad majorem Dei gloriam.* The battle is between a man of this world and one of the next; but this world has not an unworthy representative.

Muley is the typical Calderonian hero of a *comedia palaciega.* He has all Fernando's military virtues and can be his foe in battle and friend in captivity. In battle he is defeated by Fernando; afterwards Fernando makes him decide rightly in his struggle between loyalty and friendship—a struggle that again reminds us of the *comedia palaciega.* He is a conventional figure, but he plays his part in the play; a virtuous man, he shows how much more virtuous Fernando is. The convention is well exploited in the pattern of the play.

We are still left with the captives and Fénix. The first scene gives us their respective relationships. Zara, Fénix' maid, tells the captives to sing in order to please her mistress. The dialogue is worth a lengthy quotation:

CAU. 1. ¿Música, cuyo instrumento
son los hierros y cadenas,
que nos aprisionan, puede
haberla alegrado?

ZARA. Sí;
ella escucha desde aquí.
Cantad.

CAU. 2. Esa pena excede,
Zara hermosa, a cuantos son;
pues sólo un rudo animal,
sin discurso racional,
canta alegre en la prisión.

ZARA. ¿No cantáis vosotros?

CAU. 3. Es
para divertir las penas
propias, mas no las agenas.

ZARA. Ella escucha, cantad pues.

I.i

The hint for this passage was probably the 137th *Psalm:*

For there they that carried us away captive required of us a song; and they that wasted us required of us mirth, saying, Sing us one of the songs of Zion.

How shall we sing the Lord's song in a strange land?

We are given an indication, not only of the intolerable pain of lack of liberty, but also of the relation of Christian and Infidel. The speeches of the three captives bring this home, and they also prepare us for the melancholy of Fénix which is one of the undercurrents of the play. She, who could command the services of the best musicians to sing to her, takes pleasure in the singing of the slaves. They are not so much resentful as puzzled. What can be the matter with the Infanta? They have cause to sing of their troubles; they have real sufferings, hers can only be imaginary. And they make the position clear by drawing two distinctions: the first, between the animal that sings merrily in captivity because it does not understand what captivity is, and man; the second between the man who sings to give pleasure to others and the man who sings because of his own misery. The simplicity of the diction, added to this intellectual analysis is enough to make us feel deeply the plight of the captives. It is quite unnecessary to introduce references to hard tasks, cruel masters and all the apparatus of local colour that we find in Cervantes; here we know the essence of slavery. The scene, too, prepares us for what is to happen to Fernando later on.

Then the slaves are sent away. Fénix comes in

a dar vanidad
al campo con su hermosura.

I.ii

Her request for a mirror, the flattery of her maids, cannot help her. What is the matter with Fénix?

FENIX. ¿De qué sirve la hermosura
(cuando lo fuese la mía),
si me falta la alegría,
si me falta la ventura?

CELIMA. ¿Qué sientes?

FENIX. Si yo supiera,
¡Ay Celima! lo que siento,
de mi mismo sentimiento
lisonja al dolor hiciera;
pero de la pena mía
no sé la naturaleza;
que entonces fuera tristeza
lo que hoy es melancolía.
Sólo sé que sé sentir,
lo que sé sentir no sé,
que ilusión del alma fué.

I.iii

Here a nineteenth-century critic might have accused Calderón of quibbling. But there is a real distinction between her use of *tristeza* [sadness] and of *melancolía,* and the play on the words *sentir* [to feel] and *saber* [to know] is, though almost epigrammatic, terse and justified. It is like the distinctions of the first scene: poetry that arises from the analytical statement of the situation. From now on one of the principal opposites in the play is clearly situated:

Fernando will rejoice in his unhappiness, Fénix will be melancholy in her good fortune.

The cause of her melancholy is not precisely stated. We learn afterwards of her love for the then absent Muley; but absence would have been a cause for *tristeza,* and she is melancholy. Nor can it be that she is upset because her father wishes her to marry Tarudante, for she has not yet heard of it. It is a more deep-rooted trouble; though she has cause to be genuinely unhappy later on, here there seems to be only her almost neurotic sensibility to make her miserable.

At the beginning of the second act Fénix reappears in a strangely excited condition to relate to Muley the story of the old African woman's prophecy. This incident is a parallel to Enrique's stumble on landing in Africa. The stumble was an omen of misfortune which did not fall on Enrique himself; the prophecy also was one that was not to affect her adversely, although she fears it will. The woman had said to her:

> ¡Ay infelice mujer!
> ¡Ay forzosa desventura!
> ¿Qué en efecto esta hermosura
> precio de un muerto ha de ser?
>
> II.i

She and Muley both take the 'muerto' to be Muley; she is agitated, but he takes the affair calmly and with serenity. She does not realize that Fernando, and not Muley, is the 'muerto', and like the earlier Enrique she worries about the omen that does not refer to her lover. The inconstant princess, thrown out of balance by the words of an old woman, provides the contrast to the constant prince. Yet she is beautiful and pitiful, good as far as anyone can be who lacks emotional stability.

This scene is followed by the touching scene between Fernando and the captives which includes the reflections on captivity that prepare us for Fernando's final constancy:

> Temo venir desde aquí
> a más miserable estado;
> que si ya en aquéste vivo,
> mucha más distancia tray
> de infante a cautivo, que hay
> de cautivo a más cautivo.
>
> II.iv

The plot continues through the scene with Muley to the entrance of the envoys and Fernando's decision to defy the King of Fez by becoming his slave. Fénix witnesses this scene but takes little part in it. It is not until the famous scene in the garden that she once more becomes of importance in the play.

She enters the garden, having asked for flowers to be brought to her, and meditating upon this disturbing forecast. Who can the dead man be she wonders, and 'Yo' [I] answers Fernando unconsciously but truly, in a typically Calderonian *coup de théâtre* (II.xiv). This upsets her, although she cannot understand its meaning. She had asked for the flowers to distract her from her fear of her own destiny. Fernando has accepted his destiny by insisting on being the slave who should bring her the garland. They converse together about his change of fortune, and he recites the famous sonnet 'Estas que fueron pompa y alegría'; in this he shows her that her destiny is foreshadowed in the very distraction she had hoped to find. The sonnet has more than the poetic value which is apparent in it when we meet it in the anthologies; it has a dramatic purpose as well. Fénix finds herself face to face with her fears again; the dialogue proceeds:

> FENIX. Horror y miedo me has dado,
> ni oirte ni verte quiero;
> sé el desdichado primero
> de quien huye el desdichado.
>
> FERNANDO. ¿Y las flores?
>
> FENIX. Si has hallado
> geroglíficos en ellas,
> deshacellas y rompellas
> solo sabrán mis rigores.
>
> FERNANDO. ¿Qué culpa tienen las flores?
>
> FENIX. Parecerse a las estrellas.
>
> II.xiv

Here we have a very telling scene. The last line in particular is fine in a style of which Calderón's is the master: flowers in the element of the earth are the equivalent of stars in the heavenly element. But here the similarity is given force because, like the stars, flowers can reveal the terrors of the future. So Fénix in return pronounces a sonnet (to my mind a disappointing one) and goes off. Now we can see perhaps the cause of her trouble. She is afraid of Death, and she has not the resources of Christianity on which Fernando can draw, to enable her to overcome her fear.

In the last act Fénix pleads for the life of the noble captive as we might expect any Calderonian lady to do. She pleads in vain; the King is resolute (III.ii). And then, in Fernando's last hours, the Prince and Princess are brought together again, when he is lying stinking on the dunghill, visited by the King who wishes to show Tarudante his power. There is a powerful scene of the conflict of wills between King and Prince, the King remaining solid as a rock, completely justified in his own mind in his cruelty. The King and Tarudante move away; Fénix remains helpless before the horror of the dying man.

> FERNANDO. Si es alma de la hermosura
> esa divina deidad,
> vos, señora, me amparad
> con el rey.
>
> FENIX. ¡Qué gran dolor!
>
> III.vii

Then the last touches are laid on. Fernando with religious cruelty lays bare Fénix' emotional inadequacy, giving her the last, terrible revelation:

> FERNANDO. Hacéis bien; que vuestros ojos
> no son para ver enojos.
>
> FENIX. ¡Qué lástima! ¡Qué pavor!
>
> FERNANDO. Pues aunque no me miréis
> y ausentaros intentéis,
> señora, es bien que sepáis,
> que aunque tan bella os juzgáis,

que más que yo no valéis,
y yo quizá valgo más.

III.vii

Notice how deliberately Fernando's trenchant criticism is contrasted with her vague expressions of pity: burning moral indignation against her inadequate sympathy. Finally she is brought to realize her plight, and losing even this feeling of charity she exclaims:

Horror con tu voz me das,
y con tu aliento me hieres.
¡Déjame hombre! ¿qué me quieres?
Que no puedo sentir más.

Fénix goes off, Fernando dies. The most important part of the play is over, but there are still a few points to notice in the last scenes.

Most readers will agree that the scene of the *post mortem* triumph of St Ferdinand is disappointing. The verse is deliberately heightened in tone to contrast with the poignancy of the scene before, but the expression is cold and conventional (II.xi). Fernando's apparition is theatrical, probably very effective on the stage, but that is all. Then in the last scene we find that Fénix has become the prisoner of Alfonso, balancing, as it were, the imprisonment of Fernando by the King of Fez, and she is to be exchanged for Fernando (III.xiii). The King has to confess what the Christians already know, that Fernando is dead. Alfonso exclaims:

Rey de Fez, porque no pienses
que muerto Fernando vale
menos que aquesta hermosura,
por él, cuando muerto yace,
te la trueco.

III.xiii

Again Alfonso has taken over the attributes of Fernando: he continues to point out the inferiority of her beauty to Fernando's holiness. The truth at last dawns upon Fénix and she exclaims:

Precio soy de un hombre muerto;
cumplió el cielo su homenage.

But she is rewarded for her attempts at generosity when Alfonso insists that she shall marry Muley. For me the finest parts of the play are the scenes in which this contrast between Fernando and Fénix is displayed. It has often been said that Calderón was at his worst in his depiction of women; have none of the critics read this play?

In reading and criticizing this play it is necessary to avoid the hunt for characters that is the favourite pastime of so many writers on literature. We have here a number of almost conventional figures, all moving in the same world of courtly behaviour but with certain conflicts of loyalties and divisions of religion. What Muley is in himself is a matter of no importance whatever; we have met him many times before if we have read more than a few plays of Calderón. In this play, though, he is of great importance, for he is used to set off Fernando. It is the same with the others. With Fenix there is more attempt at a psychological study, but it is not until she has been placed near Fernando that we can see her in proportion, and then we are surprised at the revelation. Chivalry and pity are fine enough emotions, but here they are powerless to help the victim, not so much of evil, as of blindness (the King of Fez is wise in his own conceit) believing itself to be right. Saintliness, by their side, shows that they are entirely inadequate.

El Principe Constante is a study of how a good man becomes a saint, as ***La Vida es Sueño*** is a study of how an animal man becomes a good man. That does not necessarily mean that in order to appreciate this play we must accept the Catholic, even the Christian, values. (To justify the ending this would perhaps be necessary.) The figure of Fernando stands for any man who carries through his devotion to a belief to the end, and sacrifices to it himself and all his interests. Such a man has integrity of character, a quality that is rare in these days when so many are well-intentioned. It is in Calderón's concern for this quality of integrity that the value of this magnificent play lies. (pp. 207-17)

The figure of Fernando stands for any man who carries through his devotion to a belief to the end, and sacrifices to it himself and all his interests. Such a man has integrity of character, a quality that is rare in these days when so many are well-intentioned. It is in Calderón's concern for this quality of integrity that the value of this magnificent play lies.

—E. M. Wilson

II

I owe to E. M. Wilson the suggestion for a more sensitive approach to this piece. In essence, the *comedia* [honor play] is a great symbolic drama. Behind the human marionettes there are eternal and abstract values in conflict: Evil all-powerful in the things of this world, Good which triumphs through weakness and death. Under these circumstances the rights of history are abrogated. The mention of the disasters of Los Gelves (1510) and Alcacerquivir (1578) is fittingly introduced into an action of the year 1437 and after, because by so doing the poet raises the whole question of the apparent triumphs of the Moslem enemy of Christendom. The Constant Prince is the epitome of Christian disasters, and the proof that they are contributions to ultimate triumph on a higher plane. So other historical facts have been warped to suit the play. The opponent of the Portuguese is not the famous Çala-ben-çala but a generic Muley (Maulay 'my master' might be any distinguished Moor); Enrique is subordinated to his younger brother Fernando; and his relics are obtained by conquest in a more or less imaginary expedition of Afonso V, and not smuggled from the country by Fr. João Álvarez.

The Christianity of this play is that political Christianity of the epoch, the religious element of which we are prone overmuch to discount. The question of Ceuta arises in the play, and it is undoubtedly an element in Christian constancy that ground occupied by churches and souls won for the faith should not be surrendered to the enemy. But the question of Ceuta arises only incidentally. It occurs to the mind of the King of Fez after the Infante has surrendered, but is in no way a cause of war; and once the Infante has refused to surrender Ceuta for his own liberty, the contest between the King and Infante continues on purely personal, i.e. on spiritual, grounds. There is no doubt as to the overwhelming power of the King, to which the Infante offers no resistance. Yet the King is baffled:

Constante
te muestras a mi pesar.
¿Es humildad o valor
esta obediencia?

III.vii

In fact it is both: Christian humility is the highest kind of valour. The play reaches its climax in the lines

En el horror de la noche,
por sendas que nadie sabe,
te guié.

III.xiii

In this way Fernando, after his death, leads the Portuguese army to the victory which he had failed to achieve in his material body. The appearance of the deified Prince, 'con manto capitular y una hacha encendida', is not only a magnificent *coup de théâtre,* but the keystone of the action, which would otherwise be unintelligible. It is probably a pity that the Prince should use parry-and-thrust language as if the grave had taught him nothing: it is even a pity that he should speak at all. But the heroic silences—those of Cassandra and Prometheus, all that Lear bites back and Macbeth leaves unsaid—belong to another order of eloquence: they are not Calderón's way. He covers the moments of tension with heightened rhetoric; and what seems so disappointing to a modern reader may have seemed less so to a contemporary spectator. Whatever the language, the intention is clear enough. It is through the Valley of the Shadow of Death that Christian fortitude triumphs.

Behind the human actors, there is a tragic conflict of elementals. The Constant Prince is Christian Constancy itself, Fortitude, or perhaps most succintly La Fe. Faith, incarnate in human beings, is not always clear-sighted. It may misinterpret the omens in a carnal sense, and so look for an immediate material triumph in a work that seems to be of God's choosing, whereas the real triumph was to be otherwise. Faith may even hesitate, and suggest momentarily (only to retract) the notion of some escape from Calvary. There is ambiguity in the message

Dirásle a nuestro hermano
que haga aquí como príncipe cristiano
en la desdicha mía.

I.xix

But even before the end of that early scene, Faith has recovered from its weakness:

Dirásle al Rey . . . Mas no le digas nada.

I.xix

It is the same with succeeding trials. The Prince is on the point of accepting Muley's offer of escape, and does not do so because it becomes clear that Muley could not honourably make the offer. This is a secondary consideration really; the primary one is that to have run away would have left his task undone, and the justification of Faith incomplete. What is characteristic of Faith, however, is the ability to recognize the ultimate right in each situation and to grow in clearness of vision.

In this respect Faith is opposed to human understanding, El Entendimiento (Enrique). Human understanding may judge more accurately on a short view, as that the expedition would immediately fail, but it can see no further than the facts. The great renunciation is merely '¡Qué desventura!' The victory is inexplicable:

Dudando estoy, Alfonso, lo que veo.

III.x

The conclusion is accepted coldly and uncomprehendingly:

ALFONSO. En mis brazos os recibo,
divino Príncipe mártir.

ENRIQUE. Yo, hermano, aquí te respeto.

III.xiii

There is, incidentally, grievous historical injustice in this portrayal. Enrique was the chief mover in interpreting Fernando's death as martyrdom, and it was he who ordered the composition of Fr. João Álvarez's life.

On the other side, we have Power, or rather Tyranny.

REY. Vive muriendo; que yo
rigor tengo.

FERNANDO. Y yo paciencia.

III.vii

I am not sure that Calderón would wish to excite our indignation against the Rey de Fez for the particular history of Fernando's sufferings. The matter goes further back. As a Moslem infidel, the King of Fez could only be a tyrant, *tyrannus,* illegally occupying power. This was the regular medieval terminology, just as the equivalent word *tâgh* was applicable to even noble Christians like the Cid. But in cases of obstinacy, all kings acted more or less in the same way. When Fernando ceased to be a redeemable hostage and became a slave, he laid himself open to ill-treatment proportionate to his previous dignity. He does not complain of the humiliations cast on him. He is resisting power that is in its nature wrongful.

Alfonso to some extent duplicates his uncle, and Tarudante is a more farouche duplicate of the Rey de Fez. Fénix is another, and an unexpected character, though she fits in too. She is Beauty, La Hermosura. Beauty is satisfied with itself, yet uneasy. Beginning with an undefined melancholy, which is not yet quite unhappiness, her feelings turn to horror when she realizes her own worthlessness. She, Beauty, is to be exchanged for a corpse, a grinning death's head:

precio soy de un hombre muerto.

III.xiii

It is not merely death, but all the Baroque horrors of death, decomposition and skeletons. So it is with a growing fascination of horror (the word 'horror' is a key-note of her exits) she sees her fate linked to that of Fernando, whom she only sees in his outward aspect of ugliness; until she reaches breaking-point on seeing him lying, a living corpse, putrefying on a dunghill:

Horror con tu voz me das,
y con tu aliento me hieres.
¡Déjame, hombre! ¿qué me quieres?
Que no puedo sentir más.

III.vii

And in the end Beauty and Force, Fénix and Tarudante, are things of much less value than Constancy of Faith. Beauty does not hesitate to demand the exchange which Constancy had been bold enough to refuse.

The character of Muley, as Mr Wilson points out, is that of the Abencerraje. As a single quality it might be Bizarría. He is released by Fernando as Abindarráez by Narváez, and for the same reason. Oddly enough he carries the reader's sympathies on that occasion as the Abencerraje does; though the moral is the superior chivalry of Narváez and Fernando. Later he seeks to repay the debt, even at the cost of his own honour. Humanly he could do nothing more, and if the offer is declined, it redounds again to the superior credit of Fernando. Muley, whose love affairs might seem impertinent, fulfils one other office. In the welter of supernatural forces, he provides the human level. He is perplexed, like Segismundo in ***La Vida es Sueño,*** but he has one sound principle which can carry him through, laying the responsibility elsewhere:

Porque al fin,
hacer bien nunca se pierde.

Brito also has a foot in ***La Vida es Sueño,*** with his comic effort to escape death by feigning death, which leads to his capture (it might have been death, but he is barely named later), while others escape.

With this definition of characters and elementals it is possible to state what is the action of the play. Fernando comes leading an army to overthrow the Moroccan infidel, but his army is materially defeated. The contest continues on a new plane. Fernando, the prisoner, will conquer through patience; the King through power. Opportunities of avoiding the issue are presented to Fernando, and these he alone is clear-sighted enough to refuse. Enrique offers the surrender of Ceuta, backed by Duarte's will; it is Fernando who refuses the offer, and the King is reasonably incensed:

¿cómo así
hoy me quitas, hoy me niegas
lo que más he deseado?

II.vii

It is the first victory of Constancy over Power. Then Muley offers to facilitate an escape. The situation is not quite clear at this point until Muley is made Fernando's keeper, and so bound in honour to retain him. Then Fernando voluntarily refuses this way out. Finally there is the appeal for mercy. Muley makes it as a gentleman should: Fénix makes it, as Beauty would, to remove a horror of decay:

Horror da a cuantos le ven
en tal estado.

III.ii

Even Fernando makes the appeal to clemency as a royal virtue, but midway in his own speech he retracts the appeal; he reflects that he knows how to die, and that the appeal was a sign of weakness; he ends by proclaiming his unbending constancy. So he dies, and by dying lives to achieve the real triumph. In the reversal of fortune, Beauty is a frightened virago, and Power cannot claim for itself

que en un ánimo constante
siempre se halla igual semblante
para el bien y el mal.

I.v

Such constancy belongs only to Faith.

The element of time is essential to this great argument, for in a short space of time all Fernando's calculations run agley. Hence the insistence through the drama of the motif *En un dia* [in a day]—a motif also discernible in ***La Vida es Sueño.*** Hence also the particular appropriateness of Fénix or La Hermosura. Beauty is the type of transitory good, and is the means of measurement applied to the whole piece:

hoy cadáver y ayer flor.

Power may seem to have more permanence than Beauty; Tyranny is an evil in itself. Beauty does not harm anyone, but rather intercedes in a selfish way, to spare itself harrowing reflections. But Beauty is nothing in itself, and vanishes leaving no trace:

Estas que fueron pompa y alegría,
despertando al albor de la mañana,
a la tarde serán lástima vana,
durmiendo en brazos de la noche fría.

II.xiv

The sense of transience which the notion of beauty connotes is applied to the whole play by Fénix in the first scene. She is irresistibly attracted by—but plainly neither she nor other infidels understand—the melancholy moral of captivity:

Al peso de los años
lo eminente se rinde;
que a lo fácil del tiempo
no hay conquista difieil.

(pp. 218-22)

E. M. Wilson and William J. Entwistle, "Calderón's 'Príncipe Constante': Two Appreciations," in The Modern Language Review, *Vol. XXXIV, No. 2, April, 1939, pp. 207-22.*

LIFE IS A DREAM

PRODUCTION REVIEWS

Gwynne Edwards (review date Spring 1984)

[In the review below, Edwards encourages British theatergoers to attend the 1984 Royal Shakespeare Company's production of Life is a Dream *and highlights the drama's themes, characters, and symbolism.]*

The [Royal Shakespeare Company] production of Calderón's ***Life is a Dream,*** close on the heels of the [National Theatre's] ***The Mayor of Zalamea,*** presents the British theatregoer with the opportunity of seeing the best-known play of, arguably, the finest dramatist of Spain's so-called Golden Age. The youngest of a glittering trio, Don Pedro Calderón de la Barca (1600-1681) capped the achievements of his illustrious predecessors, Lope de Vega and Tirso de Molina—and many lesser figures—and climaxed an age of enormous accomplishment, inventiveness and vitality in the theatre. Lope, described by Cervantes as a 'prodigy of Nature', is said to have written more than a 1,000 plays, Tirso 300 or so, and Calderón, the least productive of all, some 190. Calderón's smaller output, remarkable by any standards, is a pointer to a movement in his theatre away from the vigorous, almost spontaneous inventiveness of Lope to a much more studied artistry, and it is no coincidence that he came to be known as a 'prodigy of intellect'.

The 17th century is, then, the 'classical' age of Spanish drama, though it represented at the same time a deliberate movement away from classicism. Like its Elizabethan and Jacobean counterpart, but developing quite independently, Spanish Golden Age drama mixed serious and comic elements, broke the classical unities of time and place, interwove main and subplot, and delighted in vigorous and swift-moving action. It is a theatre, therefore, that should be familiar to audiences nourished on a diet of Shakespeare.

Calderón wrote ***Life is a Dream*** in 1635, basing it on another play on which he had collaborated. The main plot centres on a young man, Segismundo, and his father, Basilio, King of Poland, who had imprisoned the boy at birth on account of an unfavourable horoscope. Years later, when the action of the play begins, Basilio has decided to release his son from his prison-tower to give him the opportunity of disproving the prophecy and showing himself to be worthy of kingship. When he awakens in the palace, Segismundo uses his newly-found freedom to avenge himself on those responsible for his imprisonment, to indulge his own desires, and to abuse those who offended him. He is soon locked up again and in his prison begins to ponder on his palace experiences, reaching the conclusion that life is indeed dream-like and its pleasures inherently illusory.

Released from the tower for a second time, Segismundo reacts with initial uncertainty but with a steadily growing resolution to the transient temptations of the world, placing his faith in the permanent values of reason and the spirit, in consequence of which he finally forgives Basilio, ascends the throne and thus completes the transition from beast to rational man. The play's subplot, focusing on the father-daughter relationship of Clotaldo and Rosaura, is concerned with her efforts to recover her honour and reputation, tarnished by her seduction by Astolfo, a claimant to Basilio's throne.

Even a brief summary of the plot points to the principal themes of ***Life is a Dream:*** above all, the fleeting and uncertain nature of life; but, in addition, the conflict of reason and passion; the flawed nature of man; the extent of human freedom; man's relationship with his fellow men; the contrast between appearance and reality, and the role of the king. Such are the concerns of Calderón's secular plays as a whole, and they are, of course, the issues that preoccupied 17th century Europe in general. The view of Calderón as an essentially Spanish and Catholic dramatist, the equivalent in the theatre of El Greco in the world of painting, is a misleading one, largely based on his religious plays, the *autos sacramentales,* and does less than justice to the broader character of his work.

The intellectual nature of Calderón's art is seen to the full in ***Life is a Dream*** in the way in which action and characters illustrate the play's themes. Segismundo and Basilio, despite their differences, pursue objectives that are ultimately similar; the former a self-centred freedom that becomes a licence for self-indulgence; the latter the continuing expression of his own authoritarian power. And both, through painful disillusionment, acquire knowledge of themselves and of the insufficiency of worldly values.

Similarly, the principal characters of the sub-plot, Clotaldo and Rosaura, are associated with self-interested passion. In his youth, Clotaldo informs us, he seduced and abandoned Violante. Now in later life he encounters Rosaura, the child of that union, a painful reminder of the past and, since she has been seduced, abandoned and thus dishonoured, an obligation which Clotaldo is obliged to recognise. Father and daughter, echoing the father and son of the main plot, likewise achieve through bitter experience a deeper knowledge of their own and the world's shortcomings. And as Segismundo recovers his true identity and status, so through him Rosaura's honour is finally restored. Main and sub-plot constantly impinge upon each other. In addition, all the minor characters—Clarin, a servant, a soldier—are facets of the play's themes, each of them aspiring to or tasting the rewards and pleasures of the world only to swallow the bitter pill of disillusionment and even death.

Another feature of ***Life is a Dream*** is its symbolism. The prison of Segismundo, prominent in Acts I and II, is, more than a physical confinement, the prison of man deprived of reason, fettered and chained by savage instinct. And although the play is not specifically Christian, it is also the prison of Original Sin. Segismundo, clearly, is Everyman embarked on the difficult journey through life, and around him are grouped the other characters, reflections of him, the prisoners of their own imperfections. Another key symbol which invests the play with the universal quality of myth is that of the labyrinth, suggested initially by the maze-like confusion of rocks and trees in which Segismundo's prison is situated. On a metaphorical plane the labyrinth represents the moral and emotional confusion of the characters, be it Segismundo plunged into the dark world of passion, or Rosaura lost in the blackness of dishonour. The two dominant symbols of the play, central to the theatre of Calderón, are closely interwoven throughout its fabric, and from them radiate a series of closely associated and suggestive metaphors and images: darkness, the grave, the tomb; and their opposites, light, the sun, the stars, dawn.

Life is a Dream is also a striking example of many of the essential features and formal characteristics of the Baroque, and in this sense typifies Calderón's theatre. From the outset dramatic contrasts of light and darkness, as in a painting by Caravaggio, are much in evidence. Great emphasis is placed on violent and dramatic movement: Rosaura's runaway horse; Segismundo's aggression in the prison and the palace; the events of the civil war in Act III. The emotions of the characters are highly charged, and the confrontations of individuals are paralleled by their inner turmoil. The dynamism and tension of the play, and the feeling it communicates of a scarcely contained restlessness, are far removed indeed from the nicely balanced symmetries of Renaissance art. Calderón's language often suggests too the ornate profusion of the Baroque, for it is rich in colourful—though meaningful—clusters of images, while its musicality, arising from the dramatist's fondness for patterns composed of verbal parallels, repetitions and accumulations, has something of the rhetoric of opera.

As far as staging is concerned, ***Life is a Dream*** would have been performed in the *corrales* or public theatres of Calderón's time. These were basically courtyards, surrounded by houses, with a stage at one end whose apron projected into the pit. The entrances and exits of the characters were made through two doors or curtains at either side of the backstage, while a part of the backstage area was generally curtained off and could be used for dramatic 'discoveries' when the curtains were suddenly drawn back. Another important feature was an upper balcony which could be connected to the main stage by ladders or ramps. In ***Life is a Dream*** Rosaura would clearly have made her initial appearance on the upper balcony—in the text a mountain top—and would then have made her way down a ramp to the prison-tower of Segismundo, situated in the 'discovery-space'. Golden Age plays, it should be noted, were performed in the public theatres in daylight, and it is interesting, therefore, to note how often the audiences were required by the dramatist to imagine a scene taking place in darkness—a true 'suspension of disbelief'. (pp. 17-18)

> *Gwynne Edwards, "The Prison and the Labyrinth," in* Drama, *London, No. 151, Spring, 1984, pp. 17-18.*

An excerpt from *Life is a Dream*

What is life? A frenzy.
What is life? An illusion,
a shadow, a fiction,
and the greatest good is small;
for all life is like a dream,
and dreams are nothing more than dreams.

Calderón, as quoted by Everett W. Hesse, in his Calderón de la Barca, *New York: Twayne Publishers, Inc., 1967.*

Martin Hoyle (review date 8 June 1992)

[*In the following review of the 1992 West Yorkshire Playhouse production of* Life is a Dream, *Hoyle extols Calderón's drama and praises this production as "intellectually the clearest and theatrically the most exciting seen . . . for years."*]

This production of Calderón's fable of reality and fantasy, destiny and free will [***Life is a Dream***], is intellectually the clearest and theatrically the most exciting seen in this country for years. That includes the 1984 Royal Shakespeare Company version and the production by Polish visitors to Edinburgh a couple of festivals ago.

The RSC saw it as a chamber piece. Here it is large-scale and dramatic. It opens with a bang: a black, starry firmament lit by occasional lightning in which a bed is seen suspended on end; the sheet falls forward, making a stairway down which a pyjama-clad figure tumbles. Life is a dream indeed. The theatrical impact stills any charge of over-literalness, and more is to come as curtains, pillars and thrones rise from the floor, swagged drapes descend and echoing off-stage voices conjure up a dream world limbo, or more properly a purgatory which leads through suffering to redemption.

The play dates from 1635, seven years after Descartes's *Discourse on Method,* but too soon for rationalism to make sense of post-Renaissance bewilderment. Man's power over his destiny and his impotence under the stars were still disputed.

In mood, the piece resembles a late Shakespeare problem play in its emphasis on self-knowledge through painful purgation. Matthew Warchus, at 25 the new resident director, makes a thrilling Playhouse debut, aided by Neil Warmington's tilting-stepped set.

Producer and designer have chosen to underline the theatricality of this black fairytale, in which a superstitious king has kept his son chained up through fear of a prophecy being fulfilled. When the king resolves to confront fate and has his drugged son clothed in finery, the young man wakes within a golden frame on a stage-like platform backed by a slanting, painted sky-scape: a set-up, artifice, the ambivalence so dreaded by the Renaissance where "nothing is but what is not".

Now the magnificent central performance becomes apparent. James Larkin was the romantically curly-haired Orlando of Renaissance Theatre Company's *As You Like It.* Here he is a crop-headed ferret-faced fury, almost yelping with bitter outrage as he realises his past mistreatment. Big emotional guns aside, the actor has the intensity and intelligence to keep the intellectual threads untangled. He underlines the parallels with *Hamlet:* both princes blunder in search of a code of values to make sense of a moral maze, the one paralysed into inertia, the other in need of a channel for his destructive energies. Larkin must try his princely ponderings in Elsinore.

"I am a man who is a beast, a beast who is a man." The difference must be discovered, painfully, as the prophetic stars assert their power and man explores his capacity to check them. Gwynne Edwards's translation is lucid and literate, keeping the rhythm of blank verse without either contrived colloquialisms or pseudo-poetics. Long speeches of exposition are crystal clear, thanks to actors such as David Killick (a veteran of the RSC [Royal Shakespeare Company] production), who even manages to make the capricious and sanctimonious old king [Basilio] understandable.

Suzan Sylvester gives a vigorous performance as a disguised noblewoman in search of her false lover [Rosaura]. The tone of plaintive rant could be more varied, but that may be the fault of the role. The production's diminuendo, as the curtain falls to the ground to reveal the back wall, the scenery stowed away, as the actors embrace and walk off, affords yet another level of reality in this energetic and committed production of a fascinating play.

Martin Hoyle, "Dazzling Journey into Moral Maze," in The Times, *London, June 8, 1992, p. 2.*

CRITICAL COMMENTARY

Albert E. Sloman (essay date 1953)

[*An English educator, Sloman has written several works on Calderonian drama. In the following essay, he rejects criticism that considers the subplot concerning Rosaura's honor in* Life is a Dream *a "useless adjunct" which "seriously detracts from the play's unity." In Sloman's view, the strength of the play's dramatic structure derives from the linking of this episode with the main action.*]

Two issues are involved in Calderón's ***La vida es sueño:*** a man's conversion and a woman's clearing of her honour. One centres on Segismundo, the other on Rosaura. The main issue is suggested by the title ***Life is a dream;*** this is Segismundo's discovery and the key to his conversion. To this central theme, with its origin in the legends of the Awakened Sleeper and of Barlaam and Josaphat, and deeply rooted in Spanish tradition, Calderón has linked the story of Rosaura, an honour episode akin to it neither in subject nor in spirit. It is this honour episode which has occasioned the most serious criticism of Calderón's famous play. Until recently, the very critics who were unanimous in placing ***La vida es sueño*** amongst the greatest of Spanish and world plays were equally unanimous in condemning its subplot, regarding it not merely as a useless adjunct, but as an action which seriously detracted from the play's unity, a parasite entwined about a noble oak.

The Rosaura episode, however, is clearly neither of the nature nor dimensions of a parasite. It is no mere afterthought to fill out the required three acts. From the play's first scene Rosaura is involved in the fate of Segismundo, and the characters among whom she moves and with whom she is concerned are those of the main plot; Clotaldo, Astolfo, Estrella and Clarín. And the lines devoted to Rosaura and to the honour motive comprise very nearly one half of the play. The Rosaura episode, that is, is so inextricably bound up with Segismundo and given such prominence throughout the play that the whole dramatic structure depends upon it. Reject the subplot, and the play itself must be rejected.

Once the significance of the subplot is recognized, it is of paramount importance to see exactly how Calderón has linked it to the main episode and related it to the play's central theme. Professor Wilson's interpretation of ***La vida es sueño*** [in *Revista de la Universidad de Buenos Aires* IV, No. 3-4, 1946] throws light on this aspect, but the point calls for a specific analysis of the play's structure. That is the object of this brief essay. It attempts to show that, as the action of the play progresses, the two plots and the two characters on which they centre are intimately related, and that despite the two centres of interest Calderón has created a single, coherent and integrated dramatic movement. This integration of the two plots was the essential problem of construction in ***La vida es sueño.*** The present essay, therefore, is primarily concerned with the parallel between Segismundo and Rosaura, and details which are not pertinent to their interrelation and which do not affect the general structural lines of the play have been omitted.

Calderón's opening scene couples Rosaura with Segismundo. Rosaura, disguised as a man, comes unawares upon the stronghold where Segismundo is imprisoned, and at once the parallel between the two characters is established. Both are dogged by misfortune: the first speech of Rosaura ends with the question '¿Dónde hallé piedad una infelice?', and Segismundo's first words, reiterated at the beginning of his soliloquy, are '¡Ay, mísero de mí! ¡Ay, infelice!' Moreover, from the start, these two victims of misfortune respect and pity each other: knowing the fate of Segismundo, Rosaura observes:

> Temor y piedad en mí
> sus razones han causado,
>
> (I.173-74)

and to Segismundo's 'Who's there?' she replies:

> No es sino un triste ¡ay de mí!
> que en estas bóvedas frías
> oyó tus melancolías.
>
> (I.177-79)

Segismundo, for his part, mysteriously moved by the presence of Rosaura, checks his natural impulse to attack her:

> tú solo, tú, has suspendido
> la pasión a mis enojos,
> la suspensión a mis ojos,
> la admiración a mi oído.
> Con cada vez que te veo
> nueva admiración me das,
> y cuando te miro más,
> aun más mirarte deseo.
>
> (I.219-26)

And when Rosaura is discovered by Clotaldo he pledges his life for her safety:

Primero, tirano dueño,
que los ofendas ni agravies,
será mi vida despojo
destos lazos miserables;
pues en ellos, vive Dios,
tengo de despedazarme
con las manos, con los dientes,
entre aquestas peñas, antes
que su desdicha consienta
y que llore sus ultrajes.

(I.309-18)

From the first, therefore, there is a bond of sympathy between Segismundo and Rosaura: they are companions in misfortune. The words of Rosaura underline the parallel:

Sólo diré que a esta parte
hoy el cielo me ha guiado
para haberme consolado,
si consuelo puede ser,
del que es desdichado, ver
otro que es más desdichado.

(I.247-52)

Clotaldo provides a further link, for as we are soon to learn he is at once Segismundo's gaoler and Rosaura's own father, and is concerned with the fortunes of both. He discovers the reason for Rosaura's visit to Poland and guesses at her identity; but, by the King's order, she must be placed under arrest. When the scene ends, Segismundo has been returned to his prison cell and Rosaura is under sentence of death.

Scene II brings hope for both Segismundo and Rosaura. King Basilio discloses the long-guarded secret that he has a son Segismundo who, because of his horoscope, has been secretly imprisoned; and he announces his decision to bring him to the palace for one day, to afford him an opportunity of giving the lie to the stars' prediction. Basilio's decision means trial freedom for Segismundo; and it means life to Rosaura, for since it no longer matters that she knows the whereabouts of Segismundo's prison she is reprieved.

And at this point the fortunes of Segismundo and Rosaura are shown to be not only closely related but interdependent. Rosaura tells Clotaldo that her grievance is against Astolfo, and one clearly that can only be removed by his marrying her:

Juzga advertido,
si no soy lo que parezco,
y Astolfo a casarse vino
con Estrella, si podrá
agraviarme. Harto te he dicho.

(I.969-73)

But Basilio has announced that, should Segismundo fail to redeem himself during his stay at the palace, he will consent to the marriage of Astolfo and Estrella, that they may be joint heirs to the Polish throne. The failure of Segismundo, therefore, since it will confirm the marriage of Astolfo to Estrella, implies the failure of Rosaura.

This parallel between the fortunes of Segismundo and Rosaura is maintained in Act II. In the first scene Clotaldo's description of the drugging of Segismundo and his transfer to the palace is followed by Clarín's announcement that his mistress Rosaura has shed her disguise and, under the name of Astrea, is maid of honour to Estrella. The way is thereby prepared for a second meeting of Segismundo and Rosaura. Of all Segismundo's palace experiences his meeting with Rosaura is the most significant. Whilst Clotaldo, Basilio, Astolfo and the second servant are the victims of his anger and passion for revenge, the feminine beauty of Estrella and Rosaura attracts and intrigues him. But with Rosaura there is something more than physical attraction, though in this respect she is evidently superior to Estrella. She is strangely familiar to Segismundo:

Pero ¿qué es lo que veo?

(l.1578)

Yo he visto esta belleza
otra vez.

(ll.1580-81)

Ya hallé mi vida.

(l.1583)

He pleads with her to stay, and only when she refuses is he provoked to attack her. That this meeting with Rosaura is something totally different from Segismundo's other palace experiences is clear from his own confession to Clotaldo in the following scene.

Segismundo has at least aired his grievance against his father Basilio, 'tryant of his freewill'; but his behaviour has served only to confirm the verdict of the stars, and he is to return to his prison tower. In the portrait incident with which the palace scene ends, Rosaura too confronts the person responsible for her misfortune, Astolfo, and she succeeds in embarrassing him and alienating him in the eyes of Estrella. But the failure of Segismundo augurs ill for the cause of Rosaura.

In scene II Segismundo is again in prison under the eye of his gaoler Clotaldo; and he is readily persuaded that his palace sojourn was but a dream. But of all his experiences, one was unique:

De todos era señor,
y de todos me vengaba.
Sólo a una mujer amaba . . .
Que fué verdad, creo yo,
en que todo se acabó,
y esto solo no se acaba.

(II.2132-37)

Rosaura has been responsible for the one occasion when he curbed his will for revenge, the experience which remains as the only truth and only reality of his palace stay. Segismundo's resolve at this point to control his cruel nature, which has been shown to be a first stage towards his later conversion, follows directly upon this recollection of his meeting with Rosaura.

Act III opens with the rescue of Segismundo. Though suspecting that this liberation is a second dream, he resolves to do good, and even spares Clotaldo, allowing him to join forces with King Basilio to oppose him. In a new scene at the palace, Clotaldo brings news of Segismundo's rescue; then, alone with Rosaura, he refuses to take the life of Astolfo to clear her honour. Segismundo himself is unwit-

Scene from a German production of Life is a Dream, *1953.*

tingly responsible for Clotaldo's refusal: Astolfo has won the gratitude of Clotaldo by coming to his rescue when he was attacked by Segismundo and, after Segismundo's behaviour at the palace, he is for Clotaldo the only acceptable heir to the Polish throne. Clotaldo at all events is not prepared to meet the demands of Rosaura.

So it is that the play comes full circle with the reuniting of Segismundo and Rosaura. The very speech in which Clarín announces the approach of Rosaura seems to parody the opening lines of the play which preceded their first meeting; and as before, Rosaura is dressed as a man and Segismundo is in skins. Rosaura delivers a long speech to Segismundo in which she recalls their two previous meetings and, for the first time in the play, gives a full account of her birth and misfortune; and she ends by laying emphasis on their common interests. As a woman she comes to plead for her honour, as a man she pledges to support him against his father:

¡Ea! pues, fuerte caudillo,
a los dos juntos importa
impedir y deshacer
estas concertadas bodas:
a mí, porque no se case
el que mi esposo se nombra,
y a ti, porque, estando juntos
sus dos estados, no pongan
con más poder y más fuerza
en duda nuestra victoria.
Mujer vengo a persuadirte
al remedio de mi honra,
y varón vengo a alentarte
a que cobres tu corona.
Mujer vengo a enternecerte
cuando a tus plantas me ponga,
y varón vengo a servirte
con mi acero y mi persona.
Y así piensa que, si hoy
como mujer me enamoras,
como varón te daré
la muerte en defensa honrosa
de mi honor; porque he de ser,
en su conquista amorosa,
mujer para darte quejas,
varón para ganar honras.

(ll.2892-917)

This reunion scene is, as Professor Wilson has pointed out, all-important in the process of Segismundo's conversion. Rosaura, and Rosaura only, can convince Segismundo that his visit to the palace was real. And only in the knowledge of this can his conversion be complete—the knowledge, that is, that life itself is as fleeting and unreal as a dream. Rosaura is the means of Segismundo's conversion.

More than that, however, Rosaura is the proof of Segismundo's conversion. Segismundo is clearly in love with Rosaura; he was strangely attracted by her at their first meeting in Act I; at the palace in Act II his arrogance leads him to attack her when she dares to stand against him. Now, too, his first reaction is force:

Rosaura está en mi poder,
su hermosura el alma adora;
gocemos, pues, la ocasión:
el amor las leyes rompa
del valor y la confianza
con que a mis plantas se postra—

(ll.2954-59)

words which recall those of Act II:

y así por ver si puedo, cosa es llana
que arrojaré tu honor por la ventana.

(ll.1644-45)

But he overcomes his natural impulse and, far from dishonouring her, resolves to be the very champion of her honour:

¡Vive Dios! que de su honra
he de ser conquistador
antes que de mi corona!

(ll.2985-87)

He calls his men to arms and abruptly takes leave of her:

Rosaura, al honor le importa,
por ser piadoso contigo,
ser crüel contigo ahora.
No te responde mi voz,
porque mi honor te responda:
no te hablo, porque quiero
que te hablen por mí mis obras:
ni te miro, porque es fuerza,
en pena tan rigurosa,
que no mire tu hermosura

quien ha de mirar tu honra.

(ll.3001-11)

In the battle which follows, Rosaura's servant, Clarín, is killed. Clarín, attempting to evade the battle, is the one person who dies. His dying words are an insistence on the inevitability of death and on the futility of trying to avoid one's fate:

pues no hay seguro camino
a la fuerza del destino
y a la inclemencia del hado.

(ll.3085-87)

These words recall those of Basilio in an earlier scene of Act III:

Poco reparo tiene lo infalible,
y mucho riesgo lo previsto tiene:
si ha de ser, la defensa es imposible,
que quien la excusa más, más la previene.
¡Dura ley! ¡fuerte caso! ¡horror terrible!
Quien piensa huir el riesgo, al riesgo viene:

(ll.2452-57)

Basilio has tried to change the course of events by imprisoning Segismundo, just as Clarín has tried to avoid his own fate, and, like Clarín, he has failed. The words of the dying Clarín convince Basilio of the error of his ways, but his inference

son diligencias vanas
del hombre cuantas dispone
contra mayor fuerza y causa!

(ll.3101-03)

is wrong, and he is corrected by Clotaldo:

Aunque el hado, señor, sabe
todos los caminos, y halla
a quien busca entre lo espeso
de las peñas, no es cristiana
determinación decir
que no hay reparo a su saña.
Sí hay, que el prudente varón
victoria del hado alcanza.

(ll.3108-15)

Segismundo is soon to give ample proof of such *prudencia.* Clarín, as servant of Rosaura, belongs, strictly speaking, to the secondary action; but his role of *graciose* has here given way to a tragic role of particular relevance to the main theme. Clarín himself provides an example of the interlinking and interrelation of the characters of the two plots in the mind of Calderón.

Basilio's error is underlined when Segismundo enters in the final scene. Basilio has failed lamentably to change the course of fate, and, as the stars decreed, finds himself kneeling before his son. One person only has the power to overcome what fate has decreed for Segismundo: Segismundo himself, by his own free will:

Sentencia del cielo fué;
por más que quiso estorbarla
él, no pudo: ¿y podré yo
que soy menor en las canas,
en el valor y en la ciencia,
vencerla?—Señor, levanta.
Dame tu mano; que ya
que el cielo te desengaña
de que has errado en el modo
de vencerle, humilde aguarda
mi cuello a que tú te vengues:
rendido estoy a tus plantas.

(ll.3232-43)

Segismundo has again triumphed over his arrogant self.

Clotaldo, Rosaura and now Basilio owe their honour and their lives to Segismundo, sure proof of his conversion. Arrogance has given way to humility, cruelty to mercy. But the greatest and final proof of his conversion is still to come. The sparing of Clotaldo, Rosaura and Basilio bears witness only to the self-restraint of the new Segismundo. Self-denial provides the crowning proof. And it is Rosaura who makes this possible. Segismundo sacrifices the woman he loves for the sake of her honour; we have his own words for it:

Pues que ya vencer aguarda
mi valor grandes victorias,
hoy ha de ser la más alta
vencerme a mí. Astolfo dé
la mano luego a Rosaura,
pues sabe que de su honor
es deuda y yo he de cobrarla.

(ll.3251-57)

Since Calderón's ***La vida es sueño*** is composed of two quite dissimilar plots, the strength of its structure depends on their combination and interlinking. Plot and subplot are perfectly blended. Rosaura not only makes possible the conversion of Segismundo, but she provides the supreme proof of his conversion; Segismundo, in turn, is responsible for the clearing of Rosaura's honour.

The problem presented by a double plot and Calderón's achievement are thrown into relief if ***La vida es sueño*** is set against Lope de Vega's *Fuente Ovejuna.* The two plots of Lope's play derive from chapter thirty-eight of the Second Part of Rades y Andrada, *Crónica de las Tres Ordenes y Cavallerías de Santiago, Calatrava y Alcántara* (Toledo, 1572): first, the capture of Ciudad Real by the Order of Calatrava and its later recapture by the armies of Fernando and Isabel, and second, the rising of Fuente Ovejuna against its Commander Fernán Gómez de Guzmán. These plots have much in common: both are historical, both show the common people supporting and protected by the Monarchy in opposition to the Order of Calatrava, and in both right is on the side of the monarchy and the people. As well as these historical links, Lope makes Fernán Gómez, the tyrant Comendador, persuade the young Maestre of Calatrava to attack Ciudad Real, and take a leading part in the actual capture of the town. Both actions of *Fuente Ovejuna* are in the same spirit. But the technique of Lope is to isolate rather than unit them. The Fuente Ovejuna episode is expanded and elaborated. The outrages of the Comendador are particularized and shown against a traditional rustic background, and every significant incident is represented on the stage in action: the reception for the Comendador, the gifts of the village, the detaining of Laurencia, Fernando's clash with the Comendador, the Comendador's protest, the molesting of Jacinta, the defence of Mengo, permission for the marriage of Frondoso and Laurencia, the wedding celebration, its interruption by the Comendador, the decision to attack the Comendador, the attack itself, the death of the Comendador, the decision for concerted action, the arrival of the investigator, the questioning, and finally the King's pardon. All this action occupies some four-fifths of the play. The Ciudad Real episode, on the other hand, is used merely as a backcloth against which the incident at Fuente Ovejuna is set. The incident is not elaborated nor do its characters assume any particular importance. And it is presented as a narrative proceeding in short scenes of its own, used by Lope to break into the all-important events at Fuente Ovejuna. The narrative is eked out to provide bridge scenes for the main action. Though linked to the main action in spirit and though providing emphasis for Lope's theme, it is by no means essential to the play. Indeed, with but minor alterations, the play could stand with the secondary action removed.

Calderón's ***La vida es sueño*** could hardly provide a greater contrast. Here the subject matter of the secondary action is totally unrelated to that of the main action; the tone of the two actions, as Sr. Valbuena has remarked, [in his *Calderón,* 1941] is often quite different. For all this, however, Calderón has achieved a unity wholly lacking in *Fuente Ovejuna.* Two plots are woven together to form a single pattern, so much so that it may be misleading to speak of two plots. From the first scene to the last Rosaura is intimately linked with the fortunes of Segismundo, and Clarín, Clotaldo and Astolfo contribute to both main and subplot. The two episodes, so unlike in character, have been carefully fitted together to form one dramatic movement; its culmination in Astolfo's acceptance of the hand of Rosaura signifies at once the clearing of Rosaura's honour and the final proof of Segismundo's conversion. (pp. 293-300)

Dian Fox on the political dimension of *Life is a Dream:*

The idea of a dream or a fiction as a teacher or a surrogate experience is basic to Calderón's own function as playwright. He *can* control the elements of his drama. As an educated courtier of seventeenth-century Spain, Calderón is surely familiar with the theoretical arguments of writers like Rivadeneira, Mariana, Quevedo, and Saavedra Fajardo on the art of kingship. He is also a dramatist with the power to convey theory about many aspects of Spanish social life in a medium accessible to all. Calderón's work entertains. It also translates sometimes extremely complex moral and political principles into a language which speaks to the common man as well as to the courtier. Such plays as ***La vida es sueño*** re-create the experiences not only of men like Basilio and Segismundo, but also the rebel soldier. The audience is shown that a significant aspect of loyalty to one's king consists in peaceful protest when he errs. The royalty in the audience learns to prize a loyal opposition. All witness the success of discourse over violence, of justice tempered with mercy, of humility.

Dian Fox, in "Kingship and Community in *La vida es sueño,*" *Bulletin of Hispanic Studies LVIII, No. 3 (July 1981): 226.*

Albert E. Sloman, "The Structure of Calderón's 'La Vida es Sueño'," in The Modern Language Review, *Vol. XLVIII, No. 3, July, 1953, pp. 293-300.*

Edwin Honig (essay date 1963)

[*An American educator, translator, and author, Honig is highly regarded as a poet and as an authority on Spanish literature. In particular, his* Calderón and the Seizures of Honor *(1972) is respected for its scholarship and deep understanding of the Spanish code of honor. In the following essay, Honig lauds Calderón's* Life is a Dream *for its clear dramatic pattern and well-defined theme of the triumph of consciousness and experience over illusion. He also analyzes the various meanings of the play which, he argues, "grow, change, even multiply with each reading."*]

One can never completely account for the appeal of [***La vida es sueño***] because it is many-faceted and the facets change as one holds it up to scrutiny. It has the appeal of a mystery in which part of the life and energy that go to make it up is withheld, always being transformed into something different from the rigid terms and forms which are meant to contain it. Though the play follows a clear dramatic pattern and a well-defined theme, its meanings are not reducible but rather grow, change, even multiply, with each reading. We expect this condition to apply to all great literary works, but it is hard to show how it applies to a particular work. We see the clear design; then, beneath it, the baffling multiplicity of effects.

Yet there is a way into everything if not a way out, and for a way into this play I would like to borrow a few sentences from the late William J. Entwistle's excellent essay on Calderón's ***La devoción de la cruz*** ["Calderón et le théâtre symbolique," *Bulletin Hispanique* LII, 1950]. He is describing how Calderón habitually founded his characters and situations according to the tenets of Suarist theology, where

> The evidence of the senses is not denied, but it is checked and corrected. The world of phenomena is, admittedly, a dream, but there is a network of realities immediately underneath the surface and embracing the correlated postulates of all the sciences. It is this world which Calderón reveals in a number of his great plays.

Accordingly, Entwistle tells us, ***La devoción de la cruz***

> is, like any of the *autos,* a *representable idea.* The characters are individual exponents of leading principles. They are seen, so to speak, beneath the epidermis, in their essential structure.

Entwistle then concludes that

> Calderón's style is based, not so much on philosophy as on an aesthetic appreciation of philosophical arguments. He is not an original thinker, but an expositor. His philosophical position can be identified in the authorities whom he never questions. What enchants him is their coherence and austere beauty as an artistic whole.

I would not follow Entwistle to this conclusion. I am made uneasy by critical arguments imputing originality solely to a philosopher's way of thinking, as though the imaginative writer could not equal it in his own work so that he must import it from the outside in order to give his work some special dignity. This comes from an old problem of aesthetics that goes back to Aristotle's ethically oriented *Poetics;* we won't resolve it here. What I would like to do is to adapt two of Entwistle's observations: first, what is implied about the realism of Calderón's view of the world, "the evidence of the senses is not denied, but it is checked and corrected"; then, what is suggested about Calderón's realistic view of character motivation: "the world of phenomena is, admittedly, a dream, but there is a network of realities immediately underneath the surface . . . (where characters) . . . are seen, so to speak, beneath the epidermis, in their essential structure."

The first observation leads to a definition of the theme (the triumph of consciousness and experience) of a play which is a series of dramatic actions and soliloquies in the form of a dream vision. The second observation leads to a confrontation with the hidden life of impulse, which if fully understood in this play, would tell us a good deal about the intricate emotional dynamics that make not only ***La vida es sueño*** but a score of other Calderón plays such absorbing documents of psychological realism.

Dramatic actions and soliloquies in the form of a dream vision:

If the life of consciousness is the only life worth living, then Segismundo is clearly the only character who succeeds in attaining it. He emerges from the dream of life, which is the condition of all the other characters, to triumph over the sleep of death, the anonymity in which he is cast to begin with. The other characters are there to aid, block and test him along the way; their only conviction, with which they ceaselessly advise, bait and even torment him, is that life is a dream, the unregenerate condition which he has still to discover before he can be regenerated. The stages of his regeneration are marked off by a number of speeches he makes which other characters strategically overhear but do nothing to answer or to further in the narrative sequence of the play. Through these soliloquies Segismundo sets up certain rationales for behavior which he subsequently enacts in the plot of the play. The other characters, including Rosaura, who is closest to Segismundo as a quest character, are there to feed him with the possibilities of experience which will confirm his own gradual acquisition of consciousness along the way. This is typically what happens in dreams as well as in dream visions which are allegorical or didactic in purpose. There is an unalterable line to be followed which only the consciousness of a single actor may pursue since it is essentially from and through his consciousness that the real business and effect of the actions takes its meaning.

The triumph of consciousness and experience:

Inside the chained man in animal pelts in the tower is the prince of humankind. Another way to say this would show the distance, moral and psychological, which Segismundo must traverse in the course of this play. He must go from the lowest form of human life, the equivalent of the cave men, to the highest—the human being who most nearly reaches the condition of being civilized by fighting for everything while believing in the worth of nothing. (How could anyone who has hardly been born believe in anything?) Others may say life is a dream; he must prove it by the example of his own life, by living it. He must fight for the power he has been destined to achieve; but he must also abjure it, at the end, by pardoning his enemies and renouncing his love. (As Shakespeare puts it, "They that have the power to hurt and will do none / . . . They are the lords and owners of their faces, / Others but stewards of their excellence.") (Or, as Donne puts it, in "Th' Ecstacie," "Because such fingers need to knit / That subtile knot, which makes us man: / So must pure lovers soules descend / T'affections, and to faculties, / Which sense may reach and apprehend, / Else a great Prince in prison lies.")

The great virtue he will attain at the end is magnanimity, the quality of the highest civilized behavior. Battle in a just cause, the pursuit of one's honor, the attainment of knowledge and intellectual pride, and the unswerving course of loyalty are other virtues possessed by characters in the play. But none of these saves them from suffering desperation, an unresolved moral dilemma. Only Segismundo's attainment of consciousness and magnanimity frees the others; or—since they are characters in name only and really dream figures—enables the lesser virtues they represent to be seen against Segismundo's fundamental moral evolution.

Segismundo's magnanimity means nothing in itself; it must be won by experience, past which, as he himself says, "Pues que ya vencer aguarda / mi valor grandes victorias, / hoy ha de / ser la mán alta / vencerme a mí." ("I have other victories to win, / The greatest of them all awaits me now: / To conquer my own self.") This is no mere reiteration of the Greek adage; in the play it comes as a shattering renunciation of power politics, the life of tooth and claw, the deceits and delusions of intellectual pride, and the emptiness of filial piety. We see that to achieve magnanimity Segismundo must attain full recognition of who and what he is, through a course of action which includes an actual murder, several attempts at murder, parricide and rape. He must learn to love, he must learn to overcome himself, he must vanquish his father. It is not an easy formula. His career is a paradigm of several millennia of human history.

Confronting the hidden life of impulse: Rosaura, Clotaldo, Basilio, Clarin:

As in other Calderón plays that are overlain by a metaphysical problem, this play draws its vitality from the life of impulse covertly motivating the characters. It is as though by his strict insistence on the problem, Calderón's casual, almost incidental, intrusion of the impulsive life would not be noticed. Only the peculiarity of the resolution leads us to reconsider the theme, until we are startled by implications which we did not—and, it would seem by the author's design, could not—at first surmise. In this way we discover, and then are able to measure, the effect which the life of impulse exerts upon the dominant problem of the play.

It is clear, for example, that the subplot involving Rosaura and the honor question she is committed to resolve is thematically related to, even crucially feeds, Segismundo's attainment of consciousness. By vanquishing the need to possess her, he takes up her cause and shows himself capable of magnanimity. Yet on the level of hidden impulse it is important that the play begins with Rosaura's helpless fall, because this puts her directly in the way of the imprisoned prince who immediately feels an affinity for her—an affinity he can never consummate and must finally cast off.

When Rosaura first appears she is dressed as a man. (When she sums up her situation for Segismundo at the end of the play she will insist on this role as one of three disguises, the others being her disguise as a lady-in-waiting to Estrella and her final appearance as a woman fighting in a war beside Segismundo.) With each appearance in a different guise she affects Segismundo strongly and unaccountably. He himself tells her that she is like the gift of life to him, who is perhaps dead, perhaps not yet born. She curbs his rage, she fills him with the sense of wonder, which is love for a fellow creature, and she gives him his first taste of inner freedom, which is the beginning of conscious life, the sense of self. Later, when he is distraught by the doubts and delusions of others and sees her as a woman and wants to rape her in order to escape his fear, we recognize that she also serves as a tabu object—someone with whom he has identified himself too closely. In this way she serves (much as Julia, his actual twin, serves Eusebio in ***La devoción de la cruz***), as a surrogate sister whom he tries to violate, as if to challenge or escape the illusion that life is a dream, that he has no identity or potency as a man. Nevertheless, it is Rosaura whose three appearances help crucially to advance his self-recognition, leading him out of the animal cage into the daylight of moral consciousness.

Like Segismundo, Rosaura has a delinquent father in Clotaldo, Segismundo's tutor and keeper. Clotaldo's constancy is his main virtue—he will not let any other cause impede his service to the King. But we are made to see that his single-mindedness, even though it is praised at the end of the play, rests on unsound motives and a guilt-ridden past. For Clotaldo raped Violante, Rosaura's mother, and Rosaura is the product of that union. The token sword he left behind is a talisman for his conscience. It is introduced by Rosaura and becomes the means of revealing Clotaldo's fears—the same Clotaldo who even now would sacrifice his daughter-son (he does not even know which she is) in any matter of loyalty to a superior. Clearly Clotaldo's constance is a virtue that stands on weak legs, though it is not for that reason less adamant. But it is Segismundo, not Clotaldo her father, who rescues Rosaura from the honor dilemma and restores her identity as a woman. And it is Segismundo's magnanimity that spares Clotaldo, allowing him to sustain his own identity in continued loyalty to the King. In practice the virtue of magnanimity makes for a communion of effects, like a chain reaction.

In the case of Basilio, Segismundo's father, the life of impulse is more overwrought by rationalization and more protected by the majesty of his position. If Segismundo's progress toward higher consciousness is marked off by his soliloquies, Basilio's decline as a potent figure of authority is noted in his long, self-justifying speeches and by his fitful behavior in the presence of his son. We see him at first as a savant and a conscientious monarch eager to assure the peaceful transition of power on resigning the throne in order to pursue his extraordinary studies. But we soon learn that it is his intellectual pride, his boastful knowledge of the stars, which caused him to imprison his infant son as a monstrous tyrant-to-be. His uneasy curiosity to discover whether he has done the right thing initiates the action of the play, bringing Segismundo the young prince out of the tower and into the palace.

The guilt behind these rationalizations reveals itself when Basilio imputes to his son the murder of his mother in childbirth, and uses this as the reason for believing in the auguries of heaven. There is also his willingness to settle the crown on Segismundo's cousins, Astolfo and Estrella, by a gratuitous public test of Segismundo's unfitness to rule. Basilio's fears and pride allow him to deny the realistic auguries of experience, proof of which is brought to bear by Segismundo's sharp arguments. But Segismundo's arguments, the strongest of those set forth in the play, do not overcome Basilio; the power of arms he wishes to abjure and his own compounded fears are what overcome him. When these defeat him, he is ready as one who wishes "hacer . . . / un remedio que me falta" ("to take a cure I've needed for some time") to yield to Segismundo and to kneel to him.

But if there are mythical reverberations in Segismundo's struggle toward higher consciousness, something similar subsists beneath Basilio's psychological tremors, something that goes to the heart of the play. For here it appears that what Basilio is fighting is the blind fear of the succession of life, which he has suppressed by imprisoning his son. The power he seems so eager to resign he is actually wishing to preserve by transferring to remoter kin, by avoiding the issue of its true passage and transmission to a natural heir whose identity he has kept a secret and against whom he gathers all the other characters to conspire. He would make this conspiracy as effective as he believes he has made his boastful challenging of the auguries of heaven. The gift of life Rosaura has bestowed upon Segismundo is what Basilio has all the time been zealously withholding from him. And subsequently, when Segismundo's experience teaches him how to understand the caution, "life is a dream," he is ready to accede to the soldier's invitation to rebel against his father and actively wrest the power which Basilio has been so scrupulously hoarding. But to do so Segismundo must first break the conspiracy which prevents him from acting, surrounded as he is like a bull by bull-baiters cautioning him to accept the illusion of life as self-explanatory. It would appear that he must break this chain, the assault against his credulity and manhood, in order to be disillusioned and thrown back into the nullity of dreaming, before he can understand the use of power necessary to subject his father, and beyond that, the use of renunciation to cast off the illusion of false victory, which is the enjoyment of power for its own sake.

To effect such a transformation, Calderón employs the *gracioso* Clarín and the rebellious soldier in the final act. (Calderón has already used the palace servant for a similar purpose in the second act, when needing a violent example of a substitute sacrifice. There, Segismundo must be shown as unbearably vexed by the conspiratorial illusion he is not yet able to withstand, but when to strike out and kill any person greater than the presumptuous servant would disqualify him from filling the role of the magnanimous prince he must attain.) The heedless and arbitrary nature of power manipulation, especially when enforced by rebellion ("the people is a great beast"), is shown through Clarín. Because he babbles too much, Clarín is imprisoned in the tower and there mistaken by the rebels for the prince. Earlier, in the second act, the prince impulsively takes Clarín as an ally—"Tu solo en tan nuevo mundo / me has agradado." ("You're the only one / of the whole crowd who pleases me.") Clarín is incapable of illusion or disillusionment—he stands outside the course of events in order to comment on them from a nonmoral point of view. But now in the final act it is just such a point of view which Calderón finds crucially useful: first, as underscoring the folly of the power drive, and secondly, as providing a victim for the substitute sacrifice that must be made for Segismundo's tabu crime: a son overcoming a father, and worse, overcoming him, as the divinely appointed king, in an act of rebellion.

So Clarín's fate, to be shot to death while hiding from the battle, accomplishes two things. It shocks the King into accepting his own vainglory in opposing the designs of heaven, hence preparing him to succumb to Segismundo; it also releases Segismundo from the offense of rebellion. And when the dissident soldier is sent to the tower, we recognize that the order of constituted authority has been restored by Segismundo. Chaos and anarchy have been consigned to the house of illusion, sleep, and death. The tower itself is preserved; it is not destroyed. What Segismundo suffered in it others will continue to suffer. Segismundo himself points to this condition in the closing words of the play:

> ¿Qué os admira? ¿Qué os espanta,
> si fue mi maestro un sueño,
> y estoy temiendo en mis ansias
> que he de despertar y hallarme
> otra vez en mi carrada
> prisión? Y cuando no sea,
> el soñario solo basta;
> pues asĩ llegue a saber
> que toda la dicha humana,
> en fin, pasa como un sueño . . .
>
> Why
> Do you wonder? Why do you marvel, since
> It was a dream that taught me and I still
> Fear to wake up once more in my close dungeon?
> Though that may never happen, it's enough
> To dream it might, for thus I came to learn
> That all our human happiness must pass
> Away like any dream . . .

I have avoided going into the implications of the title of the play because I believe that it is a motif rather than a theme, that it runs its course through the play in a great variety of ways which Calderón himself enjoys interweaving, and that its significance is all-pervasive as a source of the mystery, not as a definition of the play's meaning.

> Porque quien miente y engaña
> es quien, para usar mal dellas,
> la penetra y las alcanza.
>
> They only lie
> Who seek to penetrate the mystery
> And, having reached it, use it to ill purpose.

This is said by Segismundo in his last long speech.

I have stressed the nature of the play as a dream vision in connection with the leading thematic concern it expresses for the triumph of consciousness. This appears to point to the way in which Calderón essentializes the thought and action as well as giving them the widest possible applicability in a strict dramatic form. Though it is Calderón's best play, it is not a religious but a metaphysical and moral play. Yet it shares with a good many religious plays and comedies of his, an anti-authoritarian bias. What is more, it aligns itself with such plays (say, ***La devoción de la cruz*** and ***El mágico prodigioso*** as well as ***El alcalde de Zalamea*** and ***La dama duende***) by a persistent exploration of the humane virtues—clemency, love, magnanimity, as against the combative principles of the power drive, vengeance, absolute law. In addition, in ***La vida es sueño,*** perhaps uniquely among Calderón's plays, a metaphysical problem is supported not by appeals to faith or insistence on ideality but by the proofs of experience itself. For the virtue of magnanimity to emerge in Segismundo, it must be shown to disprove the ideals which generate false pride, rape, murder, and perverted sexuality. By implication, the play is a criticism of inflexible rule, of self-deceptive authoritarianism masquerading as benevolent justice.

Appropriate to such criticism are Calderón's disclosures of the life of impulse which underlies the motivations of characters. Such disclosures often lead in his works to a formula whereby compulsive action, moral desperation, and distraught behavior must issue from sidetracked and guilty consciences: the pursuit of vengeance and the expression of doubt from the fear of infidelity, perverted love, and incest. But from this and other examples of his psychological realism we see that Calderón in his best plays is never merely a preacher or an upholder of abstract morality. He essentializes in order to identify; he dramatizes in order to characterize; and he particularizes experience in order to show the relation of misguided motives to the espousing of false ideals, and the necessity of earned perception for the attainment of humanly practicable ideals. This seems a lesson worth having and perhaps, also, opens a way to view and review many of Calderón's plays from a larger perspective than they have been used to receiving. (pp. 63-71)

Edwin Honig, "Reading What's in 'La Vida es Sueño'," in The Theatre Annual, *Vol. XX, 1963, pp. 63-71.*

THE DEVOTION OF THE CROSS

CRITICAL COMMENTARY

Edwin Honig (essay date 1972)

[*In the following excerpt, Honig considers* The Devotion of the Cross *analogous to the biblical account of humanity's fall from grace and its redemption through the cross of Jesus Christ.*]

In ***Secret Vengeance,*** where honor's agent is the king and its instrument is Don Lope, "membered to the body" of the state, the action is largely internalized through Lope's soliloquies. The legalistic development of the theme proceeds appropriately in secret, through definition of his state of mind, implemented by his conscientious strategy. Symbolic counterparts to this action appear in the critically realistic speeches of his servant Manrique, through the recurrence of elemental symbolism throughout the play, and through the various inset actions and witnessings which other characters introduce. Dramatically we are aware of a constant balancing and symmetry of processes; the play's highly schematized structure, based on the allegorical treatment of theme, makes for sharp but discrete doubling effects, like sounds counterposed to echoes and images counterposed to mirrored reflections.

No such thing occurs in ***La devoción de la cruz,*** 1633 (***Devotion to the Cross***). For here is a play in which the honor theme is eclipsed by an incest situation and transcended by an act of supernatural mercy. What seems more prominent is a blurring of dramatic action, an impression of structural imbalance, together with a thematic resolution which shocks belief. One reason for this difference between the plays is that the action of thought in ***Devotion*** is largely externalized; there is no nice thematic complementariness set up between auxiliary characters and the principal agents. And since the allegory is revealed in what the main characters do, the course of action must be viewed more generally; it must be taken as a continuous analogue to an archetypal situation of man's fall and redemption.

Although the play is structurally ragged and esthetically less satisfying than ***Secret Vengeance,*** it is more moving. As with [William Shakespeare's] *Hamlet* or [Christopher Marlowe's] *Doctor Faustus,* the dramaturgic failure is somehow overcome by the play's resonant tone of outrage and by the depths of implication at its center. The gross melodrama enforces a pathetic and strategically delayed action of self-realization, and this is achieved by a flouting of the very credibility which the play insists upon in order to make its point.

For us the play is problematic; for Calderón's contemporaries it was perhaps mainly a religious thriller, a lesson in heavenly clemency steeped in blood and spiced with incest. Our problem is not how to swallow the melodrama with its religious message in one gulp, which is what troubled nineteenth-century critics of the play. For us as for Albert Camus, who adapted ***Devotion to the Cross*** in French, neither the dramatic tenor nor the morality is necessarily anachronistic:

> Grace transfiguring the worst of criminals, goodness weakened by excessive evil are for us, believers and nonbelievers alike, familiar themes. But it was three centuries before Bernanos that Calderón in his ***Devotion*** provocatively illustrated the statement that "Grace is everything," which still tempts the modern conscience in answer to the nonbeliever's "Nothing is just" ["Avant–propos," *La Dévotion à la croix,* 1953].

To go further: the larger problem of belief depends upon how we understand the implications of honor and incest in the play. What, we may ask, has honor to do with incest and, if a real connection exists, does this account for the resonances we feel in the play as well as the shock of poetic justice underlying the thaumaturgic actions at the end? Unless we frame the problem in some such way we must stop with a literal reading of the play, and a literal reading leads into a tangle of absurdities.

Robert Sloane on *The Devotion of the Cross:*

La devoción de la cruz is an early work and it values instinct and passion in the way that later works will value thought. Eusebio feels, rather than thinks, yet the young Calderón evidently understands him well and is able to convey with considerable vividness the course of those feelings as well as the changing human context which gives rise to them. . . . If from Curcio's error we learn to be forgiving, it is from Eusebio that we learn the difficult lesson of maintaining faith at the very edge of despair. We are made to see again, not only the origins of wrongs, but the problem of living in a fallen world where error already holds sway. Though elements of the play seem strange and extravagant, they also lend their own kind of depth and verisimilitude to the characterization of that fallen world and the men who must populate it. For Calderón the allegorist may deal in abstract truths, but he is not at odds with Calderón the humane playwright who sees and deeply understands the men forced to live by them.

Robert Sloane, in his "The 'Strangeness' of *La devoción de la cruz,*" *Bulletin of Hispanic Studies LIV, No. 4 (October 1977): 309.*

Lisardo has challenged his friend Eusebio to a duel for daring to court Julia, Lisardo's sister, without asking permission of Curcio, their father. Eusebio, as Lisardo tells him, would not qualify as her suitor anyway since he is presumably not of noble blood. So Lisardo must now redress the blight on the family honor incurred by Eusebio's rash suit, and Julia must be made to end her days in a convent. Eusebio tells Lisardo the story of his strange birth at the foot of a cross and the charmed life he has led; then, vowing to have Julia at any price, he mortally wounds Lisardo. But, in answer to Lisardo's plea to be shriven, Eusebio carries him off to a monastery. Following this, Eusebio enters Curcio's house secretly, speaks with Julia, hides when her father appears and, after the body of Lisardo is brought in and Curcio leaves, Eusebio emerges and carries on an impassioned dialogue with her over the corpse. He finally leaves at Julia's bidding, promising never to see her again.

In Act Two Eusebio is a refugee from justice and the leader of a band of highwaymen, notorious for their crimes in the mountain passes and nearby villages. Eusebio spares the life of a traveling priest, Alberto, and exacts a promise from him to be shriven before dying. Next, he breaks into Julia's convent, where he is about to rape her when he discovers that she bears the same sign of the cross on her breast which he bears on his. Now he will have nothing to do with her, and escapes. She leaves the convent to search for him, although he does not know this. Meanwhile Curcio, who has been officially directed to capture Eusebio dead or alive, leads a group of peasants and soldiers through the mountain. There he reveals the story, partly hinted at in the first act, of his mistrust and jealousy of his wife Rosmira. We learn of the ruse by which he brought her to the mountains when she was pregnant and of his attempt to kill her there. We also learn that he left Rosmira for dead at the foot of the cross where she gave birth to twins. On returning home he found her, miraculously transported there with the infant Julia, the other child having been lost.

In Act Three Julia, disguised as a man, is captured and brought before Eusebio. Left alone with him, she first attempts to kill him, then is persuaded to tell her story, which turns out to be a fantastic tale of the multiple murders she has committed since leaving the convent. She is interrupted by the report of Curcio's arrival. When Eusebio and Curcio meet they are almost immobilized by a feeling of mutual sympathy. They fight briefly without swords and are interrupted by Curcio's men who chase Eusebio, then slash at him until he topples from the cliff and falls dying at the foot of the cross—the same one where he was born. Followed there by Curcio, he is at last acknowledged as a long-lost son, Julia's twin, and dies. Meanwhile the return of Alberto the priest causes the dead Eusebio to come back to life and call out the name of Alberto. The priest confesses him and Eusebio gives up the ghost a second time in a scene witnessed by Curcio and his group and by the disguised Julia and the highwaymen. Revealing herself now, Julia publicly confesses her crimes, but as her father advances to strike her she throws herself at the giant cross, which ascends heavenward, bearing her away with the dead Eusebio.

Many readers have been annoyed with the play's hypocrisy, its crude religious propaganda, and its perverse morality which pardons the apparently devout but unsympathetic criminal. But if one recalls the allegorical patterns observed in ***Secret Vengeance,*** it may become apparent that there is a general as well as particular way of making sense out of ***Devotion to the Cross,*** despite its odd morality.

Through Eusebio, its chief character, ***Devotion*** represents the figurative fall and redemption of mankind. As a figure for the fallen Adam, Eusebio is redeemed by the cross ("tree divine"), which bears him heavenward, and thus fulfills his "secret cause"—a prefiguration, as Adam in the Bible prefigures Christ. At infancy he is abandoned (assumed to be "lost") at the foot of the cross where, we learn later, his mother fell under the hand of his jealous father. Having no identity, Eusebio takes the cross as a totemic object which corresponds to the talisman etched on his breast like a birthmark. This makes him a candidate for salvation, as it does Julia his twin, who is similarly marked. As Eve may be said to have been Adam's twin, and as both were victims of the tree of the knowledge of good and evil, so Eusebio and Julia share a common destiny, part of which is to be restored through grace by the cross, the tree of eternal life. The implication of incest, which underlies the act of original sin in Genesis, is here metaphysically, if not sacramentally, material to Calderón's allegory. The reason for this is that Eusebio must learn who he is, which he can do only by discovering and rejoining Julia, his other half. But to do so he must relive symbolically the primal scene in the garden, whose analogue in the play is the convent where Julia, as "the bride of Christ," is immured.

Another analogue suggested here is that of the body and the soul, the twin or complementary entities. The soul (Eusebio) seeks to be restored to the body (Julia) from which it has been separated. When Eusebio finds Julia in the convent and is about to re-enact the primal deed, he dimly senses in her talismanic sign some heavenly purpose linking her to his secret cause. This foreboding makes him reject her, much as a figure of the new Adam, forewarned of his cause, would reject the old sexual crime—incest, original sin. Yet he must suffer Adam's fall literally as well as symbolically; and this occurs when Eusebio falls from the ladder by the convent wall. In her turn Julia, the rejected body and spouse, is separated by means of the same wall and ladder from re-entering the garden-convent. In ignorance of her destiny, she follows Eusebio and tries to destroy him. The crimes she commits on the way are, like Eusebio's earlier crimes, committed in blind outrage at having been separated from her other half.

In the worldly terms represented by the shepherds, Eusebio's and Julia's cause is criminally absurd. But since at the play's end, worldly discretion and justice are both foiled by the twins' heavenly ascension, it seems clear that it is the spiritual significance of the action, symbolically represented, which interested Calderón.

A Christian hero, Eusebio, like the heroes of all myths, is at the start unaware of his origin, though supremely conscious of some unrevealed fate he has been designated to fulfill. While still ignorant of when and how his fate will be revealed, and because he cannot know if his duel with Lisardo will end disastrously, he tells the story of his life, ticking off each miraculous episode as if to indicate his triumphs over mere earthbound, mortal forces. To Lisardo's grim reminder of Eusebio's inferior blood, Eusebio retorts, "Inherited nobility / is not superior to / nobility that's been acquired." He can say this because he knows he has a patent to act in ways that transcend a nobleman's prerogatives; his "escutcheon" is "inherited from this Cross." He has been tested and has triumphed before; he will triumph again: in the wilderness of the mountain, in the garden-convent, and finally—to his eternal reward when he dies—at the foot of the same cross where he was born. To that cross he is to speak later as Adam might have spoken to God, remembering the paradise tree: "Forgive me the injury / of that first crime against you." And again like Adam with foreknowledge of his sin, he will say, "I do not blame / my father for denying me / a cradle. He must have sensed / the evil that was in me." Eusebio's invocation to the cross at the end is shot through with transfigured consciousness:

> Oh Tree, where Heaven chose to hang
> the one true fruit to ransom man
> for his first forbidden mouthful!
> Oh flower of paradise regained!
> Rainbow light that spanned the Flood
> and thus pledged peace to all mankind!
> Oh fruitful vine, the harp of yet
> another David, and the tablets
> of another Moses:
> Here I am, a sinner seeking grace.

Eusebio has been transformed from the human agent of his crimes into a symbolic force voicing the redemptive hope of all mankind. In this way he defeats the exactions of earthly penalties, and incidentally overcomes the harsh, tyrannical laws of honor represented by Curcio, the father who survives his wife and all his children.

Yes, but what about the honor theme which is so abruptly transcended at the end of the play by divine law? The question of honor not only bulks large throughout the play but is also curiously altered in the light of Eusebio's cause. Further inquiry tells us something about the unconscious motivations supporting the honor code as shown in the implicit incest-relationship lividly darting forth from the root situation of the play. For as they affect human motives, the impulsions and repulsions of the characters, the conventions of honor relate to certain basic though unspecified taboos concerning the sexual assault of male upon female in the same family. But we must begin with the first recorded sexual relationship, in Genesis, and then go on to the society represented in Calderonian drama.

In effect the Genesis story demonstrates an archetypal incest situation inherent in man's disobedience, his fall from God's grace, and his knowledge of good and evil. Taken as a paradigm for man's earthly condition, the sexual crime called original sin derives from a transgression against divine command, a transgression that brings with it the knowledge of guilt. Presumably instigated by Eve, man rebels against a paternal authority, Jehovah, who punishes her accordingly: "I will greatly multiply thy sorrow and thy conception; in sorrow thou shalt bring forth children; and thy desire shall be to thy husband, and he shall rule over thee." Later in Genesis (5:2), one finds, "Male and female created he them; and blessed them, and called their name Adam, in the day when they were created." The creation of man and woman out of one body, the division of interests indicated between male and female, the transgression against authority, the sorrow of sex and childbearing, and the dominance of Adam over Eve are set down as almost simultaneous events and become an archetypal situation.

It is assumed, then, that Eve's transgression is congenital and innate: as woman, she will always rebel against the authoritarian principles. Eve, "the mother of all living," will be a divisive force in fallen society, just as she was in paradise. One way to counteract her innate rebelliousness is to idealize her, as the Middle Ages did: first, symbolically, by elevating the Virgin Mary as an object of worship; secondly, by lodging the image of woman as a venerated but scarcely attainable object in the tradition of courtly love. Another way is to bind her, as the prize and victim of transgression to a code of honor—a role descending from the courtly tradition and modified by the needs of an authoritarian society, typical of seventeenth-century Spain.

The peculiarly tight, claustrophobic condition of the honor code appears to derive from an already tense, anxiety-ridden view, featured in myth and religion, of woman's unreconciled position between transgressor and idol. In addition, this view is overlaid by the historical and social exigencies of an imperial Spain warring against Protestantism as it had for centuries warred against Islam. In this struggle the impossible myth of Spanish Christian purity and pure-blooded descent would have to be sustained against the millennial evidence of intermarriage with Berbers, Moslems, and Jews, not to mention cultural assimilation with other peoples of Western and Mediterranean Europe, going back to the Phoenicians. The avowal that one is an "old Christian Catholic," repeated so often in Renaissance Spanish literature, becomes a self-defensive cry; vainglorious and perversely aggressive, it reminds one of Nazi Germany's self-conscious Aryanism. Thus, where the invasion of one's honor is sexually directed, an attack on one's personal pure-bloodedness, with social and religious implications, is also immediately assumed.

In the autocratic society of Calderón's plays, every family seems to be a miniature Spain seeking to preserve itself against the real or imagined, but always chronic, invasions of lawless forces from the outside. That the laws of honor are inhuman and tyrannical—a protest constantly being voiced by Calderón's heroes—does not prevent their being fulfilled. And as they are being fulfilled, often in strictest secrecy, we are struck by the incredible, tragic strength of will involved in acting upon an impossible ideal according to an impossible sense of justice.

The fear of incest and the fear of sexual assault become one and the same thing; particularly notable in ***Devotion to the Cross,*** the same fear is evident in most of Calderón's honor plays. In addition, the incest barrier is complemented by the religious barrier between different faiths as well as by the social barrier between classes, and behind such barriers lurks the constant fear of contamination. Life under these circumstances is seen as warfare, catastrophe, and fatality, in which the vaguest hint of misdemeanor is as culpable as any number of overt murders. Where authoritarian justice rules, whether theocratic or monarchic, to think or to be tempted as a human being (the hero in ***Secret Vengeance*** exclaims, "How is it one thinks or speaks at all?") is as dangerous as to put one's thoughts and temptations into action. What makes the honor code so strange to us is that it is a reduction (often to absurdity) of an imperialistic legal structure, from its embodiment in ecclesiastical and state authority to an individual psychological problem, without any mitigation of its impersonal emphasis. What would justify legal punishment by state or church—the impersonal need to preserve the community against assaults by criminal or heretic—becomes bizarre when voiced as a rationale by human beings following the letter of the honor code. They act as though they had set some gigantic, superhuman machine in motion, which is just what they have done. What makes for further bizarreness is the unconscious irony with which they speak in rationalizing their human pride as the cause of justice while being ignorant that they themselves are part of the machine and that their voice is actually the voice of the machine. The pride they boast of concerns the acts and strategies of will—their skill, their cunning; what they do not know is that such pride is simply the fuel that makes the honor machine run. Human pride, then, frequently becomes a sign not of personal satisfaction but of the impersonal glorification of the legal structure; and the act which the human agents engineer in its name becomes a personal *auto da fé,* a self-punishing sacrifice in the name of a superpersonal faith.

That this makes for dramatic irony in Calderón's plays may be seen in the various views, ranging from satiric to sacramental, with which the central character's situation is regarded by other characters as well as the opposing views he has of it himself. The dramatic irony is further evident in the rapid glimpse we get of the hero's fate at the end of the play, where he appears at best a Pyrrhic victor, exhausted, wrung out by the machine, and hardly distinguishable from his victim. Dramatic irony is highly schematized in Calderonian drama, being part of, if not indeed the instrument for creating, a larger moral irony. It is interesting to see how the ironic form shapes the honor-bound figure of Curcio in ***Devotion.***

An aspect of the moral irony made explicit here is that the avenger complains against the tyrannical laws of honor, though they are the only laws he can follow in exacting his revenge. But an even more pronounced irony is that the object of Curcio's revenge, Eusebio, is redeemed at the end by a higher law than that of honor, so that the matter is literally taken out of Curcio's hands. Since the action of the play is allegorical, we can no more read this final turn of events realistically than we can any other part of the play. The literal meaning is apparent: Curcio is not avenged, and in not being avenged, the course of honor which he has pursued throughout is defeated. How then are we to take his defeat and, by clear analogy, since he is its implement, the defeat of honor? The obvious answer is that honor has been superseded by a miracle; the intervention of divine powers indicates that Eusebio is not to be punished, but having entered into a state of grace is, on the contrary, given his heavenly reward along with Julia. Curcio's last speech—his final remarks to the audience are simply conventional and do not count—is clearly a revenger's furious threat addressed to Julia, an intended victim: "I shall kill you with my own two hands, / and have you die as violently / as you have lived." She pleads to the cross, and as Curcio "is about to strike her," she embraces it and so is lifted heavenward with Eusebio. Curcio could not have been more plainly foiled, and to say that his vengence, including his authority for seeking it, has been superseded by divine intervention, does not seem a full or satisfactory answer. Apparently Curcio was mistaken—just as badly mistaken here, when about to kill his daughter, as he was earlier when striking at his innocent wife, who was similarly rescued by the cross. The deeper moral irony, then, is that the laws of honor, so assiduously upheld by Curcio, are indeed defeated and their justification, as enacted by their avenger here, is shown to be reprehensible on the highest possible authority.

Is honor here defeated or merely superseded? To seek a fuller answer to the question, one must rephrase it to accord with Curcio's allegorical role in the play. In what way is Curcio, the surrogate of honor and an omnipotent figure in the community, responsible for the fate which his family suffers? First, and most generally, it is evident that by accusing his wife of infidelity and seeking to kill her on admittedly groundless evidence, Curcio touches off a series of actions which ends with the death of his three children and his wife. Secondly, it is made clear that Curcio is temperamentally handicapped: he is prodigal, rash, desperate, and overweeningly proud. Some of these attributes are inherited and reinforced to his own detriment by his children, in a way suggestive of King Lear. Lisardo's brief appearance before Eusebio kills him seems at least partly intended to characterize his father.

> My father
> was a profligate who rapidly
> consumed the great estate
> his family had left him.
> In so doing, he was heedless
> of the straitened circumstances
> to which his children were reduced.
> And yet, although necessity
> may beggar one's nobility,
> it does not lessen in the least
> the obligations one is born with.

Following his inherited obligation, Lisardo must challenge Eusebio for lacking the noble qualifications to court his sister Julia. Lisardo's pronouncement concerning his sister, considering it is addressed to her lover who is also his friend, seems precipitous and mechanical, as though echoing a catechism learnt from his father.

> An impoverished gentleman
> who finds his fortune does not meet
> the requirements of his rank
> must see to it his maiden daughter,
> rather than pollute his blood
> by marriage, is taken off
> in safety to a convent.
> In all this, poverty's the culprit.
> Accordingly, tomorrow, my sister
> Julia will quickly take the veil,
> whether she wishes to or not.

Julia's subsequent report confirms the fact of her brother's anxious nature. Lisardo's face pales, drained by suspicion; he prevaricates—"snatched the key / impulsively, and angrily / unlocked the drawer," to discover the evidence of Eusebio's courtship; then,

> without a single word, oh God!
> he rushed out to find my father.
> Then inside his room behind locked doors,

the two of them spoke loud and long—
to seal my fate . . .

Lisardo is hardly distinguished from his father, whose purpose he is serving, before he is killed. Later, when Julia questions Curcio's decision to put her into a convent, his voice seems simply a magnification of Lisardo's catechism.

Right or wrong, my will
is all you need to know.

My decision will suffice, and that
has been resolved. The matter's closed.

Rebel, hold your tongue! Are you mad?
I'll twist your braids around your neck,
or else I'll rip that tongue of yours
out of your mouth with my own hands
before it cuts me to the quick again.

Curcio immediately identifies Julia's rebellion with her dead mother's, now impulsively finding "proof" where later he admits no evidence existed.

So at last I have the proof
of what I long suspected:
that your mother was dishonorable,
a woman who deceived me.
So you attack your father's honor,
whose luster, birth, nobility,
the sun itself can never equal
with all its radiance and light.

It is henceforth apparent that Curcio, hiding his defects behind the shield of honor, is steering a course which must victimize Julia as surely as he has victimized his elder son Lisardo and his wife Rosmira. Although victimized as well, Eusebio listens to a higher law in his worship of the cross. It would be possible to show similarly that Curcio's defects of despair, pride, and simple-minded credulity also influence the course of events. And though the exemplification of such personal defects would suffice to support the action in realistic terms, this is not what we get in ***Devotion to the Cross.*** What we get is allegorical action, action by analogy, by symbolic counterpart. By such action Curcio is predominantly a type of vengeful Yahweh, the thunder god in Genesis, the creator and punisher of the incestuous pair who exceeded the commandment and attained to a knowledge of good and evil—as in their separate ways Eusebio and Julia do. In the Bible the vengeful God is superseded by a sacrificed human God, who comes as Christ and redeems the Adamic sin. The code of honor, one might say, is similarly transcended in ***Devotion.*** It is transcended and defeated as a partial truth, but without being destroyed or removed—as the Old Testament is superseded by the New.

The attraction and repulsion which lead Eusebio toward and away from Julia, and which induce her to act in complementary movements, have been discussed in terms of the Adam and Eve analogy and the body-soul analogy. Similarly, a movement from repulsion to attraction is evident in the relationship between Curcio and Eusebio, and the effect is concentrated wholly in Act Three. Two of Curcio's speeches summarize this shift:

his chilling blood cries out
to me so timidly. And if
his blood were not my own in part,
it would not beckon me,
nor would I hear it cry.
How I hated him
alive; now how I grieve his death!

As soon as father and son confront one another, there is mutual affinity between them, though they do not know they are related. It is so intense a thing that Eusebio refuses to use his sword to fight Curcio. When they struggle barehanded, the sense of their combat is dreamlike—a scene reminiscent of the more famous father-son contention in ***Life Is a Dream.*** Unwilling to surrender to the law, Eusebio will nevertheless give himself up to Curcio, out of "respect." And Curcio, though he has long hunted Eusebio, suddenly offers to let him escape. He refuses, and when Curcio's men arrive, the father intervenes, suggesting to their astonishment the alternative of a legal trial: "I'll be your advocate before the law." But it is too late; the honor machine has already moved closer to its inexorable goal: Eusebio is mortally wounded by Curcio's men at the foot of the cross.

Despair leads Curcio to recognize the inefficacy of the honor machine and to admit a guilt he can no longer hide from himself. The mystery of the twin birth at the cross is a mystery which he, as the surrogate of honor and fallen pride, is not prepared to contend with. Mercy is not a principle which autocratic honor accepts. We witness Curcio's increasing helplessness, a condition which the avenging thunder god of Genesis might experience in confronting the imminent redemption of his "son," Adam, transfig-

Scene from a French production of The Devotion of the Cross, *1953.*

ured into Christ. But overwhelmed by the clemency of the cross, Curcio again astonishes his men by telling them to

> Take up this broken body
> of Eusebio's, and lay it
> mournfully aside till there is time
> to build an honorable
> sepulcher from which his ashen gaze
> may contemplate my tears.

They reply with the outraged disbelief of men who have also become cogs in the honor machine.

> TIRSO. What? How can you think of burying
> a man in holy ground who died
> beyond the pale of Church and God?
>
> BLAS. For anyone like that, a grave here
> in the wilderness is good enough!
>
> CURCIO. Oh, villainous revenge!
> Are you still so outraged
> you must strike at him beyond the grave?
> [*Exit* CURCIO, *weeping.*]

But there is still a last and clinching irony to account for. If Curcio admits the defeat of honor before the miracle of heavenly clemency, how can he suddenly revert to the vengeance principle at the end when he tries to destroy Julia? Curcio unwittingly instigates this turn and counter-movement by recognizing the mercy principle, and this recognition on his part calls for Julia's confession.

> CURCIO. My dearest son! You were not
> so wretched or forsaken
> after all, when in your tragic death
> you merit so much glory.
> Now if only Julia
> would recognize her crime.
>
> JULIA. God help me! What is this I hear,
> what ominous revelation?
> Can it be that I who was
> Eusebio's lover
> was his sister too? Then let
> my father and the whole wide world,
> let everybody know about
> my crimes. My perversions hound
> and overwhelm me, but I shall be
> the first to shout them out.
> Let every man alive be told
> that I am Julia, Julia
> the criminal, and of all
> the infamous women ever born,
> the worst. Henceforth my penances
> will be as public as the sins
> I have confessed. I go now to beg
> forgiveness of the world for the vile
> example I have given it,
> and pray that God forgive
> the crime of all my life.

When Curcio erupts and attempts to kill her, she pledges to the cross to "atone beneath your sign / and be born again to a new life," and the cross bears her away to heaven. If we can swallow the melodrama here, Calderón's serious purpose will emerge. Desperate and defeated though he is, Curcio still incarnates the vengeance principle—a principle which survives in him, even after he has been chastened by the higher law. In this he is like Eusebio, who represents the mercy principle ordaining that he survive his own death and be revived solely to be shriven. Because he embodies the honor code, Curcio must strike out as he does, spontaneously, against Julia's offense and dishonor. And her offense in this instance is precisely her public confession of guilt instigated by Curcio's wishful remark. For according to the code, the public admission that one's honor has been wronged compounds the wrong already committed against it. And so Julia's public declaration not only constitutes the last blow against her father's crumbling defenses but also makes explicit the cruel inoperativeness of the honor code when faced with a human cry for clemency. Julia's assertion that she will make her penances public is intolerable to honor and inadmissible to a code which categorically denies forgiveness. By implication there is no forgiveness on earth but only in heaven.

If as an honor figure Curcio cannot extend mercy, he is likewise incapable, as a figure for the Genesis thunder god, of offering reconciliation to Julia. And in the final exchange between the two, we are also reminded that Julia's "crime of all my life" is, like Eve's "crime," unforgivable in terms of the old dispensation in Genesis, where the sexual act is incestuous and the original crime of the creation underlies the discovery of good and evil. Significantly, it is when she learns of the incestuous relationship with Eusebio that Julia makes her public declaration. As a type of Eve, Julia is the quintessential criminal ("of all / the infamous women ever born, / the worst"), universally damned by authoritarian law. Only the figure of a sacrificed god, according to the new dispensation, can redeem her, as Eusebio does at the end. We see, then, that honor is a form of the old, merciless, unregenerate, earthbound, dehumanized, patriarchal law, which is ultimately self-defeating. It prevails to the end and presumably will continue to exist on earth, opposing the merciful, regenerative, humane, and matriarchal law of heaven, symbolized in the cross which has vanquished it.

At the conclusion of the play, where the cross triumphs so resolutely, so providentially, and so patently as a *deus ex machina,* we are inclined to minimize its connection with the rest of the drama. Yet its function throughout is not only essential to the theme but also integral to the action. One might say that the final appearance of the cross culminates many symbolic manifestations, from the start, of an extraordinarily complex role. And that role, in fact, is to serve dramatically as a complementary mechanism, a machine working in countermotion to the honor machine.

We first hear of the cross early in the first act in Eusebio's lengthy recital of the events of his life, while holding off Lisardo. Eusebio's story is eager, rapt, proud, enthusiastic. He has been the subject of strange, benevolent miracles; he rapidly imparts his sense of wonder and mystery at these happenings—and is never so confident again. The effect of the speech, more notable for the feeling it releases than for its literal sense, is to introduce a sensation of power and authority into a tense situation. Then tension leading to an impasse is exemplified in the opening scene of the play by the peasants Gil and Menga, vainly trying to drag their stalled donkey out of the mud. When Lisardo and Eusebio arrive, the impasse is augured in their pale, silent, distraught appearance. Gil describes them:

> My, how pale
> they look, and in the open fields
> so early in the morning!
> I'm sure they must have eaten mud
> to look so constipated.

Whenever the cross is introduced subsequently, the effect is similarly to dispel an impasse, initiate a contrary action, or metaphorically to lend a new dimension to the scene. Eusebio's cross "that towered over me at birth, / and whose imprint is now pressed / upon my breast" is a talismanic object which he serves and which actively serves him, symbolic of his paternity, a charismatic "symbol of some secret cause, / unrevealed as yet." And its "secret cause" gradually begins to emerge in a series of significant actions.

Lisardo's dying plea "by the Cross Christ died on" deflects Eusebio's sword and makes him carry the fallen man away to be shriven, an action which later aids in Eusebio's own redemption. When Lisardo's corpse lies between the divided lovers, Julia and Eusebio, there is a curious dramatic effect which the theatricality of the scene emphasizes. Curcio's two living children seem here to form the horizontal appendages of a cruciform figure whose vertical stalk is the dead Lisardo. As the pair speak across the corpse we realize that it is the only time when the three children are joined together in the play. Joined but also divided by the visible presence of the dead brother. That one power of the cross is to join and another is to separate will appear significantly again.

At the beginning of Act Two, Alberto, the priest, is saved when Eusebio's bullet is stopped by the holy book the priest carries in his tunic. The metaphor Eusebio uses underlies the merciful power of the cross to deflect the course of violence: "How well that flaming shot / obeyed your text by turning / stubborn lead softer than wax!" By this token Eusebio releases the priest who will reappear only once, in the third act, to confess him. The next reference to the cross occurs in Curcio's soliloquy describing the miracle which saved his wife after she protested her innocence at the foot of the cross, where he thought he had killed her. There the twins Eusebio and Julia were born, though, as we learn later, Eusebio was left behind when Rosmira was rescued by divine intervention and brought home with Julia. Subsequently, when Eusebio forces his way into the convent to violate Julia, he discovers that she, too, bears the imprint of the cross on her breast and fearfully withdraws. Here the cross serves to prevent the incestuous act, and in so doing separates the Adamic from the Christ figure in Eusebio. Julia and Eusebio are not meant to repeat the paradisiacal crime under the Eden tree; they must now be separated from one another. They are only destined to be joined in an act of heavenly redemption at the cross where they were born.

As we observed, when Eusebio falls from the ladder leaning against the convent wall, he symbolically enacts Adam's fall. Of this fact he seems dimly aware on rising:

> Oh Cross Divine, this I promise you
> and take this solemn vow
> with strict attention to each word:
> wherever I may find you,
> I shall fall upon my knees
> and pray devoutly, with all my heart.

Julia, too, vaguely senses that her destiny is to follow Eusebio's "fall" by way of the ladder, though she is not impelled by heavenly signs nor aware, as he is, of the cross's "secret cause." At this point she may simply be following the Genesis prescription—"and thy desire shall be to thy husband, and he shall rule over thee"—when she says, "This is where he fell; then I / must fall there too and follow him." Or perhaps she is feeding her desire with a later rationalization: "Does not my creed tell me / that once I give assent in thought / I thereby commit the crime?" Yet when she continues in this vein, we see that she has clearly identified her destiny with Eusebio's, though she may not know what that destiny is.

> Did not Eusebio scale
> these convent walls for me?
> And did I not feel pleased
> to see him run such risks
> for my sake? Then why am I afraid?
> What scruple holds me back?
> If I leave now I do the very thing
> Eusebio did when he entered;
> and just as I was pleased with him,
> he'll be pleased to see me too,
> considering the risks I've taken
> for his sake. Now I have assented,
> I must take the blame. And if
> the sin itself be so tremendous,
> will enjoying it be any
> less so? Since I have assented
> and am fallen from the hand of God . . .

In modern terms the covert incest motive may be fused here with the affinity science has noted between closely related persons, particularly twins, causing similar behavior patterns because of similarities between their neuroelectrical activities. But in Christian terms it is clear that once Julia "falls"—that is, makes the choice to descend the ladder—she is seized by the chilling evil of the symbolic act:

> I find that my esteem for mankind,
> honor, and my God is nothing
> but an arid waste. Like an angel
> flung from Heaven in my demonic
> fall I feel no stirring of
> repentance.

With this admission she becomes Eve, the transgressor in Eden and cohort of the fallen angel, the eternal rebel against the patriarchal order of society. Her rebellion is an assault against man's contempt, the authoritarian abuse of her fruitful power to love and to heal the divisive prohibitions which sacrifice individual men to its order:

> I am alone in my confusion
> and perplexity. Ingrate, are these
> your promises to me? Is this
> the sum of what you called your love's mad
> passion, or is it my love's madness?
> How you persisted in your suit—
> now by threats, now by promises,
> now as lover, now as tyrant,

till I at last submitted to you.
But no sooner had you become
master of your pleasure
and my sorrow than you fled
before you had possessed me.
Now in escaping you have
vanquished me entirely.
Merciful Heaven, I am lost
and dead! Why does nature provide
the world with poisons when the venom
of contempt can kill so swiftly?
So his contempt will kill me,
since to make the torment worse
I must follow him who scorns me.
When has love been so perverse before? . . .
Such is woman's nature that
against her inclination
she withholds that pleasure
which she most delights to give.

The capacity to sin is no different from the capacity to hurt and be hurt, perversely, against one's inclination. But to tell one's hurt, confess one's sin, and be forgiven are to triumph over the corruptions of evil enforced by social law. As Julia says, this forgiveness can be extended by the restorative power of providence.

faith teaches
there is nothing which the clemency
of Heaven cannot touch or reach:
all the sparkling constellations,
all the sands of all the oceans,
every atom, every mote upon
the air, and all these joined together,
are as nothing to the sins
which the good Lord God can pardon.

Contempt, scorn, division, separation, hopelessness, despair—these are the goads to crime and destructiveness. And this is what Julia recognizes when the ladder leading back to the convent is withdrawn.

Ah, but I begin to understand
the depths of my misfortune.
This is a sign my way is barred,
and thus when I would strive
to creep back, a penitent,
I am shown my own cause is hopeless.
Mercy is refused me.
Now a woman doubly scorned,
I shall perpetrate such
desperate deeds even Heaven
will be astounded, and the world
will shudder at them till
my perfidy outrages all time
to come, and the deepest pits
of hell shall stand agape
with horror at my crimes.

Understood symbolically, according to the dialectic of fall and redemption, male and female principles, and the subversion of humanity by the authoritarian necessity of honor, Julia's intentions and subsequent crimes are not the ludicrous things they appear to be when viewed according to cause-and-effect realism. They are the dramatic epiphanies of closely interwoven lines of thought, feeling, and action rising from all that "devotion to the cross" can imply. It is only the misuse of symbolic meaning which is ludicrous. Calderón makes this clear immediately following Julia's speech, at the start of Act Three.

Gil enters "covered with crosses; a very large one is sewn on his breast." The situation is reversed: a man is now following a woman's bidding," as Gil says with regard to Menga, adding,

I go . . .
scouring the mountainside for firewood,
and for my own protection
I've concocted this stratagem.
They say Eusebio loves crosses.
Well, here I am, armed from head to foot with them.

But Gil's cross is not charismatic. He sees Eusebio, hides in a bush and is immediately stuck with thorns. Eusebio at this point is brooding over the meaning of the cross inscribed on Julia's breast:

I was driven by the impulse of a higher power
whose cause prevailed against my will,
forbidding me to trespass on
the Cross—the Cross that I respect . . .
Oh Julia, the two of us were born
subject to that sign, and thus I fear
the portents of a mystery
which only God can understand.

Then the scene where he discovers Gil is oddly discordant, mixing serious and comic elements to such effect that Eusebio's cause appears ludicrous.

GIL [*aside*]. I can't stand it any longer;
I'm stung all over!

EUSEBIO. There is
someone in the bushes. Who's there?

GIL [*aside*]. Well, here's where I get tangled in my snare.

EUSEBIO [*aside*]. A man tied to a tree,
and wearing a cross on his breast!
I must be true to my word and kneel.

GIL. Why do you kneel, Eusebio?
Are you saying your prayers, or what?
First you tie me up, then you pray
to me. I don't understand.

EUSEBIO. Who are you?

GIL. Gil. Don't you remember?
Ever since you tied me up here
with that message, I've been yelling out
my lungs but, just my luck,
nobody's yet come by to free me.

EUSEBIO. But this is not the place I left you.

GIL. That's true, sir.
The fact is, when I realized that
no one was passing by, I moved on,
still tied, from one tree to the next,
until I reached this spot.
And that's the only reason
why it seems strange to you.

[Eusebio *frees him.*]

EUSEBIO [*aside*]. This simpleton may be of use

to me in my misfortune.
—Gil, I took a liking to you
when we met the other time.
So now let us be friends.

GIL. Fair enough,
and since we're friends I'll never
go back home but follow you instead.
And we'll be highwaymen together.
They say the life's ideal—not a stitch
of work from one year to the next.

Gil's mention of "the other time" refers to the occasion in Act Two when Eusebio found Gil and Menga in the mountains, tied them to tree trunks, and left them with a crucial message for Curcio—a message Gil failed to deliver. The message is about something Curcio does not yet know and through which Eusebio hopes for a reconciliation with Lisardo's father and to clear himself from the charge of murder. Eusebio does not know that Gil did not deliver the message, nor is it certain that if Gil had done so the course of events up to this point would have been altered. Gil's appearance immediately after Julia's speech at the end of Act Two, the absurd story he tells Eusebio about progressing "still tied, from one tree to the next," and Eusebio's curiously quixotic reaction to Gil's cross are all puzzling and disconcerting details. Gil's antics are as bathetic as Eusebio's devoutness is ludicrous, and both appear to be defects of taste and dramatic emphasis.

Considered symbolically, however, the scene is anything but bathetic or implausible; on the contrary, it comes as a sharp, immediate reminder of the opposing claims of honor and mercy, of vengeance and devotion, the very theme developed in the play's movements and countermovements which we have been tracing. In effect Calderón is reminding us that Eusebio's devotion is a cause squarely opposed to Curcio's vengeance, and that one has its provenance in a heavenly mystery symbolized by the cross as the other has in the code of honor. Troubled by the symbol on Julia's breast, Eusebio is caught off-guard when Gil's presence interrupts his thoughts. He does not know it is Gil; all he sees is the cross on Gil's breast, to which he automatically responds by kneeling respectfully, according to his vow. It is the symbol and not the man he responds to. The act immediately makes him out to be a fool—not the crazy fool Gil takes him for, but the "fool in Christ," the devoted servant of the cross. Gil, of course, has correctly guessed that wearing the cross will protect him from Eusebio, just as it saved Alberto, the priest, at the beginning of Act Two. What Gil does not understand is the objective power and principle of the cross; and we may see in his being entangled in the briers until Eusebio frees him an exemplum of this mistaken view. The absurd story he tells about moving, tied, from tree to tree, is an extension of his mistaken view because it supposes that Eusebio, though dangerous, is merely simpleminded. But the effect of Gil's story is to identify him and to bring Eusebio's attention away from the symbol in order to recognize the simpleton who is wearing it. Eusebio awakes to his own situation, his self-defensive strife against Curcio's pursuit of vengeance, in which Gil "may be of use" to him as one who knows the mountain passes. On the other hand, all Gil can conclude from Eusebio's offer of friendship is that the other's addiction to crosses somehow involves the charmed life of brigandage—"not a stitch / of work from one year to the next." The fact is, however, that Eusebio's situation is narrowing and, as later events show, he is ridden by anxiety and by the burden of his cause. He is fast approaching his own end, which will entail the complete revelation of heaven's secret symbolized by the cross. But while waiting for the mystery to unfold, he must contend with Curcio's vengeance. So he acts feverishly, half terrified, half audacious, as a man aware of some impending catastrophe would act.

This is notable in his response to Julia, who has reappeared dressed as a man, and who after attempting to kill him has told the story of her crimes. He says:

I listen to you fascinated,
enchanted by your voice,
bewitched by everything you say,
although the sight of you
fills me with dread . . .

I fear Heaven's
retribution looming over me . . .
I live in such horror of that Cross,
I must avoid you.

His anxiety is also apparent in the orders he gives his men, and later in his hand-to-hand encounter with his father.

I do not know what reverence
the sight of you instills in me.
But I know your suffering awes me
more than your sword . . .
and truth to tell, the only
victory I seek is to fall
upon my knees and beg you
to forgive me.

And so it is almost with relief that he receives the mortal wound at the hands of Curcio's men. He can at last yield to his father and die; but also—and this he does not know—he is to be resurrected in order to receive absolution at the foot of the cross where he was born. In this way his destiny is fulfilled, his secret cause revealed, his life career run full cycle. But there is also the posthumous miracle of his heavenly ascent which includes the sanction of Julia. Besides proving Julia's earlier declaration about the clemency of Heaven, this last miracle reclaims her from the perversely male-dominated role of revenger ("the symbol / of terrifying vengeance") in which the honor machine has cast her. There is perhaps a conclusive irony in this last turn: that the monolithic, all-pervasive engine of the honor machine on earth can only be transcended by the more powerful, absolutist machine of heavenly mercy. (pp. 53-80)

Edwin Honig, in his Calderón and the Seizures of Honor, *Cambridge, Mass.: Harvard University Press, 1972, 271 p.*

THE DOCTOR OF HIS HONOR

CRITICAL COMMENTARY

Bruce W. Wardropper (essay date 1958)

[*Wardropper is a Scottish-born educator and linguistic scholar. In the essay below, he examines* The Doctor of His Honor *as poetry, asserting that the medical imagery of the play constitutes an extended metaphor underlining the work's tragic essence.*]

Drama criticism in the Hispanic field tends to be somewhat old-fashioned. Hispanists usually regard the theatre of the seventeenth century as though it were drama in the post-Romantic sense. They judge it by its degree of realism, by its value as a social document, by its fitness as a vehicle of ideas. If they analyze it esthetically it is to the dramatic structure or the characterization that they point. They seek in it drama, not poetry. They apply criteria which may be perfectly valid in discussing Ibsen, Shaw, or Benavente, but quite inappropriate to the later O'Neil, T. S. Eliot, or García Lorca. The fact is that twentieth-century "poetic drama" has more in common with the theatre of the Golden Age than had the theatre of ideas which preceded it. But here a possibility of confusion must be eliminated. The "poetic drama" of our day is a revival, a break with tradition; its proponents are apt to regard poetry as ancillary to drama. The theatre of Lope and Calderón, on the other hand, is a continuation of a poetic tradition established in the sixteenth century, an age when, with a few exceptions such as Torres Naharro's and Lope de Rueda's plays, dramatic performances were little more than complicated recitals of lyric poetry. In both centuries of the Golden Age—as in classical antiquity—dramatic, lyric, and epic poetry are simply species of the genus poetry. Not for nothing is the dramatist called a *poeta.* Dramatic poetry has a long, strong tradition behind it: it differs from "poetic drama" in that it makes drama—action, character, dialogue—serve poetry, and not the other way round.

Some Hispanic critics have felt pangs of conscience about neglecting the poetry in drama. But their reaction has often been misguided: they have counted verses for non-poetic reasons; or they have, following what may well be an ironic treatise by Lope de Vega, attempted to force certain phases of the action into particular metrical molds. The poetic in drama is not reducible to such mechanics and arithmetics. I suggest that dramatic poetry might be studied in much the same way as one studies lyric poetry. And this recommendation is hardly revolutionary. Our colleagues in other literary disciplines have been doing this for years. As an illustration of what I mean I should like to examine one aspect of the poetry of ***El médico de su honra***: its imagery.

This play is usually studied for the light it sheds on an area of the history of ideas: the meaning of *el honor.* No ideological problem in Spanish literature is in greater need of restatement. Américo Castro and García Valdecasas have probably, in their learned and valuable studies of this question, created as much confusion as enlightenment. The reason for this is that they start with the assumption that the honor code reflected in the theatre is a social phenomenon that can be illustrated indifferently by means of dramatic, casuistic, or sociological texts. Because they see the problem as one and indivisible—and, polemically, as an essential part of the *problema de España*—they have been baffled by its many contradictions: the variations between attested practice and the drama, and the differing interpretations as between one playwright and another, or even between one work and another in the corpus of a single writer. The student of literature, however, should be satisfied if the problem is presented coherently in each individual play he reads. The work of art is autonomous at least to this extent: that it contains its own rationale. It is probable that, without knowing what the *Siete partidas* or the sixteenth-century casuists had to say about honor, one does a better job of reading a *drama de honor.* Each play is sufficient unto itself. With this principle in mind we shall disregard the code—or sentiment—of honor in its broader implications, and concern ourselves with it only to the extent that it impinges on the imagery of ***El médico de su honra.***

Now, the first point that strikes one about the imagery is that the whole play is a complex extended metaphor. Don Gutierre, the protagonist, who suspects his wife—quite wrongly, as it turns out—of having brought dishonor on his good name, regards himself as a metaphorical physician. Influenced by this poetic vision of himself he finally concludes that, to cure his sick honor, he should call in a real—literal—blood-letter, a *sangrador,* to bleed his wife to death. Don Gutierre not only regards himself in this poetic way, but succeeds in making other characters in the play see him in the same light. A simultaneous equation, based on this fundamental image, is thus set up. Don Gutierre equals the physician; Doña Mencía, his wife, the repository of his honor, equals the patient; dishonor equals the malady. It follows that Don Gutierre makes a diagnosis and prescribes a remedy; the *sangrador,* the equivalent of the modern *practicante,* carries out his instructions. As doctors sometimes do, Don Gutierre makes a wrong diagnosis. As doctors sometimes do, Don Gutierre kills the patient with his treatment. But here the analogy breaks down: real physicians kill by accident; Don Gutierre *prescribes* death. With blood he cures the malady, but not the patient.

Calderón's plays are often, like ***El médico de su honra,*** extended metaphors, ***La vida es sueño, La dama duende, El pintor de su deshonra, El gran teatro del mundo***—in all branches of his dramatic art we can find examples. An equivalence which has no logical validity (and which, as we have seen, may not even have an absolute autonomous logic) is assumed to have a poetic validity. It is fearlessly worked out down to the last detail, including the possible analogical breakdown, which is never glossed over. This is, of course, a technique that lends itself most effectively to the elucidation of a Christian mystery in an *auto sacramental.* But since life in the world also has its mysteries (honor, love, the behavior of the other sex . . .), the same device will apply. It is nothing new either in lyric or dramatic poetry. Calderón's strength lies in the rigor with which he applies his conceit, the intellectual subtlety and ingenuity which made the *idea*—to cite a well-known phrase—*representable.*

In Calderón's *autos sacramentales* such fundamental dramatic metaphors may be so far-fetched that they strike more squeamish ages as irreverent, if not blasphemous. An intellectual consistency is the poet's only ground rule. The image often is unheard-of, new, daring. In the *comedias* of Calderón the spectator's need to recognize in the *idea representable* a world familiar to his senses and to his experience, a plausible vital situation, imposes a limit on the metaphor's scope. But even here the esthetic doctrine of *admiración*—the new catharsis, a newly accepted synthesis of Aristotelian terror and pity—requires the metaphor to be startling. And in ***El médico de su honra*** it is indeed startling, particularly in the dénouement, that is to say, in the consequences drawn from the rhetorical comparison implied in the title. This is, says the King,

> el suceso más notable
> del mundo.

And Don Gutierre himself is impressed with his own dramatic conceit. Speaking to the King he says:

> y de la mayor desdicha,
> de la tragedia más rara,
> escucha la admiración,
> que eleva, admira, y espanta.
>
> (217b)

The metaphor is what carries the tragedy with its ennobling effect and its wonder and fear.

The dramatic effect, in other words; hinges on the plausibility of the basic poetic metaphor. Calderón ensures poetic belief by establishing his more significant images on a nonmetaphorical precedent. For example, in the case of our basic dramatic metaphor Doña Mencía suffers a metaphorical fall—a fall from honor—as a result of which she needs a rhetorical, though dramatically presented, medical treatment. This ending—the *novedad,* the source of *admiración*—is, however, anticipated at the beginning of the play when the Infante Don Enrique, the cause of Doña Mencía's honor troubles, falls literally from his horse, and is in need of medical attention. In this way the rhetorical figure is carefully grounded in the literal. The polarizing of the play around the two falls implies, of course, much more than an acceptable metaphor: there is a certain irony in the whole situation which links the Prince and Doña Mencía as the two tragic victims; there is structural coherence; there is, possibly, an almost medieval sense of the allegory of human life. I am here concerned, however, only with the implications for the imagery. It is worth pointing out because it is the most significant—not the only—example of how Calderón proceeds from the real to the figure of speech. As a further illustration one might quote the compact speech of Don Gutierre in which he passes from an allusion to his actual imprisonment and temporary release to the topos of the prison of love:

> El alcaide que conmigo
> está, es mi deudo y amigo,
> y quitándome prisiones
> al cuerpo, me las echó
> al alma, porque me ha dado
> ocasión de haber llegado
> a tan grande dicha yo,
> como es a verte.
>
> (199b)

To return to the basic image of ***El médico de su honra***: it is obviously an adaptation of a traditional metaphor—love as an illness for which remedies must be prescribed. There is no need to do more than hint at the bare outline of this tradition. Ovid's amusingly ironic *Remedia amoris* popularizes the idea that lovers are sick men; Arnaldus de Villanova, the thirteenth-century physician, in his discussion of *herosis,* the lover's malady, takes Ovid seriously, and embodies his suggested remedies in a medical treatise; in Spain the *cancionero* poets repeatedly declare themselves to be love-sick, while in the same fifteenth century Celestina invokes Melibea's sympathetic aid as a physician for the stricken Calisto. In Lope, Alarcón, Tirso, the metaphor proliferates. In Calderón's play it is given some significant variations: the theme has become *Remedia honoris,* not *amoris;* the emphasis has shifted from patient to agent (the physician, not the sick man, has the problems); the metaphor is not only an embellishment of the poetic language, it is incorporated into the dramatic action. A worn cliché has been renovated by a consummate artist.

Now, in progressing from the remedies of love to the remedies of honor Calderón has moved into the territory of tragedy. The honor play, rare as it is, is the typical tragedy of the baroque. This is a fact which has escaped those critics who, ignoring dramatic poetry, restrict their attention to dramatic situations. Dramatically speaking, there is little difference between a *comedia de capa y espada* [comedy of cloak and sword] and a *drama de honor* because the same devices and motivations are used in each. Both dramatic genres rely on concealment of motivation, on eavesdropping, on mistaken identity, on confusion of all kinds. But there is one essential difference between them, a difference which prizes them as far apart as comedy and tragedy. The *comedia de capa y espada* presents unmarried couples; consequently love, not honor, is the predominant motivation; jealousy is *celos de amor,* slightly ridiculous because, even though promises may be involved, the man has no abiding claim on the woman—there is no law, civil or moral, to prevent the breaking of the troth. A confusion resulting from courtship can be resolved with no worse results than the indignity or discomfiture of the lover. There is no threat to life. What we have, then, in the *comedia de capa y espada* is the comic treatment of potential, but not actual, honor tragedies. The *drama de honor,* on the other hand, presents married couples; conjugal honor has largely replaced possessive love as the dominating motive; jealousy, *celos de honor,* is either admirable or base, but never silly. This, as Cervantes has pointed out, is because marriage involves a sacramental relationship; therefore, where honor is threatened God is interested. At the wedding two fleshes have become sacramentally one; since in the honor play this single flesh has been diseased, the only recourse open to the man—the "head" of the union—is to amputate ("And if thy hand offend thee, cut if off"—Mark 9:43), or, in human, non-sacramental terms, to kill the offending wife. Only death can sever the sacramental union of the sexes. It follows that life is endangered by the sacrament of matrimony. Tragedy, then, with its catharsis of *admiración,* its divine participation, its threat of death, is characteristic of the honor play. And this—far more than the questions that are usually raised about the nature of honor—is the poetic significance of the *drama de honor.* In the specific case of ***El médico de su honora*** we err if we fail to recognize that, in spite of the conceivable "happy ending" from Don Gutierre's point of view, it is a tragedy—a tragedy of the baroque, one not quite like that of Sophocles, Shakespeare, or Racine, but with some points of contact.

The realization that the play is a tragedy brings into focus esthetic relationships which, seen otherwise, are unrelated. Don Gutierre's dishonoring of Doña Leonor, before the action begins, is no longer seen merely as a comment on his character. This detail is a part of the tragic web of circumstance. Doña Leonor *devoutly* wishes for revenge. At the climax of Act I it is with a prayer that she expresses her hope that Don Gutierre in his turn shall be dishonored:

> ¡El mismo dolor
> sientas que siento, y a ver
> llegues, bañado en tu sangre,
> deshonras tuyas, porque
> mueras con las mismas armas
> que matas, amén, amén!
>
> (197b)

When this prayer is granted one senses an interference of God: a providential righting of accounts which brings Don Gutierre and Doña Leonor together. The play ends with Doña Leonor almost ritually accepting her role in the honor relationship, agreeing to live tragically with a suspicious man, under constant threat of death:

> D. GUT. Mira que médico he sido
> de mi honra: no está olvidada
> la ciencia.
>
> DA. LEO. Cura con ella
> mi vida, en estando mala.
>
> D. GUT. Pues con esa condición
> te la doy.
>
> (219)

The innocent Doña Mencía, when the play is seen in this light, has been nothing more than a pawn in a tragic chessgame, played under divine supervision. Savagely, but almost incidentally, she is liquidated. She has been merely an obstacle to the righteous union of Don Gutierre and the woman he has dishonored; the pathos lies in the fact that she is a human, sentient obstacle. She is, without being in the least heroic, a tragic victim.

But the tragedy has even wider scope. Don Enrique sees his fall from the horse as "agüero / de mi muerte" (190a). His tragedy, though it resides in history rather than in the scheme of the action, is as assured as Doña Mencía's. The King, too, takes Don Enrique's accidental cutting of his hand—when the dagger is being returned—as a symbol of his own assassination, a concern of history which lies beyond the limits of the action. A political dimension is in this way given to Don Gutierre's private sorrow. A hint is even given of the determinism of the stars: Don Enrique tells us that he was born unlucky, and Coquín says of Doña Mencía that she was an unhappy woman, "perseguida de su estrella" (217a). The cosmos is interested in the fate of the two tragic victims.

The action of the play is governed, as we have said, by the fundamental medical imagery, the *idea representable* of the title. But there are three other sets of images which reflect the tragic web of circumstance. One cluster is rooted in mythology and heavenly bodies. Usually, above all in the *comedias de capa y espada,* celestial images—*sol, arrebol, estrella,* and the like—are reserved for descriptions and invocations of the beloved; mythological allusions refer to anything exalted. In ***El médico de su honra*** such terms are applied only to royalty—to the King and, occasionally, to his brother—in its function as the fountainhead of honor. Inasmuch as the King supervises affairs of honor in his realm (this is his function in the play) and honor is the "patrimonio del alma" ("El honor es reservado / lugar, donde el alma asiste" [210b]) we see in this imagery of perfection reminders of divine surveillance over the action through the King's mediation. Honor is a striving for perfection in worldly terms, but it is also a reflection—a pale reflection, it is true—of a divine moral code.

Against this divine perfection, represented by celestial and mythological images, there is man's imperfection—his limitations, his errant nature, his failure to follow the light he sees. This human imperfection is conveyed by images of doors and prisons, of sport (conceived perhaps as a dilution of war), and of academies of learning. These are images of restraint and constraint: lovemaking, matrimony, and honor deprive man of his liberty; honor imprisons love. Formal virtue smothers Don Gutierre's internal guilty thoughts; his self-incrimination over his conduct towards Doña Leonor is held in check.

***El médico de su honra* is not, as it has often been taken to be, a treatise on honor or a document illustrating a social custom alien to the modern reader. It is a highly moving tragedy, thoroughly explicable in terms of the play itself, and organized around a body of poetic imagery which, though not logical in the logician's sense of the word, contains its own rationale.**

—Bruce W. Wardropper

Finally, there are the cosmic images, such as those based on meteorology and the elements. All four elements are present—as is usual with Calderón—in the description of a horse. But elsewhere the elements are taken singly. The play, after all, is ethical, not metaphysical, in its range. (In this it differs from such plays as ***La vida es sueño,*** where Wilson's typical pattern of element-imagery can be seen in its greatest rigidity [see E. M. Wilson's "The Four Elements in the Imagery of Calderón," *Modern Language Review* XXXI, 1936]. We are here not concerned with the tense truce among the four bellicose elements that so greatly fascinated Calderón. We have rather an insistence on one predominant element, Air, in its private war with Fire. A good example is Don Gutierre's explanation to his wife about the breeze that put out the light:

> ¿No has visto ardiente llama
> perder la luz al aire que la hiere,
> y que a este tiempo de otra luz inflama
> la pavesa? Una vive y otra muere
> a sólo un soplo. Así, desta manera,
> la lengua de los vientos lisonjera
> matar[te] la luz pudo,
> y darme luz a mí.
>
> (208b)

Around this basic cosmic image—*aire, viento,* etc.—are gathered reinforcing images of nature: *blood,* 'rose'; *mountain,* 'jealousy'; *basilisk,* 'love'; *weeds,* 'dishonor'; *light,* 'life'; *night,* 'death,' etc.

This imagery, which has of necessity been sketchily described, creates in the poetry of ***El médico de su honra*** a sense of tragedy, a private grief in an interested universe. But, just as the fundamental medical metaphor fluctuates between speech and action, so too does a great part of the other imagery. An important symbol in the play, for example, is the light which is repeatedly extinguished while Doña Mencía is sitting in the garden. Sometimes it is put out by the wind: Air has won a battle over Fire, rumor over reputation. At other times a human agency is responsible:

> D. GUT. Mato la luz, y llego,
> sin luz y sin razón, dos veces ciego.
>
> (207a)

In either case the extinction of the light serves to conceal the fact or the presumption of dishonor. The phrase *matar la luz* [to kill the light], presented dramatically rather than verbally, is the symbolic link between the extinction of honor and the extinction of life. "Muerte a las luces, a las vidas muerte" (208b), cries Don Gutierre. The symbolism is present to his mind, as well as to the spectator's, but Doña Mencía, in her innocence, cannot think thus ambivalently. It is a private rite that Don Gutierre celebrates when he extinguishes the light for one last time at the moment of Doña Mencía's death:

> LUD. [. . .] en este instante
> el hombre mató la luz
>
> (216a)

El médico de su honra is not, as it has often been taken to be, a treatise on honor or a document illustrating a social custom alien to the modern reader. It is a highly moving tragedy, thoroughly explicable in terms of the play itself, and organized around a body of poetic imagery which, though not logical in the logician's sense of the word, contains its own rationale. Its full flavor can be savored only when the reader casts off modern prejudice, and approaches the work as dramatic poetry. (pp. 3-11)

Bruce W. Wardropper, "Poetry and Drama in Calderón's 'El médico de su honra'," in The Romanic Review, *Vol. XLIX, No. 1, February, 1958, pp. 3-11.*

Roberta J. Thiher (essay date 1970)

[*In the essay that follows, Thiher explores ambiguity as part of the design of* The Doctor of His Honor *in an attempt to explain the genesis of this "ambivalent" and "open" tragedy.*]

Calderon's plays, though concerned with problems and dilemmas, are seldom morally ambiguous. ***El príncipe constante,*** for example, if it is read with close attention to textual detail, leaves the reader in no doubt as to Calderón's judgment of characters and events. ***La vida es sueño*** may leave him uncertain how far to press the metaphor of the title, but the moral case for altruism over selfishness is compelling. Calderón is, in the best sense of the word, a dogmatic writer. It is all the more surprising, then, when despite one's best efforts at interpretation an occasional play leaves one unsure of its moral position. Cervantes' works are usually, in this sense, open; Calderón's are closed, although his honor plays seem to invite the reader to speculate about the way in which they must be taken.

El médico de su honra is the most ambiguous of Calderón's dramas. While its dramatic cohesion is rigorously precise, the reader is left bewildered. He has difficulty in answering a number of questions. Is Mencía guilty of loving Enrique after her marriage to Gutierre? Is Pedro a cruel or a just king? Does Pedro condone or condemn Gutierre's crime? Is Leonor justified in searching for retribution for her lost honor? Whereas in ***La vida es sueño*** it is the character Segismundo who is lost in a labyrinth of *engaño* [deceit], in ***El médico de su honra*** it is the reader who is in a maze as he seeks a way out of his doubts regarding the motivation of the characters and the meaning behind their statements. The fact that ambivalence is present is obvious. A poet of Calderón's immense skill can hardly be suspected of having written a play in which the ambiguity is accidental. The ambiguity must, then, be a part of his design. The reasons for his writing such an open play need to be discovered.

The lack of clarity seems to stem from the fact that Calderón is saying to us much the same thing that he says in ***La vida es sueño*** or ***El gran teatro del mundo***: the world is a stage, often a serious, bloody, tragic one, but still a stage on which the illusion of temporal life is presented. What we men perceive, or think that we perceive, is often deceptive, but as characters required to act on that stage, we must play our roles until the curtain falls. The tragedy lies in the way we choose to play our assigned roles, whether with prudence or passion. Acting passionately compounds the deception of the temporal world itself, as Segismundo came to realize. Similarly, the one character in ***El médico de su honra*** who also learns the lesson that all men's perceptions lead to ambiguity and deception is Pedro the Cruel (or Pedro the Just). An examination of his role within the play and the reasons supporting his final pronouncement on Gutierre's crime will show how Calderón illustrates his idea that our perceptions of this world ultimately offer only uncertain knowledge.

Since Pedro, as the king, is the ultimate dispenser of earthly justice, and since it is he who must decide whether Gutierre's action is to be condemned or condoned (thereby incidentally passing judgment on Mencía's possible guilt), we must first estimate the worth of his authority as a judge. Cyril A. Jones [in his edition of ***El médico de su honra,*** 1958] has called Pedro an "odd mixture, cruel, just, and recklessly generous by turns." As we have seen, some critics, such as A. E. Sloman [in his *The Dramatic Craftsmanship of Calderón*, 1958] and Edward M. Wilson [in his "Gerald Brenan's Calderón," *Bulletin of the Comediantes* VI, No. 1, 1952], tend to view him as a cruel king; others, like Watson [in his "Peter the Cruel or Peter the Just," *Romantisches Jahrbuch* XIV, 1963], see him as a just king. The fact is that Calderón has given Pedro *both* of these possible roles, reflecting the ambiguity with which his reign has been interpreted by history. In many cases Pedro's actions are so inscrutable that the reader can find arguments to support either thesis. The opening scene provides a good illustration. When Pedro leaves his wounded brother Enrique in order to continue on to Seville, he appears to leave him in a rather cavalier manner:

no me quiero detener
hasta llegar a Sevilla.

I.23-4

Yet, at the same time, he tells everyone in his company to remain with his brother and look after him. The words "he de pasar adelante." (I.20) suggest that he is not vaguely heedless of his brother's welfare but obligated to powerful reasons of state. His "justice" and his "cruelty," being inseparable, will be differently interpreted by different observers. Later on Pedro will perform an act of kindness toward his brother by permitting him to release Don Arias, his constant companion, from prison. Indeed, Pedro never once commits an act which shows him to be an essentially cruel person. The most convincing argument for Pedro's cruelty is the wager with Coquín which threatens Coquín with the loss of all his teeth. A. Irvine Watson has disproved this argument by showing that the threat was a commonplace in the literature of the time and that it illustrates Calderón's attitude toward buffoons rather than Pedro's fundamental cruelty.

Pedro's gravest defect is his imprudence, in permitting both Leonor and Gutierre to eavesdrop on confidential testimony, but even here his intention is to be just. He permits himself this indiscretion in the hope of justly resolving their honor problems. Pedro's imprudence therefore stems from a desire to be equitable. He has the appearance of a cruel king, but in reality he seeks justice. Far from presenting him as cruel and aloof, Calderón goes to some trouble to endow Pedro with some very human qualities. He is, for instance, boyishly impulsive when he cannot resist the temptation to take on single-handedly a band of *Valientes* in the streets of Seville.

If Pedro commits no acts in the play which would cause him to be thought of as a cruel king, he does perform several acts of generosity, such as rewarding a soldier with a commission and giving a diamond to a beggar. At the same time he imposes limits on his generous impulses by giving short acknowledgment to the undeserving *pretendientes.* Such generous acts are expected of a king, and in performing them Pedro is fulfilling the kingly role that the reader expects of him. But he tempers his liberality with justice.

Pedro's dedication to justice is particularly evident when he comes to resolve problems of honor. The minute that Leonor tells him that she has an honor problem, Pedro makes everyone leave the room and gives his full attention to her. He is compassionate toward her, promising all of his help, even going so far as to permit her to overhear his conversation with Gutierre.

Since Pedro has shown himself truly desirous of doing justice when it is a question of honor, we must re-examine his final decision on Gutierre's crime in this light. Again the critics are at odds. Wilson maintains that, since Pedro was a cruel man, "it is no wonder that he approves of Gutierre's vengeance," whereas Watson states that Pedro, being a just king, shows justice tempered with mercy in making Gutierre marry Leonor, whom he should have married in the first place. But a third, hitherto unproposed, possibility exists. Pedro realizes the ambiguous nature of Gutierre's crime and the ambiguous nature of the guilt which caused it; and he is such a just king that he can do no other than mete out an ambiguous punishment.

Gutierre, a naturally suspicious man, is forced to marry a woman about whose fidelity his suspicions have long since been aroused: Leonor, as a single woman, had committed the same imprudent act that his wife has committed, that of hiding a man in her house in an attempt to allay his suspicions that she is unfaithful to him. But if Gutierre's punishment is to be mental torture, it is not the king who is responsible for inflicting this agony on Gutierre, but rather Gutierre's all-too-vivid imagination. In the eyes of the world (and the judiciary) the king lets Gutierre go scot free. In making Gutierre marry Leonor, Pedro is justly fulfilling his promise to Leonor to restore her honor, if possible.

The next question to be decided is why Pedro rendered a decision which is at best a question mark. The last scene of the play gives us the first clue. Pedro bends over backwards to be just, though he realizes that Gutierre has committed the crime:

Gutierre sin duda es
el cruel que anoche hizo
una acción tan inclemente.

(III.741-43)

Pedro also knows that prudence on his part is necessary: "La prudencia es de importancia" (III.825). The necessity for prudence and for making rational judgments in matters of honor is something he emphasizes over and over again in his last exchanges with Gutierre: "no dar crédito a sospechas" (III.858); "y apelar a la cordura" (III.864).

Pedro fully realizes that Gutierre was deceived by appearances and that the "surgeon of his honor" has become a victim of his own imagination; and Pedro is determined not to commit the same mistake.

The king could neither condemn nor condone Gutierre's crime because he knew that Mencia's guilt could not be objectively determined, since her "crime" was justified only in Gutierre's imagination. If we examine Mencía's possible guilt and Gutierre's attitude toward her, we can see the ambiguity in the nature of the guilt underlying the exoricide.

The first thing that we learn about Mencía is that she does not love her husband. She tells her servant Jacinta: "Tuve amor y tengo honor" [You have love and I have honor]. Mencía is doggedly determined to uphold her husband's honor. While she is not in fact guilty of adultery, she imprudently takes a series of fatal steps which will lead her to her death. She tells Enrique, for instance, to return to see her in order that she may vindicate herself. While dreaming, she speaks to her husband, under the impression that he is Enrique. Though it is true that Mencía speaks to her husband while dreaming, and cannot therefore be held accountable for what she says, the very fact that she mistakes a man who is in her bedroom in the middle of the night for someone other than her husband gives the reader a glimpse into the true nature of her feelings.

Gutierre, though a suspicious man, does sufficiently trust Mencía until she herself, through these imprudent acts, arouses his suspicions. Mencía clearly feels guilty about her feelings for Enrique, for twice she sees herself bathed in her own blood. It is her own idea of her guilt which becomes implanted in Gutierre's mind. Only after she tells Gutierre that she sees herself bathed in her own blood does Gutierre begin to think that his honor has been violated:

> ¡Ay, honor!; mucho tenemos
> que hablar a solas los dos.
>
> (II.381-82)

It is also Mencía herself, who, by the fact that she has extinguished the light in order to help Enrique escape, conveys to Gutierre's imagination the image of the light as symbol of life and honor. Following this episode, Gutierre, in two successive insinuating speeches, speaks of putting out the light, and in one of them he asserts that he must extinguish the light in order to regain his honor:

> la lengua de los vientos lisonjera,
> matarte la luz pudo
> y darme luz a mí.
>
> (II.988-90)

Gutierre thus takes what appear to be demonstrations of infidelity and, letting his imagination dwell upon this circumstantial evidence, convinces himself of its truth. He well knows that Mencía may, in fact, be innocent, for he tells Pedro:

> que hombres como yo
> no ven, basta que imaginen,
> que sospechen, que prevengan.
>
> (III.79-81)

The situation is just ambiguous enough for Gutierre to deceive himself. Mencía's actions activate his imagination until he begins to think of himself as the surgeon of his honor. What he has actually perceived has not been enough to confirm his wife's guilt, but, becoming caught up in his own rhetoric, he decides to play out the role he has assigned himself. He becomes possessed with the image of blood, an image that Mencía herself has suggested to him. Mencía will even helpfully suggest the very method by which her husband will cause her to be put to death:

> Al verte así, presumía
> que ya en ni sangre banada
> hoy moría desangrada.

Although technically innocent of adultery, Mencía feels guilty because she still loves a man other than her husband. Her sense of guilt is what induces Gutierre to imagine her guilt to be possibly greater than it was, and to prepare to kill her by methods she herself has conceived.

King Pedro is well aware that Gutierre, having become obsessed with the image of blood, is no longer capable of making a prudent, rational judgment. Gutierre has told him of the acts of which he might be capable:

> a mi honor desahuciara,
> con la sangre la lavara,
> con la tierra le cubriera.
>
> (III.48-50)

When Gutierre decides to play out his self-appointed role, he becomes an Othello-like figure, and Mencía becomes his sacrificial victim. Her very death scene is described in ritualistic terms: a veil is hiding her face, a cross is over her head, and a candle is placed on either side of her bed.

Pedro, however, cannot prove that Mencía was an innocent victim, though he believes she was. Coquín, who has evolved into an "hombre de muchas veras" (III.685), testifies to her innocence. Ludovico supports Coquín's statement when he reports to the king that Mencía has died proclaiming her innocence. On the other hand, the king has the external evidence of Enrique's dagger; he also hears a half-baked confession of Enrique's love from Enrique himself. But Pedro knows that the only justification for her guilt is to be found in Gutierre's imagination. There was no way for Pedro, as there was no way for Gutierre, to determine objectively the nature of the guilt. Pedro sees the conflicting evidence and realizes that what he has perceived and what Gutierre has perceived is an *engaño,* and thus at the end of the play Pedro becomes the voice of prudence, telling Gutierre that everything he has perceived was a deception. The final speeches of the play thus place Pedro and Gutierre in diametrical opposition. Gutierre's rashness is contrasted with the king's circumspection. Pedro, unlike Gutierre, will not condemn or condone on insufficient evidence. Realizing that true knowledge of what had actually happened could not be obtained, Pedro, as a just king, could only make Gutierre's punishment an open-ended one. Pedro thus comes to realize the ambiguous nature of honor. Honor cases, as ***El médico de su honra*** so amply demonstrates, are ambiguous. Judgments of these cases must, therefore, of necessity be ambiguous. (pp. 237-44)

Roberta J. Thiher, "The Final Ambiguity of 'El médico de su honra'," in Studies in Philology, *Vol. LXVII, No. 1, April, 1970, pp. 237-44.*

FURTHER READING

OVERVIEWS AND GENERAL STUDIES

Cascardi, Anthony J. *The Limits of Illusion: A Critical Study of Calderón.* New York: Cambridge University Press, 1984, 181 p.

Analyzes theater as a form of illusion, noting the conflict resulting from Calderón's professional need to employ illusion, which as a Christian, he was morally forced to abjure.

Dunn, P. N. "Honour and the Christian Background in Calderón." *Bulletin for Hispanic Affairs* XXXVII, No. 2 (April 1960): 75-105.

Explores the multiple meanings of "honor" in seventeenth-century Spain, pondering whether Calderón embraced any particular aspect of the honor code.

Greer, Margaret Rich. "Art and Power in the Spectacle Plays of Calderón de la Barca." *PMLA* 104, No. 3 (May 1989): 329-39.

Examines the symbiosis between art and power in Calderonian dramas written for the courts of Philip IV and Charles II of Spain.

Heiple, Daniel L. "Charity and Disillusionment in Calderón." *Romance Quarterly* 34, No. 3 (August 1987): 335-44.

Analyzes Calderon's *auto sacramentale Tu prójimo como a ti* (*Thy Neighbor as Thyself*) as a deviation from the traditional Christian definition of charity. The dramatist's presentation of the virtue, Heiple claims, is pessimistic, "a conscious revision of a traditional doctrine in light of contemporary values."

Hilborn, Harry Warren. *A Chronology of the Plays of D. Pedro Calderón de la Barca.* Toronto: University of Toronto Press, 1938, 119 p.

Attempts to establish a complete and accurate chronology of Calderonian dramas based on internal references, manuscripts, and production history.

Johnson, L. Carl. "Milking the Machine: The Aesthetics of Formula in Calderón." *Bulletin of the Comediantes* 42, No. 1 (Summer 1990): 119-27.

Argues that Calderón's plays are not formulaic. Johnson asserts that the dramatist did not recycle conventional thematic and organizational elements, but developed new techniques which account for the aesthetic impact of his dramas.

Kurtz, Barbara E. " 'In Imagined Space': Allegory and the *Auto Sacramental* of Pedro Calderón de la Barca." *Romanic Review* LXXIX, No. 4 (November 1988): 647-64.

Discerns an affinity between Spanish theologian St. Ignatius of Loyola's *Spiritual Exercises* and Calderón's *autos sacramentales.* Kurtz maintains that Ignatius provided Calderón with a compositional and cognitive model for his theory of allegory.

Leavitt, Sturgis. "Did Calderón Have a Sense of Humor?" In *Romance Studies Presented to William Morton Dey,* edited by Urban T. Holmes and others, pp. 119-21. Chapel Hill: University of North Carolina, 1950.

Explores the humorous elements and characters of Calderón's tragedies and *comedias capa y espada.*

McGraha, Michael D., ed. *Approaches to the Theater of Calderón.* Washington, D.C.: University Press of America, 1982, 287 p.

Collection of essays by such scholars as Bruce W. Wardropper, Everett W. Hesse, and William Whitby, offering a spectrum of approaches to Calderón's art.

Muir, Kenneth. "The Comedies of Calderón." In his *The Singularity of Shakespeare and Other Essays,* pp. 149-58. Liverpool: Liverpool University Press, 1977.

Discusses a representative selection of Calderonian comedies, noting their dramatic effectiveness.

Mujica, Barbara Louise. *Calderón's Characters: An Existential Point of View.* Barcelona: Puvill-Editor, 1980, 350 p.

Draws a parallel between Calderón's drama and the existentialist fiction of Jean-Paul Sartre and Albert Camus. Mujica argues that Calderón's characters exhibit an unequivocal belief in free will, though always plagued by doubt in the face of choice.

Nicoll, Allardyce. "The Spanish Stage Under Lope de Vega and Calderón." In his *World Drama from Aeschylus to Anouilh,* pp. 208-39. New York: Harcourt, Brace and Co., 1949.

Survey of Calderón's works and major themes. Nicoll argues that although Calderón was a skilled dramatist, he lacked the greatness of Shakespeare, since his "writing is tied to a particular place and time, thus preventing his scenes from making such appeal to all ages and races as is made by the dramatist of Elizabethan England."

O'Conner, Thomas Austin. *Myth and Mythology in the Theater of Pedro Calderón de la Barca.* San Antonio: Trinity University Press, 1988, 365 p.

Examines several Calderonian plays within broad mythological categories. O'Conner asserts that there is a continuity between Calderón's earlier serious dramas and his later myth plays, and that "these myth plays reveal what can be truly labeled a Calderonian mythology."

Parker, Alexander A. *The Allegorical Drama of Calderón: An Introduction to the "Autos Sacramentales".* 1943. Reprint. Oxford: The Dolphin Book Co., 1968, 231 p.

Introduction to Calderón's religious dramas, with analyses of particular plays. Parker insists that each *auto* is meant to be read individually as a play by itself, rather than as part of a series of dramas "enshrining a philosophical system."

Sloman, Albert E. *The Dramatic Craftsmanship of Calderón: His Use of Earlier Plays.* Oxford: Dolphin Book Co., 1958, 327 p.

Analyzes the structure of eight Calderonian dramas to determine the dramatist's creative ingenuity.

Ter Horst, Robert. *Calderón: The Secular Plays.* Lexington: University Press of Kentucky, 1982, 254 p.

Critical discussion of Calderón's eighty non-allegorical plays, which, in Ter Horst's opinion, "provide the clearest insights into Calderón's art at maturity."

Trend, J. B. "Calderón and the Spanish Religious Theatre of the Seventeenth Century." In *Seventeenth Century Studies*

Presented to Sir Herbert Grierson, edited by J. Dover Wilson, pp. 161-83. 1938. Reprint. New York: Octagon Books, 1967.

Overview of the corpus of Calderonian dramas.

Wardropper, Bruce W., ed. *Critical Essays on the Theatre of Calderón.* New York: New York University Press, 1965, 231 p.

Collection of essays by such critics as Alexander A. Parker, Edwin Honig, and Albert E. Sloman, dealing with the complexities of Calderonian drama.

Wilson, E. M. "The Four Elements in the Imagery of Calderón." *Modern Language Review* XXI, No. 1 (January 1936): 34-47.

Negatively evaluates Calderón's use of metaphors drawn from the ancient world and the cult poems of sixteenth-century Spanish poet Góngora. Wilson argues that unlike Góngora, Calderón abused literary conventions with the frequent use of repetition, formalism, and stylization.

Ziomek, Henryk. "Calderón: The Apogee of the *Comedia.*" In his *A History of Spanish Golden Age Drama,* pp. 134-68. Lexington: University Press of Kentucky, 1984.

Considers Calderón's contribution to the development of the *comedia* through an analysis of his dramatic forms and principles.

THE CONSTANT PRINCE

Sloane, Robert. "Action and Role in *El príncipe constante.*" *Modern Language Notes* 85 (1970): 167-83.

Probes the function of the character Fernando in the second half of the drama. Sloane asserts that Fernando makes himself "the constant prince," that is, he "learns to become the man he has chosen to be."

Truman, R. W. "The Theme of Justice in Calderón's *El príncipe constante.*" *Modern Language Review* LIX, No. 1 (January 1964): 43-52.

Views justice as the drama's unifying theme. Truman contends that Calderón was influenced by Aristotle's and Thomas Aquinas's definitions of justice, particularly in the creation of the character Fernando.

LIFE IS A DREAM

Buchanan, Milton A. "Calderón's *Life is a Dream.*" *PMLA* XLVII (1932): 1303-21.

Lauds the drama as a great literary creation for its "striking and original treatment" of the Spanish code of honor.

Fox, Dian. "Kingship and Community in *La vida es sueño.*" *Bulletin of Hispanic Studies* LVIII, No. 3 (July 1981): 217-28.

Considers the play in the context of seventeenth-century Spanish politics. Fox concludes that the drama is a commentary on the absolute monarchy's fallibility.

Hall, J. B. "The Problem of Pride and Interpretation of the Evidence in *La vida es sueño.*" *Modern Language Review* 77, No. 2 (April 1982): 339-47.

Contends that the central themes of free will and disillusionment are complemented in the drama by emphatic warnings regarding the danger of pride and humanity's tendency to misinterpret reality as a result of arrogance.

Homstad, Alice. "Segismundo: The Perfect Machiavellian Prince." *Bulletin of the Comediantes* 41, No. 1 (Summer 1989): 127-39.

Political interpretation of the drama focusing on the character of Segismundo as the perfect balance between good and evil, which, in Homstad's opinion, ensures his political survival.

Maurin, Margaret S. "The Monster, the Sepulchre and the Dark: Related Patterns of Imagery in *La vida es sueño.*" *Hispanic Review* XXXV, No. 2 (April 1967): 161-78.

Studies three main patterns of imagery and their relation to the plot development of *Life is a Dream.*

Nelson, Esther W. "Ellipsis in Calderón's *La vida es sueño:* The Lack of Feminine Perspectives." In *Texto y Espectaculo: Selected Proceedings of the Symposium on Spanish Golden Age Theater,* edited by Barbara Mujica, pp. 99-116. Lanham, Md.: University Press of America, 1989.

Observes the differences between male and female characters in *Life is a Dream* with regard to dynamism or lack thereof.

Paterson, Alan K. G. "The Traffic of the Stage in Calderón's *La vida es sueño.*" In *Renaissance Drama,* edited by S. Schoenbaum, pp. 155-83. Evanston, Ill.: Northwestern University Press, 1972.

Uncovers some of the traditions upon which Calderón based the psychological elements of *Life is a Dream,* citing the drama as "a succession of spectacular breakthroughs into new perceptions of consciousness and states of being, dependent nonetheless on traditional frameworks of dramatic presentation."

THE DEVOTION OF THE CROSS

Sloane, Robert. "The 'Strangeness' of *La devoción de la cruz.*" *Bulletin of Hispanic Studies* LIV, No. 4 (October 1977): 297-310.

Perceives the play's sense of miracle and estrangement as essential elements of both plot and characterization.

THE DOCTOR OF HIS HONOR

Bryans, John. "Coquín's Conversion: Honour, Virtue, and Humour in *El médico de su honra.*" *Modern Language Review* 77, No. 3 (July 1982): 597-605.

Examines Coquín's understanding of the Spanish code of honor. Bryans maintains that Coquín, unlike the humorless king, accepts the traditional value of honor but allows himself the liberty to reject it if it conflicts with higher Christian values such as clemency and charity.

Soons, A. "The Convergence of Doctrine and Symbol in *El médico de su honra.*" *Romanische Forschungen* 72 (1960): 370-80.

Discusses symbolism and imagery as constitutive elements of the tragedy.

John Dryden

1631-1700

INTRODUCTION

Regarded as the leading literary figure of the Restoration period, Dryden excelled in a variety of genres, including drama, satire, criticism, and poetry. While some critics consider Dryden's poems and essays the best examples of his powerful and lucid style, others greatly admire his plays; as Margaret Sherwood wrote in 1898, one "finds all of Dryden, both intellect and character, in his dramatic work. It is stamped everywhere by that grave, meditative genius which finds its best expression in the eloquent and sententious line."

The eldest son of a large, socially prominent Puritan family, Dryden was born in Aldwinkle, Northamptonshire. He received a classical education at Westminster School in London, where he was enrolled as a King's Scholar. At Westminster Dryden published his first poem, "Upon the Death of the Lord Hastings," commemorating the life of a schoolmate who had recently died of smallpox. In 1650, Dryden entered Trinity College, Cambridge, where he earned a bachelor of arts degree. Shortly thereafter his father died, leaving him to oversee the affairs of his family and of the elder Dryden's small estate. In 1658, following the death of Oliver Cromwell, who had taken control of the English government after the execution of King Charles I, Dryden published "Heroique Stanzas," a verse tribute in which Cromwell is portrayed as architect of a great new age. In the following years, Dryden continued to publish politically oriented poems, the most notable of which are *Astraea Redux* and *Annus Mirabilis: The Year of Wonders, 1666.* The former, which celebrates the exiled Charles II's return to England as head of the restored monarchy, incited libelous attacks in later years by detractors who openly questioned the integrity of the author's political convictions. Modern scholars, however, have asserted that Dryden maintained throughout his life a belief in political and religious tolerance, reflecting the attitudes of the majority of the English people as he shifted from a republican to a royalist view.

In 1663, following his marriage to Lady Elizabeth Howard, Dryden debuted as a dramatist. His first play, the comedy *The Wild Gallant,* was based on a Spanish source and performed at the newly established Theatre Royal at Drury Lane; it was not a success. The following year, Dryden, in collaboration with his brother-in-law Sir Robert Howard, produced a heroic tragedy, *The Indian Queen,* also derived from a Spanish original. A sequel, *The Indian Emperour, Or, The Conquest of Mexico by the Spaniards,* was Dryden's own work, and its success signaled his ascendance as a master of rhymed verse drama. Dryden offered his theoretical views on drama as a genre in his celebrated essay *Of Dramatick Poesie,* published in 1667. That same year, he composed the successful *Secret-Love, or The Maiden-Queen,* which drew upon Madeleine de Scudéry's immensely popular ten-volume novel *Le Grand Cyrus* (1649-53). Some commentators believe that the play's main characters, brilliantly acted by Nell Gwynn and Charles Hart, inspired William Congreve's Millamant and Mirabell in *The Way of the World* (1700).

Succeeding Sir William Davenant as Poet Laureate in 1668, Dryden continued writing comedies and heroic dramas, producing *Tyrannick Love, Or The Royal Martyr* and *The Conquest of Granada by the Spaniards,* a work in two parts. Following the production of *The Conquest of Granada* in 1670 (first part) and 1671 (second part), Dryden produced the comedy *Marriage A-la-Mode* and the heroic drama *Aureng-Zebe.* In his 1677 work, *All for Love; or, The World Well Lost,* Dryden abandoned the rhymed couplet as the verse form of his dramas, finding in blank verse a less constraining technique. Although adapted from Shakespeare's tragedy of Antony and Cleopatra, *All for Love* has enjoyed critical respect as an original play and is generally considered Dryden's best dramatic work.

Throughout the 1680s, Dryden devoted himself to other genres, producing works on various political and philosophical subjects that critics have hailed as his greatest literary creations. In *Absalom and Achitophel,* a poetic rendition of the biblical story concerning King David's rebellious son Absalom, Dryden alludes to the plot to prevent Charles II's Catholic brother James from succeeding to the throne. Upon his conversion to Catholicism in 1685, Dryden dedicated his poetic talent to the cause of religious and political tolerance, as evidenced by the allegorical poem *The Hind and the Panther.* The Revolution of 1688, which established a Protestant monarchy in England, brought financial ruin to Dryden, who lost his court appointments and connections. He consequently returned to the theater, producing a number of plays, but his creative energy and inspiration were diminished. However, his collaboration with the great English composer Henry Purcell resulted in the musical drama, *King Arthur: Or, The British Worthy,* first performed in 1691.

Dryden's stature as a dramatist began diminishing toward the end of his life, eclipsed by the success of such brilliant comic playwrights as Congreve and William Wycherley. With the exception of a few of his thirty-odd plays, such as *All for Love, Don Sebastian,* and *Marriage A-la-Mode,* his productions have vanished from the English stage. This, according to critics, is perhaps due to his devotion to the heroic play, a form which attained its greatest expression through him, but which subsequently declined in public appeal. In addition, Dryden's comedies, though containing fine examples of witty repartee and many memorable characters, have been found wanting in truly comic scenes and effective explorations of human emotion. Not until the early twentieth century, when T. S. Eliot's study and Montague Summers's six-volume *Dryden: The Dramatic Works* appeared, did the plays receive favorable reassessments, with Summers, in particular, extolling Dryden for his monumental contribution to Restoration drama. Yet, of most interest to the majority of Dryden's critics are the numerous prologues, prefaces, and dedications in which he expounds on the English theater, the difficulties of representing life on the stage, the merits and drawbacks of rhyme, and, most perceptively, the works of John Fletcher, Francis Beaumont, Jonson, and Shakespeare, as well as his own writings. In so doing he inaugurated the English tradition of practical criticism. Commentators have also noted that Samuel Johnson's paraphrase of Augustus's self-congratulatory phrase, stating that Dryden found the English language "brick, and . . . left it marble," also applies to his dramas, in which the sheer mellifluousness of the language contributes considerably to the overall poetic effect. In addition, historians of music have also praised Dryden's profound understanding of music, as demonstrated by his successful collaborations with Purcell.

Despite the favorable modern re-assessment of Dryden's plays, the only work enjoying even a modicum of stage popularity is his masterpiece *All for Love.* This work about a noble Roman torn between patriotism and his love for an Egyptian queen is a passionate exploration of the mysterious dialectic of love and death. In addition, as Earl Miner has written, the play's presentation of a private world of desire and will opposed to a public world of responsibility and duty reflects the playwright's own dual citizenship, in which his dramatic works treat private concerns, while his non-dramatic poems address public issues. Though seemingly incompatible, both worlds, Miner observed, "are parts of the larger world of [Dryden's] poetry, both are aspects of his values as a man," and both contribute to the power and richness of his dramatic vision.

PRINCIPAL WORKS

PLAYS

The Wild Gallant 1663
The Indian Queen [with Sir Robert Howard] 1664
The Rival Ladies 1664
The Indian Emperour, Or, The Conquest of Mexico by the Spaniards. Being the Sequel of the Indian Queen 1665
Secret-Love, or The Maiden-Queen 1667
Sir Martin Mar-All, Or The Feign'd Innocence [adaptor; from the drama *L'étourdi* by Molière; with the Duke of Newcastle] 1667
The Tempest, Or The Enchanted Island [adaptor; from the drama *The Tempest* by William Shakespeare; with Sir William Davenant] 1667
An Evening's Love, Or The Mock Astrologer [adaptor; from the drama *Le feint astroloque* by Thomas Corneille] 1668
Tyrannick Love, Or The Royal Martyr 1669
The Conquest of Granada by the Spaniards, Part I 1670
The Conquest of Granada by the Spaniards, Part II 1671
Marriage A-la-Mode 1671
The Assignation; or Love in a Nunnery 1672
Aureng-Zebe 1675
All for Love; Or, The World Well Lost 1677
The State of Innocence, and Fall of Man [adaptor; from the poem *Paradise Lost* by John Milton; first publication] 1677
The Kind Keeper; Or, Mr. Limberham 1678
Troilus and Cressida, Or Truth Found Too Late [adaptor; from the drama *Troilus and Cressida* by William Shakespeare] 1679
The Spanish Fryar, or The Double Discovery 1680
The Duke of Guise [with Nathaniel Lee] 1682
Albion and Albanius 1685
Don Sebastian, King of Portugal 1689
Amphitryon: Or, The Two Socia's 1690
King Arthur: Or, The British Worthy 1691
Love Triumphant; Or, Nature Will Prevail 1694
Dryden: The Dramatic Works. 6 vols. 1931-32

OTHER MAJOR WORKS

Astraea Redux. A Poem on the Happy Restoration and Return of His Sacred Majesty Charles the Second (poetry) 1660
Annus Mirabilis: The Year of Wonders, 1666. An Historical Poem: Containing the Progress and Various Successes of our Naval War with Holland, under the conduct of His Highness Prince Rupert, and His Grace the Duke of Albermarl. And Describing The Fire Of London (poetry) 1667

**Of Dramatick Poesie* (criticism) 1667
"The Author's Apology for Heroic Poetry and Poetic Licence" (criticism) 1677; published in *The State of Innocence, and Fall of Man*
"The Grounds of Criticism in Tragedy" (criticism) 1679; published in *Troilus and Cressida, Or Truth Found Too Late*
Absalom and Achitophel (poetry) 1681
Mac Flecknoe, Or A Satyr Upon the True-Blew-Protestant Poet, T. S. (poetry) 1682
The Medall. A Satyre Against Sedition (poetry) 1682
Religio Laici Or A Laymans Faith (poetry) 1682
Threnodia Augustalis: A Funeral-Pindarique Poem Sacred to the Happy Memory of King Charles II (poetry) 1685
The Hind and the Panther. A Poem, In Three Parts (poetry) 1687
A Song for St. Cecilia's Day, 1687 (poetry) 1687
Alexander's Feast; Or The Power of Music. An Ode, In Honour of St. Cecilia's Day (poetry) 1697
The Works of Virgil: Containing his Pastorals, Georgics, and Aeneis. Translated into English Verse [translator] (poetry) 1697
Fables Ancient and Modern; Translated into Verse, from Homer, Ovid, Boccace, & Chaucer: With Original Poems [translator and adaptor] (poetry) 1700
The Works of John Dryden. 18 Vols. (poetry, criticism, and dramas) 1808; revised 1882-93.
The Letters of John Dryden (letters) 1942

*This work is commonly referred to as *An Essay of Dramatic Poesy.*

AUTHOR COMMENTARY

Of Dramatick Poesie (1667)

[*In the following excerpt from his critical essay* Of Dramatick Poesie, *composed in the form of a conversation between individuals representing different points of view, Dryden searchingly discusses various arguments for and against the use of rhyme in dramatic works.*]

["I confess," said Crites to Eugenius and Neander, "that] I have a joint quarrel to you both, because you have concluded, without any reason given for it, that rhyme is proper for the stage. I will not dispute how ancient it hath been among us to write this way; perhaps our ancestors knew no better till Shakespeare's time. I will grant it was not altogether left by him, and that Fletcher and Ben Jonson used it frequently in their Pastorals, and sometimes in other plays. Farther,—I will not argue whether we received it originally from our countrymen, or from the French; for that is an inquiry of as little benefit, as theirs who, in the midst of the great plague, were not so solicitous to provide against it, as to know whether we had it from the malignity of our own air, or by transportation from Holland. I have therefore only to affirm, that it is not allowable in serious plays; for comedies, I find you already concluding with me. To prove this, I might satisfy myself to tell you, how much in vain it is for you to strive against the stream of the people's inclination; the greatest part of which are prepossessed so much with those excellent plays of Shakespeare, Fletcher, and Ben Jonson, which have been written out of rhyme, that except you could bring them such as were written better in it, and those too by persons of equal reputation with them, it will be impossible for you to gain your cause with them, who will still be judges. This it is to which, in fine, all your reasons must submit. The unanimous consent of an audience is so powerful, that even Julius Caesar (as Macrobius reports of him), when he was perpetual dictator, was not able to balance it on the other side; but when Laberius, a Roman Knight, at his request contended in the *Mime* with another poet, he was forced to cry out *Etiam favente me victus es, Laberi* [Even with me on your side you are beaten, Laberius]. But I will not on this occasion take the advantage of the greater number, but only urge such reasons against rhyme, as I find in the writings of those who have argued for the other way. First, then, I am of opinion that rhyme is unnatural in a play, because dialogue there is presented as the effect of sudden thought: for a play is the imitation of nature; and since no man, without premeditation, speaks in rhyme, neither ought he to do it on the stage. This hinders not but the fancy may be there elevated to an higher pitch of thought than it is in ordinary discourse; for there is a probability that men of excellent and quick parts may speak noble things *extempore:* but those thoughts are never fettered with the numbers or sound of verse without study, and therefore it cannot be but unnatural to present the most free way of speaking in that which is the most constrained. For this reason, says Aristotle, 'tis best to write tragedy in that kind of verse which is the least such, or which is nearest prose: and this amongst the ancients was the Iambic, and with us is blank verse, or the measure of verse kept exactly without rhyme. These numbers therefore are fittest for a play; the others for a paper of verses, or a poem; blank verse being as much below them as rhyme is improper for the drama. And if it be objected that neither are blank verses made *extempore,* yet, as nearest nature, they are still to be preferred.—But there are two particular exceptions, which many besides myself have had to verse; by which it will appear yet more plainly how improper it is in plays. And the first of them is grounded on that very reason for which some have commended rhyme; they say, the quickness of repartees in argumentative scenes receives an ornament from verse. Now what is more unreasonable than to imagine that a man should not only light upon the wit, but the rhyme too, upon the sudden? This nicking of him who spoke before both in sound and measure, is so great an happiness, that you must at least suppose the persons of your play to be born poets: *Arcades omnes, et cantare pares, et respondere parati* [We are all dwellers in Arcadia, ready both to sing and to reply]: they must have arrived to the degree of *quicquid conabar dicere;*—to make verses almost whether they will or no. If they are anything below this, it will look rather like the design of two, than the answer of one: it will appear that your actors hold intelligence together; that they perform their tricks like fortune-tellers, by confederacy. The hand of art will be too visible in it, against that maxim of all professions—*Ars est celare artem;* that it is the greatest perfection of art to keep itself undiscovered. Nor will it serve you to object, that however you manage it, 'tis still known to be a play; and, consequently, the dialogue of two persons understood to be the labour of one poet. For a play is still an imitation of nature; we know we are to be deceived, and we desire to be so; but no man ever was deceived but with a probability of truth; for who will suffer a gross lie to be fastened on him? Thus we sufficiently understand that the scenes which represent cities and countries to us are not really such, but only painted on boards and canvas; but shall that excuse the ill painture or designment of them? Nay, rather ought they not be laboured with so much the more diligence and exactness, to help the imagination? since the mind of man does naturally tend to truth; and therefore the nearer anything comes to the imitation of it, the more it pleases.

"Thus, you see, your rhyme is incapable of expressing the greatest thoughts naturally, and the lowest it cannot with any grace: for what is more unbefitting the majesty of verse, than to call a servant, or bid a door be shut in rhyme? and yet you are often forced on this miserable necessity. But verse, you say, circumscribes a quick and luxuriant fancy, which would extend itself too far on every subject, did not the labour which is required to well-turned and polished rhyme, set bounds to it. Yet this argument, if granted, would only prove that we may write better in verse, but not more naturally. Neither is it able to evince that; for he who wants judgment to confine his fancy in blank verse, may want it as much in rhyme: and he who has it will avoid errors in both kinds. Latin verse was as great a confinement to the imagination of those poets as rhyme to ours; and yet you find Ovid saying too much on every subject. *Nescivit* (says Seneca) *quod bene cessit relinquere* [He didn't know how to let well enough alone] of which he gives you one famous instance in his description of the deluge:

Omnia pontus erat, deerant quoque litora ponto.
Now all was sea, nor had that sea a shore.

Thus Ovid's fancy was not limited by verse, and Virgil needed not verse to have bounded his.

"In our own language we see Ben Jonson confining himself to what ought to be said, even in the liberty of blank verse; and yet Corneille, the most judicious of the French poets, is still varying the same sense an hundred ways, and dwelling eternally on the same subject, though confined by rhyme. Some other exceptions I have to verse; but since these I have named are for the most part already public, I conceive it reasonable they should first be answered."

"It concerns me less than any," said Neander (seeing he had ended), "to reply to this discourse; because when I should have proved that verse may be natural in plays, yet I should always be ready to confess, that those which I have written in this kind come short of that perfection which is required. Yet since you are pleased I should undertake this province, I will do it, though with all imaginable respect and deference, both to that person from whom you have borrowed your strongest arguments, and to whose judgment, when I have said all, I finally submit. But before I proceed to answer your objections, I must first remember you, that I exclude all comedy from my defence; and next that I deny not but blank verse may be also used; and content myself only to assert, that in serious plays where the subject and characters are great, and the plot unmixed with mirth, which might allay or divert these concernments which are produced, rhyme is there as natural and more effectual than blank verse.

"And now having laid down this as a foundation,—to begin with Crites,—I must crave leave to tell him, that some of his arguments against rhyme reach no farther than, from the faults or defects of ill rhyme, to conclude against the use of it in general. May not I conclude against blank verse by the same reason? If the words of some poets who write in it are either ill chosen, or ill placed, which makes not only rhyme, but all kind of verse in any language unnatural, shall I, for their vicious affectation, condemn those excellent lines of Fletcher, which are written in that kind? Is there anything in rhyme more constrained than this line in blank verse?—*I heaven invoke, and strong resistance make;* where you see both the clauses are placed unnaturally, that is, contrary to the common way of speaking, and that without the excuse of a rhyme to cause it: yet you would think me very ridiculous, if I should accuse the stubbornness of blank verse for this, and not rather the stiffness of the poet. Therefore, Crites, you must either prove that words, though well chosen, and duly placed, yet render not rhyme natural in itself; or that, however natural and easy the rhyme may be, yet it is not proper for a play. If you insist on the former part, I would ask you, what other conditions are required to make rhyme natural in itself, besides an election of apt words, and a right disposition of them? For the due choice of your words expresses your sense naturally, and the due placing them adapts the rhyme to it. If you object that one verse may be made for the sake of another, though both the words and rhyme be apt, I answer, it cannot possibly so fall out; for either there is a dependence of sense betwixt the first line and the second, or there is none: if there be that connection, then in the natural position of the words the latter line must of necessity flow from the former; if there be no dependence, yet still the due ordering of words makes the last line as natural in itself as the other: so that the necessity of a rhyme never forces any but bad or lazy writers to say what they would not otherwise. 'Tis true, there is both care and art required to write in verse. A good poet never establishes the first line till he has sought out such a rhyme as may fit the sense, already prepared to heighten the second: many times the close of the sense falls into the middle of the next verse, or farther off, and he may often prevail himself of the same advantages in English which Virgil had in Latin,—he may break off in the hemistich, and begin another line. Indeed, the not observing these two last things makes plays which are writ in verse so tedious: for though, most commonly, the sense is to be confined to the couplet, yet nothing that does *perpetuo tenore fluere,* run in the same channel, can please always. 'Tis like the murmuring of a stream, which not varying in the fall, causes at first attention, at last drowsiness. Variety of cadences is the best rule; the greatest help to the actors, and refreshment to the audience.

"If then verse may be made natural in itself, how becomes

it unnatural in a play? You say the stage is the representation of nature, and no man in ordinary conversation speaks in rhyme. But you foresaw when you said this, that it might be answered—neither does any man speak in blank verse, or in measure without rhyme. Therefore you concluded, that which is nearest nature is still to be preferred. But you took no notice that rhyme might be made as natural as blank verse, by the well placing of the words, etc. All the difference between them, when they are both correct, is, the sound in one, which the other wants; and if so, the sweetness of it, and all the advantage resulting from it, which are handled in the Preface to ***The Rival Ladies,*** will yet stand good. As for that place of Aristotle, where he says, plays should be writ in that kind of verse which is nearest prose, it makes little for you; blank verse being properly but measured prose. Now measure alone, in any modern language, does not constitute verse; those of the ancients in Greek and Latin consisted in quantity of words, and a determinate number of feet. But when, by the inundation of the Goths and Vandals into Italy, new languages were introduced, and barbarously mingled with the Latin, of which the Italian, Spanish, French, and ours (made out of them and the Teutonic) are dialects, a new way of poesy was practised; new, I say, in those countries, for in all probability it was that of the conquerors in their own nations: at least we are able to prove, that the eastern people have used it from all antiquity. This new way consisted in measure or number of feet, and rhyme; the sweetness of rhyme, and observation of accent, supplying the place of quantity in words, which could neither exactly be observed by those barbarians, who knew not the rules of it, neither was it suitable to their tongues, as it had been to the Greek and Latin. No man is tied in modern poesy to observe any farther rule in the feet of his verse, but that they be dissyllables; whether Spondee, Trochee, or Iambic, it matters not; only he is obliged to rhyme: neither do the Spanish, French, Italian, or Germans, acknowledge at all, or very rarely, any such kind of poesy as blank verse amongst them. Therefore, at most 'tis but a poetic prose, a *sermo pedestris;* and as such, most fit for comedies, where I acknowledge rhyme to be improper.—Farther; as to that quotation of Aristotle, our couplet verses may be rendered as near prose as blank verse itself, by using those advantages I lately named,—as breaks in an hemistich, or running the sense into another line,—thereby making art and order appear as loose and free at nature: or not tying ourselves to couplets strictly, we may use the benefit of the Pindaric way practised in *The Siege of Rhodes;* where the numbers vary, and the rhyme is disposed carelessly, and far from often chiming. Neither is that other advantage of the ancients to be despised, of changing the kind of verse when they please, with the change of the scene, or some new entrance; for they confine not themselves always to iambics, but extend their liberty to all lyric numbers, and sometimes even to hexameter. But I need not go so far to prove that rhyme, as it succeeds to all other offices of Greek and Latin verse, so especially to this of plays, since the custom of nations at this day confirms it; the French, Italian, and Spanish tragedies are generally writ in it; and sure the universal consent of the most civilised parts of the world, ought in this, as it doth in other customs, to include the rest.

"But perhaps you may tell me, I have proposed such a way to make rhyme natural, and consequently proper to plays, as is unpracticable; and that I shall scarce find six or eight lines together in any play, where the words are so placed and chosen as is required to make it natural. I answer, no poet need constrain himself at all times to it. It is enough he makes it his general rule; for I deny not but sometimes there may be a greatness in placing the words otherwise; and sometimes they may sound better; sometimes also the variety itself is excuse enough. But if, for the most part, the words be placed as they are in the negligence of prose, it is sufficient to denominate the way practicable; for we esteem that to be such, which in the trial oftener succeeds than misses. And thus far you may find the practice made good in many plays: where you do not, remember still, that if you cannot find six natural rhymes together, it will be as hard for you to produce as many lines in blank verse, even among the greatest of our poets, against which I cannot make some reasonable exception.

"And this, Sir, calls to my remembrance the beginnings of your discourse, where you told us we should never find the audience favourable to this kind of writing, till we could produce as good plays in rhyme as Ben Jonson, Fletcher, and Shakespeare had writ out of it. But it is to raise envy to the living, to compare them with the dead. They are honoured, and almost adored by us, as they deserve; neither do I know any so presumptuous of themselves as to contend with them. Yet give me leave to say thus much, without injury to their ashes; that not only we shall never equal them, but they could never equal themselves, were they to rise and write again. We acknowledge them our fathers in wit; but they have ruined their estates themselves, before they came to their children's hands. There is scarce an humour, a character, or any kind of plot, which they have not used. All comes sullied or wasted to us: and were they to entertain this age, they could not now make so plenteous treatments out of such decayed fortunes. This therefore will be a good argument to us, either not to write at all, or to attempt some other way. There is no bays to be expected in their walks: *tentanda via est, qua me quoque possum tollere humo* [I must seek a route that will take me also off the earth].

"This way of writing in verse they have only left free to us; our age is arrived to a perfection in it, which they never knew; and which (if we may guess by what of theirs we have seen in verse, as *The Faithful Shepherdess,* and *Sad Shepherd*) 'tis probable they never could have reached. For the genius of every age is different; and though ours excel in this, I deny not but to imitate nature in that perfection which they did in prose, is a greater commendation than to write in verse exactly. As for what you have added—that the people are not generally inclined to like this way,—if it were true, it would be no wonder, that betwixt the shaking off an old habit, and the introducing of a new, there should be difficulty. Do we not see them stick to Hopkins' and Sternhold's psalms, and forsake those of David, I mean Sandys his translation of them? If by the people you understand the multitude, the [*hoi polloi*], 'tis no matter what they think; they are sometimes in the right, sometimes in the wrong: their judgment is a mere lottery. *Est ubi plebs rectè putat, est ubi peccat* [The people

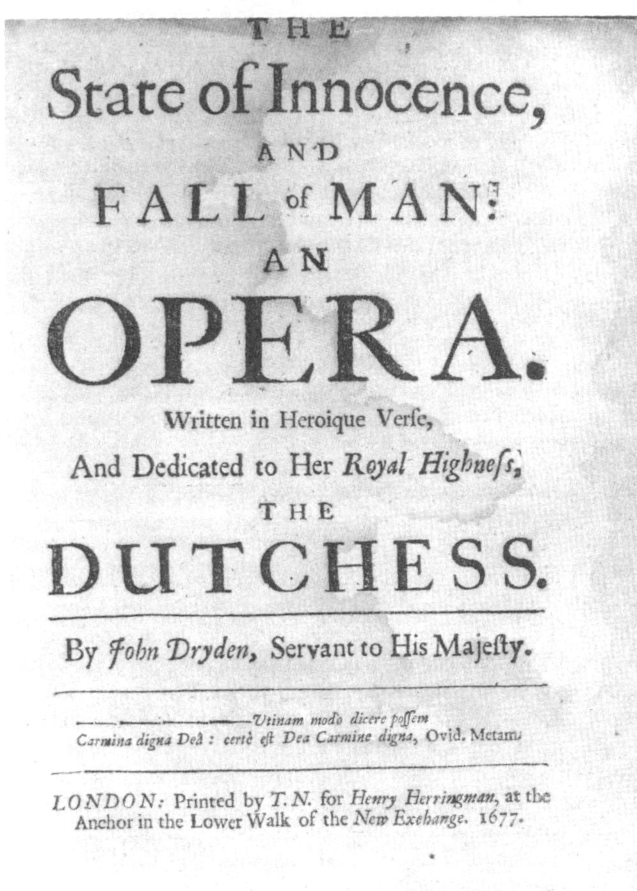

THE

State of Innocence,

AND

FALL of MAN:

AN

OPERA.

Written in Heroique Verſe,

And Dedicated to Her *Royal Highneſs*,

THE

DUTCHESS.

By *John Dryden*, Servant to His Majeſty.

——*Utinam modò dicere poſſem*
Carmina digna Deâ: certè eſt Dea Carmine digna, Ovid. Metam.

LONDON: Printed by *T. N.* for *Henry Herringman*, at the Anchor in the Lower Walk of the *New Exchange*. 1677.

Title page of The State of Innocence, *a musical show based on John Milton's* Paradise Lost.

are sometimes right in their judgment, sometimes wrong]. Horace says it of the vulgar, judging poesy. But if you mean the mixed audience of the populace and the noblesse, I dare confidently affirm that a great part of the latter sort are already favourable to verse; and that no serious plays written since the king's return have been more kindly received by them than *The Siege of Rhodes,* the *Mustapha,* ***The Indian Queen,*** and ***Indian Emperor.***

"But I come now to the inference of your first argument. You said that the dialogue of plays is presented as the effect of sudden thought, but no man speaks suddenly, or *extempore,* in rhyme; and you inferred from thence, that rhyme, which you acknowledge to be proper to epic poesy, cannot equally be proper to dramatic, unless we could suppose all men born so much more than poets, that verses should be made in them, not by them.

"It has been formerly urged by you, and confessed by me, that since no man spoke any kind of verse *extempore,* that which was nearest nature was to be preferred. I answer you, therefore, by distinguishing betwixt what is nearest to the nature of comedy, which is the imitation of common persons and ordinary speaking, and what is nearest the nature of a serious play: this last is indeed the representation of nature, but 'tis nature wrought up to a higher pitch. The plot, the characters, the wit, the passions, the descriptions, are all exalted above the level of common converse, as high as the imagination of the poet can carry them, with proportion to verisimility. Tragedy, we know, is wont to image to us the minds and fortunes of noble persons, and to portray these exactly; heroic rhyme is nearest nature, as being the noblest kind of modern verse.

> Indignatur enim privatis et prope socco
> Dignis carminibus narrari coena Thyestae
>
> [The banquet of Thyestes refuses to be related in colloquial verses, of a style suited to comedy.]

says Horace; and in another place,

> Effutire leves indigna tragoedia versus.
>
> [Tragedy, unfitted to babble rival verses.]

Blank verse is acknowledged to be too low for a poem, nay more, for a paper of verses; but if too low for an ordinary sonnet, how much more for tragedy, which is by Aristotle, in the dispute betwixt the epic poesy and the dramatic, for many reasons he there alleges, ranked above it?

"But setting this defence aside, your argument is almost as strong against the use of rhyme in poems as in plays; for the epic way is everywhere interlaced with dialogue, or discoursive scenes; and therefore you must either grant rhyme to be improper there, which is contrary to your assertion, or admit it into plays by the same title which you have given it to poems. For though tragedy be justly preferred above the other, yet there is a great affinity between them. . . . The *genus* of them is the same—a just and lively image of human nature, in its actions, passions, and traverses of fortune: so is the end—namely, for the delight and benefit of mankind. The characters and persons are still the same, viz., the greatest of both sorts; only the manner of acquainting us with those actions, passions, and fortunes, is different. Tragedy performs it *viva voce,* or by action, in dialogue; wherein it excels the epic poem, which does it chiefly by narration, and therefore is not so lively an image of human nature. However, the agreement betwixt them is such, that if rhyme be proper for one, it must be for the other. Verse, 'tis true, is not the effect of sudden thought; but this hinders not that sudden thought may be represented in verse, since those thoughts are such as must be higher than nature can raise them without premeditation, especially to a continuance of them, even out of verse; and consequently you cannot imagine them to have been sudden either in the poet or in the actors. A play, as I have said, to be like nature, is to be set above it; as statues which are placed on high are made greater than the life, that they may descend to the sight in their just proportion.

"Perhaps I have insisted too long on this objection; but the clearing of it will make my stay shorter on the rest. You tell us, Crites, that rhyme appears most unnatural in repartees, or short replies: when he who answers (it being presumed he knew not what the other would say, yet) makes up that part of the verse which was left incomplete, and supplies both the sound and measure of it. This, you say, looks rather like the confederacy of two, than the answer of one.

"This, I confess, is an objection which is in every man's mouth, who loves not rhyme: but suppose, I beseech you, the repartee were made only in blank verse, might not part of the same argument be turned against you? for the measure is as often supplied there as it is in rhyme; the latter half of the hemistich as commonly made up, or a second line subjoined as a reply to the former; which any one leaf in Jonson's plays will sufficiently clear to you. You will often find in the Greek tragedians, and in Seneca, that when a scene grows up into the warmth of repartees, which is the close fighting of it, the latter part of the trimeter is supplied by him who answers; and yet it was never observed as a fault in them by any of the ancient or modern critics. The case is the same in our verse, as it was in theirs; rhyme to us being in lieu of quantity to them. But if no latitude is to be allowed a poet, you take from him not only his licence of *quidlibet audendi* [trying anything], but you tie him up in a straiter compass than you would a philosopher. This is indeed *Musas colere severiores* [to worship Muses more severe]. You would have him follow nature, but he must follow her on foot: you have dismounted him from his Pegasus. But you tell us, this supplying the last half of a verse, or adjoining a whole second to the former, looks more like the design of two, than the answer of one. Suppose we acknowledge it: how comes this confederacy to be more displeasing to you, than in a dance which is well contrived? You see there the united design of many persons to make up one figure: after they have separated themselves in many petty divisions, they rejoin one by one into a gross: the confederacy is plain amongst them, for chance could never produce anything so beautiful; and yet there is nothing in it that shocks your sight. I acknowledge the hand of art appears in repartee, as of necessity it must in all kind of verse. But there is also the quick and poignant brevity of it (which is an high imitation of nature in those sudden gusts of passion) to mingle with it; and this, joined with the cadency and sweetness of the rhyme, leaves nothing in the soul of the hearer to desire. 'Tis an art which appears; but it appears only like the shadowings of painture, which being to cause the rounding of it, cannot be absent; but while that is considered, they are lost: so while we attend to the other beauties of the matter, the care and labour of the rhyme is carried from us, or at least drowned in its own sweetness, as bees are sometimes buried in their honey. When a poet has found the repartee, the last perfection he can add to it, is to put it into verse. However good the thought may be, however apt the words in which 'tis couched, yet he finds himself at a little unrest, while rhyme is wanting: he cannot leave it till that comes naturally, and then is at ease, and sits down contented.

"From replies, which are the most elevated thoughts of verse, you pass to those which are most mean, and which are common with the lowest of household conversation. In these, you say, the majesty of verse suffers. You instance in the calling of a servant, or commanding a door to be shut, in rhyme. This, Crites, is a good observation of yours, but no argument: for it proves no more but that such thoughts should be waived, as often as may be, by the address of the poet. But suppose they are necessary in the places where he uses them, yet there is no need to put them into rhyme. He may place them in the beginning of a verse, and break it off, as unfit, when so debased, for any other use: or granting the worst,—that they require more room than the hemistich will allow, yet still there is a choice to be made of the best words, and least vulgar (provided they be apt), to express such thoughts. Many have blamed rhyme in general, for this fault, when the poet with a little care might have redressed it. But they do it with no more justice than if English poesy should be made ridiculous for the sake of the Water-poet's rhymes. Our language is noble, full, and significant; and I know not why he who is master of it may not clothe ordinary things in it as decently as the Latin, if he use the same diligence in his choice of words: *delectus verborum origo est eloquentiae.* It was the saying of Julius Caesar, one so curious in his, that none of them can be changed but for a worse. One would think, *unlock the door,* was a thing as vulgar as could be spoken; and yet Seneca could make it sound high and lofty in his Latin:

> *Reserate clusos regii postes laris.*
>
> Set wide the palace gates.

"But I turn from this conception, both because it happens not above twice or thrice in any play that those vulgar thoughts are used; and then too (were there no other apology to be made, yet), the necessity of them, which is alike in all kind of writing, may excuse them. For if they are little and mean in rhyme, they are of consequence such in blank verse. Besides that the great eagerness and precipitation with which they are spoken, makes us rather mind the substance than the dress; that for which they are spoken, rather than what is spoken. For they are always the effect of some hasty concernment, and something of consequence depends on them.

"Thus, Crites, I have endeavoured to answer your objections; it remains only that I should vindicate an argument for verse, which you have gone about to overthrow. It had formerly been said that the easiness of blank verse renders the poet too luxuriant, but that the labour of rhyme bounds and circumscribes an over-fruitful fancy; the sense there being commonly confined to the couplet, and the words so ordered that the rhyme naturally follows them, not they the rhyme. To this you answered, that it was no argument to the question in hand; for the dispute was not which way a man may write best, but which is most proper for the subject on which he writes.

"First, give me leave, Sir, to remember you that the argument against which you raised this objection was only secondary: it was built on this hypothesis,—that to write in verse was proper for serious plays. Which supposition being granted (as it was briefly made out in that discourse, by showing how verse might be made natural), it asserted, that this way of writing was an help to the poet's judgment, by putting bounds to a wild overflowing fancy. I think, therefore, it will not be hard for me to make good what it was to prove on that supposition. But you add, that were this let pass, yet he who wants judgment in the liberty of his fancy, may as well show the defect of it when he is confined to verse; for he who has judgment will avoid errors, and he who has it not, will commit them in all kinds of writing.

"This argument, as you have taken it from a most acute person, so I confess it carries much weight in it: but by using the word judgment here indefinitely, you seem to have put a fallacy upon us. I grant, he who has judgment, that is, so profound, so strong, or rather so infallible a judgment, that he needs no helps to keep it always poised and upright, will commit no faults either in rhyme or out of it. And on the other extreme, he who has a judgment so weak and crazed that no helps can correct or amend it, shall write scurvily out of rhyme, and worse in it. But the first of these judgments is nowhere to be found, and the latter is not fit to write at all. To speak therefore of judgment as it is in the best poets; they who have the greatest proportion of it, want other helps than from it, within. As for example, you would be loth to say that he who is endued with a sound judgment has no need of history, geography, or moral philosophy, to write correctly. Judgment is indeed the master-workman in a play; but he requires many subordinate hands, many tools to his assistance. And verse I affirm to be one of these; 'tis a rule and line by which he keeps his building compact and even, which otherwise lawless imagination would raise either irregularly or loosely; at least, if the poet commits errors with this help, he would make greater and more without it: 'tis, in short, a slow and painful, but the surest kind of working. Ovid, whom you accuse for luxuriancy in verse, had perhaps been farther guilty of it, had he writ in prose. And for your instance of Ben Jonson, who, you say, writ exactly without the help of rhyme; you are to remember, 'tis only an aid to a luxuriant fancy, which his was not: as he did not want imagination, so none ever said he had much to spare. Neither was verse then refined so much, to be an help to that age, as it is to ours. Thus then the second thoughts being usually the best, as receiving the maturest digestion from judgment, and the last and most mature product of those thoughts being artful and laboured verse, it may well be inferred, that verse is a great help to a luxuriant fancy; and this is what that argument which you opposed was to evince." (pp. 472-85)

John Dryden, "An Essay of Dramatic Poesy," in his John Dryden: Selected Works, *edited by William Frost, second edition, Holt, Rinehart and Winston, 1971, pp. 428-85.*

OVERVIEWS AND GENERAL STUDIES

August Wilhelm Schlegel (lecture date 1808)

[*A German critic, translator, and poet, Schlegel is perhaps best known for founding with his brother Friedrich the periodical* Das Athenäum, *which was very influential in the establishment and development of the German Romantic movement. He is also highly regarded for his translation of Shakespeare's works into German and for his* Uber die dramatische Kunst und Literatur *(1809-11;* Lectures on Dramatic Art and Literature, *1846). In the following excerpt from a lecture that was first delivered in 1808, he identifies Dryden as the foremost representative of Restoration drama. While recognizing Dryden's technical merit, Schlegel condemns his plays as paragons of lifelessness, confusion, and bad taste.*]

The influence which the government of [Charles II] had on the manners and spirit of the time, and the natural reaction against the principles previously dominant, are sufficiently well known. As the Puritans had brought republican principles and religious zeal into universal odium, so this light-minded monarch seemed expressly born to sport away all respect for the kingly dignity. England was inundated with foreign follies and vices in his train. The court set the fashion of the most undisguised immorality, and its example was the more contagious, the more people imagined that they could only show their zeal for the new order of things by an extravagant way of thinking and living. The fanaticism of the republicans had been associated with strictness of manners; nothing therefore could be more easy and agreeable than to obtain the character of royalists, by the extravagant indulgence of all lawful and unlawful pleasures. Nowhere was the age of Louis XIV. imitated with greater depravity. But the prevailing gallantry of the court of France had its reserve and a certain delicacy of feeling; they sinned (if I may so speak) with some degree of dignity, and no man ventured to attack what was honourable, however at variance with it his own actions might be. The English played a part which was altogether unnatural to them: they gave themselves up heavily to levity; they everywhere confounded the coarsest licentiousness with free mental vivacity, and did not perceive that the kind of grace which is still compatible with depravity, disappears with the last veil which it throws off.

We can easily conceive the turn which, under such auspices, the new formation of taste must have taken. There existed no real knowledge of the fine arts, which were favoured merely like other foreign fashions and inventions of luxury. The age neither felt a true want of poetry, nor had any relish for it: in it they merely wished for a light and brilliant entertainment. The theatre, which in its former simplicity had attracted the spectators solely by the excellence of the dramatic works and the skill of the actors, was now furnished out with all the appliances with which we are at this day familiar; but what it gained in external decoration, it lost in internal worth. (pp. 476-77)

Dryden soon became and long remained the hero of the stage. This man, from his influence in fixing the laws of versification and poetical language, especially in rhyme, has acquired a reputation altogether disproportionate to his true merit. We shall not here inquire whether his translations of the Latin poets are not manneristical paraphrases, whether his political allegories (now that party interest is dead) can be read without the greatest weariness; but confine ourselves to his plays, which considered relatively to his great reputation, are incredibly bad. Dryden had a gift of flowing and easy versification; the knowledge which he possessed was considerable, but undigested; and all this was coupled with the talent of giving a certain appearance of novelty to what however was borrowed from all quarters; his serviceable muse was the resource of an irregular life. He had besides an immeasurable vanity; he frequently disguises it under humble prologues; on other occasions he speaks out boldly and confidently, avowing his opinion that he has done better than Shakespeare, Fletcher, and Jonson (whom he places nearly on the same level); all the merit of this he is, however, willing to ascribe to the refinement and advances of the age. The age indeed! as if that of Elizabeth compared with the one in which Dryden lived, were not in every respect "Hyperion to a Satyr!" Dryden played also the part of the critic: he furnished his pieces richly with prefaces and treatises on dramatic poetry, in which he chatters most confusedly about the genius of Shakespeare and Fletcher, and about the entirely opposite example of Corneille; of the original boldness of the British stage, and of the rules of Aristotle and Horace.—He imagined that he had invented a new species, namely the Heroic Drama; as if Tragedy had not from its very nature been always heroical! If we are, however, to seek for a heroic drama which is not peculiarly tragic, we shall find it among the Spaniards, who had long possessed it in the greatest perfection. From the uncommon facility of rhyming which Dryden possessed, it cost him little labour to compose the most of his serious pieces entirely in rhyme. With the English, the rhymed verse of ten syllables supplies the place of the Alexandrine; it has more freedom in its pauses, but on the other hand it wants the alternation of male and female rhymes; it proceeds in pairs exactly like the French Alexandrine, and in point of syllabic measure it is still more uniformly symmetrical. It therefore unavoidably communicates a great stiffness to the dialogue. The manner of the older English poets before them, who generally used blank verse, and only occasionally introduced rhymes, was infinitely preferable. But, since then, on the other hand, rhyme has come to be too exclusively rejected.

Dryden's plans are improbable, even to silliness; the incidents are all thrown out without forethought; the most wonderful theatrical strokes fall incessantly from the clouds. He cannot be said to have drawn a single character; for there is not a spark of nature in his dramatic personages. Passions, criminal and magnanimous sentiments, flow with indifferent levity from their lips, without ever having dwelt in the heart: their chief delight is in heroical boasting. The tone of expression is by turns flat or madly bombastical; not unfrequently both at the same time: in short, this poet resembles a man who walks upon stilts in a morass. His wit is displayed in far-fetched sophistries; his imagination in long-spun similies, awkwardly introduced. (pp. 477-79)

August Wilhelm Schlegel, "Lecture XXVIII," in his A Course of Lectures on Dramatic Art and Literature, *edited by Rev. A. J. W. Morrison, translated by John Black, revised edition, 1846. Reprint by AMS Press, Inc., 1973, pp. 475-87.*

T. S. Eliot (essay date 1932)

[*An American-born English poet, critic, and dramatist, Eliot is numbered among the seminal figures of twentieth-century English literature. His works include the poem* Four Quartets *(1943), the plays* Murder in the Cathedral *(1935) and* The Cocktail Party *(1950), and* Poetry and Drama *(1951), a collection of critical writings. In the following excerpt from his 1932 study,* John Dryden: The Poet, The Dramatist, The Critic, *Eliot assesses Dryden's contribution to English drama, remarking that, although "a great poet, who, by close application of a first-rate mind, made himself a great dramatist, . . . Dryden was not* naturally *a dramatist, as Shakespeare and Congreve were natural dramatists."*]

It is not such an easy matter to explain the utility to English letters and civilisation of Dryden's dramatic work, as it is to persuade of the importance of his poetry. Here are, in the edition of 1735 which I have, six volumes of miscellaneous plays, the chief product of twenty years of his life: it would be in a modern edition a fairly stout volume. The point is: are we to consider these plays as merely the by-product or waste-product of a man of genius, or as the brilliant effort to establish an impossible cause, or have they, perhaps, any important relation to the development of English literature? Would Dryden be as important as he is, would he have accomplished just as much as he did, if he had never written these plays at all; plays, one or two of which a small number of people to-day have had the opportunity of seeing on the stage, and three or four of which a rather larger number of people have read? (p. 25)

We begin, all of us, with every prejudice against Dryden's "heroic drama." There is one great play in blank verse, ***All for Love,*** and the difficulty about that is that Shakespeare's play on the same subject, *Antony and Cleopatra,* is very much greater—though not necessarily a much finer *play.* There are several fine plays in rhymed couplets, of which there is none better than ***The Conquest of Granada,*** and the trouble with them is that they are not in blank verse. It is extraordinarily difficult not to apply to these plays irrelevant standards of criticism, and standards, moreover, which are not exactly of play-writing or even of verse-making. We have always at the back of our minds a comparison which is not in kind. Most of us prefer the reading, not only of Shakespeare, but of several other Elizabethan dramatists to that of Dryden. And in our reading of Elizabethan plays, we are inclined to confer upon them the dramatic virtues of the most actable (on the modern stage) of Shakespeare's plays, because they have some of the *reading* virtues of these and the rest of Shakespeare's plays. I shall not venture here to investigate the nature of the *dramatic* in poetic drama, as distinguishable from the *poetic* in poetic drama; only to point out that the problem is much more of a tangle than it looks. For instance, there is *that which expressed in word and action is effective on the stage without our having read the text before:* that might be called the *theatrically dramatic;* and there is also the "poetically dramatic," that which, when we read it, we recognize to have dramatic value, but which would not have dramatic value for us upon the stage unless we had already the perception of it from reading. *Theatrically* dramatic value in verse exists when the speech has its equivalent in, or can be projected by, the action and gesture and expression of the actor; *poetic* dramatic value is something dramatic in essence which can only be expressed by the word and by the reception of the word.

Shakespeare, of course, made the utmost use of each value; and therefore confuses us in our attempt to estimate between the minor Elizabethans and Dryden, for neither they nor Dryden had such vast resources. But to make my point a little clearer I will take parallel passages from *Antony and Cleopatra* and from ***All for Love.*** In the former play, when the soldiers burst in after Cleopatra's death Charmian is made to say

> It is well done, and fitting for a princess
> Descended of so many royal kings.
> Ah, soldier!
> (dies).

Dryden's Charmion says

> Yes, 'tis well done, and like a Queen, the last
> Of her great race. I follow her.
> (Sinks down and dies).

Now, if you take these two passages by themselves, you cannot say that the two lines of Dryden are either less *poetic* than Shakespeare's, or less *dramatic;* a great actress could make just as much, I believe, of those of Dryden as of those of Shakespeare. But consider Shakespeare's remarkable addition to the original text of [Sir Thomas North's translation of Plutarch's *Life of Antony*], the two plain words *ah, soldier.* You cannot say that there is anything peculiarly *poetic* about these two words, and if you isolate the dramatic from the poetic, you cannot say that there is anything peculiarly dramatic either, because there is nothing in them for the actress to express in action; she can at best enunciate them clearly. I could not myself put into words the difference I feel between the passage if these two words *ah, soldier* were omitted and with them. But I know there is a difference, and that only Shakespeare could have made it.

One might say that Dryden was a great poet who, by close application of a first rate mind, made himself a great dramatist. His best plays are a happy marriage, or a happy compromise, between poetry and drama. You cannot say, when he is at his best, that he is less dramatic than Shakespeare, often he is more *purely* dramatic; nor can you say that he is less poetic. It is merely that there is a flight above, at which poetry and drama become one thing; of which one is often reminded in passages of Homer or Dante. We often feel with Shakespeare, and now and then with his lesser contemporaries, that the dramatic action on the stage is the symbol and shadow of some more serious action in a world of feeling more real than ours, just as our perceptions, in dreams, are often more ominously weighted than they are in practical waking life. As Chapman says

> That all things to be done, as here we live,
> Are done before all times in the other life.

Here again is a passage, from the dying words of a hero of Chapman [Bussy D'Ambois], which I will contrast presently with words of a hero of Dryden.

> Here like a Roman statue I will stand
> Till death hath made me marble; oh, my fame,
> Live in despite of murder; take thy wings
> And haste thee where the grey-eyed morn perfumes
> Her rosy chariot with Sabæan spices,
> Fly, where the evening from the Iberian vales
> Takes on her swarthy shoulders Hecate
> Crowned with a grove of oaks: fly where men feel
> The cunning axle-tree: and those that suffer
> Beneath the chariot of the snowy Bear:
> And tell them all that D'Ambois now is hasting
> To the eternal dwellers.

Here is an equally well known purple passage from ***All for Love.***

> How I loved
> Witness ye Days and nights, and all ye hours.
> That danced away with down upon your feet,
> As all your business were to count my passion.
> One day passed by, and nothing saw but love,
> Another came, and still 'twas only love,
> The suns were wearied out with looking on,
> And I untired with loving.
> I saw you every day, and all the day;
> And every day was still but as the first:
> So eager was I still to see you more. . . .
> While within your arms I lay,
> The world fell mouldering from my hands each hour
> And left me scarce a grasp. . . .
> . . . . I knew not that I fled;
> But fled to follow you.
> —What haste she made to hoist her purple sails!

Now, you cannot say that one of these passages, that of Chapman or that of Dryden, is more purple than the other, or better poetry. Both are inferior in that each does to excess one part of what Shakespeare can do. Chapman departs too far from the direct stage action into the second world which the visual symbolises; Dryden is also excessively poetic, or rather too consciously poetic, by lavishing such fine poetry *solely* in the direct action. Chapman has only overtone; and Dryden has none. But if you consider the lines of Dryden solely as poetry, or solely as drama, you cannot find a flaw in them.

As for the verse of ***All for Love*** and the best of Dryden's blank verse in the other plays in which he used it, it is to me a miracle of revivification. I think that it has more influence than it has had credit for; and that it is really the norm of blank verse for later blank verse playwrights. How Dryden could have escaped so completely the bad influence of the last followers of Shakespeare, with their dissolution of rhythm nearly into prose, and their wornout wardrobe of imagery, is as wonderful as his superiority to, and difference from the other schools of verse, that of the Senecal poets, and D'Avenant to whom he was somewhat indebted. I will hazard here an heretical and contestable opinion: that later blank verse dramatists have written better verse when they wrote more like Dryden, and worse blank verse when they were conscious of Shakespeare. When Shelley wrote in *The Cenci*

> My God! Can it be possible I have
> To die so suddenly? So young to go
> Under the obscure, cold, rotting, wormy ground!
> To be nailed down into a narrow place;
> To see no more sweet sunshine. . . .

I feel that this was not worth doing, because it is only a feeble echo of the tremendous speech of Claudio in *Measure for Measure;* but Shelley is not the only poet who has been Shakespearean by the appropriation of worms and rot and such Elizabethan stage properties. But other lines, such as

> worse than despair,
> Worse than the bitterness of death, is hope:
> It is the only ill which can find place
> Upon the giddy, sharp and narrow hour
> Tottering beneath us

are more, in their context, like Dryden—though in *The Cenci* resemblances are confused by the nature of the subject, which is more sympathetic to Ford than to either Shakespeare or Dryden. And much more obviously than in the play of Shelley—which I have chosen for mention because it is obviously of Elizabethan model—is the debt to Dryden present in the plays of Byron.

The skill of Dryden's blank verse is all the more admirable when one admits that it is a tour de force: blank verse is not natural to him. We shall see that in one of his critical essays he presents a most able defence of the rhymed couplet in heroic drama; but I always feel that here Dryden founded his reasons for what he believed upon instinct. Just as he had to defend the heroic drama because it happened to be the only form possible for the time, so I suspect that he defended the rhymed couplet because it was the form of verse which came most natural to him. There is not a line in ***All for Love*** which has, to my ear, the conversational tone of the best of Dryden's satires. As he adapted himself to drama, so he had, as far as possible, to adapt the drama to himself. Not that he was the first or the last to rhyme on the stage. But there is no other poet to whom the couplet came so naturally as the vehicle of speech as it did to Dryden; what he did not do with it cannot be done; and his couplet, miraculously, is speech. There are two reasons for the comparative success of his rhyming in drama: first, he regularly relaxed the phrasing and made his lines run on as much as possible, so that they are technically different from his satire, and though still closely packed, less compressed; and of course he helps himself out with broken lines and triplets. The other reason is that he limits himself to those dramatic effects for which the rhymed couplet is adequate. Now the kind of play that he tried to write, and succeeded in writing, was a kind which would have been in existence, whether Dryden had written or not; and as it was there, it is wholly a merit on the part of Dryden to have written that kind of play in rhymed verse. The rhymed plays, such as ***The Conquest of Granada*** and ***Aurung-Zebe,*** would *not* have been such good plays as they are, had they been written in blank verse, even blank verse as good as Dryden's. So that Dryden himself, in defending rhyme in the drama, oversimplifies the problem: for as a particular type of play modifies versification, so the play is in turn modified by the versification.

No one still supposes that Dryden made his plays out of whole cloth on the French pattern. What there is in common, including the Spanish and Oriental themes, can be enumerated. But at the same time we do not always recognise how very different is the *ethos* of either Corneille or Racine from that of Dryden. The order of French tragedy sprang from an origin which has its parallel in the Senecal drama of the Countess of Pembroke's circle, the sort of play that Fulke Greville wrote. I do not think that Dryden's drama has any essential relation to that abortive movement. The great French tragedy is classical in the sense that it is strongly *moral.* Now Dryden's plays are emphatically not "moral" in this way; they are diversified, certainly, with fine, if not very profound, *moralising,* but that is not at all the same thing. The Elizabethan tragedy was not moral either, as the French was; but Shakespeare's work as a whole, and some of the best plays of his contemporaries, explore the possibilities of human sin and suffering so profoundly as to give us something more than morals. But with Dryden I am afraid you get something less; he is a moralist only in speeches, not in plot; and the rest is a pageantry of humanity in heroic roles. And so I think that the true antecedent of Dryden is to be found in the plays of Beaumont and Fletcher. There is a similar exploitation of stage effect, the same dependence upon the strained situation for its immediate dramatic effectiveness. I cannot myself see any striking resemblance between the plays of Shakespeare's last period and the work of Beaumont and Fletcher; but the resemblance between *A King and No King* and ***Don Sebastian*** in their ethos is obvious. And if I am right in drawing this comparison, then it may be allowed that Dryden came at the right time, and that he did well to substitute for the enervated Jacobean blank verse of Fletcher his firm and masculine couplet.

We must call Dryden's plays "heroic drama" because we certainly can not call them tragedy. Even though he kills people off at the end, and though a dying queen raves in couplets better than one would conceive it possible for rhymed couplets to rave, what Dryden has is not the sense of tragedy at all. Indeed, it is from one point of view ironic to call these plays even "heroic"; for though he does not introduce the comic scene, some of his most effective passages are in a tone of witty satire, and are those in which the protagonists appear least heroic. For Dryden is an observer of human nature, rather than a creator.

I suspect that when Dryden regretted his efforts in comedy he was not merely deploring their licentiousness, which seems pretty innocent fun nowadays, but less consciously admitting their defects. Everything else that Dryden attempted, he brought to perfection in its kind, but in comedy he is a crude precursor of Congreve, and less admirable than Wycherley at his best. His is the Restoration world, certainly, not that of the simple Elizabethan humours; but his most polished figures of comedy, are, compared to the finest Restoration comedy, almost bumpkins; that delightful lady of ***Marriage à la Mode,*** Melantha, is still too "humorous" in her French affectations; and the fun of ***Mr. Limberham*** is not altogether well-bred. What I think is most noticeable, however, is that in his comedies Dryden was not able to bring his prose to perfection; it is a transition prose; and I doubt anyway whether his heart was in it. Dryden was quick enough to recognise the real right thing in prose dialogue; when young Mr. Congreve came along no one extolled him more highly than the older master of English letters. Congreve's prose is truly what we ordinarily call poetic; at any rate, I believe that the only two dramatists who have ever attained perfect prose in comedy—meaning perfect prose *for* comedy, are Shakespeare and Congreve.

But Dryden was not *naturally* a dramatist, as Shakespeare and Congreve were natural dramatists. His direct service to English drama is—apart from the value of his plays themselves—but here I am estimating the obligation of later times to Dryden, and not Dryden himself—his direct service is largely negative: had he not developed his own form of heroic play, which was suited to, and representative of his time, it is likely that a more and more etiolated Jacobeanism, with decayed versification, would have lingered on. His great service to the drama is merely incidental to his service to English letters.

We are apt to think, for convenience, and to forget that it is merely a convenience, of the development of prose and the development of verse as two parallel currents which never mingle. But Dryden's verse, for example, affects the history of English prose almost as much as his prose does. I have suggested that it is a bad sign when the written language and the spoken language drift too far apart. It is also bad when poetry and prose are too far apart; certainly, a poet can learn essential knowledge from the study of the best prose, and a prose writer can learn from the study of the best verse; for there are problems of expression common to both. But for Dryden's verse, we might not have had the perfection of Congreve's prose: though this is not demonstrable. Prose which has *nothing* in common with verse is dead; verse which has nothing in common with prose is probably artificial, false, diffuse, and syntactically weak. We commonly find versifiers who are prosaic, and prose writers who dress out their flat writing with withered flowers of poetic rhetoric, and this is just the opposite of what I have in mind. I do not believe that in any modern civilisation prose can flourish if all the verse being written is bad, or that good verse can be written in an atmosphere choked with bad prose. If I am right, the beneficent influence of Dryden's poetry cannot be confined to those poets his disciples, but is diffused over the whole of English thought and expression.

Illustration for The Indian Queen *in the 1735 edition of* The Dramatick Works of John Dryden, Esq. *(engraving by van der Gucht, after H.F.B. Gravelot).*

I cannot, finally, pretend to demonstrate that Dryden had a beneficent influence on English tragic drama—but only for the reason that since Dryden there has been no English tragic drama to influence. I have tried to affirm a belief, at least, that Dryden's dramatic work has, besides the pleasure it can give us for its merits unique in English literature, importance in the following ways: first, I believe that it strengthened his command of his verse medium for other work, and enlarged his interests; then, because of its interest for his own time, and because of the importance of the theatre in his time, it helped to consolidate his influence upon his contemporaries and successors; it is an essential member of the body of his work, which must be taken as a whole; and lastly, because it gave him the knowledge and the opportunity for some of his best critical writing—which last . . . has been of enduring value. (pp. 28-45)

T. S. Eliot, in his John Dryden: The Poet, The Dramatist, The Critic: Three Essays, *1932. Reprint by Haskell House, 1966, 68 p.*

Bruce King (essay date 1966)

[*King's scholarly works include* Marvell's Allegorical Poetry *(1977) and* The New English Literatures: Cultural Nationalism in a Changing World *(1980). In the following excerpt from his* Dryden's Major Plays, *he interprets Dryden's heroic plays as satires in which the characters' opinions "are often humorous or ironic," reflecting a crass materialism incompatible with the author's Christian worldview.*]

Since the main obstacle to an understanding of Dryden's aims as a dramatist is his heroic plays, it is best to begin with them. The usual critical approach towards the heroic plays has not changed in almost two centuries. Macaulay objected [in "John Dryden," *The Works of Lord Macaulay,* Vol. VII, 1898] "we blame Dryden, not because the persons of his dramas are not Moors or Americans, but because they are not men and women." When Cleanth Brooks says [in *Modern Poetry and the Tradition,* 1949] that Dryden's plays lack tension, he is essentially in agreement with Macaulay that Dryden failed at creating real people with real conflicts. Even critics favourable to Dryden have not argued that Macaulay was wrong in his approach, but in his judgment. [In *John Dryden,* 1949] Saintsbury said: "I am not fond of the theatre, but I should like to see one of these plays acted. The very boards might dissolve in laughter at the first scene or two; but if this danger could be surmounted. . . . " Van Doren agrees with the nineteenth-century view that the heroic plays are about creatures of "no significance as human beings" [*The Poetry of John Dryden,* 1931]. As far as the plays are concerned, we still adhere to the Whig view of history. Critics are almost unanimous in assuming that Dryden meant to portray character, but was betrayed by a literary theory which confused the epic with drama.

Certainly the discussion of such theories in his prefaces might lead one to believe that Dryden attempted to transfer the epic to the stage. In his ***Essay on Heroic Plays*** (1672) he says that "an heroic play ought to be an imitation, in little, of an heroic poem; and consequently, that love and valour ought to be the subject of it." But Dryden's early critical writings tell us little about what he really thought. As a professional dramatist Dryden had little choice in what kind of plays he wrote during the early part of his career. William Davenant and Roger Boyle had already set a fashion which might be modified, but which had to be followed. The same ***Essay*** begins: "Whether heroic verse ought to be admitted into serious plays, is not now to be disputed: it is already in possession of the stage, and I dare confidently affirm, that very few tragedies, in this age, shall be received without it." If the heroic play was already popular by the time Dryden began writing, the problem then is the uses he made of it. The question, however, has seldom been asked. Instead, critics have usually occupied themselves debating such topics as whether Dryden believed that love was more important than honour, or honour more important than love, and whether a play is an epic tragedy or a tragi-comedy. No wonder admirers of Dryden's poetry look uneasy when his plays are mentioned. It is doubtful whether Shakespeare could survive such a defence.

I would like to put forth a rather different point of view. My suggestion is that the heroic plays are a form of satire: that is, the values and sentiments of the characters are often humorous or ironic. Moreover, this irony reflects Dryden's attitudes towards many of the social, political, and intellectual ideas current in his time. If I am correct, it would be a mistake to criticise these plays for their distorted representation of human nature; the distortion would be essential to Dryden's satiric perspective. Such an approach would not only have the advantage of making the heroic plays palatable to modern taste, but it could also, oddly enough, be justified from the evidence of Dryden's contemporaries.

Dryden's early reputation as a dramatist primarily depended upon what was then called his wit. Throughout the Restoration Dryden was praised for his "wit" and his "learning." In the Prologue to John Laccy's *Old Troop* (1665) Dryden is described as "filled with wit and judgement to the brim." Lacey makes a clear distinction between his own plays and Dryden's. Dryden writes for gentlemen, wits, and the learned:

> Let wits and poets keep their proper stations;
> He writes to th' terms, I to th' long vacations.

Implicit within Lacey's remarks is the suggestion that an appreciation of Dryden's plays requires knowledge and sophisticated judgment. This was a common critical view of the period. When Rochester criticised Dryden in *An Allusion to Horace,* he acknowledged:

> But that his *Plays* embroider'd up and down,
> With *Wit* and *Learning,* justly pleas'd the *Town,*
> In the same *Paper,* I as freely own.

But what was meant by Dryden's wit? I think that D. W. Jefferson has the answer when he suggests [in his "Aspects of Dryden's Imagery," *Essays in Criticism* IV, 1954] that Dryden "did not lose the metaphysical art of using images suggestively and wittily." The imagery of Dryden's heroic plays is often intentionally humorous. Samuel Johnson understood this when he wrote that Dryden's "delight was in wild and daring sallies of sentiment, in the irregular and eccentric violence of wit. He delighted to tread upon the brink of meaning, where light and darkness begin to mingle; to approach the precipice of absurdity, and hover over the abyss of unideal vacancy." When examined closely, all of Dryden's heroic plays have an undercurrent of ironic disbelief. ***The Conquest of Granada*** is a virtuoso display in the use of comic and grotesque images:

> I'me pleas'd and pain'd since first her eyes I saw,
> As I were stung with some *Tarantula.*
> [***Part I,*** III.i.28]

> Farewell my *Almahide!*
> Life of it self will goe, now thou art gone,
> Like flies in Winter when they loose the Sun.
> [***Part I,*** V.ii.60]
> I go—but if too heavily I move,
> I walk encumbred with a weight of Love.
> Fain I would leave the thought of you behind
> But still, the more I cast you from my mind,
> You dash, like water, back, when thrown against
> the wind.
> [***Part I,*** V.ii.66]

> If from thy hands alone my death can be,
> I am immortal; and a God, to thee.
> If I would kill thee now, thy fate's so low
> That I must stoop 'ere I can give the blow.
> But mine is fix'd so far above thy Crown,
> That all thy men
> Pil'd on thy back can never pull it down.
> But at my ease, thy destiny I send,
> By ceasing from this hour to be thy friend.
> [***Part I,*** III.i.33]

Such imagery is not a poor attempt at expressing lyrical or forceful ideas. In his Dedication of ***The Spanish Friar,*** Dryden says that when he wrote such passages he "knew they were bad enough to please." Dryden's imagery is a guarantee that he has not been taken in by the exaggerated sentiments that the heroic play was supposed to express.

Dryden's wit, however, is not merely a matter of comic imagery. He gains similar effects from compressed syntax, unusual word order, surprising analogies, uneven rhythms, and shifts into colloquial diction. It would be a mistake to think that the end-stopped heroic line was the only line that Dryden could produce. The extreme flexibility of his prologues and epilogues at this time shows that he had other weapons at his disposal. We think of heroic verse as basically serious, but it is significant that throughout Augustan literature it is most commonly used for satire. The Augustan concept of the epic and Augustan satire developed together, often from the same roots. Caroline poetry abounds with writers attempting to find comic possibilities within the heroic diction which had already been established for the narrative verse tale. Sometimes writers merely lowered the tone of the narrative into mock-heroic farce. However, another form of wit was the stuffing of elaborate grammatical constructions, seemingly haphazard syntax, slipshod conversational contractions, "astonishing contortions and bizarrenesses of thought and phrase" [George Sainstbury, *Minor Poets of the Caroline Period,* Vol. I, 1905] into the prison cell of the couplet. Dryden took the characteristic features of the Caroline mock epic and further heightened its heroic and ironic qualities. By tightening the heroic couplet and giving it greater apparent regularity, he created a further absurdity of effect:

> I cannot, will not; nay I would not fly;
> I'le love; be blind, be cousen'd till I dye.
> And you, who bid me wiser Counsel take,
> I'le hate, and if I can, I'le kill you for her sake.
> [***The Conquest of Granada, Part I,*** III.i.24]

A common criticism is that the verse in such passages is stilted and mechanical. The complaint fails when we realise that the pace is intentional and part of the over-all comic effect.

It was not only the contrast of gnarled sentence-structure and comically syncopated rhythm with the apparent regularity of the couplet which Dryden heightened. To achieve a more elaborate structure of wit he also heightened the diction of the Caroline poets. There is a subtle variety in the techniques Dryden uses. For example, the coinage of a compound nonsense word at the end of a speech:

> The work is done; now, Madam, you are free:
> At least if I can give you Liberty.
> But you have Chains which you your self have chose;
> And, oh, that I could free you too from those.
> But, you are free from force, and have full pow'r
> To goe, and kill my hopes and me, this hour.
> I see, then, you will go; but yet my toyl
> May be rewarded with a looking-while.
> [***The Conquest of Granada, Part I,*** IV.ii.48]

While other early Restoration dramatists also inherited the characteristic features of Caroline narrative verse, no one else developed Caroline wit for his own use so consistently as Dryden.

A favourite device of Dryden's is to parody other poets. When Rochester praised Dryden for his "learning," he was probably referring to the various allusions and imitations in Dryden's plays. When Almanzor and Almahide explore the distinctions between spiritual and physical love, we are reminded of the discussion of angelic nutrition in *Paradise Lost:*

> ALMANZOR. Pure love had need be to it self a feast;
> For, like pure Elements, 'twill nourish least.
>
> ALMAHIDE. It therefore yields the only pure content;
> For it, like Angels, needs no Nourishment.
> To eat and drink can no perfection be;
> All Appetite implies Necessity:
>
> ALMANZOR. 'Twere well, if I could like a spirit live:
> But do not Angels food to Mortals give.
> [***The Conquest of Granada, Part II,*** IV.iii.132]

Twice in the course of ***The Conquest of Granada*** Dryden imitates Donne's *Apparition:*

> If not a Subject then a Ghost I'le be;
> And from a Ghost, you know, no place is free.
> Asleep, Awake, I'le haunt you every where;
> From my white shrowd, groan Love into your Ear.
> When in your Lovers Arms you sleep at night,
> I'le glide in cold betwixt, and seize my Right.
> And is't not better in your Nuptial Bed
> To have a living lover than a dead?
> [***Part I,*** IV.ii.50]

A later variation on the apparition theme is particularly comic:

> Thou darst not marry her while I'm in sight;
> With a bent brow thy Priest and thee I'le fright,
> And in that Scene
> Which all thy hopes and wishes should content,
> The thought of me shall make thee impotent.
> [***Part I,*** V.ii.61]

In the same play the appearance of a heavy, phlegmatic ghost has its purposefully comic aspect. Restoration audiences would remember Hobbes's claim [discussed in Dryden's ***An Essay on Heroic Plays***] that incorporeal substance is a contradiction in terms.

It is difficult to offer an exact description of Dryden's form. It is neither burlesque nor mock heroic. Burlesque occurs when a hero acts in a lowly manner. The mock heroic occurs when a low subject is portrayed in an heroic manner. Dryden's heroic plays are a form of heroic satire: the protagonists are heroes or villains, but their values and emotions are satirised or made comic. Admittedly Dryden's comic effects are often so exaggerated that the plays almost topple into burlesque. But the object of Dryden's satire is not primarily the heroic play itself; rather it is the heroic character and the sentiments associated with him.

Dryden's view of life was essentially conservative. In the ***Discourse Concerning Satire*** (1693) he said:

> The fortitude of a Christian consists in patience, and suffering, for the love of God, whatever hardships can befall him in the world; not in any great attempt, or in performance of those enterprises which the poets call heroic, and which are commonly the effects of interest, ostentation, pride and worldy honor.

In the Dedication of ***Examen Poeticum*** (1693) he describes "those ungodly man-killers, whom we poets, when we flatter them, call heroes; a race of men who can never enjoy quiet in themselves, till they have taken it from all the world." Dryden did not even approve of the idealised hero of French drama. In the Preface to ***All for Love*** (1678) he describes Racine's Hippolitus as a fool and a madman:

> Take Hippolitus out of his poetic fit, and I suppose he would think it was a wiser part, to set the saddle on the right horse, and chuse rather to live with the reputation of a plain-spoken honest man, than to die with the infamy of an incestuous villain.

While these remarks were written after the heroic plays, they can be applied to Dryden's earlier work. Dryden always believed, as he says in the Preface to ***All for Love,*** that "our passions are, or ought to be, within our power." He had no belief in heroics, whether heroical emotions or actions. Perhaps the best statement of Dryden's view of life is in the Preface to ***Sylvae*** (1685), where he justifies his translation of Lucretius:

> There are other arguments in this poem . . . which are strong enough to a reasonable man, to make him less in love with life, and consequently in less apprehensions of death: such as are the natural satiety proceeding from a perpetual enjoyment of the same things; the inconveniences of old age, which make him uncapable of corporeal pleasures; the decay of understanding and memory, which render him contemptible and useless to others.

Dryden's values are conservative and pre-Deist Christian. In the same work he argues that the fear of an after-life is the only basis for moral conduct:

> 'T is hope of futurity alone that makes this life tolerable, in expectation of a better. Who would not commit all the excesses to which he is prompted by his natural inclinations, if he may do them with security while he is alive, and be uncapable of punishment after he is dead! If he be cunning and secret enough to avoid the laws, there is no band of morality to restrain him: for fame and reputation are weak ties; many men have not the least sense of them; powerful men are only aw'd by them, as they conduce to their interest, and that not always, when a passion is predominant; and no man will be contain'd within the bounds of duty, when he may safely transgress them.

Dryden has read Hobbes, but Hobbes's theories of the natural state of mankind have made Dryden aware of the need for religion. The attitude is common to the great Augustan satirists. Swift and Johnson would have agreed.

Dryden's view of human nature shapes his dramatic satire. His heroes as well as his heroic villains represent what happens, in Dryden's opinion, when man is freed from Christian morality. The characters are aberrations, sick diseased minds, following false concepts of virtue and gain. The reason for Dryden's comic imagery is that it is meant to picture "nature in disorder." This is what he described as the correct wit of drama. In the Preface to ***Annus Mirabilis*** (1667) he says that wit "is not the jerk or sting of an epigram, nor the seeming contradiction of a poor antithesis, (the delight of an ill-judging audience in a play of rhyme,) nor the jingle of a more poor *paronomasia.*" Here Dryden refers to the word play that early Restoration dramatists inherited from Caroline drama. An example of paronomasia, or puns, is Roger Boyle's *General* (1664):

> To Conquer Empires is what force may doe,
> But 'tis your virtue must yourselfe subdue.
> If you deny my first and only suite,
> My knees shall never rise, but here take roote.

Dryden gave the wit of Boyle an ironic twist, turning it into a vehicle for dramatic satire.

When wit occurs in Dryden's heroic plays its function is to illustrate folly and excess. It is a means of defining character. The discussion of wit in the Preface to ***Annus Mirabilis*** goes on to speak of the use of Ovidian imagery to illustrate "the movements and affections of the mind, either combating between two contrary passions, or extremely discompos'd by one." Admittedly Dryden never completely freed himself from the word play of Boyle. But he did believe that Ovidian imagery "is the proper wit of dialogue or discourse, and consequently of the *drama.*" Such wit in Dryden's heroic plays is used to show that the speaker is "either combating between two contrary passions, or extremely discompos'd by one." When Maximin in ***Tyrannic Love*** is stunned by his daughter's suicide he threatens to revenge himself upon the gods by prohibiting offerings:

> What had the Gods to do with me or mine?
> Did I molest your Heav'n?—
> Why should you then make *Maximin* your Foe
> Who paid you Tribute, which he need not do?
> Your Altars I with smoke of Gums did crown:
> For which you lean'd your hungry nostrils down.
> All daily gaping for my Incense there,
> More than your Sun could draw you in a year.
> And you for this these Plagues on me have sent;
> But by the Gods, (by *Maximin* I meant)
> Henceforth I and my World
> Hostility with you and yours declare,
> Look to it, Gods; for you th' Aggressors are.
> Keep you your Rain and Sun-shine in your Skies,
> And I'le keep back my flame and Sacrifice.
> Your Trade of Heav'n shall soon be at a stand,
> And all your Goods lie dead upon your hand.
> [V.i.63–4]

This isn't the wit of Boyle or William Cartwright. The sentiments are comic, but they are also a form of inverse irony. Their purpose is to show the violent nature of Maximin's emotions.

There is a passage in Colley Cibber's *Apology* which shows that the actors knew that they were supposed to exaggerate the comic element in such speeches. Cibber says of Morat in ***Aureng-Zebe*** that there "are in this fierce character so many sentiments of avow'd Barbarity, Insolence, and Vain-glory, that they blaze even to a ludicrous Lustre, and doubtless the Poet intended those to make his Spectators laugh while they admir'd them." But by the first quarter of the eighteenth century, only a minority still understood Dryden's ironic intentions. When Booth acted

Morat, he refused to play the part for laughs. Cibber quotes him as saying:

> it was not through negligence, but by design, that I gave no spirit to that ludicrous bounce of Morat. I knew very well, that a laugh of approbation may be obtained from the understanding few, but there is nothing more dangerous than exciting the laugh of simpletons, who know not where to stop. The majority is not the wisest part of the audience, and therefore I will run no hazard.

Booth understood what Dryden was doing, but his audience was not sufficiently sophisticated to appreciate Dryden's wit. The brilliant, intellectually aware libertines of Charles's Court were replaced by the middle classes and the "understanding few" had dwindled. Unfortunately, Booth's Morat is a step in the direction towards Macaulay's naturalistic interpretations of the heroic plays. Oldmixon understood the connection between the verse of Dryden's heroic plays and metaphysical wit. But it is doubtful whether he responded to the self-consciously ludicrous twist Dryden had given to the conceit. In *An Essay on Criticism* (1728) Oldmixon wrote: "*Dryden* was so far from spying Blemishes in his Works, that he often took them for Beauties, and particularly what the *Italians* call *Concetti.*" Johnson seems to have appreciated Dryden's wit but he did not understand its function. After Johnson everything is blank. Once actors stopped exaggerating the purposefully ludicrous lines, then Dryden's mocking tone was lost, and people confused wit with bombast.

If the comic imagery of Dryden's plays derives from the metaphysical wit of Caroline drama, Dryden's treatment of character derives from Marlowe and Ben Jonson. In his ***Essay on Heroic Plays,*** Dryden cites Jonson as an authority for having dramatic characters speak in an extravagant manner. Dryden's defence of Almanzor's bombast is:

> He talks extravagantly in his passion; but if I would take the pains to quote an hundred passages of Ben Jonson's Cethegus, I could easily shew you, that the rhodomontades of Almanzor are neither so irrational as his, nor so impossible to be put in execution; for Cethegus threatens to destroy nature, and raise a new one out of it; to kill all the senate for his part of the action; to look Cato dead; and a thousand other things as extravagant.

What Dryden had in mind was such a passage as this from [Jonson's] *Catiline:*

> Would I
> Had somewhat by my selfe, apart, to doe.
> I ha' no Genius to these many counsells.
> Let me kill all the *Senate,* for my share
> He doe it at next sitting.
>
> [Act IV]

or this:

> CURIUS. I would there were more *Romes* then one, to ruine:
>
> CETHEGUS. More *Romes?* More worlds.
>
> CURIUS. Nay then, more gods and natures,
> If they tooke part.
>
> [Act III]

Dryden followed Jonson's use of extreme speech to indicate the mental contours of excessive passions. Such speeches almost always occur, during the heroic plays, when the character has lost all sense of proportion. The wildness of the speech is an indication of the psychological state of the speaker. Moreover Dryden modelled many scenes in his heroic plays on *Tamburlaine,* and Dryden's treatment of such scenes is highly revealing of his attitude towards the heroic tradition. There is a scene in Marlowe's play where, after his mistress dies, *Tamburlaine* curses the gods. In ***Tyrannic Love*** Maximin curses the gods after his son dies. Dryden turns Tamburlaine's extravagance into comedy by the impossibility of the speaker's thoughts:

> Stay; if thou speak'st that word, thou speak'st thy last:
> Some God now, if he dares, relate what's past:
> Say but he's dead, that God shall mortal be.
>
> [I.i.7]

Another passage which Dryden imitated was Tamburlaine's dying threats against the gods. In Marlowe it goes like this:

> Come let us march against the powers of heaven,
> And set black streamers in the firmament,
> To signify the slaughter of the gods.
> Ah friends, what shall I do? I cannot stand.
> Come carry me to war against the gods,
> That thus envy the health of Tamburlaine.
>
> [*Tamburlaine, Part II,* V.iii.]

In ***Tyrannic Love*** Maximin's dying words are:

> —And after thee I go,
> Revenging still, and following ev'n to th' other world my blow.
> And shoving back this Earth on which I sit,
> I'le mount—and scatter all the Gods I hit.
>
> [V.i.65.]

There is a similar violence and extravagance, but the tone is comic in Dryden's play. The scene where Tamburlaine sat upon a king especially preyed upon Dryden's imagination. In the last act of ***Tyrannic Love,*** Maximin twice sits upon the dead body of an enemy.

Where Thomas Shadwell made the mistake of simplifying Jonsonian comedy to some single eccentricity, Dryden had the genius to apply the humours technique to the heroic play. It is useful to remember Dryden's definition of dramatic wit as an illustration of minds discomposed by passions. Dryden, like Jonson, exaggerates the behaviour of his characters to reveal their emotional impulses. Dryden, not Shadwell, is the real heir to Jonson in the Restoration. Nothing could be closer to Jonson's humour than the dry savage ironies of Dryden's ***Duke of Guise. The Duke of Guise,*** however, is not of comparable quality to any of the heroic plays. Dryden's satiric sense included too much open laughter to be naturally confined within a tight Jonsonian frame. This is the main difference between Dryden's dramatic satires and those of Marlowe or Jonson. When they keep their exaggerations tightly under control within hard ironic outlines—T. S. Eliot compared their technique to caricature—Dryden's effects are often highly inflated and almost topple into burlesque. It is Dryden's sense of humour that makes the heroic plays worth reading although the wit of the allusions has somewhat faded.

Despite the humorous undercurrents of his heroic plays, Dryden, like Jonson, was concerned with depicting aberrant emotional states as they were influenced by ideas. Thomas Hobbes's theory of human nature laid the basis for his treatment of character. It enabled him to base the sentiments of his heroic characters upon a contemporary theory of motivation. Throughout the heroic plays, characters defend their actions by allusion to Hobbes's theory of natural man, to his social contract, or to his determinism. That is one reason for the materialistic imagery in the heroic plays. The imagery subverts the character's idealised explanations of his moods, and it offers a psychological analysis of the emotions. Dryden's characters may speak in an heroic manner, but his imagery warns us that they are appetitive matter in search of satisfaction. An example of this is Abdalla's description of his attraction to Lyndaraxa:

How bold our Passions are, and yet how blind!
She's gone; and now
Methinks there is less glory in a Crown;
My boyling passions settle and goe down:
Like Amber chaf't, when she is near she acts,
When farther off, inclines, but not attracts.
[***The Conquest of Granada, Part I,*** II.i.18.]

Such imagery is surprisingly frequent.

Almanzor is Hobbes's natural man who lives by his own instincts and prowess in a general state of war with others. Lyndaraxa accepts Hobbes's claim that the desire for glory is a major cause of warfare since it proves our power over others. Her actions are directed towards becoming Queen so that she may "live without controul." Zempoalla, in ***The Indian Queen,*** is a thoroughgoing Hobbist. She accepts Hobbes's claim that man is appetite in motion, and that he seeks new pleasures as quickly as he has enjoyed present ones. Dryden even based the plots of a few plays on Hobbes's theories. The rebellion that precipitates the action of ***Aureng-Zebe*** is the result of Hobbist assumptions:

When Death's cold hand has clos'd the Father's eye,
You know the younger Sons are doom'd to die.
Less ills are chosen greater to avoid,
And Nature's Laws are by the States destroy'd.
What courage tamely could to death consent,
And not, by striking first, the blow prevent?
Who falls in fight, cannot himself accuse,
And he dies greatly who a Crown pursues.

Nature's laws are those of self-preservation. The state's laws are, according to Hobbes, the absolute power that is necessary to preserve peace and to secure the government from outside threats.

The use of Hobbist ideas does not mean that Dryden was a follower of Hobbes. Dryden was a Christian. (When he wrote his heroic plays he was probably influenced by the rationalist thought of his time and was probably close to Latitudinarianism in point of view. I base my assumption on St Catharine's speeches in ***Tyrannic Love.***) Dryden's view of the human condition was traditional; he felt that appetite and imagination create greater desires than can ever be fulfilled. This is the reason why he ironically portrays extravagant sentiments and violent emotions. Hobbes had a great influence upon the seventeenth century and Dryden used Hobbes's ideas as a psychological theory to explain human behaviour. But that doesn't make Dryden a Hobbist. Many Christians, including Archbishop Tillotson, made use of Hobbes's psychological theories to describe the condition of mankind. While such Hobbists as Rochester believed that materialism proved the necessity of vice, Christians thought that man could only withdraw from the Hobbist jungle by practising resignation and by believing in God. In this difference lay the two major trends in Restoration thought: the one religious, the other materialist. Dryden's characters use Hobbes's theories as a justification for their actions because they belong to the second group.

Dryden's technique has a double edge. He mocks his characters by the use of materialistic imagery, and by having them allude to Hobbes's ideas. The characters claim to be heroes, or admirable examples of human energy, but they are shown to be merely appetite in motion. Yet looked at from another standpoint Dryden satirises Hobbes by putting his theories into the mouths of fools, madmen, and villains. In a sense, the object of Dryden's satire is Hobbes and what he represents. Where Marlowe is concerned with the breaking of traditional bounds, and Jonson with new forms of anti-social behaviour, Dryden's subject, in his heroic plays, is the new movements of thought that were forming during the later seventeenth century.

While the last vestiges of the scholastic tradition still remained alive during the later seventeenth century, the outstanding feature of the period was the concern with applying the methods of science to all spheres of human activity. As a result of new concepts of causation—based upon Galileo's experiments with matter and motion—philosophy, religion, political theory, and ethics were approached in ways which often were contrary to traditional Christian modes of thought and feeling. The scientific method influenced Descartes, and Cartesian philosophy had its effect upon religion. Descartes's attempt to prove God's existence and Lord Herbert of Cherbury's Deism are precursors of the rationalistic attitudes that led to Tillotson, Ralph Cudworth, and eventually to John Toland's *Christianity Not Mysterious.* "The role of reason was magnified, that of revelation was depressed. The scriptures were subjected to intensive and often unsympathetic scrutiny. Miracles were challenged. Prophecy was reassessed. Christian thought faced a threat which might have stripped it of all its uniqueness and its authority" [G. R. Cragg, *The Church and the Age of Reason: 1648-1789,* 1962]. John Locke, who began writing during the Restoration, is an example of the rational rather than traditional approach to political thought. The social contract began to replace the divine right of kings as a basis of government. The dead atom, postulated by science, helped strengthen the growing interest in Epicureanism and other early determinist philosophies. Gentlemen began translating Lucretius. Meanwhile the naturalistic currents of thought which first approached England from the Continent, at the turn of the century, had gained ground, and were rationalised along scientific principles, giving intellectual support to libertines.

Perhaps none of these currents in itself would have produced the particular intellectual climate which is noticeable in many Restoration writers. However, the cumulative effect of scientific thought, Epicureanism, materialism, rationalism, Deism, libertinism, and the other movements of the time, created an intense scepticism in the younger intelligentsia of the day. Rochester's great satires illustrate the way in which materialism and the influence of science were used against traditional Christian values. In Rochester's satire *Upon Nothing,* the creation of the world is told from the standpoint of that "Great Negative" from which matter is created, to which all things return. In his translation of the chorus from *Troas,* he says that after death man becomes "the Lumber of the World" and is swept back into that "Mass of Matter" from which "things unborn are kept." This is not merely Renaissance speculation but something deeper, a more fundamental questioning of the worth of morals, thought and existence. Rochester's famous *Satire Against Mankind* begins by comparing man unfavourably to the beasts. According to Rochester, the beasts at least follow their instincts, while man's false pride in his spiritual existence misleads him from the only truth, his animal emotions. Reason, to Rochester, was equivalent to physical satisfaction. Whereas to the Renaissance, right reason meant the hierarchy of mind over body, Rochester defines it as the supremacy of the instinctual, on the level of the animals. The animals at least live by their instincts, while man commits crimes because he is ruled by fear, and the desire for honour and power.

Rochester is, of course, the extreme case of an almost nihilistic sensibility formed from Restoration currents of thought. Rochester was not, however, a lonely recluse, or an eccentric philosopher out of touch with society. He was a courtier, a favourite of the King, one of Dryden's patrons, and a leader of the young wits who dominated London social life. He is well representative of the intellectual tension of his period; anyone who examines Restoration writing will find that the opinions Rochester held were also the issues upon which others felt compelled to take sides. Presenting an abstract of Stoic philosophy [in *Seneca's Morals,* 1678], Roger l'Estrange comments upon his period:

> We are fallen into an age of vain philosophy (as the holy apostle calls it), and so desperately over-run with drolls and Sceptics, that there is hardly any thing so certain, or so sacred, that is not exposed to question, or contempt. Insomuch, that betwixt the hypocrite and the Atheist, the very foundations of religion and good manners are shaken, and the two tables of the Decalogue dashed to pieces, the one against the other: the laws of government are subjected to the fancies of the vulgar, public authority to the private passions and opinions of the people, and the supernatural motions of grace confounded with the common dictates of nature.

L'Estrange's "vain philosophy" was the growing rationalism of the period. The effects it had on life during the Restoration were immense. The complete texture of the period was altered by it: the Court rakes justified their libertinism by Hobbes; the Whigs justified their Exclusionist policies by a republican interpretation of Hobbes's social contract; and, of course, Dryden's ***Religio Laici*** was written against the rationalistic religion of the Deists.

Since the best minds of the Restoration understood what was happening, it is not surprising that Hobbes's ideas appear in Dryden's plays. However, it is not merely Hobbism that is the focus of Dryden's satire. Dryden's subject is the new movement of thought: the replacing of free will by determinism, the revival of Epicurus's atoms, the belief that man is appetitive matter in motion, and the change from innate to environmental concepts of morality. In his heroic plays Dryden drew characters who reflected the new thought, and upon whom the new thought had demoralising effects—as it did on Rochester. The inner unity of Dryden's heroic plays can be defined like this: the ironic imagery suggests that his characters are aberrant and psychologically or morally defective; the characters, however, are associated with contemporary intellectual theories; these theories are, by implication, worthless except as they describe men and women who have accepted to live by them.

The heroic satires are the major work of Dryden's early career as a dramatist. The analysis of character begins with ***The Rival Ladies*** (1664) while the use of irony begins with ***The Indian Emperor*** (1665). These two elements first successfully come together in ***Tyrannic Love*** (1669), where they are used to create a magnificent satire of a Hobbist tyrant in Maximin. In ***The Conquest of Granada*** (1670) Dryden extends his irony from the treatment of villains to a satiric presentation of the majority of heroic characters in the play. ***The Conquest of Granada,*** however, represents a turning point in Dryden's development. Having created a play in which everything was wit, almost every character satirised, he reached a dead end. To exaggerate Restoration stage conventions further would have resulted in burlesque. There are, in fact, passages in ***The Conquest of Granada,*** such as the ghost scene [***Part II,*** IV.iii.], which are perilously close to burlesque. Dryden's next plays are attempts to recast the themes of the heroic plays into less extravagant forms. In ***Marriage A-la-Mode*** (1672) he uses social comedy to portray the disquietude that results from living by Hobbist ideals. In ***The State of Innocence*** (published 1674) he treats in an opera the Hobbes-Bramhall controversy over free will and necessity—L'Estrange's "the supernatural motions of grace confounded with the common dictates of nature." While Dryden occasionally uses ironic techniques in his later plays, ***Aureng-Zebe*** (1675) is his final attempt at heroic satire. Even here the characters are more supple and treated with more sympathy than before. The conventions of the early Restoration stage had outlived their usefulness. Beginning with ***All for Love*** (1677), Dryden abandoned the heroic play and sought new means of expression. (pp. 1-19)

Bruce King, in his Dryden's Major Plays, *Oliver & Boyd, 1966, 215 p.*

Kenneth Muir (essay date 1970)

[*Muir is a literary scholar whose writings include* Shakespeare's Tragic Sequence *(1979),* King Lear: Critical Essays *(1984), and* Shakespeare: Contrasts and Controversies *(1985). In the following essay, he discusses the elements of farce, satire, and even serious drama in Dryden's comedies, characterizing the plays as frequently uneven mixtures of the various genres. In Muir's view, Dryden's "importance depends on the fact that he was the only real stylist before the advent of Congreve."* Secret Love, An Evening's Love, *and* Marriage A-la-Mode *receive particular attention in this essay.*]

Dryden wrote as many plays as Etherege, Wycherley, Congreve, Vanbrugh and Farquhar together. Altogether his plays—tragedies, comedies, tragi-comedies, adaptations from Shakespeare, libretti—covered a period of more than thirty years and three reigns. But despite his varied achievement in the dramatic form, and despite such masterpieces as ***All for Love*** and ***Aureng-zebe,*** Dryden's best work was not written for the stage. And since heroic drama is unlikely ever to be seen again in the theatre, one is almost tempted to say that the heroic verse of the plays was chiefly valuable as training—training for the couplets of ***Absalom and Achitophel*** and ***The Hind and the Panther.***

Dryden had a low opinion of comedy and of his own talent for it: he wrote 'comedies rather than serious plays' simply in order to please the public. He thought that he lacked 'that gaiety of humour' necessary for comedy.

> My conversation is slow and dull; my humour saturnine and reserved; in short, I am none of those who endeavour to break jests in company, or make repartees. So that those, who decry my comedies, do me no injury, except it be in point of profit: reputation in them is the last thing to which I shall pretend [***Of Dramatic Poesy***].

It seems probable that the explanation of these views was his belief that farce was enjoyed by his audience as much as high comedy.

Dryden would, perhaps, have a greater reputation as a dramatist if we had the chance of seeing his plays on the stage. In recent years there have been revivals of ***All for Love*** and ***Marriage à la Mode,*** but not of any of the heroic plays or any of the other comedies. One difficulty is that some of Dryden's best comedy is to be found in plays which in other ways are less revivable. Dryden's earliest comedy, ***The Wild Gallant*** (1663), has little to recommend it; and four years elapsed before he returned to comic writing in ***Secret Love.*** The main plot, which is concerned with the queen's love for one of her subjects and her renouncement of it in the interests of 'glory', comes nearer, perhaps, to French classical tragedy than any play of the period. But its chief merit consists in the gaiety and wit of the comic scenes in which Florimell woos and wins the promiscuous Celadon. The two halves of the play are not unrelated. Celadon has an important function in the abortive rebellion against the queen; and, as John Loftis has pointed out [in *The Works of John Dryden,* Vol. IX, 1966], 'there is a juxtaposition of love plots in different moods':

> The plots reveal certain parallels of detail: dialogue in praise of the queen's beauty (I.iii) follows similar dialogue in praise of Florimell's (I.ii); depiction of the queen's jealousy and petulant criticism of her rival Candiope (III.i) precedes a similar depiction of Florimell's jealousy and criticism of her two rivals . . . (IV.i)

Although these observations are true, the fact remains that the Florimell-Celadon scenes are quite different in tone, a tone that was largely original and which was Dryden's great contribution to Restoration comedy.

Celadon and Florimell are early examples of what John Harrington Smith calls 'The Gay Couple' and their independence and their pretence of cynicism does not mean that they are not deeply in love with each other. Nell Gwyn's playing of the part of Florimell aroused Pepys' enthusiasm:

> So great performance of a comical part was never, I believe, in the world before as Nell do this, both as a mad girle, then most and best of all when she comes in like a young gallant, and hath the motions and carriage of a spark the most that ever I saw any man have.

Celadon is the archetypal philanderer who makes love to every pretty woman but who thinks that 'Marriage is poor folks pleasure that cannot go to the cost of variety'. He tells Florimell:

> Yet for my part, I can live with as few Mistresses as any man: I desire no superfluities; only for necessary change or so; as I shift my Linnen.

Florimell brings Celadon to the point of matrimony by her wit and gaiety, by her cunning tactics, by her acceptance of her lover's temperament, and by her refusal to accept him on easy terms. When it is pointed out that Celadon loves others, she retorts:

> There's the more hope he may love me among the rest: hang't, I would not marry one of these solemn fops; They are good for nothing but to make Cuckolds: Give me a servant that is an high Flier at all games, that is bounteous of himself to many women; and yet whenever I pleas'd to throw out the lure of Matrimony, should come down with a swing, and fly the better at his own quarry.

Florimell adopts various stratagems. She imposes a year of probation, with an extension if Celadon proves unfaithful; she sends an invitation to him in the names of Melissa's daughters and catches him kissing one of them; she dresses as a man and lures both the girls from him; and finally agrees on conditions of marriage.

> FLOR. But this Marriage is such a Bugbear to me; much might be if we could invent but any way to make it easie.
>
> CEL. Some foolish people have made it uneasie, by drawing the knot faster than they need, but we that are wiser will loosen it a little.
>
> FLOR. 'Tis true indeed, there's some difference betwixt a Girdle and an Halter.

CEL. As for the first year, according to the laudable custome of new married people, we shall follow one another up into chambers, and down into Gardens, and think we shall never have enough of one another.—So far 'tis pleasant enough I hope.

FLOR. But after that, when we begin to live like Husband and Wife, and never come near one another—what then Sir?

CEL. Why, then our onely happiness must be, to have one mind, and one will, *Florimell.*

FLOR. One mind, if thou wilt, but prithee let us have two wills; for I find one will be little enough for me alone: But how, if those wills should meet and clash, *Celadon*?

CEL. I warrant thee for that; Husbands and Wives keep their wills far enough asunder for ever meeting. One thing let us be sure to agree on, that is, never to be jealous.

FLOR. No; but e'en love one another as long as we can; and confess the truth when we can love no longer.

CEL. When I have been at play, you shall never ask me what money I have lost.

FLOR. When I have been abroad you shall never inquire who treated me.

CEL. *Item,* I will have the liberty to sleep all night, without your interrupting my repose for any evil design whatsoever.

FLOR. *Item,* Then you shall bid me good night before you sleep.

CEL. Provided always, that whatever liberties we take with other people, we continue very honest to one another.

FLOR. As far as will consist with a pleasant life.

CEL. Lastly, Whereas the names of Husband and Wife hold forth nothing but clashing and cloying, and dulness and faintness in their signification; they shall be abolish'd for ever betwixt us.

FLOR. And instead of those, we will be married by the more agreeable names of Mistress and Gallant.

CEL. None of my privileges to be infring'd by thee, *Florimell,* under the penalty of a month of Fasting-nights.

FLOR. None of my privileges to be infring'd by thee, *Celadon,* under the penalty of Cuckoldom.

CEL. Well, if it be my fortune to be made a Cuckold, I had rather thou shouldst make me one, than any one in *Sicily;* and, for my comfort I shall have thee oftner than any of thy servants.

FLOR. La ye now, is not such a marriage as good as wenching, *Celadon*?

CEL. This is very good, but not so good, *Florimell.*

This passage looks forward to the bargain scene in [William Congreve's] *The Way of the World* a generation later. The spirit of the two scenes is almost identical, although Millamant is a more subtly-realised character, and more reluctant, than Florimell. The passage also looks back, as Kathleen Lynch was the first critic to notice [in her article in the *Philological Quarterly* IV, 1925] to Honoré D'Urfé's *L'Astreé,* where Hylas and Stelle set down twelve conditions of marriage, of which the following are examples:

> That no one shall exercise over the other that sovereign authority which we say is tyranny.
>
> That each of us shall be at the same time both lover and beloved.
>
> That our friendship will be eternally without constraint.
>
> That we shall love as long as we please.
>
> That one can cease loving without any reproach of infidelity.
>
> That jealousy, complaints and sadness shall be banished from our midst as incompatible with our perfect friendship.
>
> In order that we shall not be liars or slaves, words of fidelity, servitude, and of eternal affection shall never be used by us.

As *L'Astreé* was the chief source of ***Secret Love*** there is no reason to doubt that Dryden took the idea of conditions from this passage, but, as Frank H. Moore suggests [in *The Nobler Pleasure,* 1963], the sustained banter of Celadon and Florimell may be modelled on that of Fletcher's lovers.

Since Fletcher's day the question of sexual relationships had become a matter of debate. Society, in reaction against the puritanical views of the previous age, had become more openly licentious than at any previous time; vows of eternal fidelity hardly seemed to square with the facts of life, and the Cavalier poets, no less than their successors after the Restoration, proclaimed that the satisfaction of desire was fatal to its continuance. Asteria's couplet, in one of the serious scenes of ***Secret Love,*** puts the matter neatly. She urges the queen to let Philocles marry:

> Let him possess, and then he'll soon repent:
> And so his crime will prove his punishment.

Dryden's later couple, Rhodophil and Doralice in ***Marriage à la Mode,*** have committed matrimony without taking the precautions of Celadon and Florimell who know that although they are in love and although they have similar tastes they cannot guarantee that their love will endure. But half the fun of their proviso scene, as of the one in *The Way of the World,* depends on the dichotomy between reason and emotion.

We may pass over ***Sir Martin Mar-All,*** performed in the same year as ***Secret Love,*** not because it seemed to L. C. Knights to be the stupidest play he had ever read, but because Dryden was merely revising a play by the Duke of Newcastle. ***An Evening's Love*** (1668) is one of the finest of Dryden's comedies. The dialogue is less brilliant than that of ***Secret Love*** or ***Marriage á la Mode,*** but in other respects it is superior to either; it has a clever plot and the scenes have a unity of tone—we are not made to oscillate between the heroic and the realistic, between verse and contemporary prose. The stratagem which gives the play its sub-title, ***The Mock Astrologer,*** though it strains our credulity, is theatrically effective; the disguisings of Jacinta—played, like Florimell, by Nell Gwyn—are gay and spirited; and, above all, the wit-combats of the lovers are second only to those in ***Secret Love.***

The libertine sentiments professed by Wildblood are eroded in the course of the play. In the first scene he scoffs at the very idea of marriage:

> Marriage quoth a! what, dost thou think I have been bred in the Desarts of *Africk,* or among the Savages of America? nay, if I had, I must needs have known better things than so; the light of Nature would not have let me gone [go?] so far astray.

He tells Jacinta in the second scene:

> I beseech you, Madam, trouble not your self for my Religion; for though I am a Heretick to the men of your Country, to your Ladies I am a very zelous Catholick.

In II.1, Bellamy confesses that if a woman flies he feels bound to pursue, and Wildblood replies:

> What a secret have you found out? Why 'tis the nature of all mankind: we love to get our Mistresses, and purr over 'em, as Cats do over Mice, and then let 'em go a little way; and all the pleasure is, to pat 'em back again.

When Jacinta, who pretends to share his libertine views, proposes a short love affair, Wildblood agrees with alacrity:

> Faith agreed with all my heart. For I am none of those unreasonable lovers, that propose to themselves the loving to eternity; the truth is, a month is commonly my stint; but in that month I love so dreadfully; that it is after a twelve-month's rate of common love.
>
> JACINTA. Or would not a fortnight serve our turn? for in troth a month looks somewhat dismally; 'tis a whole *Ægyptian* year.

Before the end of the play, Wildblood is desperately in love, and his quarrels with Jacinta are a proof of their mutual affection:

> WILDBLOOD. Why, are we quite broke off?
>
> JACINTA. Why, are we not?
>
> WILDBLOOD. Well, since 'tis past, 'tis past; but a pox of all foolish quarrelling for my part.
>
> JACINTA. And a mischief of all foolish disguisements for my part.
>
> WILDBLOOD. But if it were to do again with another Mistress, I would e'en plainly confess I had lost my money . . . If it were not to please you, I see no necessity of our parting.
>
> JACINTA. I protest I do it out of complaisance to you.

Dryden is alleged to have called ***An Evening's Love*** 'but a fifth-rate play' and he speaks of it in the Prologue as the result of 'ungrateful drudgery'. He may have felt that it was a piece of hack writing, based partly on Molière's *Le Dépit amoureux* and partly on Thomas Corneille's *Le Feint Astrologue.* But he surely underestimated the quality of the amalgam, and the admirable comic dialogue. It certainly does not—at least in its published form—deserve the complaints of bawdiness levelled against it by Pepys and Evelyn. 'It afflicted me', wrote Evelyn, 'to see how the stage was degenerated and polluted by the licentious times'.

Marriage à la Mode (1673) contains Dryden's finest comic scenes, although these are set in a romantic framework reminiscent of *Cymbeline* or *Philaster.* The different strains do not blend satisfactorily, not because the comic scenes are in prose and the others in verse, but because the former reflect the manners and morals of Charles II's England and seem unrelated to the Sicily, seen through literary eyes, depicted in the serious scenes. Dryden tries without much conviction to unite the two plots by making the gallants of the comedy of manners fight gallantly on behalf of the rightful king. But their previous modishness hardly prepares us for Palamedes ringing couplet:

> Or die with you: no Subject e'er can meet
> A nobler fate, than at his Sovereign's feet.

Shakespeare, of course, had successfully joined things even more incompatible, filling a wood near Athens with English craftsmen, or blending in *Cymbeline* folk-tale, pastoral, ancient history and Renaissance Italy. But in both cases the poetry acts as a solvent. In Dryden's play the quartet of lovers live in a different world from that occupied by Polydamas, the usurper, Palmyra, his daughter, and Leonidas, the rightful Prince. Both worlds, if considered separately, are successfully presented; but the realism of the prose scenes makes the poetical ones seem unreal.

The see-saw of events, which first reveals that Leonidas is the king's son and so separates him from Palmyra, and then reveals that Palmyra is the king's child and Leonidas is not, again separating the lovers, and at last reveals that Leonidas is the rightful monarch, is an effective romantic vehicle. For full measure, there is another beautiful princess in love with Leonidas. Moreover the play contains some of Dryden's most charming verse, especially the lovers' remembrance of things past:

> LEON. When Love did of my heart possession take,
> I was so young, my soul was scarce awake:
> I cannot tell when first I thought you fair;
> But suck'd in Love, insensibly as Ayre.
>
> PALM. I know too well when first my love began,
> When at our Wake you for the chaplet ran:
> Then I was made the Lady of the May,
> And, with the Garland, at the Goal did stay:
> Still, as you ran, I kept you full in view;
> I hop'd, and wish'd, and ran, methought, for you.
> As you came near, I hastily did rise,

And stretch'd my arm out-right, that held the
prize.
The custom was to kiss whom I should crown;
You kneel'd and, in my lap, your head laid
down:
I blush'd, and blush'd, and did the kiss delay:
At last, my Subjects forc'd me to obey;
But, when I gave the crown, and then the kiss,
I scarce had breath to say, Take that—and this.

LEON. I felt, the while, a pleasing kind of smart;
That kiss went, tingling, to my very heart.
When it was gone, the sense of it did stay;
The sweetness cling'd upon my lips all day,
Like drops of Honey, loath to fall away.

PALM. Life, like a prodigal, gave all his store
To my first youth, and now can give no more.
You are a Prince; and, in that high degree,
No longer must converse with humble me.

With this pastoral idealism and the heroic fidelity it inspires, Dryden contrasts the fashionable assumptions about marriage of the society of his time, just as the adulteries and gallantries of the comedy of manners contrast with the inflated virtues and passions of heroic tragedy. Rhodophil and Doralice are out of love with each other not because they are ill-matched, like the Brutes and Sullens, but because they are married. The opening song states the theme: it might, indeed, be the theme-song for many Restoration comedies:

Why should a foolish Marriage Vow,
Which long ago was made,
Oblige us to each other now,
When Passion is decay'd?
We lov'd, and we lov'd, as long as we cou'd,
Till our love was lov'd out in us both;
But our Marriage is dead, when the Pleasure is
fled:
'Twas Pleasure first made it an Oath.

If I have Pleasures for a Friend,
And farther love in store,
What wrong has he, whose joys did end
And who cou'd give no more?
'Tis a madness that he should be jealous of me,
Or that I should bar him of another:
For all we can gain, is to give our selves pain,
When neither can hinder the other.

Rhodophil admits to Palamede that he is unhappy, despite the fact that Doralice is young, gay and beautiful. Palamede replies, 'You dislike her for no other reason, but because she's your wife'. Rhodophil asks, 'And is not that enough?' and he continues with a contrast between his feelings and those he had two years ago:

All that I know of her perfections now, is only by memory. I remember, indeed, that about two years ago I lov'd her passionately; but those golden days are gone, *Palamede:* Yet I lov'd her a whole half year, double the natural term of any Mistress; and I think in my conscience I could have held out another quarter; but then the World began to laugh at me, and a certain shame of being out of fashion, seiz'd me. At last, we arriv'd at that point, that there was nothing left in us to make us new to one another. Yet still I set a good face upon the matter, and am infinite fond of her before company; but, when we are alone, we walk like Lions in a room; she one way, and I another: and we lie with our backs to each other, so far distant, as if the fashion of great Beds was only invented to keep Husband and Wife sufficiently asunder.

The key words in this speech are 'the World began to laugh at me'. Dryden is both recording and satirising the fashionable view of marriage. The scene in which Rhodophil and Doralice act out the antagonism which is expected of them is a good example of Dryden's style which for wit and polish had no rival until the advent of Congreve twenty years later:

RHO. Well, thou art the most provoking Wife!

DOR. Well, thou art the dullest Husband, thou art never to be provok'd.

RHO. I was never thought dull till I marry'd thee; and now thou hast made an old knife of me; thou hast whetted me so long, till I have no edge left.

DOR. I see you are in the Husbands fashion; you reserve all your good humours for your Mistresses, and keep your ill for your wives.

RHO. Prethee leave me to my own cogitations; I am thinking over all my sins, to find for which of them it was I marry'd thee.

DOR. Whatever your sin was, mine's the punishment.

RHO. My comfort is, thou art not immortal; and when that blessed, that divine day comes, of thy departure, I'm resolv'd I'll make one Holy-day more in the almanac for thy sake.

DOR. Ay, you had need make a Holy-day for me, for I am sure you have made me a Martyr.

It is curious, in the light of such a passage of dialogue, that Dryden believed he had little talent as a writer of comedy, since he had not the gift of repartee. Every one of these speeches proves the contrary.

[In *Dryden's Major Plays,* 1966] Bruce King suggests that Palamede and Rhodophil have 'accepted the Hobbist view of life according to which man is a series of appetites seeking new sensations', though, as King points out, Hobbes never said that married love was an impossibility. Dryden had, of course, read Hobbes; but the idea that desire is destroyed by its satisfaction was continually being expressed both by the Metaphysical poets and the cavaliers, many of whom wrote before Hobbes published anything.

Dryden in his early plays seems to express, and even share, libertinist views of sexual behaviour; but in ***Marriage à la Mode*** not merely are the prose characters placed in opposition to the poetic characters (to whom love, fidelity and heroism are meaningful), but the gallants (and their mistresses) are made to recognise the errors of their philosophy of life.

At the end of the play Rhodophil and Palamede are jealous of each other and Doralice points the moral:

> DOR. But you can neither of you be jealous of what you love not.
>
> DHO. Faith, I am jealous, and this makes me partly suspect that I love you better than I thought.
>
> DOR. Pish! A meer jealousie of honour.
>
> RHO. Gad, I am afraid there's something else in't; for *Palamede* has wit, and if he loves you, there's something more in ye than I have found: some rich Mine, for ought I know, that I have not yet discovered.
>
> PAL. 'Slife, what's this? Here's an argument for me to love *Melantha;* for he has lov'd her, and he has wit too, and, for ought I know, there may be a Mine; but if there be, I am resolv'd to dig for it.

The funniest character in the play is Melantha who combines a snobbish passion for royalty with an equal passion for everything French. She contrives to introduce at least one French word into every sentence and gets her maid to collect new words for her to use. It is a splendid acting part and as such was praised by Cibber [in his *Life*]:

> Melantha is as finished an impertinent as ever fluttered in a drawing-room, and seems to contain the most complete system of female foppery that could possibly be crowded into the tortured form of a fine lady. Her language, dress, motion, manners, soul and body, are in a continual hurry to be something more than is necessary or commendable.

Melantha has, indeed, been regarded as a forerunner of Millamant, whose faults 'serve but to make her more agreeable'. But Melantha's affectations are so exaggerated that she is more a figure of farce than of comedy and it is difficult to believe that men as intelligent as Palamede and Rhodophil should both fall in love with her. It would have been more satisfactory, if less economical, to have kept her as the subject of satire and not to have made her one of the quartet of lovers.

Mr Limberham (Dryden claimed) was 'intended for an honest satire against our crying sin of *keeping*'. Because of opposition, the play was acted only thrice and Dryden removed those things which offended the audience. These could hardly have been indecencies—since so many remain—but were probably satire of individuals. Despite Dryden's statement of his intentions, there is some ambiguity about the results. Limberham himself is certainly satirised as a doting, deluded cuckold; and the amiable pander, Aldo, is also an object of good-humoured ridicule. But Eliot's spokesman, who declares that the morality of the play is impeccable, seems to ignore the hero of the play, the cheerfully promiscuous Woodall, who has affairs with two of the women of the house, agrees with a third and marries a fourth, the only chaste one of the four, without forfeiting the sympathies of the audience. It is true that there is some attempt to return to conventional morals in the final scene of the play: Woodall's bride is determined to keep him faithful; Limberham marries his mistress; Mrs Saintly has to make do with Woodall's servant; and Brainsick is reconciled to his wife. But Woodall's previous adventures are not morally condemned as they are treated as amusing scrapes from which, with the help of others, he manages to extricate himself.

But though the play is amoral, it need not therefore be condemned. It obeys the laws of farce, not of comedy; and it should be judged by appropriate standards. Characterisation is comparatively crude; the dialogue is without any literary graces; but the action is rapid and coherent and the situations extremely funny. When Woodall is locked in a chest, or hidden in a closet, or embracing one of his mistresses while the unsuspecting husband mounts guard outside, we don't judge his conduct by any standards or morality—we simply wonder how he will escape from his various predicaments. The situations display Dryden's powers of theatrical invention, not least when one of Woodall's mistresses lies under the bed which he shares with another and the three of them are surprised by the third pretender to his favours. ***Mr. Limberham*** is a brilliant farce and, in its way, a masterpiece.

The Spanish Friar (1681), has been praised by many of Dryden's critics, including Scott and Johnson. The serious scenes contain some fine verse and some good debate and a genuine tragic situation; but the happy ending is forced, the psychology of the main character, Torrismond, theatrical, and these scenes do not harmonise with the farcical comedy of the underplot. Despite the title, the scenes involving the Friar are subordinated to the others and their main function is to exhibit the hypocrisy and greed of the Friar, and by implication of ecclesiastics in general. Friar Dominic cheerfully acts as Lorenzo's pimp while pretending all the time that his motives are pure. Bruce King admits that Lorenzo and Elvira are lacking in wit and gaiety but he argues that what he calls 'an unfortunate crudeness in the sexual comedy' was intentional because libertinism 'was going out of fashion' and because Dryden had 'developed a new seriousness'. I can see little sign that Dryden was critical of Lorenzo's licence or of Elvira's desire to cuckold her husband, who is depicted as a cowardly, impotent usurer. The revelation at the end that the lovers are brother and sister and that they had narrowly escaped committing incest is an additional bit of salaciousness. The satire of hypocrisy is funny in a crude way, but Dryden is appealing to vulgar prejudice.

The last of Dryden's comedies, ***Amphitryon,*** uses the plot which has been a favourite with dramatists from Plautus to Giraudoux. It falls outside the scope of this [essay] because it is not concerned with the manners or morals of Dryden's own age, and is written mainly in verse. But it is worth pointing out that Jupiter, after seducing Alcmena in the guise of her husband, expresses the view of marriage which is found so often on the lips of Restoration gallants. He urges Alcmena:

> I love so nicely that I cannot bear
> To owe the Sweets of Love, which I have tasted
> To the submissive duty of a Wife.
> Tell me: and soothe my Passion e're I go,
> That in the kindest moments of the Night,
> When you gave up yourself to Love and me,
> You thought not of a Husband, but a Lover?

The name of husband is dull, he tells her; his tenderness

Surpasses that of Husbands for their Wives.

When Alcmena tells him she gave him all a virtuous wife could give, he protests:

No, no, that very name of Wife and Marriage
Is Poyson to the dearest sweets of Love:
To please my niceness you must separate
The Lover from his Mortal Foe—the Husband.
Give to the yawning Husband your cold Vertue;
But all your vigorous Warmth, your melting Sighs,
Your amorous Murmurs, be your Lover's part.

It is interesting to have Jupiter sharing the prejudices of the Restoration gentleman; but there is an underlying irony in that the real and the counterfeit Amphitryon, the husband and the lover, are indistinguishable to the virtuous Alcmena.

Dryden's achievement in comedy was uneven. Only one, ***Marriage à la Mode,*** is entirely successful as a whole; but ***Mr. Limberham*** is an excellent farce; and there are fine comic scenes in several of his other plays. His importance depends on the fact that he was the only real stylist before the advent of Congreve. (pp. 41-54)

Kenneth Muir, "John Dryden," in his The Comedy of Manners, *Hutchinson University Library, 1970, pp. 41-54.*

John Loftis (essay date 1972)

[*Loftis is a literary scholar whose books include* Steele at Drury Lane *(1952),* The Spanish Plays of Neoclassical England *(1973), and* Sheridan and the Drama of Georgian England *(1976). In the following essay, he provides an analytical overview of Dryden's comedies. According to Loftis, Dryden's comedies, commonly undervalued by critics, can be enjoyed as "superb dramatic entertainments combining romantic adventure with acutely observed scenes from familiar life." In this essay he particularly focuses on* The Wild Gallant, Marriage A-la-Mode, The Spanish Fryar, *and* Amphitryon.]

Dryden began writing comedies soon after the Restoration, earlier than the other principal dramatists of his time, before the conventions of the 'comedy of manners' were established by Etherege and Wycherley in the late 1660s and the mid 1670s. When Dryden began writing comedies, a repertory of new plays had not been developed after the long intermission in theatrical production. The two companies of actors relied perforce on Renaissance plays—above all, on the plays of the dramatists whom Dryden in ***Of Dramatick Poesie*** of 1668 isolated for special attention: Beaumont and Fletcher, Jonson, and Shakespeare. These dramatists, more than any others, were his masters; and if in the thirty years that separate his first comedy from his last he followed and responded to contemporary developments, his work throughout his career has an affinity with Renaissance drama.

His comedies of London life, ***The Wild Gallant, Sir Martin Mar-all,*** and ***The Kind Keeper,*** resemble in their citizen characters and boarding house scenes the realistic comedy of Middleton and Brome as well as of Jonson; and they include characters who resemble Jonsonian humours. His tragicomedies from ***The Rival Ladies*** to ***Love Triumphant*** have a complication and resolution of potentially tragic action approximating a pattern followed in plays by Shakespeare and Beaumont and Fletcher. His lifelong predilection for tragicomedy, a form that he repeatedly defended in his critical writings, would seem to derive from his admiration for the Renaissance dramatists. Although he was the first great neoclassical critic writing in English, he was not so completely convinced by the arguments of the French theorists and of their English disciple, Thomas Rymer, that he was willing to give over the use of juxtaposed scenes with contrasting emotional impact.

He did not often write comedies of manners as that term is now usually understood. The plays of Etherege and Wycherley, of his own generation, and those of Congreve, Vanbrugh, and Farquhar, of the following, have shaped our conception of that sub-genre, with its distinctive conventions of plot, locale, character types, dialogue, and satirical objectives. The plays of those five dramatists follow the conventions with remarkable if not complete consistency. The best plays of Dryden do not follow them comprehensively enough for the conventions to be very useful in critical discussion. His affinities with Etherege and Wycherley—in the conduct of dramatic dialogue and in the probing analysis of relationships between social classes and between the sexes—are numerous and important, but the affinities are most apparent in isolated scenes of his tragicomedies, in which remote locales and action of potentially serious import produce an effect reminiscent of Beaumont and Fletcher. He was a man of his times, in writing comedy as in everything else, but he went his own way, experimenting with many forms of comedy, largely avoiding the satirical comedy of fashionable London life in which his most famous contemporaries excelled.

The variety of his comedies suggests the variety of Restoration drama and the range of literary sources from which it derived. He was a learned man, the most learned in the traditional sense of the major dramatists of the later seventeenth century. He knew the classical drama of antiquity, often referring to it in critical essays and basing one of his best comedies, ***Amphitryon,*** on a story transmitted by Plautus. He was well informed about the French drama written during his own lifetime, reading new plays as they appeared as well as the established masterpieces. He was familiar with that type of the Spanish *comedia* known as the cloak and sword play, imitating at a considerable distance its formal qualities in ***The Rival Ladies*** and ***An Evening's Love*** and once at least, in ***The Assignation,*** taking suggestions for a plot from Calderón. He knew the Italian *commedia dell'arte,* referring to it in dialogue in ***The Kind Keeper*** (I. i) and basing one of his most popular comedies, ***Sir Martin Mar-all*** (written with the Duke of Newcastle), on two French plays that in turn are closely based, both of them, on a single Italian play in that form. He took episodes and even stretches of dialogue in his plays from foreign as well as earlier English drama, drawing freely on the work of his predecessors—to such an extent, indeed, that from the 1660s until the last decade of his life he was subjected to charges of plagiarism.

There are few more eloquent tributes to the range of his literary culture than Gerard Langbaine's ill-tempered catalogue, in *An Account of the English Dramatick Poets* of 1691, of his alleged literary thefts. Langbaine provides a comprehensive account of Dryden's reading as it is relevant to his plays. Langbaine is sometimes wide of the mark in specifics, and he fails to mention some works that Dryden demonstrably knew, but the *Account* is nevertheless an inquiry, written by a very well informed contemporary, into the literary background of Dryden's plays. It provides a sobering reminder to us that he knew many books of which the modern memory is dim.

In Dryden and Langbaine, whatever the obscure personal reasons for their quarrel, we would seem to have an opposition of Renaissance and post-Renaissance literary attitudes: an opposition similar to that allegorically expressed only a little later by Swift in *The Battle of the Books,* in the debate between the spider and the bee. Within the Renaissance conception of literary property which Dryden held, he was not guilty of plagiarism in his liberal use in his plays of the work of his predecessors. Shakespeare and Jonson in England, Calderón and Moreto in Spain, Pierre and Thomas Corneille in France, among many others, provided honourable precedents for his own practice. Dryden praised Jonson in ***Of Dramatick Poesie*** for his use of the work of his predecessors, and we may apply to Dryden himself his own conclusion about Jonson: 'what would be theft in other poets is only victory in him'.

Dryden wrote, or wrote part of, a dozen comedies. He began with a comedy of London life, ***The Wild Gallant*** of 1663, a form to which he returned in ***Sir Martin Mar-all*** of 1667 and ***The Kind Keeper*** of 1678. Alone among the dozen plays these three have English locales and characters, and in the second and third of them the locales and characters seem to have been determined, not by Dryden, but by other persons: the Duke of Newcastle for ***Sir Martin*** and King Charles II himself for ***The Kind Keeper.*** The tragicomedies, by far the most important group of the plays, have settings in the Mediterranean countries. The first of them, ***The Rival Ladies*** of 1664, Spanish in setting and characters, follows at an amused distance the conventions of the currently popular 'Spanish Plot'. ***The Rival Ladies*** was a qualified success, and in ***Secret Love*** of 1667 Dryden altered his dramatic strategy, devising the pattern of tragicomedy he would thereafter follow: a two-plot pattern, with differentiation of social rank as well as of mood between the largely independent plots, only one of which includes events potentially tragic in outcome. In ***An Evening's Love*** of 1668, ***Marriage A-la-Mode*** of 1672, ***The Assignation*** of 1672, ***The Spanish Fryar*** of 1680, and ***Love Triumphant*** of 1694, Dryden worked variations on the pattern, in some plays giving primary emphasis to the comic plot, in others to the serious. These plays represent over half his production in comedy, much more than that if proper allowance is made for the quality of several of them. And traces of his distinctive pattern of tragicomedy may be seen in the two famous comic plots he reworked: ***The Tempest*** of 1667 (written with Davenant) including much that is original though it is based on Shakespeare, and ***Amphitryon*** of 1690, again including much that is original, though it is based on Plautus and Molière.

The locales of Dryden's comedies have a functional relationship to dramatic structure and tone. Without exception, the tragicomedies are set in remote places, removed from the pressing realities of English life; without exception a London locale in his comedies is accompanied by a deflation of spirit, in which the action, if not 'all cheat' (in the phrase he applied to Jonson), is largely just that. He did not, except tentatively in his first play, employ his remarkable gift for repartee, perhaps his most impressive gift as a dramatist, in his comedies of London life. The work of his left hand, these three plays are inferior to his best tragicomedies, just as they are inferior to the best plays of his great contemporaries, who achieve an actuality lightened by conversational wit, in which expressions of affection are not always excluded.

Dryden's comedies have suffered in reputation with critics from his own depreciatory references to them. 'Neither, indeed, do I value a reputation gained from comedy,' he wrote in the Preface to ***An Evening's Love,*** 'so far as to concern myself about it any more than I needs must in my own defence: for I think it, in its own nature, inferior to all sorts of dramatic writing. Low comedy especially requires, on the writer's part, much of conversation with the vulgar: and much of ill nature in the observation of their follies.' And in the Dedication of ***Aureng-Zebe*** he wrote that 'some of my contemporaries, even in my own partial judgment, have outdone me in comedy'. We are more likely to agree with him in the latter observation than in the former, and yet both of them may unfairly prejudice the case against him. Modern students have been inclined to take him at his word. David Nichol Smith, for example, used the remark in the Preface to ***An Evening's Love*** as warrant for confining to a single paragraph his comments on the comedies in an essay devoted to Dryden's plays [*John Dryden,* 1950]. This is not to say that his comedies have been ignored; rather that, in the intensity of our preoccupation with Etherege, Wycherley, and Congreve, his comedies have received less attention than they deserve—and less than he in other critical statements would seem to claim for them.

'Wit's now arriv'd to a more high degree,' Dryden wrote [in the Epilogue to ***The Conquest of Granada***] not long before ***Marriage A-la-Mode*** appeared; 'Our native language more refin'd and free'. If in 1671, before the best plays of Etherege and Wycherley had been written, the couplet was boastful hyperbole, it would have become more nearly an accurate judgment by the time Dryden died in 1700. If Shakespeare be left out of account, it is not self-evident that the *comedy* of the earlier seventeenth century is superior to that of the later part of the century. Congreve's accomplishment may equal Jonson's; Dryden's comedies are arguably better than those of Beaumont and Fletcher, which they so often resemble.

Dryden alludes in the Prologue to ***Marriage A-la-Mode*** to a character in Beaumont and Fletcher's *The Scornful Lady.* That comedy depicts a gentleman's stratagems to win a lady whom he has alienated, her love for him notwithstanding, by a public show of affection. Because in plot and in stretches of wit dialogue, the play anticipates Dryden's own preoccupation with dialogue and episodes turning on antagonism between the sexes, it provides a meaningful subject for comparison with Dryden's own work. Described by Eugene M. Waith [in *The Pattern of Tragicomedy in Beaumont and Fletcher,* 1952] as 'the best comedy written by Beaumont and Fletcher in collaboration', *The Scornful Lady* has a plot which, again in Waith's words, consists 'mainly in the brilliant battle of wits' between the two chief characters, the Elder Loveless and the reluctant lady. The play well illustrates what Dryden had in mind when, in ***Of Dramatick Poesie,*** he described the 'chase of wit' as a special excellence of Fletcher. He emulated the accomplishment, and in several of his plays, including ***Marriage A-la-Mode,*** he may be thought to have surpassed it.

Reading the latter play along with *The Scornful Lady,* we can see that Dryden's claim, 'Wit's now arriv'd to a more high degree,' was not without some foundation. Dryden's analysis of the vagaries of sexual affection is more probing, and it is much more susceptible to a generalized application to humanity at large, than is Beaumont and Fletcher's. If they occasionally provide an intimate glimpse into the divided mind of the lady, who out of caprice risks the loss of the man she loves, they more frequently confine themselves to banter arising from the ludicrous situations to which Loveless' disguises and stratagems give rise. One seeks in vain in *The Scornful Lady* for lines comparable to many in ***Marriage A-la-Mode*** in which relaxed conversation conveys profundity of psychological insight with economy and precision of statement. In elegance of style which is yet dramatically appropriate, Dryden is surely superior. His play was written some sixty years closer to our own time, after the important linguistic changes of mid-century; that is after all what he had in mind when he wrote that 'Our native language' was 'more refin'd and free'. The credit for his achievement was partially attributable, as he implied more than once, to the age in which he lived. Yet to read *The Scornful Lady* and ***Marriage A-la-Mode*** one after the other is perhaps to experience an impression that there was indeed improvement with the passage of time in seventeenth-century comedy. It is certainly to experience a sense of movement into something like the modern world. One is reminded of the aptness of Norman N. Holland's phrase, 'the first modern comedies', to describe the best of those written in the Restoration [*The First Modern Comedies: The Significance of Etherege, Wycherley and Congreve,* 1959].

Our disappointment with Dryden's comedies of London life is intensified by the expectations we take to them. If in the best of his tragicomedies he surpassed Beaumont and Fletcher, he did not in his London comedies equal, much less surpass, Ben Jonson. Reminiscences of Jonson abound in ***The Wild Gallant, Sir Martin Mar-all,*** and ***The Kind Keeper,*** but these plays cannot sustain comparison with *The Alchemist* and *Bartholomew Fair,* nor can they sustain comparison with the best London comedies written in his own time. It is curious that he was not impelled by the successes of Etherege and Wycherley to a more sustained effort in the satirical vein they had opened. Presumably he had them in mind when in the Dedication to ***Aureng-Zebe*** he wrote that he had been surpassed in comedy by some of his contemporaries. Yet after his relative failure in ***The Wild Gallant*** and his early successes in tragicomedy, he turned to the life around him only in response to commands he could not refuse. The comic scenes of his best tragicomedies, ***Secret Love, Marriage A-la-Mode,*** and ***The Spanish Fryar,*** reveal that he possessed in abundance the specialized gifts for close and witty analysis of social and emotional antagonisms needed for success in the kind of comedy Etherege and Wycherley wrote. The Sicilian or Spanish locales of his plays often seem loose disguises for the London of his own time. Yet the remote places provide an insulation against mundane actuality. His London comedies are different in impact from his own tragicomedies and from the best comedies written by his contemporaries.

The Wild Gallant, like ***Sir Martin Mar-all*** and ***The Kind Keeper,*** seems not to be altogether Dryden's own work. So much is implied in his Preface to the play: 'The plot was not originally my own: but so altered by me (whether for the better or worse, I know not) that, whoever the author was, he could not have challenged a scene of it.' Dryden apparently did not know the identity of the author, who was probably, in view of the early date of ***The Wild Gallant,*** someone who had been active before the theatres were closed in 1642. Presumably Dryden worked from an old manuscript: perhaps, as has been suggested [by Alfred Harbage in "Elizabethan–Restoration Palimpsest," *Modern Language Review* XXXV, 1940], one by Richard Brome. In any event, the supposition that he rewrote a Renaissance play would account for the resemblances of ***The Wild Gallant*** to the comedies of Massinger, Middleton, Shirley, and Brome as well as to those of Fletcher and Jonson. If it was not successful with its first audiences and is now little read, it nevertheless repays attention for the clarity with which it reveals the continuity in English comic tradition of the seventeenth century: the derivation of Restoration comedy in themes, character types, and plots from patterns well established before the civil wars. In his critical essays Dryden said little about the earlier comic dramatists other than Beaumont and Fletcher, Jonson, and Shakespeare. '*Heywood* and *Shirley* were but Types of thee,' he wrote about Shadwell in ***Mac Flecknoe,*** and his contempt seems to have encompassed most of the earlier dramatists. ***The Wild Gallant*** is the more significant in his development for the evidence it provides of a link between his own work and the generality of Jacobean and Caroline realistic comedies of English life. Yet it has much about it to remind us of the Restoration. If it resembles Dryden's later comedies—in its Jonsonian humours, its boarding house scenes, its sexuality, and its improbable episodes—it approximates more fully than the two later ones the form which the comedy of manners assumed.

For all its farcical situations, ***The Wild Gallant*** turns on the central antagonisms of Restoration comedy: between social classes, between the generations, and between the sexes. Not surprisingly in this play produced less than three years after the Restoration, the social antagonisms have political overtones. Loveby's casual allusion (I. ii) to a tradesman named Tribulation might have reminded his first audiences of Jonson's Tribulation Wholesome, but it would also have reminded them that many Dissenters of the City had supported Parliament during the civil wars.

Citizens and citizens' wives, like many before and after them in seventeenth-century comedy, are the destined victims of young gentlemen, richer in wit than in ready money. Bibber, the tailor whose love for a joke makes him an easy target, is a type of the Restoration would-be wit, aspiring to a social level above his reach, and Loveby, 'the wild gallant', is an impecunious and free-living true-wit, a foreshadowing of such a character as Congreve's Valentine, who like Loveby is finally saved by the resourcefulness of his lady. Sir Timorous, 'a bashful knight' and victim of town sharpsters, is the familiar figure of the maladroit squire, one who can be awarded to a clever girl who lacks the fortune needed for marriage to a true-wit. The Restoration practicality in marriage settlements is fully apparent: the clearheaded young are not too much in love to forget the need for a fortune, nor do they cross class lines in choosing a mate.

Lord Nonesuch has the conventional role of a father determined to marry his daughter, Constance, to a rich man, a role that as in many another comedy leads his daughter to a defensive stratagem—here a pretended pregnancy—so that she may marry the man of her choice. (It is a mark of the early date of the play that Dryden, contrary to the neoclassical principle that a character's personal qualities should be commensurate with his rank, portrayed a lord, even one with a name proclaiming his atypicality, as such a simpleton as this one.) Constance loves Loveby, but like Angelica in [Congreve's] *Love for Love* she is reluctant to admit her love for a man who has been profligate with his favours and his money. Like Angelica, she undertakes on her own initiative stratagems to aid her beloved, who is ignorant of her affection for him. Like other heroines of Restoration comedy, Angelica included, she is a reluctant mistress, in whom affection is not incompatible with a willingness to enjoy a triumph over her lover. When after she has secretly supplied Loveby with money, he, in ignorance of the source of his wealth, boasts to her and her cousin Isabelle about a pretended inheritance (II. i), the two girls draw him into yet more extravagant lies, in a conversational duel of wits. The scene is in what proved to be one of the richest comic veins of the age, one that Dryden himself later exploited with distinction. Yet he did so in his tragicomedies rather than in his later London comedies.

The Wild Gallant did not succeed on the stage to Dryden's expectations, and he is defensive about it in his Preface and in the Epilogue he wrote for a revival. 'This motley garniture of fool and farce', he called it in the Epilogue: excessively severe perhaps but not altogether inaccurate as a description of the play, which is indeed a mixture of comic styles.

The inferiority of ***Sir Martin Mar-all*** and ***The Kind Keeper*** to most of Dryden's plays may be explained by the fact that he did not have a free hand in them. Samuel Pepys referred to ***Sir Martin*** in his Diary, 16 August, 1667, as 'made by my Lord Duke of Newcastle, but, as everybody says, corrected by Dryden', a statement consistent with what can be inferred from the play itself, which retains strong traces of Newcastle's hand, even as it reveals in its excellences the professional skill of Dryden. If the radical superiority of the play to Newcastle's unaided work argues for Dryden's part in it, the presence of situations and character types taken over from obscure plays by Newcastle as well as one episode borrowed from an old play that Newcastle but not Dryden could be presumed to know provides convincing evidence that the Duke's part in the collaboration was more than nominal. ***Sir Martin*** is intermittently a farcical comedy of situation (vulnerable to the criticism of farce that Dryden included in his Preface to ***An Evening's Love***), and so is ***The Kind Keeper; or, Mr Limberham,*** in which Dryden's collaborator seems to have been the King himself. In a letter of July 1677 Dryden remarked that 'the Kings Comedy lyes in the Sudds . . . it will be almost such another piece of businesse as the fond Husband, for such the King will have it, who is parcell poet with me in the plott; one of the designes being a story he was pleased formerly to tell me'. Dryden refers, Charles E. Ward has explained [in *The Letters of John Dryden, with Letters Addressed to Him,* 1942], to ***The Kind Keeper,*** which resembles Tom D'Urfey's *A Fond Husband.* Even if the King's collaboration was confined to casual suggestions, Dryden was limited by them in writing the play, which can no more be regarded as representing his natural taste in comedy than ***Sir Martin.***

Unlike ***Sir Martin,*** one of the most popular of all Dryden's plays during his lifetime, ***The Kind Keeper*** did not succeed on the stage, a fact to which Dryden refers with a certain bitterness in his Dedication, attributing its failure to resentment of the sharpness of his satire on 'keeping' mistresses. This would seem to be less than a comprehensive explanation of the play's failure, the reasons for which, entangled as they may be with Restoration politics and personalities, we can probably never know. Dryden praises the play in his Dedication: 'I will be bold enough to say, that this comedy is of the first rank of those which I have written, and that posterity will be of my opinion.' Posterity has not been of his opinion (though the play has numbered George Saintsbury among its admirers), and, in the light of Dryden's reference to it in the letter of July 1677, it is hard to believe that his praise of it was altogether sincere. Perhaps his remark was a politic tribute to the King.

The Kind Keeper and ***Sir Martin Mar-all*** are alike in respects other than their settings in London boarding houses. Continuity of plot is subordinated in both plays to disjunctive episodes turning on audacious acts of misrepresentation and trickery; both plays have 'humours' characters, including in ***The Kind Keeper*** the distinctly Jonsonian type of the 'hypocritical' and 'fanatic' Dissenter; both plays portray the mundane realities of London life rather than the social affectations of the fashionable. Dryden includes a reference to *The Alchemist* in the dialogue of ***The Kind Keeper*** (I.i), and the mad stratagems by which the principal character, Woodall, carries out his simultaneous intrigues with the women of the boarding house are heaped one on another like the stratagems of Face and Subtle to bilk their greedy patrons. The loose-jointed plot, dependent on such a palpable absurdity as a father not recognizing his own son, is resolved by the simple device of revealing that the putative daughter of the landlady is in reality the rich heiress whom Woodall's father has picked out for his lecherous son.

King Charles's taste in comedy, it would appear, was not fastidious, nor was that of the Duke of Newcastle. Exposition and continuity of plot are if anything more casual in ***Sir Martin*** than in ***The Kind Keeper,*** and the indifference to plausibility of event is scarcely less extreme. Yet ***Sir Martin*** less frequently approaches the sordid than ***The Kind Keeper,*** which in its depiction of a father unwittingly aiding his son in whore-mongering can repel even readers who relish the uninhibited treatment of sexual subjects. It is not difficult to discover qualities in the two plays that would have won the earlier a prominent place in the repertory and removed the later from the stage after a short opening run.

A passage in the Preface to ***An Evening's Love*** would seem to express Dryden's attitude toward such comedies as ***Sir Martin Mar-all*** and ***The Kind Keeper.*** He will ignore undiscriminating applause, he insists in what must be described as a petulant tone, from a public which is insensitive to 'wit on the poet's part, or any occasion of laughter from the actor besides the ridiculousness of his habit and his grimaces'.

> But I have descended, before I was aware, from comedy to farce; which consists principally of grimaces. That I admire not any comedy equally with tragedy is, perhaps, from the sullenness of my humour; but that I detest those farces which are now the most frequent entertainments of the stage, I am sure I have reason on my side. Comedy consists, though of low persons, yet of natural actions and characters; I mean such humours, adventures, and designs as are to be found and met with in the world. Farce, on the other side, consists of forced humours and unnatural events. Comedy presents us with the imperfections of human nature. Farce entertains us with what is monstrous and chimerical: the one causes laughter in those who can judge of men and manners, by the lively representation of their folly or corruption; the other produces the same effect in those who can judge of neither, and that only by its extravagances.

A curiously strong indictment of 'low comedy' to come from a man who just four years earlier had scored a popular success with ***Sir Martin Mar-all,*** which abounds in 'forced humours and unnatural events', and yet a statement of personal preferences that helps to explain the direction his career took.

After this emphatic expression of his antipathies, he describes later in the same Preface the form of comedy he prefers.

> I will not deny but that I approve most the mixed way of comedy; that which is neither all wit, nor all humour, but the result of both. Neither so little of humour as Fletcher shows, nor so little of love and wit as Jonson; neither all cheat, with which the best plays of the one are filled, nor all adventure, which is the common practice of the other. I would have the characters well chosen and kept distant from interfering with each other; which is more than Fletcher or Shakespeare did: but I would have more of the *urbana, venusta, salsa, faceta,* and the rest which Quintilian reckons up as the ornaments of wit; and these are extremely wanting in Ben Jonson. As for repartee in particular; as it is the very soul of conversation, so it is the greatest grace of comedy, where it is proper to the characters.

We can be sure that he meant what he said because for the rest of his life, except in the single instance of ***The Kind Keeper,*** in which the King was 'parcell poet' with him 'in the plott', he wrote comedies to which this description is applicable.

Dryden wrote tragicomedies at a time when the mixed form was controversial. As early as ***Of Dramatick Poesie*** he provides an analysis of conflicting opinion on the subject, expressing through one of his interlocutors, Lisideius, the opinion that 'mirth and compassion' are 'things incompatible' and expressing through another, Neander, his own contrary opinion. On few of the subjects treated in ***Of Dramatick Poesie*** may we feel such confidence as here that we are in touch with a studied conclusion Dryden had reached. Lisideius's arguments in opposition to tragicomedy and Neander's in defence of it are closely and circumstantially applicable to ***Secret Love,*** on which Dryden was at work at about the time he wrote the essay. The play illustrates Neander's proposition that 'a scene of mirth mixed with tragedy has the same effect upon us which our music has betwixt the acts'. Unlike ***The Rival Ladies,*** in which several plot lines are interwoven, ***Secret Love*** has two largely independent plots, with separate groups of characters, who, as Lisideius derisively put it, 'keep their distances, as if they were Montagues and Capulets, and seldom begin an acquaintance till the last scene of the fifth act'. Far from regarding the separation of the groups of characters as a defect, Dryden regarded it as a valuable formal device which enabled him to present persons of exalted rank without foregoing scenes of irreverent mirth. His convictions on this subject led to the remark in the Preface to ***An Evening's Love*** that he 'would have the characters well chosen, and kept distant from interfering with each other; which is more than Fletcher or Shakespeare did'. Those Renaissance dramatists were not subject to the kind of censure Dryden sustained for ***Secret Love.*** In the final scene of that play, Dryden wrote in his Preface, 'Celadon and Florimell are treating too lightly of their marriage in the presence of the Queen, who likewise seems to stand idle while the great action of the drama is still depending', a situation that Dryden was compelled 'to acknowledge . . . as a fault, since it pleased His Majesty, the best judge, to think so'. King Charles insisted that even stage monarchs be accorded the privilege of their rank. Dryden found it convenient to keep royalty out of his comic scenes, in which he indulged his gift for 'repartee', which he regarded 'as the greatest grace of comedy, where it is proper to the characters'.

Dryden's concentration on tragicomedy resulted in his choice of characters of higher rank than those who appear in the plays of Etherege and Wycherley. In the threefold division of society to which he referred in the Prologue to ***Marriage A-la-Mode,*** 'the town, the city, and the court', he gave primary attention in the tragicomedies to the court (as in the London comedies he gave it to the city), largely ignoring the town—fashionable society, but not of its highest reaches. The other dramatists always kept royalty out of their plays and for the most part even the nobility. Dorimant of *The Man of Mode* may have 'had in him several of the Qualities' of the Earl of Rochester, as John Dennis asserted [in 'A Defense of Sir Fopling Flutter,' *The Critical Works of John Dennis,* ed. Edward Niles Hooker, 1939-43], but in the play he is not identified as a nobleman. One of the reasons for the distance we perceive between Dryden's plays and most comedies of manners lies in Dryden's minimal attention to the social group that from the time of James Shirley to that of Oscar Wilde has provided the richest subjects for the display of snobbery, affectation, and ambition.

Dryden dedicated ***Marriage A-la-Mode*** to the Earl of Rochester, who, Dryden said, read and criticized it in manuscript and recommended it to the King, who in turn 'by his approbation of it in writing, made way for its kind reception'. Dryden writes with scorn of 'City' folk in his Prologue, and he includes in the play a caricature of a social climber, Melantha—not in her case a 'cit' but a fashionable lady of wealth who aspires yet higher, to an association with royalty. She is of lower social rank than the other three principal characters of the comic plot, and it is not coincidence that unlike them her conversation is marred by her bungling fondness for French words. 'Wit seems to have lodged itself more nobly in this age, than in any of the former', Dryden writes in his Dedication, and the Sicilian setting of the play notwithstanding, he seems to have provided in his comic scenes an improved version of the conversation he heard from the Court wits.

If the tone of the serious plot is different, necessarily so because decorum forbade banter in the presence of royalty, Dryden's social assumptions as they appear in the sequence of events are again aristocratic. The train of events leading to the denouement is set in motion by the discovery of Leonidas and Palmyra, who had been reared in obscurity. The discovery comes about, not through the agency of an informer, but from the undisguisable circumstance that they are of noble appearance and bearing. 'Behold two miracles!' the usurping King exclaims on first seeing them (I.i):

> Of different sexes, but of equal form:
> So matchless both, that my divided soul
> Can scarcely ask the gods a son or daughter,
> For fear of losing one.

And Leonidas, unabashed and resourceful amid the new splendours of the court, reveals the magnanimity that is a natural consequence of his royal birth. The plot moves as though by divine plan to a restoration of legitimate succession. Dryden after all wrote the play only a dozen years after legitimacy had prevailed over usurpation in England.

The serious and the comic plots of ***Marriage A-la-Mode*** illustrate Dryden's juxtaposition of Renaissance dramatic patterns and Restoration attitudes and preoccupations. Along with the analysis of sexual passion in the conversation of his worldly young lovers, an analysis that in its concern for accuracy in physiological and psychological detail can scarcely be paralleled in earlier English drama, he includes a serious plot reminiscent of dramatic romances produced in the reigns of Elizabeth I and James I. What Samuel Johnson said [in his *Preface to Shakespeare*] about Shakespeare, that his 'comedy pleases by the thoughts and the language, and his tragedy for the greater part by incident and action', is applicable to the two plots of this single play, just as it is applicable also to the two plots of *Much Ado About Nothing.* Yet if we can find precedents in Shakespeare, and even more of them in Beaumont and Fletcher, for the improbable incidents of tragedy narrowly averted, we cannot find in the verbal duels of Benedict and Beatrice or anywhere else precedents for such an uninhibited comment on the workings of the male mind during sexual intercourse as Rhodophil's patient explanation to Doralice (III.i) that in his effort to enjoy her after three years of marriage he has imagined her to be 'all the fine women of the town—to help me out'.

Dryden examines more audaciously than had any English dramatist before him the irreconcilable tension between the urge for variety of sexual gratification, on the one hand, and the need, which in its origin is both psychological and social, for constancy. The specifics of his conversational review of the subject may owe something to the libertine philosophy of which his patron, Lord Rochester, was a distinguished exponent, but his conception of the subject is not bound by seventeenth-century speculations in moral philosophy or by the habits of life of the Court wits. In answer to a question from Palamede about his wife, Rhodophil professes ignorance (I.i): 'Ask those, who have smelt to a strong perfume two years together, what's the scent.' The seventh commandment of the Old Testament and the modern phrase about 'the seven year itch' alike testify to the strength of the temptation to which Rhodophil is subjected, a temptation not reduced by the fact that he had married a beautiful woman whom he had loved. Should he take a mistress, as Palamede suggests, the remedy could like 'cordials' be but temporary, for, as Palamede adds, 'as fast as one fails, you must supply it with another'. The licence of the Restoration Court enabled Dryden to speak frankly on the subject, but the authority with which he addressed it derived from his humanity rather than from anything he learned from other people.

Despite their longings, the two couples do not commit adultery, and the play closes with a reaffirmation of the marriage tie: not a very vigorous reaffirmation, but still an acknowledgment that social anarchy would ensue if matrimonial law should be abandoned. How seriously, we may ask, are we to take the couples' change of heart? Is it more than a conventional termination of the comic plot? Does the final agreement of Rhodophil and Palamede to respect each other's matrimonial rights constitute an answer to the famous question (*'Why should a foolish marriage vow . . . ?'*) with which the play begins? It is scarcely a convincing answer, and its force is weakened by the exhortations to erotic delight that have preceded it. The account of a sexual embrace in the song of the fourth act (IV.ii), reporting instructions exchanged in an effort to reduce differences in the timing of the male and female approaches to ecstasy, is not consonant in emotional impact with a celebration of marital fidelity. Our susceptibility to sexual stimulation conveyed in language as graceful as Dryden's is such that we cannot quickly recover a devotion to the principle of monogamy. The play is erotic in its impact, let us acknowledge it, and our pleasure in it has a sexual as well as an intellectual basis. Yet the eroticism is not incompatible with the exploration, by way of the fable of two couples whose affections are mismatched, of the perennial tension between impulse and obligation. In this play Dryden refuses to make an emphatic moral judgment, a circumstance that troubles us less in the twentieth century than it troubled Jeremy Collier in the seventeenth, Samuel Johnson in the eighteenth, or Lord Macaulay in the nineteenth century.

Jocelyn Powell's perceptive discrimination, in an essay about Etherege ["George Etherege and the Form of a Comedy," in John Russel and Bernard Harris, eds., *Restoration Theatre,* 1965], between 'comedy of experience' and 'comedy of judgment' can help us to an understanding of ***Marriage A-la-Mode.*** The comic plot of Dryden's play depicts the vagaries of sexual love, with analytical attention—unclouded by moral judgment—to the minute discriminations of passion. If we seek for a convincing sign of authorial disapproval of promiscuity, we will be disappointed. To be sure, the impact of the comic plot is softened by that of the heroic plot. Love assumes many forms, and the constancy and devotion of Leonidas and Palmyra provide a reminder that the emotion is not always a matter of lust and a roving fancy. Yet the heroic plot scarcely constitutes a judgment on the intrigues of the uninhibited couples, whose forthright reports of the state of their affections articulate the experience of common humanity.

If the moral and emotional attitudes dramatized in the two plots are complementary, there is nevertheless an extraordinary difference between them, so great a difference that it is remarkable that the two plots can coexist in harmony. The reputation of the play testifies to the fact that audiences and readers have found them compatible. There are fewer thematic and episodic parallels between the two plots than between those in ***Secret Love,*** that one of Dryden's plays which most closely resembles ***Marriage A-la-Mode.*** In ***Secret Love,*** the heroic action, like the comic, portrays the fortunes in love of a young couple, but with the difference from ***Marriage A-la-Mode*** that the heroic couple themselves suffer from vagaries of affection. When Philocles belatedly discovers that he is the beloved of the Queen, he is briefly tempted by the prospect of grandeur to abandon Candiope, his own lady. The Queen herself in the earlier play, like Florimel in the comic plot, reveals jealousy of a rival. ***Secret Love*** resembles many Renaissance and Restoration comedies portraying the parallel courtships of a serious and a witty couple, but the same cannot be said about ***Marriage A-la-Mode,*** in which the obstacles confronting Leonidas and Palmyra are political and dynastic, irrelevant to their affections, which remain constant. Rather than seek thematic links between the two plots, we should recall Dryden's musical analogy in ***Of Dramatick Poesie.*** 'A scene of mirth mixed with tragedy has the same effect upon us which our music has betwixt the acts . . . ': something less than an exhaustive account of the matter but one which places emphasis where it belongs, on the calculated and harmonious alternation of mood. Dryden's carefully planned contrasts of mood convey a sense of design or pattern which is itself a source of aesthetic pleasure.

In the Dedication of ***Marriage A-la-Mode*** Dryden referred to it as 'perhaps . . . the best of my comedies', a judgment in which critics and makers of anthologies in the twentieth century have on the whole concurred. Whether it is in fact superior to ***Secret Love,*** among his earlier comedies, or ***The Spanish Fryar*** and ***Amphitryon,*** among his later, is a question that need not engage us. Its excellencies are like those of ***Secret Love;*** they are different from, but not necessarily superior to, those of the two later plays. In any event, ***Marriage A-la-Mode*** represents in Dryden's career a climactic working out of a pattern of tragicomedy in which he projects the intrigues of eminently credible young lovers, whose attitudes toward love and marriage would seem to be those of the inner circle of Charles II's Court, against a background action of political intrigue and improbable adventure. Dryden continued to write comedies with plot lines firmly separated from one another, in which contrasts of mood and sometimes of theme are prominent; but he did not again write a play in which emphasis is so neatly divided between an heroic world of romantic love and a commonplace world of sexual passion, nor did he again provide such gifted conversationalists as three of the young lovers in this play.

In the Dedication of ***The Spanish Fryar,*** Dryden returns to the subject of tragicomedy. His defence of his two-plot pattern is not so unqualified as it is, in Neander's remarks, in ***Of Dramatick Poesie.*** We may surmise that in the dozen years since that essay was published neoclassical opinion had hardened against it. Rymer had published his influential *Tragedies of the Last Age,* and Dryden as well as other dramatists and critics had been receptive to Rymer's argument for French formalist principles. Soon after the appearance of *The Tragedies of the Last Age,* Dryden had written ***All for Love,*** that one of his plays in which he observed neoclassical precept most consistently. Whatever the reason for the modification of his opinions, in the Dedication of ***The Spanish Fryar*** he rests his case on his own and on his audiences' preferences rather than on a reasoned exposition of the advantages of the mixed form. The play includes two actions, he writes:

> but it will be clear to any judicious man, that with half the pains I could have raised a play from either of them; for this time I satisfied my humour, which was to tack two plays together; and to break a rule for the pleasure of variety. The truth is, the audience are grown weary of continued melancholy scenes; and I dare venture to prophesy, that few tragedies, except those in verse [rhymed verse], shall succeed in this age, if they are not lightened with a course of mirth; for the feast is too dull and solemn without the fiddles.

Dryden reverts to his musical analogy, but this time in a prudential appeal to taste, in opposition to the rules, and this time his remarks have a defensive ring.

Throughout the Dedication Dryden gives primary attention to the 'melancholy scenes', a circumstance relevant to our reading of ***The Spanish Fryar.*** For the serious much more than the comic plot commands attention, to such an extent that the comic scenes are likely to seem merely interludes in tragic action. In the relationship between the two plots as in much else apart from its denouement, ***The Spanish Fryar*** indeed resembles the tragedy ***Don Sebastian*** more closely than the tragicomedy ***Marriage A-la-Mode.*** That it does so is an indication of the gravity of the subjects treated satirically in the comic scenes as well as those alluded to in the heroic action. In tone, characters, sequence of events, and even in subdued echoes of Shakespeare's *The Merchant of Venice,* the comic plot anticipates that of ***Don Sebastian.*** And the serious plot hints at the tragic theme which is dominant in the later play,

> That unrepented crimes of parents dead,
> Are justly punished on their children's head,

as Dorax in the final speech of the tragedy puts it. In the opening and expository scene of ***The Spanish Fryar,*** Pedro explains of Leonora that 'Her father's crimes / Sit heavy on her, and weigh down her prayers.' Leonora's relationship with Torrismond is clouded by her dead father's usurpation of his father's throne. The tragic potential of ***Don Sebastian*** is present in this earlier play. Dryden chose to mute it in an adroitly contrived denouement.

The serious action of ***The Spanish Fryar,*** with which the play opens and closes, has a more apparent relevance to the conditions of seventeenth-century political life than those of the earlier tragicomedies. There is a fairy tale quality about the dynastic complications depicted in ***Marriage A-la-Mode,*** a remoteness from historical reality scarcely lessened by the presence of the comic scenes, with their striking psychological realism. In ***The Spanish Fryar,*** for all its medieval setting in Aragon, the struggle for political power is played out so convincingly as frequently to recall the recent history of England. The allusions to the imprisonment of King Sancho by a usurper could scarcely have failed to put the audience in mind of the imprisonment of King Charles I, and Raymond's account of the King's entrusting him with the care of his son and heir Torrismond (IV.ii)

> Till happier times shall call his courage forth,
> To break my fetters, or revenge my fate,

would have recalled Charles I's prudent concern that his own sons escape from his enemies. It is a curious tribute to the liveliness of the political themes of the play that after the Revolution, when Queen Mary commanded a performance of it, she was embarrassed by the lines about inherited sin to which I have already referred, lines that seemed to describe her own situation (I.i):

> Her father's crimes
> Sit heavy on her, and weigh down her prayers.
> A crown usurped; a lawful king deposed,
> In bondage held, debarred the common light.

This fortuitous bit of political allegory, pertaining to events still in the future when Dryden wrote the play, suggests the force of Dryden's serious plot as well as the difficulties inherent in the dramatic portrayal of conflicts involving royalty.

Queen Mary's motive in commanding a performance of

Anthony Leigh as Friar Dominic in The Spanish Fryar *(engraving by John Smith, based on a painting by Sir Godfrey Kneller).*

The Spanish Fryar, which had been barred from the stage during her father's reign, was presumably political: to display publicly her hostility to Catholicism. Dryden must have had a similar motive when, two years after the revelations of an alleged Popish Plot, he wrote the scenes in which the avaricious and hypocritical Friar Dominic appears. The incongruity of Dominic's position as priest with his pious rationalization of his role as pander provides Dryden's most effective comic resource—and it is one which in 1680 would have had political voltage. There is no reason to assume that he had wavered in his loyalty to the principle of legitimate succession in England, which at that time meant the right of succession of the Catholic Duke of York. There would have been political advantages in indicating that the Tories as well as the Whigs could be critical of Catholic duplicity. Dryden wrote ***Absalom and Achitophel*** the following year, and if the poem is much more explicit about the constitutional issues raised in the Exclusion Controversy, it is not incompatible in its political burden with ***The Spanish Fryar.*** The primary action of the play as of the poem reaffirms legitimacy, and the play like the poem glances satirically at self-serving politicians who manipulate the emotions of the common folk. 'I have no taste / Of popular applause;' Torrismond declares (I.i), and there is reason enough to believe that he speaks for Dryden:

> the noisy praise
> Of giddy crowds, as changeable as winds;
> Still vehement, and still without a cause;
> Servant to chance, and blowing in the tide
> Of swoln success.

Such sentiments were scarcely less applicable to the England of 1680 than the criticism of Catholicism implicit in the character of Friar Dominic.

The degeneracy epitomized in the Friar reinforces the tone of calculating sensuality pervading the scenes of Lorenzo's courtship of Elvira. A young colonel whose lust has been intensified by the enforced abstinence of a military campaign, Lorenzo undertakes with Dominic's paid assistance the seduction of Elvira, the young, beautiful, and receptive wife of the impotent moneylender, Gomez, who is sixty years old. Apart from the detail of Dominic's calling, the character relationships and sequence of events—at least prior to the unexpected discovery that Lorenzo and Elvira are brother and sister—parallel those in many another Restoration comedy. Yet there is no other witty couple who can provide an ameliorating note of half-idealized love. Lorenzo and Elvira are articulate in Dryden's more relaxed manner, but the willingness of Elvira to be seduced precludes a conversational duel, and the nature of their relationship, before the late introduction of the theme of incest averted, enforces an unremitting attention to the consummation of adultery.

The comic scenes lack the conversational wit of those in ***Secret Love, An Evening's Love,*** and ***Marriage A-la-Mode,*** and they are less important in relation to the serious plot. Yet they are remarkably funny—and they must have been strikingly so when they could be seen on the stage. It is easy to imagine what a gifted actor could have made of the role of Friar Dominic, described by Pedro (I. i) as a

> reverened, fat, old gouty friar,—
> With a paunch swoln so high, his double chin
> Might rest upon it; a true son of the Church;
> Fresh-coloured, and well thriven on his trade,—

a description that helps us to understand why the character has seemed to many readers to be a redaction, in priestly garb, of Sir John Falstaff [in Shakespeare's *1* and *2 Henry IV*]. Dominic is a tribute to Dryden's versatility as a comic dramatist as well as to his clearheaded awareness of the claims of the flesh in opposition to those of an idealized code of conduct, claims of the flesh including but not restricted to the imperious needs of sexual love. It is idle to assess the resemblances of Dominic to Falstaff: they are members of a famous brotherhood, to which Cervantes's Sancho Panza [in *Don Quixote*] also belongs, men in whom a conflict between earthly and spiritual desires is almost non-existent, so strong is the commonsensical awareness of the simple need of a man to live comfortably in a difficult and dangerous world. Love and lust are facts of life, and Dryden in this play makes ample acknowledgment of them, but they are less important in the totality of experience than a reading of English drama would lead one to believe. Dryden enlarges, almost in an Elizabethan manner, the spectrum of his comic targets. The variety of the targets as well as the nature of Lorenzo's intrigue to seduce Elvira results in dialogue very different from the repartee of ***Marriage A-la-Mode,*** and it results also in a deflation of mood.

Yet it is the serious plot which controls the play. Dryden writes with pride about it in his Dedication, commending the diction, which is indeed vigorous and free of the bombast that, as he acknowledges, had sometimes appeared in his heroic plays. We may feel less confidence in accepting his praise of the denouement, in which against all expectation the protagonist and his wife end in happiness and prosperity and the seeming villain reveals himself as prudent and even benevolent. 'The dagger and the cup of poison are always in a readiness;' Dryden remarks in his Dedication, 'but to bring the action to the last extremity, and then by probable means to recover all, will require the art and judgment of a writer; and cost him many a pang in the performance.' Dryden's terms are well chosen, and insofar as they mean that he has managed the action adroitly, they are accurate. Passages early in the play may be seen in the retrospect afforded by the fifth act to prepare for the revelations of the events by which catastrophe was averted. Bertran's enigmatic response to the Queen's half-articulated command to kill the imprisoned King and his suspicion that she may be using him as a tool to prepare the way for Torrismond (III.iii) provide plausibility for Bertran's ruse of falsely pretending to kill the King. So also the Queen's doubts and hesitations in her complicity in the projected crime provide plausibility for her later most sincerely experienced remorse. The vacillating and weak-willed Queen may not seem an appropriate wife for Torrismond, but, like the Queen in ***Secret Love,*** she provides a not unconvincing study in a mind torn by conflicting desires.

The tragicomic movement of the main plot is well contrived. So much we must concede. The next step in an evaluation of it brings us to decision on problems common to the form of tragicomedy, a form that has always been more popular in the theatre and with readers than with critics. The problems are too familiar, and too generalized in their application to the drama of many generations, to repay much attention here. We may acknowledge at once that Dryden's denouement inhibits an exploration of the consequences of sin: actual sin in the case of the Queen, who had indeed hinted to Bertran that she wished him to kill the King; a contemplation of sin in the case of Bertran, who had apparently refrained from the murder as much out of prudent calculation as moral compunction. And curiously the comic action proceeds analogously. Because Lorenzo and Elvira are revealed to be brother and sister, their sin remains merely one of thwarted intention. Whatever Dryden thought of Thomas Rymer's doctrine of 'poetical justice,' he manipulated the events of this play to provide a delight arising from unexpected turns of plot.

Less than a year before ***Amphitryon; or, The Two Socia's*** was performed in 1690, Dryden had defended himself in the Preface to ***Don Sebastian*** against the charges of plagiarism Langbaine made in *A New Catalogue of English Plays* of 1687. 'The *materia poetica* is as common to all writers', Dryden wrote in the Preface to ***Don Sebastian,*** 'as the *materia medica* to all physicians.' As if to illustrate that proposition, he turned in ***Amphitryon*** to one of the oldest of all comic stories, best known in the versions of Molière and Plautus but with a literary ancestry extending into antiquity far beyond Plautus: 'were this comedy wholly mine,' Dryden writes to his patron in his Dedication, 'I should call it a trifle, and perhaps not think it worth your patronage; but when the names of Plautus and Molière are joined in it, that is, the two greatest names of ancient and modern comedy, I must not presume so far on their reputation, to think their best and most unquestioned productions can be termed little.' Dryden joins an acknowledgment of literary indebtedness to a conventional compliment to his patron, and by implication he reaffirms his conception of literary property. Plautus had drawn on the writings of his predecessors; Molière—as well as Rotrou and others—had drawn on Plautus. Could anyone who knew and admired the classical tradition in comedy censure Dryden for emulating his distinguished predecessors?

Amphitryon was published too late for Langbaine to consider it in its proper alphabetical order in *An Account of the English Dramatick Poets,* but he included an entry for it in his Appendix of late additions to that work. Dryden's literary borrowings for the play presented an awkward subject to Langbaine, and his comments reveal an ambiguity in evaluation, a grudging admiration for Dryden's accomplishment undercut by the use of a depreciatory metaphor. Referring to Dryden's acknowledgment of his sources, Langbaine justly adds that he has taken more from Molière than from Plautus: 'but however it must with Justice be allowed, that what he has borrowed, he has improv'd throughout; and *Molliere* is as much exceeded by Mr *Dryden,* as *Rotrou* is outdone by *Molliere.*' A handsome compliment—but one qualified in what follows: 'The truth is, our Author so polishes and improves other Mens Thoughts, that tho' they are mean in themselves, yet by a *New Turn* which he gives them, they appear Beautiful and Sparkling: Herein resembling Skillful Lapidaries, that by their Art, make a *Bristol* Stone appear with almost the same Lustre, as a Natural Diamond.' Langbaine is more accurate in his descriptive remarks than in his critical evaluation. The 'other Mens Thoughts' that Dryden used were scarcely 'a *Bristol* Stone,' nor is his play a counterfeit diamond, but he nevertheless borrowed more liberally for ***Amphitryon*** than for any other play he wrote. Yet it is his own play, in his distinctive style, directed in many particulars to an English audience of 1690.

Dryden exploits the eroticism inherent in his subject more forthrightly than had Molière, but he is scarcely gross. Although ***Amphitryon*** is as singlemindedly preoccupied with seduction as ***The Kind Keeper,*** it has an ameliorating classical setting unlike the London milieu of the other play, which is all too convincing to permit an escape into fantasy. The quality of fantasy in ***Amphitryon,*** the vicarious experience it provides of sexual fulfilment, constitutes a special attraction of the subject. If Charles Lamb's famous defence of Restoration comedy as existing in a self-contained and amoral world of its own is applicable to any late seventeenth-century play, it would seem to be applicable to this one, in which the king of the gods employs divine powers to enjoy a wife devoted to her husband, whose love for her husband ironically intensifies Jupiter's pleasure in her embraces. The adulterous relationship has a natural consequence, but with the supreme felicity of his divinity, Jupiter can interpret Alcmena's pregnancy as a favour granted to her.

Yet for all its classical setting, its eroticism, and its sustained gaiety, ***Amphitryon*** is an audacious play, a comical study of a grave situation arising from the self-indulgent intrusion of the great into the affairs of their inferiors. The opening scene establishes a conception of Jupiter as despotic, and it suggests as well the vulnerability of common folk to the abuse of power. In an expository conversation, Jupiter explains to Mercury and Phoebus the plan he has ordained. (The mock logic of the passage, in Dryden's best philosophical style, reminds us that not long before he had written ***The Hind and the Panther.***) 'Fate is,' Jupiter declares,

> . . . what I,
> By virtue of omnipotence, have made it;
> And power omnipotent can do no wrong. . . .

When he has told Mercury and Phoebus about his intention to enjoy the wife of Amphitryon, he silences their objections with a further revelation:

> . . . yet thus far know,
> That, for the good of humankind, this night
> I shall beget a future Hercules,
> Who shall redress the wrongs of injured mortals,
> Shall conquer monsters, and reform the world.

Dryden had the warrant of classical mythology for all this, and he stops short of a sustained parallel with human affairs. He nevertheless glances at recent English history.

If the first audiences saw a double meaning in the play, they would probably have thought of Jupiter as representing Charles II (and perhaps James II also), famous for the prodigality of his favours and famous too for his generosity to his mistresses and illegitimate offspring. The Epilogue, spoken by Phaedra of easy virtue, would seem to be an ironic lament for the Restoration Court:

> When the sweet nymph held up the lily hand,
> Jove was her humble servant at command;
> The treasury of heaven was ne'er so bare,
> But still there was a pension for the fair.
> In all his reign, adultery was no sin;
> For Jove the good example did begin.

Acceptable sentiments two years after the Revolution, affectionate criticism of the late King for those who chose to find it, in the vein of half-disguised topical allusion recurrent in the play. Mercury describes in the opening scene a quarrel between Jupiter and Juno that would have put audiences in mind of the matrimonial relations between Charles and Queen Catharine. 'She threatened to sue him in the spiritual court for some matrimonial omissions; and he stood upon his prerogative; then she hit him on the teeth of all his bastards,' among whom Mercury himself was numbered. It tells much about the atmosphere of political liberality of William III's reign, in comparison with the early years of Charles II's, that a Roman Catholic dramatist who had been closely associated with the Restoration Court could treat the familiar habits of royalty jestingly. 'These are a very hopeful sort of patriots,' says Sosia in indignation against his master (II.i), 'to stand up, as they do, for liberty and property of the subject: There's conscience for you!' Gibes at the slogans of the Revolution were permissible when spoken by a serving man of ancient Thebes, who was confronted on stage by a god who had assumed his likeness.

The topical allusions testify to the inventiveness of Dryden's reshaping of the familiar story. So also does the structural pattern of the play, which approximates to the pattern of the tragicomedies more closely than may at first appear. Again Dryden introduces separate groups of characters, of different rank, engaged in largely independent intrigues, though they are frequently together on stage; and again he uses contrasts in mood and personality in successive scenes, developing thematic and episodical parallels among them. The heroic dimension of Jupiter's courtship of Alcmena is sustained by an eloquent blank verse appropriate to the king of the gods. Jupiter's lines represent Dryden's best vein of dramatic poetry, never bombastic, often ironic, and occasionally in the love scenes lyrical, expressing a tenderness undercut by our awareness of his true identity. Amphitryon sometimes speaks in blank verse, but not consistently and not with the eloquence the god can command. As in the tragicomedies Dryden turns from the verse of the heroic characters to a conversational prose when the lesser characters talk with the deflation of everyday life about their own affairs and the affairs of their betters. Phaedra returns us to a credible world when she ventures the opinion (III.i) that Amphitryon has picked a quarrel with Alcmena because she has drained him of sexual energy and he is ashamed to admit it. Phaedra, who has no parallel in Plautus or Molière, is a variant of the type figure of the coquette, more covetous and less libidinous than most of them, but still a character who can play a love game with Mercury in the manner of Dryden's earlier comic heroines. Mercury's courtship of her, in which he is aided by his supernatural powers and hindered by the physical appearance he has assumed, provides a humorous parallel to the main action, reinforcing the eroticism of it. Unlike Jupiter's relationship with Alcmena, Mercury's with Phaedra is to continue after play's end, under conditions specified in a celestial version of the Restoration 'proviso' (V.i). And Sosia's aversion to his wife and his reluctance to perform his husbandly duties, as well as his suspicion of Mercury, provides a contrast to the ardours and suspicions of his master Amphitryon.

Amphitryon's and Alcmena's sequence of experiences, as they are confused and troubled by Jupiter's intrusion into their lives, is not unlike that of the protagonists of the tragicomedies, who find themselves in difficult or desperate circumstances, which are then resolved in a final turn of unexpected events. Their plight is grave indeed, leading in fact to Amphitryon's threat (III.i) to divorce Alcmena. Yet the reader or spectator, informed from the beginning of the true relationships among the characters, cannot feel a concernment comparable to that evoked by the tragicomedies, partly because he is already informed that the troubles are transitory, and partly because the tragic potential of the situation is obscured by the cynical comments on it of the secondary characters. Dryden suggests though he does not emphasize the pathos latent in the predicament of Alcmena. 'A simple error is a real crime,' she says poignantly (V.i), 'And unconsenting innocence is lost.' If Dryden develops more fully than Plautus and Molière those possibilities which Alcmena's puzzlement presents for examining the ambiguities of emotion and even of knowledge based on personal experience, he yet stops short of such a full exposition of her doubts as that of Heinrich von Kleist in the early nineteenth century. Dryden resolves her problems—and Amphitryon's—with a reversion to classical myth when Jupiter offers such consolation as he can in his announcement that she will become the mother of Hercules. Mercury's response to the congratulations offered Amphitryon after Jupiter's announcement would seem to articulate Dryden's doubts about the nature of the divine favour granted: 'Keep your congratulations to yourselves, gentlemen. 'Tis a nice point, let me tell you that; and the less that's said of it the better. Upon the whole matter, if Amphitryon takes the favour of Jupiter in patience, as from a god, he's a good heathen.'

Like Shakespeare in *The Comedy of Errors* at the beginning of his career, Dryden at the end of his own career turned to a play of Plautus. ***Amphitryon*** is his penultimate comedy, followed some four years later by ***Love Triumphant,*** which derives in part from Beaumont and Fletcher's *A King and No King.* Although more influential than anyone else in establishing neoclassicism in England, Dryden retained his affinities—in the choice of literary sources, subjects, and dramatic forms—with his Renaissance masters. For this reason, perhaps, his comedies have often seemed to be apart from the main line of development in the Restoration. They are indeed different from the comedies of Etherege, Wycherley, and Congreve. Whether the best of them are inferior to the best written by Etherege and Wycherley, as Dryden implied in the Dedication of ***Aureng-Zebe,*** would seem to me to be an unanswerable question—or at least a question to which the answer would turn on preconceptions concerning human nature and the nature of comedy. Neoclassicism even today has not lost all its force in dramatic criticism, and we are still inclined to undervalue Dryden's plays because of his predilection for the mixed form of tragicomedy. If we can take them for what the best of them are, superb dramatic entertainments combining romantic adventure with acutely observed scenes from familiar life, and if we can suspend our neo-Aristotelian conceptions of what comedy should be, we are likely to think that he understated the claim for his own work. (pp. 27-57)

John Loftis, "Dryden's Comedies," in John Dryden, *edited by Earl Miner, Ohio University Press, 1972, pp. 27-57.*

Jean H. Hagstrum (essay date 1980)

[*Hagstrum's writings include* The Sister Arts: The Tradition of Literary Pictorialism and English Poetry from Dryden to Gray *(1958),* The Romantic Body: Love and Sexuality in Keats, Wordsworth, and Blake *(1986), and* Eros and Vision: The Restoration of Romanticism *(1989). In the excerpt below from his* Sex and Sensibility: Ideal and Erotic Love from Milton to Mozart, *he praises Dryden as a dramatist who masterfully probed the psychological complexities of love without hesitating to address its physical manifestations. Comparing Dryden favorably to French dramatists, Hagstrum declares that the playwright "endows the theme of love with the elevation, delicacy, and tenderness that antiquity lacked, and in quite un-Gallic fashion, his* oeuvres *often throb with a bold and hearty physicality." The critic pays particular attention to* All for Love, Tyrannic Love, The Indian Queen, The Indian Emperour, The Conquest of Grenada, *and* Aureng-Zebe.]

[Although contemporaries and both public defenders of the Christian religion, Milton and Dryden approached love in entirely different ways.] For Milton, a divinely ordained hierarchy governs the relations of God, man, and woman; and a gulf yawns between love and lust, between Edenic sexuality and sin. In Dryden love is hard to locate as a link in the Great Chain of Being. It is an energy within experience, a powerful drive available to the writer, an exploitable subject for comic, ironic, sensuous, heroic, even moral purposes. It does not, however, fit into a structural microcosm, as it does in [Dante's] *La vita nuova* or in the *Divine Comedy.* Dryden of course possessed a clear sense of right and wrong in love, as in other matters, but no Miltonic chasm separates the respective realms of good and evil. Dryden enjoys and transmits to his countrymen the sensuality of pagan classical verse. He is drawn to the physical heartiness of Chaucer and Boccaccio. And even the incestuous Sin, who in Milton stands with her paramours at the gate of hell, is somewhat more ambiguously placed in Dryden.

In expressing love and related emotions, Dryden was as much a pioneer, as much a creator of subsequent culture, as he was in writing satires or heroic couplets. Richardson inherited his heroic sensibility, as Pope inherited his wit and versification. My aim is to show how Dryden, under some contemporary impulses but nevertheless with great force and originality, created within a belligerent heroic world characters moved by delicate love, tender pity, and soft compassion. [In his *John Dryden: The Poet, The Dramatist, The Critic,* 1932] T. S. Eliot considered Dryden one of the creators of English culture and believed that "to him, as much as to any individual, we owe our civilization." Eliot was talking chiefly about Dryden's triumph in modernizing the English language. It is also possible to see him as a creator of modern feeling, gentler than what has usually been known before, softer and more civilized. Dryden had found England raw, bleeding, and angry after the Civil War. He left it willing to subdue its raging passions and bend its neck to a yoke of mildness. Dryden does more than Milton can to justify the ways of man to man.

Dryden's Sensuality

If love in Dryden ends up as a civilizing and social affection, the reason for this does not lie in the elimination or even the weakening of physical passion. From his earliest plays to his very late translations and adaptations from foreign tongues, sexuality continues to burn with undiminished heat. No Restoration writer has been called Romantic more often than Dryden: "It would be hard to frame a definition of romanticism that should include *Marmion* and exclude ***The Conquest of Granada***" [George R. Noyes, "Biographical Sketch," *The Poetical Works of Dryden,* 1950]. That "romanticism" embraces the treatment of love and its inescapable sexual ingredient, for Dryden in his own way was as sensual as Keats. He was of course writing for a newly liberated audience, for an age to which libertinism as a plausible philosophy and way of life was not unknown, during a century in whose middle years "pornography seems to have been born and grown to maturity" [David Foxon, *Libertine Literature in England, 1660–1745,* 1965]. But Dryden's sexuality seems to owe more to a source deep within him than to his age. His religious conversions did not extinguish it, and it survived his deeply felt poetic repentance for having added to the "fat Pollutions" of a "lubrique and adult'rate age"—more specifically to the "steaming Ordures" of the Restoration stage (***To . . . Mrs. Anne Killigrew*** [1686], 63-65). Part of Dryden's zest in writing about sex must have been related to an age-old belief that it can cure low spirits and add spice to life—and also to language, spoken and written. Benedick says to Leonato in his own penultimate speech in *Much Ado about Nothing,* "Prince, thou art sad; get thee a wife, get thee a wife: there is no staff more reverend than one tipped with horn." That venerable wand Dryden waved over his readers throughout a long career. Looking to the future, we may note that by praising the hearty male and suggesting that the man with a past who has finally decided to direct his inclination to one woman only makes the best husband, Dryden provides a possible reason why Pamela, Sophia Western, and Marianne Dashwood were able to lead happy lives after all. In the comic subplot of a very early play, ***Secret Love*** (1667), a play seen three times by Charles II and at least eight times by Pepys, Florimell scorns foppish solemnity and remains undisturbed when others tell of her wooer's previous flirtations:

> Give me a servant [that is, a *cavaliere servente*] that is an high Flier at all games, that is bounteous of himself to many women; and yet whenever I pleas'd to throw out the lure of Matrimony, should come down with a swing, and fly the better at his own quarry.
>
> [3.1.300-304]

If this [essay] were concerned with sexuality in comedy, it would dwell on what can here be noted only in passing, that the play Dryden regarded as perhaps his best comedy, ***Marriage A-la-mode*** (written in the spring of 1671 and dedicated to the Earl of Rochester), contains a vigorous subplot full of high-spirited repartee and an earthy and refreshing wisdom about love, marriage, and sexuality.

One of Dryden's tasks, writing as he did after the Puritan dominance, was to reaffirm against the dourness of the "Saints" what the Renaissance had earlier affirmed against centuries of Christian asceticism, namely, the importance of the senses in life and art. Neither Dryden nor his Renaissance predecessors could do this with an absolutely easy conscience; and they turned to antiquity, especially to translating and enjoying Ovid, as an outlet for their own sensuality. If Dryden's sexualization of the decorous Virgil does not surprise, perhaps his intensification of Ovid's already assertive sexuality will. Just as the pagan love poet was more specifically erotic than his Latin predecessors, so Dryden surpassed in sexual meaning earlier English translators, reversing the tendency to tone down the ancient to please modern Christian taste. The time had come for boldness in language, and Dryden's heightenings of sexual *entendre* undoubtedly did nothing to impede the vogue that Ovid enjoyed as the seventeenth turned into the eighteenth century. Dryden's relations to his classical mentor are more complex than my discussion has so far implied. The ancient was a psychologist, concerned with the social implications of love; so was Dryden. Ovid was a master of pathos and delicacy, and Dryden praised him for these qualities, as for his naturalness, his shrewd and passionate pictures of psychological disorder, and his fidelity to the details and concerns of ordinary life. Ovid appears to have helped create the Dryden we shall later be concerned with—the celebrant of pathetic love, the early Man of Feeling. At the very least, Dryden's translations from Ovid included many swift and buoyant lines of excited sexuality. (pp. 50-3)

In praising Ovid for possessing the dramatist's ability to create "pleasing admiration and concernment," Dryden points to three characters from the *Metamorphoses,* Myrrha, Caunus, and Biblis (***Essay of Dramatic Poesy***). These are all guilty of incest, the first as a daughter, the second two as brother and sister. And other Ovidian stories that attracted Dryden are also concerned with what in discussing Milton I have called the circle of narcissistic sins. From Ovid's *Heroides* 11, Dryden translates in 1680 the story of the daughter and son of Aeolus who loved each other (**"Canace to Macareus"**), a story which Ovid and Dryden convey with gentle pathos, the sin, which leads to death, being viewed as entirely human and deeply pathetic. In the ***Examen poeticum*** (Third Miscellany, 1693) Dryden translates the **"Fable of Iphis and Ianthe,"** from *Metamorphoses* 9, which portrays a lesbian love which is totally frustrated, the problem being solved only when Isis transforms one of the lovers to a boy.

In the adaptation of ***The Tempest,*** performed in November 1667, a hoydenish, comic view of incest is associated with Dryden's desire in that decade to humanize the devil and to shift the grotesque from the demonic realm to the sociopolitical, separating the supernatural from terror and tyranny. In adapting Shakespeare's play he gives Caliban an equally grotesque sister, Sycorax, and adds to their monstrous inhumanity the sin of incest. Trincalo comes upon the unlovely, loving pair in a *delicto* that is uncommonly *flagrante* but that is nonetheless treated in a burst of comic energy: "I found her . . . under an Elder-tree, upon a sweet Bed of Nettles, singing Tory, Rory, and Ranthum, Scantum, with her own natural Brother" (4.2.107-09).

After such roistering, the treatment of incest in two important plays seems complex indeed; it also reveals a degree of ambivalence perhaps not expected in the author of ***Religio Laici*** and ***The Hind and the Panther.*** In ***Oedipus: A Tragedy*** (performed 1678) Dryden collaborated with Nat. Lee in surrounding the parricide and incest with full-blooded Gothic imagery. The incest is regarded as an unnatural horror, an "offence to Kind," since nature abhors

> To be forc'd back again upon her self,
> And, like a whirle-pool swallow her own streams.
>
> [I.iv.369]

But in a scene of the final act Oedipus and Jocasta are left alone. This scene, following the unspeakable agonies of mind that accompanied the revelation of their crimes, considerably mitigates the horror. At first Oedipus asks Jocasta to leave, but when she persists in staying, he, the unnatural criminal, feels the "pangs of Nature" and of "kindness" and melts with "a tenderness, / Too mighty for the anger of the Gods!" She proclaims her innocence and asks him to discover his: "You are still my Husband." He replies,

> Swear I am,
> And I'll believe thee; steal into thy Arms,
> Renew endearments, think 'em no pollutions,
> But chaste as Spirits joys: gently I'll come,
> Thus weeping blind, like dewy Night, upon thee,
> And fold thee softly in my Arms to slumber.
>
> [V.iv.419-20]

This tender speech is terminated when the ghost of Lajus rises and causes Jocasta to return to the world of condign and separate punishment. It is difficult to overstress the importance of a scene that brings Oedipus and his mother-spouse together in full knowledge of their relation but also in an access of tenderness and emotional affinity. The scene is part of a tendency that reached a climax in the Enlightenment and in Romanticism, to move incest from Milton's column of evil to a position in human sensibility where the *lachrymae rerum* could water it.

The latest and best of Dryden's heroic, romantic plays, ***Aureng-Zebe*** (performed in 1675), concludes the series of wild lawless women (that scorner of weakness and virtue, Zempoalla in ***The Indian Queen;*** that unabashed libertine in love, Lyndaraxa of pt. 2 of ***The Conquest of Granada***) with the character of the Empress Nourmahal, who is carried away—ultimately to foaming madness—by her love for the title character. As in the case of Phèdre's love for Hippolyte in Racine, this passion, conceived by a stepmother for her stepson, is called "incestuous" (3.352); for the attainment of it, "You must Divine and Humane Rights remove" (3.353). Nourmahal is perfectly willing to remove them all, for she is a Hobbesian "natural" woman, power mad as well as incestuous, a dedicated libertine who believes love is a sovereign power which either washes guilt away from any action she undertakes or, when it stains, stains beautifully. In her mad scene she is all fire, a burning lake, in full possession of hell even before her death, which takes place only eight lines before the curtain. The punishment meted out to her keeps Dryden safely within convention, but he does provide her, like his other Amazonian villainesses, with an uncommon amount of dramatic vigor.

In one of his best plays, ***Don Sebastian*** (December 1689), Dryden gives to unwitting incest a sympathetic and attractive delineation. The love between the king and queen (who are brother and sister, though the fact is unknown to either) is consummated in marriage, which is tragically dissolved immediately upon revelation of the truth. Don Sebastian is ready to take his own life until he realizes what the hereafter would then hold for him. He resolves instead to become an anchorite and remain in Africa, refusing to return to Portugal and pollute its throne by making incest seem to be "triumphant" (5.1.538). While he remains in a natural cave to live out his life as a lonely vegetarian, Almeyda goes to a convent, and the fact that brother and sister have married will be kept secret. Thus the action at the end obeys all the requisite proprieties. But in a climactic place the play includes lines about the sin that remove from it the stigma which the severe punishment has given it. The young king, kindling at the sight of his sister-bride and hearing her say that she must continue to love him, declares, "Nay, then there's Incest in our very Souls, / For we were form'd too like" (589-90). Love and guilt, in an almost proto-Byronic fashion, are intrinsically intertwined:

Alas, I know not what name to call thee!
Sister and Wife are the two dearest Names;
And I wou'd call thee both; and both are Sin.
Unhappy we! that still we must confound
The dearest Names, into a common Curse.
[608-12]

The king calls the night of his nuptials

a glorious guilty night:
So happy, that, forgive me Heav'n, I wish
With all its guilt, it were to come again.
[615-17]

How can sin reside in such bliss? If the two are allowed to be together one moment longer, then

I shou'd break through Laws Divine, and Humane;
And think 'em Cobwebs, spred for little man,
Which all the bulky herd of nature breaks.
The vigorous young world was ignorant
Of these restrictions, 'tis decrepit now;
Not more devout, but more decay'd, and cold.
[629-34]

Dryden makes romantic love attractive even when it stands cursed by a powerful taboo. He both reflects the primitivism of the Restoration and anticipates defenses of the illicit by Enlightened thinkers and Romantic poets. But the incest has its dramatic antecedents. Ford, in *'Tis Pity She's a Whore,* portrays passionate love between Giovanni and his sister, who is pregnant with his child. The play has been condemned as morally monstrous by Gerard Langbaine, Vernon Lee, Stuart Pratt Sherman, and T. S. Eliot; and Ford does indeed try to make the love seem sincere and appealing. But Dryden is much more tender and forgiving than his predominantly skeptical and hard-headed predecessor. He allows the hero to express a sentiment of which the long and eloquent defense of incest by Mignon's father in Goethe's *Wilhelm Meister* is not much more than an expansion.

It is widely known that the *frisson* of much Gothic fiction and Romantic poetry arises from portrayals or suggestions of incest, but it has been thought that during the eighteenth century the theme remained out of sight. This is not true. No less than five of Dryden's plays make it prominent, and Defoe and Fielding chose not to avoid it. But of course it did not become prominent and obsessive, nor did it receive powerful literary treatment, until that soaring—or searing—of the spirit that we call Romanticism or at least until respect for institutional control declined as the French and American revolutions became imminent.

Love and the Tears of Magnanimity

Every student of Restoration drama knows that "pathos" and "pity" are among the most important critical terms of the period. [We also know that "the pathetic," a term derived from the "pathē" of Aristotle's *Poetics,* underwent a transformation] from a term that refers to all the passions, including the most vehement, to one that refers largely to the tender and the soft. . . . Not nearly enough has been made of the relation of aesthetic pathos to Christ's *passio*—a relation that is obvious in music of the baroque when a composer like Bach creates special effects of awed tenderness for the incarnation and the crucifixion. Because love can soften the flinty heart and tears can avail to a repentance that saves the soul, aesthetic love and pity must surely, in a Christian culture, resonate with religious meanings. Chaucer's *Troilus* is concerned with both love and pathos, and its portraits of love suffering are as heart-rending as its portraits of dalliance are infectiously joyous. Spenser—the "inimitable Spenser" whom Dryden early and long admired—steeps in tears those lines in *The Faery Queene* that introduce the loyal, fair, and forsaken Una (1.3.1-4). When Belphoebe comes upon the grievously wounded Timias, the author mollifies the asperities of his Diana by giving her *un coeur sensible.* The "soft passion and unwonted smart" that these lovers feel is underscored by comparing the woman with the mother of Jesus. Belphoebe was born of the morning dew, and no sin "ingenerate in fleshly slime" ever touched her (3.5.30, 3.6.3).

Dryden does not often follow Spenser in associating purity and pity. For him and his age it was more rhetorically effective and socially necessary to associate heroism and pity—a union that could best be made through the mediation of love. To explain and defend his infusion of tender, loving, forgiving feeling into heroic action, Dryden had a wide range of critical terms to draw upon—terms used to refer both to emotions he bestowed upon his characters and also to those he hoped to arouse in his audience. "Concernment" meant emotional involvement in tragedy: it could refer to fear alone but often could also invoke pity. "Compassion" was used frequently for Aristotelian pity; and "sense," which . . . did not yet mean practical, prudential reason, was "a feeling perceived in the mind, the heart." "Sensible" should be dissociated from its modern meaning and be allowed to refer to feeling, particularly (though not exclusively) of the refined, sensitive variety. As early as 1668, in ***An Essay of Dramatic Poesy,*** Dryden used "compassion" and "concernment" to describe the effects of tragedy, and in the same work he associates the "soft passion" of love with the Christian dispensation in general and with Shakespeare and Fletcher in particular. In 1679, in **"The Grounds of Criticism in Tragedy,"** prefixed to ***Troilus and Cressida,*** he reveals how much he admires pity, which works effectually to create charity, "the noblest and most god-like of moral virtues." Two years before, in the **"Heads of an Answer to Rymer"** (1677), he again specifically associated this eminently Christian quality with love: "We are not touched with the sufferings of any sort of men so much as of lovers; and this was almost unknown to the Ancients; . . . neither knew they the best commonplace of pity, which is love."

Such, then, is Dryden's idea of love. It is modern, Christian, and peculiarly relevant to the needs of his countrymen. It is adumbrated in the early plays; it develops steadily, though complexly, in the heroic drama; and it reaches a climax in ***All for Love,*** which appeared in the very years in which Dryden made his full formulation of the idea in prose. In ***The Indian Queen*** (1663) four characters, including Montezuma himself, weep openly and in concert.

> Into my eyes sorrow begins to creep;
> When hands are ty'd it is no shame to weep,

says Montezuma (5.1.160-61). But here there is no particular association of love and sentiment. In ***The Rival Ladies*** (published 1664) love springs up like a straw fire, and, though it does not go out, it is forced to yield to "Obligement" (5.3.280) and the presence of anterior passion. In reworking ***The Tempest*** (1667), Dryden and Davenant had before them an example of a delicate and tender innocent in Miranda, who is first aroused to suffer ("with those that I saw suffer," 1.2.5-6) a tender distress which ends in romantic passion. But to Shakespeare's example the collaborators respond either with coarse jokes about male and female innocence awakening to experience or by the hoariest clichés that "Agéd Ignorance" ever dreamed up about heterosexual love.

By December 1677 Dryden was able worthily, though not with full success, to challenge Shakespeare and in ***All for Love*** to give noble embodiment to the new sensibility and idealism. To the magnificent excess of Shakespeare's lovers Dryden responds by portraying a love that is sensual and death defying but also refined, pitiful, courteous, and in its own way uxorial. The refinement of the new sensibility should not obscure Dryden's daring achievement in making sexual love attractive. He was at least bold enough to offend Johnson, who censured him severely for "admitting the romantick omnipotence of love" ["Life of Dryden," in *The Works of Samuel Johnson, LL.D.,* 1825].

As if to anticipate one feature of the eighteenth-century landscape he helped to create, Dryden introduces Antony as a "Commoner of Nature" (1.132), a deeply melancholy man now "turn'd wild" (232) and inhabiting a Gothic setting. The "horrid Scene" (31) portrays a priest walking "a lone Isle o' th' Temple" (18) at midnight and also rising whirlwinds, opened graves, an armed ghost—and a ruin, the ruin being Antony, who paints himself in the red color of shame and the black of despair. His preeminent quality appears at once, his loyal love to the one who "deserves / More World's than I can lose" (368-69). Cleopatra is also temporarily without her lover, but not without her love, which she calls "a noble madness," a "transcendent passion" (2.17, 20). Giving the play a modern sentimental touch absent in Shakespeare, Dryden makes Cleopatra emphasize that, though Julius Caesar first possessed her person, Antony was her first true love. The lovers are mature and experienced, but their love is eager and untired, obsessive and exclusive. Consider the uninhibited, joyous, and poetic speech of Antony, "How I lov'd, / Witness ye Dayes and Nights" (2.281-82). Here no cynical Enobarbus mocks the passion; instead, Cleopatra, rejecting Augustus's offer of place and power and thinking only of death in Antony's absence, is all "that's excellent! / Faith, Honor, Virtue" (2.439-40). Dryden, reconceiving the values of the play, has made passionate love honorable without depriving it of sensuality: Antony is "a greater *Mars*" who "grow[s] rich by giving," and Cleopatra is a "brighter *Venus*" in a "perpetual Spring" (3.11, 12, 25, 28).

Shakespeare's lover is seen on the world stage, but Dryden's is not without heroic virtue, which coexists with a friendship for Dolabella that is almost Shelleyan and one for Ventidius that comes close in rivaling in intensity the love for Cleopatra. Of his love for the younger man, Antony says, "I was his Soul," "We were one mass," "For he was I, I he"—words that anticipate Heathcliff [in Emily Bronte's *Wuthering Heights*] as well as Shelley (3.91, 96, 97). Both friendships of Antony, however, are transcended by romantic love; as is the uxorial, which is so far from being despised in this play that Antony bestows on his wife the heroic phrase "the greatness of your Soul" (3.314). The loyalty of Octavia is surpassed not only by the passion of Cleopatra but also by its union with those wifelike and gentle qualities that Shakespeare's generally greater heroine lacked. Antony too is a gentler being than history or myth would warrant, although Shakespeare's hero is also a generous man of tender feeling, over whom his comrades in arms shed tears and who insists that the defected Enobarbus receive the treasures that had been his own. In Dryden's apotheosis love also transcends war, and, in behavior that looks ahead to the antiheroism of the eighteenth century, Antony chooses a love death full of rich human emotion over an empty military conflict. For Cleopatra that love death is a spousal rite. The tableau at the end is carved in noble institutional marble, for Antony and Cleopatra sit in death as though they were the unacknowledged legislators of mankind. Dryden has indeed glorified tender and passionate love. To what it traditionally possessed he adds order, pity, kindliness, and a mitigated fury. ***All for Love*** is the purest embodiment of Dryden's love pathos. It drove Shakespeare's greater play off the boards for over a century, for more reasons than can be accounted for in the somewhat bland term "classical." Neither respect for the dramatic unities and decorous discipline nor manageability as a piece of stage business alone can account for the eighteenth-century vogue of ***All for Love.*** Surely its expression in noble blank verse of a love ideal that was entirely human, at once passionate and tender, better explains its high place in the age of sensibility and humanism.

The Heroic Hero in Love

However important the stage history of ***All for Love,*** it was the earlier heroic plays in rhymed couplets that touched the hearts of the broadened reading public who supported sensibility. If the tastes of Richardson's characters can be thought of as typical, it was Almanzor and other heroic lovers who caught the fancy of later generations and established models for conduct, not the civilized Antony, who "bates of his mettle; and scarce rants at all" (prologue, 11). Perhaps it was because the great Roman and Egyptian lovers indulged an illicit affection and were allowed to die that it became the lot of heroes who fought, forgave, and in the end married to provide examples of nobility to the sentimental eighteenth century.

In [Plato's] *Cratylus* (398C-D) Socrates, in one possible etymology of the term, derived the word "hero" [herōs] from "eros" [erōs] and so established an association between the two that lasted for centuries. That link Dryden did not break in his heroic plays, where love is omnipresent and constitutes one of the basic themes. It will repay our effort to observe the nuances and trace the developments of this theme. In a collaboration with Robert Howard, ***The Indian Queen*** (performed 1663/4), "the first fully formed heroic play to be acted in London" [John Harrington Smith and Douglas MacMillan, *The Works of John Dryden,* Vol. 8], Dryden develops a contrast between the raging, passionate love of Montezuma and the virtuous, gentle love of Acacis, both of whom court Orazia the daughter of the "Inca of Peru," for whom Montezuma now fights. The contrast influences the conduct of Montezuma himself, who, though he begins in passion and fury, ends as a well-tempered, magnanimous hero. His rival and ultimate model is a Mexican prince, son of the usurping Zempoalla, whose violent blood he has not inherited, and of a dead father, a mild and gracious ruler, from whom his heritage was nothing less than civilized virtue. This virtue appears in his release of captives and his display of chivalry toward his rival Montezuma. But it appears most strikingly in his noble love of the good Orazia, to whom he remains loyal unto death, a death administered by his own hand. The pagan Acacis is an *anima naturaliter Christiana* in an ambiguous world of loss and gain, violence and gentleness. He stands as an example of delicate and forgiving love to the once violent Montezuma, whose character he surely helps to form.

In the sequel, his own ***Indian Emperour*** (performed 1665), Dryden has continued the basic contrast between two noble characters in the pagan Montezuma and the Christian Cortez. Both are in love. Montezuma woos Almeria (the daughter of the now deceased savage Indian queen), who spurns him in haughty language that causes him to lament that his lion heart is caught in the toils of a passion for an unyielding woman. Cortez also falls in love with a pagan beauty, Cydaria, daughter of Montezuma, a girl who feels strangely and deeply stirred by the affection of a Christian conqueror. This love deepens on both sides, because the lovers are mature enough to discuss its nature and the social conditions that govern it. It is quite otherwise with Montezuma, who in his frustration over unsuccess with Almeria, seeks superstitious advice from a pagan high priest and even considers accomplishing the violent death of Cortez, of whom he is mistakenly jealous. It is the misfortune of the Indian emperor that he should love a woman in love with his rival, Cortez, who does not reciprocate her love, whom she had thought she hated, and to whom she does in fact administer a stab wound in the anger that follows the frustration of her love. In the end this violent woman dies by her own hand, still loving Cortez and receiving that good man's commendation, though not his love. Both Acacis the pagan of the earlier play and Cortez the Christian represent something more fundamental than doctrinal belief, and that is goodness of heart and civility in love. Cortez leads a band of greedy Christians, whose degeneracy of character the noble Montezuma exposes in a pitiless light. But in the end Cortez surpasses in moral dignity the pagan, whose death he survives. He is not a simple conqueror but a good and noble man who thanks the power above for the double blessing of "Conquest" and "Love" (5.2.379). In the end he wins his beloved because of his goodness as much as his passion. Once more Dryden rewards a love that consists of moderation and decency, of forgiveness and chivalry. Admirable though he is, the passionate Montezuma knows only frustration in love, partly, no doubt, because the object of it was a woman of impiety and violence.

Tyrannick Love (performed 1669) presents a contrast between baroque Christianity and paganism, the one as exalted as the other is base. On the Christian side, at its most ideal, "the least immodest thought" (2.1.218) is proscribed; when Saint Catharine goes to hideous torture, she goes "bare and naked," fearing most for her sacred modesty and praying, "Let not my body be the Tyrant's spoil" (5.1.307). Against so austere and unworldly an ideal (which was doubtless unrealistic even to Dryden), the romantic love present in the Roman court displays the frustrations of a real life torn between pagan and Christian values. That life is not without idealism, which the rantings of Maximin and the sapphire-studded glories of Catharine's apotheosis tend to obscure. The successful general Porphyrius is in love with the wife of Maximin, Berenice; but the emperor wishes to reward the general's valor with the gift of his daughter. Unfortunately, the young Valeria is more than willing and so supports her father's plan by offering herself to Porphyrius. He remains steadfast in his love of the empress, but Placidius, a trusted confidant of the emperor, adds to the complication by loving Valeria. The situation is at sixes and sevens, and the frustration that thwarts almost everyone is bound to end in violence. Catharine is delivered to her horrible-glorious death. Valeria stabs herself in the presence of her beloved Porphyrius; a love martyr, she "sighs her Soul into her Lovers eyes" (5.1.577). Placidius, deprived of Valeria by her death, stabs the tyrannical emperor, who retaliates in a series of counterstabs so fierce as to be ridiculous and decrees the death of his wife and her lover. But these two survive—the empress, who is revealed to be a Christian, and Porphyrius, who inclines toward Christianity. Dryden allows them to live because during the life of her husband, monstrous though he became at the end, Berenice would not hear of infidelity and looked to the hereafter for the fulfillment of her love. In the tangled world of tyrannic and sensual passion it is Christian mildness and civility in love that are rewarded. Catharine's love is of course too noble for this world and is appropriately rewarded with a martyr's crown. But the love of Berenice and Porphyrius survives violence and passion to be fulfilled on earth because it respects law and civil society and is moderate and mature, decent and forgiving.

These lovers indeed point the moral that Dryden constantly makes about love in the decade of the 1660s. It is approved when it is disciplined, orderly, civil; and it is opposed when it is passionate, wild, and excessively individualistic. In the comedies, love in real life can be racy and amusing. In the mythic world of heroism, love must obey the conventions of society and religion. Berenice passed the test triumphantly. While her husband lived, she was "Too ill a Mistress, and too good a Wife" (5.1.448); her love for Porphyrius while Maximin lived was pure, chaste, passionless, "As light transmitted through a Crystal glass" (460). But with the creation of the greatest of the heroic plays, a more comprehensive ideal than that of social, civil love is developed. Love becomes intenser, more individual, more ennobling; by it the heroic hero is redeemed because it contains the saving ingredient of pity. Pity does not of course drive out terror, as the continuing presence of powerful and destructive villains demonstrates. Nor is pity swallowed by admiration, that new objective added to the purposes of serious drama by Minturno in the sixteenth century, an objective that became prominent in the Restoration and was specifically associated with love: Hobbes said that the "work of an heroic poem is to raise admiration, principally for three virtues, valour, beauty, and love" [quoted by Bonamy Dobrée in *Restoration Tragedy: 1660–1720,* 1929]. For Dryden, as for most playwrights of the period, it is extremely difficult to define precise dramatic aims and to ascertain what emotions in the audience a particular play is intended to arouse. But if we concentrate on content and character within the plays rather than on putative responses, it is not far from the truth to say that the last and best of the heroic plays all embody pity, fear, and admiration—these three—and that the greatest of these is pity. There is now no need for an Acacis or a Cortez separated from a Montezuma. The new hero has himself absorbed the values that Dryden had earlier found it necessary to distribute. If this analysis is right, we may have the clue to why the heroic play lived on in the newer sensibility of the eighteenth century. It united those qualities that later came to be regarded as the two chief nerves of poetry, pathos and sublimity (the latter concept including both terror and admiration).

I shall now trace what Dryden himself approvingly termed the "pathetic vehemence" (**"The Grounds of Criticism in Tragedy"**) that characterizes his portrayal of love in the major heroic plays. It has not been sufficiently considered that the notorious exaggerations and bombastic violence of these plays may in fact be marks of struggle—a struggle within Dryden's own soul as he tried to forge an ideal for himself, for his age, and for the age to come. Certainly the canon of naturalism with which Dryden himself later judged his heroic achievement does not—perhaps cannot—do it justice. What Dryden had tried to accomplish in his serious drama was to redefine greatness of soul in terms useful to a Christian society recovering from civil strife and turning toward unity, order, and civilization. His own contemporaries were aware that they were in the presence of a lofty ideal. Mrs. John Evelyn said of ***The Conquest of Granada*** that it is "so full of ideas that the most refined romance I ever read is not to compare with it; love is made so pure, and valour so nice, that one would imagine it designed for a Utopia rather than our stage." Mrs. Evelyn admired someone who could "feign such exact virtue" in an age of declining morality [quoted by Eugene M. Waith in his "Dryden and the Tradition of Serious Drama," in *Writers and Their Background: John Dryden,* ed. Earl Miner, 1972]. Dryden himself said of his hero Almanzor that he possessed "a frank and noble openness of nature, an easiness to forgive his conquered enemies, and to protect them in distress; and, above all, an inviolable faith in his affection." He was a romantic Christian knight—forgiving, sensitive to suffering, and primarily a believer in the heart's affections.

In part 1 of this ten-act play (performed December 1670) Almanzor, a "noble Stranger" (1.1.235) of mysterious origins falls in love with the future queen Almahide, now a captive, who conquers him with one glance ("As I were stung with some *Tarantula,*" 3.1.329), and he sinks immediately into a "Lethargy of Love" (3.1.337). We wonder if this man, whom Almahide finds "roughly noble" and even "Divine" in his "unfashion'd Nature" (3.1.305, 306) will go the way of Montezuma, forced to die frustrated, by his own hand. But another way is being prepared for the magnanimous but proudly and fiercely independent hero, who declares, "I alone am King of me" (1.1.206), for he now burns more for the beauteous captive's freedom than for her body. Almanzor is great, but that heroic quality is being redefined: "Great Souls by kindness onely can be ti'd" (4.1.54). Under a woman's influence, this "brave bold man" learns to damp his "inborn fire" (4.2.456, 469). He does not yet fully succeed: seizing his beloved's hand, he provokes the king to sentence him to death, a sentence changed to banishment through Almahide's entreaties. The fiery, eccentric, manly hero departs full of redemptive promise but not yet fully reclaimed, for he dreams of erecting empire on the "Conquer'd Necks" of the "best and bravest Souls" he can find (4.2.478, 479).

Part 2 (performed January 1671) reveals that Almanzor achieves the ideal stated at the outset by Queen Isabella:

> Love's a Heroique Passion which can find
> No room in any base degenerate mind:
> It kindles all the Soul with Honours Fire,
> To make the Lover worthy his desire.
> Against such Heroes I success should fear,
> Had we not too an Hoast of Lovers here.
> An Army of bright Beauties come with me;
> Each Lady shall her Servants actions see:
> The Fair and Brave on each side shall contest;
> And they shall overcome who love the best.
> [1.1.145-54]

To the achievement of that ideal (which the popularity of this passage helped to propagate during the eighteenth century) there remain grave obstacles. Almahide is now married to Boabdelin and reigns with him as queen. Almanzor's own nature is as fiery as ever, a prey to a "quick imagination," a "boundless fancy" (2.3.73, 79) that believes the queen is still available. Of her continuing love there is no doubt: at one point death seems the only way out for one who loves another but is determined to remain loyal to her spouse. The obstacles to union are formidable, but they are all overcome. After Almanzor's banishment, his vows of poverty and separation from the world, and his sentence to death, the king and husband dies in battle, the discovery is made that Almanzor is of noble Christian birth, Granada is conquered by Ferdinand and Isabella, and the hero and heroine marry. Long before Dryden so rewards them, the values that justify the reward have been established. These constitute a pattern repeated again and again in the sensibility of the following century: a powerful imagination, irrepressible impulses for good, magnanimity, pity, and above all, passionate love.

The Conquest of Granada is a public play, displaying on a world canvas the conflict between Muslim and Christian. Its values are those of a Christian civilization, freshly imbued with a new, highly individualistic sense of love, realizing itself against fanatical and old-fashioned self-will. Love is thus given an international and interfaith setting. ***Aureng-Zebe,*** whose portrayal of incest I have already mentioned, is confined to the world of Muslim India, and the emotions are more narrowly focused on the primal and the domestic. Such wars and conquests as take place are almost entirely within the family, and [in his Dedication to John Sheffield, Earl of Mulgrave] Dryden says that "true greatness, if it be anywhere on earth, is in a private virtue; . . . confined to a contemplation of itself." In this, his last and best heoric play, Dryden has clearly anticipated the domestication of heroism, which in Johnson's criticism, as throughout the eighteenth century, was transferred from the field of battle to the hearth and the heart. But in this intense familial setting there is no normative Christian character like Cortez or Isabella to establish sentimental, religious values. These—or at least a version of them—are learned anyhow: the lustful, power-hungry Morat, under the tutelage of a woman he loves illicitly, learns the truths of virtue, honor, mercy. The emperor, at first unnaturally lustful and as reckless as King Lear, is in the end softened by filial love. And Indamora, the heroine beloved of so many, is a plausible human being, not an automaton of ideal love and beauty. She contrasts strongly and favorably with the abject Melesinda, Morat's wife, a Muslim Griselda. Indamora loves but also wishes to live: she presents a contrast not only to Melesinda in this play but to Benzayda of the ***Conquest*** (pt. 1), a girl as faithful to her father as to her lover, her breast often and eagerly exposed to the avenging daggers of justice. Indamora, very humanly, fears death. Though completely innocent herself, she will dart a flirtatious glance at another man to gain a practical advantage, and she can pity the dying and formerly monstrous Morat while continuing loyal to her lover. This Kashmiri princess is a modern woman—beautiful, charming, decent, worldly, moderate, and virtuous. She is worth the winning.

And she is won by a hero, who is not so dramatically interesting as she but who, intellectually considered, is Dryden's completest union of the pathetic and the heroic. In a world of threatening parricide, fraternal rivalry, wounded minds, and unnatural affection, Aureng-Zebe establishes admirable human values. Unconquerable on the battlefield, he is also kindly and forgiving. A dutiful son and loving brother, he must win his prize against the rivalry of his father and brother. And he must also resist the amorous fury of his power-mad stepmother. His one fault (Dryden seems to make the point here and elsewhere that his heroes all do—indeed must—have blemishes) is that he is excessively and sexually emotional, a defect that he shares with others in the play, even the villainous Nourmahal.

> Love mounts, and rowls about my stormy mind,
> Like Fire, that's born by a tempestuous Wind.
> Oh, I could stifle you, with eager haste!
> Devour your kisses with my hungry taste!
> Rush on you! eat you! wander o'r each part,
> Raving with pleasure, snatch you to my heart!
> Then hold you off, and gaze! then, with new rage,
> Invade you, till my conscious Limbs presage
> Torrents of joy, which all their banks o'rflow!
> So lost, so blest, as I but then could know!
> [4.533-42]

Is this fustian pure and simple? Or is it, rather, the dramatic expression of forgivable emotions in a man who loves with his body—humanly, physically, as Adam did in paradise? Dryden, who believed greatly in moderation and who had made civil conformity the dominant virtue in the earlier heroic plays, here, at the climax of his heroic inspiration, has chosen to deemphasize the value of moderation per se and to exalt what needs to be moderated, that is, energy and vitality. Aureng-Zebe is no plaster saint, no blue stocking sentimentalist, certainly no Saint Catharine, and not even a Christian hero like Cortez. But he is very much worth redeeming. His sexual energies make him susceptible to jealousy, and when this normally kind and forgiving man sees his beloved supporting the head of his dying brother, who kisses Indamora's hand, his anger blazes. The heroine leaves, too large spirited to abide a permanently jealous man, only to be brought back by a forgiven and forgiving father, who quickly restores Aureng-Zebe to his senses and his prize. This chapter began by considering Dryden's sensuality; it is tempting to see in this last of the heroic heroes (a passionate and sensual man whose excesses are fully forgiven) the lineaments of a self-portrait.

The approach taken in my reading of the heroic plays is somewhat different from that of those critics [such as Anne T. Barbeau in *The Intellectual Design of John Dryden's Heroic Plays,* 1970] who have praised the ratiocinative in Dryden and found him weak in sentiment and passion. It is diametrically opposite to the view of those who believe Dryden wishes to laugh at the absurd sentiments he allowed his characters to utter: Almanzor lives on ground dangerously enchanted by the self-indulging fancy, a victim of the notion that love is an enthusiastic fit. It also differs from the view stated with such force by Samuel Johnson, who put emphasis on the "romantick heat" of these plays and on the "dramatic wonders," the "illustrious depravity, and majestick madness" of the characters and scenes. Johnson, though he grudgingly admires Dryden's bold treading on the brink of nonsense, denies to him a knowledge of gentle love, of "effusions purely natural," of "the simple and elemental passions, as they spring separate in the mind" ("Life of Dryden"). Dryden's rhetoric does indeed tend toward rhodomontade, and even his most human ethical insights are expressed in hearty and overly rhythmic verse that tends to belie delicacy and gentleness. His characters are volatile and sometimes violent. Goodness is set off against an array of melodramatic

OF

HEROIQUE PLAYES.

An Eſſay.

Hether Heroique verſe ought to be admitted into ſerious Playes, is not now to be diſputed: 'tis already in poſſeſſion of the Stage: and I dare confidently affirm, that very few Tragedies, in this Age, ſhall be receiv'd without it. All the arguments, which are form'd againſt it, can amount to no more than this, that it is not ſo near converſation as Proſe; and therefore not ſo natural. But it is very clear to all, who underſtand Poetry, that ſerious Playes ought not to imitate Converſation too nearly. If nothing were to be rais'd above that level, the foundation of Poetry would be deſtroy'd. and, if you once admit of a Latitude, that thoughts may be exalted, and that Images and Actions may be rais'd above the life, and deſcrib'd in meaſure without Rhyme, that leads you inſenſibly, from your own Principles to mine: You are already ſo far onward of your way, that you have forſaken the imitation of ordinary converſe. You are gone beyond it; and, to continue where you are, is to lodge in the open field, betwixt two Inns. You have loſt that which you call natural, and have not acquir'd the laſt perfection of Art. But it was onely cuſtome which cozen'd

a 2 *us*

First page of Dryden's preface to The Conquest of Granada, *from the 1672 quarto edition.*

sinners. But none of these qualities of characterization or versification should obscure the fact that primitive passion is combined with "Mercy, Pity, Peace, and Love" to make Almanzor and Aureng-Zebe heroes of moral culture, forerunners of even Sir Charles Grandison. Through the mediation of Richardson, the villa at Clarens in Rousseau's best novel is organically connected with the benevolent aspects of Dryden's Agra and Granada.

It is possible to argue that Dryden's heroic plays are dramatically redeemable only by their vigorous, though monstrous, villains—Morat, Nourmahal, Lyndaraxa, and Maximin—and that their values of benevolence and love are kept alive only by their association with diabolical energy. Two considerations keep this approach from being fruitful. The first is that Dryden was no Milton, and his Satans, for all their raw power, lack the humanity or the negative moral coherence to make them fully plausible. The other is that, quite apart from intrinsic merit, Dryden's influence had waned by the time of Byron and Blake, who in *Manfred* and *The Marriage of Heaven and Hell* were eager to join the devil's party but were in no way tempted by Dryden's villains. It was different, however, at the beginning of the eighteenth century, when, though there was no identification with the diabolical energy in Dryden, there was a keen appreciation of the poet of both erotic and ideal love—of the translator of Ovid, the author of ***The Conquest of Granada,*** the creator of the adulterous but otherwise admirable Antony.

Apposite quotations from Dryden introduce works as diverse as the anonymous *Illegal Lovers; A True Secret History, Being an Amour Between A Person of Condition and his Sister* (London, 1728) and Jane Barker, *A Patch-Work Screen for the Ladies; or, Love and Virtue Recommended: In a Collection of Instructive Novels* (London, 1723). Charles Hopkins in *The Art of Love: . . . Dedicated to the Ladies* (2d ed., London, 1704) refers to the "great *Dryden,*" the "Sacred *Dryden*" (p. 3), urging his beloved to place him first in the list of writers to be read, ahead of Congreve, Wycherley, Cowley, Otway, and Lee. Thus Dryden was revered not only by Pope and the satirists, by witty users of the elegant and barbed heroic couplet; he was also remembered by Rowe, Richardson, and that "other" eighteenth century of tenderness and sentiment. Johnson called him "the father of English criticism." He may also be called the father of English sensibility.

Dryden is of the highest importance because he embodied *both* sex and sensibility. The love he presents is *both* ideal and erotic—ideal in the sense that it is associated with a forgiving, humanizing pathos. For each of these, the full-bodied sensuality and the sensibility, there are abundant precedents. But for his combination of the two—a yoking of antithetical qualities that was at once powerful and prolific—Dryden must be credited with being something of a pioneer. [In his *Mimesis: The Representation of Reality in Western Literature,* 1953] Erich Auerbach has shown that the ancients, though they often treated love in literature, rarely made it the subject of elevated verse; he has also shown that the French, though they made love a tragically sublime and noble motif, presented it with barely a trace of overt sexual passion. How different is Dryden, who owes much to both ancient and French drama! He endows the theme of love with the elevation, delicacy, and tenderness that antiquity lacked, and, in quite un-Gallic fashion, his *oeuvres* often throb with a bold and hearty physicality. (pp. 54-71)

Jean H. Hagstrum, "John Dryden: Sensual, Heroic, and 'Pathetic' Love," in his Sex and Sensibility: Ideal and Erotic Love from Milton to Mozart, *The University of Chicago Press, 1980, pp. 50-71.*

Paul Hammond (essay date 1991)

[Hammond is a literary scholar and editor whose writings include John Oldham and the Renewal of Classical Culture *(1984) and* John Dryden: A Literary Life *(1991). In the following excerpt from the latter book, he provides an overview of Dryden's dramatic oeuvre, concluding that the playwright, despite his apparent acceptance of political stability based on power, asks "far-reaching questions about the operations of power, and the strategies which it uses to give itself authority." Hammond gives special attention to* Secret Love,

Aureng-Zebe, The Conquest of Grenada, *and* The Indian Emperour.]

The writing of poetry could not secure a living for Dryden. It is unlikely that he earned anything much from his poems of the early 1660s, and it is probable that these pieces served chiefly to establish his name before the reading public and the men of power. If he was to make a reasonable income solely as a writer, Dryden would have to turn to the theatre, for no man of letters before Pope was able to make a living from poetry alone. Dryden's involvement with the theatre was often to prove burdensome and disillusioning, but there were several reasons why the theatre might have seemed attractive in these early years. The status of the playwright was no longer as disreputable as it had been when Shakespeare and Jonson had begun their careers: under Elizabeth playwrights had often been working actors, and actors were regarded at best as servants, at worst as vagabonds. The achievement of Jonson in gaining recognition for his plays as works of literature through their publication in a handsome folio collection in 1616 had helped to secure a similar recognition for Shakespeare in 1623 and for Beaumont and Fletcher in 1647. Without the canonisation of pre-war playwrights many play-texts would have been lost, and the literary reputations of their authors would have been harder to establish. For Dryden and his contemporaries this body of work was an impressive and even intimidating literary achievement. But the plays of the half-century before the civil war could not simply be revived for the new public, which had had few or no opportunities of theatre-going for twenty years. For reasons of taste as well as reasons of copyright a new repertoire had to be created, and those who were involved in this enterprise were men of substance and distinction. The two companies licensed by the King to perform plays were headed by Sir William Davenant, who had succeeded Jonson as poet laureate and already had an established record as a dramatist and producer, and Thomas Killigrew, diplomat and groom of the bedchamber to Charles II. New plays were provided by Abraham Cowley, at that time England's most celebrated poet, by the diplomat and Fellow of the Royal Society Sir Samuel Tuke, by the Earl of Orrery, an Irish grandee, and by Dryden's ambitious brother-in-law Sir Robert Howard. These new playwrights were gentlemen and aristocrats, and the creation of a new dramatic repertoire was an opportunity to fashion Restoration culture, building on and rivalling the early Stuart achievement, and thus helping to write out the Interregnum from public memory.

From the start Killigrew and Davenant were fierce competitors, and this competition shaped the course of Restoration drama. Killigrew had experienced actors and a large repertoire of pre-war plays; Davenant's troupe were novices and his repertoire meagre. With a monopoly shared by two companies, and a fairly limited London audience to draw upon, novelty would be vital. The quest for novelty led to the commissioning of new plays and to the development of more lavishly equipped theatres. Davenant's first theatre, the Duke's Playhouse, opened in 1661 in an adapted tennis court in Lincoln's Inn Fields which accommodated changeable scenery and machines: spectacle, song and dance were to be crucial in attracting audiences. Killigrew was forced to follow suit, and in 1663 he moved from his own converted tennis court in Vere Street to a new Theatre Royal between Bridges Street and Drury Lane. Although Cosimo III of Tuscany commented on a visit that 'the scenery is light, capable of a great many changes, and embellished with beautiful landscapes', it was evidently not lavish enough, and while the theatres were closed by the plague in 1666 Killigrew took the opportunity to widen the stage; Pepys picked his way through the debris to inspect 'the inside of the Stage and all the tiring roomes and Machines; and endeed it was a sight worth seeing.' The Duke's Company, now managed by Thomas Betterton, moved in 1671 to a new theatre at Dorset Garden which had arrangements for even more elaborate scenic effects. Their mastery of spectacle was never matched by the King's Company, particularly after a fire destroyed the Theatre Royal in 1672; the replacement building, designed by Wren, was only 'a Plain Built House.'

The development of Restoration drama was determined to a large degree by this rivalry between the two companies. As Robert Hume says [in *The Development of English Drama in the Late Seventeenth Century,* 1976]:

> Experienced writers almost invariably wrote specifically for one company or the other; consequently, they knew precisely what actors would be available and for what sort of roles. When one house did well, the other might try to steal its thunder (in Dennis's phrase) by imitation, or produce a novelty as a counter-attraction, or mock the success.

There is, therefore, a strong element of self-consciousness in Restoration theatre. The redesigning of the playhouses away from the Elizabethan model, where an audience sat round three sides of the stage, to the proscenium arch design emphasised a formally framed spectacle, but this did not result in a loss of intimacy. Indeed, the audience was highly conscious of itself as a social group, and engaged in banter, intrigue and occasional brawls. The theatre's physical lines of demarcation mapped out social distinctions: the pit (the modern stalls) was dominated by the trendsetters who wished to display their wit and their fashions; the boxes (running above the pit, behind and alongside it) were occupied by the King, the courtiers and gentry; the middle gallery was the preserve of the middle classes; and the upper gallery was used by servants. The social composition of audiences was often played upon in prologues and epilogues which established a teasing relationship between playwright, actors and audience; sometimes the teasing descended to ritualised abuse, but it was always part of a well-recognised technique of audience management.

Many of the prologues and epilogues to Restoration plays challenge the audience on the subject of judgment, exposing the vulnerability of the dramatist and actors to the audience's inattention or disapproval. In his early prologues Dryden dwells upon the difficulty of writing anything, since his predecessors have exhausted the available subjects:

> Our Poet yet protection hopes from you,

But bribes you not with any thing that's new.
Nature is old, which Poets imitate,
And for Wit, those that boast their own estate,
Forget *Fletcher* and *Ben* before them went,
Their Elder Brothers, and that vastly spent:
So much 'twill hardly be repair'd again.
('Prologue to ***The Wild Gallant***, ll.41-7)

The audience's criticism that the play lacks novelty is forestalled by the observation that nature itself (the subject of any writer) is old, and therefore does not admit of novelties; moreover, any wit has been used up by the earlier generation. This is more than a pre-emptive strike against hostile critics, for it expresses a real predicament for these new dramatists inheriting, as they put it, an estate which is virtually bankrupt. The desire for novelty led to an interest in the exotic, as the 'Epilogue to ***The Indian Queen***' explains:

You see what Shifts we are inforc'd to try
To help out Wit with some Variety;
Shows may be found that never yet were seen,
'Tis hard to finde such Wit as ne're has been:
You have seen all that this old World cou'd do,
We therefore try the fortune of the new,
And hope it is below your aim to hit
At untaught Nature with your practic'd Wit:
Our naked Indians then, when Wits appear,
Wou'd as soon chuse to have the Spaniards here:
'Tis true, y'have marks enough, the Plot, the Show,
The Poets Scenes, nay, more the Painters too:
If all this fail, considering the cost,
'Tis a true Voyage to the Indies lost:
But if you smile on all, then these designs,
Like the imperfect Treasure of our Mindes,
'Twill pass for currant wheresoe're they go,
When to your bounteous hands their stamps they owe.
(ll.1-18)

While this epilogue is a teasing reminder to the audience that the company has a large financial investment in these spectacular dramas set in Latin America, it is also an admission that spectacle may have to compensate for lack of 'wit'—a word which means here both 'intelligence' and 'liveliness of thought'. The naivety of the drama is like the naivety of the Indians it depicts; and the company is at the mercy of the sophisticated and financially powerful audience, just as the Indians are vulnerable to the conquering Spaniards. It is an image which, for all its playfulness, admits the subservience of art to the judgment of those who have the money. The epilogue is delivered from a position of superiority: few in the audience could match its witty couplets, none of the audience commands the actor's elevated position on the stage. Yet the command is temporary and precarious, for the audience may heckle, may doze off, may not return. Here the only independence seems to lie in continual play with the admissions of dependency. Dryden's 'Epilogue to ***The Indian Emperour***' catalogues the various kinds of wit which different sections of the audience are allowed to judge—a classification which is at once flattering and sarcastic. As Dryden says in the 'Prologue to ***Secret Love***',

Each Puny Censor, . . . his skill to boast,
Is cheaply witty on the Poets cost.
(ll.26-7)

yet at the same time

. . .you think your selves ill us'd
When in smart Prologues you are not abus'd.
(ll.35-6)

But none of this play can alter the poet's fundamental dependence upon the audience. In his 'Prologue to ***An Evening's Love***' Dryden reflects upon the changing relationship which he has had with the theatre:

When first our Poet set himself to write,
Like a young Bridegroom on his Wedding-night
He layd about him, and did so bestir him,
His Muse could never lye in quiet for him:
But now his Honey-moon is gone and past,
Yet the ungrateful drudgery must last:
And he is bound, as civil Husbands do,
To strain himself, in complaisance to you:
To write in pain, and counterfeit a bliss,
Like the faint smackings of an after kiss.
(ll.1-10)

The dramatist is bound by contract, and powerless to abridge his audience's freedom:

Though now he claims in you an Husbands right,
He will not hinder you of fresh delight.
He, like a Seaman, seldom will appear;
And means to trouble home but thrice a year:
That only time from your Gallants he'll borrow;
Be kind to day, and Cuckold him to morrow.
(ll.30-5)

This is not quite Dryden's own voice: it is the company's dramatist speaking through an actor, extending the repertoire of the bantering relationship between servant and master. Yet it is also the voice of the playwright struggling for artistic integrity and financial survival.

Dryden's contract with the King's Company stipulated that he should deliver three plays a year. As a shareholder he would receive a portion of the company's profits, rather than having the playwright's third night's profits on each of his plays; and if he supplied prologues and epilogues for his colleagues' plays he could earn a few extra guineas. Dryden was a professional, bound by the practical limitations of his playhouse and company, and by the need to satisfy his audiences. If he was to satisfy himself artistically and intellectually it could only be through the use of—and creative play with—the conventions of the drama, which were in part dictated by audiences. Nevertheless, we should not imagine that Dryden was a frustrated romantic, longing for the opportunity for self-expression which the theatre denied him: convention enables speech, as well as limiting it, and for twenty years Dryden was influential in shaping both the forms and the ethos of Restoration drama, using it to make far-reaching enquiries into the ideologies and practices of his society. His work was generally successful commercially, and it is only in the mid 1670s that there is evidence that he had tired of the stage. He produced his plays at a steady rate, though not three a year: there were twenty-two plays between 1663 and 1683. With ***The Wild Gallant*** (1663) he made an uncertain start: in its first version it was apparently insufficiently rakish, and Pepys commented that he did not know which of the characters was supposed to be the wild gallant. Yet the assistance of the King's mistress, Lady Castlemaine, seems to have brought it to the attention of Charles himself, who had it acted at court. Little is known of the fate of ***The Rival Ladies*** (1664). ***The Indian Queen*** (1664) and its sequel ***The Indian Emperour*** (1665) successfully exploited exotic costumes and sets, and helped to set a fashion for the rhymed heroic play. The comedies ***Secret Love*** and ***Sir Martin Mar-all*** (both 1667) were unusually successful—Pepys saw the latter ten times. In the same year the demand for music and spectacle prompted a reworking of ***The Tempest.*** Dryden himself thought ***An Evening's Love*** (1668) merely a fifth-rate play, yet it ran for a remarkable nine consecutive days. A further three heroic plays were also well received: ***Tyrannick Love*** (1669) and the two-part ***The Conquest of Granada*** (1670-1). Evidence is lacking about the reception of what is now Dryden's best-known comedy, ***Marriage A-la-mode*** (1671), though the subsequent comedy ***The Assignation; or, Love in a Nunnery*** (1672) did not find favour, despite its titillating setting. After the crude topical anti-Dutch play ***Amboyna*** (1672?) Dryden, tiring of the stage, wrote his final heroic play ***Aureng-Zebe*** (1675). Evidently he was casting around for new directions at this period. He tried an operatic adaptation of *Paradise Lost* (as ***The State of Innocence***) which was never staged, and in 1677 produced ***All for Love,*** a version of the Antony and Cleopatra story written with an eye on Shakespeare. His comedy ***Mr Limberham*** (1678) was banned, though whether for political or moral reasons is still unclear. Then ***Oedipus*** (1679) and ***Troilus and Cressida*** (1679) continued Dryden's emulatory engagement with his great dramatic predecessors. His last three plays before a decade away from the stage were politically topical: ***The Spanish Fryar*** (1680) includes anti-papist satire, ***The Duke of Guise*** (1682) is a commentary on Monmouth and the Whig cause, while the masque-like ***Albion and Albanius*** (1685) celebrates the triumph of Charles II over his enemies.

The audience for which Dryden was writing these plays was not a self-conscious participant only during the recital of prologues and epilogues. The style of performance encouraged an awareness of different levels of theatrical representation. Audiences were, first of all, aware of themselves, observing who sat with whom and taking part in their own drama of critical and sexual by-play. (pp. 44-50)

The private lives of the actors and actresses could hardly be separated from their public performances when both men and women were displayed as objects of sexual interest, the women's allure often being enhanced and complicated by cross-dressing. The audience's awareness of the players' sexuality could produce intriguing use of both appropriate and unexpected casting. Nell Gwyn, at a time when she was the King's mistress, played the Emperor's daughter Valeria in ***Tyrannick Love,*** a play which was supposedly a compliment to Charles' Queen Catherine. At the end of the play as she is carried off stage dead, she rises and stops the bearers:

> Hold, are you mad? you damn'd confounded Dog,
> I am to rise, and speak the Epilogue.
>
> (ll.1-2)

And the epilogue plays teasingly with the mismatch between the reputations of actress and character:

> . . . I dye
> Out of my Calling in a Tragedy.
> O Poet, damn'd dull Poet, who could prove
> So sensless! to make *Nelly* dye for Love . . .
> But, farewel Gentlemen, make haste to me,
> I'm sure e're long to have your company.
>
> (ll.15-26)

The invitation backstage is blatant. Blatant too was the way in which the play had earlier invited the audience to contemplate not merely the display but also the possible dismemberment of the woman's body, when the wheel on which St Catharine is to be martyred is revealed and Maximin orders:

> Go, bind her hand and foot beneath that Wheel:
> Four of you turn the dreadful Engine round;
> Four others hold her fast'ned to the ground:
> That by degrees her tender breasts may feel,
> First the rough razings of the pointed steel:
> Her Paps then let the bearded Tenters stake,
> And on each hook a gory Gobbet take;
> Till th' upper flesh by piece-meal torn away,
> Her beating heart shall to the Sun display.
>
> (V.i.245-53)

The audience's delight in the spectacle of stage machinery is tempered by their complicity in Maximin's sadistic erotic pleasure. The woman's body is available for sexual use, both on and off stage.

The game which Nell Gwyn played with the audience in that epilogue, and the teasing game which runs through ***Tyrannick Love*** when she is cast as a princess, are part of a self-conscious and stylised form of acting which characterises Restoration drama generally. Such a playing style should not be confused with the affected voices and camp gestures which pass for authentic period style in some modern productions of Restoration comedy. It is true that comedy often quoted and parodied the foppish displays which were performed in the pit, but stylisation more importantly shapes the form of dramatic exchanges and the relationship between actor, words and audience. Restoration drama tended to prefer the exemplary: plots often have a diagrammatic shape which concentrates certain dilemmas for the characters, who are examples of particular forms of vice and virtue or the site where conflicting desires and duties struggle for mastery. Such plays tend therefore to neglect individual quirks and the particularities of experience; naturalistic presentation of character is not required. What is required instead is the rhetorical demonstration of states of mind. Words are not private utterances, but the typical language of a particular passion or dilemma, and they are voiced more for the benefit of the audience than for the other characters on stage; indeed, characters may often move downstage to speak lines out into the theatre away from their supposed interlocutors. Even when the drama is one of witty repartee or serious philosophical debate, the lines have a formality which marks them out as contributions to a dialectic which the audience is assessing, rather than to a naturalistically plausible confrontation with another person. Such a drama encourages the analysis of serious issues in generalised terms, and the dramas of individual lives are exemplifications of the forces which shape each human life: notably sexual passion, the power of the state, and the gods, fate or fortune.

Dryden's analysis of sexuality generally keeps away from any overt engagement with the particular sexual politics and *mores* of his own society; his analysis of contemporary sexuality proceeds at a deeper level because it declines to engage with the immediate social vocabulary. He avoids the apparent topicality of time, place and fashion which Etherege and Wycherley manipulate so discomfortingly. Instead of mapping the play of social conventions through which sexual desire is exhibited, controlled and satisfied, Dryden dramatises the force of the body's passions, the way in which women and men are bound by their physical selves, even while mind and spirit may aspire to lofty ideals or may attempt to impose moral and social duties which are at odds with the raw urgency of desire. It is not only in his heroic plays that Dryden shows an awareness of the power of physical desire, for many of his translations from Ovid, Lucretius and Homer will explore that also. In his stage characters we already see how tragically human beings are bound to their bodies, and how fruitlessly they attempt to transcend their limitations. It is not simply that 'desire is boundless, and the act a slave to limit' [Shakespeare, *Troilus and Cressida* III.ii.81-2], but that the body is subject to the demands of political expediency, the call of honour and duty, and the taboos which society places upon the accomplishment of some desires. The question of social taboo fascinated Dryden. Why does a particular society forbid sexual intercourse in certain cases? It is the complaint of Myrrha in [Ovid's] *Metamorphoses,* desiring her father Cinyras; and incest is the trap which awaits the unwitting lovers in ***Don Sebastian*** (1689). But of special interest to Dryden is the uneasy relationship between the mind and the body. This is a philosophical concern which he may have encountered in Descartes, but certainly found in his avid reading of Montaigne. In the essay 'Upon some Verses of Virgil' Montaigne addresses the question of the representation of sexuality: intercourse 'is an action we have put in the precincts of silence, whence to draw it were an offence . . . Nor dare we beare it but in circumlocution and picture'. Why is this? Does not the concealment of sexuality in circumlocution, like the hiding of the genitals by clothing, arouse interest and desire rather than suppress them? Montaigne shows that the evasive means through which sexuality is represented are themselves problematic, perhaps even defeating the social ends which they claim to serve. In another essay, 'Of the force of imagination', Montaigne explores the ways in which the mind influences the body, causing impotence when it fears impotence, and performing successfully when reassured by some talisman. It was Montaigne who opened up for Dryden a world of different social customs, societies whose habits and taboos are so different from our own that they suggest that what we think of as being an eternal law of nature is only temporary human custom. Dryden was well aware that the drama of mind and body is a source of both comedy and tragedy for individuals, and a continual challenge to the writer who uses language to analyse and represent passion. But he also knew that in any society—and particularly in the Restoration—sexuality is always already politicised: there is no private space which is immune from governmental and social interference, no language of love and desire which is not already appropriated by society for its own ends of exploitation and control. That Dryden chose to set most of his plays abroad does not distance them from the sexually charged politics and politicised sexuality of his day: rather, it is this dislocation which enables his analysis.

In many of Dryden's heroic plays the drama arises precisely from the inevitable location of sexual desire within a political realm. ***Secret Love*** shows that sexual passion in a ruler (in this case the Queen of Sicily) is potentially a source of cruelty and tyranny. Philocles and Candiope are in love, but the Queen is also in love with Philocles. In Act III scene i the Queen contemptuously describes to Philocles and other courtiers the deficiencies in Candiope's beauty, and when the Queen leaves, Candiope responds to this tyranny by reflecting that

> The greatest slaves, in Monarchies, are they,
> Whom Birth sets nearest to Imperial sway.
> While jealous pow'r does sullenly o're spy,
> We play like Deer within the Lions eye.
> Would I for you some Shepherdess had been;
> And, but each May, ne're heard the name of
> Queen.
> (III.i.166-71)

Philocles then proposes that they escape from court into a pastoral paradise away from the Queen's surveillance:

> Since happiness may out of Courts be found
> Why stay we here on this enchanted ground?
> And choose not rather with content to dwell
> (If Love and we can find it) in a Cell?
> (III.i.182-85)

But, unknown to Philocles, the Queen is herself eavesdropping on the couple: even this talk of retirement is being policed. In any case, Candiope realises the hold which political ambition has over those who have once experienced power:

> Those who, like you, have once in Courts been
> great,
> May think they wish, but wish not to retreat.
> They seldom go but when they cannot stay;
> As loosing Gamesters throw the Dice away:
> Ev'n in that Cell, where you repose would find,
> Visions of Court will haunt your restless mind;
> And glorious dreams stand ready to restore
> The pleasing shapes of all you had before.
> (III.i.186-93)

Though Philocles makes the expected rejoinder that 'All my Ambition will in you be crown'd', the audience which is watching this debate about ambition and retirement is likely to agree with Candiope that 'Thus hope misleads it self in pleasant way.' And they would be right. The pull of ambition in Philocles is strong. He has enough honesty to admit that 'Int'rest makes all seem reason that leads to it' (IV.i.317), and contemplates abandoning Candiope to marry the Queen. In soliloquy he observes:

> Wheree're I cast about my wond'ring eyes,

Greatness lies ready in some shape to tempt me.
The royal furniture in every room,
The Guards, and the huge waving crowds of people,
All waiting for a sight of that fair Queen
Who makes a present of her love to me:
(V.i.164-69)

and he asks an imaginary Stoic philosopher a rhetorical question:

Now tell me, Stoique!—
If all these with a wish might be made thine,
Would'st thou not truck thy ragged vertue for 'em?
If Glory was a bait that Angels swallow'd
How then should souls ally'd to sence, resist it?
(V.i.170-74)

The audience knows, of course, that a true Stoic philosopher *would* resist such temptation, and that it was only the fallen angels who swallowed the bait. The play of passion, the dilemma of souls 'ally'd to sence', is performed as an exemplary drama for the spectators to analyse.

At the end of the play the Queen announces that she will reward Philocles for his military service on her behalf; he imagines that she means to offer him herself in marriage, but instead she offers him Candiope, and he is struck silent. In an aside which exhibits his state of mind to the audience he admits how attractive the Queen appears to him; she has the attraction of power:

I'm going to possess *Candiope,*
And I am ravish'd with the joy on't! ha!
Not ravish'd neither.
For what can be more charming then that Queen?
Behold how night sits lovely on her eye-brows,
While day breaks from her eyes! then, a Crown too:
Lost, lost, for ever lost, and now 'tis gone
'Tis beautiful!—
(V.i.426-33)

The Queen announces that she will remain unmarried and devote herself to the care of the people:

As for my self I have resolv'd
Still to continue as I am, unmarried:
The cares, observances, and all the duties
Which I should pay an Husband, I will place
Upon my people; and our mutual love
Shall make a blessing more than Conjugal.
(V.i.456-61)

It is only when Philocles hears the Queen's resolution not to marry that he masters his jealousy and ambition, feelings which are political but expressed in sexual terms:

Then, I am once more happy:
For since none can possess her, I am pleas'd
With my own choice, and will desire no more.
For multiplying wishes is a curse
That keeps the mind still painfully awake.
(V.i.468-72)

Here tragedy is averted by renunciations, by the deliberate limitation of desire. Yet the accommodations which this ending arranges are not simply to be accepted by the audience without demur. The Queen's final action may be exemplary, but she has earlier been a disturbing example of the manipulative power which rulers may exercise, and an ending which suggests that the safest course is for a ruler's sexuality to be completely denied is hardly comforting to subjects of Charles II. In Philocles we see the mind torn between love and ambition, rewriting ambition as love, and expressing contentment in love only when ambition has been finally thwarted. As if to underline the arbitrariness of the truces which are made between reason and passion, the play does not end with this edifying spectacle, but moves on to a spirited negotiation between the lovers Florimell and Celadon (played by Nell Gwyn and Charles Hart) over the terms of their marriage contract:

CEL. *Item,* I will have the liberty to sleep all night, without your interrupting my repose for any evil design whatsoever.

FLOR. *Item,* Then you shall bid me good night before you sleep.

CEL. Provided always, that whatever liberties we take with other people, we continue very honest to one another.

FLOR. As far as will consist with a pleasant life.

CEL. Lastly, Whereas the names of Husband and Wife hold forth nothing but clashing and cloying, and dulness and faintness in their signification; they shall be abolish'd for ever betwixt us.

FLOR. And instead of those, we will be married by the more agreeable names of Mistress and Gallant.
(V.i.540-52)

This exchange was given a special character by the fact—known of course to Dryden and to many in the audience—that Gwyn and Hart had been lovers, and perhaps, early in 1667, still were. Nell Gwyn was in the process of being handed over to Lord Buckhurst, and in 1668 would be passed on to Charles II. ***Secret Love*** may draw back from explicit contemporary comment, but its depiction of the transactions between sexual desire and political ambition is not confined within the safe framework of the proscenium arch.

In ***Aureng-Zebe*** the lustful monarch is male, and here Dryden focuses on the image of the king as father of his people, which is one of the period's dominant ideological tropes. Aureng-Zebe loves Indamora, but so too does his father the Emperor. The Emperor confuses his roles: his instincts as a sexually predatory male lead him to want Indamora, and he is determined to have her—by force if necessary. Here the kingly power is entirely at the service of the private man's lust. The result is not only a misuse of power, but a neglect of the interests of his people and his son: fatherly care for country and child are subordinated to sexual passion. The Emperor's wife is also a victim of the despotic power which he insists husbands have over wives. Dryden repeatedly stresses this distortion of the traditional language, holding up the idea of patriarchy for sceptical scrutiny. Through showing the links which metaphor makes between these various areas of control,

Aureng-Zebe makes visible the structures of power in a way which defeats the operation of ideology, which would use metaphor to have us accept the naturalness of these structures. We see the image as an image, a construction which performs a special service on behalf of those who have power. In ***Aureng-Zebe*** the Emperor's sexual licence is coercive of private bodies and destructive of the body politic. In an exchange between the Emperor and his son Morat, different ideas are voiced about power and pleasure. Morat likes fighting, and he also likes the display of kingly power:

> Methinks all pleasure is in greatness found.
> Kings, like Heav'n's eye, should spread their beams around,
> Pleased to be seen while glory's race they run;
> Rest is not for the chariot of the sun.
> (III.i.166-69)

The Emperor, however, is a degenerate form of Epicurean, preferring pleasure without the pains of government (either of the state or himself):

> Had we but lasting youth and time to spare,
> Some might be thrown away on fame and war.
> But youth, the perishing good, runs on too fast,
> And, unenjoyed, will spend itself to waste;
> Few know the use of life before 'tis past.
> Had I once more thy vigor to command,
> I would not let it die upon my hand.
> No hour of pleasure should pass empty by;
> Youth should watch joys, and shoot 'em as they fly.
> (III.i.157-65)

This is more than an ironic representation of Charles II, for it keeps close to Lucretius, and is a dramatised version (albeit in a bastardised form) of a particular philosophy, one element in a theatrical and ethical dialectic for the audience to assess. Yet it is also a reflection on Charles, and when Morat remarks that

> Luxurious kings are to their people lost;
> They live like drones upon the public cost.
> (III.i.176-77)

or again,

> Women emasculate a monarch's reign,
> And murmuring crowds, who see 'em shine with gold,
> That pomp as their own ravished spoils behold.
> (IV.i.200-02)

many in the audience must have murmured agreement. But this is not an allegory; the Emperor is not Charles II; Morat is no virtuous critic of excess. Morat's words have a sharp, epigrammatic force, but they are also compromised by the character of their speaker. We are watching a play between different ways of living, one which through its philosophical generality and geographical distance can analyse the forces which shape the Restoration ethos, and through suggestive, discontinuous allusion can establish repeated contacts with the world just outside the theatre while maintaining an air of innocence.

This form of drama can often create for itself a space in which the political theories of Restoration England can be debated philosophically, and given particular practical exemplification. In ***The Conquest of Granada*** the king, Boabdelin, whose authority is dubious since he has sworn an oath of allegiance to Ferdinand and Isabella of Spain, against whom he is in revolt, seeks to punish Almanzor for his intervention in a factional riot. Almanzor replies with a claim which provokes a debate on the nature of government:

> ALMANZ. No man has more contempt than I of breath
> But whence hast thou the right to give me death?
> Obey'd as Soveraign by thy Subjects be,
> But know, that I alone am King of me.
> I am as free as Nature first made man
> 'Ere the base Laws of Servitude began
> When wild in woods the noble Savage ran.
>
> BOAB. Since, then, no pow'r above your own you know,
> Mankind shou'd use you like a common foe,
> You shou'd be hunted like a Beast of Prey;
> By your own law, I take your life away.
>
> ALMANZ. My laws are made but only for my sake,
> No King against himself a Law can make.
> If thou pretend'st to be a Prince like me,
> Blame not an act which should thy pattern be.
> I saw th' opprest, and thought it did belong
> To a King's office to redress the wrong:
> I brought that Succour which thou oughtst to bring,
> And so, in Nature, am thy Subjects King.
>
> BOAB. I do not want your Councel to direct,
> Or aid to help me punish or protect.
>
> ALM. Thou wantst 'em both, or better thou wouldst know
> Then to let Factions in thy Kingdom grow.
> Divided int'rests while thou thinkst to sway,
> Draw like two brooks thy middle stream away:
> For though they band, and jar, yet both combine
> To make their greatness by the fall of thine.
> (Part I, I.i.203-29)

The debate here is a play between extreme positions. Almanzor claims that man was born free, anticipating Rousseau. Civil society's laws are base servitude, and the savage is noble. Here Dryden is recalling the image of the noble and innocent natives which Montaigne offers (without fully endorsing) in his essay 'Of the Cannibals'. Boabdelin's rejoinder posits a different, Hobbesian, notion of the state of nature, which is a war of every man against every man, with no overall power to keep the peace. Since Almanzor claims to be outside civil society, he can be hunted to death as an outlaw. Almanzor retorts that the law is made for the benefit of the individual, not to his detriment, and he then uses Hobbes against Boabdelin: since he rather than Boabdelin has provided these people with protection, he is their true sovereign. Neither character holds a theoretical position which Dryden or his audience would necessarily accept, but the argument succeeds in laying out the foundations of a debate about the legitimation of political authority in terms other than those of the divine right of kings, which was still the primary legitimising strategy in Restoration England. The remote setting, together with Boabdelin's uncertain status, enables Dryden to try out these arguments.

The reflections on government which these plays offer extend to a consideration of the imperialist adventure. Dryden's early plays ***The Indian Queen*** and ***The Indian Emperour*** use their setting in the Americas to mount a debate on nature and civilisation, taking their bearings partly from Montaigne. Queen Zempoalla provides several epigrammatic opinions on the way in which ideas of legitimacy may simply be a cover for the naked exercise of self-interest. The right of hereditary monarchs has its origin in violent usurpation:

> Let dull successive Monarchs mildly sway:
> Their conquering Fathers did the Laws forsake,
> And broke the old e're they the new cou'd make.
> (***The Indian Queen*** III.i.113-15)

But the observation is part of Zempoalla's attempt to excuse her own cruelty. Later, when her general observes that 'Princes are sacred', she replies:

> True, whilst they are free.
> But power once lost, farewell their sanctity.
> (III.i.157-58)

Once princes diminish their power by taking advice from their subjects, they 'but like publick pageants move', reduced to player kings without power and so without sanctity. Divine right is but a rhetorical legitimation of power. Zempoalla's outburst here is due to an infatuation which prevents her taking advice, so once again the ideas are qualified by their speaker's interest. Nevertheless, the ideas are spoken.

The Indian Emperour takes this questioning further, and dramatises the clash between two cultures, that of the Mexican Indians under Montezuma, and that of the invading Spaniards led by Cortez. The hypocrisy of the Spaniards is evident in the formula by which Vasquez demands Montezuma's submission:

> *Spain's* mighty Monarch, to whom Heaven thinks fit
> That all the Nations of the Earth submit,
> In gracious clemency, does condescend
> On these conditions to become your Friend,
> First, that of him you shall your Scepter hold,
> Next, you present him with your useless Gold:
> Last, that you leave those Idols you adore,
> And one true Deity with prayers implore.
> (I.ii.266-73)

The interweaving of political, religious and economic imperialism could hardly be more blatant. Montezuma's reply exposes the duplicity of Vasquez's claim:

> You speak your Prince a mighty Emperour,
> But his demands have spoke him Proud, and Poor;
> He proudly at my free-born Scepter flies,
> Yet poorly begs a mettal I despise.
> Gold thou may'st take, what-ever thou canst find,
> Save what for sacred uses is design'd:
> But, by what right pretends your King to be
> This Soveraign Lord of all the World, and me?
> (I.ii.274-81)

The Spaniards reply that the Pope has given Mexico to their king, and Montezuma comments:

> Ill does he represent the powers above,
> Who nourishes debate not Preaches love;
> Besides what greater folly can be shown?
> He gives another what is not his own.
>
> VASQ. His pow'r must needs unquestion'd be below,
> For he in Heaven an Empire can bestow.
>
> MONT. Empires in Heaven he with more ease may give,
> And you perhaps would with less thanks receive;
> But Heaven has need of no such Vice-roy here,
> It self bestows the Crowns that Monarchs wear.
>
> PIZ. You wrong his power as you mistake our end,
> Who came thus far Religion to extend.
>
> MONT. He who Religion truely understands
> Knows its extent must be in Men, not Lands.
> (I.ii.285-98)

The Spaniards never manage to muster convincing replies, and Montezuma's incisive, epigrammatic speeches carry the day (at least in terms of argument: the Spaniards eventually win by murder). This debate about religious imperialism is skewed against the Spaniards partly to provide comfortable anti-catholic material for a protestant audience, but the argument also reflects generally upon the European imperialistic adventure, showing the ways in which self-interest is legitimised. At the beginning of the play Vasquez had commented on the poverty of the country:

> Corn, Wine, and Oyl are wanting to this ground,
> In which our Countries fruitfully abound:
> As if this Infant world, yet un-array'd,
> Naked and bare, in Natures Lap were laid.
> No useful Arts have yet found footing here;
> But all untaught and salvage does appear.
> (I.i.5-10)

Cortez corrects him:

> Wild and untaught are Terms which we alone
> Invent, for fashions differing from our own:
> For all their Customs are by Nature wrought,
> But we, by Art, unteach what Nature taught.
> (I.i.11-14)

And Pizarro contradicts Vasquez's assertion that Spain is fruitful:

> In *Spain* our Springs, like Old Mens Children, be
> Decay'd and wither'd from their Infancy:
> No kindly showers fall on our barren earth,
> To hatch the seasons in a timely birth.
> (I.i.15-18)

There is a recognition here that European ways are not normative, and as the play develops we see clearly the hypocrisy of imperialist rhetoric. Cortez claims:

> Heaven from all ages wisely did provide
> This wealth, and for the bravest Nation hide,
> Who with four hundred foot and forty horse,

Dare boldly go a New found World to force.
(I.i.31-34)

The emphasis appropriately falls on 'force'.

At the beginning of ***The Conquest of Granada,*** Part II, King Ferdinand has a curious speech on the growth and decay of empire:

When Empire in its Childhood first appears,
A watchful Fate o'resees its tender years;
Till, grown more strong, it thrusts, and stretches out,
And Elbows all the Kingdoms round about:
The place thus made for its first breathing free,
It moves again for ease and Luxury:
Till, swelling by degrees, it has possest
The greater space; and now crowds up the rest.
When from behind, there starts some petty State;
And pushes on its now unwieldy fate:
Then, down the precipice of time it goes,
And sinks in Minutes, which in Ages rose.
(I.i.5-16)

Ferdinand intends to say that heaven and earth are joining to free Spain from Islam, but the terms which he uses imply that the growth and decay of empire is like that of a human being, who will in due course be rudely jostled aside by some more thrusting competitor. Oblivion is its ultimate fate. Dryden's plays often end with gestures which reassure: the legitimate ruler is triumphant at the end of ***The Conquest of Granada,*** the true heir is recognised and restored in ***Marriage A-la-mode.*** But during the course of the plays, through the licence given by the dialectic of drama, Dryden has asked some far-reaching questions about the operations of power, and the strategies which it uses to give itself authority. (pp. 52-66)

Paul Hammond, in his John Dryden: A Literary Life, *Macmillan Academic and Professional Ltd, 1991, 184 p.*

ALL FOR LOVE

CRITICAL COMMENTARY

Eugene M. Waith (essay date 1962)

[*Waith is a literary scholar known for his book* The Herculean Hero in Marlowe, Chapman, Shakespeare and Dryden, *in which he traces a literary tradition of heroes modelled after the mythological figure. In the following excerpt from that work, he discusses Dryden's approach to the hero motif, with particular emphasis on* All for Love. *The moral of Dryden's play, Waith suggests, is not the condemnation of blind love, "but the tragic limitations imposed on human existence on the infinite aspirations of heroic passion." The critic's quotations from* The Conquest of Granada *and* All for Love *are from* Selected Dramas of John Dryden, *edited by G. R. Noyes, 1910; quotations from Dryden's essays are from* Essays of John Dryden, *edited by W. P. Ker, 1926; quotations from* Aureng-Zebe *are from the Scott-Sainstbury edition (1883) of Dryden's complete works.*]

•

Yours is a Soul irregularly great,
Which, wanting temper, yet abounds with heat . . .

The Herculean hero in Dryden's plays is both the sum of all his predecessors and a new creation, suited to the ideals and the stage conventions of a new age. In Dryden's major contributions to serious drama, ***The Conquest of Granada, Aureng-Zebe*** and ***All for Love,*** certain elements present in all the earlier "Herculean" plays stand out with the dazzling clarity of points made by a good debater, fully aware of the significance of his material. As Chaucer in *Troilus and Criseide* and the *Knight's Tale,* while in certain respects modifying the medieval romance, produces a distillation of its essential character, Dryden seizes upon the essentials in the tradition . . . , and in the very process of transforming, gives them a kind of ideal statement by making explicit what was before implied.

The hero's extraordinary stature is never more emphatically clear than in these plays. "Vast is his courage, boundless is his mind," says an admiring observer of Almanzor (***I Conquest,*** I.253), and Ventidius expatiates on the "vast soul" of Antony (***All for Love,*** I.125). In **"A Parallel of Poetry and Painting"** Dryden writes, "When we view these elevated ideas of nature, the result of that view is admiration, which is always the cause of pleasure."

The protagonists of these plays are prime examples of the Herculean hero's self-reliance and determination to guard his own integrity at whatever cost. Each of them is imbued with the areté of an Achilles or a Coriolanus. In the dedication of ***All for Love*** Dryden is eloquent on this subject, and the words he addresses to his noble patron apply perfectly to his heroes:

> The highest virtue is best to be trusted with itself; for assistance only can be given by a genius superior to that which it assists; and 'tis the noblest kind of debt, when we are only oblig'd to God and nature. This, then, my Lord, is your just commendation, that you have wrought out yourself a way to glory, by those very means that were design'd for your destruction. . . .

In one of the most famous passages of ***The Conquest of Granada,*** Almanzor proclaims: "I alone am king of me. / I am as free as nature first made man" (***I Conquest,*** I. 206-07). As [Marlowe's] Tamburlaine plays fast and loose with Cosroe and [Shakespeare's] Coriolanus deserts Rome for the Volsces, Almanzor changes sides so often that it was easy for Dryden's enemies to ridicule the fickleness of the hero. Dryden replied by asking, "what tie has he on him to the contrary?" Though the reply does not settle the question of artistic propriety, it stresses the main point: Almanzor has a freedom of action granted only to gods and heroes. His only obligations are those which he chooses to recognize.

The superiority to ordinary mortals, such a conspicuous trait in Tamburlaine and Coriolanus, is again illustrated in Almanzor, whose contempt for the "unthinking crowd" is matched only by his power over them. In the first scenes of ***The Conquest of Granada*** a sentence or two and a few sword-strokes suffice to establish his absolute authority. Aureng-Zebe, also, is distinguished from the average by something approaching the supernatural—"Sure *Aureng-Zebe* has somewhat of Divine" (III.249).

As to the fierceness of the Herculean hero, it was doubtless impossible to surpass Marlowe either in degree or in the clarity of presentation, but Dryden has not skimped on this characteristic in his portrayal of Almanzor, who inspires terror by his very looks (as do Tamburlaine and Coriolanus), and flies into a rage whenever his purpose is thwarted. The fierceness of Morat in ***Aureng-Zebe*** is equally conspicuous. In these two instances Dryden may fairly be accused of exaggerating a Herculean trait almost to the point of caricature.

His essays—particularly the essay **"Of Heroic Plays"**—reveal Dryden's awareness of the confluence of traditions which produced this genre and also his preference for the kind of heroic character which I have called Herculean.

Illustration for All for Love *in the 1735 edition of* The Dramatick Works of John Dryden, Esq. *(engraving by van der Gucht, after H.F.B. Gravelot).*

His often-quoted genealogy of Almanzor is the core of his ideas on this subject:

> I must therefore avow, in the first place, from whence I took the character. The first image I had of him was from the *Achilles* of Homer; the next from Tasso's *Rinaldo* (who was a copy of the former), and the third from the *Artaban* of Monsieur Calprenède, who has imitated both.

By emphasizing his debt to Homer and Tasso Dryden wishes to dissociate himself from a tendency in the French romance which seems to him a falsification of the heroic tradition, the exaggerated importance of the "point of honour". Of Homer and Tasso he says:

> They made their heroes men of honour; but so as not to divest them quite of human passions and frailties: they contented themselves to show you, what men of great spirits would certainly do when they were provoked, not what they were obliged to do by the strict rules of moral virtue. For my own part, I declare myself for Homer and Tasso, and am more in love with Achilles and Rinaldo, than with Cyrus and Oroondates.

Although Dryden goes on to say that Almahide, Ozmyn and Benzayda are "patterns of exact virtue" which may challenge comparison with the best of the French, Almanzor is deliberately excluded from this category. The distinction Dryden is making brings out his love for a greatness which is irregular. This is the greatness of Antony, for whom virtue's path is too narrow (***All for Love,*** I.124-25). It is equally Almanzor's:

> A soul too fiery and too great to guide:
> He moves eccentric, like a wand'ring star
> Whose motion's just, tho' 'tis not regular.
> (***I Conquest,*** V.3.37-9)

But this attribute is never more succinctly put than in Indamora's lines to Morat:

> Yours is a Soul irregularly great,
> Which, wanting temper, yet abounds with heat . . .
> (***Aureng-Zebe,*** V.281)

Dryden's heroes are legitimate descendants of the earlier Herculean heroes. However, it requires no argument to persuade any reader of the plays that these descendants speak and behave very differently from their forebears. One of the reasons why they do so is the acknowledged influence of the romance, and especially of the French romance. The emphasis on the theme of love is the most obvious contribution of the romance tradition . . . [A] romantic concept of love does not occur at all in the Hercules plays of Sophocles, Euripides and Seneca. In *Tamburlaine* it is distinctly secondary, but considerably more important in [Chapman's] *Bussy D'Ambois.* In *Coriolanus* it is again almost non-existent, but so important in [Shakespeare's] *Antony and Cleopatra* that the play cannot be considered exclusively as the tragedy of a Herculean hero. At the outset, then, it might seem that the romance influence, which largely accounts for the major roles of the women in Dryden's plays, makes the hero too much a lover to be a Hercules. In Dryden's hands, however, the love of the hero is often a means of completing his heroic duty, rather than an alternative or an obstacle. The presence of such an element modifies, but does not destroy the Herculean pattern. The case of ***All for Love,*** like that of *Antony and Cleopatra,* is a special one, but I shall argue that Dryden's play is even more affected than Shakespeare's by the concept of the Herculean hero.

The emphasis on romantic love may be traced all the way back to Virgil and Heliodorus, but for Dryden it was the more recent examples of the tradition which counted most. He had the opening pages of [Ariosto's] *Orlando Furioso* open before him when he reflected that

> . . . an heroic play ought to be an imitation, in little, of an heroic poem; and, consequently, that Love and Valour ought to be the subject of it.

but the courtliness of some of the speeches and actions of his lovers comes more directly from French romance than from Ariosto or Tasso. Artaban [from Gauthier de Costes la Calprenède's heroic romance *Cléopâtre*] is one of the models for Almanzor, and despite Dryden's primary allegiance to Achilles and Rinaldo, the influence of Artaban is powerful.

The romance not only increases greatly the importance of love in the hero's life. Sometimes it also leads to the resolution of a major paradox in the situation of the Herculean hero, the opposition between his freedom and the demands of society. In *Tamburlaine, Bussy D'Ambois* and *Coriolanus* this paradox is left unresolved. We can sympathize with Zenocrate's pleas for Damascus and at the same time respect Tamburlaine's refusal to heed them—see that Bussy has no right to Tamyra, yet wish for his victory over the French court which seeks to restrain him—respond to Volumnia's arguments while perceiving that they are aimed at the destruction of the hero's integrity. In ***The Conquest of Granada*** the same opposition is again dramatized, but at the end Almanzor, who has boasted that "I alone am king of me", has come to acknowledge not only certain moral obligations but even fealty to King Ferdinand. In the character of Aureng-Zebe a careful balance of personal honour and filial duty is preserved. In both cases the influence of the heroine is largely responsible for the reconciliation of these opposites. (pp. 152-56)

All for Love

The comparison of ***All for Love*** with Shakespeare's *Antony and Cleopatra* has been an exercise for innumerable students, the subject of at least one German dissertation, and of a few sentences in every history of the drama. Here, aside from an occasional reference to Shakespeare, the context will be Dryden's other plays. It is easy to exaggerate the differences between ***All for Love*** and [***The Conquest of Granada*** and ***Aureng-Zebe***]. Dryden himself led the way towards putting it in a category apart not only by abandoning couplets to "imitate the divine Shakespeare" [as he says on his Preface to ***All for Love***], but by his comment in the late essay, **"A Parallel of Poetry and Painting"**, that he never wrote anything (presumably meaning any of his plays) for himself but *Antony and Cleopatra.* Since Dryden's time critics have considered it exceptional in having an artistic merit which they deny to ***The Conquest of Granada*** or ***Aureng-Zebe,*** and one of the most astute of the recent critics [John Winterbottom, in the *Journal of English and Germanic Philology* 52, 1953] has seen it as an exception in Dryden's thematic development. There can be no doubt that there are differences, but the resemblances which bind ***All for Love*** to its predecessors, if less obvious, are very strong. The verse is certainly much freer; yet it retains often the antithetical balance common to heroic couplets, as when Cleopatra says of Caesar:

> He first possess'd my person; you, my love:
> Caesar lov'd me; but I lov'd Antony.
> (II.353-54)

Though emotion is presented with more immediacy in this play than in ***The Conquest of Granada,*** the basic concerns from which the emotions arise remain very similar, and the entire framework of feeling and thought within which the characters discuss their problems is the same. If the characters of ***All for Love*** are less stylized in presentation, they are still of the same family as the characters in Dryden's other heroic plays.

One of the family connections is seen in the traits of the Herculean hero which reappear in Antony. Though the title of the play leaves no doubt about the primacy of the theme of love, the hero, like his prototype in Shakespeare's play, is a warrior whose nobility and generosity are combined with strong passion and a contemptuous disregard for the mores of his society. Dryden's Antony manifests these characteristics in ways which relate him even more closely to Almanzor and Morat than to Shakespeare's hero. And Cleopatra is much more closely related to other Dryden heroines than to Shakespeare's Cleopatra. These relationships must now be examined in more detail.

The first extended description of Antony is given by his general, Ventidius, who is known to the Egyptians as one who does not share in Antony's debauches, "but presides / O'er all his cooler hours" (I.103-04):

> Virtue's his path; but sometimes 'tis too narrow
> For his vast soul; and then he starts out wide,
> And bounds into a vice, that bears him far
> From his first course, and plunges him in ills:
> But, when his danger makes him find his fault,
> Quick to observe, and full of sharp remorse,
> He censures eagerly his own misdeeds,
> Judging himself with malice to himself,
> And not forgiving what as man he did,
> Because his other parts are more than man.
> (I.124-33)

Here again is an "irregular greatness" which cannot be quite contained within the bounds of virtue. Antony is farther than Almanzor from being a "pattern of perfect virtue", much farther than Aureng-Zebe, and not so far as Morat. The admiration of Ventidius is apparent, but equally so is his Roman attempt to distinguish neatly between what is to be praised and blamed in Antony. As Aureng-Zebe tries to dissect the paradox of Morat into man and brute, Ventidius divides Antony into erring man and "more than man", but in spite of this logical division the implication of the speech is that virtue and vice are distinctions of secondary importance when discussing so vast a soul. Later in the play, echoing the "taints and honours" speech of Shakespeare's Maecenas, he says:

> And sure the gods, like me, are fond of him:
> His virtues lie so mingled with his crimes,
> As would confound their choice to punish one,
> And not reward the other.
>
> (III.48-51)

The impossibility of confining Antony's spirit is the essence of his heroic individuality. When his fortune has ebbed to its lowest point, he compares his fortitude to a "native spring" which again fills the dried river-bed to overflowing:

> I've still a heart that swells, in scorn of fate,
> And lifts me to its banks.
>
> (III.133-34)

The image recalls Shakespeare's Antony, but echoes Almanzor more closely:

> I cannot breathe within this narrow space;
> My heart's too big, and swells beyond the place.
>
> (***I Conquest,*** V.3.23-4)

In Ventidius' initial description Antony's love is sharply differentiated from his virtue. It is obviously the vice into which the great man has "bounded"—an unruly, excessive infatuation. It may be compared with the "wild deluge" of the opening lines of the play, where Serapion is talking of "portents and prodigies". To stem this disastrous flow is the task which Ventidius has set himself, regardless of the admiration he has for Antony's largeness of spirit.

It is a commonplace of criticism that the first act of Dryden's play is dominated by Ventidius. Never again are we so completely in the warriors' world. From a dramatic point of view the showpiece of this act, and indeed one of the best scenes of the entire play, is the quarrel and reconciliation of Antony and his general. It has always been thought to derive from the famous quarrel and reconciliation of Brutus and Cassius [in Shakespeare's *Julius Caesar*], and [Charles] Hart and [Michael] Mohun, who took these parts in Shakespeare's play, distinguished themselves as Antony and Ventidius. Dryden preferred the scene, as he states in the preface, to anything he had written "in this kind". It bears a certain resemblance to the reconciliation of ***Aureng-Zebe*** with his father and more to the quarrel and reconciliation of Dorax and Don Sebastian, written many years later. In all of these scenes the generosity of the heroic mind triumphs over *amour propre.*

The significance of Antony's scene with Ventidius, however, is totally different from that of Aureng-Zebe's scene with the Emperor. Not only is the hero in this instance more sinning than sinned against, but the result of the dialogue is to arouse, not to pacify, the party at fault. The Emperor had to be induced to give up the senseless persecution of his son; Antony has to be roused from the torpor of remorse. Antony's change is presented in a highly dramatic contrast. At the beginning of the scene he throws himself on the ground, calling himself the "shadow of an emperor" and thinking of the time when he will be "shrunk to a few cold ashes". At the end, standing with Ventidius, he says:

> O, thou has fir'd me; my soul's up in arms,
> And mans each part about me.
>
> (I.438-39)

The vital spark which makes him great has been restored.

In ***All for Love*** appears again the contrast between the fiery spirit and the cold one, analogous . . . to Dryden's familiar contrast between wit and dullness. Though Antony is cold and torpid at the beginning, he is by nature fiery, and is brought to himself by the force of friendship. Caesar, his opposite, is "the coldest youth", who gives "so tame" an answer to Antony's challenge, has not even warmth enough to die by a fever, and rather than risk death will "crawl upon the utmost verge of life" (II.113-30).

> O Hercules! Why should a man like this,
> Who dares not trust his fate for one great action,
> Be all the care of heav'n?
>
> (II.131-33)

The task that Ventidius accomplishes in the first act may be looked at in two ways. It is in one sense a curbing and controlling of Antony. This aspect is suggested early by Ventidius' stern disapproval of Cleopatra's lavish plans for celebrating Antony's birthday. But it is also the firing of Antony's soul, and this is the aspect which is emphasized. To Ventidius the enemy is, of course, Cleopatra, but the worst of her effect on Antony is to have made him a "mute sacrifice" and "the blank of what he was". The state of mind which Ventidius has to combat directly is a paralysing remorse:

> You are too sensible already
> Of what y'have done, too conscious of your failings;
>
> (I.312-13)

> you sleep away your hours
> In desperate sloth, miscall'd philosophy.
>
> (I.336-37)

In fact, Antony is at this time in a state very similar to Samson's when Manoa comes, in the second episode of *Samson Agonistes,* to warn him against being "over-just" with himself. The maintaining of the inner fire is so important a part of Dryden's concept of the heroic that it is stressed even in the depiction of Cleomenes, the nearly perfect hero of Dryden's last tragedy. The words of Cleomenes' mother might be almost as well applied to Antony:

> This melancholy flatters, but unmans you.
> What is it else, but penury of soul,
> A lazy frost, a numbness of the mind,
> That locks up all the vigour to attempt,
> By barely crying,—'tis impossible!
>
> [***Aureng–Zebe,*** I.8.276]

Only when Cleomenes assures her that his is a grief of fury, not despair, is his mother satisfied. "Desperate sloth", "penury of soul", "a lazy frost"—by the heroic code these are the true sins, beside which other forms of moral deviation pale.

Cleopatra is first seen as the cause of Antony's unmanning. The theatrical strategy of this first unfavourable impression, established only to be radically altered later on, is almost the only similarity between Dryden's treatment of his heroine and Shakespeare's. After exposure to the charms of Shakespeare's Cleopatra, who manages to remain marvellously attractive even at her most hoydenish and deceitful ("holy priests bless her when she is riggish"), one is apt to find the Cleopatra of Dryden shockingly tame and stiff. While it is easy to picture Shakespeare's Cleopatra in anything from Egyptian dress to the bodice and farthingale she probably wore on the Elizabethan stage, Dryden's Cleopatra belongs in late seventeenth-century court dress, complete with train. Passion never quite robs her of dignity. There is no haling of messengers by the hair, no riggishness. To understand this Cleopatra is an essential preliminary to understanding the play.

She dominates the second act as Ventidius does the first. In her initial appearance with Iras and her eunuch, Alexas, she proclaims her love a "noble madness" and a "transcendent passion" which has carried her "quite out of reason's view" till she is "lost above it" (II.17-22). Force and excessiveness combine here with nobility as they do in Ventidius' first description of Antony. The heroine is no mere temptress to lure the hero from the path of virtue. She is herself carried away by a passion of heroic proportions like his. Serapion's description of the flood, already suggested as an analogue for Antony's love, may be associated even more properly with Cleopatra's:

> Our fruitful Nile
> Flow'd ere the wonted season, with a torrent
> So unexpected, and so wondrous fierce,
> That the wild deluge overtook the haste
> Ev'n of the hinds that watch'd it . . .
>
> (I.2-6)

Dryden has taken over Shakespeare's insistence on the resemblances between the lovers and added another in giving Cleopatra a heroic stature like Antony's. Grandeur and largeness of mind are hers as much as they are his. In fact it is her high-mindedness rather than her sensual attraction which persuades Antony not to leave her. The telling blow is her announcement that she refused a kingdom from Caesar because of her loyalty to Antony (in her noble contempt for wealth she resembles the Cleopatra of Fletcher and Massinger's *The False One*). By the end of the act these similar lovers have been brought together to the dismay of Ventidius, but it is to be noticed that Antony's conviction that Cleopatra is worth more than all the world does not alter his heroic determination to fight with Caesar. There is now the additional motive of revenge for Caesar's attempt to corrupt Cleopatra. Love for her is not entirely the effeminizing passion Ventidius thinks it to be, and despite her dignified bearing she is far from tame.

One sentence of self-description has exposed Cleopatra to a great deal of unfriendly laughter:

> Nature meant me
> A wife; a silly, harmless, household dove,
> Fond without art, and kind without deceit.
>
> (IV.91-3)

The comparison is not apt, and it is particularly unfortunate that the incongruity blocks the understanding of a crucial point—Cleopatra's attitude towards being a wife. In Shakespeare's play "Husband I come" owes its brilliance as much to its unexpectedness as to its rightness. It signals a transformation in Cleopatra matching the reemergence of the heroic Antony. In Dryden's play the change is a much smaller one, and so thoroughly prepared that it is no shock to hear:

> I have not lov'd a Roman, not to know
> What should become his wife; his wife, my Charmion!
> For 'tis to that high title I aspire . . .
>
> (V.412-14)

Her first reference to marriage is contemptuous, as one might expect. Charmion has brought a message that, though Antony is leaving, he will always respect Cleopatra, and she picks up the word with obvious irritation:

> Is that a word
> For Antony to use to Cleopatra?
> O that faint word, *respect!* how I disdain it!
> Disdain myself, for loving after it!
> He should have kept that word for cold Octavia.
> Respect is for a wife: am I that thing,
> That dull, insipid lump, without desires,
> And without pow'r to give 'em?
>
> (II.77-84)

The speech not only expresses Cleopatra's pique but establishes an attitude towards the cold and the dull exactly like that of Antony (the speech precedes Antony's comments on Caesar by only thirty lines). Though Cleopatra in other moods and other circumstances speaks more favourably of being a wife, she retains to the end her scorn of a "dull, insipid lump". Immediately after vowing to follow the dead Antony as a dutiful wife, she adds:

> Let dull Octavia
> Survive, to mourn him dead: my nobler fate
> Shall knit our spousals with a tie too strong
> For Roman laws to break.
>
> (V.415-18)

The opposition between "spousals" and "Roman laws" provides the necessary clue here. Cleopatra considers her love above and beyond law as it is above and beyond reason, yet she borrows from marriage law the terms which distinguish this love from an infatuation of the senses. Her unfortunate self-comparison to a household dove (the context of which will have to be examined later) is part of this process of distinguishing her feelings both from the dullness of the routine and every-day and from the purely sensual and transient.

A glance back at ***The Conquest of Granada*** will make the distinction clear. Cleopatra's love (and Antony's too) is the sort that Queen Isabella defines:

> Love's a heroic passion which can find
> No room in any base degenerate mind:
> It kindles all the soul with honor's fire,
> To make the lover worthy his desire.
>
> (***2 Conquest,*** I.1.145-48)

The fire and honour of such a love distinguish it from the "lethargy" to which Abdalla succumbs under Lyndaraxa's spell and also from the mere legality of Almahide's relationship to Boabdelin, "When all I knew of love, was to obey!" Almanzor at first takes love for a "lethargy", but by the time of his debate with Lyndaraxa he has learned that though it is not controlled by reason it is both constant and strong:

> 'Tis an enchantment where the reason's bound;
> But Paradise is in th'enchanted ground . . .
> My love's my soul; and that from fate is free;
> 'Tis that unchang'd and deathless part of me.
> (*2 Conquest,* III.3.146-47, 179-80)

Similarly, Antony is lethargic at the opening of the play, seemingly unmanned by love. He is "fired" first by Ventidius, though still half unwilling to leave Cleopatra. When she has persuaded him of the nobility of her love, he identifies his passion with his heroism, much as Almanzor does, and prepares with a whole heart for his battle with Caesar. The spectacle of triumph with which the third act opens presents the momentarily successful fusion of warrior and lover.

When Cleopatra compares herself to a household dove she is explaining to Alexas why she does not want to adopt his plan of flirting with Dolabella to arouse Antony's jealousy: she is opposed to all deceit. Repeatedly during the play her plainness is brought out. Though she finally takes the advice of Alexas, she is unable to maintain the counterfeit. Later, when the false news of her death is carried to Antony, she, unlike Shakespeare's heroine, is unaware of the ruse. Antony, too, has a transparent nature, and both of them in this respect resemble Almanzor, who compares his heart to a crystal brook. Antony complains of his "plain, honest heart", and compares himself to "a shallow-forded stream" (IV.432-40). Plainness is another heroic trait which Dryden has given to Cleopatra; his desire to emphasize it in the scene with Dolabella leads him to force the comparison of his heroine to a wife, who is further compared to a fond and artless dove. If Cleopatra lacks the dullness of a wife, she hopes to prove that she lacks the meretriciousness of a mistress.

The comparison of two kinds of love is best seen in Cleopatra's interview with Antony's legal wife, who is hardly more like a household dove than Cleopatra. Dryden was well aware that the unhistorical introduction of Octavia in Act III was his most daring innovation. I doubt whether it has the effect which Dryden most feared, of dividing the audience's sympathies (and he notes that no critic made this objection), but it has other consequences, very likely unintentional, though by no means damaging to the total effect of the play. Briefly stated, they are the shift from the contrast between Cleopatra and Caesar to the contrast between Cleopatra and Octavia and the resulting transfer of heroic values to the realm of love.

In Shakespeare's play Caesar remains throughout the chief embodiment of the Roman point of view as Cleopatra of the Egyptian. Caesar's ideal of heroic man is a Stoic concept of the warrior, whereas Cleopatra's includes both warrior and lover. The same might be said of the ideals of these two characters in ***All for Love,*** but from the moment that Octavia appears, she usurps her brother's antipodal position. The confrontation with Cleopatra establishes her firmly as Antony's alternative choice. Even Ventidius, who represents Roman values though qualified by his admiration for Antony, relies on Octavia to make the Roman ideal compelling. Thus, though the issue remains Antony's choice of love or his responsibilities in the world, the stage presents as the dramatic symbols of these alternatives two women, Cleopatra and Octavia, and the choice at the centre of the play becomes one between love and marriage. The turn of the third act which determines Antony for the second time to leave Cleopatra is not, as it was in the first act, the responsibility to fight Caesar in order to show the world who is master, but duty to a wife, through whom he may reach a peaceful understanding with Caesar. Octavia's weapons are her unrequited love and her children. Cleopatra, who was portrayed in the first act as a deterrent to heroic action, now appears as an alternative to domestic love. When the two women meet, they naturally quarrel over which one of them loves Antony more, and Cleopatra stakes her claim on the very extravagance of her love, which has made her give up her good name in order to become Antony's mistress. The fourth act in effect tests the truth of this love in the episode of Dolabella, showing that it is too great to be concealed. Octavia's love, in this same act, is overwhelmed by outrage. When she leaves in the midst of angry (though justifiable) accusations, it is reduced to duty, its basic component all along.

In the fifth act Antony is separated from both women. Octavia has left and he has quarrelled with Cleopatra over her supposed liking for Dolabella. The problems of empire are raised again but only to be reabsorbed in the problems of love. Though the Egyptian fleet has deserted and Caesar is at the gates, Antony is primarily concerned with Cleopatra's feelings towards him. When he thinks that she has fled, his first thought is that she has "fled to her Dolabella"; the accusation that she has turned to Caesar comes second. The idea of a heroic last stand is banished in an instant by the false news of Cleopatra's death, which seems to prove her innocence. The only possible heroic action now is suicide, since

> I was but great for her; my pow'r, my empire,
> Were but my merchandise to buy her love . . .
> (V.270-71)

The structure of the play has been called episodic. Noyes says that "like that of ***The Conquest of Granada,*** it deals with successive adventures in the life of one man, not with one central crisis." Jean Hagstrum says the play "is not a closely concatenated action that unfolds moral justice. It is a gallery of related heroic poses intended to arouse our sympathy . . . and our admiration . . . " (*The Sisters Arts*). The second judgment is much the more acceptable, and surely the relatedness which Hagstrum recognizes is provided by the crisis in the love-relationship of Antony and Cleopatra, the concern of each act in the play. It is strange to complain of looseness of structure in a play whose strength resides in concentration upon one problem. In this respect the structure is a refinement upon that of ***The Conquest of Granada*** and ***Aureng-Zebe.*** The three plays constitute a series in progressive tightness and simplification.

In ***All for Love*** the Herculean hero's quest for unbounded power is replaced by a quest for unbounded love. In ***The***

Conquest of Granada a noble love modifies the masculine drive for power, redirecting it towards a goal acceptable to society. In ***Aureng-Zebe*** Indamora tries to exert a similar modifying and redirecting influence, but without achieving the same results as Almahide. Aureng-Zebe's love for her is his one unruly passion, and Morat gives up his ambition for "unjust dominion" only to replace it by a love which ignores marital bonds. We never see Antony, as we do Almanzor and Morat, at a time when military conquest is his chief aim. In spite of the efforts of Ventidius, the problems of empire rapidly sink to a position of secondary importance, hardly competing in Antony's mind with his desire for Cleopatra. At the end of the play, instead of the heroic image of him conjured up by Shakespeare's Cleopatra, we are presented with a stage picture of the bodies of the two lovers, regally attired and seated next each other in throne-like chairs. When Serapion finds them he says:

> See, see how the lovers sit in state together,
> As they were giving laws to half mankind!
> (V.507-09)

Only in this paradoxical image is the idea of world-conquest restated, and even here it is subordinated to the triumph of love.

It is a curious fact that this play, which is so thoroughly a love-tragedy, is in one important respect closer to the pattern of Herculean plays than either ***The Conquest of Granada*** or ***Aureng–Zebe.*** In both of these plays the final emphasis is on a reconciliation of heroic energies with the laws of society. Almanzor remains an invincible hero but in the service of Ferdinand and Isabella. Morat's case is more ambiguous, but at the end death has removed his irregular greatness, and the compelling image of the hero lying at Indamora's feet gives way to tableaux of orderly family relationships. Aureng-Zebe, after a quarrel, is reconciled to Indamora. Melesinda marches in a religious procession to her husband's funeral pyre, where she will commit suttee. Nourmahal, the spirit of restless disorder, dies on the stage. Aureng-Zebe, having succeeded in restoring his father to power, receives the crown from his hands. In ***All for Love*** the effort to tame or redirect the hero's energies is totally unsuccessful. The love which the play celebrates soars beyond reason and legality, leading the lovers to defiance of the world and a final self-assertion in suicide. In his unrepentant commitment to a highly individualistic ideal Antony is a logical successor to Morat, but far more Herculean than Almanzor or Aureng-Zebe.

For different reasons, the play as a whole is more like the other Herculean plays than is Shakespeare's *Antony and Cleopatra.* There Antony's love is more clearly an alternative to heroic action, however attractively that alternative is presented. In ***All for Love*** it is not merely that the world is well lost for such a love, but that Dryden, largely through his treatment of Cleopatra, has elevated the love and made its truth and strength unquestionable, though to attain it the world must be defied. Thus presented, it becomes a suitable enterprise for a hero.

In the preface Dryden makes it clear that the lovers are to be blamed for not controlling their passions and finds the attraction of the story in the "excellency of the moral", but he also states that he has drawn the characters of the hero and the heroine as favourably as his sources would permit him. His emphasis on the greatness and nobility of their love is obviously part of this process. The result is a powerful claim on the sympathy of the audience and perhaps less moral instruction than Dryden liked to think. In fact, the love of Antony and Cleopatra, elevated to the level of a "heroic passion", contains the very sort of contradictions which make a moral judgment of Tamburlaine or Bussy so difficult. The love itself is an extravagant, fiery force, knowing no obligations, and yet ennobling in spite of its extra-legality. It is a pattern of loyal commitment. One might say that the moral is not (as Dryden implies) the punishment of lovers who fail to control their passions, but the tragic limitations imposed by human existence on the infinite aspirations of heroic passion. (pp. 188-200)

Eugene M. Waith, "Dryden," in his The Herculean Hero in Marlowe, Chapman, Shakespeare and Dryden, *Chatto & Windus, 1962, pp. 152-201.*

Earl Miner (essay date 1967)

[*Miner is a noted scholar and editor whose writings include* The Japanese Tradition in British and American Literature *(1958),* Dryden's Poetry *(1967), and* The Restoration Mode from Milton to Dryden *(1973). In the following excerpt from the second-named work, he analyzes* All for Love *in the context of Dryden's drama and poetry. According to Miner,* All for Love, *as a play about tragically conflicting interests, brilliantly and insightfully reflects Dryden's struggle throughout his literary career to define a balance between individual needs and public obligations.*]

•

> What is the race of humankind your care
> Beyond what all his fellow creatures are? . . .
> Nay, worse than other beasts is our estate;
> Them, to pursue their pleasures, you create;
> We, bound by harder laws, must curb our will,
> And your commands, not our desires, fulfil.
> —Palamon to the "Eternal deities,"
> ***Palamon and Arcite,*** I.

In ***Annus Mirabilis*** Dryden had succeeded in creating a public world and the means of expressing it. That world is one fashioned of the ideals of Christian humanism, imbued with history, public beyond merely private concerns, and affirmative of life for its potential. That world is the very one well lost in ***All for Love: Or, The World Well Lost*** (1678). It is lost with some regrets but triumphantly. What is gained is another world fashioned of the ideals of pagan passion, affirmative of an ecstatic moment above time, private in its exclusion of the larger world, and laudatory of gain in death. The two worlds seem as incompatible as might be; yet both are parts of the larger world of his poetry, and both are aspects of his values as a man. To the extent that they are contraries, they represent conflicting motives in the man, and themes that found expression in different genres.

The opposite pole to Dryden's public poetry is love poetry. Although he wrote a number of love lyrics, mostly songs for plays, that affirm the passions of private individuals, no one has ever taken them as the overflowings of his heart. The intimacy and ecstasy of private poetry at its intensest are absent, in part because the private individuals are dramatic fictions in the situations of plays, in part because the songs have a public audience.

> You charm'd me not with that fair face,
>   Tho' it was all divine:
> To be another's is the grace
>   That makes me wish you mine.
>
> The gods and Fortune take their part,
>   Who like young monarchs fight,
> And boldly dare invade that heart
>   Which is another's right.
> [**"An Evening's Love"**]

The private address is qualified by the awareness of others implied in the generalizing second stanza, and the public world is conveyed by the religious diction and political metaphor.

If Dryden's plays show similar qualifications of the private motive, the matter is a highly complex one. The drama is a represented genre, sharing at once in the private world of its characters and in the public of its audience. To the extent that the mode of his plays is private, his is a drama of the human will challenging the standards expressed in ***Annus Mirabilis.*** To the extent that it is public, the larger movements of his plays, like those of his poetic career, challenge and at last harmonize the will with other forces. In practice, the distinctions are not so easily drawn, and two extremes must be avoided. The common, and I think mistaken, notion that the claims of passion and will had no appeal to Dryden is one whose testing must await consideration of the development of ***All for Love.*** The contrary idea, known better to the pages of scholarly journals than to popular opinion, that because his characters espouse strongly voluntarist behavior Dryden is therefore a Hobbist, a Puritan, or libertin has been fully answered by the scholarly essays of John A. Winterbottom ["The Place of Hobbesian Ideas in Dryden's Tragedies," *JEGP* LVII, 1958; "Stoicism in Dryden's Tragedies," *JEGP* LXI, 1962].

Some twenty-eight plays make up Dryden's dramatic canon, a few of them falling outside generalizations that may be made about the majority. Among the lot there are such diverse forms as tragedy, comedy, tragi-comedy, the heroic play, and opera or masque. Although such variety precludes a characterization at once simple and adequate, we may say that the major subjects of most of the plays are related in some fashion to those Dryden thought proper to the heroic play: "Love and Valour ought to be the subject of it" [**"Of Heroic Plays,"** prefixed to ***The Conquest of Granada***]. The love is usually that known in the century as heroical love, the passion overriding the limits that might bound it. Usually caught at first sight, it overturns reason and charges the will to seek its object, whatever the cost. "Valour" is similarly unbridled in its claims, and is often less a legitimate search for public trust than an exercise of its own pleasure. Dryden declared his grand fire-eater Almanzor to be descended from Achilles, through Tasso's Rinaldo and Calprenède's Artaban. It has been suggested [by Eugene M. Waith, in his *The Herculean Hero,* 1962] that such a character is a type of the Herculean hero owed to remote antiquity through Roman drama and such earlier Renaissance types as Marlowe's Tamburlaine. Whatever his ancestry on one side or the other, Almanzor is—in love and valor—as voluntaristic a creature as ever lived on fire and words. Coextensive with his will, he resembles such other of Dryden's own characters as "little" Maximin, the tyrant of ***Tyrannic Love.*** The chief protagonists in the comedies match wills and words, usually brandishing challenges at the conventions of sexual behavior in the century.

At their worst, such characters will huff and puff. At their best, they are borne by the currents of their passionate wills. They are the very kinds of person who were to rouse Dryden to his one angry poem, ***The Medal,*** where he says sarcastically of the crowd,

> Pow'r is thy essence, wit thy attribute!
> Nor faith nor reason make thee at a stay,
> Thou leap'st o'er all eternal truths in thy Pindaric way! . . .
> Ah, what is man, when his own wish prevails!
> How rash, how swift to plunge himself in ill;
> Proud of his pow'r, and boundless in his will!
> (92-4; 132-34)

The passage ironically parodies Dryden's own belief that God's essence is reason, His will but an attribute, and that man's reason should in correspondence control his will. The same assumptions underlie the plays, although their expression is so greatly complicated that Dryden the critic does not always seem to get those matters straight.

His description of ***All for Love*** in the Preface is not of a play in which the claim of passion is accepted. Speaking of the various writers who had dramatized the story of Antony and Cleopatra, he writes:

> I doubt not but the same motive has prevailed with all of us in this attempt: I mean the excellency of the moral. For the chief persons represented were famous patterns of unlawful love; and their end accordingly was unfortunate. . . . I have therefore steered the middle course [between perfect and wicked characters]; and have drawn the character of Antony as favourably as Plutarch, Appian, and Dion Cassius would give me leave: the like I have observed in Cleopatra. That which is wanting to work up the pity to a greater height was not afforded me by the story; for the crimes of love which they both committed were not occasioned by any necessity, or fatal ignorance, but were wholly voluntary; since our passions are, or ought to be, within our power.

The description of the play is inaccurate. It accords with the sort of tragedy that Thomas Rymer might have written. Or, alternatively, Dryden has described what he might have written in a historical poem expressive of his public values. His Preface speaks a public, his play a private, language. He recognized as much himself twenty-three years later, when he raised the very same issue of characterization in the play.

> . . . my characters of Anthony and Cleopatra,

> though they are favourable to them, have nothing of outrageous panegyric. Their passions were their own, and such as were given them by history; only the deformities of them were cast into shadows, that they might be objects of compassion; whereas if I had chosen a noon-day light for them, somewhat must have been [revealed] which would rather have moved our hatred than our pity.

This is very much more to the point: it speaks of the play we have read. It distinguishes between the "shadows" of private treatment and the "noon-day light" of public knowledge. In effect, the shadows obscure the public world, allowing private experience and the private motives of passion to make their claim. The "noon-day light" is that of the Preface to ***All for Love.*** There is no doubt that the actions of Antony, unshadowed and open to public view would rouse us into the shock we would feel if similar "crimes" had been committed by an Alexander in Egypt or a MacArthur in Japan. But it is precisely the scope given to private desires that distinguishes the world of the play from that of ***Annus Mirabilis.*** In writing of the similar proclivities of Charles II in ***Absalom and Achitophel,*** Dryden was sorely pressed to admit them without arousing condemnation. Only the brilliant wit of the opening lines and the biblical metaphor were to save that day.

So natural is it for all men to invoke separately the one standard of shadows or the other of noonday light, that we are scarcely conscious of any contradiction. Dryden seems to have been no exception. His Antony dismisses normative "nature" and the public "world" in frequent grand gestures.

> Die! rather let me perish: loosened nature
> Leap from its hinges! Sink the props of heav'n,
> And fall the skies to crush the nether world!
> My eyes, my soul, my all!—
> [*Embraces Cleopatra.*]
> VENTIDIUS. And what's this toy,
> In balance with your fortune, honor, fame?
>
> ANTONY. What is't, Ventidius?—it outweighs 'em all.
>
> (II.424-29)

The private claim is accepted: "*My* eyes, *my* soul, *my* all!" But Dryden would not be himself if he failed to recognize, or in some manner to accommodate, the public as well. The exchange echoes an earlier speech by Ventidius, who is given to the imagery of scales and the public judgment it implies.

> Behold, you pow'rs,
> To whom [Antony] you have intrusted humankind;
> See Europe, Africa, Asia, put in balance,
> And all weighed down by one light, worthless woman!
> I think the gods are Antonies, and give,
> Like prodigals, this nether world away
> To none but wasteful hands.
>
> (I.369-75)

Antony as well as Ventidius is aware of the "nether world" of public values, and Ventidius as well as Antony of a realm of private values at once transcendent and destructive of rival claims. As the two speeches together suggest, the play works out the claims of both in its imagery and structure. These aspects of poetry are important to every poet, but they are of special weight in Dryden's writing, where repeatedly diverse interests—old and new, public and private, temporal and eternal, or literal and figurative—are given, or seek, harmonious expression by their embodiment in careful structures grounded in figurative language. Examination of these matters in ***All for Love*** should reveal the nature of the drama. It also helps explain the cast of values in most of his plays and Dryden's artistic maturation leading to the great nondramatic poetry of the 1680's.

All for Love opens with ambiguous expression of alternatives—of the public, historical, and ethical values—and of the death-creation of passion. The famous opening speech by the Egyptian priest, Serapion, sets the possibilities in a way characteristic of Dryden's imagistic handling.

> Portents and prodigies are grown so frequent,
> That they have lost their name. Our fruitful Nile
> Flowed ere the wonted season, with a torrent
> So unexpected, and so wondrous fierce,
> That the wild deluge overtook the haste
> Ev'n of the hinds that watched it: men and beasts
> Were borne above the tops of trees, that grew
> On th' utmost margin of the water-mark.
> Then, with so swift an ebb the flood drove backward,
> It slipt from underneath the scaly herd:
> Here monstrous phocæ panted on the shore;
> Forsaken dolphins there, with their broad tails,
> Lay lashing the departing waves: hard by 'em,
> Sea-horses flound'ring in the slimy mud,
> Tossed up their heads, and dashed the ooze about 'em.
>
> (I.1-15)

The initial line is one of those tragic portents our older playwrights use for poetic convenience; the next seven, concluding the first sentence, relate the rise of the Nile in its forward motion, as the second seven and another sentence its fall and backward motion. We begin with a "fruitful Nile"; we end with "slimy mud" and "ooze." A later appreciation of Cleopatra by Antony realizes the first alternative.

> There's no satiety of love in thee;
> Enjoyed, thou still art new; perpetual spring
> Is in thy arms; the ripened fruit but falls,
> And blossoms rise to fill its empty place;
> And I grow rich by giving.
>
> (III.24-8)

His reply to Ventidius, welcoming the fall of "loosened nature" upon "the nether world" realizes the second alternative. The general air of threat in Serapion's speech is part of the tragic tone, but it foretells even such imagistic steps along the way as Antony's declaration to Ventidius at the close of the first act:

> thou and I,
> Like Time and Death, marching before our troops,
> May taste fate to 'em; mow 'em out a passage,

And, ent'ring where the foremost squadrons
yield,
Begin the noble harvest of the field.
(449-53)

Serapion's descriptions of the Nile naturally suggest the usual idea of fertile creation, but his emphasis upon the monstrous implies destruction as well. The paradox is temporarily resolved at the end of the first act by turning the imagery of a "fruitful Nile" into that of "the noble harvest of the field." Antony has revived his *honestas,* his personal and public integrity. Ventidius is the agent, having, as we say, called upon all that is best in Antony. The public resolution of the first act has also been foreshadowed in the emphasis given Serapion's first speech by his second. In this he recalls the portents within the temple's

iron wicket, that defends the vault,
Where the long race of Ptolemies is laid . . .
From out each monument, in order placed,
An armed ghost [starts] up . . .
. . . a lamentable voice
Cried, "Egypt is no more!" My blood ran back.
(21-8)

The realms invoked are those of history, discipline, religion, and art. They are conveyed by the temple, which is girded in iron, the sanctuary of Egyptian history, and the monuments *in order placed.* The blood runs backward, like the Nile. The issues are such that they could be resolved in a number of ways. In the first act, they are treated as public values for the larger part, and the balance is that of Ventidius' scales. As Egypt or the Nile falls, Rome and "intrusted humankind" rise in the triumph of normal human experience heightened and glorified, or guaranteed, by the hero's honor, *honestas.*

The first act also concerns the past and present. Antony's analysis of the past, in the imagery he employs, speaks for itself in terms of the imagery we have been following.

I have lost my reason, have disgraced
The name of soldier, with inglorious ease.
In the full vintage of my flowing honors,
Sat still, and saw it pressed by other hands.
Fortune came smiling to my youth, and wooed
it,
And purple greatness met my ripened years.
When first I came to empire, I was borne
On tides of people, crowding to my triumphs.
(293-300)

This is the public response to the disturbance of the public realm by merely private affairs. It would be a foolish person who argued that great men cannot be destroyed in such fashion. Yet the imagery of flowing, of wines, of the regal purple, and of tides combine both halves of Serapion's initial speech in a Roman version whose values are public, but whose expression suggests a powerful undertow in an opposed direction. Similarly, Ventidius speaks of Antony's past in Roman terms employing the imagery of creativity. The difference between his speech and Antony's is that his figures and diction are completely harmonious with the public values they espouse:

you, ere love misled your wand'ring
eyes,
Were sure the chief and best of human race,
Framed in the very pride and boast of nature;
So perfect, that the gods, who formed you, won-
dered
At their own skill, and cried, "A lucky hit
Has mended our design." Their envy hindered,
Else you had been immortal, and a pattern,
When heav'n would work for ostentation sake,
To copy out again.
(403-11)

It is this version, of creation in the immortal terms proper to classical gods and according to the *perfect,* the *design,* and the *pattern,* that represents the main current of the first act. Such an assessment of Antony's past is a Roman assessment and, confirmed as it is by the structure of the play, is a very real alternative for those eyes of Antony, wandering in error to Cleopatra and private delights. The imagery makes us feel we know the values. These are powerfully reinforced by the scene of reconciled *amicitia*—by the resolution in heroic friendship of the quarrel between Antony and Ventidius, itself strengthened by the precedents in Homer and in [Shakespeare's] *Julius Caesar.* By the second act, it has become necessary to return to Egypt, for Cleopatra to enter, her values much in doubt.

Her first words offer a passive, defenseless version of Antony's inability to comprehend his proper sphere of action: "What shall I do, or whither shall I turn?" Her complaints voice a pathos from which she soon recovers. Antony had berated himself: "I have lost my reason, have disgraced / The name of soldier, with inglorious ease" (I. 293-94). When the issue of reason is raised again by Iras, "Call reason to assist you," Cleopatra justifies herself for intensity of feeling in language that gives a new aspect to the imagery of motion at the opening of the play.

I have none,
And none would have: my love's a noble mad-
ness,
Which shows the cause deserved it. Moderate
sorrow
Fits vulgar love, and for a vulgar man:
But I have loved with such transcendent pas-
sion,
I soared, at first, quite out of reason's view,
And now am lost above it.
(II.16-22)

Here in the transcendent soaring of passion, with a logic of causes known only to the heart, is the origin of a triumph "out of reason's view" with which the play will leave us. Cleopatra's opposition to the public claims of Ventidius is clear, in fact too simply clear to satisfy Dryden. Most of the second act takes as its thematic and imagistic business the qualifying, countering, and even parodying of Cleopatra's claim. It begins with Iras telling Cleopatra to forget about it: "Let it be past with you: / Forget him, madam." Cleopatra shakes her head.

Never, never, Iras.
He once was mine; and once, though now 'tis
gone,
Leaves a faint image of possession still.
(29-31)

Her love soars—it cannot march in public myth as the resolutions of Antony and Ventidius do at the end of the first act. The soaring is that of "transcendent passion," but its base is a physical one like that of the beasts in the Nile. Antony offers such a version in reproaching Cleopatra with their past love.

I loved you still, and took your weak excuses,
Took you into my bosom, stained by Cæsar,
And not half mine: I went to Egypt with you,
And hid me from the bus'ness of the world,
Shut out enquiring nations from my sight,
To give whole years to you.

(275-80)

"Shut out enquiring nations from my sight" is the public version of "Quite out of reason's view." But Antony, whose birthday this last day of his life is, has introduced time as a consideration. He continues:

How I loved,
Witness, ye days and nights, and all your hours,
That danced away with down upon your feet,
As all your bus'ness were to count my passion!
One day passed by, and nothing saw but love;
Another came, and still 'twas only love:
The suns were wearied out with looking on,
And I untired with loving.

(281-88)

These lines must be treated with some care. One of their purposes is to show in their "poetry" the extent of Antony's love still, for all he may say. But more importantly, they convey a languor, a timelessness of time, sterile in a deadening ceaselessness, a static dance. And yet this treatment of time, too, will be absorbed into the final affirmation.

The reproach of shared love is always cruelest, but Antony's emotions lead him to mistake in his rhetoric. He has chosen to emphasize the sterility of their time together by parodying the imagistic strains of ripeness and fruitfulness.

When I beheld you first, it was in Egypt,
Ere Cæsar saw your eyes; you gave me love,
And were too young to know it; that I settled
Your father in his throne, was for your sake;
I left th' acknowledgment for time to ripen.
Cæsar stepped in, and with a greedy hand
Plucked the green fruit, ere the first blush of red,
Yet cleaving to the bough.

(262-69)

In rhythm and diction and imagery, the passage conveys Antony's intention marvelously, but it also shows how his reproaches can betray him. Once his imagination is committed too far to re-creating memory and passion, even in parody, the physicality and 'over-ripeness will begin to seem glorious in their very decadence.

While within your arms I lay,
The world fell mould'ring from my hands each hour,
And left me scarce a grasp (I thank your love for't).

(295-97)

Cleopatra need do little more now than speak to reclaim him. However ironic his intention and bitter his tone, he has too feelingly recalled the past.

Give, you gods,
Give to your boy, your Cæsar,
This rattle of a globe to play withal,
This gewgaw world, and put him cheaply off:
I'll not be pleased with less than Cleopatra.

CLEOPATRA. She['s] wholly yours. My heart's so full of joy,
That I shall do some wild extravagance
Of love, in public.

(442-49)

Antony in his image of payment, and Cleopatra in hers of defiance, could not more clearly reject the "world." "Some wild extravagance / Of love, in public" expresses it perfectly. Antony's lines closing the act seem to suggest that he believes he has found a way to accommodate his military resolution to his love—a belief his own and Cleopatra's words have just shown to be impossible in any workable terms. Yet the phrasing is exact and moves us forward to the last images of the play:

How I long for night!
That both the sweets of mutual love may try,
And once triúmph o'er Cæsar [ere] we die.

(459-61)

The gods must have attended his remarks, because Antony gets exactly what he asks for, if not what he intends. The interval between the second and third acts is that of his triumphant battle. Dryden was inspired to have it follow that speech of Antony just quoted rather than that to Ventidius closing the first act. His victory is now entangled in his love: the tragic web is woven by its prey. In order to make a tragedy out of human disaster, Dryden has needed to conceive characters and issues of unusual scope. His style is, then, crucial to the experience molded in the play, and some consideration of it will lead to a firmer understanding of the final affirmations of the play. There are a number of passages like Antony's "rattle of a globe" speech. In the first act he had questioned,

Why was I raised the meteor of the world,
Hung in the skies, and blazing as I travelled,
Till all my fires were spent; and then cast downward
To be trod out by Cæsar?

(I.206-09)

And yet, "How I long for night!" The imagery of light, time, and worlds echoes throughout the play with each echo taking on a new meaning. Such imagery is of uncommon scope, as in Antony's remarks upon Octavius.

He would live, like a lamp, to the last wink,
And crawl upon the utmost verge of life. . . .
Fool that I was, upon my eagle's wings
I bore this wren, till I was tired with soaring,
And now he mounts above me.
Good heav'ns, is this—is this the man who braves me?
Who bids my age make way, drives me before him,
To the world's ridge, and sweeps me off like rubbish?

(II.129-30; 138-43)

The imagistic relations of this to other passages in the first two acts is clear. The image of the lamp, even in itself, is splendid, especially as its "last wink" is followed by the "utmost verge." The eagle of the Roman legions is similarly well fused with the Æsopian fable of the Eagle and the Wren.

Many readers find such imagery highly pleasing for its stylistic resemblance to Shakespeare's. There are resemblances, which should not be surprising, but it is equally true that one does not get very far comparing other writers to Shakespeare at his greatest. Dryden is best appreciated for himself. As is his structure, so is his style reined in tightly. A phrase like, "her darling mischief, her chief engine" (I.191) possesses that exploration of the range of disciplined English syntax which was to become a stylistic basis of Pope's greatness. Often the discipline conceals the imagistic conceits in clarity.

> A foolish dream,
> Bred from the fumes of indigested feasts,
> And holy luxury.
> (I.37-9)

The ironic parallelism gives a complexity to the direction taken by the alliteration; the sexual image, emphasized by the initial stress upon *Bred,* is rather felt than observed. There is a special kind of wit in this, the same that plays over the four chief words of "cooler hours, and morning counsels" (I.104). The larger design is made up of numerous closely woven details.

The stylistic span of the play is from the simple to the complex; it ranges from poetry of a high order to one excruciating passage. In the third act, Ventidius looses Antony's children by Octavia upon him, saying,

> Was ever sight so moving?—Emperor!
>
> DOLABELLA. Friend!
>
> OCTAVIA. Husband!
>
> BOTH CHILDREN. Father!
>
> ANTONY. I am vanquished; take me.
> (III.362-63)

It is a painful, even ridiculous tableau, a morality play of the public world exerting its series of claims upon Antony, but so baldly that it is positively good manners on Antony's part to give in with as little delay as possible. The public tone is much to be preferred in so simple a sentence as Ventidius' "I have not wept this forty year" (I.263), which carries its proper emotion. At times the style has a sinuous winding through repetitions and patterned rhythms that recalls Milton.

> Set out before your doors
> The images of all your sleeping fathers,
> With laurels crowned; with laurels wreathe your posts,
> And strow with flow'rs the pavement; let the priests
> Do present sacrifice; pour out the wine,
> And call the gods to join with you in gladness.
> (I. 144-49)

At other moments, a passage seems, like many in ***Annus Mirabilis,*** to be a microcosm of the imagery running through the play as we have followed it in the first two acts. Such a passage is Antony's "But I have lost my reason" speech (I.293-300). Again, also as in ***Annus Mirabilis,*** often the imagery of a passage anticipates major imagistic or thematic motifs that subsequently come into the play. A fine example, which sets into the motion the theme of manliness and its ruin, can be found in the first act.

> Does the mute sacrifice upbraid the priest?
> He knows him not his executioner.
> Oh, she has decked his ruin with her love,
> Led him in golden bands to gaudy slaughter,
> And made perdition pleasing; she has left him
> The blank of what he was;
> I tell thee, eunuch, she has quite unmanned him.
> Can any Roman see, and know him now,
> Thus altered from the lord of half mankind,
> Unbent, unsinewed, made a woman's toy,
> Shrunk from the vast extent of all his honors,
> And cramped within a corner of the world?
> O Antony!
> Thou bravest soldier, and thou best of friends!
> Bounteous as nature; next to nature's God!
> (168-82)

Antony excels in such manliness but, according to Ventidius, the exercise of his virility with Cleopatra has unmanned him. It is easy to see what he means, yet difficult to understand how Antony, and Dryden, are going to show the hero a man among men as well as with one woman. The style creates a complex of alternatives requiring resolution and so is congruent with the structure and thematic development of the play.

The beginning of the third act offers a solution in imagery of language, of the stage, and of myth. For much of the third and fourth acts, especially in their middle sections, the imagery of the stage will dominate. That is, what we see on the stage or imagine visually in reading becomes at times imagistically more important than the language. The transition in the first thirty lines of the scene is splendid. To represent his hero and heroine Dryden recalls the song of Mars and Venus in the *Odyssey;* and Rome and Egypt, enemies for two acts, are joined in full, if not lasting, harmony. The degree to which this masque evokes the preceding two acts can be more easily declared than demonstrated. We may posit a few images, however, and compare them with the opening lines of the third act.

> [He] leaves a faint image of possession still.
> (II.31)
>
> While within your arms I lay.
> (II.295)
>
> I shall blush to death
> (I.269)
>
> The conqu'ring soldier, red with unfelt wounds.
> (I.275)

. . . .

At one door enter CLEOPATRA, CHARMION, IRAS, *and* ALEXAS, *a train of Egyptians: at the other,* ANTONY *and Romans. The entrance on both sides is prepared by music, the trumpets first sounding on* ANTONY'S *part, then answered by timbrels, etc., on* CLEOPATRA'S. CHARMION *and*

IRAS *hold a laurel wreath betwixt them. A dance of Egyptians. After the ceremony,* CLEOPATRA *crowns* ANTONY.

ANTONY. I thought how those white arms would fold me in,
And strain me close, and melt me into love;
So pleased with that sweet image, I sprung forwards,
And added all my strength to every blow.

CLEOPATRA. Come to me, come, my soldier, to my arms!
You've been too long away from my embraces;
But, when I have you fast, and all my own,
With broken murmurs, and with amorous sighs,
I'll say, you were unkind, and punish you,
And mark you red with many an eager kiss.

ANTONY. My brighter Venus!

CLEOPATRA. O my greater Mars!

ANTONY. Thou join'st us well, my love!
Suppose me come from the Phlegræan plains,
Where gasping giants lay, cleft by my sword,
And mountain-tops pared off each other blow,
To bury those I slew. Receive me, goddess!
Let Cæsar spread his subtile nets, like Vulcan;
In thy embraces I would be beheld
By heav'n and earth at once;
And make their envy what they meant their sport.
Let those who took us blush; I would love on
With awful state, regardless of their frowns,
As their superior god.

(s.d. and 1-23)

It is no small part of the dramatic irony of the play that Antony has unknowingly summed up the preceding two acts while consciously describing a present earned by his actions in the immediate past. But the "awful state" he predicts (cf. V.505 ff.) is one that must be earned before our eyes and suffered through. Only so will this lovely myth come to life.

Acts III and IV bring this about largely through dramatic imagery. The language itself does not cease to be imagistic, but the crucial imagistic role is dramatic or theatrical, consisting as it does of images made by actors in action. The Restoration playhouse was ideally suited for such visual imagery. Although the exact nature of the theatres of Shakespeare's day is in dispute, surviving inventories show that it was in some sense symbolic but that it also made use of such rude, realistic devices as a flowery bank, a view of Rome, and a "machine" for seemingly true decapitation. The Restoration stage is not symbolic in the same way. It maintains some of the emblematic features of Jacobean masque, but for the most part develops a stage idiom in a ground intermediate between symbol and realism. Audiences had to imagine less (Hieronimo [in Thomas Kyd's *Spanish Tragedy*] does not bite out his tongue any more), but they had to see more—both with the eyes and the understanding. Such visual effects cannot of course be regarded apart from the language of the play: ***All for Love*** is not a dumb show. But it is a carefully created play. Although the evidence for this is to be found for the looking, a letter from Dryden to Walsh in 1693, written about his last play, ***Love Triumphant,*** shows how concerned he was with the purely theatrical aspects of drama.

> I have plotted it all; & written two Acts of it. This morning I had their chief Comedian whom they call Solon, with me; to consult with him concerning his own Character; & truly I thinke he has the best Understanding of any man in the Playhouse.

As usual, Dryden anticipates the shift to visual imagery in ***All for Love*** by means of a striking instance, the stage ceremony opening Act III.

The pageantry at the beginning of the third act is, then, a masque marking a turning point in the play, both in the action and the kind of language of drama employed. It is the play's climax insofar as all that follows is a turning away from this triumph (in both the private and public realms) through action and myth. As a step forward towards the tragic triumph, however, it is the first of three tableaux, and the first as well of a number of closely knit scenes of wishful hopes and of an ever-growing illusion that leads Antony in the end to clear-sighted truth. The beginning of the third act naturally grows immediately from the close of the second in the mythic reconciliation between Antony and Cleopatra. No sooner is the myth created, however, then we find a visual image repeated from the first act. Once again Ventidius enters, standing apart in the chill glow of Roman armor. There stands the surrogate of Roman Antony. As in the first act, the Egyptian Antony is awed by the "virtue" of his other self and wishes to flee. Nothing makes clearer the ill success of the masque of Mars and Venus in harmonizing Antony's two worlds: we observe that the myth was devised by Cleopatra. Rome, which is to say the public, ethical, and historical sides of human experience, must perforce challenge the strange pact Antony tries to make between Rome and Egypt, between war and love. In under a hundred lines later, Dolabella enters for the first time, a Roman fresh from Cæsar's camp but with the graces of Antony. From this point, the alternatives which had seemed so simple—Cleopatra or Ventidius, the private or the public world—become increasingly qualified by each other. The imagery Antony uses to greet his younger friend seems familiar enough to us.

Thou hast what's left of me;
For I am now so sunk from what I was,
Thou find'st me at my lowest water-mark.
The rivers that ran in, and raised my fortunes,
Are all dried up, or take another course.
What I have left is from my native spring;
I've still a heart that swells, in scorn of fate,
And lifts me to my banks.

(127-34)

The imagery of the opening of the play has been rephrased in reverse form.

Antony senses in Dolabella, who resembles him in many more ways than Ventidius does, a more dangerous version of his native world than the older general. Without knowing why, but with strong subconscious compulsion, he justifies himself by sharing with Dolabella the memory of his first sight of Cleopatra. The vision rises from Antony's reproach of his younger friend to an implicit self-justification.

> Her galley down the silver Cydnos rowed,
> The tackling silk, the streamers waved with gold;
> The gentle winds were lodged in purple sails;
> Her nymphs, like Nereids, round her couch were placed,
> Where she, another sea-born Venus, lay.
> (162-66)

"My brighter Venus! O my brighter Mars!" Antony may well chide his friend for finding in Cleopatra an appeal he feels even more strongly.

> She lay, and leant her cheek upon her hand,
> And cast a look so languishingly sweet,
> As if, secure of all beholders' hearts,
> Neglecting, she could take 'em: boys, like Cupids,
> Stood fanning with their painted wings the winds
> That played about her face: but if she smiled,
> A darting glory seemed to blaze abroad,
> That men's desiring eyes were never wearied,
> But hung upon the object. To soft flutes
> The silver oars kept time; and while they played,
> The hearing gave new pleasure to the sight,
> And both to thought. 'Twas heaven, or somewhat more . . .
> Then, Dolabella, where was then thy soul?
> Was not thy fury quite disarmed with wonder?
> Didst thou not shrink behind me from those eyes,
> And whisper in my ear, "Oh, tell her not
> That I accused her with my brother's death?"
> (168-87)

The lush passage, with its undertone of niggardly eroticism, takes in neither Dolabella nor Ventidius—although it is instrumental in having Dolabella fall to Cleopatra's pretended blandishments in the next act. For the moment, he urges home to Antony the values of the public world.

> But yet the loss was private that I made;
> 'Twas but myself I lost: I lost no legions;
> I had no world to lose, no people's love.
> (199-201)

These are some of the clearest distinctions in the play. Here we begin to see the wellsprings of Antony's tragedy—his public grandeur has deprived him of the opportunity to obtain private pleasure. Dolabella has lost himself; Antony has lost a self that desires a private as well as a "people's love."

What follows is presented in more vivid stage imagery than linguistic. Ventidius is out and back in a moment (III.238) with Antony's wife and two daughters. Rome plays its three female characters against the three Egyptian. Growing desperate, Antony strives repeatedly and unsuccessfully to bring back the reality shown by Ventidius into manageable symbols—in particular to Octavius—so that it may seem his enemy. Octavia's appeal is generous, warm, noble, and in fact possessed of every grace. But Antony feels no passion; he tells her with honesty and a new insight into himself,

> Octavia, I have heard you, and must praise
> The greatness of your soul;
> But cannot yield to what you have proposed;
> For I can ne'er be conquered but by love;
> And you do all for duty.
> (313-17)

Rome has still to exert its claims; these come in the act's second tableau, which is again one of relationships, in the passage quoted earlier as the stylistic nadir of the play.

Dryden has another surprise in the wings. "*Enter* ALEXAS *hastily*" (372 s.d.). Now Egypt comes to exert its attraction, and just as the ambassadresses of the public realm had been those who might excite *personal* feeling, so now the viceroy of passion is the eunuch.

> ALEXAS. The queen, my mistress, sir, and yours—
>
> ANTONY. 'Tis past.— . . .
>
> . . . .
>
> VENTIDIUS. There's news for you; run, my officious eunuch,
> Be sure to be the first; haste forward;
> Haste, my dear eunuch, haste!
> (373-78)

What follows is remarkable. Dryden clears the stage for the traditional soliloquy of the villain, but the effect is to humanize Alexas, to give him humanity and passions that we are made to feel. He becomes for himself a potential statesman and lover, a might-have-been Antony, now that the real one has left the stage, and he speaks of Ventidius with considerable insight.

> This downright fighting fool, this thick-skulled hero,
> This blunt, unthinking instrument of death,
> With plain dull virtue has outgone my wit.
> Pleasure forsook my earliest infancy;
> The luxury of others robbed my cradle,
> And ravished thence the promise of a man.
> Cast out from nature, disinherited
> Of what her meanest children claim by kind,
> Yet greatness kept me from contempt: that's gone.
> Had Cleopatra followed my advice,
> Then he had been betrayed who now forsakes.
> She dies for love; but she has known its joys:
> God, is this just, that I, who know no joys,
> Must die, because she loves?
> (379-92)

The depth of understanding makes this one of the great humane passages of the play. Antony has created his tragedy; Alexas has his inflicted on him. This solitary anguish yields to yet a third pageant in this act, the encounter between Cleopatra and Octavia. Once again it is a matter of relationship, as wife and mistress exert their claims and credentials to each other rather than to their usual object, Antony. Skirting comedy as it does, the encounter releases our tensions with the abuse. We think Octavia to be right, and sympathize with Cleopatra. Although matters are not decided in this scene, Cleopatra wins the world-engagement and loses the battle. She who had been described in imagery of eternal fruitfulness now speaks of herself in terms altering the endurance to death and the mature fertility to childhood. Egypt is again sinking.

> My sight grows dim, and every object dances,
> And swims before me, in the maze of death.
> My spirits, while they were opposed, kept up;
> They could not sink beneath a rival's scorn . . .
> Lead me, my Charmion; nay, your hand too,
> Iras:
> My grief has weight enough to sink you both.
> Conduct me to some solitary chamber,
> And draw the curtains round;
> Then leave me to myself, to take alone
> My fill of grief.
> There I till death will his unkindness weep;
> As harmless infants moan themselves asleep.
> (470-73; 477-84)

The act is a triumph (with one accompanying blemish in the language) of stage metaphors and of a nearly total shifting in roles through three pageants dealing with relationships. We feel the need for the ironies to clear and for the "complexities of mire and blood" to simplify.

Instead of filling the need, the fourth act heightens it. Antony wishes Dolabella to be his ambassador to Cleopatra to bid her farewell, which is of a piece with his earlier trying to accuse Dolabella of loving Cleopatra. The responsibility is properly his own. As he leaves Dolabella with his charge, Antony has four exits in about fifteen lines (IV.26-42), on each entry trying to soften the blow for Cleopatra. Now Roman Dolabella is left to make the traditional soliloquy of the hero's surrogate. The resemblance is not to Shakespeare's Enobarbus, but to Alexas, for Roman Dolabella is even more of a would-be Antony. The imagery is that of the chamber and childhood with which Cleopatra had ended the preceding act.

> Men are but children of a larger growth;
> Our appetites as apt to change as theirs,
> And full as craving too, and full as vain;
> And yet the soul, shut up in her dark room,
> Viewing so clear abroad, at home sees nothing;
> But, like a mole in earth, busy and blind,
> Works all her folly up, and casts it outward
> To the world's open view: thus I discovered,
> And blamed the love of ruined Antony;
> Yet wish that I were he, to be so ruined.
> (43-52)

Curiously, Antony seems better matched against the ruin spoken of by Dolabella than against the unsexed tragedy of Alexas.

What follows is a rapid succession of intrigue and pretense, whose effect is to ennoble Antony's consideration and even his softness by making it plain-dealing. Ventidius enters after Dolabella's soliloquy, again unseen, and very like Alexas in the opening scene of the play. He has designs of getting Dolabella in love with Cleopatra, so to rouse Antony's anger against them for their betrayal. Alexas has the same scheme, but with the opposite motive of arousing Antony's jealous concern. Cleopatra, dizzy on her sinking ground, yields to the counsel, perhaps because it has so much of death in it. Alexas urges:

> Believe me; try
> To make him jealous; jealousy is like

Portrait of Nell Gwynn, c. 1675.

> A polished glass held to the lips when life's in
> doubt:
> If there be breath, 'twill catch the damp, and
> show it.
> (70-3)

Cleopatra protests. Adversity has made her regard herself in new terms, terms which make us come to see that Alexas' condition, Dolabella's dilemma, and her role are alike in being examples of what is tragic and inscrutable in the roles men find they must play.

> Nature meant me
> A wife, a silly, harmless, household dove,
> Fond without art, and kind without deceit;
> But Fortune, that has made a mistress of me,
> [Has] thrust me out to the wide world, unfur-
> nished
> Of falsehood to be happy.
> (91-6)

This is what she says before acting a falsehood, and it is in any event too simple a picture of herself. She will not rise to true tragic dimensions till she learns to act, nor Antony till he can no longer act. We are given a courtship scene that involves pretense on all sides, and the self-pretense of all concerned.

Cleopatra cannot sustain the role of coquette through the abuse Dolabella reports Antony to have thundered at her. (He betrays the conditions of his charge in every way.) As she sinks, Dolabella recovers himself and calls upon his absent friend in Cleopatra's imagery of childhood.

> My friend, my friend!
> What endless treasure hast thou thrown away,

And scattered, like an infant, in the ocean,
Vast sums of wealth, which none can gather thence!

(204-07)

She responds with Roman imagery. She is

Like one who wanders through long barren wilds,
And yet foreknows no hospitable inn
Is near to succor hunger, eats his fill,
Before his painful march.

(210-13)

Ventidius brings in Octavia to see Dolabella take her hand as a pledge of their truth to Antony and his abortive love for her. The watching eyes think it a new affair for Cleopatra. The delusions of the characters grow apace, and in that growth begin to give the play a clarity of ironic outline that is taking us steadily on to an end. Ventidius' remarks on Cleopatra and her dangers are parallel to the soliloquies of Alexas and Dolabella. What we learn about him is that no little part of his hatred for her grows from jealousy of her rivalry for Antony's affection, and indeed from her claim upon his own.

I pity Dolabella; but she's dangerous:
Her eyes have pow'r beyond Thessalian charms
To draw the moon from heav'n; for eloquence,
The sea-green Sirens taught her voice their flatt'ry;
And, while she speaks, night steals upon the day,
Unmarked of those that hear. Then she's so charming,
Age buds at sight of her, and swells to youth:
The holy priests gaze on her when she smiles;
And with heaved hands, forgetting gravity,
They bless her wanton eyes: even I, who hate her,
With a malignant joy behold such beauty;
And, while I curse, desire it.

(233-44)

The revelations of such depths and alterations in the characters suggest a time span of many years in the scheme of the play. In fact, we have moved simply from early morning to afternoon of the same day. In truth, the play's unity of time is artificial, and anyone could be forgiven for presuming that several days go by in the action. Somewhat differently, unity of place seems to be strictly adhered to—but it also seems to make no difference, to be so natural as to be unimportant. It is the unity of action which we all know to be the important thing, and in which Dryden took pride, and which in the third and fourth acts achieves special importance.

The unity of the action—and included in that is not only the direction of details to a single end but a sense of that end towards which all moves—contrasts with the growing confusion and delusion from which the characters suffer. As we come to understand them better in the fourth act, they understand each other less. Similarly, in the rest of this act and in much of the last we begin to understand the nature of the tragedy and its destination, while the characters find the action is getting out of their control. The scene of Alexas' entry (IV.319 s.d., ff.) is a masterpiece of clear confusion, cross-purposes, self-deluded intrigue, and ironic confidence. Ventidius catches sight of him, thinks (wrongly) that Alexas does not wish to be seen, and calls him in. Alexas begins a mock-humble series of addresses couched in a marvelously oriental vagueness and flattery, at last getting round to the suggestion that Cleopatra (full of measured consideration for everybody's feelings in this difficult matter) has decided she might as well fall in love with Dolabella. Only the self-deluded could believe such a tale. Ventidius is so very pleased ("On, sweet eunuch; my dear half-man, proceed," 376), thinking quite wrongly that now Antony will be cured. Antony, who alone has no plans working under cover, is also taken in. His protestations upset Octavia, and while Alexas is delighted to find himself thrust out by the jealous emperor, she leaves voluntarily, never to see Antony again. Antony has a soliloquy which shows him, like Cleopatra, reduced to simplicity. The speech (431-40) echoes Dolabella's descriptions of Cleopatra, rephrasing his imagery of the transparent soul (IV.202-03) and applying to her (205-06) the river/marine imagery so prominent in the play. It is now Antony's turn to misconstrue the situation and everyone involved in it. Confident, but wrong, that he now for the first time clearly sees himself and the world, he indulges in self-pity. At this stage, Dryden brings back once more the linguistically complex imagery that he had for the most part foregone in the latter half of Act III and the first two-thirds of Act IV. Such construction is very typical of his art: a change in imagery prefigures a change in other matters. For although the action has not yet started its tragic rise, the imagery of scope and complex values that alone can make suffering positive is introduced while the characters are continuing to fall into dismal confusion. It is notable that the self-delusions and the complexity of intrigue in this portion of the play employ like, say, *Othello* and *King Lear,* a manipulation of plot and characters, of motive and action, that seems more the stuff of comedy than tragedy, as it is usually conceived. Like them, too, it is concerned with seeing, that is, understanding, both passion and the world in which men find themselves.

The return of the imagery of language to a dominant role in the play re-introduces the imagery of ripeness, which now comes to achieve prime importance. Antony reproaches Cleopatra and Dolabella:

you have ripened sin,
To such a monstrous growth, 'twill pose the gods
To find an equal torture. Two, two such!—
Oh, there's no farther name, two such!—to me,
To me, who locked my soul within your breasts,
Had no desires, no joys, no life, but you;
When half the globe was mine, I gave it you
In dowry with my heart; I had no use,
No fruit of all, but you: a friend and mistress
Was what the world could give. O Cleopatra!
O Dolabella! how could you betray
This tender heart, which with an infant fondness
Lay lulled betwixt your bosoms, and there slept,
Secure of injured faith?

(478-91)

The image of infancy is remarkably developed here. Antony treats his heart as the child of the bosoms of Dolabella and Cleopatra, lying innocently asleep between them while they plan adultery. This is indeed to ripen sin, if it be true. Cleopatra admits to her degree of guilt and so starts the action upwards—and gives the imagery of flood one of its last expressions.

> Ah, what will not a woman do, who loves!
> What means will she refuse, to keep that heart
> Where all her joys are placed? 'Twas I encour-
> aged,
> 'Twas I blew up the fire that scorched his soul,
> To make you jealous, and by that regain you.
> But all in vain; I could not counterfeit.
> In spite of all the dams my love broke o'er,
> And drowned my heart again. Fate took th' oc-
> casion;
> And thus one minute's feigning has destroyed
> My whole life's truth.
>
> (513-22)

The act concludes with Antony trying, still unsuccessfully, to control his world by telling Cleopatra and Dolabella how they must all live. His last speech (586-97) shows him giving orders more out of habit than desire, as much out of weariness as self-pity. Only death can lie ahead, death renewed into life by feeling expressed in language, by the knowledge of truth, and by some symbol that will both contain and express the experiences endured.

The last act opens with a new kind of question being asked—and the wrong answer given. Charmion exclaims,

> Be juster, heav'n: such virtue punished thus,
> Will make us think that chance rules all above,
> And shuffles, with a random hand, the lots,
> Which man is forced to draw.
>
> (V. 1-4)

To Dryden this is obviously irrational fatalism. In its psychological import it is also a gesture towards death, as is shown in a moment by a stage image, Cleopatra's gesture of suicide. She is restrained, and in her reproaches of Alexas for his central guilt, and in his reply, we get the last changes rung upon the imagery of the waters, if not upon that of motion accompanying it.

> Thou, thou, villain,
> Has[t] pushed my boat to open sea; to prove,
> At my sad cost, if thou canst steer it back.
> It cannot be; I'm lost too far; I'm ruined!
>
> (32-5)

Alexas accepts the imagery but would correct its application.

> Suppose some shipwracked seaman near the
> shore,
> Dropping and faint, with climbing up the cliff,
> If, from above, some charitable hand
> Pull him to safety, hazarding himself
> To draw the other's weight; would he look back,
> And curse him for his pains? The case is yours;
> But one step more, and you have gained the
> height.
>
> (39-45)

To this Cleopatra's reply is "Sunk, never more to rise" (47), a judgment confirmed too soon by news that the Egyptian fleet has gone over to Octavius, that Antony's cause with Egypt is doomed. (The handling of this, the second military action reported in the play, leaves Cleopatra absolved of the guilt attributed to her in some versions of the story.) Significantly, it is Serapion who brings the news, using her word, *sunk* (one of the play's many variants on Latinate meanings of *ruin*), and recalling his second speech at the beginning of the play.

> Egypt has been; our latest hour is come:
> The queen of nations, from her ancient seat,
> Is sunk for ever in the dark abyss:
> Time has unrolled her glories to the last,
> And now closed up the volume.
>
> (71-5)

As the play moves closer towards its affirmation of passion, the public realm, now of Egypt, is introduced. Indeed we are beginning to see what is to a considerable extent a reversal of roles. The most attractive Romans become attractive in their private selves, the Egyptians most attractive in their public dignity. The reversal is not whole; perhaps it is not half. But it establishes that balance of experience which the action and the characters have been seeking. This opening scene of the last act cannot be left without reference to the second, and again sympathetic, villain's soliloquy of Alexas.

> O that I less could fear to lose this being,
> Which, like a snowball in my coward hand,
> The more 'tis grasped, the faster melts away.
> Poor reason! what a wretched aid art thou!
> For still, in spite of thee,
> These two long lovers, soul and body, dread
> Their final separation.
>
> (131-37)

It is ignominious of him to wish to save himself "No matter what becomes of Cleopatra," but his talk of these "two long lovers" inevitably calls to mind the central love theme of the play.

The next scene, between Antony and Ventidius, is one of Dryden's microcosmic views of the play which yet moves the whole forward. Beginning (149-56) with the imagery of Serapion's opening speech, they go through the will to do battle that had come from their resolved friendship at the end of the first act. Next, first Ventidius and then Antony take over the imagery of transcendence Cleopatra had introduced at the beginning of the second act.

> Now you shall see I love you. Not a word
> Of childing more. By my few hours of life,
> I am so pleased with this brave Roman fate,
> That I would not be Cæsar, to outlive you.
> When we put off this flesh, and mount together,
> I shall be shown to all th' ethereal crowd,—
> "Lo, this is he who died with Antony!"
>
> ANTONY. Who knows but we may pierce
> through all their troops,
> And reach my veterans yet? 'Tis worth the
> tempting,
> T' o'erleap this gulf of fate,
> And leave our wond'ring destinies behind.
>
> (178-88)

That what is expressed here is personal cannot be doubted. The spirit seems Roman and, we might think, therefore public. There is no reason why the public values cannot be personal, but the emphasis upon the emotional strength of *amicitia*—"Now you shall see I love you"—suggests private values as well. Ventidius is saying after all that he loves Antony so much that he will die for him. We can only say that the public and private are beginning to lose some of their distinctions. It is a characteristic bit of management on Dryden's part to have Ventidius make his declaration just as Alexas is on his way to give Antony the (false) news that Cleopatra has taken her life out of love for him.

This lesser irony is as nothing to the handling of Antony's approach to death. Dryden still refuses to allow him adequate insight into himself or his world. Unwilling to give Alexas a chance to tell the (false) news he brings, Antony assumes that Cleopatra is untrue and his life meaningless. Time comes to be a major consideration now that there is so little of it.

> . . . my whole life
> Has been a golden dream of love and friendship.
> But, now I wake . . .
> Ingrateful woman!
> Who followed me, but as the swallow summer,
> Hatching her young ones in my kindly beams,
> Singing her flatt'ries to my morning wake;
> But, now my winter comes, she spreads her wings,
> And seeks the spring of Cæsar.
> (204-13)

Upon allowing Alexas at last to tell him that Cleopatra has committed suicide Antony's thoughts tend at once to the same act. Alexas leaves pleased with himself if anxious—"But, oh! the Romans! / Fate comes too fast upon my wit, / Hunts me too hard" (254-56). Antony is simply exhausted in public will—"I will not fight: there's no more work for war"—but the exhaustion brings a reconciliation. "The bus'ness of my angry hours is done" (261-62). The decision made, his emotions are all with Cleopatra. What reason could not decide and action not achieve has been managed by the lie of Cleopatra's death. The price he pays for a clear mind is the sacrifice, over a lie, of half the world. He thinks of Octavius.

> 'Tis time the world
> Should have a lord, and know whom to obey.
> We two have kept its homage in suspense,
> And bent the globe, on whose each side we trod,
> Till it was dinted inwards. Let him walk
> Alone upon't; I'm weary of my part.
> My torch is out; and the world stands before me
> Like a black desart at th' approach of night:
> I'll lay me down, and stray no farther on.
> (280-88)

When he extracts from Ventidius a promise to kill him but finds that his friend has slain himself instead, Antony falls on his own sword and is mortally wounded though not at once killed.

His earlier hope of resolving the contradictions and dilemmas that faced him had been vain because he was unwilling to face up to the truth of a world governed, not by Charmion's celestial lottery, but by men's own freedom of action, and also to the related truth that such freedom is assured and rendered intelligible only by laws of human affairs. Antony had tried to be emperor at the courts of both arms and love. Unlike Æneas, who gave up most of his private desires and so succeeded in the public world, Antony wished to accommodate his military valor to the myth of Mars and have his Venus, too. The play shows that it is impossible to sustain such a life. That it is possible to live it in delusion for a moment, upon condition of dying, it also shows—in the vision at the beginning of the third act, as again truly at the end of the play. The tragic irony that he founds his truth on the basis of Alexas' lie is transcended by the merger, in death, of the private and public values. The Roman death in suicide which saves the soldier's honor is invoked—as he falls on the field of love. There is therefore no need of further adjustment or bickering when Cleopatra hurries in to reassure him, and then to vow her own death. Calm and reconciled for the first time on this long last day of his life, he can reassure her.

> But grieve not, while thou stay'st[,]
> My last disastrous times:
> Think we have had a clear and glorious day,
> And heav'n did kindly to delay the storm,
> Just till our close of ev'ning. Ten years' love,
> And not a moment lost, but all improved
> To th' utmost joys,—what ages have we lived!
> And now to die each other's; and, so dying,
> While hand in hand we walk in groves below,
> Whole troops of lovers' ghosts shall flock about us,
> And all the train be ours.
> (387-97)

Just as the play's unity of time is a formal symbol of a man's adult life, so Antony has had "a clear and glorious day" and yet has lived "ages." Living, then to die, and then to live below forever; dying for love, they shall lead a lovers' army of "troops."

Cleopatra completes the harmony of values. She becomes a Roman—"I have not loved a Roman not to know / What should become his wife" (412-13), and with the marriage returns the myth of Venus and Mars, and religion. She dresses with "pomp and royalty"

> As when I saw him first, on Cydnos' bank,
> All sparkling, like a goddess: so adorned,
> I'll find him once again . . .
> For I must conquer Cæsar too, like him,
> And win my share o' th' world.—Hail, you dear relics
> Of my immortal love!
> Oh, let no impious hand remove you hence.
> (457, 459-61, 465-68)

The imagery of the fruitful yet destructive Nile with which the play opens, like the imagery of ripeness and of death that develops from it, receives one last brilliant expression in language as well as in dramatic imagery when Iras hands Cleopatra the basket with the serpent: "Underneath the fruit / The aspic lies" (471-72). By themselves the six words are simple enough, but at the end they carry much of the weight of the play's configuration of experience. Charmion and Iras die with her, and it is left, with great artistic propriety, for Serapion to close, as he had begun the play, with the choral voice.

> See how the lovers sit in state together,

As they were giving laws to half mankind!
Th' impression of a smile, left in her face,
Shows she died pleased with him for whom she lived,
And went to charm him in another world.
Cæsar's just ent'ring: grief has now no leisure.
Secure that villain [Alexas], as our pledge of safety,
To grace th' imperial triumph.—Sleep, blest pair,
Secure from human chance, long ages out,
While all the storms of fate fly o'er your tomb;
And fame to late posterity shall tell,
No lovers lived so great, or died so well.
(508-19)

The march of Roman feet leaves grief no leisure. We are reminded at the moment of the lovers' triumph of their defeat, for unlike some earlier dramatists, Dryden does not dissolve all into a mist. The nature of his art, here as elsewhere, depends upon seeing clearly even when that requires the admission of dissident elements or mixed feelings. It would be difficult to demonstrate that clarity better than in the exactness of Serapion's observation that the lovers sit, "As they were giving laws to *half* mankind," to half of that complex of public and private values that makes up our lives and sometimes divides them. But which half is it?

Octavius, Rome, and all that is as it were near at hand offstage cannot break their "spousals," "a tie too strong / For Roman laws to break." By the same token, however, there is the other half of mankind whose laws have proved too strong for them. They have lost the world, or rather one world. There is no doubt of that. And yet they have equally certainly won. Ventidius has not been converted to their love, but he has shared with them their resolution of conflicting claims at the price of tragedy. Looking back over the play, we see that the resolution has grown from the contradictory decisions of the first two acts, from the delusions of the third and the fourth acts, and from a deceit that no longer matters in the fifth. We also see how other seemingly contradictory elements have been accommodated to each other—"ages" within a single day, imagery of great scope rendered very nearly intimate, and even to some extent the private with the public. The imagery ennobles the action, but also gives it a manageable proportion, what one would call tenderness if it were not accompanied by something like irony. Antony's speech—

Give to your boy, your Cæsar,
This rattle of a globe to play withal,
This gewgaw world—

shows how the scope is encompassed in little, in that which is manageable (II.443-45). Antony's first speech in the play suggests as much.

Why was I raised the meteor of the world,
Hung in the skies, and blazing as I travelled,
Till all my fires were spent; and then cast downward
To be trod out by Cæsar?
(206-09)

But for its change from agony to assurance, a speech of his in the last act suggests much the same.

I'm weary of my part.
My torch is out; and the world stands before me
Like a black desart at th' approach of night.
(285-87)

The large lodges in the small, energy in extinction, day in night.

Think we have had a clear and glorious day,
And heav'n did kindly to delay the storm,
Just till our close of ev'ning.
(389-91)

The gain is loss, their day ends well only with the dark. And so the Roman feet march in to claim a different triumph.

The fact of tragedy is plain; the loss it represents is quietly conveyed. But what kind of tragedy has occurred? What has been finally affirmed? If the world lost is the public one in a "noon-day light" of vitality, continuity, and achievement, it is because in imagery as well as in other respects the play leads to the dark. The tragic gain accrues from an identification with this dark, this death of that creative yet doubtful love. Most of the imagery of the play can be referred to the central integration of love and death. In this Dryden presents a version of one of the most abiding images of human experience, one that in Western literature may be called Romantic in view of its most characteristic expression in the medieval romances. (There are of course religious and patriotic analogies, but even in such Latin phrases as *amor patriae* or *dulce est pro patria mori* we sense the analogy to two comparable features of experience.)

The sense of the relatedness of death and love is to be found throughout the literature of the century, whether in the familiar quibble upon "death" and "dying" or in the emotional climaxes of the Jacobean and Caroline stage. The Aspatias who seek death at the hands of those Amintors who do not return their love are not always credible creatures, but their motives have a genuine basis in psychological truth. Although in expressing the same truth so well in ***All for Love*** Dryden was to be more essentially the "Romantic" dramatist than in any other important play, Romantic elements have been discovered in more plays than this. The usual reasons for speaking of his plays as Romantic have been their sources in romances and their cultural primitivism. To read Dryden's prefaces is sufficient to demonstrate his familiarity with the Scuderys and the Calprenèdes. Cultural primitivism, that fascination with another, simpler civilization contemporary with one's own, marks a number of his plays, especially those situated in the New World. Significantly, it is Dryden who, in ***The Conquest of Granada,*** gave the language the phrase, the Noble Savage. These are matters in which it is difficult to speak briefly without claiming too much. Certainly, in the century there is much at Versailles or London that could not be termed Romantic in any sense, and Dryden is often to be found putting what is sentimental coin in other writers to calculated use.

Yet Noyes was very perceptive in speaking of "Romantic tragedy" in the Restoration and in deriving it from Beaumont and Fletcher, the French romances, and the romantic epics of Tasso, Ariosto, and Spenser. "It would be hard," he observed, "to frame a definition of romanticism that should include [Sir Walter Scott's] *Marmion* and exclude ***The Conquest of Granada.***" He felt that this side of Dryden was "a distorted survival of medieval romance" and that it had "no future before" it. But in that he judged hastily. Dryden's plays indeed had little influence, since there is no actable tragedy and little comedy to be found fifty years after his death. But they assisted in a continuity of thought, as did also his similar images of experience in another genre, the narrative poetry of ***Fables,*** which did in fact have influence upon the nineteenth century.

The important fact is that in such historical senses some of Dryden's plays have a character that can conveniently be termed Romantic. More importantly some of them, notably ***All for Love,*** identify and affirm two kinds of experience that will seldom be found identified, much less affirmed, in his other writing. Clearly, the special esthetic conditions of drama (as also of lyric . . .) provided Dryden with the opportunity to explore new kinds and images of experience. Certainly without the "Romantic" identification in ***All for Love*** the play could not exist. There is nothing whatsoever in the play to show that death is a punishment of the two lovers; on the contrary, it brings their final and most exalted union. That fact is not controverted but modified by the presence in the play of a contrary image identifying the public world with life. This public image is not as significant to the play as the Romantic, but it is of great importance to a full view of it, and to our sense of the consistency of Dryden's interests. To pose the matter in terms of dramatic choice, Antony is faced with the alternatives of a vital public honor he has tired of and a mortal private desire which is insatiable. It is a question of will, of choice, of the extent to which—in the old faculty psychology—the will is directed by passion or reason. Yet, partly to make the lovers' triumph the magnificent thing it is, and perhaps partly as well to avoid a total commitment to the passionate will, Dryden makes the vital public honor and the mortal private desire accommodate themselves to each other part way by exchanging some of their values. What in the great nondramatic poems is a force of personal and even private feeling energizing a public mode, is in this play the private dignified by the public. This larger motion of the play is one factor in its claim to be Dryden's greatest, but it is typical of the motions of most of his plays. In all the will is to be seen choosing rightly or wrongly a private or public course, whether for a testing time or, with the finality of tragedy, choosing culpably, nobly, or in tragic ignorance of its true range of choice.

The special acclaim given ***All for Love*** may make it seem that the play is an exception in its affirmations and in the kind of human drama it presents. Such an attitude can only be countered by attention, however brief, to other of the plays. The reader, whether of them or of criticism in the last century and a half, will soon discover that ***All for Love*** is not the exception it is commonly thought to be. Scott and others have advanced good reasons for considering ***Don Sebastian*** to be Dryden's greatest play, and other titles have a way of making their way into criticism, if seldom with claims of superiority to ***All for Love.*** If Dryden's version of the story of the famous lovers has some special claim as the center of quality in his dramatic work, it is not, like ***Annus Mirabilis*** in the public realm, his first success in fashioning the other world of private will in his writing. Fifteen plays had preceded it, and twelve were to follow. Even granting the success which the earlier fifteen had brought him, it is not easy to explain why he should wish to treat a subject in which our greatest poet should have anticipated him. He knew that "Shakespeare's magic could not copied be; / Within that circle none durst walk but he." The only explanation to make full sense is one that covers his other plays as well: that he felt a personal attraction to a kind of human experience not readily seen in most of his nondramatic work. Perhaps something must be granted to what he says in the Preface to ***All for Love;*** perhaps attempts by other writers than Shakespeare gave him "the confidence to try myself in this bow of Ulysses amongst the crowd of suitors." But he was not given to courting the failure the allusion implies to be inevitable and total. He later claimed it as the only play he had written for himself, and whether that be true or not, it is difficult not to believe—in the context of nearly thirty plays—that his own heart to some measure sanctioned the lovers' rejection of the "world" for passion. It is evident to anyone that he devoted much of his genius and his feeling to such tragedies as ***Aureng-Zebe, Don Sebastian, Cleomenes,*** and even ***Oedipus.*** It seems equally evident that for all his lament of his saturnine humor he enjoyed laughing at, or even mingling with, the absurdities of man as he revealed them to be in ***Marriage A-la-Mode,*** in ***Amphitryon,*** and even in so mindless a *jeu d'esprit* as ***Sir Martin Mar-All.***

What is at issue is not the high opinion of Dryden's plays that my remarks imply but his own attitude toward them. The protests that all but one were given to the public, like his doubts of comic gifts, are often quoted as if they ended the matter. I think them defensive comments betraying uneasiness. The bulk of the evidence, after all, is on the other side. His single essay in what Dr. Johnson termed elaborate criticism is the ***Essay of Dramatic Poesy.*** His plays were accompanied into print with prefaces of theoretical or practical criticism, or both, designed in no small part to justify his dramatic work. Except for the "Account" prefixed to ***Annus Mirabilis,*** almost all his prose criticisms are in fact joined either to plays, to translations, or to collections. ***MacFlecknoe*** is a gay satire, if there ever was one to come from a saturnine disposition, of a playwright who had offended his standards of drama as much as of personal behavior and political principle. Unless we are prepared to think Dryden alone an exception to normal ways of assessing human nature or to literary rules of evidence, we must conclude that his plays, and the kinds of experience they treat, were of great emotional importance to him. It may well be that he felt something akin to embarrassment or guilt over them, perhaps for their occasional though much exaggerated indecency, perhaps for the rant of some of the heroic plays, or perhaps for the unevenness resulting from too hasty work. Beyond such reasons, however, there was a better one. In the plays, he challenged with will and passion what his faith and reason supported. It is as though the absence of critical prefaces to his nondramatic works showed that they needed no apologia to the world and himself, while his plays required the best efforts of justification, whether literary or personal.

If so, it is a fine irony that he should feel the need to justify to the world plays whose values come closer to those of that world from his birth to the present than do the values of his nondramatic works. The affirmation of passion, the preoccupation with boundless will, the opposition of private interest to public care, and the exaltation of the moment over history and eternity as he understood them, are harmonious with the voluntarism of most writers of his generation and since. It is further ironic that his plays violate his own "rationalist" or "realist" position less than he had reason to fear. The limiting of conscious will by the irrational passion of heroical love and the opposition to love by the code of honorable behavior afforded some small but significant qualification. His conscience should have been yet more assuaged by the larger movements of his plays, from freeing to limiting the will, or from attacking public values to absorbing them. That such qualifications of the voluntaristic concerns of his plays did not quiet his doubts testifies to the power of will, passion, and the irrational in a man whom other emotions and the force of his mind bore in an opposed direction. It was not until these but barely subdued ideas could be translated into the emotional force of religious faith, love of his sons, and the secure admiration of his contemporaries that he gained full composure.

His greatest play after ***All for Love*** and after his conversion is ***Don Sebastian*** (1690), and it shows the extent to which he has at last understood himself. Sebastian describes his beloved Almeyda, who, only later he learns, is his sister, as one "Strong in her passion, impotent of reason." And even the embittered Dorax can say, "Why, love does all that's noble here below." The claim of the heart is heard and set into its place alongside the public values in a larger whole. Upon learning of his incest, he has a parting scene with Almeyda, an experience once again rousing his love and with it the will to break "laws divine and human." But the reason judges, and will submits.

> One moment longer
> And I should break through laws divine and human,
> And think them cobwebs spread for little man,
> Which all the bulky herd of nature breaks.
> The vigorous young world was ignorant
> Of these restrictions; 'tis decrepit now;
> Not more devout, but more decayed, and cold.—
> All this is impious, therefore we must part,
> [V.i.]

The speech is very like the passage quoted from ***Palamon and Arcite*** as the epigraph to this [essay]. Palamon in his suffering also questions the constitution of things, protesting man's tragic place in it. Like Palamon, Sebastian challenges all that Dryden's public world held firm, giving rise to a sense of tragedy and of the blind night of fate in which men steer like that of ***Annus Mirabilis,*** but more wholly realized. Only, the sense has been absorbed, even while being allowed fuller expression, by a Stoic acceptance of suffering. *Lacrimae volvuntur inanes,* the Virgilian sense of the tearful nature of experience is harmonized with the greater sense that the natural human protest must yield to acceptance of the nature of things. The tragedy, like its resolution, is heightened by the fact that the suffering originates not in the willful actions of Sebastian and Almeyda but in their father's adultery and concealment of their relationship. Caught like Oedipus in a tragic web woven by forces beyond his power of will, Sebastian naturally rebels. But with implicit faith and in affirmation of "laws human and divine" he accepts a world in which will and such laws break man's heart in their clash.

In other plays, the drama of the will undergoes different, although kindred motions. The play in which "will" is most often mentioned is ***Tyrannic Love*** (pub. 1670), with its ranting Maximin totally voluntaristic and its composed St. Catharine wholly true to reasoned faith. The play moves very simply from the dominance of the one to that of the other. In ***The Indian Emperour*** (pub. 1667), ***Secret Love*** (pub. 1668), and other heroic plays, the major good characters learn to alter the private will of their desires to a will choosing the public value of a "heroic" world. In the comedies, the "gay couples" move from an initial "perfect balance, in which the absurdity of the antimatrimonial mode is so delightfully heightened" to "another perfect balance, as the facts of basic human nature weigh the [antimatrimonial] mode and find it wanting," [John Harrington Smith, *The Gay Couple in Restoration Comedy,* 1948]. Whether married or seeking, such characters in the comedies willfully hunt out the fruits forbidden them by public convention and, just before burning their fingers, come to terms with the public world, usually by accepting its most important social expression, marriage. The force of the public world is not usually given the full expression of ***Marriage A-la-Mode*** (1673), where it is conveyed in what may best be called a serious sub-plot. Nor is there always in the tragedies, as there is in ***Don Sebastian,*** a comic subplot ridiculing the indulgences of private will. Yet in plays of all kinds there is a form of reconciliation managing by insight, acceptance, or yielding to bring into "perfect balance" a tragic or comic action of the human will. So much are these motions basic to Dryden's plays that it is difficult to find that conflict between a prevailing libertinism in most of the play and a final acceptance of convention which makes the tone of some Restoration comedies so difficult to assess. In his best plays, the reconciliation mingles the two worlds of private will and public reason or with opened eyes affirms the disparity between them.

In like fashion, the course of Dryden's dramatic career shows an increasing degree of protest and of awareness of the chasm between will and reason, even while leading to a higher reconciliation. The development from ***The Indian Emperour*** to ***All for Love*** and to ***Don Sebastian*** shows that he gradually found means of absorbing his own contrary motives in that blind tragedy, or comedy, of human life he had glimpsed as the fate of others in ***Annus Mirabilis.*** Similarly, his nondramatic poetry after his conversion affirmed in faith a faculty superior to reason and yet harmonious with it. Until that time he argued the reasons of the heart most eloquently in his plays and felt in his poetry outside the theatre the emotions of hope for a world meaningful in its rationality. In the plays we often find, whether in imagery of language, of action, or of both, that ages-old identification of love and death, the world of shadows and private desires. In works other than the plays, in their imagery and tone, we usually find a very different identification of meaningful action and civilized life, of the noonday world of light and personal achievement in a public arena. It may seem, then, that Dryden has two literary worlds, the dramatic and the nondramatic. Yet for all their concern with private shadows the plays finally submit to light, and for all their bright publicity the nondramatic poems take form in the obscure private reaches of Dryden's personality, whether his concern be with fate as in ***Annus Mirabilis,*** with that which causes bristling anger as in ***The Medal,*** or the salvation of his soul as in ***Religio Laici*** and ***The Hind and the Panther.*** For in both his dramatic and nondramatic works there is but one man responding, attempting to define his interests by exploring the limits of his forms and by searching for a "perfect balance" that could be struck in the writing only to the extent that it held between Dryden's inner needs and the values he could discover in his world. (pp. 36-73)

Earl Miner, in his Dryden's Poetry, *Indiana University Press, 1967, 354 p.*

Bruce King (essay date 1968)

[*In the following excerpt, King examines* All for Love *in the context of French and English seventeenth-century drama. Praising Dryden's aesthetically pleasing distillation of emotions in his dramas, King declares that in* All for Love *one finds "a classical economy of emotion and detail which will be appreciated by those who are concerned with art for its own qualities rather than as a mirror of contemporary anxieties."*]

All for Love (1677) is one of the few English tragedies written between the mid-seventeenth and late nineteenth centuries which still commands critical attention. While it was seldom performed during Dryden's lifetime, it has steadily gained in popularity; during our century it has often been seen on the university and professional stage.

The story of Antony and Cleopatra had been treated of course by English dramatists previous to Dryden, but not in the same way. Shakespeare's *Antony and Cleopatra,* for example, contains a wide-ranging mixture of scepticism, irony, and grandeur. Dryden's play is smaller in scope, more polished, and has a different theme. It is a study of the psychology of love and holds up for our inspection the emotions of two people who, having found satisfaction together, are threatened by moral obligations and society. Dryden depicts an idealized love; his theme is neither the deep, one-sided passions of lust portrayed in *Antony and Cleopatra,* nor the refined, spiritual love portrayed in many seventeenth-century plays. The story shows the varying pressures on Antony's affections and on the decisions that he makes. The plot has a pendular motion as Antony oscillates from one allegiance to another. Love, war, empire, friendship, family, and wife make their appeals to Antony. He recognizes the justice of each claim, and after each confrontation he temporarily accepts the point of view offered, but he finally chooses to live with and die for Cleopatra. Each important character may be said to be representative of some value, such as honor (Ventidius), friendship (Dollabella), and family (the children); each act is designed to illustrate Antony's attachment to and eventual rejection of such values for the sake of his love.

The design of ***All for Love*** contributes towards the idealization of emotion into its pure state. The suicide of Ventidius shows the depth of his friendship; it is a noble act, but is of lesser value than the love which Antony has found in Cleopatra. Cleopatra's rejection of the offers made to her by Caesar demonstrates the purity of her love and makes her worth Antony's sacrifice of the world. Her suicide shows Roman courage, symbolically bringing together Roman and Egyptian values. The eunuch Alexas might be said to offer the most complete contrast to Antony. His jealousy of Antony's potency provides a center of psychological interest for the reader, and his attempt to save his own skin sharply contrasts with Antony's decision to die for Cleopatra. While Antony has all the world if he leaves Cleopatra, Alexas has nothing of worth, except his life. He is completely despiritualized, yet it is his intervention which causes the final tragedy.

It is only necessary to compare the steadfast love of Antony and Cleopatra with the conduct of others in the play to see how strongly our sympathies are directed towards them. Caesar is cold, passionless, and a coward; emotionally he is an Alexas with an army at his command. Octavia, though noble, is also cold, and there is perhaps a little of the shrew in her character. Judged, however, by Roman values, Octavia is admirable. She is even capable of forgiving Antony, but is otherwise limited. Dollabella, though Antony's best friend, easily succumbs to the temptation to supplant Antony in Cleopatra's affections. Although it is true that he loved Cleopatra in the past, and that similarities between his character and Antony's make a similar choice of mistress probable, his attempt to seduce Cleopatra is still dereliction from his duties as a friend. An even more interesting study of personality is presented to us in Ventidius. While he remains constant to his Roman values throughout the play, the limitations of such ideals eventually corrupt his honesty. He begins by disapproving of Antony's lapse from Roman virtue, but ends by cooperating with corrupt Alexas to deceive the lovers. While Alexas and Ventidius have different aims, they temporarily reach the same level of dishonesty.

In ***All for Love*** the characters often criticize each other's language. The play begins with a bombastic prophecy by the priest Serapion; this is mocked by Alexas. At least thirteen times during the course of the play characters comment upon the imagery, rhetorical style, or tone others use. While such questioning of false rhetoric is appropriate to a play in which the hero and heroine's deaths are brought about by duplicity and a succession of lies, it also implies a concern with the relation of language to truth. The language we use embodies the values of our culture. But what happens when we feel or perceive something of value beyond commonly accepted cultural standards? This is Antony's problem. Through his sensual delight in Cleopatra he has discovered love of more value than

Roman ideals. But just as the eunuch Alexas is physically debarred from knowing love, so Antony lacks a vocabulary permitting the valuation of love over Roman duty. When Ventidius and Octavia appeal to his sense of honor and family, Antony temporarily accepts the values involved, but he need only see Cleopatra to realize that their love is more valuable than anything he could gain by redeeming his fortunes. The meeting between Octavia and Cleopatra illustrates this opposition of values. Octavia considers Cleopatra little better than a trollop, whereas Cleopatra scorns the frigid, dutiful love, legitimatized by society, which Octavia represents. But Cleopatra has no culturally acceptable means to defend the nature of her love, which is neither mere Egyptian sensuality nor stern Roman virtue. In a later scene we see her lamenting that fate has deprived her of a lawful relationship with Antony. Throughout the play it is asked whether Antony and Cleopatra are honest in their love, or whether it is merely a combination of lust, infatuation, self-interest, and dotage. Their deaths prove, and therefore symbolically legitimatize, their love.

The imagery of ***All for Love*** is appropriate to its theme. Throughout the play Rome is associated with images of coolness, reason, warfare, manliness, and duty, while Egypt is associated with images of night, heat, sensuality, allurement, and effeminacy. But unlike the grand contrast between Roman and Egyptian qualities in Shakespeare's play, the imagistic opposition in ***All for Love*** is less important and the contrast is blurred. An atmosphere of grey, decaying grandeur is appropriate to a story concerned with the last stages of Antony's life, when all the world has been sacrificed for love. Images of grandeur, the world, and space consequently are found side by side with images of decay, ruin, age, and the passing of time.

Even more important, Dryden uses imagery to define the point of view of the speaker. If Shakespeare's imagery has similarities with the expanded analogies of lyric poetry, Dryden's imagery, which reflects a character's point of view, looks forward to later novelistic techniques. Dryden uses imagery as it is applicable to each specific situation rather than to create expanding patterns. As Moody Prior points out [in his "Tragedy and The Heroic Play," in *Dryden: A Collection of Critical Essays,* edited by Bernard Schelling, 1963], whenever Ventidius speaks of Cleopatra he uses words suggestive of tainted allurements ("gaudy slaughter," "poisoned gifts," "infected"), whereas in Antony's speeches Cleopatra appears in imagery free from any suggestion of taint. From Ventidius' point of view, Cleopatra and Egypt represent "lascivious hours," whereas Charmion sees the Romans as "iron statues."

All for Love is a socially subversive play. While recognizing social obligations, it challenges their omnipotence by holding up for our admiration an unlawful but fully achieved love. Dr. Johnson was well aware of the radical moral nature of ***All for Love:*** "it has one fault equal to many, though rather moral than critical, that by admitting the romantic omnipotence of love, [Dryden] has recommended as laudable and worthy of imitation that conduct which, through all ages, the good have censured as vicious and the bad despised as foolish." Johnson's comment, with its awareness that Dryden was recommending neither the values of conventional marriage nor the libertine indulgence of the flesh, is one of the best interpretations of the play.

The success of ***All for Love*** hinges on Dryden's ability to convince us of the fulfillment Antony found with Cleopatra. On the whole he is convincing. Some of Antony's speeches offer us a pure distillation of mature love unmixed with any lesser emotions:

> How I lov'd
> Witness ye Dayes and Nights, and all your hours,
> That Danc'd away with Down upon your Feet,
> As all your business were to count my passion.
> One day past by, and nothing saw but Love;
> Another came, and still 'twas only Love:
> The Suns were weary'd out with looking on,
> And I untyr'd with loving.
> I saw you ev'ry day, and all the day;
> And ev'ry day was still but as the first:
> So eager was I still to see you more.

Other speeches picture the fulness of love:

> Think we have had a clear and glorious day;
> And Heav'n did kindly to delay the Storm
> Just till our close of Ev'ning. Ten years love,
> And not a moment lost, but all improv'd
> To th' utmost Joys: What Ages have we liv'd?
> And now to die each others; and, so dying,
> While hand in hand we walk in Groves below,
> Whole Troops of Lovers Ghosts shall flock about us,
> And all the Train be ours.

Some speeches seem sentimental and almost adolescent in the feelings they represent. The following passage mars, but does not ruin, Dryden's play:

> Go; leave me, Soldier;
> (For you're no more a Lover:) leave me dying:
> Push me all pale and panting from your bosome,
> And, when your March begins, let one run after
> Breathless almost for Joy; and cry, she's dead:
> The Soldiers shout; you then perhaps may sigh,
> And muster all your *Roman* Gravity;
> *Ventidius* chides; and strait your Brow cleares up:
> As I had never been.

Antony's melancholy and tears are overdone. The conversation between Cleopatra and Dollabella is too reminiscent of the seduction scenes of Restoration comedy, although it is possible Dryden meant it to be so. The final speech of the play is awkward and sentimentalized:

> See, see how the Lovers sit in State together,
> As they were giving Laws to half Mankind.
> Th' impression of a smile left in her face,
> Shows she dy'd pleas'd with him for whom she liv'd,
> And went to charm him in another World.

Dryden seems at times less poised than we might expect from such a craftsman. But if ***All for Love*** has faults—and it does—they are minor in comparison to its total effect.

All for Love is supposedly the only play that Dryden

wrote for himself. Although it shares several characteristics with the new sentimental drama developing in the mid-1670s, it represents a radical departure from Dryden's previous work. The major form of English drama after the restoration of Charles II to the throne in 1660 was the heroic play, an attempt to turn the Renaissance epic into theatre. The heroic play was usually written in rhymed heroic couplets and was notable for its exotic settings, larger than life characters, violent action, extravagant speeches, variety of character, and overriding concern with questions of valor, honor, and other highly stylized forms of noble conduct. In ***Tyrannic Love*** (1669) and ***The Conquest of Granada*** (1670) Dryden carried the heroic play to new heights of violence and extravagant behavior. Although such plays were fashionable and in great demand, it is probable that Dryden had his tongue in his cheek while writing them and that they were seen in a humorous light by the more sophisticated members of his audience. It is not surprising that Dryden wearied of the heroic style and began to search for a more natural, more serious form of drama.

Before writing ***All for Love*** Dryden had already transferred his allegiance to a set of critical principles opposed to those upon which the heroic play was based. In his prologue to ***Aureng-Zebe*** (published 1676) Dryden confessed that "he has now another taste of wit" and has grown "weary of his long-loved mistress, rhyme." Dryden was aware that the artificiality of the heroic play represented a severe limitation. He also confessed: "Passion's too fierce to be in fetters bound, / And Nature flies him like enchanted ground . . . A secret shame / Invades his breast at Shakespeare's sacred name."

If English drama was to take a new direction, in what direction should it go? Previously the heroic play had imitated the Corneillean hero who, although not consistently virtuous, was admirable for his physical prowess and noble actions. During the 1670s English drama was influenced by the growing popularity of Racine in France. The Restoration courtiers, always up-to-date in their appreciation of French fashion, were supplied with plays in which, as in Dryden's ***Aureng-Zebe,*** the hero illustrated a pattern of almost blameless conduct. But Dryden soon moved on from the imitation of French drama and, as shown by his attack on Racine in the preface to ***All for Love,*** decided that tragedy should hold up for compassion a criminal love.

The most influential English critic of the day was Thomas Rymer, whose *Tragedies of the Last Age Considered* taught the necessity of poetic justice in drama. According to Rymer the task of tragedy was to illustrate moral truths; good should be rewarded, evil punished. Rymer, for example, condemned Shakespeare's *Othello* for showing a world in which evil seemed unchecked by divine intervention. While it is easy to mock Rymer's theory of poetic justice, such views were common to medieval and Renaissance criticism. Neo-classical criticism had no way of justifying drama in which characters develop outside a moral framework, and offer convincing alternative moral and religious views to those accepted by society. While Renaissance epic theory permitted admiration for valiant if ethically erratic heroes, Dryden in ***All for Love*** goes beyond Renaissance critical theory in creating pity for a hero who, for the sake of love, eventually rejects all social obligation.

At a time when Rymer claimed that plot, decorum of manners, and poetic justice were the most important aspects of drama, Dryden found an alternative theory of tragedy in Rapin's *Réflexions sur la poétique d'Aristote* (1674). According to Rapin (as interpreted by Dryden), the purpose of tragedy is to raise pity and compassion for the faults of the hero. The emotions raised in the audience towards the protagonist are of more importance than the formal structure of the drama. But how are the emotions to be raised? Dryden's notes, written as a reply to Rymer's *Tragedies of the Last Age Considered,* provide the answer:

> Rapin attributes more to the *dictio,* that is, to the words and discourses of a tragedy, than Aristotle had done, who places them in the last rank of beauties; perhaps only last in order, because they are the last product of the design, of the disposition or connection of its parts; of the characters, of the manners of those characters, and of the thoughts proceeding from those manners.
>
> Rapin's words are remarkable: " 'Tis not the admirable intrigue, the surprising events, the extraordinary incidents that make the beauty of a tragedy; 'tis the discourses when they are natural and passionate." So are Shakespeare's.

Rapin offered a justification for Dryden's replacing the heroic couplet with the Shakespearean-influenced blank verse of ***All for Love.*** Rapin also wrote that while pity and terror may in the past have been the mainsprings of drama, love is now the passion "which most predominates in our souls." Whereas Dryden's heroic plays had been concerned with the rise and fall of empires, the deeds of warriors, and displays of artificial, idealized conduct, ***All for Love*** shows that love is the passion which "most predominates in our souls."

Dryden's decision to use blank verse in ***All for Love*** indicates a fundamental change of attitude towards his material, especially towards his characters. Whereas the heroes of the rhymed verse plays were held up for admiration (or, as I believe, for our sophisticated laughter), Antony and Cleopatra earn our sympathy. We do not judge the hero and heroine. Their actions seem inevitable and correct. At the play's conclusion they receive our pity, and their passion is vindicated by the depth of feeling and nobility shown through their deaths.

Dryden makes our response to Antony and Cleopatra pitying and compassionate by pointing to their nobler and softer qualities. Myris says that Antony dreams out his hours; Alexas says that Cleopatra "dotes, She dotes . . . on this vanquish'd Man." Antony "eats not, drinks not, sleeps not, has no use / Of any thing, but thought;" "He censures eagerly his own misdeeds." He observes his birthday with "double pomp of sadness." Ventidius finds this "mournful, wondrous mournful!" and comments: "How sorrow shakes him! / So, now the Tempest tears him up by th' Roots, / And on the ground extends the noble ruin." When Ventidius and Antony meet, the former weeps: "This is no common Deaw, / I have not wept this forty year." When Ventidius upbraids his passion for Cleopatra, Antony replies that "She deserves / More Worlds than I can lose."

If the loves of Antony and Cleopatra represent a higher value than any other in the play, why does Dryden's preface say that he wrote the play for the excellency of its moral? "For the chief persons represented, were famous patterns of unlawful love; and their end accordingly was unfortunate." ***All for Love*** does not picture criminal love deservedly punished for its sins; rather it illustrates a transcendent love for which the world is well lost. Dryden was fully aware that ***All for Love*** flouted current critical tastes in portraying a genuine tension between conventional morals and some private emotion, such as love. If Dryden contradicts himself by saying that ***All for Love*** illustrates a moral, it is probably because Rymer's book had just been published and was highly influential among the courtiers. Dryden's preface deviously pretends that ***All for Love*** does in fact illustrate a moral; having given the slip to his critics, he then, under the guise of attacking French drama, rejects Rymer's claim that the characters in a play must always act nobly and with decorum.

All for Love lacks an involved moral intelligence which judges the actions and emotions of the hero and heroine. This once seemed to me a limitation when compared with the critical pressure we can feel operating through Dryden's other plays and satires. But I now feel that such a judgment must be modified in that it demands from Dryden's play something totally opposed to his purpose. Dryden, like most of the great Augustan satirists, was suspicious of romantic feelings. He usually portrayed men as self-seeking and egotistical, deluded by vain fancies, and only saved from worse corruption by the limitations imposed by society and religion on the indulgence of emotion. In ***All for Love*** Dryden ignores the pessimistic view of human nature common to the Augustan conservative tradition. Instead he depicts a love which, although neglecting social obligations, rises above selfishness and corruption. Perhaps the best way to show the difference in attitude between ***All for Love*** and the heroic plays is to compare a few passages from each. In the heroic plays love is represented as farcical jealousy:

> Who dares touch her I love? I'm all o'er love:
> Nay, I am Love; Love shot, and shot so fast,
> He shot himself into my breast at last.
> I, ***The Conquest of Granada,*** III.i

Heroic love is also represented as wild imaginings, sensual desire, and fulfilment of such excess that it borders on comedy:

> Oh, I could stifle you, with eager haste!
> Devour your kisses with my hungry taste!
> Rush on you! eat you! wander o'er each part,
> Raving with pleasure, snatch you to my heart!
> Then hold you off and gaze! then, with new rage,
> Invade you, till my conscious Limbs presage
> Torrents of joy, which all their banks o'erflow!
> So lost, so blest, as I but then could know!
> ***Aureng-Zebe,*** IV.i

In ***All for Love*** Dryden excludes any humorous element in Antony's descriptions of Cleopatra:

> There's no satiety of Love in thee;
> Enjoy'd, thou still are new; perpetual Spring
> Is in thy armes; the ripen'd fruit but falls,
> And blossoms rise to fill its empty place;
> And I grow rich by giving.

It is possible that our age, steeped in the ambiguities of human behavior disclosed by Freud and Dostoievsky, will not find ***All for Love*** fully satisfying. The intense subjectivity of Donne's poetry with its attempt to delineate particular feelings may seem preferable to Dryden's more generalized reflections upon love. We are more interested in complex psychological states, such as Shakespeare's Egyptian bitch-goddess, than in Dryden's simplification of problems into neat categories of love versus duty. It would be unfortunate if this were so. ***All for Love*** offers an unusually fine example of the distillation of emotions, with all impurities removed, arranged into a formal dramatic pattern. The over-all effect is closer to the warmly colored, clear abstract designs in a painting of Mondrian or Rothko than the expressionism often found in modern drama. There is a classical economy of emotion and detail which will be appreciated by those who are concerned with art for its own qualities rather than as a mirror of contemporary anxieties. (pp. 5-13)

Bruce King, in an introduction to Twentieth Century Interpretations of "All for Love": A Collection of Critical Essays, *edited by Bruce King, Prentice-Hall, Inc., 1968, pp. 1-13.*

FURTHER READING

OVERVIEWS AND GENERAL STUDIES

Drydeniana. (The Life and Times of Seven Major British Writers: Dryden, Pope, Swift, Richardson, Sterne, Johnson, Gibbon). New York: Garland, 1975.

Facsimile reprints of numerous early critical writings on Dryden's works.

Ehrenpreis, Irvin. "Dryden the Playwright." In his *Acts of Implication: Suggestion and Covert Meaning in the Works of Dryden, Swift, Pope, and Austen,* pp. 20-50. Berkeley: University of California Press, 1980.

Examines several themes and techniques in Dryden's dramas, including the playwright's "willingness to suspend probability and simplify character; his apparent wavering between the comic and tragic modes; his fascination with modulations of tone; his employment of the play . . . as a vehicle for political theory; his readiness to use spectacle to imply meaning but his preference for rhetoric and poetic" as well as his views on religion and sexual passion.

Grace, Joan C. "John Dryden's Theory of Tragedy: 'They, Who Have Best Succeeded on the Stage, Have Still Conform'd Their Genius to Their Age'." In her *Tragic Theory in the Critical Works of Thomas Rymer, John Dennis, and John*

Dryden, pp. 89-128. London: Associated University Presses, 1975.
Analyzes Dryden's theory of tragedy. Maintains that "all the central ideas in Dryden's criticism concerning probability, characterization, verisimilitude, the unities, and the use of rhyme are connected with the problem of what to imitate nature means in his age."

Hall, James M. *John Dryden: A Reference Guide.* Boston: G. K. Hall, 1984, 424 p.
Annotated bibliography of writings on Dryden from 1668 to 1981.

Hartsock, Mildred E. "Dryden's Plays: A Study in Ideas." In *Seventeenth Century Studies,* second series, edited by Robert Shafer, pp. 71-178. Princeton, N. J.: Princeton University Press, 1937.
Examines the intellectual background of Dryden's plays, with particular emphasis on the influence of Thomas Hobbes and Michel de Montaigne.

King, Bruce. *Dryden's Mind and Art.* Edinburgh: Oliver and Boyd, 1969, 211 p.
Collection of essays on several topics, including "Dryden and the Heroic Ideal," "Anne Killigrew: Or the Art of Modulating," and "Dryden's Imagery."

Kinsley, James, and Kinsley, Helen, eds. *Dryden: The Critical Heritage.* London: Routledge and Kegan Paul, 1971, 414 p.
Annotated selection of essays, from first reviews to early nineteenth-century criticism; contains a cross-section of Dryden's own criticism of his works.

Krutch, Joseph Wood. *Comedy and Conscience after the Restoration.* New York: Columbia University Press, 1924, 271 p.
Includes numerous references to Dryden's dramas and dramatic theory. Krutch considers him a pioneer of Restoration Comedy.

McFadden, George. *Dryden: The Public Writer, 1660-1685.* Princeton, N. J.: Princeton University Press, 1978, 305 p.
Focuses on Dryden as a poet and public figure, emphasizing in particular his dramatic works.

Moore, Frank Harper. *The Nobler Pleasure: Dryden's Comedy in Theory and Practice.* Chapel Hill: The University of North Carolina Press, 1963, 264 p.
Traces Dryden's development as a comic dramatist, with particular emphasis on his theoretical views on comedy.

Myers, William. *Dryden.* London: Hutchinson University Library, 1973, 200 p.
Survey of Dryden's works.

Nicoll, Allardyce. *Dryden as an Adapter of Shakespeare.* 1922. Reprint. New York: AMS Press, 1975, 35 p.
Compares *The Tempest, All for Love,* and *Troilus and Cressida* with their Shakespearean antecedents.

Saintsbury, George. "John Dryden the Dramatist." In *A Saintsbury Miscellany: Selections from His Essays and Scrap Books,* pp. 74-88. New York: Oxford University Press, 1947.
Overview of Dryden's dramatic work. According to Saintsbury, Dryden's plays are important literary works despite their technical faults.

Sherwood, Margaret. *Dryden's Dramatic Theory and Practice.* 1898. Reprint. New York: Russell & Russell, 1966, 110 p.
Compares Dryden's plays to his theoretical writings, remarking that in the latter, "Dryden's mind shows to better advantage than in the creation of plays."

Smith, David Nichol. "Plays." In his *John Dryden,* pp. 23-43. Cambridge: Cambridge University Press, 1950.
General overview of Dryden's dramatic career, including references to the playwright's literary models.

Verrall, A. W. *Lectures on Dryden.* Edited by Margaret de G. Verrall. New York: Russell & Russell, 1963, 271 p.
Comprehensive discussion of Dryden's works.

Ward, Charles E. *The Life of John Dryden.* Chapel Hill: University of North Carolina Press, 1961, 380 p.
Overview of Dryden's life and literary career.

Winn, James Anderson. *John Dryden and His World.* New Haven, Conn.: Yale University Press, 1987, 651 p.
Comprehensive and richly documented biography. Winn also provides the social, cultural, political, and literary backgrounds of Dryden's dramatic works.

Young, Kenneth. *John Dryden: A Critical Biography.* London: Sylvan Press, 1954, 240 p.
Study of Dryden's life and works. Young regards him as "a Conservative in politics and an innovator in poetry; but the one explains the other, for Conservatism brought peace, and only in peace could the pursuit of poetry be successfully undertaken."

ALL FOR LOVE

King, Bruce. "Dryden's Intent in *All for Love.*" *College English* XXIV (1963): 267-71.
Identifies the literary sources of some of the ideas incorporated into Dryden's best known play.

———, ed. *Twentieth Century Interpretations of* All for Love: *A Collection of Critical Essays.* Englewood Cliffs, N. J.: Prentice-Hall, 1968, 120 p.
Includes essays on various aspects of Dryden's play by Bonamy Dobrée, Kenneth Muir, David Nichol Smith, Jean H. Hagstrum, Arthur C. Kirsch, and others.

Kloesel, Lynn F. "The Play of Desire: Vulcan's Net and Other Stories of Passion in *All for Love.*" *The Eighteenth Century: Theory and Interpretation* 31, No. 3 (Fall 1990): 227-44.
Analysis of the various representations of desire in Dryden's drama. "Desire—human passion, its sources and its consequences—is," Kloesel affirms, "the subject of *All for Love.*"

Leavis, F. R. " 'Antony and Cleopatra' and 'All for Love': A Critical Exercise." *Scrutiny* V, No. 2 (September 1936): 158-69.
Focusing on the unexpected difficulties inherent in any attempt to compare Dryden's work with its Shakespearean source, Leavis concludes that neat textual correspondences clearly demonstrating Dryden's inferiority to Shakespeare cannot be easily established.

HEROIC DRAMAS

Chase, Lewis Nathaniel. *The English Heroic Play: A Critical*

Description of the Rhymed Tragedy of the Restoration. New York: Russell & Russell, 1965, 250 p.

Analysis of English heroic drama, with numerous references to Dryden's works.

Hughes, Derek. *Dryden's Heroic Plays.* Lincoln: University of Nebraska Press, 1981, 195 p.

Critical study of the heroic plays, with particular reference to earlier interpretations.

Kirsch, Arthur C. *Dryden's Heroic Drama.* Princeton, N. J.: Princeton University Press, 1965, 157 p.

Explores a variety of formal, theoretical, and historical issues connected with Dryden's heroic plays.

Waith, Eugene M. "Dryden and the Tradition of Serious Drama." In *John Dryden,* edited by Earl Miner, pp. 58-89. Athens: Ohio University Press, 1972.

Detailed analysis and appreciative review of Dryden's heroic plays.

MUSICAL DRAMAS

Altieri, Joanne. "Dryden's Recapitulation." In her *The Theatre of Praise: The Panegyric Tradition in Seventeenth-Century English Drama,* pp. 131-55. Newark: University of Delaware Press, 1986.

Includes a discussion of Dryden's role in the history of English opera. According to Altieri, Dryden and Henry Purcell masterfully employed the "operatic resources of their time."

Price, Curtis A. *Henry Purcell and the London Stage.* Cambridge: Cambridge University Press, 1984, 300 p.

Includes comments on Dryden and Purcell's collaborative works.

———. "Political Allegory in Late-Seventeenth-Century English Opera." In *Music and Theatre: Essays in Honour of Winton Dean,* pp. 1-29. Cambridge: Cambridge University Press, 1987.

Examines the role of political motifs in *Albion and Albanius.*

Additional coverage of Dryden's life and career is contained in the following sources published by Gale Research: *Dictionary of Literary Biography,* Vols. 80, 101; *Literature Criticism from 1400 to 1800,* Vols. 3, 21; *World Literature Criticism,* Vol. 2.

Athol Fugard

1932-

INTRODUCTION

The author of *Blood Knot* and *"Master Harold". . . and the boys,* Fugard is South Africa's foremost dramatist. Combining social protest with a deep concern for humanity in his plays, Fugard focuses on victims of the South African system of apartheid, which denies basic rights to nonwhite residents, without overtly propagandizing his political beliefs. He expresses the somewhat controversial view that white South Africans as well as black and mixed-race residents can suffer from the debasing and divisive nature of apartheid. His plays typically center on a small number of characters, drawn from the fringes of South African society and viewed as a microcosm of the country's poor and dispossessed. The South African government considers many of Fugard's dramas subversive, and has periodically attempted to prevent the publication or production of his plays; Fugard, however, insists that his work is "nonpolitical" and sees himself simply as "bearing witness" to the notion that "all human beings are in some sense victims."

Fugard was born in Cape Province. When he was three his family moved to Port Elizabeth, which has been his home ever since and has served as the setting of many of his plays. His father was English and his mother, the more dominant presence in his life, was an Afrikaner, a white South African descended from European settlers. He describes his father as a man "full of pointless, unthought-out prejudices," while his mother felt an "outrage and anger over the injustice of [South African] society." In 1950 Fugard received a scholarship to study philosophy at the liberal University of Cape Town, where he first became acquainted with the writings of Albert Camus, whose ideas concerning the absurdity of the human condition influenced him greatly. His interest in writing for the theater developed several years later, coinciding with his marriage to Sheila Meiring, a South African actress. Dismissing his early theatrical works as "imitative exercises," Fugard acknowledges that it was the time spent in Johannesburg in 1958 that inspired him to write his more substantial plays. During this time he worked at the Native Commissioner's Court, which tried cases against nonwhites who had been arrested for failing to carry identification. He has said of this experience: "I knew that the system was evil, but until then I had no idea of just how systematically evil it was. That was my revelation." Also while in Johannesburg, he began spending time in the township of Sophiatown with a group of black writers and actors. Out of these experiences came *No-Good Friday* and *Nongogo,* both of which were written in the late 1950s and first performed for small private audiences by black amateur actors and Fugard himself. These dramas portray poverty and hopelessness as perpetual aspects of South African existence, a theme that recurs throughout Fugard's works. *The Blood Knot,* Fugard's first major success, centers on the oscillating sense of conflict and harmony between two nonwhite half-brothers, one of whom is light-skinned enough to pass for white. In this work, Fugard dramatizes the ambivalence and racial hatred that characterize most South African relations, which have perverted the "blood knot," or common bond of humanity, among its people. Commenting on the play's 1985 revival, Jack Kroll called it "one of the wisest, sweetest, even noblest plays about the balked brotherhood of racism ever written."

The major concerns of Fugard's subsequent dramas of the sixties are hopelessness, the effect of the past on the present, and the individual's search for identity in a country which denies essential human rights. In *Hello and Goodbye* and *People Are Living There,* Fugard compassionately examines the lives of characters made grotesque by poverty and circumstance. *Boesman and Lena* is the story of a homeless couple's aimless wanderings. While Boesman's hatred of the South African political system assumes the form of violence toward his wife, Lena retains her basic humanity and compassion. Both, however, are revealed to be victims of the unjust nature of the human condition. Reminiscent of Samuel Beckett's *Waiting for Godot* in its stark staging and confrontation with the ultimate nature of human existence, *Boesman and Lena* secured Fugard's reputation as a major dramatist.

Experiencing a fallow period after *Boesman and Lena,* Fugard embarked on a new path in the form of collaborative theater. In *Orestes,* he juxtaposed the Greek tragedy of Orestes with a contemporary incident of violent protest in South Africa. Developed in the rehearsal room by Fugard and the actors, the play defied transcription into a formal text. In what Fugard has described as "a series of strange dream images," *Orestes* depicted "a metaphor of innocence [meeting] a metaphor of evil." Despite its limited number of performances, *Orestes* has been cited by critics and Fugard himself as a significant work which profoundly affected his ensuing plays. *Statements after an Arrest under the Immorality Act,* which concerns the discovery by government authorities of a biracial couple's love affair, was Fugard's first play written for the Serpent Players, a nonwhite theater company which Fugard, together with blacks living in a township outside Port Elizabeth, had helped establish in the early sixties. His work with these actors allowed for further exploration of the relationship between actor and playwright: *Sizwe Bansi Is Dead* and *The Island,* one-act plays developed in collaboration with two actors from the Serpent Players, Winston Ntshona and John Kani, explore the consequences of apartheid by allowing the actors to respond naturally to the scenarios presented. The first play portrays the degrading experiences of a man who, through no fault of his own, has been denied official papers that would allow him to work and earn a living to support his family. In the second drama, two men serving sentences in a political prison perform a version of Sophocles' play *Antigone* as a means of expressing solidarity and resistance. Performed together in repertory in New York, both works received overwhelmingly positive reviews.

Although his concern with despair, ambivalence, and the struggle between freedom and political restrictions persists, the characters and situations of Fugard's plays written since the mid-1970s differ markedly from those of his early dramas, reflecting the playwright's increased tendency toward introspection and autobiography. The white protagonists of *A Lesson from Aloes* debate whether to remain true to their political beliefs and face their country's growing racial tension or flee their homeland, a question Fugard has wrestled with in his own life. *"Master Harold". . . and the boys,* Fugard's most autobiographical work to date, is widely considered one of his best plays. The drama revolves around Hally, a white youth who, like Fugard, is embittered by the neglect of his alcoholic, racist father. In the end, the boy vents his anger on Sam, the black servant who has acted as his substitute father and friend throughout his life. *The Road to Mecca* depicts several days in the life of an eccentric and rebellious elderly woman who seeks self-discovery through artistic expression after the death of her husband. *A Place with the Pigs,* described by Fugard as a personal parable, marks a departure from his preceding works in its affirmative ending and its avoidance of dramatic realism. Set "somewhere in the author's imagination," the play depicts Pavel, a Soviet soldier who abandons his post. To avoid punishment from the army, he hides in a pigsty, where he remains for forty years. Despite the bleakness of the situation, the drama contains elements of slapstick and concludes with Pavel pulling himself out of the sty and reentering the world with his wife by his side. In *My Children! My Africa!,* Fugard returns to the realistic drama of many of his earlier works. In this play an elderly black schoolteacher places all of his faith in the power of education as a tool for social change. Reflecting what Fugard has described as his own frustration over his inability to effect significant change in South Africa, the play presents the teacher's growing awareness that a purely intellectual approach and a policy of nonviolence may be ineffective in a turbulent society.

Highly acclaimed for his sensitive and thoughtful depictions of human anguish, Fugard has achieved worldwide recognition. Although faulted by some for his failure to denounce the injustices of apartheid in a more confrontational manner, he nevertheless commands respect for his unfailing opposition to the racial policies of the South African government and for his sophisticated explorations of their subtly destructive effects. Critics note that by powerfully and skillfully describing the impact of apartheid on a personal level, Fugard persuasively argues against its continuation.

PRINCIPAL WORKS

PLAYS

The Blood Knot 1961
People Are Living There 1969
Boesman and Lena 1969
Orestes 1971
Hello and Goodbye 1971
Statements: Two Workshop Productions Devised by Athol Fugard, John Kani, and Winston Ntshona: "Sizwe Bansi Is Dead" and "The Island"; and a New Play: "Statements after an Arrest under the Immorality Act" 1974
Three Port Elizabeth Plays [including *The Blood Knot, Hello and Goodbye,* and *Boesman and Lena*] 1974
"Dimetos" and Two Early Plays [including *Nongogo* and *No-Good Friday*] 1977
A Lesson from Aloes 1981
"Master Harold" . . . and the boys 1983
The Road to Mecca 1986
Selected Plays [including *"Master Harold" . . . and the boys;* a revised version of *Blood Knot; Hello and Goodbye;* and *Boesman and Lena*] 1987
A Place with the Pigs 1988
My Children! My Africa! 1990

OTHER MAJOR WORKS

The Guest: An Episode in the Life of Eugene Marais [with Ross Devenish] (film) 1977
Tsotsi (novel) 1980

Marigolds in August (film) 1982
Notebooks: 1960-1977 (nonfiction) 1983

AUTHOR COMMENTARY

The Art of Theater: Athol Fugard (1985)

[*The following is the text of an interview conducted by Canadian-born actor and director Lloyd Richards. He was artistic director of Yale Repertory Theater at the time of the interview, which took place in connection with the twenty-fifth anniversary revival of Fugard's* The Blood Knot *in 1985. In a discussion covering several of his plays, Fugard explains his writing process and his view of the relationship between art and politics in his native South Africa.*]

[*Richards*]: *When did you realize that you wanted to become a writer? Was there some precipitating event, or did it grow naturally out of a commitment to literature?*

[Fugard]: There was no one moment, but you could see it growing. You can see it in ***"Master Harold" . . . and the boys***—that gauche young schoolboy playing around with words. Young Hallie talking about what would be a good title for a novel, thinking about writing a short story. From early on there were two things that filled my life—music and storytelling, both of them provoked by my father. He was a jazz pianist and also a very good storyteller, an avid reader. He passed both those interests on to me. Thoughts about being a concert pianist or a composer started to fall away from about the age of fifteen. By eighteen, by the time I went to university, I knew that somehow my life was going to be about putting words on paper. Originally I thought I was going to write the great South African novel, then poetry, and only when I was twenty-four or five did the thought of theater come into my head. That obviously relates to my meeting my wife Sheila, who, when I met her, was an out-of-work actress.

What is your reason for writing?

Well, it's a convergence of two things. I can't think of a single one of my plays that does not represent a coincidence between an external and an internal event. Something outside of me, outside even my own life, something I read in a newspaper or witness on the street, something I see or hear, fascinates me. I see it for its dramatic potential. That external event affords me the opportunity to deal with what has been building up inside me. For example, the writing of ***The Bloodknot.*** I remember the genesis of that, even though it happened twenty-five years ago. I am singularly prone to that most human of all diseases—guilt. I've had my fair measure of it. But the image that generated ***The Bloodknot*** had absolutely nothing to do with the racial situation in South Africa. The seminal moment was my returning home late one night and going into the room where my brother was sleeping. My brother is a white man like myself. I looked down at him, and saw in that sleeping body and face, all his pain. Life had been very hard on him, and it was just written on his flesh. It was a scalding moment for me. I was absolutely overcome by my sense of what time had done to what I remembered as a proud and powerful body. I saw the pain: that is the seminal image in ***The Bloodknot.***

And that translated into the injection of race and whiteness?

I was trying to examine a guilt more profound than racial guilt—the existential guilt that I feel when another person suffers, is victimized, and I can do nothing about it. South Africa afforded me the most perfect device for examining this guilt without going into the area of the absurd as Ionesco did by giving a man a rhinoceros's horn.

Can you describe the conjunction of external and internal events in **A Lesson from Aloes?**

The external provocation is very simple: I got to know an Afrikaner in Port Elizabeth who had been committed to the struggle for decency and dignity and human rights, but who was suddenly suspected of being a police informer. His name was Piet. Piet's story gave me a chance to deal with the fact that you cannot simply dispose of the Afrikaner as the villain in the South African situation. If that's the only sense you have of the Afrikaner in South Africa at this moment, your thinking is too naive, and you are never really going to understand what is happening in that country. You'll never understand how we landed in the present situation or what's going to come out of it. The terrible and challenging thing about the Afrikaner is his complexity: he is not just bad; there's good as well. The case of Piet Bezuidenhout occurred at a time when I was ready to put an Afrikaner—not a hero, but a survivor—up on the stage. That was my internal provocation.

Why do you use the symbol of aloes? I have an image of the aloe as tangled in the roots of South Africa. It can either be strangled, or survive to produce a flower. . . .

Yes, I think the aloe is one of South Africa's most powerful, beautiful and celebratory symbols. It survives out there in the wild when everything else is dried. At the end of one of our terrible recurrent droughts, the aloe is still there.

You once told a story about being in England for a while and saying you had to go back to South Africa because you could not look at the people on the street and identify where they had come from. . . .

That is true. That one little corner of South Africa, Port Elizabeth and its immediate surroundings, is a region which I know like the back of the hand which holds my pen as I write about it. I can stand on a street corner in Port Elizabeth, look at anybody and put together some sort of biography. I know where they come from, where they're going. I have a feel of the textures of their life. If I stand on a street corner in New Haven, which is a place I've gotten to know as well as any place outside of South Africa, I am still at a total loss to identify the people passing me on that street.

Do you identify with Piet's inability to leave South Africa?

I don't think I could. Of course I'm saying this on American soil. I'm facing a few more months of work in this city, but at the end of it, I will be returning to South Africa. I would like to believe that if for some reason the situation deteriorated to the point where I was told, "If you leave South Africa, you can never come back," I'd stay there. There were periods in my life when I could have been seduced away. I am incredibly fortunate that the government took away my passport at the point when I was most open to seduction. With my passport gone, I could have left on a one-way ticket. But the issue was so starkly highlighted that I had no problem in saying, "No."

Why was your passport taken away?

I don't know. I think they identified me as a liberal. And in the late sixties a liberal was a dangerous animal. Liberals aren't dangerous animals anymore, so they don't hassle me too much. I know they open my mail, I know my telephone is tapped—but I have a passport, a perfectly normal passport. The likes of myself aren't seen as a threat to the establishment anymore. Now they have to deal with men and women who make bombs and set them off. Of course this could change—the government doesn't seem to pursue any sort of consistent policy. Their attitude toward me depends on how they feel when they wake up in the morning. Nadine Gordimer, J. M. Coetzee, Andre Brink are as baffled by how and why the government does things as I am. There just doesn't seem to be any logic to it.

What about the government and censorship?

I have never had trouble publishing my work in South Africa. Although there've been a couple of occasions when school authorities threw my books out of their libraries.

That seems pretty serious to me. Don't you have any reservations about going back to a country where that sort of thing goes on?

No. Nobody can take what I love away from me. I would like to believe that love is the only energy I've ever used as a writer. I've never written out of anger, although anger has informed love. When I return, that love will still be there, even if the South Africa I go back to in five months' time is radically different from the one I left. I would like to believe that my absence from South Africa won't affect my relationship to that country, which has been the source of my inspiration, the soul of my writing.

Is pain a part of that?

Yes. One wishes that pain weren't the potent achemical element that it is.

You tend, in your plays, to take a few crucial people, put them into a space and let them thrash out their lives. Is that a part of your own way of functioning?

Yes. How one human being deals with another remains the most critical fact in history. You can kill a man, or you can bless him. We all know about our potential to kill; we have dangerously lost sight of the fact that each of us can also bless.

At the end of the last performance of **The Bloodknot** *at the Yale Repertory Theatre, you and Zakes Mokae stood at the front of the stage, with the audience standing and applauding. You held hands and raised them. There was something about the event that was more than just the applause of an audience for a performance.*

In my country there's an Athol Fugard trying to kill a Zakes Mokae at this very moment, and there's a Zakes Mokae who wants to kill an Athol Fugard. But Zakes and I were together on that stage.

Does hope still exist today? Where does it reside?

My faith in human nature, in the capacity to change, grows with every year. My faith in the essential goodness of life increases. Yet my faith in politics has withered.

If you ever lost that sense of hope, would that be the moment at which writing became impossible? Could you write out of despair?

That would be a moment at which a lot of things would become impossible. I don't know what I would do with my life if I lost faith in human nature.

What was the conjunction between the external event and the internal impetus with **"Master Harold" . . . and the boys**?

For fifteen years I kept thinking to myself, when am I going to get around to writing about those two extraordinary men, Sam and Willie, who were literally my closest and virtually my only friends for a period of my childhood. Suddenly one day I put a white boy, Hallie, in with them. There it was. I had it. I was locked in to the tensions, the polarity, the dynamic. I had the chance and the courage to deal with something that I had never dealt with in my life. The particular moment was the spitting event—Hallie spits in the black man's face. Before that I was convinced I'd created the necessary dynamic simply by putting Hallie in there with Sam and Willie, and that I could write the play without resorting to anything like the vulgarity of spitting on stage. I thought I could deal with all my problems, my guilts, and wash my dirty linen in a place of public entertainment without having to resort to that. But I just couldn't avoid it. The moment came: I wrote, "Hallie spits in Willie's face."

How did you feel after that?

Well, there's a vulgar aspect to the craft. Even when you're dealing with the most private, intensely personal moment of pain, if you do it well enough, if you handle it correctly, you immediately pat yourself on the back. . . . I might as well be honest about it.

Did the writing of the play absolve any feeling of guilt?

No, but it was necessary for me to deal with it, I've realized your life can be stained so deeply that you can never get rid of it. It's soaked into the fabric.

What was the background of **The Road to Mecca**? *Was it guilt?*

No, quite different. An extraordinary sculptress, Helen Martins, lived in the little village in the Karroo where my house is. For twenty-two years of her life, starting at the age of fifty, she handed herself over to an incredible creative energy. She sculpted away, single-mindedly, with a total obsession. Then, mysteriously, her creativity dried up and she committed suicide. From time to time I'd say to myself, "Come on, deal with it. You're a writer; this is extraordinary." But I kept pushing her aside. Then her story became such an urgent reality inside me, I needed to examine it. ***The Road to Mecca*** focuses on the possibility that creative energy can exhaust itself, probably the most frightening reality an artist can face. Every artist lives in total fear of that—I know I do. I kept wondering whether, with an act of terrible prescience, in describing the end of Helen Martins's creative energy, I was in fact writing my own epitaph.

Is **The Road to Mecca** *your favorite play?*

I think every writer has a special relationship with his most recent work. In my case that would be ***The Road to Mecca.*** Firstly, the process of writing it, creating it, the traumas or difficulties that you live through in order to get it written—those are close to you still. Also the most recent play says something about where you are in your life. It still needs a certain protection; it is very young. Its life has just been started, and you feel very paternal about it. ***The Bloodknot*** is also a very recent experience in my life, but I see it primarily as the work which launched my career in theater, the work in which I found my own voice for the first time. ***A Lesson from Aloes*** has a very special meaning for me because it was the first play I wrote after two or three agonizing years of writer's block, when I just couldn't get anything down on paper.

How does a play come from you as a craftsman? How do you write?

I write by dealing with what I lovingly describe as the inquisition of blank paper—lovingly despite the terror that it's had for me in the past, and no doubt will continue to have in the future. My most important tool is my notebook. I've been a bit careless these past two or three weeks, but even while producing ***The Bloodknot*** at Yale, I spent a few minutes with it every day. I jot down random images, thoughts, ideas, speculations, and a little bit of personal misery. It's a five-finger exercise. Every one of my plays started off a long time before the actual writing took place as an image in those notebooks. There comes a point when one of these images from the past, such as Sam or Piet or Helen Martins, presents itself again. If it is the right moment, and if, as I tried to describe earlier, there is a coincidence between the external and the internal, the things start happening. First I just free associate. It's almost as if the seminal image has a certain magnetic power of its own which helps me focus on the things of daily living that relate to it. This is the first step. It usually results in an accumulation of ideas, scraps of dialogue, rough structures for scenes and a mass of paper. I can lift up that paper and feel its weight metaphorically and think, "Yeah, there's enough here now." Next it's got to be ordered and organized. I never actually start to write a play—by that I mean put "1" up at the top of a blank sheet of paper and open a bracket for my first stage direction—until I have completely structured the play. I have never started to write a play without knowing with total certainty what my final image is. Other writers work differently, I know. They say, "Oh, the material did this to me, I got surprised, it sent me off in a different direction." That has never happened to me. While it may be a flaw, I am absolutely brutal about my disciplining of the material before I write the words "page one" and get to work.

When you begin to write, does the dialogue flow in your head as you write it down?

It's a very slow and painful process. I'm very conscious of how faltering the first few steps are, how much stalling and drowning in the blankness of paper there is. Nothing flows in my head. There have been occasions when I've found my head working away quite energetically with my hand a foot behind, watching in amazement. But there have never been sustained outpourings. If I've got three full pages done, longhand, that's a good day. That's a damn good day in fact. Sometimes there is nothing, or what I have written goes into the wastepaper basket. I tear up and throw away furiously when I write. I don't accumulate a lot of paper. For something to stay on paper longer than two days it has to pass some very critical tests. I usually work through three drafts, longhand, in the course of writing a play; it takes about nine months.

Are your plays ever revised during rehearsal? Do you know how good a line or a scene is before you hear it spoken, or is your ear so developed that there's no need to revise?

I've had varying experiences. Some plays have gone through rehearsal and ended up on the stage without even so much as the punctuation having changed. Others have benefited substantially from the rehearsal process. Sometimes the actors have made me aware, in the course of the rehearsal process, of moments that needed fleshing out and points that hadn't been made strongly enough.

What, do you feel, is the relationship of a playwright to politics?

I think it varies. There are as many answers to that as there are playwrights. It is a facile, glib thing to say—but I think I am fortunate in that my relationship to politics is resolved very simply: I come from a country which is so highly politicized that there is no act, even the most private you can think of, which does not resonate politically. Obviously when it comes to the question of telling stories about other people's lives in a situation as political as South Africa, you get to be political. So political commitment isn't really something I've had to look for; it was an automatic by-product of my being a storyteller—one who is going to try to tell stories truthfully and through them bear witness to the South African situation. Talking with young students at Yale recently, I was asked whether I agreed with a fellow South African writer—I am going to be cowardly and not name that writer—who said that all writers in that country had an obligation to make a political stand. I got angry about this because I don't think any writer should presume to give orders to another. The place from which you take your orders is probably the most secret place you have. If you have a word like "God" in your vocabulary, then that is an area in which you and God deal with each other. So, no writer must ever presume to tell another writer what his or her political responsibilities are. It is a poet's right in South Africa to write a poem which seemingly has no political resonance.

Is the duty of a playwright in South Africa to his society different than the duty of an American to his?

I don't think so. This is really just a way of asking about the relationship of the artist to his society. Some writers do nothing but talk about the objective moral obligations that artists must live up to. If you're Brecht, you're going to write as Brecht writes; you're going to be as committed as Brecht. There may be pale imitations, but there will only be one Brecht. Every artist does as he needs to. There is a desperate tendency to try to legislate artists, to try to lay down rules for their obligations to society. Just leave artists alone. If you are a true artist, you will have a very finely tuned moral mechanism. If you're a Georgia O'Keeffe, a Bertolt Brecht or a Harold Pinter, you'll do it your way.

You have chosen not to leave your country, for various reasons. Do you consider yourself, even there, in exile to any extent? How does exile fit into your art, or does it?

Exile is a phenomenon I have watched with morbid curiosity over the years because it is a fate that has befallen a lot of my friends. It is something I have watched but not experienced. I do not consider myself to be in exile. I could play around with words and say that I consider myself an exile from the society that I believe South Africa should be, but that's just being clever. No, I don't really know what exile means.

You said your faith in politics has withered. How did this happen?

My faith in politics and politicians has withered, but as I was saying my faith in human nature grows stronger. But politicians screw up so often now—when did we last have a decent statesman? Let's not even talk about South Africa; let's look at America, England. Where's the statesmanship? The mess is global. My skepticism is something that has come with experience, a certain world-weariness as I have looked at the past decades. The world wasn't getting better. I don't think the moral tone of the Western world has significantly improved in the fifty-odd years that I've been alive. Technologically it has, but morally it damn sure hasn't.

How do you feel the role of art in bringing about social change compares to that of politics and persuasion?

Art has a role. Art is at work in South Africa. But art works subterraneanly. It's never the striking, superficial cause and effect people would like to see. Art goes underground into people's dreams and surfaces months later in strange, unexpected actions. People bring a sort of instant-coffee expectation to art; they'd like the results to be immediate. It doesn't work that way. I like that image of art dropping down through the various layers of the individual's psyche, into dreams, stirring around there and then surfacing later in action.

In a recent article you spoke about the role of alcohol in your life, and its subsequent absence. Does alcohol open up new channels of access to the muse? How was your work affected when you quit drinking?

Oh God, I'm only too prepared to talk about that. For a long time I thought that drinking had a great influence on my imagination. Not that I've used alcohol at any of the few desks where I've done my writing; I've always sat down at my desk very sober, but alcohol was there as a part of my life. Especially at night, after a day working, I used to enjoy my whiskeys, my wines, my beer. And then with the last carafe at night I brainstormed, putting down ideas for the next day. It was a critical aspect of my writing cycle and it led me to believe that if I decided to give up drinking I would end up not writing any longer. I won't go into the circumstances that led me to give up drinking, except that obviously one of the reasons was the recognition that I would become an alcoholic. Another was its effect on relationships that were very important to me. Anyway, one day three-and-a-half years ago I decided to stop. In the course of that time I have written ***The Road to Mecca*** and directed it in South Africa, America and London. I also returned to the anniversary production of ***The Bloodknot*** with Zakes Mokae, which started at Yale and ended up on Broadway. The three-and-a-half years prove I can get on with a creative life even though I don't drink. I must confess that I had moments of unbelievable terror, fear and panic, with the devil inside me trying to persuade me that the reason that I hadn't done any writing that day was that I hadn't been able to get any drinking in; that the real reason the rehearsal had gone so badly and I hadn't gotten any sleep and had a headache was because I wasn't drinking; that I had made a mess of a number of critical moments in the past several years while honoring my resolve to stay sober. Fortunately, I was able to resist those low moments. Starting three-and-a-half years ago, life has become a most extraordinary adventure. I didn't ever believe I would have such a sense of rebirth, of rediscovery.

Would you share with us what your family means to you as a writer, and how your relationship with your family either facilitates, implements or impedes your work? I ask this knowing that your wife Sheila was in the theater before you were.

Yes, and now Sheila is a novelist. Theater didn't turn out to be what she wanted to do. Prose and poetry have become her life. We have lived together as two writers. The marriage has survived on the basis of one absolute rule: total privacy. It came about quite unconsciously, without any fuss; we never addressed ourselves to the issue. I think two writers living together can be dangerous. I never know what Sheila is writing, what her novel is about, until the first copy comes from the publisher. And she, by and large, knows nothing about the play that I'm working on until she sits down in a preview or a first-night audience. We exchange sighs of relief or groans of despair at the end of the day, but it's as general as that. They are noises, like two draft animals stabled together, blowing and groaning away. That makes the work possible. Obviously, there is incredible mutual respect and support. And Lisa, my daughter, is very inspirational. I think that she's a major reason for a lot of what I do.

You have been at once both the playwright and the director. Is the relationship between these two roles an easy one?

It started out of economic necessity. The blunt and simple reality was that twenty-five years ago, when I wrote ***The***

Bloodknot, nobody in South Africa wanted to touch it. If I hadn't got hold of Zakes, whom I had already known from some previous work we had done in the theater, and said, "Let's do it," and then tried to sort out the traffic on the stage—in addition to taking on the role of Morris—the play wouldn't have got done. It was the same with ***Hello and Goodbye, People are Living There, Boesman and Lena, Sizwe Bansi is Dead, The Island*** and ***Statements after an Arrest under the Immorality Act.*** I only started enjoying the luxuries so taken for granted in the American theater when I came to Yale. I had never had designers in my life. I had never had dramaturges—I'm still trying to discover what to do with that animal; what do you *do* with a dramaturge? I think they are asking themselves that question as well. God knows I have no conceits as a director. Someone has to organize the traffic. That's what I do: I see that people don't bump into each other on the stage. I look after the six-foot rule.

Forgive me, what is the six-foot rule?

The six-foot rule is that no two actors must come nearer to each other than six feet unless there is a crisis. Get closer than six feet and you've got a crisis in the action. So I organize the traffic. I also understand the text, because I wrote it. With those two contributions to the event, I have discharged my responsibilities as a director.

Would you lose a certain amount of the autonomy you feel as a writer if you turned a play over to another director?

I've no experience with that. I make very certain that I handle the first productions of the play in South Africa, in London and in New York. When those three events are behind me, I cut the umbilical cord, and the play looks after itself. Once or twice I've dropped in on other productions of my work and had varying experiences—some good, some bad, quite a few indifferent. I've no working relationship with other directors and I think it will probably stay that way.

What about the experience of acting in your own plays? When you're writing do you have it in mind that certain words will be for you to speak?

I'm glad I'm an actor. I'm glad I've had acting experience, because I think it has sharpened my craft as a playwright. Acting has made the writer realize what actors need up there on stage to make a moment work. I feel that's the reason actors have such a good time with my plays—they often tell me they do. I often think of my plays as being written with three characters sitting at the desk: the writer himself, and then behind his left shoulder is the actor, watching as he writes and nudging his arm, and behind the other shoulder is the director who's eventually going to be responsible for the staging of it. There's a triple psychology that functions when I write a play. I don't want to become too conscious of this aspect of my writing in case it interferes with its progress, but it seems there is a three-pronged attack on the blank paper when I sit down to write a play.

You said earlier that you gather your material before you set out to write. Could you talk a little about the plays that were worked on improvisationally?

My work with the actors during one stage of the rehearsals is for both rehearsing and improvising. With ***The Island,*** when I got together with John Kani and Winston Ntshona, I always came prepared with questions, ideas, provocations. This would set them up; they are both consummate personal storytellers who love acting out their lives. I fed them a constant stream of provocations relating to the central idea on which we had decided.

How were John and Winston involved in the genesis of **Sizwe Bansi is Dead***?*

Yes, very simple, easy to talk about that. I had been working with John and Winston in an amateur context, a black drama group from New Brighton, the black ghetto of Port Elizabeth. They approached me one day and said that they wanted to turn professional. I listened to them with disbelief. At that point in South Africa's theater history, twelve years ago, the notion that a black man could earn a living being an actor in South Africa was just the height of conceit. But they were insistent, and so we looked around for a play for them to do. We couldn't find anything that really excited us, anything that I wanted to direct them in. Then John said, "Couldn't we *make* a play?" We tried various ideas, all of which petered out, and then I remembered something: it was a photograph I'd once seen in the display window of a pokey little backstreet photographer in Port Elizabeth, an extraordinary photograph of a man wearing what was obviously a new suit, seated on a chair, smiling broadly, a hat on his head. I think there was even an umbrella across his knees. In one hand he had a pipe and in the other a cigarette. It was an extraordinary photograph, a great celebratory moment captured by that backstreet photographer. I finally put this down as a mandate; I said to these chaps, "Come on now, for that chap to be smiling like that, he's got to have a reason. Maybe that's the story we're looking for. Maybe that's where our play lies." I asked them why he was smiling. Again it was John who said, "One reason why a black man smiles as broadly as you've suggested is if his reference book, his much-hated passbook, is in order, or if he's just managed to get some problem in connection with it sorted out." That was the start of it, that stupid question. In fact, the passbook does lie at the core of ***Sizwe Bansi is Dead.*** That question, and a whole series of others—all concerning the man in the blue suit with the umbrella, smiling at the camera, with the cigarette in one hand and a pipe in the other—was the start of ***Sizwe Bansi.*** He was our seminal image, I fed John and Winston constant provocations from what I knew about them and their lives. It was my job to take home whatever had happened in the rehearsal room and start shaping it. I used my craft to structure and define and dramatically shape what they had provided by way of raw improvisation. That was my process. I am a great believer in architecture, in structuring. It's my discipline.

Can you talk about the original production of that play in Johannesburg? Was there censorship involved?

We felt that the play was far too dangerous for us to go public with it; there was the problem of mixed audiences.

So we launched the play by underground performances to which people had to have a specific invitation—a legal loophole in the censorship structure in South Africa, and one we continued to exploit for many years. During our underground period, we had a lot of police interference. They rolled up once or twice and threatened to close us down, arrest us—the usual bully tactics of security police anywhere in the world. We just persisted, carried on and survived it. We eventually did go public with ***Sizwe Bansi,*** many years later, but only after it had played in London and New York. After that, we felt that the play's reputation protected us.

What are some of the limits you perceive in the American theater? You spoke recently about the difficulties of producing an off-Broadway show.

Well, I could talk endlessly about the limits of Broadway theater. Broadway, oh God, what a pain! It is going through a long process of dying—it should just get on with the business and do it. Broadway's become one hell of a mess, but then Broadway isn't American theater. If Broadway wants to die, and if legitimate theater, straight theater, hasn't got a place on Broadway, well then good. Theater's flourishing out in the regions. I look around and all sorts of very exciting things are happening.

Did you seek out a relationship with the New York theater world and the Yale Rep?

Not any more than any writer or playwright who tries to get his work done. When it gets done, you earn a living, you earn royalties, you can pay the rent. Fortunately American audiences and American actors go for the same sort of theater that I try to write. I don't think it's an accident that I earn eighty or ninety per cent of my living as a playwright in America. In England it's only about ten or fifteen per cent. The English don't tune in to my plays as strongly as American audiences and critics. This relationship between New York, American theater and myself is one which I'm very happy with and hope to continue.

How has your relationship with Zakes changed through all this? What was it like working with a very unprofessional actor twenty-five years ago as opposed to the experienced actor he is now?

Oh, I've got a lovely answer to that question: I was as unprofessional as Zakes then. We both thought we were as good then as we think we are now. Zakes had seen five plays twenty-five years ago; I had seen six.

So the ego does not change.

The ego does not change. Now we've seen a dozen each. (pp. 131-51)

Athol Fugard and Lloyd Richards, in an interview in The Paris Review, *Vol. 31, No. 111, Summer, 1989, pp. 128-51.*

OVERVIEWS AND GENERAL STUDIES

Chris Wortham (essay date 1983)

[*In the excerpt below, Wortham focuses on four of Fugard's plays set in the playwright's hometown of Port Elizabeth, attempting "to demonstrate some of the ways in which Fugard achieves his vivid presentations, so rich in vitality and distinctive local colour."*]

Athol Fugard has experimented with a variety of dramatic modes. Since some of his plays are founded less in text than upon improvisation, it seems that his enduring achievement will be measured by those plays which may be most fully recreated from the printed word. Among his fully scripted plays are three works which originally appeared independently, but which were later perceived by Fugard himself to be related and were published together as ***Three Port Elizabeth Plays.*** To this group—consisting of ***The Blood Knot*** (1961), ***Hello and Goodbye*** (1965), and ***Boesman and Lena*** (1969)—I would add his latest work, ***A Lesson From Aloes*** (1979).

The four Port Elizabeth plays have much in common. Their subject matter is a world that is ugly, painful, and bitter; and yet one responds to them with delight in their aesthetic qualities, for they are skilfully constructed, the work of an artist who is also an accomplished craftsman. Speech, gesture, visual and verbal symbolism, and a rhythmic line of action moving simply and strongly towards its conclusion—all these complement and enrich each other. These attributes do not adequately account for the psychic force of the Port Elizabeth plays, a force or power which can be described and demonstrated, in so far as such things can be demonstrated, only as emanating from an overwhelming sense of place.

Not all Fugard's plays are equally successful and it is invariably this sense of place which marks his best work. Fugard's early plays, ***No-Good Friday*** (1958) and ***Nongogo*** (1959), are set in the satellite African townships which ring Johannesburg. Their failure to convince cannot be attributed entirely to apprenticeship, for only two years after ***Nongogo*** came ***The Blood Knot,*** by common consent one of Fugard's finest achievements. And then there is ***People Are Living There,*** with which Fugard himself has expressed dissatisfaction, which comes between ***The Blood Knot*** and the next major success, ***Hello and Goodbye.*** Like the early plays, ***People Are Living There*** is located in Johannesburg. The manifold iniquities of apartheid are no less distressing in Johannesburg than in Port Elizabeth but, concerned as Fugard is about social justice, he is much more than a protest marcher under a dramatic banner: he sees the human predicament fully and he sees it whole. Herein lies his greatest strength. In Johannesburg Fugard came to recognise the horrors of the South African system, working in the courts which send Africans to gaol every day in their hundreds for breaches of the pass laws that restrict their movements. But in Johannesburg Fugard was a sojourner; Port Elizabeth has always been his home—and it is well to remember that the two cities are as different as any two cities eight hundred miles apart. Fugard writes with greatest assurance and authority when creating scenes from the lives of Cape coloured people and poor whites in the Eastern Cape: Johannesburg he has known as a visitor in adulthood; Port Elizabeth he has experienced with his whole being.

Fugard's Port Elizabeth is a city viewed idiosyncratically, to the extent that it is a place of the lost, the lonely, and the forsaken. Not for him are the equally real joys and suffering of the rich, the successful, and the privileged. Solly, the rich liberal living 'in his nice Humewood house', and all his kind are present only by allusion or passing reference. Idiosyncratic or not, Fugard brings his city to life. It is my purpose in this essay to demonstrate some of the ways in which Fugard achieves his vivid presentations, so rich in vitality and distinctive local colour. I hope further to demonstrate that there is an unpretentious but definite philosophical purpose behind Fugard's choice of subject.

What is place to Athol Fugard? He accepts and works from the common everyday reality that a place is somewhere in time and space, but that is only a starting-point: place is much more than a spot on a map. Fugard sees place in general and Port Elizabeth in particular much as William Blake saw London: as something that is perceived not in absoluteness but through the refracted light of human consciousness. Man's identity in place is defined less by where he is in a topographical sense than by whom he is with; his existence is necessarily social. Fugard talks of one of his protagonists confronting 'the absurdity of himself, *alone*' and in the same passage goes on to declare that 'A man's scenery is other men'. Fugard's notebooks, which have in part been published, disclose what he calls 'generative images'. From these images his plays have taken shape. What is particularly striking as a common factor in the plays is that in each case the generative image has emerged from meditation on the interpenetration of person and place.

Fugard speaks of writing ***The Blood Knot*** as 'a compulsive and direct experience' and in his Introduction to ***Three Port Elizabeth Plays*** gives an entry from his notebook on Korsten, where ***The Blood Knot*** is set:

> Korsten: the Berry's Corner bus, then up the road past the big motor-assembly and rubber factories. Turn right down a dirt road—badly potholed, full of stones, donkeys wandering loose, Chinese and Indian grocery shops—down this road until you come to the lake. Dumping ground for waste from the factories. Terrible smell. On the far side, like a scab, Korsten location. A collection of shanties, pondoks, lean-to's. No streets, names, or numbers. A world where anything goes.
>
> When the wind blows in from the east the inhabitants of Korsten live with the terrible smell of the lake.
>
> In one of these shacks the two brothers—Morrie and Zach.

It is instructive to see how Fugard integrates the action on stage with this pre-informing image that can only partially be recreated in the theatre. One way is through the set itself, the shack with its patchwork walls of 'corrugated iron, packing-case wood, flattened cardboard boxes, and old hessian bags'. The visual effect is one of a monstrous collage, not unlike the collage-work of Kurt Schwitters and other Modernists: what we see is a collection of waste products cast off by a dehumanised industrial society, accidentally gathered and rearranged haphazardly into an arbitrary pattern out of the need to make a home. The set speaks eloquently for what Morris and Zach are, for what they have become.

In retrospect, Fugard thinks that ***The Blood Knot*** is overwritten. One may indeed find some awkwardness, some improbably poetic and finely articulated imagery in speeches given to two men whose lives epitomise deprivation. Furthermore, some of the imagery seems false, the symbolism strained and contrived. There is, perhaps, in this still quite early work, an over-anxious desire to communicate ideas rather than to let dramatic action speak for itself, a fault also evident in some plays by the best dramatists of our century—among them Eugene O'Neill and Arthur Miller. Nevertheless, ***The Blood Knot*** has much to commend it in dialogue and in action. Its special strength is a cohesiveness which the earliest plays, and one or two of the later ones, lack.

In ***The Blood Knot*** and the later Port Elizabeth plays the set is complemented by a mood that is established through

Athol Fugard and Zakes Mokae in the 1985 New York revival of The Blood Knot.

time of day and time of year. The time of day in the Port Elizabeth plays, with the exception of one scene from ***The Blood Knot,*** is late afternoon stretching into night; the season is autumn descending into winter. This mood projects itself upon and at the same time reflects the state of mind of Fugard's characters in their landscape. They are loneliest, most anxious, and have the deepest sense of their alienation as night comes in the cold time of year. In the first scene Morris muses upon the lake, 'the smell of the rotting waters', noticing that 'On blue days or grey days it stays the same dirty brown. And so calm, hey, Zach! Like a face without feeling.' In the same speech, quite a long one, he continues: 'Have you noticed, Zach, the days are getting shorter again, the nights longer? Autumn is in our smelly air'. At the end of the same scene Morris recalls what called him home from his wanderings:

> I remember turning off the road and coming this way across the veld. The sun was on my back. Yes! I left the road because it went a longer way around . . . and I was in a hurry . . . and it was autumn.
>
> I needed comfort. It's only a season, I said bravely. Only the beginning of the end of another year.

In Scene Three, which takes place only a few days later, Zach's depressed state of mind on discovering that Ethel, his new-found pen-friend, is white is so intense that he speaks of its being winter already. He writes to her, through his amanuensis, Morris:

> It's winter down here now. The light is bad, the lake is black, the birds have gone. Wait for spring, when things improve.

Through the descent into black wintry night, Morris and Zach identify their racial and political plight. Only in whiteness is there hope, but it is unattainable. For a fanciful moment Zach allows himself an impossible dream: 'I like the thought of this little white Ethel better than our future . . . It's a warm thought for a man in winter'. They identify their plight as a lack of whiteness and of light. Later, recalling the flight of moths and birds, Morris says:

> . . . there were moths. Then I had that deep thought. You see they were flying in out of the darkness, out of the black, lonely night . . . to the lamp . . . into the flame. Always to light, I thought. Everybody always flying, or growing, or turning, or crying for the whiteness of light. Birds following the sun when winter comes; trees and things standing begging for it; moths hunting it; Man wanting it. All of us, always, out of darkness and into light.

Whether or not the moths symbolise the non-whites is one of the minor problems of the play—they may be taken as allusions to Morris's dangerous attempt to use the relative paleness of his skin to 'try for white'—but the brutal fact which emerges through the imagery is that, as Cape coloured people in a land dominated by white people with an ideology of their own racial superiority, Morris and Zach in some measure accept the spurious symbolic associations made by their oppressors. They long with part of their being for the whiteness which would give them self-respect and which in fact denies it to them.

This dualistic attitude towards the white people manifests itself in a characteristic behaviour pattern among coloured people of the Eastern Cape: they have a tradition of elaborate self-parody, at once mocking the whites by affecting exaggerated servility and mocking themselves in their degradation. Fugard has brought this distinctive tradition of behaviour into his Port Elizabeth plays most effectively. In ***The Blood Knot*** there is a devastating scene when Morris puts on the European clothing bought by Zach to impress Ethel, and the two act out a scene of South African racial interaction. Morris for the time being pretends to be white and humiliates Zach in front of her in order to enhance the impression. Zach, acting the part of a coloured vendor on the street, approaches Morris and is cut off with the vicious taunt, 'Swartgat!' Morris realises that he has gone too far and apologises, but they both know that this coarse rejection is all too close to what Morris had done earlier in his life by deserting Zach and trying for white. Theatrical and metatheatrical role-playing routines have become commonplace in modern drama, the most noted exponents probably being Harold Pinter and Edward Albee, whose work has been concurrent with and almost certainly influenced by a whole generation of social psychologists—R. D. Laing, Eric Berne, and Erving Goffman, to name but a few. Fugard has not been an innovator in using impersonation in a role-playing motif—after all, it goes back to the great tavern scene in *1 Henry IV* and probably much farther—but what he has done is to bring to life the special qualities of the role-playing mechanism among Cape coloured people in confrontation with white society. In ***The Blood Knot*** and in his other plays dealing with the plight of the coloured people, ***Boesman and Lena*** and ***A Lesson From Aloes,*** Fugard has strengthened the sense of place with the mutually reinforcing speech patterns and gestures of the people.

The Blood Knot is not primarily a political play. For people like Morris and Zach, the way things are in South Africa is not so much a special case as evidence that the universe is at worst hostile and at best indifferent. What afflicts them most is not belonging in the only land they know. And so their need to find some way of being at home in the world is acute. Morris recalls how he had wandered like Cain after abandoning Zach to try for white, and that it was the need to feel at home somewhere which impelled him to return; in half-mocking tones he recounts the experience as though given in a revelation from God:

> 'And he said: What hast thou done? The voice of thy Brother's blood crieth unto me!' (Morris drops his head in an admission of guilt). Oh Lord! Oh Lord! So he becomes a hobo and wandered away, a marked man, on a long road until a year later, in another dream, He spake again: Maybe he needs you, He said. You better go home, man!

Alienated man asks how far brotherhood might extend in a world of better people and better prospects; an inquiry which has engaged many writers, particularly those with an existentialist cast of mind. Among these are Sartre and

Camus, whose influence Fugard has acknowledged. The quest for home, for a wider sense of relatedness, has been put succinctly, if somewhat sententiously, by another twentieth-century dramatist, Arthur Miller: 'How may a man make of the outside world a home?' At one moment in ***The Blood Knot*** Morris hopes for redemption from isolation in shared labour, reciting:

> No smell does stink as sweet as labour.
> 'Tis joyous times when man and man
> Do work and sweat in common toil,
> When all the world's my neighbour.

and Zach echoes antiphonally, 'When all the world's my neighbour.' This hope is evanescent, however, for in the next scene Morris comes to the conclusion that in our world brotherhood is by definition exclusive. He invokes the word 'Brother', to which Zach responds, 'A warm word,' and Morris continues:

> Ah! Now you're on to it. A woolly one. Like old brown jackets a size too big. But what does that matter, as long as it keeps out the cold, and the world.

It is sad to reflect that the play will end with the brothers affirming their relationship, but in isolation.

However imperfect the world and however reduced the terms on which men may feel at home in it, the need remains. Apart from the intensity which the South African situation adds to a universal human issue, Fugard has a number of ways of intensifying feeling in the play. One which we have already noticed is the seasonal and diurnal mood which settles down upon the people of Port Elizabeth in Fugard's plays. The onset of darkness takes them deeper into a dark night of the soul where the only consolation is the possibility of a home—whatever that may mean. As Morris puts it:

> It hits you when the sun goes. That's when you really know why men build homes, and the meaning of the word 'home', because the veld's gone grey and cold with a blind, bad feeling about you being there.

Place in time, brotherhood, home: the effect in the play is cumulative and borne upon its rhythmic flow, to end with Morrie and Zach's final words:

> ZACHARIAH: What is it, Morrie? The two of us . . . you know . . . in here?
>
> MORRIS: Home.
>
> ZACHARIAH: Is there no other way?
>
> MORRIS: No. You see, we're tied together, Zach. It's what they call the blood knot . . . the bond between brothers.

In ***Hello and Goodbye*** Fugard turns his attention to poor whites of the Valley Road area in Port Elizabeth. Johnnie Smit is white, but the terms on which he endures life are hardly more favourable than those enjoyed by Morris and Zach. The room in which the action takes place is starkly spare: it has some rudimentary trappings of domestic comfort—a kitchen table and four chairs—but isolation and poverty are oppressively evident from the moment the play begins. The four chairs suggest a family, yet all but one remain eloquently vacant throughout the play. I am reminded of Ionesco's use of the empty-chair motif in his play, *The Chairs.* On stage there is one man, one jug, one glass, and one spoon. This man's world is lit by 'a solitary electric light'. The only sound heard is the sound of the spoon tapping slowly on the glass.

Johnnie is alone. The only person in his world, his long-widowed father, has recently died; Johnnie is trying to come to terms with his grief. The time is evening, the time for being at home. Johnnie recalls:

> And sooner or later it starts to get dark in the square, the sun sets, and the last light goes riding away on the backs of the buses, and then it's twilight with a sky stretching all the way down Main Street and beyond who knows where, the ends of the earth . . . Bringing peace, the end of the day . . . Until the lights go on . . . Suddenly like a small fright, ON, which is my sign to think of going . . . I pull up my roots as the saying goes and go . . .

And yet, as Johnnie dimly recognises through his grief, a lonely house is not a home:

> As I was saying, back in the twilight . . . Back home. No place like here. That's a lie.

His limited consciousness fails to perceive that the lie is not in the adage but in his changed situation: the house is no longer a home. As in ***The Blood Knot,*** darkness intensifies isolation. When Johnnie's sister, Hester, comes in the dark to the house, she tells of her alienation in a way that reminds us of what Morris had said about nightfall and the need for a home:

> All my life I been noticing this, the way night works, the way it makes you feel home is somewhere else.

In his maundering opening monologue, Johnnie evokes what is most immediately distinctive about Port Elizabeth to a listener, the names of localities and suburbs:

> Summerstrand Humewood Cadles Walmer Perridgevale Newton Park Mount Pleasant Kensington . . . Jetty Street . . . Baakens Bridge . . . Valley Road.

These names are familiar to Johnnie in this order from his accustomed bus routes, and they form an accidental litany. As in a litany, the names in themselves give some order and comfort, but there is something just a little disturbing to the ear in these Port Elizabeth names. They are not like the place-names in England, which have grown and developed organically over the centuries; they are imposed names, in which strangely assorted particles are united, e.g. Summer-strand, Hume-wood, and Perridge-vale; some of them are apparently English-derived and yet seem strangely unEnglish, e.g. Cadles: and the transported English names like Kensington remind us that they are displaced when juxtaposed with names from Afrikaans, or half from Afrikaans, like Baakens Bridge. The names, then, have a double effect, which is to draw one uncomfortably in opposite directions: on the one hand they assert familiarity in place; on the other they awaken a sense of alienness and alienation. It is in this carefully prepared context of disjunctive feelings that Johnnie and Hester reveal their distress, their sense of homelessness.

There is one great difference between Johnnie and Hester which makes it impossible for them to understand each other, to form a mutually redemptive relationship: Johnnie is obsessed with the purposeful life that he has lost, that of caring for his disabled father; Hester is obsessed with finding compensation—literally and metaphorically—for what she never had. Fugard creates subtle irony by investing the clichés of their earliest moments of conversation with significance beyond their comprehension. When Hester comes in she says, 'I thought nobody was home.' Shortly afterwards, Johnnie, suspicious but unsure of himself, says, 'Make yourself at home!' At every stage of their brief coming-together (one could hardly call it a reunion), home is the *leitmotif* in all their defensiveness, derision, and pained recollection. When Johnnie asks, 'Why have you come back?', Hester replies, 'It's also my home'. Again he asks the same question, and she retorts, 'Must I have a reason to visit my own home?' The need for home, Fugard implies, is beyond reason—it is an existential reality. At the present moment, however, neither Johnnie nor Hester has the capacity to form the kind of relationship which transforms mere place into home. Throughout Act One Hester pleads for some recognition of her loneliness from her brother, but he is unmoved, locked into his private world of the past. Finally they communicate, but only to reach a compromise that will reinforce their separateness: he will keep the house and she will take the money from the compensation paid to their father for his accident.

Act Two centres on Hester's increasingly frantic search for the compensation. As she rummages through the boxes that contain the tattered past of the Smit family, she forgets her purpose, becoming confused between the monetary compensation and her indignant demand for compensation for the bitter youth she spent in the house that was never a home to her. There are no religious consolations in Fugard's own world and he does not allow them to Hester either. At the end of her fruitless search she cries:

> *There is no God! There never was!* We've unpacked our life, Johannes Cornelius Smit, the years in Valley Road and there is no God. Nothing but rubbish. In this house there was nothing but useless . . . second-hand poor-white junk!

All that she uncovers is hatred, self-disgust and pain. 'Pain?', asks Johnnie, ' . . . Home ground'. For him, home has meant living with hate and hardship, subjugating the pain of living to relatedness.

As a prostitute living in Johannesburg, which is just about as far away from Port Elizabeth as she can get, Hester knows loneliness in its bleakest form: in an isolation broken only by joyless sexual encounters, she has neither place nor relationship to sustain her. In response to Johnnie's promise to write to her when she has found a new place, she cries:

> There's no address! No names, no numbers. A room somewhere, in a street somewhere. To Let is always the longest list, and they're all the same. Rent in advance and one week's notice—one week to notice it's walls again and a door with nobody knocking, a table, a bed, a window for your face when there's nothing to do . . . And I'm Hester. But what's that mean? What does Hester Smit mean?

There can be no meaning for her there. At the end of the play she decides in her confusion to return to Johannesburg, saying:

> I'm too far away from my life. I want to get back to it, in it, be it, be me again the way it was when I walked in.

Mistaking the accidental circumstances of her terrible situation for the deeper and necessary reality of her life, she decides to go back to the pointlessness, the despair, which she feels to be her spiritual lot in a Godless world. Her speech sounds like an existentialist set-piece spoken by someone truly in search of authentic existence; Fugard's irony, a sad irony, reveals the extent of her lostness, for the life she is going back to seek out is a living death.

Johnnie's decision to stay at home and look after his father rather than go to the railway school at Kroonstad is open to more than one interpretation. It is at one level an act of self-sacrifice and commitment to another person. Unfortunately, Johnnie's need to be at home in the world after his father's death is too much for him to bear, so he devises a pseudo-resurrection of his father by adopting his father's disability:

> They'll say shame, buy me a beer, help me on buses, stop the traffic when I cross the street . . . Birth. Death. Both. Jesus did it in the Bible. Resurrection.

Ironic biblical references, of which there are many in Fugard's work, are beyond the scope of this essay, but one can't pass over a passage like this one without noting that homelessness is a dramatic given in much of Fugard's work.

Hello and Goodbye shows little overt concern with South Africa's racial politics. There is general concern with social and economic forces, which are recalled through the fortunes of the Smit family. What Johnnie calls 'our inheritance' is shown to be a combination of private disasters and catastrophic public events during the years of the Depression. There are Sartrian implications in Hester's nausea—she frequently talks of vomiting—but the closest Fugard comes to a specifically South African hell for the homeless is in Johnnie's recital of his bus rides through the suburbs, the full text of which reads:

> Summerstrand Humewood Cadles Walmer Perridgevale Newton Park Mount Pleasant Kensington Europeans only and all classes double deckers with standing prohibited spitting prosecuted and alighting while in motion is at your own risk . . .

The animosity of the environment, the specifically human environment, is expressed through imperatives and negatives. It is the sense of living in a hostile place that drives

Johnnie to the desperate subterfuge with which the play ends—acting the part of the cripple to gain sympathy on those buses which permit Europeans only, and which prohibit and threaten to prosecute persons who dare to stand or spit.

The Blood Knot and ***Hello and Goodbye*** are both set indoors; to some extent both plays offer the small consolations of human habitation, if not the larger ones. In Fugard's next play, ***Boesman and Lena,*** even the minimal assurances given by four walls and a roof have gone. The play opens on an empty stage. Onto this bare set stagger two grotesquely burdened human creatures, carrying between them all that they have in the world in the way of food, clothing and shelter. The influence of many aspects of Samuel Beckett's plays on Fugard is self-evident here as elsewhere: two pitifully reduced characters in a featureless landscape, at the end of their tether, but carrying on because there is nothing else to do. Fugard's debt is of the best kind, for he has used what he has learned from Beckett—and others—to create his own distinctive drama.

It is in his sense of place that Fugard has diverged from his Beckettian model in ***Boesman and Lena.*** An audience accustomed to modern expressionistic drama that has broken away from the Naturalism of Zola and Ibsen will not be dismayed by ***Boesman and Lena,*** but it will be in for a surprise if it is expecting the unlocalised landscape of *Waiting for Godot.* The silent actions of the two people in the first moments of the play confirm the symbolism that one has learned from Beckett, but when one of the figures speaks, the opening line immediately identifies a place that is a local habitation and has a name: 'Here? Mud! Swartkops!' We learn that the mud-caked fringes of the Swartkops River are a wasteland, a place where discarded black people go to die. Boesman and Lena have arrived at nightfall. Lena looks for the direction of the sun to orientate herself, but the sun has gone down. They set about lighting a fire: as in ***The Blood Knot,*** it is evening in the cold time of the year.

Boesman and Lena have come to the mudflats of Swartkops following the demolition of their shanty in Korsten earlier that day in the interests of slum clearance. Boesman rehearses the mighty deeds of the bulldozer:

> Slowly it comes . . . slowly . . . big yellow *donner* with its jawbone on the ground. One bite and there's a hole in the earth. Whiteman on top . . . In reverse . . . take aim! . . . *maak sy bek oop!* . . . then horsepower in top gear and smashed to hell. One push and it was flat. All of them. Slum clearance! And what did we do! Stand and look.

The monstrous combination of man and machine joined in an awesome but inhuman partnership of power has been a recurrent motif in twentieth-century art. From the First World War poets to the paintings of George Grosz and the sculpture of Raoul Haussman, technologically enhanced cruelty has appalled and yet fascinated the creative imagination. Having been cast out of Korsten, Boesman and Lena seek refuge in the cold, inhospitable world of Swartkops. Appropriately, Boesman fashions their latest makeshift home from 'an old sack, a few pieces of wood, a piece of corrugated iron, an old motor-car door', for they are themselves 'whiteman's rubbish'; and so they put together a home from the leftovers of the technologically advanced society which dispossessed them only a few hours before.

The sense of place is sustained in many ways in this finely textured play. I shall concentrate upon three of them. The first, which is already quite highly developed in ***The Blood Knot*** and ***Hello and Goodbye,*** but taken further here, resides in the kind of language spoken. Not only is the speech of the Port Elizabeth coloured people unique and quite unmistakable, but what Fugard has done in ***Boesman and Lena*** is to heighten the distinctive qualities, stopping just short of caricature. Fugard acknowledges having had difficulty with the language of ***Boesman and Lena,*** having thought it out first in Afrikaans and then later translated it into English. The result is an English which incorporates a number of Afrikaans words and phrases without any disjunction because the syntactic patterns and style of speech accord as much with Afrikaans as with English. The blend, almost a patois of its own, belongs to the Eastern Cape. Fragments of Xhosa, justified by Outa's presence, confirm the locality, and the juxtaposition of the three languages in the play is skilfully managed so that language itself comments upon the racial, social, and more generally political issues of the play. One could quote many instances, but the effect is gained through the play as a whole rather than in particular instances. One brief, but effective, moment of interplay between the languages comes when Lena, who is trying desperately to find words that will communicate with the dying Outa, calls—first in English, then in Afrikaans, and finally in Xhosa—the one word that signifies life's most basic necessity, 'Water. *Water! Manzi!'*

Intensified action complements intensified language in ***Boesman and Lena.*** This is the second way in which the sense of place in this play becomes a vivid reality. It is a particular kind of action found in the Eastern Cape—a capering self-parody that is simultaneously comic and bitter. We have already noticed Fugard's use of this behaviour in ***Blood Knot,*** but in ***Boesman and Lena*** it is more fully developed and less self-conscious. It may be argued here that Fugard owes much to Brecht in the use of mimed and danced scenes from the life of ordinary people. Be that as it may, Fugard's interposition of such scenes in this play accentuates the humour and the horror of South Africa's racial politics through the grotesque capering dances of Boesman and Lena.

The third attribute which sustains the sense of place is the use of place-names themselves. In ***The Blood Knot*** place-names are only incidental; in ***Hello and Goodbye,*** Fugard has begun to explore the resonances of names in themselves; in ***Boesman and Lena*** names recur as a *leitmotif* that contains in itself the essence of the Eastern Cape. Over and over again Lena repeats the names of the places where they have set up home after ramshackle home, trying to work out where they are and where they have come from:

> Coega Kop to here . . .

> Redhouse—Swartkops—Veeplaas—Korsten . . .
> Here! Where I am.

To which Boesman adds, delighting in her confusion:

> Go on! But don't forget Bethelsdorp this time. You've been there too. And Missionvale. And Kleinskool.

As with the suburban place-names of ***Hello and Goodbye,*** these names of shanty-towns and non-white areas on the fringes of Port Elizabeth have in common the fact that they are of relatively recent origin and have been imposed on places rather than growing out of long settlement. Beyond this common factor and, I believe, more significant, is the tension between the names in their linguistic and allusive diversity. For example, in the names Redhouse and Swartkops there is not only the opposition between languages but the primal opposition in colour—red and black.

The resonances of some of the names may be adventitious, but they are real none the less. In ***A Lesson From Aloes*** Fugard will postulate that names have an iconic value in themselves. Bethelsdorp suggests the ancient city of Bethel in Palestine, but it is qualified by the prosaic Afrikaans 'dorp' to suggest a small, deracinated modern town of no distinction. Missionvale evokes what the name of Bethelsdorp just hints at—an apostolate of religious white men who persuaded themselves and some of their black catechumens that their purpose was to bring Christian civilisation to a savage land. Kleinskool witnesses to an educational enterprise, but a diminutive one. Amid these reminders of a European influence, the Khoi name of Coega stands alone to insist upon a more distant past.

Boesman and Lena bear their mixed ancestry in their names as well as in their appearance and social condition. Lena's European name could equally well come from English or Afrikaans stock; Boesman's is almost allegorical, stating that the coloured's African heritage is not only Bantu, but also from the dying race of the Bushmen. Yet further echoes from the remoter past are heard through the belittling word 'Hotnot', a term for coloured people that is an uncomfortable reminder of the Hottentots, whose extinction the white newcomers helped to complete.

In ***Boesman and Lena,*** Fugard's landscape is compounded of topographical and human features, and again there is the yearning for home in homelessness. Though Boesman and Lena are both homeless in terms of their material poverty, they are not equally bereft in spirit. While Boesman has navigated their hikes from one encampment to the next, and while Lena is confused about her bearings, in spiritual terms it is Boesman who is more lost than Lena. It is Lena who tries to care for Outa, albeit out of her own need for company. She offers him a meal and there is a socially if not supernaturally sacramental quality in her sharing: she has a sense of being with others, whereas Boesman himself suffers from the white man's desire to distance himself from others. Lena resorts to saying simply, without holding onto names, over and over again, 'Here! Where I am.' and 'I'm here!' Boesman taunts her, 'Lena! You're lost', but he is more lost than she is, even though he knows the names and the places. On encountering the old man, she finds an existential authenticity that is quite beyond Boesman's understanding. She says:

> I'm on this earth, not in it . . . It's here and now. This is the time and place. They've ended *now.* The walks led *here.* Tonight.

In a letter written during the time when he was working on ***Boesman and Lena,*** Fugard stated:

> The issue is people—it's the fact that men can be good, that the good must be sustained, and that it's almost impossible to imagine a situation on this earth where it is harder to survive with any decency than here and now in South Africa.

What he goes on to say in this letter is about his own work, his own creative activity in drama, but it applies equally well to what Lena has decided to do on this one night of her life:

> But to sit in moral paralysis while the days of my one life, my one chance to discover the brotherhood of other men, pass is obviously so futile and pointless it is not worth talking about. So without the support of reason, or a clear conviction as to consequences—relying only on an instinct (blind as it is) at the core . . . I have chosen to act.

Lena discovers the brotherhood of other men this night; acting on impulse, her own plight being scarcely less desperate, she cries out to Boesman:

> Do something. Help him . . . It's another person, Boesman.

Boesman is unmoved and rejects Outa—as Lena calls him, employing the white man's condescending term but affirming the relatedness it literally asserts—rejects him in precisely the terms in which he, Boesman, has been rejected on racial grounds by the inhumane white society:

> *Kaffer!* . . . He's not brown people, he's black people . . . You'll end up with a tribe of old *kaffers* sitting here. That's all you'll get out of that darkness . . . Turn my place into a *kaffer nes!*

Iniquity is learned by its victims as well as by the members of an oppressing faction. As the Jewish psychiatrist in *Incident at Vichy,* Arthur Miller's play about Nazi persecution, puts it, 'Even the Jew has his Jew.' Fugard's point is that the individual's integrity is not determined by his racial, social or cultural identity, but by his commitment to making the world more tolerable for others. If Boesman is no worse than the white man with his machine who knocked over his shack in Korsten, he is no better. The desolation of Swartkops is appropriate to his own spiritual condition.

In Fugard's three Port Elizabeth plays of the 1960s, the sense of place—place in the broader, existential sense—has been a dominant motif, partly because Port Elizabeth is a place which Fugard has lived in and experienced for himself, and partly because it has a rich diversity of peoples and situations. If Port Elizabeth is a paradigm for, or a microcosm of, South Africa, so is South Africa for the world: the inhumanity of man is a constant quality and to the extent that all societies are thus guilty, Fugard's plays have universal application. Fugard's retrospective grouping of the three plays as a trilogy under the cognate title of *The Family* is apt. His characters are brothers, brother and sister, and husband and wife in successive plays; and these primal relationships suggest that Fugard's ultimate concern is less with the particularity of South African evils than with those besetting the whole family of man. The lack of relatedness—homelessness—is, in part at least, of human making, and it is universal.

Like its predecessors, ***A Lesson From Aloes*** is a small-cast play centring on a single family relationship, that of husband and wife, though with the addition of the husband's strained relationship with his single friend. Piet, the husband, is white, and his friend Steve is coloured. Piet is Afrikaans, his wife English. As one might expect, a Fugard play with this admixture is overtly political, and it is indeed more overtly political than any of the other Port Elizabeth plays—a reminder that other plays, chiefly ***Statements, The Island*** and ***Sizwe Banze Is Dead,*** have intervened. In ***A Lesson From Aloes,*** the protagonist, Piet Bezuidenhout, is a political activist whose marriage and sole friendship have been threatened as a direct result of political events. What is at stake in the play is not only Piet's political commitment, but also his spiritual survival in a parched environment—and for his will to survive the aloe becomes a symbol.

As in the previous Port Elizabeth plays, it is late afternoon fading into evening when the play begins, and it is autumn. Very early in the first scene Piet says to his wife, who is afraid of being sunburnt:

> No danger of that on an autumn afternoon. This is the start of our gentle time, Gladys . . . our season of mists and mellow fruitfulness, close bosom friend of the maturing sun.

Piet, who is much given to quoting English poets, offers these lines from Keats's hymn of praise to natural harmony in the way of comfort, but the truth of their lives is so different that the lines acquire a sad irony in this context: there is no fruitfulness in their childless marriage, and no empathetic rapport breathes from their Port Elizabeth backyard, cluttered with tins of aloes. From his flights of romantic fantasy, Piet always returns to the real world of his aloes, however, and his admiration for this hardy genus contains within it Fugard's sense of interpenetration of person with place:

> Aloes are distinguished above all else for their inordinate capacity for survival in the harshest of possible environments. In writing this play I have at one level tried to examine and question the possibility and nature of survival in a country for which 'drought', with its harsh and relentless resonances, is a very apt metaphor.

As ***A Lesson From Aloes*** opens, Piet is trying to find the name of an aloe he has been examining, but the specimen does not conform to any known species. Taken symbolically, this seems to be an existentialist statement of the uniqueness of individual human response to adversity. His meditation, half addressed to Gladys and half to himself, sounds disconcertingly like the beginning of a phenomenological discourse; it is soon resolved, however, into the straightforward assertion that 'Names are more than just labels and that they signify identity:

> For better or for worse, I will remain positively identified as Petrus Jacobus Bezuidenhout; Species, Afrikaner; Habitat, Algoa Park, Port Elizabeth, in this year of our Lord, 1963 . . . and accept the consequences.

We recognise again an iconic significance in names and their juxtaposition. Piet's own name is plainly and quite relentlessly Afrikaans; the defining and categorising terms 'Species' and 'Habitat' affirm a European cultural heritage from which Afrikanerdom dissociated itself early on; Algoa recalls the place on a then-unknown continent where Portuguese sailors made landfall on their way to Goa. The coupling of the English word Park with the Portuguese is quaint in itself, but the opposition in concept within the two words—Algoa is merely a wild place on the way to somewhere else, whereas Park implies a long-tamed and cultivated habitation on the estate of a former country mansion—sets up ironic reverberations. Later in the same scene, another litany of names evokes the unique ambience of Port Elizabeth and of these unique inhabitants:

> Peter and Gladys Bezuidenhout, Xanadu, 27 Kraaibos Street, Algoa Park.

Fugard allows a touch of dramatic irony, for he makes Gladys go on to say of this extraordinary medley, 'It sounds very ordinary to me.' We notice the subtlety with which Fugard exposes her need to modify her South African experience to fit her essentially English cultural identity, for she anglicises her husband's name fully to Peter. Conversely, Piet, whose taste in poetry is clearly behind the name of Xanadu for their little suburban house, has his own need to modify reality, but this Xanadu remains as irremediably in Kraaibos Street as her Peter is Petrus, for better or for worse.

Names are revealing in ***A Lesson From Aloes***: they reveal how people see themselves and others and how they feel about where they are. In this play there is a significance in names that Fugard may have implied but has not specifically stated before. When meditating on the impressive array of names that aloes have, Piet goes on to say this of their names:

> And knowing them is important. It makes me feel that little bit more at home in my world.

For a man as isolated as Piet, who has lost his wife's affection in the trauma of her ill-treatment by the police, as well as the trust of his only friend, the hope of feeling at home in the world is sadly diminished and for that reason is more desperately needed. The desire to find a new species of aloe and to name it Gladysiensis after his wife shows a totemic sense of association through name. He hopes that through it he will confer upon her the capacity to survive; this hope is to be dashed, for at the end of the play she prepares to return to the mental hospital and he will be entirely alone.

A Lesson From Aloes has a clarity and firmness of dramatic line beyond Fugard's achievement in his earlier plays, possibly the result of the influence of Grotowski and the years of practical experience with the Serpent Players. Unfortunately, there is a tendency to force significance, a tendency which is evident in the exchange wherein Piet recalls Gladys's maiden name of Adams. Not content that the name itself should lightly suggest a lost home in a paradisal world, Fugard has Piet say:

> What's the first thing we give a child when it's born? A name. Or when strangers meet, what is the first thing they do? Exchange names. According to the Bible, that was the very first thing Adam did in Eden. He named his world.

Overstated or not, this at least explains another aspect of naming the names in the earlier plays—by Johnnie in ***Hello and Goodbye*** and by Lena in ***Boesman and Lena***—which is the attempt to domesticate an alien environment and to make it home.

The difference between Piet and Gladys emerges most clearly in their later discussion about Piet's friend Steve, who is preparing to leave for England on an exit permit, South Africa's one-way pass to exile:

> PIET: He's leaving on an exit permit, Gladys.
>
> GLADYS: So?
>
> PIET: He can't come back.
>
> GLADYS: So?
>
> PIET: I don't think it's all that easy for him. This is his home as much as it is ours.
>
> GLADYS: No. I know I was born here, but I will never call it that.

And then, when Steve is trying to communicate his troubled feelings about leaving, Gladys interposes:

> You see, there is no chance of persuading him to leave. I must confess I don't really understand why. It's all got to do with him being an Afrikaner and this being 'home' . . . because like you, Steven, I'm more than prepared to call some other place that. But not Peter. If those aloes can survive droughts, so can he!

In stating the central theme of the play, she speaks more truth than she knows. Piet will survive; she will not. The damage done to her mind has precluded that.

Gladys's lostness, her total inability to find a home in the real world of men, is revealed when she finally answers Steve's question about whether she has ever been to England. In the last terrible moments, as Steve prepares to go for ever, she struggles to explain:

> Please . . . please . . . I promised to tell him about England. I was taught to keep my promises. It's very green. There are mountains in the distance, but you can't see them too clearly because of a soft, soft mist and the rays of the setting sun. There's a lovely little cottage with a thatch roof, and flowers in the garden, and winding past it an old country road with tall trees along the side. An old shepherd and his dog are herding a little flock of sheep along it and watching them, at the garden gate, is a little girl . . . It's called 'Sunset in Somerset' and it hangs on a wall in a room where you sit and wait for your turn. I always tried to forget what was coming by looking at it and imagining that I was the little girl and that I lived in that cottage.

The place where she has sat waiting her turn is the antechamber to the room where patients are given shock treatment. Ironically, the mental hospital to which Gladys was sent after her shattering experience with the police is called Fort England. Her England, her home, is a fiction, a lie even, told by sentimental art. In different ways Gladys and Steve have given up the struggle: he is retreating to England by ship; she in her imagination. For Piet, the ability to be at home in South Africa, to survive there and to make his little Port Elizabeth backyard a Xanadu that is part-escape and part-fantasy without losing touch with the overwhelming fact of everyday reality, is the lesson he has learned from aloes. His important capacity is to learn from aloes without losing consciousness of the point where the analogy between vegetable nature and human nature, with its powers of thought and deliberate action, breaks down:

> An evil system isn't a natural disaster. There's nothing you can do to stop a drought, but bad laws and social injustice are man-made and can be unmade by men. It's as simple as that. We can make this a better world to live in.

And so Piet commits himself to stay in South Africa, in Port Elizabeth, to work in whatever way he can—however limited the prospects of success—rather than to accept the certain failure of exile.

However much South Africa may change in future times, Fugard has faithfully recorded in his Port Elizabeth plays what it was to be in and a part of a particular place at a particular time, what it meant in terms of human needs and sufferings that never change in themselves but only in intensity. The authentic, living world of the Port Elizabeth plays will assuredly continue to hold the attention of audiences and to move them to recognition of themselves, long after apartheid has become the record of an evil hour in which men acted perversely and, not for the first time and not for the last, excluded themselves from the hope of making the world a home. (pp. 165-83)

Chris Wortham, "A Sense of Place: Home and Homelessness in the Plays of Athol Fugard," in Olive Schreiner and After: Essays on Southern African Literature in Honour of Guy Butler, *edited by Malvern Van Wyk Smith and Don Maclennan, David Philip, 1983, pp. 165-83.*

Dennis Walder (essay date 1984)

[*Walder is a South African educator and critic. In the excerpt below, he details Fugard's career, describing his work as "extreme [theater] . . . in response to an extreme situation."*]

Sunday is not generally a day when anything happens in South Africa. But on Sunday, 3 September 1961, in a cramped, unventilated room on the third floor of an abandoned factory in Eloff Street, Johannesburg, something did happen. A new South African play was performed in which, for the first time, a white man and a black man appeared together on stage. And for nearly four hours the two held their invited, multiracial audience spellbound. Traffic noises drifted up from the front of the building, drumming and chanting from an African miners' hostel at the back penetrated the empty egg-boxes pinned to the windows. But the journalists, theatre people and assorted friends who packed the new 'Rehearsal Room' of the African Music and Drama Association in Dorkay House were gripped as never before by a passionate duet which probed and revealed the feelings associated with that perennial South African subject—race.

The play was ***The Blood Knot,*** by Athol Fugard; the actors, 'Arrie Potgieter' (Fugard himself, using his maternal grandfather's name) and Zakes Mokae. Fugard also directed, using Barney Simon as a 'third eye'. When the performers awoke the next morning, the event was all over the newspapers. Oliver Walker devoted his entire 'Arts and Entertainment' column in the *Star* (usually dominated by fulsome accounts of productions such as *The Amorous Prawn*) to praise for the new work. On 8 November, cut to two-and-a-half hours, the play reopened under professional management at the Intimate Theatre, Johannesburg. Approval was unanimous, and a tour practically sold out before it began. From the barely known author of two 'township' plays—***No-Good Friday*** (1958) and ***Nongogo*** (1959)—Athol Fugard had become a national figure, virtually overnight. Successful production and publication in London and New York followed in due course and, slowly but surely, an international reputation. With twelve plays (including joint ventures such as ***Sizwe Bansi Is Dead,*** 1973) currently in print, and his latest—***'Master Harold'. . . and the boys*** (1982)—a phenomenal success both at home and abroad, Fugard may be said to have become a major modern playwright. His plays now command an audience whenever and wherever they are performed. He has transformed the limitations of his South African background into theatre of great power and lasting implication.

Fugard's theatre is radical, even extreme; but this is in response to an extreme situation. He lives in a society familiar the world over for its unique system of racial oppression. Brutality and degradation are, of course, to be found elsewhere than in South Africa. But there is a level and quality of humiliation, suffering and despair present in the lives of millions of ordinary South Africans—mostly, but not exclusively black—which demands recognition. Fugard's plays help obtain that recognition. His plays make us aware not only of the South African dimension of man's inhumanity to man, but also of the secret pain we all inflict upon each other in the private recesses of our closest relationships. His works all focus upon two or three people inextricably entangled by the ties of blood, love or friendship. He shows them struggling to survive in an arbitrary, bleak and almost meaningless world. This does not mean his plays lack feeling: on the contrary, they are filled with anger and compassion. It is his great strength to move us deeply by showing the plight of ordinary people caught up in the meshes of social, political, racial and even religious forces which they are unable to understand or control. It is his weakness that he cannot reflect upon or analyse these forces himself. He is like the actor in Brecht's *Messingkauf Dialogues* who provokes 'all sorts of passions, but a passion for argument—oh no'. For Fugard, the message is too urgent. This does not mean that he is simply a propagandist—although propaganda has its place. What it does mean is that there is a characteristic intensity of effect gained by his work, an effect of painful, shared awareness, which it is perhaps uniquely possible to create in the theatre. And Fugard is, above all, in the clichéd phrase, a man of the theatre. As actor, director and playwright, he is obsessed with the idea that what he has to say can only be said indirectly, as an *image,* embodied in the 'living moment' on stage.

He began by going back to the so-called 'Method' school, according to which actors authenticate their roles by finding in them some relation to their own experience. In the—mainly American—development of this approach, the tendency has been to rely on naturalistic performances of pre-existing texts, constructed according to the familiar hierarchy of writer, director, producer and actor. But, although naturalism remains an important thread in Fugard's work, he has moved away from it, towards a more characteristically modern, symbolic realm. Surface reality, or the 'facts' of everyday experience, are never entirely ignored; but the suggestive 'sub-text' is often more important. He is fundamentally opposed to the parochial consumer art with which most Western playgoers are, alas, all too familiar: that mode of drama which pushes the performers into a well-lit picture frame behind a proscenium arch, where they converse with one another according to a given script, while the audience looks on passively. Like such influential and innovative directors as Peter Brook and Jerzy Grotowski, whose work and ideas (especially Grotowski's) have been important for him, Fugard is inspired and sustained by the actuality of performance, by live actors before a live audience, 'flesh and blood, sweat, the human voice, real pain, real time'. For him, as for that great progenitor of 'living theatre' in our day, Antonin Artaud (1896-1948), the trappings of the institutionalised, illusionistic theatre—buildings, props, costumes, lighting and so on—only interest in so far as they aid the primary function of drama: to find the 'truth' of the 'living moment'.

The living moment in a Fugard play tends to emerge as the climax of a shifting pattern of emotions of gradually increasing strength, a moment of revelation, expressed as an image. Words are only a part of what he defines—in terms borrowed from Ezra Pound—as the 'image': 'the presentation of a psychological and emotional complex in an instant of time'. Any script which has not stood the test of production is 'provisional' and 'rough'; and, whatever else may change during workshops, rehearsals or production, he does not concede 'any alteration with the central image—once that happens you have a new play'. Most of Fugard's plays begin life as, and finally focus on, one central image or cluster of images. The climax of ***Hello and Goodbye*** (1965), for instance, occurs when Johnnie, unable to leave home and face life, takes up his father's crutches: 'Why not? It solves problems. Let's face it, a man on his own two legs is a shaky proposition.' A chilling and disturbing moment: the crippling inadequacies of family life are exposed simultaneously with—on the deeper, sub-textual level—the failure of the 'poor white' Afrikaner to come to terms with his past. And, when, in ***Sizwe Bansi Is Dead,*** the central character sits frozen in a grotesquely comic pose, a 'studio' cigarette balanced nonchalantly in one hand, his own pipe gripped firmly in the other, the photographer's studio backdrop of city skyscrapers behind him, while a beatific smile spreads slowly across his features . . . the image sums up the truth of his life: Robert/Sizwe is a naïve dreamer, a simple man who wishes to survive with dignity, but it is a wish as far out of reach as those skyscrapers, for a black man in his situation.

The dramatic impact of the living moments in Fugard's plays represent a stage on a journey, when the 'external story' he has found in the lives and circumstances of those around him coincides with his own 'inner dynamic'. He is engaged in a 'slow trek through the detours of art', as it was put by a writer he resembles as well as admires, Albert Camus (1913-60)—a trek to rediscover 'those two or three great and simple images in whose presence his heart first opened'. Without the coincidence of 'external' and 'internal' in an image, Fugard's plays could not be written. For all the 'external', even documentary detail of his work, it always demonstrates a deeply personal concern for the fate of the 'ordinary', anonymous, *little* people with whom he most closely identifies. The opening entry of Camus's notebooks reads, 'I must bear witness. When I see things clearly, I have only one thing to say. It is in this life of poverty, among these vain or humble people, that I have most certainly touched what I feel is the true meaning of life.' Similarly for Fugard: his 'true meaning', he says in *his* notebooks, his 'life's work', is 'just to witness' as 'truthfully' as he can 'the nameless and destitute' of his 'one little corner of the world'. For Camus, that 'corner' lay in North Africa, among the white *colons* and their despised local helotry; for Fugard it is the Eastern Cape region of South Africa, among the 'poor whites', the 'Coloureds' (mixed race) and, occasionally, members of the subject African majority. Like Camus, Fugard belongs by birth and upbringing to the relatively underprivileged sector of the white group which rules his country, a lower middle-class, verging on 'poor white', group, which tends to provide the strongest anti-black feelings and which therefore considers him a 'traitor' for turning against their own apparent interests. Camus was led to exile; Fugard insists on staying, believing that only while living where he is can he testify to the lives of those around him, the disinherited and the lost—whether it is Morris and Zach, the two 'Coloured' brothers of ***The Blood Knot,*** or Sizwe Bansi, or Johnnie, or Milly (***People Are Living There,*** 1968) or ***Boesman and Lena*** (1969)—or even, in her way, which is the way of insanity, Gladys Bezuidenhout, the bus-driver's wife in ***A Lesson from Aloes*** (1978). When Fugard leaves these 'small' people, as in ***Dimetos*** (1975), and attempts to create and study a character who is heroic, even mythical, he loses his way, becoming abstract and unsympathetic.

Yet, like other modern artists (including Camus, whose notebooks provided the story of Dimetos), Fugard frequently returns to the mythical—or, at least, to the early myths of the classical Greek era, the bloody family feuds dramatised by Aeschylus, Sophocles and Euripides. Hence the little-known work entitled ***Orestes*** (1971); hence the use of *Antigone* in ***The Island*** (1973). He feels he is touching on the basic drives which motivate us all, and so is naturally drawn to the most powerful and lasting embodiment of them, in the Greek drama. Is there then no closer tradition which might have provided him with a source of inspiration? Where is the South African tradition?

There is no systematic or comprehensive account of drama in South Africa—much less of South African literature as a whole, incorporating (as it should) the various strands, oral and written, in African as well as European languages, going back to the earliest times. The only half-decent book on the subject, Stephen Gray's *Southern African Literature* (1979) begins by confessing the impossibility of his task: he refers to the fact that by the late 1960s at least half South Africa's English-speaking writers of all colours had been expelled from the country into 'an international diaspora' with the result that South African literature in English had split so 'irremediably and bitterly into two' that it only makes sense to talk of 'two distinct literatures at present'. And this is while focusing only on South African writing *in English.* Gray goes on to identify what he calls an 'archipelago' of literatures, somehow associated merely by being where they are. He omits not only the writers to whom he cannot have access as a scholar working in South Africa, but also the larger framework which might make sense of his material: that is, *history.* But, as Dan Jacobson once remarked [in his introduction to *Olive Schreiner's Story of an African Farm*], a colonial culture is precisely one in which the sense of history is 'deficient'. This deficiency means that the enmities engendered by the conditions which first brought the colony into existence tend to be regarded 'as so many given, unalterable facts of life, phenomena of nature, as little open to human change or question as the growth of leaves in spring'. Typically, the members of such a culture delude themselves into believing that things have always been the way they are, and always will be. South Africa is a good example: it is a fragmented ex-colonial culture; and it is a culture in which the potential for unity and integration has not only been resisted by the dominant white minority, but has been corrupted according to an ideology which emphasises and exploits difference, so as to manipulate and control the vast majority. Even apart from the specific effects of apartheid laws—of censorship, of bannings, imprisonment and exile—there is a history of division and isolation which has made it difficult, if not impossible, for people to know what is going on in their own country. For writers and artists, this leads to the common feeling that they are operating in a vacuum.

When Fugard was asked what dramatists he had met during the early years of his career in the 1950s, he replied, 'There were none around.' In fact there was taking place at the time a so-called 'renaissance' of English drama, including plays by Alan Paton, James Ambrose Brown and

Lewis Sowden—the last of whom wrote a play, *Kimberley Train* (1958), which anticipates the subject of ***The Blood Knot.*** But in terms of quality and relevance Fugard may seem right to have presumed 'There were none around.' On the other hand, there was also a less well documented or known 'renaissance' in the urban black 'townships', an upsurge of popular theatre, of song and dance, of satire and jazz, which white entrepreneurs in Johannesburg at least were aware of, and which became more familiar with the emergence in 1959 of the jazz opera *King Kong. King Kong* was essentially urban, and should not be confused with such dubious successors as *uMabatha* (1970) or *Ipi Tombi* (1973), all-black musical productions designed by their white managements to present the impression of black South Africans as a crowd of smiling, dancing, bare-breasted rural illiterates. The last decade has, in fact, seen a flood of 'township' drama, ranging from the sensational accounts of everyday urban life purveyed by Gibson Kente and Sam Mhangwani (the latter's unpublished *Unfaithful Wife* remains a hit after twenty years) to the more serious, politically committed work of writers such as Maishe Maponya (*The Hungry Earth,* 1979) and Matsemela Manaka (*Egoli,* 1980)—to name only a few from Soweto alone.

Fugard has acknowledged his debt to black *performers:* those first befriended in Sophiatown, the multiracial Johannesburg ghetto, in the late fifties, and whose talents and experiences were embodied in his first full-length plays, ***No-Good Friday*** and ***Nongogo;*** as well as those who came to him from New Brighton, Port Elizabeth, in 1963 to form the Serpent Players, a remarkable group whose collaborative work led to (amongst other plays) ***Sizwe Bansi Is Dead*** and ***The Island.*** Fugard's own influence upon 'township' theatre is recognised and is continuing. Playwrights in the townships have had to learn a tough lesson in survival, a lesson they articulate in a variety of forms, using whatever means they can—including the aid of those few, such as Fugard and writer—director Barney Simon, willing and able to 'cross over' from the white side to offer the knowledge and experience to which they have privileged access. But such contact barely deflects the pressures of the situation. Dramatists still feel they must start from scratch, unable to draw on the fragmented, unknown or unacknowledged traditions of their own country.

So it is not altogether surprising that Fugard's acknowledged mentors should not be South African. One of the few playwrights to whom he admits he owes anything is Samuel Beckett—an allegiance confirmed by his small casts, sparse sets, flat, seemingly pointless dialogue and inconsequential plots. But, even if some such influence can be traced, Fugard's plays are all ultimately derived 'from life and from encounters with real people', as he put it in the Introduction to his published notebooks. These notebooks reveal the secret, slow and painful germination of his plays over many years, culminating in ***'Master Harold' . . . and the boys***—which, based upon an incident in his adolescence, has had the longest incubation of them all, no doubt because it is the most personal, and has been the most difficult to expose. Evidently ***'Master Harold'*** was a cathartic experience for him; and so it is for his audiences, too. There is nothing 'literary' about this: it is primarily a matter of transferring emotions, of arousing in us a powerful and deep emotional awareness, which burns into our consciousness the imagery of a group of individual human beings caught within the conflicting tensions of their specific situation. The nature of their relationships suggests the profound forces at work in their society; the characters in his plays are revealed struggling to survive with some shred of dignity the almost intolerable burden of suffering imposed upon them by an apparently irresistible fate. If this seems to suggest an endorsement of suffering, of passivity in the face of oppression, that seems to be true; but it is not the whole truth. Fugard's work also contains a potential for subversion, a potential which, I would suggest, is the hallmark of great art, and which qualifies his best work to be called great.

Art is often called revolutionary if it represents a radical quality in style or technique; but there is a more important sense in which it can be revolutionary—or, as I would prefer to put it, subversive. This lies in its potential to undermine the status quo, a potential revealed in its tendency to make us realise that things need not be the way they have been, or the way they are. If racialism and exploitation seem natural as 'the growth of leaves in spring', then it is in the capacity of art to show us that this is not so. As Brecht said, to make the ordinary extraordinary. Before a word was uttered in that first performance of ***The Blood Knot*** in September 1961, the audience was presented with a curious sight: a pale-skinned man, shabbily dressed (Morris, played by Fugard), coming in and setting about preparing a footbath, timing his actions (which are evidently routine) by means of an old alarmclock; an equally shabby man, of African appearance (Zach, played by Mokae) but wearing a greatcoat and obviously returning from a hard day's work, then enters, and makes a great show of being surprised at the footbath, testing the water with one toe, and so on, before finally and luxuriously resting his calloused feet in it. In that 'living moment', that 'image', a relationship was suggested which thrilled the audience with disturbing implications: revealing a white man behaving like a housekeeper, a servant, to a black. The relationship at the centre of the structure of South African society was being subverted before their eyes. ***The Blood Knot*** went on to reveal that the two were mixed-race brothers, outcasts tormented by the fact that one of them was more 'European' in appearance than the other; and the alternating pattern of dominance and dependence between them which this generated in a racialist society. But it is the lasting, subversive resonance of that initial image and the variations upon it which follow that provide the play with the possibility of its continuing power and relevance.

All Fugard's plays approximate to the same basic model, established by ***The Blood Knot:*** a small cast of 'marginal' characters is presented in a passionately close relationship embodying the tensions current in their society, the whole first performed by actors directly involved in its creation, in a makeshift, 'fringe' or 'unofficial' venue. This is 'poor theatre', although less as a matter of theory (Grotowski's *Towards a Poor Theatre* only came to Fugard in 1970) than as a matter of preferred practice. With few resources and impelled to operate under rough, workshop conditions, relying on actors to impart their own experiences, Fugard has always worked outside the conventional, mainstream theatre, implicitly challenging by his conditions of production the prevailing assumptions about theatre—i.e. that it is a form of packaged entertainment which confirms the status quo. Despite the subsequent, inevitable assimilation of his most well-known works into that mainstream theatre, as far as he is concerned all that the theatre, *his* theatre needs is (as he put it at the time of ***The Blood Knot,*** and has repeated ever since)

> the actor and the stage, the actor *on* the stage. Around him is space, to be filled and defined by movement and gesture; around him is also silence to be filled with meaning, using words and sounds, and at moments when all else fails him, including the words, the silence itself.

This helps explain his reliance upon his chosen actors, as well as his determination always to have a controlling hand in the production of all his plays; the end product is not so much a written text, which may only be a record of a performance, but an existential moment, in a particular place at a particular time. What his plays mean is determined less by their written words than by the total conditions of performance. This became especially important to him when, under the impact of the ideas of Grotowski and the workshop practice developed with the Serpent Players, he attempted his most 'extreme excursion' into radical communication by means of image and gesture, rather than pre-established text: ***Orestes,*** which defies translation into a script, and the separate performances of which are 'scored' in three large drawing-books, a pale shadow of the eighty minutes of strange, somnambulistic action which took place at the time. Here Fugard attempted an apparently total reliance upon the 'creative' as opposed to merely 'illustrative' abilities of his cast, two women and a man. Yet the 'truth' discovered was the result of the performers responding to the director—scribe's challenges, expressed as a complex of images Fugard derived from ancient and modern sources; the playwright himself remained in charge. This 'new' type of theatre focused on an event very close to South Africans—and, especially, white liberals: the explosion of a bomb as an act of protest on Johannesburg station, which killed an elderly white woman and led to the execution of its perpetrator, a white schoolteacher. If ***Orestes*** represents an extreme, even a limit, to what Fugard has been able to do in the theatre, this may have more to do with its subject, than with what ideas about the theatre released in him. The play explored the effect of violence upon those who carry it out: the central image was created by the slow, deliberate and silent destruction in each performance of a unique, irreplaceable and innocent object—a chair—by the actress, who sank down eventually into the debris, exhausted and terrified by what she had done. In a context in which violence is breeding more violence, this image is important; but, if Fugard persistently condemns violence, he is also careful to show its inevitability in a society which has adopted violent means to stifle opposition and prevent change. (pp. 1-13)

The South African experience which emerges in his plays is bitter and painful to contemplate; but, at the same time, there is a deep faith in the potential for survival of the individual human being. He wants to 'bear witness' to what is happening in his time. This is another way of saying that, as he puts it,

> as a South African I want to talk to other South Africans about what is happening here and now. Now, being a South African means that I have got to acknowledge the fact that my whole style of living, everything, comes down to . . . how many decisions have I got that are not related to my white skin? I can only acknowledge that these exist, that they are facts. . . . Thorn trees don't protest the endless drought of the Karroo. . . . They just go on trying to grow. Just a basic survival informs the final, mutilated, stunted protest. . . .

Fugard's plays are all, on some level, more or less explicitly, a protest about the quality of life in South Africa. To ignore this would be to render them meaningless. Many critics (especially in South Africa) prefer to stress their 'universitality'; and so help maintain the status quo. He himself prefers not to be called a 'political playwright'; nor am I suggesting that he is; but, in embodying what he sees as the 'truth' of his place in his work, in his textures and imagery, he cannot help but also embody its politics. Failure to recognise or admit this involves a failure to respond to his kind of theatre, as well as to what he is saying. (pp. 17-18)

Dennis Walder, in his Athol Fugard, *Macmillan Publishers Ltd., 1984, 142 p.*

THE BLOOD KNOT

PRODUCTION REVIEWS

Time (review date 13 March 1964)

[In the following review of a New York production of The Blood Knot *featuring James Earl Jones and J. D. Cannon as Zachariah and Morris, the critic praises Fugard, asserting that he "shuns preachments and never oversimplifies the human equation."]*

The Blood Knot, by Athol Fugard, links two South African half-brothers in a fierce, funny, tender, scalding love-hate relationship. Though both are sons of the same dark-skinned mother, one brother is white and the other is dark. They live in a tin shack in the colored ghetto outside Port Elizabeth, South Africa. The white brother, Morris (J. D. Cannon), an intense, broody, mothering sort, keeps house for the pair. The black brother, Zachariah (James Earl Jones), is one of nature's children, openfaced and openhanded. He tends a park gate where he shoos away any colored child who tries to enter. Every night Morris readies a ritualistic footbath for Zach's raw, swollen feet.

But in the realm of color, skin-deep is heart-deep and there is no balm for those abrasions.

Morris speaks feelingly of brotherhood, but what he practices is more like Big Brotherhood, the slightly proprietary snobbism of a global planner confined to one squalid room and one underdeveloped mentality. He is a demon of uplift ("talking helps") and tries to tempt Zach's palate with a wedge of pie in the sky—a farm the two brothers will buy and work. But Zach, a man of profound instinctual sanity, is slow to sublimate. "I'm sick of talking, man, I want a woman," he says. Morris fobs him off with a pen pal ("18 years old and well-developed") to whom Morris will write. When the girl, who is white, promises to appear, each brother panics for opposing reasons. Zach yearns for the girl, but he dares not violate the racial taboo, and must violate his feelings instead. Morris is tempted to meet the girl, except that he has passed for white before and knows the self-loathing he felt at the ugly pleasure of renouncing the black within him, and spurning the blacks around him.

In a full-length two-character play, each actor has to be at least an actor and a half. Both J. D. Cannon and James Earl Jones are enormously skillful. At first Cannon seems considerate, practical, matter-of-fact, and then his nerves start to sing like high-tension wires. The playgoer senses that he is watching a man hiding from the beast in himself. James Earl Jones can be as quiet as an extinct volcano one moment, and spewing emotional lava across a stage the next. With some actors, words clothe feelings; with Jones, feelings unclothe words so that joy, rage, wonder and sadness radiate nakedly through the theater.

An off-Broadway production, ***Blood Knot*** sometimes echoes with echoes, and speaks in the voices of Genet, Pinter, and even the John Steinbeck of *Of Mice and Men.* But Athol Fugard, a white South African, shuns preachments and never oversimplifies the human equation. His symbols are the kind that laugh, cry and bleed.

"In the Prison of Color," in Time, *New York, Vol. 83, No. 11, March 13, 1964, p. 73.*

Zakes Mokae and Ian Bannen in The Blood Knot *at the New Arts Theatre, London, 1963.*

Edith Oliver (review date 14 March 1964)

[*Oliver began her career as an actress and television writer and producer, and joined* The New Yorker *in 1948, becoming the magazine's off-Broadway theater critic in 1961. In the review below, she gives a negative assessment of* The Blood Knot, *describing the plot as "obvious and predictable and soggy with significance."*]

The best, though not the only, thing that can be said for Athol Fugard, the South African author of ***The Blood Knot,*** at the Cricket, is that he has provided a good part for James Earl Jones, who is wonderful in it, and a pretty good, if not entirely believable, part for J. D. Cannon, who does it justice. He has also provided, during the play's more human and matter-of-fact moments, which get sparser as it proceeds, a close look at the strain and hair-trigger passion that exist between the races in South Africa. Mr. Jones and Mr. Cannon play a pair of half brothers named Zachariah and Morris, the first a full-blooded Negro, the second half-white and entirely white in appearance. The setting is Zachariah's miserable shack, which Morris has shared for the past year or so, acting as housekeeper and, as it turns out, total spirit dampener, saving all Zachariah's earnings for a farm they will buy someday, and cutting him off from his old friends. Zachariah has no interest in a future farm or future anything; what he wants is a woman. Morris, who is unable to do anything directly but must make a game of it, suggests that they pick someone from a lonely-hearts ad in a newspaper to be Zachariah's pen pal. Morris will write the letters for Zachariah, who is totally illiterate, and read the replies. Zachariah agrees, in a puzzled kind of way. A letter is sent, and one comes back with a snapshot enclosed. The girl is white. Morris is terrified, but Zachariah thinks it a great joke and persuades Morris to continue the correspondence. When the girl announces that she is coming to their town and would like to meet Zachariah, he insists that Morris take his place. Morris is at first reluctant, then agreeable, and then eager. Zachariah uses the accumulated savings to buy him a white man's outfit, and rehearses him for the part. As soon as Morris puts the dudish clothes on, trouble starts—for the brothers and, unfortunately, for the playwright.

All becomes obvious and predictable and soggy with significance.

The play—depending, as it does, on a device—is awkward, and Mr. Fugard's hand is too much in evidence. Even so, there are comic and effective moments here and there throughout. Mr. Jones is an actor with great reserves of energy and brilliance, and the part of Zachariah gives him a chance to put them to use. His performance of this inarticulate African is varied and subtle and always under control. He is very funny in brief scenes within scenes—in pantomime, taking the unknown girl for a ride in his nonexistent car and grandly shifting away at nonexistent gears, or impersonating a frisky monkey-nut vender ("I'm ignoring you, son. I'm the cheeky sort") and then, menacing and sullen, reenacting his daily job as gatekeeper and trash collector in a public park. The part of Morris is more subdued and devious and, I think, synthetic than that of Zachariah. Mr. Cannon makes him almost credible, though. The two men play together very well indeed. They were directed by John Berry. (pp. 110, 112)

Edith Oliver, in a review of "The Blood Knot," in The New Yorker, *Vol. XL, No. 4, March 14, 1964, pp. 110, 112.*

Harold Clurman (review date 30 March 1964)

[*A celebrated director and theater critic, Clurman founded, in association with Lee Strasberg and Cheryl Crawford, the Group Theatre in 1931. For the next ten years, as its managing director, he helped create many notable productions, particularly of American plays. He served the* Nation, *the* New Republic, *and the* Observer *as drama critic from 1949 to 1963. His publications include* The Fervent Years: The Story of the Group Theatre *(1945),* Lies Like Truth: Theatre Reviews and Essays *(1958),* On Directing *(1973), and* The Divine Pastime: Theatre Essays *(1974). In the review below, he praises the skill with which Fugard links South African racial policies and universal human concerns in* The Blood Knot.]

On the surface [***The Blood Knot***] is a "race" play, situated in the, to us, still unfamiliar region of South Africa. Apart from its individual merits, the play is important because, while the "color question" is one of the few topical themes capable of renewing the impetus of our theatre, it has thus far stimulated hardly any dramatic expression commensurate with its possibilities and demands. ***The Blood Knot,*** comparatively modest in its scope, gives some idea of what may be developed in this vein.

There are only two characters, Negro half-brothers: Morris, son of an unknown white father, and Zachariah, all black. Morris, sufficiently light-skinned to "pass," had disappeared from his native village, leaving Zach in the wretched isolation of the unskilled black laborer. When the play opens, he has returned, frightened and disillusioned by his encounter with the whites in the big cities. Now he acts the protector and mentor to his still illiterate and more "savage" brother. Zachariah works as a sort of park watchman while Morris keeps house and guards the budget, forcing Zach to give up his pastimes in order that they may save enough money to buy a little green land in the open country.

Zach must forgo his fun with women, and much of the play concerns itself with Morris' arrangements to supply him, in compensation, with a "pen pal," a girl from another town who advertises in a local paper her desire to correspond with someone of the opposite sex. There are humorous and frightening developments from this device because the girl who answers Zach's letter (written by Morris) is white. Morris foresees terrible consequences, even in such a disembodied connection between black and white. I have never seen the horror of the South African racial situation so vividly revealed as in this essentially comic episode.

The play goes still deeper. The vicarious correspondence and its subterfuges trigger a conflict between the brothers. Each has a different memory of his mother. To Morris she represents something traditionally tender; to Zach, the less favored son, she remains a grimly threatening figure. At bottom, both men think of her as the cause of their suffering, someone whom they secretly revile.

The two men, brothers as all men are "brothers," seek mutual consolation and protection from the hostile world; their sense of fraternity, however, is complicated by blood and color differences which, despite their need, separate them in ill-disguised hatred.

The play is constantly absorbing. At times it is somewhat too studied in its effects, too forced in its symbolic overtones. Yet it has the power to penetrate our consciousness. What has seemed at first only the picture of a special situation in a distant land develops into something much subtler. The separation of black and white results in a tension within each Negro's soul. This is ultimately converted into the depiction of the tension between all human beings—between man and man, white or black. "Hell is the other." The Negro problem is part of the universal dilemma of man's commerce with himself and of his dealing with every other man: the fundamental need to reconcile his identity and desire for independence with the equally unconquerable urge to overcome that which separates him from his "brother."

John Berry's direction is not only vigorous but endowed with remarkable variety, in this instance a noteworthy technical accomplishment. The acting by J. D. Cannon as Morris and by the American theatre's most prevalent actor, James Earl Jones, except for fleeting moments of overstrenuousness, is admirable. (pp. 334-35)

Harold Clurman, in a review of "The Blood Knot," in The Nation, *New York, Vol. 198, No. 14, March 30, 1964, pp. 334-35.*

CRITICAL COMMENTARY

Russell Vandenbroucke (essay date 1985)

[*In the excerpt below, Vandenbroucke examines themes and characterization in* The Blood Knot.]

Fugard's first thoughts about ***The Blood Knot,*** indeed the first entry he made in his notebook, include the following: "No streets, names or numbers. A world where anything goes. . . . In one of these shacks the two brothers—Morrie and Zach. Morrie is a light-skinned Coloured who has found out that to ignore the temptations to use his lightness is the easiest way to live. . . . In contrast, his brother Zach—dark-skinned Coloured, virtually African in appearance. . . . Zach can never be anything other than what he is—a black man. There are no choices for him." Fugard recalls that writing ***The Blood Knot*** "was a compulsive and direct experience and this note is the only reference I can find to it."

His note reflects the setting and nucleus of the play. Its story runs as follows: Having returned home to Zach after some years apart, Morrie fosters the dream of their purchasing a farm together. Zach has adapted to Morrie's manipulations and the changes he has effected, but he still remembers a past that was not limited to the womanless world of a Korsten shanty. Morrie suggests he get a pen-pal, Ethel. She turns out to be white. When she writes that she is planning to visit, Zach proposes that Morrie pass himself off as a white man and pretend that *he* is her pen-pal. Their farm savings pay for the fancy clothes Morrie will need, and Zach convinces his finely-dressed brother to learn "whiteness" by playing the role of the condescending *baas.* Even after Ethel cancels her visit, the role-playing continues until Morrie and Zach abandon their dreams of an illusory future and embrace their brotherhood.

The initial image for the play, according to Fugard, was "a man on the road and all the possibilities. He was a Coloured man. He was possibly even myself, confused, going somewhere." Fugard has also admitted that ***The Blood Knot*** "is really a personal statement. It is basically myself and my brother . . . when I developed an enormous guilt thing about him because he was going through a hard time. . . . There was just the sense of responsibility for another man, for another existence." He has added, "Zach did not need Morrie and my brother did not need me." Royal Fugard had been a slow learner who failed his major exams.

The Blood Knot explores new themes even as it reflects Fugard's previous interest in hopes, dreams, and the presence of the past. The brothers are temporarily uncertain about their shared distant past, their childhood. Morrie is additionally troubled by those years from the recent past that he spent away from Zach; he hopes to expiate the guilt he feels for ever having left him. Connected to this uncertainty about his past is Morrie's insecure identity as either Coloured or white. Morrie imposes on Zach his own desires for the future, especially the two-man farm, as a means to escape an unaccommodating past and present. Through the use of imaginary games and role-playing, Morrie and Zach reconcile themselves to their personal histories and true identities, discard illusory dreams of an ideal future, and learn to live in the present.

Morrie precipitates most of the play's action: His return to the Korsten shack has caused its disruption, the guilt is his, and the farm and pen-pal are his ideas. When Zach mentions his old drinking friend Minnie, Morrie tries to change the subject; he is so jealous of anyone or anything that might threaten the marvelous future he has planned that he tries to destroy Zach's memories of his old friend with lies and speculations. Early in the play it is Morrie who persistently deflates Zach's reveries of a golden past; later, Zach will help destroy Morrie's dream of an ideal future.

Zach's past life of sensual pleasures had been wholly different from the monasticism Morrie has imposed. Zach's recollection of Minnie quickly leads to memories of women. Again Morrie tries to change the subject. The intrusion of any outsider might usurp his position or diminish his function. Zach is the breadwinner, but Morrie is the head of the household. Zach ignores Morrie's attempts to make him forget his palpable past experiences with women. It is these memories, these perceptions of an absence in Zach's life, that lead Morrie to suggest a pen-pal.

He manipulates Zach to insure the future he has planned. Morrie's behavior can also be explained by his personal history before his return to the Korsten shack. The facts of his immediate past are gradually revealed throughout the play, especially towards its end. At first Morrie's musings are opaque and obscure. Although Zach is asleep, Morrie cannot forthrightly admit what he has done because his guilt is too oppressive. What he cannot openly admit to himself cannot yet be revealed to the audience, although the vagueness of his words arouses curiosity about his apparent piety, sense of guilt, and feelings of responsibility. This obscurity is Morrie's, not Fugard's. The way Morrie gradually accepts what he has done and explains and admits it directly is the same deliberate process by which Zach and the audience are led to understand his past.

At first Morrie mutters and stammers. He wants to escape or at least forget his past, but he later admits. "There is no whitewashing away a man's . . . facts." After counseling Zach to remember *his* facts, however difficult they are to accept, Morrie finally admits openly that he had used his light complexion to "pass" as a white man until he was caught—not by the law, but by his burdensome guilt and the sense of responsibility it had engendered. By caring for Zach he seeks atonement for what he perceives to be the betrayal of a Cain, the desecration of a blood relationship. The guilt living on in him is only one indication of the presence of the past. Sublimation, however often attempted, is impossible.

Whereas Zach wants to escape the consuming ennui of his life through immediate satisfaction of his senses, Morrie believes in delayed gratification—saving money for the future. His dream is so compelling that he has been able to foist it onto Zach, thus altering Zach's inclination to live for the day. Morrie has apparently traded the illusion of passing as white for the illusion of the farm, but he fails to recognize that he has only switched dreams and not transformed the dreamer. Morrie is initially unable to objectify his experience and learn from it; his self-consciousness is limited. He thinks he has forsworn his past games, but he will soon play them again.

Imaginary games and role-playing are the primary means by which Morrie and Zach finally affirm the present and their true identities. Morrie had made his debut in the role of the white man many years before, but within the play Fugard also indicates the ability of Morrie and Zach to perform, as in, for example, their reenactment of a childhood game, a scene that also advances the theme of time.

Their imaginary car ride triggers the memory of other childhood games, but Morrie and Zach have done more than rediscover their youth and distant past. They have also verified the present, their fraternal bond: Although they had different fathers, which explains their different pigmentation, they had the same washerwoman mother. Without this blood relationship Morrie might not suffer from the guilt of his presumed betrayal, but without a brother he would also lose a purpose for existence. After acknowledging their bond, calmness reigns; the struggle for dominance and to impose one will on another ceases, at least temporarily. Morrie and Zach have not yet fully accepted themselves, but they are adjusting to each other.

The car ride is a pivotal scene because it affirms the present. It is also stylistically important. Morrie and Zach self-consciously play themselves. They relive their childhood imaginatively and begin to indicate an objectivity towards themselves, an ability to be self-critical, that was not previously evident. Self-deception gives way to reflection and insight. As in art itself, imagination makes truth accessible.

Morrie and Zach do not write their own play, the way Hamlet does, nor are they as theatrically self-conscious as many of Pirandello's and Beckett's characters. ***The Blood Knot*** is not anti-illusionistic, but Morrie and Zach do collaborate, in a sense, with Fugard in their own dramatization. From the car ride on, Morrie and Zach "play" with increasing frequency; they repeatedly use their imaginations, ephemeral internal means to escape concrete external circumstances. Merely corresponding with Ethel is a kind of game, as is Morrie's planned imitation of a white man. Sometimes they simply mimic: Zach coyly keeps one of Ethel's letters from Morrie, who responds with his own childish tricks and feigned indifference; while explaining the way a man courts a woman, Morrie mimes a tea service; and upon returning with the new clothes, Zach acts out the roles of customer and salesman. However, these are mere sophomoric turns, audition pieces, compared to the role-playing that lies ahead. Twice they reenact the South African ritual of the arrogant white *baas* abusing the black "boy."

The first of these is undertaken to teach Morrie "whiteness," but before this Morrie himself takes on the role of teacher in helping Zach understand his identity. Morrie has wanted to help Zach and be needed by him for so long that he cannot quite believe Zach's plea for help. For perhaps the first time since Morrie's return, Zach truly needs his brother. What follows is an incisive Socratic inquiry in which Morrie's hard questions and exhortations lead Zach to understand his "facts." The scene is between tutor and pupil. Zach is coached and coaxed until his dream of meeting a white woman is exorcised and he realizes he can never have her. Zach understands and accepts, "I'm black all right." He finally recognizes that, "after a whole life I only seen me properly tonight." It remains for Morrie to discover and accept his true identity.

The identity that Zach has found with Morrie's help may be a limiting one defined primarily by his race, but Zach at least has the security of that identity: "Black days, black ways, black things. They're me. I'm happy. Ha Ha Ha! Do you hear my black happiness?" Morrie envies that certainty and happiness.

Morrie dominates the early scenes, but Zach can also get his way. Despite Morrie's objection, Zach replies to Ethel's letter. This letter is truly Zach's in a way the introductory one was not. (In playing Zach's Cyrano, Morrie had initially all but appropriated the pen-pal for himself.) Zach gets his way again after suggesting they use the money saved for the farm to buy "white" clothing. Despite his initial opposition, Morrie begins to warm to the idea. By the end of the scene he has switched from resistance, through passivity, to an active desire to meet Ethel and once again try passing.

With his appropriation of the "future tin" in which they keep their savings, Zach takes charge. In the first scene Morrie had interrupted Zach's memories of Minnie. Now, in an exact reversal, Zach interrupts Morrie's musing on his own past. Morrie's acquiesence in spending the farm money is the first sign of his willingness to live in the present. He is ready to don the costume of a white man and play the role of the white man on the dirt floor stage of a Korsten shack.

After purchasing the new outfit, Zach plays tutor: Morrie had taught Zach "blackness," now Zach will teach Morrie "whiteness." In the past Morrie had not discovered the "inner whiteness" that supposedly pervades the white man's demeanor. Every actor knows that a costume helps create a character, and ***The Blood Knot*** audience has also been alerted to the link between the clothes and the man: As Zach sleeps, Morrie puts on his brother's coat and says, "You get right inside the man when you can wrap up in the smell of him."

Until Morrie unleashes an abusive taunt, he and Zach rehearse a brief episode of a white man purchasing nuts from a black man. The derision Morrie directs at Zach is a kind of self-hate. The role-playing ends, but Morrie finally explains to Zach in the clearest terms yet exactly why he had left home. The scene is wonderfully ironic and complex. Morrie and Zach are playing—and they are not. Illusion and reality meld to the point where it is impossible to ascertain where one stops and the other begins. Their games are always deeply rooted in an external reality; their wakeful, everyday life is dominated by dreams of escape. They have thoroughly learned the black and white roles by observing and playing them in the outer world—Morrie by passing, Zach by kowtowing to his boss.

Morrie has sworn at his brother and been forced to recognize the persistence of his desire to pass. This old dream remains, as does the new one of pastoral retreat, but the farm money has been spent. Morrie decides to leave Korsten again. He has been unable to expiate the old remorse and thinks he has again betrayed his brother by abusing him. To meet Ethel would be to invite additional feelings of guilt.

Zach perceives only part of the cause of Morrie's dejection, the threat of Ethel's visit. When they learn she is not coming, the worry about discovery is removed and Morrie is ecstatic. His readiness to resume the old illusions seems to indicate he has learned nothing. Zach even suggests he dress again in the white man's costume and that they repeat their game: "We're only playing now." However, it is not really the same game since before they had been preparing for Ethel; now it appears to be play for its own sake, just for fun. It is actually no such thing. When initiating this game Zach says—"*slyly*" according to the stage direction—"You looked so damn smart in that suit Morrie. It made me feel good." Zach is disingenuous for the first time. Instead of interacting spontaneously, he is now consciously plotting.

This game starts where the last one ended, with Morrie abusing Zach, but now the game is different. As teacher in the fifth scene, Zach had delivered a lesson about whiteness. He now has another lesson and shows Morrie an additional side of the stereotyped black man Zach had played. In response, Morrie pretends to walk and walk, fervently believing that he has left Zach, Korsten, and his past behind. But Zach follows. He is as inescapable as Morrie's past and the true identity Morrie will soon discover and accept.

Throughout much of the play Morrie has had an answer for everything. Now Zach answers each of Morrie's questions and rebuffs his attempts at escape. As Morrie becomes cold, lonely, and afraid, he prays for forgiveness and Zach prepares to attack him. The foreboding and tension of the confrontation are finally broken by the alarm clock; as in their previous game, Morrie and Zach are shocked back to reality.

Through Zach's instruction, Morrie recognizes and understand's the inner meaning and implication of his hopes, not simply their external form. He abandons the fantasy of the farm, the illusion of living in the future, and says, "It's a good thing we got the game. It will pass the time. Because we got a lot left, you know! (*Little laugh.*) . . . I mean, other men get by without a future. In fact, I think there's quite a lot of people getting by without futures these days." Morrie will live in present time.

The most obvious symbol of ***The Blood Knot***'s time theme is Morrie's alarm clock, which breaks the silence of the play's opening and catapults Morrie into one of his housewife routines. The clock dictates life in the shack. It fails to command immediate attention only after the brothers become disoriented by the first dress-up game. The calendar is another way Morrie regiments life. He serves fish every Thursday and polony (baloney) on Friday. A break in the routine indicates something important has transpired. The disheveled appearance of the room at the beginning of the last scene, an objectification of Morrie's befuddlement, suggests the turmoil to come. This signal of a change in Morrie, both past and impending, is strengthened when he holds up the clock: "It's stopped. Like me. What time shall we make it?" Morrie is in control of the clock instead of it being in control of him. Time becomes subjective rather than objective.

The time theme is also implied elsewhere, as in the moths Morrie describes. In addition to flying into the whiteness of light where they are burned, both Morrie and the moths undergo transformation through time. The latter end up ugly moths, but there is always the possibility that a plain caterpillar will evolve into a beautiful butterfly. Morrie ponders the human equivalent: "worms lying warm in their silk to come out one day with wings and things! Why not a man?"

By the play's conclusion Morrie and Zach begin to live in the present, brother and brother. Should they continue to play their little game, they will do so without taking it seriously, without deluding themselves through the illusion of true or final escape. The game will simply be part of the routine, along with footsalts and the alarm clock. The game is recognized as a game, an end in itself rather than a means.

Morrie and Zach will live in the present with the one certainty that has existed throughout their lives, but that was sometimes unrecognized. Morrie speaks the last lines of the play: "You see, we're tied together, Zach. It's what they call the blood knot . . . the bond between brothers." When all else fails, the symbiotic bond of blood and love remains. Meager as this may be, it is more than many of Fugard's subsequent characters will have.

"Brother" is not the only word emphasized in ***The Blood Knot.*** Morrie teaches Zach the meaning of terms such as "insult," "injury," "inhumanity," "prejudice," and "injustice." Fugard has a penchant for such loaded words: In ***Tsotsi,*** Boston stresses "decency;" Boesman is fond of "freedom."

Zach also likes to listen to the lines Morrie has memorized, and he responds to Zach's requests with short recitations of sentimental verse Fugard has made up. (He says, "It's easier to write something yourself than to scour about and find the right quotation from someone else.") In contrast to Morrie's verse, Zach's words, even in the song "My Skin is Black," tend to be assembled into simple, declarative statements of fact.

Quoting lines and learning new words are games the brothers play to pass the time. Morrie truly believes talking helps and that words are an adequate—indeed ideal—substitute for action, the thing itself. He has faith in the word as purgative and suggests that Zach satisfy his need for female companionship through a pen-pal, more words. When he first hears Ethel's self-description, Zach complains, "I can't get hot about a name on a piece of paper. It's not real to me," but Morrie quickly recaptures Zach's interest by quoting Ethel's words, "I am eighteen years old and well-developed." Morrie relies on words for their impressionistic and euphonious sense, but also by attempting to argue with Zach logically. After discovering Ethel is white, Morrie wants to throw away her letter, but Zach successfully counters with, "What sort of chap is it that throws away a few kind words? Hey, Morrie? Aren't they, as you say, precious things these days?" These letters are as important as those Willie must write in ***No-Good Friday.***

The language of Morrie and Zach is often metaphorical, but there are problems with it—not its pitch or lyricism, but its sheer quantity. Some scenes are too long. Moments of delightful humor—selecting a pen-pal, writing Ethel, and the car ride, for example—provide respite from emotional self-indulgence. Morrie's reveries and speeches are often repetitious. Unsure of the evocative power of his language, or, perhaps, because he had fallen in love with it, Fugard often repeats himself, as if afraid the audience would otherwise mistake his intentions. ***The Blood Knot*** is not his last play to have this problem, but over the years Fugard gradually diminishes it. From ***The Blood Knot*** through ***Statements after an Arrest under the Immorality Act,*** an eleven-year period, each of Fugard's major plays is more condensed than its predecessor.

This process of refinement has been conscious. In 1980 Fugard admitted that in ***No-Good Friday*** and ***Nongogo*** he was concerned not so much with language but with the craft of dramatic structure, his models being O'Neill, Williams, and Odets: "Somehow the question of dramatic structures was, after I'd written those two plays, not exactly solved, but I was able to find it instinctively. I didn't have to work away at it like an apprentice making a chair. But a different apprenticeship started with ***The Blood Knot*** and continues even now with ***A Lesson from Aloes***. . . . I see this apprenticeship in terms of working on the *word,* making that line as spare as it needs to be."

Fugard is aware of the excesses of ***The Blood Knot*** and says, "Anybody who was to do that play as written now would be an absolute lunatic. It's overwritten, monstrously overwritten." For the first American production, director John Berry cut some of the text, and Fugard realized that he was absolutely right, but that he hadn't been bold enough and that a lot more had to go. In 1966, as he was preparing a second London production, Fugard cut the text by twenty-five percent, rearranged its seven scenes into three acts (the second scene, for example, was inserted into the first), and severely trimmed Morrie's long rhetorical turns. His part is now more nearly equal to Zach's. (None of the lines or actions Fugard cut has been cited.) The revised text has only recently been published by Samuel French, in an acting edition. It is an unusual writer who would throw his first novel into a lagoon in Fiji, forget entirely about his first plays, and presume his second novel had been discarded. It is not unusual, however, for a playwright to be more concerned with the performed text than the published one.

Fugard was apparently aware of other inadequacies, since the play contains unsuccessful attempts to solve them. Most of these relate to plot developments. With one exception, Fugard's plots are never of the mystery-story, what-will-happen-next variety. He does not cleverly complicate stories or situations, then unravel them in the last scene in order to impress with his deftness. Ethel, the threat of her visit, the clothes purchased to meet her, and the relief that settles when she does not come, are not so much plot elements as character ones. (They are catalysts that elicit from the brothers their differing reactions.) However, ***The Blood Knot*** does tell a story as it develops, and its "revelations" are sometimes awkward, especially regarding Ethel's race and Morrie's light complexion.

Despite these problems, ***The Blood Knot*** is an astonishing work from a twenty-nine-year-old playwright active in theatre for only five years. Its promise and craftsmanship are especially impressive because the theatre has often been a medium for the mature writer: It was not until Ibsen and Shaw were in their late thirties, and Pirandello and Beckett in their late forties, that they indicated the full range of their dramatic skill.

Fugard attributes the improvement of ***The Blood Knot*** over his earlier plays to his encounter with European theatre. In addition: "Those one-acts and ***Nongogo*** and ***No-Good Friday*** were written ready-made for a group. ***The Blood Knot*** was the first time that, as a playwright, I sat down and faced a very private situation, without there being any prospect of a production. It was what I call 'the inquisition of blank paper.' I just wrote. For myself."

The Blood Knot dramatizes a psychological and ontological condition. In one of his introductions to the play Fugard writes, "If there is a human predicament, this is it. There is another existence and it feels, and I feel it feels, yet I am impotent. . . . I don't feel innocent. So then how guilty am I? . . . Maybe guilt isn't all *doing.* Maybe just *being* is some sort of sin. I'm sure Morris says that somewhere. If he hasn't, he should." Morrie has suffered because he tried to pass, because he does not accept himself, because he has indulged in illusory dreams, but most of all he suffers because he exists. To suffer is, in part, the meaning of his life, as it is for many of Fugard's characters.

Morrie and Zach will not live happily ever after, but their illusions have ended. They are resigned, but not defeated. Naïve optimism, unfounded faith, and self-delusion give way to perspicuity and consciousness. It is this self-reflection that indicates their kinship to tragic rather than comic characters. Throughout the play, action and cognition are opposed—distinguished by the very personalities of Zach and Morrie—but thought and deed are finally joined through their role-playing. Action leads to cognition. They recognize and accept their true identities.

Morrie and Zach finally possess the lucidity of Sisyphus on the way back down the hill. Camus has influenced Fugard so profoundly that it is impossible to record every cross-current, but two years after completing ***The Blood Knot,*** Fugard himself noted one connection: "Far from 'leaping,' Morrie and Zach wake up to find themselves heavy, hopeless, almost prostrate on the earth. . . . What is more obvious than that I should be drawn, be overwhelmed by Camus? Morrie and Zach at the end of ***The Blood Knot*** are two men who are going to try to live without hope, without appeal. If there is anything on that stage before the curtain drops it is lucid knowledge and consciousness. In effect, Morrie says: 'Now we know.' " (pp. 36-45)

Russell Vandenbroucke, in his Truths the Hand Can Touch: The Theatre of Athol Fu-

gard, Theatre Communications Group, 1985, 252 p.

THE ISLAND and *SIZWE BANSI IS DEAD*

PRODUCTION REVIEWS

Clive Barnes (review date 14 November 1974)

[*A British-born American drama and dance critic, Barnes has been called "the first, second and third most powerful critic in New York." He has refrained from exploiting his influence, however, and has adopted an informal, conversational writing style in his reviews. Barnes insists that criticism of the arts is a public service; therefore, the function of a reviewer is to advise and inform audiences rather than determine a production's success or failure. As a result, Barnes has also earned the reputation of being "the easiest critic to please." His commentary has appeared regularly in the* New York Times *and the* New York Post. *In the following review of a New York performance of* Sizwe Bansi Is Dead, *which was being staged in repertory with* The Island, *he describes the former play as "a joyous hymn to human nature."*]

Theatrical power is a curious thing. It can start small, like a murmur in a chimney, and then build up to a hurricane. It can slide into you as stealthily as a knife. It can make you wonder, make you think. The South African play ***Sizwe Banzi Is Dead*** starts almost slower than slow. A black South African photographer from Port Elizabeth wandered onto the stage at Edison Theater last night and started chatting to the audience, talking nonchalantly about Ford, Kissinger, Nixon and the like.

It was beautifully acted, mildly amusing, but I must admit that I thought this improvisatory and, I now believe, deliberately low-key introduction boded a strange evening. I realized that this play, when at London's Royal Court Theater, had been triumphantly received by audiences and critics alike, but there was a moment there when I thought that this was just a tribute to liberal Britain's guilt over South Africa. But slowly it happened, like a train gathering speed. The play, the theme, the performances, gradually took over, and the sheer dramatic force of the piece bounced around the theater like angry thunderbolts of pain. From this slow, kidding beginning there comes a climax that hits and hurts. You will not forget ***Sizwe Banzi*** easily.

The play comes from South Africa, was performed in South Africa, and apparently following its fantastic international success, official South Africa—by which, of course, I mean white South Africa—is rather proud of it. Which is fantastic, for this is a terrible and moving indictment against the South African Government and the horrifying way it treats its black majority. Interestingly, a government that can let a play like this be shown and even exported, doesn't know its behind from its elbow, or perhaps doesn't even have the miserable courage of its own evil convictions.

The play, like ***The Island,*** which joins ***Sizwe Banzi*** in repertory next week, has been devised by the white South African playwright Athol Fugard and two black South African actors, John Kani and Winston Ntshona. Mr. Fugard has directed the play and presumably acted as some kind of umpire to its creation.

Styles, the jokingly ironic photographer, gets a customer and takes his picture, which is to be sent to the man's wife. They get into conversation, and the man tells him that he is staying with Buntu, a textile worker. And so the story of Sizwe Banzi and his death is told in flashback.

"The world and its laws leave us nothing but ourselves." This is the awful message of the play. Buntu and Sizwe are what South Africans call Bantus. As recently as 1969, the South African Deputy Minister of Justice referred to these 15 million black South Africans as "appendages." They are forced to carry a passbook, which has stamps on it saying where these "appendages" can or cannot work.

Sizwe's passbook is wrong. Coming to Port Elizabeth for work, he will have to go back to the country or face arrest. Already he is overdue, but without getting a job in the city he has no way of supporting his wife and four children. Sadly, he and Buntu go to a bar and get drunk. Coming home, they find the dead body of a stabbed man. Buntu removes the dead man's passbook. All they have to do is change around the photographs—and Sizwe Banzi is dead, and Sizwe himself, under a new identity, is free to live and work. After all to South African officials a black man is not a name but a number, not a man but a boy, not a creature but a worker.

A stirring moral message is one thing; a good play is another. And in its strange way ***Sizwe Banzi Is Dead*** is an astonishingly good play. From its satirically sly opening—with its corrosive remarks on the Ford factory in Port Elizabeth—to its slashing climax, where, echoing Shylock, Buntu and Sizwe insist on their human dignity, the play has a style, manner and grace of its own.

You can hardly talk about the play without talking about the two actors and its staging, because it is all of one piece. John Kani, sleek and flashing, is dynamite as both the cynical Styles and the embittered Buntu, while Winston Ntshona has just the right puzzled dignity and despair as Sizwe. Mr. Fugard's staging is inseparable from them and the play.

There is a great deal of fun here as well as tragedy. It is human nature to fight disaster with laughter, and this play is a joyous hymn to human nature.

Clive Barnes, " 'Sizwe Banzi' Is a Message from Africa," in The New York Times, *November 14, 1974, p. 56.*

Winston Ntshona and John Kani in the 1972 production of Sizwe Bansi is Dead *in Cape Town.*

Clive Barnes (review date 25 November 1974)

[*In the following review, Barnes asserts that the extraordinary acting in, and the subtle direction of,* The Island *result in a compelling, "terrifyingly realistic" production.*]

The other South African play that runs in repertory with ***Sizwe Banzi Is Dead*** opened last night at the Edison Theater. It is called ***The Island*** and it is probably the most terrifyingly realistic play of prison life I have ever seen. It is not for the weakhearted, or even the weakstomached, but this extraordinary dramatic essay on the rigors of prison life from boredom to hope, from fantasy to misery, make Arrabal and Genet seem romantics. But most of all it is a play to stir compassion, and to remind us of man's unending inhumanity to man in many parts of the world. No man is an island.

The island in question is Robben Island, which is apparently a small island in the Atlantic about seven miles from Cape Town. It is used as South Africa's maximum security prison for political offenders.

John and Winston are two such offenders. They have also annoyed one of the guards, who has them running around on the beach, shoveling sand and pushing heavy wheelbarrows. They run back to the prison manacled together. Here, locked in their cell, they attend to their bruises and start to talk.

As with ***Sizwe Banzi, The Island*** is a collaborative effort of John Kani and Winston Ntshona, black South African actors, and the white South African playwright Athol Fugard, who has also directed. And, as with ***Sizwe Banzi,*** it has resulted in a strange dramatic form that is hardly structured enough to be regarded as a conventional play, while the tone and texture of the dialogue, to say nothing of the almost unbelievable spontaneity of the acting, produce a degree of actuality that while common enough in the cinema is extraordinarily unusual, arresting and at times even embarrassing in the theater.

As they talk, we get to know John and Winston a little. We never, in fact, discover precisely what political offenses landed them in jail, and they never talk about politics. Each night before bed, one fantasizes for the other. He might fantasize over a film, with, say, Glenn Ford as "the fastest gun in the West," or perhaps, another night, over a telephone call home. They are also planning a performance of *Antigone*—that's right, *Antigone*—for a prison concert, making up the play, scrounging props, learning the lines. *Antigone*—the question of the rights of the state over the claims of humanity.

John and Winston have been together on the island for two years and nine months. Then, one night, John bursts his bombshell. His lawyer on the mainland has successfully appealed his sentence. He will be released after three years. He will be released in three months. Three months—92 days. It is a great measure of the success of the evening that the impact of this move, this sudden, unfathomable division between two friends, is talked out in the most penetrating fashion. It is a theatrical masterstroke. Finally they act their homespun *Antigone,* with a bitter, satiric irony, for their lords and masters.

It is an unusual evening. The mimetic opening with the convicts on the beach seems hopelessly prolonged, until slowly one realizes one is being given a touch of tedium, a small, painless hint of the boredom that is the prisoner's most constant companion. At times the lack of theatrical artifice becomes trying, but once again this lack is surely deliberate.

The acting is extraordinary—so extraordinary that you do not notice it, which is precisely why it is extraordinary. The baffled honesty of Mr. Ntshona and the more spirited, wittier shafts of Mr. Kani seem totally natural to them, as is their concern for each other, their momentary hatreds, and remarkable self-knowledge. Mr. Fugard's direction—presumably his role was largely that of umpire—is similarly unobtrusive.

I find both ***The Island*** and ***Sizwe Banzi*** most compelling experiences in the theater that have very little precedent. In compass, they are achieving what Brecht often sought—a kind of didactic realism, but didacticism is the last quality you think of with these South African plays. The first quality is compassion.

Clive Barnes, " 'The Island', a Powerful Tale of Prison Life," in The New York Times, *November 25, 1974, p. 37.*

CRITICAL COMMENTARY

Patrick O'Sheel (essay date 1978)

[*In the essay below, O'Sheel discusses Fugard's works, focusing on the creative process and effect of* Sizwe Bansi *and* The Island.]

This article gives a brief account of the shaping impulses of ***Sizwe Bansi Is Dead*** and ***The Island,*** two plays devised by Athol Fugard in collaboration with John Kani and Winston Ntshona, and takes a critical look at the first of them, concluding with observations on Fugard's representation of life in South Africa and his achievement as a dramatist.

Although black South Africans are in a four-to-one majority, government policy has degraded their identity and made them all but voiceless. This fact permeates public life in South Africa, but few authors have been able (or been allowed, under repressive laws) to probe deeply into its significance. Black writers of the post-war era made a brave beginning, only to be banned or forced into exile. Their published work is a testament of thwarted promise, the best of which speaks with an enduringly authentic voice. Among white writers, the voice of Alan Paton (in *Cry, the Beloved Country*) is authentic from a white Christian liberal point of view, but not, according to many blacks, in representing the realities lived by Africans. The fiction of Nadine Gordimer and Dan Jacobson shines with acute perceptions of South African life, including the situation of blacks; but essentially they write of whites, despairingly.

A single powerful voice, that of the playwright Athol Fugard, has won recognition for what he has had to say of life as experienced on both sides of the colour line, but especially the black. He himself is a white hybrid, his father English-speaking, his mother Afrikaans, born into the lower middle class of the eastern Cape Province. His first plays, ***No Good Friday*** (1958) and ***Nongogo*** (1959), are commentaries on the scene in Johannesburg's black townships. His first great success, ***The Blood Knot*** (1961), investigates the alienating effects of officially prescribed racial discrimination. It deals specifically with two brothers, both 'coloured' but one light and the other dark-skinned, whose poverty and torment are a refraction of the larger alienation that divides South African society into privileged whites and disfranchised blacks.

Omitting certain lesser works, the two plays which consolidated Fugard's reputation were ***Hello and Goodbye*** (1965) and ***Boesman and Lena*** (1969). The first tells of poor-white Afrikaners, a brother and sister caught in a dense field of psychological forces arising from family misfortunes and human weakness. The second is a poetic and scarifying, Beckett-like portrayal of a coloured man and wife who exist as 'white man's rubbish'. Like ***The Blood Knot,*** both these plays have been well received in South Africa and abroad; ***Boesman and Lena*** has been successfully filmed; and the three have been published together as ***Three Port Elizabeth Plays,*** with a Fugard introduction commenting on his methods and motivations. In the circumstances of South Africa, this local and international acclaim is an astonishing achievement.

The sequel has been equally astonishing—the performance of ***Sizwe Bansi Is Dead*** (1972) and ***The Island*** (1973), presented as 'two workshop productions devised by Athol Fugard, John Kani and Winston Ntshona'. These collaborative plays were enthusiastically received in London and New York, and ***Sizwe Bansi*** also made its mark in South Africa.

The story of the creation of these productions is itself uncommon drama, heightened by the fact that Kani and Ntshona constituted the entire cast of both plays in the early performances. They are members of Port Elizabeth's Serpent Players, a group of amateur black actors. The two actors found themselves contributing to a new kind of authorship, made possible by Fugard. They may also be seen, I think with fairness, as surrogates for South Africa's black majority. Fugard has thus had a hand in a creative feat of major proportions.

In Johannesburg, Fugard was a leading force in establishing the Rehearsal Room, a club-style theatre sponsored by the African Music and Drama Association; ***The Blood Knot*** was its first production. Returning to Port Elizabeth, where he has remained, he was approached by a group of blacks from New Brighton, the city's segregated 'township' for Africans. It was the beginning of Serpent Players. Their first production, in May 1963, was Machiavelli's *The Mandrake;* typically, it was a highly experimental affair, an adaptation to a black-township setting. Later productions included works by Beckett, Buchner, Brecht, Shakespeare, and Sophocles, and a number of improvised original works. In his Introduction to ***Three Port Elizabeth Plays,*** Fugard gives this picture:

> We function as an amateur group—that is, nobody gets paid and we do most of our rehearsing at night. At the moment Serpent Players consists of myself and another white as non-acting members, and ten members from the township. Of the latter one is a school teacher, one a social worker, four are factory workers, two messengers and two domestic servants. Most of our performances take place in the townships . . . We would not be given permission to perform publicly for whites . . . Serpent Players has had to cope with the imprisonment of some of our members on political charges, police harassment, isolation . . . Africans are given virtually no chance to see any of the white theatre that is staged in Port Elizabeth . . . We work under the most primitive conditions imaginable. Apart from one talent in white theatre, the work of this group is the only significant provocation and stimulus to myself as writer and director that I have encountered in South Africa . . .

Sizwe Bansi and ***The Island*** are outgrowths of that stimulus, and of a separate, even more radical play-making experiment (with three white actors) which resulted in Fugard's ***Orestes,*** first performed in Cape Town in 1971. He has described the interweaving of these influences, in his introduction to ***Statements,*** citing in particular how Serpent Players had improvised a sixty-minute play, ***The Coat,*** based on an incident in one of the political trials of the mid-1960s. In that work, Fugard's reading of Brecht's *Messingkauf Dialogues* provided a spur. The fact is mentioned to underscore how, in the relative isolation of South Africa, Fugard takes a deep interest in the most advanced work of the theatre abroad; Beckett and Camus are among his other mentors.

Then during a period of even greater isolation (he was deprived of his passport for four years, 1967-1971) he wrote ***Boesman and Lena*** while brooding over means to achieve deeper effects in his work with Serpent Players. The works of McLuhan, Lowell, and other American writers, and especially of R. D. Laing were usefully stimulating. But it was Grotowski's *Towards a Poor Theatre* which became 'in every sense the *agent provocateur* at that moment in my career'. Grotowski, who may be thought of as a Polish successor to Stanislavsky, was lecturing in New York in 1969, where his book had just been published; friends on the spot sent Fugard the book and notes of the lectures, by mail. He has never seen any of Grotowski's own productions.

A many-sided man of the theatre (actor and director as well as playwright) Fugard was already an exemplar of 'poor theatre'. But it was Grotowski's intensity, and his insistence on the actor as 'holy' and creative, that led to what Fugard calls 'my most extreme excursion into a new type of theatrical experience'. In the Introduction to ***Statements*** he tells of it:

> I had an idea involving an incident in our recent South African history . . . a young man took a bomb into the Johannesburg station concourse as an act of protest. It killed an old woman. He was eventually caught and hanged. I superimposed, almost in the sense of a palimpsest, this image on that of Clytemnestra and her two children, Orestes and Electra. There was no text. Not a single piece of paper passed between myself and the actors. Three of them. Anyway, after about twelve weeks of totally private rehearsals we got around to what we called our first 'exposure'. This was an experience that lasted for sixty minutes, had about 300 words, a lot of action—strange, almost somnambulistic action—and silence. It was called ***Orestes*** . . .

Which explains why ***Orestes,*** which had a limited run before small audiences in Cape Town and Johannesburg, has not been published.

In relation to ***Sizwe Bansi*** and ***The Island*** (and to a lesser extent, ***Statements After an Arrest***), what ***Orestes*** did was 'to suggest techniques for releasing the creative potential of the actor'. The starting point in the case of ***Sizwe Bansi*** was Fugard's fascination with 'a studio photograph I had once seen of a man with a cigarette in one hand and a pipe in the other'. The play grew from challenge and response between Fugard—offering a 'mandate' and acting as 'scribe'—and Kani and Ntshona, who reacted with their personal truths to the dramatic possibilities implicit in the situation. The final structure of the play was Fugard's responsibility. Such a creative process calls for great courage and trust, for as Grotowski puts it, 'even in a theatre based on the art of the actor', the actor's work is:

> . . . thankless because of the incessant supervision it is subject to: . . . urging him on to increasing efforts which are painful to him. This would be unbearable if such a producer did not have a moral authority . . . if mutual confidence did not exist beyond the barriers of consciousness. But even in this case he is nevertheless a tyrant.

Fugard readily admits to 'harrowing experiences in the rehearsal rooms'.

Sizwe Bansi Is Dead, in the words of John Kani, is a play about 'what it means to be a black man in South Africa'. As with Fugard's other principal plays, two actors carry the entire burden (a third actor appears in ***Boesman and Lena*** but is essentially mute), and a single austere set is used. Performance is correspondingly demanding and intense, embracing a full register of despair, self-discovery, raucous humour, and didactic 'messages', the language and images now harsh, now strongly poetic.

The play begins with a forty-five-minute monologue delivered by Styles (John Kani), who runs a photographic studio patronized by blacks. He is reading aloud from the daily newspaper, a device to define his sagacity and establish contact with the audience. A news item about the Ford car factory leads him to recall his days as a worker there, notably the day when Henry Ford II ('the big bastard' from America) came to inspect the assembly line. He pictures the white managers master-minding a Potemkin Village reception, in hilarious contrast to the normally unsafe and dehumanizing conditions the African work force must endure. It was to escape those conditions that Styles broke away to set up his own business, an epic achievement in the conditions faced by blacks.

Styles recounts that epic, including a mad battle against cockroaches in his slum premises, and then rattles off examples of how his picture-taking caters to the sad/funny dreams of his customers. Among the old photos on his display board is one of his father, who, at Tobruk in the Second World War, had enjoyed the brief dignity of fighting for 'something called freedom'. At this point, an unsophisticated African (Winston Ntshona) enters. The visitor has come for a 'snap' to send to his wife back in the Ciskei African homeland, giving his name as Robert Zwelinzima. By the device of having him 'dictate' a letter to the wife, the play reveals that the man is in fact Sizwe Bansi. The second half of the play recounts how Sizwe came to switch passbooks with a dead African in order 'legally' to remain in the urban area.

Sizwe's mentor in this identity masquerade is Buntu, a friend of Styles and, like him, a sophisticate in outwitting the pass-laws. Kani (Styles) now shifts into the role of Buntu, to whose house Sizwe has come as a lodger. He listens to Sizwe's hurt, baffled story of being caught in a police raid with an invalid pass. Is there no way to avoid being sent back to the dusty dead-end of the Ciskei? No way to get employment to support his wife and four children?

The dialogue here meticulously, and with graphic examples, brings out the Kafka-like, pain-inflicting bondage of South Africa's apartheid legislation—the pass laws, job permits, labour contracts, travel limitations, and residence restrictions that apply to blacks. When Sizwe asks: 'Why is there so much trouble?', Buntu tells of attending the funeral of Outa Jacob, an old itinerant farm worker whose last white employer had moved off to the city during a drought, leaving him to die: 'That's it brother. The only time we'll find peace is when they dig a hole for us . . . '

To relieve such bleak thoughts, Buntu takes Sizwe on a drinking spree. On the way back Buntu stumbles across a dead body: 'I thought I was just pissing on a pile of rubbish, but when I looked carefully I saw it was a man. Dead. Covered in blood. Tsotsis must have got him.' He wants to go on but Sizwe thinks they should report the death or 'carry him home'; the man's pass-book gives the address of a barracks-like quarters used to house contract labourers. Buntu holds forth on the danger and futility of any such actions. Shocked by this callousness, Sizwe turns to the audience and delivers a peroration against conditions which drain a man's life of value. During this metaphorical stripping he tears his clothes off (until, at least in the New York production, he is holding up his penis as proof of his own value).

Buntu hits on the idea of using the dead man's pass-book, which contains a valid work-seeker's permit. With Sizwe's photo pasted in it, Sizwe will become Robert Zwelinzima; they will burn his own book—and 'Sizwe Bansi . . . is dead'.

This idea opens a dialogue in which Sizwe protests 'I cannot lose my name', and 'How do I live as another man's ghost?' Buntu rubs in the depressing alternative of banishment to the bush, and points out the ghost-like, pride-destroying characteristics of all pass-books. As for eventual discovery of the fraud, Sizwe is able to rationalize that trouble will come anyway: 'Our skin is trouble'. With that, he agrees to the plan.

The play ends with a reversion to the photographic studio. Kani is again Styles, behind his camera: 'Hold it Robert . . . Just one more. Now smile, Robert . . . Smile . . . Smile . . . '

Into the spare framework of this 'poor theatre', a great deal has been packed. The performance runs about an hour and forty-five minutes, nearly half given to Styles's opening monologue before what might be called the play proper is launched.

In content the play turns on the ironies of Sizwe Bansi's 'death', a death that opens the prospect of a job, and hence a life, for a black family. It is a life that costs the sacrifice of name and honour; a life bearing the ghostly identity of the real dead man, whose death epitomizes the lawless violence of the black townships, themselves ironically creations of South African law. It is a splendid and hopeful thing that Styles and Buntu have been able to pull themselves some way up from the general facelessness imposed by the system. Their stories are a trenchant condemnation of that system, often transmuted as mockery. But Sizwe Bansi provides the dominant image, of hounded lives in a politically-exacerbated struggle for survival. The will to survive is the source of the dreams brought to the photographic studio.

The *Guardian* called it a 'profoundly political play' [9 January 1974]. Yet the elements of hope and humour—and irony, which permits a dimension of ambiguity—save it from becoming a mere polemical preachment.

There is very little explicit action. The events are recounted, are conjured up. Clive Barnes observed that 'you can hardly talk about the play without talking about the two actors and its staging, because it is all of one piece' [*The New York Times,* 14 November 1974]. (The staging, as Barnes noted, is by Fugard.) The actors very nearly *are* the play, as is suggested by John Elsom's description of the opening [in *The Listener,* 3 January 1974]: 'a *tour-de-force* of solo acting . . . in which Kani manages to people the stage in a manner unmatched since the days of the great Ruth Draper.' A further tribute to the acting was that

Kani and Ntshona shared the 1975 Tony Award for the best actor of the New York theatrical season.

An obvious question is whether the play can be equally successful without Kani and Ntshona, and without Fugard's own staging. Time will tell; and of course good plays survive later, less-good productions. One wonders, too, whether novelty was not an exceptional advantage in the earliest reception of the plays, an advantage subject to diminishing returns. Here a lot may depend on which audiences are being considered. London and New York audiences and critics were largely white, and their reactions are tinged with a liberal readiness to shoulder the white man's burden of guilt toward blacks, at least in the theatre. It is an over-welcoming reaction, found also in white audiences in South Africa, and Fugard himself is aware of it. But the play has also appealed strongly to black audiences in South Africa, which speaks well for its faithfulness to black concerns. It is, of course, highly topical; given political change in South Africa, it may 'date'. In that event ***Sizwe Bansi*** (along with other Fugard plays) may be reckoned among the influences facilitating change, a reckoning that would no doubt please its three authors more than conventional theatrical honours.

The text, in my reading, has its lapses. At various points there is something close to padding, as in Styles's account of cleaning out the premises for his studio ('When the broom walked in the Sahara Desert walked out.') and his battle with cockroaches that talk. Some lines flirt with banality: 'This is a strong-room of dreams . . . ' or 'My passbook talks good English, too . . . big words that Sizwe can't read and doesn't understand'. We are near to bathos in Styles's tale of a group photograph made in honour of a wise old grandfather, who dies before the prints are ready. When the eldest son has collected these, 'I thought of him going back to his little house . . . filled that day with the little mothers in black because a man had died . . . I saw hands wipe away tears . . . ' If there is a weakness here it is, as with other examples in the play, retrieved by a following and highly effective passage: 'You must understand one thing. We own nothing except ourselves. This world and its laws, allows us nothing, except ourselves. There is nothing we can leave behind when we die, except the memory of ourselves . . . '

Such shortcomings may all be seen as forms of excess, to say nothing of the opening monologue and Sizwe's stripping off his clothes. But the word 'excess' has also a positive meaning, given the influence of Grotowski, who has written:

> If the actor, by setting himself a challenge publicly challenges others, and through excess, profanation, and outrageous sacrilege reveals himself by casting off his everyday mask, he makes it possible for the spectator to undertake a similar process of self-penetration . . . The performance engages a sort of psychic conflict with the spectator. It is a challenge and an excess, but can only have any effect if it is based on human interest and . . . sympathy, a feeling of acceptance . . .

Certainly the author-actors in ***Sizwe Bansi*** deal provocatively with the audience. One senses the strain in the text; in performance, it would appear, the strain is bearable (and fruitful) because the actors are able to approach the 'holiness' prescribed by Grotowski. Future productions, with mere human beings on stage, may well suffer from what Dorrian McLaren sees as a 'looseness and verbosity' in the script [*Athol Fugard and His Work,* 1974], 'those moments when the play drifts', as Martin Gottfried put it in *The New York Post* [14 November 1974].

Of a dozen reviews I have seen, Stanley Kauffman's in *The New Republic* [21 December 1974] is the only one that is plainly negative; 'disappointing' is his word. Compared to ***Boesman and Lena,*** which he had hailed for its universality, he saw this play as 'superficial' and 'only about the troubles of South African blacks'. The 'convenience of the dead man', and Sizwe's stripping, he thought were distracting 'contrivances'. Moreover, speaking of ***Sizwe Bansi*** and ***The Island*** together, he held that, 'the facts of South African apartheid are as well known, in essence, as they are ever going to be to those who are interested in knowing them; and these plays do little more than elaborate, without deepening our insight into, those facts'.

Kauffman's is a minority view; more typical is Clive Barnes's report that ***Sizwe Bansi*** is 'an astonishingly good play' [*The New York Times,* 14 November 1974]. (I should add, I agree that ***Boesman and Lena*** is the stronger work.) As for Kauffmann's knowledge of 'the facts about South African apartheid', it rather carelessly overlooks the point that theatre has its special ways of stating important truths; those in ***Sizwe Bansi*** had not hitherto been explicitly staged.

But Kauffmann raised another question of importance. Sympathizing with Fugard's 'passionate reasons' for helping to devise these plays, he called him 'a director of strengths, but a writer of much greater strengths . . . I hope Fugard, the writer, will write'.

There is something poignant in this remark. Fugard has sought contact across the colour line to an extent rare among South African whites, and for nearly twenty years his writing has been a sort of extended report on the truths he has been able to discover there—and in himself. Animated by literary purposes, he has been drawn into a deeper involvement, a more personal and helping response. Working with Serpent Players has perhaps been at the expense of his writing *per se.* But on the other hand, it is in keeping with the importance attached by two of his mentors, Grotowski and Brecht, to working with amateur groups and learning the language of the people. Certainly it appears that he has gained from this involvement as much as he has given.

Fugard's situation, then, is unique. He has helped make something correspondingly unique in his works of collaboration. ***Sizwe Bansi,*** he has said, came as 'an attempt to break the conspiracy of silence that surrounds our day-to-day relationship with black people'. Few writers, as writers, take on such extraordinary tasks. Nevertheless, Kauffmann has a point. Speaking of the two devised plays, Fugard writes:

> I have lived constantly with the fear of our work

> degenerating into a dangerous game with personalities. This might well be one of the reasons why at this point I feel I have exhausted for myself personally the experience that started with ***Orestes,*** and that the time has now come to return to the privacy of blank paper.

The actress Yvonne Bryceland, who has appeared with Fugard in several of his plays and is a close friend, reports that he has long threatened to give up acting and directing, fearing the dissipation of energies he needs for writing.

> He wants to protect his privacy—the great model is Beckett—but his generosity won't allow him to. He has been very much at the disposal of those who need him; we pull lumps off him because we need him. He is the core of theatre in South Africa. What he has done for it has inevitably been at the expense of going into himself, the writing, which is the most important thing.

Where will resumed writing lead?

Except in ***Orestes,*** Fugard has always taken his bearings from personal experiences, in his particular corner of the world; he has always been the 'scribe', taking that role farther than most playwrights. His achievement shows an intimate, down-to-earth sense of place; of common speech in all its harshness and poetry; of the psychological pressures and injustices felt in a society surrealistically divided. But he has stayed on one side of that dividing line, writing almost entirely of 'the lower depths', often with the ambiguous imagery associated with the Theatre of the Absurd. But whereas in Absurd theatre despair is inescapable and deserved, the characters self-victimizing, in Fugard's plays despair is subordinate to a struggle for survival that holds positive implications.

The question seems to be whether those implications will animate Fugard's further writing. To depict grievances raises, implicitly, the whole question of redress, which Fugard has not tried to deal with. The woes of the victims clamour for attribution, specifically to the victimizers—who do not appear in his work. This is political territory, of course, and it is exactly the complaint of black writers like Lewis Nkosi and Dennis Brutus that Fugard's plays fail to follow out the implications posed by their politically-charged subject matter. Writing some years ago about ***The Blood Knot,*** Nkosi objected to its 'implicit quietism' which he attributed to 'Fugard's distrust of politics' [*South Africa: Information and Analysis,* May 1968]. Even ***Sizwe Bansi,*** he feels, contains false images that betray a shying-away from political truth. Where white critics acclaim the effectiveness of understatement in Fugard's work, black writers say this is precisely its failing: it is too palatable. It is this, they say, that accounts for the South African government's tolerance of Fugard, despite the ravages of its policies that he has held up to view.

Fugard admits to concern over these strictures, sometimes feeling 'rotten with compromise'. Believing it essential to remain in South Africa, close to his roots, he acknowledges the inhibiting effect of censorship laws and the state's proclivity for banning writers. Yet he has been relatively bold; he has taken risks; he has been harassed. He has never seen himself as a political writer, yet he prides himself on the honesty of his writing, which forecloses overt propagandizing. He has indeed 'broken the conspiracy of silence' in the theatre about the conditions forced upon blacks.

Lewis Nkosi calls Fugard 'an important writer, whose work has profound insights into human nature'. But in the conditions of South Africa this, he argues, is not enough. The dilemma is a cruel one. It is reflected in Fugard's notebooks where he cries out: 'How do I align myself with a future, a possibility, in which I believe, but of which I have no clear image? . . . Like everyone else in [South Africa], black and white, my horizons have shrunk . . . Today's future barely includes tomorrow.' (pp. 67-76)

Patrick O'Sheel, "Athol Fugard's 'Poor Theatre'," in Journal of Commonwealth Literature, *Vol. XII, No. 3, April, 1978, pp. 67-77.*

Albert Wertheim (essay date 1987)

[*In the following essay, Wertheim praises the dramatic effect of "the conflation of ancient and contemporary, of Greek legend and the apartheid state" in* The Island.]

Athol Fugard works with spare materials in his powerful play ***The Island:*** an audience, two black actors, the barest of stage properties and an empty playing space. From these he transforms both theatre and playing space into the interior of South Africa's infamous Robben Island Prison, a brutal and brutalizing place just off the coast of Cape Town where many political prisoners have been held in dehumanizing captivity and without known term to their incarceration. ***The Island*** is a play not so much written by Fugard as devised jointly by Fugard and the two original actors of the piece, John Kani and Winston Ntshona. And these two actors use the stage powerfully to enact the existence, routine and human relationships on Robben Island.

It is singularly important that the two characters of the play, John and Winston are acted respectively by John Kani and Winston Ntshona, for this enables Fugard to use his performance technique in order to transform his playhouse into a large playing space. Kani and Ntshona are not two actors portraying two black fictive characters. They are instead playing themselves incarcerated. The stage does not *represent* the prison, it *is* their prison and their particular prison cell. Similarly, the audience is not a disengaged body watching a representation of a prison; it is, instead, transformed through the dramaturgy into John and Winston's fellow prisoners and guards. In short, the playing space of Athol Fugard's ***The Island*** is not the actual stage area of the theatre where John and Winston's prison cell is located. Rather the playing space is the playhouse as a whole which becomes Robben Island.

Carefully orchestrating the opening segment of ***The Island,*** Athol Fugard sees to it that theatre quickly becomes a prison. Even as the audience file into the theatre, revealed to them on stage is a Robben Island prison cell with the two black prisoners asleep on the floor. There are no beds on Robben Island. Only a single blanket and a tin

Winston Ntshona and John Kani in a 1973 production of The Island.

drinking cup for each prisoner plus a shared bucket of water make up the stage props. And from these the two men in the course of the play will fashion an existence and a political statement.

The action of the play begins with a siren, stage lights coming on and the two men, heads shaven and dressed in shorts, in an extended, seemingly endless mime lasting perhaps ten painful minutes during which the two prisoners engage in a Sisyphusian labor of pointlessly digging sand, filling a wheelbarrow with it, pushing the wheelbarrow to another side of the stage and emptying the sand. The stage directions make a point of saying, *'Their labour is interminable.'*

That exhausting, pointless mime serves as a warm-up exercise for the play, at once conditioning the actors and the audience to the dehumanizing spirit of a South African prison. Ten minutes is a long time in the theatre, and ten minutes of repeated, wordless action is an eternity particularly when the audience does not know what the point of the monotonous action is supposed to be. But that of course is the point! The restiveness and the failure to understand why actions are taking place or punishments being inflicted is at the core of the existence created in the South African prisoners. The theatre consequently becomes for the audience a microcosm of a South African prison, for they do not know when the playwright will end his play and release them, they do not see the point of the scenario the playwright has created, and they undoubtedly ask themselves what they have done to deserve the treatment they are receiving from the play.

The seemingly interminable mime with which ***The Island*** commences transforms the theatre into Robben Island and provides an excruciatingly moving dumb show from which the drama that follows can be built. With the blowing of a prison whistle, a second mime immediately ensues: John and Winston are handcuffed, joined at the ankles and forced to run in tandem. Brilliantly, Fugard portrays the subhuman race with the stage directions, *'They start to run . . . John mumbling a prayer, Winston muttering a rhythm for their three-legged run.'* With dramatic concision, Fugard indicates the way the tedium, animal degradation and torture work upon the prisoners, serving to evoke the very things that raise men above bestiality: a reliance upon the spirit, manifested in John's prayer, and a reliance upon reason, manifested in Winston's creating a rhythm so that the two men may with dignity run in unison. At the same time, the audience are made voyeurs either suffering along with the two actors or sadistically enjoying their labors. And it is important here that the mime is not merely punishing, hard physical labor for the characters of John and Winston but is so as well for the actors, John Kani and Winston Ntshona. The sweat and pain shown by the actors is earned on stage. In their short traffic on the stage, the actors are meant to undergo as well as enact what hundreds of men undergo every day of their lives in South African prisons.

What Fugard's opening mimes poignantly show is the way the South African authorities have created a system that is meant to reduce men to beasts, to annihilate the last shreds of their humanity. Their humanity, however, remains intact, even flowers amid a situation that is meant to be death in life or living death. And it does so because the two men continue to act as humans by using dramatic acting as the means for sustaining their humanity. Improvisation—that tool through which an actor learns to understand and practice a role—becomes the means through which John and Winston understand, practice and enact their humanity. Acting, moreover, becomes both shield and sword to the two prisoners: a means for self-protection, for protection of the self, and a means for taking action or acting against their captors, against the State. Fugard thus asserts that acting is no idle art, no end in itself, but the very essence of life and of being human.

Finally, after the men are beaten and returned wounded to their cell, dumb show yields first to sounds and then to words of rage and pain. Nevertheless, the situation in all its intense physicality creates moving words and pictures enunciating spiritual strength. Winston's pain causes John to act: to urinate and wash Winston's wounded eye. And with the consciously chosen terminology of the theatre, Fugard's stage directions indicate, *'In a* reversal of earlier roles *Winston now gets John down on the floor so as to examine the injured ear'* (emphasis mine). As the two men thus act to assuage each other's bodily injuries, Winston exclaims, *'Nyana we Sizwe,'* 'brother of the land,' affirming the power of brotherhood and the indomitability of the two men's human spirit.

In his recent plays, ***A Lesson from Aloes*** and ***Master Har-***

old, Athol Fugard has explored the ways in which the South African apartheid system is equally and perhaps, finally, far more damaging to the psyche of Whites than it is to Coloureds and Blacks. ***The Island,*** likewise, and with great intensity, shows the backfiring of a system that wishes to rob John and Winston of their humanity and reduce them to beasts. To show this, Fugard has John and Winston appear on stage constantly affirming their brotherhood. Their white guard, by contrast, is unseen. Only his irritating noises and the sting of his blows are heard. The guard is named *Hodoshe,* an Afrikaans word meaning 'the green carrion fly'; and like Ben Jonson's Mosca, whose name also means 'flesh fly', it is the white Hodoshe who is reduced by Fugard to a character in a mean-spirited beast fable. John and Winston remain triumphantly human.

Hodoshe exemplifies the prison guards whose humanity devolves into animal behavior whereas the prisoners create their humanity out of the very bestiality that has been forced on them. John and Winston receive beatings and wounds from their guards. They were transported to Robben Island in vans, crammed and shackled to one another like animals, urinating on one another as they traveled. And yet it is their care for one another's wounds that brings forth and italicizes John and Winston's humanity, and no more painfully so than when Fugard's stage directions read, '*John urinates into one hand and tries to clean the other man's* [*wounded*] *eye with it.*' The mimed stage action brilliantly portrays the transilience of inhumanity and animal function into human caring, of Sisyphus' punishment transformed into Antigone's triumph. Such humanity rising from the depths of degradation is reminiscent of the spirit that survived in Nazi concentration camps. And the similarity, as Fugard's recently published notebooks make clear, is not accidental.

Having turned his theatre into Robben Island Prison, Fugard writes a play in which the main action is concerned with John and Winston's turning the prison into a theatre. For the 'entertainment' of their fellow prisoners and their guards, John and Winston plan to present their dramatized version of an ancient drama: the confrontation between Antigone and Creon. Like the devisers of ***The Island***—Fugard, Kani and Ntshona—the prisoners are not merely actors but playwrights. They forge drama, an art that is an affirmation of their humanity. And they fashion it from the basic artifacts of their prison life and from the basic resources of their imagination. Using a few rusty nails and some string, John devises Antigone's necklace; with a piece of chalk he has treasured away, he lays out on the cell floor the plot of the *Antigone* skit he has created. Similarly, the two prisoners have in the past produced recreations, have re-*created* their spirits by taking each other to the bioscope, creating cinema without film or screen but through the combination of imagination, narration and physical gesture. And in the course of the first scene, they reach out from the isolation of their island prison in Cape Town to friends and family in Port Elizabeth using an empty prison tin cup transformed into a telephone receiver and using the power of fictive imagination, rhetoric and gesture to create the two-sided conversation. Through acting, in short, comes their survival. And clearly for Fugard, acting in the sense of making theatre and acting in the sense of making a commitment are not two separate meanings for a single word but essential identities.

When Winston and John begin to rehearse their *Antigone,* Fugard reveals his master's touch as a dramatist. Winston appears dressed in false wig, false breasts and necklace all wrought from the scraps the two prisoners have been able to store away or find in their restricted, repressive, bare essentials environment. He is ludicrous not only for John but also for the audience, both of whom laugh freely at the grotesque sight Winston presents. But Fugard and John both know that once the audience has had its laugh at the comic figure Winston cuts, the joke will be over and they can go beyond their laughter to perceive Antigone, not a 'drag' Winston, and to take the meaning of Antigone and *Antigone* seriously:

> This is preparation for stage fright! I know those bastards out there. When you get in front of them, sure they'll laugh. But just remember this brother, nobody laughs forever! There'll come a time when they'll stop laughing, and that will be the time when our Antigone hits them with her words . . . You think those bastards out there won't know it's you? Yes, they'll laugh. But who cares about that as long as they laugh at the beginning and listen at the end. That's all we want them to do . . . listen at the end!

What Winston does not at this point in the play realize is that the story of Antigone and his own story are congruent. He exclaims, ' . . . this Antigone is a bloody . . . what do you call it . . . legend! A Greek one at that. Bloody thing never happened. Not even history . . . Me? . . . I live my life here! I know why I'm here, and it's history, not legends.' The audience, however, begins to realize that John and Athol Fugard have chosen the Antigone story because it is a legend that embodies the history of protest; and Winston's life is thus history and legend in one. And as he ruminates about his imprisonment at Robben Island for having burned his passbook, the obvious parallelism of his defiance of the state and Antigone's is hidden for him but understood by the audience.

The Island forces its characters and its audiences to grow. It is only at first a simple play merely about incarceration and about time 'Experienced,' as Fugard says in his ***Notebooks,*** 'as a loss of Life, as a Living Death. You are no more.' But, to evoke the absurdity of life on Robben Island, Fugard swings his play around, moving it from a depiction of imprisonment to a consideration of the meaning of freedom: measuring freedom against the absurdity of incarceration. When John suddenly learns that his case has been reviewed and that he will be freed in a matter of months, clock time—counting the months and weeks and days—returns to him, separating him from Winston who has only the time without end of open-ended imprisonment.

For Winston, John's forthcoming release serves to underline the pointlessness, the absurdity of his own lot; and with that, his spontaneous joy for his friend is transformed into temporary jealousy and hatred. A jealousy and hatred that he releases through playwriting; and it is a playwriting that is meant at once as a self-defense and as a pointed attack on John. Whereas John and Winston's earlier creative efforts had been written for mutual entertainment or, as in the case of their imaginary telephone call to Port Elizabeth, had permitted joint creativity, Winston now implies his divorce from John by writing a monologue, using the same subject matter as their telephone call, taunting John with very graphic descriptions of relationships and events that will soon be, but are still not, within his reach.

But writing and acting out a dramatic monologue about John's freedom creates heuristic experiences on several levels for Winston. He is able to give vent to his envy and purge it. He is able to punish John for his good fortune. He is able to recognize his own absurdity. And, at last, he comes to terms with that absurdity, sensing for the first time its power. Here Fugard adeptly brings Camus' *The Myth of Sisyphus* directly to bear on ***The Island*** and does so without a heavy hand. After concluding his dramatic monologue, Winston sees himself projected in old Harry, a seventy-year-old prisoner serving a life sentence and working in the quarries:

> When you go to the quarry tomorrow, take a good look at old Harry. Look into his eyes, John. Look at his hands. They've changed him. They've turned him into stone. Watch him work with that chisel and hammer. Twenty perfect blocks of stone every day. Nobody else can do it like him. He's forgotten himself. He's forgotten . . . why he's here, where he comes from. That's happening to me John. I've forgotten why I'm here.

The picture of old Harry, like the opening stage picture of Winston and John with the sand and wheelbarrow, is a version of Camus' picture of Sisyphus. Camus writes: ' . . . Sisyphus is the absurd hero. He *is* as much through his passions as through his torture. His scorn of the gods, his hatred of death, and his passion for life won him that unspeakable penalty in which the whole being is exerted toward accomplishing nothing.

Yet Camus argues that Sisyphus, each time he descends from the heights to find his stone and his eternal torment, gains a special consciousness:

> At each of those moments when he leaves the heights and gradually sinks toward the lairs of the gods, he is superior to his fate. He is stronger than his rock . . . [he] knows the whole extent of his wretched condition: it is what he thinks of during his descent. The lucidity that was to constitute his torture at the same time crowns his victory.

Camus concludes his description of Sisyphus saying, 'The struggle itself toward the heights is enough to fill a man's heart. One must imagine Sisyphus happy.' Elsewhere in his essay, Camus addresses the question of freedom and absurdity. And what he says there is precisely what Fugard shows as Winston's situation:

> The only conception of freedom I can have is that of the prisoner or the individual in the midst of the State. The only one I know is freedom of thought and action. Now if the absurd cancels all my chances of eternal freedom, it restores and magnifies, on the other hand, my freedom of action. That privation of hope and future means an increase in man's availability.

In short, Winston looks with fright at old Harry who, like Camus' Sisyphus, 'loves stone'; but after his drama is over, Winston, as Fugard's stage direction makes clear, reflects upon his fate and for the first time understands it: *'Winston almost seems to bend under the weight of the life stretching ahead of him on the Island. For a few seconds he lives in silence with his reality, then slowly straightens up. He turns and looks at John. When he speaks again, it is the voice of a man who has come to terms with his fate, massively compassionate.'* The result is the repeated exultation of brotherhood and renewed commitment, *'Nyana we Sizwe!'*, brother of the land.

In the final scene of ***The Island,*** John and Winston present their *Antigone* play, but it is a presentation that is informed simultaneously by John's understanding and Winston's new understanding of the Antigone legend on the one hand and by their understanding of the Sisyphus legend in much the way that Camus understood it on the other. And in his last scene, Fugard pulls out all his stops to create a *coup de théâtre* that is not an end in itself but a means to enlightenment and political engagement.

As John and Winston take the stage to provide the closing act for the prison entertainment with their *Antigone* play, the role of the audience, of the prisoners and guards, is played by the members of the actual theatre audience, who are addressed as though they were guards and prisoners. And thus the connection between the Antigone story and the story of apartheid in South Africa, between the stage and life, is made immediately, stunningly clear. John's address to the audience in his role of Presenter or Prologue is one filled with the irony of Fugard's dramatic situation:

> Captain Prinsloo, Hodoshe, Warders, . . . and Gentlemen! Two brothers of the House of Labdacus found themselves on opposite sides in battle, the one defending the State, the other attacking it. They both died on the battlefield . . . But Antigone, their sister, defied the law and buried the body of her brother Polynices. She was caught and arrested. That is why tonight the Hodoshe Span, Cell Forty-two, presents for your entertainment: 'The Trial and Punishment of Antigone'.

The pause indicated in the text of the first sentence—'Captain Prinsloo, Hodoshe, Warders, . . . and Gentlemen!'—pointedly endows the prisoners with gentility while separating them from the officials of State power. Furthermore, using the word *arrested* to describe Antigone's situation raises the spectre of the modern polity, and in particular the South African state. It is a word that succinctly captures the bond between the ancient Antigone legend and the events of contemporary history. It fixes the Antigone story as a symbol for John and Winston's plight as well as for all who protest and resist in South Africa. This is nicely and pointedly italicized when after his exposition of Antigone's actions and subsequent arrest, John states that *'that is why'* they are presenting their play.

The conflation of ancient and contemporary, of Greek legend and the apartheid state, continues as Creon becomes the symbol for the State as well as for compliant blacks: 'Creon's crown is as simple, and I hope as clean, as the apron Nanny wears. And even as Nanny smiles and is your happy servant . . . so too does Creon—your obedient servant!—stand here and smile.' Creon, moreover, as he does in Sophocles' play, upholds the letter of the law of the State. Antigone upholds a higher law, but relates the issue at once to the dilemma in Sophocles as well as to that in South Africa by declaiming, 'What lay on the battlefield waiting for Hodoshe to turn rotten, belonged to God. You are only a man, Creon. Even as there are laws made by men, so too there are others that come from God.' Antigone's defiance of the laws of the Greek state justifies the defiance of the passbook and apartheid laws of the South African state. Antigone, like Sisyphus and like the Robben Island prisoners, knows the consequences of her deeds, knows that her defiance will cause her to be immured; but she thereby comes to know an existential, happy transcendence over tragedy. Winston playing Antigone can say to Creon, 'Your threat is nothing to me.'

John and Winston take the Antigone story only as far as her trial. But with the words, 'You will not sleep peacefully, Creon,' Winston as Antigone hints at the remainder of Creon's story for Fugard's audience. As a result of his unjust treatment of Antigone, Creon's own son, Haemon, and his wife, Eurydice, die; and at the close of Sophocles' drama, it is Creon who loses power and is reduced to nothingness:

> This is my guilt, all mine. I killed you, I say it clear.
> Servants, take me away, out of the sight of men.
> I who am nothing more than nothing now.

The tragic nothingness awaiting the inflexible upholders of the State's laws in South Africa is obviously foreshadowed.

As John and Winston's Antigone leaves to be immured, she goes not to the tomb of the ancient story but to an all too familiar South African fate. John as Creon exclaims, 'Take her from where she stands, straight to the Island! There wall her up in a cell for life, with just enough food to acquit ourselves of the taint of her blood.' And Antigone acknowledges that on the Island she will, like the other prisoners there, 'be lost between life and death.' Having said this, however, Winston goes beyond Antigone's tragedy, stepping out of his costume movingly to assert his own renewed defiance and to reaffirm his absurdity as he returns, like Antigone, to his cell and to the pointless existence he must bear for having had the courage to honor a law of mankind higher than South African civil law.

In forging the connections between ancient myths and modern history, Fugard relates the plights of Sisyphus and Antigone to those of prisoners on Robben Island. As John and Winston play Creon and Antigone, they feel the immediacy of the Greek legend. But ***The Island*** has another dimension, a dimension that is there at the beginning in John and Winston's names and is there at the end as Fugard forces the theatre audience consciously to recognize that it is also the prison audience.

Fugard's actors and co-dramatists, John Kani and Winston Ntshona, themselves black South Africans, have kept their own names. The play in which they act is a metaphor, as is *Antigone,* the play in which the two prisoners act. The Island is not merely Robben Island but South Africa itself, an absurd prison with absurd rules enforced by absurd officials. South Africa's citizens, be they non-white or white, are as much immured and imprisoned as the heroine in Sophocles' play or the prisoners in Fugard's. If Fugard's play has been effective, the audience will come to recognize that they have been part of the cast and that their seats have been part of the playing space of ***The Island.*** The enactment of the imprisonment of Antigone is a microcosm of John and Winston's situation which is in turn a microcosm of the theatre as prison, which is in turn a microcosm of South Africa. In the course of ***The Island,*** we come to realize that John will soon be released from prison and we wonder whether, when he returns to normal life, he will repress his Robben Island experience or whether, as seems likely, he will be energized to work with zeal for an end to the inhumanity he knows his friend and brother Winston as well as other South African prisoners continue to face. Similarly, by extending the playing space from stage to theatre, Fugard suggests that the audience, like John, is released from prison back into normal life when ***The Island*** concludes. Will we, Fugard implicitly asks then, repress our theatre experience or will we use it to know that we must work to end a polity that transforms society into a prison? (pp. 229-37)

Albert Wertheim, "The Prison as Theatre and the Theatre as Prison: Athol Fugard's 'The Island'," in Themes in Drama, *Vol. 9, 1987, pp. 229-37.*

"MASTER HAROLD". . . AND THE BOYS

PRODUCTION REVIEWS

Frank Rich (review date 5 May 1982)

[*In the review below of an American production featuring Zakes Mokae, Danny Glover, and Lonny Price, Rich describes* "Master Harold" . . . and the boys *as a drama "lyrical in design, shattering in impact."*]

There may be two or three living playwrights in the world who can write as well as Athol Fugard, but I'm not sure that any of them has written a recent play that can match ***"Master Harold" . . . and the Boys.*** Mr. Fugard's drama—lyrical in design, shattering in impact—is likely to be an enduring part of the theater long after most of this Broadway season has turned to dust.

Master Harold, which opened at the Lyceum last night following its March premiere at the Yale Repertory Theater, may even outlast the society that spawned it—the racially divided South Africa of apartheid. Though Mr. Fugard's play is set there in 1950, it could take place nearly anywhere at any time. The word "apartheid" is never mentioned; the South African references are minimal. The question that Mr. Fugard raises—how can men of all kinds find the courage to love one another?—is dealt with at such a profound level that ***Master Harold*** sweeps quickly beyond the transitory specifics of any one nation. It's not for nothing that this is the first play Mr. Fugard has chosen to open away from home.

What's more, the author deals with his issue without attitudinizing, without sentimentality, without lecturing the audience. ***Master Harold*** isn't another problem play in which people stand for ideological positions. By turns funny and tragic, it uncovers its moral imperatives by burrowing deeply into the small, intimately observed details of its three characters' lives.

We meet those characters on a rainy afternoon, as they josh and chat in a fading tea room. Two of them, Sam (Zakes Mokae) and Willie (Danny Glover), are black waiters who rehearse for a coming ballroom dancing contest while tidying up the restaurant. Because they only have enough money for bus fare home, they can't put Sarah Vaughan on the jukebox: they imagine the music, as well as their Ginger Rogers-like partners, as they twirl about. Eventually they are joined by Hally (Lonny Price), who is the son of the tea room's owner. A precocious white prep-school student on the verge of manhood, Hally has stopped by to eat lunch and work on an English essay.

The black servants are the boy's second family: they have been employed by his parents since Hally was in short trousers. But, for all the easy camaraderie and tender memories that unite master and servants, there's a slight distance in their relationship, too. As the waiters practice their steps, Hally playfully but condescendingly calls them "a pair of hooligans." To the boy, such dancing is a "simple-minded" reflection of "the culture of primitive black society"—only now "the war dance has been replaced by the waltz."

But the articulate Sam, an unacknowledged mentor to Hally since childhood, patiently sets the boy to thinking otherwise. Dancing, Sam contends, "is like being in a dream about a world where accidents don't happen"—where white and black, rich and poor, men and women don't bump into one another. Hally is so taken with this theory that he decides to write his essay about it. Maybe, he postulates, "the United Nations is a dancing school for politicians." Maybe "there is hope for mankind after all."

It's a lovely, idyllic metaphor, and there is much joy in ***Master Harold*** as the characters imagine their utopian "world without collisions." Yet the joy soon dissipates. Mr. Fugard has structured his intermissionless 100-minute play much as Sam describes a dance contest: "a relaxed atmosphere changes to one of tension and drama as the climax approaches." When the tension erupts in ***Master Harold,*** it rips through the audience so mercilessly that the Lyceum falls into an almost deathly hush.

The drama is catalyzed by a series of phone calls Hally receives from his real-life family offstage. Hally's father, we learn, is a drunk, a cripple and a racist; his mother is his long-suffering victim. Hally is caught between them, and, as old wounds are ripped open, the bitterness of his entire childhood comes raging to the surface. The boy is soon awash in tearful self-pity and, in the absence of his real father, takes out his anger on his surrogate father, Sam. What follows is an unstoppable, almost unwatchable outpouring of ugliness, in which Hally humiliates the black man he loves by insisting that he call him "Master Harold," by mocking their years of shared secrets, by spitting in his face.

Mr. Fugard's point is simple enough: Before we can practice compassion—before we can, as Sam says, "dance life like champions"—we must learn to respect ourselves. It is Hally's self-hatred that leads him to strike at the black man and his crippled Dad and, in this sense, the boy is typical of anyone who attacks the defenseless to bolster his own self-esteem.

But ***Master Harold,*** unlike many works that deal with the genesis of hatred, forces us to identify with the character who inflicts the cruelty. We like Hally so much in the play's early stages, and emphathize with his familial sorrow so keenly later on, that it's impossible to pull back once he lashes out. And because we can't sever ourselves from Hally, we're forced to confront our own capacity for cruelty—and to see all too clearly just who it is we really hurt when we give in to it.

Mr. Fugard can achieve this effect because he has the guts to face his own shame: Hally, a fledgling artist who believes in social reform, is too richly drawn not to be a ruthlessly honest portrait of the playwright as a young man. But if Mr. Fugard's relentless conscience gives ***Master Harold*** its remarkable moral center, his brilliance as an artist gives the play its classic esthetic simplicity.

This work is totally without pretension. As Sam says that the trick of dancing is to "make it look easy," so Mr. Fugard understands that the same is true in the theater. The dialogue is light and easy, full of lilting images that gradually warp as the darkness descends. After Hally relives the exultant childhood experience of flying his first kite with Sam, the kite comes down to the ground, "like something that has lost its soul." Sam's description of graceful waltzers is usurped by the boy's vision of "cripples dancing like a bunch of broken spiders."

Like the script, the production has been deftly choreographed by the author: you don't know you're entering the center of a storm until you're there. The one newcomer to the cast since Yale, Mr. Price, will be at the level of his predecessor, Zeljko Ivanek, as soon as he tones down his overly cute youthful friskiness in Hally's early scenes. Once the protagonist falls apart, Mr. Price takes the audience right with him on his bottomless descent to self-immolation.

As the easygoing Willie, Mr. Glover is a paragon of sweet

kindliness—until events leave him whipped and sobbing in a chair, his low moans serving as forlorn counterpoint to the play's main confrontation. Mr. Mokae's Sam is a transcendental force—an avuncular, hearty figure who slowly withdraws into dignified serenity as Hally taunts him. Though the boy has repaid the servant's life-long instruction in tolerance by making him feel "dirty," Mr. Mokae still glows with his dream of a world of perfect dancers—one that's like "a love story with a happy ending."

The author doesn't provide that happy ending, of course—it's not his to confer. But if ***Master Harold*** finally lifts us all the way from pain to hope, it's because Mr. Fugard insists that that ending can be—must be—ours to write.

Frank Rich, " 'Master Harold', Fugard's Drama on Origin of Hate," in The New York Times, *May 5, 1982, p. C21.*

John Simon (review date 17 May 1982)

[*Simon is an American film and drama critic whose reviews have appeared in the* New Leader, New York, *the* Hudson Review, *and the* New York Times. *In the following review, he lauds Fugard for his complex characterizations and subtle expression of the effects of apartheid on both the victim and the oppressor in* "Master Harold" . . . and the boys.]

Except for the overexplicit title, all is well with Athol Fugard's ***"Master Harold" . . . and the boys.*** Fugard has now perfected his way of writing plays about the tragedy of apartheid; he avoids the spectacular horrors and concentrates instead on the subtle corrosion and corruption, on the crumbling of the spirit for which the cure would be heroic action that may not be forthcoming, and which the blacks try to assuage with the salve of dreams, the whites with the cautery of oppression. For Fugard, the ultimate evil is the weakness, the cowardice, that is one of the constituents of so much human nature. When, rarely, unalloyed nobility does occur, its chances of prevailing are slim. Yet it exists, and its mere existence is reason enough for not wiping the name of mankind off the slate. The play springs two wonders on us: It is devastating without being depressing, and it is pungently specific without any loss in universality.

The sixteenish son of white parents who own a tearoom in Port Elizabeth in 1950, "Master" Harold has a tricky, touchy relationship with Sam and Willie, the two black employees. Sam is wise, even philosophical, and hopes for a better world; although Harold has passed on some of his book learning to him, Sam has been more of a father to the boy than his real father, a physical and moral cripple. Willie is a simple soul, seemingly content with funny-sweet fantasies of winning in a ballroom-dancing competition. Not only are the relations between the white boy and the black men who helped him grow up an intricate network of generosities and withholdings, of frustrations and humiliations (not entirely one-sided, though the boy is selfish and the men are a trifle, just a trifle, too good), but even the interaction between Sam and Willie has its curious yet credible complexities. The psychological sharpness, dramatic scope, and existential suggestivity that Fugard wrests from humble but never trite ingredients are a precious, precarious compensation for the ills of being. The author cannot legislate justice for South Africa or the rest of the world, but his plays are among the few small, doughty justifications for carrying on.

The two black actors are exhilarating. Danny Glover, as Willie, demonstrates with thrilling straightforwardness that the unlikeliest beings can harbor staunch talents for learning and endurance; his movements are patience translated into motion, his eyes teem with dormant ardor. As Sam, Zakes Mokae gives a performance stripped of everything that smacks of effect, technique, acting; the only reason for calling it a performance is that life can hardly be that undiluted—that sheerly, overwhelmingly to the point. Only Lonny Price is disappointing as Master Harold, as young Hally vindictively wishes to be called; his effects are big, but seldom let you forget that they are effects.

This production—originally by the Yale Repertory Theatre—has correctly self-effacing scenery by Jane Clark, costumes by Sheila McLamb, and lights by David Noling. And Mr. Fugard directs with the same insight and control with which he writes. There is, despite the noble metaphor of life as ballroom dancing, a certain dearth of language here: These characters, almost by definition, cannot talk poetry, which only a few masters, such as Beckett, have been able to extract from rock-bottom prose. O'Neill, for instance, never quite could, yet it did not finally keep him from greatness. What Fugard offers is wave upon wave of comprehension, compassion, and achingly autobiographical honesty that create a poetry of their own. (p. 76)

John Simon, "Two Harolds and No Medea," in New York *Magazine, Vol. 15, No. 20, May 17, 1982, pp. 76, 79.*

The 1982 production of "Master Harold" . . . and the boys, *starring Zakes Mokae, Lonny Price, and Danny Glover.*

Robert Brustein (review date 23 June 1982)

[*Brustein is an American drama critic whose dedication to improving the quality of the American theater has led to both respect and controversy. In the following review, Brustein describes* "Master Harold" *as the "quintessential racial anecdote," and ascribes to Fugard's writing "a sweetness and sanctity that more than compensates for what might be prosaic, rhetorical, or contrived about it."*]

Athol Fugard's ***"Master Harold" . . . and the boys*** (Lyceum Theater), like this South African playwright's other works, is distinguished more by his majestic spirit than by his artistic gifts. Fugard is not a dramatist of the first rank in a class with Beckett, Brecht, or even the late O'Neill—he makes no deep metaphysical probes, he fashions no striking poetic images, he doesn't change our way of looking at the world. His theatrical impulses are similar to those of Jean-Paul Sartre, Arthur Miller, Arnold Wesker—writers who put their craft at the service of an idea. Like them, Fugard is more interested in identifying social injustices and inequities than in transforming consciousness, which is to say that he is less a visionary poet than a man of great liberal conscience. Fugard's conscience, however, is a judicious instrument—scrupulous without being paralyzed, partial without being simplified. He avoids self-righteousness—the customary pitfall of such writing—by acknowledging that he may be implicated in his own indictments. If not the most inspired of contemporary playwrights, he certainly has the greatest heart, which makes him the most attractive character in his plays.

Fugard's compelling subject is the corrosive effect of apartheid on the spirit of South Africa; in ***Master Harold,*** he may have found his quintessential racial anecdote. The play takes place in a grubby tea room in Port Elizabeth, tended by two black men, the sedate, dignified Sam and the slower-witted Willy. After a desultory opening during which Sam advises Willy about a dancing contest, they are joined by Hally, the schoolboy son of the white woman who owns the tea room. Hally is obviously very fond of Sam, who was a surrogate father to him during his childhood; he just as obviously detests his own father, a crippled, insensate barfly, now preparing to return home after an extended hospitalization. Although Hally believes in social progress and admires humanitarian reformers, the prospect of his father's return triggers extraordinary aggression in him. In the scorching concluding moments of the play, he insists that "the boys" call him "Master Harold," then tells a brutal racist joke and spits in Sam's face.

Though sorely tempted, Sam does not strike Hally. Instead, he exposes him as a coward and a weakling, a creature riddled with self-hatred: "You've hurt yourself, I saw it coming. . . . You've just hurt yourself bad and you're a coward." Sam tries to turn the occasion into a positive learning experience about how one becomes a man; Hally is too ashamed to accept instruction. Sam offers reconciliation; Hally equivocates. The two part with a shared sense of failure and a shared conviction that the dream of racial brotherhood has suffered a damaging, perhaps irreparable blow. The play ends with Sam and Willy locked in each other's arms, inconsolable, dancing to a jukebox tune.

Fugard arranges his anecdote as if he were placing tiles in a mosaic. This sometimes creates an impression of contrivance—twice the phone rings, for example, with information that turns Hally vicious right after he has made fervent humanitarian affirmations. Then, perhaps because Sam's insights into the self-hatred motivating Hally's behavior are so cogent, you are left with a sense that everything has been said, that there is nothing more to be revealed, which robs the evening of ambiguity and suggestiveness. Still, there is no denying the explosive impact of that ending, and Fugard has directed a performance from the three players that is muscular and powerful. Casting Lonny Price as Hally may have exposed the author's hand a little prematurely—Price acts the role with sniveling authority, but if he didn't look and behave so much like a weasel from the beginning, the shock of the ending might have been even greater. As it is, there is no contest, especially when Danny Glover plays Willie with such tender simplicity and Zakes Mokae brings such extraordinary grandeur to the part of Sam.

But the real spiritual beauty of the play comes from Fugard. ***Master Harold*** seems to be a much more personal statement than his other works; it also suggests that his obsession with the theme of racial injustice may be an expression of his own guilt, an act of expiation. Whatever the case, his writing continues to exude a sweetness and sanctity that more than compensates for what might be prosaic, rhetorical, or contrived about it. At this rate, Athol Fugard may become the first playwright in history to be a candidate for canonization. (pp. 30-1)

Robert Brustein, "Coming at History from Two Sides," in The New Republic, *Vol. 186, No. 25, June 23, 1982, pp. 30-1.*

CRITICAL COMMENTARY

Errol Durbach (essay date 1987)

[*In the excerpt below, Durbach asserts that* "Master Harold" . . . and the boys *is not an overtly political play, but a depiction of "a personal power-struggle with political implications."*]

In [***"Master Harold" . . . and the boys***], dredged out of Athol Fugard's painful memories of a South African adolescence, at least one event stands out in joyous recollection: the boy's exhilarating, liberating, and ultimately transcendent experience of flying a kite made out of tomato-box slats, brown paper, discarded stockings, and string. From the scraps and leavings of the depressingly mundane, the boy intuits the meaning of a soul-life; and he responds to the experience as a "miracle." "Why did you make that kite, Sam?" he asks of the black servant whose gift it was—but the answer is not given until much later in the play. Nor can Hally recollect the reason for Sam's failure to share in the experience of high-flying delight:

> HALLY: . . . You left me after that, didn't you?
> You explained how to get it down, we tied it to

the bench so that I could sit and watch it, and you went away. I wanted you to stay, you know. I was a little scared of having to look after it by myself.

SAM: (*Quietly*) I had work to do, Hally.

In the final moments of the play Sam provides the simple explanation: the kite had been a symbolic gift to console the child against the degrading shame of having to cope with a drunken and crippled father—an attempt to raise his eyes from the ground of humiliation:

That's not the way a boy grows up to be a man! . . . But the one person who should have been teaching you what that means was the cause of your shame. If you really want to know, that's why I made you that kite. I wanted you to look up, be proud of something, of yourself . . .

The second question has an answer more readily understood by one familiar with apartheid's so-called "petty" operations:

I couldn't sit down there and stay with you. It was a "Whites Only" bench. You were too young, too excited to notice then. But not anymore. If you're not careful . . . Master Harold . . . you're going to be sitting up there by yourself for a long time to come, and there won't be a kite in the sky.

This, in essence, is the psychopathology of apartheid. Growing up to be a "man" within a system that deliberately sets out to humiliate black people, even to the point of relegating them to separate benches, entails the danger of habitual indifference to the everyday details that shape black/white relationships and, finally, pervert them. It is not merely that racial prejudice is *legislated* in South Africa. It insinuates itself into every social sphere of existence, until the very language of ordinary human discourse begins to reflect the policy that makes black men subservient to the power exercised by white children. Hally, the seventeen-year-old white boy whose affectionately diminutive name is an index of his social immaturity, is "Master Harold" in the context of attitudes fostered by apartheid. And the black man who is his mentor and surrogate father is the "boy"—in all but compassion, humanity, and moral intelligence.

This, finally, is the only definition that the South African system can conceive of in the relationship of White to Black; and Hally, with the facility of one habituated to such power play, saves face and forestalls criticism by rapidly realigning the components of friendship into the socio-political patterns of mastery and servitude. Like quicksilver, he shifts from intimate familiarity with his black companions, to patronising condescension to his social inferiors, to an appalling exercise of power over the powerless "boys" simply by choosing to play the role of "baas":

Sam! Willie! (*Grabs his ruler and gives* WILLIE *a vicious whack on the bum*) How the hell am I supposed to concentrate with the two of you behaving like bloody children! [. . .] Get back to your work. You too, Sam. (*His ruler*) Do you want another one, Willie?

(SAM *and* WILLIE *return to their work.* HALLY *uses the opportunity to escape from his unsuccessful attempt at homework. He struts around like a little despot, ruler in hand, giving vent to his anger and frustration*)

Within the culture portrayed in the play there is nothing particularly remarkable about a white child hitting a black man. It would have been unheard of on the other hand for a black man, in the South Africa of the 1950s, to strike back. *His* anger and frustration could be unleashed only upon those even more pitifully dispossessed of the human rights to dignity and respect. The white child hits the black man, and the black man hits the black woman. It is a system in which violence spirals downwards in a hierarchy of degradation—as Fugard shows in Willie's relationship with his battered dancing partner who can no longer tolerate the abuse.

A very simple racial equation operates within apartheid: White = "Master"; Black = "Boy". It is an equation which ignores traditional relationships of labour to management, of paid employee to paying employer, or contractual relationships between freely consenting parties. And Sam's attempt to define the nature of his employment in conventional terms is countermanded by Hally's application of the equation:

HALLY: You're only a servant here, and don't forget it. [. . .] And as far as my father is concerned, all you need to remember is that he's your boss.

SAM: (*Needled at last*) No, he isn't. I get paid by your mother.

HALLY: Don't argue with me, Sam!

SAM: Then don't say he's my boss.

HALLY: He's a white man and that's good enough for you.

What needles Sam is the thought of being paid for his work by a bigot who shows him none of the simple human respect that is everyone's most urgent *need* in Fugard's world—the white child's in a family that shames him, and the black man's in a culture that humiliates him. It is the common denominator that Sam and Hally share; and the ultimate goal of "Master" Harold's power-play is to secure his own desire for self-respect at the expense of a man whose native dignity proves all but impervious to these attempts to "boy" him. It is a self-defeating and self-destructive ploy, imposed by threat and blackmail upon a relationship which has all the potential for mutual comfort, support, and love. It is the human content of their shared affection that Hally is about to petrify into the equation of apartheid:

HALLY: To begin with, why don't you also start calling me Master Harold, like Willie.

SAM: [. . .] And if I don't?

HALLY: You might lose your job.

> SAM: (*Quietly and very carefully*) If you make me say it once, I'll never call you anything else again. [. . .] You must decide what it means to you.
>
> HALLY: Well, I have. It's good news. Because that is exactly what Master Harold wants from now on. Think of it as a little lesson in respect, Sam, that's long overdue. [. . .] I can tell you now that somebody who will be glad to hear I've finally given it to you will be my Dad. Yes! He agrees with my Mom. He's always going on about it as well. "You must teach the boys to show you more respect, my son."

"Teaching respect" loses all semantic value in the context of apartheid. It means coercion by threat, just as "showing respect" means acquiescence through enforced abasement. It is easy to teach Willie respect—one does it with the stick, and with impunity because Willie lacks the necessary sentiment of self-regard to oppose such treatment. His predictable response is to insist that Hally whack Sam as well—the sole comfort of the wretched being to recognise fellow-sufferers in distress. But Hally cannot *command* Sam's respect; and if he cannot *win* it, his only recourse is to humiliate Sam to the point where, by default, his own pathetic superiority supervenes. Finally, the only power left to Hally is the wounding power of bigotry supported by a system in which "black" is, *ipso facto,* base. Echoing his father's words, associating himself with the very cause of his shame, he spreads the "filth" he has been taught in a racist joke—the penultimate weapon in his arsenal of power. It is a crude pun about a "nigger's arse" not being "fair"; and one senses, in the numb incredulity of the two black men, an irreversible redefinition of their relationship with their white charge. In the ensuing silence, he belabours the pun—the double meaning of "fair" as light in colour *and* just and decent—and is ensnared in the moral implications of his bid for respect through insult and abuse:

> SAM: You're really trying hard to be ugly, aren't you? And why drag poor Willie into it? He's done nothing to you except show you the respect you want so badly. That's also not being fair, you know . . . and *I* mean just or decent.

And to underscore the embarrassment that Hally has brought upon himself, Sam performs an action of rebuke through self-abasement that reveals both the reality and the vulnerability of the "nigger's arse"—the thing that the Master feels at liberty to mock at and kick: *"He drops his trousers and underpants and presents his backside for* HALLY*'s inspection."* His nakedness is clearly no laughing matter. It calls in question the justice and decency and fairness of an entire system which can encourage a child so to humiliate a man. Its indictment is Dostoievskian in its power to shame.

Hally's countermeasure is to exercise his power to degrade with impunity: he spits in Sam's face, saving his own by fouling another's and, in so doing, placing Sam forever in the role of "boy" to his "Master". It is a gesture of contempt and angry frustration, the adolescent's protest against his own sense of degradation—horribly misdirected against the wrong source, as Sam instantly realises: "The face you should be spitting in," he says, "is your father's . . . but you used mine, because you think you're safe inside your fair skin . . . and this time I don't mean just or decent." It is Hally's "white" father who ensures the "principle of perpetual disappointment" in the boy's life—the crippled alcoholic who must be dragged out of bars fouled in his own excrement, whose chamber pots must be emptied by the boy, and whose imminent return from the hospital provokes in Hally the thought of further humiliating servitude. But it is Hally's black "father" who must bear the brunt of his anguish and his shame. Sam has become his "spitting boy" just as Willie had been his "whipping boy", the recipient of a contempt which he cannot reveal to his father whom he both loves and despises. This is the moment, Fugard admitted in an interview, "which totally symbolised the ugliness, the potential ugliness waiting for me as a White South African."

The overwhelming shame of the actual event is recorded in the section of Fugard's ***Notebooks*** dealing with his childhood memories of growing up in Port Elizabeth. But he sets the play five years later, in 1950, that *annus mirabilis* of Apartheid legislation; and Fugard's political point of view is nowhere more clearly revealed than in his location of the encroaching ugliness of South Africa's destiny in a *personal* rather than a *national* failure of moral decency. Despite the statutory enforcement of racist laws in the 1950s, apartheid (like charity) is seen to begin *at home,* in the small details of everyday existence. There is no sense, in the play, of the Nationalist Government's Population Registration Act of 1950 with its racial system of classification by colour, the Group Areas Act of 1950 which demarcated the areas of permissible domicile for the races and controlled the ownership of property in those areas, the 1950 Amendment to the Immorality Act which prohibited sexual contact across the colour bar, or the Suppression of Communism Act of 1950 which empowered the minister of Justice to ban suspect individuals without trial or right of appeal—indeed, without even notifying the detainee of the nature of his offence. There is nothing of Kafka's nightmare about Fugard's world, nothing of the political absurdity of Václav Havel's vision of man's soul under totalitarianism. Nor does he invoke the ridiculous terms of the Separate Amenities Act which, in 1953, would subject a black man sitting on a "Whites Only" bench ("reserved for the exclusive use of persons belonging to a particular race or class, being a race or class to which he does not belong") to a fine not exceeding fifty pounds or imprisonment not exceeding three months, or to both.

Fugard's is not a drama of political protest nor an exposé of a corrupt regime entrenched in its position of power. His detractors on the militant Left call him bitterly to task for failing to fight against the system, just as his Right-wing detractors point to the obsolescence of his political vision—to the disappearance of "Whites Only" signs on South African benches in the 1980s. Plays like ***Statements after an Arrest under the Immorality Act*** or ***Sizwe Bansi is Dead*** may, indeed, seem anachronistic after the rescinding of the Immorality Act and the Pass laws with which they deal. But the psychopathology of apartheid in Fugard's drama is quite distinct from Government policy.

There is no guarantee, when the letter of all the 1950's legislation has passed into oblivion, that the *attitudes* which informed its spirit will disappear as well. The Laws are crucial historical background to Fugard's world, but these attitudes are the substance of his most insistent misgivings about apartheid's operation upon human relationships.

In the absence of explicit political comment, it might seem tendentious to equate the social awkwardness of a troubled teenager with government policy. Hally's condescending attitude towards his "boys", his failure to share with them any of the chocolate and cake and ice-cream that he is constantly consuming—these may be evidence of an ingrained arrogance and selfishness rather than a culturally conditioned attitude to an "inferior" race. But these unobtrusive details underscore the more overt acts of insulting racism in the play. Having whacked one "boy" with a ruler and spat in the other's face, his last shamefaced act is to remove the wretched day's takings from the cash register—essentially small change—and tell Willie to lock up for him. One entrusts the "boy" with the keys to the tearoom, but not with the few coins which might tempt him to play the juke-box or take the bus home. One may *give* a "boy" some cake or chocolate, but never *offer* it. Every social gesture, within the South African context, becomes an affirmation or a negation of the principle of apartheid; and every act is more or less political.

Against the petty and unconscious cruelties of Hally, Fugard juxtaposes the magnanimity of Sam: the compassionate father, the good friend, the moral teacher. He offers a solution to the predicament, again in *personal* rather than *political* terms—a response so lacking in revolutionary fervour as to alienate, once again, the new generation of post-Sowetan critics of Athol Fugard's drama. Mastering his violence and the desire to strike Hally for spitting at him, Sam carefully considers the strategy of aggression with Willie, and they both agree to suffer the indignity in stoical resignation:

> WILLIE: [. . .] But maybe all I do is go cry at the back. He's little boy, Boet Sam. Little *white* boy. Long trousers now, but he's still little boy.
>
> SAM: (*His violence ebbing away into defeat as quickly as it flooded*) You're right. So go on, then: groan again, Willie. You do it better than me.

Though struck to the quick, they endure the insult with weeping and groaning rather than striking back. There is no revolution in the St. George's Park Tearoom—but not because the black man is culturally conditioned to patience, nor for fear of putting his job in jeopardy. In Fugard's world, as in Prospero's, the rarer action is in virtue than in vengeance, in humane reasoning rather than fury; and Sam trusts, once again, to his capacity for moving Master Harold to shame through moral suasion and exemplary behaviour. He forgives the little white boy who knows no better, and behaves like a "man" in order to teach him the rudiments of "manly" behaviour. Turning the other cheek may not be politically expedient as a response to apartheid, but where problems are engendered at the personal level it is only at the personal level that they may be resolved.

"I oscillate," says the precocious Hally early in the play, "between hope and despair for this world. . . . But things will change, you wait and see." On the whole, Sam's politics are ranged on the side of hope—the hope born, initially, of a naive vision of reform and racial harmony but modulating, in the final scenes, to the more sombre hope of salvaging the scrap of value remaining in his relationship with the little white master. He dreams of a world transformed by some benevolent reformer—a saviour like Napoleon for whom all men were equal before the law, or another Abraham Lincoln who fought for the oppressed, or a Tolstoy, or Gandhi, or Christ; and he envisions life as a celestial ballroom in which no accidents occur, in which powers are harmoniously aligned on the global dance floor. But, like Hally, he is forced to acknowledge the harsh reality of things: we go on waiting for the "Man of Magnitude", he admits, bumping and colliding until we're sick and tired. All that remains is the small gesture, the little act of decency that may turn a fragment of the dream into something real. This, finally, is what he hopes for. He takes off his servant's jacket and returns in clothes that no longer distinguish him as a "boy"; he addresses Hally by the affectionate diminutive once again; and he offers, very simply, the chance to "fly another kite." "You can't fly kites on rainy days," says Hally—and the rain and the wind squalling beyond the windows of the tearoom assume the depressing and hopeless condition of the entire South African situation. Better weather tomorrow? No one is sure.

At this point in the Yale Repertory production of the play, the excellent Zakes Mokae playing Sam extends his hand tentatively towards Hally in a gesture of appeal and reconciliation as important to his well-being as to the boy's; and he challenges him to change the situation through an act of personal transformation which flies in the face of his cultural and political conditioning: "You don't *have* to sit up there by yourself," he says, recalling the boy's isolation on the "Whites Only" bench. You know what that bench means now, and you can leave it any time you choose. All you've got to do is stand up and walk away from it". But ingrained attitudes dic hard. Paralysed by shame but incapable of extending himself towards the black man, Hally hesitates and then walks out into the rain as Sam's hand crumples in its gesture.

If anyone has learned a lesson from this bleak afternoon of moral instruction it is the simple, inarticulate Willie who, in his effort to comfort Sam, endorses his dream-ideal of life as a ballroom. He vows never to beat up his partner again, and slips his bus fare into the juke-box which *"comes to life in the gray twilight, blushing its way through a spectrum of soft, romantic colours"*. "Let's dream," he says. And the two men sway through the room to Sarah Vaughan's melancholy lullaby to an unhappy child—"Little man you're crying". The final dramatic image is suffused with the ambiguous tonalities typical of Fugard's best work: the rain of despair beyond the windows, the wind in which no kites fly, the hopelessness of a situation where people are driven apart by racist attitudes, the consoling music which evokes our compassion for children who are casualties of their upbringing, the hope that shame and embarrassment might induce change in a morally receptive child, the delusory political vision of racial harmony on the South African dance floor, and the image of a world where "Whites Only" leave two black men dancing together in an act of solidarity. It is a typically Fugardian oscillation between hope and despair, qualified only by the realisation that "Master Harold" grows up to be Athol Fugard and that the play itself is an act of atonement and moral reparation to the memory of Sam and "H.D.F."—the Black and the White fathers to whom it is dedicated.

It would clearly be misleading to claim that ***"Master Harold" . . . and the boys*** addresses the growing complexity of apartheid politics in the South Africa of 1987. It is a "history" play—a *family* "history" written, like O'Neill's *Long Day's Journey into Night,* as an exorcism of the tormented ghosts of his childhood; but it is also a phase of South African "history", an anachronistic backward glance to a time when black men in their stoical optimism still dreamed of social change and when white boys might have been able to grasp the implications of "Whites Only" benches and choose to walk away from them. It deals with a rite of passage clumsily negotiated, a failure of love in a personal power-struggle with political implications. Alan Paton, writing in the same time-frame of history, projects a similar vision of tenuous hope for racial harmony—and also the dreadful consequences of its deferment. Msimangu, the black priest in *Cry, the Beloved Country,* speaks the powerful subtext beneath the action of Fugard's play:

> But there is only one thing that has power completely, and that is love. Because when a man loves, he seeks no power, and therefore he has power. I see only one hope for our country, and that is when white men and black men, desiring neither power nor money, but desiring only the good of their country, come together to work for it.
>
> He was grave and silent, and then he said sombrely, I have one great fear in my heart, that one day when they are turned to loving, they will find we are turned to hating.

(pp. 505-12)

Errol Durbach, " 'Master Harold' . . . and the boys: *Athol Fugard and the Psychopathology of Apartheid,*" *in* Modern Drama, *Vol. XXX, No. 4, December, 1987, pp. 505-13.*

FURTHER READING

AUTHOR COMMENTARY

Benson, Mary. "Keeping an Appointment with the Future: The Theatre of Athol Fugard." *Theatre Quarterly* VII, No. 28 (1977): 77-83.

An interview in which Fugard addresses both personal and professional issues.

Fugard, Athol. Introduction to his *Statements,* pp. vii-xiii. London: Oxford University Press, 1974.

Examines his experiments in improvisational theater.

———. Introduction to his *"Boesman and Lena" and Other Plays,* pp. vii-xxv. London: Oxford University Press, 1978.

Discusses himself "as a South African and a writer." Fugard includes several excerpts from journals outlining his writing process.

———. *Notebooks: 1960-1977.* New York: Alfred A. Knopf, 1984.

Reveals the genesis of Fugard's plays and theater activities as well as his reflections on literary, political, and autobiographical topics.

OVERVIEWS AND GENERAL STUDIES

Benson, Mary. "Athol Fugard and 'One Little Corner of the World'." *Yale/Theatre* 4, No. 1 (Winter 1973): 55-63.

Examines several of Fugard's plays and the dramatic theories behind them.

Cohen, Derek. "Drama and the Police State: Athol Fugard's South Africa." *Canadian Drama/L'Art Dramatique Canadien* 6, No. 1 (Spring 1980): 151-61.

Surveys Fugard's works, describing him as "the poet of pain for our times, making of the pain of his small but vital world a rich and varied truth about existence."

Collins, Michael J. "The Sabotage of Love: Athol Fugard's Recent Plays." *World Literature Today* 57, No. 3 (Summer 1983): 369-71.

Focuses on plot and characterization in *A Lesson from Aloes* and *"Master Harold" . . . and the boys,* asserting that, "while neither of the plays is perfect . . . , the faults seem small ones finally, and the plays are both inordinately effective on the stage."

Green, Robert J. "The Drama of Athol Fugard." In *Aspects of South African Literature,* edited by Christopher Heywood, pp. 163-73. London: Heinemann, 1976.

Outlines Fugard's early works, tracing his development from the trilogy of plays known as The Family to his collaborative efforts in the early 1970s with particular attention to the influence of South African politics on his work.

Gussow, Mel. "Profiles: Witness." *The New Yorker* LVIII, No. 44 (20 December 1982): 47-94.

Comprehensive biographical and critical essay, including extensive quotes from conversations with Fugard.

Mshengu. "Political Theatre in South Africa and the Work of Athol Fugard." *Theater Research International* VII, No. 3 (Autumn 1982): 160-79.

Reassesses commonly held views of Fugard, including the idea that he is "the lone individual playwright of talent battling singlehandedly in the 'forbidding environment of apartheid South Africa'." Mshengu describes the accomplishments of black South African writers and actors and argues that Fugard's anti-apartheid ideology is less radical than is generally imagined.

Post, Robert M. "Victims in the Writing of Athol Fugard." *Ariel* 16, No. 3 (July 1985): 3-17.

Surveys Fugard's dramatic works, examining the effects of apartheid on the citizens of South Africa.

Wells, Ronald A., ed. *Writer and Region: Athol Fugard.* New York: The Anson Phelps Stokes Institute for African, Afro-American, and American Indian Affairs, 1987, 42 p.

Comprises a biographical sketch, an address Fugard made at the Anson Phelps Stokes Institute's Africa Roundtable on 21 May 1984, excerpts from the discussion following his speech, and an essay on the importance of region to his works.

THE BLOOD KNOT

Freedman, Samuel G. "*Blood Knot*: Creators Play Roles Again at Yale." *The New York Times* (2 October 1985): C21.

Reviews the 1985 production of *The Blood Knot* at the Yale Repertory Theater. Freedman sketches the history of the relationship between Fugard and actor Zakes Mokae from their work on the South African premiere of *The Blood Knot* to its revival twenty-five years later.

Green, R. J. "South Africa's Plague: One View of *The Blood Knot.*" *Modern Drama* 12 (February 1970): 331-45.

Praises Fugard for transcending "immediate and topical issues" in *The Blood Knot* by "writing a play that has universal resonances."

McKay, Kim. "*The Blood Knot* Reborn in the Eighties: A Reflection of the Artist and His Times." *Modern Drama* XXX, No. 4 (December 1987): 496-504.

Analyzes the changes Fugard made to *The Blood Knot* for the twenty-fifth anniversary production.

THE ISLAND

Durbach, Errol. "Sophocles in South Africa: Athol Fugard's *The Island.*" *Comparative Drama* 18, No. 3 (Fall 1984): 252-64.

Addresses Fugard's use of *Antigone* in *The Island* "as the indictment of a political system which devalues human dignity in the name of law and order."

Kauffmann, Stanley. Review of *Sizwe Bansi Is Dead* and *The Island. The New Republic* 171, No. 25 (21 December 1974): 16, 26.

Maintains that the collaborative efforts between Fugard and actors John Kani and Winston Ntshona in *Sizwe Bansi* and *The Island* were unsuccessful, and resulted in works that are "artistically insecure and essentially didactic."

Mackay, E. Anne. "Fugard's *The Island* and Sophocles' *Antigone* within the Parameters of South African Protest Literature." In *Literature and Revolution,* edited by David Bevan, pp. 145-62. Amsterdam: Rodopi, 1989.

Analysis of *The Island* in which Mackay asserts that, "while Fugard did not intend to write protest literature, . . . without doubt [*The Island*] does achieve a certain protest resonance."

OTHER PLAYS

Green, R. J. "Athol Fugard's *Hello and Goodbye.*" *Modern Drama* 13 (September 1970): 139-55.

Studies *Hello and Goodbye,* maintaining that Fugard "has extracted the full tragedy and comedy of everyday life, everywhere."

Kauffmann, Stanley. "*Boesman and Lena.*" *The New Republic* 163, No. 4 (25 July 1970): pp. 16, 25.

Describes *Boesman and Lena* as "a drama of all human beings in their different captivities, suffering from and inflicting hate."

MEDIA ADAPTATIONS

"Master Harold" . . . and the boys. Iris Merlis, 1984.

Made-for-cable production of Fugard's drama starring Matthew Broderick. Distributed by Lorimar Home Video. 90 minutes.

Sizwe Bansi Is Dead. Miami Dade Community College, BBC, 1978.

Shown as it was staged at the Royal Court Theatre in 1974, with Ruby Dee and Ossie Davis commenting and reading from the works of African-American authors. Also hosted by Jose Ferrer. Distributed by Films Inc. 60 minutes.

Additional coverage of Fugard's life and career is contained in the following sources published by Gale Research: *Contemporary Authors,* Vols. 85-88; and *Contemporary Literary Criticism,* Vols. 5, 9, 14, 25, and 40.

Langston Hughes

1902-1967

INTRODUCTION

Full name James Mercer Langston Hughes.

A seminal figure of the 1920s Harlem Renaissance, a period marked by unprecendented artistic and intellectual achievement among African Americans, Hughes devoted his versatile and prolific career to portraying the urban experience of working-class blacks. Called "the Poet Laureate of Harlem" by critic and art patron Carl Van Vechten, Hughes incorporated the rhythm and mood of jazz and blues music into his work and used colloquial language to reflect African-American culture. While a poet first and foremost, Hughes experimented, with varying degrees of success, in almost every literary genre, including drama. Although he never achieved fame as a major American playwright, his output was considerable: fifteen dramas in addition to numerous playscripts for opera, radio, and film. His most notable drama, *Mulatto,* is a symbolic commentary on black America's failure to achieve the American dream of freedom and equality. Regarded by critics as an innovative dramatist for his implementation of audience participation and theater-in-the-round, Hughes was instrumental in establishing the black drama as a hallmark of American theater.

Hughes was born in Joplin, Missouri, to James Nathaniel and Carrie Mercer Langston Hughes, who separated shortly after their son's birth. His father left the United States for Cuba and later settled in Mexico, where he lived the remainder of his life as a prosperous attorney and landowner. In contrast, Hughes's mother lived a transitory life, often leaving her son in the care of his maternal grandmother while searching for a job. Following his grandmother's death in 1910, Hughes lived with family friends and various relatives in Kansas and, in 1914, joined his mother and new stepfather in Cleveland, Ohio. Hughes attended Central High School, where he excelled academically and athletically. He also wrote poetry and short fiction for the *Belfry Owl,* the high school literary magazine, and edited the school yearbook. In the summer of 1919 Hughes visited his father in Mexico for the first time but soon became disillusioned with his father's materialistic values and contemptuous belief that blacks, Mexicans, and Indians were lazy and ignorant. Upon graduating from high school in 1920, Hughes returned to Mexico. He taught English for a year and wrote poems and prose pieces for publication in *Crisis,* the magazine of the National Association for the Advancement of Colored People. With the help of his father, who had originally urged him to study engineering abroad, Hughes enrolled at Columbia University in New York City in 1921, favoring classes in English literature. Subjected to bigotry on campus—he was assigned the worst dormitory because of his color—and teachers he found boring, Hughes often skipped classes in order to attend shows, lectures, and readings sponsored by the American Socialist Society. After his freshman year, Hughes dropped out of college and worked a series of odd jobs while supporting his mother, who had recently moved to Harlem. Hughes also published several poems in *Crisis* during this period. In 1923 he signed on as a cabin boy on a merchant freighter, the *S. S. McKeesport,* bound for West Africa.

Hughes spent the majority of the following year overseas. After resigning his position on the freighter in the Netherlands, he lived in virtual poverty in France and Italy. Returning to the United States in 1925, he resettled with his mother and half-brother in Washington, D. C. He continued writing poetry while working menial jobs, experimenting with language, form, and rhythms reminiscent of the blues and jazz compositions he had heard in Paris nightclubs. In May and August of 1925, Hughes's verse garnered him literary prizes from both *Opportunity* magazine and *Crisis.* In December, Hughes, then a busboy at a Washington, D. C., hotel, attracted the attention of poet Vachel Lindsay by placing three of his poems on Lindsay's dinner table. Later that evening Lindsay read Hughes's poems to an audience and announced his discovery of a "Negro busboy poet." The next day reporters and photographers eagerly greeted Hughes at work to hear more of his compositions.

Shortly thereafter, with the help of Van Vechten, Hughes published his first book, *The Weary Blues,* a collection of poems that reflect the frenzied atmosphere of Harlem nightlife. In 1927, while enrolled at Lincoln University in Pennsylvania, he met Zora Neale Hurston, with whom he later composed the drama *Mule Bone: A Comedy of Negro Life.* Together with other writers they founded *Fire!,* a literary journal devoted to African-American culture. The venture was unsuccessful, however, and, ironically, a fire eventually destroyed the editorial offices. In the spring of that same year, Hughes published a second collection of verse, *Fine Clothes to the Jew,* in which he included several ballads describing Harlem's lower class. While some black intellectuals felt that Hughes's depiction of crap games, street brawls, and other "unsavory" activities would undermine their efforts to improve race relations, Alain Locke contended that *Fine Clothes to the Jew* "is notable as an achievement in poetic realism in addition to its particular value as a folk study in verse of Negro life." With the support of his literary patron and friend, Mrs. R. Osgood Mason, Hughes wrote his first novel, *Not Without Laughter,* in 1930. Their relationship, however, was severed soon thereafter, when Hughes realized that Mrs. Osgood, an elderly white widow, was determined to dictate what he should write.

Hughes showed some interest in drama as early as 1921 when his first play, *The Gold Piece,* appeared in *The Brownie's Book,* a children's magazine established by American educator W. E. B. Du Bois and the editors of *Crisis.* In 1932 his interest heightened when he joined a group of Harlem artists for a filmmaking venture in Moscow. Though the movie was unsuccessful, Hughes was intrigued by the innovative theater-in-the-round that he encountered in the Soviet cities of Samarkand, Ashkhabad, and Bukhara. Over the next three years he traveled extensively throughout the Soviet Union and the Far East, composing poetry, short stories, essays, and dramas. In an effort to advance his career through the promotion of his recent stories and essays, he went to New York in September 1935; there he was surprised to find that his play, *Mulatto,* was scheduled to open on Broadway the next month. Despite receiving mixed reviews, it ran for a year on Broadway and toured the country for another two seasons, setting an American performance record among plays written by blacks. Considered autobiographical, *Mulatto* interweaves the themes of miscegenation and paternal rejection, a tragic interplay of love and hate culminating in patricide, suicide, and insanity. The best-drawn character, the black woman Cora, is mother to Bert and mistress to Bert's white father, Colonel Norwood. Cora, who loves both men, is ultimately a tragic character, since at the play's end she loses her mind after her son kills his father and then himself. Described by some critics as melodramatic because of its propagandistic oversimplification of racial issues, *Mulatto* is universally commended for its emphasis on the dignity and strength of black Americans in the face of adversity.

In 1938 Hughes, inspired by the success of *Mulatto,* undertook the challenge of establishing the Harlem Suitcase Theater, with unsalaried community actors and technicians. Using the techniques of arena staging he had encountered in the Soviet Union, Hughes premiered *Don't You Want to Be Free?,* an historical play that elicited audience participation and achieved a record of one hundred thirty-five weekend performances in Harlem over a two-year period. Focusing on black America's enslavement, emancipation, continuing persecution, and assimilation into the white working class, the drama ponders a socialist solution to racial and economic problems in America. Like many other young African-American writers of the 1930s and 1940s, including novelist Richard Wright, Hughes saw hope for the oppressed masses—black and white—in the Marxist, proletarian system. Depicting black oppression, *Don't You Want to Be Free?* reveals how the merchants and landlords of the Depression years repeat in variation the practices of slave overseers and plantation owners. By fusing spirituals, jazz, blues, and workers' chants taken from the labor movement, Hughes created a distinctive drama that concludes, unlike *Mulatto,* on an optimistic note with black and white workers united to defeat an oppressive economic and social system. Described by one critic as a kind of "street theater," *Don't You Want To Be Free?* was the inspiration for the black freedom-fighter dramas produced some thirty years later.

By 1938 several of Hughes's plays had been performed by the Gilpin Players of Cleveland's Karamu House. These plays constitute a core of works that developed two of Hughes's major dramatic themes: urban life and black history. For example, in *Little Ham* Hughes exposed the poverty and corruption that lie beneath the comic behavior and amorality of an overcrowded urban community. Peopled with characters living lives of quiet desperation, the drama reveals the insecurities of ghetto blacks and their frustration in dealing with the corrupt white authorities who control them. Likewise, *Soul Gone Home,* a satirical fantasy, centers on the mutual hatred of a mother and her deceased son. Described by Arthur Davis as "macabre and bitter" but "effective," the drama relates the debilitating effect of the urban environment on transplanted rural African Americans unprepared for its deprivations and temptations. In the play a prostitute and her illegitimate son, who has just died from consumption and malnutrition, discuss their impoverished lives. Sustaining a precarious balance between irony and outrage, Hughes portrays a mother who feigns mourning, secretly relieved that her financially burdensome son is now dead. Understated and stark, the play is acclaimed for its simplicity and power. As Webster Smalley has observed, *Soul Gone Home* "bristles with implications and reverberates with connotations."

Hughes achieved dramatic success with his play *Simply Heavenly* in 1957. Based on the character of Jesse B. Semple, the principal figure in four of Hughes's acclaimed books, *Simply Heavenly* satirically and humorously conveys black America's frustration with white oppression and minority stereotyping. An urban-transplanted Southerner, Semple speaks of "Uncle Toms" and "Aunt Thomasinas" in a biting manner, conveying a strategy that African Americans have used to transcend and survive the failure of the American democratic experiment. Critical reception of *Simply Heavenly* has been mixed. While scholars have lauded the play's humorous elements, they have also cited its loss of effectiveness in the transformation of one literary medium to another. In the Semple books, the character overcomes his oppression to become a folk hero; in *Simply Heavenly,* critics have contended, the dramatic action replaces philosophical reflection, reducing Semple to a comic figure who overshadows the play's serious thematic concerns. In a similar drama, *Tambourines to Glory,* Hughes constructed a plot against the background of a storefront church in order to explore the struggle between good and evil. Essie and Laura, the major characters, are strong women—Essie in virtue, Laura in vice. A morality play involving larceny and murder, *Tambourines to Glory,* like Hughes's gospel musicals and Christmas cantata *Black Nativity,* makes use of hymns and spirituals to depict the conflict between love of God and love of money.

Though Hughes's poetry has received greater critical attention, his dramas are one with his verse in theme, structure, and plot. Utilizing the idiom of the ordinary African American of the urban North, his plays appeal to the common people with whom he identified and for whom he wrote. As Davis has observed, Hughes had "great faith in the essential worth and the indomitable spirit of the black man in the street, and this faith comes through in his dramatic works." Even more significant, Hughes was a forerunner of present-day avant-garde playwrights such as Amiri Baraka, Ed Bullins, and Sonia Sanchez who believe in street theater's positive impact and responsibility for showing African Americans an image that reflects the experiences and problems of their own lives. While scholars generally find his plays melodramatic and weak in characterization and dramatic structure, they universally praise Hughes's use of theater as a forum to give immediate and striking voice to the concerns of the black community.

PRINCIPAL WORKS

PLAYS

The Gold Piece 1921
**Mule Bone: A Comedy of Negro Life* [with Zora Neale Hurston] 1930
Scottsboro Limited: Four Poems and a Play in Verse 1932
Little Ham 1935
Mulatto 1935
The Drums of Haiti 1936
Joy to My Soul 1937
Soul Gone Home 1937
Don't You Want to Be Free? 1937
Front Porch 1938
The Sun Do Move 1942
†*Troubled Island* [with William Grant Still] 1949
The Barrier (libretto) 1950
Simply Heavenly 1957
Black Nativity 1961
Gospel Glow 1962
The Emperor of Haiti 1963
Tambourines to Glory 1963 [adapted from his novel *Tambourines to Glory*]
‡*Five Plays by Langston Hughes* 1963
Jericho-Jim Crow 1964
The Prodigal Son 1965

OTHER MAJOR WORKS

"The Negro Artist and the Racial Mountain" (essay) 1926; published in periodical *The Nation*
The Weary Blues (poetry) 1926
Fine Clothes to the Jew (poetry) 1927
Not Without Laughter (novel) 1930
Dear Lovely Death (poetry) 1931
The Negro Mother and Other Dramatic Recitations (poetry) 1931
The Dream Keeper and Other Poems (poetry) 1932
Popo and Fifina: Children of Haiti [with Arna Bontemps] (juvenilia) 1932
The Ways of White Folks (short stories) 1934
A New Song (poetry) 1938
The Big Sea: An Autobiography (autobiography) 1940
Shakespeare in Harlem (poetry) 1942
Freedom's Plow (poetry) 1943
Jim Crow's Last Stand (poetry) 1943
Lament for Dark Peoples and Other Poems (poetry) 1944
Fields of Wonder (poetry) 1947
One Way Ticket (poetry) 1949
Simple Speaks His Mind (short stories) 1950
Montage of a Dream Deferred (poetry) 1951
Laughing to Keep from Crying (short stories) 1952
Simple Takes a Wife (short stories) 1953
The Sweet Flypaper of Life [with Roy De Carava] (nonfiction) 1955
The Langston Hughes Reader (poetry and short stories) 1958
Tambourines to Glory (novel) 1958
Selected Poems of Langston Hughes (poetry) 1959
Ask Your Mama: 12 Moods for Jazz (poetry) 1961
The Best of Simple (short stories) 1961
Something in Common and Other Stories (short stories) 1963
Simple's Uncle Sam (short stories) 1965
The Panther and The Lash: Poems of Our Times (poetry) 1967

*This comedy, completed by Hughes and Hurston in 1930, was first staged in 1991 with a prologue and epilogue by George Houston Bass.

†This work, a musical adaptation of *The Drums of Haiti,* was later revised again as *The Emperor of Haiti.*

‡Included are *Little Ham, Mulatto, Simply Heavenly, Soul Gone Home,* and *Tambourines to Glory.*

OVERVIEWS AND GENERAL STUDIES

Webster Smalley (essay date 1963)

[*An American educator, playwright, and producer, Smalley edited the 1963 edition of* Five Plays, *the first available printed version of Hughes's major dramas. In the following excerpt from his introduction to that work, Smalley assesses* Mulatto, Soul Gone Home, Little Ham, Simply Heavenly, *and* Tambourines to Glory.]

[Langston Hughes] began writing during the Harlem literary renaissance of the twenties and is today, at the age of sixty, America's outstanding Negro man of letters. . . . No writer has better interpreted and portrayed Negro life, especially in the urban North, than Langston Hughes. . . .

From his plays it is evident that Hughes has more and more identified with and written about the Negro community in Harlem. This crowded section of New York City, its vitality and variety, is his favorite setting. . . . (p. vii)

Not all of his writing is about Harlem and its inhabitants, of course. . . . His strong feeling for the Negro race and for the past and present problems of the Negro in America made inevitable his concern with the lot of the Negro in the South. This concern is strongly reflected in his first full-length play, ***Mulatto,*** for which Hughes chose as his subject the still explosive problem of racial intermixture and based the story on the plight of the son of a Negro housekeeper and a white plantation owner. (p. viii)

[***Mulatto***] was Langston Hughes' first professionally produced play and its text appears for the first time in [***Five Plays by Langston Hughes***]. (p. x)

While reading ***Mulatto,*** one should remember when it was written. It is very much a play of the thirties, an era when sociopolitical plays dominated American drama. The tendency was to oversimplify moral issues as in melodrama. . . . In ***Mulatto,*** the injustices suffered by Bert, by Cora, and by all the Negroes in the rural South are clearly and forcefully presented. The thesis is there clearly enough. But then the characters of Bert and Cora begin to dominate the action, and the play becomes something more than mere thesis drama. Bert Lewis, the rebellious son of a white plantation owner and his Negro mistress, is placed in an unhappy, untenable situation, but it is his own stubborn, unbending pride—inherited, ironically, from his father—that brings about his downfall and death. The patient love and rich dignity of Cora and Bert's final recognition of the totality of his tragic situation raise ***Mulatto*** above the level of a mere problem play. One forgives Hughes the sometimes obvious exposition of the opening scenes (as one does the early O'Neill in *Beyond the Horizon*) for the tragedy and power of the play's final scenes. If the reader finds "melodramatic" elements in the play, let him look to the racial situation in the deep South as it is even today: it is melodramatic.

Mulatto is the only play included [in ***Five Plays by Langston Hughes***] in which a white character is more than peripheral. In the other plays, where white characters do appear, they are little more than symbols—evil, good, or, as in the one-act ***Soul Gone Home,*** indifferent. The conception of ***Soul Gone Home*** is that of fantasy, and it contains some ironically comic moments, but its impulse is far removed from comedy. In a vignette-like episode, Hughes creates with great economy the kind of play [French dramatist Émile] Zola called for in his preface to *Thérèse Raquin.* Although a fantasy in concept and structure, its atmosphere and effects are those of naturalism. Like one of Hughes' poems, ***Soul Gone Home*** bristles with implications and reverberates with connotations. That which is unsaid becomes almost more important than what is put into the dialogue. The repressive dominance of the white culture is suggested only by the arrival of ambulance attendants, who are white as the mother knew they would be. The tragedy is that of a people so repressed that they can no longer love, and the ironic implications build to a shocking climax. Its impact is stark and uncomplicated, and it is a difficult play to forget.

Hughes does not always write in a serious vein, as readers of his stories and poems well know. His folk plays of urban Negro life, at once humorous and revealing, are a true contribution to American folk drama. The three included [in ***Five Plays by Langston Hughes***]—***Little Ham, Simply Heavenly,*** and ***Tambourines to Glory***—are, if one must define them, comedies. But the triple specters of poverty, ignorance, and repression can be seen not far beneath the surface of the comedy. The "numbers racket," "dream books," and the "hot goods man" in ***Little Ham,*** Simple's wistful sadness that no Negro has seen a flying saucer, and Laura's attitude toward the "religion business" in ***Tambourines to Glory,*** all indicate the near poverty, the ignorance, and the superstition that prevail in the world of which Hughes writes. Nevertheless, it is a colorful, wonderful world he presents to us, and we cannot but admire the spirit and vigor of his characters. He gives us a dynamic view of a segment of life most of us will never know and can discover nowhere else. At times he may sacrifice dramatic action for the sake of portraying nothing more than the people of Harlem absorbed in living out their lives from day to day, but if the humor of the scene and Hughes' infectious interest in his characters carry us along with him, what more can we ask?

Little Ham, "a play of the roaring twenties," is the first of Hughes' urban folk comedies. Its setting is Harlem at the time of the "Negro Renaissance," of *Shuffle Along,* and of the Cotton Club, but it is unlikely that any of its characters knew the meaning of "renaissance," had seen *Shuffle Along,* or had been inside the Cotton Club (which catered to a white clientele). Completed in 1935, ***Little Ham*** is a period piece, and one should remember the short skirts, tassels, brocades, and bell-shaped trousers of the era as he reads.

The play concerns the affairs (the word is intentionally ambiguous) of Hamlet Jones, a fast-talking, colorful, pint-sized Negro who shines shoes for a living. Little Ham's world is crowded, almost too crowded at times, with Harlemites of every sort except those of conventional respectability and education. It is a lively world, a society of casual morality that the white community either ignores or makes no attempt to understand. Hughes understands it, and this is the Harlem he has made into a literary land exclusively his own. One should not search too hard for profundity in ***Little Ham;*** it is a high-spirited revel and should be accepted as just that. Little Ham, Madam Bell, Lulu, and generously proportioned Tiny Lee are of the Harlem Hughes remembered as a young man, but are persons clearly recognizable today. If the characters in these folk comedies seem uncomplex, it is simply because these people are, in reality, direct and lacking in subtle complexity. Since they are unaware of the existence of Freud and Jung, Hughes has not hampered them with a burden of subconscious motivation.

The dramatic world of Langston Hughes is a quite different world from that of any other playwright, and the discovery of that world is, in itself, an entertaining, wonderful, and enlightening experience.

—Webster Smalley

Hughes creates his characters from life. He does not create character to fit a preconception, so he is not frightened if some of his creations do things and like things that Negroes are reputed to do and like. There is probably no group of people he dislikes more than the "passers" and pretenders of this world. He accepts, loves, and enjoys every aspect of his heritage and has the wisdom to recognize its richness. He does not write for those Negroes who have turned their backs on the spirituals and blues, nor for the people, Negro and white, who would bowdlerize [Mark Twain's] *Huckleberry Finn.* He writes of what he sees, in his own way. (pp. xi-xiii)

Langston Hughes is a most eclectic writer. In his "Simple" books and in his play, ***Simply Heavenly,*** he has created a hero who is almost no hero at all. Jesse Semple, or "Simple," yields to temptation so innocently but means so well, that any audience will forgive him more quickly than does his fiancée. Simple is Hughes' most memorable comic creation. He is of the same dramatic stripe as Figaro in [French dramatist Pierre-Augustin Caron] Beaumarchais' *Figaro's Marriage*—both constantly skirt calamity and get into a good deal of trouble before they finally succeed in marrying the girls they love, and each has a unique dignity in spite of their comic weaknesses. Like his comic compeer, Simple has more than his share of these. His power of reasoning is wonderful to follow, even when his conclusions are unanswerable. . . . Simple, like most of his friends in Paddy's Bar, seldom has much money. What the inhabitants of this "neighborhood club" lack in affluence, they make up for in high spirits and good humor. There are no villains in ***Simply Heavenly***. . . . The values of this play are not built on dramatic clash and suspense, rather, they are inherent in Hughes' intimate and warmly affectionate picture of the unique inhabitants of this city within a city. (p. xiv)

Essie and Laura, in ***Tambourines to Glory,*** are presented as simply and forthrightly as are Ham and Simple, but there is no similarity of character. Essie and Laura are both strong individuals—Essie, in her goodness, and Laura, in her predilection toward chicanery. Symbolically, they represent two very real aspects of all revivalist, perhaps all religious, movements. The saint and the charlatan often live side by side, even in established religions, and sometimes exist in a single personality. Hughes chose to write a rousing musical melodrama about some aspects of Harlem religion. The result is a skillfully created, well-integrated musical play, written with humor, insight, and compassion. (p. xv)

Villains are not plentiful in Hughes' Harlem plays. Big-Eyed Buddy Lomax (who informs us that he is really the Devil) is unique. Even he is a threat only through Laura's weakness for him (and all he represents). Hughes is not as interested in a conventional conflict between protagonist and antagonist as in revealing the cracks in the self-protecting façades humans erect to conceal their weaknesses. His characters are never merely subservient to plot. Thus, even within the confines of melodrama, he is able to write a moving and honest play.

Tambourines to Glory is more than musical melodrama; it is a play of redemption. It is a Faust-like tale, told with the simplicity of a medieval morality play. Hughes tells the story with great good humor, but he never asks us to laugh derisively or to smile sardonically. Behind the laughter is a touch of pity and a great quantity of warm understanding. As broadly and simply as the characters are sketched, they are utterly believable. When they show weakness, their frailties stem directly from problems that plague the average Negro in our largest metropolis. Laura's grasping drive for material things, for example, is a natural reaction to the deprivation and poverty she has suffered all her life, and Essie's honest faith is a triumph over tribulation and temptation. Both characterizations are true.

Finally, this play is in effect a "dramatic song," to use one of Hughes' descriptive terms. It has a pervasive rhythm. The integration of action, original lyrics, traditional spirituals, and the gospel music of Jobe Huntley, adds to the richness of the drama and contributes to characterization. Music is central to the lives—one might say, even to the spiritual being—of these characters. Nowhere has Hughes more skillfully interwoven and integrated music into the fabric of drama. (p. xvi)

The dramatic world of Langston Hughes is a quite different world from that of any other playwright, and the discovery of that world is, in itself, an entertaining, wonderful, and enlightening experience. (p. xvii)

Webster Smalley, in an introduction to Five Plays *by Langston Hughes, edited by Webster Smalley, Indiana University Press, 1963, pp. vii-xvii.*

Darwin T. Turner (essay date 1968)

[An American educator, editor, poet, and author, Tur-

Playbill for the 1957 Broadway production of Simply Heavenly.

ner was a recognized authority on African-American literature. In the essay below, he commends Hughes's contribution to the development of African-American drama but contends that Hughes is not a major American playwright.]

Throughout his professional writing career of forty-six years, Langston Hughes maintained keen interest in the theater. He published his first play, ***The Gold Piece,*** in 1921. In 1935, he had his first Broadway show—***Mulatto,*** which established a record by remaining in production on Broadway longer than any other play which had been written by a Negro. During the Thirties and early Forties, he founded three Negro dramatic groups—The Suitcase Theater in Harlem, the Negro Art Theater in Los Angeles, and the Skyloft Players in Chicago. As late as 1963, Hughes was still polishing ***Emperor of Haiti,*** which had been produced as ***Drums of Haiti*** twenty-seven years earlier.

Langston Hughes took pride in his achievements in the theater. Truly, for a Negro writer, they were remarkable. In addition to the record-setting ***Mulatto*** and ***Simply Heavenly,*** which appeared on Broadway in 1957, he wrote seven other plays which were produced professionally. He also wrote musicals, a movie script, radio drama, a passion play, and the lyrics for the musical version of Elmer Rice's *Street Scene.* Nevertheless, despite his extensive efforts, Hughes never became outstanding as a dramatist. The reasons for his failure are evident in a close examination of his works.

Produced in 1935, but written in 1930, ***Mulatto*** is an emotionally engaging drama, marred by melodrama, propaganda, and crudities common to inexperienced playwrights. Developed from a short story, **"Father and Son,"** ***Mulatto*** dramatizes the conflict between Colonel Norwood, a wealthy white man, and Robert, his "yard child." Since he was seven years old, Robert has hated his father for refusing to recognize their relationship, of which he himself had been proud. During his summer's vacation from college, Robert has strained tension to a breaking point by defying the morés of his father and of the Georgia town in which they live. Finally, on the scheduled day of Bert's return to college, the tension snaps. Incensed to learn that Bert has defied a white woman, has sped past a white man, and has entered the front door of the house regularly, Norwood threatens to kill Bert. Bert kills his father and flees; but, chased by a posse, he returns to the house, where he kills himself.

Much of the power of the play derives from the subject itself. A traditional subject in drama, father-son conflict inevitably generates excitement and frequently produces memorable characters and confrontations: Oedipus and Laertes, Hamlet and Claudius, Theseus and Hippolytus are only a few. In this instance, the excitement was intensified for American audiences by the first professional dramatization of a conflict between a mulatto and his father.

The play gains strength also from Hughes' characterizations of Bert and Cora. Although he is obviously modeled on the proud and noble slaves of Negro literary tradition, Bert is an interesting character. His contempt for other Negroes, his stubborn insistence that he be recognized as a man, and his arrogant defiance of custom symptomize a fatal *hubris.* In his deliberate provocation of trouble, a manifestation of what seems almost a suicidal complex, he anticipates [American author] James Baldwin's protagonist in *Blues for Mr. Charlie,* written a generation later.

Cora too seems a familiar figure from American stories about the antebellum days. At first, she is merely the docile servant who, for many years, has lived with the master, nurtured him, and borne his children without concern for herself and without complaint. After Norwood's death, however, Cora assumes more significant dimensions. Revealing that love had caused her to excuse Norwood's faults and cling to him, she now repudiates him because his death threatens her son, who is even more precious to her. Unfortunately, as Hughes has written the scene, a reader is uncertain whether Cora is insane or is, for the first time, rationally aware of the manner in which she has been abused by Norwood. Regardless of the reason for her transformation, Cora, like all of Hughes' other heroines, appears more carefully delineated and more admirable than the male figures who dominate her life.

Even Colonel Norwood is interesting as a character. Although Hughes, writing protest drama, stereotyped him from racial bigots of his own day and slave masters of the previous century, Norwood gains reality in his final confrontation with Bert. Transcending racial identity, he becomes, like Hughes' own father, a man in conflict with his son. When Norwood cannot pull the trigger of his gun to kill Bert, Bert strangles him. Although Bert could only wonder why Norwood did not fire, a reader suspects, romantically perhaps, that, at the critical moment, Norwood realized that Bert was actually his flesh and blood, not merely a "yard child" whom he could ignore.

Despite the subject and the interesting characterizations of Bert and Cora, the play is weak artistically in plot structure, language, and thought. From the moment of Norwood's death, the action moves with the rapidity and inexorability of Greek tragedy. Prior to the death, however, it too frequently seems painfully slow and digressive. For example, Bert's sister Sally appears in Act I, talks, and then leaves for college. Rather than contributing to the plot or background, she merely distracts the reader, who puzzles about the reason for her existence. One can almost argue artistic justification for the play's producer, who revised the play to cause Sally to miss her train in the first act and be raped in the third. Even though the producer was motivated by the commercial possibilities of sensationalism, he at least provided dramatic reason for Sally's presence and carried to their logical conclusion hints which Hughes planted casually and forgot.

Hughes forgot some other matters in the drama. From the opening scene onward, he reiterated the fact that Norwood does not permit Negroes to use the front door. Negro servants who haul a huge trunk down the front hall steps are required to carry it out the back door. When Norwood learns that Bert frequently enters through the front door, he threatens to break Bert's neck. Nevertheless, only a few moments after Norwood has voiced his threat, a Negro servant helps his master enter through the front door and leave through the same portal. Nothing in the stage directions indicates that Norwood pays any attention to this dark transgression of his hallowed sill.

Because Hughes was a talented poet, it is difficult to understand his apparent insensitivity to language and to effective usage in ***Mulatto.*** His faults are various. "Kid" and "old man" seem inappropriate slang for rural Georgia of the early 1930's. Even more incongruous is the use of "papa." Norwood slapped seven-year-old Bert for calling him "papa." One wonders how the word came into Bert's vocabulary since no one else in the play uses it. Cora uses "daddy" and "pappy." Bert's brother says, "Pa." Norwood says, "Pappy." Even Bert himself fails to use the counterpart when addressing his mother. He calls her, "Ma."

Other words are questionable. It is doubtful that a Southerner would use "lynching" to describe an activity in which he participated. It is improbable that Norwood would emphasize his own immorality by calling his son a bastard. It is unnecessary for the overseer to inform the audience that he will form a posse from *white* men.

Quibbling about words may seem petty criticism of a writer. Nevertheless, one assumes that a poet, more than other writers perhaps, would exercise care in selecting words. Occasionally but too infrequently, Hughes demonstrated ability to use language effectively when he chose to. The most appealing scene in the play is that in which Cora, in a monologue, recalls her early relationship with Norwood. The speech rings true in every respect. It is colloquial, faithfully representative of the dialect of Southern Negroes, and poetic. Hughes also demonstrated incisive use of language in the ironic moment at which a Negro servant, disregarding Norwood's five Negro children, agrees with a white undertaker's assertion that Norwood had no relatives.

Part of Hughes' difficulty with language resulted from his desire to be certain that spectators understood the full implications of the characters' statements. In order to assure himself that no one would miss the point, Hughes sometimes overstated it. For example, Norwood, explaining his financial security, says that he has "a few thousand put away." A wealthy man who is not boasting would probably say merely that he has a few *dollars* put away. But Hughes wanted the spectator to realize Norwood's wealth. Similarly, Higgins, a white man, says, "All this postwar propaganda on the radio about freedom and democracy—why the niggers think it's meant for them." Psychologically, the statement is false. A bigot would not verbalize his awareness of a difference between the condition of the Negro and America's promise to its citizens. In fact, he probably would not be aware of any difference. But Hughes, using a white man as mouthpiece, wanted to emphasize the discrepancy in the minds of his audience.

Finally, in ***Mulatto,*** Hughes slipped into improbable contradictions which sometimes are amusing. For instance, to emphasize the sacredness of the Colonel's library, Cora says that even she has never been permitted to enter it in thirty years. Surely someone, however, cleaned the room at least once during that time. Certainly, Colonel Norwood was not a man to clean and dust a room; certainly also, the individual who most probably would be assigned the task would be Cora, the most trusted servant.

Not amusing, but even more improbable, is the picture of life in the Norwood house. Except for allusions to contemporary personalities and inventions, one might assume that the story was set in the antebellum South. For instance, there is never any mention of paying the servants. Surely, however, most working Negroes in Georgia in 1930 at least touched the money they earned even if they immediately handed it on to a creditor.

Little Ham, written during the Thirties, is set in the Harlem Renaissance of the Twenties. Webster Smalley [in ***Five Plays by Langston Hughes,*** 1963] has described it as a folk comedy. To a Negro reader, however, it is a slow-moving, frequently dull, artificial attempt to present within a single play all of the exotic elements which distinguish life in Harlem from life in the rest of America. Here, jumbled together like the animals in a box of animal crackers, are shoe shiners, beauticians, numbers runners, homosexuals, West Indians, followers of Father Divine, gangsters, middle-class Negroes. They cut, shoot, drink, make love, gossip, play numbers, flirt, but rarely utter a significant thought.

The slight and confused story, better suited for musical comedy where it might be obscured by attractive songs and dances, recounts the adventures of Hamlet Hitchcock Jones, a "sporty" ladies' man. When Little Ham, who flirts with all women, meets fat Tiny Lee, a beauty parlor owner, his conversation ends in a promise to escort her to a Charleston contest the following evening. Soon afterwards, he purchases a stolen coat for his new girlfriend, wins $645 playing the numbers and is given a job as a number runner. When he visits Tiny at her shop, he is surprised to find Mattie Bea, his married girlfriend, who, expecting to accompany him, bought the contest tickets which Ham has given to Tiny and who believes that Ham will give her the stolen coat which he has already given to Tiny. When she discovers the true situation, she attacks Tiny; but Ham is arrested by the police, who assume that he is beating her. Later, Gilbert, Tiny's former boyfriend, visits her apartment to take her to the Charleston contest. His efforts are interrupted by the arrival of Ham, who has secured his release from jail by charming a female judge. To forestall trouble, Tiny hides Gilbert in a closet and locks him in. Still later, at the dance, Mattie Bea and Gilbert, both arriving late, threaten to continue their quarrels with Tiny and Ham. Coincidentally, however, it is revealed that Mattie Bea and Gilbert are husband and wife. Finding themselves together for a change, they become reconciled, and all the couples participate in a frenzied Charleston contest, which is won by Ham and Tiny.

A play with such insignificant action needs to be redeemed by characterization, language, humor, or thought. ***Little Ham,*** unfortunately, is weak in each of these.

The language probably is the most effective element of the play. In the Harlem dialect and slang, with which he was familiar, Hughes wrote more freely and more accurately than in ***Mulatto.*** The language constitutes a significant source for the humor of the play. Hughes wrote effective quips: "She is just a used blade, and I got a new razor"; "I don't duel, I duke"; "love is taking 'til you can't give no mo." Hughes also drew comedy from the strangeness of the Harlem dialect—"she-self," "perzactly"—and from such malapropisms as "reverted" (instead of "converted") and "prostitution" (instead of "prostration").

Like [African-American author] Zora Neale Hurston he assumed that non-Negro audiences would be amused by the colorful language of Negroes, especially the language of invective. This is effectively illustrated by Tiny's tirade directed towards Mattie Bea:

> TINY. I'm a real good mama that can shake your peaches down. . . . I hear you cluckin', hen, but your nest must be far away. Don't try to lay no eggs in here.

Unfortunately, however, some of the expressions already had been overworked by the time Hughes wrote the play. Now they seem hackneyed: "I'm from Alabam, but I don't give a damn"; "God don't love ugly."

Hughes based his comedy almost as much on slapstick actions and situations, such as that in which Gilbert, locked inside a closet, quarrels with and shoots at Ham, who is outside. Hughes found humor in low comedy, such as the ridicule of the effeminate movements and cowardice of a homosexual and Tiny's accidental burning the head of a middle-class woman who is her client. In general, the comedy is heavy rather than subtle.

The characterization too is heavy and stereotypic. Ham is a wise-cracking, fast-talking ladies' man. Tiny is fat, pleasant, and undistinguished. The other characters are such obvious types that Hughes frequently did not even name them. They are listed merely as "West Indian," "Staid Lady," "Youth," "Shabby Man," etc.

The action is heavily foreshadowed and overly dependent upon chance and coincidence. For example, the complicated love triangles of Tiny and Ham are eased by the improbable coincidence that their former lovers are married to each other. Motivation is puzzling. For example, although love is reputed to work marvels, a critical reader might wonder what attracts Ham to Tiny. Is he enchanted by her money, or is he conquered by her dominance? Without the necessary explanation, the incongruous pairing seems comic rather than sentimental.

Although serious ideas do not intrude upon the apparently continuous gaiety of the Harlemites, shadows of a troubled world appear at the edge of the gay and the comic. Such a shadow is the pathetic joy of the Shabby Man, who has secured a job for the first time in two years. Such a shadow appears in the wish-fantasies and self-delusions of the numbers players who, praying for the one wonderful windfall, overlook the vast sums which they are dribbling away by daily dimes and quarters. Shadowy too are social protests: a janitor's complaint about long hours, the silence of Madam Lucille and Ham when police, without a warrant, search the shoe shine parlor for evidence of gambling.

Don't You Want To Be Free? also written in the Thirties, is a poetic drama—or, more appropriately, a pageant—which traces the history of the American Negro from the original enslavement to the Depression. The scenes are predictable—a slave auction, a slave rebellion which ends in massacre. Nevertheless, effective narration provides pride for Negro spectators by recounting Negroes who struggled for freedom—Nat Turner, Denmark Vesey, Harriet Tubman, Sojourner Truth. Furthermore, Hughes effectively underscored the emotion by using lyrics and melodies of spirituals and the blues. A product of the Thirties, however, the pageant overemphasizes a call for a uniting of the workers of the world. In language and in thought, the play was the most artistic which Hughes had written, but its obvious aiming at a Negro audience made it unsuitable for commercial production on Broadway.

The Sun Do Move (1942) echoes, expands, individualizes, and dramatizes the thought which was narrated in ***Don't You Want To Be Free?*** After two Negro porters strip to reassume their identity as Africans, the play begins with the auction of two young Africans, Rock and Mary. After a period of time Rock is sold before he has time to see the birth of his child. On the new plantation, he becomes friends with Frog and resists the advances of Bellinda,

Hughes with Nicolás Guillén, Mikhail Koltzov, and Ernest Hemingway, Madrid, 1937.

who has been chosen as his new mate. When they attempt to escape, Frog is killed and Rock is recaptured. Meanwhile, on the other plantation, Mary, Rock's wife, has reared their son. When Little Rock attempts to protect his mother from her mistress's brutality, he is sent to another plantation, where he dies. Escaping again, Rock this time reaches Mary and, with her, flees to the North, where, assisted by Quakers, they become free.

Despite structural weaknesses caused by cinematic flashes from scenes of Rock to those of Mary or Little Rock and despite Hughes' characteristic interpolations of irrelevant low comedy, the play is much more forceful and dramatically interesting than the earlier one. The dispassionate historicity of the pageant is emotionalized by Hughes' focus upon Mary and Rock, struggling to live as human beings rather than chattel.

Simply Heavenly (1957), designed for the commercial theater, reached Broadway in a state weaker than ***Simple Takes a Wife,*** the book upon which the play was based. The major sufferer in the adaptation is Jesse B. Semple himself. In the tales and dialogues of the Simple books, Jess assumes the dimensions of a folk hero. Even though he drinks, cavorts with women, has difficulty paying rent, talks ungrammatically and excessively, his foibles never detract from his dignity; for, like the Greek gods and the heroes of various myths, he is larger than life. It may be appropriate even to say that he, like Joseph Conrad's Kurtz, is remembered primarily as a voice, in this instance a voice which utters common sense even when the speaker seems emotional and illogical. Reduced to actable dimensions, however, Simple, losing his grandeur, shrinks into a more sincere, more conservative, and more thoughtful Ham. In the play, he peeks beneath his legs to watch Joyce, his fiancée, change clothes; he turns somersaults; he is thrown from a car to land on his "sit-downer"; he is propped comically in a hospital bed with his legs in traction; sentimentally and pathetically, he tries to reform and to win Joyce. In short, Simple's reality as the embodied spirit of the Negro working class is reduced to the Harlem barfly; the Chaplinesque Comic Hero shrinks to a farcical fall guy of the pattern of Stan Laurel and Lou Costello.

The second major injury resulting from the transformation from the book to the play is suffered by the material itself. Even though incidents occur in the book, they generally serve merely as acceptable devices to generate Simple's philosophizing. Consequently, what matters is not what happens but what reaction it stimulates from Simple. For a Broadway musical, however, it was necessary to emphasize action and to minimize Simple's reflections. As a result, undue attention is given to Simple's unsuccessful efforts to seduce Joyce, to the Watermelon Man's pursuit of Mamie, and to the domestic difficulties of Bodidilly and Arcie.

Judged merely in its own terms, however, without reference to the Simple material which it distorts and cheapens, ***Simply Heavenly*** is vastly superior to ***Little Ham.*** Simple is more likable than Ham. Joyce and Zarita are less grotesque than Tiny, whose type reappears in Mamie, a secondary lead.

Similarly, the ideas of ***Simply Heavenly*** have significance missing from ***Little Ham,*** where Harlemites seemed to concern themselves only with numbers, gossip, parties, sex, and killing. In fact, the differences in ***Simply Heavenly*** underscore the fact that ***Little Ham*** was intended as a commercial exploitation of Harlem's exoticism rather than as a presentation of its actuality. In ***Simply Heavenly,*** the people occupy the same socio-economic level as those in ***Little Ham;*** they take interest in numbers, gossip, parties, and sex; but they also think and talk about racial problems, economic problems, and domestic problems.

Hughes reacted sensitively to the allegation that he had stereotyped the characters of his earlier books and plays. When a middle-class man says that the denizens of Paddy's bar are stereotypes, Mamie, defender of the race, answers furiously:

> Why, it's getting so colored folks can't do nothing no more without some other Negro calling you a stereotype. Stereotype, hah! If you like a little gin, you're a stereotype. You got to drink Scotch. If you wear a red dress, you're a stereotype. You got to wear beige or chartreuse. Lord have mercy, honey, do-don't like no blackeyed peas and rice! Then you're a down-home Negro for true—which I is—and proud of it! I didn't come here to Harlem to get away from my people. I come here because there's more of 'em. I loves my race. I loves my people. Stereotype!

Nevertheless, it is true that Hughes generally created stereotypes. Ham, Tiny, Robert Norwood, Cora Norwood—all are stereotypes. Even in ***Simply Heavenly,*** Hughes clung to gross, time-honored models. Joyce is a loving but prim heroine, who probably will become a shrew. A good-hearted, fun-loving girl, who wears her morals loosely, Zarita is from a tradition as old as literature itself.

Both comedy and language seem improved in ***Simply Heavenly.*** In addition to writing better quips, Hughes, writing lyrics for songs, was able to display his poetic talent more persuasively than in earlier plays. Using the contemporary idiom of Harlem, he created a free and natural dialogue, sometimes rising to colloquial eloquence, as in Simple's recollection of his aunt's efforts to reform him.

Despite the improvement, Hughes continued to relish sentimentality and farce which too frequently detracts from the reality of the characters. For example, it is difficult to believe Boyd's honesty when he describes Simple's crying at night.

During the Sixties, Hughes worked on his two best plays—***Emperor of Haiti*** and ***Tambourines to Glory. Emperor of Haiti*** was a generation old. Hughes first presented it as ***Drums of Haiti*** (1936), rewrote it as ***Troubled Island,*** an opera, revised it further, and completed his final revisions in 1963, shortly before he presented a script to the Schomburg Collection in Harlem.

Emperor of Haiti is the story of Jean-Jacques Dessalines' progress from slave to emperor to corpse. Beginning during the Haitian blacks' rebellion against their French masters and treating historical fact freely, the play focuses on the economic and personal problems of Dessalines' rule as emperor. Economically, the kingdom suffers because Dessalines refuses to require labor from the liberated blacks. When he finally realizes the need, they turn against him. Personally, Dessalines fails in Hughes' play because, after becoming emperor, he rejects his uneducated wife Azelea, who loves him. In her place, he takes Claire Heureuse, a pawn of the mulattoes who seeks to overthrow him. The play climaxes and ends when, riding to crush a rebellion, Dessalines is killed in the trap set by mulattoes. Melodramatically, Azelea, now a penniless street seller, discovers his body and mourns his death while Claire flees with her mulatto lover and two passing Haitians fail to recognize their emperor.

The play has artistic and historical flaws. As in much of Hughes' drama, low comic relief is overworked while the plot lags. For instance, prior to the climactic arrival of Dessalines at the trap, street sellers talk and joke interminably. Furthermore, history is distorted. Although Toussaint is mentioned, the play suggests that Dessalines is the only leader of the slaves' rebellion. Moreover, Dessalines' character is given a moral bath. The libertinism which characterized Dessalines after his becoming emperor is reduced to his affair with Claire Heureuse.

Nevertheless, the historical events provided Hughes with plot, thought, and character superior to those which generally emerged from his imagination. Although Azelea is perhaps idealized as a devoted, self-sacrificing wife, Dessalines is well-drawn, even in outline.

Hughes' final play, ***Tambourines to Glory,*** was adapted from his novel of the same name. It is a modernized morality play and, as such, is surprisingly good. To make money, Laura Reed, a gay girl like Zarita, persuades staid, religious Essie Johnson to join her in establishing a church. They are assisted and protected by Big-Eyed Buddy Lomax, who actually is the Devil. Gradually Laura slips further and further into sin as Buddy's mistress. She swells membership by giving tips on numbers; she sells tap water as holy water. Vainly, she tries to thwart Buddy's pursuit of Gloria, a singer, and Marietta, Essie's teen-aged niece. Finally, fearing him, Laura stabs Buddy. Essie is arrested but released when Laura confesses. Laura is charged with self-defense.

There is more development in this plot than in any Hughes had written previously; and, although the action is tinged with melodrama, it is free from the irrelevant comedy and improbable coincidence which characterize most of Hughes' work. The characters are not new, but they are smoothly delineated—perhaps because Hughes' frequent recreation of the same types enabled him to know them fully. As has been explained, Laura is modeled after Zarita, and Essie is a quieter, more mature, less attractive Joyce.

More than in any work since ***Don't You Want To Be Free?*** Hughes used poetry to develop thought. Instead of being entertaining diversions, as in ***Simply Heavenly,*** the lyrics of the songs explain the motivation and personalities of the characters. For example, Laura sings her love for Buddy; Buddy sings the blues characterizing life in Harlem; Marietta sings her purity.

Perhaps the chief reason for Hughes' success is that the musical morality play permitted him to display his major talents without straining the credulity of the audience. Stereotyped characters and heavy underlining of ideas are accepted in morality plays, and colloquial poetry and broad comedy have a place in musicals.

As Webster Smalley has pointed out, Langston Hughes must be credited with establishing several all-Negro professional dramatic groups. In doing so, he contributed significantly to the development of drama among Negroes. In his own work, however, even though he continued to write and to be produced through two generations, he never developed the artistry of [African-American dramatists] Louis Peterson or Lorraine Hansberry. Least successful when he catered to the predictable taste of Broadway audiences, he was most artistic when he wrote simply and lyrically of the history and aspirations of Negroes. (pp. 297-309)

Darwin T. Turner, "Langston Hughes as Playwright," in CLA Journal, *Vol. XI, No. 4, June, 1968, pp. 297-309.*

An excerpt from "The Negro Artist and the Racial Mountain" (1926)

We younger Negro artists who create now intend to express our individual dark-skinned selves without fear or shame. If white people are pleased, we are glad. If they are not, it doesn't matter. We know we are beautiful. And ugly too. The tom-tom cries and the tom-tom laughs. If colored people are pleased we are glad. If they are not, their displeasure doesn't matter either. We build our temples for tomorrow, strong as we know how, and we stand on top of the mountain, free within ourselves.

Langston Hughes, as quoted by Dudley Randall in The Black Aesthetic, *edited by Addison Gayle, Jr., Doubleday and Co., 1971.*

Edward J. Mullen (essay date 1986)

[Mullen is an American educator who has written several works on African-Cuban literature. In the following excerpt, he surveys Hughes's dramatic output, noting his plays' mixed critical reception.]

Although Langston Hughes's contributions in the area of poetry and prose fiction have received the most critical attention, his work in the theater was extraordinarily rich and varied and meant a great deal to him personally. Although he never achieved the reputation of a major American playwright, his output was considerable. He wrote nine full-length plays (***Mulatto, Little Ham, Troubled Island, When the Jack Hollers, Joy to My Soul, Front Porch, The Sun Do Move, Simply Heavenly,*** and ***Tambourines to Glory***), two one-act plays (***Soul Gone Home*** and ***Don't You Want to Be Free?***), four gospel song-plays (***Gospel Glow, Black Nativity, Jericho-Jim Crow,*** and ***The Prodigal Son***), and more than twenty other scripts for opera, radio, and film.

In spite of the lukewarm critical reception of many of his plays and a seemingly endless series of personal traumas associated with his work in the theater (especially the rift with [African-American dramatist] Zora Neale Hurston over the authorship of ***Mule Bone*** and the legal entanglements related to the production of ***Mulatto***), Hughes did achieve a number of real commercial successes.

Langston's interest in the theater began early in his youth; while living in Topeka, Kansas, his mother took him to plays such as *Buster Brown, Under Two Flags,* and *Uncle Tom's Cabin.* As Faith Berry reports [in *Langston Hughes: Before and Beyond Harlem,* 1983], "When most pre-teen boys in Lawrence were playing ball, Langston Hughes was going to the theater. The interest in plays, which he had acquired from his mother, soon developed into a favorite diversion." His apprenticeship in the theater was a long one stretching back to the summer of 1926 when he wrote lyrics for a projected revue, *O Blues,* which, although it never materialized, provided Hughes with invaluable experience in theater production and put him in touch with important practitioners of the art. That same year in **"The Negro Artist and the Racial Mountain,"** he spoke directly about the emergence of a black theater:

> Now I await the rise of the Negro theater. Our folk music, having achieved world-wide fame, offers itself to the genius of the great individual American Negro composer who is to come. And within the next decade I expect to see the work of a growing school of colored artists who paint and model the beauty of dark faces and create with new technique the expressions of their own soul-world. And the Negro dancers who will dance like Flame and the singers who will continue to carry our songs to all who listen—they will be with us in even greater numbers tomorrow.

His work in theater paralleled his activities in other areas, and he frequently borrowed thematic material from his poems, short stories, and novels and rewrote it as plays. ***Mulatto*** and ***Tambourines to Glory*** are cases in point. His first play, entitled ***The Gold Piece,*** appeared in 1921 in *The Brownie's Book,* a magazine for children established by [African-American educator and author] W. E. B. Du Bois and the editors of *Crisis.* In addition to writing plays, Hughes also founded three important dramatic groups: the Suitcase Theater in Harlem, the Negro Art Theater in Los Angeles, and the Skyloft Players in Chicago.

Critical reaction to Hughes's work as a dramatist is sketchy and, when compared to his work in other genres, appears almost nonexistent. This may be explained by the fact that, until the appearance of Webster Smalley's 1963 edition of ***Five Plays by Langston Hughes,*** no printed versions of his plays were available. Smalley's edition contains the texts of five plays: ***Mulatto, Soul Gone Home, Little Ham, Simply Heavenly,*** and ***Tambourines to Glory.*** Smalley's introduction, although not a book-length critical study, effectively highlights Hughes's role as one of the premier interpreters of black urban life in North America. Although Hughes's work did not have the full impact of a text like [African-American author Richard] Wright's *Native Son,* it nonetheless conveyed in a powerful and direct way a sense of life in black urban America.

It is important to note that five of Hughes's plays were written during the thirties—a turbulent period in his life and a time when he received few accolades from white or black critics. His first play, ***Mulatto,*** based on the miscegenation theme and on Hughes's short story, "**"Father and Son,**" was a commercial but not an artistic success. It opened on Broadway on 24 October 1935 and had the longest run of any play by a black author until the production of [African-American dramatist] Lorraine Hansberry's *A Raisin in the Sun* broke the record in 1959. Initial critical response was spotty and Hughes was frequently accused of artlessness. Brooks Atkinson's review of ***Mulatto*** for the *New York Times* is a telling document:

> To judge by ***Mulatto*** Mr. Hughes has little of the dramatic strength of mind that makes it possible for a writer to tell a coherent, driving story in the theatre. His ideas are seldom completely expressed; his play is pretty thoroughly defeated by the grim mechanics of the stage. What gives it a sobering sensation in spite of its artlessness is the very apparent earnestness of Mr. Hughes's state of mind. He is writing about the theme that lies closest to his heart.

Edith J. R. Isaacs, writing in *Theatre Arts Monthly,* echoed much the same view:

> More, too, might have been expected of ***Mulatto,*** a drama by Langston Hughes, who is a good poet and a leader in negro [*sic*] affairs. In this first play he is concerned with the state of the negro [*sic*] in the south today—a problem that welcomes restatement by a man who knows his subject through training and sympathies. Unquestionably negro [*sic*] life in the south is today little less complex than it ever was; the negroes [*sic*] in ***Mulatto*** are, as they have ever been, "someone to rape or to lynch," "good for workin' and lovin' "—good for nothing else. So far, the picture is searing; what destroys its effectiveness is Mr. Hughes' weak, amateurish writing, and the unvarnished fact that the negro [*sic*] protagonist is as ingrate and obnoxious as the villainous whites believe. When Mr. Hughes has his next play produced, he should make sure that Rose McClendon is again present. After what seemed like a heedless beginning—actually a thoughtful statement of the character's submissive, selfless quality—Miss McClendon's rare sensitivity and beautiful voice made her scenes glow like bright lights in shoddy surroundings.

In his *Black Drama* Loften Mitchell described the opening of the play in the following terms: "Teeth gnashed and people squirmed when Langston Hughes' ***Mulatto*** opened on Broadway in 1934. Many critics complained that the play was too realistic, too bitter and too hostile. Nevertheless, audiences flocked to it, and the play enjoyed a long run."

More recent critical reaction is mixed. Darwin Turner [in his "Langston Hughes as Playwright," *CLA Journal* 11 (June 1968)] considers that the play is "weak artistically in plot, structure, language, and thought," and Webster Smalley warns readers that ***Mulatto*** "is very much a play of the thirties, an era when sociopolitical plays dominated American drama." Doris E. Abramson is considerably more sympathetic, noting [in her *Negro Playwrights in the American Theater 1925-1959,* 1969] that "there is a universality about ***Mulatto*** that other plays of the period lack." In an engaging comparison of Hughes's play with Edward Sheldon's *The Nigger* ("Miscegenation on Broadway: Hughes' ***Mulatto*** and Edward Sheldon's *The Nigger*"), Richard K. Barksdale adds another link in the chain of evidence supporting a critical reappraisal of ***Mulatto*** as a play rich in psychological nuances.

Don't You Want to Be Free?, a folk pageant that traced the history of the American black from slavery to the depression, was Hughes's second most successful drama of the 1930s. Produced by the Harlem Suitcase Theater (1937-38), it was performed 135 times in two years, making it one of the longest running plays in Harlem during Hughes's lifetime. In 1938 Edward Lawson [in "Theater in a Suitcase," *Opportunity* 26 (December 1938)] spoke of

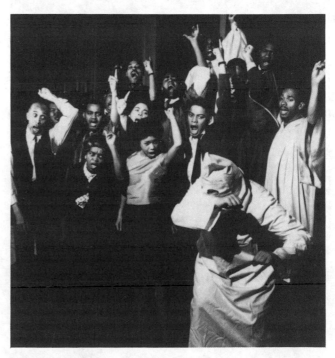

A scene from the 1964 production of the gospel drama Jericho-Jim Crow.

it enthusiastically as an "interesting compendium of poetry, song, and drama combined in a manner that is engagingly new." His views were not shared by contemporary critics. Hilda Lawson [in her disstertation "The Negro in American Drama," 1939] felt that Hughes overstated the facts of black life in order to support his thesis that "the overseer of slave days still confronts the Negro in every phase of his present life," and Norman MacLeod [in "The Poetry and Argument of Langston Hughes," *Crisis* 46 (1938)] concluded that "Unfortunately, however, ***Don't You Want to Be Free?***—even as a sustained piece of 'agit-prop' writing does not reach the level of Langston Hughes' best work or approximate the excellence we have come to expect of him."

Although Darwin Turner concedes that "in language and in thought the play was the most artistic which Hughes had written, its obvious aiming at a Negro audience made it unsuitable for commercial production on Broadway." Doris E. Abramson is considerably more positive, crediting Hughes's blending of poetry and drama with raising "agit-prop" "to a rare level of literary value."

One other play from this period merits review—***Emperor of Haiti.*** First presented as ***Drums of Haiti*** (1936), Hughes rewrote it as an opera, ***Troubled Island,*** and further revised it in 1963 as ***Emperor of Haiti,*** Turner noted that the play has both artistic and historical flaws: "As in much of Hughes's drama, low comic relief is overworked while plot lags." Hughes's reputation as a dramatist was heightened by Helene Keyssar's detailed reevaluation of this play. In her study, *The Curtain and The Veil: Strategies in Black Drama* (1981), she expanded upon and refined some of Darwin Turner's earlier assessments of ***The Emperor of Haiti,*** Keyssar argued that, by employing one of the oldest tricks of drama, that of historical distance, Hughes was able in ***The Emperor of Haiti*** to confront a complex of issues that no contemporary American location could contain. He was thus able to seduce both black and white viewers to a recognition of persons who might otherwise have been dismissed as abhorrent, unbelievable, or both.

Evelyn Quita Craig [in her *Black Drama of the Federal Theater Era,* 1980] further enriched Hughes's reputation as a dramatist through the discovery of a script entitled ***Troubled Island*** that Hughes had submitted to the Federal Theater. An examination of scripts indicates that it is based on ***Emperor of Haiti*** (originally ***Drums of Haiti***) and that it is "a brilliantly polished version of the former." Craig writes, "***Troubled Island*** flows more smoothly, concentrates more sharply on essentials, and is usually more brilliantly, wittily, or poetically phrased than ***Emperor of Haiti.***"

In the last two decades of his life Hughes turned away from serious drama and concentrated on musicals, often rewriting and adapting his fiction to the popular stage. For example, ***Simple Takes a Wife*** was transformed into ***Simply Heavenly,*** which enjoyed a brief run on Broadway in 1957. Similarly, ***Tambourines to Glory,*** based on the novel of the same name, had a short run at New York's Little Theater in November 1963. Although Turner considers ***Tambourines*** to be one of Hughes's stronger plays, it was unfavorably reviewed in the popular press. Hughes's greatest success appears to have been the gospel song-play, a genre that permitted him greater flexibility as a writer and allowed him to use poetry. ***Black Nativity*** (1961), a gospel song-play first performed at New York's 41st Street Theater, was extraordinarily successful both in the United States and Europe. Writing in the *Nation,* Robert Shelton reported:

> ***Black Nativity*** has taken the volcanic energy of Negro gospel music and channeled it skillfully toward theatrical ends. It has already introduced new audiences to gospel music in Spoleto, London and seven other European centers. It will return to the Continent for six months and tour the United States for forty weeks. There is even some talk of taking it to Russia and Eastern Europe.

For a complex set of reasons, such as the state of the black theater in the twenties and thirties, the explosive nature of the race question itself, and his inability to adapt forms that had originated as poems or short stories (***Mulatto*** and ***Scottsboro Limited*** are cases in point), Hughes never achieved the same critical acclaim for his playwriting that he did for his poetry and prose fiction. In addition, there is the question of his reputation as a poet, which seemed to haunt him critically. Thought of primarily as a poet, his work in other genres seemed necessarily to pale in comparison. Once during the production of ***Tambourines to Glory*** in 1963 he remarked to Lewis Nichols, drama critic for the *New York Times,* that "I keep going back to poetry to make a living."

Despite their reservations, however, Hughes's critics have noted the enormous variety of dramatic form and situation in his plays and credit him with being one of the fountainheads for what was to be called in the 1970s "Black Theater." In his 1971 doctoral dissertation, "Langston Hughes as American Dramatist," Edwin Leon Coleman offered the following assessment:

> Hughes' contribution to the theatre, then, lies in the fact that his plays, while representing a personal growth, also parallel the development of the Civil Rights movement in the United States and the flowering of the black cultural philosophy. Besides his dual role as the progenitor for many black artists today and spokesman for his race, Hughes has served as an educator for white audiences who are unfamiliar with the world of the ghetto. He has given to all a realistic portrait of a segment of America, and in a pluralistic society it is vital that each part know what the other is thinking and feeling and wanting. This was Hughes' gift.

(pp. 22-7)

Edward J. Mullen, in an introduction to Critical Essays on Langston Hughes, *edited by Edward J. Mullen, G. K. Hall & Co., 1986, pp. 1-35.*

MULE BONE

PRODUCTION REVIEWS

Henry Louis Gates, Jr. (review date 10 February 1991)

[In the following preview of Mule Bone, *American educator and noted critic Gates anticipates the drama's debut by detailing its background. Noting that Hughes and Hurston considered the play "the first real Negro folk comedy," Gates laments the long delay in its production, pondering the effect the drama might have had on black theater if it had been produced in the early 1930s.]*

For a people who seem to care so much about their public image, you would think blacks would spend more energy creating the conditions for the sort of theater and art they want, rather than worrying about how they are perceived by the larger society. But many black people still seem to believe that the images of themselves projected on television, film and stage must be policed and monitored from within. Such convictions are difficult—even painful—to change. And never more so than in the case of ***Mule Bone,*** the controversial 1930 Langston Hughes-Zora Neale Hurston play that is only now being produced for the first time, almost 60 years to the day after it was originally scheduled to open.

Why should a folk comedy about the residents of a small Florida town in the 1920's cause such anxiety? Because of its exclusive use of black vernacular as the language of drama.

In analyzing the discomfort ***Mule Bone*** has aroused over the decades, the playwright Ntozake Shange has said that Hurston's language "always made black people nervous because it reflects rural diction and syntax—the creation of a different kind of English."

"Are we still trying to figure out what is real about ourselves that we know about that makes it too dangerous to say it in public?" she asked.

Ms. Shange was speaking at a 1988 forum at Lincoln Center at which the play was read and the merits of staging it debated—"in a post-Tawana Brawley decade," as the theater's artistic director, Gregory Mosher, put it. Few occasions have brought together more prominent black actors, directors, writers and critics than that November reading: the actors Ruby Dee, Paul Winfield, Giancarlo Esposito and Joe Morton, and the playwrights Ed Bullins and Ron Milner were among the nearly 100 people present, along with Hughes's biographer, Arnold Rampersad, the literary executor of the Hughes estate, George Houston Bass, who died last September, and myself.

As each speaker commented, often passionately, it seemed incredible that the debate was occurring in the first place. Why would anyone believe there are still aspects of black culture that should be hidden because they are somehow "embarrassing"?

Mule Bone is a revelation of life "behind the veil," in the words of [African-American educator and author] W. E. B. Du Bois. It portrays what black people say and think and feel—when no white people are around—in a highly metaphorical and densely lyrical language that is as far removed from minstrelsy as a Margaux is from Ripple. It was startling to hear the play read aloud and enjoyed by actors who weren't even alive when it was written. The experience called to mind sitting in a black barbershop, or a church meeting—any one of a number of ritualized or communal settings. A sign of the boldness of Hughes (1902-1967) and Hurston (1891-1960) was that they dared to unveil one of these ritual settings and hoped to base a new idea of theater on it. Would the actors and writers in the late 1980's find poetry and music in this language, or would it call to mind minstrelsy, vaudeville and Amos 'n' Andy? Was it Sambo and Aunt Jemima, or was it art?

Sixty years after ***Mule Bone*** was written, many black Americans still feel that their precarious political and social condition within American society warrants a guarded attitude toward the way images of their culture are projected. Even a work by two of the greatest writers in the tradition cannot escape these concerns, concerns that would lead some to censorship, presumably because of "what white people might think," as if white racists attend black plays or read black literature to justify their prejudices. While the causes of racism are legion, literature hardly looms large among them.

Yet much of the motivation for the creation of what is now called the Harlem Renaissance—that remarkable flowering of black literature and the visual arts that occurred during the 20's, when ***Mule Bone*** was conceived—was implicitly political. Through the demonstration of sublime artistic capacity, black Americans—merely 60 years "up from slavery," as [African-American educator] Booker T. Washington described it—could dispel forever the nagging doubts that white Americans might have about their innate intellectual potential. Then, the argument went, blacks could easily traverse the long and bumpy road toward civil rights and social equality.

Given this burdensome role of black art, it was inevitable that debates about the nature of that art—about what today we call its "political correctness"—would be heated in black artistic circles.

These debates have proved to be rancorous, from that 20's renaissance through the battles between social realism and symbolism in the 30's to the militant black arts movement in the 60's. More recently, there have been bitter arguments about sexism, misogyny and the depiction of black women and men in the works of Alice Walker, Toni Morrison, Michele Wallace and Ms. Shange, as well as controversies about the writings of such social critics as Shelby Steele and Stanley Crouch. "The Negro in Art: How Shall He Be Portrayed?"—the subject of a forum published by Du Bois in *Crisis* magazine in the mid-20's—can be identified as the dominant concern of black artists and their critics for the last 70 years.

Black art in the 20th century, then, is a pivotal arena in

which to chart worries about "political correctness." The burden of representing "the race" in accordance with explicitly political programs can have a devastating impact on black creativity. Perhaps only black musicians and their music, until rap arose, have escaped this problem, because so much of what they composed was in nonverbal forms and because historically black music existed primarily for a black market. Categorized that way, it escaped the gaze of white Americans who, paradoxically, are the principal concern of those who would police the political effects of black art.

But such fears were not for the likes of Zora Neale Hurston. In April 1928 she wrote Hughes about her interest in a culturally authentic African-American theater, one constructed on a foundation of black vernacular: "Did I tell you . . . about the new, the *real* Negro theater I plan? Well, I shall, or rather we shall act out the folk tales, however short, with the abrupt angularity and naïveté of the primitive 'bama Nigger." It would be, she assured him, "a really new departure in the drama."

Hurston and Hughes did more than share the dream of a vernacular theater. They also established themselves as creative writers and critics by underscoring the value of black folk culture, both in itself and as the basis for formal artistic traditions. But the enormous potential of this collaborative effort was never realized, because, as Hughes wrote on his manuscript copy of the play's text, "the authors fell out."

Exactly why they "fell out" has never been clear, but the story of this abortive collaboration is one of the most curious in American literary history. For whatever reason, Hurston would copyright ***Mule Bone*** in her own name and deny Hughes's role in its writing.

The action of their play turns on a triangle of desire between a guitarist, Jim Weston (played by Kenny Neal), and a dancer, Dave Carter (Eric Ware), who are best friends as well as a musical duo, and their growing rivalry for the affections of Daisy Taylor (Akosua Busia). Directed by Michael Schultz, ***Mule Bone*** has a score by Taj Mahal, who has set five Langston Hughes poems to music and composed four songs for the Lincoln Center production.

Eventually, the two friends quarrel and Weston strikes Carter with the hock bone of an "ole yaller mule." He is arrested and his trial forms the heart of the play. The trial, and most of the second act, takes place in the Macedonia Baptist Church, converted into a courthouse for the occasion, with Mayor Joe Clark (Samuel E. Wright) presiding. The resolution of the case turns upon an amusing biblical exegesis: Can a mule bone be a criminal weapon? If so, then Weston is guilty; if not, he is innocent.

Using Judges 18:18, Carter's "attorney" (his minister, played by Arthur French) proves that since a donkey is the father of a mule, and since Samson slew 3,000 Philistines with the jawbone of an ass, and since "de further back you gits on uh mule de more dangerous he gits, an' if de jawbone slewed 3,000 people, by de time you gits back tuh his hocks it's pizen enough tuh kill 10,000." Therefore, "I ask y'all, whut kin be mo' dangerous dan uh mule bone?" Weston is banished from the town, which was based on Hurston's own Eatonville, Fla. The final scene depicts the two friends' reconciliation after both reject Daisy's demand that her husband get a proper job.

What is so controversial about all this? Hughes and Hurston develop their drama by imitating and repeating historical black folk rituals. Black folklore and Southern rural black vernacular English served as the foundation for what they hoped would be a truly new art form. It would refute the long racist tradition, in minstrelsy and vaudeville, of black characters as ignorant buffoons and black vernacular English as the language of idiots, of those "darkies" who had peopled the American stage for a full century before ***Mule Bone.***

This explains why they subtitled their play "**A Comedy of Negro Life**" and why they claimed that it was "the first real Negro folk comedy." By using the vernacular tradition as the basis of their play—indeed, as the basis of a new *theory* of black drama—Hurston and Hughes sought to create a work that would undo a century of racist representations of black people.

It is clear that Hurston and Hughes believed the time had come to lift the veil that separates black culture from white, allowing black art to speak in its own voice, without prior restraint. Had they not fallen out, one can only wonder at the effect that a successful Broadway production of ***Mule Bone*** in the early 1930's might have had on the development of black theater. (pp. 5, 8)

Henry Louis Gates, Jr., "Why the 'Mule Bone' Debate Goes On," in The New York Times, *February 10, 1991, pp. 5, 8.*

Randall Short (review date March 1991)

[*In the following preview of* Mule Bone, *Short relates the drama's genesis and the controversy that delayed its arrival on the Broadway stage.*]

•

> I never heard from Miss Hurston again. Unfortunately, our art was broken, and that was the end of what would have been . . . the first real Negro folk comedy—***Mule Bone.***
>
> [Langston Hughes, ***The Big Sea: An Autobiography,*** 1940]

Until recently, those were the final words on one of the stranger episodes in American theatrical history. In 1930, two of the Harlem Renaissance's leading lights—poet Langston Hughes and novelist Zora Neale Hurston—sequestered themselves in Hurston's New Jersey rooming house to write a play. Based on a folktale that Hurston, a doctoral student in anthropology at Columbia, had transcribed during researches in her hometown of Eatonville, Florida, the story depicts a comic wrangle between two young men whose fight for a girl's attention divides their community along Baptist and Methodist lines. Its vivid use of Negro slang was intended to strike a new note in the black literary movement. From a suitcase bursting with notes, Hurston supplied characters, situations and language; Hughes knit the material into a dramatic whole.

"Langston, Langston," enthused Hurston, "this is going to be big . . . "

Then things miscarried. A year later, news of plans for an unauthorized production persuaded Hughes that Hurston was cutting him out of the picture; she responded bitterly that ***Mule Bone*** was her work, not his. The legal battle that followed made it impossible for either to present the play during the other's lifetime, and copies of the never-published script gradually vanished into desk drawers and archives. The play's existence was known to few people beyond a handful of scholars. "The first real Negro folk comedy" seemed fated to remain a footnote in the annals of the American stage.

Fate, however, had not reckoned with Henry Louis Gates. A celebrated scholar/detective whose labors have restored many neglected and forgotten works to the canon of African-American literature, Gates came across the play while at Yale in the early eighties. Struck by its power and originality, he approached his friend Gregory Mosher, then at the helm of Chicago's Goodman Theater, about a production. Shortly after being named director of New York's Lincoln Center Theater in 1985, an enthusiastic Mosher set the project in motion. That's the story of how, after more than half a century, ***Mule Bone,*** a funny, gentle evocation of rural black life in the South of the 1920s by two American masters, is receiving its world premiere this month. The play's brilliant comedy should make it popular with contemporary audiences. Its rediscovery may change perceptions of the history of black theater in this country.

Producing a sixty-year-old theater piece for the first time with neither author on hand is not without complications. "What we had to do, more or less, was finish the play," says Anne Cattaneo, Lincoln Center's dramaturg. "As Hughes and Hurston left it, it's a good going-into-rehearsal script. It was our job to complete the fine-tuning they would have had to do if it had been staged." Using the authors' correspondence and manuscripts as a guide, Cattaneo and her associates—Gates, Hughes scholars George Houston Bass and Arnold Rampersad and director Michael Schultz—made the sort of minor cuts any new play receives during previews. More significantly, they replaced the traditional blues lyrics punctuating the text with several of Hughes's own blues-style poems; contemporary blues artist and historian Taj Mahal provided original, period-accurate music to accompany Hughes's jazzy riffs. ("Man," he said when jamming a few exploratory licks to the poems during an early brainstorming session, "this guy is in the groove.")

Ironically, ***Mule Bone*** has reawakened a controversy that dogged both writers when they were first published in the 1920s. Unlike many of their Harlem Renaissance colleagues who wanted to create a noble, high-flown literature embodying lofty spiritual and political aspirations, Hughes and Hurston drew inspiration from the voices of ordinary people doing ordinary things; their shared genius lay in capturing the beauty and humor of unsophisticated talk. ("He was so skinny you could do a week's washin' on his ribs for a washboard and hang 'em up on his hipbones to dry.") Writing like that left them open to angry complaints about representing their fellow Negroes in a less-than-ideal light, and it can be reasonably wondered whether this production revives stereotypes that blacks have worked hard to destroy.

It's a legitimate concern, admits Schultz, "especially in these reactionary times—if you don't handle it right, the play can sound like it's straight out of *Amos 'n' Andy.*" But the respected black director, who turned down an earlier offer to direct ***Mule Bone*** for just that reason, believes he's overcome the problem. A passage from a Hurston book used as prologue makes explicit what the play is trying to achieve; a Brechtian performance style emphasizes the distinction between its modern African-American actors and the characters they're portraying.

Schultz had no choice in the matter; he says ***Mule Bone*** was too important not to be done. "The first time I heard of the play," he says, "was when Greg held a reading at Lincoln Center in 1988, to which just about every black theater person in New York was invited. Afterwards over half the people there said [the play] should stay in the trunk, that it would be too easy to misinterpret. But I felt it needed to be seen. I didn't want the work of these artists to suffer the same fate it experienced early on because of people's reluctance to deal with this stuff." It's taken a while for the theater to get its act together but . . . Langston, Zora, welcome back.

Randall Short, "Just Folks," in Mirabella, *March, 1991, p. 72.*

MULATTO

PRODUCTION REVIEWS

Brooks Atkinson (review date 25 October 1935)

[*Hughes's* Mulatto *premiered on Broadway in 1935. In the following review, Atkinson declares that though Hughes "has little of the dramatic strength that makes it possible for a writer to tell a coherent, driving story in the theatre," his sincere and candid treatment of miscegenation accounts for the drama's ultimate success.*]

After a season dedicated chiefly to trash it is a sobering sensation to sit in the presence of a playwright who is trying his best to tell what he has on his mind. In ***Mulatto,*** which was acted at the Vanderbilt last evening, Langston Hughes, the Negro poet, is attempting to describe the tragic confusion of the people whose blood is half black and half white. To judge by ***Mulatto,*** Mr. Hughes has little of the dramatic strength of mind that makes it possible for a writer to tell a coherent, driving story in the theatre. His ideas are seldom completely expressed; his play is pretty thoroughly defeated by the grim mechanics of the stage. What gives it a sobering sensation in spite of its artlessness is the very apparent earnestness of Mr. Hughes's state of mind. He is writing about the theme that lies closest to his heart.

His mulattoes are the children of Cora Lewis, Negro housekeeper, and Colonel Thomas Norwood, a widower and a wealthy planter of Georgia. Since Colonel Norwood is the immediate instrument of oppression Mr. Hughes might easily have drawn him as a white villain. As a matter of fact, the colonel is according to his code a rather decent citizen; he has always treated his field Negroes honestly and he has been generous with the illegitimate children Cora has borne him. But that merely intensifies their mental anguish and makes their race bondage the more difficult to endure. Finally one of the boys, who has been educated in the North, gets completely out of control, kills the colonel and stirs up a lynching party to conclude the play.

Obviously, Mr. Hughes is immediately concerned with the code of ethics that keeps his race in subjection—the casual begetting of illegitimate children who are denied the prerogatives of their paternity, scorned by the whites, hated by the blacks. But the writing of ***Mulatto*** has set Mr. Hughes so many problems that it often seems like a moral retribution drama about the misery of a white man plagued by the social misdemeanor of having illegitimate mulatto children. For Colonel Norwood is always in trouble with his neighbors and the members of his own household, and is finally killed by a boy so cocky and impudent that he seems more like an ungrateful son than a martyr to race prejudice. The sympathies evoked by Mr. Hughes's story are muddled and diffuse.

If the material the actors have to work with is taken into consideration, some of them give a pretty good account of themselves. Stuart Beebe does well by the harassed colonel's state of mind. Jeanne Greene, playing the part of a terrified mulatto girl, does an excellent job. Hurst Amyx has something to give the part of a mulatto boy when he is in flight in the last act. Morris McKenney gives a good performance as an obedient Negro servant. As for Cora Lewis, she has the honor to be played by Rose McClendon, who is an artist with a sensitive personality and a bell-like voice. Plays are not very numerous for Miss McClendon but it is always a privilege to see her adding fineness of perception to the parts she takes.

In spite of its fatal weaknesses as a drama, ***Mulatto*** offers the combination of Rose McClendon and a playwright who is flaming with sincerity. After a fairly shabby season a professional playgoer is grateful for at least that much relief.

Brooks Atkinson, in a review of "Mulatto," in The New York Times, *October 25, 1935, p. 25.*

CRITICAL COMMENTARY

Doris E. Abramson (essay date 1969)

[In the following excerpt, Abramson explores Hughes's treatment of miscegenation in Mulatto. *She concludes*

THE VANDERBILT THEATRE

WEST 48th STREET Tel. BRyant 9-0134

DIRECTION

ALFRED E. AARONS and HARRY G. SOMMERS

FIRE NOTICE: The exit, indicated by a red light and sign, nearest to the seat you occupy, is the shortest route to the street.

In the event of fire or other emergency please do not run—WALK TO THAT EXIT.

JOHN J. McELLIGOTT, Fire Chief and Commissioner

THE · PLAYBILL · PUBLISHED · BY · THE · NEW · YORK · THEATRE · PROGRAM · CORPORATION

BEGINNING MONDAY EVENING, NOVEMBER 11, 1935

MATINEES WEDNESDAY AND SATURDAY

MULATTO

A New Drama

By

LANGSTON HUGHES and MARTIN JONES

Produced and Staged by MR. JONES

"CROSS"

My old man's a white old man
And my old mother's black.
If ever I cursed my white old man
I take my curses back.

If ever I cursed my black old mother
And wished she were in hell,
I'm sorry for that evil wish
And now I wish her well.

My old man died in a fine big house.
My ma died in a shack.
I wonder where I'm gonna die
Being neither white nor black.
—Langston Hughes

CAST

(In the order in which they speak)

CORA LEWIS .... Played by .... ROSE McCLENDON
WILLIAM LEWIS .... " " .... MORRIS McKENNEY
COLONEL THOMAS NORWOOD ..... " " .... STUART BEEBE

GEORGE WASHINGTON'S OVERSEER MADE IT FIRST

Mount Vernon

Straight Rye Whiskey—Bottled in Bond

NATIONAL DISTILLERS

THIS EMBLEM PROTECTS YOU

THE AMERICAN MEDICINAL SPIRITS CORPORATION, Baltimore, Md.

Executive Offices: 120 Broadway, New York, N.Y.

Playbill for the Broadway premiere of Mulatto, *1935.*

that Hughes possessed an aesthetic distance that enabled him to compose a drama whose universality is of greater significance than its subject matter.]

When five of [Hughes's] plays, with copyright notations ranging from 1931 to 1962, were published in 1963, the editor [Webster Smalley, ***Five Plays by Langston Hughes***] called Langston Hughes "America's outstanding Negro man of letters." He went on to say of Hughes's subject matter, the Negro in America:

> The position of the Negro in the United States is one of the facts that any Negro must face if he is to write at all. No one has more faith in the strength and dignity of his people than does Hughes, but only a few of his works can be called militant or didactic. Some few readers might wish that he were more belligerent, but he is an artist, not a propagandist.

The last statement seems, at first glance, to contradict what the author said of himself in a radio symposium in 1961: "I am, of course, as everyone knows, primarily a—I guess you might even say a propaganda writer; my main material is the race problem." But is it really a contradiction in terms—artist and propagandist? It seems an unnecessary separation. Art that has at its center a social problem, in this case all the social problems related to race, has almost an obligation to be propaganda. Unless one reserves the term "propagandist" to describe someone who is part of a movement organized to spread information, Langston Hughes may, without casting doubt on his artistic merit, be called a propagandist. As an individual he seemed intent upon letting his readers, and in the theatre his audience, in on what it is like to be a Negro in America. (pp. 67-8)

Edith Isaacs once observed [in her *The Negro in the American Theater,* 1947] that "Negro poets, although not many of them are writing plays as yet, seem to turn spontaneously toward the dramatic, in form or content, in situation, or character, or mood." When she wrote of envying the "many play-kernels that are buried in short poems," she might have been thinking of Langston Hughes's **"Cross"** [1931]:

> My old man's a white old man
> And my old mother's black.
> If ever I cursed my white old man
> I take my curses back.
>
> If ever I cursed my black old mother
> And wished she were in hell,
> I'm sorry for that evil wish
> And now I wish her well.
>
> My old man died in a fine big house.
> My ma died in a shack.
> I wonder where I'm gonna die,
> Being neither white nor black?

The subject of this early poem, miscegenation, was to be the subject of several short stories and at least one other poem as well as the kernel for Hughes's play ***Mulatto,*** which opened on Broadway, October 24, 1935, and had the longest run of any play by a Negro until [American dramatist] Lorraine Hansberry's *A Raisin in the Sun* broke the record in 1959.

In 1935 he was addressing himself as a poet to "Comrade Lenin of Russia," but it was a more commercially-minded Hughes who brought the subject of miscegenation to Broadway. Audiences proved to be as intrigued by it as the readers of nineteenth-century novels on the subject had been. Langston Hughes himself acknowledged [in his autobiography, ***The Big Sea,*** 1940] that "the problem of mixed blood in America is . . . a minor problem, but a very dramatic one." Writers before and after him, recognizing the dramatic value of the problem, have played upon both the fears and the fascination engendered in American society by this subject. (pp. 69-70)

The subject of ***Mulatto,*** then, was not a new one in literature or on the stage. What was new was that a Negro was writing about miscegenation for predominantly white audiences. Langston Hughes was not writing for the Negro unit of the Federal Theatre; ***Mulatto*** was not to be produced at the Lafayette Theatre. He set himself the task of writing a tragedy about miscegenation in the Deep South of his own time (between World War I and World War II) for audiences accustomed, on the one hand, to [American dramatist Marc Connelly's] *Green Pastures* and, on the other, to Frank Wilson's *Walk Together Chillun.* Langston Hughes did not write anything like *Green Pastures,* which one occasion he had called "a naïve dialect play about a quaint funny heaven full of niggers," nor even a play interspersed with spirituals and minstrel material. He wrote a successful tragedy that had elements of melodrama, and he dealt, to a surprising degree of honesty, with an old problem in a contemporary setting.

Mulatto is a well-constructed play in two acts. The setting is the same in each act, and the action proceeds during an early fall afternoon and evening. The setting immediately suggests a naturalism akin to that of [Norwegian dramatist Henrik] Ibsen's. If it were possible to imagine [Ibsen] describing "the Big House on a plantation in Georgia," he might well have done so in these details:

> Rear center of the room, a vestibule with double doors leading to the porch; at each side of the doors, a large window with lace curtains and green shades; at left a broad flight of stairs leading to the second floor; near the stairs, downstage, a doorway leading to the dining room and kitchen; opposite, at right of stage, a door to the library. The room is furnished in the long outdated horsehair and walnut style of the nineties; a crystal chandelier, a large old-fashioned rug, a marble-topped table, upholstered chairs. At the right is a small cabinet. It is a very clean, but somewhat shabby and rather depressing room. . . . The windows are raised. The afternoon sunlight streams in.

Just as there is nothing in this description that is not used, ultimately, in the action of the play, so there is no action that is not pertinent to exposing the problems peculiar to miscegenation in American society.

Mulatto has obvious exposition at the beginning, with speeches designed to tell a great deal in a short space of time. It has a kind of retrospection by means of which past actions are revealed in present ones, something similar to Ibsen's analytic exposition. Early in the play, for example, Cora, the brown woman who has been Colonel Norwood's housekeeper-mistress for some thirty years, tries to justify the actions of their son: "He don't mean nothing—just smart and young and kinder careless, Colonel Tom, like ma mother said you used to be when you was eighteen."

This is not an answer calculated to please Colonel Tom, who has been complaining about the boy's impudence, but it lets him know that she does not forget whose children she has borne, and it lets us know that she is in a privileged, if sometimes uncomfortable, position in this household. In a very short time we learn from the Colonel's outbursts that he has fathered mulatto children by Cora Lewis; that the oldest son, William, stays in his place among the plantation laborers; that one girl is away, working up North; that another, Sallie, is about to go back to school; and that Robert, the one who most resembles the Colonel in looks and fiery temperament, is home from college and home to stay. Robert, or Bert as he is usually called, is the immediate focus of attention and cause for conflict in the play. Incidentally, it is only by indirection that we know that these children are the Colonel's. He always refers to them simply as Cora's, except for one slip that is nearly buried in a long speech:

Just because Bert's your son, and I've been damn fool enough to send him off to school for five or six years, he thinks he has a right to privileges, acting as if he owned this place since he's been back here this summer. . . . There's no nigger-child of mine, yours, ours—no darkie—going to disobey me. . . . Schools for darkies! Huh! If you take that boy of yours for an example, they do 'em more harm than good. He's learned nothing in college but impudence, and he'll stay here on this place and work for me awhile before he gets back to any more schools.

The Colonel's contention is that he sent "Cora's kids" to school because he could not bear to see them stay as dumb as the other "darkies." Of course, as soon as Bert begins to act like something other than a dumb "darkie," he is stepping out of line. There is no doubt that each race has its role and its place. When the old Negro retainer, Sam, asks if he may move Sallie's trunk down the front stairs, because it will not fit down the back, Colonel Norwood replies:

No other way? (*Sam shakes his head*) Then pack it on through to the back, quick. Don't let me catch you carrying any of Sallie's baggage out of the front door here. You-all'll be wanting to go in and out the front way next. (*Turning away, complaining to himself*) Darkies have been getting mighty fresh in this part of the country since the war. The damn Germans should've . . . (*To Sam*) Don't take that trunk out that front door.

This speech not only helps to characterize the Colonel and place the scene in terms of time, but it also gives Sam a chance to tell the Colonel that Bert has been using the front door, an act which gains symbolic importance as the plot develops. The first act curtain, for instance, will fall on Bert walking defiantly out that door. But before that occurs, there are two scenes that further develop the characterization of the Colonel, of Bert, and of Cora. These scenes also move the action of the play ahead with an inexorable air of tragedy.

In a scene between Colonel Norwood and his friend Fred Higgins, the latter reports that Cora's boy, "that young black fool," is speeding in Colonel Norwood's Ford and acting as if he were as good as a white man. Even worse, Bert has been boasting "to the wall-eyed coons" of his parentage, that his name is Norwood, that his money is as good as a white man's any day. If Colonel Norwood is a stereotype of the Georgia plantation owner, Fred Higgins is even more a stereotype of the fat, elderly county politician. He huffs and puffs as he is helped in and out of a chair by his Negro chauffeur, Mose. He drinks too much, speaks crudely, and divulges a great deal of information as well as vulgar comment upon it. His remarks about how a Negro should act in the South are particularly striking:

A darkie's got to keep in his place down here. Ruinous to other niggers hearing that talk, too. All this postwar propaganda on the radio about freedom and democracy—why the niggers think it's meant for them! And that Eleanor Roosevelt, she ought to been muzzled. She's driving our niggers crazy—your boy included. Crazy! Talking about civil rights. Ain't been no race trouble in our country for three years—since the Deekin's lynching—but I'm telling you, Norwood, you better see that that buck of yours goes away from here. I'm speaking on the quiet, but I can see ahead.

Colonel Norwood is furious, not only with Bert, significantly, but at the white man's dependence upon the Negro. "Everything turns on niggers, niggers, niggers!" he exclaims. It is obvious, of course, that Colonel Norwood has been dependent on Cora for some years for many favors. Higgins disapproves not of the favors but of what living with only Negroes can do to a man:

Nothing but blacks in the house—a man gets soft like niggers are inside. (*Puffing at cigar*) And living with a colored woman! Of course, I know we all have 'em—I didn't know you could make use of a white girl till I was past twenty. Thought too much o' white women for that—but I've given many a yellow gal a baby in my time. (*Long puff at cigar*) But for a man's own house you need a wife, not a black woman.

Colonel Norwood agrees with him but observes that it is too late for him to marry again. Their short scene contains one statement after another in support of white supremacy.

In a scene that serves as a transition to Cora's scene with Bert, and that adds to the suspense growing all through the act, she reminisces with her son William about the time that Bert called the Colonel "papa." He was then seven years old, and the Colonel beat him unmercifully. Bert is home now only to please Cora, who is fast changing her mind about the visit. She is frightened for her boy. "Something' gonna happen to my boy," she tells William. "I had a bad dream last night. . . . I seed a path o' living blood across this house, I tell you, in my sleep."

When Cora is alone with Bert—who enters through the

C. W. E. Bigsby on *Mulatto:*

[The] most successful Broadway production by a black writer in the 1930s was Langston Hughes's ***Mulatto*** (1935). Hughes was a major talent. A leading figure of the Harlem Renaissance, he was in turn a poet, a novelist, a short-story writer, a dramatist and a journalist. ***Mulatto*** was a melodrama set in the South. It concerned the dilemma of the mulatto, poised uneasily between two cultures. Faced either with acquiescence or with self-destructive revolt, the principal character destroys himself. A brutal play, resting uneasily on familiar figures from literary tradition and public myth, it established a record run for a black play on Broadway not rivalled for twenty-four years. And if it did little to advance the cause of drama, it did constitute an assertion of the role of the theatre in literally dramatising a primary moral issue of the day.

C. W. E. Bigsby, in his A Critical Introduction to Twentieth-Century American Drama 1900-1940, *Cambridge University Press, 1982.*

front door, announcing that "*Mister* Norwood's here!"—she tries to reason with him, to remind him of the ways of the South. He stubbornly defies those ways and announces his intention to have his rights, to be a Norwood and not a "field-hand nigger." Cora answers him quietly from the depths of her experience:

> I knows, honey, you reads in de books and de papers, and you knows a lot more'n I do. But, chile, you's in Georgy. . . . This ain't up North—and even up yonder where we hears it's so fine, yo' sister has to pass for white to get along good.

She tells about moving up to the Big House when the Colonel's wife died, of how good he was to let her keep her children with her in the house when they were little, and of how he sent them to school:

> Ain't no white man in this country done that with his cullud chilluns before, far as I can know. But you—Robert, be awful, awful careful! When de Colonel comes back, in a few minutes, he wants to talk to you. Talk right to him, boy. Talk like you was colored, 'cause you ain't white.

Bert's angry answer, "And I'm not black either," hits at the center of the play's theme.

The climax of the first act occurs when Colonel Norwood enters the front door just as Bert is preparing to leave by it. The Colonel raises his cane to strike the boy. Cora screams. The boy looks insolently into his father's eyes, and the Colonel, unable to strike him, orders the boy to leave the house. As Bert walks proudly out the front door, the Colonel takes a pistol from the cabinet and starts to follow him. Cora intervenes with the moving, if melodramatic, line: "He's our son, Tom. Remember he's our son."

In spite of lengthy speeches, the action moves ahead rapidly in the two scenes in the second act of ***Mulatto.*** At sunset, after supper, the Colonel and Bert confront each other. After a long speech in which Colonel Norwood tells Bert about all the advantages he has given Cora's children and how kind he is to all his "darkies," he concludes with the comment that he is going to give this impudent boy a chance to explain himself. He adds that he wants Bert to "talk right." When Bert asks what he means by that, the Colonel answers in a way that sets off the violence that has been stirring just under the surface of the scene.

> NORWOOD. I mean talk like a nigger should to a white man.
>
> ROBERT. Oh! But I'm not a nigger, Colonel Tom. I'm your son.
>
> NORWOOD. (*Testily*) You're Cora's boy.
>
> ROBERT. Women don't have children by themselves.
>
> NORWOOD. Nigger women don't know the fathers. You're a bastard.

(One remembers the refrain from an early poem by Langston Hughes:

> A nigger night,
> A nigger joy,
> A little yellow
> Bastard boy.)

This particular "boy" will not accept his bastardy. He flings accusations and challenges at the Colonel, who answers him in kind. After heated words on both sides, the Colonel draws his pistol to prevent Bert from leaving by the front door, but Bert twists the gun from his father's hand. There is a struggle, and the younger man strangles the older one. Cora enters the room and finds Colonel Norwood dead. When we read that Bert drops his father's body at his mother's feet "in a path of flame from the setting sun," we remember her dream of the house bathed in blood.

There is only one course for Bert to take. He must run away to avoid being lynched by the white men who are on their way to visit Colonel Norwood. He sets out for the swamp, promising Cora to return to the house if he finds he cannot make it that far: "Let them take me out of my father's house—if they can. (*Puts the gun under his shirt*) They're not going to string me up to some roadside tree for the crackers to laugh at."

The white men, on discovering Colonel Norwood's body, form a posse to get Bert. Cora is left alone with the corpse. In a long, emotional speech she moves from tenderness to outright hatred of the Colonel:

> He's your boy. His eyes is gray—like your eyes. He's tall like you's tall. He's proud like you's proud. And he's runnin'—runnin' from po' white trash that ain't worth de little finger o' nobody what's got your blood in 'em, Tom. (*Demandingly*) Why don't you get up from there and stop 'em, Colonel Tom? What's that you say? He ain't your chile? He's ma bastard chile? Ma yellow bastard chile? (*Proudly*) Yes, he's mine. . . . He's ma chile. . . . Don't you come to my bed no mo'. I calls you to help me now, and you just lays there. I calls you for to wake up, and you just lays there. Whenever you called me in de night, I woke up. When you called for me to love, I always reached out ma arms fo' you. I borned you five chilluns and now one of 'em is out yonder in de dark runnin' from yo' people. Our youngest boy out yonder in de dark runnin'. (*Accusingly*) He's runnin' from you, too. . . . You are out yonder in de dark, runnin' our chile, with de hounds and de gun in yo' hand. . . . Damn you, Colonel Norwood! (*Backing slowly up the stairs, staring at the rigid body below her*) Damn you, Thomas Norwood! God damn you!

This is less than half of the speech that brings the curtain down on the scene. Cora is released by madness to cry out what she has suppressed over the years.

Cora's fantasy persists in the last scene. Her madness mounts, and after she has said goodbye to William, she reports to Colonel Tom:

> Colonel Tom! Look! Bertha and Sallie and William and Bert, all your chilluns, runnin' from you, and you layin' on de floor there, dead! (*Pointing*) Out yonder with the mob, dead. And

> when you come home, upstairs in my bed on top of my body, dead.

This outburst is followed by a long speech of reminiscing, repetitious but charged with lively images. The sounds of the approaching mob are growing stronger and stronger. By the end of the speech Cora knows that Bert is coming home.

He bursts into the room, exchanging shots with the loud mob outside. Voices can be heard shouting, "Nigger! Nigger! Nigger! Get the nigger!" Cora bolts the door after Bert and sends him upstairs to hide in a hole in the floor under her bed. He has one bullet left, which they both agree he must use for himself. They bid each other good night almost formally, glad to reach this ending with dignity.

Cora is on the stairs when the white mob bursts into the living room with guns, knives, rope, clubs, flashlights. She turns on the stairs and tells them to be quiet. Her boy is going to sleep. Before they can get past her, a single shot rings out. "My boy . . . is gone . . . to sleep!" are Cora's last words. Her last action, however, comes just as the curtain falls. It is not an action so much as a lack of one. Talbot, the overseer, furious at having been cheated of a chance to lynch the boy, "walks up to Cora and slaps her once across the face. She does not move. It is as though no human hand can touch her again."

Cora Lewis wins. Her kind of dignity gives the play a special dimension. Webster Smalley put it this way.

> The patient love and rich dignity of Cora and Bert's final recognition of the totality of his tragic situation raise ***Mulatto*** above the level of a mere problem play. One forgives Hughes the sometimes obvious exposition of the opening scenes (as one does the early [Eugene] O'Neill in *Beyond the Horizon*) for the tragedy and power of the play's final scenes.

It may very well be that Broadway audiences in 1935 were moved by the production more than they were by the script and the ideas expressed in it. Rose McClendon played the part of Cora, and this great Negro actress brought power and dignity to the role, the last one she played before her untimely death the following year. There was, however, along with the intensity provided by the script and the actors, a touch of sensationalism added by a producer with an eye on the box office. Sallie, in the Broadway production, was made to miss her train back to school so that she could later be raped by the wicked overseer. This bit of melodramatic action was added without the consent of the author. Whatever the reasons for its success, ***Mulatto*** ran for nearly a year on Broadway and then toured the country—with the exception of the South, which included even Philadelphia—for eight months. (pp. 71-9)

Langston Hughes . . . was the first Negro playwright of any stature, a writer by profession, a man who traveled in his own country and abroad. It seems only fair to guess that, through these activities, he gained an objectivity that enabled him to interpret Negro life and, at the same time, to write a soundly constructed play.

There is a universality about ***Mulatto*** that other plays of the period lack. The play goes beyond the problem of miscegenation, which is still a real or imagined issue in our time. Bert symbolizes all educated Negroes when he demands his rights of Colonel Norwood, who so obviously symbolizes the old South. The Colonel educated Bert and then asked him to go back into the fields, to return to "his place." The South is just beginning to feel the results of Negroes coming of age, questioning their place in the scheme of things. The front door still belongs to the white man, but Langston Hughes predicted as early as 1935 the bloodshed that might occur if the Negro were not allowed to go in and out that door at will.

Critics [like T. J. Spencer and Clarence J. Rivers in "Langston Hughes: His Style and Optimism," *Drama Critique* VII (Spring 1964)] have spoken of Langston Hughes's tolerance in dealing with characters, whites as well as Negroes: "In ***Mulatto*** it is not only Robert Lewis who suffers from tragic *hybris* and who involves our sympathy; it is also Colonel Norwood—trapped by the assumptions of his own society and too proud to defy them altogether." Only recently has the public begun to realize that in abusing the black man the white man is doing terrible things to himself. (p. 87)

Doris E. Abramson, "The Thirties," in her Negro Playwrights in the American Theatre: 1925-1959, *Columbia University Press, 1969, pp. 44-88.*

SOUL GONE HOME

CRITICAL COMMENTARY

William Miles (essay date 1970)

[*In the following excerpt, Miles analyzes the effects of forced isolation on the African-American culture as portrayed in* Soul Gone Home. *He maintains that by skillfully combining situation, structure, character, and symbol, "Hughes has produced a compact and powerful play of a people so isolated that even the ordinarily secure relationship between mother and son is impossible."*]

(Few writers) have been as prolific in their attempt to describe and interpret Negro American life as Langston Hughes. Poet, novelist, short story writer, and dramatist, "he writes to express those truths he feels need expressing about characters he believes need to be recognized," [Webster Smalley, ed., ***Langston Hughes: Five Plays,*** 1963]. One such truth is the forced isolation of the majority of black people by the culture within which they are forced by circumstance to exist. The intensity and repressiveness of such isolation alienates the black person not only from the culture at large, but frequently from his own brothers as well. This is the theme of Hughes' powerful one-act play, ***Soul Gone Home.*** In less than four pages of text he presents a tragic and poignant picture of a people so isolated from each other that the establishment of meaningful emotional relationship is no longer possible.

The theme of isolation is not, of course, original with Hughes. What is original in ***Soul Gone Home,*** however, is the manner in which this theme is treated. The play is a fantasy in both situation and structure. Reality as we commonly experience it is replaced by the unreal, the dreamlike; the usual physical laws governing life and death are suspended. Yet the emphasis of the play is clearly on things as they exist in actuality. The play is about a situation resulting from the condition of black people in America. The immediate situation explored within the fantastic world of the play is itself unreal: a conflict between an uncaring mother and the ghost of her dead son in which the latter condemns his mother ("You been a hell of a mama! . . . I say you been a no-good mama.") because she failed to provide him with the necessities of life, food, clothing, "manners and morals."

This internal conflict in the realm of fantasy forms the center of the drama, but the structural limits are defined by reality. ***Soul Gone Home*** begins with the mother grieving over her son's body and concludes with his removal by the ambulance drivers. However, Hughes has constructed even these two apparently real incidents in such a way as to render them unreal. For example, the opening stage direction informs us that the mother is "loudly simulating grief" and the play ends on the same note with her again feigning grief in the presence of the indifferent ambulance drivers.

The importance of both this underlying structure and the unreality of the situation is that they immediately establish the fact of the isolated condition of the mother and son. The boy is, of course, apart from the real world in the sense that he is dead, and, likewise, the mother is removed by the very fact that she can openly converse with him. Indeed, the mother is actually doubly removed: her "real" life, or what glimpses we get of it, is characterized by a sense of unreality. Symbolically, therefore, she is not a part of the reality defined by the general society, and her being outside in large part is the result of her race. To emphasize this fact, Hughes underlines the isolated condition of both mother and son through their lack of relatedness to the white ambulance drivers. Both are completely oblivious and indifferent to the dead boy and the tears of the "grieving" mother, and their lack of responsiveness to the situation is a measure of the vast gulf separating black and white.

Structurally, therefore, fantasy functions to establish the complete physical isolation of the two main characters from the real world. The focal point of the play, the inability of mother and son to relate on the emotional level, exists in a cause-and-effect relationship with their isolation from the society: forced and repressive physical isolation of one group by another results in severe emotional alienation among members of the persecuted group. In developing and emphasizing this emotional element, Hughes superimposes upon his fantasy clear implications of stark reality. Thus the total effect of ***Soul Gone Home*** is realism, and while the central conflict may be internal, the implied commentary relates wholly to the external world.

The conflict itself takes place in appropriate surroundings: it is night and the scene is "a tenement room, bare, ugly and dirty." Such a setting is explicitly illustrative of the type of life which the dead boy was forced to live and with keen insight into his once human condition, he attacks his mother for her lack of concern. Always in need of food, he had grown up "all bowlegged and stunted from undernourishment," and had died at sixteen of tuberculosis brought on by a lack of "milk and eggs" in his diet. Furthermore, he has come to realize that his "home" totally lacked an atmosphere of love and failed to provide him with examples of proper "manners and morals." Sickly and treated as nothing more than a burdensome bastard, he was forced out on the streets to grub out whatever money he could find. However, refusing to recognize her existence for what it really is, the mother sadly defends her actions and is quick to point out that the boy *was* nothing more than a burden to her. As this argument is developed, one can easily see that the gulf between white and black is as great and unbridgeable as the one existing between this mother and son.

Hughes does not explicitly explore the causes of such a situation nor the reasons it is permitted to persist. Why should a sixteen-year-old boy have to die from the lack of necessary foods; why should a mother be forced to view her child in terms of how much monetary help he can be; and, indeed, why should a mother herself be forced to turn to prostitution in order to scratch out an existence? Such questions are left unanswered, but Hughes does indicate responsibility. All the implications of ***Soul Gone Home*** point directly to the white world as the source of the problems of the majority of Negro Americans. Two incidents in the play illustrate this fact: the complete indifference of the white ambulance drivers, and the mother's symbolic whitening of her face before she goes out to prostitute her body.

It is interesting to note that the son, ironically, gains his great insight into the essential condition of life and his true relationship with his mother only upon dying. When the mother demands to know where he learned "all them big words" such as "manners and morals," he replies, "I learn't 'em just now in the spirit world." "But you ain't been dead no more'n an hour," the mother counters. "That's long enough to learn a lot," he says. In less than an hour of death the son has learned more about life than he did in sixteen years of real existence on earth. This new insight into and knowledge of what his and his mother's life has been is symbolically represented by the throwing off of the pennies (the material world) which cover his eyes.

> SON. I'm dead now—and I can say what I want to say. (*Stirring*) You done called on me to talk, ain't you? Lemme take these pennies off my eyes so I can see.

Hughes' implicit comment that only death (or some type of escape from existing conditions) can provide true insight into the human condition of the black American in a closed white society is closely paralleled in the work of

Richard Wright. When Bigger Thomas commits the accidental murder of Mary Dalton in *Native Son* [as Constance Webb states in "What Next for Richard Wright?" *Phylon* X (1949)],

> he blossoms into full consciousness as a personality. He is at once free of the society in which he lives. He can now analyze the relationship between the Negro and white world. He can probe into his own personality reactions and those of the people around him. For the first time in his life he lives as a whole human being.

Likewise, the son in the play is able truly to see and assess his situation only when he is free from the constraints of the white-dominated physical and material world; only then can he "see" and "talk." Only in death has he found a home and a "real" life; he is a "soul gone home."

It is also an ironical but poignant consequence of the conflict between the mother and son that the mother utterly fails to comprehend what her son is talking about. Always on the defensive, she not only justifies her own position and actions, but even attempts to shift the blame for them to the boy.

> MOTHER. (*Proudly*) Sure, I could of let you die, but I didn't. Naw, I kept you with me—off and on. And I lost the chance to marry many a good man, too—if it weren't for you. No man wants to take care o' nobody else's child. (*Self-pityingly*) You been a burden to me, Randolph.
>
> SON. (*Angrily*) What did you have me for then, in the first place?
>
> MOTHER. How could I help havin' you, you little bastard? Your father ruint me—and you's the result. And I been worried with you for sixteen years. (*Disgustedly*) Now, just when you get big enough to work and do me some good, you have to go and die.

The mother's complete isolation from her son is firmly implanted in the minds of the audience by her final gestures. She again feigns grief over the loss of her son; she smooths out the bed where he lay, thus seemingly blotting out any signs of his former existence; and she makes a final statement which indicates that her love for her son is less than complete.

> MOTHER. Tomorrow, Randolph, I'll buy you some flowers—if I can pick up a dollar tonight. You was a hell of a no-good son, I swear!

Through the skillful combination of situation, structure, character and symbol, Hughes has produced a compact and powerful play of a people so isolated that even the ordinarily secure relationship between mother and son is impossible. And while this thematic consideration is immediately relevant to the Negro American, ***Soul Gone Home*** does achieve a sense of universality in that its social commentary relates to any oppressed minority. Furthermore, the play also fulfills the criteria for "high art" laid down by LeRoi Jones [in "Problems of the Negro Writer," *Saturday Review* XLVI (20 April 1963)].

> High art, first of all, must reflect the experience, the emotional predicament of the man, as he exists, in the defined world of his being. It must be produced from the legitimate emotional resources of the soul in the world. It can *never* be produced by evading these resources or pretending that they do not exist. It can never be produced by appropriating the withered emotional responses of some strictly social idea of humanity. It must issue from *real* categories of human activity, *truthful* accounts of human life, and not fancied accounts of the attainment of cultural privilege by some willingly preposterous apologists for one social "order" or another.

As Jones would have it, ***Soul Gone Home*** "tells it like it is," but in such a way as to create an impact and effect not soon nor easily forgotten. (pp. 178-82)

William Miles, "Isolation in Langston Hughes' 'Soul Gone Home'," in Five Black Writers: Essays on Wright, Ellison, Baldwin, Hughes, and LeRoi Jones, *edited by Donald B. Gibson, New York University Press, 1970, pp. 178-82.*

BLACK NATIVITY

PRODUCTION REVIEWS

Howard Taubman (review date 12 December 1961)

[*In the following review, Taubman offers a mixed evaluation of* Black Nativity, *judging the production's narrative inferior to its "kinetic" and fervent gospel music.*]

There is a lot of song but hardly any play in Langston Hughes' Christmas songplay, ***Black Nativity,*** which opened last night at the 41st Street Theatre.

What play there is might well be dispensed with. It takes the form of amateurish choreography, which gets in the way of the gospel singing. If there is any justification for ***Black Nativity,*** it is in the singing.

The first half of ***Black Nativity*** is devoted to telling the story of "The Child Is Born," and here the intrusive efforts at miming occur. The second half, "The Word Is Spread," moves into our time. The singers, taking over entirely, observe the injunction to make a joyful noise unto the Lord, and it is as if one has wandered into a jubilant revival meeting.

For cultivated musical ears a little gospel singing may go a long way, but how these singers can belt out a religious tune! They sing with the afflatus of jazzmen in a frenzy of improvisation. The rhythms are so vibrant that they seem to lead an independent existence. The voices plunge into sudden dark growls like muted trombones and soar in ecstatic squeals like frantic clarinets.

When Marion Williams and the Stars of Faith, gowned in black, explode into "We Shall Be Changed," they can scarcely contain their elation. As they sing, they beat time with their hands and feet, and one of the women moves into the aisle, dancing and shouting the great hope of immortality. Some of the parishioners in the audience clap their hands, too, and a voice up front cries out, "That's right!"

Alex Bradford and his singers turn "Said I Wasn't Gonna Tell Nobody" into a surging syncopated hymn of joy. Princess Stewart, a blind singer, attempts a graver mood. For the most part the singing has a kind of wild, pounding rapture. A stately hymn like "Joy to the World" is transformed into a pulsing jubilee. The familiar Christmas songs become a singular kinetic experience.

Mr. Hughes has provided a slim narration, and Howard Sanders reads it. It is merely an excuse to cue in the gospel singers. With uninhibited spirits and unlimited lung power—at times they are deafening—they celebrate the Christmas story. It is not always art—and the occasional organ sounds are embarrassingly cloying—but it is overflowing in fervor.

Howard Taubman, "Langston Hughes Work at the 41st Street," in The New York Times, *December 12, 1961, p. 54.*

Hughes as a busboy at the Wardman Park Hotel, Washington, D.C., 1925.

Robert Shelton (review date 5 January 1963)

[*In the excerpt that follows, Shelton extols the New York Philharmonic Orchestra's 1963 production of* Black Nativity *as a masterful blending of gospel music and theater. Describing it as a "simple" drama ornamented with narration and dance, the critic encourages other black dramatists to imitate Hughes and "use gospel music to tell of other aspects of Negro life in America."*]

A Christmas gift for Philharmonic Hall audiences was provided the week ending December 30 by the return of ***Black Nativity.*** The gospel song-play by Langston Hughes, after critical and popular success on the Continent, won a standing ovation at its Lincoln Center opening.

Black Nativity has taken the volcanic energy of Negro gospel music and channeled it skillfully toward theatrical ends. It has already introduced new audiences to gospel music in Spoleto, London and seven other European centers. It will return to the Continent for six months and tour the United States for forty weeks. There is even some talk of taking it to Russia and Eastern Europe.

All this *réclame* has centered on a show that is the essence of simplicity. A narrator, three dancers, three featured singers, two vocal quartets and an off-stage pianist and organist make up the cast. The first act, "The Child Is Born," recounts the travail of Mary and Joseph and the birth of Jesus. The second act, "The Word Is Spread," is little more than a gospel concert, albeit a most exciting concert. Mr. Hughes's narration, read by Gilbert Adkins, ties the old thread of the Christmas legend together loosely, while Christyne Lawson and Kenneth Scott dance and mime the roles of Mary and Joseph. On this simple scaffolding of narration and dance is hung the flesh of the show—singing by Marion Williams, Alex Bradford and Princess Stewart and of the two groups, the Stars of Faith and the Bradford Singers.

Therein lies the key to the show's impact, novelty and popular appeal. The singing is gospel joy at its freest. Vibrant rhythms, wild hand-clapping that soon involves the audience, tambourine-playing and surging vocal athletics make the musical elements of the show almost irresistible.

Modern gospel music began to assume its present form after World War I. It is a startlingly successful marriage of the tempos, cadences and improvisations of jazz, the blues and even rock 'n' roll with lyrics that are either Biblical or rudimentary homiletic words of religious praise.

Heretofore, gospel music had to be experienced in a church situation to savor the tremendous emotional impact it conveyed. Many a congregation has been moved to near-hysteria by the timing, repetitions and shouting abandon of the gospel singers. Efforts to transplant this sensuous and compelling style to concert halls and to such settings as last fall's three-day Gospel Festival at Randall's Island have often failed.

Mindful of this, the producers of ***Black Nativity,*** Barbara Griner and Michael R. Santangelo, and its director, Vinnette Carroll, have staged this gospel production with attention to pacing, movement, variety and continuity.

At first glance, the childlike naïveté of ***Black Nativity*** could bring to mind *Green Pastures.* The flowing robes of the singers might seem to those who are vigilant about stereotypes to be damaging to the dignity of Negroes. But in actuality the show does truly reflect a church atmosphere, a form of worship in song that is widespread among the Negro communities of the North and the South. Appreciation of a folk art or folk culture presupposes a sympathetic attitude on the part of the viewer from a more sophisticated background. In this context, ***Black Nativity*** is not promulgating stereotypes.

But the show is just a beginning. It will continue to overwhelm audiences with the abandon of gospel singing, but the next logical step is to use gospel music to tell of other aspects of Negro life in America—the integration struggles and the whole role of protest in music that has dominated Negro religious and musical life for 150 years. Having successfully used the vibrant qualities of gospel song to tell the most familiar of religious stories in a theatrical situation, Langston Hughes and the others involved with ***Black Nativity*** could easily find a fitting sequel in the story of the rebirth of the Negro people in the South today. With gospel music setting the tempo, the world would listen.

Robert Shelton, in a review of "Black Nativity," in The Nation, *New York, Vol. 196, No. 1, January 5, 1963, p. 20.*

Darwin T. Turner on the changing function of the black dramatist:

The changes in the Negro dramatist's image of his hero, his attitude toward education, his attitude toward the North, and his image of his society and its problems parallel those which can be observed in other media utilized by Negro literary artists: from idealization of Negroes to efface the caricatures created by white authors, to strident, self-conscious defense of the vices of Negroes, to objective appraisal. Unlike the Negro novelist, the dramatist cannot escape easily into a world of racelessness. If he employs Negroes to enact his stories, he identifies the characters with Negroes. For that reason, perhaps, the Negro dramatists, more than the novelists, have continued to emphasize problems unique to the Negro race. As reasons for protest have faded, however, they have become more concerned with dilemmas of individuals rather than of the entire race. They have created individuals in the confidence that America has become educated to a stage at which audiences will not assume these characters to typify the Negro race. The Negro dramatists of the present and of the future are no longer compelled to regard themselves as spokesmen for a race which needs educated and talented writers to plead its cause. Now they can regard themselves as artists, writing about the Negro race only because that is the group with which they are the most familiar.

Darwin T. Turner, in his "The Negro Dramatist's Image of the Universe," CLA Journal *V, No. 2 (December 1961).*

Jennifer Dunning (review date 30 December 1980)

[In the review below, Dunning assesses Hazel Bryant's 1980 production of Black Nativity. *Although noting its physical shortcomings, Dunning deems it worthy of being considered a "holiday classic."]*

It has been 19 years since ***Black Nativity,*** Langston Hughes's "gospel song-play," celebrated Christmas on Broadway with joyous gospel shouts. There have been a number of "all-black" versions of classics since then, of course, but the impact of ***Black Nativity*** has not lessened. It has only changed, or so Hazel Bryant's new production of the musical—at the Richard Allen Center for Culture and Art through Sunday—suggests.

Some leading gospel singers of the time appeared in Vinnette Carroll's original. Miss Bryant has assembled a cast of shining youngsters, who for the most part are the products of the Broadway musical tradition rather than the earthier, more formal style of gospel song developed in black churches. Howard A. Roberts and Esteban Vega, the directors of this production, have reworked ***Black Nativity,*** now a streamlined one-act version.

Using a narrator, two dancers and a chorus of singers, the musical still tells the story of the nativity, starting with the wandering of Joseph and Mary from inn to inn on a cold winter night, and ending with the arrival of the Three Kings at the stable. Mr. Roberts has kept the best, like the exuberant "What You Gonna Name Your Baby." And two of his additions heighten the vibrant, deceptively naïve spirit of Mr. Hughes's conception, catching the rich blend of sly humor, affection and muted pain in Mr. Hughes's own underrated poetry.

"Last Month of the Year" establishes the time of Jesus' birth in a rousing, teasing, rhetorical strut for the company, led by the big-voiced Stan Lawrence. And Gayle Turner's slow, almost murmured singing of "Silent Night" is a spellbinding showstopper. With her agile, filigree voice, Miss Turner is a major reason for seeing ***Black Nativity.*** But the entire cast is good, from its huge, cherubic bass singer, P. L. Brown, and an equally tall wildman named Gary Gibbs, to the smokey come-hitherishness of Val Eley. Deborah Lynn Sharpe comes closest to pure gospel singing in her "Most Done Traveling," Lillias White is the company's red hot mama in "Rise Up, Shepherd," and Vanessa Shaw brings a touch of concert-hall class with her lullaby, "Sweet Little Jesus Boy." Dwayne Grayman's big, easy voice is one of the show's most powerful elements, as is the intricate and precisely balanced rhythmic layering of the chorus singing throughout.

Christophe Pierre has a touchingly wistful quality as the narrator. Agnes Johnson is a luminous Mary and Thomas Reid a quietly tender Joseph. And if one misses the rolling, traditional gospel organ of the original, Frank Anderson, William Foster McDaniel and Ivan Hampden add a touch of dry jazz wit to the keyboard and percussion accompaniment.

The production's only shortcoming is a physical one. Mr. Vega and Charles Moore, the choreographer for this ***Black Nativity,*** make inventive enough use of the cramped, multileveled stage. Myrna Colley-Lee's costumes, which range from sari bazaar to attic velvets, do not make a virtue of simplicity, at least at this close range. And, a week after the musical opened, it was surprising to see a number of unsewn hems among the costumes.

Black Nativity deserves to become a holiday classic. Isn't there a church in the city that could invite Miss Bryant and her fine singers, dancers and musicians in next Christmas?

Jennifer Dunning, "Streamlined Song-Play," in The New York Times, *December 30, 1980, p. C5.*

TAMBOURINES TO GLORY

PRODUCTION REVIEWS

Lewis Nichols (review date 27 October 1963)

[*In the following excerpt, Nichols recounts comments made by Hughes about* Tambourines to Glory *when he spoke to Nichols prior to the Broadway production of the play.*]

On a sunny afternoon of Indian summer, there came through the open windows of a West Side warehouse building the spirited, rhythmic chant of gospel singing. On the street, this formed an oddly apt background for stick-ball playing, exhortations down there being both sacred and profane. Inside, and up two flights, there was no nonsense. With a Broadway opening due at the Little on Saturday, the cast and singers of the play with music called ***Tambourines to Glory*** were in rehearsal, and each beat sounded like a warning of the crack of doom.

Seated with the directors at his table was the man who, in effect, had blown up this storm of sound. Nodding in time to the rhythm—and it was hard not to do so—was Langston Hughes, poet, playwright, lyricist, general all-around man of letters. Stocky, now 61, with a receding hair line and a frontal bulge that suggested defiance of the physical fitness program, he was watching the coming to bloom of a flower that had undergone even more vicissitudes than usual. Chain-smoking cigarettes and brushing ashes from the bulge during a rehearsal break, he gave out the suggestion that he felt like a merry-go-round rider, coming around at stated intervals to the same bit of scenery.

Tambourines is based on the store-front churches that dot Harlem, churches that anyone can start by declaring himself a minister and opening for business, he said. "Most of them are run by men of good will, pious, trying to help the community and area, but there's an occasional bad seed that mars the record. Gospel singing is a feature of the store-front church, and it was with this idea that ***Tambourines*** began.

"Gospel songs are written out, unlike spirituals, which are folk songs. I'd been interested in them for a long while, and one night went to a concert at the Golden Gate. Afterwards outside, I met Jobe Huntley, who said he was a gospel singer. I said, 'Good, I'll come and hear you.' I had three or four poems that I thought would lend themselves to the gospel idiom, and I asked him if he'd like to make up some music. He did. Mahalia Jackson went over a couple of them and liked them, and there was talk of her making a record, but nothing came of it.

"So now I had some gospel songs. It seemed a pity to waste them, so I sat down and wrote a play around them—then couldn't sell the play. I sent it out to every producer I could think of. Some kept it, some lost it—every six months there would be $75 or $80 spent on more copies to go out. No takers. This went on two or three years.

"Then one night I was cleaning out my files and came across the play. I read it again, said to myself, 'Look here, this has a good story.' So I wrote the story as a novel, following the play closely.

"The novel came out in '58, was pretty well received, and all the producers who had paid no attention to the play called up and said to dramatize the novel. Among the early callers was Lawrence Langner for the Theater Guild. The guild had had the play, but I guess Langner never saw it. He worked on it with me for two or three months—gave very good theatrical suggestions—and it was tried out in Westport in the summer of '60. Every fall, we'd say we'll go ahead and put it on, but we didn't. But it was Lawrence's pet project when he died a year ago."

Joel Schenker and associates are the producers now, such players as Clara Ward and Hilda Simms are in the cast, and ***Tambourines*** will present the oddity of being one of the few nonintegrated shows in town. Such is the present temper of the day that several potential backers refused to participate on the ground there are no whites in the company, thus might be subject to white picketing. Mr. Hughes, who keeps a level head when dealing with extremes, offered to let a white actor play the role of a chauffeur, but nothing came of that. He also can be down-to-earth and realistic as to where extremes should stop.

"In the field of art, there is such a thing as a regional theater, an ethnic theater. I hope one day there will be a Negro theater up in Harlem. There are both a place and a need for it. But in a play about Harlem—well, if you're doing "The Playboy of the Western World,' Negroes shouldn't go picket the Irish either."

Mr. Hughes has been involved in sundry ways with four Broadway attractions, three off Broadway, and the chances seem good this morning that ***Tambourines*** really will open on Saturday. Nevertheless, he remains a little moody about the theater. "I keep going back to poetry to make a living," he remarked. To his composer, who has the build of a halfback and is a nurse in charge of a floor at Harlem Hospital, he ordered, "Keep your job!" One reason for the moodiness—

"There was a whole long period from [Marc Connelly's] *The Green Pastures* to [Lorraine Hansberry's] *Raisin in the Sun* when it was most difficult to get a play about

Negro life on the stage. When they did come along, they were written by whites. There were some very good Negro writers and composers around, but they were disregarded. The gospel songs give another case in point. They were around, but now that they've gotten known commercially, they have non-Negro arrangers. I kept telling Lawrence, 'Let's get this play on before gospel singing gets so commercial Mitch will have it.' "

Lewis Nichols, "Poems to Play: Langston Hughes Describes the Genesis of His 'Tambourines to Glory'," in The New York Times, *October 27, 1963, p. 3.*

Howard Taubman (review date 4 November 1963)

[In the review below, Taubman negatively appraises Hughes's Tambourines to Glory. *Though he lauds the production's gospel music and singing, he faults its narrative, characterization, and staging, judging it a dramatic embarrassment.]*

Almost any excuse, you would think, would justify a company gathered for gospel singing. But it's hard to condone ***Tambourines to Glory,*** even though its gospel singing has the beat and fervor of hallelujah time.

For this "gospel singing play," which Langston Hughes has adapted from his novel, has the look of something slapped together. As drama it is embarrassing; it cannot make up its mind to a point of view, and it shifts carelessly from comedy to satire to melodrama to piety. Its characterization is as casual as a comic strip's. And the story drags foolishly and gets in the way of the singing.

The singing and songs, particularly the gospel numbers, are better than all right. When the Little Theater, which was reclaimed for the living stage when ***Tambourines to Glory*** opened Saturday night, becomes the Tambourine Temple and the company beatifically pounds out "I'm Gonna Testify," a theatergoer feels like joining in the rejoicing. For this company knows how to communicate the jubilation of a gospel song's ecstatic rhythms.

But by this time ***Tambourines to Glory*** has lost its narrative way. At the outset Mr. Hughes's play behaves as if it will be something more than an outlet for gospel singing. Despite an absence of tight writing and staging, the work begins as if it means to be ironic as well as warmhearted.

In the opening scene we meet Rosetta Le Noire as devout, deep-voiced Essie Belle Johnson who, though evicted with her battered valises and birdcage onto a Harlem sidewalk, trusts in the Lord to help her. At this point Hilda Simms as Laura, a trim chippie, arrives and suggests that there is money to be made in starting a street-corner church.

Laura meets the fancy of Louis Gossett as Big-Eyed Buddy Lomax, an evil Harlem hustler. Buddy is a sharpie who has quick ideas for turning a dishonest buck. He also has a line to Marty, the man behind the man behind the man who can arrange everything, and he is wise enough in the ways of the world to know that a fellow like Marty "can't be colored." With his fringe of beard and his sinuous way Mr. Gossett's Buddy is delightfully Mephistophelean.

But ***Tambourines to Glory*** refuses to hold fast to style. Its attitude even to the gospel songs is confused, shuttling between spoof and earnestness. However, there are some fine solo and ensemble numbers, with music by Jobe Huntley that is hauntingly blue and bouncingly joyous.

Among the performers who do what they can to keep up the spirits of ***Tambourines to Glory*** are Clara Ward, a formidable gospel singer; Robert Guillaume and Micki Grant as attractive youngsters in love, Anna English and Joseph Attles. The leading players are supported by an ensemble overflowing with energy and a zest for song. Like their play, they'd all be more usefully employed if they had more gospel songs to sing and less story to tell.

Howard Taubman, in a review of "Tambourines to Glory," in The New York Times, *November 4, 1963, p. 47.*

FURTHER READING

Arvey, Verna. "Langston Hughes: Crusader." *Opportunity* XVIII, No. 12 (December 1940): 363-64.

Laudatory essay on Hughes and his ideals.

Barksdale, Richard K. "Miscegenation on Broadway: Hughes's *Mulatto* and Edward Sheldon's *The Nigger.*" In *Critical Essays on Langston Hughes,* edited by Edward J. Mullen, pp. 191-99. Boston: G. K. Hall and Co., 1986.

Compares Hughes's treatment of miscegenation to Sheldon's as found in two of their principal dramas. Barksdale contends that Sheldon viewed the theme from a "racially exterior" perspective "as just another regional foible bespeaking the legendary moral turpitude of the sinful South," whereas Hughes's "racially interior view" is based on his own personal experience of paternal abandonment.

Clark, VèVè. "Restaging Langston Hughes' *Scottsboro Limited:* An Interview with Amiri Baraka." *The Black Scholar* 10, No. 10 (July-August 1979): 62-9.

Interview in which producer Baraka discusses the question of national oppression in the famed Scottsboro Trial (1931), describing his plans to revive Hughes's "revolutionary" drama based on the case.

Cohn, Ruby. "Less than Novel." In her *American Drama,* pp. 170-225. Bloomington: Indiana University Press, 1971.

Acknowledges Hughes's sustained interest in African-American theater, praising his dramatic range and skill in dialogue.

Davis, Arthur P. "The Tragic Mulatto Theme in Six Works of Langston Hughes." *Phylon* XVI, No. 2 (1955): 195-204.

Concludes that Hughes unconsciously employed the tragic mulatto theme to express the disappointment and rejection that he himself felt as a rejected son.

Emanuel, James A. *Langston Hughes.* New Haven, Conn.: College & University Press, 1967, 192 p.

Biographical and literary survey that provides understanding of Hughes's achievements in all genres, particularly concentrating on the major themes and stylistic variations in his works.

———. "The Literary Experiments of Langston Hughes." *CLA Journal* XI, No. 4 (June 1968): 335-44.

Examines the black aesthetic in Hughes's plays, humorous prose, short stories, and poetry.

Embree, Edwin R. "Shakespeare in Harlem." In his *Against the Odds,* pp. 117-38. New York: Viking Press, 1944.

Biographical profile of Hughes.

Hughes, Langston. "The Twenties: Harlem and Its Negritude." *African Forum* 1, No. 4 (Spring 1966): 11-20.

Hughes's personal recollections of the Harlem Renaissance.

Meltzer, Milton. *Langston Hughes: A Biography.* New York: Thomas Y. Crowell Company, 1968, 281 p.

Overview of Hughes's life and career.

Randall, Dudley. "The Black Aesthetic in the Thirties, Forties, and Fifties." In *The Black Aesthetic,* edited by Addison Gayle, Jr., pp. 224-34. Garden City, N.Y.: Doubleday and Co., 1971.

Discusses the black artist's function in American society. Randall cites Hughes as the first to break from the school of black writers who desired to be part of mainstream American literature in order to establish his own literary style.

Taylor, Patricia E. "Langston Hughes and the Harlem Renaissance, 1921-31." In *The Harlem Renaissance Remembered,* edited by Arna Bontemps, pp. 90-102. New York: Dodd, Mead and Co., 1972.

Recognizes Hughes's literary contributions to the Harlem Renaissance.

Turner, Darwin T. "The Negro Dramatist's Image of the Universe." *CLA Journal* V, No. 2 (December 1961): 106-20.

Traces the African-American artist's progression from crusader and denouncer of racial injustices to delineator and psychologist concerned with individual dilemmas.

Vidal, David. "What Happens to a Dream? This One Lives." *New York Times* (24 March 1977): B 1-2.

Praises Hughes's literary accomplishments on the occasion of his seventy-fifth birthday.

Additional coverage of Hughes's life and career is contained in the following sources published by Gale Research: *Black Literature Criticism,* Vol. 2; *Children's Literature Review,* Vol. 17; *Contemporary Literary Criticism,* Vols. 1, 5, 10, 15, 35, 44; *Dictionary of Literary Biography,* Vols. 4, 7, 48, 51, 86; *Poetry Criticism,* Vol. 1; *Short Story Criticism,* Vol. 6.

Thomas Kyd

1558-1594

INTRODUCTION

Also known as Thomas Kid, Kidde, and Kydd.

Primarily known for *The Spanish Tragedy,* Kyd is recognized as an innovative and transitional figure in Elizabethan drama. In *The Spanish Tragedy,* Kyd developed previously unrefined dramatic devices and conventions to a new level of maturity, and his masterful use of classical tragic models far surpassed the efforts of preceding dramatists. Kyd was the first playwright in English literature to feature revenge as the central focus of a tragedy, introducing to the popular stage a literary form which has become known as the revenge tragedy and which has been characterized by Deborah Rubin as, "the most perfect vehicle for the portrayal of man's struggle to harmonize his spontaneous need for retribution with his religious and ethical beliefs." Kyd's form was widely imitated throughout the Elizabethan era and the theatrical success of *The Spanish Tragedy* lasted well into the seventeenth century. Moody E. Prior has credited Kyd with "greatly [advancing] the art of verse drama," claiming that with *The Spanish Tragedy,* "English tragedy had been clearly started in the direction of its artistic destiny."

Kyd was born in London in 1558. A record of his baptism on November sixth of that year still exists, identifying him as the son of Francis Kyd, a scrivener of good standing. Francis Kyd enrolled his son in the newly established Merchant Taylors' school in 1565, where he was a classmate of Edmund Spenser. Kyd's later life and career are not well documented. There is no evidence that Kyd pursued a university education and some scholars have speculated that he may have temporarily practiced his father's trade before he began writing for the stage. It is known that Kyd entered the service of a lord in some capacity in 1587 but was released in 1593. According to London records, Kyd was arrested that year in a city-wide search for the author of discriminatory publications against foreigners residing in London. Authorities who searched Kyd's room for proof of his involvement in this matter instead found papers that they considered atheistic and sacrilegious. During his imprisonment, Kyd was subjected to what he described in a letter to his previous employer as "paines and undeserved tortures," but he would not confess to writing the heretical essays. In fact, Kyd attributed them to his friend and fellow playwright, Christopher Marlowe, with whom he had shared the searched quarters. Before this accusation could be fully investigated, however, Marlowe was murdered. Although Kyd was eventually freed from prison, he was never wholly cleared of the charges, and he died destitute little more than a year later at the age of thirty-six.

Although Kyd's reputation is based solely on *The Spanish Tragedy,* the play was not published under his name until several centuries after it was written. Literary historians have assigned the work to Kyd in large measure because Thomas Heywood attributed it to him in his 1612 *Apology for Actors.* The date of the tragedy's composition, however, is the subject of much debate. Scholars have generally agreed that the tragedy may have been written as early as 1582, when published material that *The Spanish Tragedy* alludes to was first printed, or as late as 1592, the year in which the play was staged for the first time. Although critics have suggested many theories for their estimations, there is no consensus of opinion on an actual composition date. Frederick S. Boas concluded that *The Spanish Tragedy* was written around 1586 or 1587, basing his arguments on apparent references to its subject matter by Thomas Nashe in his preface to Robert Greene's *Menaphon* (1589). Arthur Freeman has seconded Boas's opinion and has reasoned further that Kyd's treatment of the Spanish milieu in his tragedy indicates that it was writ-

The Spanish Tragedie:
OR,
Hieronimo is mad againe.

Containing the lamentable end of *Don Horatio*, and *Belimperia*; with the pittifull death of *Hieronimo*.

Newly corrected, amended, and enlarged with new Additions of the *Painters* part, and others, as it hath of late been diuers times acted.

LONDON,
Printed by W. White, for I. White and T. Langley, and are to be sold at their Shop ouer against the Sarazens head without New-gate. 1615.

Title page from the 1615 edition of The Spanish Tragedy.

ten before the destruction of the Spanish Armada in 1588. Philip Edwards, however, has disagreed with Boas and Freeman, positing that 1590 is a more accurate composition date; his contention is founded on the work's thematic and stylistic parallels with other dramas from that period.

Kyd's *Cornelia* is the only play that has been definitely ascribed to him and that has a precise composition date. A translation of Robert Garnier's *Cornélie* (1585), Kyd's play was registered for publication in early 1594 under his name. Scholars have characterized *Cornelia* as an attempt by Kyd to compose a tragedy for academia, rather than for the popular stage. They also believe that Kyd translated Torquato Tasso's *Il Padre di Famiglia* (1583) as *The Housholder's Philosophie,* a small pamphlet espousing rural wisdom and offering strategies for running a successful household. This work was published in 1588 under the initials T. K. and resembles Kyd's *Cornelia* in its method of translation and certain peculiarities of style. Literary historians have also posited that Kyd is the author of *Soliman and Perseda,* a play that was anonymously registered for publication in 1592 but was most likely written earlier. The attribution of *Soliman and Perseda* to Kyd primarily rests on the appearance of a virtually identical story in the play-within-the-play of *The Spanish Tragedy* also entitled *Soliman and Perseda.* Similarities in dramatic technique, melodramatic elements, and dramatic irony in these two works have led many critics to conclude that they were both written by the same playwright.

Many commentators have further speculated that Kyd produced a dramatic work, now lost, of significance equal to or greater than that of *The Spanish Tragedy.* Several references in Elizabethan literature suggest that Kyd may have created a well-known version of the Hamlet story at least a decade before Shakespeare's great tragedy. The probable source for this drama was Saxo Grammaticus's *Historiae Danicae* (c. 1200), a rendering of the Norse legend of *Amloth.* In the above-mentioned preface to Greene's *Menaphon,* Nashe alluded to "the Kidde in Aesop" who would "afford you whole *Hamlets,* I should say handfulls of tragical speeches." This and other vague comments in Nashe's preface have led critics to ascribe the so-called *Ur-Hamlet* to Kyd. They also cite parallels in dramatic style and plot between *The Spanish Tragedy* and an early quarto edition of Shakespeare's *Hamlet* as proof of Kyd's authorship of the *Ur-Hamlet.*

As the first significant tragedy on the Elizabethan stage in which the central action is linked to the progression of revenge, Kyd's *Spanish Tragedy* introduced a new type of tragedy to the English theater. The genre of revenge tragedy is generally characterized by the revenge of a son for the death of a father or vice versa, sensational brutality, intrigue, the occurrence of insanity and suicide, a scheming villain, and the ghost of a murdered man who urges vengeance. *The Spanish Tragedy* centers on the character of Hieronimo, who seeks to avenge the death of his son Horatio, who has been murdered by Lorenzo, the nephew to the King of Spain, and Balthazar, son of the Viceroy of Portugal. The murder was committed to end Horatio's affair with Bel-Imperia, Lorenzo's sister who is loved by Balthazar. At various points in the play, the ghost of the nobleman Andrea—who had earlier been killed by Balthazar—appears, acting as a "chorus" figure, commenting on the action and promoting the idea of revenge. The tragedy is particularly memorable for its enactment of great horrors; by the end of the play, nearly everyone of the main characters has been violently killed onstage. Kyd's focus on violence and bloodshed in *The Spanish Tragedy* has further led scholars to classify the play as a tragedy of blood, an intensely morbid version of the revenge tragedy in which retribution is achieved through murder, assassination, and mutilation. In addition, because Hieronimo avenges the death of a blood relative, Kyd introduces yet another motif, identified as blood-revenge, into *The Spanish Tragedy.*

The plays of Seneca—a first century Roman dramatist, philosopher, prose writer, and statesman—are considered among the leading sources for *The Spanish Tragedy,* for Kyd's drama exhibits many characteristics of Senecan tragedy, including the use of a chorus, stock characters such as the ghost and the tyrannical villain, sensational themes and the explicit depiction of horrors, and a highly rhetorical style marked by both sharp dialogue and tragic soliloquies. Imitations of Seneca's themes and techniques were prevalent in the English theater in the decades before *The Spanish Tragedy* was composed, and Senecan tragedy became the subject of great academic and popular interest throughout the Elizabethan era. However, while revenge had appeared in Seneca as an important vehicle for the culmination of tragedy, it was never exploited in his plays as fully as in Kyd's *Spanish Tragedy.* Some scholars have suggested that Kyd adopted this added emphasis from popular Italian tragedy. Italian theater as well as Italian and French novellas often treated vengeance and horror as central plot concerns. Furthermore, the ruthless Machiavellian villain resembling Kyd's Lorenzo and the revengeful female character similar to Bel-Imperia in *The Spanish Tragedy* were common features in French and Italian fiction. Most importantly, critics have claimed that the carnage associated with the vendetta tradition in Italian tragedy could easily have enhanced Kyd's principal theme. Other commentators have presumed that Kyd may have borrowed the blood-revenge motif in *The Spanish Tragedy* from the source for his *Ur-Hamlet,* asserting that the two works treated a markedly similar theme.

Critics have speculated that Renaissance audiences relished performances of *The Spanish Tragedy,* having a decided fondness for such entertainment as bear-baiting and public executions. Nevertheless, a decade after its appearance on the stage, theater owner and manager Philip Henslowe commissioned another dramatist to revise Kyd's tragedy, presumably to make the play conform with the audience's changing tastes. Ben Jonson has generally been acknowledged as the author of these additions, although John Webster and even Shakespeare have been suggested as well. This version engendered a great number of enlarged and emended editions of *The Spanish Tragedy,* although Kyd's original text still survives. Later generations of theatergoers were less attracted to the overt melodrama and violence of Kyd's tragedy of blood, and *The Spanish Tragedy* became the object of parody and ridicule by subsequent playwrights. It has rarely been produced on stage since the seventeenth century, but Kyd's most successful play has not failed to receive a great deal of scholarly interest. Curiously, because significant critical attention has been devoted to Kyd's impact on the development of English tragedy, commentators have often neglected the artistic value of his dramaturgy. Recent critics such as Prior, however, have stressed Kyd's innovative use of dramatic speech in *The Spanish Tragedy,* noting that Kyd skillfully mastered an elegance of expression and a complex but various use of rhetoric and blank verse. Prior has also demonstrated how Kyd used symbols and images to accentuate the central action of the tragedy and to reveal the progression of Hieronimo's emotions. After Horatio's death, images of darkness and night evoke Hieronimo's sorrow and the beginning of his insanity, while contrasting images of heaven and hell later in the narrative express Hieronimo's inner turmoil and doubt about obtaining justice for his son's murder. When Hieronimo eventually succumbs to the lure of revenge, images of blood and violence serve as reminders of his son's death and as indicators of his determination to avenge Horatio and secure justice.

Although Prior has argued that Kyd used imagery and symbolism to reveal Hieronimo's thoughts and emotions, he has concluded that Kyd's work is technically immature and suffers from his attempt to merge the play's unrestrained violence with the stylized and ornamental speech common to drama of that period. Other critics have maintained that the greatest flaw of *The Spanish Tragedy* is Kyd's failure to convey Hieronimo's motives for exacting private revenge rather than obtaining public justice. Furthermore, some commentators have contended that the complexity of the play's action and its seemingly extraneous episodes and subplots are also signs of Kyd's technical immaturity. Fredson Bowers has voiced both of these complaints, asserting that the disorganization and diffusion of the various subplots in *The Spanish Tragedy* detract from the central theme of revenge and thus deprive the tragedy of the impression of a unified whole. He has also claimed that Hieronimo does not seek justice through the proper channels and that, by deceitfully satisfying his need for retribution through private revenge, he would appear as a villain in the eyes of Elizabethan audiences. Other scholars have disagreed with Bowers, suggesting that, if Kyd's main concern was justice, rather than revenge, these perceived faults could be reconciled. These critics have argued that Hieronimo does in fact attempt to secure justice for Horatio's murder, but Lorenzo successfully outmaneuvers him in each of his efforts to approach the king. Further, Hieronimo's judgment is impaired by his lapse into insanity toward the end of the play. Ejner J. Jensen has commented that if one accepts justice as the chief unifying theme that links each of the characters and their actions in *The Spanish Tragedy,* then the "various disparate themes and elements combine to create a skillful dramatic unity." Some commentators who have given special attention to the episodes involving the ghost of Andrea contend that the principal theme of *The Spanish Tragedy* is divine justice, emphasizing Kyd's use of dramatic irony in depicting each character as a particular tool of destiny. In these assessments, Hieronimo is seen not as a villian, but as an instrument of the gods, who have granted Andrea's request for revenge against Balthazar. Herbert R. Coursen has provided yet another perspective on the theme of revenge and justice in the play by considering the Castile family—Lorenzo and his father the Duke—not Hieronimo, as the focus of Kyd's attention in *The Spanish Tragedy.* He has proposed that the mechanism of revenge is triggered by the machinations and crimes of the House of Castile, which range from the Duke and Lorenzo's engineering of Andrea's murder to Lorenzo's killing of Horatio. Coursen maintains that this theory explains Kyd's inclusion of the ghost of Andrea and other elements of the tragedy which had previously been viewed as unnecessary distractions from the main plot.

While critics continue to debate over the ambiguous nature of Kyd's plot and character development in *The Spanish Tragedy,* they generally concede his skill in creating an exciting and absorbing theatrical spectacle. Kyd's dramatic achievement has largely been overshadowed by that of his contemporaries Marlowe and Shakespeare, but he is nevertheless accorded a significant place in the history of English drama. *The Spanish Tragedy* remains a testament to Kyd's innovative cultivation of dramatic techniques, representing, as Philip Edwards has summarized, "a most ingenious and successful blending of the old and the new in drama."

PRINCIPAL WORKS

PLAYS

* *Ur-Hamlet* 1587?
† *The Spanish Tragedy* 1590?
‡ *Soliman and Perseda* 1592?
Cornelia [translator; of the play *Cornélie* by Robert Garnier] 1594

OTHER MAJOR WORKS

§ *The Housholder's Philosophie* [translator; of Torquato Tasso's *Il Padre di Famiglia*] (essay) 1588
The Works of Thomas Kyd (dramas and essays) 1901

* The hypothetical *Ur-Hamlet* is not extant. Its existence and date have been inferred from several contemporary essays, poems, and dramas, most notably Thomas Nashe's prose preface to Robert Greene's *Menaphon* (1589). The work has been attributed to Kyd on the basis of these references and on parallels between *The Spanish Tragedy* and Shakespeare's first quarto version of *Hamlet.*

† This date is based on Philip Edward's estimate in his 1959 edition of *The Spanish Tragedy.* Most scholars agree that *The Spanish Tragedy* was written between 1582 and 1592. This ten-year range is inferred from the appearance in 1582 of material alluded to in Kyd's famous tragedy and from the first recorded performance of *The Spanish Tragedy* in 1592. Although *The Spanish Tragedy* was published anonymously, Thomas Heywood ascribed it to Kyd in his *Apology for Actors* (1612).

‡ *Soliman and Perseda* was entered in the Stationer's Register in 1592 as *The Tragedye of Solyman and Perseda.* The date above is derived from that entry, although the play may have been written earli-

er. Kyd's possible authorship of this play has been suggested by similarities in dialogue, plot, and style between *Soliman and Perseda* and both *The Spanish Tragedy* and its play-within-the-play also entitled *Soliman and Perseda.*

§ Although scholars have not been able to attribute this work to Kyd with absolute certainty, it bore the initials T. K. when it was first published in 1588. *The Housholder's Philosophie* has also been ascribed to Kyd because the style of translation closely resembles that of Kyd's *Cornelia.*

THE SPANISH TRAGEDY

Fredson Bowers (essay date 1940)

[*Bowers was an American scholar and educator whose works include* Elizabethan Revenge Tragedy *(1940) and* Hamlet: A Guide to the Play *(1965). In the following excerpt from the former work, the critic argues that* The Spanish Tragedy *"is far from a perfect working-out of the revenge theme." In Bower's opinion, the Andrea–Revenge episodes bear little relation to the rest of the tragedy, Kyd fails to unify the numerous revenge plots in the play, and Elizabethan audiences would have perceived Hieronimo as a villain for exacting lawless, private revenge on Lorenzo and Balthazar. For a response to this thesis, see the excerpt dated 1965 by Ejner J. Jensen.*]

With the production of ***The Spanish Tragedy*** Elizabethan tragedy received its first great impetus. The immediate and long-lasting popularity of the play stamped it as a type, a form to be imitated. Thus it is of the highest significance that ***The Spanish Tragedy*** first popularized revenge as a tragic motive on the Elizabethan popular stage by using blood-vengeance as the core of its dramatic action. True, earlier English tragedies, leaning heavily on Seneca, had utilized revenge to a certain extent for dramatic motivation. But in *Gorboduc* (1562) any incipient interest in the characters' motives of revenge is stifled under the emphasis on the political theme and the general classical decorum, and the ancient classical story of revenge in John Pikeryng's *Horestes* (1567) is so medievalized that it loses all significance except as a basis for comedy and pageantry. *Gismond of Salerne,* acted at the Inner Temple in 1567/8, borrows various revenge trappings from Seneca and the Italians but the pathetic love story usurps the main interest.

Elizabethan revenge tragedy properly begins with Thomas Kyd's extant masterpiece, ***The Spanish Tragedy*** (1587-1589) which presented revenge in kind—blood-revenge, the sacred duty of the father to avenge the murder of his son—and from that sensational theme derived its popularity. Sensational though the central motive proved, it was a universal one, appealing to all classes of people and to all time. As in the law-abiding Athens of Aeschylus, the Greek audience saw enacted in the Orestes trilogy events of a more turbulent past but now outmoded, so the English spectators viewed dramatic action at once somewhat foreign to their present stage of society yet still within their range of sympathy and understanding. The realism was clinched when the scene was laid in another country where, to their knowledge, the people were crueler and more revengeful, and where, as in Italy, the individualistic spirit still flourished among the nobility in despite of the law.

The Spanish Tragedy is far from a perfect working-out of a revenge theme. Kyd started to make a Senecan imitation adapted to the popular stage. Someone has been killed, and the slayer is to suffer the revenge of the ghost, presumably by becoming tangled in his own misdeeds as in *Hercules Furens,* or, as in *Thyestes,* through the malign influence of the supernatural chorus. Curiously, this Senecan ghost's reason for revenge is extraordinarily weak as seen through English eyes. The parallel with the ghost of Achilles in *Troades* which rises to demand vengeance for death in battle is obvious, but an English popular audience could not become excited over a ghost seeking vengenance for a fair death in the field. No very personal interest can be aroused in the early action of the play if it proceeds solely from the point of view of an alien ghost, and with Horatio as the successful avenger of his friend.

The first human note is struck when Bel-Imperia resolves to use second love, in the person of Horatio, to revenge the death of her first lover. If this resolution had furnished the plot, the sequence of events would still have revolved about the ghost but with greater logic. Bel-Imperia is more closely connected with Andrea than Horatio, and some semblance of justification is added when Balthazar begins his suit, for the audience can visualize a forced marriage with the slayer of her lover, an impossible situation. Furthermore, at the moment she was the logical revenger since women were noted for their revengefulness in Elizabethan life and the Italian *novelle.* The whole first act is devoted to the exposition and to the resolution of the beloved to revenge the death of her lover. The rising action is begun when Bel-Imperia starts to charm Horatio, her chosen instrument for the revenge, and some hint is given of an opposing force in the person of her brother Lorenzo who has sided with Balthazar's suit.

Still the situation is dramatically almost impossible. Horatio has no thought that Andrea's death requires vengeance; consequently, if he is intended for the revenger of blood, he will prove no more than the weak tool of Bel-Imperia, who, by her insistence in driving him to the deed, will become a villainess. And if Horatio is not to be made this anomalous revenger, Bel-Imperia's only course would be so to set Balthazar and Horatio at odds over her love that one or the other is killed. If Balthazar falls, the play is no tragedy. If, on the other hand, Horatio is killed, his position as Bel-Imperia's tool precludes the sympathy of the audience, and forces Bel-Imperia herself to kill Balthazar, a course she might have followed in the beginning without causing the death of an innocent man. If Horatio is not conceived as a mere instrument for the unscrupulous Bel-Imperia but as a real and requited lover, his position as revenger for a preceding lover grows even more anomalous, and the revenge for Andrea loses all ethical dignity.

The only solution lies in developing the strength of the opposing force. The second act, therefore, is given over entirely to showing the ascendancy of Lorenzo. Necessarily the revenge theme lies dormant while Kyd devotes himself to painting an idyllic picture of the love of Horatio and Bel-Imperia, and its fatal end. Bel-Imperia is ostensibly carrying out her avowed intention to love Horatio and thus spite Balthazar, but since her passion for Horatio (which has rapidly passed from pretense to reality) seems to have replaced her desire to revenge Andrea, the central theme of revenge is dropped in the emphasis on the happy lovers. Balthazar now has a tangible reason for a revenge: first, because Horatio took him prisoner in battle, and second because Horatio has preempted his intended bride. With Lorenzo as the guiding spirit, the two slay Horatio. The deed is presumably the revenge of Balthazar, but Lorenzo's cold determination to brush aside all obstacles to his sister's royal marriage makes him the real murderer.

At this point the tragedy has strayed its farthest from the main theme as announced by the chorus composed of Revenge and the ghost of Andrea. This time, however, a real revenger of blood appears. Hieronimo does not know the murderers of his son, but he plans to dissemble until he learns and then to strike. At the finish of the second act, with Bel-Imperia imprisoned, and a new revenger for a new crime appearing, the play actually disregards the revenge for Andrea and settles down to dramatize a revenge among men for a crime already seen and appreciated by the audience, no longer a revenge for an unreasonable ghost. From this point the ghost and his theme, which was to be the core of the play, are superfluous; and, indeed, need never have been introduced.

The third act, which begins the second half of the play, works out two lines of action: the progress made by the revenger Hieronimo, and the efforts of the murderer Lorenzo to consolidate his position in order to escape detection. The difficulty of appropriate dramatic action for the revenger posed a nice problem for Kyd. A revenger with no knowledge and no possible clues to investigate is a static figure since action is impossible. Yet a revenger with complete knowledge would normally act at once, and the play would be over. Kyd solved the problem brilliantly. The note from Bel-Imperia which gives him the names of the murderers is so startling that Hieronimo suspects a trap, for he knows of no motive why Lorenzo and the foreign prince should have killed his son. He must therefore assure himself of the truth before he acts, and since Bel-Imperia has been removed from court a delay is unavoidable. At one stroke Kyd has given the necessary information to the revenger, and then tied his hands until the plot has further unfolded.

Hieronimo's projected investigation has provided him with some dramatic action, particularly when the course of his inquiries sets the opposing force once more in motion. Lorenzo, believing his secret revealed, endeavors to destroy all proof by ridding himself of his accomplices Serberine and Pedringano. Ironically, it is this deed which finally gives the revenger his necessary corroboration in the incriminating letter found on Pedringano's dead body. The doubts of Bel-Imperia's letter are now resolved; his delay ended, Hieronimo rushes to the king for justice. It is important to note that Hieronimo first endeavors to secure his legal rights before taking the law into his own hands. Again a problem in plotting occurs. Hieronimo with his proof will gain the king's ear; Bel-Imperia will second Pedringano's letter; the murderers will be executed. Another impossible dramatic situation looms, for there would be no conflict of forces and no tragedy except of the most accidental sort.

It is evident that the revenger must be made to delay once more. Fear of deception cannot be employed again, and clearly the only possible means is either to delay Hieronimo's interview with the king or else to introduce some motive that would lead the king to discredit him. Once again Kyd brilliantly solved the problem by introducing the motive of madness. Isabella, Hieronimo's wife, runs mad, and Hieronimo next appears so stunned by grief for her and for his son that his own wits have been unsettled. He answers a request for information so wildly that his questioners think him wholly insane. Realizing that his madness has made him impotent, he meditates suicide but thrusts the thought aside before the reviving sense of his duty to revenge. His distraction, however, keeps him from gaining the king's ear, and when he recovers his senses he realizes that he can never find legal justice but must act as the executioner himself.

At this point the reasons for delay, previously logical, break down. Hieronimo says simply that he will revenge Horatio's death, but

> not as the vulgare wits of men,
> With open, but ineuitable ils,
> As by a secret, yet a certaine meane,
> Which vnder kindeship wilbe cloked best.
> Wise men will take their opportunitie,
> Closely and safely fitting things to time.
> But in extreames aduantage hath no time;
> And therefore all times fit not for reuenge. . . .
> *Remedium malorum iners est.*
> Nor ought auailes it me to menace them
> Who as a wintrie storme vpon a plaine,
> Will beare me downe with their nobilitie.
> (III,xiii,21-38)

These are scarcely valid reasons for delay in the execution of his private justice, since he admits that open and inevitable ills exist (without the necessity for delay) by which he could overthrow his enemies. Of course, his intention to dissemble patiently and to wait until he can consummate his vengeance at the right time and place heightens the interest in the inevitable catastrophe. The speech, in its entirety, would nevertheless irretrievably weaken the logic of the plot and the conception of Hieronimo's character were it not that it marks the turning point from Hieronimo the hero to Hieronimo the villian.

The fourth and last act opens with Bel-Imperia, now entirely forgetful of Andrea, swearing that if Hieronimo neglects his duty to revenge Horatio she herself will kill the murderers. Hieronimo presumably has a plan in mind, for the manuscript of the tragedy is ready when Lorenzo asks for an entertainment. Isabella, tortured by the thought of the unrevenged death of her son, kills herself in a fit of madness. Hieronimo braces himself for his revenge, and the fatal play is enacted. Even with Lorenzo and Balthazar slain and Bel-Imperia a suicide, the Viceroy, Balthazar's father, interposes for Hieronimo. Then occurs a scene which is useless except as it leads to the final culmination of horrors and the eventual conception of Hieronimo as a dangerous, blood-thirsty maniac. Hieronimo from the stage has already rehearsed his reasons for the murders, but the king orders him captured and inexplicably tries to wring from him the causes (already explained) for the deed, and the names of the confederates (already revealed as Bel-Imperia alone). Without this senseless action Hieronimo would have had no opportunity to tear out his tongue or to stab the duke, Lorenzo's father. His own suicide closes the play.

An analysis of the play reveals the basic Kydian formula for the tragedy of revenge:

(1) The fundamental motive for the tragic action is revenge, although the actual vengeance of Hieronimo is not conceived until midway in the play. This revenge is by a father for the murder of his son, and extends not only to the murderers but also to their innocent kindred. The revenger is aided by a revenger accomplice, and both commit suicide after achieving their vengeance.

(2) Hieronimo's revenge is called forth by the successful revenge, conceived for a supposed injury, of the villains on his son.

(3) The ghost of the slain Andrea watches the revenge on the person who killed him and on those who hindered his love, but the action of the latter half of the play does not spring from the motive of a revenge for him nor is this revenge directed chiefly at his slayer. Consequently the ghost has no real connection with the play. This loose use of a vengeance-seeking ghost was not repeated in later plays.

(4) An important dramatic device is the justifiable hesitation of the revenger, who requires much proof, and, on the failure of legal justice, supposedly lacks a suitable opportunity for straight-forward action. Hieronimo finds his task difficult; he is burdened with doubt and human weakness and delayed by his madness. The letter from Bel-Imperia, Pedringano's posthumous confession, the exhortations of Bel-Imperia and her offers of assistance, and the death of his wife, are all required to spur his resolution to the deed.

(5) Madness is an important dramatic device. Hieronimo is afflicted with passing fits of genuine madness brought on by his overwhelming grief and the overwhelming sense of his obligation and his helplessness to revenge which saps his will. It is not probable that in Kyd's original version Hieronimo ever pretended madness. There are two scenes in which his words are too glib and flighty (the reconciliation with Lorenzo and the plans for the play-within-a-play), but in both his nerves are under pressure owing to the rôle he is acting, and his wild talk shows the intense strain on a mind already somewhat weakened rather than a pretense to lure his opponents into false security.

(6) Intrigue used against and by the revenger is an important element. Lorenzo's machinations fill a considerable portion of the play. Hieronimo secures his revenge by elaborate trickery.

(7) The action is bloody and deaths are scattered through the play. Ten characters are killed, eight of these on-stage.

(8) The contrast and enforcement of the main situation are achieved by parallels. Andrea requires revenging, as does Horatio. Hieronimo's grief for his son is reenforced by the grief of the Viceroy for the supposed death of Balthazar and later for his actual slaying. More particularly, Hieronimo is paralleled by the petitioner whose son has been killed. His madness finds a counterpart in Isabella's, and his hesitation is contrasted to Bel-Imperia's desire for action.

(9) The accomplices on both sides are killed. Bel-Imperia falls a suicide, and the villain with keen irony destroys Serberine and Pedringano in order to protect himself.

(10) Lorenzo, the villain, is an almost complete Machiavellian, as full of villainous devices as he is free from scruples.

(11) The revenge is accomplished terribly, fittingly, with irony and deceit. Once his resolution is screwed to the point, the revenger becomes exceedingly cunning, dissembles with the murderers, and adroitly plans their downfall.

(12) Minor characteristics are: the exhibition of Horatio's body; the wearing of black; reading in a book before a philosophical soliloquy; a letter written in blood and a handkerchief dipped in blood and kept as a memento to revenge; the melancholy of the revenger, who struggles with the problems of revenge, fortune, justice, and death; the sentimental but desperately revengeful woman.

A specific source is customarily presupposed for ***The Spanish Tragedy,*** but it has never been found, and very probably no detailed source for the entire story ever existed; for if this hypothetical source be disregarded, the roots of the play are found in Seneca's tragedies, the Italian and French *novelle,* possibly in the Renaissance Italian tragedy, and certainly in the old Teutonic story of Hamlet as told by Saxo Grammaticus and translated by Belleforest.

Senecan influence there is undoubtedly in the penning of the lines. The machinery of the ghost of Andrea and Revenge is also Senecan in construction, although the function of the two as chorus is not classical. The Spirit of Revenge is presumably influencing the actions of the characters in much the same fashion in which the ghost of Tantalus casts his malign influence over the house of Pelops in *Thyestes.* Such a pulling of the strings from without, therefore, is wholly Senecan, as is the parallel to *Thyestes* where a particular revenge enacted on the stage satisfies the debt to an unrelated crime from the past. Senecan, too, are the bloodshed and horrors, though typically Renaissance in their form. Seneca usually emphasizes one great passion; ***The Spanish Tragedy*** is a study of the overwhelming passion of revenge. Revenge either moderately forthright, as in *Agamemnon,* or else by secret, deceitful means, as in *Thyestes,* had already appeared in Seneca as a proper subject for tragedy.

To a certain extent, however, the debt to Seneca has been

exaggerated. Actual insanity in Seneca is limited to the madness sent by Juno upon Hercules, a situation which has no possible parallel in ***The Spanish Tragedy.*** Somewhat closer to Kyd's conception are the divine "madnesses" of Medea and Deïanira, but the origin of Hieronimo's insanity does not actually come from the Roman tragedian. The hesitation of the revenger had appeared momentarily when Medea once falters in her resolve and when Clytemnestra requires the goading of Aegisthus. Neither of these plays, however, utilized the motive of hesitation to prolong the plot, as does Kyd, but instead merely to fillip the interest of the audience for a moment with the possibility that the revenge might be abandoned. The true source for Hieronimo's dramatically important hesitation is not there. Again, the suicides of Bel-Imperia and Hieronimo have no relation to the expiatory suicides of Seneca's characters who have caused the death of some beloved person. The most specific contribution of Seneca to the dramatic form of ***The Spanish Tragedy*** is the ghost; yet it has been noted how Kyd was gradually led away from the Senecan construction so that his supernatural chorus became superfluous and even intrusive. The interest in the play is on the revenge on Lorenzo (and only incidentally on Balthazar) for a Horatio murdered in plain view of the audience, not the revenge on Balthazar for the ghost of Andrea, with whom Hieronimo is entirely unconnected.

Yet the general influence of Seneca on the writing and the original conception of the play cannot be denied, for such an influence was unavoidable at the time. Classical tragedy had gained an enormous prestige in England because of the great value set on classical learning, of which tragedy was supposed to be the highest expression; and knowing little of the Greeks the Elizabethans came to regard Seneca as the most tragic, the most perfect of ancient writers. Senecan tragedy was dominant on the Continent; Seneca was read freely in the English schools and universities where his plays were acted, as were Latin imitations. His methods of treating tragic situations were akin to Elizabethan temperament, for the men of the time were well equipped to understand his philosophy, which held that man, the individual, was more than the puppet of medieval scholasticism and was, indeed, to some extent the master of his fate. Even the fatalistic Senecan passages found a ready echo in the breasts of Englishmen already afflicted with the melancholia which sometimes turned them to practising malcontents. Seneca's cosmopolitanism was near to the Elizabethans, who were starting an empire and were beginning to cast off their insular provincialism.

The crudity hidden beneath the superficial polish of the Elizabethans made them less sensitive to the fundamental emptiness of much of Seneca. They were delighted with his rhetoric, for they were still so intellectually young as to be impressed by bombast and flamboyance. Introspection had become a national trait, and fed agreeably on the elaborate Senecan philosophizing, with its spice of stoicism suitable to a hard-bitten age. The long Senecan descriptions were suited for imitation on the bare English stage. Finally, Seneca's emphasis on sensationalism, on physical horrors to stimulate emotion, appealed to the English taste, for blood and horror on the stage could not be offensive to the spectators at cruel executions. Ghosts were accepted as fact, and forewarnings were everyday affairs, as with Ben Jonson's on the death of his son. Except for his classical subject-matter and his rigid classical form involving the use of choruses, there was no single element of Seneca that could not be accepted immediately by the spectator in the pit.

With such a tradition it was inevitable that ***The Spanish Tragedy*** should ring with Seneca in its rhetoric. Kyd, however, was no humble slave in his dramatic craftmanship. Admitting freely that it would be difficult to conceive ***The Spanish Tragedy*** without Seneca, we find, when details are sought for specific sources of plot and characterization, that the way leads beyond Seneca. It is highly probable that Kyd, uninfluenced specifically save by Belleforest's story of Hamlet, drew his main inspiration for the working out first of Lorenzo's and then of Hieronimo's and Bel-Imperia's revenges not from Seneca but from the ethics and incidents in the Italian and French stories and from English ideas about the Italian character.

So closely allied with the villainous characters of the Italian novels that the two cannot be separated is the Elizabethan's creation of the Italian villain based on Machiavelli's principles. Lorenzo in ***The Spanish Tragedy*** is the first of the long line of Elizabethan villains who owe their sole inspiration to Machiavelli. Although Lorenzo is not the protagonist of the play, he is so extremely active as the opposing force that he is almost as prominent as Hieronimo, and just as necessary to the extension of the dramatic action. Except that he is not a prince relying upon the doctrines of Machiavelli to rule and hold his state, every one of Lorenzo's actions reads like a exemplum of Machiavellian "policy." Even though the boundless Machiavellian ambition which produced the bloody Italian despot is absent, yet the ambition to raise his house by a royal marriage for his sister is the motivating spring of his murder of Horatio. His fundamental likeness to the Machiavellian comes in his ruthlessness toward all who stand in the way of his plans, in his perfect indifference to the sufferings he causes others, in his mania for secrecy and willingness to employ other men as catspaws, and in the tortuous and deceitful means he uses to attain his ends. Lorenzo is fundamentally cold-blooded and unsentimental, a practical man after Machiavelli's own heart. What lends particular interest to his character is the weighty evidence for believing that he was partly drawn from scandalous accounts of the Earl of Leicester, who was naïvely believed by his enemies to be the foremost exponent in England of the hated Machiavellian doctrines.

Although several are found in the French, the Italian *novelle* contain few stories of actual blood-revenge. Terrible revenges for other reasons are plentiful, however, and these influenced ***The Spanish Tragedy*** not only in incident but also in character and motivation. The type of revengeful woman exemplified by Bel-Imperia is a commonplace in Italian and French fiction, as is the brutal intriguing Lorenzo. In particular, his disposal of accomplices is partly drawn from the forty-fifth novel of the first part of Bandello. Balthazar, swearing revenge the moment he learns Horatio has won Bel-Imperia's love, fits the conception of touchy Italian pride which motivated so many tragic *novelle.* Above all, the atmosphere of the vendetta was unassailably Italian.

It is, indeed, the carrying-out of the vendetta tradition which turns Hieronimo from a hero to an Italianate villain. So long as he is pitiful in his grief for Horatio and in search of his murderers, so long the English audience would give him full sympathy. When, at last spurred to action by complete knowledge, he rushes to the king for legal justice, he would still be the hero whose actions, according to the best Elizabethan ethics, were those of an honorable man. But when Lorenzo foils him in his attempt at legal redress and he consciously gives up an open revenge in favor of a secret, treacherous device, according to English standards he inevitably becomes a villain. Indeed, so transparently weak is his sophistry and so open-eyed his turning from God's to the devil's means in the soliloquy opening Act III, scene xiii, that it is evident Kyd is deliberately veering his audience against Hieronimo.

Hieronimo begins,

> *Vindicta mihi,*

and, pursuing this promise from the Bible, consoles himself with the thought that Heaven never leaves murder unatoned; therefore he will await Heaven's decree. A quotation from Seneca then comes to his mind, and, swayed by the materialistic Senecan philosophy, he reflects that one crime opens the way for another, and he should repay wrong with wrong, for death ends both the resolute and the patient man and the end of destiny for each is merely the grave. Fortified by this un-Christian sophistry, he determines to anticipate Heaven's slow justice and to revenge for himself at his own appointed hour. Having decided to cast off Heaven, he cannot now expect a divinely awarded opportunity and so must carve the occasion for himself. He scorns acting

> as the vulgare wits of men,
> With open, but ineuitable ils,

(the only formula with which his "vulgar" audience could sympathize) and therefore, from his Machiavellian superiority to common humanity, he chooses a secret, albeit certain, plan, which he will conceal under the cloak of pretended friendship with Lorenzo. Since his project is of so great weight, he cannot hasten the hour but must bide the proper time for his revenge; delay, and dissemble his true feelings, hoping by his feigned ignorance to deceive his wary opponents. He then weakly excuses his planned hypocrisy by arguing that, even if he revealed his true feelings, he is too helpless to prevail merely with threats against his enemies' high position. Therefore he must deceive until opportunity offers revenge.

Since the next scene with Bazulto shows Hieronimo led by his grief into a fresh fit of insanity, it might be held that he is not responsible for his actions, that his weakened mind has forced him into the winding channels of his soliloquy, and that the subsequent scenes of deceit leading to the final slaughter are the actions of an insane person holding himself so rigidly in check that his madness is not visible. Such a view might, to the Elizabethans, mitigate his deed, but it would not release him from the consequences of his blood-guilt, since he would then be merely a villainous madman. Whether Kyd had enough psychological subtlety to portray Hieronimo's conversion according to this line of thought may well be a matter of opinion. A careful examination of the text leads to the view that, except for certain well defined scenes, Hieronimo is entirely sane in his revengeful plans—as sane certainly as Shakespeare's Hamlet when he stabs Claudius—although the actor may well have chosen to play him as unbalanced.

This change marked by the soliloquy from open to dissembling action was forced upon Hieronimo by the absolute necessity for Kyd to evolve a final reason for delay, and also, one may suspect, by Kyd's leaning toward the Italianate, the sensational, for the dramatic catastrophe. Once Hieronimo adopted the Italianate Machiavellian tactics, he immediately lost the absolute admiration of his audience. The English insistence on straightforward action by open assault or formal duel, which they would be inclined to view as manslaughter, refused to tolerate treacherous Italian plots. The Bible said, "Cursed is he that smiteth his neighbour secretly," and they heartily agreed. The Machiavellian breach of faith was not to be endured, for it led only to the total destruction of the breaker, and Hieronimo's pretended reconciliation with Lorenzo, with its reminiscence of Judas's kiss, was branded with the brand of Cain and of Machiavelli. With all allowance for the fact that, owing to Kyd's delight in wholesale slaughter, it was unlikely even an innocent Hieronimo would have survived the play, the fact that he was guilty of murder made it absolutely necessary for him to die. No slayer in Elizabethan drama escaped some penalty, and that penalty was usually death.

If the means by which Hieronimo ensnared and killed Lorenzo and Balthazar were not sufficient to label him a villain, the débâcle which ends the play (when, after promises of immunity if his cause has been just, he refuses all questions and wilfully stabs Lorenzo's father) certainly transported him beyond the pale. While collective revenge was understood in Elizabethan times, it was universally decried:

> "Farre be the first from God, farther be this; to strike the godly sonne for the godlesse Sire, to punish innocencie for Iniquitie. . . . Man is so just, *Amagias* slew the men, that kill'd his Father: but their children he slew not, 2 *Chron.* 14. and mans law provides for it, that *factum unius* doe not *nocere alteri,* one mans fact hurt another, saith old *Vlpian.*"
>
> [Richard Clerke, *Sermons,* 1647]

The act would have been serious enough if Hieronimo had wreaked his revenge on the duke alone, according to the primitive custom where, in a state of family solidarity, any member of a family is as acceptable as the criminal; but when, after killing Lorenzo, Hieronimo refuses a pardon and stabs the duke also, he is departing so far from the English sense of justice as finally to withdraw all sympathy. (pp. 65-81)

Hieronimo's act is . . . either the culmination of his villainy (mad or sane), or else Kyd, swept away by a passion for violence, wrote the scene with no motive in mind but the wish to portray more bloody deeds. It is faintly possible that the duke's death satisfies in some roundabout manner the justice demanded by the ghost of Andrea—long since forgotten in the play's action—for the duke had apparently discouraged with considerable emphasis Andrea's love-affair with Bel-Imperia. It might be argued that Kyd was possibly following too closely his hypothetical source with its different morality, and so confused the ethics of the play. But the theory that Kyd followed one main source is very uncertain, and there is hardly a doubt that, mad or sane, Hieronimo was a villain to the English audience at the end and was forced to commit suicide to satisfy the stern doctrine that murder, no matter what the motive, was never successful.

Bel-Imperia shares the blood-guilt with Hieronimo, but the audience probably viewed her with a more lenient eye. Her suicide, thus, was not so necessary to satisfy morality as it was the usual move of the woman in romantic fiction who refused to outlive her slain lover after seeing vengeance done. The women of Elizabethan drama did not bear the guilt of blood, as did the men, unless they were portrayed as unmistakable villainesses from their position in the plot. That they, too, often perished after staining their hands with blood or assisting in the revenge, is owing more to their refusal to live after their slain lovers than to the demands of contemporary ethics. When the reason for their revenge is not romantic, they customarily enter a convent to purge themselves.

The characters of Lorenzo, Hieronimo, and Bel-Imperia, the whole atmosphere of brutal and Machiavellian vendetta, together with part of the Pedringano incident, thus were the outgrowth of the Italian and French *novelle* and the Elizabethan's hostile view of Machiavelli and the Italian character. (pp. 81-3)

There is no definite proof that Kyd had ever read an Italian tragedy. Indeed, with the exception of the translation of *Jocasta* from Dolce by Gascoigne and Kinwelmarsh, and some borrowings by the author of *Gismond of Salerne* from Dolce's *Didone* (not omitting the debt to the Italian of the academic *Progne* and *Roxana*), no direct relationship between Italian and English tragedy has been established. Dubious parallels there are, to be sure, to indicate that early Elizabethan tragedy was perhaps following Italianate Seneca more than Seneca himself in the elaborate use of dumb shows, the rejection of the traditional Latin and Greek stories, and the extension of the scope of the action and of the list of characters. The motive of sexual love, the intensification of physical horrors and their performance on the stage, all had been paralleled in Italian tragedy; and in *Gismond of Salerne* and its later revision had been deliberately adopted from the Italian. With ***The Spanish Tragedy*** and *Locrine* the mingling of classical and popular traditions ended with the fixation of the English form of tragedy. The most suitable elements of Seneca were completely naturalized by incorporation with the main stream of popular drama, and henceforth Seneca or his Italian and French derivatives had really nothing more to teach.

Moreover, even the few early parallels were all the work of men of the Inner Temple or of the universities, and, being learned performances, were no true indication of a diffused knowledge of the Italian tragic art. In Italy itself Neo-Senecan tragedy was not a popular form, and there is no evidence that more than a handful of Englishmen were at all familiar with Italian tragedies. Certainly the typical sixteenth century Italian tragedies were not of a type to exercise any especial influence on ***The Spanish Tragedy,*** although certain rough parallels may be drawn. The Italian tragedy interested itself chiefly in the depiction of villainy and horrors. Horrors are emphasized in ***The Spanish Tragedy*** and Lorenzo is extremely important as a villain. The sources for Lorenzo's character, however, have been noted, and he bears little relation to the bloody tyrants of Italian tragedy. Furthermore, the horrors of ***The Spanish Tragedy*** are honest English horrors based on the copiousness with which blood is shed and the resulting emotional response of the audience, and have little to do with the unnaturalness of the crude Thyestean banquets and elaborate dissection and poisoning scenes of the Italian.

The most important point of similarity to Italian tragedy lies in the ghosts. In none of Seneca's plays does the ghost of the recent dead rise to demand vengeance for his own murder, as Andrea does, although such a demand is common in Italian tragedies like Cinthio's *Orbecche* (1541) and Decio da Orte's *Acripanda* (1591). The rather important parallel between the spirit of Revenge in ***The Spanish Tragedy*** and the spirit of Suspicion in Groto's *La Dalida* must be noticed, and there may possibly be an authentic borrowing here. For the rest, Seneca's tragedies, while bloody, are not the slaughter-houses of the Italian, where hardly a character remains alive. In this respect Italian tragedy is paralleled in Kyd.

Here the general resemblance ceases, for the action of Italian tragedy and ***The Spanish Tragedy*** is vitally dissimilar. No Italian play depends for its plot, like ***The Spanish Tragedy,*** upon blood-revenge for a person slain on the stage. The Italian usually revolves about a villain protagonist and a heroine, with lust ever in the foreground. This villain is usually a tyrannous king, who is portrayed in some incident of his private life (like a love-affair where he is either the lover or the father of the lover) in which he exercises the powers of his kingship for a terrible revenge. "Tragic error" is expanded to include even the ordering of a Thyestean banquet. There is little in common between such a type and ***The Spanish Tragedy.*** Possibly a detail or two in Kyd came from the Italian, but there is no argument for any general, thoroughgoing influence. (pp. 83-5)

Fredson Bowers, "The Spanish Tragedy and the Ur-Hamlet," in his Elizabethan Revenge Tragedy, 1587-1642, *Princeton University Press, 1940. Reprint by Princeton University Press, 1969, pp. 62-100.*

Moody E. Prior (essay date 1947)

[*In the excerpt below, Prior asserts that while* The Spanish Tragedy *reflects a certain "technical immaturity" on Kyd's part, the dramatist, "confronted by the need of introducing a wholly new style to satisfy the special demands of his plot and characters, and at the same time of retaining the established artifices of manner which were features of the tragic pieces up to his time, solved the problem by admitting a variety of styles through a kind of principle of decorum which suited the style to person or occasion." The critic then analyzes Kyd's dramatic technique, focusing on such elements as language, imagery, and symbolism.*]

The Spanish Tragedy . . . occupies an intermediate position between the academic experiments of the middle years of the sixteenth century and the fully developed Elizabethan tragedy. Its contribution to this development was very great, though it was different from that of *Tamburlaine.* In comparison with that play, it is distinguished by a scheme of construction conventionally described as an intrigue plot. The principal action is set in motion by the love of Bel-Imperia for Horatio, shortly after Horatio returns victorious from battle bringing home captive the Portuguese prince, Balthazar, who had slain her former lover in the combat. This love ends in the murder of Horatio by Lorenzo, Bel-Imperia's brother, who is promoting the suit of Balthazar for his sister's favor. From this point on, the principal episodes are taken up with the attempts of Hieronimo, Horatio's father, to discover the murderers and obtain justice and revenge. But the thread which started the play is not neglected. Bel-Imperia comes eventually to Hieronimo's aid, partly to secure her own vengeance and partly to forestall the plans to have her marry the Portuguese prince in a politically advantageous match. The revenge is not accomplished until the offending persons are killed during the performance of a tragedy staged by Hieronimo as part of the celebrations for the forthcoming state wedding. If the play fails at times to maintain a close progression of events through a systematic dovetailing of the episodes it is not through any weakness in the nature of the design as such, but through faults in craftsmanship—for example, the introduction of the story of the treacherous noble in the Portuguese court, which has no bearing on the main action, and the disproportionate amount of preliminary preparation necessary before Hieronimo is introduced as the avenging agent. Nevertheless, close integration of episodes is inherent in the design of ***The Spanish Tragedy.*** The play provides for continuous excitement on the stage within a restricted and progressive narrative framework. It was not too bad a model for other dramatists to learn from.

The distinctive feature which later dramatists borrowed from ***The Spanish Tragedy*** was the use of revenge as a motive for the principal character. Whatever the merits of this formula as a basis for tragedy, it had the advantage of imposing a fairly strict pattern on the play. It thus assisted in discouraging multiple narratives and irrelevant episodes, and, in general, acted as a check on the tendency toward diffuseness and digression which was a common defect of populuar Elizabethan drama. Comparison might be made with the influence toward concentration which the detective story and the "western" have had on the wayward tendencies of the motion picture. The revenge formula, however, possessed another advantage in the fact that through the practical and moral dilemmas which it forced on the main character, it was not incompatible with serious and exhaustive exploration of character, as *Hamlet* alone will indicate. In Hieronimo, Kyd made a brilliant choice. Hieronimo is a marshal, the principal officer of justice, with a highly developed sense of right and a reputation for humanity and integrity. Great probability is thus established, on the one hand, for the delay of the revenge—his suspicion of Bel-Imperia's secret letter, his attempts to get justice through the king, and his belief that the heavens are just and will not permit cruelty to go unpunished, a point reiterated throughout the play. Probability is also established for Hieronimo's madness or near-madness: he is appalled at the wanton injustice of the murder and inveighs against the "monstrous times" and a world which is a "mass of public wrongs"; he is driven to frenzy at the calculating way in which the avenues to justice are blocked to him and concludes finally that there can be none for him, "for justice is exiled from the earth." He is thus forced to rely on himself, and when Bel-Imperia joins with him as a confederate, he concludes

> . . . that heaven applies our drift,
> And all the saints do sit soliciting
> For vengeance on those cursed murderers.
> (4.1.32-34)

That Hieronimo is not one of the great dramatic figures is chiefly due to the technical immaturity of Kyd; the brilliance of the conception, not wholly apparent in Kyd's early play, is to be seen in its progeny.

In view of the remarkable originality of so much of this play, the presence of the conventional rhetoric of the older tragedies seems surprising. The appearance of balanced and alliterative lines recalls again the early experiments in blank verse:

> To *gracious fortune* of my *tender youth*
> For there in *p*rime and *p*ride of all my years,
> By *d*uteous service and *d*eserving love. . . .
> (1.1.7-9)

But the rhetorical artifice of the style of ***The Spanish Tragedy*** has variety and complexity beyond these devices. The repeated line-pattern is very common, the following lines being the most notorious because Jonson subjected them to ridicule in *Every Man in His Humour:*

> O eyes, no eyes, but fountains fraught with tears;
> O life, no life, but lively form of death;
> O world, no world, but mass of public wrongs.
> (3.2.1-3)

Kyd uses stychomythia, and the variant of it in which the statement and reply occur within the same speech, as in the following lines of Balthazar:

> Yet might she love me for my valiancy—
> Ay, but that's slandered by captivity.
> Yet might she love me to content her sire—
> Ay, but her reason masters his desire.
> (2.1.19-22)

And so on for almost ten lines. Another device is the telescoping of one line into the next by the use of the last word of one line to introduce the idea in the succeeding one:

First, in his hand he brandished a sword,
And with that sword he fiercely waged war,
And in that war he gave me dangerous wounds,
And by those wounds he forced me to yield. . . .
(2.1.118-22)

In this particular instance the device is sustained for eleven lines. In addition to the common appearance of such artifices of style the effect of studied eloquence is conspicuous in sustained speeches like the Induction spoken by the ghost of Andrea, or the General's description of the battle, or Horatio's report of the death of Andrea. A comparison of Bel-Imperia's soliloquy about her new love (1.4.58ff.) with soliloquies in later plays will also show some of the pervasive effects of the rhetorical style: it is constructed more like a formal debate or brief of the issues than a reflection on an emotional crisis.

What is not at once apparent is that in spite of his preoccupation with such elegances of expression, Kyd did a great deal in this play to liberate dramatic blank verse from the patterns of the fashionable rhetoric. While still within the discipline of a fairly regular meter, many lines have the flexibility that suggests ordinary speech:

Then shalt thou find that I am liberal.
Thou know'st that I can more advance thy state
Than she; be therefore wise, and fail me not.
Go and attend her as thy custom is,
Lest absence makes her think thou dost amiss.
(2.1.102-6)

More striking is the use of varied and flexible rhythms to suggest Hieronimo's distraction and antic disposition before Lorenzo (3.2.61-63). Such a shift in the handling of the verse and in the phrasing necessarily implies an equally radical shift in the diction, and, in fact, the play proves on examination to have accomplished some remarkable developments in that respect. Kyd could not have come to anything like satisfactory terms with his plot structure and characters otherwise. The transitional nature of the play is therefore to be seen in the retention of the older style in spite of the original advances. The older features were retained, no doubt, because such formalized enhancements of language had become established through the academic tragedies fostered by *Gorboduc* as the traditional signs of the tragic art, just as in a similar way the reflections on Fortune in the irrelevant Portuguese episodes presumably acknowledge the expectation of sententious or eloquent expression of certain conventional themes, though the idea of fickle Fortune has no essential bearing on anything involved in the main action. The survivals appear, however, not merely as vestigial remains. The variations in style seem to conform to some vague principle of appropriateness to the speaker or the kind of situation involved. Thus, the Induction, spoken by the Ghost, is done in the style of the imitations of the Virgilian descent to hell common to the metrical tragedy, of which Sackville's Induction to *The Mirror for Magistrates* is the best known example. The reports of battles are rendered with an epic stateliness combined with the turgid sensationalism of reference to broken bodies and bloodshed which had become the characteristic manner of the conventional Nuntius, and was retained for such accounts in later plays—for instance, in Chapman's plays where they are conspicuous, and less obviously in the report of the battle by the Sergeant in the second scene of *Macbeth.* The speeches of Balthazar are almost invariably marked by greater artifice than those, for instance, of his Machiavellian companion Lorenzo. Certain of the speeches in which a character is represented as probing for himself the personal aspects of some situation are, as we have already noted, marked by a patterned formality. It appears as though Kyd, confronted by the need of introducing a wholly new style to satisfy the special demands of his plot and characters, and at the same time of retaining the established artifices of manner which were features of the tragic pieces up to his time, solved the problem by admitting a variety of styles through a kind of principle of decorum which suited the style to person or occasion.

The solution, though ingenious, is not, however, wholly satisfactory, for, the two methods being essentially incompatible, one must sometimes succeed at the expense of the other. Those passages in which both methods appear distinctively in the same speech demonstrate at once the technical skill with which Kyd effected his compromise, and the extent to which it weakened his originality:

Alas, it is Horatio, my sweet son.
O, no, but he that whilom was my son.
O, was it thou that call'dst me from my bed?
O, speak, if any spark of life remain.
I am thy father. Who hath slain my son?
What savage monster, not of human kind,
Hath here been glutted with thy harmless blood,
And left thy bloody corpse dishonored here,
For me, admidst these dark and deathful shades,
To drown thee with an ocean of my tears?
O heavens, why made you night to cover sin?
By day this deed of darkness had not been.
O earth, why didst thou not in time devour
The vile profaner of this sacred bower?
O poor Horatio, what hadst thou misdone,
To leese thy life ere life was new begun?
O wicked butcher, whatsoe'er thou wert,
How could thou strangle virtue and desert?
Ay me most wretched, that have lost my joy,
In losing my Horatio, my sweet boy!
(2.5.14-33)

The opening lines are patterned, as though in formal introduction of the emotional outburst; the central portion is more flexible in its rhythms and more rich in its imagery; the closing lines, a sort of miniature peroration, return to a formalized pattern again, emphasized not only by the systematic repetition in phrasing, but by the couplet rhymes. The immediate effect of the patterned sections is to bring this speech in stylistic conformity with the rest of the play. In a sense, the presence of these artifices tends to soften the raw physical impression of blood, violence and death, and of wild grief; and it might be argued for these professed formalities of style—in this as in certain other Elizabethan plays of violence—that in the absence of other means to that end, they tend to give to the expression of horror and outrage a semblance of art. But ostentatiously rhetorical art of any sort endows almost any sentiments with an academic, generalized quality. Consequently, where, as in the passage just quoted, other means are also used, such devices tend to undercut their effect and limit their operation. It becomes necessary in ***The Spanish Tragedy*** to isolate them from their rhetorical environment, as it were, in order to understand their function. Omission of the first four and last eight lines will show to what extent they weaken the most effective part of the speech.

The necessity for effecting such an isolation for purposes of analysis in the case of this play can be illustrated by means of the allusions to classical mythology with which it abounds. Such typical lines as "Ere Sol had slept three nights in Thetis' lap," "Now while Bellona rageth here and there," and "Till Phoebus waving to the western deep," are obviously devices of ornament and stylistic elevation. They come early in the play, the first in the Induction, the others in the General's report of the battle; they appear, that is, in set speeches which by convention are formal and deliberately elevated in manner. There are others like them, and they establish the expectation that all the mythological references will be of the same sort. The fact is that they are not. In the love scenes and in the speeches of Hieronimo following his son's death they occupy quite a different role. Indeed, with the declaration of affection between Horatio and Bel-Imperia, the love episodes become for a moment the focus of the play and a new manner of handling the diction is introduced; with the discovery of the body of his son by Hieronimo, the focus of the play shifts to the Marshal and the diction once more enters a new phase. The mythological references become a feature of the new treatment and there is a consistency in each instance in the way they are selected: in the love scenes appear Vesper, Flora, Cupid, Venus and Mars; the mythological allusions in Hieronimo's speeches almost without exception are to characters and features of the underworld or to persons who were associated at some time with it—Furies, Orpheus, Aeacus, Proserpine, Pluto, and the like. Particularly in the latter case, these are a part of a sustained and homogeneous development of images.

The first scene in which Bel-Imperia and Horatio acknowledge their love is complicated by the presence of the spies, Lorenzo and Balthazar, whose asides are worked into the main dialogue with due consideration for the artifices of phrasing in the whole development. It contains Bel-Imperia's extended similitude of the storm-tossed bark and the harbor, and the likening of love to war. The latter figure plays a part in the next love episode, but it is only in the closing line of the scene that the poetical development of the subsequent scene is suggested as in miniature:

> Then be thy father's pleasant bower the field,
> Where first we vowed a mutual amity.
> The court were dangerous; that place is safe.
> Our hour shall be when Vesper gins to rise,
> That summons home distressful travelers.
> There none shall hear us but the harmless birds;
> Haply the gentle nightingale
> Shall carol us asleep, ere we be ware,
> And, singing with the prickle at her breast,
> Tell our delight and mirthful dalliance.
> (2.2.42-51)

The scene in which the lovers next meet is little more than an amplification of this speech—the darkness that brings pleasure to lovers, the beauty and safety of the bower, the singing of the nightingale, and the allusions to Venus and Mars which introduce the artful playing with the similitude of war and love. These elements are fairly skillfully blended into a kind of idyll to suggest the beauty and happiness of the lovers, and provide a moment of tense quiet before the murderers burst in. The tenseness is introduced not merely in the passing apprehension of Bel-Imperia, but in the infusion of irony in the symbols; the darkness brings not happiness but sorrow and the bower holds not safety but death, and since we are aware of the plot against the lovers, we know this from the start and the images take on a double aspect. For instance, in the opening speech of Horatio—

> Now that the night begins with sable wings
> To overcloud the brightness of the sun,
> And that in darkness pleasures may be done,
> Come, Bel-Imperia, let us to the bower
> And there in safety pass a pleasant hour
> (2.4.1-5)

—it is the words "sable wings," "overcloud," and "darkness" which take on a sinister prominence, and all the later references to Flora decking the arbor with flowers and the birds which "record by night" for Bel-Imperia are insufficient wholly to remove these suggestions and other similar ones lurking in the speeches. It is through this ironic strain that the language of this scene is tied in to what follows. When Hieronimo runs out in response to the cries for help, he exclaims, "This place was made for pleasure, not for death," and in his first outburst of grief at discovering the body to be Horatio's,

> O heavens, why made you night to cover sin?
> By day this deed of darkness had not been.
> (2.5.24-25)

There is thus a complete reversal in direction of the imagery used in the arbor scene. The ironic overtones in Horatio's line, "The more will Flora deck it with her flowers," are brought out in full in the scene during which Isabella tears down the arbor:

> Fruitless forever may this garden be,
> Barren the earth, and blissless whosoever
> Imagines not to keep it unmanured.
> An eastern wind, conmixed with noisome airs,
> Shall blast the plants and the young saplings;
> The earth with serpents shall be pestered,
> And passengers, for fear to be infect,
> Shall stand aloof, and, looking at it, tell:
> "There, murdered, died the son of Isabel."
> (4.2.14-22)

In the speeches of Hieronimo, darkness and night become central sources for the imagery of sorrow, indignation, and madness. Combined in a supplementary relationship with the mythology of the underworld, and touched up with reiteration of the violence of the murder and the pity of Horatio's death and of the sighs and tears of the parents, these images become important means through which we are enabled to follow the tortured disorder of Hieronimo's mind.

In their simplest function the "dark" suggestions project

the horror of the deed and the gloom of death. They make their appearance, heightened by the sanguinary references to the corpse, in Hieronimo's first outcry on discovering the dead Horatio (quoted above). The "dark and deathful shades," the "deed of darkness," "the night to cover sin," mingle with the other impressions to underscore the horror of the murder. There is an elaborate extension of this later when Hieronimo in his madness imagines an old man to be his son:

> Sweet boy, how art thou changed in death's black shade!
> Had Proserpine no pity on thy youth,
> But suffered thy fair crimson-colored spring
> With withered winter to be blasted thus?
> (3.13.145-48)

The same images are used to impress the wanton cruelty of the murder in Hieronimo's long speech of explanation following the accomplishment of his revenge in the play-within-the-play:

> But night, the coverer of accursed crimes,
> With pitchy silence hushed these traitors' harms.
> (4.4.101-2)

> There merciless they butchered up my boy,
> In black, dark night, to pale, dim, cruel death.
> (4.4.106-7)

This entire speech is singular in the direct forcefulness of its expression, and in its relative freedom from ornament; moreover, with the exception of the two excerpts quoted, some references to wounds, and sanguinary expressions accompanying the display of the bloody handkerchief which Hieronimo has carried with him as a token of his duty to revenge, there is very little in the way of the characteristic figures which are prominent in the middle portions of the play. The directness of the speech may be considered a sign of Hieronimo's calm of mind with the completion of his task and of freedom from the "brainsick lunacy" which he had to struggle against while he was working toward his goal. The presence in these lines of such figures of speech as are concerned only with the expression of the horror of the crime is a hint, however, that the fuller development of the principal images in the central portion of the play serves another function than to underline the physical violence of the events, and that from the moment Hieronimo resolves on his revenge they are no longer needed.

After the first shock of realization, the force of the images shifts and is focused on the turmoil in Hieronimo's mind. They become expressive of his inability to reconcile the violence of the act with the innocence of his son, of his gloomy conviction that the world is a "mass of public wrongs," of his growing doubts whether the justice of men or of heaven can be depended upon, and of his increasing turmoil and harassment of mind verging upon madness. As these conflicts come to occupy his mind, the opposition of dark and light imagery becomes involved with other suggestions:

> O sacred heavens, if this unhallowed deed,
> If this inhuman and barbarous attempt,
> If this incomparable murder thus
> Of mine, but now no more my son,
> Shall unrevealed and unrevenged pass,
> How should we term your dealings to be just,
> If you unjustly deal with those that in your justice trust?
> The night, sad secretary to my moans,
> With direful visions wake my vexed soul,
> And with the wounds of my distressful son
> Solicit me for notice of his death.
> The ugly fiends do sally forth of hell,
> And frame my steps to unfrequented paths,
> And fear my heart with fierce inflamed thoughts.
> And cloudy day my discontents records,
> Early begins to register my dreams,
> And drive me forth to seek the murderer.
> (3.2.5-21)

There will be noticed implied here a new opposition between heaven and hell. As Hieronimo's frustration grows, as he becomes increasingly skeptical of finding justice, as his mind becomes more disordered, this opposition is more elaborately phrased and "the fierce inflamed thoughts" are reflected in imagery derived from the classical underworld. Such imagery is first introduced into the play in the Induction, spoken by the Ghost, but whereas its presence in the Induction is clearly for the purpose of describing the horrors of Hades, in the speeches of Hieronimo it is symbolic of horrors within. His fierce lamentations, he complains, have blasted the trees and meadows and "broken through the brazen gates of hell"—

> Yet still tormented is my tortured soul
> With broken sighs and restless passions,
> That winged mount, and, hovering in the air,
> Beat at the windows of the brightest heavens,
> Soliciting for justice and revenge.
> But they are placed in those empyreal heights,
> Where, countermured with walls of diamond,
> I find the place impregnable; and they
> Resist my woes, and give my words no way.
> (3.7.10-18)

Nevertheless, though he subsequently finds indisputable evidence of who the murderers are, he reflects that heaven cannot be denied and has its own ways. It is this idea which forms the basis for the elaborate description of a guilty conscience which Hieronimo gives to the Portuguese who ask him to direct them to Lorenzo's house; in a mad conceit, he directs them to the path that leads from a guilty conscience through darksome forests to despair and death—

> Whose rocky cliffs when you have once beheld,
> Within a hugy dale of lasting night,
> That, kindled with the world's iniquities,
> Doth cast up filthy and detested fumes—
> Not far from thence, where murderers have built
> A habitation for their cursed souls,
> There in a brazen caldron, fixed by Jove
> In his fell wrath, upon a sulphur flame,
> Yourselves shall find Lorenzo bathing him
> In boiling lead and blood of innocents.
> (3.11.69-78)

This effort to find satisfaction in the thought of punishment for the murderer through the terrors of a guilty conscience, symbolically represented by the shifting of the infernal images to Lorenzo with a change in emphasis, is momentary: it is not justice and revenge, and in the next scene Hieronimo, with rope and poniard in hand, contemplates suicide, and the infernal images focus again on him:

> Hieronimo, 'tis time for thee to trudge.
> Down by the dale that flows with purple gore
> Standeth a fiery tower. There sits a judge
> Upon a seat of steel and molten brass,
> And twixt his teeth he holds a fire-brand,
> That leads unto the lake where hell doth stand.
> Away, Hieronimo! To him be gone;
> He'll do thee justice for Horatio's death.
> (3.12.6-13)

The absence of heavenly images reveals the implicit rejection of the justice of heaven. The piling up of the infernal images from this point on reflects the full bitterness of Hieronimo's mind and his growing resolution that he must secure justice through vengeance. Thus in the next scene:

> Though on this earth justice will not be found,
> I'll down to hell, and in this passion
> Knock at the dismal gates of Pluto's court,
> Getting by force, as once Alcides did,
> A troop of furies and tormenting hags
> To torture Don Lorenzo and the rest.
> (3.13.108-13)

To the old man whom in his madness he mistakes for his son, he says,

> Go back, my son; complain to Aeacus,
> For here's no justice. Gentle boy, begone,
> For justice is exiled from the earth.
> (3.13.137-39)

> What, not my son? Thou then a Fury art,
> Sent from the empty kingdom of black night
> To summon me to make appearance
> Before grim Minos and just Rhadamanth,
> To plague Hieronimo that is remiss,
> And seeks not vengeance for Horatio's death.
> (3.13.152-57)

Only when he discovers a spur and an ally in Bel-Imperia and determines on the one course left him do these infernal images leave the play:

> But may it be that Bel-Imperia
> Vows such revenge as she hath deigned to say?
> Why, then I see that heaven applies our drift,
> And all the saints do sit soliciting
> For vengeance on those cursed murderers.
> (4.1.30-34)

Private vengeance is now identified with the justice of heaven, and the torment of his mind is over. In the episodes which follow he is calculating and self-possessed. In his speech of explanation, images of blood and darkness return, but here they are clearly distinct from those which were the index of a troubled mind and are a repetition in kind of those initial images which gave emphasis to the recognition of the horror and violence of the crime. The bloody handkerchief is the symbol of the determination to secure justice which had kept him from final despair and death.

Since the action of the play is centered in Hieronimo's attempt to secure justice and in his final success through private vengeance, and since the probability of the delay and the final execution of the revenge thus resides chiefly in the character of Hieronimo, the diction of the play is quite properly ordered to cooperate with the exploration of Hieronimo's mind, which occupies the central portion of the play. The imagery is in this way brought into intimate relationship with the action. The means Kyd used are less complex and less subtle than those of certain later dramatists, and his compromise with the precedents in style established by such plays as *Gorboduc* helps to conceal the originality with which he freed the blank verse line from its dependence on rhetorical design and made it answerable to his purposes. Nevertheless, ***The Spanish Tragedy*** greatly advanced the art of verse drama and represents a genuine break with Kyd's immediate dramatic past; it was still a long way from the tragedies of Shakespeare, but it was essentially like them in kind. (pp. 46-58)

Moody E. Prior, "The Elizabethan Tradition," in his The Language of Tragedy, *1947. Reprint by Indiana University Press, 1966, pp. 16-153.*

Philip Edwards (essay date 1959)

[*Edwards, an English educator and literary scholar, has edited several of Shakespeare's plays and has published such works as* Thomas Kyd and Early Elizabethan Drama *(1965). In the essay below originally published in 1959, the critic examines Kyd's use of the revenge theme in* The Spanish Tragedy, *asserting that the various revenge plots exist to satisfy one purpose only: retribution by the gods for Andrea's death. Edwards especially focuses on Hieronimo as an agent of his own revenge as well as of divine justice.*]

One of the most popular and influential of plays in its own day, ***The Spanish Tragedy*** became the object of affectionate derision in the succeeding generations—or of derision without affection, as with Jonson. Such elements of the play as Hieronimo's outcries and the sallies of his madness, the elaborately patterned verse, Andrea's sombre prologue, were constantly parodied and guyed by Jacobean and Caroline dramatists. This attention to the play, however scornful, shows the hold which Kyd's work had; a hold demonstrated by the successive editions of the play, and the desire to keep it fresh by adding new scenes. It was looked on as an extravagant and crude work, and yet a bold work, holding a special position as the best that could be done in an age which had not learned to produce a polished play. And it may be said that the attitude has stuck, and still prevails. Once the play had sunk into oblivion, after the mid-seventeenth century, it was not rehabilitated in the Romantic period, as so many other "forgotten" plays were. Lamb (1808) was interested only in the Additions: he gave the "Painter's Scene" in his *Specimens of English Dramatic Poets* and remarked that these scenes were "the very salt of the old play (which without them is but a caput mortuum, such another piece of flatness as Locrine)." With the growth of evolutionary criticism, historians of drama found the play a seminal work in tragedy and the revenge play, in spite of the crudity which they did not gloss over. Mild merits of various kinds were proposed by various critics, chiefly skill in maintaining suspense and in working out a complicated plot. There have been wide differences of opinion on Kyd's powers of characterization. But although there has been general recognition of Kyd's unusual ability in contriving a theatrically effective play, no one has made a serious claim that Kyd has much to offer as a poet or tragic dramatist. It is significant that the most exhaustive and sympathetic study of ***The Spanish Tragedy,*** the monograph by Biesterfeldt published in 1936, is a study in structure (*Die dramatische Technik Thomas Kyds*). A standard view of Kyd is Gregory Smith's summing-up in *The Cambridge History of English Literature* (vol. v, 1910):

> The interest of Kyd's work is almost exclusively historical. Like Marlowe's, it takes its place in the development of English tragedy by revealing new possibilities and offering a model in technique; unlike Marlowe's, it does not make a second claim upon us as great literature. The historical interest lies in the advance which Kyd's plays show in construction, in the manipulation of plot, and in effective situation. Kyd is the first to discover the bearing of episode and of the "movement" of the story on characterization, and the first to give the audience and reader the hint of the development of character which follows from this interaction. In other words, he is the first English dramatist who writes dramatically.

The historical position of Kyd has been the chief concern of criticism, and that is one reason why the brief account of the play which follows avoids questions of what Kyd borrowed and what he gave to others. Another reason is that our uncertainty about the date of the play makes it extremely difficult to mark Kyd's place in a fast-moving development of the drama. Was Lorenzo the first great Machiavellian villain? Did Kyd invent the Elizabethan revenge play? Yet Kyd's play is a most ingenious and successful blending of the old and the new in drama, and the fact that a comparative method is not followed here will not, I hope, obscure the obvious point that no good verdict can be made on Kyd's achievement which does not take into account what was achieved in plays written or performed at the same period.

The Spanish Tragedy is a play about the passion for retribution, and vengeance shapes the entire action. Revenge himself appears as a character near the beginning of the play, a servant of the spiritual powers, indicating what a man may find in the patterns of existence which are woven for him. Retribution is not only the demand of divine justice but also a condescension to human wants. Andrea seeks blood for his own blood; though he died in war, Balthazar killed him in a cowardly and dishonorable fashion, and not in fair fight (I.iv.19-26, 72-5; I.ii.73). The gods look with favor on Andrea and are prepared, by destroying his destroyer, to bring him peace. When all is completed, he exults: "Ay, now my hopes have end in their effects, / When blood and sorrow finish my desires . . . Ay, these were spectacles to please my soul!" Men lust for retribution, and the gods, assenting to this idea of satisfaction as only justice, can and will grant it. Marlowe never wrote a less Christian play than ***The Spanish Tragedy:*** the hate of a wronged man can speak out without check of mercy or reason; when a sin is committed, no-one talks of forgiveness; the word "mercy" does not occur in the play.

Once Proserpine has granted that Balthazar shall die (I.i.81-9), everything that happens in the play serves to fulfil her promise. To bring about what they have decreed, the gods use the desires and strivings of men. Hieronimo and Bel-imperia and Lorenzo, as they struggle and plot to bring about their own happiness, are only the tools of destiny. The sense of a fore-ordained end is strongly conveyed by Kyd by his constant use of dramatic irony. The characters always have mistaken notions about what their actions are leading them towards. Bel-imperia believes that "second love will further her revenge," but only, it turns out, through the murder of her second love. As Horatio and Bel-imperia speak of consummating their love, they are overheard by those who are plotting to destroy it. And as the unwitting lovers go off the stage, the King enters (II. iii) complacently planning the marriage of Bel-imperia with Balthazar. By the very means he chooses to make his crime secret, the liquidating of his accomplices, Lorenzo betrays the crime to Hieronimo. Pedringano is secure in his belief in the master who is about to have him killed. The King and the court applaud the acting in a play in which the deaths are real. And there are very many other examples. In a way, the play is built upon irony, upon the ignorance of the characters that they are being used to fulfil the decree of the gods.

The play seems to move in a rather leisurely way from the entry of Andrea's Ghost to the killing of Horatio, the deed which opens the play's chief interest, Hieronimo's revenge. There is the description of the underworld by Andrea, two long reports of the battle in which Andrea was killed (one by the General to the King, and one by Horatio to Bel-imperia), Hieronimo's "masque," and the introduction of the sub-plot concerning Villuppo's traducement of Alexandro at the Portuguese court. These prolix early scenes should not be dismissed without taking into account Kyd's use of the long speech in general throughout the play. Two recent and most interesting brief studies of the play's language have put Kyd's "antiquated technique" in a new light. Both Moody E. Prior [in his *The Language of Tragedy,* 1947] and Wolfgang Clemen in his [*Die Tragödie vor Shakespeare,* 1955] demonstrate how Kyd converts the techniques and conventions of an academic and literary drama with considerable skill to new dramatic ends: the long speech becomes more dramatic in itself and is used more dramatically. A good example used by both critics is that the most elaborately stylized rhetoric issues from the mouth of Balthazar, and these studied exercises in self-pity are used as a means of characterization; the more practical people, like Lorenzo and Bel-imperia, are impatient of his roundabout utterance (e.g., I.iv.90-8, II.i.29, II.i.134). Clemen has particularly valuable things to say about how Kyd controls the tempo of the play through his use of the long speech, and how purposefully he knits together (each mode serving its own function) the long speech and dialogue; a long speech, for example, will introduce, or sum up, issues which are to be or have been set out in dialogue. But although Clemen, like Biesterfeldt before him, can find the early scenes in some measure artistically justified, and an improvement on what Kyd's predecessors achieved in long "reports," it is the very absence of that artistry which Kyd shows in his handling of the long speech in the later parts of the play which makes the early scenes seem so labored. And, long speeches apart, it is very hard to justify the sub-plot. The Portuguese court could have been introduced more economically and the relevance of theme is very slight. Few readers of ***The Spanish Tragedy*** resent the clamant appeals and laments of Hieronimo and the rest once the play is under way, but few readers fail to find the early scenes tedious, and I think the common reaction is justified. It is as though Kyd began to write a literary Senecan play, and, even as he wrote, learned to handle his material in more dextrous and dramatic fashion.

But the opening of the play will seem far more dilatory than it really is to those who take it that the real action starts only with the death of Horatio. It is Balthazar's killing of Andrea which begins the action—the news being given by the ghost of the victim. The avenging of Andrea, is, as we have seen, the supernatural cause of all that follows; but in terms of plot, too, or of direct, human causes, all flows from Andrea's death. For Andrea's mistress wishes to revenge herself on the slayer of her lover. Bel-imperia is a woman of strong will, independent spirit, and not a little courage (witness her superb treatment of her brother after her release, first furious and then sardonic, making Lorenzo acknowledge defeat; III.x.24-105); she is also libidinous. Kyd has successfully manœuvered round a ticklish necessity of the plot (that Bel-imperia and Horatio should be lovers) by making Bel-imperia a certain kind of woman; what *has* to be done, is credibly done, naturally done. There is no question about her relations with Andrea (see I.i.10, II.i.47, III.x.54-5, III.xiv.111-12); and, with Horatio, she does not appear to be planning an early wedding; the two are entering upon an illicit sexual relationship, and it is Bel-imperia who is the wooer (II.i.85, II.ii.32-52).

But, not to anticipate, Bel-imperia, while wishing to avenge Andrea, finds herself conceiving a passion for Horatio (I.iv.60-1). She is momentarily ashamed of her lightness and tries to rationalize her affection as being a sign of her love for Andrea (62-3); then she repents and decides that revenge must come before she is off with the old love and on with the new (64-5) and then (triumphant ingenuity!) realizes that to love Horatio will in fact help her revenge against Balthazar, since it will slight the prince, who is a suitor for her love (66-8). So character and plot are married, and the action drives forward on its twin pistons of love and revenge.

Bel-imperia's scheme brings about her lover's death. Balthazar has new cause to hate the man who took him prisoner, but his hate would be nothing were it not given power by the hate of Lorenzo, whose fierce pride has twice been wounded by the lowly-born Horatio: once over the capturing of Balthazar, and now in his sister's preferring Horatio to his royal friend. Bel-imperia's revengeful defiance brings about the simple reaction of counter-revenge—the murder of Horatio in the bower. Horatio is hanged and the *fourth* of the interlocked revenge-schemes begins: Andrea's the first, then Bel-imperia's, then Lorenzo's and Balthazar's, and finally Hieronimo's. Kyd may seem to take some time to reach this most important of his revenge-schemes, but he chose to set layer within layer, wheels within wheels, revenge within revenge. The action is a unity (the Portuguese scenes excepted), and in engineering the deaths of Balthazar and Lorenzo, Hieronimo satisfies not only himself, in respect of Horatio, but Bel-imperia in respect of Horatio and Andrea, and Andrea in respect of himself. And Hieronimo's efforts to avenge his dead son are the means by which the gods avenge Andrea. The presence of the Ghost of Andrea and Revenge upon the stage throughout the play, with their speeches in the Choruses, continually reminds us of this fact, which is indeed so central to the meaning of the play that it is astonishing that it is occasionally overlooked.

Hieronimo's motives for revenge are several. (i) Revenge will bring him emotional relief; (ii) it is a duty; (iii) a life for a life is the law of nature, and (iv) is, in society, the legal penalty for murder.

Hieronimo's first remark about revenge is to tell Isabella that if only he knew the murderer, his grief would diminish, "For in revenge my heart would find relief." The therapeutic virtues of homicide may seem doubtful, but Hieronimo insists:

> Then will I joy amidst my discontent,
> Till then my sorrow never shall be spent.
> (II.v.55-6)

Closely associated with this odd and selfish cue for revenge is the idea of revenge as an obligation. We are to imagine (because it is hardly stated explicitly) that Horatio's peace in the world beyond depends, like Andrea's, upon his obtaining the life of his murderer as a recompense for, and a cancellation of, his own death. For Hieronimo to assume the duty of securing this price is a tribute to his son and a measure of his love:

> Dear was the life of my beloved son,
> And of his death behoves me be reveng'd.
> (III.ii.44-5)

Hieronimo takes a vow to avenge Horatio and, of course, the notion of a vow to be fulfilled, with the bloody napkin as a symbol of it, provides a good deal of the play's dramatic force, particularly as regards Hieronimo's sense of insufficiency, failure, or delay. But, it may be noted, delay itself is not an issue in the play. That Hieronimo's conscience should accuse him for being tardy (III.xiii.135) is a measure only of the stress he is under and the difficulties he faces, and of the depth of his obligation; that Bel-imperia and Isabella should speak of delay (III.ix and IV.ii.30) is a measure only of their understandable impatience and does not mean that Hieronimo *could* have acted more quickly. It is the sense of delay which is real, and not delay itself. Hieronimo does everything possible as quickly as possible.

The idea of revenge as a personal satisfaction for wrongs endured is enlarged into the idea of revenge as punishment, a universal moral satisfaction for crime committed, or the demands of divine justice. Though Hieronimo's wrongs are personal, he sees his claims for satisfaction as the claims of the Order of Things. The mythology chosen to represent the governance of the world is rather muddled in ***The Spanish Tragedy;*** paganism sits uneasily with—something else; but the gods (whoever they are) hate murder and will, through human agents, punish the murderer. There is morality among the gods, or so Hieronimo (somewhat anxiously) trusts:

> The heavens are just, murder cannot be hid.
> (II.v.57)

> If this incomparable murder thus
> Of mine, but now no more my son,
> Shall unreveal'd and unrevenged pass,
> How should we term your dealings to be just,
> If you unjustly deal with those that in your justice trust?
> (III.ii.7-11)

> Murder, O bloody monster—God forbid
> A fault so foul should scape unpunished.
> (III.vi.95-6)

When things go wrong with Hieronimo, he pictures himself beating at the windows of the brightest heavens, soliciting for justice and revenge (III. vii. 13-14). When things go well, he has the sense of divine support. But the nexus between Hieronimo's plans for revenge and the workings of providence is a somewhat controversial matter, and must be discussed with other facts in mind.

Punishment of murder is the course of human law, and Hieronimo's revenge is to be within the framework of law. Yet he goes about to discover the murderer in a manner curious to modern eyes. He sees it as his personal duty to find the criminal, and he conceals the crime. But this is no usurpation of the law; there is no C.I.D. to call in and he must act himself. The secrecy is to be explained by Hieronimo's fear that someone is contriving against his family so that it behoves him to move warily. Bel-imperia's letter seems to confirm his suspicions; nothing could be less credible than its news, and, should there be a plot against his family, what more suitable means to entrap him than to get him to lay an accusation for murder against the King's own nephew (III.ii.34-43)? He will find out more, still keeping his mission secret (III.ii.48-52). Confirming evidence comes via Pedringano, and Pedringano's arrest and punishment are an important accompaniment of Hieronimo's vendetta. For here is an orthodox piece of policework, as it were. Pedringano commits murder, he is arrested *flagrante delicto* by the watch, tried by a court, and executed. There is law in Spain, and, once a murderer is known, he can be brought to account by due process of law. Hieronimo's anguish at the trial of Pedringano is not because for him justice has to be secured by different means, but because the course of justice which is available cannot be started since he, the very judge, cannot name the murderer of his son. It is not the least part of Hieronimo's design to indulge in Bacon's "wild justice"; it does not enter his head to "put the law out of office."

But, now that Hieronimo has Pedringano's letter and the clinching evidence which he needed, he may proceed to call in the aid of law and get justice. To lay an accusation, however, proves to be the heaviest of Hieronimo's difficulties. The protracted battle of wits between Hieronimo and Lorenzo (so excellently handled by Kyd and so unfortunately obscured in the Additions) comes to a head, and, more powerful obstacle still, just as Hieronimo is ready to call down punishment on the criminals, the strain on his mind begins to tell, and his madness begins. The unsettling of Hieronimo's mind is well done; it has been prepared for long ago, in Hieronimo's excessive pride in his son when he was alive, and it is made more acceptable in that Isabella ("psychologically" unimportant as a character) has already been shown to be going out of her mind with grief. Hieronimo's frenzy makes Lorenzo's task of keeping him from the King easy; Hieronimo really prevents himself from securing justice. Thwarted, he plots to be his own avenger.

At this point, we may bring in again the question of divine justice. Momentarily, and most awkwardly, Jehovah assumes a role in the play; Hieronimo remembers that the Lord says, "Vengeance is mine, I will repay (III.xiii.I). He acknowledges that "mortal men may not appoint their time" (1. 5). But since "justice is exiled from the earth" he persuades himself that private vengeance is justified. Bowers is of the opinion that the play condemns Hieronimo for taking it upon himself to be the executioner instead of waiting for God's will to be done, and that "Kyd is deliberately veering his audience against Hieronimo" [F. T. Bowers, in his *Elizabethan Revenge Tragedy, 1587-1642,* 1940]. The problem is far from simple. It has been seen that the gods of the play like revenge. More important, after the *Vindicta mihi* speech, Hieronimo is convinced that his private course is congruent with the morality of heaven. When he is joined by Bel-imperia, he interprets his good fortune as a sign of the approval of the gods, and feels that he is a minister of providence:

> Why then, I see that heaven applies our drift,
> And all the saints do sit soliciting
> For vengeance on those cursed murderers.
> (IV.i.32-4)

Moody Prior (*Language of Tragedy*) sees this outcry as a turning point in the drama. "Private vengeance is now identified with the justice of heaven, and the torment of his mind is over. In the episodes which follow, he is calculating and self-possessed." This seems a most sensible view, but the question must be asked, Is Hieronimo deluding himself in supposing he now has divine support? To answer "yes" to this question must suggest that there is a clash in the play between the dominant pagan morality and a Christian morality. The only overt introduction of the Christian morality on revenge is in the brief allusion to St. Paul; where, in other parts of the play, the mythology for Providence seems to be Christian—as in the passage just quoted, with its reference to heaven and saints—we almost certainly are faced with inconsistency and confusion on Kyd's part and not a dualism. We could, indeed, make no sense out of a dualism which meant that every reference to powers below was a reference to evil and every reference to powers above a reference to good. The clash, if it exists, must be between the ideas which Hieronimo has and ideas not expressed in the play, except in the *Vindicta mihi* speech. In other words, the argument must be that Hieronimo is condemned because the Elizabethans condemned revenge, however strongly the play's gods support him.

But what an Elizabethan might think of Hieronimo's actions in real life may be irrelevant to the meaning of ***The Spanish Tragedy.*** Hieronimo may still be a sympathetic hero in spite of Elizabethan indignation against private revenge. The cry of *Vindicta mihi,* and the pause it gives Hieronimo may be more of a dramatic than a moral point. Hieronimo, robbed of the law's support, rocks for a moment in indecision before determining that at all costs the murderers must die. The indecision, and then the determination, are dramatically most important and effective; but the cause of the indecision (the inappropriate promptings of Christian ethics) is not important. Kyd has won sympathy for Hieronimo in his sufferings; there is no sign, at the end of the third and the beginning of the fourth Act, that Kyd now wishes the audience to change their sympathetic attitude, even though orthodoxy would condemn the private executioner. Kyd creates, and successfully sustains, his own world of revenge, and attitudes are sanctioned which might well be deplored in real life. The moral world of the play is a make-believe world; the gods are make-believe gods. In this make-believe world, the private executioner may be sympathetically portrayed and his Senecan gods may countenance his actions. And all this may be, however, strongly Kyd himself disapproved of private vengeance. I remarked that ***The Spanish Tragedy*** was an un-Christian play, and so it is. But it is not written to advocate a system of ethics, or to oppose one. If its moral attitudes are mistaken for the "real life" attitudes of the dramatist, then the play has an appalling message. But if the play is seen as a thing of great—and skilful—artificiality, with standards of values which we accept while we are in the theatre, there is no problem at all about sympathizing with the hero. The play had power enough to lull an Elizabethan conscience while it was being performed.

It could well be said, however, that it is a poor play which depends on the audience suspending its belief in law and mercy. And yet a swingeing revenge-play has its own emotional satisfaction for the audience. Vengeance is exacted from evil-doers by a man whose wrongs invoke pity; in enabling an audience to forget their daily docility and to share in Hieronimo's violent triumph, it may be that Kyd has justified himself as an artist more than he would have done in providing a sermon on how irreligious it is to be vindictive.

It would be foolish to gloss over the difficulty of siding with Hieronimo to the very end, after the punishment of the criminals. As Bowers points out, he seems in the final scene little more than a dangerous and blood-thirsty maniac. Although I have suggested that the crudities of Hieronimo's departure from life might have been much less apparent in Kyd's original version of the play, no theory of revision can explain away what seems to be the pointless savagery of the murder of the unoffending Castile. It may be that Kyd was trying to give a Senecan touch of the curse upon the house, but there are other considerations which make *condemnation* of Hieronimo rather irrelevant. In the first place, Castile was Andrea's enemy (see II.i.46-7 and III.xiv.111-13) and Hieronimo is the agent of destiny employed to avenge Andrea; Castile's death appears to make Andrea's peace perfect. Revenge is satisfied, and we had best try not to worry about the bloodthirstiness of it all.

Much more important, however, is the reflection that ***The Spanish Tragedy*** is, after all, a tragedy of sorts. Hieronimo has gone mad with grief, with the stress of observing his vow, and with the long war between himself and Lorenzo. As Castile falls, horror is mingled with pity that this should be the end of Hieronimo's life. If we cannot take Senecan revenge very seriously, or the somewhat contrived idea of destiny, we can take Lorenzo's machinations and Hieronimo's sufferings without embarrassment. ***The Spanish Tragedy*** has most merit in its study of the hero's grief and final distraction, and, when at the end the innocent man suffers at the hands of the hero whose innocence was not in question, it is probable that an audience feels a more complex emotion than revulsion against extra-legal revenge. (pp. 46-55)

Philip Edwards, "The Theme and Structure of 'The Spanish Tragedy'," in Shakespeare's Contemporaries, *edited by Max Bluestone and Norman Rabkin, Prentice-Hall, Inc., 1961, pp. 46-55.*

Ejner J. Jensen (essay date 1965)

[*In the excerpt below, Jensen strongly objects to Fredson Bowers's interpretation of* The Spanish Tragedy *as an unfocused and unethical work (see excerpt dated 1940). Jensen counters that if the play is viewed as an exploration of "the problem of justice" rather than as a revenge tragedy, its various disparate themes and elements combine to create a skillful dramatic unity.*]

Fredson Bowers' *Elizabethan Revenge Tragedy* has long been a useful guide to the study of a specific type of drama in the context of Elizabethan attitudes toward its central theme. The book, like others of its kind, helps us to read the plays of an earlier period with greater knowledge of the probable reaction of the audience to the presentation of certain ideas and attitudes. Professor Bowers' book, however, has had an unfortunate influence on later views of Kyd's ***Spanish Tragedy.*** Bowers points out certain conditions in which revenge could be taken with impunity according to the Elizabethan moral code; he then assumes that the Elizabethan audience would have kept these conditions in mind and would have rejected anyone who overstepped them. He insists that, according to the Elizabethan ethic, Andrea and Revenge are not essential to the play; that the revenge which interested the audience is the blood revenge of Hieronimo on Lorenzo and Balthazar, a revenge which is in no way connected with revenge for Andrea; and that Hieronimo became, in the eyes of the audience, a villain who was forced to take his own life in compliance with the doctrine that vengeance was the concern solely of God.

Certain arguments have been advanced against the case presented by Bowers, but no one has dealt with all three of his charges; furthermore, no one has replied effectively to the charge that seems implicit in his argument—that ***The Spanish Tragedy,*** though of great historical interest, is flawed by lack of focus, extraneous characters, and a hero who becomes a villain.

The critical arguments advanced by Bowers may be answered most readily if we examine in detail the specific faults he imparts to the play. The assumption that there is an excess of contingent elements in the play attributes to it faults which grow not from Kyd's drama itself but from its failure to square with Bowers' theory of revenge. The play is in reality highly organized. Its chief unifying theme is not revenge but the problem of justice. From first to last ***The Spanish Tragedy*** is filled with discussions of the nature of justice, its machinery and its operation. Hieronimo, as Knight Marshal, is himself a judge.

Andrea's ghost introduces the theme of justice in his opening speech when he recounts his journey to the underworld. His approach to Minos, Aeacus, and Rhadamanth is unsuccessful, for they are unable to reach a decision. Minos effects a compromise, and Andrea is sent on to Pluto for judgment. When he arrives at Pluto's court Proserpine asks to be given the power of decision; it is her verdict, whispered to Revenge, which sends Andrea's ghost back to the world above. Thus divine judgment summons Andrea as spectator of the action; and Revenge, who has been informed of the decision, announces to him:

> thou art arriv'd
> Where thou shalt see the author of thy death,
> Don Balthazar the prince of Portingale,
> Depriv'd of life by Bel-imperia.
> (I.i.86-89)

In the next scene the victorious Spanish army returns, and the king is faced with a problem of judgment. He must decide who is to receive the honors for the capture of Balthazar. Like Minos, he determines upon a compromise, awarding Horatio the ransom and Balthazar's armor and giving Lorenzo the prisoner's horse and weapons. Lorenzo is to provide accommodations for Balthazar because Horatio is not in a position to entertain the Portuguese and his retinue.

The Portugal scenes, which, except for the Alexandro-Villuppo plot, are filled primarily with the sending and receiving of emissaries, are often dismissed as inconsequential; yet they serve to point up a significant lesson on the problem of justice. Alexandro narrowly escapes death when the ambassador from Spain returns just in time with the news that Balthazar is alive. Villuppo is then given suitable punishment for his false accusation. Later in the play, when Hieronimo delays his revenge even after he has received the letter from Bel-imperia, the lesson of the Portuguese subplot might be remembered and would suggest the reasonableness of Hieronimo's initial delay.

Immediately before the accusing letter falls, Hieronimo delivers his famous "O eyes, no eyes" speech (III.ii.1-23). The speech is a plea to the incomprehensible divine powers who are apparently willing to allow the existence and even the success of evil in this world. It is the address of a man defeated by evil, of a man who is unable to reconcile his experience of an evil world with the concept of a beneficient deity:

> How should we term your dealings to be just,
> If you unjustly deal with those that in your justice trust?
> (III.ii.9-10)

In spite of his perplexity in the matter of divine justice, Hieronimo subdues his confusion and faces up to his own responsibilities as the dispenser of public justice in his capacity as Knight Marshal:

> Thus must we toil in other men's extremes,
> That know not how to remedy our own;
> And do them justice, when unjustly we,
> For all our wrongs, can compass no redress.
> (III.vi.1-4)

And he makes a direct comment on the principle of that justice; crimes of blood are to be avenged in kind:

> For blood with blood shall, while I sit as judge,
> Be satisfied, and the law discharg'd;
> And though myself cannot receive the like,
> Yet will I see that others have their right.
> (III.vi.35-38)

Pedringano is hanged for the murder of Serberine, a deed to which he readily confesses; and the rapid execution emphasizes by contrast the difficulties faced by Hieronimo in his attempt to discover and punish the murderers of his son just as the self-assuredness of Pedringano emphasizes the craftiness of Lorenzo.

The difficulty of his position begins to have serious effects on Hieronimo; justice and revenge, he says, "Resist my woes, and give my words no way" (III.vii.18). But when the hangman presents to him the letter from Pedringano to Lorenzo, his reaction indicates that he hopes to obtain redress through legitimate channels. It is also clear that blood for blood is the legal punishment for murder, for Hieronimo stresses that only the death of the conspirators will satisfy him. He realizes that he has been given, for the first time, both proof and the opportunity for action; and he moves to take immediate advantage of the situation:

> But wherefore waste I mine unfruitful words,
> When naught but blood will satisfy my woes?
> I will go plain me to my lord the king,
> And cry aloud for justice through the court.
> (III.vii.67-70)

Hieronimo's attempts to find justice, however, are not successful; Lorenzo effectively blocks the accepted legal channels and makes it impossible for Hieronimo to present his suit. Once again he bemoans the lack of justice in this world, and he seems ready to take his own life; but he recalls himself to reality when he comprehends that Horatio's death will then go unavenged (III.xii.1-19). He shouts three times for justice while the king continues to conduct state business with the Portuguese ambassador (III.xii.27, 63, 65); and once again Lorenzo is able to keep Hieronimo from securing an audience, this time discrediting him by the imputation of lunacy.

And, in fact, Hieronimo is mad. His scene with the four petitioners reveals the extent to which he has lost his reason. Yet in his madness he reveals the same concern with justice that he has evinced throughout the play. Fancying that Bazulto is his son, he addresses a question to the old man:

> And art then come, Horatio, from the depth,
> To ask for justice in his upper earth?
> (III.xiii.133-34)

And he suggests that this is not the place to seek justice, that it would be better to return and "complain to Aeacus" (III.xii.138-39). When Bazulto protests that he is not Hieronimo's son, the Knight Marshal imagines that the old petitioner is a fury sent by the judges of the underworld to rebuke him for not obtaining revenge for Horatio. When Bazulto finally explains to Hieronimo that he has come to seek justice in the matter of his own son's death, Hieronimo names him correctly, "the lively image of my grief" (III.xiii.162).

Hieronimo's obsessive concern with the problem of justice reflects the informing theme of ***The Spanish Tragedy.*** When Isabella dies she echoes this concern:

> For sorrow and despair hath cited me
> To hear Horatio plead with Rhadamanth.
> (IV.ii.27-28)

The play ends as it began, with Andrea's ghost and Revenge providing the focus of the drama. The sentence pronounced by Proserpine at the beginning of the action has been extended to give Andrea further power. He has seen Bel-imperia kill Balthazar; now he is to superintend the dispensing of rewards to all of the characters in the drama. He is to be the judge when he descends with Revenge, who encourages him in this role:

> Then haste we down to meet thy friends and foes,
> To place thy friends in ease, the rest in woes.
> (IV.v.45-46)

In the case of ***The Spanish Tragedy*** it is not a tautology to say that we are dealing with a revenge play whose theme is justice. Justice comprehends revenge; justice is the whole system of rewards and punishments, judgments of good and evil, and ethical decisions of which revenge forms only a part. Incident after incident echoes the theme of the tragedy, and the revelation by Andrea and Revenge of the judgments to come demonstrates the essential orderliness of divine justice.

Justice in Kyd's play is delivered by the characters themselves with the approval of those agents of divinity, the ghost and Revenge, who watch over the entire action. ***The Spanish Tragedy*** is not based on the moral order which the Elizabethan thought of as controlling his world. The justice of that order, as Lily B. Campbell has shown [in her "Theories of Revenge in Renaissance England," *Modern Philology* XXVIII (1931)], was grounded on the text of Romans, "Vengeance is mine, I will repay, saith the Lord" (12:19). In this Christian view of justice, "private revenge was forbidden alike by God and by the state as his representative." To the Elizabethan, then, revenge was condemned both on religious and political grounds. But Miss Campbell's treatment of Renaissance theories of revenge also provides a suggestion which should direct the reader to a clearer understanding of Kyd's play. She grants that those plays which are dependent on Seneca present a special problem of interpretation. The obvious debt to Seneca in ***The Spanish Tragedy*** indicates that the Christian principles which formed the Renaissance attitude toward revenge, justice, and mercy cannot satisfactorily be applied to this play. Philip Edwards declares [in his edition of ***The Spanish Tragedy,*** 1959,] that "Marlowe never wrote a less Christian play than ***The Spanish Tragedy;*** the hate of a wronged man can speak out without check of mercy or reason; when a sin is committed, no one talks of forgiveness; the word 'mercy' does not occur in the play." Although it is possible to say of the Elizabethan dramatists generally that "in solving their dramatic problems—which are inescapably the problems of justice—they had all the data of the Graeco-Jewish-Christian civilization in which they were born" [see Marion Hope Parker, *The Slave of Life: A Study of Shakespeare and the Idea of Justice,* 1955], it should be clear that Kyd ignores (or perhaps defies) that tradition in ***The Spanish Tragedy,*** a play in which "retribution is not only the demand of divine justice but also a condescension to human wants" [Edwards]. The revenge approved by the gods and secured by Hieronimo is just only when considered in the context of the moral order revealed in the play.

The theme of justice runs throughout Kyd's tragedy. It is introduced by Andrea, reflected in the Portuguese scenes, repeated with variations by Hieronimo, touched upon in Isabella's death scene, and brought in to provide the conclusion of the drama. There is, in this respect, neither a lack of focus nor a failure to establish and justify relationships of parts of the play to the whole. But the element of revenge is part of the larger pattern, and it is in the treatment of this element that Bowers would say Kyd had failed to make his drama whole. Bowers would claim that the audience would be concerned only with Hieronimo's revenge for Horatio, revenge for a murder committed in their sight; and he maintains that Andrea's ghost has no part in the play after the second revenge motif is begun. This attitude fails to give due importance to the larger theme of justice; it also ignores some of the more obvious connections which bind the play together and make Andrea an essential part of the drama.

To begin with, it is significant that Andrea and Revenge are on stage during the entire play; as the chorus they have certain duties to perform. In addition, Bel-imperia represents a link between Andrea and Horatio, declaring as she does that she is able to love her second lover because of his affection for her first (I.iv.58-76). The attitude of Lorenzo seems to have been the same toward both Andrea and Horatio; perhaps their similarity in social standing may be seen as another element unifying the two revenge themes. Howard Baker has provided additional justification for considering Andrea's ghost (and Revenge also) essential to the play [in "Ghosts and Guides: Kyd's ***Spanish Tragedy*** and the Medieval Tragedy," *Modern Philology,* XXXIII (1935)]. He suggests that both the ghost and Revenge derive from stock characters in medieval metrical tragedy. Thus they would be familiar to the audience, and they would have a specific and necessary share in the proceedings.

There may be still another link relating Andrea and Horatio and establishing their common interest in revenge on Lorenzo and Balthazar. Horatio relates to Bel-imperia the circumstances attending the death of Andrea; at the close of his account he shows her the scarf which he took off the arm of the dead Andrea and which he now wears in remembrance of his friend. Bel-imperia recognizes the scarf:

> For 'twas my favour at his last depart.
> But now wear thou it both for him and me.
> (I.iv.47-48)

When Hieronimo discovers his murdered son he finds a handkercher:

> Seest thou this handkercher besmear'd with blood?
> It shall not from me till I take revenge.
> (II.v.51-52)

Thus the handkercher is to be a reminder of the need for revenge. Percy Simpson has stated [in "The Theme of Revenge in Elizabethan Tragedy," *Studies in Elizabethan Drama,* 1955] that the handkercher belongs to Hieronimo and that he has merely dipped it in Horatio's blood as a token. But the handkercher is surely Horatio's; Hieronimo draws it out (according to the stage direction "He draweth out a bloody napkin") to offer the weeping Bazulto when he suddenly recognizes the memento:

> O no, not this: Horatio, this was thine,
> And when I dy'd it in thy dearest blood
> This was a token 'twixt thy soul and me
> That of thy death revenged I shall be.
> (III.xiii.86-89)

The importance of the handkercher is stressed again in Hieronimo's long speech of explanation when he draws the curtain to reveal the body of his son:

> And here behold this bloody handkercher,
> Which at Horatio's death I weeping dropp'd
> Within the river of his bleeding wounds:
> It is propitious, see, I have reserv'd,
> And never hath it left my bloody heart.
> (IV.iv.122-26)

The handkercher is for Hieronimo an objective reminder of his duty as a revenger. Might it not also be a symbolic link, joining the revenge for Horatio to that for Andrea? We have no stated evidence that the handkercher displayed by Hieronimo is the scarf given by Bel-imperia which Horatio uncovered from the body of Andrea. But *scarf* and *handkercher* were interchangeable terms, and it appears from the stage direction cited above that *napkin* was another word for the same article. It is impossible to say that Hieronimo's handkercher is the scarf of the first act, but one might suggest that it could well have been. If it were, Kyd might be credited with more skill as a dramatist than he is now conceded. Furthermore, the play would appear as a more unified whole; for the handkercher-scarf would symbolize the connection between two revenge motifs. In the absence of proof that the handkercher-scarf was employed to achieve these ends we may at least suggest that it would provide a singularly effective piece of stage business; perhaps its use in a modern production might serve to counteract those critics who charge that the play lacks focus, or that its revenge themes are never successfully joined, or that Andrea is a superfluous character.

Two of the objections to ***The Spanish Tragedy*** have been answered; the play does have a focus; it is unified, and Andrea is essential to its wholeness. It now remains to deal with the final charge, the claim that Hieronimo would have been rejected by the Elizabethan audience and that in securing vengeance by private means and with Italianate method she lost all claim to the sympathy of the spectators. In the consideration of this claim it might be well to keep in mind the questions with which Miss Campbell concluded her investigation of Elizabethan attitudes toward revenge: "Does the dialogue make clear whether the avenger has the right to take upon himself the prerogative of public vengeance, executing God's justice upon others? Does the plot make clear whether or not God executes vengeance upon the avenger?"

Bowers insists that Hieronimo became a villain in the eyes of Kyd's Elizabethan audience and that he was forced to commit suicide because the accepted doctrine forbade murder. He even maintains that "The audience is sympathetic with his [the dramatist's] revenger so long as he does not become an Italianate intriguer, and so long as he does not revenge." But does Hieronimo become a complete villain? To say no is to reply to Miss Campbell's first question in the affirmative. Hieronimo retains his belief in the need for justice even when he is unable to receive justice in his own case; he continues to fulfill his duties as Knight Marshal. He does not contemplate action against Horatio's murderers until he has certain proof. Even then he does not consider taking private vengeance; instead he determines to put his case before the king (III.vii.69-70).

Hieronimo seeks to obtain redress through every legitimate means, but Lorenzo effectively prevents him from gaining even a hearing. Hieronimo is forced to resort to secret ways because all other avenues seem closed to him, and he does not seem capable of gaining revenge by direct violent methods. Thus Hieronimo's revenge scheme is the product of necessity, for he finds that he must fight policy with policy. Hieronimo's actions should not be regarded as a violation of moral standards, nor should one assume that he lost the sympathy of his Elizabethan audience. Kyd's play is not based on the Christian morality which, in theory, would provide the basis for Renaissance ideas of justice; and the device of the Soliman-Perseda play is just as much an example of common sense, give-them-their-own-medicine morality as it is an example of Italianate intrigue.

Even if it were granted that Hieronimo does become a plotter to achieve his ends, it is doubtful that this alone would alienate the audience. Malevole, in Marston's *The Malcontent,* employs subterfuge and guile throughout the play; but he is restored to his dukedom at the end, and the play comes to a joyful conclusion. Of course, Malevole does not commit murder; nevertheless, his case appears to demonstrate that the use of Italianate intrigue would not disqualify a hero from receiving the sympathy of the audience. Another of Marston's heroes, Antonio, is not only an intriguer but the perpetrator of acts of violence which are among the most horrible ever presented on the stage.

After cutting out Piero's tongue, binding him to a chair, and serving him a platter containing the remains of his son, Antonio leads his accomplices in the raging butchery of their helpless foe. Yet Antonio is offered both riches and public office by the Venetian senators, and he rejects their offer because he has chosen to retire to religious solitude. Against these examples one might set *The Revenger's Tragedy* and point to Vindice as a revenger who transgressed the bounds of justice; but it is just that transgression which makes Vindice a different case. It is possible to judge the revenger only with respect to the context of the play. When he is forced to employ intrigue it is usually because he must contend with policy on its own terms. Perhaps there is in Elizabethan tragedy a "hero as villain" just as there is a "villain as hero" [Clarence Valentine Boyer, *The Villain as Hero in Elizabethan Tragedy,* 1914], and perhaps this "hero as villain" is, in every case, a man who must contend with those whom he is unable to defeat in direct conflict and who depend for the security of their positions upon the employment of policy. Such a hero is Hieronimo, whose concern with justice is everywhere in evidence but who must himself resort to policy and intrigue in order to gain the revenge which is his legitimate due.

It is now necessary to inquire into the fate of Hieronimo. The answer to Miss Campbell's second question is also affirmative; not only does the play reveal the judgment on Hieronimo, it also makes it quite clear that he is to suffer no punishment for taking his revenge. "Good Hieronimo" is to enjoy the blessing of everlasting delights, for Andrea promises:

> I'll lead Hieronimo where Orpheus plays,
> Adding sweet pleasure to eternal days.
> (IV.v.23-24)

The principle of justice controls the play's conclusion; and even an Elizabethan audience, I think, would not have condemned an Hieronimo whose revenge was sanctioned by the gods of his world in ***The Spanish Tragedy.***

I do not wish to quarrel unnecessarily with the work of Professor Bowers. It seems important, however, to point out some of the limitations of his theory and some of the difficulties involved in the application of social and ethical values, however admirably derived, to literary works. The effect of attempts at historical reconstruction should be illuminating, not restrictive. My general disagreement with Bowers has taken the specific form of objections to his treatment of ***The Spanish Tragedy,*** for his criticisms of Kyd's play are primarily the result of his attempt to make the play fit his theory. The rigid observance of theoretical strictures would discard large parts of the work as superfluous and make its conclusion ethically untenable. But Kyd's tragedy is a unified whole, and it supplies all of the solutions to the moral and ethical questions which it raises. Elizabethan attitudes toward revenge notwithstanding, ***The Spanish Tragedy*** is a greater play than Professor Bowers would lead us to believe. (pp. 7-16)

Ejner J. Jensen, "Kyd's 'Spanish Tragedy': The Play Explains Itself," in The Journal of English and Germanic Philology, *Vol. LXIV, No. 1, January, 1965, pp. 7-16.*

Nashe on Kyd's writing style (1589):

I'le . . . talke a little in friendship with a few of our triuiall translators. It is a cōmon practise now a daies amongst a sort of shifting companions, that runne through euery arte and thriue by none, to leaue the trade of *Nouerint* whereto they were borne, and busie themselues with the indeuors of Art, that could scarcelie latinize their necke-verse if they should haue neede; yet English *Seneca* read by candle light yeeldes manie good sentences, as *Bloud is a begger,* and so foorth: and if you intreate him faire in a frostie morning, he will affoord you whole *Hamlets,* I should say handfulls of tragical speaches. But ô griefe! *tempus edax rerum,* what's that will last alwaies? The sea exhaled by droppes will in continuance be drie, and *Seneca* let bloud line by line and page by page, at length must needes die to our stage: which makes his famisht followers to imitate the Kidde in *Æsop,* who enamored with the Foxes new fangles, forsooke all hopes of life to leape into a new occupation; and these men renowncing all possibilities of credit or estimation, to intermeddle with Italian translations: wherein how poorelie they haue plodded, . . . let all indifferent Gentlemen that haue trauailed in that tongue, discerne by their twopenie pamphlets: and no meruaile though their home-born mediocritie be such in this matter; for what can be hoped of those, that thrust *Elisium* into hell, and haue not learned so long as they haue liued in the spheares, the iust measure of the Horizon without an hexameter. Sufficeth them to bodge vp a blanke verse with ifs and ands, and other while for recreation after their candle stuffe, hauing starched their beardes most curiouslie, to make a peripateticall path into the inner parts of the Citie, and spend two or three howers in turning ouer French *Doudie,* where they attract more infection in one minute, than they can do eloquence all dayes of their life, by conuersing with anie Authors of like argument.

Thomas Nashe, in his preface to Robert Greene's Menaphon, *edited by G. B. Harrison, 1927.*

G. K. Hunter (essay date 1965)

[*In the following excerpt, Hunter contends that Kyd's ironic treatment of the concept of justice in* The Spanish Tragedy *serves to unify the play structurally and thematically. The critic argues that in this tragedy justice represents the illusion of free will in lives already determined by destiny, and while the enactment of revenge results in a morally satisfying conclusion, it is at the expense of the characters' humanity.*]

The assumption that ***The Spanish Tragedy*** is usefully categorized as a "revenge play" and that this categorization gives us a means of differentiating what is essential in the text from what is peripheral—this has governed most that has been said about Kyd's play. And this is a pity, because the play when looked at in these terms shows up as rather a botched piece of work.

It is no doubt an inevitable part of the tendency of literary historians that they should look everywhere for indications of historical progress. Certainly this has caused them to search among the "amorphous" (i.e., nonmodern) dramatic forms of the Elizabethans for signs and portents of the coming of Scribe and the "well-made" play. The revenge motif, in particular, has been seen as important because (to quote Moody Prior [in his *The Language of Tragedy,* 1947]) it

> had the advantage of imposing a fairly strict pattern on the play. It thus assisted in discouraging multiple narratives and irrelevant episodes, and, in general, acted as a check on the tendency toward diffuseness and digression which was a common defect of popular Elizabethan drama.

Percy Simpson [in his 1935 British Academy Shakespeare Lecture entitled "The Theme of Revenge in Elizabethan Tragedy"], in the same general terms, sees the revenge motif as imposing on Elizabethan dramaturgy the Aristotelian virtues of beginning, middle, and end: "The beginning is effectively supplied by the murder; the end should be effectively supplied by the vengeance. The problem for the working dramatist was skilfully to bridge the gap between the two."

Unfortunately this pattern of progress shows the actual products it seeks to explain as rather unsatisfactory parts of the very progression which is adduced to explain them. Prior finds ***The Spanish Tragedy*** to be ensnared in the very "multiple narratives and irrelevant episodes" that the revenge motif was supposed to discourage. He speaks of "the disproportionate amount of preliminary preparation necessary before Hieronimo is introduced as the avenging agent," and also of "the introduction of the story of the treacherous noble in the Portuguese Court, which has no bearing on the main action." Fredson Bowers tells us [in his *Elizabethan Revenge Tragedy,* 1940] that "the ghost has no real concern with the play" and that "the fundamental motive for the tragic action . . . is not conceived until midway in the play." Simpson has much the same attitude. After the passage quoted above, he goes on to apply it to Kyd:

> Now Kyd, who had a keen eye for dramatic situation and, in his happy moments, a powerful style, does at critical points fumble the action. His main theme, as the early title-page announces, is "the lamentable end of Don Horatio," avenged at the cost of his own life by his aged father Hieronimo. But the induction brings in the ghost of Horatio's friend, Don Andrea, and the personified figure of Revenge.

Later Simpson speaks more unequivocally of

> the disconnectedness, the waste of opportunity, and the dramatic unevenness of much of the writing.

This attitude toward the revenge play in general and ***The Spanish Tragedy*** in particular has persisted in criticism. Philip Edwards' recent and excellent edition of the play (1959) speaks of the "prolix early scenes" and tells us that "it is very hard to justify the sub-plot . . . the relevance of theme is very slight." But at the same time as these attitudes persist, their historical foundations are disappearing. The assumption that the Elizabethan play inherited from the Tudor interlude a diffuse form which reflects mere incompetence—this becomes increasingly difficult to sustain in the light of recent studies of the interlude by Craik [in his *The Tudor Interlude,* 1958], Spivack [in his *Shakespeare and the Allegory of Evil,* 1958], Bevington, [in his *From* Mankind *to Marlowe,* 1962], and Habicht [in his *Sénèque et le théâtre de la Renaissance,* ed. Jacquot, 1964]. These, in their different ways, present the interlude as a serious form, in which flat characterization, repetitiveness, and dependence on a multiplicity of short episodes are not defects, but rather means perfectly adapted to express that age's moral and religious (rather than psychological or social) view of human destiny. Persons are seen to be less important than theme; they exist to illustrate rather than represent; and narrative lines gives way to the illustration of doctrine. I may quote Bevington's remarks on the late morality, Lupton's *All for Money* (*c.* 1577):

> The unity of *All for Money,* as in so many popular "episodic" plays, is the singleness of theme (man's greed) manifested in a variety of episodes. This theme becomes more important than the fate of individuals. Characters are drawn to illustrate a single motif of human behavior, and are given no more depth than is necessary to make a point. The full course of their lives has no relevance here. It is the course of the moral formula that is all-important: the genealogy of sin, the analysis of its origins, motivations, and processes, the depiction of its worldly success and ultimate downfall—all seen in the perspective of moral uprightness, the beginning and end of virtuous living. The parts succeed each other as *exempla* to a homily, written for an audience that perceived a rich totality in matters of faith. The success of the play lies in varied illustration, in "multiple unity" and gathering of impact, not in the crisis of the individual moment.

If ***The Spanish Tragedy*** is seen not so much as the harbinger of *Hamlet* (not to mention Scribe), but more as the inheritor of a complex and rich tradition of moralizing dramaturgy, the actual structure of the play begins to make more sense, and the traditional strictures that Prior and Simpson re-echo lose much of their relevance. The text of the play does not appear to give its complete attention to the enactment of revenge. True. But this may be because the play is not centrally concerned with the enactment of revenge. Much more obsessive is the question of justice. Indeed we may hazard an initial statement that if revenge provides the plot line of the play (i.e., play structure as seen from Scribe's point of view), justice provides the thematic center of the play (i.e., play structure as seen from the point of view of the Tudor interlude).

The centrality of the concept of justice serves to explain much of the so-called "preliminary preparation" of the first two acts. The play opens with Don Andrea, who has been slain in the late war between Spain and Portugal. Don Andrea's journey after death is through an infernal landscape devoted to working out justice. He is set before Minos, Rhadamanthus, and Aeacus, the judges of the classical afterlife; they are unable to resolve his legal status and refer him to a higher authority—to the monarchs of the underworld, Pluto and Proserpine. On his way to their court he passes through the enactments of Hell's precisely organized justice—horribly poetic justice indeed:

Where bloudie faries shakes their whips of steele,
And poore *Ixion* turnes an endles wheele;
Where vsurers are choakt with melting golde,
And wantons are imbraste with ouglie Snakes,
And murderers grone with neuer killing wounds,
And periurde wightes scalded in boyling lead,
And all foule sinnes with torments ouerwhelmd.
(I.i.65-71)

But Don Andrea is not allowed to complete his search for justice amid the palpable abstractions of Hell. What the higher court orders is that he should be sent back to earth to observe how the gods operate *there,* and for this purpose he is given Revenge as his companion and guide:

Forthwith, *Revenge,* she rounded thee in th' eare,
And bad thee lead me through the gates of Horn,
Where dreames haue passage in the silent night.
No sooner had she spoke, but we were heere,
I wot not how, in twinkling of an eye.

REVENGE. Then know, *Andrea,* that thou art ariu'd
Where thou shalt see the author of thy death, . . .
Depriu'd of life by *Bel-imperia.*
(I.i.81-87, 89)

Revenge here seems to bear the same relation to justice as Talus (in Book V of *The Faerie Queene*) does to Artegall—that is, he is the emotionless and terrifyingly nonhuman executive arm of the legality that is being demonstrated. But Revenge, unlike Talus, does not act in his own person; his presence guarantees that the human action will work out justly, but he is not seen to make it do so. The departure of Andrea and Revenge through the gates of horn, Virgil's *porta—*

Cornea, qua veris facilis datur exitus umbris—

and their arrival at the Spanish court, can indeed be seen as dramatic equivalents to the introductory sequences of medieval dream allegory. The play may be viewed in this sense as what Andrea dreams, as an allegory of perfect justice: "The gods are indeed just; and now you shall see how their justice works out." We are promised a mathematical perfection of total recompense, where justice and revenge are identical. From this point of view the human beings who appear in Andrea's dream—the characters of the play, scheming, complaining, and hoping—are not to be taken by the audience as the independent and self-willed individuals they suppose themselves to be, but in fact only as the puppets of a predetermined and omnicompetent justice that they (the characters) cannot see and never really understand. But *we* (watching the whole stage) must never lose sight of this piece of knowledge.

The concern with justice in the opening scenes establishes an ironic set of responses for the audience and an ironic mode of construction for the play. The structure, indeed, may remind us of a Ptolemaic model of the universe, one level of awareness outside another level of awareness and, outside the whole, the unsleeping eye of God.

The disjunction between what the audience knows and what is known in the Spanish court is established straightaway when the "play proper" starts. The Spaniards congratulate themselves on the late victory and stress the unimportance of the losses:

All wel, my soueraigne Liege, except some few
That are deceast by fortune of the warre.
(I.ii.2-3)

And again: "Victorie, my Liege, and that with little losse." *We,* seeing Andrea sitting on the stage, know that the "little losse" can be too easily discounted and that the "some few" may yet blemish the complacency of the court and the overconfident assumption that justice is already achieved:

Then blest be heauen, and guider of the heauens,
From whose faire influence such iustice flowes.
(I.ii.10-11)

We now see assembled before us the characters who are to be involved in the final demonstration of justice, centrally Don Balthazar, who is to die (we have been told) by the hand of Bel-imperia. But what we see in the opening scenes is no movement that can be understood as leading toward the death of Balthazar. What happens involves Balthazar with a variety of different kinds of justice, but the play is obviously more interested in exploring thematic comprehensiveness than in moving toward any narrative consequence.

The problem of deciding justly between competing claims to truth, which has appeared already in the dispute between Aeacus and Rhadamanthus, recurs in the contest between Lorenzo and Horatio, who dispute which of them, in law, has Balthazar as prisoner; and the king shows a Solomon-like wisdom in making a just decision:

Then by my iudgment thus your strife shall end:
You both deserue, and both shall haue reward.
Nephew, thou tookst his weapon and his horse:
His weapons and his horse are thy reward.
Horatio, thou didst force him first to yeeld:
His ransome therefore is thy valours fee; [etc.].
(I.ii.178-183)

Expectation is tuned into a competency of human justice that *we* know cannot finally be sustained against the meddling of divine justice in this human scene.

The next scene introduces the Portuguese episode so famous for its irrelevance to the main action. The first scene of the "play proper" showed the Spaniards rejoicing over their victory and absorbing Balthazar into their court life. What the second (Portuguese) scene does is to show us the other side of the coin—the Portingales bewailing their defeat. And actually the Portuguese scenes serve as a continuous counterpoint against the earlier stages of ***The Spanish Tragedy,*** not only setting Portuguese sorrow against the Spanish mirth of the first scene, but later inverting the counterpoint and setting the viceroy's joy at his son's recovery against Hieronimo's cry of sorrow and demand for vengeance. Moreover, the long aria of grief put into the viceroy's mouth in I.iii gives the first statement of what is to become the central theme of ***The Spanish Tragedy,*** certainly the central and most famous impulse in its rhetoric—that frantic poetry of loss and sense of universal injustice which was to give Hieronimo his fame. We can see that, in spatial terms, the viceroy prepares the way for Hieronimo by living through the same class of experience—the loss of a son. Hieronimo makes this point quite explicitly when he says at the end of the play:

> Speake, Portaguise, whose losse resembles mine:
> If thou canst weepe vpon thy *Balthazar,*
> Tis like I wailde for my *Horatio.*
> (IV.iv.114-116)

The viceroy does not weep at this point, when Balthazar is really dead, but the opening scenes and the speeches in which he bewails his supposed death sustain our sense of what Hieronimo is referring to. Moreover, the connection between national sin and individual sorrow which seems to be implied in the main story of Hieronimo and Horatio is quite explicit in the Portuguese episode:

> My late ambition hath distaind my faith;
> My breach of faith occasiond bloudie warres;
> Those bloudie warres haue spent my treasure;
> And with my treasure my peoples blood;
> And with their blood, my ioy and best beloued,
> My best beloued, my sweete and onely Sonne.
> (I.iii.33-38)

But this scene of sorrow does more than prepare for the second and central lost son, Don Horatio; it establishes an ironic countercurrent inside the framework of the general information that has been given us by Andrea and Revenge. Not only is it deeply ironic to see the viceroy bewailing the death of a son, who is at that moment involved in the murder of another son, Horatio, and the bereavement of another father (and we should note that this second bereavement is one which cannot, this time, be avoided as if by a miracle [see III.xiv.34]). But more, the general framework of the play tells us that it is ironic even when the viceroy changes from lamentation to rejoicing; for *we* know that the relationship with Bel-imperia which looks so auspicious from inside the play will be the actual cause of his death.

The short fable of human fallibility and divine concern which supplies the narrative (as against the thematic) substance of the Portuguese episode—this feeds into the main plot an expectation that " . . . murder cannot be hid: / Time is the author both of truth and right, / And time will bring this trecherie to light" (II.v.58-60); it strengthens the expectation which Revenge and Andrea arouse by their very presence—that wrong must soon, and inevitably, be followed by retribution. It is no accident that places the second Portuguese scene (III.i)—which shows Alexandro rescued from death, as if by miracle, at the very last moment—immediately after the death of Horatio and the first sounds of Hieronimo's passion: "What out-cries pluck me from my naked bed, [etc.]" (II.v.1) The discovery of Horatio is the center of the main plot, being the reenactment in real life of the death which began the action of the play; for Don Horatio is, as it were, the living surrogate for the ghost Andrea. As he was friend and revenger to Andrea on the battlefield, so he has taken on the role of lover to Bel-imperia, and so too he falls victim to Balthazar (and his confederates). And this is the point in the play where the sense of just gods directing a revenge on Balthazar is at its lowest ebb. As Andrea understandably exclaims to Revenge:

> Broughtst thou me hether to encrease my paine?
> I lookt that *Balthazar* should haue beene slaine:
> But tis my freend *Horatio* that is slaine,
> And they abuse fair *Bel-imperia,*
> On whom I doted more then all the world,
> Because she lou'd me more then all the world.
> (II.vi.1-6)

The reinforcement of the justice theme at this point is, therefore, particularly useful. Even if the Portuguese episode had no other function, this one would seem to justify it.

Andrea was returned to earth by the just gods, to witness a parable of perfect recompense, a parable which would reenact the story of his life, but cleared of the ambiguities and uncertainties that had surrounded him. The death of Horatio re-presents the death of Andrea, but presents it as a definite crime (as the death of Andrea was not) and makes Balthazar into a definite criminal (as in the battle he was not). More important, the death of Horatio raises up an agent of recompense who has the best claim to justification in his action—the father of the victim and a man renowned for state service, the chief judicial functionary of the court. Kyd goes out of his way to show Hieronimo in this function and to make the first citizen tell us that

> . . . for learning and for law,
> There is not any Aduocate in Spaine
> That can preuaile, or will take halfe the paine
> That he will in pursuit of equitie.
> (III.xiii.51-54)

Hieronimo is justly at the center of ***The Spanish Tragedy*** because he is constructed to embody perfectly the central question about justice that the play poses: the question, "How can a human being pursue the path of justice?" Hieronimo is constructed to suggest both complete justification of motive (his outraged fatherhood) and the strongest advantages in social position. And as such he is groomed to be the perfect victim of a justice machine that uses up and destroys even this paragon. Herein lies the truly cathartic quality of ***The Spanish Tragedy:*** If this man, Kyd seems to be saying, fails to find any secure way of justice on earth, how will it fare with you and me? For Hieronimo, for all his devotion to the cause of justice, is as much a puppet of the play's divine system of recompense as are the other characters in the action. He is stuck on the ironic pin of his ignorance; we watch his struggles to keep the action at a legal and human level with involvement, with sympathy, but with assurance of their predestinate failure:

> Thus must we toyle in other mens extreames,
> That know not how to remedie our owne;
> And doe them iustice, when uniustly we,
> For all our wrongs, can compasse no redresse.
> But shall I neuer liue to see the day,
> That I may come (by iustice of the heauens)
> To know the cause that may my cares allay?
> This toyles my body, this consumeth age,
> That onely I to all men iust must be,
> And neither Gods nor men be iust to me.

DEPUTY. Worthy *Hieronimo,* your office askes
A care to punish such as doe transgresse.

HIERONIMO. So ist my duety to regarde his death,
Who, when he liued, deserued my dearest blood.
(III.vi.1-14)

He calls on heavenly justice; what he cannot know is that his agony and frustration are part of the process of heavenly justice. As his madness takes him nearer and nearer the nightmare world of Revenge and Andrea, this mode of irony is reinforced. Hieronimo tells us:

Though on this earth iustice will not be found,
Ile downe to hell, and in this passion
Knock at the dismall gates of *Plutos* Court, . . .
Till we do gaine that *Proserpine* may grant
Reuenge on them that murd <e> red my Sonne.
(III.xiii.108-110, 120-121)

What he cannot know is that this is precisely what Don Andrea has already done—indeed the explanation of the whole action of the play up to this point. Again and again he calls on the justices of Hell:

Goe backe, my sonne, complaine to *Eacus,*
For heeres no iustice; gentle boy, be gone,
For iustice is exiled from the earth:
Hieronimo will beare thee company.
Thy mother cries on righteous *Radamant*
For iust reuenge against the murderers.
(III.xiii.137-142)

. . . thou then a furie art,
Sent from the emptie Kingdome of blacke night,
To sommon me to make appearance
Before grim *Mynos* and iust *Radamant,*
To plague *Hieronimo* that is remisse,
And seekes not vengeance for *Horatioes* death.
(III.xiii.152-157)

But these infernal judges have already acted. All that Hieronimo can see is that he, the justice, the magistrate, the proponent of civil order, is living in a world where justice is impossible, where

. . . neither pietie nor pittie mooues
The King to iustice or compasion,
(IV.ii.2-3)

and where heavenly justice does not seem to be filling in the lacuna left by the failure of civil justice:

O sacred heauens, if this vnhallowed deed,
If this inhumane and barberous attempt,
If this incomparable murder thus
Of mine, but now no more my sonne,
Shall vnreueald and vnreuenged passe,
How should we tearme your dealings to be iust,
If you vniustly deale with those, that in your iustice trust?
(III.ii.5-11)

The heavens are not asleep, in fact, but their wakefulness has a different aspect from that which mortals expect. Hieronimo knows the orthodox Christian doctrine of Romans XII.19, which tells us ("Vindicta mihi, ego retribuam, dicit Dominus") to leave revenge to God:

Vindicta mihi.
I, heauen will be reuenged of euery ill;
Nor will they suffer murder vnrepaide.
Then stay, *Hieronimo,* attend their will:
For mortall men may not appoint their time.
(III.xiii.1-5)

But no more than Andrea can he apply this knowledge or relate it to what is happening to himself and to those around him. Andrea feels that everything is going the wrong way:

I lookt that *Balthazar* should haue beene slaine:
But tis my freend *Horatio* that is slaine.
(II.vi.2 ff.)

And when (in the next act) he finds that Revenge has actually been sleeping while the wicked continued their triumph, Heaven's conspiracy with injustice seems to be complete. But Revenge is coldly contemptuous of these passionate human outcries:

Thus worldlings ground, what they haue dreamd, vpon.
Content thy selfe, *Andrea;* though I sleepe,
Yet is my mood soliciting their soules. . . .
Nor dies *Reuenge,* although he sleepe awhile;
For in vnquiet quietnes is faind,
And slumbring is a common worldly wile.
Beholde, *Andrea,* for an instance, how
Reuenge hath slept, and then imagine thou
What tis to be subiect to destinie.
[*Enter a dumme shew.*]
(III.xv.17-19, 22-27)

The menace and even horror of Revenge's outlook, for those who are "subject to destiny," needs to be stressed. The presence of a justice machine in this play is no more cozily reassuring than in Kafka's *Strafkolonie.* For the irony of its operation works against Andrea and Hieronimo no less than against Lorenzo and Balthazar.

All in ***The Spanish Tragedy*** are caught in the toils of their ignorance and incomprehension, each with his own sense of knowledge and power preserved intact, and blindly confident of his own (baseless) understanding, even down to the level of the boy with the box (III.v). This episode—the only clearly comic piece of business in ***The Spanish Tragedy***—catches the basic irony of the play in its simplest form. The boy's preliminary explanation of the trap set up, and his key sentence, "Ist not a scuruie iest that a man should iest himselfe to death?" establishes the usual Kydian disjunction in the levels of comprehension. Throughout the following trial scene (III.vi) the boy stands pointing to the empty box, like a cynical emblem of man's hope for justice; and yet the irony has also (as is usual in the play) further levels of complexity. For Lorenzo, the organizer of the ironic show which seals Pedringano's lips even while it betrays his body to the hangman, is himself a victim, not only in the larger irony of Revenge's scrutiny but also in the minor irony that it is his very cleverness that betrays him: It is Pedringano's letter that confirms Hieronimo's knowledge of the murderers of Horatio. Lorenzo, indeed, as Hieronimo remarks, "marcht in a net and thought himselfe unseen" even at the time he was entrapping others.

Hieronimo prides himself on his devotion to justice and

his thoroughness as a judge, but he serves divine justice by ceasing to be just at all in any human sense. The feeling of incomprehension, of not knowing where he is, in terms of the standards by which he has ordered his life—this drives him mad; but even here he reinforces the play's constant concern with justice by his mad fantasies of journeys into the hellish landscape of infernal justice.

> *Hieronimo,* tis time for thee to trudge:
> Downe by the dale that flowes with purple gore,
> Standeth a firie Tower; there sits a iudge
> Vpon a seat of steele and molten brasse, [etc.]
> (III.xii.6-9)

His incomprehension is inescapable because it is a function of his humanity. His madness is a direct result of the collision of his human sense of justice with the quite different processes of divine justice; for it is a fearful thing to fall into the hands of a just God. The absorption of the human into the divine justice machine is the destruction of the human, and Hieronimo becomes the instrument of Revenge by becoming inhuman. He becomes part of the hellish landscape of his imagination. In the play of Soliman and Perseda that he organizes we have yet another reenactment of the situation that began with Don Andrea. Bel-imperia (certainly resolute even if not certainly chaste) plays the part of "Perseda chaste and resolute." Balthazar, the princely lover who hoped to win Bel-imperia from her common lovers (Andrea, Horatio), plays the Emperor Soliman, who hopes to win Perseda from her common love. The crimes and killings in the play are organized by the Bashaw or Pasha, and this is the part to be played by Hieronimo himself. When asked, "But which of us is to performe that parte?" he replies:

> O, that will I, my Lords, make no doubt of it:
> Ile play the murderer, I warrant you,
> For I already haue conceited that.
> (IV.i.130-133)

The Spanish Tragedy as a whole has continuously set the marionette-like action of the man whose destiny is predetermined against the sense of choice or willpower in the passionate and self-confident individual. Continuously we have had actors watching actors but being watched themselves by still other actors (watched by the audience). *We* watch Revenge and Andrea watching Lorenzo watching Horatio and Bel-imperia; we watch Revenge and Andrea watching Hieronimo watching Pedringano watching the boy with the box; and at each point in this chain what seems free will to the individual seems only a predetermined *act* to the onlookers.

In the play within the play, in Hieronimo's playlet of Soliman and Perseda, this interest reaches its climax. The illusion of free will is suspended. The four central characters are absorbed into an action which acts out their just relationships *for them.* The net has closed, character has become role, speech has changed to ritual; the end is now totally predetermined. The play itself is a flat puppet-like action with a total absence of personal involvement; but as the characters intone their flat, liturgical responses to one another there is an enormous *frisson* of irony or disparity between what they say and what *we* know to be meant.

Hieronimo himself has become *instrument* rather than agent. *He* knows that his life has been absorbed into the ritual and that he cannot escape back into humanity, and he accepts this Hegelian kind of freedom (freedom as the knowledge of necessity) with a resolution at once noble and inhuman. At the end of his play he comes forward to speak his own epilogue:

> Heere breake we off our sundrie languages, . . .
> And, Princes, now beholde *Hieronimo,*
> Author and actor in this Tragedie,
> Bearing his latest fortune in his fist;
> And will as resolute conclude his parte
> As any of the Actors gone before.
> And, Gentles, thus I end my play.
> (IV.iv.74, 146-151)

Commentators on the denouement of ***The Spanish Tragedy*** usually concentrate on the human *mess* which follows Hieronimo's failure to complete his life in ritual, noticing the break in the pattern rather than the pattern itself. But I think that the nature of the final actions is only kept in focus if we see them as measuring the gap between the dream of justice and the haphazard and inefficient human actions that so often must embody it. This is a recurrent interest of a writer like Seneca. When he describes the suicide of Cato Uticensis, his greatest hero, he is not content to relate his fortitude in doing the deed; he stresses the horror of Cato's failure to finish himself off in one clean blow. What he is concerned to show is the persistence of Cato's will to die, in spite of his own inefficiency. And I think a similar concern to contrast the will to martyrdom with the *mess* of actual martyrdom can be seen at the end of ***The Spanish Tragedy.***

A martyr is rather exceptional if his suffering is not prolonged and humanly degrading; a martyr whose soul had been antiseptically abstracted from his body would be rather unlike those whose histories thronged the Elizabethan imagination, whether from *The Golden Legend* or from its local equivalent, Foxe's *Acts and Monuments.* We should remember that it was not simply Zeno who anticipated Hieronimo by biting out his own tongue, but St. Christina as well. Much ink has been spilled in sympathy for Castile, who is struck down at the end of the play, simply because he stands too close to the protagonist. But Castile is, of course, identified with the tormenters who seek to interrupt the ritual and prevent it from completing itself. It is Castile who suggests that torture is still of use, to compel Hieronimo to *write* the names of his confederates. And the death of Castile confers another dramatic advantage: It transfers mourning to the highest personage on the stage. The king of Spain has hitherto been concerned with the miseries of existence only at second hand. Now, at the end of the play, he himself becomes a principal mourner, as is indicated well enough in the final stage direction:

> *The Trumpets sound a dead march, the* King of Spaine *mourning after his brothers body, and the* King of Portingale *bearing the body of his sonne.*

In the final episode we return to the justice of Hell, where the characters of the play now supply the classical examples of sin and wickedness with which the play began ("Place *Don Lorenzo* on *Ixions* Wheele," [IV.v.33]). A last judgment places everyone where he morally belongs (as in the *Last Judgment* play at the end of the mystery cycles), but we would do less than justice to the complexity of this play if we did not notice that humanity has been sacrificed so that justice can be fulfilled. Revenge has been completed; we have seen what Fulke Greville describes as the mode of modern tragedy: "God's revenging aspect upon every particular sin to the despair and confusion of mortality." (pp. 89-104)

> *G. K. Hunter, "Ironies of Justice in 'The Spanish Tragedy'," in* Renaissance Drama, *Vol. VIII, 1965, pp. 89-104.*

Herbert R. Coursen, Jr. (essay date 1968)

[*Coursen is an American poet, educator, and Shakespearean scholar. In the excerpt below, the critic maintains that Hieronimo's actions are not the central focus of* The Spanish Tragedy; *rather it is Andrea's revenge for the crimes and ambitious machinations of the House of Castile. According to Coursen, the play follows a pattern of hidden actions and their subsequent revelations, which ultimately expose the family's guilt.*]

Modern interest in ***The Spanish Tragedy*** has been primarily historical. The play is viewed quite rightly as a tremendously significant departure from preceding drama, a departure which opened up new areas for the playwrights who came after. Kyd's handling of the revenge theme, his introduction of the Machiavellian, and his use of the play-within-a-play, for example, would evolve richly in the two decades following the appearance of his play. Those who resist the temptation to place the play in an historical context find little to praise in the play *per se.* Typical is the response of Robert Heilman, who finds it "merely an accumulation of spectacular happenings," calculated "to arouse confusion and astonishment." Heilman discerns in ***The Spanish Tragedy*** the one fault bound to lead to its dismissal by modern academic critics; he finds it impossible to relate "a bewildering complexity of actions . . . to a coherent pattern of meaning" [Introduction to *An Anthology of English Drama Before Shakespeare,* 1962]. In other words, whatever it may be, ***The Spanish Tragedy*** is not art.

One of the few efforts to approach the play as a unified whole is that of William Empson. "Andrea," he says, "has suffered the fate of Uriah; the father and the brother of Bel-imperia, that is, the Duke of Castile and Lorenzo, had arranged to have him killed in battle so that they could marry her to Balthazar. Presumably they informed the enemy Prince, who killed him in the battle, where he was going to be sent and how he could be recognized" ["The Spanish Tragedy," *Elizabethan Drama: Modern Essays in Criticism,* ed. R. J. Kaufman, 1961]. According to Empson, this is not made clear at the outset because Proserpine has arranged that Andrea discover what happened to him without being told. Thus the "frame" of the play—the Ghost and Revenge—has dramatic value; it represents Andrea's education. Thus the debate in Hades (I,i,38-53) about whether Andrea died a lover or a warrior is explicable. The primary problem with Empson's theory is that Don Cyprian's involvement in the plot against Andrea is never clearly established.

Empson does little more than advance his speculation. He even admits that the one line which seems to support it will not bear the meaning he initially assigns to it. He deflects his essay into the seemingly inevitable discussion of Hieronimo and revenge. The major problem with the criticism of ***The Spanish Tragedy*** has been its too exclusive focus on Hieronimo. If, as Moody E. Prior [in his *The Language of Tragedy,* 1947] and others claim, "the action of the play is centered in Hieronimo's attempt to secure justice," then indeed the play is badly balanced, its center of gravity located almost exclusively in the final two of its four acts. It would be foolish to deny Hieronimo's importance to the play, but if we make him the whole story, we must agree with Bowers that "From this point on [Hieronimo's discovery of Horatio's body at the end of Act Two] the ghost and his theme, which was to be the core of the play, are superfluous; and indeed, need never have been introduced" [Fredson Bowers in his *Elizabethan Revenge Tragedy,* 1940]. We must agree with Prior that Villuppo "has no bearing on the main action," that the Portuguese scenes are "irrelevant." We must agree, then, that until he had Horatio murdered about half way through his play, Kyd simply did not know what he was doing.

Rather than make Hieronimo the play's center, Howard Baker suggests [in his *Induction to Tragedy,* 1939] that "In elemental terms, [the play] can be said first of all to depict the wicked deeds and just downfall of a villainous prince, Lorenzo." I do not wish to argue Lorenzo's primacy over Hieronimo. I do suggest, however, that Baker tells us more about the play than do those dealing solely with Hieronimo. The motivating force of the play—the plot in the sense Aristotle uses the term—is the dynastic ambition of the House of Castile. The murder of Horatio and Hieronimo's subsequent efforts at justice are one result, albeit the primary one the play shows us, of the effort to marry Bel-imperia to Balthazar. In his machinations to achieve this marriage, Lorenzo commits crime after crime. ***The Spanish Tragedy*** is as much a play about crime as about revenge for crime. Like *Hamlet,* Kyd's play concerns *hidden* crime. It is full of lines which anticipate the words which echo along the corridors of Elsinore ("For murder, though it hath no tongue . . . "):

> 'Tis hard to trust unto a multitude,
> Or anyone, in mine opinion,
> When men themselves their secrets will reveal.
> (III,iv,47-9)

> O sacred heavens, may it come to pass
> That such a monstrous and detested deed,
> So closely smother'd, and so long conceal'd,
> Shall thus by this be venged or reveal'd?
> (III,vii,45-8)

> This that I did was for a policy
> To smooth and keep the murder secret.
> (III,x,9-10)

> But night, the coverer of accursed crimes,
> With pitchy silence hush'd these traitor's harms.
> (IV,iv,101-2)

Like *Hamlet*, ***The Spanish Tragedy*** concerns secrets (both secret love and secret crime), and if a coherent pattern exists beneath the play's seemingly unrelated actions it is that all of the actions involve either concealment or discovery. As Eliot says [in his *Essays on Elizabethan Drama,* 1956], "***The Spanish Tragedy,*** like the series of Hamlet plays, including Shakespeare's, has an affinity with our contemporary detective drama." Revenge—Hieronimo's, for example—is a response to his discovery of the perpetrators of crime. Murder—Horatio's, for example—is a response to the discovery of a love-affair. The final discovery is not Hieronimo's, nor that of the immediate spectators of his play. It is Andrea's. And his is the final revenge.

If we grant for the moment that the play concerns the hopes of the House of Castile and the crimes committed in pursuit of those hopes, we can do what Empson neglects to do—give his theory about the fate of Uriah a chance to breathe (or suffocate) in the atmosphere of the play itself. Its vitality in that climate will show that far from being a crude contriver of sensational events, Kyd has the ability, invariably granted Shakespeare, to place in his play many analogues to his central action. What is the central action springing time and time again from Castilian ambition?—a form of secret crime, a man betrayed, sent like Uriah unknowingly to his death. The play is full of variations of this situation. Andrea dies because his presence, like that of Uriah, blocks a marriage desired by a powerful personage. Horatio dies for the same reason. As a footnote to his plan to marry his sister to Balthazar, Lorenzo sends Serberine and Pedringano blindly to their deaths. The fictitious betrayal of Balthazar (as depicted by Villuppo) and the betrayal of Alexandro which Villuppo's lie represents are also politically motivated. Ultimately, as at the end of the Alexandro episode, concealed crime is exposed. Andrea will see that he has suffered the fate of so many of the play's characters and will lead the criminals to their final punishments.

The ghost, then, is part of the drama, not merely a spectator of a play; what happens within the frame is a play-within-a-play. The two young men are linked from the outset. Horatio fought for his friend's body and buried it. Horatio returns wearing Andrea's scarf, "pluck'd from off his liveless arm" (I,iv,42). Horatio is not dressing himself in borrowed robes but assuming Andrea's identity. The scarf which could have made Andrea a marked man on the battlefield becomes emblematic of Horatio's danger. Bel-imperia confirms the identification (and the danger) by allowing Horatio to take Andrea's place as her lover:

> Yet what avails to wail Andrea's death
> From whence Horatio proves my second love?
> Had he not lov'd Andrea as he did,
> He could not sit in Bel-imperia's thoughts . . .
> I'll love Horatio, my Andrea's friend.
> (I,iv,60-7)

As Bel-imperia's lover, Horatio becomes like Andrea, "Though not ignoble, yet inferior far / To gracious fortunes of [his] tender youth" (I,i,6-7). Very early in the play, Horatio becomes the personification of the Ghost observing the action.

Gracious fortunes turn to youthful ashes, of course. If the equation between the two young men is valid, then Horatio's death should reflect back on Andrea's, suggesting that Andrea died for the reason Horatio does. Horatio is killed because he blocks Balthazar's marriage to Bel-imperia. As Lorenzo says, "Her favour must be won by his remove" (II,i,146). According to Bowers, however, "Andrea was killed by Balthazar in fair battle. True, a feeble effort is made to put Balthazar in a bad light by having his soldiers unhorse Andrea before he is slain, but that is not sufficient to justify a vengeance-seeking ghost." Andrea's "reason for revenge is extraordinarily weak as seen through English eyes." There are some suggestions, however, that Andrea's death, if not the result of the "murd'rous cowardice" (I,iv,73) Bel-imperia imputes to Balthazar, was questionable. The fight was even ("Their strength alike": I,iv,15) while it was *mano a mano.* Then, however, a band of Portuguese unhorsed Andrea, and Balthazar "Did finish what his halberdiers begun" (I,iv,25). The Prince needed help.

Even if it was a fair fight, what of Lorenzo's strange role in all this? He appears before the King as co-claimant in the capture of Balthazar. But his behavior in battle was markedly different from that of Horatio. Lorenzo "took [Balthazar's] courser by the reins" (I,ii,155), while Horatio's "lance did put him from his horse" (156). According to Balthazar, Lorenzo "spake me fair . . . promis'd life . . . won my love," while Horatio "gave me strokes . . . threat'ned death . . . conquered me" (162-4). Horatio behaved like a soldier, Lorenzo like a courtier (Balthazar yielded "To him in courtesy": 161). Lorenzo apparently meant to bring Balthazar back alive, and certainly this view is consistent with his vigorous promotion of the match with Bel-imperia. Lorenzo's battlefield activities support Empson's speculation that all of this had been prearranged with Balthazar.

But suddenly another Andrea stands between Balthazar and Bel-imperia. And Horatio suffers the fate of Andrea; Horatio, too, dies on a kind of battlefield. Immediately before his murder, Horatio and Bel-imperia develop a series of war-love equations:

> BEL. Let dangers go, thy war shall be with me,
> But such a war, as breaks no bond of peace . . .
> Be this our warring peace, or peaceful war.
>
> HOR. But gracious madam, then appoint the field
> Where trial of this war shall first be made.
> (II,ii,32-40)
>
> BEL. If I be Venus thou must needs be Mars,
> And where Mars reigneth there must needs be wars.
>
> HOR. Then thus begin our wars: put forth thy hand,
> That it may combat with my ruder hand.
>
> BEL. Set forth thy foot to try the push of mine.
>
> HOR. But first my looks shall combat against thine.
>
> BEL. Then ward thyself, I dart this kiss at thee.

HOR. Thus I retort the dart thou threw'st at me.

BEL. Nay then, to gain the glory of the field,
My twining arms shal yoke and make thee yield.
(II,iv,34-43)

This is standard Petrarchan talk, of course, but the linkage of love and war seems hardly accidental. We remember that Andrea went into battle "For glorious cause still aiming at the fairest" (I,iv,11). If the equation between the two deaths holds, we can infer that Andrea was undone by someone he had reason to trust; Horatio and Bel-imperia are "betray'd" (II,iv,50) by Pedringano, whom Bel-imperia believes "as trusty as [her] second self" (II,iv,9). The fusion of love and war just before Horatio's death reminds us of the confusion in Hades about the manner of Andrea's death. He went to war and was killed because he loved Bel-imperia. Horatio goes to love Bel-imperia and is killed when the war conceit becomes more than metaphor. As love was carried onto a battlefield, now death comes to a lover's bower. "These are the fruits of love" (II,iv,55), snarls Lorenzo as he stabs Horatio. The words refer back to Andrea's death as well, as do Hieronimo's on discovering his son's corpse: "not conquer'd but betray'd" (II,v,47).

The equation between Horatio and Andrea is reemphasized following the murder. Lorenzo explains the murder of Horatio to Bel-imperia by telling her that the King and the Duke were approaching the bower and that he shielded her from the Duke's wrath, previously demonstrated in his anger at her liaison with Andrea:

Now when I came, consorted with the prince,
And unexpected in an arbour there
Found Bel-imperia with Horatio . . .
Why then, remembering that old disgrace
Which you for Don Andrea had endur'd,
And now were likely longer to sustain,
By being found so meanly accompanied,
Thought rather, for I knew no readier mean,
To thrust Horatio forth my father's way.

Removing Horatio is clearly paralleled with removing that other mean companion, Andrea. Empson admits that the last line cannot mean, "I murdered Horatio as my father murdered Andrea," but it *can* mean, "I removed a hindrance to my father's policy." Here, as in the battlefield episode, Lorenzo is busily about his father's business.

Hieronimo supplies another parallel between the careers of Andrea and Horatio: "Proserpine may grant / Revenge on them that murdered my son" (III,xiii,120-1). This might be merely another Senecan echo were it not that Proserpine has already done precisely what Hieronimo wishes—except that she assigned revenge to Andrea. Andrea's revenge will include Horatio's.

Any doubt that Andrea suffered the fate of Uriah would be dispelled, I believc, by the many analogues to betrayal the play provides. One of the more maligned aspects of the play is the subplot involving Villuppo and Alexandro. I will not attempt to defend it, but will try to show how much it tells us about the main plot. Villuppo claims that Balthazar has been betrayed. Like Andrea, Balthazar fought "amidst the thickest troups" (I,iii,61) until

Alexandro, that here counterfeits
Under the colour of a duteous friend,
Discharg'd his pistol at the prince's back.
(I,iii,65-7)

Villuppo lies "for guerdon of [his] villainy" (I,iii,95). Actually, Alexandro is being betrayed, of course, and that truth emerges when ambassadors bring word that Balthazar lives. Villuppo is led off to "bitterest torments and extremes" (III,i,100), while Alexandro is honored. "With public notice of [his] loyalty" (III,i,104). Whatever its limitations, the subplot provides a microcosm of the main plot. Villuppo tells of treachery on the battlefield, pointing back to Andrea's death in the same battle and ahead to Horatio's death on a metaphoric battlefield. The Viceroy's sharp grief for his son and his desire to punish Alexandro anticipate Hieronimo's response. Villuppo's story turns out to be a betrayal of its own, designed to bring him "reward and hope to be preferr'd" (III,i,95). The truth is revealed and the betrayer is punished, the betrayed rewarded. The assignment of rewards and punishments by the Viceroy at the end of the Villuppo episode points ahead to those meted out by Andrea in the context of eternity at the play's end.

Another complex pattern of betrayal culminates in the deaths of Serberine and Pedringano (and by extension in the final catastrophe, since Pedringano's letter accusing Lorenzo falls into Hieronimo's hands after Pedringano is hanged). Serberine goes to Saint Luigi's Park on Lorenzo's orders (III,ii,94-6). Lorenzo dispatches Pedringano to kill Serberine and sends the guard to apprehend the killer. It is a trap within a trap (and one which ultimately traps its contriver). The equation between the two marked men and Andrea-Horatio is suggested by Lorenzo: "better it's that base companions die, / Than by their life to hazard our good haps" (III,ii,115-6). All pawns impeding the Castilian march to dynasty are expendable. Serberine waits patiently to be assassinated and, in a wonderfully effective scene, Pedringano goes impudently to his death, certain that his pardon is at hand.

The closest analogue to the story of Uriah that ***The Spanish Tragedy*** provides is Hieronimo's play, "The Tragedy of Soliman and Perseda." Here, Erasto, a knight of Rhodes,

Was betroth'd and wedded at the length
To one Perseda, an Italian dame,
Whose beauty ravish'd all that her beheld,
Especially the soul of Soliman,
Who at the marriage was the chiefest guest.
By sundry means sought Soliman to win
Perseda's love, and could not gain the same.
Then gan he break his passions to a friend,
One of his bashaws whom he held full dear;
Her had this bashaw long solicited.
And saw she was not otherwise to be won
But by her husband's death, this knight of Rhodes,
Whom presently by treachery he slew.
(IV,i,110-21)

Hieronimo's play will reenact the story of Andrea and Horatio and then move on to avenge them. It is, then, a concise version of ***The Spanish Tragedy.*** It recapitulates all that has happened and within its framework concludes the play around it—with the important exceptions of the killing of Don Cyprian and the Ghost-Revenge frame. Hieronimo exacts vengeance within a context portraying the *reason* for that vengeance.

Hieronimo's play is a version of the Uriah story. Here, however, unlike Lorenzo's manipulations, deception serves revenge, not policy. It is ironic, of course, that Hieronimo has been asked to produce a play by Lorenzo and Balthazar. Like Hamlet in the duel scene, Hieronimo translates the occasion into a vehicle for vengeance. It is even more deeply ironic that Hieronimo is able to employ the primary tactic of the criminals against them—tricking them into a deadly situation. Now controlling the mechanism of revenge, Hieronimo casts Lorenzo in the role Lorenzo had created for Andrea and Horatio—that of Erasto, hapless husband of Perseda. Hieronimo assumes the role of the murderer, while in the outer play, of course, he is the revenger. The conflict between the two roles comments subtly on the moral ambiguity of revenge. Bel-imperia and Balthazar play roles identical to those of the outer play:

> BEL. Erasto! see, Soliman, Erasto's slain!
>
> BAL. Yet liveth Soliman to comfort thee.
> Fair queen of beauty, let not favour die,
> But with a gracious eye behold his grief,
> That with Perseda's beauty is increas'd,
> If by Perseda grief be not releas'd.
>
> BEL. Tyrant, desist soliciting vain suits,
> Relentless are mine ears to thy laments,
> As thy butcher is pitiless and base,
> Which seiz'd on my Erasto, harmless knight.
> (IV,iv,53-62)

Here, as in the Villuppo–Alexandro episode, is a miniature version of ***The Spanish Tragedy.***

In Hieronimo's play, a fictional rendering of the truth, the four parts are read in different languages, a perhaps labored way of suggesting that some of the actors and all of the spectators on the stage, King, Viceroy, and Duke, cannot understand what the play means. His play over, Hieronimo breaks away from "our sundry languages" and speaks in "our vulgar tongue" (IV,iv.74-5). It is an important transition from what seemed "counterfeit" (IV,iv,77)—both the fable of Hieronimo's play and the deaths suffered within it—to a revelation of "this tragedy" (IV,iv,147)—in which Horatio *was* killed and in which the actors who seemed so convincing in their death throes actually *were* dying. Although the audience in the theater knows all this, the effect of Hieronimo's emergence from his play is to eliminate one layer of complexity, one level of fiction. He shifts the plane of action to that of the spectators of his play. A further step in this process of simplification and clarification is the projection of the truth to the Ghost. He must learn who is *really* responsible for his death—not merely Balthazar or the sinister Lorenzo, but the Duke of Castile.

It would be strange for Kyd to introduce a superfluous death into his carefully wrought play. That Don Cyprian has been interested in advancing his daughter there can be no doubt (II,iii; III,xii,52-7; III,xiv,40-115). His brother, the King, in fact, orders Castile to promote Balthazar's suit (II,iv,41-50). Nor is there any doubt of Castile's rage at Bel-imperia's affair with Andrea (II,i,45-8; III,x,54-9, 68-70; III,xiv,108-14). Clearly, Andrea was Cyprian's enemy. While it is never shown that Lorenzo's actions are ordered by Cyprian, it *is* clear that they are dictated by the Duke's interest. If Lorenzo did arrange for Andrea's death, his warrant was his father's infuriation at Andrea's relationship with Bel-imperia, an anger clearly based on Cyprian's desire to see his daughter better matched (III,xiv,106-13). Obviously, Cyprian would have been similarly incensed had he learned of Horatio's assumption of Andrea's role. Lorenzo tells us as much in his explanation to Bel-imperia of the bower episode (III,x,54-9). Cyprian's rage, in fact, would have been augmented in Horatio's case, since Balthazar was on the premises yearning for Bel-imperia's hand. Whether Cyprian orders the murders or not, his policy demands them. Thus his death at Hieronimo's hand is symbolically appropriate. Hardly the "unoffending" [Philip Edwards, in his Introduction to *The Spanish Tragedy,* 1959] or the "innocent" [F. S. Boas, in his Introduction to the *Works of Thomas Kyd,* 1901] Castile, he represents the ambitious and powerful families who make ghosts of the humbler men who threaten their designs.

This truth is transmitted to Andrea when Hieronimo stabs Cyprian. Why doesn't Hieronimo include an indictment of Cyprian in his long speech after his play? There can be no certain explanation. Hieronimo has no evidence to bring against the duke. Furthermore, were he to accuse Cyprian, the Duke would simply deny the charges and have Hieronimo dispatched (as Villuppo tried to do with Alexandro, and as Lorenzo almost succeeded in doing with Pedringano). Hieronimo bites out his tongue because he *can not* inform effectively against the Duke. He can express his knowledge of Cyprian's guilt only in action. Castile's guilt is left unsaid; that does not mean it must also go unperceived. That all has *not* been said in Hieronimo's exegesis of his play is suggested by Hieronimo's further words (IV,iv,152, 180-82, 184-91), by his biting out of his tongue, and by the reiterated questions and demands of King, Viceroy, and Duke (IV,iv,157-8, 163-7, 176, 179, 183-4, 192-200). This insistence on a further meaning indicates that the stabbing of Castile is not merely another of the play's "supererogatory and unconvincing horrors" [Leslie Fiedler, "The Defense of the Illusion and the Creation of Myth," *English Institute Essays, 1948,* 1949], not merely another example of "pointless savagery" [Edwards], or "mere massacre" [Boas]. The stabbing must be Hieronimo's answer to the repeated questions. The emphasis on a further secret should incite us to seek it, not merely to complain that, after Hieronimo's long speech, "there is nothing more to say" [Fiedler].

Hieronimo's stabbing of Cyprian reveals the truth about the Duke to Andrea, thus moving it a step closer to the audience. As the fiction of Hieronomo's play has been erased for its immediate spectators by his revelation, so the fiction of Cyprian's innocence is exposed for Andrea by Hieronimo's action. Truth moves from Hieronimo's play (a play-within-a-play-within-a-play) to the spectators on the stage (a play-within-a-play) to the frame (a play). All fictive levels are erased until only the the frame remains. Andrea's final words suggest the truth about Cyprian. Andrea describes his "revenge" as "just" (IV,v,16) and punishes Cyprian first, as the source of the policy which dictated his death and that of his friend, Horatio. He punishes Lorenzo next, as the agent of that policy, then Balthazar, as the element which would have completed the Castilian design. Balthazar is accused of a "bloody love" (IV,v,37). The words suggest that if Andrea has *not* been betrayed because his love for Bel-imperia, then he is revenging himself on Balthazar merely for the deaths of Horatio and Bel-imperia. If so, he has forgotten his own revenge for his death at Balthazar's hands, the revenge mentioned so often during the earlier parts of the play (I,i,86-8; I,v; II,iv). "Bloody love" can only be interpreted, I believe, as a comprehensive term including the deaths of both Andrea *and* Horatio (and Bel-imperia, Hieronimo, *et al.*).

It is not that Kyd has revived a frame fallen into meaninglessness as the play develops new directions. The frame represents the play's most comprehensive level; the final truth is to be perceived there. The frame encompasss more than the play it surrounds; it raises judgments to a higher power. Hieronimo may have exacted vengeance on a temporal level; Andrea projects it beyond time. That the frame is meant to cast the final light on the darknesses of the play within it is implied by Revenge's echo of his first couplet. When he emerged with Andrea from Hades, he said,

> Here sit we down to see the mystery,
> And serve for chorus in this tragedy.
> (I,i,90-1)

"Mystery," according to Edwards, means "events with a hidden meaning . . . [an] allegorical significance." Indeed the events observed by Andrea have had another level of significance—they have told him not only what happened to his friends after his death, but what happened to *him.* As he returns to Hades with Andrea, Revenge makes a final choric comment suggesting that all concealed crimes have been exposed (there is no more "mystery"). A last layer of fiction—that of life on this earth—merges with the context of the frame, that of eternity:

> For here though death hath end their misery,
> I'll there begin their endless tragedy.

The two characters of the frame disappear into eternity and, finally, all levels of fiction erased, the play is over. (pp. 768-82)

Herbert R. Coursen, Jr., "The Unity of 'The Spanish Tragedy'," in Studies in Philology, *Vol. LXV, No. 5, October, 1968, pp. 768-82.*

Peter B. Murray (essay date 1969)

[*In the excerpt below, Murray examines the structure of* The Spanish Tragedy, *discussing Kyd's development of various levels of reality through the use of such devices as the chorus and the play-within-the-play. The critic also explores the close relationship between love and hate in the tragedy and how it affects the principal characters' actions.*]

What kind of play is ***The Spanish Tragedy?*** If we say that it is a work of theatrical genius, sensational and melodramatic in its manipulation of externals, do we deny it all possibility of having tragic depth and internal power? We may note at the outset that, whatever the limitations of Kyd's dramatic technique, his insistence on having his themes arise from characters in action on the stage is in one way, at least, an advance over Senecan tragedy, in which too often there is a great deal of "philosophy" that needs the test of characters in action. Moreover, Kyd has manipulated his "external" theatrical elements to create complex patterns of action, character, and language that have complex and profound implications even though they are made up of simple units; and the audience must perceive these patterns in order to understand the play.

For example, the play depends for both effect and meaning on parallels and contrasts between its different lines of action. Hieronimo's mistrust of Bel-imperia's letter accusing Lorenzo and Balthazar of the murder of Horatio is only developed superficially in psychological terms, and we in the audience accept his mistrust chiefly because, in the preceding scene, in parallel circumstances having nothing to do with Hieronimo, *we* have seen that such accusations can be false (III.i-ii). Kyd has thus sought to achieve the effect he desires by manipulating the audience as well as the characters of his play. The characters tend to speak as much to the audience as to one another; and the reason may be that Kyd means to exploit the arts of language not only to develop character and action but also to persuade and affect the audience so that it will be more immediately involved with his play than is usual.

Indeed, ***The Spanish Tragedy*** goes beyond Hamlet's assertion that a play is an image of reality to suggest that the play world *is* the real world or its symbolic equivalent. Perhaps the most striking feature of this play, as of *Hamlet,* is the play-within-the-play; but, whereas in *Hamlet* the playlet is only a pretended re-enactment of a murder, the playlet in ***The Spanish Tragedy*** is also a *vehicle* for murders. At its conclusion, Hieronimo tells his audience that it was mistaken to think it had watched "fabulously counterfeit" action, for the murders have been "perform'd" in two senses (IV.iv.77, 129). From *Hamlet* we may infer that, if the play-within-the-play is a mirror of the *Hamlet* world, perhaps the *Hamlet* world is likewise a mirror of our world. When the royal audience for Hieronimo's play sees that the play world is a real part of Spain, we may suddenly see that events in Spain are part of our world, that the characters have been made to work on our emotions because Kyd wants us to feel their passions directly, and not only as part of an esthetic whole from which we maintain a large degree of detachment. We are to see the characters in Kyd's play as people whom we might almost accept as part of our world at the same time that we recognize the artifice that has created them and know that we are at a higher level of awareness because we are in an audience.

The idea of an intimate relation between those in the play and those outside it is implicit in the use Kyd makes of

Andrea and Revenge. Andrea has precipitated the action he now watches as an audience, and Revenge both directs and witnesses the working out of the plot. Andrea even seems to enter the action of the play in the person of Horatio who, like Andrea, becomes the clandestine lover of Belimperia, is killed by Balthazar and his cohorts, and so causes a bloody revenge. It is no coincidence that revenge for Andrea is accomplished through revenge for Horatio in a play-within-the-play: just as the playlet contains murders for revenge of Horatio, with Hieronimo both "author and actor in this tragedy," so the whole play is an enactment of murders for revenge of Andrea who, if not its author, is its inspiration and a key participant both in spirit and in the person of Horatio (IV.iv.147).

The relation between the playlet and the play has still more implications than these. When Hieronimo says he is the author as well as an actor in his tragic playlet, he is claiming that he controls his own fate. He is not aware that above the level of his will and his authorship of action is another author, Revenge, who is using him for his own ends (or that above Revenge may be other authors like Pluto and Proserpina or Thomas Kyd; this last author is of course using everyone on the stage and in the audience for his own ends). Through this pattern we can see that the question the play asks is the one that all tragedies ask in one way or another: What are the forces that govern human destiny? Can men govern their own actions, joining the powers of author and actor to exercise complete freedom of will? Or is the freedom of the will only partial, so that man is less an author than an actor governed by a script created by his previous actions, by the passions of his character, and by the powers of heaven and hell, of chance and circumstance?

Kyd invites us, as Revenge invites Andrea, to "imagine thou / What 'tis to be subject to destiny" (III.xv.27-28) and to sit down and "see the mystery" of tragic fate (I.i.90). Of course the mystery of man's fate is, in part, what makes it tragic. If we knew the whole truth about our situation, we could use our reason to act in accordance with that truth; but, as it is, we do not know whether we live in an absurd universe having no order and no justice, whether we can author our own fates, or whether we are governed by powers whose wills we can only guess and may fulfill only unconsciously and ironically, against our own wills.

Repeatedly, the play gives us scenes of men who are unable to understand the powers above them. The most ingenious of these is the scene in Act III when Pedringano kills Serberine and is arrested by the Watch. Pedringano and Serberine were Lorenzo's accomplices in the murder of Horatio, and Lorenzo fears that they will betray him to Hieronimo. He decides, therefore, to destroy them. Serberine is told to go to the park behind the palace at eight o'clock; Pedringano is sent there to kill him; and the Watch is also told to be there. And not one of the men knows why he has really been sent to the park. Serberine's awareness is the least of all; he has no idea why he has been sent for, although he is instinctively afraid of the forces that may look down on him in the dark (III.iii.23-27). Pedringano knows that he is to kill Serberine, but does not suspect that this act is to result in his own death. Like Serberine, he is afraid, but he appeals to the goddess Fortune and places his faith in Lorenzo's rewards and promises. The men of the Watch know only that they have been commanded to guard where they have never been sent before, and they do not dream that they are the key part of a pattern of crime and retribution prearranged by Lorenzo.

In fact, no one comprehends the pattern in its entirety. Serberine sees nothing but the command of his master. Pedringano sees Serberine and his reward, but he does not see the Watch or the real plan of Lorenzo. The Watch see Serberine and Pedringano, and they know the power of the rulers, but they do not see how that power is being used in this case. Lorenzo is not on stage, but we must imagine him exulting as the clever stage manager who has masterminded the scene. But even Lorenzo does not see the final level of control: the persons of Revenge and Andrea, who have really arranged this pattern of crime and retribution, and have arranged it chiefly to destroy Lorenzo and Balthazar. There is no evidence that either Serberine or Pedringano would ever have willingly betrayed Lorenzo; but, after his arrest, Pedringano writes to Lorenzo reminding him of his crimes and begging his master to save him as he had promised to do. When Pedringano has been hanged, the executioner finds this letter and takes it to Hieronimo. Thus, although Lorenzo thinks he is the master of fate, the very means he employs to save himself are his ruin. His unreasonably fearful self-love has betrayed him to Revenge, an unseen power that destroys men by preying upon such passions through a pattern that is in every way ironic, as we shall see.

The central image of man in ***The Spanish Tragedy*** is thus a figure standing alone in semi-darkness, able to see and apparently able to control those below him in the hierarchy of power, although without understanding them, but often unable even to *see* those above him. If men could see those above themselves, they might realize that they are manipulated in the same way that they manipulate others; and they might then learn to treat other men more humanely. Humans destroy each other and are destroyed in turn because they do not understand that they are related to others not as superior to inferior, not as person to object or other, but as images of each other, or, most deeply of all, as forms of each other. If Lorenzo could see Revenge destroy him as he destroys Pedringano, he might know that what he does to Pedringano he really does to himself.

Hieronimo may progress toward a blind and isolated egotism like Lorenzo's, in which he thinks he is both author and actor of fate and does not rightly look above himself, but for most of the play he is desperately aware of the need to see:

> O eyes, no eyes, but fountains fraught with tears;
> O life, no life, but lively form of death;
> O world, no world, but mass of public wrongs,
> Confus'd and fill'd with murder and misdeeds;
> O sacred heavens! if this unhallow'd deed,
> If this inhuman and barbarous attempt,
> If this incomparable murder thus
> Of mine, but now no more my son,
> Shall unreveal'd and unrevenged pass,

How should we term your dealings to be just,
If you unjustly deal with those that in your justice trust?
(III.ii.1-11)

This speech is in many ways a key to the themes and structure of the play. Hieronimo, alone on the stage, is crying out to the unseen powers of heaven and hell, asking the questions that tragic action raises: Is there any order in the world? Are the heavens just? At the end of the speech, a letter falls at his feet that accuses Lorenzo and Balthazar of the murder of Horatio; but Hieronimo suspects the letter, and his loneliness, doubts, and fears are not allayed. The fearsome isolation of the tragic individual is expressed in every word he utters. Hieronimo is blinded by the tears of his passionate grief, and in his blindness he leaves unclear or else denies the true relations of things, even their very identities: "eyes, no eyes." If Hieronimo were not blinded by tears, he might be able to see Andrea and Revenge who are sitting right in front of him with an answer to his question. His inability to see them gives his speech a level of meaning of which he is not aware, again implying a failure to perceive identities and relations. He says "O life, no life, but lively form of death," meaning that his life is a painful living death; but the ghost of Andrea is another "lively form of death," almost an alternate form of Hieronimo, like him writhing in agony for revenge.

Although Hieronimo cannot see the parallel or identity of his level of action with the one above him, these ironies make *us* feel the relations of the two. In another way, also, the speech makes us feel that the parts of reality are related by parallels and identities of structure. The rhetoric itself, as so often in the play, implies that such a pattern underlies reality, that it is necessary to perceive parallels as well as patterns of cause and effect in viewing the ascending planes of reality. Since there are no logical connectives between the major units of the speech, its logic is entirely expressed through the implicit relations of its parts:

O eyes, no eyes, but . . .
O life, no life, but . . .
O world, no world, but . . .
O sacred heavens [implied: no sacred heavens, if there is no justice] . . .

We must grasp the logic of this structure of parallels in much the same way that we grasp the logic of the parallels between the induction of the ghost and Revenge, the play, and the play-within-the-play; between Serberine, Pedringano, Lorenzo, and Revenge; or between the story of Alexandro and Villuppo and that of Hieronimo. The speech builds upon the traditional parallels or correspondences between the various levels of reality. "Eyes" epitomize in microcosm the problem that "life" also develops. The individual "life" is a microcosm of the life of the body politic or the "world," and the order of the world should conform to the order of the cosmos, governed by "heavens." These significant parallels stress the point that Hieronimo, believing the proper relation of life, world, and heavens to have been destroyed, is tempted to deny their very identities. "Eyes, no eyes"—perhaps we are to see that his emotions blind him not only to Andrea and Revenge but to whatever order and hope of justice there might be in his world, and to the truth contained in the letter that drops at his feet in response to his plea for help.

It may be that there is an important denial of relationship and identity in Hieronimo's statement that Horatio is "now no more my son" (III.ii.8). He means only to say that Horatio is dead, but perhaps Kyd also means to imply that for Hieronimo his son's death has in some sense ended or transformed their relationship. The two lines of his speech just after he discovers Horatio's body are much like the denials of the "Eyes, no eyes" speech: "Alas, it is Horatio my sweet son! / O no, but he that Whilom was my son" (II.v.14-15). This could give a clue to one of the most puzzling of the mysteries of human destiny the play is concerned with: How are love and hatred related to each other?

One might blindly think of love and hate as unrelated opposites, but they are related in many ways in ***The Spanish Tragedy*** and in life. Hieronimo loved his son Horatio. But now Horatio has been murdered, and for Hieronimo the positive relationship to his son is ended. Love for his son is now to be expressed negatively in hatred of the murderers. From this ironic reversal of emotion the motive of revenge arises. Yet, at a different level, the motive for revenge arises out of the complete irreconcilability of love and hate. Don Andrea loves Bel-imperia, and for love of her goes off to war, an expression of hate. There he is killed, and, when his soul comes before Minos, Aeacus, and Rhadamanth, the judges in Hades, Minos describes his fate:

"This knight," quoth he, "both liv'd and died in love,
And for his love tried fortune of the wars,
And by war's fortune lost both love and life."
"Why then," said Aeacus, "convey him hence,
To walk with lovers in our fields of love, . . . "
"No, no," said Rhadamanth, "it were not well
With loving souls to place a martialist,
He died in war, and must to martial fields, . . . "
Then Minos, mildest censor of the three,
Made this device to end the difference.
"Send him," quoth he, "to our infernal king,
To doom him as best seems his majesty."
(I.i.38-42, 45-47, 50-53)

The *judges* are thus frustrated, and Andrea is sent to Pluto's palace, where Proserpina turns him over to Revenge. The revenger, like the chivalric warrior, is a role that combines the lover and the killer into one: "Awake, Revenge, if love, as love hath had, / Have yet the power or prevalence in hell!" (III.xv.13-14). Revenge thus comes into play when ordinary justice is impossible because a man has committed acts of violence for love. And revenge fatefully repeats this ironic pattern of motivation, yielding a series of murders for love. . . . [The] solution Revenge provides for Andrea's problem is hardly equitable: in order to destroy Balthazar, he will add murder to murder, finally killing no fewer than nine people, of whom none but Balthazar is one of the Portuguese who had anything to do with the death of Andrea.

We find love and hate linked together in every part of the play's chain of motivation. The love of Bel-imperia for

Andrea dies with him, but it inspires both her hatred of his slayer and her love for Horatio, who, as a friend, also loved Andrea. Bel-imperia clearly perverts love when she says she will use Horatio's love to further her revenge for Andrea (I.iv.60-68). Since it is partly a shared hatred of Andrea's slayer that brings Bel-imperia and Horatio together as lovers, it is quite appropriate that they should talk of love in the language of war, speaking of it paradoxically as "our warring peace, or peaceful war" (II.ii.38). When they meet to make love, this loving sex-war reaches its ironic catastrophe in the Elizabethan pun that joins the killer and the lover, the symbolic use of "die" for the sexual climax (II.iv.47–48). At the very moment of sexual "death" the lovers are torn apart and Horatio literally dies at the hands of the jealous and vengeful Balthazar and Lorenzo. Balthazar, a study in the way unrequited love can make a person kill for jealousy, knows that this murder will frustrate his love for Bel-imperia, but he cannot help himself. He is caught between erotic love and a self-loving hatred of his rival in which one of them must die: "she'll fly me if I take revenge. / Yet must I take revenge or die myself, / For love resisted grows impatient" (II.i.115-17).

The murder of Horatio is, then, brought on by tangled motives of self-loving hatred and erotic love, but in the murders that follow, the fearful self-love of Lorenzo is pitted chiefly against the frustrated and sometimes self-pitying paternal love of Hieronimo that joins with the frustrated erotic love of Bel-imperia to destroy Balthazar and Lorenzo in the play-within-the-play. This playlet is a microcosm of the whole play in its motive forces of hate, love, and egotism:

> BAL. Ah Bashaw, here is love between Erasto
> An fair Perseda, sovereign of my soul.
>
> HIER. Remove Erasto, mighty Soliman,
> And then Perseda will be quickly won.
>
> BAL. Erasto is my friend, and while he lives
> Perseda never will remove her love.
>
> HIER. Let not Erasto live to grieve great Soliman.
>
> BAL. Dear is Erasto in our princely eye.
>
> HIER. But if he be your rival, let him die.
>
> BAL. Why, let him die, so love commandeth me.
>
> (IV.iv.39-48)

Love commands a man to kill: this epitomizing line is echoed by Hieronimo speaking in his own person a little later when he reveals the corpse of Horatio: "The cause was love, whence grew this mortal hate, / The hate, Lorenzo and young Balthazar, / The love, my son to Bel-imperia" (IV.iv.98-100).

At times the play seems to suggest that men who lose their love may be so blinded by passion that they seek a perverse satisfaction in killing as a substitute for loving. Lorenzo is capable only of this perverse satisfaction, and Balthazar is driven to it in his frustration. Hieronimo describes thus his expectation of revenge: "Then will I joy amidst my discontent, / Till then my sorrow never shall be spent" (II.v.55-56). This emotional transformation can even be seen in Andrea. At the outset, he does not seem to care about revenge; at the end of Act II, he wants only his enemies to suffer and laments that Horatio and Bel-imperia have been hurt; but in the final chorus he exults in all the killings as the fulfillment of his desires (IV.v.1-12).

The imagery of the transformation of Andrea is the basis for the transformations of the characters who dramatize the action caused by the relationship of Andrea and Revenge. As frustrated love changes the heart and soul of a man, he goes on a pilgrimage along strange pathways in the underworld of his spirit. Andrea, who craves a passage for his wandering ghost, finds it only with Revenge. Hieronimo tries to avoid this evil conductor, grieving that men should destroy their souls by their perversions of spiritual values:

> O monstrous times, where murder's set so light,
> And where the soul, that should be shrin'd in heaven,
> Solely delights in interdicted things,
> Still wand'ring in the thorny passages
> That intercepts itself of happiness.
>
> (III.vi.90-94)

Balthazar describes his pursuit of Bel-imperia in terms of an erring or wandering pilgrimage:

> Led by the loadstar of her heavenly looks,
> Wends poor oppressed Balthazar,
> As o'er the mountains walks the wanderer,
> Incertain to effect his pilgrimage.
>
> (III.x.106-9)

A moment after Balthazar says these words, three men ask Hieronimo what path to take to find Lorenzo. Hieronimo's reply describes the psychology of Lorenzo's response to guilt as a journey, but the description is also colored strongly by Hieronimo's own journey of despair as a result of Lorenzo's crimes:

> There is a path upon your left-hand side,
> That leadeth from a guilty conscience
> Unto a forest of distrust and fear,
> A darksome place and dangerous to pass:
> There shall you meet with melancholy thoughts,
> Whose baleful humours if you but uphold,
> It will conduct you to despair and death.
>
> (III.xi.13-19)

Hieronimo thinks of both revenge and suicide as hellish spiritual journeys; but, as long as his appeals to heaven or his journeys to the court of the King are fruitless, he feels he must choose between evils: "Where shall I run to breathe abroad my woes, / My woes, whose weight hath wearied the earth?" (III.vii.1-2). His cries of woe have

> . . . broken through the brazen gates of hell.
> Yet still tormented is my tortur'd soul
> With broken sighs and restless passions,
> That winged mount, and, hovering in the air,
> Beat at the windows of the brightest heavens,
> Soliciting for justice and revenge:
> But they are plac'd in those empyreal heights
> Where, countermur'd with walls of diamond,
> I find the place impregnable, and they
> Resist my woes, and give my words no way.
>
> (III.vii.9-18)

If he cannot make his way into heaven, it is clear enough that he has reached hell: "The ugly fiends do sally forth of hell, / And frame my steps to unfrequented paths, / And fear my heart with fierce inflamed thoughts" (III.ii.16-18).

Hieronimo knows that going to see the King for justice will be a fruitless pilgrimage, and he is tempted to kill himself so he can go a journey to hell for revenge (III.xii.1-13). Nevertheless he chooses the path that leads to the King; and, when his demand for justice goes unheeded, he gives powerful expression to the force behind all the journeys of the play: "Needs must he go that the devils drive" (III.xii.82).

In the very next scene the situation is reversed when Hieronimo, who has just decided to seek private revenge, is confronted with other men's appeals for justice, including Bazulto's for his murdered son. Hieronimo is driven temporarily insane, and this loss of control of his spirit sends him on a quest very much like that of the dead spirit of Andrea:

> Though on this earth justice will not be found,
> I'll down to hell, and in this passion
> Knock at the dismal gates of Pluto's court,
> Getting by force, as once Alcides did,
> A troop of Furies and tormenting hags
> To torture Don Lorenzo and the rest. . . .
> Then will I rent and tear them thus and thus,
> Shivering their limbs in pieces with my teeth.
> *Tear the papers.*
> (III.xiii.108-13, 122-23.I)

It is most important that Hieronimo denies justice to others as he despairs of justice for himself and turns to revenge: the "limbs" he shivers are actually papers brought to him by men seeking his help in cases at law. All this suggests that a too-obsessive quest for good may be ironically reversed into a journey toward its evil opposite. Just as Balthazar's lust for love leads him to hate and kill, so Hieronimo's love for his son leads to a lust for justice that makes him unjust.

Hieronimo's treatment of Bazulto is even more significant than what he does to the other appellants and their papers. He sees that Bazulto is an image of himself—a "lively portrait"—but this recognition, though it makes him offer pity, does not enable him to help the old man find justice. He regards Bazulto more as a mirror in which he sees his own need than as another man having great importance in his own right. Hieronimo is ashamed to be shown up by a "lesser" man's love for a son (III.xiii.99). He gives his purse to Bazulto and proposes that they go and sing discordant songs with Isabella, yet for all his pity he cannot respond to the old man's repeated request:

> SENEX. I am a grieved man, and not a ghost,
> That came for justice for my murder'd son.
>
> HIER. Ay, now I know thee, now thou nam'st thy son,
> Thou art the lively image of my grief:
> Within thy face, my sorrows I may see.
> (III.xiii.159-63)

In his madness Hieronimo seems to assume that justice is impossible in Bazulto's case since he feels that it is in his own. Perhaps we are to see that Hieronimo's pity and his grieving for the lost sons is the only response that is truly meaningful under the circumstances, that revenge and justice are equally unsatisfactory. But Hieronimo's pity itself is in part brought on and confused by his mad rage for revenge, and we must therefore also see the way obsessive, self-pitying vengefulness makes him unable to give the help to another man that he asks as an individual in his own right. Hieronimo can see the parallel between his own level and the one "beneath" him, but he cannot consistently see that the levels are really the same. And when he does see a sameness he confuses its real nature.

A man of Hieronimo's high position must see that the "levels" may be a distortion of reality imposed by the ego and by his society's misunderstanding of the traditional idea that a monarchy is a divinely ordained hierarchy in which men are separated in levels according to social class. It must always be remembered that this concept was balanced by the idea that from the *higher perspective* of God in eternity, all men are equal, and particularly so in the face of death.

Hieronimo's conduct is illuminated through the parallel with the Portuguese Viceroy's response to the charge that Alexandro has killed Balthazar. The Viceroy is more self-pitying, perhaps because he is evading his own guilt, and it is clear that his self-concern helps to intensify his vengeful anger to the point where he is unjust to Alexandro. He blames not only this innocent inferior but also Fortune, who he assumes is above him in power. In Act I. iii he attacks Fortune with personal bitterness when he has not yet found any person to blame but himself. Later, when his guilty self-concern is somewhat assuaged by having Alexandro to punish, he speaks in less personal terms, making his complaint against Fortune a universal statement of the tragedy of the man who stands at the highest level of human action:

> Infortunate condition of kings,
> Seated amidst so many helpless doubts!
> First we are plac'd upon extremest height,
> And oft supplanted with exceeding heat,
> But ever subject to the wheel of chance:
> And at our highest never joy we so,
> As we both doubt and dread our overthrow.
> So striveth not the waves with sundry winds
> As fortune toileth in the affairs of kings.
> (III.i.1-9)

The conception of the tragic as a condition that puts man in the "extremest" depth or height is essential to this play. We are repeatedly called upon to visualize the terrifying extremes of madness and despair, of love and hate, whether on the field of war or in the arbor of peace. Typically, man is brought to the peak of passion and the edge of death, and there we are invited to ponder his fate as he is caught between the extremes of heaven and hell. Andrea is slain in the crisis of the battle. Horatio is brought to a passionate sexual climax and is then killed. The supposed "extreme hate" of Alexandro's heart brings him to the "extremity of death," but, at the latest possible moment, the truth is revealed; and Villuppo is instead made to suffer "the bitterest torments and extremes" (III.i.16, 31-32,

40, 100). Alexandro is tested and then saved, but Pedringano is deceived to think that he is being tried by extremes and will be saved at the "uttermost" moment:

> LOR. Tell him his pardon is already sign'd,
> And thereon bid him boldly be resolv'd:
> For were he ready to be turned off
> (As 'tis my will the uttermost be tried),
> Thou with his pardon shalt attend him still:
> Show him this box, tell him his pardon's in't.
> (III.iv.67-72)

The play asks whether man is governed by a benign destiny that lets him suffer only to test and save him if he is patient, or whether destiny is figured forth instead in such men as Lorenzo, such forces as Revenge, who only *seem* to be interested in human welfare. We are asked to ponder this question most deeply in the case of Hieronimo, who is called upon to be just to other men who are in extremes while the failure of justice for his own son's murder drives him to extremes of hatred and of despairing madness:

> Thus must we toil in other men's extremes,
> That know not how to remedy our own,
> And do them justice, when unjustly we,
> For all our wrongs, can compass no redress.
> (III.vi.1-4)

(pp. 28-41)

Peter B. Murray, in his Thomas Kyd, *Twayne Publishers, Inc., 1969, 170 p.*

J. R. Mulryne (essay date 1970)

[*In the following excerpt, Mulryne offers a general overview of themes, structure, and characterization in* The Spanish Tragedy, *maintaining that while interpreting the work as "a revenge play successfully identifies the mainspring of [its] action," "the securing of justice . . . might be named the play's central preoccupation."*]

In the scene that closes the third Act of ***The Spanish Tragedy*** the Ghost of Andrea upbraids Revenge for neglecting his office. Revenge's answer might serve as gloss on the whole play:

> Thus worldlings ground, what they have dreamed, upon.
> Content thyself, Andrea: though I sleep,
> Yet is my mood soliciting their souls; . . .
> Behold, Andrea, for an instance how
> Revenge hath slept, and then imagine thou
> What 'tis to be subject to destiny.
> (III,xv,18-20, 26-28)

All in the play's main action ground their thoughts and deeds on 'dreams'; most are solicited by Revenge's mood; all are subject to destiny. Within the ironic co-ordinates defined by these terms the play's meaning takes shape.

The Spanish Tragedy stands among the first of a group of Elizabethan plays now known as tragedies of Revenge. In an obvious way, the play's action is set in motion and sustained by revenge-intrigues: Andrea seeks revenge for his death in battle at the hands of Balthazar; Bel-imperia looks for vengeance for Andrea's, her lover's, death; Balthazar and Lorenzo seek revenge on Horatio for winning Bel-imperia's love; Hieronimo pursues vengeance for the murder, by Lorenzo and Balthazar, of his son Horatio. From these intrigues develops all the rest of the play's narrative; as Philip Edwards writes, '***The Spanish Tragedy*** is a play about the passion for retribution, and vengeance shapes the entire action.' But quite as remarkable as this dominance of plot is the range of attitudes that prompt the characters to vengeance: the slight to of Andrea's honour, and the ending of his love-plans, that come with death in battle; the aversion Bel-imperia feels for her lover's deathsman; the envy Balthazar cherishes for a successful rival in love and war; the outrage felt by Hieronimo on the assassination of his innocent son. Each of these characters is in some sense injured by one or more of the others, and each seeks to amend the injury. Revenge is central to ***The Spanish Tragedy,*** as to others among the great Elizabethan plays, because it offers a convenient way of dramatising human conflict and competitiveness; blood-revenge merely exaggerates, makes more dramatic, familiar antagonisms. Criticism of Kyd's play has sometimes complained that it is structurally weak and morally unallowable because the action that sets it off, and to which it returns, involves vengeance for an incident—Andrea's death in formal, if uneven, battle—which does not fitly ask vengeance; the tragedy gets under way, it is said, only when the murder of Horatio provides a more allowable cause for revenge. Such criticism is misguided because Kyd's interests lies in the consequences, proportionate or not, of human enmity. When the play concludes in the satisfaction of Andrea and Revenge, we may well feel that morally there is a good deal to excuse or deplore: the waste and deaths that minister to that satisfaction. We shall feel equally the bitter consistency of motive and action that has led to this point. Kyd has dramatised, through the revenge idiom, one full and tragic episode in the satisfaction of a human ego.

Seeing the play in this light explains the pertinence of the Vergilian framework within which Kyd has placed the main action. Andrea's search for a resting-place in the classical underworld stands for the disappointed man's thirst for satisfaction. Thwarted by death of fulfilment as lover or 'martialist', he is unable to find rest in the underworld. Only when the goddess Proserpine bids Revenge to sponsor his privileged view of subsequent events can he achieve rest. The gods in the play are gods that watch over, and promote or thwart, human desires—or dreams. Only by circumstance do they become gods of morality (when we think the desires and their realisation justified); even more rarely do they come within an acceptable Christian sense of the word God. Almost all the play's major characters appeal at one time or other to Aeacus, Minos, Rhadamanth, Pluto or Proserpine; when they do so they are supplicating the amoral overseers of Fortune. Heaven in this tragedy is normally the province of such gods as these; fittingly in a play that concerns itself with the working-out of Revenge.

Interpretation of ***The Spanish Tragedy*** as a revenge play successfully identifies the mainspring of the play's action. It fails, however, on the surface at least, to account for certain of the play's scenes, especially those that take place in Portugal. 'The Portuguese court', writes Philip Edwards, 'could have been introduced more economically and the relevance of theme is very slight.' Recent studies by Ejner Jensen ["Kyd's *Spanish Tragedy:* The Play Explains Itself," *Journal of English and Germanic Philology,* 1965] and G. K. Hunter ["Ironies of Justice in *The Spanish Tragedy,*" *Renaissance Drama,* 1965] have tried to demonstrate the pertinence of these and other scenes by displacing the play's focus from revenge to justice. The tragedy's 'chief unifying theme', according to Jensen, 'is not revenge but the problem of justice'; Hunter agrees that 'the play is not centrally concerned with the enactment of revenge. Much more obsessive is the question of justice.' Justice, or judgment, serves indeed as a major preoccupation. Not only is Hieronimo himself a judge but instances of judging and misjudging occur repeatedly. Andrea seeks judgment from Aeacus, Rhadamanth and Minos, and, on their reaching deadlock, from the higher court of Pluto and Proserpine. The King of Spain is called on to arbitrate the rival claims to Balthazar of Lorenzo and Horatio. The Viceroy of Portugal is led into, and then narrowly avoids, a miscarriage of justice in the case of Alexandro and Villuppo. Hieronimo questions the 'justice' of the Heavens, while himself administering justice in others' causes. Pedringano is hanged despite promises to subvert the course of justice. Hieronimo's playlet of *Soliman and Perseda* may be construed as a kind of last judgment, its sentences interpreted by Andrea and confirmed, we expect, by Proserpine. Justice, then, or rather the securing of justice, might be named the play's central preoccupation. But justice and revenge are not really separate issues. In the judgment Andrea seeks they are identical; Revenge sponsors the decisions of Proserpine's court. For Hieronimo the only problem is the straightforward practical one of arranging circumstances so that justice brings about revenge. In other cases, justice, though in danger of mistake, is the simple instrument of vengeance: the Viceroy condemns Alexandro for, as he thinks, the murder of his son; Pedringano is condemned and executed for the killing of Serberine. When Lorenzo and Balthazar die, Hieronimo's vengeance serves in place of the justice they have till then averted. Sometimes, as in the King's arbitration or in Hieronimo's promises to the suitors, justice is a matter of 'fair play', a situation that falls between justice as retribution and justice in the emotionally-loaded sense that Andrea, Bel-imperia and sometimes Hieronimo mean the word. For to say that revenge and justice are not separate issues is not to say that they are always identical. Justice in the familiar sense can scarcely be said to be done in the killing of Castile at the play's end (even though he was Andrea's enemy) nor in the deaths of Hieronimo nor Bel-imperia nor Horatio, all of them sanctioned by Revenge. Justice satisfies us in a play because it reflects a situation we desire in our everyday lives: order upheld by the correcting of socially-unacceptable behaviour. Revenge is a more personal matter, a matter more of emotional satisfaction, to which justice may contribute, but which may not always involve, may even contradict, the interests of law and of society. When Hieronimo protests the seeming absence of Heavenly justice, he is protesting certainly the failure of human courts to bring to justice his son's murderers. But he is really talking about a far larger issue, and one that becomes a leading preoccupation of dramatists like Shakespeare and Webster:

> Yet still tormented is my tortured soul
> With broken sighs and restless passions,
> That winged mount, and hovering in the air,
> Beat at the windows of the brightest heavens,
> Soliciting for justice and revenge;
> But they are placed in those empyreal heights,
> Where, counter-mured with walls of diamond,
> I find the place impregnable; and they
> Resist my woes, and give my words no way.
> (III,vii,10-18)

The bafflement of the individual before the ways of Heaven (or Fortune) becomes more embittered in plays later than this. Here the justice Hieronimo seeks is one that operates (as line 14 suggests) through revenge, and the whole play ministers to their eventual triumph. ***The Spanish Tragedy*** might be termed an optimistic tragedy, despite its killings, in that it is structured to show that Heaven is not deaf, even if the Heaven that listens is one that sometimes disregards the claims of equity in favour of the more selfish and emotional satisfactions of Revenge.

Kyd's play is held together by instances of judging that finally contribute to the success of revenge; or, in the case of the Portuguese scenes and those that deal with Pedringano, that shadow revenge's ultimate triumph. But judging is by no means always done in full knowledge of the facts. On the contrary, ***The Spanish Tragedy*** is remarkable for the extent to which Kyd exploits the ignorance of the characters for ironic effect. By virtue of the framing action in particular we in the audience enjoy knowledge hidden from participants in the main play. We know that the play's outcome will be disastrous for anyone who opposes Andrea's revenge, even though the path to vengeance may be tortuous and revenge delayed. Andrea's doubts and Revenge's reassurance (in the scenes that close Acts I, II and III), as well as their continued presence as spectators, merely dramatise overtly the relationship the audience adopts to the events on stage. We are held between concern and detachment as the plot moves forward: concerned, like Andrea, that Horatio is killed, Bel-imperia sequestered, and Hieronimo thwarted, but detached like Revenge because we know that Andrea's cause, under his sponsorship, must eventually win through. The effect of this is to place us in an ironic relationship with almost everything that happens: all action takes place within a determined framework to which we, but not the actors, hold the key. We feel in I, i, for instance, the threat of oncoming disaster behind the boastful self-confidence and military display of the Spanish court, even if we cannot exactly predict the catastrophe that at the play's end destroys the whole Spanish succession. When the Spanish King overweeningly exclaims

> Then blest be heaven, and guider of the heavens,
> From whose fair influence such justice flows.
> (I,ii,10-11)

we recognise that heavenly justice may not be as simple nor, for him, as comprehensible as he thinks: the battle he gives such easy thanks for is the battle of Andrea's death.

Equally, we sense behind every movement Balthazar makes, or Lorenzo or Bel-imperia or Hieronimo, the long shadow of Andrea's revenge, sometimes aiding, sometimes threatening. But besides such general ironies as these Kyd cultivates more particular and overt ironic moments. As Horatio courts Bel-imperia in II,ii, for instance, we know that Pedringano has already betrayed their love; while the two lovers confess their affection and anticipate love's pleasures the hidden Balthazar and Lorenzo contradict all they say: the intricate structure of statement and counterstatement provides a grim version of the overhearing scenes of intrigue comedy. When in a later scene (II,iv) they invoke night and darkness to countenance their love-making we scarcely need the sombre if crude irony of Horatio's

> O stay awhile and I will die with thee

to underline the equivocal sense in which we have been observing the whole episode. Ironies can run in a contrary direction also, most complexly perhaps in the Portuguese scenes (I,iii and III,i). There we see the Viceroy mourning, while we know his son is in fact alive; and yet the mourning is pertinent too for we know the son's life is threatened ineluctably by Andrea. When the mourning turns to joy in a later scene we appreciate that under the superficial cause of joy lie causes of dread: for by now the Viceroy's son has committed the murder of another son, Horatio, a crime which must inevitably lead to his own destruction. Ironies multiply elsewhere; we are always conscious of the ignorance, sometimes greater, sometimes less, of the characters. Each of them attempts to clear a little space for himself, to impose his will a little, without being able to escape the pattern of consequence established by Revenge. Even the intriguers, the Machiavels, like Lorenzo and his shadow Villuppo, are only attempting, in their own bad way, to control the movements of Fortune. Villuppo is cheated by the merest coincidence: the Ambassador returns from Spain moments before Alexandro is to be executed; Lorenzo's schemes, at first successful, are ultimately defeated by Hieronimo's persistence and Bel-imperia's, and by the operations of chance. Hieronimo is himself another intriguer, a wily revenger forced by circumstances to adopt unlawful tactics; an intriguer favoured, however, by the prevailing Fate, as Bel-imperia's letter and then Pedringano's lead him to apt and successful action. Kyd provides us with an almost emblematic, near-burlesque, statement of the whole situation: Pedringano jesting with death (or Fate) as the boy points to the box—empty, despite Pedringano's confidence that it contains his pardon. Each of the play's characters is as vulnerable to an engrossing Fate as Pedringano; and almost all are as blithely unaware as he that they lack the power to turn that Fate aside, whether their purposes are good or ill. The experience of watching ***The Spanish Tragedy*** is the ironic one of seeing 'truth' gradually vindicated over the ignorance or devising of the characters, whether it is vindicated in the matter of Villuppo, or the death of Serberine, or the main-plot killing of Horatio. 'Truth' is, of course, as we have seen, a concept that in this play serves the interests of Revenge.

To present his theme Kyd has structured the play masterfully. Not only are the ironies brilliantly cultivated, but episodes are contrived with striking skill to reflect and balance each other. The Viceroy's mourning for his son anticipates and extends Hieronimo's mourning; both weep the death of a son and protest Fortune's injuries: the subtleties of the Elizabethan sub-plot are predicted. Andrea's revenge, the Viceroy's revenge on Alexandro or Villuppo, Lorenzo's witty disposal of Pedringano, Hieronimo's revenge for his son—these serve like angled mirrors to reiterate but never exactly repeat similar concerns and situations. Alexandro, the Viceroy, Isabella, Bel-imperia, Hieronimo, Pedringano all see themselves at one time or another the victim of an oppressive Fortune, and each in his different way tries to rationalise his position; the author's devising hand has so contrived the action that we discover a whole range of linked but dissimilar attitudes. To keep the plot firm, Kyd has arranged that Horatio becomes quite explicitly a second Andrea (I,iv,58ff.); he may even (the evidence is not quite conclusive) make use of a convenient hand-prop to connect visually the two revenges: the scarf Bel-imperia gave Andrea to wear in battle was taken from his dead body by Horatio and confirmed by Bel-imperia for her new lover's wearing; it may be the same 'bloody handkercher' that Hieronimo takes from his dead son's body and keeps to the end as revenge-token. A contrivance equally deft operates within scenes and episodes: Wolfgang Clemen has shown [in his *English Tragedy before Shakespeare,* 1961] how scene after scene observes carefully-planned, almost geometrical, patterning, a structural cunning that reflects on the level of plot the rhetorical niceties of the characters' language. Act two, scene one, for instance, is structured on the 'corner-posts' of Balthazar's twin speeches, at beginning and end, about Bel-imperia and Horatio; 'thus the two goals of Balthazar's future endeavours are brought into sharp relief, not only in dialogue enlivened by action, but also through the rhetorical emphasis of the set speeches'. So too Kyd has shown he knows how to use stage-action to underline the symmetries of the plot: Balthazar first enters with Lorenzo and Horatio on either side, each laying claim to being his captor, and thus predicting the dissensions the whole play is about to elaborate. Even the two plays-within-the-play reflect and echo each other: the first, though counselling humility, written in honour of Spain's military glory, the second contriving the destruction of the royal house. And this second play itself provides one of the best examples of Kyd's structural cunning, as it reflects and interprets the play's governing theme. There is a certain, though not exact, appropriateness in Bel-imperia playing Perseda, Balthazar playing Soliman and Hieronimo playing the 'Bashaw': they enact in these parts roles that parallel their actions in the main play. More telling is the episode's general bearing. There has been disagreement about whether the 'sundry languages' of the polyglot play were ever spoken on stage; there can scarcely be any disagreement over the almost surrealist manner in which the action of the play—death stealing in unperceived amidst a Babel-like confusion of tongues—repeats the major idiom of the whole tragedy. By this point Hieronimo has become virtually Fate's representative dealing to ignorant victims the consequences of Revenge. The manner in which this playlet, three fictional levels distant from a theatre-audience, crystallises Kyd's ironic intentions indicates why Kyd became so fruitful an influence on later dramatic craftsmen.

The perils of a tragedy conceived as ***The Spanish Tragedy*** is conceived are that the audience may become *mere* spectators, the plot-structure *merely* contrived and the ironies *merely* patronising. The figure of Hieronimo ensures that such dangers are slipped. Hieronimo is the play's centre because he tries more persistently and with more emotion than anyone else, within the limits imposed by this play, to find truth and establish equity—though of a crude kind. In so doing he draws an audience's sympathy and involvement, despite arguments, now largely discounted by critics, that he forfeits our respect when he begins to act unlawfully. Hieronimo engages our interest as the beleaguered man who tries in all honesty, and with outstanding pertinacity, to set right the wrongs of his time. In this he of course anticipates Hamlet, the character with whom he has notoriously been linked by literary historians. It is true that for Hieronimo the world is not as question-fraught as it is for Shakespeare's hero, largely because Kyd scarcely allows Hieronimo to question his own nature and motives, nor is he skilled enough to make the environment within which Hieronimo exists anything like so disturbingly equivocal as the world of *Hamlet.* Yet the seeds of self-questioning are there (the soliloquy in II,xii, for example, anticipates Hamlet's musings on suicide), and so are the first signs of a difficult if not quite equivocal world: the intrigues of Lorenzo, the hints of a double standard for judging strong and weak, the business-preoccupied mentality that thwarts justice and revenge in the latter part of III, xii. If Hieronimo is nothing so complex and fascinating a character as Hamlet, he does share many of the same challenges, and he does pursue his similar quest with comparable unwillingness to prevaricate or compromise, except on the surface. And unlike Hamlet he raises an issue very fruitful for tragedies written later in the Elizabethan decades: his anguished sense that Heaven itself is deaf:

> Where shall I run to breathe abroad my woes,
> My woes whose weight hath wearied the earth?
> Or mine exclaims, that have surcharged the air
> With ceaseless plaints for my deceased son? . . .
> (III,vii,1 ff.)

Hieronimo's quest soon slips off into less demanding matters of tactics and practicality, but here at least—the whole speech should be studied—Kyd succeeds in writing a poetry of the theatre that adequately conveys Hieronimo's sense of a world wholly occupied by his new-found sorrow, a sorrow made more intense because at this stage he can summon no comforting belief that a supernatural order oversees his experience or will in any way alleviate his pain. It is true that even a sympathetic critic must find moments in this speech of over-emphasis and cliché; and what is true here is true *a fortiori* of other among Hieronimo's soliloquies. A modern reader finds it difficult to adjust to the larger-than-life emphasis, as well as the self-conscious artificiality of structure, in Kyd's stage-rhetoric. Exaggeratedly deep emotion wedded to exceptional artifice of structure appears to us contradiction and even insincerity; we react all too gratefully to those parodies of Hieronimo's speeches that Elizabethan authors soon began to invent. Yet we miss the point of Kyd's dramatic skill if we do not see how subtly he has calculated, in the quoted speech, the alliterative patterns: not so emphatic as to call undue attention to themselves, but strong enough to afford the actor some purchase for moulding the speech-pattern; or if we do not see how naturally, and yet with seeming inevitability, he has ordered the tempo of the speech: noting particularly the way in which urgent exclamation is reined in at the natural pauses of lines 9, 14 and 18. Kyd's strengths as a writer of dramatic verse are at their most remarkable in this and other soliloquies put into Hieronimo's mouth. Even the notorious 'O eyes, no eyes' soliloquy (III,ii,1-52), the most formally patterned and among the most emotional of all Hieronimo's speeches, need not prove impossibly difficult on the modern stage; Kyd's instinct for dramatic speech ensures that here too the cadences of his rhetoric are such as can be turned to account: the rise and fall of emotional intensity, and the implied tempo of individual sentences, never forget stage-requirements, but rather provide opportunities for the actor's virtuosity. And Kyd can be affectingly simple where simplicity seems in place:

> Ay, now I know thee, now thou nam'st thy son;
> Thou art the lively image of my grief:
> Within thy face my sorrows I may see.
> Thy eyes are gummed with tears, thy cheeks are wan,
> Thy forehead troubled, and thy muttering lips
> Murmur sad words abruptly broken off
> By force of windy sighs thy spirit breathes;
> And all this sorrow riseth for thy son:
> And selfsame sorrow feel I for my son.
> (III,xiii,161-9)

Bazulto as the emblem, the 'lively image', of Hieronimo's sorrow is a somewhat 'literary' device, part of that self-conscious patterning that spans the whole tragedy. But Hieronimo's encounter with him provides an opportunity for the expression of genuine unforced emotion, and Kyd shows that he possesses the theatrical tact to take advantage of it. The character of Hieronimo, and especially his soliloquies, provided not only theatre-experience so vivid, and so popularly successful, that later dramatists were forced, almost in self-defence, to write parodies of them; they also provided the growth-points for a whole generation of tragic heroes and of tragic verse.

To speak of Hieronimo as a fully-realised character is perhaps to mis-state the realities of Kyd's play. ***The Spanish Tragedy*** stands at the turning-point between a drama of statement and a drama of experience (or exploration), and Hieronimo remains largely a typical rather than an individual figure: the lamenting father, and wily avenger. Characterisation of the other persons is both slighter, emotionally, and, in one or two cases, more helpful to the actor. The Spanish king and the viceroy of Portugal, it is true, remain figureheads; Isabella utters a few speeches of lament and protest without becoming any more than a mouthpiece for lament and protest. Bel-imperia, on the contrary, appears as a woman with definite characteristics. Consider, for example, how freely her nature emerges during Kyd's masterly re-handling of the Senecan device of stichomythia (line-by-line dialogue), a device utterly dead in the hands of earlier and contemporary playwrights:

> LORENZO. Sister, what means this melancholy walk?
>
> BEL-IMPERIA. That for a while I wish no company.
>
> LORENZO. But here the prince is come to visit you.
>
> BEL-IMPERIA. That argues that he lives in liberty.
>
> BALTHAZAR. No madam, but in pleasing servitude.
>
> BEL-IMPERIA. Your prison then belike is your conceit.
>
> (I,iv,77-82)

The excellence of this does not lie in any of the elaborately decorated verbal schemes we normally associate with Kyd, but rather in a sparseness that gives the actor ample opportunity. Again a much longer passage should be read to drive the point home. Bel-imperia's icy reserve, her barely-veiled hatred of Balthazar, comes across sharply in the stilted, glacially-polite exchange. Her formidable qualities emerge even more clearly as she confronts Lorenzo and Balthazar after her release from confinement (III,x,24 ff.); her protests are only less vigorous than the sardonic double-talk she offers in pretended acceptance of their explanations. No actress need have difficulty in playing Bel-imperia as a strong-willed—and sensually-inclined—woman. Lorenzo, important as the first (certainly among the first) of a line of stage-Machiavels so worthy of note in concentrating Elizabethan delight in guile, nevertheless remains a more conventional figure than his sister. Yet he is a distinctly playable figure, astute, self-willed and slippery. His companion Balthazar is more thoroughly characterised, a rather ineffectual young man, deeply conscious (see II,i,118-33) of his inferiority to Horatio. And his feelings of inferiority register themselves in his language; as Clemen has pointed out, his repetitive style of utterance, and his tedious dependence on rhetorical figures, 'is exactly in keeping with the irresolute, dependent, puppet-like role' he fills. His antagonist Horatio suffers from being the ideal young man, perfectly adapted to being the victim of a horrid murder; yet while he lives he does at least engage with Bel-imperia in sufficiently lively, and sufficiently sex-conscious, dialogue to show that he is no prig. And his love-poetry is, at the lowest, better than Balthazar's. The other figures in the tragedy are largely supporting cast without distinct characterisation.

The Spanish Tragedy has too often been discussed for its historic significance, too often plundered for the first example of this or that device; and above all, too often regarded merely as an example of a dead or moribund tradition, the mine where Senecan device and rhetorical figure could be first quarried and then docketed. What is most remarkable in fact is not Kyd's debt to the past nor even what his play holds for development in the future by others, but the extent to which it is already a moving, successful stage-play in its own right. More noticeable than the display of academically-correct rhetorical devices is the extraordinary range of dramatic styles Kyd employs, from the most elaborate and artificial to the simplest and most economical. More significant than the borrowed Senecan plot-devices, like the Ghost and Revenge, is the swift and sure way in which Kyd communicates necessary information, in the early scenes especially; the play moves forward most boldly and satisfyingly. Above all, perhaps, ***The Spanish Tragedy*** is remarkable for the astonishingly deft and complete way in which Kyd has transmuted his theme into drama, by way of the intricate tactics of his play's structure. It would indeed be satisfying to see the tragedy well produced, though the production would almost certainly have to be in the hands of one of the great professional companies, for the conventions of Kyd's play, and the demands it makes on an actor's resources of voice and gesture, are well beyond the range of most amateurs. ***The Spanish Tragedy*** could I believe be shown to deserve its place as one of the first important English tragedies. (pp. xix-xxx)

J. R. Mulryne, in an introduction to The Spanish Tragedy, *by Thomas Kyd, edited by J. R. Mulryne, Hill and Wang, 1970, pp. xiii-xxxii.*

Deborah Rubin (essay date 1976)

[*In the essay below, Rubin assesses Hieronimo's conception of justice and revenge in relation to those of other characters in* The Spanish Tragedy *in an attempt to determine a moral perspective for the play. The critic contends that Hieronimo's rationalization of his actions and his justification for private revenge exempt him from the category of villain.*]

> Our corrupt nature, which ever striveth against thy blessed will, seeketh all means possible to be revenged, to requite tooth for tooth and eye for eye, to render evil for evil, when vengeance is thine and thou wilt reward; and by this means we grievously offend thee, and break the order of charity, and the bond of peace.
>
> Thomas Becon
> "The Flower of Prayers" (1551)

Perhaps the most perfect vehicle for the portrayal of man's struggle to harmonize his spontaneous need for retribution with his religious and ethical beliefs is the dramatic genre of the revenge tragedy. As a participant in the accumulating tangle of plots and counter-plots, murders and attempted murders, each character is provided with an opportunity to create discrepancies between his own actions and the abstract system of religious and secular ethics that he possesses. For the character who does not concern himself with conceptual abstracts, carrying out actions which are simply expedient or pleasure giving is easy; but for the character who wishes to behave by a given code and yet finds that code antithetical to his most urgent need for retributive action, the resultant tension and frustration add an extra burden to his often already fragile mental state.

This study is a discussion of the various ways in which the characters in Thomas Kyd's ***The Spanish Tragedy*** relate their own actions and thoughts to the concepts of revenge and justice in the light of the broader action of the play. Also the bearing which Hieronimo's fluid interpretation of revenge and justice has on the question of his possible villainy will be considered. And finally, Hieronimo's constant juxtaposing of these concepts in reaction to his internal states and external events will be traced.

Since it is helpful to consider Hieronimo against the background of the other characters in the play, their reactions and mental processes will be outlined briefly before examining Hieronimo. Upon the initial discovery of Horatio's body, Isabella expresses faith in the tenet of heavenly justice: "The heavens are just, murder cannot be hid, / Time is the author both of truth and right, / And time will bring this treachery to light." At this point her restrained behavior and words of comfort to Hieronimo are reflections of what she intellectually believes will be the course of events resulting from this incident. With virtuous passivity she reminds Hieronimo that time is on their side, that only the passage of time is required before justice spontaneously takes place. But as this standardized rationalistic formula becomes increasingly more inadequate in satisfying the intensifying irrational needs created by Isabella's grief, the congruence between what she initially accepted intellectually, and her subsequent behavior breaks down. Gradually, the concept of heavenly justice as verbalized by Isabella at the outset proves to be an inaccurate description of the reality confronting her during the play. This revelation combined with her building emotional necessity for action renders her incapable of waiting for heavenly justice any longer.

Contrary to her original assessment of the role of time, in her last speech when she urges Hieronimo to "make haste" in his revenge (IV,ii,26-30), time has become a negative quality for her, seen as causing her to prolong her psychological suffering rather than assuring her of eventual retribution. Finally, in a state of madness she discards the injunction to wait for heavenly justice (which conceivably still could come), and succumbs to her grief by tearing down the arbor and killing herself. Isabella is a character who has attempted to act according to the concept of heavenly justice, but by her last appearance her need to explain her actions through abstract concepts is superseded by her need to deal with her grief. It is most significant, however, that she excuses her infraction of her original belief by citing the fact that " . . . neither piety nor pity moves the king to justice or compassion . . . " (IV,ii,2-3); therefore, in her own eyes she is entitled to vent her feelings irrationally. Although more could be said about the relationship between justice and revenge in Isabella's mind, it is the fact that she has tried to reflect the concept of heavenly justice in her behavior, and finds a rationalization necessary when she cannot, that will be useful later in defining Hieronimo's place among the other characters.

For Bel-Imperia revenge is an end sufficient in itself not requiring any further justification. She is not tortured by deeper concerns or paralyzed by philosophical contradictions. Since she simply views revenge as an acceptable goal, she is able to satisfy herself emotionally and intellectually by her actions. Even less concerned with ethical dictates is Pedringano. He has no compunction about "strain[ing] his conscience" (III,iii,8) for monetary remuneration. The only interest Pedringano has in justice is that he be protected from its sanctions by Lorenzo. Ironically, this character who tries so conscientiously to avoid Justice, is eventually served with it most appropriately.

Villuppo, the Portuguese courtier, delights in the breaking of ethical concepts and is quite pleased with himself in the following enumeration of his actions: "Thus have I with an envious forged tale / Deceiv'd the king, betray'd mine enemy, / And hope for guerdon of my villainy" (I,iii,93-95). Through his false accusation of his rival Alexandro (III,i), Villuppo attempts to pervert the process of reward and punishment by manipulating the king into disposing of Alexandro. In this scene Villuppo takes advantage of the fact that the other characters will react according to their belief in the concept of justice and gambles the success of his plan on the predictability of their responses.

Similarly, Lorenzo exploits the official system of justice by allowing Pedringano to be executed thereby eliminating the possibility of being implicated in Horatio's murder himself. Not only is Lorenzo totally unconcerned with ethical concepts in relation to his own behavior, but like Villuppo, he uses the belief of others in these concepts to control their behavior. For example, when Lorenzo hires Pedringano to spy on Bel-Imperia, he adds to his promises of reward the argument that Pedringano is indebted to him and therefore cannot refuse his "just demand" (II,i,54). By appealing to Pedringano's sense of fair play Lorenzo hopes to insure Pedringano's sense of fair play Lorenzo hopes to insure Pedringano's loyal service. The very different ways that Isabella, Bel-Imperia, Pedringano, Villuppo and Lorenzo relate themselves to the concepts of revenge and justice must be kept in mind because these characters comprise the moral spectrum on which Hieronimo will be located.

In approaching the problem of Hieronimo's moral position in the play, one must first define the criteria by which Hieronimo is to be evaluated. Fredson T. Bowers author of *Elizabethan Revenge Tragedy 1587-1642* measures Hieronimo's actions against the legal and ethical values of Elizabethan society when he reminds us that "Blood-revenge for the murder of a close relative . . . falls in the same legal category as any other murder with malice aforethought" Professor Bowers continues to build a case for Hieronimo's villainy in the eyes of the Elizabethan audience by emphasizing the duplicitious and deceptive nature of Hieronimo's quest for revenge (established in III,xiii,38-44): "When, at last spurred to action by complete knowledge, he rushes to the king for legal justice, he would still be the hero whose actions, according to the best Elizabethan ethics, were those of an honorable man. But when Lorenzo fails him in his attempt at legal redress and he consciously gives up an open revenge in favor of a secret, treacherous device, according to English standards he inevitably becomes a villain."

On the other hand, in his article "Hieronimo Explains Himself" [*Studies in Philology* 54 (1957)], John D. Ratliff contends that the famous "Vindicta mihi" speech (III,xii,1-45) serves " . . . to explain Hieronimo's behavior carefully so as to keep any suspicion of villainy from him." Professor Ratliff, then, clears Hieronimo of villainy on the basis of the character's rhetoric rather than his actions.

From yet a third point of attack, Ernst De Chickera views Hieronimo's actions within the framework of the alternatives offered to Hieronimo by the situation: " . . . Hieronimo's inhuman behavior in his role of revenger only indicates the nature of the choice forced on him by the dilemma he faces: either to ignore God's justice that cries out for a revenger, or to assume that role and become part of the very evil he is called upon to destroy" ["Diving Justice and Private Revenge in *'The Spanish Tragedy',*" *Modern Language Review* 57 (1962)]. Of course the crucial question arising from this interpretation of Hieronimo's alternatives is whether or not Hieronimo consistently believes that revenge is truly the expression of "God's justice."

Strong arguments for and against Hieronimo's villainy can very well be established on the basis of the legality of his actions in the eyes of the audience, or the competence with which he explains his actions, or the difficulty of the situation within which he finds himself. But perhaps it is also useful to consider Hieronimo's actions and reactions through the moral perspective that exists in the play itself and is created by the actions and reactions of the other characters. Rather than superimposing externally derived values and definitions on the play, there is an ethical scale of behavior, that can be distilled from the play itself.

One way to identify this scale is to examine the individual interior processes of the characters as revealed in Kyd's rhetoric and to evaluate these processes as they compare with each other. As has been shown in the brief discussions of Isabella, Bel-Imperia, Pedringano, Villuppo and Lorenzo, each individual relates himself to the potential problem of the discrepancy between the concept of justice and the reality of his own actions in a different way. It is possible to establish degrees of villainy on the basis of the degree of the characters' concern with the harmony or dissonance between the concepts he holds intellectually (particularly of justice) and his own actions. As will be seen, the emotional pressure under which the character functions of course also determines the amount of difficulty the character will have in creating a congruence between his beliefs and his behavior, as well as the accuracy with which he perceives reality. In the previously cited article, Professor Chickera makes use of the character's varying intensity of concern with the concept of "God's justice" as a criterion for identifying what he calls "good" and "bad" characters:

> The King publicly acknowledges belief in the justice of God, thus setting up expectations that he will execute God's justice should the occasion arise. Others in the play who show their awareness of God's justice are Hieronimo, Isabella and Alexandro (III,i,35-7). By contrast, the bad characters, the evil-doers, never once refer to God. The manner in which each character shows his awareness of God's justice varies with the situation of each.

In Hieronimo's case the need to harmonize his beliefs, emotional needs and actions manifests itself in a most interesting juggling of the concepts of revenge and justice. Until the last few speeches, his concern with judicial values and the necessity of seeing himself as upholding those values remains almost constant. His initial response to Horatio's death, however, is not typical (although prophetic of the final outcome). Upon the discovery of his son's body, Hieronimo states simply that " . . . in revenge my heart would find relief" (II,v,40-41) and it is Isabella who mentions heavenly justice. But by Act III scene ii, Hieronimo is attempting to resist the temptation of man-made retribution:

> O sacred heavens! If this unhallow'd deed, . . .
> Shall unreveal'd and unrevenged pass,
> How should we term your dealings to be just,
> If you unjustly deal with those that
> in your justice trust?
> The night, sad secretary to my moans,
> With direful visions wake my vexed soul,
> And with the wounds of my distressful son
> Solicit me for notice of his death.
> The ugly fiends do sally forth of hell,
> And frame my steps to unfrequented paths,
> And fear my heart with fierce inflamed thoughts.
> The cloudy day my discontents records,
> Early begins to register my dreams
> And drive me forth to seek the murderer.
> (III,ii,5-21)

There is no question in this speech that, whether by heavenly means or the revenger's hand, justice will only be done when Horatio's murderers are punished. Yet the qualitative distinction between revenge and heaven's justice remains clear. Significantly, revenge is associated with hell and characterized as the product of a wild irrational compulsion in the form of "ugly fiends" and "fierce inflamed thoughts". This aspect of revenge is repugnant to Hieronimo who is imploring heaven not to force him to follow "unfrequented paths" in search of justice. At this point obsessive revenge is an unacceptable means to the end of true and proper justice.

Hieronimo's position as Knight Marshal simultaneously increases his awareness of both his responsibility to obtain justice through official channels and the cruel irony with which his desire to do so is frustrated. At Pedringano's sentencing Hieronimo insures that legal revenge is properly expedited when he says "For blood with blood shall, while I sit as judge, / Be satisfied, and the law discharg'd" (III,vi,35-36). Then, conceiving of himself as an outcast from justice he adds, in a burst of righteous self pity, "And though myself cannot receive the like, / Yet will I see that others have their right" (III,vi,37-38). Although he is building up fuel for the emotional fire that will burn out of control later, Hieronimo thinks of himself in this scene as a guardian of the official legal and ethical system in which he believes. It is revealing also that Hieronimo is horrified by Pedringano's flippant attitude and apparent failure to grasp the gravity of his crine. Beyond being mystified by such behavior from a man who is about to die, he finds it impossible to understand how a person can be so totally insensitive to moral issues (III,vi,89-94).

In the next scene, as the urgency of Hieronimo's emotions mounts and his rhetoric becomes more elaborate, he resolves to "cry aloud for justice through the court" (III,vii,70). But this time he adds the ultimatum that he will " . . . either purchase justice by entreats / Or tire them all with . . . revenging threats" (III,vii,72-73). This couplet is the logical extension of the previously cited speech in which Hieronimo mentions private revenge as the undesirable alternative to heavenly justice. Although still pledging to try to seek legal redress, the desperation of emotional necessity has modified Hieronimo's disgust for private revenge. The seriousness with which Hieronimo contemplates private revenge increases proportionately with his frustrated grief, while the need to create an authentic congruence between the cause of legitimate justice and the emotionally mandatory retributive action becomes eclipsed.

Four scenes later, the recognition that the justice gained through immoral means is better than no justice at all (which is an integral part of Hieronimo's changing attitude toward revenge) is revealed in the images of his mad ravings:

> Hieronimo, 'tis time for thee to trudge:
> Down by the dale that flows with
> purple gore,
> Standeth a fiery tower: there sits a judge
> Upon a seat of steel and molten brass,
> And 'twixt his teeth he holds a firebrand,
> That leads unto the lake where hell
> doth stand.
> Away, Hieronimo, to him be gone:
> He'll do thee justice for Horatio's death.
> (III,xii,6-13)

While revenge was previously associated with hell, now, in a maniacal reversal, a judge appears in the infernal landscape. Where heaven and justice had been rhetorically linked, and represented as incompatible with demonic revenge, now it is the judge of hell who is the agent of justice. It is most significant, though, that instead of simply abandoning the cause of justice, which remains a positive value throughout, Hieronimo forces an artificial parallel between that cause and the retributive action he had so abhorred at the outset. Rather than renouncing justice, Hieronimo becomes insanely obsessed with it, while his ability to relate the civilized meaning of that concept accurately to reality all but disappears. Because Hieronimo still needs to view his actions within the framework of what is acceptable to him intellectually, he irrationally seeks to nullify the inherent evil of the private revenge he must have by equating it with justice.

Despite all his talk of hellish revenge, Hieronimo has not forgotten heaven by any means. In the famous Vindicta mihi speech (III,xiii) he says " . . . heaven will be reveng'd of every ill" (III,xiii,1). Since this sentence follows the declaration that "revenge is mine," the implication is that heaven will be avenged through Hieronimo's planned actions—an implication which will be elucidated later. In the latter part of the speech, Hieronimo decides to assume a facade of congeniality to insure the success of his plan. As was mentioned before, for Professor Bowers this secrecy qualifies Hieronimo as a villain, but in his article "Kyd's ***Spanish Tragedy:*** The Play Explains Itself" [*Journal of English and Germanic Philology* 64 (1965)], E. J. Jensen suggests that because of the secrecy Hieronimo fits C. V. Boyer's definition of the villain functioning as a hero. Professor Jensen presents the definition and his own interpretation of Hieronimo in the following statement:

> [The villain as hero is a man] . . . who must contend with those whom he is unable to defeat in direct conflict and who depend[s] for the security of . . . [his] position upon the employment of policy . . . Such a hero is Hieronimo, whose concern with justice is everywhere in evidence, but who must himself resort to policy and intrigue in order to gain the revenge which is his legitimate due.

Professor Jensen's identification of Hieronimo is useful in that it accommodates both Hieronimo's concern with ethical concepts and the less than forthright way he chooses to achieve his usually rationalized or justified goals. Although not descriptive of Hieronimo in all situations, Professor Jensen's interpretation is a solution to the question of the relationship between Hieronimo's means and his possible role as villain. When Hieronimo is evaluated in the context of the behavior of the other characters, however, his concern with justice becomes the more crucial factor.

By the middle of scene thirteen revenge has become "sweet" (III,xiii,107) and is again associated with a court of hell. Thus, the positive value of official justice becomes further mingled with the barbarian lust for private revenge. In a critical speech at the beginning of Act Four, heaven once more becomes part of Hieronimo's rhetoric when he takes Bel-Imperia's thirst for revenge as a sign that " . . . heaven applies our drift, / And all the saints do sit soliciting / For vengeance on those cursed murderers" (IV,i,32-34). Now, in a complete about face, the revenge with which "ugly fiends" of hell had tempted him (III,ii,16) has become the expression of heavenly will. As M. E. Prior writes in his book *The Language of Tragedy,* "Private vengeance is now identified with the justice of heaven, and the torment of his mind is over."

It is impossible for Hieronimo to see that his craving for revenge is a product of his shattered emotional state. He must perceive of his motives as consistent with the most revered statutes of religious and legal authority. In contrast to Bel-Imperia, revenge alone is insufficient motivation in Hieronimo's eyes, unless it is seen as an expression of higher abstract concepts. " . . . only by seeing himself as the instrument of divine justice can he bring himself to do the deed" [Chickera]. Peter B. Murray also makes the point in his book *Thomas Kyd* that "Hieronimo thinking that he is heaven's agent does not mean that . . . he *is* heaven's agent; it means that a man of Hieronimo's character in his dire circumstances needs desperately to think he is such an agent." How ironic it is that Hieronimo's spontaneous statement at the very beginning that in revenge his "heart would find relief" (II,v,41) will prove to be a much more accurate explanation of his final behavior than all the intervening rhetorical contortions.

Breaking with previous behavior, at the moment of revenge all attempts at logical or even illogical rationalization are cast aside and the prophecy inherent in the foregoing statement is fulfilled. Again the inverse relationship between the strength of the emotional reaction and the need to create congruence between behavior and abstract formuli holds true. Elinor Prosser, author of *Hamlet and Revenge* describes this disintegration of the rationalization process in Hieronimo's final speech when she writes:

> His revenge is as total and as bloody as we now expect. His defense to the court makes no mention of the law's failure, of his duty to his son, of his authorization as Marshal to punish, or of any other conceivable justification. He speaks only of his own pain. He does not declare his satisfaction that justice has triumphed; he says rather that his "heart is satisfied," that he is "eas'd with their revenge"
>
> (IV,iv,129, 190).

It is almost as if once the act is accomplished Hieronimo no longer needs the courage he gained by invoking society's values. The emotional core of his motivation appears naked at last, an echo of those simple words he uttered soon after his son's body was first discovered.

Despite this final lapse, with the only possible exception of Isabella, no other character in ***The Spanish Tragedy*** is as concerned with creating a compatibility between his behavior and the concept of justice as Hieronimo. On this basis alone, Hieronimo cannot be condemned to total villainy within the universe of characters created by the playwright. In one respect, Isabella's need to rationalize her behavior remains stronger than her husband's because she does mention the failure of the King's justice immediately before she succumbs totally to her madness. In contrast, Hieronimo's process of justification is abundantly manifest throughout his speeches but evaporates at the final moment. But in the final analysis, it is the cynicism of Lorenzo and Villuppo that exempts Hieronimo from the simple category of villain. Where they use the belief of the other characters in legal justice to further their own criminal purposes, Hieronimo, as a private citizen and Knight Marshal, only seeks to have the judicial system function properly.

Any eventual perversion of the concept of civilized justice that Hieronimo is guilty of results from the very need to explain his behavior to himself in moral terms, while Lorenzo and Villuppo pride themselves on their respective misuses of justice. A distinction in character type must be made to account for the fundamentally different processes of self conception exhibited by these characters. It must be remembered too that the purpose underlying Hieronimo's tortured juxtapositioning of justice and revenge is an effort to associate his emotionally motivated illegal behavior (revenge) with that which is an intellectually and socially positive value (justice). Since Hieronimo is psychologically incapable of following what he knows is the only proper course of action, he creates an aura of righteousness about the inherently evil private revenge he is compelled to commit.

Another prominent factor which separates Hieronimo from Lorenzo and Villuppo is his madness. The calculating, clear mindedness of Lorenzo and Villuppo implies that their behavior is free of compulsion and psychological disintegration; whereas Hieronimo's behavior is a pathological outgrowth of his grief. Whether or not his madness can be viewed as an excuse for his behavior, it does create another qualitative difference between Hieronimo and Lorenzo or Villuppo, the two true villains in the play. One characteristic of villainy which Hieronimo does share with these two characters, however, is the adoption of intrigue. Yet, Hieronimo's rationalizations for resorting to this modus operendi prevent him from fitting neatly into a category with Villuppo and Lorenzo. As Professor Jensen points out in the previously mentioned article, Hieronimo's all-pervasive consciousness of justice signifies that (if viewed as a villain) Hieronimo is a different type of villain, not to be confused with the more clearly motivated Lorenzo and Villuppo.

Finally, then, if each character in this play is placed in his ethical niche according to the psycho-moral processes he undergoes. Hieronimo cannot be viewed simply as a villain. Although what Hieronimo eventually does is both irrational and wrong, when his moral dynamics are compared to those of the other individuals who populate the world of ***The Spanish Tragedy,*** he emerges as a tragically perverted hero. (pp. 3-13)

Deborah Rubin, "Justice, Revenge and Villainy in Kyd's 'Spanish Tragedy'," in Thoth, *Vol. 16, No. 2, Spring, 1976, pp. 3-13.*

FURTHER READING

BIBLIOGRAPHY

Tannenbaum, Samuel A. *Thomas Kyd (A Concise Bibliography).* Elizabethan Bibliographies Number 18. New York: Samuel A. Tannenbaum, 1941, 34 p.

Bibliography of the Kyd canon and the body of criticism surrounding it.

OVERVIEWS AND GENERAL STUDIES

Boas, Frederick S. Introduction to *The Works of Thomas Kyd,* edited by Frederick S. Boas, pp. xiii-cvii. Oxford: Clarendon Press, 1901.

Seminal study of Kyd's life and works, outlining the major issues regarding his career and influence on Elizabethan drama.

Edwards, Philip. *Thomas Kyd and Early Elizabethan Tragedy.* London: Longmans, Green & Co., 1966, 48 p.

Briefly discusses Kyd's biography and the minor works attributed to him but primarily "concentrates on *The Spanish Tragedy,* and places it in the perspective of the development of Elizabethan tragedy."

Freeman, Arthur. *Thomas Kyd: Facts and Problems.* London: Oxford University Press, 1967, 200 p.

Exhaustive study of Kyd's life and career, attempting to clarify the uncertainties surrounding *The Spanish Tragedy* and other works ascribed to him.

THE SPANISH TRAGEDY

Baker, Howard. "Ghosts and Guides: Kyd's *Spanish Tragedy* and the Medieval Tragedy." *Modern Philology* XXXIII, No. 1 (August 1935): 27-35.

Attempts to show that the Ghost of Andrea and Revenge in *The Spanish Tragedy* are characters adapted from medieval metrical tragedies rather than Senecan figures.

Barish, Jonas A. "*The Spanish Tragedy,* or The Pleasures and Perils of Rhetoric." In *Stratford-upon-Avon Studies 9: Elizabethan Theatre,* edited by John Russell Brown and Bernard Harris, pp. 59-85. London: Edward Arnold, 1966.

Analyzes Kyd's use of rhetorical models to accentuate the action and themes of *The Spanish Tragedy.*

Clemen, Wolfgang. "Kyd." In his *English Tragedy Before Shakespeare: The Development of Dramatic Speech,* translated by T. S. Dorsch, pp. 100-12. London: Methuen & Co., 1961.

Praises the technical virtuosity of *The Spanish Tragedy.*

De Chickera, Ernst. "Divine Justice and Private Revenge in *The Spanish Tragedy.*" *Modern Language Review* LVII, No. 2 (April 1962): 228-32.

Asserts that the theme of revenge in *The Spanish Tragedy* reflects the Elizabethan conception of private revenge as an instrument of divine justice.

Edwards, Philip. "Thrusting Elysium into Hell: The Originality of *The Spanish Tragedy.*" In *The Elizabethan Theatre XI,* edited by A. L. Magnusson and C. E. McGee, pp. 117-32. Ontario, Canada: P. D. Meany Company, 1990.

Examines Kyd's use of pagan deities and the question of whether divine justice is a central concern of *The Spanish Tragedy.* The critic's comparison of Kyd's work to three contemporary plays leads him to conclude that the tragedy's message is that men and women are totally subject to destiny.

Empson, William. "*The Spanish Tragedy.*" In *Elizabethan Drama: Modern Essays in Criticism,* edited by R. J. Kaufmann, pp. 60-80. New York: Oxford University Press, 1961.

Reprint of a 1956 essay arguing that the Ghost of Andrea is the principal agent of revenge in *The Spanish Tragedy.* According to Empson, Hieronimo's quest for revenge is a mere facet of Andrea's desire for retribution against the Duke of Castile and Lorenzo.

Harbage, Alfred. "Intrigue in Elizabethan Tragedy." In *Essays on Shakespeare and Elizabethan Drama in Honor of Hardin Craig,* edited by Richard Hosley, pp. 37-44. Columbia: University of Missouri Press, 1962.

Asserts that Kyd dealt with the difficulties of introducing the element of intrigue to *The Spanish Tragedy* by using comic techniques, "thus creating a species of comitragedy."

Johnson, S. F. "*The Spanish Tragedy,* or Babylon Revisited." In *Essays on Shakespeare and Elizabethan Drama in Honor of Hardin Craig,* edited by Richard Hosley, pp. 23-36. Columbia: University of Missouri Press, 1962.

Posits that Hieronimo's play-within-the-play was meant to recall the biblical fall of Babylon.

Levin, Michael Henry. " 'Vindicta mihi!': Meaning, Morality, and Motivation in *The Spanish Tragedy.*" *Studies in English Literature 1500-1900* IV (1960): 307-24.

Discusses the morality and motivation of Kyd's characters in *The Spanish Tragedy.* Levin claims that the "positions of the central characters with respect to the morality of vengeance pinpoint the question which is the thematic keystone of the play. Is revenge justifiable in the name of goodness, right, and truth?"

Ratliff, John D. "Hieronimo Explains Himself." *Studies in Philology* 54 (1957): 112-18.

Asserts that Hieronimo's "*vindicta mihi*" speech reveals to the audience the reasons for his private revenge.

Righter, Anne. "The World and the Stage." In her *Shakespeare and the Idea of the Play,* pp. 64-88. 1962. Reprint. Westport, Conn.: Greenwood Press, Publishers, 1977.

Maintains that Kyd's use of a chorus and the play-within-the-play serves to emphasize "the idea of the world as a stage" and to demonstrate the relationship between illusion and reality.

Stockholder, Kay. " 'Yet can he write': Reading the Silences in *The Spanish Tragedy.*" *American Imago* 47, No. 2 (Summer 1990): 93-124.

Psychoanalytical study of identity, romance, honor, and relationships between fathers and sons in *The Spanish Tragedy.*

Talbert, Ernest William. "Aspects of Structure and Serious Character-Types." In his *Elizabethan Drama and Shakespeare's Early Plays: An Essay in Historical Criticism,* pp. 61-131. New York: Gordian Press, 1973.

Examines Kyd's use of Elizabethan dramatic conventions in *The Spanish Tragedy.*

Additional coverage of Kyd's life and career is contained in the following sources published by Gale Research: *British Writers,* Vol. 1 and *Dictionary of Literary Biography,* Vol. 62.

Menander

c. 342 B.C. - c. 292 B.C.

INTRODUCTION

One of the foremost dramatists of ancient Greece, Menander is considered the greatest writer of New Comedy, a dramatic form that significantly influenced the development of romantic comedy and comedy of manners throughout western Europe. *Dyskolos* (*The Dour Man*), *Samia* (*The Girl from Samos*), and other Menandrian plays depict the domestic lives of middle-class Athenians and commonly center around love, marriage, and social intrigues. Audiences and critics since classical times have recognized Menander as an original comic playwright whose works, while following many of the conventions of Old Comedy (c. 435-405 B.C.) and Middle Comedy (c. 400-323 B.C.), introduced numerous important innovations. Reworking the stock characters and plots of his predecessors, Menander offered realistic characterizations and urbane, ironic wit in place of the raucous hilarity of such Old Comedy dramatists as Aristophanes. In addition, he provided his characters with common everyday language that helped to individualize them and make them seem true to life.

Few facts are known about Menander's life. He was born around 342 B.C. and lived through the reign of Alexander the Great (336-323 B.C.), having witnessed Macedon's conquest of Greece in 338 B.C. Some scholars believe that Alexis, the major dramatist of Middle Comedy, was Menander's uncle and that he may have provided his nephew with some training in dramatic composition. In his early years Menander studied under Theophrastus, a former pupil of Aristotle and the head of the Peripatetic school. As a student he also met two figures who would later be highly influential: the philosopher Epicurus and the future governor of Athens, Detrius Phalereus. Menander's early training and connections likely enabled him to take part in the dramatic competition in the Dionysian festival in the city of Lenaea in 321 B.C. (The festival was an important annual event in which rival playwrights staged their new plays in a competition for prizes.) Menander won first place for his *Orgē* (*Anger*). He continued to compete in the festivals, winning the prize a total of eight times, including one in 316 B.C. for *The Dour Man.* Despite this relatively small number of victories—he wrote over one hundred plays in his lifetime—Menander achieved fame both in and outside Athens, receiving invitations to stage his works in Egypt and Macedon. He declined the offers, however, preferring to remain with his longtime mistress Glycera in his villa in Piraeus, a seaport five miles southwest of Athens. Menander drowned in the harbor in 292 B.C. at the age of fifty.

Performances of Menander's comedies continued well into Roman Imperial times and some of his works were adapted by the Roman dramatists Plautus and Terence. While copies of his plays were made as late as the fifth and sixth centuries A.D., all but fragments were lost sometime between the seventh and ninth centuries. For over a thousand years, Menander's plays were known only through these fragments, the Roman adaptations, and ancient quotations from them (including one by St. Paul in 1 Corinthians 15:33: "Evil companionships corrupt good morals"). In 1905 the French archaeologist G. Lefebvre found Egyptian papyrus scrolls containing one half of *Epitrepontes* (*The Arbitration*), about two-fifths of each *Perikeiromenē* (*The Shearing of Glycera*) and *The Girl from Samos,* and parts of scenes from two other plays. The first essentially complete play by Menander, *The Dour Man,* was discovered in 1957 in an Egyptian manuscript that also contained substantial portions of *Aspis* (*The Shield*) and *The Girl from Samos.* More fragments were discovered throughout the 1960s.

To help clearly establish the nature of Menander's achievement, scholars often compare him to his predecessors. Since little survives from the Middle Comedy period, precise comparisons between Menander's works and those of that time are difficult to make; but when placed beside Old Comedy plays, such as Aristophanes's, Menander's works display striking innovations as well as similarities.

The structure of Menander's plays resemble their earlier models with their five-act framework: act one establishing the situation and theme, two and three developing complications, four providing the climax, and act five resolving any remaining problems. The Menandrian chorus, however, is reduced from the extensive, integral part of the drama in Aristophanes's plays to a type of interlude between acts. He assigned it no particular dramatic significance, and in fact often presented it as a boisterous interruption by slightly drunk revellers.

Menander also utilized stock comic plots and characters, borrowing from his predecessors such situations as thwarted love and unfaithful spouses and employing typical characters such as abandoned children, clever courtesans, young lovers, scheming servants, and cantankerous masters. *The Shearing of Glycera* and *The Arbitration,* for example, both feature foundling children as well as the figure of the wise concubine, a character type also found in Chrysis, the title character of *The Girl from Samos.* All three of these plays in addition to *The Dour Man* involve complications surrounding marriage and all conclude in joyful weddings. Despite their contrived, traditional plot situations, Menander's comedies transform the characters into unique figures by providing them with highly individualized speech patterns and plausible motives and actions. What is more, Menander placed them in urban, middle-class settings that were immediately recognizable to his Athenian audiences. Characteristically, Menander's works show less concern for the will of the gods and less interest in political affairs than do those of the Old Comedy writers; his works revolve around everyday conflicts between rich and poor, city and country life, masters and servants, and they comment on the fashions, manners, and outlook of contemporary Athenians. This so-called "realism" of Menander's comedy is in marked contrast to Aristophanes's fantastic plays featuring mythological figures and heroes who travel to other worlds.

With the recovery of nearly the whole of *The Dour Man* and substantial portions of *The Girl from Samos* scholars and critics have been able to investigate the overall construction of Menander's plays, to analyze the relation between plot and character, and to examine more thoroughly the playwright's reworking of traditional comic devices. In his discussion of *The Girl from Samos,* Sander M. Goldberg points out that the play's "obstructed marriage" plot greatly improved upon the typical formula: "the dramatist's ability to impart to [the traditional plot] a diverse range of coloration makes the result truly original and intriguing. . . . If the tradition is one of many elements, it is also one of many possibilities. Menander mixes the serious and the light, makes character a source of action, and subordinates one situation to another." Similarly, E. W. Handley considers *The Dour Man* an "admirable illustration" of a well-designed comedy; it is, he states, "a play planned as a whole, to progress from beginning through dramatic climax to light-hearted conclusion, with its detail taking a place in the main design and contributing to it."

T. B. L. Webster and others observe that plays like *The Dour Man* also differ from earlier comedies by infusing the humor with distinctly tragic qualities, which gives Menander's works a curiously modern sensibility. According to Webster, Menander's comedy is capable of taking on a serious tone. Knemon in *The Dour Man,* for instance, has rejected the world "because he saw that all men were governed by purely mercenary motives"; thus his actions take on a greater dignity, and he is presented as an "idealist" and something of a philosopher. Menander's realistic presentation of plot and character make his works comparable with "modern social comedy" in Webster's view. Summing up the relevance of Menander to the present age, Geoffrey Arnott asserts that Menander is "modern," "because he writes about the recurrent problems of families, young and old alike, as they wrestle with love and greed, worry about status and reputation, and flounder in a morass of misconceptions." More important, Arnott adds, Menander's plays effectively utilize irony, ambiguity, and other "dramatic and stylistic techniques . . . which our modern critics love to label as undisputedly modern."

PRINCIPAL WORKS

PLAYS

Orgē (*Anger*) 321
Samia (*The Girl from Samos*) c. 321-08 B.C.
Dyskolos (*The Dour Man*) c. 316-17 B.C.
Aspis (*The Shield*) c. 314-13 B.C.
Perikeiromenē (*The Shearing of Glycera*) c. 314-10 B.C.
Epitrepontes (*The Arbitration*) c. 304 B.C.

PRINCIPAL ENGLISH TRANSLATIONS

Menander: The Principal Fragments (translated by F. G. Allinson) 1921; revised edition 1930
Three Plays: The Girl from Samos, The Arbitration, The Shearing of Glycera (translated by L. A. Post) 1929
Two Plays: The Rape of the Locks, The Arbitration; The Fragments (translated by Gilbert Murray) 1945
Dyskolos; or, The Man Who Didn't Like People (translated by W. G. Arnott) 1960
The Plays of Menander (translated by Lionel Casson) 1971
The Girl from Samos; or, The In-Laws (translated by E. G. Turner) 1972
Dyskolos; or, The Feast of Pan (translated by R. N. Benton) 1977
**Menander: In Three Volumes* (translated by W. G. Arnott) 1979-
Samia (translated by D. M. Bain) 1983
Plays and Fragments: Menander (translated by Norma Miller) 1987

*Only the first volume has been published.

OVERVIEWS AND GENERAL STUDIES

Gilbert Murray (essay date 1933)

[*A British educator, humanitarian, translator, author, and classical scholar, Murray has written extensively on Greek literature and history and is considered one of the most influential twentieth-century interpreters of Greek drama. In the following excerpt, he presents a comprehensive overview of Menander's works, the condition of Athenian society in the playwright's time, the conventions of New Comedy, and Menander's influence on succeeding comic writers.*]

Menander, son of Diopeithes, the chief poet of the Athenian New Comedy, is a figure difficult to estimate. He was born in the year 342 B.C., only some forty years after the death of Aristophanes, but into an Athens which was greatly changed. He must have heard Aristotle; he was on friendly terms with Epicurus. He lived practically all his life under the rule of the Macedonians, and died in 290 when the first Ptolemy was already king in Egypt and the first Seleucus in Syria. His fame was immense. He is constantly quoted by later authors, including of course St. Paul: 'Evil communications corrupt good manners' [1 Corinthians, 15:33]. But until lately he was known only through these quotations and through the Latin imitations of his work by Plautus and Terence; even now, after the great discoveries of papyri, though we have seven hundred lines of one play and considerable remains of several more, we have no single comedy complete.

But the mystery does not come merely from lack of information. The things that we do know about Menander are hard to combine. The quotations have a quality of their own. They not only show simplicity and distinction of language; they also seem to be the expression of a refined, thoughtful, and very sympathetic mind, touched with melancholy but remarkably free from passion or sensuality. Let us consider a few:

> Whom the gods love die young.
>
> I am man, and nothing that belongs to man
> Is alien from me.
>
> How sweet life is, can we but choose with whom
> To live! 'Tis no life, living for oneself.
>
> All sufferers have one refuge, a good friend,
> To whom they can lay bare their griefs and know
> He will not smile.
>
> Poor mortal, never pray to have no griefs,
> Pray to have fortitude.

An attitude towards life comes out in the lines:

> We live not as we will, but as we can.
>
> Nay, Gorgias, I call him the bravest man,
> Who knows to suffer the most injuries
> With patience. All this swiftness of resentment
> Is proof of a little mind.
>
> Fight not with God, nor to the storm without
> Add your own storms.
>
> What stings you is the lightest of all ills,
> Mere poverty . . . a thing one friend can cure. . . .

This spirit of resignation leads to a sort of theoretic anarchism or antinomianism:

> The man who does no evil needs no law.

It is character that shapes a man's life. This is expounded at length in the chief extant play, ***The Arbitration*** (ll. 659-72); and briefly in [fragment 594].

> Fortune is no real thing.
> But men who cannot bear what comes to them
> In Nature's way, give their own characters
> The name of Fortune.

Lastly, to keep the true savour of Menander in one's mind, there is the great passage in fr. 481:

> I count it happiness,
> Ere we go quickly thither whence we came,
> To gaze ungrieving on these majesties,
> The world-wide sun, the stars, water and clouds,
> And fire. Live, Parmeno, a hundred years
> Or a few months, these you will always see,
> And never, never, any greater things.
>
> Think of this lifetime as a festival
> Or visit to a strange city, full of noise,
> Buying and selling, thieving, dicing-stalls
> And joy-parks. If you leave it early, friend,
> Why, think you have gone to find a better inn;
> You have paid your fare and leave no enemies.

Or again:

> My son, you do not see,
> How everything that dies, dies by its own
> Corruption: all that injures is within.
> Rust is the bane of iron, moths of wool,
> And worms of wood; in you there is a bane
> Most deadly, which has made you sick to death
> And makes and shall make—envy

How comes it that the man who writes these gentle refined thoughts, full of self-restraint and philosophy, is the chief author of the Athenian New Comedy, known to us mainly by the grotesque comic masks found on vases and frescoes, and by the rather coarse-grained and dissolute imitations of Plautus and Terence: plays in which the heroines are generally either prostitutes or girls who have illegitimate children, and the heroes worthless young rakes, while the most amusing character is often a rascally slave engaged in swindling the hero's father or uncle out of large sums of money to pay to brothel-keepers, or else in burgling the brothels themselves; in which foundlings and exposed children are recovered and recognized with bewildering monotony, and the list of stock characters so limited and mechanical, that an ancient writer on the Theatre can give you a list of all the masks that a company needs to stock in order to produce any play? It all seems at first sight so coarse, so stupid and lacking in invention, so miserably shallow in its view of life.

The ordinary explanation is that Menander was just an elegant but dissipated person with a fine style but no ideals, writing for a corrupt society which had lost all its sense of freedom, religion, and public duty. Let us quote, as typical of the best current criticism, Professor Wilhelm Schmid:

> While recognizing fully the aesthetic and technical merits of these plays, we must not pass over their ethical flatness, invertebracy, and lack of temperament. All forms of strength are transformed into elegance and smoothness for the amusement of a generation which can stand nothing rude or harsh, and is equally averse to all impetus, idealism, or artistic daring. . . . All is indulgence and hushing up, a frivolous trifling with all moral conceptions, with truth and honour; . . . a moral twilight, in which all sound standards of value become invisible.

Other critics have compared the New Comedy to the Comedy of the English Restoration, and Menander to Congreve or Wycherley, with their wit, their grossness, their narrow range, and their 'hearts like the nether millstone'. But I venture to think that all this criticism, like much else that is written about the Hellenistic period, errs through neglecting an important clue.

One cannot understand the thought of this period, particularly that of the Stoic or the Epicurean school, except as a response of the human soul to an almost blinding catastrophe of defeat and disenchantment [the domination of Athens by the Macedonians]. All that a fifth-century Athenian had believed in had failed and been found wanting. The gods could neither save their worshippers nor bear the criticism of their rejectors. As for Athens, her continued attempt to be a Tyrant City was ridiculous: she was barely strong enough to 'stand alone in the strenuous conditions of modern life'. She could no longer be regarded as a unique object of almost religious devotion. She was not sufficiently important, in a world where there were millions of human beings, nor, if it comes to that, sufficiently superior in 'wisdom and justice' to the average run of unsatisfactory mankind. Nay, wisdom and justice themselves did not seem to matter as much as the philosophers had pretended. Unlettered scoundrels with large mercenary armies behind them seemed mostly to be inheriting the earth, at least until their throats were cut by others of the same kind.

The reaction of Hellenistic Athens to this moral and civil chaos, produced by the long scrambles for empire among the generals who divided Alexander's inheritance, seems almost always to start with some admission of the vanity of human wishes and the deceitfulness of this world. The general wreck was admitted, but each school sought to save something out of the wreck on which to support the human soul. 'All is vanity except Virtue;' said the Cynic and the Stoic, 'Man can at least do his duty until death.' 'All except pleasure;' said the Epicurean, 'that man should be happy at least is indisputably good.' 'All except success;' said the military adventurers, 'let fools talk about justice or religion; the one solid good is to have power and money.' It was in much the same spirit that Demosthenes, after the crash of all his efforts, had discovered that he could at least still die for Athens, and Plato that amid a raving world he could at least try to keep his eyes on eternal truth.

The response of Menander is more complicated, and consequently less impassioned. He is not a professional philosopher; he is a writer of Comedy, an Athenian gentleman, a product of high civilization and culture, whose natural world has been broken up and is under the heel of soldiers and money-lenders. What remains to him out of the wreck is a sense of keen interest in the spectacle of life, and an infinite belief in patience, affection, and sympathy. He is always urging that men are not so bad as they would seem from their actions. 'They do not what they will, but what they can.' Their antics make him smile, but seldom alienate him, except when some one makes bad things worse by harshness to others, or envy or pride.

True, there is very little religion in his plays; and there seems to have been a good deal of satire against superstition. There is little or no Athenian patriotism: he was fellow-citizen to all humanity. His love of Athens showed itself in practice by his steadily refusing all the invitations to leave it that came to him from Ptolemy and perhaps from other kings. His moral judgements possibly err on the side of indulgence, but it is not the indulgence of indifference or of cynicism. They have the same kind of refinement and sensitiveness that has made famous his literary style. At least so it seems to me. Yet I know that the orthodox critics will ask how I can say such a thing, when his plays are all about dissipated young men and illegitimate children, cheating slaves, brothel-keepers, and prostitutes.

I will explain why I venture to say it. In the first place all these crude terms are inexact. And to understand Menander one has first of all to realize the strange conditions of the time and the hardness with which they bore upon women.

In the old City-State there were theoretically only two kinds of women: the citizeness who could be lawfully married to a citizen, and the slave or foreign woman who could not. The slave might be owned by the citizen with whom she lived, or she might belong to a speculator, a *leno,* who kept her for sale or hire. In practice there were also resident foreigners with their perfectly respectable wives; there were also women of good birth and character, but foreign nationality, who were not legally able to marry a citizen, but could contract a free union with him.

In the age of Alexander and his successors this state of affairs, already difficult, was further complicated by constant wars, sieges, and transfers of population. When a town was taken, there was not, indeed, a massacre of the men and a wholesale violation of the women, such as was common in the Middle Ages or the Thirty Years' War; but there was often a great *andrapodismos,* or sale of slaves. The slave-dealers and *lenones* were waiting behind the lines, and bought human flesh cheap. It was in this period that the great slave markets of Delos and Rhodes came into existence, and after every campaign there were hundreds of women and children sold hither and thither about the Greek world, or held by the *lenones* for the purpose of their infamous traffic. It is women of this sort, the victims of war, mostly friendless and the sport of circumstance, whom Menander so often chooses for his heroines. The titles of many plays—*The Woman of Andros, of Olynthus, of Perinthus, of Samos*—tell the story plainly enough; and the harp-player, Habrotonon, in **The Arbitration,** with her generous recklessness and her longing for freedom, probably had the same history behind her. In many plays the woman is the property of a soldier: he bought her cheap on the spot, no doubt, or perhaps got her as a prize. The facts are brutal, but the human beings are much the reverse. In one play ***(Hated)*** the Soldier has fallen in love with his captive, but will not touch her or trouble her because the frightened girl has told him that she hates him. He walks out alone at night and thinks of suicide. In others some generous or amorous youth tries desperately to collect the necessary sum to buy the girl's freedom from the *leno* who owns her, or to outbid or forestall the soldier who has arranged to buy her. In others, despairing of lawful purchase, he gets together a band of friends who storm the *leno's* house and carry the girl off by force. It is all for her good, and every *leno* deserves worse than the worst he gets. No doubt sometimes these women showed one sort of character, sometimes another; and sometimes they just lapsed into the ways of vice serenely, with a professional eye to the main chance: the two *Bacchides* of Plautus are an instance, and they are taken from Menander. But it is quite misleading to talk without further explanation of 'prostitutes' and 'brothels'. One might better compare these people with the great populations of refugees scattered about the world of recent years, the Russian 'whites' in Constantinople, the exiles from the Baltic Republics, or the 'stateless persons' of eastern Europe. There would probably be the same variety of fortune and character, though the absence of professional slave-traders has doubtless left our present refugees in a condition of greater hope, if perhaps of less security.

Another of Menander's favourite characters is the exposed child, who is eventually discovered and recognized by its repentant parents. It was an old mythical motive: the Oedipus story made use of it; Euripides' *Ion, Antiopê, Augê, Melanippê, Alopê* and other tragedies, were based upon it. It survived to shape the story of Romulus and Remus, and the many foundling-heroes of medieval romance. I have little doubt, though of course the point cannot be proved, that this baby is merely a humanized form of the divine Year-Baby which is the regular hero of the traditional 'Mummers' Play' and of many Greek rituals. Now it is likely enough that in this matter Menander was led away by the attractions of a romantic motive which was already canonized in ancient tradition, and which provided plenty of dramatic thrill with a minimum of trouble. But of course it is to be remembered also that the exposure of children was all through antiquity permitted by law, if generally condemned by public opinion. And if permitted by law, it was certain in a time of great changes of fortune to be practised. The commonest reason for exposing a child then, as now, was the desire to conceal an illegitimate birth. But there were others. Pataecus, in the ***Perikeiromenê (He clips her Hair)***, finds seventeen or eighteen years later the children whom he had exposed in their infancy. They cannot believe that he, who has always seemed so kind, would have done such a thing. But he explains that his wife had died in giving birth to them, and the day before her death he had learned that the ship which contained his whole fortune had been wrecked. He could not rear the children, so he put rich gifts with them and left them beside a shrine.

These foundlings—who in imitation of their mythical or semi-divine prototypes are apt to be twins—cause the humane playwright a good deal of trouble. In heroic legend the father is normally a god, and of course nobody as a rule ventures to characterize the action of the god as it deserves. Even the angry father who is about to kill the princess for her breach of chastity is softened when he learns the high rank of her accomplice. But Menander, in taking over the legendary motive into common contemporary life, has to give the bastard a human father, and yet not make the father a scoundrel. Sometimes he evades the difficulty by putting the false step into the distant past, and letting the guilty old gentleman drop a quiet tear over the errors of his youth. But his commonest device is a nocturnal religious festival. We have enough evidence about May-day festivals in Europe as late as the seventeenth century to show us that these ancient celebrations of the fertility of the spring retained through thousands of years, in the teeth of all law and decorum, strong traces of that communal marriage-feast in which they originated. And it is likely enough that in the wild emotion of the midnight dances in wood and on mountain many an excited girl met her ravisher. In the only scene extant which treats fully of such an incident, what strikes one most is the bitter repentance of the youth. In ***The Arbitration (Epitrepontes)*** it so happens that Charisius learns that a few months after marriage his wife Pamphilê has secretly given birth to a child. He is reluctant to publish his dishonour, and he still loves his wife. So he treats her with marked neglect and spends most of his time away, pretending to enjoy himself, but really eating his heart out. Then he discovers that last year, at the midnight festival of the Tauropolia, Pamphilê, who had got separated from her companions, was ravished in the dark by an unknown man; and he knows, by his memory of that night, that he must have been the man! A Congreve hero would have concealed the fact and doubtless handsomely forgiven the lady; but Menander's young scapegrace is wild with self-reproach. He does not merely recognize that he is in the same boat with Pamphilê; he sees that he is guilty and she is innocent, and furthermore that he has behaved like a bully and a prig and a hypocrite, while she has steadily defended him against her indignant father.

Let us take one more case to illustrate both the brutality of the times and the delicacy of feeling with which the cultivated Athenian confronted it. When Pataecus, as mentioned above, exposed his two children, they were picked up together with their tokens, or means of recognition, by an old woman. She passed the boy, Moschio, on to a rich woman, Myrrhinê, who was pining for a child, and who brought the foundling up as her own son. As for the girl, Glycera, the old woman kept her, and eventually, as she felt death approaching, revealed to her the facts of her birth, told her that Moschio was her brother, and advised her, if ever she wanted help, to go to the Rich Lady, Myrrhinê, who knew all. Then, since the girl needed a protector, and a respectable soldier was in love with her, the old woman gave her to the soldier. She was not his wife: probably a legal marriage was not possible. She was certainly not a slave. She was free, as we find stated in the play, either to live with him or to leave him.

All goes well till one evening Glycera, standing at her door, sees her brother Moschio looking at her with interest. She guesses—wrongly—that he has been told that she is his sister, and this guess is confirmed when he runs up and kisses her. She returns the kiss. Her soldier sees her; Moschio, who is a young fop and had merely kissed her because she looked pretty and smiled, runs away. The soldier is transported with rage. Had he been an Englishman, at most periods of history he would have beaten her. Had he been an Italian, he might have murdered her. Being an Athenian, he cuts her hair off. This outrage gives the play its name (***Perikeiromenê, He clips her Hair***), and from our present point of view it is interesting to see how it is regarded by the people concerned. The soldier goes away furious with himself and everybody else; he drinks in order to forget his grief, and is divided between a wish to humble himself and make it up and a wish to kill Moschio. Glycera herself considers the insult unpardonable, leaves the soldier's house, and takes refuge with the Rich Lady, as her old guardian had told her to do. When the soldier tells the story, as he understands it, to Pataecus, that quiet man of the world tells him that he has behaved disgracefully: Glycera is not his slave. She has a perfect right to leave him if she likes, and also a right to take up with Moschio; and that in any case no self-respecting woman will live with a person who may at any moment cut her hair off.

> PATAECUS. Of course, if she had been your wife . . .
>
> SOLDIER. What a thing to say! If!
>
> PAT. Well, there is a difference.
>
> SOL. I regard Glycera as my wife.
>
> PAT. Who gave her in marriage to you?
>
> SOL. She herself.

'Very good,' says Pataecus. 'No doubt she liked you then, and now she has left you because you have not treated her properly. . . . '

'Not treated her properly!' cries the poor soldier, 'That hurts me . . . ', and he goes on later to explain how entirely well and respectfully he has treated her, except for this one act of madness. 'Just let me show you her wardrobe,' he adds; and by that ingenious device Pataecus is made, later on, to see the signet ring and the necklace that he had left with his exposed child.

Meantime, since the soldier is genuinely penitent, Pataecus will try to persuade Glycera to return. When he does so, Glycera is outraged to find that he also has misinterpreted the kiss she gave to Moschio, and even imagined that it was in pursuit of Moschio that she fled to his supposed mother's house. 'You knew me, and you thought me capable of that!'

The point which I wish to make clear is this. Menander is not merely the ingenious favourite of a corrupt and easy-going society. Athenian society in his day, I would suggest, had as a whole assimilated the liberal sensitiveness that was confined to a few exceptional personalities in the previous century; the average cultivated Athenian now felt instinctively much as Plato or Euripides felt. But the ordered world of the fifth century, precarious even then, had now crumbled away. The ordinary Athenian gentleman, who had formerly lived a strenuous life in patriotic military service, in domestic or imperial politics, in the duties of his hereditary priesthoods, in the management of his estates, now found his occupation gone. Politics consisted in obeying the will of a foreign military governor; military service meant enlistment as a mercenary under some foreign adventurer; local priesthoods were little more than antiquarian hobbies, things of no reality and no importance; and the Athenian landed proprietor was, by the new standards, only a poor farmer. All public activity was dangerous. 'Keep quiet and study; keep quiet and practise virtue; keep quiet and enjoy yourself: but at all events keep quiet. And remember that even then you are not safe.' When Menander was a boy of seven, Thebes, one of the greatest of Greek cities, was razed to the ground by the Macedonians and the whole population sold into slavery. The horror of the deed range through Greece. When the poet was about twenty, Antipater put a garrison into Athens, and deported all citizens who possessed less than 2,000 drachmae, which meant exile for more than half the citizen body. Next year, Antipater being dead, one of his rivals changed the constitution again; the exiles swarmed back, only to be crushed and driven out once more by Antipater's son, Cassander. Samos was depopulated twice. It became, for some two generations at least, a common incident of war that cities should be sacked and populations sold into slavery; and this is probably the reason for the immense increase in the proportion of slaves to free citizens which we find at this period. What can a civilized and sensitive man hope to do when flung into such a world? Only to be gentle, Menander seems to say: to remember that he is human, and nothing human is outside his range of sympathy. He can comfort his soul with the contemplation of 'sun and stars, water and clouds and fire', eternal beauties which remain while puny man strives and passes; he can possess his soul in patience and in kindliness, and remember always that here we have no abiding city.

That is the philosophic background of Menander's thought. But of course it is only the background. He is not a philosopher. He is a writer of comedy, a wit, an ingenious inventor, above all an observer of the oddities and humours of mankind. He is the maker, or at least the perfecter, of a new form of art.

The New Comedy is descended both from the Old Comedy of Aristophanes and from Euripidean tragedy. From Old Comedy it took its metres and scansion and the general style of its dialogue: also the idea of using an invented situation and imaginary characters, whereas Tragedy had been content to tell and re-tell the stories of the heroes as tradition had given them. It kept also much of the underlying atmosphere of the Old Comedy. It dealt with the present, not the past. It always contained a Kômos or Revel, always a Gamos, or Union of Lovers. Some elements in it, such as the unescapable babies or twins, seem to go back to the primitive fertility rites out of which the Old Comedy developed. On the other hand, it rejected many of the most characteristic features of the Old Comedy. It rejected the phallic dress, the free indecency of the language, the dances and the songs; it rejected completely the political diatribes and the criticism by name of public men. There seems to have been no word in the New Comedy of satire against the Macedonians, just as there was never a word of flattery. The Chorus it treated in a peculiar way. Apparently the public expected a Chorus, but a poet like Menander did not condescend to write for it. Sometimes towards the end of the First Act one of the characters observes that he sees a band of young men revelling or dancing, or perhaps drunk, and proposes to get out of their way. The Chorus then enters and performs. It is not mentioned again, but it performs in the intervals between the Acts.

In most other ways the New Comedy belongs to the tradition of Tragedy, especially the tragedy of Euripides. It took from there its elaborate plots; for Euripides, though he kept religiously to the traditional heroic legends, worked them out with an ingenuity which amounted to invention. As his biographer, Satyrus, expresses it, Euripides showed invention in passionate scenes 'between husband and wife, father and son, slave and master; in reversals of fortune; in ravished maidens and supposititious children, and recognitions by means of rings and necklaces. And out of these the New Comedy is built up. Euripides had found these elements already existing in the myths and rites which lie at the back of Greek drama. The Year-God is commonly a baby who grows up; he is commonly a foundling, a child of unknown parents; he is discovered or recognized as the child of a god. But one can see that Euripides was always depending and enriching his traditional motives by the observation of real life. The saga gave him Ion as the son of Apollo and the princess Creusa, a distinguished and satisfactory parentage. He made of it a tragedy of lust and betrayal, the untroubled and serene cruelty of the perfectly strong towards the weak. Menander, going farther on the same road, takes the decisive step of making his characters no longer gods or heroes or even princes, but middle-class Athenian citizens of his own day. His comedy belongs to what Diderot called *le genre sérieux;* it was a comedy with thought and with tears in it.

It is this affiliation . . . that also explains the masks and stock characters of the New Comedy. The tragic heroes by the end of the fifth century, if not earlier, had their characters known and fixed. Oedipus, Odysseus, Clytemnestra and the rest were known figures, as Cromwell, Mary Queen of Scots, or Joan of Arc would be now. They required no exposition or explanation, but each could proceed at once to act or speak according to his traditional nature. They seem also to have had recognizable masks, so that as soon as Ajax or Orestes appeared, most of the audience knew him. The New Comedy dropped the traditional heroic names. It used fictitious names and characters; but it wanted still to use the technique of the traditional subject. The audience was accustomed to it. It avoided the tedium of beginning every play with scenes or even whole acts of mere explanation and exposition. So it used typical characters and typical masks. It is significant that both in Greek and in Latin the word for mask is also the word for character; and *Dramatis Personae* means, strictly speaking, 'The Masks needed in the Performance'. The cross elderly uncle had one sort of mask, the indulgent elderly uncle another. The Obstinate Man, the Flatterer, the Bragging Soldier and the Modest Soldier were got up in such a way that the audience could recognize each type, whatever his name or adventures might be in the particular play, almost as easily as the tragic audience could recognize Ajax. Of course this standardization of the masks tended to limit the writer's invention. But it was not rigid. There are ancient wall-paintings which represent a playwright criticizing a set of masks and having them altered.

One often wonders that the masks of the New Comedy, except for the conventional good looks of the hero and heroine, were so far removed from realism. To our taste they seem suited well enough to an Aristophanic farce, but most odd in a refined and perhaps touching Menandrian comedy. Part of the explanation lies, no doubt, in the conditions of the great open-air theatre and the absence of opera glasses. Only very strong lines were visible; and after all the audience had been accustomed to masks from time immemorial. But I think that perhaps there was deliberate intention in the avoidance of realism or life-likeness in the masks. We must remember that it was forbidden to satirize real persons on the stage. The rule was plain; but supposing a mischievous playwright, without mentioning any names, put some offensive character into a mask which closely resembled the face of some real person, what then? It is just what Aristophanes had tried to do in the *Knights,* when he wanted the mask-makers to make his Paphlagonian look like Cleon, and they prudently refused. That such a thing should be possible would make it suspected. If a comedian put a character into any realistic mask, he might discover that the Macedonian authorities thought it was too like the Governor's cousin, and would come down on him with a fine or a sentence of exile. The only safe course, when your characters were not meant for pictures of real persons, was to put them in masks which could not possibly be mistaken for any real person.

Of course modifications would or could always be made in the masks to suit the particular conception of the type-character. One cross uncle was not necessarily the exact image of another. And we must always be on guard against the mistake of imagining that the types were as limited and rigid when the New Comedy was alive and growing as they seemed to the grammarians who classified them after it was dead. When any form of art is dead, it is easy to catalogue its points and fix its boundaries. When Dickens or Shakespeare was alive, it probably seemed to contemporaries that there was no limit to the creative imagination of either: when their work is finished, we can go through it and set down the limits within which it moved. We must also realize that our remains are too scanty to admit of a confident judgement, and that the adaptations of Plautus, and even, I should say, those of Terence, are lacking in that sensitiveness and flexibility which were characteristic of Menander. Still, when all these allowances are made, the impression left is that on the whole Menander and his fellows, in spite of their great originality

Mosaic of the Muse of Comedy, Glycera (Menander's longtime mistress—center), and Menander, now in the art museum of Princeton University.

and large productiveness, did mostly operate by making different combinations of a limited number of motives. A betrayed maiden, a foundling and a recognition, a clever slave, a severe father and an indulgent father, took them a long way. Nevertheless, if one compares the subjects treated by Menander with those of Aristophanes on the one hand and Euripides on the other, the impression of diversity and abundance of invention is overwhelming. Let us take, as an indication, the names of a score or so of his lost plays.

Several seem to deal with the fate of women from captured cities: ***The Woman from Andros, The Woman from Perinthus, from Samos, from Olynthus, from Thessaly, from Boeotia, from Leucas:*** though doubtless the ***Woman from Leucas*** was based on the old love-story of one who threw herself into the sea from the Leucadian cliff, and the ***Woman from Thessaly*** must have been given to witchcraft. The ***Man from Sicyon*** was apparently a sort of Tartarin, what the French call a Gascon, in type, a talker and planner and promiser of great things. The ***Man from Carthage*** we know was a barbarian, talking broken Greek, pitifully searching the world for his two sons who had been captured in war, and eventually finding them. The ***Perikeiromenê,*** or ***He clips her Hair,*** has been discussed above; so has the ***Misoumenos*** or ***Hated.***

A great mass of plays deal with what the seventeenth century would have called 'humours'; the quaint characteristics of human nature. The titles are often impossible to translate owing to the differences in mere grammar between Greek and English: 'Ανατιθεμενη is perhaps ***She Changes Her Mind.*** But what is 'Ραπιδομενη? Perhaps ***He Boxes Her Ears!*** will do it, though possibly it is a theatrical or musical term and means 'Hissed Off'. ***In Mourning for Himself,*** Αυτον Πενθων suggests a play like Arnold Bennett's *Great Adventure.* ***The Man who Punished Himself*** did so, we happen to know, because his harsh discipline had made his son run away to the wars. ***The Rustic, The Heiress, The Treasure, The Slanderer, The Flatterer, The Woman-hater, The Sea Captain, The Recruiting Officer, The Widow*** seem fairly clear. So do ***False!*** (Απιστοδ), ***Bad Temper,*** and ***Twice Deceived*** (though in Greek the participle is active); we know something of the last from a brilliant scene in Plautus's *Bacchides,* where the slave Chrysalus, who has just cheated his master's father out of 200 Philippi, been found out and compelled to restore the money, is then required to deceive the old man again and get it back! ***The Imbrians*** or ***Gone to Imbros*** was supposed to refer to the fact that that island was the nearest place in which to escape extradition for debt and small offences: there is an old English farce with the title *A Bolt to Boulogne.* A new fragment, however, throws doubt on this. ***Thais*** and ***Phanion*** are named from their heroines, and the names are not the names of respectable citizens. Other plays are almost impossible to translate: Κωνειαξομεναι describing women who for some reason threaten to drink hemlock; Συναριστωσαι or ***Ladies Lunching together;*** Συνερωσα, which seems to mean ***She Also Loved Him;*** Συνεφηβοι, ***Both Were Young;*** Προγαμοι or Προγαμια, ***Before the Marriage.*** There seems an immense variety, and of course I have taken only a few out of the many titles preserved. Tradition says that Menander was a friend, and perhaps a follower, of Epicurus. If so, we need not be surprised to find a group of plays dealing with superstition: ***The Superstitious Man, Trophônius***—a reference to the famous and somewhat ridiculous oracle in Boeotia—***The Begging Priest, Inspired,*** and ***The Priestess.*** In ***The Apparition*** the plot presents us with a widower who has married again: his new wife has a grown-up daughter whose existence she has concealed, but from whom she cannot bear to be parted. She constructs a shrine in her house, with a curtain in front and a secret exit, and here her daughter visits her. Her step-son, who is surprised at his step-mother's extreme piety, catches sight in the shrine of a mysterious figure, which is explained by those interested as being a divine apparition. One sees the start for a comedy of mystification.

The titles form, of course, a slender foundation on which to rest any very definite belief about the qualities of the plays; but the impression which they make is greatly strengthened by what little we know of the plots. We have, for example, on a fragmentary papyrus part of an account of the plot of ***The Priestess.*** A man's wife or mistress had left him long ago—perhaps for religious reasons—and become a priestess. He does not know what she did with their son, and the Priestess is unapproachable. She is, however, an adept at exorcisms; so the man's confidential slave pretends to be possessed by a demon, has a fit on the temple steps, and is taken in by the Priestess for treatment. He finds out that the boy is being reared as their own by some people called *X,* and tells the father, who goes at once to claim his son. But it so happens that the *X*'s have also a son of their own, and by mistake the excited old gentleman lights on him and claims to be his father by telling a story which is obviously absurd. The boy decides that the old gentleman is mad, and tells his foster-brother; who consequently, when his father, now better informed, approaches him on the same subject, humours him as a lunatic. I omit some minor complications; but even thus one sees what an immense advance in the mechanism of plot-construction and entanglement has been made since the fifth century.

In the ***Woman of Samos,*** again, we can make out from the 340 lines now extant the outlines of a lively and intricate, though doubtless highly artificial plot.

The characters belong to two families. One consists of Demeas, a rich citizen, his adopted son Moschio, and his concubine Chrysis, the 'Samian Woman', free-born but enslaved through war, who has just lost her first child. There are also a household slave Parmeno, a Nurse and a comic Cook. Next door lives Nicêratus, poor but proud, with his portionless daughter, Plangon. Moschio and Plangon love each other, but both fathers have forbidden the marriage. Meantime the young people, left alone, have come together secretly, and, while the fathers are away on a voyage, Plangon has a baby, which has to be concealed, and which Chrysis, mourning for her dead child, is persuaded to take and rear as her own. The two fathers return; something has happened—there is here a gap in the papyrus—to change their minds, and they have agreed to the marriage of Moschio and Plangon. Demeas is pleased with the baby which Chrysis shows him, and the wedding feast is ordered, when suddenly things begin to go wrong. Demeas overhears the nurse speaking of the baby as if it was Moschio's child. Much upset, he questions the slave Parmeno, whose frightened prevarications convince him of the worst. Moschio, whom he loved as a son, has seduced Chrysis, whom he trusted as a wife! His world crumbles about his ears, and he jumps to the conclusion that it is all the fault of Chrysis! Sweeping aside the Cook, who has come to talk at length about the wedding breakfast, he dashes into the house, and drives Chrysis and the baby out into the street. Chrysis herself, Parmeno, and even the Cook try to get some explanation from the furious and broken-hearted old man; but he will not publish his own dishonour, and gives none. At this moment Nicêratus appears on the scene, tries in vain to check his friend's madness, and at last, defying him, takes the weeping Chrysis into his own house.

At the opening of the next act, Moschio, who knows nothing of what has happened, has made up his mind to go to his adopted father, confess his fault and humbly beg forgiveness. Demeas is in the blackest mood and difficult to approach, but, as the confession proceeds, cheers up in a surprising way, forgives and almost congratulates the sinner, and is left beaming. Chrysis and Moschio were not false to him after all. His honour is saved! Nothing is wrong—except for this little indiscretion of Moschio and Plangon, naughty young things! He meets Nicêratus, and tells him the facts with laughter and self-congratulations. 'Congratulations!' roars the other old gentleman, 'when my daughter has disgraced my name for ever!' He will punish the girl and put to death the bastard. Rushing in to do so he finds Chrysis, who valiantly claims the baby as hers, makes Plangon and her mother refuse to admit anything, and, in a scene exactly parallel to that in the last act, is driven out by her former protector and protected by her former persecutor. The two old men are again left together, with their roles reversed. Demeas first fights, then reproaches, then comforts his proud and choleric old friend, and at last formally asks, on behalf of Moschio, for the hand of Plangon in marriage.

All is ending happily, when a new complication occurs. Moschio, who had been surprised at the beaming satisfaction with which Demeas had accepted his confession of sin, has learnt meantime the explanation and is deeply hurt. How could his father have dreamed that the would be capable of such villainy? He cannot forgive him. He will not be reconciled. He will leave the country. He will go and enlist . . . at least he would if it was not for Plangon!

At this tantalizing point the papyrus breaks off. One may conjecture that poor Demeas finds he has to apologize not only to his adopted son but to a much more formidable and more deeply wronged person, the Samian Woman. Chrysis has had enough of the two half-lunatic old men; they have both driven her out with the child. 'Good!' she may say, 'the child has been given her; she will take it and not come back!' . . . How the peace is made we cannot say, but no doubt in the end the two old gentlemen are found kneeling for pardon to their respective families, the citizenship of Chrysis is somehow discovered or re-established, and the play ends with a double marriage, Demeas and Chrysis, Moschio and Plangon.

Tragedy, to use the old Roman division, dealt with *Res Sacra;* the Comedy of Aristophanes dealt with *Res Publica;* that of Menander was occupied with *Res Privata,* a region in which the emotions and changes of fortune may be smaller in extent, but are infinitely more various.

No less marked than the development of plot is the development of technique in points of detail. The number of actors is no longer limited to three. The metres are those of Comedy, though the musical and lyrical element is entirely absent. It is notable that Menander is more concerned with metrical euphony and with a skilful ordering of the words in the sentence than his contemporaries. He avoids, for example, the so-called 'pause after a dactyl', and seldom admits inversions of order for merely metrical reasons. The language though strikingly natural is never slangy or vulgar. He avoids scrupulously forms of words that were not really colloquial, such as Datives in -οισι or -αισι, while he elides freely the verbal termination -αι, which at this time was pronounced like ε. In sum one may say that while he has built up a most scrupulous and delicate style of his own, he is wonderfully free from the influence of professional rhetoric. Then there are great variety and flexibility in the composition. People enter 'talking off stage': or conversing with each other; they enter in the middle of a sentence or a line. The soliloquies, which are not uncommon, are real soliloquies, in which embarrassed persons try to get things clear by talking to themselves: they are not, except in the Prologues, mere devices for telling a story. Sometimes the soliloquies are overheard: a device which is suitable enough when the speaker has really been talking to himself aloud, though very bad when the soliloquy is only the playwright's artifice for revealing a character's unspoken thoughts. Conversations are overheard and interrupted: there are misunderstandings which lead to results; there are motives of action based deliberately on odd or over-subtle points of psychology. Thus Moschio, when all his wishes are granted, is nevertheless so hurt at having been previously misunderstood, that he determines not indeed to enlist but to pretend that he intends to enlist, so that his father may be sorry and beg him to stay. And, though the play there breaks off, we may hazard a guess that the father is either too stupid or too clever, or too full of self-reproach to do what he is expected to do. Such refinements are more in the style of the Parisian stage in the nineteenth century than that of classical Athens.

At times it would seem that a complication is invented chiefly for the sake of the psychology. It gives the opportunity for some one to act not in the ordinary way but in some strange way that illustrates the oddity of human nature. In ***The Samian Woman,*** when the baby, with the diabolical ingenuity that distinguishes Menander's babies, contrives to make Demeas believe that it is the child of the Samian Woman and his adopted son, the deceived man breaks out into a fury of rage and curses, but instantly checks himself. 'Why are you shouting? Fool, why are you shouting? Control yourself. Be patient. . . . It is not Moschio's fault. He did not mean it. He would never want to wrong me. He has always been good to me and to every one. She must have taken him in a weak moment. Fascinated the boy as she fascinated me . . . who am much older and ought to be wiser. She is a Helen! A siren! A harlot!' The unnatural gentleness of his first reaction leads to the violent explosion of his next.

Then the method of exposition, if not altogether new—for both Comedy and Tragedy had not merely their prologues but their scenes with two characters in conversation indirectly explaining the situation of the play—is nevertheless far more varied and ingenious than any in the fifth century had tried to be. Menander contrives to amuse you in a dozen different ways while he makes his explanation. Let us take the scene which gives its name to the ***Epitrepontes,*** the scene of the Arbitration. What is needed for the plot is to explain that a certain exposed baby has been reared, and will prove to be the child of Charisius. But the way the story is told is this.

Enter two slaves, a charcoal-burner and a shepherd, quarrelling, followed by a woman with a baby. 'You are cheating.' 'No, it's you.' 'Oh, why did I give him anything?' 'Will you agree to an arbitration?' 'Yes; where shall we find the arbitrator?' 'Any one will do. Try this old gentleman.'

The old gentleman, Smicrines, is just returning in an angry temper from the house of his son-in-law, Charisius.

> THE CHARCOAL-BURNER. Please, Sir, could you spend a few minutes on us?
>
> OLD GENTLEMAN. On you? Why?
>
> CHARC. We are having a dispute.
>
> O.G. What is that to me?
>
> CHARC. We are looking for an arbitrator. If there is nothing to prevent you, you might settle . . .
>
> O.G. Bless my soul! Peasants in goatskins walking about and litigating as they go!

The Charcoal-burner pleads with him, and pleads so eloquently that the Shepherd is alarmed.

> SHEPHERD. How he does talk! Oh, why did I ever give him anything?
>
> O.G. You will abide by my decision?
>
> CHARC. Yes, whatever it is.
>
> O.G. All right, I will hear the case. . . . You begin, Shepherd, as you have not spoken yet.

Every line so far is slightly unexpected and therefore amusing. You cannot help wanting to hear what comes next.

The Shepherd begins:

About a month ago I was watching my sheep alone on some wooded ground, when I found a baby lying on the grass with a necklace and some ornaments.

> CHARC. (*interrupting*). That is what it's all about.
>
> SHEP. (*turning on him*). He says you are not to speak!
>
> O.G. If you interrupt I will hit you with my stick.
>
> SHEP. Quite right too. (*The Charcoal-burner subsides.*)
>
> SHEP. (*continuing*). I brought the baby home. Then at night I thought it over. How was I to bring up a child? Next day this charcoal-burner met me and I told him what had happened, and he begged me to give him the child. 'For God's sake', he said, 'let me have it, and I will bless you. My wife has had a baby, and it has died.'
>
> O.G. (*to Charcoal-burner*). Did you ask him for it?
>
> CHARC. I did.
>
> SHEP. He spent the whole day beseeching me. When I gave it to him he kissed my hands.
>
> O.G. Did you kiss his hands?
>
> CHARC. I did.
>
> SHEP. So he went off. Then next day suddenly he came back with his wife and demanded the ornaments and things—not that they are of any value—which had been exposed with the child. Now, obviously, they have nothing to do with the case. He asked for the baby and I gave him the baby. What I found belongs to me, and he ought to be grateful that I gave him part of it. That is all I have to say. (*A pause.*)
>
> CHARC. Has he quite finished?
>
> O.G. Yes. Didn't you hear him say so?

CHARC. Very good. Then I answer. His account is perfectly correct. He found the child. I begged him to give me the child. All quite true. Then I heard from one of his fellow-shepherds that he had found some trinkets with the child. Those trinkets are the child's property, and here is the child claiming them. (Bring him forward, wife!) They are his, not yours; and I, as his guardian and protector, demand them on his behalf. His whole fortune in life may depend on those trinkets. They may enable us to identify his parents, like Neleus or Pelias in the tragedies.—Now please decide.

O.G. All that was exposed with the child belongs to the child. That is my decision.

SHEP. Very good; but in that case whom does the child belong to?

O.G. Not to you who tried to rob it. I award the child to this Charcoal-burner who has tried to protect it.

CHARC. God bless you!

SHEP. A monstrous judgement. Good Lord, I found everything, and it is all taken from me! . . . Have I got to give the things up?

O.G. Certainly.

SHEP. Monstrous! Plague take me if it isn't!

CHARC. Be quick.

SHEP. Heracles, what treatment!

CHARC. Open your bag and let us see the things. . . . Please don't go yet; wait, Sir, till he hands them over.

SHEP. (*handing the things slowly over*). Why did I ever trust this man to arbitrate?

O.G. Hand them over, rascal.

SHEP. I call it disgraceful.

O.G. Have you got them all? Then good-bye!

One might think the scene was now exhausted of all its dramatic points; but not at all. The Shepherd goes off grumbling. The Charcoal-burner sits down with his wife to look through the trinkets one by one. While they are doing so, Onesimus, the slave of Charisius, happens to come out of the house, and naturally looks to see what the pair are doing.

'A seal with a cock on it', proceeds the Charcoal-burner.

A transparent stone. An axe-head. A signet ring with the stone set in gold, the rest of it iron; the figure of a goat or a bull, I can't see which. Name of the carver Cleostratus. . . .

ONESIMUS. Let's have a look!

CHARC. Hullo, who are you?

ON. That's it!

CHARC. What's it?

ON. The ring.

CHARC. What about it?

ON. It's the ring my master lost.

There we may stop. Of course, by strict standards the scene is an artificial one, though the incidents are not impossible nor outside the range of common life. But the treatment shows a light touch and a variety of incident which mark a complete change from the style of the fifth century. Every line has a certain unobtrusive wit, the quality that was called in antiquity 'Attic salt', and the situation is made to yield its full harvest of amusement.

If this scene is leisurely in movement, let us take another from the same play to show how swift Menander can be, when he wishes, with his big emotional effects.

A harp-player named Habrotonon, moved partly by pity, partly by a wish to get her freedom, pretends that the child is hers. This gives her a hold over Charisius. Meantime she is looking for the real mother. She remembers seeing a girl with torn clothes, crying bitterly at the feast of the Tauropolia, and is sure that there she has a clue. Charisius's young wife, Pamphile, who is distracted between the unkindness of her husband and the fury with which her father takes her part against him, comes out of her house just as Habrotonon with the baby comes out of the next house.

PAM. (*to herself*). My eyes are sore with crying.

HAB. (*to the baby*). Poor thing! Did it keep whining? What did it want, then?

PAM. (*to herself*). Will no god take pity on me?

HAB. Dear baby, when will you find your mother?—But who is this?

PAM. (*to herself*). Well, I will go back to my father.

HAB. (*staring at her*). Madam, wait one moment!

PAM. Did you speak to me?

HAB. Yes. Oh, look at me! Do you know me?—This is the girl I saw. . . . (*impulsively*) Oh, my dear, I am so glad.

PAM. (*frightened*). Who are you?

HAB. Give me your hand. Tell me, dear, last year you went, didn't you, to the Tauropolia . . .

PAM. (*noticing the baby*). Woman, where did you get that child?

HAB. Poor darling, do you see something you know, round its neck? . . . (*Drawing back*) Oh, madam, don't be frightened of me.

PAM. It is not your own child?

HAB. I have pretended it was. Not that I meant to cheat the real mother. I only wanted to find her. . . . And now you are found! You are the girl I saw that night.

PAM. (*Only one thought in her mind*) Who was the man?

HAB. Charisius.

PAM. Oh joy! . . . Do you know it? Are you sure?

A scene could hardly be more rapid, and every word tells.

The literary fate of Menander has been curious. He was apparently a little too subtle, too refined, too averse from rhetoric, or possibly too new and original, for the popular taste of his own day. With over a hundred plays he only obtained the first prize eight times. He was obviously not a best-seller. But his fame was immense, and he was recognized soon after his death as the incontestable chief of the writers of the New Comedy. Almost alone in his age he ranked as a classic; and the Atticist grammarians of Roman times have to labour the point that Menander, however illustrious, did not really write the perfect Attic of Plato or old Aristophanes.

More than this, the style of drama which he brought to perfection proceeded immediately to dominate the ancient stage. The Hellenistic theatre knew no other form of comedy: the Roman theatre lived entirely on translations and adaptations of Menander and his school, Philêmon, Diphilus, Posidippus, and the rest. He was read and praised by Cicero and Quintilian; by Plutarch, Lucian, Alciphron, Aelian; he is quoted in anthologies, and his apophthegms were made up into anthologies of their own. But in modern times, when the Renaissance scholars proceeded to look for his plays, it was found that they had all perished. They were only represented by the Roman adaptations of Plautus and Terence, the former much rougher, coarser, and more boisterous in form, the latter showing much delicacy of style, but somewhat flattened and enfeebled.

Yet through these inferior intermediaries Menander conquered the modern stage. There is not much of him in Shakespeare except the *Comedy of Errors.* But Molière with *L'Avare* and *Le Misanthrope,* with *Les Femmes savantes* and above all *Les Fourberies de Scapin,* comes straight out of the Menander tradition. So does Beaumarchais with his *Figaro* and his *Don César de Bazan.* And the style of both has the Menandrian polish. The great Danish comedian Holberg confessedly went back to Plautus for some of his plays, and adopted Menandrian formulae for others. In England there is a touch of him in Ben Jonson. There are whole blocks of him in Congreve, Farquhar, and Vanbrugh—the same dissipated young men, the same clever and knavish servants, the same deceiving of parents and guardians, the same verbal courtliness and wit, the same elaboration of the story. Sheridan, though more of a gentleman than the Restoration Dramatists, belongs to the same school, and has built Sir Anthony Absolute and the Captain [in *The Rivals*], Charles Surface and Joseph Surface [in *The School for Scandal*], quite on the Menandrian model. Of course these writers only knew Plautus and Terence, and were doubtless content with their models. They had little of Menander's philosophic spirit, nothing of his interest in distressed women; nothing of his inexhaustible human sympathies and profound tenderness of heart. But, directly or indirectly, no one who writes polite comedy can avoid the influence of Menander.

It is a curious thing, this power of world-wide and almost inexhaustible influence. A price has to be paid for it, and a heavy price. A writer cannot be so popular unless he is, I will not say, vulgar himself, but at least capable of being read with pleasure by vulgar people. All great writers and thinkers need interpreters: otherwise the difference between them and the average lazy public is too great. And it is likely enough that Menander has gained in influence rather than lost through his dependence on his Roman imitators. They had left out his delicacy of thought, his reflectiveness, and much of his beauty of style, but they kept the good broad lines that were easy for every one to understand.

Thus the interpreters and inheritors were provided. But, to justify such a long life for Menander's influence, there must have been something to interpret, some inheritance precious enough to compel the interest of successive generations. And I think we can see what there was. There go to the greatest imaginative work normally two qualities: intensity of experience and the gift of transmuting intensity into beauty. Menander had both. Gibbon speaks somewhere of the intense suffering which is caused when a refined and sensitive population is put under the control of brutal and uneducated conquerors, or, what comes to much the same thing, exposed to the brutal play of chance. He was thinking of the highly civilized Byzantines put at the mercy of the Turks: we may think of the many sensitive natures who were broken or driven mad by the stain of service in the late war. Menander belonged to just such a refined and sensitive generation—the most civilized known to the world before that date, and perhaps for two thousand years after it—flung suddenly into a brutal and violently changing world. He interpreted its experience in his own characteristic way: not by a great spiritual defiance, like the Stoic or Cynic; not by flight from the world, like the Epicurean; but by humour, by patience, by a curious and searching sympathy with his fellow mortals, in their wrigglings as well as their firm stands; and by a singular power of expressing their thoughts and their strange ways in language so exact and simple and satisfying that the laughter in it seldom hurts, and the pain is suffused with beauty. (pp. 221-63)

Gilbert Murray, "Menander, and the Transformation of Comedy," in his Aristophanes: A Study, *Oxford at the Clarendon Press, 1933, pp. 221-63.*

Allardyce Nicoll (essay date 1949)

[*Called "one of the masters of dramatic research," Nicoll is best known as a theater historian whose works have proven invaluable to students and educators. He was also a popular lecturer on Shakespearean drama and the author of several studies of Shakespeare's works. Nicoll's* World Drama from Aeschylus to Anouilh *has been highly praised as a thorough and perceptive commentary on dramatic literature from all time periods. In the following excerpt from that work, he surveys the state of Greek theater in Menander's time and provides an introduction to* The Girl from Samos, The Shearing of Glycera, *and* The Arbitration.]

The style known as the Middle Comedy endured from the first quarter of the fourth century to about 330 B.C., but concerning its qualities we can but make broad guesses. The literary evidence consists of no more than a number of fragments, and our chief guide is a set of statuettes which evidently reproduce the stage appearance of its characters. From these we may hazard the conjecture that the Middle Comedy was basically a transitional form of drama, inheriting some of the features of the Old Comedy, but definitely tending towards an entirely different concept of the comic.

The costumes worn by the characters still bear traces of the attire of the actors in the fifth century, with the padded stomachs, the tights, the short cloak, but when we examine the figures in greater detail we realize that the exaggeration of feature has been softened and that the characters represented must have been much closer to the living persons to be seen on Athens' streets than the grotesques beloved by Aristophanes. There are still some burlesque mythological persons, such as the braggart Herakles, but most of the statuettes represent a series of stock types of the day—an old woman holding a child, a modest-seeming courtesan, old men and young men, rascally slaves, some seated in impertinent attitude on altars where they have sought sanctuary. We receive the impression—fortified from other sources—that the actions in which these characters were involved must have been of a more domestic kind than the earlier fantasies and that their behaviour must have been much more realistic.

A Changing Theatre

Meanwhile both audience and theatre were in process of change. The old gusty days of the Athenian democracy were gone, and a bourgeois civilization had taken its place. Civic interests had ceded to domestic. Having argued the gods out of existence, men had no other deity than Plutus, god of wealth. The ancient culture was sufficiently strong to leave its deep impress on all the peoples of the Mediterranean basin, but its vitality had been dissipated; the culture had become polite.

Gradually Athens ceased to be the core of this civilization. Power passed from state to state, and it was not to be long before Alexander the Great, Greek in outlook but a monarch of Macedon, became lord of the ancient world. Nor was it to be long after that before this civilization was to find its chief home in Egypt, at Alexandria under the Ptolemies.

All over the Greek countries there was the building of new theatres and the remodelling of old during this time, for the impetus of the three great Athenian tragic dramatists and of Aristophanes was powerful enough to maintain prime interest in the stage; but the forms assumed by these new theatres were different from those of the fifth century. True, the Greek playhouse to the very end retained its chief characteristic feature—the combination of three essentially separate parts, auditorium, orchestra, and scene-building. At the same time the functions of these parts were being altered. The great sweep of stone seats tended to approach more nearly to the shape of a semicircle. Although the orchestra still kept its central position, the reduced importance of the chorus permitted an encroachment upon its area, with the *skene* [scene-building] pushing itself forward; in some theatres, even, such as those at Assos and Priene, the circular form was deliberately abandoned, and the new orchestra took the shape of a semicircle extended by lines drawn at right angles to the diameter.

It was, however, the scene-building that altered most, taking shape as a structure clearly modelled on the richer domestic architecture of the time. Because the chorus and the actors were now separate, with more emphasis placed upon the individual characters in the dramas presented, the way was open for the erection of a high stage. Normally, this high stage was placed upon a long line of low pillars and jutted out in front of the *skene* proper: it was, accordingly, styled the proscenium (*proskenion*), literally signifying that which was before the *skene.* Behind it was the second storey of the *skene,* with a row of columns supporting a roof and providing a kind of rear or inner stage in the space between the columns and the front wall of the scene-building.

In this new type of theatre scenery could be, and was, more freely used than in the past, and we must think of the actors appearing against backgrounds of panels (*pinakes*), painted either to give the suggestion of walls and doors or more elaborately to convey an impression of buildings in perspective. We must think, too, of these actors becoming more and more important, until Aristotle could observe that in theatrical productions they were generally of greater consequence than the dramas they interpreted. This is a playhouse intended not for those who have come to a religious exercise, intent upon listening to rich words, but for those who see in the theatre a place of entertainment merely, whose interests are more mundane and whose eyes need showy scenes.

The New Comedy: Menander

The characteristic dramatic genre in this theatre was the New Comedy, established, during the time of Alexander the Great, about 330 B.C. Even had we possessed nothing but the terracottas and other visible records of the actors in these plays, we could have made a fair guess at its tone and contents. Gone is the old grotesque comic dress; the mythological types have vanished. Instead on the stage now appear figures garbed in the costumes of the day. Here are the fathers and sons of Hellenistic society, the slaves and the cooks and the musicians, the old gossips and the parasites, the young wives, and, above all, the courtesans. Some of the masks still retain an element of grotesquerie, but in general the features are closely modelled on the real.

Happily some literary record also remains, and this enables us to corroborate the impression received from contemplation of the little histrionic statuettes and to round out our imaginative reconstruction of the productions. Apart from fragments from a number of authors of the New Comedy style, a happy discovery at Cairo has given us some four thousand lines of the writing of the most famous of these authors, Menander, amply sufficient to allow us to shape general conclusions concerning the entire development of this comic style.

One of a group of playwrights including Philemon, Diphilus, Poseidippus, and Apollodorus, Menander was born in 343 B.C. (he died in 292), the nephew of a Middle Comedy dramatist, Alexis. Well-born, he was interested in social manners and the graces of culture; the life of the city appealed to him, and its types he studied with sympathetic care. The contemporary and friend of Epicurus, he imbibed some of that philosopher's ideas, while from Theophrastus he probably acquired his interest in the delineation of character types.

Before turning to an examination of those works of his which are still, though fragmentarily, extant, we may do well to consider, in general terms, the style of play which he was largely responsible for establishing on the stage. This style of play is essentially realistic. Aristophanes' fantasies are forgotten, and the characters are familiar; nor need we be surprised, since the comedies were penned for a bourgeois civic audience, to find that, despite the changed conventions of life, a peculiarly 'modern' note is struck in the dialogue. When we hear the persons of New Comedy speaking about 'gold-digging' and 'shop-keeping minds' we recognize the world we are in.

With the fantastic has vanished, too, the old uproarious laughter. Menander seldom allows more than a smile to curve his lips. Indeed, we encounter here a quiet, contemplative mood which might almost have seemed more proper to the tragic stage.

> When you wish to know what you are, look at the tombs in the cemeteries. There are bones there, and the ashy dust of men who were monarchs, tyrants, sages, men proud of their birth and their riches, their estates and their handsome figures. Naught of these defended them against Time: Death comes to all things mortal. Look on these and learn what you are.

Passages such as this remind us that we are far off from boisterous comedy, that we are in the world of a realistic, reflective, sentimental comedy of human manners.

And here the influence of Euripides upon the New Comedy becomes clearly apparent. From Euripides two great streams of influence are to be traced. His inspiration was a dominant influence on all the tragic playwrights who followed him. This was a direct channel, but no less direct was the passage from his dramas to those of Menander. In Euripides' plays certain characteristic features attract attention: his suppression of the chorus, his emphasis upon character (particularly the characters of women), his carefully wrought plots with their complications, his reflective, rhetorical tone, his introduction of love-themes, his development of a kind of tragi-comedy. The chief trend of his art was from the heroic to the realistic, from the ideal to the ordinary, from the rigours of tragedy to the sentimentalities of the drama of ideas. Already, in *Helen* and other plays, these features have been amply revealed, but there still remains at least one of his works to be considered, and this may now be glanced at, since it demonstrates in an extreme form qualities later on to be taken up by the comic playwrights of the fourth century. The date of *Ion* is unknown, but almost certainly it came late in Euripides' career; with one or two changes its plot might easily have been the plot of one of Menander's plays. The familiar situation is here—a girl ravished in the dark and a child exposed with trinkets; only here the girl is a princess, Creusa, the ravisher is a god, Apollo. As the plot proceeds we find Creusa married to a king, Xuthus; the couple are childless and go to Delphi for aid. Apollo's oracle declares that the first person whom Xuthus meets as he leaves the temple will be his son; this person is, in reality, Ion, the child of Creusa. Not knowing who he is, Creusa, enraged, determines to destroy him, is prevented, and discovers the boy's real paternity by means of the jewels she herself had left with the exposed babe. Gods appear in this story, and princesses, but they behave like middle-class citizens; bourgeois romance surrounds them, sentimentalism colours their actions, the atmosphere in which they dwell is not that highly charged mountain air out of which tragedy is wrought, but the quiet, reflective comic air of the plains. Tragedy is rapidly becoming drama.

Fundamentally, then, we may say that the style of Menander and his fellows was wrought out of the Euripidean manner. In their structure, in their romantic theme, in their concentration on the domestic, and in their rhetorical quality a direct link exists between the tragedies of the one school and the sentimental comedies of the other.

The first play from which we have fragments of Menander's writing is ***Samia* (*The Girl from Samos*)**, which, although more carefree, perhaps one might almost say farcical, than his other extant works, nevertheless reveals the typical features of his art. Only a small portion of the text has come down to us, sufficient, however, for a reconstruction of the plot. Romantic love is the core, with misunderstandings complicating the action, providing opportunity for character portrayal and creating scenes of laughable disorder. Moscion, son of the kindly, good-willed Demeas, is deeply in love with Plangon, daughter of the poor, irascible, touchy Niceratus. She has a child, and, fearing her father's wrath, has it taken by Chrysis, Demeas' mistress and housekeeper, who gives out that it is her child by her guardian. The complications may be imagined: Demeas suddenly rendered jealous when he imagines that Chrysis has been unfaithful with his own son; Niceratus so hasty in his passions that he will not listen to reason; slaves trying to conceal secrets and making confusion worse confounded by their efforts. There is in some lines a sort of brittle wit, as when the slave Parmeno addresses the Cook:

> Cook, I'm damned if I know why you carry knives with you. Your chatter would reduce anything to mincemeat.

There is abundance of comic irony when characters blunder over issues quite plain to the audience. There is pathos, as in the scene where the unfortunate and falsely suspected Chrysis is driven out-of-doors by her protector.

Misunderstandings—symbolized by the abstract figure of Misapprehension—teem also in ***Perikeiromene* (*The Girl with Shorn Hair*)**, a comedy of separated twins, Glycera and Moschion. Abandoned in infancy, the former has been brought up by a poor woman and later finds a protector in the soldier Polemon, while the latter has been adopted and lavishly cared for by a wealthy old lady, Myrrhine. From the scene in which Polemon, enraged by ill-founded jealousy, shears off Glycera's hair the play takes it title, but jealous rages of such sort do not long endure in Menander's comedies, and, of course, the pair are reconciled; of course Glycera and Moschion discover their relationship; of course the pair are united to their long-lost father. It is all very pretty, very romantic, and yet at the same time very close to real life.

How far Menander carried the comic drama along these lines is revealed even more patently in ***Epitrepontes*** (***The Arbitration***), still another play of love, in which pathos battles with laughter as to which shall win. Since more of this comedy has been preserved than of any other of Menander's works, and since in this New Comedy the true basis is to be found for the characteristic modern theatre, its plot may be more fully summarized.

In the first act we are introduced to a young wife, Pamphila, daughter of the hard-fisted Smicrines, and her strait-laced husband, Charisius, a very serious and proper youth. There has just been a crisis in the household. Barely five months after her marriage Pamphila has borne a son, and we learn that this was the result of an attack made upon her, before her wedding, by a drunken man at one of the city's festivals: since the assault was in the dark, she has no idea of the identity of her seducer. The child has been taken by a slave to be exposed, and all would have been well had not Onesimus, Charisius' slave, revealed the secret. Charisius is shocked, but, being genuinely in love with his wife, he does not cast her off: instead, he leaves the house and indulges in extravagant orgies in which a girl harpist, Habrotonon, figures largely.

The second act opens with the appearance of Smicrines, who, not knowing about the child, is in a rage at his son-in-law, not so much for having deserted Pamphila as for squandering his fortune on riotous living. His reflections are interrupted when a slave, Davus, and Syriscus, a charcoal-burner, enter in lively and acrimonious argument. They agree to put their case to arbitration and beg Smicrines to be the judge. Davus explains that some time ago he found an exposed babe along with some trinkets:

> I picked it up and went back home with it and was going to raise it. That's what I intended then. In the night, though, like everybody else, I thought it over to myself and argued it out: "Why should I bring up a baby and have all that trouble? Where am I to get all that money to spend? What do I want with all that worry?" That's the state I was in. Early next morning I was tending my flock again, when along came this fellow, he's a charcoal-burner, to this same spot to get out stumps there. He had made friends with me before that. So we got talking together and he saw that I was gloomy and said: "Why so thoughtful, Davus?" "Why indeed," said I, "I meddle with what doesn't concern me." So I tell him what had happened, how I found the baby and how I picked it up. And he broke in at once, before I had finished my story, and began entreating me: "As you hope for luck, Davus," he kept saying, "do give me the baby, as you hope for fortune, as you hope for freedom. I've a wife, you see," says he, "and she had a baby, but it died." Meaning this woman who is here now with the child. Did you entreat me, Syriscus?

The charcoal-burner admits this, but, having heard about the trinkets, he claims he ought to have them. In a spirited speech he argues that these trinkets must go with the child:

> Perhaps this babe is better born than we. He may, though brought up among labourers, look down on our condition, seek his own native level, have pluck to ply some noble occupation, hunt lions, bear arms, take part in races at the games. You have seen actors, I am sure, and all these things are familiar to you. A certain Neleus and Pelias, the famous ones, were found by an aged goat-herd clad in a goat-skin just like mine. When he saw that they were nobler born than he, he told them all, how he found and picked them up, and he gave them a wallet full of tokens and from that they found out everything about themselves for certain and, goatherds before, now became kings.

Convinced by such arguments, Smicrines immediately commands Davus to hand over the trinkets. As Syriscus examines his booty Onesimus enters, and at once recognizes a ring as belonging to his master, Charisius.

The third act reveals, through the words of Onesimus and Habrotonon, that Charisius, despite his semblance of rioting, is really pining for his wife and curses the day he was told her secret—so much so that Onesimus is afraid to reveal the secret of the ring to him. He knows Charisius lost it at a festival, and he is almost sure he must have assaulted some girl there; before taking further action he wishes to find that girl. Here Habrotonon comes to his aid: she was at the festival, she says, when a young girl was apparently attacked:

> ONESIMUS. You were there?
>
> HABROTONON. Yes, last year at the Tauropolia. I was playing the lute for some young ladies, was joining in the sport myself; at that time I hadn't—I mean I didn't know yet what a man is. (ONESIMUS *smiles knowingly.*) Indeed I didn't, by Aphrodite.
>
> ONESIMUS. Yes, but do you know who the girl was?
>
> HABROTONON. I could ask. She was a friend of the women that I was with.
>
> ONESIMUS. Did you hear who her father was?
>
> HABROTONON. I don't know anything about her except that I should recognize her if I saw her. A good-looking girl, goodness, yes, and rich too, they said.
>
> ONESIMUS. Perhaps it's the same one.
>
> HABROTONON. I don't know about that. Well, while she was with us there, she strayed off and then suddenly came running up alone, crying and tearing her hair. She had utterly ruined a very fine Tarantine shawl, and delicate, my goodness. Why, it was all in tatters.

Plutarch on Menander and Aristophanes:

Coarseness, in words, vulgarity and ribaldry are present in Aristophanes, but not at all in Menander; obviously, for the uneducated, ordinary person is captivated by what the former says, but the educated man will be displeased. I refer to antitheses and similar endings and plays on words. For of these Menander does make use with proper consideration and rarely, believing that they should be treated with care, but Aristophanes employs them frequently, inopportunely, and frigidly. . . . Moreover, in his diction there are tragic, comic, pompous, and prosaic elements, obscurity, vagueness, dignity, and elevation, loquacity and sickening nonsense. And with all these differences and dissimilarities his use of words does not give to each kind its fitting and appropriate use; I mean, for example, to a king his dignity, to an orator his eloquence, to a woman her artlessness, to an ordinary man his prosaic speech, to a market-lounger his vulgarity; but he assigns to his characters as if by lot such words as happen to turn up, and you could not tell whether the speaker is son or father, a rustic or a god, or an old woman or a hero.

But Menander's diction is so polished and its ingredients mingled into so consistent a whole that, although it is employed in connexion with many emotions and many types of character and adapts itself to persons of every kind, it nevertheless appears as one and preserves its uniformity in common and familiar words in general use; but if the action should anywhere call for strange and deceptive language and for bluster, he opens, as it were, all the stops of his flute, but then quickly and plausibly closes them and brings the sound back to its natural quality. And although there have been many noted artisans, no shoemaker ever made the same shoe, no mask-maker the same mask, and no tailor the same cloak, that would be appropriate at the same time for man and woman and youth and old man and domestic slave; but Menander so blended his diction that it comports with every nature, disposition, and age, and he did this although he entered upon his career while still a young man and died at the height of his powers as playwright and poet, when, as Aristotle says, writers make the greatest progress in the matter of diction. If, therefore, we were to compare Menander's earliest dramas with those of his middle and final periods, we should perceive from them how many qualities he would, had he lived longer, have added to these.

Some dramatists write for the common people, and others for the few, but it is not easy to say which of them all is capable of adapting his work to both classes. Now Aristophanes is neither pleasing to the many nor endurable to the thoughtful, but his poetry is like a harlot who has passed her prime and then takes up the rôle of a wife, whose presumption the many cannot endure and whose licentiousness and malice the dignified abominate. But Menander, along with his charm, shows himself above all satisfying. He has made his poetry, of all the beautiful works Greece has produced, the most generally accepted subject in theatres, in discussions, and at banquets, for readings, for instruction, and for dramatic competitions. For he shows, indeed, what the essence and nature of skill in the use of language really are, approaching all subjects with a persuasiveness from which there is no escape, and controlling every sound and meaning which the Greek language affords. For what reason, in fact, is it truly worth while for an educated man to go to the theatre, except to enjoy Menander? And when else are theatres filled with men of learning, if a comic character has been brought upon the stage? And at banquets for whom is it more proper for the festive board to yield its place and for Dionysus to waive his rights? And just as painters, when their eyes are tired, turn to the colours of flowers and grass, so to philosophers and men of learning Menander is a rest from their concentrated and intense studies, inviting the mind, as it were, to a meadow flowery, shady, and full of breezes.

Plutarch, "Summary of a Comparison between Aristophanes and Menander," in Plutarch's Moralia, *Vol. X, translated by Harold North Fowler, Harvard University Press, 1936.*

It is arranged between them that Habrotonon will wear the ring and, if Charisius notices it, will profess to have been the wronged maiden. The plot works: Charisius acknowledges the child and is prepared to pay heavily in order to secure Habrotonon's liberty; while Smicrines, outraged, determines to take his daughter home with him.

In the fourth act Pamphila protests to her father (Charisius overhearing her words) that, despite all the ill-usage she has received, she will not desert her husband. A moment later she meets Habrotonon and receives the joyous news that Charisius is the father of her child, while as for Charisius himself, the words of Onesimus are sufficient testimony:

> He's not quite sane. By Apollo, he's mad. He's really gone mad. By the gods he *is* mad. My master, I mean, Charisius. He's had an atrabilious stroke or some such thing. How else can you explain it? He spent a long time by the door inside just now craning his neck and listening. His wife's father was having a talk with her about the business, I suppose. The way he kept changing colour, gentlemen, I don't even care to mention. Then he cried out: "O darling! what a wonderful thing to say!" and beat his head violently. Then again after a while: "What a wife I had and now have lost, alas!" And to cap it all, when he had heard them to the end and had gone in at last, inside there was groaning, tearing of hair, continual frenzy. Over and over again he's repeat: "Criminal that I am, when I had myself done a thing like that, when I had myself got an illegitimate child, to be so unfeeling, so utterly unforgiving to her in the same unhappy situation. No humanity; no mercy." He calls himself names as hard as he can, his eyes are bloodshot with fury. I'm shaking in my shoes; I'm all wilted with terror. If he catches sight of me, who told on her, anywhere, while he's in this state, he'll maybe kill me. That's why I've quietly slipped out here. Where am I to turn though? What can I think of? It's all over. I'm done for. He's at the door coming out. O Zeus Saviour, help me if you can.

Poor Charisius now comes in, berating himself for his superiority and determining to make amends to Pamphila. Learning that she is really the mother of the child, his self-abasement knows no bounds, his new-found resolve no limits.

The last act shows the discomfiture of Smicrines, who, arriving in a passion to abduct his daughter by force, is suddenly deflated by the truth. "By all the gods and spirits," he cries, and Onesimus cynically questions him:

> ONESIMUS. Do you believe, Smicrines, that the gods can spare the time to mete out daily to every individual his share of good or evil?
>
> SMICRINES. What's that?
>
> ONESIMUS. I'll make it quite plain. The total number of cities in the world is approximately a thousand. Each has thirty thousand inhabitants. Are the gods busy damning or saving each of them one by one? Surely not, for so you make them lead a life of toil. Then are they not all concerned for us, you'll say. In each man they have placed his character as commander. This ever present guardian it is that ruins one man, if he fails to use it aright, and saves another. (*Indicating himself*) This is our god, this is the cause of each man's good or evil fortune. Propitiate this by doing nothing absurd or foolish, that good fortune may attend you.

Thus ends ***The Arbitration,*** on a strangely modern note. All the ingredients are here for the drama of to-day—the emphasis on manners, the mingled smiles and tears, the growth of character in the persons represented, the concept of the single moral law for men and for women alike, even, we may say, the building of the entire play about an idea, for Menander's comedy is, in essence, a problem drama. (pp. 107-15)

Allardyce Nicoll, "From Menander to the Mimes," in his World Drama: From Aeschylus to Anouilh, *George G. Harrap & Company Ltd., 1949, pp. 107-37.*

T. B. L. Webster (essay date 1965)

[*Webster was a British classical scholar, educator, and the author of* An Introduction to Menander *(1974). In the following excerpt he reviews Menander's varied use of stock New Comedy plot structures, stage conventions, costuming, and masks to transcend the limitations of the genre and create complex, realistic characters.*]

The long line of writers of social comedy from Shakespeare and Goldoni to Galsworthy, A. A. Milne, and their present-day successors have, partly consciously and partly unconsciously, been writing in a tradition which goes back to Plautus and Terence. But Plautus and Terence themselves were adapting and translating Greek New Comedy, which has only recently become known to us from considerable stretches of original text. The approach of the two Roman writers to their Greek originals was very different. Terence translated texts accurately but often flattened out the colour of the original and twice at least combined scenes from two different Greek plays; certainly also he sometimes converted monologues of the original into dialogues. Plautus seems to have been an actor himself and it is a reasonable conjecture that he translated actors' texts rather than library texts; such texts probably preserved the original much less carefully than the library texts which Terence used, and it is at least possible that some of the elements which we regard as Plautine, particularly the expansion of the slave parts, may have been due to Greek actors during the century or so which separates Plautus from his originals. As long as our knowledge of Menander and his contemporaries depended on the adaptations of Plautus and Terence and the numerous short fragments preserved in quotations, we could not appreciate the flavour of Menander's comedy. At the very end of the last century large portions of a papyrus roll were discovered giving two-thirds of Menander's ***Arbitrants,*** about half of his ***Rape of the Locks,*** about a third of his ***Samian Woman,*** and the first scene of his ***Hero.*** The succeeding years have added considerable fragments from a number of plays, but we only gained a complete play, when in 1959 Professor V. Martin published the first edition of the papyrus of the ***Dyskolos*** (or ***Grumpy,*** to borrow the title of an early twentieth-century comedy).

Let us review some of the general characteristics of this kind of social comedy. Aristotle would have said that the characters were people 'like ourselves', and if he had lived to express himself about the earliest productions of Menander, would have so distinguished them from the characters of mid-fourth century and earlier comedy, whom he calls 'worse than ourselves' in the *Poetics.* The heroes and their families belong to the upper middle class. They move in the same sort of world as we do, even if they have rather more leisure and are more lavishly equipped with butlers, nurses, and housemaids. Comparison with fourth-century Athenians as they appear in the speeches of the Attic orators suggests that Menander probably exaggerates their wealth just about as much as the modern writers of social comedy. The characters are clearly divided into old and young: parents and grandparents are lumped together as old, and the young consist of grown up children. (Young children do not have speaking parts in Menander, although his babies may exercise, as Gilbert Murray said, a devilish ingenuity.) There is also a clear division between masters and servants; it is curious that in the original texts of Menander slaves are not particularly efficient, and it looks as if the really masterful slaves of Roman comedy were developed on hints given in Menander's text by actors who played his comedies between his death and the time of Plautus. Neither action nor language strays far outside the conventions of middle-class life. It is true that Menander writes in verse, because this is the tradition of Greek drama. His spoken iambics are stricter than those of Aristophanes, and though he uses a considerable range from the earthy utterances of slaves to the almost tragic solemnity of love-sick young men and deceived fathers, he does not proceed nearly so far outside the possibilities of conventional speech as Aristophanes. When Menander changes from spoken iambic trimeters to intoned trochaic tetrameters for the scene which contains Knemon's self-defence in the ***Dyskolos*** he is probably following a tragic rather than a comic model. The final ballet-like scene in iambic tetrameters is a survival from a more boisterous form of comedy.

No one undertakes anything very adventurous or fantastic or villainous; no one has any very wild political or anti-social dreams. In Aristophanes Dikaiopolis [in *Acharnians*] makes his private peace with Sparta and Peisthetairos [in *Birds*] builds Cloudcuckoo land to escape from Athenian politics; Menander's soldier who cuts off his mistress's hair because he believes her unfaithful and the kindly uncle who pretends to die so that his property may form a dowry for a penniless girl are pale remnants of such fantastic actions, and their relevance is private not political. The world proceeds on a fairly even and predictable course, but an unexpected event like the shipwreck which lost Pataikos the means to support his orphaned twin-babies in the ***Rape of the Locks*** or Knemon's disaster of falling down the well in the ***Dyskolos*** may be introduced to throw a character off balance so that he can gradually recover equilibrium; more often the characters of Menander are thrown off balance by the gossip of their slaves. The only emotion to which one may devote oneself wholeheartedly is the emotion of love, and conjugal felicity is the normal end of this kind of play: its plot consists therefore of the gradual overcoming of the obstacles in the way of conjugal felicity.

The standard obstacle is the disapproval of parent or guardian on either or both sides. Knemon in the ***Dyskolos*** is the obstacle to his daughter's marriage to the young townsman Sostratos who has fallen in love with her. Knemon so hates the commercial motives which govern the world that he works his considerable farm with no one to help him: 'he likes it best if he can see nobody. He works with his daughter beside him for the most part; he only speaks to her; he finds it difficult to say anything to anybody else; and he says he will only marry her off when he finds a young man exactly like himself'. Sostratos' slave who has tried to make a date for his master is chased off the farm; his helpful friend deserts him; he himself wilts before the torrent of fury which Knemon pours upon him. He has the good luck to help the girl draw water from the spring of the Nymphs, but this action is reported to the girl's half-brother Gorgias as an attempt by the corrupt rich to exploit the honest poor. He convinces Gorgias of his honest intentions and works a day on the farm in the hope that Knemon may accept him as a working man. But Knemon dare not leave his house when he sees a procession approaching the shrine of the Nymphs: Sostratos' mother wishing to sacrifice to avert a bad dream about Sostratos, her daughter, and several slaves; the cook had arrived just before with the sheep for the sacrifice. The cook tries to borrow pots from Knemon but is driven off with contumely. Sostratos returns frustrated and joins his family in the sacrifice. Knemon falls down his well in the attempt to get out the bucket and the mattock which his old slave-woman has dropped in earlier in the play. Gorgias and Sostratos rescue him. He is so shattered that he tells Gorgias to provide for his daughter. Gorgias introduces Sostratos, and Knemon accepts him as a sun-tanned labourer and therefore a suitable son-in-law. Arrangements are made for Sostratos to marry Knemon's daughter and Gorgias to marry Sostratos' sister. The play ends with the cook and a fellow slave taking vengeance on Knemon for his meanness.

The obstacle need not be parental disapproval. In the ***Rape of the Locks*** the first obstacle is the soldier's jealousy of a supposed rival, which makes him treat the girl like a slave, cutting off her hair, and the second obstacle is the girl's pride, which makes her refuse to be reconciled until her own status as a citizen is established. In the ***Arbitrants*** the pair are already married but the young husband has deserted his wife because a slave has told him that she has borne a child which he thinks cannot be his; her father tries to persuade her to leave her husband on the ground that he is spending her dowry on a prostitute.

A great many variations can be played on this general theme, and the emphasis can be laid on the plot or the characters, on the lovers themselves, or on the nature of the obstacles, or on the ingenuity with which the obstacles are overcome. Such comedy is optimistic because we see people we like achieving an end which we desire for them; in addition to our satisfaction with their happiness we may also, if the author is skillful and the acting is good, feel some sympathy for the obstacle which has been overcome, for Hornblower in the *Skin Game* [of John Galsworthy], for Shylock in the *Merchant of Venice* [of Shakespeare], and for Knemon in Menander's ***Dyskolos.*** The essence of this kind of comedy is that it shows us a world like our own, which in the modern theatre we view across the footlights, separated from us but moving on a course like our own.

The ancient dramatist lacked the obvious resources of the modern dramatist for making drama realistic in this way. Menander had three different sorts of experience which helped him when he started producing in 322 B.C. at the age of 18 (he was only 24 when he produced the ***Dyskolos***): comedy, tragedy, and philosophy. Several elements in the ***Dyskolos*** show Menander's debt to earlier comedy, particularly the ragging of Knemon with its descriptions of eating and drinking in the last act, but also the breathless arrival of Sostratos' slave in the first act and the arrival of the cook with the sheep on his shoulders in the second act. We can only reconstruct the kind of comedy which intervened between Aristophanes and Menander from the fragments of plays quoted by later authors and with the help of terracotta statuettes of comic actors and representations of comic scenes on vases. It is possible that young lovers, who are the essential element in social comedy, were first introduced in mythological comedy, which parodied tragedy and was very popular in the first half of the fourth century. The fragments make it certain that the love affairs of imaginary contemporaries occurred in comedy soon after 350 B.C. and well before the earliest plays of Menander; but the actors still wore the old obscene costume that they wore in the plays of Aristophanes.

Tragedy, by which I mean largely but not exclusively the tragedy of Euripides, was a classic for Menander in the same sense that Shakespeare is a classic for us, a classic constantly performed in the theatre and used for illustrations in lectures on ethics and as the basis of literary criticism. The transformation of *Romeo and Juliet* into *West Side Story* would have won Menander's approval, even if he himself preferred to transpose the single tragic scene or situation into terms of contemporary life rather than a complete play. He could also count on his audience taking an allusion to tragedy, whether the allusion was employed by a slave adding verisimilitude to the deception of his master, by a young man in a solemn moment of self-discovery, or by a father when he reached a tragic agony of self-deception.

Menander was a pupil of Theophrastus, the philosopher who succeeded Aristotle as the head of the Peripatetic school when Aristotle died in 322 B.C. We do not know what he learnt from Theophrastos, but it is a reasonable guess that he learnt literary criticism and ethics. Aristotle had laid down that the tragic poet should construct his plot in general terms as a sequence of necessary or probable incidents with a beginning and middle and end, and he meant, partly at least, by necessary or probable incidents, incidents which resulted from the mental qualities of the characters. This is exactly the kind of play which Menander wrote; he adapted the Aristotelian rules for tragedy to the comic stage. It is easy to see this already in the youthful ***Dyskolos.*** The main events occur because Knemon is grumpy and mean (he would not have fallen down the well if he had not been too mean to provide an extra bucket, a special hook to recapture a lost bucket, and a well-head to make the top of the well safe), because Sostratos is too much in love to bother about propriety, because Gorgias has a charity which can charm Knemon out of his grumpiness for a moment, because the slave Daos realistically sees that Sostratos is good for a free day's work on the farm, and because the pompous cook cannot forgive Knemon's refusal to lend him a cooking-pot. Menander's plays are good drama in Aristotle's sense and he is also aware of Peripatetic ethics. In the ***Rape of the Locks*** he adopts a form of opening which he used in several other plays: instead of starting with a prologue speech to give the audience the essentials of the situation (like the speech of Pan at the beginning of the ***Dyskolos***) he starts with a scene of action: the soldier in fury at his slave's mistaken report of his mistress's unfaithfulness cuts off her hair. Then personified Ignorance (or perhaps Misunderstanding would be a better translation for this situation) explains that she is responsible for his action, besides giving the audience an outline of the preceding story. The conception that a crime committed in ignorance of facts relevant to the situation is less heinous than a premediated crime is elaborated in Aristotle's *Ethics* and quoted in his *Poetics.* The introduction of Ignorance to speak the prologue is therefore an indication that the poet knew Peripatetic Ethics and that the audience would do well to remember them. Two other early plays were called ***Anger*** and ***Drunkenness:*** Aristotle links them with Ignorance as causes of unpremeditated crime, and it seems likely that Menander personified them too as prologue speakers in the plays named after them and there too made explicit reference to Peripatetic Ethics.

I shall return later to Polemon, the soldier hero of the ***Rape of the Locks.*** The bare outline given of the ***Dyskolos*** must suffice to show the efficient mechanics of Menander's plot-construction. A good verse translation like J. H. Quincey's [*The Old Curmudgeon of Menander,* 1962] gets something of the felicity of his language (at least the difference between the iambic trimeters of the dialogue, the trochaic tetrameters of Knemon's self-defence, and the iambic tetrameters of the final ragging scene stand out clearly). Here I want to consider how Menander used the modest scenic resources at his disposal to achieve a realism which was far greater than that of his predecessors and comparable, when due allowances are made, with the realism of modern social comedy.

The modern dramatist gives his audience a programme which tells them the names, status, and sometimes the relative ages of the characters; status and relative ages Menander could show to some extent by his masks (and this I shall consider further later) and convention seems to have established separate sets of names for old men, young men, soldiers, parasites, slaves, wives, daughters, and prostitutes.

The modern dramatist also uses the programme to give the time, date, and place of every scene; moreover, he can change the scene as often as he likes and rely on having a realistic setting for any place that he likes to imagine. Menander's possibilities were much more restricted. Conventionally the prologue speech only summarized events up to the beginning of the action and only gave the most general intimation as to the future: Ignorance in the ***Rape of the Locks*** prophesies that the exposed children will find their father, but Pan makes no prophecy in the ***Dyskolos*** Menander seems to have accepted Aristotle's dictum that the events of tragedy should be confined within a single day and to have applied it to comedy. The glaring unrealities of Aristophanes, who makes Amphitheos [in *Acharnians*] get from Athens to Sparta and back in the space of forty lines of dialogue, have been abandoned; time experienced in the ***Dyskolos*** is a single long day. Within this single long day the time-table has no regard for geographical distances. The action takes place at the shrine of the Nymphs and Pan, which (in defiance of the terrain) is between the house of Knemon and the house of Gorgias. Athens is in fact fifteen miles away, but Getas has time to leave home in the morning walk to Athens, hire the cook in the agora, walk back with him, pick up the picnic gear and the sheep and arrive at the shrine before the end of the second act, during most of which time Knemon, who is said to spend the maximum of time on his farm, is doing nothing in his house. But Menander can disregard geography because already by the time of the ***Dyskolas*** the convention is established that town, country (and in other plays the harbour) are too far from each other to be visited between scenes but near enough to be visited between acts, and this convention overrides the audience's knowledge of the actual distances.

Realistic lighting and realistic scenery were also impossible for the ancient dramatist. Menander does occasionally want to make a young man pass a sleepless night because he cannot get hold of his beloved. The words and a lamp in the hands of his slave create the illusion; but here we can trace the convention back to the time of Aristophanes. For scenery all the evidence suggests that at any one time a Greek theatre only possessed three sets: one for tragedy, one for satyr play, one for comedy. Menander produced his early plays in the theatre as rebuilt by the statesman Lycurgus soon after 330 B.C. In this reconstruction the theatre had a stone stage-building with projecting wings, between which was a façade containing three doors: only the large central door was used for tragedy: comedy could use either the two smaller side doors or all three doors; the intervening panels were painted with the scenery. (Early in the third century and probably before Menander's death the action was moved on to the roof of the stage-building, but essentially the same background was then repeated at that level.) The set for tragedy gave buildings in perspective; the set for satyr play gave rocks and caves; the set for comedy was decorated with garlands, libation bowls, and other symposion equipment, the kind of decoration that would be found on the walls of a men's dining-room in a rich house. There is a little evidence that for a tragedy (like the *Philoctetes* [of Sophocles]) or for a comedy with a country scene (like the ***Dyskolos***) the set for the satyr play could be used. The dramatist had to create in words the particular locality which he wanted his audience to imagine, but he also knew that they had before their eyes a real locality of three doors in a row, which he could exploit when he needed it.

In the ***Dyskolos*** the action is put in Phyle, an area which Menander and many of his audience would know from their period of military service. The 'famous shrine' with the hard country, 'the rocks that bear only thyme and sage-apples', and the richer land below which is farmed by Sostratos' father, the road along the bottom of Knemon's farm, the pear trees, the fig tree and the olive trees, the scrub which Knemon shares with Gorgias, are all verbal aids to the audience's imagination. What they saw was a façade with a large central door and two smaller side doors and intervening panels decorated with rocks, and altar, and perhaps also a statue of Pan (since wooden statues were easily obtainable and easily brought on between one play and the next). The central door belongs to the 'famous shrine' of the Nymphs and Pan, and the two side doors to the houses of Knemon and Gorgias. In fact the 'famous shrine' was much too inaccessible to have any houses near it and much too small to accommodate a large picnic party. But once Menander had translated the shrine and the two houses into terms of conventional stage setting, the central door was obviously capable of admitting any number of people and the contiguity of the three doors made it possible to interweave the actions in the two houses and the shrine. When Knemon's daughter comes out of his house to fetch water, Sostratos can take her pitcher to the shrine and the slave Daos, coming out of Gorgias' house, can overheat what is going on. When Knemon falls down the well inside his own house, his old slave-woman can fetch Gorgias from his house and Gorgias can fetch Sostratos from the shrine in a moment, and the cook outside the shrine can hear and comment on what is going on in Knemon's house. Both are good dramatic moments which are made possible by the setting.

The normal Greek house had its rooms grouped round a courtyard into which the front door opened. The stage doors would therefore naturally open into the courtyards of the houses to which they belong and this house-plan is described in some detail by Demeas, who owns one of the stage-houses in the ***Samian Woman.*** Moreover, Menander establishes the stage doors as front doors by sometimes making characters knock on them when they are going in and slide the bolts back noisily when they are coming out. He has therefore no easy way, like the modern dramatist, of playing interior scenes. Yet he cannot do without interior scenes. There are, however, two mitigations of the improbability of intimate conversations between members of the family taking place in the street. One is that, although the stage doors are established as front doors, the traditional decoration of the panels with libation bowls, etc., is an interior decoration and suggests the walls of the dining-room, so that the comic set is itself a mixture of outside and inside. The other mitigation is to arrange the interior scene so that one of the participants is a visitor; thus the intimate conversation becomes a protracted greeting or farewell, which is not so unnaturally performed on the doorstep.

In the ***Dyskolos*** most of the action can take place outside quite naturally because all three doors are in action and people come and go between them, Knemon's farm, Gorgia's farm, and Sostratos' family farm. But it is extremely unnatural that, when Knemon has been rescued from the well, he should be carried outside his front door to make his final dispositions. The arrangement is made a little easier by the fact that his wife has to be fetched from Gorgias' house to hear him.

Given the convention Menander exploits it. In the ***Arbitrants*** Smikrines and his daughter discuss the infidelities of her husband Charisios on her doorstep; he is going back to fetch her old nurse in the hope of persuading her to return home, and so the scene can be played as a protracted farewell. But Charisios, who has deserted her and is supposedly enjoying a prostitute in his friend's house next door, puts his head out of that front door and listens to the conversation. In real life the conversation between father and daughter would take place in the women's quarters of her house, and Charisios would be endeavouring to drown his sorrows in the men's quarters of the next house. But given the stage-necessity of a conversation on the doorstep, Menander takes advantage of it to allow Charisios to overhear it.

Menander shows himself a master in using the conventions of the Greek stage, but there is no reason to suppose that he invented them: tragedy had long established the convention of intimate conversations outside the palace door in the presence of the chorus. But the decisive change in costume which made comic actors look like contemporary Athenians was either due to him or was carried through in the early years of his production. At the same time (and perhaps at his instigation) the stock masks of New Comedy were systematized so that he could predict the faces of his characters far more accurately than the modern dramatist who has to use unmasked actors. It is worth while trying to sketch the history of this change in costume and masks, so as to have the material to ask a final question: how far did Menander's characters run true to the form predictable by the audience from their masks?

Aristotle in the *Poetics* describes the characters of comedy as 'worse than the average' and says that 'the mask which excites laughter is something ugly and distorted without causing pain'. A glance at Athenian comic terracottas and South Italian comic vases of the second quarter of the fourth century, when this passage was written, explains Aristotle's judgment and shows that 'worse than the average' applies even more to costume than masks. But about the time that Aristotle was writing, the new intrigue comedy was coming in and included new characters as well as new situations, the lover, the parasite, the young hetaira (or prostitute), the free girl, the procurer and procuress, and the heavy father. In the new young masks there is little distortion, and some of them can be shown to be derived from contemporary fashions. Some of the young women's masks which on the monumental evidence were introduced rather before or rather after the middle of the fourth century, the girl with a peek of hair over the forehead, the girl with a scarf round her hair, the girl with a pony-tail, and the girl with melon hair, can be paralleled in everyday life as represented by Attic vases and terracottas dating from the same period: the mask-maker evidently copied the hair styles of contemporary hetairai (and because hetairai are servants of Aphrodite some of these hairstyles are also found on contemporary figures of Aphrodite). All of these continue into the New Comedy period. The mask of a young man with hair waving up from his forehead appears late in the Middle Comedy period and is a favourite in the New Comedy period; the style must have appeared in the earliest portraits of Alexander and from that time became extremely popular.

But although from the middle of the fourth century or even a little earlier the masks of young women and slightly later the masks of young and old men might reasonably be termed 'like the average' rather than 'worse than the average', Aristotle's judgment was still valid as long as men normally showed a large phallus and both men and women were grotesquely padded. The photographs of Middle Comedy terracottas are often taken from the front view and do not show the padding clearly, but in side view it can at once be seen on figures of old men, young men, slaves, old women, and young women alike. In New Comedy only slaves are fat, and they are neither abnormally fat nor are they always fat. Unfortunately the evidence is weakest for the last quarter of the fourth century, and we cannot tell whether the reduction of padding for free men and women was gradual or sudden. It must, however, have been a sudden decision to give men a chiton [tunic] which reached half-way down the thighs or nearly to the ankles instead of stopping at the hips. Two preliminary changes are significant. From the middle of the fourth century the phallus worn by slaves becomes much less obtrusive, and about the middle of the fourth century clean-shaven men, who are presumably the lovers of intrigue comedy, sometimes (as old men earlier) wear a long himation [outer garment draped over the left shoulder and wrapped around the body] which conceals the phallus. The exuberant obscenity of Old Comedy evidently decreased in Middle Comedy as the interest shifted to plot and characters. In the third century there is plenty of evidence for the long chiton; and a rough terracotta group from the small Boeotian town of Halai, dated between 335 and 280 B.C., surely implies an Attic original of the fourth century—both the young man and the slave have chitons which cover the thighs. The plays of Menander show no trace of obscenity, though the scene at the end of the ***Dyskolos*** gave opportunities which Aristophanes would not have missed. It is therefore a reasonable assumption that the longer chitons for male characters were introduced early in the New Comedy period, but we do not know whether one poet introduced longer chitons and the others followed or whether some reformer such as Demetrios of Phaleron gave instructions to the costume makers.

With the new costumes and naturalistic masks, either inherited from Middle Comedy or newly introduced, Menander's characters looked like the Athenians of his day. For the masks the likeness to real life has been sufficiently demonstrated already and we shall have more to say about them later. The costumes can in some cases be compared with contemporary and later terracottas and other monuments. The man about town, young and old, wore long chiton and himation. On Attic grave reliefs and statues the himation is shown but the chiton is often omitted by convention; occasionally, however, it can be seen. The *chlanis,* worn by an older man in the ***Orge*** and by Sostratos in the ***Dyskolos*** was a particularly fine and fashionable kind of himation. The *tribon* or *tribonion* was a much coarser and smaller himation worn by poor men, usually without a chiton, and by philosophers who affected to be poor. Gorgias in the ***Georgos*** is said 'to belong to the class of *tribon* wearers'; on this evidence his namesake in the ***Dyskolos*** and Knemon would also wear it, and we can form a good idea of Knemon from a terracotta in Boston of the earliest third century, probably a philosopher.

Sostratos wore the fashionable *chlanis* but with it a thigh-length chiton because he was an energetic young man. The thigh-length chiton is the dress of the soldier, but he wears over it a *chlamys* or military cloak; when Polemon changes into civilian clothing in the ***Perikeiromene,*** he sends Sosias to fetch him a *himation* to put on instead of his military *chlamys,* which he has been wearing with his sword. A very fine terracotta mould of the last quarter of the fourth century from the Agora represents a soldier wearing the *chlamys* pinned on the right shoulder and hanging diagonally across the body, and the chiton shows beneath the breastplate.

It is much more difficult to find representations of slaves in real life to match the slaves of comedy. The very fine third-century terracotta from the Agora of an actor playing the part of a running slave in short chiton and fringed himation gives us a good idea of Pyrrhias' first entry in the ***Dyskolos*** and there is no reason to suppose that slaves in real life looked any different. Country slaves, like Daos in the ***Dyskolos,*** wore the *diphthera:* 'you with the diphtherai, have you time for law suits?' says Smikrines in the ***Epitrepontes.*** This is a chiton made of skin. A short form was worn by Middle Comedy actors. A Roman marble figure of a fisherman wears a short skin-chiton girt round the waist and pinned on the right shoulder. This, but probably less exiguous, is the kind of garment which would be worn by the rustic slave of comedy.

The characters looked like ordinary Athenians and their clothes told the audience their sex, their age, and in some cases their social position. The masks confirmed all these points and added rather more. Beyond that the poet had to rely on gestures and words. We can say nothing useful of gestures, but we can ask what expectations the masks aroused and whether Menander fulfilled or contradicted them, what in this sphere was the interplay between production and imagination. The list in the late lexicographer Pollux gives the common stock of New Comedy masks in the third century B.C. The forty-four masks are partly new additions, partly known already in the Middle Comedy archaeological material. Here it will suffice to state the principles which can be observed in the changes. It looks very much as if families could be recognized by the hair-style of their male members. Thus we find a neat-haired old man, four neat-haired young men (in a descending sequence of age), an older and a younger neat-haired slave; a wavy-haired old man, two wavy-haired young men (the older a soldier), an older and a younger wavy-haired slave; a curly-haired old man (who is also characterized by Pollux as 'interfering'), a curly-haired young man, and a curly-haired slave. Wavy hair (derived from Alexander) suggested impetuosity; curly hair suggests energy. Further characterization is given by colour of hair and of complexion, forehead (wrinkled or smooth), brows (raised or level), nose (aquline, straight, or snub). New Comedy families are mostly better off than their predecessors and therefore the scrubbier masks of old men and women have been dropped. New Comedy adds a curly-haired wife and a grey-haired wife, but takes over the types of young women which had been developed in Middle Comedy. The great increase is in young men, largely because of the great interest in the various types of male lover.

On the evidence of the archaeological material the stock masks of New Comedy seem to have been established by the middle of the third century B.C. What part Menander himself played in this and whether he invented the hypothetical grouping of families by hair-style we cannot say. Such a prolific poet, so concerned with differentiation of character, is unlikely to have left the invention to others. In any case the new masks passed quickly into stock.

Occasionally a character in Menander is described by another character and the description includes or implies a judgment. Raised brows are the mark of a person who regards himself as superior, often a philosopher so in the ***Arbitrants*** Smikrines, the father-in-law of the young husband Charisios, 'has a scowl on his face like a miserable philosopher'—Smikrines as an interferer should wear the old curly-haired mask, which has raised brows; the cook in the ***Dyskolos*** tells Sostratos' slave Getas to relax his brows at last because he is going to have a good feed: as the leading wavy-haired slave he has raised brows and lives up to them in his anger at the women, his fury that Sostratos should invite the yokels to the sacrifice, and his readiness to join the cook in ragging Knemon at the end of the play. Knemon also looks 'not very beneficent' to Sostratos as he appears shouting his soliloquy; again brows are part of the reason. If the division of families by hair-styles is accepted, Gorgias must be the rustic youth, who has neat hair; Sostratos, his father, and their slaves, Pyrrhias and Getas, will form the wavy-haired group and this suits Sostratos as the wild young man about town; but Knemon cannot wear the old curly-haired mask, which Pollux characterizes as interfering. This is right for Smikrines in the ***Epitrepontes*** but entirely wrong for Knemon; on the other hand Knemon could very well wear the wedge-beard mask of Middle Comedy, which survives into the New Comedy period: 'raised eyebrows, pointed beard, rather bad tempered'. This would give him an old-fashioned as well as an angry air. But how can Gorgias decide immediately that Sostratos is 'a scoundrel to judge by his looks'? Sostratos should be the second young man with wavy hair, and the wavy hair on the top of the fine *chlanis* and of Daos' insinuations awake Georgias' prejudices against the rich.

These descriptions, which are preserved with their contexts, show that Menander did expect other characters, and therefore the audience, to make the obvious predictions from the masks. Mask and costume give the audience a good general idea of the age, sex, social position of the character, and tell them something about how the character may be expected to behave. Many characters run true to type but are individual because they take part in individual events: these individual events are part of the plot, and this is what Plutarch's story (*Moralia*) means when Menander says that he has made the comedy because he has finished the plot. The younger man with wavy hair may be expected to fall helplessly in love and to flout conventions in getting what he wants: Chaireas in the ***Eunuch*** seizes the chance of changing clothes with the eunuch so as to be introduced into his girl's house, and Sostratos in the ***Dyskolos*** seizes the chance of working as an agricultural labourer so as to make himself acceptable to his future father-in-law. The events are completely individual and beautifully realized, but both young men run true to predictable form.

There are, however, three young men who do not run true to form: Gorgias in the ***Dyskolos,*** Charisios in the ***Arbitrants,*** and Polemon in the ***Perikeiromene.*** Gorgias is an incredibly virtuous young man, who supports his mother on a tiny farm, who works so hard that he has no knowledge of love, who construes the report of Sostratos' approach to his half sister as the exploitation of the hard-working poor by the idle rich, but immediately accepts Sostratos' self-defence as genuine, if also misguided, and immediately leaps into the well to rescue Knemon without a thought for cavalier treatment in the past. At the end his pride flares up again when a marriage with Sostratos' sister is proposed, and he is naturally embarrassed at joining the rich man's party in the shrine of the Nymphs. Yet the rustic mask has a snub nose and thick lips, which should betoken sensuality and cowardice. The mask is well attested early (and is carried by the skeleton of Menander on a silver cup from Boscoreale). Menander here contrasts appearance and reality.

Charisios in the ***Arbitrants*** is a different case. Robert [in his *Masken der neueren attischen komödie,* 1911] assigned him the mask of the dark young man, who is studious rather than athletic. Perhaps the studious young man in comedy was always liable to forsake philosophy at least temporarily for love. What however is individual in Charisios is his whole course of action after he finds out that his wife Pamphile has been, as he thinks, unfaithful to him and has borne a child. He tries to drown his sorrows in drink and women, and fails. He then receives the shattering piece of news that he is himself the father of the baby, which he believes to be the child of the prostitute Habrotobon. Then by the convenient arrangement of the three-

Painting possibly depicting the last scene of Menander's The Arbitration, *now in a museum in Bonn.*

door stage he overhears his wife telling her father that she refuses to leave him in spite of this. The slave Onesimos thinks he has gone mad and describes him groaning, tearing his hair, changing colour, and abusing himself as a hypocrite. Then at last the audience sees him and hears him express his conclusion, perhaps as startling to a Greek as to a Victorian audience, that he should judge his wife's act by the same standard as his own and accept her willingness to stay with him. Perhaps we should say not so much that he does not run true to form as that two shattering experiences made him aware of a new truth on which he acts. But Menander has given something more than the label on the mask 'studious rather than athletic' predicts.

In the ***Rape of the Locks*** Menander himself almost tells us not to trust the label. Polemon wears the mask of the first wavy-haired young man, 'soldier and braggart', and we expect arrogance and irascibility. Our expectations are fulfilled in the first scene when Polemon immediately believes the report that his mistress has been unfaithful, cuts off her hair with his sword, and leaves her to drown his sorrows in drink. But then personified Ignorance tells the audience that this 'all flared up because of the future, that Polemon might fly into a rage—for I led him, though this was not his true character'. The rest of the play shows his repentance and ends with reconciliation. The pride and irascibility which the mask proclaims is short-lived, and his true character is to be a faithful husband.

Slaves in Menander are mostly individualized by their situations, but two stand out as individual people: Daos in the ***Hero*** and Syriskos in the ***Arbitrants.*** In the first scene of the ***Hero,*** Daos is described by his fellow-slave Getas rather as Charisios is described by Onesimos in the ***Arbitrants.*** 'Why do you keep beating your head? Why do you stop and tear out your hair? Why do you groan?' The realistic Getas supposes that Daos has committed some major misdemeanour for which he expects to be punished. But Daos has fallen in love with a poor girl, who is working wool in the house. He has made no attempt to seduce her but has told his master, and his master has promised that she shall live with him but at present he has gone to Lemnos. A slave not only in love but prepared to wait for his girl is startling; and in the sequel, which we only know from the brief summary preserved at the beginning of the papyrus, Daos, discovering that the girl is pregnant, claims that he is responsible, to the fury of his mistress; a fragment of his speech is preserved: 'Mistress, nothing is stronger than Eros, not even Zeus himself, Lord of the Gods in Heaven; even he does all that Eros commands.' This beginning is strongly reminiscent of a fragment of Euripides' *First Hippolytus.* Like Syriskos in the ***Arbitrants*** (and other slaves in Menander) Daos has seen tragedy, but nothing in the mask distinguishes this educated highly individual slave from his earthy friend Getas. In the ***Arbitrants*** the charcoal burner Syriskos is similarly contrasted with the realistic shepherd Daos. Syriskos is a slave, but he is out on his own as a charcoal burner and has come in to pay what is due from his takings to his master. His wife had lost her baby, and so he gladly accepted the foundling from Daos, but he also demands the trinkets with which the child had been exposed, because they are the baby's property and may prove his birth, as indeed they do. Syriskos is entirely disinterested and in fact acts against his own interest, because the baby is immediately recognized by its trinkets as Charisios' child and is therefore taken from him. He pleads his case with considerable skill and idealism. Again the contrast between appearance and reality is clear.

Of the older men only Demeas in the ***Samian Woman*** and Knemon in the ***Dyskolos*** need discussion. Both are contrasted with more ordinary old men, Demeas with the straightforward Nikeratos (who would wear the leading old man's mask) and Knemon with the rich, hasty, complacent Kallippides, the father of Sostratos (who would wear the wavy-haired old man's mask). Demeas is drawn in much more detail than Nikeratos and stands out as a completely individual figure. His two big preserved speeches are brilliantly written. The first is a detailed narrative of what he saw, ending with the horrible suspicion that his son Moschion and not he is the father of the baby, which he wrongly believes his mistress Chrysis to have borne. He tries to interrogate the slave Parmenon, but when he threatens him with a whip Parmenon escapes. By his second speech he tries to convince himself that Moschion was the innocent victim of his mistress Chrysis, and at the end he rushes into the house to turn her out; 'Demeas, now you must be a man. Forget your desire for her, be through with love, and hide the disaster, as far as possible, for your son's sake'. The cook thinks he is mad and fears for his pots. Demeas drives Chrysis out of the door with the old nurse and the baby: she did not know how to behave herself when he gave her a comfortable home; now she can go on the streets and drink herself to death or starve. Like Charisios, Demeas does not speak out of character; we should rather say that Menander has exposed his character to unexpected depths.

Knemon has his own ancestry in a line of Comedies which go back to the *Hermit* of Phrynichos, produced in 414 B.C. Nothing suggests that the heroes of these plays were anything more than bad-tempered men who objected to extravagance and human society. This then was the obvious forecast for the audience to make of Knemon, and if we are right in supposing that he wore an old-fashioned, bad-tempered looking mask, the mask would confirm their views. In the first three acts this forecast seems to be confirmed again and again, not least when it appears that Knemon is not a poor man at all but insists on living as a poor man although he is quite well off. But when he makes his, as he supposes, death-bed speech to his family, he justifies his conduct; he had withdrawn into solitude because he saw that all men were governed by purely mercenary motives. Gorgias' disinterested action in saving him has charmed him out of his isolation far enough to make his dispositions for his wife and daughter and to make his final proclamation of faith: 'if all men were like me, there would not be law courts nor would they hale each other to prison nor would there be war, but each would have his modicum and be content'. This is true, unpractical perhaps but undeniably true; it restamps Knemon as an idealist and suggests that the comparison which we made earlier with the statuette of a philosopher was not wholly unjustified.

Masks and costumes can give a much closer approximation to reality than the stage-building and its modest possibilities of scenery. But the reality to which they approximate is only external appearance. Imagination has to supplement production is creating a detailed picture of the characters themselves as well as of the world in which they live, and may succeed in giving them a reality which not only completes but also transcends their external appearance. This is a subtle and civilized form of comedy. The wedding-bells ring at the end and the young lovers at least are happy. But they have not achieved their happiness without a considerable struggle, and in the course of the struggle a depth and complexity of character is revealed, either in them or in those who help them or hinder them, which goes beyond what could be predicted even from the diversified and ingenious masks of New Comedy, and in the revelation a truly humane ideal is asserted. Menander's fertility of invention and the complexity of his plots survive translation into Latin. Plautus has heightened the colours and altered the emphases so much that the original outlines of the characters can only be perceived with difficulty. Terence is at best like a Roman copy of a Greek statue; the outlines are well preserved but the bloom and life is largely lost. To appreciate them we must turn to what survives in the original Greek. (pp. 1-20)

T. B. L. Webster, "The Comedy of Menander," in Roman Drama, *edited by T. A. Dorey and Donald R. Dudley, Basic Books, Inc., Publishers, 1965, pp. 1-20.*

Geoffrey Arnott (essay date 1975)

[*Arnott considers the ways in which Menander anticipated such modern literary techniques as the use of dialogue to link scenes, verbal idiosyncracies to aid characterization, and dramatic irony.*]

Is Menander, in any sense of the word, 'modern'? And if he is, what relevance does this have to the quality of his plays? Such questions will perhaps be asked more in our present age, when some of our critics appear to idolize modernity in art, literature, or music at the expense of quality; and they are questions capable of a wide variety of positive answers. In one way Menander is modern because a large section of his work—the ***Dyskolos,*** several hundred lines complete of the ***Aspis*** and the ***Samia,*** significant fragments of several other plays—has been discovered in Egypt and printed for the first time during the last sixteen years. Or again, Menander is modern because indirectly at least he has influenced the modern world's comedy of manners down to the time of Oscar Wilde and P. G. Wodehouse. He is modern, too, because he writes about the recurrent problems of families, young and old alike, as they wrestle with love and greed, worry about status and reputation, and flounder in a morass of misconceptions. But the aspect of Menander's modernity that interests me most of all is his *apparent* concern with certain dramatic and stylistic techniques which living writers deliberately apply in their novels and plays, techniques which our modern critics love to label as undisputedly modern.

Before we examine this aspect of Menander's modernity, however, there is a danger that must be recognized. When we observe one example of a particular technique in a modern novel, we can relate it to a host of other examples in other novels and plays, and adjudge its intention and function by comparing the intentions and functions of those other examples. And if, despite all our comparisons, we are still doubtful about our original example, we can always write to the author for clarification or alternatively burrow ourselves in the extensive background material—notes, earlier drafts, essays, interviews and the like—that modern authors drown themselves in.

Let me illustrate this point from a novel about the life of some American artists and intellectuals first published in 1955, Mary McCarthy's *A Charmed Life.* In the fifth chapter there is a conversation in Dolly Lamb's shack between Dolly, an unmarried painter of 32, and her friend Martha Sinnott, the heroine of the novel, who is one year older and twice married. This chapter closes with the following words:

> Dolly drew her thumb slowly across her jaw. She frowned. Her neat dish face wore a mazed look of consternation. She shook herself, dog style, and went on, still frowning, to pick up the tea things. 'You must not be *shocked*', she said to herself aloud, in stern bell tones, as she headed towards the little kitchen.

The following chapter opens with a conversation between Dolly and another character of the novel in that same shack next morning:

> 'You mustn't be shocked by anything. That's the first lesson for the artist', said Sandy Gray, seriously. He was a tall Australian with a brown beard who had formerly been an art critic on an English magazine.

The repetition of those apologetic words 'You must not be shocked', in two different contexts at the end of one chapter and the beginning of the next, is an effective little trick of technique. Two otherwise disparate conversations are thus unobtrusively linked together, and continuity is achieved. But how do we know that this particular repetition *is* deliberate, and not just a casual freak lacking all significance? We know, of course, because this one example from a Mary McCarthy novel is not an isolated phenomenon. Nowadays we are persistently bombarded with examples of this literary device in one television play after another. The technique has become a literary cliché, and it is unlikely that a careful writer like Mary McCarthy would have descended to the cliché without deliberate intention. There is a further point. The authoress focuses our attention on the phrase which is going to be repeated by italicizing its dominant word 'shocked' on its first occurrence.

But what has this to do with Menander? Let me cite two parallel instances from the ***Dyskolos,*** a play first published from the Bodmer codex just three years after the novel by Mary McCarthy. In the third act of the ***Dyskolos,*** Sikon the butcher-cook tries to borrow a skillet from Knemon, and is violently rebuffed. Before he goes off at the end of the scene into the shrine of Pan, he muses on his experience:

> Must one try another door? Though if
> They're *so* quick with their boxing lessons here,
> I foresee snags!—Will it be best to roast
> All this meat? That's the answer! I've a dish.
> Farewell to Phyle (Φυλασιοισ) ! I'll use what
> I've got.

Sikon departs. The stage is empty. Next Sostratos enters, trudging stiffly on to the stage after his unaccustomed labours under the hot Mediterranean sun. Sostratos' opening words are:

> If anybody's short of troubles, let
> Him come to Phyle ('επι Φυλην) for the hunting.

Is this double mention of Phyle, at the end of one scene and the beginning of the next, also a calculated effect, designed like the example in the novel to link in its unobtrusive way two otherwise disparate scenes? Or is it just an insignificant accident, something that Menander never intended and may not even have noticed? Differing answers have been given to these questions. Some scholars have assumed the intention, describing the repetition as 'a delicate and clever device' [Max Treu, in the appendix to his edition of ***Dyscolos***]; others have been more sceptical. As Bishop Thirlwall wrote [in *Philological Museum,* II (1833)] over a hundred and forty years ago, 'it is a most difficult and delicate task, to determine the precise degree in which a dramatic poet is conscious of certain bearings of his words, and of the ideas which they suggest to the reader.' Literary critics always run the risk of overinterpreting, of being misled by enthusiasm and prejudice into explaining subtleties that the author never put into his text; and when that author is an ancient dramatist like Menander, whose texts are unsupported by scholia or any evidence of contemporary detailed interpretation, the risk of chasing will-o'-the-wisps into treacherous bogs is all the greater.

And yet it can, I think, be argued convincingly that Menander's repetition of Phyle was a deliberate linking device: and not only because the two mentions come in succeeding lines (521-2 of the Greek text), in the very last line of one scene and the very first one of the next. The corroborating argument expands into the whole of Menander's literary environment, but it begins most appropriately with two successive scenes of the play we have already considered, and with those two same characters, Sostratos and Sikon. In the second act of the ***Dyskolos,*** Sostratos has persuaded Gorgias that his designs on Gorgias' stepsister are strictly honourable, and now he plans to spend a day in the sun thrusting a heavy mattock in the hard-baked Attic earth. Soliloquizing about his situation, he says:

> O honoured gods! The arguments you've used
> To put me off now, so you think, have made me
> twice
> As eager for the venture. If the girl
> Hasn't grown up in a horde of women, if
> She's ignorant of the vices in this life, and all
> The fears trumped up by aunts or nurses, if her
> life's
> Been, well, sincere, just with a father who's
> A natural foe to vice—why then, it *must*
> Be bliss to win her! But this mattock weighs
> Four talents, it'll kill me first. No slacking,
> though,
> Once I've begun to sweat at this affair!

With such disgruntled words about the mattock he is carrying, Sostratos leaves the stage. The scene is ended. And on to the empty stage comes Sikon with a sheep. His opening words are also a soliloquy:

> This sheep here is no ordinary beauty—damn
> And blast it to perdition! If I lift it up
> And carry it in the air, its teeth lock on a shoot,
> It wolfs the fig-leaves, pulling hard away
> From my grip. If you lower it to the ground,
> Though, it won't budge. So here's a parodox:
> this sheep's
> Got me, the cook, all in a stew, through hauling
> it
> Along the road!

The technique, as you will have observed, is a more sophisticated variety of the one we noticed earlier in the third act, in a parallel dramatic situation. Sostratos leaves the stage with a soliloquy which ends virtually with a disgruntled reference to his mattock, the tool which is going to cause him so much trouble later. Then Sikon enters, and begins his soliloquy with a curse on the sheep he has with him, the animal which has already caused him so much trouble. Once again an unobtrusive little device links two disparate scenes together, although this time the echo is partly visual, partly implicit in the tone of the words spoken.

These two related instances of the link device come within two hundred lines of each other. Does this look like the accidents of chance? But whether my second example was already blueprinted in Menander's creative imagination long before he wrote out the text in detail, or whether it was a happy (dare I say even a semi-conscious?) inspiration of the last moment, one fact should be clear. It is a fact that close perusal of all Menander's work brings repeatedly to light. Menander, at whatever level of his mind, responded eagerly to patterns and parallelisms, both in word and in structure.

This will seem less surprising if we view Menander's work against its cultural background. The debt of Menander to fifth-century Attic tragedy is as well known as those of Manzoni to Scott or of Tolstoy to Dickens. Verbal and visual patterning was a literary device at least as early as Aeschylus. Aeschylus, for example, was fond of ending long speeches with a verbal or sense echo of their beginnings, in the technique that scholars now call 'ring composition'. Or again, Aeschylus and Euripides on occasions in their choral odes would balance significant themes against each other by placing the same or an emphatically contrasted word in the identical metrical position of both strophe and antistrophe. And there is a further point that critics of ancient comedy neglect at their peril. Menander was a poet of the Hellenistic period, and it would be only natural if he was infected with some of the mannerisms which characterize the Alexandrian poetry of his near-contemporaries. The song competitions in Theocritus are loaded with parallelisms and deliberate echoes. Transitions from one section to the next in Callimachus' *Hymns* are regularly marked by instances of verbal legerdemain. Is a parallel preoccupation with scenic links and balances so unexpected then in Menander?

At the same time it is necessary to observe that Menander's experiments with link devices and echo techniques are not limited to the ends and beginnings of successive scenes, or exploited only in the ways I have already discussed in this paper. Three further examples of these devices in the Bodmer plays will indicate clearly, I hope, the variety and subtlety of Menander's aims.

The first example is taken again from the ***Dyskolos.*** It comes towards the end of the first act. Young Sostratos is in love, you will remember, and the sudden appearance of his sweetheart before him leads him first to rhapsodize and secondly to offer his help. The girl is in difficulties. She needs to draw some water for Knemon's bath, and she cannot use the well. Sostratos offers to fill her jar from the spring in the shrine of Pan, and she agrees. As he leaves the stage to get the water, he bewails his enslavement by Eros:

> O honoured gods,
> What heavenly power could save me?

The girl is now alone. Immediately she hears a door opening. She is terrified:

> Woe is me,
> Who made that noise? Is daddy coming out?
> I'll get a hiding if he finds me here
> Outside!

There is a pleasant irony in the tonal echo here. Two young characters, whose marriage will end the play, bewail their individual miseries in what I take to be a deliberate juxtaposition of balancing exclamations. 'What heavenly power could save me?' says Sostratos, going off; 'Woe is me' echoes the girl, in the same line of verse. Each of the pair is totally absorbed in his and her own emotion, and the juxtaposition of the exclamations lightly underscores the parallelism of their separate reactions.

For my second example I shall turn to that memorable opening scene in the ***Aspis,*** the third play in the Bodmer codex. The faithful slave Daos has returned from Lycia with his master's booty and a buckled shield. Daos has good reasons for believing that his master was killed in action against the natives. In this scene, Daos describes the aftermath of the battle, and is quizzed by the elderly miser Smikrines, whose eyes linger covetously on the wealth Daos has brought home with him. It is important to notice how, in the following dialogue, Daos focuses attention on Smikrines' covetousness by two deadly last words in successive remarks:

> SMIKRINES. You say you've brought
> Six hundred gold staters?
>
> DAOS. Yes.
>
> SMIKRINES. Silver cups as well?
>
> DAOS. Perhaps weighing forty minas, hardly more, O heir apparent (Κληρονομε)!
>
> SMIKRINES. What? Tell me, do you think
> That's why I ask? Apollo! And the rest
> Were seized?
>
> DAOS. About the biggest part, except for what I got at first. In there we've clothes and cloaks. There's this crowd you see here—all yours (οικειον)!

In both of his last remarks Daos modulates his tone of objective description into a direct attack on Smikrines' greed, by appending on each occasion a final word (Κληρονομε οικειον) that calls attention to Smikrines' craving for the booty. Smikrines is the head of the family to which the missing warrior belongs, and has plans to acquire the inheritance himself. The word-placing in Daos' remarks is delicately effective, and I believe we may safely argue that it was not an accidental *trouvaille* [lucky hit]. By Menander's time, poetry of several different genres had been exploiting for many generations the effectiveness of surprise last words. These produce, in Aristophanes, the παρα προσδοκιαν joke; in Anacreon, the stinging *double entendre;* in Asclepiades, clarification of a previous designed ambiguity. And in Menander—let us consider one final example of the technique.

In the fourth act of the ***Dyskolos*** Sostratos is once again alone on the stage, explaining how Knemon was rescued from the well by Gorgias, while he himself behaved like a moonstruck Michael Crawford up above:

> Gentlemen, by Demeter, by Asclepius,
> By all the gods, I've never in my life
> Seen anybody choose a better time
> For getting drowned—*nearly!* What paradise
> It's been! You see, we'd hardly got inside
> When Gorgias jumped right in the well, and up
> Above the girl and I—*did nothing!*

Twice in succession the final phrase in a sentence humorously qualifies the assertion in a slightly surprising way: 'a . . . time for getting drowned—nearly'; 'the girl and I', instead of helping, just 'did nothing'. Such delicacies must not, of course, be pressed too hard, or emphasized too much; they are minor details in the multiplex skills of a dramatist who recognized the importance of holding an audience's attention by a series of slight surprises, and who capitalized on his effects in a variety of ways. In my last quotation, for instance, those final words 'nearly' and 'did nothing' are partly mild examples of παρα προσ δοκιαν [contrary to expectations] humour, but partly also they add a delicate touch to the characterization of a man who is unaware that the self-absorption of a teenager in his love is always comic to an audience.

This last remark leads us appropriately to consider Menander's method of characterization, and to ask whether this too is an aspect of his modernity? Let us begin to answer this question by looking at a technique of characterization that has been appreciated more and more in the last few years: I refer to the individualizing touch given to characters in literature by their habitual use of certain words and phrases. We all observe examples of this in real life, and are consequently ready to assume that when novelists of the last two centuries have exploited such personalized tricks of speech, they have been imitating an aspect of real life. There is Dick Fletcher's fondness for the word 'howsomdever' in Scott's *The Pirate;* Edward Rochester's habit of beginning his addresses to Jane Eyre with the questioning oath 'What the deuce' in Charlotte Brontë's novel; Daniel Peggotty's favourite exclamation 'I'm gormed' in Dickens's *David Copperfield;* the list could be endless. I should like, however, to add just one more modern example to it, for a reason that will emerge directly. It comes in *A Charmed Life,* that novel of Mary McCarthy's to which I referred at the beginning of this paper. One of the heroine's friends is an innocent painter called Warren Coe, who has the habit of introducing his artless questions with the nonsensical cliché 'Pardon my French'. In this case we know for certain that Mary McCarthy took the trick of speech from real life. She herself [as quoted in Doris Grumbach's *The Company She Kept,* 1967] has confessed that

> the original of Warren, after the publication of the novel, was struck dumb for some time. He was unable to ask his usual questions or say things like, 'Pardon my French.' This left him without conversation.

If the linguistic mannerisms of Warren Coe are based on the observation of real life, what is the position of Menander in this respect? There certainly appears to be a group of Menandrean characters who are individualized by similar quirks of expression, as Professor Sandbach [in *Entretiens Hardt,* XVI (1970)] and other scholars have noted. In the ***Samia,*** for example, Demeas has the habit of attaching an unnecessary 'Tell me' (ειπε μοι) to his questions; in the ***Dyskolos*** the cook Sikon has a Micawberish preference for highly-coloured language and unusual words, and Knemon is the only character in Menander so far to address people with the insulting vocative 'Unholy villain' (ανοσιε). We cannot *prove* that such idiosyncrasies of language were deliberately planned by Menander on each occasion in order to individualize a character, just as we cannot *prove* that in doing what he did Menander was imitating real life. It will be more profitable, I think, to turn the present investigation into a rather different direction. If Menander was attempting to create a character's individuality only by giving him a unique set of speech mannerisms, we should be mildly interested, as literary critics, to note this and then pass on to topics of greater importance. But in fact Menander seems to have been attempting something far more complex: the creation of a dramatic character by a whole series of methods, partly linguistic and partly non-linguistic, but with the methods so interlocking that even a mannerism of speech becomes important not because it is an idiosyncratic mannerism, but rather because the significance of what is said in the mannerism may (not must) reveal something of the speaker's character.

Let me explain this intricate claim by the example of old Knemon in the ***Dyskolos.*** In addition to his penchant for the abusive phrase 'Unholy villain', he seems to have at least two other noticeable peculiarities of speech. First, in his descriptions and reflections, Knemon is an exaggerator. He prefers the universal black and the absolute white to moderating greys. When he appears on stage for the first time, before the terrified Sostratos, his opening words are charged with the ideas of 'all' and 'nothing'. Perseus, he says (153-9), met *no* pedestrians, but could turn *all* vexatious people to stone, and if Knemon possessed Perseus' gimmick, there'd be *nothing* more common than stone statues *everywhere.* Knemon had just previously been accosted on his lonely hill farm by a single slave: this he exaggerates into:

> Today men trespass on my land and—talk!
> You think I usually spend my time along
> The roadside? I don't cultivate at all
> That part of my land, I've abandoned it because
> Of all the travellers. Now, though, they chase me up
> On to the hill-tops. Oh, the teeming, swarming crowds!

When Sostratos plucks up courage to address him a moment later, Knemon accuses Sostratos of turning his lonely hill road into a portico or the shrine of Leos (173), two places where crowds gathered and jostled; exaggeration once again. Indeed it is noticeable that hereabouts Knemon addresses Sostratos not as an individual but always in the second person plural, five times (173, 175 twice, 176 twice), before storming angrily off-stage. These details must not individually be overstressed; some of them may have been formulated only in the semi-conscious intuitions of Menander; but they all tend in one direction, the individualization of a character by his choice of expressions.

The second linguistic mannerism in Knemon's role is revealed not so much by what he says, but by how he says it. In the prologue of the ***Dyskolos*** Knemon is described as a man not given to conversation:

> He's lived a good long time
> And never spoken willingly to anyone
> In his life, never been the first to greet a man,
> With one exception: me, his neighbour, Pan.
> He's forced to greet me when he passes, and
> *That* makes him rueful right away, I know for sure!

Then later, in his long fourth-act speech of self-justification, Knemon characterizes himself in similar terms: 'the man who didn't say "Good morning", didn't speak a friendly word' (726), and 'I don't think a man should say more than he needs to' (740 f.). Here, of course, Menander has a problem. How can a dramatist portray Knemon's taciturnity when at the same time he wants to write a long speech for him which justifies his past life? Menander's answer to this question, I venture to think, is given by the shape of the climactic section of Knemon's speech. The old man's instructions for the disposal of his estate are couched in laconic clauses. Unnecessary words are excluded. Even connecting particles are reduced to a minimum. The following translation attempts to reproduce the style of the original as closely as possible:

Treat all I possess as yours.
I appoint you guardian of my daughter here. And find her a
Husband. Even if I did get better, I could never track
One down. Nobody will ever satisfy *me.* All the same,
If I do live, let me live as I like! You take over and
Run the rest. You're sensible, the gods be thanked, and you are your
Sister's natural protector. Split my property in two;
Give the girl half for her dowry, with the other half provide
For your mother and me.

But where does this catalogue of linguistic idiosyncrasies get us? Details of this kind may be as useful as the Identikit drawing of a criminal for identification purposes, but usually they touch only the surface of a personality. In Menander, however, they penetrate more deeply. Knemon's use of the vocative 'Unholy villain', for example, marks him off from the play's other characters as distinctively as Mr. Peggotty's 'I'm gormed' or Warren Coe's 'Pardon my French'; but it also reflects Knemon's despairing isolation from the rest of mankind—all his interlocutors seemed to him 'unholy' because he believed that the world had rejected real friendship (718 f.), had sold its soul to Mammon (721), and so had become an unholy world. And all the other linguistic traits that I have illustrated—Knemon's fondness for absolute words like 'all' or 'nothing', his tendency to exaggerate single instances into general rules—all these are merely the external symptoms of the malaise of a fanatic, a man whose image of life is clearly outlined to him in simple black and white, an image that is uncomplicated and universally applicable. Such men as Knemon, says Menander, do exaggerate, do oversimplify, do produce their blunt solutions.

Thus far we have considered Menander's exploitation of language, tone, and word-placing for the linkage of scenes, the pointing of emphasis, and the creation of individuality of character. I should like to turn now away from these in a new but obviously related direction, towards Menander's use of language for certain types of dramatic irony. Here Menander has some interesting extensions of earlier techniques, although his debts to both comic and tragic forebears must never be disregarded.

Theater ticket from Alexandria, Egypt, one side depicting Menander holding a mask, the other side inscribed with his name.

Let me begin with two instances, perhaps trivial in themselves but, if my interpretations are correct, suggestive of the subtlety of Menander's art. Both instances are taken from the ***Aspis.*** The first comes towards the end of the first act. When news of the death of that soldier in action was received at the house of Chairestratos, the wedding that was going to take place that day between the soldier's sister and her fiancé had to be postponed, and a cook who had been hired for the occasion was sent packing. Here is that cook, grumbling to Spinther, his assistant:

This job I took ten days ago;
My fee, three drachmas. I came and thought these were
Already mine. A corpse has come from Lycia
And snatched them clean away. A blow like this
Falls on the house, you temple-robber (ιεροσυλε), you
See women crying and beating their breasts—
And then you leave with your case empty! Just
Remember what a chance you had! I've got a help
Who's honest—Aristides, not Spinther!

Ancient cooks, on the comic stage at least, had a bad reputation for pilfering from their employers. Here Menander's cook refers directly to that reputation when he pours scorn on Spinther for not removing some of his employer's property in his case, but behaving instead like Aristides the Just. But the insulting name that the cook calls Spinther is 'Temple-robber' (Ιερογυλε); and although this seems to have been a contemporary insult in Athens of very general application, an appealing irony clearly emerges out of this choice of epithet. Spinther is called a 'temple-robber' precisely because he has failed to rob his employers.

It is a well-known fact that the tradition of upside-down humour goes back at least as far as Aristophanes and Old Comedy, but Menander's custom is to exploit such irony implicitly rather than explicitly, lightly with a passing hint rather than heavily by emphatic underlining. It is Menander's normal way with hackneyed techniques. When predecessors had been content with the traditional patterns of humour, Menander preferred to develop, to imply, and to reverse the comic clichés.

For an example of irony on a grander scale than this one comic detail, we must turn to the third act of the ***Aspis.*** Daos has now transformed himself into a prototypal

Jeeves. Smikrines has announced that he intends to marry the lost soldier's sister himself, and by so doing he will acquire all the wealth that the soldier had won on his campaign. A plan is needed to foil Smikrines' design, and Daos' fertile brain invents one. Smikrines' brother, Chairestratos, is far wealthier than the missing soldier. If Chairestratos pretends to die, Daos suggests, Smikrines will be deflected from the intention of marrying the soldier's sister, and will make a beeline for Chairestratos' much wealthier daughter. The plan is put into action. Chairestratos pretends to be at death's door. When the third act opens, Daos finds Smikrines alone on the stage. The charade begins. Daos pretends not to see Smikrines at first, as he soliloquizes about the dreadful calamity, the crashing, smashing thunderbolt that has struck the house; and Smikrines pricks up his ears. Daos was the lost soldier's *paedagogus* [slave who escorted him to school], and now he shows himself to be an infuriatingly educated man, as he quotes line after line of Greek tragedy, all apposite to the sad occasion:

> DAOS. 'There lives no man who prospers over
>   all':
> Again, supremely good! Most [reverend gods],
> How unforeseen and [grievous] an affair!
>
> SMIKRINES. Daos, you devil, where's the rush?
>
> DAOS. This too, perhaps:
> 'The affairs of men not providence but chance':
> Superb. 'God plants the guilt in mortal men
> When he will blight a house completely': Aes-
>   chylus,
> Of noble words the—
>
> SMIKRINES. Citing mottoes, you
> Pathetic worm?
>
> DAOS. 'Creditless, senseless, dread'—
>
> SMIKRINES. Won't he stop, ever?
>
> DAOS. 'What, of mortal woes,
> Is past belief?' So Carcinus says. 'In
> One day god brings the victor to defeat':
> All these are jewels, Smikrines!
>
> SMIKRINES. What do
> You mean?
>
> DAOS. Your brother—O Zeus, how shall I
> Tell it?—is at death's door!

It is tempting to continue quoting, just as in fact Daos does; but this is an essay on Menander, not a dramatic performance. We must stick to the point; and one point of all these tragic quotations is their veiled irony. There are, of course, other points, too; Menander is a one-man band. The passage I have just quoted is openly comic, and exploits a favourite trick of comic writers—delaying tactics in order to frustrate a premature climax of revelation. The passage also serves to characterize Daos as a learned *paedagogus.* And then there is the irony—irony of a particularly Hellenistic kind, that we find exploited in the epigrams of Meleager's *Garland* and the longer poems of Callimachus, for example. The technique is to place a phrase or sentence which is susceptible of two different meanings at an early stage in the poem or drama, and then later on to clarify the ambiguous potentialities in one or both ways.

In Menander the ambiguity was presented in a scene shortly before Daos appeared with his tragic quotations. It was the time when Daos first introduced the details of his stratagem for hoodwinking Smikrines. Here Daos says to Chairestratos (329 f.), 'You must perform a sombre tragedy' (δει τραγωδησαι παθοσ αλλοιον υμασ). Professor Sandbach translates the words τραγωδησαι παθοδ αλλοιον with the phrase 'stage a tragic unpleasant performance', and of course the uppermost reference here is to the charade of Chairestratos' pretended death and the consequent mourning around the corpse. That constitutes a true paratragic παθοσ. But language may operate for Menander, just as it does sometimes for more modern poets like Donne or Empson, at two levels simultaneously; and I should like to think that with this phrase Menander is also subsuming a reference to the scene in which Daos hurls that volley of tragic quotations at the bemused Smikrines. After all, τραγωδησαι παθοσ is also capable of the translation 'surround a sad event with tragic language'. Such designed ambiguities abound in Hellenistic poetry, and it is not just my admitted fondness for Ximenes's crossword clues that leads me to see a possible ambiguity in Menander's words here. Menander did play this game elsewhere, and nowhere more elegantly than in the final speech of the ***Dyskolos,*** where the speaker asks the audience to applaud if they have enjoyed 'the way we've triumphed over this troublesome humgruffin' (965 f.: κατηγωνισμενοισ ημιν τον εργωδη γεροντα); but these same words are intended to mean 'the way we've acted the ***Dyskolos*** to the end'.

And in discussing Menander's modernity I have left one final topic to the end, too. This is Menander's ability to focus attention on the vivid, significant detail that lays bare a labyrinth of feelings and emotions. Menander, like Charles Dickens, could have said, 'I feel the story to its minutest point' [Q. D. and F. R. Leavis, in their *Dickens the Novelist,* 1970]. One such minute point reveals a world of emotion in the third act of the ***Perikeiromene.*** Polemon has been deserted by Glykera, the girl whom he loves, and suddenly he is overcome by the sight of the wardrobe of clothes that she has left behind:

> POLEMON. Pataikos, please, just look!
> You'll sympathize more with me.
>
> PATAIKOS. O Posidon!
>
> POLEMON. Come over here. What dresses! How
>   she looks
> When she's slipped one of these on—you might
>   not
> Have seen her?
>
> PATAIKOS. Yes, I have.

It is a small, precisely observed detail, the way that a lover betrays his emotion by making a small fetish of his beloved's clothes. The same detail, oddly enough, turns up again in F. Scott Fitzgerald's novel *The Great Gatsby.* In chapter five of this novel Daisy is similarly overcome by seeing the shirts of the man she loves:

> He took out a pile of shirts and began throwing them, one by one, before us, shirts of sheer linen and thick silk and fine flannel, which lost their folds as they fell . . . Suddenly, with a strained sound, Daisy bent her head into the shirts and began to cry stormily.
>
> 'They're such beautiful shirts', she sobbed, her voice muffled in the thick folds. 'It makes me sad because I've never seen such—beautiful shirts before.'

Had Fitzgerald come across a translation of the ***Perikeiromene*** and noted the detail, or was it a simple coincidence of two dissimilar authors 'feeling the story to its minutest point'?

Whatever the answer to this question, let us take our leave of Menander with a final glance at another small, precisely observed detail, the more gruesome one of dead bodies on the battlefield. It comes in the ***Aspis,*** where Daos is describing what he did after the battle in which his master was thought to have died:

> SMIKRINES. And did you see him lying there among the dead?
>
> DAOS. His body I couldn't identify for sure.
> They'd been out in the sun three days, their faces were
> Bloated.
>
> SMIKRINES. Then how could you be certain?
>
> DAOS. There
> He lay, with his shield. Buckled and bent—that's why
> None of the natives took it, I suppose.

Of course, one very important reason why Menander bloated the faces of the corpses and buckled the soldier's shield was simply the mechanism of the plot. It was necessary for Daos to be plausibly misled by the presence of his master's shield on the arm of an unidentifiable corpse into believing that his master was dead. But was this the only reason for Menander's gruesome picture? On a previous occasion [in *Leeds University Review* XIII (1970)] I suggested that Menander had another purpose in view, as well. Because Menander lived in an Athens tortured by war, famine, and disease, he chose a vivid detail that brought home the harsh reality of war, and thus stripped off for a moment the veneer of conventional comedy in order to bare the skeleton beneath the fine clothes. This was my own personal reading of the passage, but not everybody has interpreted it in the same way. Professor Lloyd-Jones claims [in *Greek, Roman, and Byzantine Studies* XII (1971)] that it is wrong to read such harsh realities into the light entertainment of Menander, and his view deserves the most serious consideration. It is impossible to say how many of Menander's audience had fought as mercenaries, like Daos' master, in Asia, or even as citizen soldiers in battles fought as near to Athens as Rhamnus. What would their reaction have been to Daos' description of bloated corpses and a buckled shield? I cannot unfortunately call up from the dead any such member of Menander's audience, not even for the annual spring meeting of the Classical Association; but I can at least produce a more modern Greek as a witness of impeccable credit. In his novel *The Fratricides,* which deals with the bitter Greek civil war of the 1940s, Nikos Kazantzakis similarly embeds a vivid, precisely observed detail of harsh realism in more idyllic surroundings:

> The snow on the hilltop had begun to melt, the sun became stronger, the frozen earth began to thaw. The first green blades of grass fearfully pierced the earth. A few humble wildflowers peeped from underneath the stones, anxious to see the sun. Great silent powers were at work beneath the earth. Winter's tombstone lifted—it was the resurrection of Nature. A mild breeze blew, bringing at times the scent of wildflowers from the moss-covered rocks, at times the stench of decaying bodies.

It is a small, perhaps even a trivial point of contact between two Greeks who both lived through civil war and had seen, at least with the eye of imagination, decomposing corpses on quiet battlefields. Such points must be given their due notice, but not, of course, be overemphasized, whether as details in much grander wholes, or as evidence for any parallelism of view between modern and ancient Greece, or even as the final argument in support of my brief on the modernity of Menander. (pp. 140-53)

Geoffrey Arnott, "The Modernity of Menander," in Greece & Rome, *Vol. XXII, No. 2, October, 1975, pp. 140-55.*

THE GIRL FROM SAMOS

CRITICAL COMMENTARY

Sander M. Goldberg (essay date 1980)

[*In this study of* The Girl from Samos, *Goldberg demonstrates how Menander uses complex characterization and other dramatic techniques to transform the traditional comic plot of an obstructed marriage into a poignant and original play.*]

Like most Menandrean prologues, the speech with which young Moschion opens the ***Samia*** introduces the central characters, provides necessary background information, and indicates the direction of the action to come. It functions much like Pan's prologue to the ***Dyskolos*** or the speeches by Misapprehension and Fortune in the ***Perikeiromene*** and ***Aspis,*** except for one significant detail. Menander generally uses a divine prologue speaker to colour our perceptions of his characters and situations and to shape our expectations, often by including a piece of information human characters do not know: Glykera was actually embracing her brother, Kleostratos is alive, Sostratos' love has been engineered by a god. Divinities who speak prologues emphasize the distance between audience and actors by sharing their omniscience and by reminding us that the figures on stage are subject to their greater power. There is no suggestion of a greater power in the ***Samia*** and no distance fostered between audience and actors. The figures of this play are all too responsible for their own actions, and our perceptions are coloured not so much by our omniscience as by our frustration at the sight of good intentions continually hampered by weakness of character. Moschion's marriage to the girl next door, a universally desired union, is jeopardised by his reluctance to admit an embarrassing truth. Moschion's father Demeas suddenly disrupts his own relationship with the Samian woman Chrysis because of hasty, ill-founded suspicions. The action combines the obstructed marriage found in the ***Dyskolos*** with the disrupted union of the ***Perikeiromene*** and ***Misoumenos.*** The sequence of misunderstandings that weaves the two situations into a plot develops not so much from lack of knowledge as from the fear to use it. The action of the ***Samia*** is preeminently a product of character, and the need for special care in characterisation leads Menander to abandon the divine prologue and open his play with an expository speech by Moschion himself.

Strepsiades' complaint about his son at the beginning of Aristophanes' *Clouds* reminds us that the relationship between father and son—the main theme of Moschion's narrative—is a common motif in Greek comedy. Having married the niece of an aristocrat, a 'Megakles' Megakles', the plain and hard-working Strepsiades has produced a son of extravagant, sophisticated tastes. Strepsiades must now deal with the resulting debts, and his resentment and desire to avoid payment eventually lead him to Socrates' Reflectory. In *The Wasps* Aristophanes builds a different set of actions around a similar dilemma by reversing roles; the son cannot control the father. The old man Philokleon, like the young Plautine lovers Strabax in the *Truculentus* and Philolaches in the *Mostellaria,* must woo a flute girl with promises contingent upon the death of his son, who is a harsh cress-shavingcuminsplitter. As in *The Clouds,* the dramatic action develops out of the conflict between generations. For the ***Samia*** Menander inverts the dilemma and refashions the expository device of *The Clouds.* Like Strepsiades' wife and son, Moschion has been raised in luxury, but it is with his father's encouragement. Demeas adopted Moschion as a child and gave him every advantage. Whereas Strepsiades complained about sophisticated living, Moschion's prologue glows with the vocabulary of urbane virtues. He prides himself on his sophistication. He has been cheerfully granted horses and dogs, and he has learned to be generous in his turn. The possessor of all these virtues and advantages has nevertheless got himself into a terrible fix, and his explanation shows far better then he realizes both how he got into it and why he will be unable to extricate himself unaided.

While Demeas was away Moschion got the neighbour's daughter pregnant and promised to marry her. The girl bore a child, which Chrysis is now raising as her own, and he awaits his father's return with understandable anxiety. But Moschion cannot state matters so baldly. He is suffering keenly from a shame and embarrassment that colour his entire narrative. He delays telling the crucial facts, first by describing Demeas' character, and then by describing the festive circumstances under which the rape took place. He uses the story of the festival to work up to the main point, which he then hurries over as quickly as possible: 'The girl became pregnant. In telling this I also say what went before' (49-50). Then he buries the admission in an emphatic declaration of responsibility and of honourable intentions. The difficulty he foresees is in securing Demeas' agreement to the marriage, and to show why this is so, Moschion attempts to explain what Demeas is like. Moschion's real source of difficulty, however, is his inability to see beyond his own limited perspective, and this is what the description of Demeas actually demonstrates. He speaks of Demeas only in terms of himself. His verbs are almost entirely first person singulars; adjectives refer to himself. 'Through him', says Moschion, 'I was somebody' (17). He offers hismelf as the measure of what Demeas is, and in doing so he turns an analysis of the father into a portrait of the son. Nor, when speaking of Demeas' liaison with Chrysis, can he keep himself out of the picture. Foremost in Moschion's mind is the embarrassment of his own current predicament.

> I hesitate to tell the rest. Perhaps I'm ashamed.
> There's no help for it, yet I *am* ashamed.
> (47-8)

This kind of embarrassment is fairly common among the indiscreet young men of comedy. 'I'm only afraid to face the father,' a lover tells his friend in an unidentified fragment of Menander. 'I won't be able to look him in the eye, since I've wronged him.' In ascribing a similar feeling to his father, however, Moschion is simply projecting his own sense of shame onto Demeas. Similarly, his condescension in explaining Demeas' attachment as 'a human enough occurrence' and his claim to have encouraged the liaison stamp the account with his own personality. That Demeas was reluctant to have his son involved is certainly credible, but we have only Moschion's testimony for the reason.

This speech demonstrates three things about Moschion. First is his remarkable egotism. He tells us his story because *he* has the time, and he explains every character and action in terms of his own feelings and conduct. Second is his moral cowardice. He hesitates to speak of the rape and shrinks from telling his father. Even his protestations of honourable intentions is suspect because of its very earnestness, and indeed, his slave Parmenon must soon remind him quite bluntly of his obligations (67-9). Third is his foolishness. His attempt to avoid one charge will involve the innocent Chrysis in a second, more serious one. Moschion can neither see the implications of his acts, nor is he willing to take responsibility for them. By having him speak for himself, Menander enables these aspects of his personality to permeate the narrative. When divinities portray character their terse descriptions are subordinate to a greater design. The portrait of that other Moschion in the ***Perikeiromene,*** of Smikrines in the ***Aspis,*** and even Pan's description of Knemon are accorded due, but limited place in a sequential narrative. Though these figures may influence the play's direction, they will be overcome by events turning not exclusively on their personalities but on the emergence of an unsuspected truth or a sudden catastrophe. Moschion's loquaciousness here in the ***Samia*** and the lack of anything entirely unknown create a different set of priorities.

The personalities of the fathers Demeas and Nikeratos will also shape the action, and their first appearance delineates and distinguishes between them. They enter from the harbour with their baggage train, newly arrived from Pontos and very glad to be home (96ff.). Demeas clearly commands. He instructs the porters and leads the conversation, changing topics from their safe arrival to the marriage between their children that they have previously discussed. His is the quick-witted, dominant personality, and Nikeratos looks to him for answers. Nikeratos himself is slower, and so more comic. He replies to Demeas first with a disjointed complaint about the food, drink, and people of Pontos that probably embodies stock jokes about the undesirability of the place. When Demeas answers his question about the weather there facetiously, Nikeratos takes him literally, and he must make Demeas' indirect reference to the proposed marriage explicit. Nikeratos is the first character presented as overtly and entirely comic. [Elsewhere] Menander uses such stock figures as a cook in the ***Aspis*** and ***Dyskolos*** to pace outbreaks of humour as the action requires. In the ***Samia,*** this function will reside largely in Nikeratos. This initial scene, in which Demeas' control of the conversation provides opportunities for Nikeratos' comedy, has a kind of structural parallel at ***Aspis*** 216-49, where Daos controls the action but becomes a foil for the cook and caterer. The dominance of Demeas' personality is countered by the humour in Nikeratos', and in the action to come Menander will draw upon his comic potential to control the emotional temperature of Demeas' most dramatic moments.

Demeas influences events largely through the quick temper and tendency toward precipitous action that are his main weaknesses. Both faults surface at once in Act II as he responds to the news of Chrysis' 'child' with a very ill grace. He refers to her with sardonic irony as a 'married hetaira' (130) and, if the restoration is correct, calls the child 'secret' (132). Since Chrysis' social position and that of any children by her union with Demeas depend upon his attitude toward them, the repudiation implied by his language is particularly serious. By calling the child clandestine, though he was certainly informed of it at the earliest possible moment, he presumably means that it was not conceived with his prior consent, an unreasonable but not unheard of attitude for a father to adopt. He wishes to put all the blame on Chrysis and to sever their relationship. At line 135 he refers to her in the masculine to emphasize her remoteness. Moschion meets this tirade first with feigned ignorance of its cause, and then with a studied glibness.

> [MOSCHION.] For heaven's sake, who among us is legitimate and who a bastard? We're all born men.
>
> [DEMEAS.] You're joking.
>
> [MOSCHION.] Dionysos! I'm entirely serious. I don't think birth determines breeding. Good character is the test. The honest man is legitimate, and the wicked one a bastard.
>
> (137-42)

The poignancy of these statements on legitimacy coming from an adopted son is gently undercut by our knowledge that Moschion has been off practising speeches (94-5). Though his mind drifted in other directions, fine phrases remain on the tip of his tongue. The papyrus is torn away at this point, but his arguments, whatever they were, must have been successful. Demeas apparently agreed to keep Chrysis and the child in his house, and when the text resumes after a gap of some sixteen lines, Moschion is winning his agreement to his own quick marriage. These expository scenes concentrate not on action but on character drawing to make the rapid sequence of actions to come seem credible and perhaps even inevitable. Demeas' display of anger in Act II engenders no immediate action, but it prefigures the attitude and action one further piece of information will cause him to take toward Chrysis.

The pace quickens in Act III as we begin to see the influence character will have on action. Demeas has had a shock, which he explains in a monologue similar in length and impact to Moschion's introduction. Just as Moschion's prologue centred on his embarrassment, so Demeas' monologue hinges on a central image, a nurse fondling an infant. In the bustle of preparations for the wedding the child was momentarily left unattended, and Demeas has overheard Moschion's old nurse soothe it with 'the sort of things nurses say' (242). Unfortunately for his peace of mind, one of these things indicated that the child is Moschion's. This central vignette is depicted in considerable detail and perhaps gains impact from its visual associations. Precisely such images of an old woman with a baby on her lap are common among the terracotta figurines of this period. As a structural unit in the monologue, it picks up the earlier mention of the child and looks ahead to Deméas' later, damning report that he has seen Chrysis herself nursing it. The monologue dramatises the growing impact of the discovery on Demeas. He begins with a solemn, ominous prologue to raise our expectations. A sudden storm at sea can turn a smooth voyage into a catastrophe, and this is what has happened to him. He then slips into domestic details. At the end of Act II we saw Demeas shouting instructions for the wedding preparations, and he now sketches the resulting turmoil (216ff.). We learn that the child was abandoned, that the nurse found it, and that she spoke indiscreetly. The impact of the news on Demeas is first indicated indirectly by his description of a second servant's alarm and haste to silence the nurse. Demeas himself struggles to maintain an outward calm. He wants to avoid hasty judgements, but he cannot really do so. His immediate, cold reference to 'the Samian woman' (265) recalls his earlier attempt at detachment from her, and his haste to reassure himself about Moschion's character implies an intention to fix the blame elsewhere. His temper is barely under control, and precipitous action is again in the offing.

The monologue's skillful construction provides this lucid description of offstage action simultaneously with the insight into Demeas' present mental state. Several techniques contribute to its effectiveness. *Oratio recta* enlivens the account as Demeas imitates the shouts of slaves, the nurse's chatter, and the anxious dialogue between nurse and servant. Such opportunities for mimickry add needed colour to the eighty odd lines of narrative, just as the messenger's speech in the ***Sikyonios,*** which was perhaps a hundred, requires the actor to imitate the pleas of litigants and the shouts of a crowd. A second technique is the blending of static and dynamic portraits. The detailed description of the nurse, previously unmentioned and never again more than a *muta persona,* and the second servant's anxious whispers are striking, isolated images. *Oratio recta* gives them momentary, independent life, but they are soon submerged in the rising tide of Demeas' indignation. As the old man mulls over what he has heard his verbs become almost entirely first person (265-79). Like Moschion, he instinctively subordinates others to himself. A third device is the direct appeal to the audience, marked here by the interjected vocative 'gentlemen' (*andres,* 269). This type of address is common in comedy, but in the extant parts of the ***Samia*** only Demeas uses it consistently. The informality of Moschion's opening speech created a certain rapport with the audience, and the immediacy of his prologue hinted at a special relationship to be developed with him. Menander, however, has played with the expectation. Demeas' frequent appeals to the audience establish that rapport with *him,* for the action is beginning to focus on Demeas.

Still from a 1954-55 production of Menander's The Girl from Samos *presented with fragments of his* The Arbitration *at Everyman's Theatre in New York City.*

Moschion left the stage at line 162 and will not appear again until Act IV. His concealment of the truth set the action in motion, and once he gained his father's approval of the marriage—a simple enough task since Demeas and Nikeratos both desired it—he can have little effect on the resulting complications. Demeas' discoveries and actions further the plot, and this monologue signals the increasing emphasis on his role. The familiar device of the overheard conversation both advances the action and alters its focus. Its use here makes a significant contrast with Menander's dramatisation of the analogous situation at ***Epitrepontes*** 878-932. An overheard conversation is the basic ingredient there, too, but the structure is rather different. Charisios has overheard Smikrines and Pamphile discussing him. Onesimos first enters as an *exangelos* to explain what has happened and how his master has reacted. Then Charisios appears to reveal the depth of his distress and his determination to save his marriage. Both monologues make considerable use of direct speech, Onesimos' reported and Charisios' projected, and both are lively and dramatic. Yet by dividing the scene between Charisios and Onesimos, Menander has effectively reduced the young man's role. Attention moves from Onesimos to Charisios and will soon move again from Charisios to Habrotonon. Because the action of the ***Epitrepontes*** turns on surrogates, Charisios' appearance is integrated into theirs. In the ***Samia*** Menander combines the function of the *exangelos* and soliloquist in a single monologue. Demeas speaks entirely for himself, and by having him do so Menander puts him at the very centre of the action.

There is, of course, a certain comic irony in Demeas' situation as he claims certain knowledge of Chrysis' maternity, the one thing about which he is actually in error. Yet there is also the potential for considerable poignancy. Because the relationship between Demeas and Moschion is only by adoption, it must depend on trust and good will between them. The possibility that Moschion has betrayed him with Chrysis threatens the very basis of their relationship, and that is why Demeas is reluctant even to voice that possibility. The anguish of his position is genuine, and, as we know from Euripides' *Hippolytos,* it can be tragic. Menander is moving his play close to the border between serious and light, and we may wonder for a moment which way things will turn. The entrance of Parmenon with a cook, however, is an unmistakable signpost (283ff.).

The cook, as so often in Menander, immediately introduces the broad humour characteristic of his type. There are the familiar jokes on making mincemeat, and his self-importance threatens a tiresome loquacity as he strings five if-clauses together in rapid succession. Parmenon answers in kind ('*if* you haven't noticed', 293), and the two trade insults. There is also the more subtle humour of Parmenon's blithe self-assurance on the threshold of disaster as Demeas waits to be recognized. The comedy of the following encounter is built from those weaknesses of Demeas' character that Act II revealed. He taxes Parmenon with the piece of truth he has just acquired without pausing to listen to an explanation that might reveal the rest. He is also violent, and his threats drive Parmenon off before he can speak. This refusal to listen confirms Demeas in his error. He resolves upon action, but where as his earlier monologue was balanced between serious and light, the speech in which he announces his resolve is predominantly light (325ff.).

What makes this second monologue comic? It is certainly not the content. As Demeas seeks to exonerate Moschion and save their relationship his willingness to judge his son by past conduct without extending the same generosity to Chrysis is manifestly unfair. He turns savagely on her, calling her 'my Helen' (337) and 'whore, creature, plague' (348). He is about to throw her out, and he announces his intention in a sentence marked by biting sarcasm and harsh alliteration: επι κεφαλην εσκορακασ ψσον την καλην Σαμιαν ('shove the handsome Samian on her head to Hell', 353-54). Yet the style and context undercut the seriousness of the content. Demeas begins with a string of tragic-sounding exclamations, but he interrupts himself in midcourse:

> O city of Kekrops' land,
> O outspread aether, O—Demeas, why are you shouting?
>
> (325-26)

The effort to master his emotions leads him away from tragic diction, and as he begins talking his manner becomes increasingly comic. His short, choppy sentences are characteristic of comic figures in distress, and he again addresses the audience directly. Sandwiched between these displays of emotion is the torturous chain of logic that works him up to this agitated pitch. He interprets Moschion's eagerness to marry as an attempt to escape from Chrysis, who must have seduced him when drinking.

> I just can't believe that a boy
> so well-bred and moderate in everything
> to others would do such a thing to me,
> not if he were adopted ten times over and no
> son by birth. It's not his way. I know his character.
> The woman's a whore, a plague.
>
> (343-48)

By making this chain explicit Menander enables us to identify its errors. Demeas has misinterpreted both Chrysis' character and Moschion's motive for wanting a quick marriage, and our ability to pinpoint these mistakes begins to develop the distance necessary for us to treat Demeas' anger as comedy. Context too strengthens the comic tone. We cannot take as entirely serious an old man who has just routed his slave with shouted threats. He appeals to us to see the logic of his position, but because we know both that his reasoning is faulty and that his farcical rage has just eliminated an opportunity to correct it, we are more aware of its comic lack of logic. The serious mode introduced by the dilemmas of Moschion and Demeas and the light mode represented by such characters as Nikeratos and the cook are beginning to converge as Demeas' anger turns toward action.

His expulsion of Chrysis is accompanied, as was his decision to do it, by a certain cruelty and harshness of expression. He bundles her unceremoniously out of the house with a few possessions and the baby in her arms. To avoid mentioning Moschion, Demeas can give her only an allusive explanation and finally hides his lack of coherent excuse in a torrent of abuse. It is a highly dramatic and potentially ugly scene. The frankness of his monologue and our awareness of his error, however, have created an amused sympathy for his predicament that is incompatible with harsh action. Menander therefore tempers the scene with a touch of comedy. The cook returns just as Demeas is about to charge inside to rout Chrysis. His glimpse of 'some crazy old man' puts the required comic perspective on Demeas' behaviour while his aborted effort to intervene softens the drama with farcical action (383ff.). Once Demeas has slammed the door on Chrysis comedy resumes with the appearance of Nikeratos, whose offer of refuge is necessary for subsequent developments. Introducing the old man with a sheep facilitates the transition from the cook's comedy to Nikeratos', for complaints about an animal are a motif common to cook's speeches (399ff., cf. ***Dys.*** 393ff.). Like the cook, Nikeratos also passes judgement on the madness of Demeas' behaviour, and the silliness of his explanation—the unfavourable climate of Pontos has affected him—recalls the humour of their arrival and ends the act on a note of simple-minded charity. He is again the foil to Demeas, who is acquiring attributes of the angry old man familiar in comedy.

Act IV opens with the characters in these same apparent roles. Nikeratos remains simple and benign as he announces his intention to remonstrate with Demeas. Moschion, who has spent his day at the baths waiting for sundown, is as self-centred as ever. He does not return Nikeratos' friendly greeting, but voices his impatience in a continuation of his private thoughts (428-33). When Demeas joins them on-stage he is still angry and abusive. He again addresses the audience directly, and frequent asides will signal his growing confusion. Convinced that he knows 'everything', Demeas will become increasingly exasperated by Moschion's defence of Chrysis. Moschion does not seem to appreciate the sacrifices he has made to save their relationship, and Demeas' outrage at the young man's apparent shamelessness makes him abusive and willful as he finally challenges Moschion to admit the 'truth' to Nikeratos. The seriousness of Demeas' anguish is eclipsed by the comic irony of his misapprehension and the predicament into which he has unwittingly thrust his son. Only Nikeratos' slowness of wit saves the young man. Nikeratos has finally grasped the essence of Demeas' suspicion, and the combination of his over-stated denunciation and Moschion's bewilderment at what he can possibly have in common with such sinners as Tereus, Oedipus, Thyestes, and Phoenix turns the scene toward farce (495ff.). Nikeratos' speech is a jumble of the highflown and the mundane. *He,* he says, would immediately sell such a mistress and disinherit such a son,

> . . . so that no barbershop is empty,
> no, nor stoa, but everyone will sit around from dawn
> chattering of me, saying what a man Nikeratos
> has become, who rightly prosecutes a murder.
>
> (510-13)

Nikeratos consistently sprinkles his speech with the language of high poetry. He shows a tendency to call his bed a fourposter (λεκτρον, 507) and his house his hall (μελαθρα, 517). Here he attaches a tragic set of negatives to the mundane image of gossipers in barbershop and stoa, and the colloquial 'chatters' contrasts with the overblown 'murder' to describe the subject of their talk. Equally significant is Nikeratos' desire to be thought 'a man', for this was also Demeas' thought as he steeled himself to expel Chrysis (349). Nikeratos' indignation parodies Demeas' earlier indignation, and he will soon re-enact the earlier drama as farce.

With Nikeratos safely inside, Moschion at last tells his father the truth, but only to avoid the more serious charge (526ff.). He is as reluctant as ever to face his responsibility, and when Nikeratos returns evidently upset, Moschion scurries away. Sight of the baby being nursed has again caused a crisis as the outraged bystander suddenly discovers he is the true victim. Nikeratos has seen his daughter with the infant. The news confirms the truth of Moschion's confession but raises a new set of difficulties. Having recognised and repented over his error, Demeas now reverts to his quick-witted, reasonable self; Nikeratos becomes the madman. He is beside himself with rage, and once thwarted in an attempt to destroy the evidence by burning out his family, he reverts to the idea of expelling Chrysis. Whereas Demeas' expulsion of Chrysis was saved from complete seriousness only by the presence of the cook and Nikeratos' timely arrival, this second expulsion is farcical from the beginning. Nikeratos races to and from his house in agitated confusion. There are sounds of pandemonium within, and the scene will end in slapstick with the two old men coming to blows as Demeas protects the woman and child (574ff.). Secure in his newly acquired knowledge of the true situation, Demeas holds himself aloof from events as he comments on Nikeratos' character and actions (548-56, 563-67). Menander uses the rapport established with Demeas to heighten the comedy by contrasting his calm with Nikeratos' excitement. This calm eventually prevails as Nikeratos abandons his plan to burn the baby and murder his wife. Demeas exerts the same control over him that he demonstrated in the first act, making Nikeratos walk off his anger and turning his extravagant language against him with the argument that the child was fathered by Zeus, though Moschion will certainly marry the girl.

By reversing the roles of Act III Menander moves the play towards broad comedy. A change of metre signals this alteration in tone at the outset as the increased length and regularity of the trochaic tetrameter quickens the tempo. Nikeratos' simplicity makes him a far more comic angry old man than Demeas, and the contrast between his constant motion and Demeas' stationary calm heightens the effect. The pace of the action itself increases as the web of misunderstanding woven over the previous three acts unravels in a single act with the truth brought home to both fathers. This linear progression is attended, as in the ***Dyskolos*** finale, by an internal parallelism. Menander builds this rapid, farcical act out of the comic potential present from the beginning in Nikeratos' character and from elements of the earlier drama repeated with the opposite mode dominant. Sight of the child being nursed is again the catalyst, but this time announced by Nikeratos' hysterical shouts. Chrysis is again expelled, but this time by a foolish rather than anguished old man. Demeas calms his neighbour with an explanation of events as deft and facetious as his earlier explanation of the weather in Pontos, and the act ends with the two of them reaching the same accord they had reached in their first appearance. The emergence of the truth, attended by a progression from Demeas' anguish to Nikeratos' farce, returns us to the equilibrium with which the play began.

This combination of progression and parallelism to weave elements of the play together appears again in the finale as the dramatic focus returns to Moschion. His scheme to punish his father by feigning to enlist in military service abroad is a further manifestation of his characteristic egotism. He refuses to admit to himself that Demeas' momentary injustice to him was a natural consequence of his own irresponsible desire to hide the truth. Moschion affects indignation to avoid this admission, and the resulting speech, for all its tragic overtones, has a hollow ring. Despite his claim to be almost beside himself with emotion, he can still balance long clauses, and whereas Demeas' claim of indignation had steeled him to do something 'manly', Moschion expressly eliminates that possibility (630-31, cf. 349-50). All he really seeks is to shift the blame from himself, a desire Parmenon promptly articulates in a parallel monologue of his own (641-57). Parmenon's initial oath echoes Moschion's solemnity, but he goes on to disavow responsibility in the short sentences and self-address of comedy. His quick summary of the preceding action voices Moschion's implicit desire, and it echoes Demeas' earlier effort to excuse his son.

> My young master attacked a free-born
> girl. Parmenon certainly did nothing wrong.
> She got pregnant. Parmenon's not responsible.
> The little baby came into our own
> house. *He* brought it in, not I.
> Someone inside confessed the birth.
> What wrong did Parmenon do there?
> None.
>
> (646-53, cf. 328, 537)

The absurdity of Moschion's plan is brought home by Parmenon's ignorance and the resulting slapstick, by Moschion's own doubts, and by his sudden fear that nobody will prevent his going. Its foolishness is underscored by Demeas' reaction, which Moschion was entirely unable to foresee. As Demeas quietly observes, Moschion is once again in the wrong. Whereas Demeas had sought to hide Moschion's error, Moschion's action will publicise his; whereas Demeas had sought to excuse Moschion on the basis of past conduct, Moschion apparently puts one day's wrong over a lifetime of kindness (706-10). Moschion has once again put himself in a position which threatens the play's happy resolution. Nikeratos' appearance releases this tension as once again Menander uses his presence to alter the tone of a scene. Nikeratos' ignorance of the true situation makes his abrupt questions comic, and his momentary loss of temper threatens a repetition of his earlier, overblown denunciations (715ff.). Similarly, his version of the customary betrothal formula has an unexpected comic twist as he promises a dowry only when he dies . . . which he hopes may never happen (726-28). As in Act IV, Nikeratos' bluster saves Moschion from making an embarrassing admission. All is at last ready for the celebration, and Demeas again addresses the audience directly, this time with iwth the formal appeal for the audience's favour that announces the play's close.

But what of Chrysis? Demeas' call to have her make the necessary preparations draws attention to her silent presence in this final tableau, and of course she gives the play its title. She may have had a self-characterising monologue in the gap after line 57, and the two scenes of expulsion so crucial to the action derive power from the pathos of her bewilderment as she is thrust from house to house clutching the baby. In a larger sense, the repeated nursing motif gives a certain prominence to the otherwise invisible female influence on events. The chatter of Moschion's old nurse first aroused Demeas' suspicions, and the sight of the baby being suckled by Chrysis and Plangon goaded the old men to action in turn. Similarly, isolated allusions to Nikeratos' household open a small window on domestic arrangements and suggest a strong wife and an admirable solidarity in the face of his impetuosity (421-26, 558-61). As in the ***Epitrepontes,*** an infant is the catalyst that sets the action in motion, and the woman's dilemma receives sensitive treatment. Yet these elements form only a background, and any further questions suggested by them are strictly outside the play: did Chrysis and Demeas resume their relationship as before; what did Plangon think of Moschion; who raised the baby? There is ample material here for a sub-plot, and Menander's refusal to develop one is a significant aspect of his technique. It is not due to an inability or reluctance to create strong female roles, for such women as Habrotonon of the ***Epitrepontes*** and Glykera of the ***Perikeiromene*** certainly control events. Rather, it is an indication of Menander's freedom in using the situations from which he makes his play. Moschion unwittingly becomes his own obstructor by concealing the truth, and the resulting complications establish the obstructed marriage situation as the play's primary source of action. The disrupted union of Demeas and Chrysis is a momentary consequence and is not expanded for its own sake. Woman and child are among the elements available for strengthening the development and impact of the main action, and Menander uses them freely without incurring any responsibility to grant them an independent, fully developed existence. We have seen how the lost water jar of the ***Dyskolos*** and Sikon's shortage of crockery become crucial to the action, while Knemon's daughter receives no name, Chaireas and Daos vanish from the scene, and Sostratos' sister is created out of thin air to provide a bride for Gorgias. Here in the ***Samia,*** though Chrysis' presence at the wedding celebration presumes a reconciliation with Demeas, its details are not the dramatist's concern, much as Nikeratos' scrawny sheep and leaky roof spice his characterization with comic hints of penury without developing a contrast of thematic significance with Demeas' wealth. Menander may be lavish in his use of situations to build or colour action, but he is highly selective in choosing which of them to develop.

This freedom of choice raises a final question of dramatic priorities. The ***Samia*** combines subtle and broad humour, pathos and drama, comic convention and plausible motivation, but not in equal measure. Menander uses poignancy and characterisation as tools for making stock elements individual and memorable. The play may derive its greatest comic moments from a boy's conventional indiscretion and the familiar sight of raging old men, but by setting their actions against a background of poignancy and sympathy, he creates a unique effect. Moschion's foolishness stems from a heart-felt embarrassment. Demeas is moved to action by genuine anguish, while Chrysis' calm puts his anger in sharp relief. The pain of characters in the ***Dyskolos*** was largely external, caused by working in a field or falling down a well. Hints of mental turmoil are subordinate and, . . . resolved mechanically. Unease in the ***Samia*** is internal. Moschion's reluctance to tell the truth and Demeas' misapprehension and fear for their relationship generate the action and control its direction from within. Menander dramatises their pain as comedy by juxtaposing against it the irony of their misunderstanding and the figure of Nikeratos as a consistently comic mirror of Demeas' anguish. This combination of serious motivation and comic action creates the inner tension that gives the play its interest and dramatic effect. It also suggests something further.

The play is a deliberate construction, and our investigation has led us to examine its material and the way Menander has chosen to arrange and join it. The obstructed marriage that provides a basic structure was furnished by the tradition; only the dramatist's ability to impart to it a diverse range of colorations makes the result truly original and intriguing. Yet the arrangement he chose is neither fixed nor inevitable. If the tradition is one of many elements, it is also one of many possibilities. Menander mixes the serious and the light, makes character a source of action, and subordinates one situation to another. Different priorities applied to the same set of elements may produce a play of quite different effect. (pp. 92-108)

Sander M. Goldberg, in his The Making of Menander's Comedy, *University of California Press, 1980, 148 p.*

Mario Prosperi (essay date 1982)

[Prosperi details the masks employed in Menander's time to represent New Comedy characters in performance. He then discusses a recent staging of The Girl from Samos *utilizing the masks. Significantly, Prosperi notes, "each mask wants to be 'animated' in its own way. Whomever assumes the role is not supposed to change it."]*

A recent excavation in the Greek nekropolis of Lipari brought to light almost the complete repertory of masks of the *nèa,* or "new" comedy. The Greek grammarians considered Menander's model of comedy "new" (as well as that of Dyphylos and Philemones, whose plays have been lost) to distinguish it from the *archàia,* or "old" (from Epicarmos to Aristophanes), and the *mèse,* or "in the middle" (covering the period between Aristophanes and Menander).

Menander lived in Athens at the end of the fourth century B.C., during the period of Macedonian rule. Athens was ruled by Demètrios Phalerrèos, whose concern for morals seems to have been shared by the playwright. In the Aristotelian school, then prominent in Athens, Theophrastos had just written his famous book of *Characters,* a study of human typology where a series of 30 different "characters" were analyzed on the basis of the "moral defect" characterizing each of them (*e.g.* the flatterer, the idle talker, etc.). Famous for his descriptive works on plants and minerals, Theophrastos also had a naturalistic approach to human psychology: Considerations of physiognomy and complexion were part of the description of each character. When Menander renewed and, in a certain sense, standardized the repertory of traditional masks to fit the characters of his own "new" plays, he had to take into consideration the naturalistic study of human typology that had arrived in Athens at this time. In addition, he had to make the morals of each character conform to the corresponding physical "types."

The legend says that it was Glykera, the *etàira* (mistress) who shared his life, who actually modeled the masks, probably according to his design. These masks, with few variations, were in use for centuries, until the late epoch of the Roman empire. Plautus and Terentius adopted them for their own plays, which were mostly translations and reelaborations of Menander's plays.

These masks cover the entire face, the top of the head, and the ears. They are painted in different colors, the eyes are fully designed so that the actor peeps through invisible holes, and the hair and beard, made of fiber, is actually combed. Often, especially in the case of female characters, the mask's coiffure is the main means of identifying the character.

As for complexion, men are usually red and women are white. What might be seen as purely conventional has, however, a naturalistic explanation. The "Delicate Young Man," for example, is white because, like a woman, he has lived at home and has not been in the sun. Old men are paler than young men, and their color has grey or violet nuances according to their humor. (The violet is associated with a choleric temper, the grey with a melancholic temper.) A blackish nuance distinguishes the soldiers or the cooks, both "burned" by the sun or by the fire. Red hair indicates a quarrelsome attitude and ill-humor (it is characteristic of most slaves), and chipped ears are a result of quarrels. The snub nose indicates roughness, the hooked nose rapacity. Wrinkles on the forehead manifest thoughtful attitudes, worries or stubborness. An absence of wrinkles shows the absence of thought, typical of the Parasites. Raised eyebrows can indicate excitement, anger, or effrontery, but also courage, as in the "Perfect Young Man." Heavy eyelids mark a benign nature. Some masks, such as the "Principal Elderly Man" and the "Principal Servant," have one eyebrow raised in anger and one lowered in suspicion.

The Catalog

A complete list of new comedy masks has been preserved in the second century A.D., writings of Julius Pollux, who briefly describes 44 types. They are divided into five main categories.

One: Masks of Old Men. These are characterized by their beard. Few of them are old as the category also includes middle-aged men. 1) *Pàppos pròtos* (the "First Old Man") is the good-natured, hollow cheeked old man, with a shaved head and a benign look; 2) *Pàppos dèuteros* (the "Second Old Man") is the ill-humored old man, with a vigorous look, red hair and pale color; 3) *Hegemon Presbytes* (the "Principal Elderly Man") keeps one eyebrow raised in anger, the other lowered in suspicion; 4) *Presbỳtes makropògon* (the "Elderly Man with a Long Beard") does not raise his eyelids and looks sleepy; 5) *Hermonèios* ("Created by Hermonèios," a writer of the Old Comedy) is bald, has a beautiful beard and raises both eyebrows; 6) *Sphenopògon* (the "Man with a Pointed Beard") is bald, has raised eyebrows and a stubborn expression; 7) *Lycomèdeios* ("created by Lycomèdes," a writer of the Old Comedy) has a curly beard, a raised left eyebrow, and looks sneaky; 8) *Pornoboscòs* (the "Pimp") looks like the Lycomèdeios, but curls his lips, knits his eyebrows and is bald; and 9) *Hermonèios dèuteros* (the "Second One Created by Hermonèos") looks like the first one, with a pointed beard.

Two: Masks of Young Men. 10) *Pànchrestos* (the "Perfect Young Man") is fearless, athletic and has raised eyebrows; 11) *Mèlas neaniskos* (the "Black-Haired Young Man") is studious, worried, has tented eyebrows and wrinkles on his forehead; 12) *Oulos neanìskos* (the "Curly Haired Young Man") has red hair, raised eyebrows, one wrinkle on his forehead, and is the rash, quarrelsome, cheeky young man; 13) *Apalòs neanìskos* (the "Delicate Young Man") is as white as a woman because he lives at home and does not participate in athletic and military training; 14) *Agròikos* (the "Rustic Young Man") is thick-lipped and snub-nosed; 15) *Epìseistos* (the "Young Man Who Shakes His Hair") has a blackish color, and is the "Miles Gloriosus," the braggart soldier; 16) *Dèuteros epìseistos* (the "Second One Who Shakes His Hair") is more delicate than the first braggart, has red hair, and is probably a dandy; 17) *Kòlax* (the "Flatterer") is fat, has a smooth forehead and smiles maliciously; 18) *Paràsitos* (the "Parasite") has a bump on his nose and raised eyebrows; 19) *Eikonikòs* (the "Iconic Young Man") transforms himself into an "image" for others, and is an elegant, hollow-cheeked foreigner, and 20) *Sikelikòs* (the "Sicilian") is the third parasite.

Three: Masks of Slaves. Nearly all these masks have red hair, are quarrelsome and undisciplined. 21) *Pàppos theràpon* (the "Old Servant") has white hair, smiles, and is the good-natured pedagogue; 22) *Hegemòn theràpon* (the "Principal Servant") contorts the line of his eyebrows by raising one and lowering the other; 23) *Kàto Trìchias* (the "Bald-Pated Servant") is bald and raises his eyebrows; 24) *Oulos theràpon* (the "Curly Haired Servant") is cross-eyed and is the most restless servant; 25) *Theràpon mèsos* (the "Servant in the Middle") is one of the cooks. He is bald, presumptuous and takes a professional air; 26) *Tèttix* (the "Cicada") is the garrulous cook. He is cross-eyed, has three curls on his forehead and three more on his beard; and 27) *Hegemòn epìseistos* (the "Principal Servant Who Shakes His Hair") tries to seduce women.

The Cook, Demèas, and Chrỳsis from the third act of a production of The Girl from Samos, *utilizing masks based on ancient models recently uncovered in Lipari.*

Four: Masks of Old Women. 28) *Graìdion ischnòn* or *Lukàinion* (the "Dried-Up, Little, Old Woman" or the "Little She-Wolf ") is grumpy, has many wrinkles and an oblique look; 29) *Gràus pachèia* (the "Fat Old Woman") has deep wrinkles in her fleshy face and wears a ribbon in her hair; 30) *Graìdion oikuròn* (the "Little Old Woman of the House") is probably an old slave. She is snub-nosed, has two upper and two lower teeth, looks benign and smiles.

Five: Masks of Young Women. These are divided into two main groups: the respectable women and the *etàirai* (mistresses). 31) *Leptikè* (the "One Who Wants to Receive") is the talkative and petulant wife. She has a large mass of hair; 32) *Oule* (the "Curly Haired woman") is mature, has begun to put on weight and has a few wrinkles. She is a wife and mother; 33) *Kòre* (the "Pure Young Woman") wears her hair parted in the middle, and has straight black eyebrows; 34) *Pseudokòre* (the "False Virgin") has been seduced. Her hair is tied around her head, like a bride's; 35) *Pseudokòre dèutera* (the "Second False Virgin") does not wear her hair parted in the middle; 36) *Spartopòlion leptikè* (the "Grey-Haired Woman Who Wants to Receive") is the talkative mistress, who was formerly a prostitute; 37) *Pallacheè* (the "Concubine") looks like number 36 but is younger. She has a mass of dark hair elaborately combed in the form of an amphora; 38) *Tèleion etairikòn* (the "Refined Lover") has curls around her ears; 39) *Oràion etairìdion* (the "Good-Looking Little Prostitute") is fresh and attractive. She wears a simple coiffure with only one ribbon; 40) *Dìachrysos etàira* (the "Mistress Wearing Gold") wears gold in her elaborate coiffure; 41) *Diàmitros etàira* (the "Mistress with a Scarf Around Her Head") wears a scarf (*mitra*); 42) *Lampàdion* (the "Mistress With a Hair-do Like a Lamp") wears her hair combed into the shape of a flame; 43) *Abra perikùros* (the "Young Servant with Short Hair") is a pretty, adolescent slave; and 44) *Terapainìdion paràpseston* (the "Little Servant of the Prostitutes") has a snub nose and straight hair.

The Discovery

Before the 1960s and 1970s, when archeologist Luigi Bernabò Brea discovered terracotta models of the masks in the Greek tombs of Lipari, Pollux's list could not be referred to a corresponding series of known masks. Greek and Roman bas-reliefs and mosaics frequently show scenes from comedies, but it was difficult, without the necessary references and comparisons within the system, to identify even the masks that were known. The discovery at Lipari was crucial to the identification of most characters. At this point, we know 32 characters out of the 44, and since the digging continues, new discoveries can be expected.

Why in Lipari? The masks and other funeral objects were preserved there by the unique soil conditions. The presence of the *nèa* masks in the tombs is the result of unique historical circumstances. Menander died around 290 B.C., and after his death his fame spread throughout the Hellenized world. The Greek colony of Lipari enjoyed, at the time, a position of neutrality in the conflict between Rome and Carthage. The island's neutrality was of interest to both contenders, and resulted in an extraordinary accumulation of money in Lipari. In the days of its wealth, Menander's plays were at the center of the cultural interest of Lipari's elite. People who had been passionate about the characters in his theatre were buried with masks representing those characters.

Terracotta models of the masks were sculpted for various reasons. The most important reason was to transmit the models to theatre companies throughout the world, to enable the faithful rendering in a lighter material (such as papier-mâché) of the actual masks that were to be worn by the actors. The "face" of each was transmitted to ensure the faithfulness and the homogeneity of the different interpretations.

The second reason was economic. The models were sold to spectators as souvenirs, ornaments, toys, or funeral objects. The cult of Dionysos, in whose context the theatre events took place, was related to the cult of the dead. It was considered a good recommendation for a dead person if they carried the symbols of their passion for the theatre to the beyond. Through the masks, Dionysos would recognize the soul as one of his followers and favor it.

The rich community of theatre-goers was disbanded when the Romans conquered Lipari in 251 B.C., and the exceptional conditions that favored this kind of cultural life ceased to exist. The models of the masks found in the tombs of Lipari are first-hand evidence of the first wave of Menander's fame in the 40 years from his death in Athens in 290 B. C. to the Roman conquest of Lipari in 251 B. C.

The Use of the Masks

Luigi Bernabò Brea—who found the models and founded the Eolian Museum in Lipari, where they are kept—took the initiative to reproduce the masks in the necessary size and material for actual use by actors on the stage. Silvio Merlino, a Neapolitan artist, created painted masks in canvas-mâché with woolen hair and beards. With these, Bernabò Brea promoted the actual staging of one of Menander's plays in the Greek theatre he had had built himself on the acropolis of Lipari.

Coincidentally, in fact, while Brea was digging in Lipari, three plays by Menander were brought to light by the discovery of an Egyptian papyrus. Suddenly, we had three almost-complete plays (***Dỳskolos, Samia, Epitrepontes***) by an author who up to this point was known only for his fame and his Latin imitators, and the almost-complete repertory of the masks. The text chosen for Brea's experiment was the ***Samia*** (***The Woman from Samos***). I was entrusted with the translation of the text into Italian and with the mise-en-scène. The piece was presented to an audience of Greek scholars gathered in Lipari for a conference on the subject.

The first problem was casting the masks. Since we did not have Menander's directions, we had to figure out what mask corresponded to each character. Demèas, the father, was an old man who kept Chrỳsis, the woman from Samos, as his concubine. Since he was the protagonist, he could only be one of the first three old men in the list; the others were character roles. Demèas was vigorous, overbearing, passionate, and choleric. He could not, therefore, be the placid and melancholy "First Old Man" (no. 1). The only possibility seemed to be the "Principal Elderly Man" (no. 3). The other old man in the script, Nikèratos, who was especially choleric, seemed to fit perfectly the mask of the "Second Old Man" (no. 2).

We started rehearsing. Since the mask *is* the character, different actors tried the same mask and said the lines belonging to it. The actor started by looking at himself, masked, in the mirror and developed improvisational gestures to fit the character. The mask first appeared to possess an extraordinary power of psychological conditioning. No matter how diverse the actors were in age, physical type or social background, the same voice, the same gestures and the same rhythm came from each of them when they wore the same mask.

Then a contradiction was found between the character suggested with a powerful immediacy by the mask to different actors and the character in the play for whom the mask had been cast. The suspicious look of the "Principal Elderly Man" did not fit Demèas' grandiose attitude. The voice of the mask sounded like the voice of an angry oppressed person; his anger did not sound like the indignant anger of a dominant character. When the masks were finally exchanged between characters, everything suddenly sounded right. Changing actors behind each mask only provided irrelevant variations; only casting the masks differently produced a consistent image for each character.

Casting a mask for Moschìon, the stepson of Demèas, was accomplished after a few attempts. The character describes himself in the play as always behaving like the perfect young man. It seemed natural to cast him in the mask of the "Perfect Young Man" (no. 10). But in the text his attitudes were worried and anxious; the proud attitude of that mask seemed unable to credibly express these feelings. Only when we tried the Mèlas (the "Black-Haired Young Man," no. 11), did we find the correct correspondence between the psychology suggested by the mask and that implied by the character in the play.

Casting the actors, once the masks had been cast, was easier. After Sophocles added another actor, there were three actors with roles in the Greek theatre. They are usually indicated as actors A, B, and C. In the ***Samia,*** each of them plays one of the protagonist roles. The characters of Moschion (the young man who seduces the daughter of his father's neighbor), of Demèas (his father), and Nikèratos (the neighbor) are each played by a separate actor. The actor cast in the role of Moschion will be actor A; the actor cast in the role of Demèas will be actor B; the actor cast in the role of Nikèratos will be actor C.

There are three more speaking roles in the play, played by the same three actors changing their masks and costumes. Chrỳsis (mask no. 37, the concubine of Demèas who pretends to have given birth to the baby of the seduced girl) is played by actor B in the first act and by actor A in the rest of the play; Pàrmenon (mask no. 22, the chief of Demèas' servants) is played by actor C in the first and the fifth acts, and by actor A in the rest of the play; the Cook (mask no. 26) is played by actor C in the third act, the only time he appears.

Secondary mute roles are Plàngon (mask no. 34, the seduced girl—in the end, the bride), Plàngon's Mother (mask no. 31, the petulant wife), the Old Nurse (mask no. 30), and a few servants (masks no. 21, 23, 24, 43).

It appears, then, that each mask wants to be "animated" in its own way. Whomever assumes the role is not supposed to change it. The actor must conform to the authority of a code. Although the mask's main features are found instinctively, defining their codes is a work of profound dedication. We realized that the masks could have many expressions. Some, like the "Principal Elderly Man" (Nikèratos in the ***Samia***) and the "Principal Servant" (Pàrmenon in the ***Samia***), have one eye wide open in anger, the other peering in suspicion. One eyebrow is an arch, the other a horizontal line. By slightly rotating the head to the right or left, the actor could show more or less anger, more or less suspicion. The mask of the "Black-Haired Young Man" (Moschìon in the ***Samia***) changes expression by rotating the head up and down: When it looks upward, it shows heroic determination; when it looks forward, it shows worry; when it looks downward, it shows embarrassment.

Another method of adding to the mask's expression is to associate the movement of the head with the expression of the hands. By touching the mask's bottom lip with his forefinger, an actor makes it look thoughtful, but by introducing his hand in the mask's mouth, he makes it look frightened. By grasping its beard, he makes it look desperate; by caressing its beard, the character looks pleased with himself. The hands are not enough to animate a mask. The movement of the feet is also indispensable in keeping a mask alive. A mask cannot sit still; it can never entirely stop moving. Movement can be discreet, or minimal, but it must be continuous and must involve the actor's entire body. As soon as the actor stops moving, the mask dies. The mask is, in fact, a symbol of mortality. It is the imprint of someone's face, the memory of someone's life, frozen in a certain expression. The "person" behind it, as in the funeral masks, is dead. But the mask is also a symbol of immortality since the imprint contains the code of an existence, and through it that existence can be brought to life again. Interpreting a mask is very much like incarnating a soul; this may be partly why masks are associated with the cult of the dead.

Moschion in the Prologue of The Girl from Samos.

The Style of the Reconstruction

Everyone who saw the play noticed a natural similarity to the masks of the Commedia dell'Arte. But a basic difference was also noticed. The masks of the *nèa* represent characters, not stereotypes. They are detailed in physiognomic design and have specific psychological references. The masks of the Commedia dell'Arte are monochromatic, do not have eyes (they have holes through which the actor's eyes are visible), and do not cover the chin or the ears. The Commedia masks are light (mostly leather) and allow the actor maximum agility. Psychologically, in fact, they are the "negative" of the human face and, with regressive simplification, give the body the abstract expressiveness of an ideographic pantomime, where the gags are hyperbolic and the buffoonery is as abstract as that of clowns. The cultural trend moved away from naturalism in the late sixteenth century, toward the bizarre and the marvelous of the baroque. Menander's movement is, on the contrary, toward realism, and is more accurately comparable to the reform initiated by Goldoni when he humanized the characters of the Commedia.

Menander humanized the masks, forcing the actors to harmonize "animating the mask"—and subsequent pantomime—with the demands of a naturalistic reference and a detailed, articulated character. Actors who were trained in the Commedia dell'Arte style had to submit to Method techniques of identification, then transfer their emotions again into a code of pantomime. The resulting style was a tempered pantomime in which the gags conformed to the thematic needs of a realistic play, and functioned as "critical" estrangement, with humorous moralistic characterizations, of human behavior. (pp. 25-36)

Mario Prosperi, "The Masks of Lipari," in The Drama Review, *Vol. 26, No. 4, Winter, 1982, pp. 25-36.*

Norma Miller (essay date 1987)

[*Miller comments on the plot, characterization, and other aspects of Menander's dramatic technique in* The Girl from Samos. *The critic particularly stresses the playwright's economical style: "Characters reveal themselves and others, provide information and entertainment, and advance the action."*]

To the ancient world [Menander] was a poet 'second only to Homer', a 'mirror of life', a writer whose 'polished charm exercises a reforming influence and helps to raise moral standards', a writer 'of great invention, with a style adapted to any kind of circumstances, character and emotion'—a style which was recommended as a model for aspiring public speakers in Rome in the first century A.D. He is all these things. But he is also a practical playwright of considerable skill, and his dramatic preoccupations and techniques are worth attention. ***The Girl From Samos*** illustrates many of them well. It presents two fathers, one mild and reasonable, the other choleric; the son of the first, in the absence abroad of both, has seduced the daughter of the second; there is a good-hearted courtesan, a slave in the know, and a cook. The ingredients are standard. But the play is far from the 'mixture as before'.

'Demeas' is usually the name of a father in New Comedy (other examples can be found in Menander's ***The Man She Hated*** and Terence's *The Brothers*), but he is not always mild and reasonable: far from it in Terence's play, which is based on a lost play by Menander. In *The Brothers*, Demeas is the choleric father, and the adoptive father in that play (Micio) is a very different character from our Demeas. Demeas in ***The Girl From Samos*** has no 'philosophy of education', and has his moments of quick temper and ill-considered action, as when he ejects Chrysis from his house. But his temper springs not from a choleric nature, but at least partly from a guilty desire to remove blame from his adopted son. Both father and son tread warily in the adoptive relationship, and that is what causes much of the trouble. The fact that the relationship *is* adoptive provides not only an interesting variation on a basic theme, but interesting possibilities of dramatic action and dramatic comment, as father and son have to work their own way out of the situation. Standard procedures do not necessarily apply here.

Nikeratos, the neighbour, is not only choleric, he is foolish with it. His staccato conversation in Act One mirrors his butterfly brain; he is slow on the uptake, and over-violent in reaction in Act Four. But these characteristics are necessary to move the action as Menander wants it to move. Nikeratos must not learn the truth before Demeas does; and his ejection of Chrysis helps to secure her safety and to move the action to its desired climax.

'Moschion', to judge from the parts played by characters of that name in ***The Rape of the Locks, The Sikyonian, The Harpist*** and the play of ***Title Unknown,*** is usually a young and somewhat irresponsible man, who either fails to get his girl or incurs considerable difficulty in doing so. The Moschion of ***The Girl From Samos*** is no exception, but he is also different. He is adopted and (perhaps because of his attitude to this) he is weak, unable to face responsibility, willing to involve others in his difficulties, and anxious always to shift the blame from himself. His actions (and inactions) cause the initial situation and the initial complications, and in the final act produce sheer but plausible farce. He is the first character we see, because he speaks the Prologue which, although it tells us facts we have to know, tells us more about the self-centred, irresponsible (and so potentially dangerous) young man who delivers it.

Chrysis, the girl from Samos who gives the play its name . . . is not a common courtesan. She has a stable and affectionate relationship with Demeas (she could not, as a non-Athenian, hope for marriage with him); she is good-natured and loyal, she risks real hardship and danger, because an "unprotected' alien woman would find life hard in fourth-century Athens, and Nikeratos in a temper might well inflict physical injury upon her. She has to be what she is, to be what Menander wants her to be, the catalyst of the action. Her good nature and frustrated maternal instinct lead her originally to help Moschion; Demeas's affection for her as well as for Moschion makes his reaction particularly violent; her need for shelter causes her to accept Nikeratos's offer and so introduces his as yet unknown grandchild into his house; and her protection of the baby precipitates the crisis and the resolution.

Parmenon, the slave who knows all, contributes to the plot mainly by his absence. Menander likes sometimes to confound the conventions of his comedy, and here his slave does not manipulate or organize, but timidly and prudently removes himself (and his information) from possible involvement. But his rare appearances are dramatically significant. In Act One, his attitude highlights Moschion's weakness and indecisiveness; in Act Two, his 'shopping slave' role provides comic bustle and comic tone; in Act Three, his scenes with the cook and Demeas lower the tension after Demeas's monologue, and complicate the action by allowing Demeas to associate the baby with Moschion and Chrysis; and his final appearance in Act Five with Moschion gives him the traditional slave role in knockabout farce, but also helps to underline the folly of his young master.

The cook fulfils his traditional role of providing low comedy, but he provides it at significant points of the play. With Parmenon in Act Three, he provides comic reassurance after Demeas's potentially tragic monologue-cum-messenger speech, and he does the same thing later in the Act, after Demeas's second monologue. Here, too, he points the irrationality of Demeas's behaviour and of his treatment of Chrysis.

Menander's dramatic style, like his literary style, is economical. Characters reveal themselves and others, provide information and entertainment, and advance the action. That action results from what the characters are in their peculiar circumstances. And what they are is often complicated and contradictory, just like real people. Menander uses character to create misunderstanding, and misunderstanding to create comedy. He does not present 'character studies' in our sense of the words; his interest in character is ethical rather than psychological, but his people are shrewdly observed, and plausible. His presentation of the quirks of human nature is thoughtful as well as entertaining. The comment on human behaviour is not overt, but it is certainly there.

He puts the five-act structure to good dramatic use. New characters enter or a new situation emerges before each break, so that our interest is held. The fathers come home, so double trouble is likely (Act One); a marriage is being arranged—too early in the play, there must be further complications to come (Act Two); the baby is introduced into Nikeratos's house, that could be dangerous (Act Three); all appears to be settled, so what is yet to come? (Act Four); and what comes in Act Five is the release of farce, a farce which has wry undertones. Within this structure, he uses variety of tone (misunderstanding, pathos and low comedy), of presentation (monologue and dialogue), and of metre (the whole of Act Four, which is the emotional climax of the play, is in the emotionally heightened 'recitative' long metre). He also employs parallelism of scene and structure, to underline effects: Chrysis is forcibly ejected from both stage houses (Acts Three and Four), Demeas's monologues bracket a passage of comic dialogue in Act Three, and both fathers declaim like tragic heroes (Acts Three and Four), but with very different effect.

Vivid details add realism to the text: Chrysis's confidence that she can handle Demeas; her attitude to the child; Moschion's day-dreaming and his attitude to legitimacy; Demeas's story of the baby, the nurse and the servant-girl; all these are memorable, and they all contribute to our understanding of the characters, and therefore of the action. Menander gets a lot into nine hundred lines of text. We are still in process of recovering at least part of the text of his plays. It does not seem likely that future discoveries will be to his dramatic disadvantage. (pp. 12-15)

Norma Miller, in an introduction to Menander: Plays and Fragments, *translated by Norma Miller, Penguin Books, 1987, pp. 3-17.*

THE DOUR MAN

CRITICAL COMMENTARY

E. W. Handley (essay date 1965)

[*In the following excerpt from the introduction to his edition of* The Dour Man, *Handley provides an overview of the play, discussing its structure, characterization, and realism. He also offers a tentative reconstruction of an early performance.*]

If Menander ever expounded his views of drama in detail, we have no record of the fact; but among the stories told of him there is one which at least gives a lead to what he thought important. According to Plutarch (*Moralia*), a friend is said to have remarked 'Well, Menander, the festival's nearly here, and you haven't composed your comedy, have you?' 'Composed my comedy?', replied Menander, 'I most certainly have: I have my treatment of the theme worked out—I just have to set the lines to it.' Designing the play was the vital and difficult part; once that was done, the dialogue would follow. One should not of course go too far in deducing a literary doctrine from what is after all a neat and possibly half-ironical way out of a friendly social challenge; but there is a recognizable core of truth in the remark, which may well have helped to make it memorable in the first place.

In being virtually complete, the ***Dyskolos*** offers an admirable illustration of this concept of comedy: a play planned as a whole, to progress from beginning through dramatic climax to light-hearted conclusion, with its detail taking a place in the main design and contributing to it. By some modern standards of dramaturgy, this is an unpopular quality; when narration or commentary attempts to bring it out in an ancient play, one is apt to feel either that the obvious is being laboured at length, or that the conclusions drawn from the text are too calculatedly academic to be real in terms of the dramatist's own practical intentions: but it is the general fate of commentators to follow with labour where original writers go by genius. A good example of detailed planning in the ***Dyskolos*** will present itself later when we consider how Menander brings out the rustic setting of the play through the words of the text . . .; here it is perhaps useful to call attention to one striking general feature of the design.

The central feature of the ***Dyskolos*** is the character who gives it its title, Knemon, the 'Angry Old Man', the misanthrope. We see him on stage for roughly a quarter of the time the play would take to act, over half of this in two scenes which come late on—the predominantly serious scene of Act IV, from 691 to about 760, which brings the climax of dramatic interest, and the scene in Act V from 909 onwards, where a situation from earlier in the play is taken up and refashioned to provide a finale of lively comic revel. For much of the time, Knemon remains in the background, dominating the play through what we hear of him from others, until his long scene in Act IV brings the moment for him to reveal himself, and in revaluing his way of life to resolve most of the dramatic tension which has been built up around and about him; with that, the pattern of the plot is worked out almost to completion. The main line of the action begins from, and follows, the attempts of young Sostratos to approach Knemon for consent to marry his daughter, and it is through the lover's story, complicated and diversified by the presence of unreliable helpers and unexpected allies, that the portrait of Knemon is built up: the audience sees him as he is seen by different characters, whose reactions to Knemon are intended, in different proportions, to reveal both him and them. This example of a central character portrayed to a high degree by indirect means finds an interesting contrast in a close dramatic relation of Knemon's, the self-centred old miser Euclio of Plautus, *Aulularia;* to make the point by arithmetic, Euclio is on stage for something over half, and possibly near to three-quarters of the time the play would take to act, calculating approximately from the incomplete Latin text: he and his affairs are largely in the foreground, and the lover's story, analogous to that of Sostratos in the ***Dyskolos,*** is correspondingly made to recede. Since the Greek original of the *Aulularia* was almost undeniably a play by Menander, it seems hard to avoid the conclusion that the two plays were seen by the author as complementary variations in the study of a similar central character—not of course exclusively, but at least to some extent consciously.

From Antiquity onwards, Menander has been much praised for his realism: the unaffected naturalness of his language, the likeness of his characters to real people, the true portrait he gives of life in fourth-century Athens. After what has been said already, it is perhaps not necessary to spend long in remarking that realism is a relative term, and that Menander's realism is not only the product of acute observation, but of a refined art working in a traditional medium. His subjects, while less limited than one might believe from those who listen too closely to Ovid's assertion that 'there is no play of Menander's without love', are chosen and treated with a regard for the conventions of civilized high comedy: so far as we know, Menander excluded from his plays a whole range of grave events and permanent misfortunes (such as murder and distressing illness) to which real human beings are unfortunately prone; nor, as a rule, does he indulge in realistic detail purely for realistic detail's sake: his plays are plays and not documentary records. We may judge his characters to be drawn with acute psychological insight, yet he is not, as a modern dramatist might be, concerned to explore the inner depths of their personalities; his analysis of character is ethical rather than psychological, and it is striking in the ***Dyskolos*** that Knemon's major speech of self-revelation leaves the old man's emotions almost entirely to the audience's imagination. Menander's Greek can still appeal to modern critics, as it did to ancient ones, by its air of aptness to character and situation, and its range of effects from seriousness and high emotion to easy colloquial familiarity: from it, one seems to hear real people speaking; yet one suspects that Menander would not have dissented strongly from the modern dramatist who argued that 'it is not the purpose of dialogue to reproduce conversation naturalistically but rather, in the guise of conversation, to supply conversation's deficiencies—to be amusing where conversation is dull, to be economic where conversation is wasteful, to be articulate and lucid where conversation is mumbling or obscure' [Charles Morgan, in his *Dialogue in Novels and Plays,* 1954]. The mirror in which Menander is said to reflect life filters, concentrates, and sometimes distorts the impression it receives; often, we may think, it thereby shows more than the superficial truth; but if we expect it to reflect life in too literal a sense, the result will not be gratification. (pp. 10-14)

. . . . .

Although we cannot hope to reconstruct the first performance of an ancient play in detail, our understanding of the text remains incomplete if we ignore the theatrical conditions in which the author worked, or equate them uncritically with modern practice in one place or another. For all who wrote Attic drama, a general standard of practice was set by the conditions of production in the Theatre of Dionysus at Athens and the conventions which grew up there; for Menander, this means the theatre as it stood after the extensive rebuilding credited to Lycurgus. Since at least the major part of the work is likely to have been completed while Lycurgus was in charge of Athens' finances (ca. 338-326 B.C.), Menander can hardly have known the earlier theatre except as a childhood memory, and though much in the history of the building is disputed, it seems not to have undergone any other substantial alteration until after his death.

We may therefore use what is known of the 'Lycurgan' period of the theatre to form an idea of the environment in which Menander expected his ***Dyskolos*** to be performed. The following paragraphs offer an outline. Against this background, it seems useful to consider the dramatic setting as presented in the play itself, and to note how that presentation relates to the design as a whole and to the real place in which the action is supposed to happen.

For the present purpose, Menander's stage may be thought of as a space about 66 feet wide, framed by colonnaded wings which gave a depth of some 15 feet. It communicated, probably by a low step or steps, with a circular orchestra, again of about 66 feet across: there the chorus still held its place. Actors could enter from either side past the wings; between them, the main block of the stage building provided three doors, a large centre one and two flanking. Its architecture (which is very differently reconstructed) must have given at least some features of background common to all kinds of plays, but hangings and painted panels were used to add to the decorative effect, and it is a fair presumption that they also served to provide different scenic arrangements (for instance by masking doors not in use), and could be modified or changed to suggest different kinds of set. We should not however expect great elaboration in a large open-air theatre, nor prolonged intervals for changes of scene between plays within the limited time of the dramatic festivals.

One thinks of a street in Athens or some other town as the natural background for a New Comedy, and certainly at a later period a standard comic set consisted of painted 'urban' scenery. Such a background could hardly have been acceptable for comedies where the action took place out of town, and for these it may have been the practice to set the scene as for tragedies played in remote places (like *Ajax* and *Philoctetes* [by Sophocles]), or as for satyr plays, with whatever individual variations the available resources allowed. At all events, Menander was not averse to a change from urban surroundings. Apart from the ***Dyskolos,*** plays set in the Attic countryside include ***Heautontimoroumenos*** ('at Halai', frg. 127) and ***Heros*** ('at Ptelea', 22); at the beginning of ***Leucadia*** (frg. 258), the scene is set at the temple of Apollo on the cliffs of Leucas, from which Sappho was supposed to have thrown herself for love of Phaon. The more individual character a setting had, the more need to augment what could be shown in the theatre through the words of the text. The ***Dyskolos,*** by virtue of its completeness, shows well what care Menander took to create the background he required in the audience's imagination.

The place of the action is to be Phyle in Attica: Pan says so in the opening lines. In the theatre it is obvious at once who the speaker is (though presently he will mention his name); the central door from which he enters is a shrine of Pan and the Nymphs, but no nondescript one: 'it belongs', we are to think, 'to the people of Phyle and those who can farm the rocks here—a most distinguished shrine.' Already we know the setting and something of its character. The prologue speech is to give the essential information, in this as in other respects; the rest will appear as the play goes on.

On the left, as the audience sees it, is the door of Knemon's farmhouse, where he lives a life of morose isolation, alone but for his daughter and the old slave woman, Simiche; his wife has left him and now lives in the house on the right of the shrine, with Gorgias, her son by a former marriage, and their one slave, Daos—a household of three, barely supported by Gorgias' small farm.

Inside the shrine, the Nymphs have their spring, and there is room for a sacrifice and celebration; this the audience cannot see, and does not need to be told: it will be accepted when necessary (197ff and later *passim*). By one of the house-doors—let us say Knemon's—Apollo Agyieus is represented by his altar or emblem, a familiar object which matters only when it is referred to (see 659). Behind Knemon's door, again invisible but imagined, is his yard with its well (first mentioned 191), and its dung-heap (584f).

Off stage right, the road, bordered by trees (395f), goes past Kallippides' large estate, where young Sostratos is with his family for the hunting; then on 'down to Cholargos', and so to Athens. Off stage left, it goes up the valley past Knemon's land, and Gorgias' much smaller holding nearby. From near his house, Knemon can be pointed out 'up on the ridge there collecting wild pears' (99ff); below it and nearer to hand, a thicket is supposed to be visible, where Pyrrhias says he escaped from the old man after a hill-and-dale chase of what seemed like nearly two miles (117ff). The isolation of the place is brought to mind not only by direct reference, as in Daos' words at 222ff, but more often and more effectively by indirect means: it is reflected, for instance, in the hostility to strangers which is shown in violent form by the misanthrope Knemon, but also present in the reactions of Daos and Gorgias to Sostratos; Sostratos arrives there 'by chance' while hunting some way from home; when the shrine is visited by his mother, who 'goes all round the district sacrificing', her advance guard arrives sorely tried by the journey, and the main party is late. The hard rocky landscape figured in Pan's first sentence; it reappears conspicuously in the portrait of the farmer's life there—a typically Attic 'battle with the rocks' among wild thyme and sage, with the dry-walling to attend to for a change, a battle which is nearly too much for Sostratos, as an active young man who is unused to it.

Apart from his audience in the Theatre of Dionysus and those who would see the play restaged elsewhere, Menander could probably expect a considerable reading public. In making the play convey its own scenery and atmosphere through the words, he may have had readers in mind as well as the conditions imposed by relatively simple standards of production; but we shall be disappointed if we look for passages of picturesque description, or expect the setting to be as fully mapped out as it might be in a novel. The most striking feature of the verbal scene-painting is one with a less obvious appeal—the extreme economy and regard for dramatic relevance with which it is done. Once the action begins, the portait of Phyle is built up gradually and naturalistically, by a method similar to that of the character portraits; like them, it is also carefully integrated with the whole design, so that details which appear at first hearing to be no more than casual touches of realism generally prove to have been selected to serve other purposes as well. A good example is Pyrrhias' phrase about Knemon 'up on the ridge there, collecting wild pears'. This helps to portray the setting, as we noted; but there are two other points of immediate importance

Mosaic portrait of Menander found in a fourth-century A.D. Roman villa on the island of Lesbos.

in the context: it matters that Pyrrhias should see Knemon at a distance before they meet, and that he should see him doing something which will naturally provoke the reaction 'wretched old peasant'. Presently the ridge will become the scene of the two-mile chase; and, by a neat stroke of comedy, the pears will become missiles hurled by Knemon when his fury has exhausted everything else (120f). When Knemon appears, we learn that he works on the ridge because working the lower part of his land by the public road is more than his misanthropy can bear (162-6): in other words, in order to be inaccessible, he farms uneconomically. The original vivid detail of Knemon at work is thus made to lead up to the point that his hardships and poverty, unlike those of Gorgias, arise not from circumstance but by his own misguided choice; this emerges with full emphasis when Gorgias remarks to Sostratos on the extraordinary behaviour of the old man: he owns a valuable farm ('worth about two talents'), but insists on working it alone, with no help from neighbours, hired labour, or slaves.

The imagined setting goes beyond the physical limitations of the theatre, as we have seen; but it sometimes compromises with them. For instance, Knemon's house in the theatre must be literally next door to the shrine; accordingly Menander makes dramatic capital of the fact, as at 10ff, 442ff and 663. The lands of Knemon and Gorgias need to be off stage on the same side, so that characters may come and go that way without seeming to meet those who arrive from further off; accordingly, the plot makes a point of having the two work close by each other, and the audience must accept the result that while Knemon's house in on the same side as his land, the house of Gorgias is not (see on 24f).

Another kind of compromise is imposed by the nature of the real place which lends its identity to the dramatic scene. To an Athenian audience, the real Phyle was a district of the northwestern borderland of Attica, a journey of some thirteen miles from town, remote among mountains. Some presumably knew the place personally from service in the fort there, or from travelling the pass through Parnes which it guarded, the most direct of the three ancient routes to Thebes and Delphi; others may have lived or worked in the district, or visited it for the hunting, like Menander's Sostratos—but anyone who knew or knew of Phyle as more than a name could well have known something of its celebrated Nymphaeum. It is a cave in the side of a gorge, with a high and narrow entrance framed in an angle of cliff; all round and opposite there is steep rock, breaking into patches of scree and rough scrubby slope with scattered low trees; one arrives by scrambling precipitously down the mountainside from above, or by a sharp ascent from the torrent-bed below, having reached it from a place where the crags on the side facing the cave relent enough to allow a way down. Secluded by nature from the ancient village of Phyle and from the main branches of the pass, this forbidding valley is an ideal place for the home of an imaginary misanthrope; but for dramatic purposes the cave must become a wayside shrine like any other, where people can come and go without climbing, which can have houses built next to it, and where, at any rate notionally, a family party with music and dancing can be held. We need not ask whether the gorge was ever in fact inhabited, what sort of cultivation can have gone on there, or what sort of road or track ever led through. The eye accustomed to the documentary realism of the cinema may regard Menander's Phyle as a creation of fancy; but the standards to be adopted are those of artistic representation, not literal or would-be literal record. If patterns were needed for the tree-bordered country road, the narrow lonely valley, cultivation among the rocks, thyme, sage, pear-trees and so on, the district of Phyle could still offer them: its likeness in the play is (and presumably was) acceptable as a generalized one made to fit the author's dramatic requirements; it can seem realistic without being topographically real. (pp. 20-5)

E. W. Handley, in an introduction to The Dyskolos of Menander, *edited by E. W. Handley, Cambridge, Mass.: Harvard University Press, 1965, pp. 3-19.*

David Konstan (essay date 1983)

[*Konstan examines Knemon in* The Dour Man *as a "misanthrope" who rejects society. He argues, however, that the character is depicted as a "tough, hard-working peasant" and, although he is surly, "Knemon represents an ideal as well as a vice."*]

The misanthrope is not merely different from other men; he judges them, and does so on what he takes to be their own terms. He perceives himself as the representative of a social ideal which others have betrayed, and condemns his fellows for their perversity and hypocrisy. And yet society abides, and it is the misanthrope who cannot fit. He is rigid and surly, a natural target for comic deflation. Were he asocial, like the cyclops or the anchorite, the codes of communal life would not be an issue for him. But he is antisocial, and bears within him the image of the thing he opposes. This tension demands dialogue, as Cicero perhaps divined when he said [in *De amicitia*] of Timon, the renowned misanthrope of Athens, that even he "could not endure to be excluded from one associate, at least, before whom he might discharge the whole rancour and virulence of his heart." The misanthrope comes on as a satirist, and is kin to the stern Umbricius in Juvenal, who delivers his tirade against the corruption of Rome as he lingers by its gates, before abandoning the city forever. Juvenal had vision when he named his spokesman after shadows (*umbra*), for the railer shapes his critique of society according to its own occluded ideals.

The misanthrope, then, is an ambiguous figure. His complaint is in principle with the failures of society, not its existence as such. But by his isolation he relinquishes the authority of those social ideals which are the grounds of his reproach against others. The virtues which he demands lose their meaning in a society of one. For the rigor of his ideals, there is something heroic about him, but he is also the victim of his humor. He can rail but he refuses to engage—it is this which distinguishes him from the prophet. The misanthrope is a contradiction, society's own self-denial. He is, so to speak, the thing in the moment of its otherness. In this misanthrope, society presents both itself and its own negation.

It is precisely this social character of the misanthrope, however, which should warn us against taking him as an abstract type. His withdrawal is not simply a function of individual personality, but a relation to the norms and conduct of the world. (pp. 97-8)

Menander's misanthrope [in the ***Dyscolos***] lives with his daughter and an elderly slave who keeps house for him on his rural property which he farms himself. The estate is large and fertile enough to enable him to be economically independent, and its worth is not negligible. He is exceedingly shy of company, enough to have abandoned tilling a portion of his land near the public road; and his hostility to strangers finds missiles in clods or stones should anyone trespass on his domain. He discovers the speciousness of his pretended self-sufficiency, however, when, in pursuit of a bucket that had dropped from a rotten cord, he falls down his own well and requires the kind assistance of neighbors to get him out again. It is two young men who come to his rescue: his stepson, who lives nearby in relative poverty with his mother, the estranged wife of Knemon, as the misanthrope is called; and Sostratos, a young, elegant, wealthy city-lad who has fallen in love with Knemon's daughter, and has, from the beginning, been trying to earn the confidence of the old man in order to gain his consent for marriage with her. The rescue at the well does it. Knemon submits, or rather, he turns the girl over to the authority of her stepbrother, Gorgias, who gladly gives his approval. Knemon is now prepared to withdraw into complete solitude, but is prevented from doing so by the antics of a cook and slave who earlier had suffered from his ill temper. Preparations are in process for a double wedding, since, in a kind of coda to the main romantic action, Sostratos has persuaded his father to give his daughter to the worthy, if impoverished, Gorgias. The cook and slave tease and manhandle Knemon, who is still weak and battered from his fall, oblige him to dance, and, finally, to join in the general festivities despite his protestations.

It is possible to pick out two strands or themes in this story, "the romantic love-interest (involving Sostratos and Knemon's daughter) demanded of New Comedy, and a character-study of the misanthropic Knemon" [Michael Anderson, "Knemon's *Hamartia,*" Greece and Rome, 17 (1970)]. Armin Schäfer, in an exhaustive monograph on the play [*Menander's* ***Dyskolos,*** 1965], argued that "Menander comes near to a solution . . . but these two elements are basically irreconcilable, and the play consequently fails to achieve complete unity of action." Schäfer's division ignores, however, the logic, implicit in the social relations of the ancient city-state, which makes a single issue of Knemon's isolation and the fate of his daughter. I do not mean the mere contingent circumstance that Knemon's fierce temperament stands in the way of Sostratos' desire and of any conjugal union with his child. To put the matter that way is simply to posit Schäfer's distinction. It is rather that Knemon and his daughter, who is a demure but vague figure of whom we see little in the play (she has about a dozen lines in all) together constitute a household or *oikos,* and this is the unit which Knemon's misanthropy segregates from the social world. Such households, which were perceived as potentially autonomous, were bound together into a community of feeling by collective rituals, on the one hand, and by the bonds of marriage on the other. The social significance of Knemon's withdrawal is the disintegration of those bonds, beginning with the breach between himself and his wife, but achieving a categorical expression in his daughter's sequestration which marks a permanent lapse of kinship ties between his household and the larger community. From this point of view, the essence of Knemon's misanthropy is his abdication of responsibility for his household, and specifically for the next generation.

The theme of responsibility or authority is broached early in the play, when Sostratos indicates that he has sent his slave to seek out the girl's father or "whoever it may be who is in charge of the household" (73-4). The person in charge is in Greek the *kyrios,* who in Attic law had legal authority over his wife, children, and property, as well as others, such as unmarried sisters, who are subject to no other responsible adult male. At this point in the action, of course, Sostratos simply does not know who the girl's *kyrios* happens to be. But the hint of ambiguity is soon developed in connection with an encounter between Sostratos and Knemon's daughter, the only scene in which she appears. She has emerged from her house to fill a jug with water, since the bucket, which I mentioned earlier, has by now fallen into the well. Sostratos offers to fetch some for her, and a slave of Gorgias, who has overheard the exchange, curses Knemon for his carelessness in allowing a virtuous young girl to go out by herself, without a chaperone. He decides to report the matter to Gorgias, so that they at least can assume the care (*epimeleia*) of her (220-29). When Gorgias appears, he reproaches the slave for having stood by like a stranger (*allotrios,* 238). One may not, he says, run away from relationship, employing here a word (*oikeiotēs,* 240) whose normal sense, as we are told by a Byzantine lexicographer, denotes ties by marriage, although Menander used it loosely of blood-relations. . . . Her father, Gorgias continues, wishes to be a stranger toward them, but they must not imitate his churlishness. Later, Knemon will acknowledge his failure as head-of-household, accept Gorgias as his son, and place him in charge of his estate and his daughter, entrusting him to find a husband for her, since no one, he realizes, is likely to find favor with him (729-35; cf. 737-39).

At this point in the play, a kind of denouement has been achieved, because Knemon's household has been liberated from the constraints of his irascible nature and is restored to the community of families. This is exhibited at once in Gorgias' consent to his half-sister's marriage to Sostratos; and, from this point of view, we may understand the function of Sostratos' passion as a sentimental or personal vehicle of the objective kinship code of Athenian society, which may be described as a closed conjugal group—that is, one in which citizens married citizens, while strangers were strictly excluded from this relation. To put it another way, Sostratos' love for Knemon's daughter is a manifestation of the city-state's claim on Knemon's *oikos,* which he, by his isolationism, was in effect renouncing. The theme of misanthropy and the love-interest, then, may be regarded as the obverse and reverse of the same coin.

Knemon himself, to be sure, remains aloof from the new arrangements, disclaiming any interest in the man his daughter is to marry (752) and demanding for himself and his wife simply provision for their support (739). His intransigence may seem a blemish on the spirit of comic resolution, although an easy conversion of the misanthrope would undercut the representation of his character, and neither Timon [in Shakespeare's *Timon of Athens*] nor Molière's Alceste [in *Le Misanthrope*] submits to such reform. What is more, such a transformation would compromise the essential dignity of Knemon, for he, like Timon and Alceste, has a kind of virtue or nobility about him. I have intimated that a double nature pertains to the essential idea of the misanthrope; we need to explore the way Menander brings it into play.

Early in the action, when Sostratos' slave returns breathless from his unfortunate interview with Knemon, Sostratos ventures, if not a defense, at least a generous interpretation of Knemon's conduct: "A poor farmer is a bitter sort, not only this one, but practically all of them" (120-31). Sostratos' own courage deserts him when Knemon himself arrives, but the suggestion that Knemon represents a general type of tough, hard-working peasant is echoed and amplified throughout the drama. Gorgias later observes that Knemon's vehemence is directed against the idle lives that people lead (355-57), and Knemon himself reveals this side of his surliness when he observes of a party preparing a festive sacrifice to Pan, who shares a shrine with the Nymphs next door to Knemon's house, that such lavish piety is for their own sakes, not the gods'. The god himself would be content with some ritual cake and incense; the roasted animals serve the people's gluttony (449-53). Finally, after Knemon has been rescued from the well, largely through the efforts of Gorgias with the distracted assistance of Sostratos, he delivers, along with his confession that man needs the help of others and cannot be independent of everyone, and explanation and an apologia for his ways. Having observed, he says, the calculating greed of human beings, he had imagined that no one was really considerate of anyone else (718-21). The example of Gorgias, especially in light of Knemon's former treatment of him, upsets this judgment. But still he ventures in his own defense: "If everyone were like me, there wouldn't be courts, they wouldn't be taking each other off to jail, there'd be no war, and each would be content with his fair share" (743-45). The sentiment is a Greek commonplace: trouble starts when people stop minding their own business. Nevertheless, it is a fine moment. One critic [Anderson] observes: "It is Menander's considerable achievement that after spending three acts building Knemon into a monster (a comic monster, maybe, but one for whom the audience's sympathy is not invited for a moment), he is able to transform him into a human being whose ill-guided attempt to live without assistance from others, *autos autarkēs* (714), is not merely touching but has a trace of nobility about it." We have seen that this side of Knemon's character had in fact already been adumbrated. There are other such indications too. The god Pan, who delivers the prologue, describes Knemon's daughter as "like her breeding, ignorant of pettiness" (35-6). The implied approval of Knemon's household has seemed anomalous enough to cause some editors to emend the text, but Sostratos himself speaks later of the somehow liberal or decent rearing (*eleutheriōs,* 387) she enjoyed with her boorish father, which sheltered her from the corrupting influence of nannies, and when he sees the girl he is struck at once by the liberal style of her rusticity (*eleutheriōs ge pōs agroikos estin,* 201-02).

One shcolar [Edwin S. Ramage, in "City and Country in Menander's ***Dyskolos,"*** *Philologus,* 110 (1966)] suggests that faults of Knemon are patterned not only on the type of the misanthrope proper but on the rude rustic as well, the "unattractive *agroikos* of Theophrastos or Aristotle," and that Menander "has used him to portray an excess of rustic harshness." But the image of the rustic cuts both ways, carrying connotations of sturdy independence, straightforwardness, hard work, and honesty alongside those of taciturn or uncouth unsociability. Knemon represents an ideal as well as a vice. In the words of a scholar who adores Menander for his ethics and didacticism [L. A. Post, in "Some Subtleties in Menander's ***Dyscolos,"*** *American Journal of Philology,* 84 (1963)], "Rusticity is a fault in Theophrastus. In Menander it is coupled with noble independence and innocence."

The fact that the misanthrope in Menander may be seen as a version, however exaggerated, of the type of the Attic farmer suggests that his autarky too is not simply a personal delusion, but a real, or at least an ideologically credible, possibility. Indeed, it was both. Knemon's style was perfectly viable. A freeholder could support himself by his own labors, and such a way of life left little enough reason for an affable disposition. Menander's picture of Knemon's property and circumstances is probably a fair one. More important, the vision of a perfectly autonomous family unit was old and deep in the city-state society. Aristophanes captured it best in his play, the *Acharnians,* produced about a century before the ***Dyscolus.*** The hero, Dicacopolis, whose name means "Just City," in disgust at the corruption of his fellow citizens, who will do nothing to secure an honorable peace with Sparta, withdraws to his own farm in the country and signs a private peace treaty with the enemy. The whole fantasy that follows is based on the notion that an individual household could function like a city, autonomous and self-sufficient. There is, of course, a vast difference in spirit between the two dramatists. Where Aristophanes' hero succeeds exuberantly in his bold enterprise and has the Athenians begging for a share in his treaty, Menander's is humbled. But not entirely: there abides a tension between autarky and community which is manifest both in the two aspects of his character and in his stubborn pride.

This tension was real for the ideology of the city-state, even while—perhaps because—accelerating class differentiation in the Hellenistic epoch, together with political changes in favor of large landowners that were supported by the Macedonians, was rendering the ancestral image of a community of citizen-farmers ever less actual. To overcome it, and at the same time to defuse the very real problems of social and class antagonisms, Menander proceeds, as I see it, on several fronts. First, on the moral level, he suggests a principle of generous regard for others, of *philanthrōpia* in the large sense which the Greek term possesses, to stand against the disintegrative misanthropy of Knemon. Because ethical criticism is still very much in fashion among classicists, this feature of the play has often been observed. One writer [Ramage] sums up his argument: "Menander, then, in the ***Dyskolos*** has pictured very vividly for us the schism existing between city and country in Athens in the late fourth century B.C. At the same time he has shown us that the seeds of philanthropia which can solve this problem lie in the refinement of the city and the practical experience of the country. He shows us also the great binding influence that this feeling can have." This fine sentiment, it must nevertheless be conceded, does not lighten the testy suspiciousness of Knemon.

A second strategy involves the introduction of Kallipides, Sostratos' father. Gorgias is in awe of him: he is a wealthy man, but an honest one and an incomparable farmer (774-75). He consents graciously to Sostratos' marriage with Knemon's daughter, but balks at his demand, raised rather abruptly at the beginning of Act V, that his own daughter be given in matrimony to Gorgias. A double wedding with paupers is too much (795-96). I believe that Kallipides' resistance, brief as it is, is meant to balance the obstacle which Knemon represented. Both sides, rich and poor, urbane and surly, are made to yield something. Implicitly, the scene acknowledges the grounds of Knemon's wariness and thus the rational side of his behavior. At all events, his rudeness is not the only barrier to full and free ties of kinship among all citizens. Sostratos caps his plea with an elevated homily on the right use of wealth, over which one is master (*kyrios,* 806; cf. 800) for a brief span of years; the noble thing is to assist all, render as many as one may prosperous through one's efforts. Such generosity is immortal, and from it benefits will return in time of need (805-10). This moralizing is at a sublime level of abstraction, and my guess, which could perhaps be substantiated by a stylistic analysis, is that Kallipides hears this earnest lecture with respect and kindly amusement. In any case, he gives in at once, gently reminding his son: "You know me, Sostratos" (813).

Still, Knemon remains outside the charmed circle. To bring him in, Menander resorts to plain boisterousness. In a farcical finale, with new rhythms, music, and a slap-stick dance with an unwilling Knemon, the curmudgeon joins the party. Here is the spirit of the city-state at the level of festival, collective rituals of community. Knemon's continued resistance is perhaps significant; but it may also be that the identity of the group is at this level no longer a matter of individual will. One ought at least to be aware of a certain ecstatic element in Athenian civic life, not out of place, certainly, in the theater of Dionysus. The poet might dip down, so to speak, into this stratum of the ideology in order to provide a resolution to the narrative tension. Festival, the civic bond of marriage, and the autonomy of the individual household thus constitute the ideological matrix for the action of the play. In these terms the misanthrope is defined, with his virtues and his faults, and in these terms, specific to the culture of the ancient city-state, his secession is resolved. (pp. 99-106)

David Konstan, "A Dramatic History of Misanthropes," in Comparative Drama, *Vol. 17, No. 2, Summer, 1983, pp. 97-123.*

FURTHER READING

OVERVIEWS AND GENERAL STUDIES

Andrewes, M. "Euripides and Menander." *The Classical Quarterly* XVIII, No. 1 (January 1924): 1-10.

Demonstrates the influence of tragedy on Greek New Comedy by comparing the works of Euripides and Menander.

Arnott, W. Geoffrey. Introduction to *Menander: Volume I—"Aspis" to "Epitrepontes,"* pp. xiii-xlv. Cambridge, Mass.: Harvard University Press, 1929.

Discussion of Menander's life, critical reception, and use of language, plot, and character development.

———. "Young Lovers and Confidence Tricksters: The Rebirth of Menander." *The University of Leeds Review* 13, No. 1 (May 1970): 1-18.

Investigates the figures of young lovers and conniving slaves in Menander's plays to demonstrate the dramatist's innovative use of linguistic and stylistic devices to create well-defined and highly individualized characters.

———. "Menander." In his *Menander, Plautus, Terence,* pp. 5-27. Oxford: At the Clarendon Press, 1975.

Explores Menander's historical context and his dramatic techniques.

———. "Time, Plot, and Character in Menander." *Papers of the Liverpool Latin Seminar* 2 (1979): 343-60.

Investigates Menander's debt to Aristotle's concept of "unity" of time and the relationship between plot and character.

Fantham, Elaine. "Sex, Status, and Survival in Hellenistic Athens: A Study of Women in New Comedy." *Phoenix* XXIX, No. 1 (1975): 44-74.

Presents "an account of the social roles available to different categories of women in the everyday world of around 300 B.C.," using Menandrian comedy as evidence.

Frost, K. B. *Exits and Entrances in Menander.* Oxford: At the Clarendon Press, 1988, 125 p.

Study of Menander's use of stage exits and entrances in an exploration of "how these ways were used both to create certain effects in performance and on occasion to permit dramatic short cuts to be taken."

Gassner, John. "Menander, Plautus, and Terence." In his *Masters of the Drama,* pp. 92-104. New York: Dover Publications, 1951.

Judges *The Arbitration* Menander's best work, deeming it "quite modern in its implications."

Gomme, A. W. and Sandbach, F. H. *Menander: A Commentary.* Oxford: At the University Press, 1973, 760 p.

Comprehensive analysis of Menander's life, social and historical contexts, and dramatic works.

Henry, Madeleine Mary. *Menander's Courtesans and the Greek Comic Tradition.* Frankfurt am Main, Germany: Verlag Peter Lang, 1985, 140 p.

Examines the use of courtesans in Greek comedy, particularly in the plays of Aristophanes and Menander.

Lever, Katherine. "Athenian New Comedy: 338 to 290 B. C." In her *The Art of Greek Comedy,* pp. 186-205. London: Methuen & Co., 1956.

Identifies the formative influences on Menander's comedy, discussing the nature of the playwright's realism and his use of stock dramatic conventions.

MacCary, W. Thomas. "Menander's Characters: Their Names, Roles, and Masks." *Transactions and Proceedings of the American Philological Association* 101 (1970): 277-90.

Suggests that Menander's characters were not merely "typed" but identical in his plays by noting the similarities and variations in several of his figures.

Norwood, Gilbert. "Menander." In his *Greek Comedy,* pp. 313-64. Boston: John W. Luce & Co., 1932.

Surveys the style, dramatic techniques, and recurring theme of love in several of Menander's plays, including *The Girl from Samos, The Shearing of Glycera,* and *The Arbitration.*

Perry, Henry Ten Eyck. "The First Literary Comedy: Aristophanes and Menander." In his *Masters of Dramatic Comedy and Their Social Themes,* pp. 44-8. Cambridge, Mass.: Harvard University Press, 1939.

Praises Menander's ability to sketch varied characters in fine detail but notes that, since his plays are not concerned with social or political problems, they represent the work of "an admirable creator of character" rather than that of "a first-rate comic dramatist."

Post, L. A. "The Comedy of Menander." In his *From Homer to Menander: Forces in Greek Poetic Fiction,* pp. 214-44. Berkeley: University of California Press, 1951.

Examines plot and character development in *The Girl from Samos, The Shearing of Glycera,* and *The Arbitration.* Post concludes that Menander transformed comedy into "a serious and moral commentary on what men do and what they ought to do."

Sandbach, F. H. "Menander." In his *The Comic Theatre of Greece and Rome,* pp. 76-102. London: Chatto & Windus, 1977.

Discusses the structure and characterization of Menander's plays. Responding to the criticism that the playwright's universe is immoral, Sandbach argues that Menander represented a world in which crime and greed were discouraged in favor of kindness and understanding.

Webster, T. B. L. *Studies in Menander.* Manchester, England: Manchester University Press, 1959, 252 p.

Examination of Menander and his dramas in which Webster divides the works into plays of reconciliation, social criticism, adventure, and satire. He also examines Menander's output in relation to philosophy and earlier drama.

———. *An Introduction to Menander.* New York: Barnes & Noble Books, 1974, 211 p.

Discussion of Menander's plays from historical, thematic, social, and philosophical perspectives. Webster also includes an appendix summarizing what is known of the playwright's surviving fragmentary plays.

THE GIRL FROM SAMOS

Turner, Eric G. Introduction to *The Girl from Samos; or, The In-Laws* by Menander, pp. 1-16. London: The Athlone Press, 1972.

Argues that Menander best represents reality in his depiction of relationships among his characters.

THE DOUR MAN

Graves, Robert. "*The Dour Man.*" In his *Food for Centaurs: Stories, Talks, Critical Studies, Poems,* pp. 224-29. Garden City, N. Y.: Doubleday & Company, 1960.

Derides *The Dour Man* for its ineffective dialogue, excessive moral platitudes, and weak plot. Graves notes that the existence of only a few of Menander's plays does not "stir much regret for the loss of [his] other plays."

Lever, Katherine. "The *Dyskolus* and Menander's Reputation." *The Classical Journal* 55 (n.d.): 321-26.

Hails the discovery of the first complete play by Menander, exploring the characterization and structure of *The Dour Man* and calling for a critical reassessment of the dramatist's overall reputation.

Lloyd, Robert B. "Two Prologues: Menander and Plautus." *American Journal of Philology* LXXXIV, No. 333 (April 1963): 146-61.

Examines the similarities between the prologues of Plautus's *Rudens* and Menander's *The Dour Man.*

Lloyd-Jones, Hugh. "A Greek Dramatist Rediscovered." *The Listener* LXI, No. 1527 (14 May 1959): 837-38.

Remarks on the discovery of *The Dour Man,* claiming that although the play suffers from weak characterization, an audience "cannot fail to respond to its youthful freshness and unsophisticated charm."

Moulton, Carroll. Introduction to the *Dyskolos* by Menander, pp. xiii-xxiii. New York: New American Library, 1977.

Illustrates how Menander enlivened the dramatic conventions of New Comedy by individualizing his plots and characters, particularly in *The Dour Man.*

Reckford, Kenneth J. "The *Dyskolos* of Menander." *Studies in Philology* LVIII, No. 1 (January 1961): 1-24.

Considers the theme of town and country and the subordination of plot to character development in *The Dour Man.* Reckford claims that, by transforming the characters from stock comic types to fully realized individuals, Menander "holds up life to his audience not so much as it is, but as it ought to be."

Webster, T. B. L. *The Birth of Modern Comedy of Manners.* Adelaide: The Australian Humanities Research Council, 1959, 13 p.

Contends that *The Dour Man* is the first modern social comedy and notes its sympathetic treatment of a traditionally unsympathetic character.

THE SHIELD

MacDowell, Douglas M. "Love Versus the Law: An Essay on Menander's *Aspis.*" *Greece and Rome* XXIX, No. 1 (April 1982): 42-52.

Examines *The Shield* in relation to Athenian family law. MacDowell maintains that in the confrontation between love and legal considerations, Menander sides with love.

THE ARBITRATION

Harsh, Philip Whaley. "Menander: *Arbitration* (*Epitrepontes*)." In his *A Handbook of Classical Drama,* pp. 322-27. Stanford, Calif.: Stanford University Press, 1963.

Presents an overview of *The Arbitration,* considering plot, structure, and the influence of Euripidean tragedy on the comedy. Harsh concludes that, as the play fails to satirize or criticize the morals of its day, it remains a comedy of errors and essentially a farce.

Additional coverage of Menander's life and career is contained in the following source published by Gale Research: *Classical and Medieval Literature Criticism,* Vol. 9.

Joe Orton

1933-1967

INTRODUCTION

Born John Kingsley Orton.

An influential playwright in England during the 1960s, Orton wrote anarchic comedies illustrating his view of life as ludicrous. *Entertaining Mr. Sloane, Loot,* and *What the Butler Saw* shocked audiences with their portrayal of people who affect mannered language and a dignified demeanor as they participate in ignoble or violent acts. Characters in Orton's plays repeatedly refer to their grotesque situations euphemistically, heightening the disparity between their pretensions to gentility and the harsh realities of the situations portrayed on stage. Although Orton died at the age of thirty-four, his comedies have influenced many other dramatists with their satirical approach to complex themes. "It is remarkable," John Russell Taylor has written, "that though they seem to start from the material of camp fantasy, Orton's plays manage completely to transform that material into a serious vision of life, which, however eccentric—and however comic in its chosen forms of expression—carries complete conviction as something felt, something true."

The son of working-class parents, Orton was raised in Leicester, an industrial city eighty miles northwest of London. In 1951 he won a place at the Royal Academy of Dramatic Arts (RADA), where he studied for two years. At the Academy, Orton met Kenneth Halliwell with whom he had a prolonged homosexual relationship. Halliwell, seven years Orton's senior, introduced Orton to classical drama and encouraged his literary aspirations. After working as the assistant stage manager for the Ipswich Repertory in 1953, Orton returned to London. There, he and Halliwell collaborated on several novels, working for six months out of the year to earn enough money to live and write during the other six. In 1962 Orton and Halliwell were convicted of malicious damage to eighty-three library books and with removing 1,653 plates from art books which they had used to decorate their apartment. During the six-month prison sentence he served separately from Halliwell, Orton began to write plays. His solo literary career began with the 1964 BBC radio broadcast of *The Ruffian on the Stair,* which was followed by a three-year period in which he completed two full-length plays, the draft of another, and three one-act plays for television. Orton achieved critical recognition, popular success, and also notoriety with the London production of *Loot* in 1966, but his career ended a year later when Halliwell, jealous of his lover's success and in a deep depression, beat Orton to death with a hammer, committing suicide immediately afterwards by consuming a lethal dose of sleeping pills.

Critics have noted that several of Orton's early plays were influenced by the works of Harold Pinter, which feature unusual individuals who disrupt the lives of other characters. Like Pinter, Orton also relied on fractured dialogue to develop what commentators call the absurdist qualities of his works. His 1964 radio play, *The Ruffian on the Stair,* concerns the efforts of Wilson, a despondent young man, to avenge the death of his older brother, with whom he was incestuously involved. Wilson tries to provoke his brother's killer into murdering him as well, thus incriminating the killer in both murders and saving himself from committing the sin of suicide. This play includes elements found in many of Orton's subsequent works, including farcical treatment of incest, homosexuality, murder, and sexual ambiguity; the playwright's trademark witty and urbane dialogue; and the presentation of bizzare situations in a naturalistic manner.

The title character of Orton's next work, *Entertaining Mr. Sloane,* is an intruding stranger, a murderer who is blackmailed by the son and daughter of his latest victim into granting each of them sexual favors. In typical Ortonesque fashion, the siblings' carnal opportunism outweighs all ethical considerations regarding their father's murder. The play opened in May 1964 to mixed critical response: Terrance Rattigan called it "the best first play" he had seen in thirty years, while other reviewers referred to Orton's work as "a dirty highbrow play" that should never have been allowed on stage. Orton delighted in the controversy and even contributed to the critical debate by taking both sides in pseudonymous letters to London newspapers. Under the guise of "Alan Crosby," he praised *Sloane:* "I myself consider—a) the dialogue brilliant; b) the comedy breath-taking; c) the drama satisfying; d) the play as a whole well-written if not profound . . ."; as "Edna Welthorpe" he denounced his own play and, by extension, all contemporary dramatists: "I myself was nauseated by this endless parade of mental and physical perversion. And to be told that such a disgusting piece of filth now passes for humour. Today's young playwrights take it upon themselves to flaunt their contempt for ordinary decent people. I hope that the ordinary decent people will shortly strike *back!*"

In *Loot* Orton continued to satirize contemporary morality by portraying corrupt and avaricious individuals from all levels of society, this time through more overt use of farce. The play recounts the efforts of two bank robbers, Hal and Dennis, to hide stolen money in the coffin of Hal's recently deceased mother. The two men undress the body and hide it upside-down in a closet, losing the mother's false teeth and glass eye in the process. When a police inspector, Truscott, discovers the criminals, Hal's father, McLeavy, trusts him to make the proper arrests, only to find himself apprehended on false charges after the unscrupulous inspector accepts a portion of the money from the thieves. Despite its initial failure in regional theaters, *Loot* became a critical success when it opened in London in September 1966; it was voted the best play of the year by the journals *Evening Standard* and *Plays and Players.*

The convoluted logic and exaggerated situations of *Loot* foreshadow Orton's last play, *What the Butler Saw.* Set in a psychiatric clinic, the play features not only the traditional farcical elements of mistaken identities and physical humor, but also the themes of homosexuality, transvestism, lesbianism, nymphomania, and incest. In this piece, Dr. Prentice is discovered by his wife while he is trying to seduce a woman who has applied for a position as secretary. The doctor attempts to conceal his indiscretion and, as the complications multiply wildly, it is eventually revealed that the doctor and his wife have both been unknowingly seducing their own children. The comedy was unsuccessfully staged in London in March 1969; it was labeled pointless and needlessly filthy by its first reviewers. But, as John Lahr wrote, "critics mistook the flaws in the production as limitations in the play and Orton's best work became the most underrated." Later revivals were better received, and *What the Butler Saw* is now recognized as one of Orton's finest works.

Orton's one-act plays, *The Erpingham Camp, The Good and Faithful Servant,* and *Funeral Games,* originally written for television, are regarded as less significant works. *The Erpingham Camp* is a retelling of Euripides's *Bacchae,* set in a British vacation resort. *The Good and Faithful Servant* centers on the usurpation of personal identity by authority figures. The protagonist, Buchanan, has worked in a large factory for more than fifty years but retires virtually unnoticed by his employers. The play ends with Buchanan's son seeking a job at the same factory, thus beginning the cycle anew. Orton also wrote *Funeral Games,* a satire on religion, generally considered the least focused of his plays,.and *Until She Screams,* a sketch that was included in the musical *Oh! Calcutta!*

In recent years, Orton's comedies have generated renewed interest, largely due to the work of Lahr, the editor of Orton's complete plays and diaries, and the author of *Prick up Your Ears,* the definitive biography of the playwright. Recent critics consistently praise Orton's plays, calling attention to his masterful handling of farce in exposing the hypocrisy and greed underlying "respectable" behavior. Lahr summarized Orton's significance to contemporary drama: "Nobody came closer than Orton to reviving on the English stage the outrageous and violent prankster's spirit of comedy and creating the purest (and rarest) of drama's by-products: joy. In showing us how we destroy ourselves, Orton's plays are themselves a survival tactic. Orton expected to die young, but he built his plays to last."

PRINCIPAL WORKS

PLAYS

Entertaining Mr. Sloane 1964
**The Ruffian on the Stair* 1964
Loot 1965
**The Erpingham Camp* 1966
The Good and Faithful Servant 1967
† *Funeral Games* 1968
† *What the Butler Saw* 1969
† *Until She Screams* 1969
Joe Orton: The Complete Plays 1976

OTHER MAJOR WORKS

Head to Toe (novel) 1971
Up against It (screenplay) 1979
‡ *The Orton Diaries* (diaries) 1986

*These works were performed as *Crimes of Passion* in 1967.

†These works were first produced after Orton's death.

‡Orton wrote the diaries between December 1966 and August 1967.

AUTHOR COMMENTARY

The Biter Bit (1964)

[*In the following interview with Simon Trussler, Orton discusses some influences on his writing in general and on his play* Entertaining Mr. Sloane *in particular. Denying that* Mr. Sloan *is a black comedy, Orton maintains that "it's just a play, which happens to make people laugh about sodomy and nymphomania. It's a comedy insofar as the whole world and the whole human situation are comic and farcical."*]

[Trussler]: *Before meeting Joe Orton the dramatist, there's Joe Orton the man. Your past, your likes and dislikes . . . ?*

[Orton]: Well, I hate all animals with tails and my favourite play is the *Andromeda* of Euripides. I was born in Leicester 25 years ago. My father was a gardener and my mother a machinist—both are still alive and working. I failed my eleven-plus, and went to a secondary modern: after that I was sacked from various jobs for incompetence, and ended up with a two-year scholarship at RADA. Then I worked in rep for four months, but haven't been on the stage since. During the next few years I was married, divorced, operated on for acute appendicitis, photographed in the nude and arrested for larceny. Then came a six-month spell in prison.

And this was when you began to write plays?

Yes. All I had written before prison was a dialogue, set in a hospital, between a very old, dying man and his 70-year-old daughter. The BBC and the Royal Court both reacted favourably to it, but they both said it wasn't a play: it had no dramatic interest. My first real play was ***The Ruffian on the Stair***—it's about a young hooligan who terrorises a middle-aged woman, and provokes jealousy and violence between the woman and her husband, wreaking a rather devious kind of revenge. It's to be produced on the radio this August, but I've had to do a lot of cutting and rewriting. ***Entertaining Mr Sloane*** was written very soon after ***The Ruffian,*** actually while I was living on National Assistance.

Did your time in prison influence your writing?

It must have done, though I couldn't say *how* very precisely. More than anything, it affected my attitude towards society. Before, I had been vaguely conscious of something rotten somewhere: prison crystallised this. The old whore society really lifted up her skirts, and the stench was pretty foul. Not that actual prison treatment was bad: but it was a revelation of what really lies under the surface of our industrialised society.

You feel yourself, then, basically out of tune with the existing social set-up?

Yes, and with the political alternatives that are usually offered. I suppose I'm most in sympathy with D H Lawrence's standpoint. Now *Lady Chatterley's Lover* fails in its presentation of sex, but the basic attitude is right: if you have the kind of sexual freedom Lawrence advocated, the kind of corrupted industrial society he detested would automatically be smashed.

And yet all your plays are written about this society: are they also written against *it?*

Not specifically, they simply show what *happens* within it. One must write about those things with which one is most familiar, and in this sense all my plays are realistic. Particularly in the dialogue—I'm told that's the best part of my writing, and I suppose it's why I'm a dramatist rather than a writer of novels.

Apart from Lawrence, who has most influenced your writing?

Strindberg has been a strong influence, particularly in his later works like the *Ghost Sonata.* And I've read and been very impressed by all the Ben Travers farces, which I should say are ripe for revival. But I don't know how these very different dramatists have *affected* my own writing: the acquisition of a style begins in imitation, of course, and I used to parody other writers as well as imitate them. But I think I've developed beyond that kind of imitation now.

There does seem to be something Strindbergian in the conflict between the sexes in your plays: particularly in that between Ed and Kath in **Entertaining Mr Sloane.**

Yes: but besides conflict ***Mr Sloane*** has humour: it's a funny play. I suppose it's *about* the biter bit—this very attractive young man Sloane trying to dominate both brother and sister, play them off against one another, and ending up as a helpless victim of them both. Actually the original ending was quite different, and much more complex: and it was wrong. Many writers I think compromise themselves with over-subtle endings—Tennessee Williams is an obvious example. The new ending to ***Mr Sloane*** is a very simple, but a very natural outcome. This is how I always work: letting a situation emerge and develop gradually, without a preconceived plan—letting the characters take over.

Perhaps we could discuss these characters more specifically. How do you see Sloane himself?

I originally saw him as physically rather small and stocky—though now, of course, Dudley Sutton towers over Peter Vaughan, who plays Ed. What many people have found difficult to understand about Sloane is his combination of innocence and amorality. The English always tend to equate innocence with ignorance, which is nonsense.

The first murder of which Kemp accuses him: is this fact or fantasy?

Oh, I'm always very honest in my writing. I don't try to lead the audience up a garden path of fantasy. What my characters say is always true (or at least subjectively true), except where the contradictions or lies are made obvious to the audience. Ed, too, is speaking the truth when he says he's had birds—he *has* had birds, decided he doesn't fancy them, and prefers young lads instead. He's sexually quite capable with women, and highly potent. That's why he so positively *dislikes* women: only a man who's had experience of women can dislike them. The adorers of women tend to be impotent: the priests of the mother-goddess were always eunuchs. But Ed's hatred isn't violent or vitriolic, he's had the sense simply to see the obvious alternative.

And only when Kath's desire for Sloane comes into conflict with Ed's does the situation reach crisis point?

Yes. All the characters are basically likeable and should be sympathetically portrayed. Much of this sympathy can be achieved through humour: the scene of Kath's seduction of Sloane is very funny, and it should also be very sexy. But sex doesn't just consist in undressing or wiggling as appropriate: sexiness can be just *there* without anyone moving a muscle. Just as the humour should make the sex more real, so too it should make Sloane's murder of Kemp more real. Put a murder on the stage with a straight face, and it's just a whodunnit and nobody takes it seriously. Make it funny and you make people think about it.

Surely Kemp is scarcely a sympathetic character—a thoroughly vindictive, irritating old man?

Kemp is literally tottering on the edge of the grave, and as a character he is, of course, very much smaller than the other three.

The play is funny: but surely not strictly a comedy?

Well, certainly, not a black comedy, or whatever the currently fashionable label is. It's just a *play,* which happens to make people laugh about sodomy and nymphomania. It's a comedy insofar as the whole world and the whole human situation are comic and farcical.

Joe Orton and Simon Trussler, in an interview in Plays and Players, *Vol. 11, No. 11, August, 1964, p. 16.*

OVERVIEWS AND GENERAL STUDIES

John Bull and Frances Gray (essay date 1981)

[*In the excerpt below, Bull and Gray explore some biographical and literary influences on Orton's drama. They maintain that the connection between Orton's upbringing and his plays is indeed significant, calling Orton "the least impersonal of the modern dramatists." Bull and Gray also examine Orton's two main sources for dramatic models: the European and English Absurdists, especially Harold Pinter, and the genre of farce.*]

Joe Orton died between 2.00 and 4.00 on the night of the 9th of August 1967. He was thirty-four years old, and on the brink of the recognition and financial success as a playwright that had eluded him since he had left R.A.D.A. in 1953. He was found in bed with his entire skull smashed in, the result of nine manic blows with the hammer that had been placed neatly on the bed-cover on his chest. The blows had been struck by his friend, Kenneth Halliwell, with whom he had lived for 15 years. Halliwell was naked on the floor, a glass and a can of grapefruit-juice by his side. The twenty-two Nembutal tablets that he had swallowed had killed him considerably quicker than Orton.

Orton's funeral took place at the Golder's Green Crematorium on the 18th August. The two dozen mourners watched the coffin being carried down the aisle to the accompaniment of a tape-recording of the Beatles' song *A Day in the Life* (from the *Sergeant Pepper's Lonely Heart's Club Band* album), from which the drug references had been tastefully removed. One of the mourners suggested to Joe Orton's brother, Douglas, that the ashes should be mixed with those of Halliwell who had been cremated at Enfield the previous day. He thought hard before agreeing: "Well," he said, "as long as nobody hears about it in Leicester" [quoted in John Lahr's biography of Orton, *Prick up Your Ears,* 1978].

At the time of his death Orton must have appeared to the public as a complete embodiment of the 1960's London scene. His exploits were those of an outrageous social nonconformist. He was colourfully and promiscuously gay, a constant experimenter with drugs, possessed of a demonic sense of humour—at the time of his first London production he had written to the press complaining about the obscenity in his own play, under the pseudonym of a 'Mary Whitehouse' figure, Edna Wellthorpe (Mrs)—and in receipt of the ultimate fashionable accolade for a 60's writer, a commission to write the screenplay for a Beatles' film. Increasingly his plays reflected his involvement in this world, but always he wrote with a bleak awareness of his past as an inescapable spectre. Douglas was not alone in worrying what Leicester thought about it all.

Orton's death and his funeral were in perfect keeping with the facts of his London life, a bizarre episode that could not have been better calculated to appeal to a popular English press intent on the creation of the myth of an exciting but dangerous 'alternative' society. But there is an uncanny link with the plot of one of his major plays, ***Loot,*** which is concerned with the macabre events surrounding the funeral of the wife of a Mr McLeavy whose attitudes and obsessions are very like those of Orton's own father, William. Early in the play, the son, Hal, tells his father that another wreath has arrived, and McLeavy goes off to check the contents. The nurse, Fay, who plans to marry the widower in the seventh of her suspiciously brief unions, is left alone with Hal.

> FAY. I sometimes think your father has a sentimental attachment to roses.
>
> HAL. Do you know what his only comment was on my mother's death?
>
> FAY. Something suitable, I'm sure.
>
> HAL. He said he was glad she'd died at the right season for roses. He's been up half the night cataloguing the varieties on the crosses. You should have seen him when that harp arrived. Sniffing the petals, checking, arguing with the man who brought it. They almost came to blows over the pronunciation. If she'd played her cards right, my mother could've cited the Rose Grower's Annual as co-respondent.
>
> FAY. The Vatican would never grant an annulment. Not unless he'd produced a hybrid.

William Orton was a refugee from the modern world. He had retreated early into a peaceful world of modest horticultural activity, into his own brand of suburban pastoral. After a series of false-starts he had settled for 35 years as a gardener for Leicester City Council, and in addition devoted most of his leisure-time to the allotment and greenhouse to which he cycled 15 miles most mornings before work. Evenings and weekends were spent in this quiet refuge, away from the inarticulate demands of an unsatisfied and embittered wife, and from the growing family with whom he had little contact. "Gardening kept you busy. You always looked forward to something coming up, you see. It was exciting to see if they came up and see how they were doing every year." William Orton was the model for the succession of weak father-figures that inhabit his son's plays. McLeavy's sole ambition on the death of his wife is to construct a Rose Garden; in ***Loot*** the roses celebrate death, not life or love: "I've ordered four hundred roses to help keep memory green. On a site, only a stone's throw from the church. I intend to found the 'Mrs Mary McLeavy Memorial Rose Garden.' It will put Paradise to shame." Orton had a total contempt for his father, presenting him not only as weak but as the representative suburban man, timorous, dutiful and completely shackled by conformity. In ***Loot,*** McLeavy is rewarded for his honest and dull citizenship by being the only character to be punished by the due processes of the law he so reveres; while in the earlier television play, ***The Good and Faithful Servant*** he had appeared as Buchanan, the unquestioning employee who retires from his firm after fifty years employment, with an electric clock and an electric toaster, both of which immediately cease to function. When he learns that his newly discovered grandson, Ray, has never worked, he sets out to make him see the error of his ways:

> BUCHANAN. Not work! What do you do then?
>
> RAY. I enjoy myself.
>
> BUCHANAN. That's a terrible thing to do. I'm bowled over by this, I can tell you. It's my turn to be shocked now. You ought to have a steady job.
>
> EDITH. Two perhaps.

Still haunted by Leicester, Orton has Ray succumb to marriage, work and respectable dȯmesticity—at which point Buchanan immediately dies, the continuity having been established; in his later plays, Orton would increasingly move away from the savage presentation of his past to a riotously threatening version of the alternatives. The other side of Ray—"I enjoy myself"—came to preoccupy Orton more and more. But Orton never really escaped.

In the final, unrevised play, ***What the Butler Saw,*** Geraldine declares, "I lived in a normal family. I had no love for my father," a remark which owes as much to his own memories as it does to the character's denial of unnatural practices around which so much of the action of the play revolves. The married couple in this play become as farcically obsessed with the significance of a vase of roses as McLeavy had been with his flowers in ***Loot.*** Having persuaded his prospective secretary, Geraldine, to undress, under the pretext of giving her a medical examination, the psychiatrist, Prentice, is thwarted in his attempt at seduction by the unexpected return of his wife. He crams Geraldine's underwear into the vase and presents a surprised Mrs Prentice with the roses. Later he trims the stems to fit them on top of the concealed clothing. The visual joke is of course reinforced by the fact that the roses—which are, as the visiting psychiatrist, Rance, points out, a 'poetically' Jungian symbol of woman—are presented, and then mutilated, to hide a rather more prosaic symbol, the unfortunate Geraldine's knickers. Much of the verbal humour of ***What the Butler Saw*** derives from the absurd attempts of the supposed expert on human behaviour, Rance, to explain, in an anarchic parody of psychoanalytical terminology, the farcical results that follow Prentice's concealment of the attempted seduction; the intellectual complexity of the explanation is always at war with the physical simplicity of the cause. But the parody has a perfectly serious side for Orton. What is being parodied takes us away from the chaotic celebration of 60's excess—when Mrs Prentice believes her husband to have become a transvestite, she tells him "I'd no idea our marriage teetered on the edge of fashion"—and back into the articulated traumas of his early life.

The connection between Orton's upbringing and his plays is important, more important than for any other English playwright. He is the least impersonal of the modern dramatists. Had he lived, doubtless the connections would have become less vital; indeed in ***What the Butler Saw,*** there is strong evidence that Orton was beginning to move towards a more generalised analysis of his world. But most of his earlier writing is a straightforward attempt to exorcise through comedy the ghosts of his past; so that it is very easy to make direct links between his plots and characters, and the life of his pre-R.A.D.A. days. This obsessional re-working of his life gives the plays much of their energy, but it also points to essential weaknesses. For instance, the original version of ***The Erpingham Camp*** was as a television play for Rediffusion in 1966. It is a freewheeling attack on the British Holiday Camp, complete with regimented fun, and grotesque competition:

> ERPINGHAM. The Mother and Child competition resulted in a dead heat. Mrs J M Nash of Palmers Green and Mrs Susanne Mitchell of Southampton both win cash prizes . . . Our disability bonus was won by Mr Laurie Russell of Market Harborough. Both Laurie's legs were certified 'absolutely useless' by our Resident Medical Officer. Yet he performed the Twist and the Bossa Nova to the tune specified on the entrance form.
>
> TED. He fell over, though. Twice.
>
> LOU. They help them a lot, don't they? That blind woman would've never found the diving-board if the audience hadn't shouted out.

As a television play it is moderately successful; the problem is that the severe limitations of the selected locale make the targets too easy. It is a play rather obviously aimed at the television viewers of the Ortons' Council Estate, at a Mrs McLeavy who included among her wreaths one from "the Friends of Bingo." Orton attempts to widen the scope of the play with the abortive revolt of the holiday-makers, but the overall mood is patronising rather than anarchic in the sense of using the Camp to question larger issues. Its limitations were made apparent when, in a revised version, it was produced at the Royal Court the following year. It was too obviously playing at the wrong audience. "***The Erpingham Camp*** has the advantage of being an assault on holiday-camps intended to provoke those who attend them, rather than a sneer to flatter those who wouldn't be seen dead in one; but it retains the mealy-mouthed obviousness of the small screen, and is not yet ready to be shown to the elite" [D. A. N. Jones, in "Common Indecencies," *New Statesman* (16 June 1967)].

Much of the intended impact of Orton's plays derives from an insistent assault on a series of such British institutions as the Holiday Camp, the monarchy, the church, the mysterious workings of the public bureaucracy of police, water-board and the like. They are on the whole, in post—'Beyond the Fringe' days, fairly safe targets whose comic demolition is unlikely to surprise, let alone offend, an even casually enlightened theatre-goer. It is difficult not to feel that, when mounting such attacks, Orton was still looking back over his shoulder at Leicester. They are at their most effective, particularly in ***Loot,*** when they are presented as a confused, almost surrealistic, collage of attitudes; as when Inspector Truscott finally discovers the stolen banknotes in the coffin. The absurd moral outrage is even more comic when we realise that Truscott's distaste is simply a preamble to allowing himself to be bribed:

> TRUSCOTT. Who is responsible for this disgraceful state of affairs?
>
> HAL. I am.
>
> TRUSCOTT. (*stoops and picks up a bundle of notes*) Would you have stood by and allowed this money to be buried in holy ground?
>
> HAL. Yes.
>
> TRUSCOTT. How dare you involve me in a situation for which no memo has been issued. (*He turns the notes over*) In all my experience I've never come across a case like it. Every one of these fivers bears a portrait of the Queen. It's dreadful to contemplate the issues raised. Twenty thousand tiaras and twenty thousand smiles buried alive! She's a constitutional monarch you know. She can't answer back . . . (*He picks up another bundle and stares at them*)
>
> MCLEAVY. Well, Inspector, you've found the money and unmasked the criminals. You must do your duty and arrest them. I shall do mine and appear as witness for the prosecution.
>
> HAL. Are you married, Inspector?
>
> TRUSCOTT. Yes.
>
> HAL. Does your wife never yearn for excitement?
>
> TRUS. She did once express a wish to see the windmills and tulip fields of Holland.
>
> HAL. With such an intelligent wife you need a larger income . . .
>
> TRUS. Where is this Jesuitical twittering leading us?
>
> HAL. I'm about to suggest bribery. (*TRUSCOTT removes his pipe, no one speaks*)
>
> TRUS. How much?
>
> HAL. Twenty per cent.
>
> TRUS. Twenty-five per cent. Or a full report of this case appears on my superior's desk in the morning.
>
> HAL. Twenty-five it is.
>
> TRUS. (*shaking hands*) Done.
>
> DENNIS. (*to TRUSCOTT*) May I help you to replace the money in the casket?
>
> TRUS. Thank you, lad. Most kind of you.

Here, the pious platitudes of the Inspector are not left hanging in the air for a quick and obvious laugh; they are a surface beneath which Orton carefully reveals the face of unlicensed authority—in this instance comically corrupt, but elsewhere genuinely threatening:

> TRUS. Understand this, lad. You can't get away with cheek. Kids nowadays treat any kind of authority as a challenge. We'll challenge you. If you oppose me in my duty, I'll kick those teeth through the back of your head. Is that clear?
>
> HAL. Yes. (*Door chimes*)
>
> FAY. Would you excuse me, Inspector?
>
> TRUS. (*wiping his brow*) You're at liberty to answer your own doorbell, miss. That is how we tell whether or not we live in a free country. (*standing over HAL*) Where's the money?
>
> HAL. In church. (*TRUSCOTT kicks HAL violently. HAL cries out in terror and pain*)
>
> TRUS. Don't lie to me!
>
> HAL. I'm not lying. It's in church!
>
> TRUS. (*shouting, knocking HAL to the floor*) Under any other political system I'd have you on the floor in tears!
>
> HAL. (*crying*) You've got me on the floor in tears.

The comic policeman draws real blood. Truscott is Orton's most successfully realised character; the false logic of his bureaucratic mind takes us back to a real world and not away from it. He owes much to Orton's own experiences at the hands of the legal machinery when he and Halliwell were arrested, fined and imprisoned for defacing Public Library books." ' I wasn't actually beaten up,' he said. 'But they hovered around . . . I found that the best thing was to be as nice as possible because it was no use standing on your rights once they've got you in their power.' Privately, Orton contended that their severe sentence was 'because we were queers.' " The comically outrageous defacement of the collection of the Islington Borough Council Library thus brought Orton suddenly in conflict with the establishment in two related 'outsider' roles, as criminal and as homosexual. In the original production of ***Loot,*** Kenneth Williams tried with some success to combine Truscott's comic potential with the real violence that Orton had written into the part. In the more successful revival, Michael Bates turned Truscott into a harmless funny copper, and totally lost the desired effect.

The character of Truscott which came to dominate ***Loot,*** at the expense of Fay who is clearly intended at first to be the major figure, moved Orton away from the limitations of his usual source material. His is, played properly, not a two-dimensional part; he is paranoia made flesh. This brilliant creation is a possible indication of the way in which Orton might have developed beyond a witty, but essentially superficial, analysis of the contemporary world, to suggest the real horror that lies beneath the skin. As it is, Orton is at his best when he makes play with family archetypes. His mother's confusion of sexual energy and Council Estate propriety is captured in Kath in ***Entertaining Mr Sloane;*** as Orton's sister, Leonie, recognized immediately when she saw the 1975 Royal Court revival of the play: "That's my mum! That's her! Its like seeing a ghost. She was always over-dressing. Once she got dressed in gold lamé and painted her shoes gold just to go to the pub. The paint cracked when she walked. There were gold flakes all the way to the City Arms." Kath's attitude to Sloane is that of mother as well as lover; in both roles Orton makes it clear that Ed and Sloane find her physically repellant:

> KATH. (*to SLOANE*) Baby, my little boy . . . mamma forgives you.
>
> ED. What have you got to offer? You're fat and the crowsfeet under your eyes would make you an object of terror. Pack it in. I tell you. Sawdust up to the navel? You've nothing to lure any man.
>
> KATH. Is that the truth, Mr Sloane?
>
> SLOANE. More or less . . .
>
> KATH. Mr Sloane, I believed you were a good boy. I find you've deceived me.
>
> SLOANE. You've deceived yourself.

Whilst even during her initial seduction of Sloane, a certain maternal propriety is in order: "I don't think the fastening on this thing I'm wearing will last much longer . . . (*Pause: he attempts to move; she is almost on top of him*) Mr Sloane . . . (*Rolls on to him*) you should wear more clothes, Mr Sloane. . . . I believe you're as naked as me. And there's no excuse for it. (*Silence*) I'll be you mamma. I need to be loved. Gently. Oh! I shall be so ashamed in the morning. (*Switches off the light*) What a big heavy baby you are. Such a big heavy baby." In Sloane, Orton created a role for himself in a rearranged 'family,' first killing off the unwanted 'Dadda,' and then being willingly coerced into servicing both the handsome Ed and his sister, the peculiar mixture of spinsterly lust and maternal coyness.

There is much of Orton in Wilson, the intruder from Mike's homosexual past, who disturbs his and Joyce's unmarried domesticity, in the earlier ***The Ruffian on the Stair;*** but above all it is in ***Loot,*** with the character of Hal, the son who, unlike Orton, has not learnt to lie, that Orton comes nearest to confronting his past. The mother is dead before the play begins, but her body carries the burden of the farcical action of the play. Hal removes the corpse from the coffin, and places it upside-down in a cupboard, so that he and his bi-sexual lover, Dennis, can utilize the container to smuggle out the proceeds of their bank raid. Initially, only Dennis has scruples:

> HAL. Has anybody every hidden money in a coffin? . . .
>
> DENNIS. Think of your mum. Your lovely old mum. She gave you birth.
>
> HAL. I should thank anybody for that?
>
> DENNIS. Cared for you. Washed your nappies. You'd be some kind of monster. (*HAL takes the lid off the coffin*)
>
> HAL. Think what's at stake. (*He goes to wardrobe and unlocks it*) *Money.*

However, when, faced with the potential problem of getting rid of the body, Dennis argues that it will be safer to undress it. Hal is for the first time perturbed:

> HAL. (*pause*) Take her clothes off?
>
> DENNIS. In order to avoid detection should her remains be discovered.
>
> HAL. Bury her naked? My own mum? (*He goes to the mirror and combs his hair*) It's a Freudian nightmare.

By a curious coincidence, Orton's mother died whilst the first production of ***Loot*** was in rehearsal. Orton described his plans in his diary: "I'll have to send a telegram to find out details of my mother's funeral. I can't go home if there's nowhere to stay. And I don't fancy spending the night in the house with the corpse. A little too near the Freudian bone for comfort." His description of events is almost indistinguishable in content from the dialogue of the play. "As the corpse is downstairs in the main living room it means going out or watching television with death at one's elbow. My father, fumbling out of bed in the middle of the night, bumped into the coffin and almost had the corpse on the floor." What is different, however, is the tone. Whether he is describing a casual sexual encounter, or the sleeping arrangements during the funeral, the diary entries are objective and dispassionate, though never without humour. Orton's energy and his displays of subjective emotion were reserved for the plays. Orton wrote at length about the funeral in his diary; it was clearly an important event, representing the removal of the last ambivalent tie to his previous existence. And certainly his female characters, never very attractively presented, become in subsequent plays the victims of a no longer thinly disguised sexual disgust on Orton's part:

> SGT. MATCH. Only women are permitted to examine female suspects.
>
> PRENTICE. Doesn't that breed discontent in the force?
>
> SGT. MATCH. Among the single men there's a certain amount of bitterness. Married men who are familiar with the country are glad to be let off extra map-reading.

Orton took back to London with him one memento of his mother, a memento that emphasises the reality that the world of ***Loot*** was for him. "Leonie and I spent part of the afternoon throwing out cupboards full of junk collected over the years; magazines, photographs, Christmas cards. I found a cup containing a pair of false teeth and threw it in a dustbin. Then I discovered they belonged to my father. I had to rescue them. I found my mother's teeth in a drawer. I kept them. To amaze the cast of ***Loot.***" This strange legacy—their falsity and their appetite, Rance, in ***What the Butler Saw,*** might well argue, representing the sexual duality of Orton's mother—was a deliberately coarse affront to finer sensibilities, a head-on collision between his old world and his new. The urge to shock is apparent in all Orton's work, but it is not until the final, unrevised play, ***What the Butler Saw,*** that he really begins to concentrate his attention on a 60's London audience without a backward glance at Leicester. "I'm from the gutter," Orton once told Peggy Ramsay, his agent, "and don't you ever forget it because I won't."

Orton was not a great structural innovator. In general he used and abused the theatrical models that were to hand, and most of his recorded comments on his own dramatic techniques give the feeling of being written after the event, of being rationalisations rather than pointing towards any cohesive theory. The plotting of plays perplexed rather than interested him, and he would frequently make major changes up to and beyond the first night. Kenneth Williams was reduced to despair as the opening of ***Loot*** approached: "I'm now worried about the play—it seems a random collection of bits with no sense of wholeness . . . I can't see any sense of construction in the piece." What was happening in this instance was that Orton's increasing fascination with the figure of Truscott altered the balance of the plot almost daily; and this obsessive rewriting, in particular involving radical changes of the plays' endings, assumed ever larger proportions as his career developed. The problem was, in essence, that he was far more interested in the first part of the comic game, turning the world upside-down in a festive interlude, than he was in its traditional counterpart, putting the pieces together again at the end. Orton's fascination with the anarchic potential of human behaviour made any firm resolution of the plot narrative difficult. There is a plot which must be resolved, but it does not appear that it matters much what the conclusion is, as long as it brings the particular events to a point of *stasis.* Orton does not wish us to see his plays as moral structures, still less in terms of a process of discovery about the characters and their motivations. The plot is simply a convenient peg on which to hang his own obsessions.

The point is emphasised if we consider the two main areas that Orton turned to for his dramatic models. They are, chiefly for his early work, the plays of the European and, to some extent, the English "Absurdists," and above all to the first produced plays of Harold Pinter; and, in his later work, a broad tradition of farce. Orton's first production, ***The Ruffian on the Stair*** and ***Entertaining Mr Sloane*** (1964) owe much to Pinter's *The Birthday Party* (1958) and *The Room* (1960); indeed the opening of the original radio version of ***The Ruffian*** is taken almost word for word from that of Pinter's first play, and the format of the room taken over by sinister intruders is broadly that of Orton's first two plays. However, it is likely that Pinter, at the beginning of *The Birthday Party,* is himself evoking the opening of Ionesco's *The Bald Prima-Donna* (1956), which opens with the middle-class Mr and Mrs Smith discussing their supper: "Goodness! Nine o'clock! This evening for supper we had soup, fish, cold ham and mashed potatoes and a good English salad, and we had English beer to drink. The children drank English water. We had a very good meal this evening. And that's because we are English, because we live in a suburb of London and because our name is Smith." Certainly the supposedly logical way that Truscott establishes Fay's guilt in ***Loot*** is reminiscent of Mr and Mrs Martin's tortuous process of deduction later in the play by which they conclude that they must be married to each other. It is not important to establish particular links; from 1956 onward, the French and European 'Absurdists' were beginning to be produced in London, and there are many examples of the absurd deflation of suburban life that were available to both Pinter and Orton.

The most significant one is probably Max Frisch's *The Fire-Raisers* (1961 at the Royal Court), a play in which the respectable burghers invite the mysterious arsonists to share their house, keeping up their respectable life in spite of their certain knowledge of the consequences of their invitation. The connections with Pinter's contemporaneous work are obvious enough: "The world is full of surprises. A door can open at any moment and someone will come in. We'd love to know who it is, we'd love to know exactly what he has on his mind and why he comes in, but how often do we" [quoted in Martin Esslin's *The People Wound,* 1970]. But the intrusion into the room in Orton's plays is not into a world that could be remotely described as respectable, suburban or middle-class, nor is there any attempt, as in Pinter, to cloak the motives of the intruders in mystery. Orton stressed the point in his production notes to the Royal Court when the revised ***Ruffian*** was being staged: "The play is not written naturalistically, but it must be directed and acted with absolute *realism* . . . Unless it's real it won't be funny. Everything the characters say is true. MIKE has murdered the boy's brother, JOYCE is an ex-call girl, WILSON has an incestuous relationship with his brother, WILSON does provoke MIKE into murdering him. The play mustn't be presented as an example of the now out-dated 'mystery' school—*vide* early Pinter. Everything is as clear as the most reactionary *Telegraph* reader could wish. There is a beginning, a middle and an end." Orton's use of the model rejects the idea of the settled norm being invaded by a sinister abnorm; disorder, in conventional societal terms, is already present, and the doors open, as they do increasingly regularly, on clearly articulated explanations.

Given this, it is not surprising that the 'invaded room' model, which is to some extent still in evidence in ***What the Butler Saw*** (1969), would be further modified towards farce—the ridiculous mechanics of plot moving the audience away from any possibility of a moral evaluation of the characters' acts or motivations. On his first entrance in the last play, Rance asks, "Why are there so many doors. Was the house designed by a lunatic?" It is a question which not only emphasises the function of the psychiatric clinic in the play—a mad-house with doors for all tastes; it takes us back to the play's epigram, from Tourneur's *The Revenger's Tragedy:* "Surely we're all mad people, and they / Whom we think, are not." Farce, as Orton understood it, was a perfect medium. It allowed for a complete abandonment of a naturalistic paraphernalia of plot and character—although he continued to insist that the plays should be performed naturalistically—in favour of a world in which the repressions and sublimations of life are allowed fully-articulated play. The world that he first presented in ***What the Butler Saw*** is a true Freudian nightmare of unleashed sexual repression, free from the burdens of respectability or convention. It is civilisation without its clothes. Indeed it is Dr Prentice's inability to admit to his attempt at the only comparatively straightforward heterosexual act in the play that sets things in motion. The wife he would deceive has just returned from a meeting of a club "primarily for lesbians," during the proceedings of which she has availed herself of the body of the hotel porter, Nicholas Beckett, who is about to demand money from her for photographs taken during the event; having himself spent a large part of the previous evening molesting an entire hotel corridor of school-girls. Normality is never the norm in this play; as in the brothel in Genet's *The Balcony,* the clinic converts hidden fantasy into living reality. "Marriage excuses no one the freaks' roll-call," the policeman, Match, assures Prentice when he protests his status as a proof of his innocence. What follows is a sort of sexual *Bartholomew Fair* in which clothing is first removed and then redistributed in a confusion of sexual roles—the whole business being presided over by a lunatic bureaucrat, Rance, who offers a succession of psychoanalytical explanations of the characters' behaviour, the unlikelihood of which is only outreached by the truths of the case.

What the Butler Saw is a flawed play. It needs, and would certainly have received, considerable rewriting—in particular, the tedious running gag about the lost penis from the statue of Winston Churchill which is eventually used to bring proceedings to a halt, takes us back to the world of sacred cows, and could easily be removed. However, what it promises is a redefinition of farce, a complete liberation of *libido* in a glorious celebration of chaos and *fin-de-civilisation.* " 'It's the only way to smash the wretched civilisation,' I said, making a mental note to hot-up ***What the Butler Saw*** when I came to re-write . . . Yes. Sex is the only way to infuriate them. Much more fucking and they'll be screaming hysterics in next to no time." But sex is both the subject of the play and the vehicle which suggests potentially more serious matters. The tradition of farce which Orton had inherited was diluted and trivial; it confirmed rather than questioned the assumptions of its audience. Orton's unusually perceptive analysis of the situation suggests that, given time, he might well have developed into a major dramatist.

> I am a great admirer of Ben Travers, in particular, but the boundaries he set to present-day farce are really very narrow. As I understand it, farce originally was very close to tragedy, and differed only in the *treatment* of its themes—themes like rape, bastardy, prostitution. But you can't have farce about rape any longer. French farce goes as far as adultery, but by Ben Travers' time it was only *suspected* adultery, which turned out to have been innocuous after all . . . A lot of farces today are still based on the preconceptions of half a century ago. But we must now accept the fact that, for instance, people *do* have sexual relations outside marriage: a 30's farce is still acceptable because it is distanced by its period, but a modern farce which merely nurses the old outworn assumptions is cushioning people against reality. And this, of course, is just what the commercial theatre usually does. In theory there is no subject which could *not* be treated farcically—just as the Greeks were prepared to treat any subject farcically. But in practice farce has become a very restricted form indeed.

Orton's awareness of the proximity of farce and tragedy, both as theatrical modes and as mirrors of psychological reaction to chaos, points to what he was attempting in ***What the Butler Saw;*** but it also highlights the structural weakness, in particular its lack of any resolve. Orton seems only fascinated by the chaos and with a sense of personal liberation achieved by its embracement. Whilst the plays of such as Tourneur and Webster move easily from farce to tragedy, the presentation of chaos counterpointed by a sense of moral order, in Orton's work the possible transition to a tragic sense of farce is never a possibility. The characters do end the play bloodied, if unbowed, but that transition is purely mechanical. As Orton argues, farce has become a purely escapist medium, on the run from precisely that which it had originally presented—the disturbing manifestations of the human consciousness which threaten the stability of the social order. Farce, from the 30's through Brian Rix's Whitehall antics, no longer really explored the subconscious fears of public self-revelation; it provided a safety-valve, allowing the audience to laugh off nothing more important than losing one's trousers in public. Thematically, Orton moves farce towards a properly Freudian consideration of its roots, but the connection between plot and character is never satisfactorily made. In the end, we cannot take any of it very seriously. It may offend, it may amuse, but it does not involve. Orton has frequently been compared to Wilde, and it is an instructive comparison. In one respect at least he

John Russell Taylor on Orton's style:

The key to Orton's dramatic world is to be found in the strange relationship between the happenings of his plays and the manner in which the characters speak of them. The happenings may be as outrageous as you like in terms of morality, accepted convention or whatever, but the primness and propriety of what is said hardly ever breaks down. And the gift of Orton's characters for intricate and inventive euphemism, so far from toning down the outrageousness of their actions and ideas, only places it in even stronger relief. Orton was, perhaps first and foremost, a master of verbal style—or of his own particular verbal style. And even during his short public career his mastery of that style may be observed increasing and refining itself.

John Russell Taylor, in his The Second Wave: British Drama for the Seventies, *Hill and Wang, 1971.*

is completely different. Where Wilde invites us to see beyond the brittle and studied brilliance of his characters' dialogue, the hollowness underneath, Orton presents all his cards directly at the audience. What we are being shown is the underneath. What Orton is moving towards is the presentation of a pre-civilised world in which the awakened subconscious at large in a decadent society makes each individual a 'minority group.' The problem is that the action takes place entirely on the surface, and it is as a manipulator of the restricted codes of opposing languages of ordinary discourse that Orton, on what he has left us, has finally to be measured. (pp. 71-84)

John Bull and Frances Gray, "Joe Orton," in Essays on Contemporary British Drama, *edited by Hedwig Bock and Albert Wertheim, Max Hueber Verlag, 1981, pp. 71-96.*

Joan F. Dean (essay date 1982)

[Dean is an American educator and critic who writes on modern drama. In the following essay, she explores how Orton's comedies extend the accepted boundaries of farce as a genre. Rather than present his plays as light entertainment, Dean maintains, Orton portrayed selfishness, unbounded desires, and hypocrisy as typical of human nature.]

The critical prejudice against farce as an intellectually and artistically valid dramatic genre is probably as old as the word itself. "Farce" derives from the Latin verb *farcire,* meaning "to stuff"; its etymology recalls its early use as referring to an amplification, often impromptu and buffoonish, of medieval church liturgy. Writing about Italian comedy of the sixteenth and seventeenth centuries, K. M. Lea epitomizes critics who suggest the intrinsic inferiority of farce as a dramatic genre [in *Italian Popular Comedy: A Study in the Commedia dell'Arte 1520-1620 with Special Reference to the English Stage,* 1934]: "Farce is comedy reduced to commercialism. The best farce is what gives the maximum of amusement for the minimum of intellectual efforts." This presistent critical bias against farce also underlies Barbara Cannings's criteria for identifying farce [in "Towards a Definition of Farce as a Literary 'Genre,'" *Modern Language Review,* 56 (1961)]:

> The vital question to ask, then, is: 'What is this play about?' And it is safe to say that if it is about people it is a farce, whereas if it is about political, historical or religious ideas, if its significance is symbolic rather than personal, or if it is merely a display of verbal pyrotechnics, it is not a farce.

Cannings's attempt to distinguish farce from medieval *débat,* parody, and *sotie* produces an extreme generalization, but like many critics she assumes that farce is primarily an entertainment not to be taken seriously. In writing specifically about the works of Joe Orton, Simon Shepherd evinces a similar critical aversion to farce [in "Edna's Last Stand, or Joe Orton's Dialectic of Entertainment," *Renaissance and Modern Studies,* 22 (1978)]: "To perpetuate the belief that [Orton's] plays are merely rather outrageous farces is . . . to tuck them behind the proscenium and silence them." Even the *Oxford English Dictionary* in its definition of farce as "a dramatic work (usually short) which has for its sole object to excite laughter" confirms the critical prejudice against farce.

Another basis for the disparaging use of the term farce is the belief that such plays are populated by caricatures rather than fully drawn, well-developed characters capable of growth and change. The prevailing assumption is that the farceur is not so much unwilling as unable to create three-dimensional characters. The gross physical action and slapstick violence of farce seem better suited to simple, readily identifiable characters than to complex or sophisticated ones. Consequently, some definitions of farce emphasize the inferior social, economic, or intellectual status of its characters. From the time of the *fabula Atellena,* farce has been linked with buffoons, rustic yokels, and lower-class characters—characters who populate what Mikhail Bakhtin, in writing about Rabelais, [in his *Rabelais and His World,* 1968], describes as "a boundless world of humorous forms and manifestations opposed to the official and serious tone of medieval ecclesiastical and feudal culture." Even in the works of Shakespeare, Molière, and Wilde, the inhabitants of the best households behave primitively, ludicrously, or even impolitely—thereby severing the link between man's economic status and his potential for farcical or ridiculous behavior. But in modern drama, farce frequently crosses economic lines to acknowledge the mechanistic or animalistic nature potential in all men. Absurdist theatre, as in the plays of Beckett and Ionesco, also stresses the psychology that reduces man to an animal or a machine; so does silent-film comedy. Especially in the twentieth century, farce cuts across class barriers to show that any one might act barbarically.

Among recent critics of farce as a dramatic genre, Eric Bentley and Leonard C. Pronko are especially important. Bentley's famous defense of farce, "The Psychology of Farce" [*The New Republic* (6 January 1958 and 13 January 1958)], cogently argues for the genre's primitive vitality and psychological validity.

> Farce in general offers a special opportunity: shielded by delicious darkness and seated in warm security, we enjoy the privilege of being totally passive while on stage our most treasured unmentionable wishes are fulfilled before our imagination. In that application of the formula which is bedroom farce, we savor the adventure of adultery, ingeniously exaggerated in the highest degree, and all without taking the responsibility or suffering the guilt.

Pronko's study of Feydeau [in his *Georges Feydeau,* 1975] records the connection between Feydeau's farces and the theatre of the absurd, and, like Bentley, stresses the darker side of human nature suggested by farce:

> Lurking beneath the frenetically joyous surface, however, is a vision of the world in explosion which was to go almost unnoticed until the mid-twentieth century—a vision which gives depth and bite to comedies and farces which might otherwise have perished along with the halcyon days they depict.

In Feydeau's work, Pronko recognizes the possibility that

farce can accommodate a vision of man's animality and selfishness. In the works of Joe Orton this possibility was fully realized.

The dark side of the comic vision, the side explored by Orton, has its own precedents and traditions among both playwrights and theorists. The plays of Aristophanes, Euripides, Shakespeare, Jonson, Molière, and Congreve all consider man's potentially limitless animality, lust, greed, and selfishness. As their subjects, these dramatists take areas of human experience often considered beyond the limits of art, let alone the conventions of their genres: those unbounded realms of Dionysiac frenzy, anarchy, and even nihilism. In pursuing these subjects, these playwrights frequently expand or redefine the boundaries of their genre—sometimes bursting them completely. For Aristophanes, as Cedric Whitman observes [in his *Aristophanes and the Comic Hero,* 1964], "bawdry . . . serves merely to illustrate vividly the poet's devotion to the limitless, that kind of world view which . . . is almost the exact opposite of what we term morality. Boundlessness itself, one might say, is the essence of the Aristophanean comic impulse. . . ." Similarly, glimpses of the limitless potential of man can be seen in Euripides's *The Bacchae,* Shakespeare's *Measure for Measure,* Jonson's *Volpone,* Molière's *The Misanthrope,* or Congreve's *The Way of the World.* In those profoundly disquieting moments, the perimeters of dramatic genres were redefined. But however disquieting a perception of man's nature is offered by these authors, it is counterbalanced by a more optimistic vision of the human condition in other characters or other works. Moreover, goodness usually foils—in both senses of the word—the villainy of those who would persecute or victimize. In *Alcestis,* the ostensible self-sacrifice of the title character contrasts with her husband's willingness to let her die in his place; in *Measure for Measure,* the healthy sexuality of Claudio and Julietta is sanctioned while Angelo's hypocrisy is exposed; in *Volpone,* the predatory schemes of Volpone and Mosca turn back upon their perpetrators while the virtue of Celia is preserved. But in Orton's plays, virtue, if it can be found, is a sham.

Among aestheticians and philosophers who have discussed comedy, there is an even greater emphasis on its dark and disquieting dimension. From the time of Aristotle, descriptions of comedy have stressed the superiority that the audience enjoys over the play's characters. Hobbes's definition of laughter [in his essay "Of Human Nature"] accentuates this aspect of comedy:

> The passion of laughter is nothing else but sudden glory arising from some sudden conception of some eminency in ourselves, by comparison with the infirmity of others, or with our own formerly.

Baudelaire writes [in his essay "On the Essence of Laughter, and, in General, On the Comic in the Plastic Arts"] that "the comic is one of the clearest tokens of the satanic in man." For him, the laughter elicited by the violent and the grotesque, which he calls "the absolute comic," is not only man's assertion of his own superiority but close to the truth of human nature. For Nietzsche [in his *Thus Spoke Zarathrustra*], laughter which could transcend morality was the crowning glory offered by Zarathustra: "This laughter's crown, this rose-wreath crown: to you, my brothers, do I throw this crown! I have canonized laughter; you Higher Men, *learn*—to laugh!" While taste, decorum, and the desire for commercial success may have restrained other playwrights, Orton seeks the laughter described by Hobbes, Baudelaire, and Nietzsche—a laughter that redefines the boundaries of farce as other authors had redefined the nature of their genres.

As a British author of farce in the 1960s, Orton faced a tradition that was commercially oriented and inhospitable to his limitless vision. Pronko argues that French farce at the beginning of this century was more complex and disturbing than its British counterpart: "The truth is that English farce blunted its edge with sentimentality and at least the suggestions of moralizing. Like melodrama and thesis plays in both countries, English farce affirmed the status quo and entrenched the public more securely in its comfortable beliefs."

Updated by Rattigan, Coward, and Simpson, British farce had specific boundaries dictated by popular mores, taste, and decorum that Orton's plays transgressed. In the mid-sixties, farce flowered in London: Brian Rix's run of farces at Whitehall Theatre continued to draw audiences throughout two decades; there were several revivals of works by Feydeau, Sardou, and Ben Travers, as well as new farces by the likes of Peter Shaffer and Orton. But for the preponderance of these dramatists, the climate in which farce thrives—the reign of the Lord of Misrule, the Dionysian revels of hedonism, the period of suspended morality—is ultimately an exception, at best a temporary condition; eventually the return to the responsibilities and conventions of society must be made. At this crucial point Joe Orton departs from his predecessors and contemporaries by refusing to acknowledge a fundamental difference between the bizarre circumstances of his plays and the course of mundane reality.

Orton's decision to write farce not only capitalized on the popularity it enjoyed in the 1960s, but was also a reaction against the drama by and about the angry young men of the 1950s. In 1964, with specific reference to ***The Ruffian on the Stair,*** he recognized the vast possibilities of farce as opposed to the limited opportunities of issue-oriented drama:

> Ten years ago this theme would have provided an addition to that moribund theatrical genre, Strong Drama. Since the mid-fifties, playwrights have forsaken the inshore fisheries for the ocean proper. Today it is farce [Quoted in John Lahr, *Prick Up Your Ears,* 1978].

As Orton perceived farce in the mid-sixties, it was not only commercially but also artistically viable as a vehicle to accommodate his perception of the boundless. While other playwrights accepted the boundaries of farce, Orton evoked the spirit of Euripides's *The Bacchae* by delving into the darkest recesses of the comic vision. His brief career as a playwright, ended by his lurid murder, at the age of thirty-four, left three full-length dramatic works (***Entertaining Mr. Sloane,*** 1964; ***Loot,*** 1966, and ***What the Butler Saw,*** 1969), two short plays (***The Ruffian on the***

Stair, 1967 and the ***The Erpingham Camp,*** 1967), two television dramas (***The Good and Faithful Servant,*** 1967 and ***Funeral Games,*** 1968), a novel (***Head to Toe,*** 1961), and an unproduced screenplay (***Up Against It,*** 1967).

With conventional farces, Orton's plays share themes that have remained remarkably consistent over the past four centuries: selfishness, lust, and greed. His plays are also characterized by the frenetic physical activity that is regularly associated with farce. Yet the term farce, even in its most sophisticated manifestations, still carries the perjorative connotations of facile amusement and limited vision—connotations distinctly unsuited to Orton's work. His farce neither provides nor suggests a safe, orderly world to which his characters (or audience) can retreat.

Orton's deeply disturbing vision of man's animality implies that perhaps the best thing we can do is to recognize the vacuity of categorical morality. Perverse and healthy, right and wrong, rational and irrational are polarities which coalesce in his plays. Hypocrisy seems to be the only or at least the cardinal sin in Orton's cosmos—and it manifests itself in myriad forms. Most obvious are the societal institutions that ensnare his worst (i.e., most despicable) characters: the Catholic Church, the police, the welfare state.

Orton is an anarchist who calls into question the most essential source of identity—sexual identity. As John Lahr observes [in his biography of Orton, *Prick up Your Ears,* 1978], "Orton had a clown's appetite for political anarchy; but for him this was impossible without sexual anarchy." The anarchy that he depicts draws its strength from the polymorphous perversity that is latent and potential in every human subconscious. His landscapes are decidedly Hobbesian in their bleakness and sterility where the best chance for an individual lies in his devotion to himself and his own pleasures. Orton's anarchy is more dangerous than the pity or fear (or whatever other tragic emotion) he might have generated, at least partially because the comedy that it elicits is always grounded in laughter.

While Orton rarely uses the sophisticated drawing rooms or boudoirs of the upper class that were so popular in nineteenth-century farce, in his earlier works he does employ domestic settings that are at least superficially conventional. Typically, his first works use a domestic situation with some jarring curiosity: an unstable common-law marriage (***The Ruffian on the Stair***); a family composed of an aged father, an unmarried and nymphomaniacal daughter, and a homosexual son (***Entertaining Mr. Sloane***); the belated marriage of a couple whose illegitimate children have already produced illegitimate grandchildren (***The Good and Faithful Servant***). What is distinctly unconventional is not so much the setting of these plays, but the dearth of institutional sanctions (especially concerning marriage) in his sitting rooms. In his later works, Orton's settings are more hyperbolic but more complementary to his thematic concerns: ***The Erpingham Camp,*** for instance, is a masochistic resort for holiday makers. As Lahr notes [in "Artist of the Outrageous," *Evergreen Review,* 14, No. 2 (Feb. 1970)]: "Orton takes farce past Feydeau. He moves the laughter out of the parlor and puts it in a mortuary (***Loot***) and a psychiatric clinic (***What the Butler Saw***)."

The settings of his works move from the lower-class environment of ***The Ruffian on the Stair*** to the upper-class ambience of ***What the Butler Saw,*** but regardless of the poverty or wealth of his characters, their motives and desires remain essentially the same. By employing increasingly bourgeois and affluent settings, Orton did not seek to deny his own lower-class background but rather to extend his perception of man's animality by cutting across all class lines.

The atmosphere invariably generated by these settings is one of claustrophobia and entrapment. Characters find themselves cornered in their own living rooms, imprisoned in Erpingham's vacation camp, or straight-jacketed in a mental institution. These are, of course, Orton's microcosmic depictions of contemporary society; in them, characters are driven by private fantasies and desires that are, at least in polite society, neither acknowledged nor pursued. But for Orton, polite society is itself a ruse.

The claustrophobia and entrapment evident at the end of Orton's plays are antithetical to the freedom and power that one character usually enjoys at the outset. That freedom or power enables a character to pursue his fantasy and to subjugate at least one other character. Oblivious to the possibility that each can hoist himself on his own petard, Kath seduces Sloane, Nurse McMahon orders Mr. McLeavy to propose to her, and Dr. Prentice orders Geraldine Barclay to undress for her physical examination. Yet in each instance as soon as someone of greater authority appears (Kath's brother Ed, Inspector Truscott of the Yard, or Dr. Rance from the mental branch of Her Majesty's Government) the potential victimizer is at a distinct disadvantage and in a position to become the victim of blackmail.

Blackmail, in fact, is the single vicious circumstance that appears most often in Orton's work. In ***The Ruffian on the Stair,*** the intruder, Wilson, attempts to blackmail both Joyce and Mike with the knowledge that she is or was a prostitute and that Mike murdered Wilson's brother. By the play's end, the final blackmail might be mistaken for love by the romantic as Joyce and Mike find themselves bound to each other in their murder of Wilson. Their interdependence hinges upon mutually corroborating alibis; so does whatever relationship they may have in the future.

Intruders like Wilson are a staple of Orton's plotlines. In ***Entertaining Mr. Sloane*** the intruder, Sloane, begins in the familiar position of power since he manages to control others because their lusts are at least momentarily stronger and more unmanageable than his own. But, like Wilson in ***Ruffian on the Stair,*** by the end of the play Sloane is the one controlled. If he was the victimizer early in the play, he has become the victim in its final moments; the trickster has been tricked.

The difficulty in using terms such as victim or victimizer is that they imply moral categories—categories beyond power relationships—which are not applicable to the vast majority of Orton's characters. Certainly, for instance, none of the three characters in ***The Ruffian on the Stair*** is "better" or more virtuous than the others. In ***Entertaining Mr. Sloane,*** this point is complicated by Kemp, the

Dadda, who (might) appear less (overtly) dangerous or (perhaps) only weaker than the other characters. Orton himself risks no such moral judgments. His characters all have something to hide, some complicity or secret that exposes them to the threat of blackmail.

Sloane appears a reasonably typical example. He seems to be little more than a body with the fitness of youth, the strength to murder, and bleached-blonde hair: unreflective, non-introspective, guiltless, and conscienceless. His past, which includes at least one murder, means nothing to him except as he might use it to rationalize his actions. Sloane is the product of a state and a society that has come to believe in behavioralism: Sloane is what he is because society has made him that way and will, most likely, forgive or at least accommodate him for his deeds. And yet, by the play's end, Sloane has lost his freedom; he will be shuffled between Kath and Ed for as long as they want or can tolerate such an arrangement or until he kills one or both of them. Power, in Orton's grotesquely yet comically Hobbesian vision, enriches any given character's freedom while simultaneously diminishing another's. Finally, everyone in ***Entertaining Mr. Sloane*** is compromised in an intricate web of blackmailing. Sloane, Kath, and Ed are all interdependent: Kath is pregnant with Sloane's child; Ed is infatuated with Sloane; Sloane, having murdered the Dadda, is at the mercy of Kath and Ed.

The Good and Faithful Servant, a television play, is the last of Orton's works to deal with the lower or lower-middle class. Like ***The Ruffian on the Stair*** and ***Entertaining Mr. Sloane,*** it lacks the verbal pyrotechnics, broad physical humor, and manic intensity that characterizes Orton's later and more incisive farces. As his most naturalistic work, ***The Good and Faithful Servant***'s potential for farce is diminished by an overpowering system, a socialistic industrial complex, which dominates the lives of its characters. But no matter how touched we may be by the thwarted romance between Buchanan and Edith, Buchanan is presented as a hypocrite who would deny his doubly illegitimate grandson the carnal pleasures he himself enjoyed. Whatever heartstrings are tugged in the opening scene of Buchanan's and Edith's mutual rediscovery after fifty years of enervating employment, Buchanan cannot see that he perpetuates the very system that he should despise. The claustrophobic and in this case asphyxiating atmosphere in the play is inextricably bound to Orton's social commentary—the likes of Buchanan are trapped in drudgery because they accept it as a given of modern life and thereby perpetuate it.

With ***Loot*** Orton moves beyond the comparatively naturalistic style of his earlier plays and into the arena of Dionysiac farce. Indeed, the rebellion of Ray, Buchanan's grandson in ***The Good and Faithful Servant,*** is entirely ineffectual when compared with Hal's abandon in ***Loot.*** The sanctimoniousness of McLeavy, a prominent Catholic layman, is less attractive than the perverse vigor of Fay, Hal, and Dennis. These three characters display human desires unmitigated and unfettered by decorum, mores, or even morality. Orton does nothing in ***Loot*** to vitiate the depravity of Fay, Hal, and Dennis, and yet they vigorously hold the audience's affections. Fay has murdered several previous husbands and patients; Hal, who passes the time by "thieving from slot machines and deflowering the daughters of better men," plans to open an extravagently decadent brothel blasphemously called the Consummatum Est; Dennis has spent considerable time in prison.

If Orton lapsed into any fatalistic vision of the human condition in ***The Good and Faithful Servant,*** he makes light of such sentimentality and determinism in ***Loot.*** Early in the play, Hal and Dennis are faced with the task of undressing Hal's mother in order to hide the booty from a bank robbery. In light of what Hal himself perceives to be "a Freudian nightmare," he tells his cohort:

> HAL. *Turning from the mirror.* I am a Catholic. *Putting his comb away.* I can't undress her. She's a relative. I can go to Hell for it.
>
> DENNIS. I'll undress her then. I don't believe in Hell. *He begins to screw down the coffin lid.*
>
> HAL. That's typical of your upbringing, baby. Every luxury was lavished on you—atheism, breast-feeding, circumcision. I had to make it my own way.

In Orton's world, a sound, religious upbringing is hardly an advantage.

In ***The Erpingham Camp*** Orton's portrayal of the microcosm demonstrates not only the fascistic and repressive nature of society but also the farcical willingness with which its members accept and perpetuate that system. As in ***The Good and Faithful Servant,*** Orton shows that such pyramidical structures, hierarchies in general, draw strength from their members' acquiescence. The program of fun and games for holiday makers at Erpingham's camp includes a regimen of humiliation—a humiliation they accept and, in fact, seek out. When the Entertainments Organiser drops dead and Riley receives his big opportunity to emcee the evening's festivities, the campers do not hesitate to comply with his bizarre orders. Riley tells Ted to take off his clothes and do the can-can, and Ted willingly consents. Riley tells Eileen, who is pregnant, to enter in the loudest scream competition and when she does, he slaps her face. Riley's ludicrous failure as Entertainments Organiser grows out of his inability to distinguish light-hearted humiliation from blatant degradation. Once the campers are driven to rebellion by Riley's lack of discernment, Erpingham disdains Riley's plan for negotiations and lapses into political metaphors:

> I won't have your rubbishy ideas brought into my camp. If it's your ambition to be Secretary General of the United Nations, you're at liberty to apply for the post. Personally I think you're better employed blowing up balloons for the underfives. (*He draws himself up with dignity.*) This whole episode has been fermented by a handful of intellectuals. If we stand firm by the principles on which the camp was founded the clouds will pass. To give in now would be madness. (*He takes a deep breath. He has recovered his composure.*) Behave as though nothing had happened. It's my intention to defy the forces of Anarchy with all that is best in twentieth-century civilisa-

> tion. I shall put a record of Russ Conway on and browse through a James Bond.

Erpingham is finally lynched by the outraged campers, and order is restored as Riley takes over the camp with full intentions of emulating Erpingham's administration. In ***The Erpingham Camp,*** which Lahr identifies as Orton's "version of *The Bacchae,*" there is no order of promise to supersede the failures of the old.

Funeral Games continues Orton's preoccupation with reversible hierarchies as he returns again to religion in this television play. Pringle, having gained notoriety as well as propriety by supposedly murdering his adulterous wife, preaches a brand of Christianity dependent upon the lack of forgiveness. As he puts it, "I won't tolerate forgiveness. It's a thing of the past." But Pringle's acclaim as a popular if not populist preacher is threatened because he has not actually murdered his wife; she, in fact, is living with McCorquodale, who did murder his wife when he discovered her adultery with, of all people, Pringle. Once again, the blackmail situation dominates the plot, for if the public learns that Pringle has not exacted the bloody retribution from his wife and that he was guilty of the very crime for which he allegedly murdered her, his newly found wealth will perish along with his prestige.

What the Butler Saw, Orton's final and best play, is confirmation of Bentley's statement [in his *The Life of the Theatre* 1967] that "outrage to family piety, and propriety is certainly at the heart of farce." Set in a psychiatric clinic whose purpose "isn't to cure, but to liberate and exploit madness" the play deals with the most serious themes of literature—incest, madness, birth and death—with astonishing irreverence. At the play's core is a quartet of characters, Geraldine Barclay, Nicholas Beckett, and Dr. and Mrs. Prentice, who, under other circumstances, might have comprised the quintessential nuclear family. But the fact that Geraldine and Nicholas are the twin offspring of the Prentices is not revealed until the libidinal depths of each character have been plumbed.

The play begins as Dr. Prentice's attempt to seduce Geraldine is interrupted by his wife's unexpected return from the Station Hotel, where Nicholas Beckett attempted to blackmail and rape her. Into this tidy psychological nightmare walks Dr. Rance, representative of Her Majesty's Government and, as he says, "of order," "obviously a force to be reckoned with." Rance's presence confuses the power structure because Prentice is now in danger of being accused of professional misconduct.

Within moments of his entrance Rance commits Geraldine on the strength of Prentice's statement that she sexually provoked him. Unwittingly, Rance seizes upon the notion that "this child was unnaturally assaulted by her own father. I shall," he says, "base my future actions upon that assumption. . . . It's obvious to the meanest amateur, Prentice, that you resemble the patient's father. That is why she undressed herself. When I arrived on the scene she was about to re-enact that initial experience with her parent." Blundering upon what is not revealed as the truth until the play's final moments, Rance plans to make a fortune with a lurid sensationalistic " 'documentary-type' novelette [that] will go into twelve record-breaking reprints."

Rance's voyeuristic delight in applying his psycho-sexual theories to this situation underscores Orton's faith in man's rampant and polymorphous sexual appetites. Rance can be seen as the ultimate extension of the Vice character in that he has been sanctioned and even empowered by society itself. He is directly responsible for several of the most grotesquely funny incidents (e.g., the shaving of Geraldine's head) and indirectly responsible for most of the others (e.g., the attempt of Geraldine to disguise herself as a page from the Station Hotel).

What the Butler Saw moves beyond the previously defined boundaries of farce in that it shows us that the bizarre goings-on at Prentice's clinic are not a temporary aberration from the orderly course of events, but that disorder and confusion grow immediately out of normal conditions. The sole unusual circumstance is the arrival of Rance. Otherwise, Orton is careful to suggest, everything is as perverse as it normally is. Perversion, in this instance, is not something out of the ordinary, but a daily reality: Mrs. Prentice has cavorted with what her husband describes as a coven of witches for some time; Prentice himself has regularly misbehaved with job applicants; Nicholas Beckett has often molested guests at the Station Hotel.

At the end of his plays, Orton presents society as a threat that will uncover and consequently compromise his characters. The police are called in at the end of ***Ruffian*** and ***Sloane*** only after the proper alibis have been concocted. At the end of ***Loot,*** Fay tells Hal that he will have to give up Dennis because "people would talk"; ***Funeral Games*** brings on the police with the threat of prison for Pringle, but his acclaim as a righteously indignant husband and minister will most likely sustain him through whatever charges are brought against him. ***Butler*** probably has the most striking of Orton's endings as the "larger than life-sized" bronze phallic fragment of Churchill's statue is brandished and the characters reluctantly accept their need to return to a society of duplicity.

The endings link the characters as participants as well as accomplices in some deed that society finds improper. As their deeds remain their own and the audience's secret, Orton's characters are together in having seen and shown the animalistic, and often unsavory side of human selfishness, desires, and out-and-out lust. Orton's endings, like Shakespeare's or Jonson's, do not invariably see justice done, good rewarded, and evil punished. That Mr. McLeavy is hauled off to the police station and, we assume, to prison, is fundamentally no different.

Orton's farces have appeared so appalling because they refuse to return the audience to the safety and stability of the status quo. By taking the standard characteristics of farce—man's unregenerate and unbounded lusts, his animality, his avarice, his willingness to indulge in patently ridiculous action, and the reign of Misrule—and taking them seriously, in fact giving them to us as the human condition, Orton has outraged nearly everyone and stood true to his claim that his are moral plays. By not compromising, not showing that the action of the play is a "temporary truancy from the family pieties" [Bentley, "The Psychology of Farce," *The New Republic,* 13 January 1958], but rather a relatively typical episode, Orton approximates the Nietzschean "all-too-human" vision of man.

Orton's claim that he is a moralist is predicated upon his refusal to undercut the picture of man's insatiably aggressive nature by sleight-of-hand at the end of the plays. At the end of ***What the Butler Saw,*** the double incest between mother and son, father and daughter is greeted not with the horror that moved Oedipus to blind himself but with the serene recognition that even one's own son may be good in bed (specifically, in this instance, in a linen closet). None of the characters feel the need for any atonement, principally because they feel no sense of sin, guilt, or immorality.

In writing about farce Eric Bentley mused that "It is hard to imagine what true indifference to morals could produce, if anything at all" ["The Psychology of Farce," *The New Republic,* 6 January 1958]. Orton's indifference to morals, at least as the term morals is conventionally used, produced a decidedly bleak and deeply disquieting yet vigorous insight into humanity's truest wishes and most closely guarded desires. His perception of human nature is neither attractive nor optimistic, but by embodying it in farce, Orton realized the possibility for farce to convey a sense of the boundless, the unlimited, the Dionysiac. Like the works of some earlier dramatists who considered man's unbridled desires, Orton's plays redefine his genre to accommodate his insight into the unbounded desires and energies in man. Orton moves farce beyond banality and toward a vision of the infinite. (pp. 481-92)

Joan F. Dean, "Joe Orton and the Redefinition of Farce," in Theatre Journal, *Vol. 34, No. 4, December, 1982, pp. 481-92.*

ENTERTAINING MR. SLOANE

PRODUCTION REVIEWS

The Times, London (review date 7 May 1964)

[*In the review below, the critic characterizes the original London staging of* Entertaining Mr. Sloane *as lively and comical. Although he praises the production, the critic questions Orton's intentions, especially whether he sees the world as "an interesting pattern of personal relationships he wished to study or a darkly comical account of sides of human nature he detests."*]

The critic's standard procedure, respected text books have informed us, is to examine a work in relation to its writer's intentions. Style, characterization, the structure and dynamics of its story and, in the case of a play, the quality of production and acting take what validity they have from their fidelity to an original intention. The text books do not instruct us in the detection of purposes which seem obscure.

Mr. Joe Orton's play sends a belated and delinquent adolescent, aged 20, to lodge at the house of Kath and Kemp, her father. It seems to be irrelevant that the house is built on and almost engulfed by a rubbish dump, but it is relevant that Kath has furnished it with a horrid, semi-refined vulgarity. Sloane, the lodger, happens to be a murderer; Kemp happens to know this; Ed, Kath's successful wealthy brother, happens to be a homosexual. As Sloane is prepared for anything that gives him money and comfort, the precise nature of the triangle that results defies geometrical definition, but a resolution of a sort is achieved when Sloane erupts into delinquent violence and, no longer able to bargain, becomes the subject of bargaining between the two unfortunates who depend emotionally on him.

Mr. Patrick Dromgoole's production gains liveliness and numerous laughs by placing Mr. Dudley Sutton's cold, vigilant and humourless young criminal, played with restraint and chilly egotism, between Miss Madge Ryan's at times almost embarrassing caricature of sloppy, possessive middle-aged sexuality and Mr. Peter Vaughan's patient, hinting but unmistakable and heavily played man hunter.

The resulting dissonances and occasional concords are cleverly calculated and reveal what character the play offers. All three performances, and Mr. Charles Lamb's senile malignancy, are good, and Mr. Orton can make an audience laugh; his jokes are either rudely outspoken or depend upon a sudden elevation of conversational style into what Mr. Ivor Brown some years ago christened "Jargantuan". The coarseness is sometimes offensive but it is characteristic of the offensive people who use it; it is theatrically valid.

Is this the world as Mr. Orton sees it, an interesting pattern of personal relationships he wished to study or a darkly comical account of sides of human nature he detests? There is sufficient natural theatricality about his first play to encourage belief that we shall soon find his activities less obscure.

"Hard to Define Triangle," in The Times, *London, May 7, 1964, p. 20.*

Norman Nadel (review date 13 October 1965)

[*Nadel is an American drama critic and writer on the arts. In the following review, he praises the Broadway debut of* Entertaining Mr. Sloane *for Alan Schneider's strong direction and for the inspired performances by the cast. Nadel concludes, however, that the play itself is not believable and contains "morosely dull" passages.*]

Entertaining Mr. Sloane has the sprightly charm of a medieval English cesspool. In pointing this out I have no wish to offend the cesspool people, British or domestic, who serve an honest function, which is perhaps more than can be said for the play by Joe Orton which opened last night at the Lyceum.

Conscience also bids me add that as cesspools, or plays,

go, this one is fashioned of strong materials. Acting is fascinating, set is appropriately dismal, dialogue is bizarre. Only the subject matter and the characters are apt to unsettle the stomach, but actually, they are quite enough. However, let me tell you about young Orton's play (a contraversial success in London) on the remote chance that it might be (you'll forgive the expression) your dish of tea:

Sloane is the handsome, young man who comes to look at a room in a desolate London house which is set in the middle of a rubbish heap. He is received caressingly by the 40-year-old landlady, who explains she is nude under her housedress, changes to a nightie and negligee and seduces him.

Before they consummate their passion on the sitting room sofa, however, the landlady's somewhat cracked old father stabs the lad in the leg with the crumpet-toasting fork. This is not entirely inhospitable as it might seem. "The Dadda" had recognized Sloane as a murderer.

Also intervening between first overture and fulfillment in the opening act is a scene involving the boy and Ed, the landlady's brother, a successful businessman. This first exploratory verbal encounter between two homosexuals (Sloane, as events prove, is sexually adaptable) is as distasteful as it is honest.

What with pregnancy, jealousy and murder, one could hardly say that nothing happens in the second act. It is nontheless, dreary, in that it merely emphasizes through repetition the unpleasant traits introduced earlier. The third act does come alive, and the play, true to its own form, concludes as a macabre, decaying kind of comedy.

A pungent play under any circumstances, its aroma comes forth that much stronger because of the heat which director Alan Schneider has applied to it. Schneider is right in treating it this way; to suppress it, or dilute it, would be unfair to the playwright. Whatever its faults or virtue, ***Entertaining Mr. Sloane*** has to be presented with such an emphasis.

What audiences will remember and most admire about Orton's play is the role of the landlady and the performance by Sheila Hancock. She slops about the stage, sometimes with her upper left front teeth in and sometimes with them out, an appalling and somehow enchanting female derelict with a moron's mind and delusions of gentility. The nasal voice is superbly appropriate.

Lee Montague is oily, pompous and sly as brother Ed, whose disposition is as gamey as some aspects of the play. There is an aura of evil to the stupid and self-indulgent Sloane, in Dudley Sutton's portrayal. George Turner's futile anger as The Dadda evokes more pity than humor, though the play manages to make even him repulsive.

Orton's characters fascinate us, but we don't really believe them. In overreaching for ways to offend an audience, he has blotted out credulity and acceptance. He has even made passages of his play morosely dull, and that is the worst offense of all.

Norman Nadel, "'Entertaining Mr. Sloane' Opens," in New York World-Telegram & The Sun, *October 13, 1965.*

Mel Gussow (review date 21 May 1981)

[*Gussow is an American drama critic. In the following review of the 1981 off-Broadway revival of* Entertaining Mr. Sloane, *he praises director John Tillinger's naturalistic approach to staging the play, noting that with Orton's comedies "the most bizarre events and comments must be made to seem matter-of-fact." He adds that Tillinger "assembled a first-class company that is precisely in tune with [Orton's] idiosyncratic rhythms."*]

Joe Orton's first full-length play, ***Entertaining Mr. Sloane,*** is a blissfully perverse comedy of bad manners, in which everyone is entirely motivated by self-interest. After three acts of sexual power play and a case of homicide, one of the characters calmly observes, "Well, it's been a pleasant morning." With Orton, the grotesque is regarded as pleasant, immorality as an accepted mode of behavior and delirium as the root of domestic comedy.

After an initial success in London, ***Mr. Sloane*** was a quick failure on Broadway in 1965, with critics treating the play as an example of urban blight. Actually, the blight and the moral decay are the corrosive subjects of the author as social critic. Today, posthumously, Orton's reputation is secure, and at the core of his small, significant body of work is the very entertaining ***Mr. Sloane.***

In performance, Orton demands the careful handling that one would bring to works by Noël Coward or Oscar Wilde. The most bizarre events and comments must be made to seem matter-of-fact, which is John Tillinger's approach in his articulate revival at the Westside Mainstage Theater. For this Off Off Broadway production, Mr. Tillinger, an actor as well as literary manager of the Long Wharf Theater, has assembled a first-class company that is precisely in tune with the author's idiosyncratic rhythms.

The title role is played by Maxwell Caulfield as a smooth, rude upstart who has graduated to adult games. Joseph Maher and Barbara Bryne, experienced character actors, are brother and sister, each of them competing for possession of Mr. Sloane, who is her tenant, his employee and their manipulative pawn. The three form an equilateral triangle with each using the others to his or her purpose.

As a suave entrepreneur of indeterminate occupation, Mr. Maher, in an extremely polished performance, is a most composed and unflappable individual, tempting young Mr. Sloane with worldly delights. In contrast, Miss Bryne is a motherly homebody with sexual designs that seem to contradict her dowdy presence. The actress veers clear of the tasteless; she makes the woman's flirtations seem natural. Brother and sister alternately "entertain" Mr. Sloane, and he craftily and with cocksure humor plays one against the other, while holding out for the highest bidder.

The trio of actors is expert at handling the author's argot, a special comic blend of common platitudes, advertising slogans and case-history jargon. Mr. Sloane, for example, is an orphan of "no fixed abode," which is a euphemism for an Oliver with a punk twist. His protectors praise him as cultured and refined, and he preens at the compliment. Actually, he is a certified Orton ruffian on the stairs, and in Mr. Caulfield's confident portrayal there is a constant threat of violence. The strangest things are happening in this mad house "in the midst of a rubbish dump," but, as depicted by the author, everything appears to be as cozy as afternoon tea.

There is a fourth member of the ménage—the cynical father of the family. At the performance I attended, because of an actor's sudden illness this supporting role was assumed on short notice by Richard Russell Ramos. Mr. Ramos was so exactingly in character that the script he was carrying seemed more of a prop than an actor's aid. In common with the other characters, Mr. Ramos's father is tinged with malice and etched in acid.

Mark Haack's set design effectively conveys the seediness of the environment and Bill Walker's costumes suit each character's vision of himself. On a tiny stage, on what is clearly a minuscule budget, Mr. Tillinger and company have performed a sizable theatrical service.

Mel Gussow, in a review of "Entertaining Mr. Sloane," in The New York Times, *May 21, 1981, p. C28.*

Edith Oliver (review date 6 July 1981)

[*Oliver began her career as an actress and television writer and producer. She joined the* New Yorker *in 1948 and became its off-Broadway theater critic in 1961. In the review below, she praises John Tillinger's 1981 Cherry Lane production of* Entertaining Mr. Sloane, *finding the play's sexually sinister elements still present, though less shocking to contemporary audiences than in its original 1967 staging.*]

Entertaining Mr. Sloane was the first of Joe Orton's high comedies of lowlife. It was produced in London, to great acclaim, in 1964 and here, to general and critical dismay, a year later. Since then, it has become a minor classic, and the dramatist, who was murdered by his homosexual partner in 1967, has become not only a cult hero but a real, literary hero, as he deserves to be. Now, given the chance to see the play again, in a revival at the Cherry Lane, under the capable direction of John Tillinger, one wonders how so many people in New York could have failed to recognize its quality at once. The lowlifes of ***Entertaining Mr. Sloane*** are Mr. Sloane himself, a young man with a criminal past and a high potential for criminality; a middle-aged woman with whom he comes to lodge, and who seduces him within minutes of his entrance; her middle-aged brother, a prosperous businessman of some kind, who has an eye and a yen for handsome young men; and her father, a rickety old dotard, who half recognizes Mr. Sloane as the murderer of his former boss and makes the fatal error of accusing him of the crime. The plot deals with the struggle of brother and sister for Mr. Sloane, which ends, perforce, in a tie.

The performance is fine. Every moment is clear, but the sinister element—for this is a horror comedy—that seemed so important fifteen years ago is almost gone now. Perhaps the main difference lies in today's audience, familiar with the play and with Orton's style, and no longer shocked by homo- or heterosexual greed. The other night, everybody accepted the doings onstage with immediate laughter, although things quieted down a bit—just a bit—when Sloane stomped the old man to death. The actors, responding to Mr. Tillinger's sure touch, are very good. Barbara Bryne (new to me but not, apparently, to audiences in Canada or at the Guthrie, in Minneapolis) plays the lady of the house with merciless gentility and merciless innocence, at one point, when her false teeth are supposed to be soaking in the kitchen, giving her lines (what lines!) an extra, mysterious fillip. The stalwart Joseph Maher is subtle and strong and very funny as her avid brother. Gwyllum Evans couldn't be better as their senile, foolhardy father; nor could young Maxwell Caulfield as the handsome, childish, dangerous Mr. S. Mark Haack's setting of the fussy "lounge" of the house looks exactly right, and so do the costumes, by Bill Walker. In the three years that Joe Orton lived after ***Entertaining Mr. Sloane,*** he wrote the great ***Loot, What the Butler Saw,*** and a couple of one-acters—but what a début! (pp. 51, 54)

Edith Oliver, "Reënter Mr. Sloane," in The New Yorker, *Vol. LVII, No. 20, July 6, 1981, pp. 51, 54.*

John Simon (review date 7 September 1981)

[*Simon is an American film and drama critic. His reviews have appeared in the* New Leader, New York Magazine, *the* Hudson Review, *and the* New York Times. *In the following excerpt, he calls John Tillinger's 1981 production "by far the best* Sloane *I or anyone can hope to see." In characterizing the staging, the critic claims that Orton's comedy is "played more for farce than for sinisterness, more for an often choreographic absurdity than for the bleak misanthropy still evident enough under the laughter."*]

With his later plays, notably ***Loot*** and ***What the Butler Saw,*** Joe Orton grew into a highly accomplished playwright who could niftily juggle epigrammatic satire, homosexual camp, and characterizations so jaundiced that the stage seemed to be populated by evil, human-sized canaries. Had his life not been snuffed out in a way that rather justified his view, Orton should have become a major force in our theater. But ***Entertaining Mr. Sloane,*** his first performed play, struck me as being still much too immature and schematic in its London premiere, and still less persuasive on Broadway and at the movies. So when an Off Broadway revival opened a couple of months ago, even good notices failed to drag me to it.

Having wended, belatedly, my wary way to the Cherry Lane, I can happily (and repentantly) report that this is by far the best ***Sloane*** I or anyone can hope to see, what with well-nigh impeccable ensemble acting and bang-up direction from John Tillinger, not to mention a theater intimate enough to make this intramural bit of nastiness look less pretentiously overblown than heretofore. This ferocious farce about a psychopathic, murderous young punk who ends up as the shared sexual possession of a Jesuitical middle-aged homosexual and his equally middle-aged, sexually voracious, stupid yet also shrewd sister is here played more for farce than for sinisterness, more for an often choreographic absurdity than for the bleak misanthropy still evident enough under the laughter. And it works.

Joseph Maher, cynical yet oddly scoutmasterish; Maxwell Caulfield, vicious yet also ingenuous; Gwyllum Evans, an old-timer upholding justice with self-destructive meanspiritedness and improvidence—these could scarcely be bettered. As a ludicrous frump both maternal and infantile, both guileless and Machiavellian, Barbara Bryne is perfection itself. She carries off one of the hardest histrionic tricks: to make a character come alive and be, with all the inconsistencies intact, an immaculate, seamless whole. (p. 49)

John Simon, "Summit Meeting," in New York *Magazine, Vol. 14, No. 35, September 7, 1981, pp. 47-9.*

Robert Asahina (review date Winter 1981-82)

[*In the following excerpt, Asahina commends Tillinger's "absolutely deadpan" staging of* Entertaining Mr. Sloane *and cites the success of the production as proof that Orton's play "is still an insightful commentary on the sexual and social role confusion that is considerably more widespread now than when it was written."*]

Orton's ***Entertaining Mr. Sloane,*** first produced in London in 1964, has just been restaged by John Tillinger at the Cherry Lane Theatre, and it is easy to see why Terence Rattigan called it "the best first play" he had seen in thirty years.

"Like all great satirists, Joe Orton was a realist," claims his biographer, John Lahr [in his *Prick up Your Ears,* 1978], whose assessment is a variation on the adage that the essence of comedy is playing straight. And the chief virtue of the new production of ***Sloane*** is that, for the most part, it is played absolutely deadpan. [British playwright Caryl Churchill] could have learned a thing or two from Orton's shrewd understanding of how the most vicious satire can be combined with the most conventional, realistic form to produce the blackest comedy.

From the moment that Sloane (Maxwell Caulfield) appears at the home of Kath (Barbara Bryne) and her elderly father, Kemp (Gwyllum Evans), it is clear that the production is strictly in keeping with Orton's perversely deadeye view of the awful desperation of lower-middle-class British life in the early sixties. The parlor (wonderfully designed by Mark Haack) is a nightmare of petit bourgeois gentility: horrible flocked wallpaper, tattered doilies on the arms of worn velvet furniture, a glass-door cabinet proudly displaying vulgar china. Kath, all aflutter in a worn, pink-and-blue-striped housecoat, is a repulsive embodiment of every middle-aged female's worst image of herself. Kemp, irascible and rude, makes old age seem as disgusting as he obviously finds it. Ed (Joseph Maher), the estranged brother, a homosexual, would rightly be labeled oily if his lubricity hadn't made him so elusive. And Sloane is such a blank cipher that it comes as no surprise when he quickly becomes the focus of the other characters' twisted fears and desires.

Orton builds his bizarre drama of lust (heterosexual and homosexual), furtive sex, illegitimacy, sibling rivalry, jealousy, generational conflict, bullying (psychological and physical) and blackmail—which climaxes first in Sloane's murder of Kemp and then in Kath's and Ed's breathtakingly amoral and grotesquely motivated coverup of the crime—by piling revealing detail upon detail: Kath's pathetically genteel inverted sentences ("That I could not say"); Kemp's obsessive concern with the "felony" of masturbation; Ed's sentimental recollections of his "mate," stolen years before by his sister.

And when Caulfield says "wont" for "want," or Bryne turns "food" into a two-syllable word, or Maher sinuously repeats Caulfield's "no" (Sloane's answer to Ed's asking if he has any girlfriends), making it convey equal parts of curiosity, lust and invitation, we know that the cast is attuned not just to Orton's language (even convincingly ending their declarative sentences with the characteristic rising inflection of the lower-middle-class Englishman) but to its social and cultural connotations. Likewise, when Maher automatically plucks at the crease of his trousers after sitting down or instinctively polishes his briefcase with the sleeve of his jacket, we see that the players understand how the smallest gesture can convey a lifetime of exaggerated concern for the superficial.

To be sure, there are a few lapses in the acting and directing. Although Orton clearly stipulated that his intention was to "break down all the sexual compartments that people have"—that Kath, Ed and Sloane should not be regarded as "the nympho," "the queer" and "the psycho" (as he called them)—the cast occasionally falls back on stereotyped gestures and readings. Maher is the worst offender—stammering, interrupting the arc of his sentences with all too noticeable breaths, and even limply extending one hand while burying the other in his pocket. And Tillinger errs badly (though it is the only time) at the end of the play by allowing the satire to degenerate into slapstick. Kath and Ed are quarreling about whether to turn Sloane over to the police, and Ed shakes his sister violently, jarring loose her false teeth. After she scrambles on her hands and knees to find them, Tillinger for no good reason has her retrieve them near Ed's feet and then rise to her knees between his legs. To say the least, this staging gives an odd slant to the pleas Sloane makes during her mad activity that Ed "persuade her" to join in a coverup.

On the whole, however, this production more than satisfactorily reveals the force of Orton's writing. Seventeen years after it was first staged and fourteen years after the playwright's death, ***Entertaining Mr. Sloane*** is still an insightful commentary on the sexual and social role confusion that is considerably more widespread now than when it was written. (pp. 567-68)

Robert Asahina, in a review of "Entertaining Mr. Sloane," in The Hudson Review, *Vol. XXXIV, No. 4, Winter, 1981-82, pp. 566-68.*

Beryl Reid as Kath and Malcolm McDowell as Sloane in a production of Entertaining Mr. Sloane *which opened at the Royal Court Theatre, London, on 17 April 1975.*

CRITICAL COMMENTARY

Maurice Charney (essay date 1984)

[*Charney is an American educator, critic, and author of* Joe Orton *(1984). In the following excerpt, he explores Orton's manipulation of the levels of discourse in his plays. Focusing on* Entertaining Mr. Sloane, *Charney elucidates how Orton deliberately used clichéd vernacular expressions in order to expose his characters' naked greed, complacency, and lust.*]

In its root sense, the occult is that which is hidden, concealed or covered over in order to protect arcane truths from the eyes of the uninitiated. In other words, there is a sharp contrast between the manifest and the latent meanings. 'Contrast' may be too mild a word because the most likely form of relation between surface and implied meanings is one of contradiction. The stated meaning is bland, polite, innocuous, even vacuous, in order to conceal a violent, chaotic and painful truth. To formulate this double effect in a different way, we may say that the language is deliberately and systematically occulted in order to sustain a continuous irony between what is said and what is meant. In popular parlance, language as an expressive vehicle is rendered meaningless, banal and jejune so that the real tenor and purpose of that language may be safely protected. Harsh truths are insulated by the trite formulae of social discourse. The characters speak an amusing and titilating babble of stock phrases, trite moralising (often of a proverbial turn), and pre-packaged emotional clichés drawn from the stockpot of daytime television serials. When this style is cultivated self-consciously by the author, the effect is that of collage, because the author is aiming at an occult contrast between the nonsense that is revealed and the deeper meanings that lie hidden. In this limited sense, the author is using a secret language for his surface discourse.

We are speaking of a general tendency in contemporary literature to appropriate non-literary materials and to employ them in disguised and ironic ways. No modern playwright uses this occulted discourse (or threatening nonsense) more brilliantly than Joe Orton. It is completely natural for a working-class lad from Leicester, a homosexual without any gifts or talents that anyone had ever noticed, to disguise his rage and disappointment with life in a jokester's or trickster's blank discourse. There is no way to deal directly with the monolithic society from which one has been forcibly excluded. As the self-appointed 'fly on the wall', Orton's buzzing was not overtly aggressive or harmful; it was merely intended to disturb the complacency of its targets. The image is emphatically a fly and not a wasp or mosquito.

It is in this area that one may understand how superficial Orton's relation is to Pinter, the model for his early plays. Orton ruthlessly cuts away Pinter's 'significances', so that comedy of menace would seem a pretentious and misguided term for Orton's savage, anarchic and turbulent farces of daily life and its empty deceptions. His sense of language as farcical exhibitionism undercuts and neutralises any feeling of menace. Orton does not write comedies of menace, but rather comedies of need and greed, where the only truths behind a façade of epigrammatic and pointless discourse are those generated by the blind instincts of self-preservation and self-aggrandisement. In this sense, unthinking egoism and self-expression are the only realities in Orton's world.

Entertaining Mr. Sloane (1963) is so distressingly autobiographical that it offers the most explicit illustrations of Orton's occulted discourse. We know from Lahr's biography [*Prick up Your Ears*] that the old and more or less useless Dadda, Kemp, is modelled on Orton's own father, that the sentimentally lascivious housewife Kath draws largely on Orton's mother, and that the idle, violent and bisexual drifter, Sloane, has many qualities of the playwright himself. The play is suffused with a sense of grandiloquence, a heightened style that is the language of a preposterous self-love. In other words, the style is continuously inflated as the tired platitudes of middle-class respectability are trolled out to decorate the naked lust, greed and aggression of the characters. The thin and shabby veneer of civilisation very imperfectly hides the monstrous truths on which the action is based.

The central event of the play is that Sloane brutally kills Ed's and Kath's old father, who happens to know about an earlier murder that Sloane had committed. The homosexual brother, Ed, and the whorish-motherly Kath both desperately need Sloane as confidant and lover, so that Sloane's murder of their father has absolutely no moral resonance. There is no real question of turning Sloane over to the police—only a question of Ed's and Kath's bargaining with each other to 'find a basis for agreement'. The negotiations are conducted under a barrage of meaningless assertions about law, order and decency. As a street-wise kid, Sloane knows that Ed and Kath are only spouting worn-out formulae that have no relevance to the present situation. Their mechanical moralising will cosset and flatter their own respectable consciences while Sloane can choose the best deal that will keep him out of prison and provide for his material comfort. He can rely on Ed's and Kath's rampant sexuality to protect him. The language of the play is only a bubble and froth of words meant to embellish the harsh, implicit truths that cannot be spoken. It all sounds like a parody of the empty slogans of welfare state paternalism, and the painfully moralistic phrases are no more than babble. As Orton wrote in his diary, 'The whole trouble with Western society today is the lack of anything worth concealing'.

Although Orton's work was undoubtedly shaped by early Pinter, ***Entertaining Mr. Sloane,*** written a year before Pinter's *The Homecoming* (1964), seems to have influenced that play. Pinter's Ruth develops the mother-whore stereotype of Orton's Kath and, more pointedly, Pinter's overbearing hustler, Lenny, has a type resemblance to Orton's hollowly successful and vaguely criminal Ed. Both are full of insufferable pretensions to middle-class manners and style. Both Lenny and Ed speak a language that is peculiarly synthetic and literary—a language of disguise that is entirely stripped of any affect, emotion or human resonance. Thus, when Ed learns that his sister is having sexual relations with Sloane and is, in fact, pregnant, he reacts with a cool and vituperative eloquence:

> What a little whoreson you are you little whoreson. You are a little whoreson and no mistake. I'm put out my boy. Choked. (*Pause.*) What attracted you? Did she give trading stamps? You're like all these layabouts. Kiddies with no fixed abode.

The stilted diction, including the archaic 'whoreson', and the posed emotions—'Choked'—contain the violence. It is all very stagey and histrionic, but threatening nevertheless. Ed is speaking for his own pleasure rather than from any need to communicate with Mr Sloane. The message is fixed for Sloane by Ed's icy detachment.

The formulaic quality of the speech in ***Entertaining Mr. Sloane*** emphasises the isolation of the characters for each other. Everyone seems to be talking to himself or herself, except perhaps for the old father, Kemp, who has a dangerous secret to tell about Sloane's past and who winds up dead for his troubles. Orton seems to deny any possibility of communication, so that language is almost by definition occult, because it serves chiefly as a way of concealing meaning. Once this assumption is accepted, it becomes easier to feel the strength of Orton's sardonic playfulness. For the staging of ***What the Butler Saw,*** we know that Orton typed up a list of phrases that could be used *ad libitum* by the cast for comic putdowns: 'You revolting fur-covered bitch!'; 'You shoulder-length prick!'; 'He likes women—you know, strip clubs, menstruation, mothers-in-law'; and the Wildean epigram: 'A word not in current use except in the vernacular'. Orton could afford to be in love with language for its own sake, because the words are so separated from any determinative meaning.

Some of Sloane's speeches are detachable arias, little pop culture vignettes of hard-boiled sentimentality, such as his extravagant narration to Kemp of the circumstances leading to his first murder:

> It's like this see. One day I leave the Home. Stroll along. Sky blue. Fresh air. They'd found me a likeable permanent situation. Canteen facilities. Fortnight's paid holiday. Overtime? Time and a half after midnight. A staff dance each year. What more could one wish to devote one's life to? I certainly loved that place. The air round Twickenham was like wine. Then one day I take a trip to the old man's grave. Hic Jacets in profusion. Ashes to Ashes. Alas the fleeting. The sun was declining. A few press-ups on a tomb belonging to a family name of Cavaneagh, and I left the graveyard.

This is fashioned in the mock-pastoral, mock-poetic mode, with air 'like wine', bits and pieces of tombstone inscriptions, and a part-line from 'The Rose of Tralee' ('The sun was declining'). Sloane is exuberant as he leads up to his encounter with the erotic photographer who liked 'certain interesting features I had that he wanted the exclusive right of preserving'. The blatant sexuality is always guarded and disguised—not part of a system of pleasure or hedonism, but only an expression of need and greed, the overpowering desire to use and possess another person.

Sloane's style collects fragments and puts them together in a pattern that has no relation at all to any meaningful context of ordinary discourse. The fragments are displaced and juxtaposed so that they have what Orton called a 'collage quality'. His room with Halliwell was an enormous collage of pasted-up images, and they both were sent to prison in 1962 for their extraordinary collage effects in public library books, especially on the altered dust jackets. In the bewildering welter of media inputs and pop culture imagery, Orton took seriously his role as collagist:

> Shakespeare and the Elizabethans did the same thing. I mean you have absolute realism and then you get high poetry, it's just language. I think you should use the language of your age and every bit of it. They always go on about poetic drama and they think you have to sort of go off in some high-flown fantasy, but it isn't poetic, it's everything, it's the language in use at the time.

But Sloane's eloquence and Orton's eloquence are extremely self-conscious. The comparison with Shakespeare and the Elizabethans is apt because Orton wrote with such bravado. In its exuberance and flamboyance, his style is certainly closer to Marlowe's than to Shakespeare's, but perhaps closest of all to the mysterious Cyril Tourneur of *The Revenger's Tragedy* (*c.* 1607).

Orton delights in collecting sentimental clichés for the part of Kath, the fading, mock-voluptuous mother-whore, who seduces Sloane and mothers him without any feeling of contradiction. Kath is the consumerist *par excellence* of the ladies' magazines, and she lives in a world of tawdry, commercialised romance. Her knick-knacks define both her respectability and her illusions about the existence of a larger world outside her own house, which is pointedly located in the middle of a garbage dump. Her 'sophisticated' conversation with Sloane is all mindless twaddle, civilised foreplay leading up to the sex act:

> KATH. Isn't this room gorgeous?
>
> SLOANE. Yes.
>
> KATH. That vase over there comes from Bombay. Do you have any interest in that part of the world?
>
> SLOANE. I like Dieppe.
>
> KATH. Ah . . . it's all the same. I don't suppose they know the difference themselves.

Kath's Bombay and Sloane's Dieppe are both cities of the mind, high-sounding words for places that have no reality. Kath's discourse has no relation to her transparent negligee, with which she is teasing Sloane: 'I blame it on the manufacturers. They make garments so thin nowadays you'd think they intend to provoke a rape'. By the time she is rolling on top of Sloane, he has become her baby: 'What a big heavy baby you are. Such a big heavy baby'. Kath dresses up her naked need for Sloane's body in a variety of genteel clichés, but the language moves on an entirely separate plane from the realities of seduction. When Sloane threatens to leave the pregnant Kath after the murder of Kemp she trolls out all the warmed-over tag lines of soap opera: 'I've a bun in the oven', 'Mr. Sloane was nice to me', 'He's free with me', 'Can't manage without a woman'. Kath is the archetype of all injured women, both long-suffering and unappreciated mother and jilted torch-lady who has no regrets. She speaks in the parodic formulae of domestic tragedy. 'Who tucks him up at night? And he likes my cooking. He won't deny that'. 'I gave him three meals a day. Porridge for breakfast. Meat and two veg for dinner. A fry for tea. And cheese for supper. What more could he want?'. A lascivious Mrs Portnoy, who has managed to preserve the integrity of English family life. What more could anyone possibly want? We know that Orton had ambiguous feelings about his cold, sexless, very respectable, but nevertheless seductive mother. Kath projects a powerful incest fantasy of the omnipotent mother who is sexual and nurturing at the same time, but whose overwhelming love must ultimately be rejected by her guilty, adolescent son. According to Freud's formulation in 'The Most Prevalent Form of Degradation in Erotic Life' (1912), the fear of incest in the mother-whore situation often produces male impotence.

Orton dramatises his own sexual ambiguity in the struggle between Kath and Ed for the control of Sloane's body. The play has a surprising bisexual conclusion, but the language throughout is intensely misogynistic. Ed has a whole series of apothegms for putting women in their place: 'Women are like banks, boy, breaking and entering is a serious business. Give me your word you're not vaginalatrous?'. 'Vaginalatrous' is an Orton coinage on analogy with 'idolatrous'; it indicates a perverse attachment. To Ed, women are essentially frivolous vamps intent on deceiving men: 'The way these birds treat decent fellows. I hope you never get serious with one. What a life. Backache, headache or her mum told her never to when there's an "R" in the month'. This is an old formula, on analogy with the popular prohibition against eating oysters except in months with an 'R', that seems to turn on disgust at menstruation. When Ed is grappling with Kath for Sloane in the last act, he is not above insulting her physically, as if she were the archetypal woman: 'Flabby mouth. Wrinkled neck. Puffy hands.' 'Sagging tits.' 'Sawdust up to the navel'. Her genitalia are scored off in a parody of Dante: 'You showed him the gate of Hell every night. He abandoned Hope when he entered there'. As a sexual being, Kath can only be shown histrionically. In an exaggerated gesture, she offers Sloane her hand: 'Kiss my hand, dear, in the manner of the theatre', and Ed's final insult is to Kath as an actress, falsely evoking theatrical sentiment: 'What a cruel performance you're giving. Like an old tart grinding to her climax'. The old tart, of course, mocks both sexuality and the theatre. Ed's language of vituperation seems the most expressive idiom in the play, but he himself assumes a position of moral and social superiority to Kath that is based only on vigorous but hollow assertion. No moral positions are possible in this play. Everyone is wholly occupied by the narcissistic struggle for survival.

Entertaining Mr. Sloane is hardly occult in any of the popular meanings of that term, yet there is a pervasive irony by which the surface action of the play is radically different from what is really happening. On the one side we see a parody of middle-class English values, full of vain moralising and empty social gestures. On the other are power and greed nakedly striving to fulfil themselves without regard to human values. Behind the comedy of manners façade, aggressive lust dominates the play. The nonsense in this play is still very threatening; it has not been neutralised by farce. We still feel the tremendous effort at concealment by which the deeper meanings have been occulted and trivialised, so that turbulence and chaos are only imperfectly mastered. It is gradually becoming apparent that Orton belongs in the classic tradition of English comedy that includes Swift, Wycherley and Wilde. In his own disguised and farcical way, Orton sought to make contact with bitter truths. Beneath the occulted and at times nonsensical collage of pop culture dialogue, Orton tried for an emotional effect like Swift's savage indignation. (pp. 70-9)

Maurice Charney, in his Joe Orton, *Grove Press, Inc., 1984, 145 p.*

LOOT

PRODUCTION REVIEWS

Clive Barnes (review date 19 March 1968)

[*A British-born American drama and dance critic, Barnes has been called "the first, second and third most powerful critic in New York." He has refrained from exploiting his influence, however, and has adopted an informal, conversational writing style in his reviews. Barnes insists that criticism of the arts is a public service; therefore, the function of a reviewer is to advise and inform audiences rather than determine a production's success or failure. As a result, Barnes has also earned the reputation of being "the major newspaper critic easiest to please." His commentary has appeared regularly in the* New York Times *and the* New York Post. *In the following review of the 1968 Broadway debut of* Loot, *he asserts that Orton's comic jabs at the police and the Roman Catholic Church appear pointless at times, but that they are nevertheless meant seriously: "Mr. Orton is like a little boy trying to shock his elders but—here's the rub—wielding, albeit clumsily, a real knife."*]

There is something for everyone to detest in Joe Orton's outrageous play, ***Loot,*** which opened last night at the Biltmore Theater. To like it I think you might have to have a twisted sense of humor. I liked it. But I do trust it's not for you, for you would be a far nicer person if it were not.

Before the curtain rises we hear the Roman Catholic mass for the dead, but this is broken into by some extraordinarily cheap and tawdry rock 'n' roll. Such irreverence is all too sadly typical of a play that leaves no stone unthrown and no avenue undefiled.

The quite deplorable story is about death, religion, money and the police, and it is soon apparent that the late Mr. Orton held sadly unconventional views about all four of these highly regarded human institutions. The work is sacrilegious and blasphemous, and, indeed, some of it is also distasteful. The fashionable thing to say of it will be: "No, I was not shocked, but merely bored." Nothing is such a fine defense against the shocking as a plea of boredom, as it sounds so agreeably worldly.

The play is in fact a kind of artificial drawing room comedy—in some respects not unlike those of Oscar Wilde—although the drawing room has been replaced by a front parlor, the principal object in which is a coffin. A freshly bereaved husband is mourning his wife, assisted by a pretty nurse who attended the good lady to the end. The scene of mourning is joined by the dead woman's son. He is preoccupied to some extent because, together with his best friend, an undertaker's assistant, he has just robbed a bank.

The two accomplices are also disturbed by the presence of a sinister pipe-smoking gentleman who is snooping around the house and claims to be an official of the Metropolitan Water Board. Since they have both had the misfortune to have been beaten up by him in the police station, they suspect him of being a police officer. Where then to hide the loot? They decide to put it in the coffin—first, of course, removing the corpse, which is placed, upside down, in a convenient closet.

Orton's comedy is not merely voguishly black. It is distinctly dirty. Its attacks on the Catholic Church and the police have a touch of madness in them; yet there is method in it.

Mr. Orton—and for this some will never forgive him—is being deadly serious. He clearly hated the Catholic Church and all it stands for, and this hatred gives the play an uncomfortable cutting edge. It wounds even to think that an author could have so much bile in him. The bitter, jeering wit is all the more corrosive because at times it snakes out like a serpent in pointless anger. Here Mr. Orton is like a little boy trying to shock his elders but—here's the rub—wielding, albeit clumsily, a real knife.

His attacks on the police, coming at a time when both Britain and America might well use a little skepticism concerning the police's fulfillment of their traditional function, have a light-hearted anger beneath a sometimes heavy handed humor. The police officer trying to get a confession out of a suspect knocks him down, twists his arm and kicks him viciously.

"Under any other political system I'd have you on the floor in tears," he shouts. The victim replies: "You've got me on the floor in tears."

Mr. Orton's style of writing varies between the ornately polished, with all the bedeviled and devastating comedy of statements taken beyond logic, and strange carelessness, where the director has had to make good the gaps in the text.

Orton was a tragic loss to the English-speaking theater because of his lively sense of the absurd. Almost any conventional sentiment he turns inside out to shock. The boy, for example, does not worry about using his mother's coffin to hide the loot, but is horrified at having to bury her naked.

"It's a Freudian nightmare," he murmurs. And the beautifully contrived farcical situations Orton managed: Here the corpse and the money go in and out of doors with the precision of the participants of a bedroom farce.

Strangely, Orton's savage disgust never affects a kind of sunny and stylish good humor that occasionally lights up his darkest powers: touches such as the bit when the nurse, with murder in her heart and a red smile on her lips, drops a book on the corpse, with the words: "Here, the Ten Commandments. She was a great believer in some of them."

That is a comic line that few playwrights could aspire to, for it is not a slick wisecrack but offers an insight.

Had Orton ever acquired more polish, had he disciplined his talent with technique, he might have written a comedy masterpiece. ***Loot*** is not that, and does make severe demands upon the director, which Derek Goldby, much helped by a superior cast, sustains better than did the London production last season.

Mr. Goldby keeps the mannered, staccato dialogue stabbing across the scene like machine-gun fire, and the sheerly mechanical farce business is adroitly handled. The play, moreover, in William Ritman's authentic seeming set, looks better than it did in London.

Of the actors, George Rose, as the mad Scotland Yard inspector, as corrupt as he is foolish, is superlative, double-taking on his double-takes, mugging like a vaudeville comic, and never losing his matchless comic authority.

Carole Shelley, all deadly composure, was acid-sweet as the nurse, Liam Redmond piously apoplectic as the father, while Kenneth Cranham and James Hunter had a kind of terrible mod poetry as the ruthless boys who would do anything for money or a laugh.

You will either hate ***Loot*** or like it a lot. But don't take your Aunt Mildred—especially if she has just died.

Clive Barnes, "Black Comedy Attacks Church and Police," in The New York Times, *March 19, 1968, Section 2, p. 40.*

Walter Kerr (review date 31 March 1968)

[Kerr is an American dramatist, director, and critic who won a Pulitzer Prize for drama criticism in 1978. A long-time drama critic for the New York Times *as well as the author of several book-length studies of modern drama, he has been one of the most important and influential figures in the American theater since the 1950s. Below, Kerr criticizes the tone of Orton's* Loot, *asserting that it "is determinedly sick for the simple pleasure of being sick." The play's satirical targets are unclear, Kerr maintains, and Orton rides "on manner alone, indifferent to where it leads him or whether it ever leads him anywhere." The reviewer praises George Rose's Inspector Truscott, however, calling his performance appropriately "earnest, fierce, sober, utterly reasonable in the unreasonable circumstances."]*

Loot is determinedly sick for the simple pleasure of being sick. It insists upon its tone whether the tone has a point or not.

The insistence is unflagging. Long after we have accepted the shuttle of corpses and the crunch of glass eyes, and have even begun to take a certain geometric amusement in the hopefully blood-curdling merry-go-round, Mr. Orton keeps at us: It is now time to wipe up the last traces of mother's entrails, stuck to a box they've been stored in. Where does intercourse between a naughty boy and a greedy nurse take place? Under a picture of the Sacred Heart. What has an underprivileged lad to complain about? "Every luxury was lavished on you," he pouts to a friend, "atheism, breast-feeding, circumcision. I had to make it my own way." We mustn't lose a word or a blood clot that might entertain us.

And, in point of fact, roughly half of the evening is *almost* entertaining. We'd like to like the play as its murderous, money-minded nurse bats eyelashes long enough to brush her chin at a widower whose wife she has just dispatched, as two earnest lads worry terribly about whether money they've stolen from a bank will fit into mother's coffin, as Police Inspector George Rose blows into the parlor as though propelled by a March wind, there to purse his moustache, transfix one and all with his baleful eye, and kick some in the groin. Total iconoclasm can be agreeably heady, as bald irrationality can warm the overworked psyche. When Mr. Rose, asked to explain how a limbless woman could have committed a murder, solemnly replies that he would rather not say because letting the news out might lead to many carbon-copy crimes, we are poised smack on the edge of delectable lunacy. Poised, and toppling.

But the closer the evening gets to success the more it explains why it is ultimately forced to subside into a weary sigh. It is closest to success with Mr. Rose's manic inspector (though everything about Derek Goldby's production here is superior to the shabby London original). Mr. Rose has the very good sense to know that he cannot be cute in the part, because part and play are already cute. He must be earnest, fierce, sober, utterly reasonable in the unreasonable circumstances. Thus, when he is identifying a culprit because her wedding ring is eroded (which means she's been near salt water, which means that she must have been at a certain beach at a time a particularly nasty crime was committed) or when he is ostentatiously revealing himself to be the policeman everyone has known he was from the beginning (he has a notion that wearing a hat disguises him), he is on the verge of delighting us with his owlish mismanagement of the obvious.

But what, we now wonder, is being satirized? Sherlock Holmes? If so, what has Sherlock Holmes to do with the very 1960ish malaise that has produced this particular black comedy, these bisexual boys, the coffin humor that abounds? *Does* the evening have a target, or even an environment? Or is it simply a random improvisation intended to make us amiably, fashionably ill (while snickering) in all directions?

Eventually it is plain that the assault on our conventional expectations is not headed for any real goal. The assault itself is expected to occupy us, and good enough for us. The play gasps, backed to the wall. Its antic furies falter, repeat themselves, reach for any old joke or no joke at all.

Any old joke:

"I'm a woman. Only half the human race can say that without fear of contradiction."

No joke at all:

"We shared the same cradle."

"Was that economy or malpractice?"

When we hear the sound of comedy without the substance of comedy we very quickly respond—with alarm. In the end, what alarms us at ***Loot,*** and makes the second half expire in agony, is not the jolly brutalities that have been thrown at us but the sense that they are without direction. Mr. Orton has adopted a manner, and forced it for all and more than it is worth, but he is riding on manner alone, indifferent to where it leads him or whether it ever leads him anywhere.

Walter Kerr, in a review of "Loot," in The York Times, *March 31, 1968, p. D3.*

John Lahr on the development of Orton's comic voice:

Loot brought Orton's craft to its maturity. Confident, independent and now successful, Orton was growing free of the fear that weighed down his early prose and forced it to revel in all that was dark, inferior and culpable in others. He was no longer oppressed in the same way by guilt and inferiority; and his plays, which were projections of these fears, took on an expansive good humour. There was a hint of forgiveness in his high spirits. Even Orton's handwriting changed from its cramped, adolescent jaggedness to an open, fluid, authoritative hand. The ten months between October 1966, when ***Loot*** made its London debut, and August 1967, when he died, would be Orton's most fecund literary period. He wrote his ghoulish capriccio about the Church and Christian charity, ***Funeral Games;*** a film script, ***Up Against It;*** the major revisions on ***Ruffian*** and ***Erpingham Camp,*** published, as they were produced, under the title *Crimes of Passion;* and his farce masterpiece, ***What the Butler Saw.*** Almost his entire œuvre was either written or rewritten in the comic voice he'd acquired through ***Loot.*** Orton's was a unique voice whose echoes invoked the descriptive comparisons to Wilde and Firbank; but it was indubitably his own.

John Lahr, in his Prick up Your Ears, *Vintage Books, 1987.*

Harold Clurman (review date 8 April 1968)

[*A celebrated director and theater critic, Clurman founded, in association with Lee Strasberg and Cheryl Crawford, the Group Theatre in 1931. For the next ten years, as its managing director, he helped create many notable productions, particularly of American plays. He served the* Nation, *the* New Republic, *and the* Observer *as drama critic from 1949 to 1963. Below, Clurman objects to Orton's apparent emotional detachment in* Loot. *Although the play boasts the author's trademark "fleet and spanking" dialogue, "*Loot *makes the impression of having been written without any feeling at all," Clurman comments, adding that "it seems disengaged even from the objects of its scorn. Orton's coldness leaves me cold."*]

Joe Orton's ***Loot*** was a hit in London and the winner of a critics' prize there three seasons ago. I have no very strong feelings about it. Its black humor did not offend me, its boldness provoked no great gusts of laughter in me. I came, I saw and I tried to understand why it left me very nearly indifferent.

It is a well-written play: its dialogue is fleet and spanking. Though its plot and technique are farcical, the play may be thought a satire. A couple of young men—one an undertaker's assistant, the other the son of a woman who has just died—have robbed a bank. They have hidden the booty in a wardrobe in the widower's home where the deceased is also lying in state. When a detective threatens to inspect the wardrobe the two culprits contrive to remove the loot by placing it in the coffin, having first wrapped the corpse in a blanket to make it look like a tailor's dummy and thrust *it* into the wardrobe. From this point the corpse—which has been undressed—is trundled back and forth, like a piece of troublesome luggage, in a series of imbroglios too frequent to enumerate.

Besides the youthful scamps and the stupidly brutal and corrupt sleuth from Scotland Yard, there is present a notorious killer who in the guise of a nurse has murdered the lady in the bundle as a first step toward marrying the widower, who would himself eventually be knocked off. At the final curtain it is arranged that the lethal lady will instead marry the undertaker's assistant who will probably fare no better than the other men whom she has wed.

The police are the butt of most of the jokes. Religion—especially the Catholic—is almost equally derided. Nor are love, sex, death spared mockery. The English, being a most respectful and respectable people, enjoy kicking over the traces in *play.* They make the best audiences for every sort of buffoonery, every "game" which permits them to loosen the braces of their etiquette. Hence the success of this play in London, where its whacky irreverence conveyed in smart speech meets with special appreciation.

Just as bedroom farce has almost disappeared from the stage because nowadays adultery is no longer of particular moment, so it seems to me that amorality can induce only a slight tremor of mirth in a time when a sense of morality has become more residual than real.

Loot makes the impression of having been written without any feeling at all; it seems disengaged even from the objects of its scorn. Orton's coldness leaves me cold. The horror in Pinter is cutting or funny because for all his air of detachment he is horrified. His jokes provide a mask to hide his hurt.

A further cause for my lack of response to ***Loot*** is the peculiar flaccidity in the production by Derek Goldby. Rapid-fire movement and delivery do not, as commonly supposed, make for pace. There is plenty of bustle in the show but little comic spirit. For all the dashing about the effect is one of inertia.

A capable cast—George Rose, Carole Shelley and others—ought to be hilarious, so the audience behaves as if they were. They aren't. (pp. 484-85)

Harold Clurman, in a review of "Loot," in The Nation, *New York, Vol. 206, No. 15, April 8, 1968, pp. 484-85.*

John Simon (review date 19 April 1968)

[In the excerpt below, Simon asserts that the direct objects of Orton's jokes in Loot, *namely the Catholic Church, the police, the family, and love, belie his true targets of greed and hypocrisy. Underneath Orton's black humor, the reviewer maintains, is "the recognition of a fundamental, horrid injustice disguising itself as respect for the accepted decencies."]*

In the theater—at least, in the establishment theater—it takes courage to be against ordinary things. ***Loot,*** a scrappy little English farce that hits out against everything (even the final curtain goes down fighting), has not found an audience on Broadway. I did not care for Joe Orton's first comedy, ***Entertaining Mr. Sloane,*** which, for all its thematic unconventionality, was structurally a commonplace, well-made play. In ***Loot,*** Orton loosened his form and borrowed, rather successfully, some devices from the absurdist theater. But then the absurdity of life caught up with the homosexual playwright: at the age of 34, Orton was gruesomely murdered by his roommate.

The plot of ***Loot*** is unimportant. It involves a brand new Catholic widower about to marry the sweet Catholic nurse who actually killed his wife and who, after marrying him, will kill him, too—she has a record of such crimes. It also involves the man's son, who, with his equally bisexual chum working for the undertaker, has robbed a bank, and must hide the loot in his mother's coffin. And there is the idiot-savant policeman, doggedly sleuthing and bullying away, but ultimately most interested in getting the lion's share of the loot. The play takes the form of a crazy juggling act, with the money and the corpse continually switching hiding places, if not actually flying through the air. The characters are all Catholics, policemen, or criminals, or a combination of these, plus that flying, incessantly undressed or wrapped-up, and otherwise manhandled cadaver. And, as you might expect, the jugglers of our lady's corpse end up thriving in direct proportion to their wickedness.

The immediate butts of Orton's humor, which is a curious amalgam of virulence and ingenuousness, are Catholicism, the police, the family, and what in this world passes for love. Some of the jokes carry lethal laughter, some collapse with a dull, albeit iconoclastic, thud, and some are quite wholesomely silly. But underlying all the humor—black, brazen, or merely blatant—is not anti-Catholicism or anti-policism or whatnot; rather, the recognition of a fundamental, horrid injustice disguising itself as respect for the accepted decencies. If the swinish police inspector proclaims, "It is for your own good that authority behaves in this seemingly alarming manner" (in view of his Gestapo tactics, that "seemingly" is richly comic); or if the nurse declares, "I would have practiced euthanasia if my religion did not forbid it, so I decided to murder her"; these and other such sallies are all finally attacks on hypocrisy and greed, which are seen as the stuff of life.

Take a gag described by Walter Kerr as "no joke at all"; when the son says of his pal and himself, "We shared the same cradle," the nurse inquires, "Was that economy or malpractice?" At the lowest level, this illustrates the nurse's dirtymindedness. But, on second thought, the boys did apparently grow up to be sexually involved with each other—may not the child be father to the fag? And, further, is this not a highly suggestive bracketing of economy and malpractice—of economics and malfeasance—which become casual, almost synonymous, alternatives? But Kerr sees no joke at all there, and "no goal" in the play. No doubt, to a theatergoer who cannot, or will not contemplate the possibility of a universe whose repertoire ranges from immorality to amorality—not even from A to B, only from Y to Z—and in which the one decent soul, the father, comes to grief, ***Loot*** is a pointless play. But to those who have been looking around them and have come to wonder about the grotesque farce that is being so dramatically enacted just about everywhere except on the Broadway stage, ***Loot,*** in its imperfect way, may seem neither unfunny nor unmeaningful. (pp. 142, 144)

John Simon, in a review of "Loot," in Commonweal, *Vol. LXXXVIII, No. 5, 19 April 1968, pp. 142-43.*

CRITICAL COMMENTARY

Maurice Charney (essay date 1981)

[In the essay below, Charney explores Loot *as a "quotidian farce," demonstrating how Orton employed everyday elements of popular culture, to satirize "all the values that straight middle-class society most cherishes."]*

After his mother died, one of the few remembrances Joe Orton wanted was her false teeth: "I found my mother's teeth in a drawer. I kept them. To amaze the cast of ***Loot*** . . ." [*Prick up Your Ears: The Biography of Joe Orton,* by John Lahr, 1978]. Orton's diary for January 4, 1967, supplies more details about the incident:

> I'd taken my mother's false teeth down to the theatre. I said to Kenneth Cranham [who played Hal], "Here, I thought you'd like the originals." He said, "What?" "Teeth," I said. "Whose?" he said. "My mum's," I said. He looked very sick.

Sheila Ballantine (Fay), Gerry Duggan (McLeavy), Kenneth Cranham (Hal), and Michael Bates (Truscott) in the first London production of Loot *which opened on 29 September 1966 at the Jeanetta Cochrane Theatre.*

> "You see," I said, "It's obvious that you're not thinking of the events of the play in terms of reality if a thing affects you like that." Simon Ward [who played Dennis] shook like jelly when I gave them to him. . . .

Orton insisted that ***Loot*** should be thought of "in terms of reality," and not as a stylized, mechanized farce.

The dentures of the dead Mrs. McLeavy figure importantly in a bizarre scene in Act One of ***Loot*** where the homicidal nurse, Fay, is undressing the corpse and has already handed across the screen, "*in quick succession, a pair of corsets, a brassiere and a pair of knickers.*" She asks: "Are you committed to having her teeth removed?", and Hal, the homosexual, bank-robbing son answers, "Yes." Meanwhile, Hal is fantasizing about the two-star or three-star brothel he will run with the loot from the bank robbery:

> I'd advertise "By Appointment." Like jam. . . . I'd have a French bird, a Dutch bird, a Belgian bird, an Italian bird—
>
> FAY *hands a pair of false teeth across the screen.*
>
> —and a bird that spoke fluent Spanish and performed the dances of her native country to perfection. (*He clicks the teeth like castanets.*) I'd call it the Consummatum Est. And it'd be the most famous house of ill-fame in the whole of England.
>
> FAY *appears from behind the screen.* HAL *holds up the teeth.*
>
> These are good teeth. Are they the National Health?
>
> FAY. No. She bought them out of her winnings. She had some good evenings at the table last year.

We can readily understand why Kenneth Cranham, who played Hal, looked very sick and Simon Ward, who played Dennis, shook like jelly when Orton handed around his mother's teeth "like nuts at Christmas," as the hard-boiled detective Truscott says in a comparable scene in ***Loot***—"Your sense of detachment is terrifying, lad. Most people would at least flinch upon seeing their mother's eyes and teeth handed around like nuts at Christmas." Orton was cutting through the artificialities and the stilted conventions of West End farce to make a point about what we might call "quotidian farce," which is much closer to black comedy than to the upper-class, comedy-of-manners assumptions of Restoration comedy, or even the middle-class gentility that Feydeau so deftly titillated in his brilliant social comedies. Orton is returning farce to its roots in Plautus and the Italic fertility and harvest rituals that farce celebrates. Like Plautus, Orton is crude and vulgar, although in Orton the language and the action seem to be moving in two entirely opposite directions. Thus Hal speaks with affected chic (and a learned pun) of his new brothel, the Consummatum Est, while clicking his mother's false teeth like castanets. Death as the ultimate tabooed subject (with sex a close second) is also the optimum subject to energize a vulgar, realistic farce cloaked in the empty, genteel clichés of the English Welfare State. We remember that Ronald Bryden called Orton the "Oscar Wilde of Welfare State gentility."

Apparently Orton's mother, Elsie, was very fastidious about her dentures, which she kept soaking in bleach in order to produce a blindingly white, million dollar smile. As Kath, the mother/whore surrogate of ***Entertaining Mr Sloane,*** apologizes to the young lodger/sex object Sloane,

> My teeth, since you mentioned the subject, Mr Sloane, are in the kitchen in Stergene. Usually I allow a good soak overnight. But what with one thing and another I forgot. Otherwise I would never be in such a state. (*Pause.*) I hate people who are careless with their dentures.

Everywhere in Orton's life and in his work he is mocking insufferable pretensions to middle-class propriety. This is quotidian farce in its most literal sense, since the plays feed on the endless preoccupations of daily life. The lewd, possessive Kath, moving through the play by amoral animal instinct, spends most of her aimless day keeping up appearances. That is the beautifully ironic curtain line of ***Loot,*** as the nurse/murderer Fay insists sharply that once she is married to Dennis they will have to move out of Hal's house. "People would talk. We must keep up appearances." And the play ends with a sanctimonious tableau: "*She returns to her prayers, her lips move silently.* DENNIS *and* HAL *at either side of the coffin.*"

Loot is still highly autobiographical, but less consistently so than ***Entertaining Mr Sloane*** of a year earlier. Orton was trying to work through his realistic materials and to fashion them into literature. Like Synge, he was constantly copying phrases and anecdotes of street life into his abundant notebooks. And Orton thought of himself as radically different from Pinter in this respect. He wanted his first play, ***The Ruffian on the Stair,*** a very Pinteresque attempt at implied profundities, to be as unlike Pinter as possible:

> The play is clearly not written naturalistically, but it must be directed and acted with absolute *realism.* No "stylization," no "camp." . . . Everything the characters say is *true.* . . . The play mustn't be presented as an example of the now out-dated "mystery" school—*vide* early Pinter. Everything is as clear as the most reactionary *Telegraph* reader could wish. There is a beginning, a middle and an end. . . .

Orton was preoccupied with the "realism" of dentures and dialogue because traditional farce was so highly stylized. The realism would contribute to the abrasive juxtaposition of black comedy and daily life. The point, of course, is that black comedy by its very nature as comedy is abstracted from daily life and insulated from any sense of pain and injury. Orton's quotidian farce is a contradiction in terms, or at least a paradox of the comic imagination, since farce is traditionally an unreal, highly mannered, dreamlike management of our more naked aggressions. Orton enjoyed working against the grain.

Quotidian farce has its roots in pop culture. We are not surprised to find Dennis, the luxurious undertaker's assistant, putting a piece of chewing gum in his mouth at a critical moment, then later sticking it "*under the coffin.*" Hal says that he got the idea of hiding the money in a coffin from "the comics I read." Wherever we turn in ***Loot,*** we are assaulted by the vulgar bits and pieces of daily life, usually fantasticated by Orton's impudent imagination. Hal, for example, wants to celebrate his success by taking Dennis to "a remarkable brothel I've found. Really remarkable. Run by three Pakistanis aged between ten and fifteen. They do it for sweets. Part of their religion. Meet me at seven. Stock up with Mars bars." It is curious that among the pseudonymous letters Orton wrote under the outraged housewife persona of Mrs. Edna Welthorpe is one dated April 14, 1967, attacking ***Loot*** for the second act discussion "upon the raping of children with Mars bars. . . ." These, and "other filthy details of a sexual and psychopathic nature . . . ," do not, of course, appear in ***Loot,*** but Orton took particular delight in outraging the insatiable popular longing for and loathing of pornography.

Loot has its quota of homosexual "in" jokes. Dennis, for example, refuses to go to a brothel with Hal: "I'm on the wagon. I'm trying to get up sufficient head of steam to marry." Dennis would like to get married because "It's the one thing I haven't tried," but Hal upbraids him: "I don't like your living for kicks, baby. Put these neurotic ideas out of your mind and concentrate on the problems of everyday life." When Fay insists that Dennis is "more relaxed in the company of women," Truscott takes this as gay innuendo: "He'll have to come to terms with his psychological peculiarity." These are admittedly easy reversals, but they depend on a pop culture awareness of sexual clichés.

Like Wilde in *The Importance of Being Earnest,* Orton as homosexual playwright assumes the stance of alien, outsider, critic, and satirist of *all* the values that straight middle-class society most cherishes. There is a cheerful anarchy about all of Orton's works, in which nothing can be assumed, and in which all values—including all the shibboleths of sexuality—are up for grabs. This endows his plays with a "carnivalesque" quality (in Bakhtin's terms), so that if he works with the quotidian materials of pop culture and daily life, these resources are transformed by the powers of farce. Thus all ideology in Orton becomes a collection of meaningless formulas. When McLeavy, the only honest, solid citizen of ***Loot,*** protests against his false arrest, he uses the cant phrases of democratic, civil liberties sermonizing: "You can't do this. I've always been a law-abiding citizen. The police are for the protection of ordinary people." Inspector Truscott of Scotland Yard recoils from McLevy's sentimental pronouncements with genuine disingenuousness: "I don't know where you pick up these slogans, sir. You must read them on hoardings." In other words, these are the advertising slogans of democracy one reads on hoardings, or billboards, the mediamessage, doublespeak, psychobabble that has nothing whatsoever to do with life as it is actually lived. In Fay's terms, McLeavy is "such an innocent," "Not familiar with the ways of the world"; to Truscott he is "a thoroughly irresponsible individual."

Loot begins with popular clichés, and the whole play is a collage of stereotyped banalities that pay lip service to the prevailing values of society. No one is more polite or thoughtful or sensitive to the needs of others than nurse Fay, the patient killer, who has "practised her own form of genocide for a decade and called it nursing." In a reversal of the Bluebeard legend, she now has her sights set for McLeavy, the bereaved widower. As the play opens, she has brought McLeavy a flower:

> MCLEAVY. That's a nice thought. (*Taking the flower from her.*)
>
> FAY. I'm a nice person. One in a million.

"Nice" is a politely formulaic word that covers so many possible meanings and social implications that it is virtually meaningless.

Orton chooses to begin his play with the mechanized dialogue of daytime serials and soap operas in order to conceal the viciousness that lurks just below the surface. Is Fay really "a nice person," "One in a million"? To all intents and purposes she is a devoted and devout Catholic woman of about twenty-eight, but the next bit of mindless dialogue already begins to plant seeds of doubt in our minds:

> MCLEAVY. Are those Mrs McLeavy's slippers?
>
> FAY. Yes. She wouldn't mind my having them.
>
> MCLEAVY. Is the fur genuine?
>
> FAY. It's fluff, not fur.
>
> MCLEAVY. It looks like fur.
>
> FAY. (*standing to her feet*) No. It's a form of fluff.
>
> They manufacture it in Leeds.

Fluff or fur? Why Leeds and not Leicester (where Orton was born)? Does it really matter? But why is the nurse already wearing the dead woman's slippers? Our suspicions run in the familiar channels of grade B movies, in which fluff has an entirely different symbolic value from genuine fur.

Fay's assertions of innocence are just as sloganistic as those of McLeavy; they are the empty phrases of an egalitarian society, which do not impress the very practical Truscott:

> FAY. You must prove me guilty. That is the law.
>
> TRUSCOTT. You know nothing of the law. I know nothing of the law. That makes us equal in the sight of the law.
>
> FAY. I'm innocent till I'm proved guilty. This is a free country. The law is impartial.
>
> TRUSCOTT. Who's been filling your head with that rubbish?

This is Gilbert and Sullivan dialogue in the tradition of musical comedy; it has no conceivable relation to beliefs or ethics. When Fay finally confesses, Truscott is all admiration for her judiciousness and professionalism: "Very good. Your style is simple and direct. It's a theme which less skilfully handled could've given offence. . . . One of the most accomplished confessions I've heard in some time." In ***Loot*** we are constantly shifting from meaning to style, from content to form, and the whole play is delightfully self-conscious about its own means of expression. The actors are always performers, and we are never permitted to get caught up in the action. We are always aware that the epigrammatic dialogue is a script.

The lines of ***Loot*** are often the gag lines of old-fashioned radio comedy, as the characters make witty repartee that has nothing to do with their characterization; the play is divided into jokers and straight men without regard to other character functions. Thus Truscott, while questioning Hal about his mate Dennis, wants to know about the five pregnancies Dennis has on his police record:

> Where does he engender these unwanted children? There are no open spaces. The police patrol regularly. It should be next to impossible to commit the smallest act of indecency, let alone beget a child. Where does he do it?

Hal caps the questions with unexpected extravagance:

> On crowded dance floors during the rhumba.

This is zany but it also puts down the officious Inspector Truscott; it is among many sendups in Orton of the received traditions of heterosexuality. Dennis is represented as "A very luxurious type of lad," on whom every luxury was lavished: "atheism, breast-feeding, circumcision"—again a swipe at the appurtenances of middle-class respectability. Everyone in the play speaks in epigrams, gags, witty repartee, one-liners, and put-downs, so that the dialogue has a strongly exhibitionistic flavor. Everyone is always on display.

Loot relies on the popular format of the detective story or whodunit, although it is basically a parody of that genre—Truscott is a mock-Sherlock Holmes detective. Tom Stoppard was to parody the same genre a few years later in *The Real Inspector Hound.* Proud of his accomplishments, Inspector Truscott of Scotland Yard emerges from his disguise as an official of the Water Board and formally introduces himself to McLeavy:

> You have before you a man who is quite a personage in his way—Truscott of the Yard. Have you never heard of Truscott? The man who tracked down the limbless girl killer? Or was that sensation before your time?

Hal plays straight man for Truscott's gag:

> HAL. Who would kill a limbless girl?
>
> TRUSCOTT. She was the killer.

Like the psychiatrist Rance in ***What the Butler Saw*** and the puffed-up camp director Erpingham in ***The Erpingham Camp,*** Truscott is a burlesque figure of authority who, like Jarry's Père Ubu, is grotesquely menacing. These capricious and tyrannical authority figures seem to fascinate Orton, and they appear in virtually every play he wrote.

Truscott's superlogical methods of detection are an obvious take-off of Sherlock Holmes. With Nurse Fay he knows immediately that she has a crucifix with a dent on one side that is engraved on the back: "St Mary's Convent. Gentiles Only." The following explanation comes almost directly from the pages of Conan Doyle:

> My methods of deduction can be learned by anyone with a keen eye and a quick brain. When I shook your hand I felt a roughness on one of your wedding rings. A roughness I associate with powder burns and salt. The two together spell a gun and sea air. When found on a wedding ring only one solution is possible.

Namely, that her first husband damaged it, after which she shot him at the Hermitage Private Hotel. As Truscott explains later, "The process by which the police arrive at the solution to a mystery is, in itself, a mystery."

We see the Inspector in action when he comes upon Mrs. McLeavy's glass eye at the end of Act One:

> *He puts his pipe into the corner of his mouth and picks up the glass eye. He holds it to the light in order to get a better view. Puzzled. He sniffs at it. He holds it close to his ear. He rattles it. He takes out a pocket magnifying-glass and stares hard at it. He gives a brief exclamation of horror and surprise.*

Orton is poking fun at the detective story as a genre, since it takes Truscott such an awfully long time to arrive at the horror and surprise with which any ordinary mortal would have immediately greeted the discovery of the glass eye.

Truscott is an amoral entertainer like all of Orton's authority figures, who are exceedingly articulate, assertive, and self-important. He also shares with them a penchant for violence that has its roots in the gangster movies that Orton and Pinter saw in their youth. As Orton understands the Pinter influence, "I think there are other influences on my work far more important than Pinter, and of course you always have to remember that the things which influenced Pinter, which I believe are Hollywood movies in the forties, also influenced me." The gangster figure derives his power not only from the gun but also from his commanding rhetoric. Thus Truscott teases Hal with sadistic glee, as in the following dialogue:

> TRUSCOTT. (*shouting, knocking* HAL *to the floor*) Under any other political system I'd have you on the floor in tears!
>
> HAL. (*crying*) You've got me on the floor in tears.

This kind of violent scene gives a special edge to Orton's quotidian farce, since the physical cruelty denies one of the major premises of traditional farce: that the blows do not hurt and that the characters are, by convention, insulated from pain and punishment.

The physical violence in ***Loot*** drives a wedge between the extravagant language and the more prosaic action. It has its own special ironies because it is necessary to preserve appearances at all costs, and especially by verbal artifice, no matter what is actually going on. Thus Kath in ***Entertaining Mr Sloane*** cloaks her seduction of Sloane in the comforting platitudes of domestic solicitude, while Truscott insists that everyone observe the proprieties of the English code of good manners. He insists strenuously, as in the scene at the end of Act I where he cautions Dennis:

> You want to watch yourself. Making unfounded allegations. You'll find yourself in serious trouble.
>
> *He takes* DENNIS *by the collar and shakes him.*
>
> If I ever hear you accuse the police of using violence on a prisoner in custody again, I'll take you down to the station and beat the eyes out of your head.

As small-time hoodlums, both Dennis and Hal have a certain warm feeling for Truscott, who represents to them a high level of professional accomplishment. Thus, early in the play, Dennis acknowledges being questioned by Truscott, who gave him "A rabbit-type punch": "Winded me. Took me by the cobblers. Oh, 'strewth, it made me bad." The mild oath, " 'strewth" ("By his truth"), is a wonderfully mannered survival of middle-class affectation, and Hal and Dennis would be virtually silent if we discounted their high-toned euphemisms. They both speak an artificial and highly artful language that thoroughly disguises what they mean to say. Truscott's sadistic style is the subject of Hal's mock-admiration, as he reacts to Dennis's report of the rabbit-type punch—not, mind you, a real rabbit punch—"Yes, he has a nice line in corporal punishment. Last time he was here he kicked my old lady's cat and he smiled while he did it." Corporal punishment is made respectable by being well administered. Like a salesman showing his samples, Truscott has a "nice line" in corporal punishment, of which the ability to kick smilingly the late Mrs. McLeavy's cat and the rabbit-type punch to Dennis are two convincing demonstrations.

Truscott is full of mock-indignation at the violation of proprieties. When Hal acknowledges that he would have buried the loot in holy ground, Truscott pretends to be scandalized:

> Every one of these fivers bears a portrait of the Queen. It's dreadful to contemplate the issues raised. Twenty thousand tiaras and twenty thousand smiles buried alive! She's a constitutional monarch, you know. She can't answer back.

The picture of the tiaraed, smiling queen on the five pound note is invoked as an alternative to the sewing-dummy corpse of the late Mrs. McLeavy and the satirical issue of *lèse-majesté* is propounded with patriotic fervor.

We know, of course, that Truscott is a jester and entertainer, the comic Vice of the morality plays, but everything in ***Loot*** clearly anticipates the conclusion, in which Hal, Dennis, Fay, and Truscott seal their alliance with the stolen bank notes and a legalistic oblivion about poor Mrs. McLeavy's murder. There are ultimately no hard feelings between the criminals and the law, who understand each other perfectly. The only victim is poor, priggish, smug, and complacent Mr. McLeavy, the only innocent in the play, who is already considered a corpse by the final tableau. It is on the fate of McLeavy that ***Loot*** turns sardonic. He suffers for his foolish faith in authority, but even more for his own exaggerated confidence in himself and the empty shibboleths of law and order and a rational society. When he first hears of the bank robbery, he churns out the sort of moralistic and religious twaddle that can only be offensive to the other characters:

> They'll have it on their conscience. Even if they aren't caught, they'll suffer. . . . [S]uch people never benefit from their crimes. It's people like myself who have the easy time. Asleep at nights. Despite appearances to the contrary, criminals are poor sleepers.

Proverbially, however, the bad sleep well, and one of the morals of ***Loot*** is that crime pays handsomely and criminals are uniformly wittier and more charming than law-abiding persons.

McLeavy is an insufferable apologist for the status quo, a man totally lacking in imagination and generosity. His ironic fate is set up almost from the beginning of the play, as we see him violate human values for the sake of the abstract slogans of Welfare State benevolence. When the father intones his pious and hypocritical platitudes about the police—"I'd like to see them given wider powers. They're hamstrung by red tape. They're a fine body of men. Doing their job under impossible conditions"—his son can only cut him off with a little common sense: "The police are a lot of idle buffoons, Dad. As you well know." McLeavy, of course, is the archetypal law-abiding citizen who is really a fascist at heart. Before he is caught up in the trammels of the law, he is exceedingly cooperative and wants to be of maximum assistance to authority: "We must give this man [Truscott] every opportunity to do his duty. As a good citizen I ignore the stories which bring officialdom into disrepute."

We are not surprised, therefore, when the self-satisfied McLeavy refuses Truscott's very reasonable offer to share in the loot. Truscott, the respectable police officer, wishes to avoid scandal at any cost:

> Now then, sir, be reasonable. What has just taken place is perfectly scandalous and had better go no farther than these three walls. It's not expedient for the general public to have its confidence in the police force undermined. You'd be doing the community a grave disservice by revealing the full frightening facts of this case.

But McLeavy is not a "reasonable" man who can recognize the theatrical conventions of the fourth wall as audience, or "general public." Truscott's "three walls" set up a teasing irony between stage and audience, and McLeavy is ceremoniously arrested with the words of the notorious Detective Sergeant Harold Challenor, who was much in the news at the time ***Loot*** was written: "You're fucking nicked, my old beauty." Orton must also have been thinking of his own spectacular arrest for defacing books in the Islington libraries.

Simon Shepherd has recently reminded us, in an excellent essay, how much Orton's plays conceal their moral horror behind a "dialectic of entertainment" ["Edna's Last Stand, *Or* Joe Orton's Dialectic of Entertainment," *Renaissance and Modern Studies,* 22 (1978)]. The plays show us a stultification of society, in which "people talk in received phrases, which contain their own received values, often despite what the individual really means or wants to say." "Everybody seems to speak journalese, to use second-hand phrases. The spoken language is so arranged that as we listen to it we hear a written text. . . . We are in the presence of the public language of Britain. Characters speak not as individuals, but as citizens, their morals are not their own but the ones they are supposed to have, they respect what they ought to respect." Without using the phrase, Shepherd gets to the heart of what I have been calling quotidian farce.

But this public language is consistently mocked in ***Loot.*** It is the background against which the wit, originality, and initiative of the criminals are applauded, with the mad police inspector Truscott as their natural leader, while the pitifully and platitudinously law-abiding citizen, McLeavy, suffers a well-deserved martyrdom. This is as it should be in farce, where wish-fulfillment values replace the tedious assumptions of the official, patriotic pieties. The quotidian rut of daily life is exploded by the wild imagination of something else, like the sudden intrusion into the dialogue of those three Pakistani girls aged between ten and fifteen who do it for sweets—part of their religion.

To return to our original example of the dentures of Orton's deceased mother clicking like castanets in ***Loot,*** we may ask again in what way Orton wanted the events of the play to be thought of "in terms of reality"? John Russell Taylor [in his *The Second Wave: British Drama of the Sixties,* 1978] is surely on the wrong track when he calls ***Loot*** "a little arid, a play about plays and play conventions rather than a play which is, however remotely, about (if you will pardon the word) life." Albert Hunt rightly takes Taylor to task for failing to perceive that, despite all of its farcical and surrealistic merrymaking, ***Loot*** has a high degree of social consciousness. Orton points up, with some degree of bitterness and pain, the absurdities that we take for granted in our real world.

Orton was fond of the terms "reality" and "realistic" as a way of explaining how to stage his plays. He must surely be using these ambiguous words in the traditional sense of Synge's preface to *The Playboy of the Western World:*

> in countries where the imagination of the people, and the language they use, is rich and living, it is possible for a writer to be rich and copious in

his words, and at the same time to give the reality, which is the root of all poetry, in a comprehensive and natural form.

Drawing on very different sources from Synge, Orton nevertheless affirms his characters' reality by the lively, histrionic, and extravagant style in which they express themselves. If the public reality is stultified, in Shepherd's sense, and the public language of Britain is torpid and dehumanizing, there is an inner reality where farce intersects with black comedy and the characters can assert, even as a form of protest, that they are still alive. We must recognize that Orton is a social satirist like the early Shaw, and ***Loot*** is a play that attacks, in the words of Albert Hunt, "the criminal lunacy of social institutions that are generally accepted as reasonable and beneficial" ["What Joe Orton Saw," *New Society,* 32 (17 April 1975)]. (pp. 514-24)

Maurice Charney, "Orton's 'Loot' as 'Quotidian Farce': The Intersection of Black Comedy and Daily Life," in Modern Drama, *Vol. XXIV, No. 4, December, 1981, pp. 514-24.*

WHAT THE BUTLER SAW

PRODUCTION REVIEWS

Irving Wardle (review date 7 March 1969)

[*In the following review, Wardle calls the London debut of* What the Butler Saw *"a calculated exercise in bad taste, running to the . . . formula of coupling a disreputable action with punctilious $10 dialogue." Noting the play's occasional wittiness, he nevertheless concludes that it is "a deadeningly rigid trick of simple reversal."*]

Rumors about Joe Orton's last play, ***What the Butler Saw,*** have been circulating since he was murdered two years ago.

The play has now arrived at the Queen's Theater after raising controversy in the provinces, notwithstanding the presence of Ralph Richardson in the cast.

Like all of Mr. Orton's work, it is a calculated exercise in bad taste, running to the (now much imitated) formula of coupling a disreputable action with punctilious $10 dialogue. But it compares lamentably with his earlier work, ***Loot,*** and suggests a rough draft that he would never himself have released for public performance.

In ***Loot,*** Mr. Orton took the pants off the police; here he tries to do the same for psychiatrists, ignoring the fact that the popular theater already holds them in low esteem.

The play is set in a private clinic run by a shifty Dr. Prentice. He is in the act of stripping a gullible secretary when he is surprised by an inspector from the Ministry of Health. Prentice passes her off as a patient, whereupon the clinic turns into a real madhouse, with most of the cast exchanging clothes and taking flight from the inspector, who certifies all who come within his reach.

Although there are some good lines and running gags, the comedy follows a deadeningly rigid trick of simple reversal. Churchill is a national idol, so he gets one in the teeth; psychiatrists are the custodians of sanity, so they must be shown as mad. The characters are socially respectable, so they must be credited with every sexual deviation in the book.

Ralph Richardson supervises these extravagances with blandly authoritarian derangement; otherwise it is rather a dim party.

Irving Wardle, "Richardson Stages Orton's Final Play, Flailing Psychiatry," in The New York Times, *March 7, 1969, p. 27.*

Clive Barnes (review date 5 May 1970)

[*In the following review of the 1970 Broadway debut of* What the Butler Saw, *Barnes admires the comic brilliance of Orton's play, "a black comedy of manners—funny, outrageous and almost terrifying in its anarchistic acceptance of logic as a way of life." He predicts that it will become a theatrical classic along with Orton's two other major plays,* Entertaining Mr Sloane*, and* Loot.]

When the British playwright Joe Orton was murdered in 1967 at the age of 34, one of the most promising talents of our time passed from the English-speaking theater. Last night at the McAlpin Rooftop Theater, Orton's last play, ***What the Butler Saw,*** had its hilariously bitter American premiere.

In common with all of Orton's work, this is a black comedy of manners—funny, outrageous and almost terrifying in its anarchistic acceptance of logic as a way of life. It is a wonderfully verbal play, toying with words as if they were firecrackers, and sentences as if they were bombs.

And Orton is a master of the compelling phrase, such as describing a girl as being "as sad as a dressed animal," or the quite unexpected yet familiar shaft of wit expressed by a lady, confronted with a threat of pornographic pictures, announcing grandly: "When I gave myself to you the contract did not provide for cinematic rights." There is an absurd and magnificently sensible nonsense here.

It is quite common nowadays to compare Joe Orton with Oscar Wilde, and the comparison is not altogether unjustified. There is the same regard for glittering language, arrogantly outrageous situations, and sugar-candy architecture by a master confectioner. Orton's plays are not so well crafted as Wilde's, his sense of nonsense sometimes overtopples the flimsiness of his comic constructions, yet in his constant confrontation between order and chaos he has the heart and soul of classic comedy in him.

Of all his plays, I'm inclined to think ***What the Butler Saw*** is the most riotously funny. The title—for reasons best known to Orton—is taken from those British peep-show machines offering modest voyeuristic lubricity at the end of every seaside pier. The plot is an error of comedies.

A psychiatrist tries to seduce a girl sent from the Friendly Faces Employment Bureau for a job as his secretary. He gets her undressed when his wife, who has just been assaulted in a hotel closet by a bellhop, arrives distraught. Add to this mixture, the bellhop himself, Dr. Rance (a government inspector) and a police sergeant, and it will soon be evident that misunderstandings are not only likely but also positively imperative.

Orton knows that everything is possible in comedy—his denouement including even twins, rivals those of the Greeks, Shakespeare or Mozart—as long as he keeps his own mad logic continually teasing the audience's sense of sanity. The play has its rough moments—I believe it was not in its final draft at Orton's death—but as a whole it dazzles. Orton's three major plays will, I think, become classics, and Joseph Hardy is to be particularly congratulated for the cool and classic approach of his staging, which makes this by far the most successful Orton production seen in New York.

The cast, although once in a while tongue-tied on the first night by Orton's Houdini-like linguistics, jumps through the comic hoops with properly startled aplomb. Laurence Luckinbill has just the right hopeful yet vanquished approach to the beleaguered psychiatrist; Jan Farrand is equally comically adept as his strictly wayward wife, and Diana Davila makes a beautifully wispy little ingenue caught up in comic disaster. And Lucian Scott, Tom Rosqui and Charles Murphy all score as the brilliantly mad inspector, the impenetrably stupid policeman, and the enormously resourceful bellhop, respectively, if not respectably.

Nothing is quite respectable about Orton's play, unless it be the wittily contrived elegance of William Ritman's stylish setting. Style is also what Orton has.

Clive Barnes, "'What the Butler Saw,' by Orton, Arrives," in The New York Times, *May 5, 1970, p. 56.*

Walter Kerr (review date 17 May 1970)

[*Kerr analyzes Orton's particular brand of farce in* What the Butler Saw, *suggesting that the true purpose in his plays was to "kill comedy." The critic explains by pointing out that Orton's jokes begin in a traditional manner but end by going in an entirely different direction, thereby constantly reminding audiences of the absurdity of the farce they are observing.*]

When people laugh at Joe Orton's comedies, as indeed some of them sometimes do, I wonder if they aren't doing exactly what Mr. Orton wished them not to do. There was something in the late Mr. Orton that hungered to kill comedy.

There is a malice, a bias against what is meant to be genuinely amusing, almost an anger at the notion of laughter itself, that haunts the plays and constitutes, I think, their true character. This isn't easy to explain, but let's try. In ***What the Butler Saw,*** Mr. Orton's last play now being well performed by Laurence Luckinbill, Jan Farrand and assorted others under Joseph Hardy's as-good-as-can-be direction off Broadway, the formula that once served *Charley's Aunt* and *Getting Gertie's Garter* and dozens of other farces up to 100 years old is trotted out for fresh examination. Stripped girls slip into bellhops' uniforms, stripped bellhops slip into dresses, everyone fails to recognize everyone else, policemen and psychiatrists spin toward the exits as though caught in a revolving door at center stage, guns go off in the garden. You remember it all. Probably you once liked it all.

Liking it requires a certain pretense, though. The underpinnings are unreal, preposterous, and in *Charley's Aunt* we know that. But in order to enjoy what is enjoyable about *Charley's Aunt* we *pretend* that it is not so preposterous by concentrating on a minute-by-minute surface logic. Maybe none of it could have happened, from the beginning. But if it had begun, the rest of it would go like this. The first joke is a contrivance, but the second is utterly reasonable. So we bury the first beneath the second, and go happily on our way.

Mr. Orton will not permit us to go happily on our way. Constantly, naggingly, unflaggingly, he keeps reminding us of how preposterous it all is through the second joke, through all the jokes. Every two-line exchange must contain its own exact interior contradiction, taking us back to the base in the false. It works like this. A patient in a psychiatric clinic is about to be examined before being certified. The government analyst insists that she must be certified *before* being examined. End of joke, if it is one any longer. "He broke the law," someone says. "And for that he is to be treated as a common criminal?" comes the kicker. (A kicker that was used, by the way, in ***Loot*** and does not, to my mind, bear so much repetition.)

Mr. Orton's practice is always to bring us to the edge of a traditional joke and then to take the edge off it. "A bellhop tried to rape me." "Did he succeed?" "No." "The service in this hotel is dreadful." You can almost hear Bobby Clark or Groucho Marx finding a way to make that kind of riposte work. But both would have done it obliquely, so that you wouldn't catch the gap in the thought process. Groucho's most outrageous lines always seem plausible at the split-second. They become outrageous, hilariously so, in the next split-second, after reflection. But he almost got it past you.

Here again, same subject (the evening is single-minded, and could stop anywhere, but doesn't): "You put me in an impossible position." "No position is impossible when you're young and healthy." (Dear Groucho: can you get the lead out of that line?) Or again, "It was very sensible of you to confiscate his clothes. If more women behaved as you did, we would have less rape. Or more." By incorporating the unreasonable into every line. Mr. Orton denies us surprise and idiot pleasure. And why he should have had a character add "or more" to the last jest simply baffles me.

But then he was after something other than jokes, and laughter. I think he may have felt that it was wrong of us to be reacting blithely to the nonsense around us, that he felt the essential ugliness of life was too close for us to be allowed our small comforts. I think he wanted to step on jokes, so that we could hear the crunch and feel them shatter. He didn't get to finish his work, dying young, and we can't say where the grotesquerie might have ended or in what way a self-flagellating form might have matured. We are left with the process under way. It is no laughing matter, unless we are willing to laugh at the old jokes after the heart of them has been deliberately carved out.

Walter Kerr, in a review of "What the Butler Saw," in The Sunday Times, *London, May 17, 1970.*

Jack Kroll (review date 18 May 1970)

[In the following review, Kroll characterizes Orton's What the Butler Saw *as a distorted reflection of contemporary sexual attitudes and practices, emphasizing that "the play has a fantastic physical and metaphysical speed, in which the lightning transvestite changes, disappearances, collisions and misconstructions become a hilarious metaphor for the metamorphic insanity of human drives, sexual and otherwise."]*

As everyone knows, homosexual playwrights have been major figures in the contemporary theater, a situation not without its equivocations. In this light, Joe Orton is almost a kind of tragic hero; he was murdered in 1967 at the age of 34 by his roommate. England thus lost a rare natural playwright, as original in his way as Pinter, though less obviously so. Like all of his plays, ***What the Butler Saw*** uses, almost casually, conventional theatrical forms to contain a savage satirical energy and invention.

Sex was the distorting mirror that Orton held up to human nature, and in this play, with its echoes of Shakespeare, Congreve, Wilde, Rattigan drawing rooms, potboiler farces, "Goon Show" absurdity and burlesque knockabout, he uses the consulting room of a posh private psychiatric clinic to poke ferocious fun at sexual roles and shibboleths. Dotty, lustful psychiatrist attempts to seduce Betty Boop typist, is surprised by his cool, lustful wife, who has her own bellhop paramour concealed about the premises. Enter, additionally, mad, lustful inspector of madhouses and putty-brained constable, and you have the funniest show of the season.

The play has a fantastic physical and metaphysical speed, in which the lightning transvestite changes, disappearances, collisions and misconstructions become a hilarious metaphor for the metamorphic insanity of human drives, sexual and otherwise. Orton's dialogue is blackheartedly funny, its impudent elegance inlaid with glittering, half-hidden parodies and send-ups. Rebuffing an accusation of inversion by pointing out his married state, the psychiatrist is sternly advised: "Marriage excuses no one the freaks' roll call." "Take your trousers down," says the inspector to a thoroughly bewildered character, "and I'll tell you what sex you belong to." "I'd rather not know," is the weary reply.

This type of careening super-farce calls for the Royal Shakespeare Company with its hair-trigger precision. This, of course, is not forthcoming, but under Joseph Hardy's direction the cast produces an amiable, mauling sort of rhythm which has its own charm. Best are the psychiatrist and his wife, played by Laurence Luckinbill and Jan Farrand, for whose ravishing legs one would almost be willing to fight in Cambodia. William Ritman's handsomely clinical set matches Orton perfectly with its witty suggestion of a giant aviary to contain these madly fluttering goonybirds. (pp. 121-22)

Jack Kroll, "Goon Show," in Newsweek, *Vol. LXXV, No. 20, May 18, 1970, pp. 121-22.*

CRITICAL COMMENTARY

William Hutchings (essay date 1988)

[Hutchings is an English educator and critic. In the following essay, he asserts that the plot of What the Butler Saw *depends primarily on Jacobean stage conventions transposed into a modern context, particularly the "assimilation of such standard motifs as the changeling, inadvertent incest, madness, and tragicomic violence." Hutchings concludes that the violent motifs in Orton's last completed play confirm his "status as a master farceur who, transforming specific literary traditions*

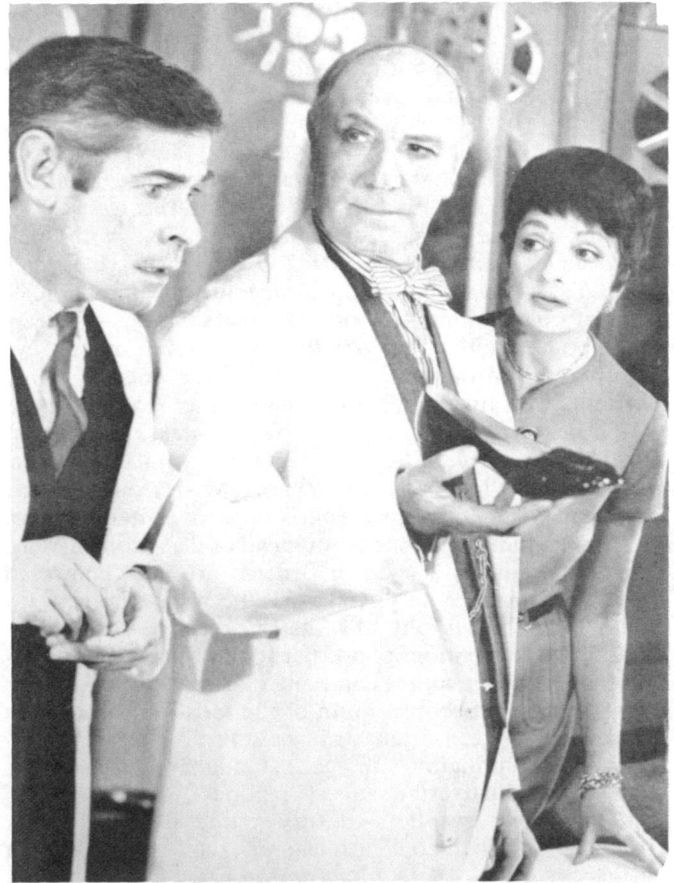

Stanley Baxter as Dr. Prentice, Ralph Richardson as Dr. Rance and Carol Browne as Mrs. Prentice in the first London production of What the Butler Saw, *which debuted at the Queen's Theatre on 5 March 1969.*

through his unique and inimitable talent, willingly dared to defy audience expectations and to outrage conventional proprieties—and did both with evident and unparalleled delight."]

•

> There is a grotesque horror about [life's] comedies, and its tragedies seem to culminate in farce.
> (Oscar Wilde)

With the possible exception of Tom Stoppard, no contemporary English playwright has written with more conscious awareness of the literary tradition within which he works than the late Joe Orton—and nowhere is this consciousness more evident than in ***What the Butler Saw,*** the controversial playwright's last and most controversial play. Denounced by some critics as nearly incoherent, it is acclaimed by many others as his masterpiece—a wild and outrageously bawdy farce which combines brilliantly polished epigrammatic wit and an elaborately contrived, maniacally fast-moving plot. Set in a contemporary psychiatric office, the play's action involves multiple mistaken identities, numerous disguises, repeated allegations of madness, and a surprisingly violent conclusion in which the text calls for copious bloodshed that is often omitted or downplayed in production. When the play opened in London in 1969, nineteen months after the author's untimely death at the age of thirty-four, audiences and critics alike were shocked by the outrageousness of its characters and by their blithe but clinical frankness in discussing a panoply of sexual practices and preferences: cross-dressing (both male and female), nymphomania, necrophilia, exhibitionism, voyeurism, sado-masochism, hermaphrodism, lesbianism, various fetishes, bondage, double incest, and rape. Even when the theatre was becoming increasingly daring and uninhibited with such plays as *Hair* and *Oh! Calcutta!,* Orton's play seemed unprecedented in its flaunted outrageousness and its violation of conventional taboos. Yet, as the play's admirers have pointed out, ***What the Butler Saw*** is in many ways comparable to the works of many of the greatest comic writers of all time; thus, the brief chapter on the play in Maurice Charney's study of Orton's works, [*Joe Orton,* 1981], for example, cites precedents and parallels from Aristophanes, Plautus, Shakespeare, Molière, Congreve, Feydeau, Wilde, Lewis Carroll, Stoppard, Pinter, Ionesco, Beckett, and Brecht. Even though all of these comparisons are quite valid and such precedents are now known to have been familiar to Orton when he wrote the play (as John Lahr's biography of him, *Prick Up Your Ears,* reveals), the conventions of one particular literary period supersede all other sources and analogues: ***What the Butler Saw*** is a virtual compendium of the most outrageous excesses of Jacobean drama transposed into a modern context—an assimilation of such standard motifs as the changeling, inadvertent incest, madness, and tragicomic violence into a twentieth-century setting. Orton's interest in parodying such conventions and excesses is clear even in his first play, ***The Ruffian on the Stair*** (1966); in that play, as Lahr indicates, 'Mike's revenger's "aria" was meant as a parody of Jacobean tragedy.' In ***What the Butler Saw,*** the prevalence of such Jacobean motifs not only helps to explain the unity and cohesion of the text in a way that other analyses of the work have not done, but it also provides ample precedent for both the outrageousness of the characters' actions and the violence of the play's ending.

Orton's most obvious acknowledgment of the Jacobean tradition is found in the play's epigraph from Cyril Tourneur's *The Revenger's Tragedy* (1607): 'Surely we're all mad people, and they / Whom we think are, are not' (III, v). The inherent theatricality of madness, with its potential for bombast and startling action, had long been exploited by Elizabethan dramatists, beginning with Hieronymo's madness in Kyd's *The Spanish Tragedy* (1586), but feigned or *misapprehended* madness was a more prevalent Jacobean theme—following the first production of *Hamlet* in 1602, the year before James I assumed the throne. The assertion embodied in Tourneur's line, however—that both sanity *and* madness are misapprehended—inverts the usual 'normal' order and invites a riotous moral and sexual anarchy that is especially conducive to farce. In Orton's play, such misapprehensions not only prevail but also compound each other; the more a character attempts to represent reason and authority or to take control of a chaotic situation, the less able he or she is to recognize madness *or* sanity when he or she sees it. Accordingly, the play's representative of the highest authority of the state—an inspector of psychiatric hospitals—identifies himself as 'represent[ing] Her Majesty's government[,] your immediate superiors in madness'; even his name, Dr Rance, contains an obvious pun on 'rants'—that most frequent of all symptoms of theatrical madness in the Renaissance. To such 'superiors in madness' who represent the prevailing social order, the most innocent will naturally appear to be the most guilty, and the most sane appear the most mad—even (or *especially*) to the psychiatrists, whose clinical training itself dismisses or precludes usual concepts of 'normality'. Thus, as the play's central character, Dr Prentice, assures his prospective secretary as he attempts to seduce her at the beginning of the play, 'What I see upon the couch isn't a lovely and desirable young girl', though that is precisely what she is; instead, he insists, 'It's a sick mind in need of psychiatric treatment'. As in Jonson's plague-infested London in *The Alchemist* (1610), the prevailing 'sickness' that is thus presumed to be pandemic allows rogues and charlatans of every sort—but especially 'mad' psychiatrists—to flourish. Like Celia in *Volpone* (1605) or the title character of Middleton's *A Chaste Maid in Cheapside* (1611), the prospective secretary in Orton's play, Geraldine Barclay, finds her virtue almost immediately assailed in a world where lechery, cunning, and deceit prevail. When she protests to Prentice's superior that she is not a mental patient but a job-seeker from the Friendly Faces Employment Bureau, she is immediately assumed to be suffering delusions, and committal papers are hastily signed.

In many ways, the psychiatrist's office in which Orton's play takes place is the modern counterpart of the Jacobean stages's Italianate court. Each is a place where—amid elaborate intrigues, disguises, and self-serving duplicities—all sorts of passions and lusts, however forbidden or illicit, flourish outside any norms of moral judgment, unrestrained by social taboos and regarded with clinical detachment by both the perpetrators and the authorities in charge. The play's intricate plot begins as Dr Prentice's attempted seduction of his new secretary is interrupted by the arrival of his wife, from whom he tries to conceal his liaison; she too, however, has had an illicit relationship with the page-boy of a local hotel, who demands money and a job before turning over incriminating photographs taken by the hotel manager. Within the opening minutes of the first act, therefore, a number of favorite Jacobean conventions have been brought into play: seduction and concealment, cuckoldry, a secretly observed assignation, and the threat of disclosure of incriminating evidence. The photographs in question are the modern technological counterpart of the 'ocular proof' of assignations on which so many Jacobean intrigues depend; like the child's horoscope intercepted in *The Duchess of Malfi* (1613), the photographs are directly incriminating—and far less subject to misinterpretation than Desdemona's lost handkerchief, for example. As Orton's intricate plot advances, both the prospective secretary and the hotel page disguise themselves in clothing belonging to other characters. Like Euphrasia in Beaumont and Fletcher's *Philaster* (1610), who also disguises herself as a *page* (called Bellario), Geraldine Barclay presents herself as a male, having donned the uniform of Nicholas Beckett, the hotel employee whom Mrs Prentice wants her husband to employ: Beckett, in turn, puts on the clothing that Miss Barclay has shed. This use of disguise, like the comic concealment (and confusion) of sexual identities, is among the foremost conventions that Orton has adapted from the Renaissance stage.

After many complications and mistaken assumptions, this portion of the plot of ***What the Butler Saw,*** like that of Jonson's *Epicoene,* is resolved when the character mistaken for a young woman is revealed to be a man (Nicholas Beckett in a disguise); then, as in *Philaster, Twelfth Night,* and numerous other plays, the person thought by many of the characters to be male is found to be female. However, in the final moments of the play, Orton adds further contrivances which compound the coincidence—and the outrageousness—of their situation, exceeding and parodying the excesses of the most melodramatic Jacobean plots. Because they bear the two halves of a unique charm given them by their unknown mother at birth, the two are revealed to be the long-separated twin children of Dr and Mrs Prentice, begotten in the linen closet of the Station Hotel where, years later, Mrs Prentice and her unknown son were intimately—and incestuously—reunited. Similarly, Geraldine Barclay, whom Rance has long assumed (without reason) to have been the victim of an incestuous attack in her childhood, is in fact revealed to have been the object of such an attempt by her then-unknown father when the play began. Orton's double-incest plot (father-daughter, mother-son) embodies the ultimate taboos of repressed desire in a way that is particularly appropriate for a play set in a psychiatric clinic, but it exceeds even the various forms of incest that provided a recurrent motif in Jacobean theatre—occurring, for example, between brother and sister in John Ford's *'Tis Pity She's a Whore* (1627) and in Beaumont and Fletcher's *A King and No King* (1611), as well as between uncle and niece in Middleton's *Women, Beware Women* (1623). Yet where as in Ford's play, for example, the incest of Giovanni and Annabella brings bitter remorse to her and leads to madness for him, Orton's characters face the situation with the sort of modern aplomb of their counterparts in Ivy Compton-Burnett's *Darkness and Day* who, confronting an Oedipal situation within their own upper-middle-class family, contend that their ancient counterpart did tend to react rather excessively—blinding himself, talking about it in public, wandering from town to town repeating the story, and becoming a burden on the daughters who must provide his care. 'Perhaps we are [more] fortunate' than those who lived in earlier, less civilized times, as one of Compton-Burnett's characters remarks [in her *Darkness and Day,* 1951], 'Or perhaps fashions have changed.' Rather than being based on changes of fashion, however, the aplomb of Orton's characters is a product of their recognition that their relationships are merely the fulfillment of impulses which are, in psychiatric terms, presumed to be universally human (and therefore nothing to be particularly ashamed of). Appropriately, in the final line of the play, Rance encourages all to 'put our clothes on and face the world' in much the same way that Compton-Burnett's intend to do. Nevertheless, this reconciliatory aspect of the plot also has direct Jacobean affinities; as Orton himself wrote in 1967 [in *The Orton Diaries,* ed. John Lahr, 1987], 'the ending works as "all is forgiven"—just as in the later Shakespeare plays'.

As the complex plot of ***What the Butler Saw*** becomes increasingly manic in the second act, several startling incidents in the final minutes of the play contribute to a seemingly radical shift in tone. Amid frantically rapid entrances and exits of characters in assorted disguises and various states of undress, the action is punctuated with gunshots—certainly a standard device in comic alarums of various kinds. However, the shots in Orton's play hit their targets with potentially fatal accuracy. Sergeant Match, the policeman investigating a number of rapes that young Beckett allegedly committed in a girls' school, enters with 'blood *pouring* down his leg' after the first shot is fired by Mrs Prentice (emphasis mine). Shortly thereafter, Beckett too enters 'moaning and clutching his shoulder', 'anguished [and] fainting' with 'his wound streaming blood, his face white and ill'. Suddenly, unexpectedly, the madcap antics and wild confusions of the play's characters become far more serious and sinister; theirs is clearly not the usually 'painless' violence of most farce, whose characters typically display a certain Punch-and-Judy resiliency if not an apparent imperviousness to pain. Amid the characters' illusions of madness and Orton's witty legerdemain with the plot, the pain and bloodshed are intended to remind the audience abruptly of what is 'real': 'If the pain is real, I must be real,' Nick insists, though Rance replies that he would 'rather not get involved in [such] metaphysical speculation'. Neither, apparently, would many directors of the play—or at least not at the climax of a frantically active farce; for this reason, as a reviewer of Lindsay Anderson's 1975 successful 'unexpurgated' revival of the play remarked [Frank Marcus, *The London Sunday Telegraph,* 20 July 1975], the final ten minutes of ***What the Butler Saw*** are 'arguably the trickiest in modern drama'. The omission of the bloodshed from many productions of the play, as if the shots have simply missed their targets, enables the director to avoid many of these problems—

and particularly the radical shift in tone. Unlike the punishments meted out at the end of *Volpone,* which cause a similarly problematical shift in tone, the gunshot wounds in ***What the Butler Saw*** are unrelated to any righting of a 'moral balance' or any reestablishment of justice (whether civil or poetic); neither are they 'necessary' for any apparent thematic intent, since equally 'guilty' characters do not suffer alike. Such seemingly gratuitous violence, with such blatantly gory effects, will surely only discomfit the audience as the enjoyably madcap antics of Orton's outrageous but likeable and witty characters suddenly become potentially lethal for no *apparent* reason.

Yet, however effective—or even *necessary*—directors may find the omission of the bloodshed to be in wholly pragmatic *theatrical* terms, such as alteration seriously distorts the playwright's *literary* conception of the play. Though it has been given scant attention by most critics, Orton's insistence on blood is neither capricious nor extraneous to an understanding of the work; it is clearly a central and carefully considered aspect of the plot. Repeatedly, the stage directions specify that copious amounts of blood are to be shed, with it 'pouring down [Match's] leg' and 'oozing between [Nick's] fingers' until both are 'streaming with blood' in the final minutes of the play. Such bloodshed, without which no Jacobean tragedy would be complete, is in fact an *essential* part of the action of any play set in the modern counterpart of the Jacobean theatre's Italianate court. There, tragi*comic* actions as well as tragic ones frequently result in characters' loss of blood—as in Beaumont and Fletcher's *Philaster,* the subtitle of which is *Love Lies A'Bleeding.* The fact that Orton's stage directions repeatedly insist on the presence of blood at the end of his farce demonstrates the depth of his commitment to the assimilation of Jacobean motifs, no matter how radically the bloodshed seems to alter the modern audience's mood or violate the director's conception of the production's tone.

When the play's events reach their most anarchic point, as the characters grapple to confine each other in straitjackets in their various drunken, drugged, wounded, half-dressed states, Dr Rance sets off the clinic's security alarm, causing sirens to wail and metal grilles to fall over the doors. Prentice's clinic, like the asylum run by Alibius and Lollio in Rowley and Middleton's *The Changeling* (1622), is ultimately and literally a cage, a profit-based prison in which the keepers can hardly be distinguished from the kept and the sane are mistakenly perceived to be insane; indeed, as Nicholas Brooke has remarked in his study of Jacobean theatre entitled *Horrid Laughter,* 'the only distinction between the inhabitants of Alibius's asylum is that the Fools are harmless and the Madmen are dangerous'. There, like Isabella in *The Changeling,* Mrs Prentice finds that she needs not leave home in order to 'stray from virtue'; repeatedly, as the play nears its climax, she encounters (and shoots at) panic-stricken, half-clad, partially disguised men whom she believes to be pursuing her. In the darkness of the power-failure caused by an overloaded circuit when the alarm is tripped, 'the room is lit only by the glare of a bloody sunset shining through the trees in the garden'; when the characters can no longer flee each other, the plot's multiple misunderstandings are quickly resolved and the play's 'darkest' secret—its double incest motif—is brought to light, confirmed by the matching pieces of the long-lost siblings' lucky elephant charm. Then, in what Orton referred to in his diaries as the play's ' "Golden Bough" subtext . . . [including] the descent of the god at the end' for a 'Euripidean ending', Sergeant Match enters through the room's skylight; clad in a leopard-skin gown originally worn by Mrs Prentice, he leads them 'weary, bleeding, drugged and drunk, [up] the rope ladder into the blazing light' as the play ends.

The play's *other* final classical obeisance—a decidedly 'Aristophanean' moment at the end of the play—was edited out by Sir Ralph Richardson before the first production of the play in 1969. A search for the 'missing part' of an exploded statue of Winston Churchill culminates in the discovery of the 'part' in a gift-wrapped box that Geraldine Barclay brought on stage at the beginning of the play. In Orton's original script (though not in the original printed edition of it, nor in any production until Lindsay Anderson's 'unexpurgated' one in 1975), the missing part—a 'larger-than-life-size bronze' phallus—is pulled from the box, held aloft before the audience, and hailed as 'an example to us all of the spirit that won the Battle of Britain'. In the altered version, the contents of the opened box remain unseen by the audience, and Dr Rance and Geraldine Barclay give predictably different characterizations of what the 'missing part' really is. Though Orton's original ending makes a wholly appropriate obeisance towards the origins of all farce in phallic fertility rites and Aristophanean Old Comedy, and though most critics have approved its 'restoration' as the clearest indication of Orton's intent, the posthumously altered version may well sustain the overall tone of the play more effectively than the one the author intended. For all its Fraserian subtext and 'Euripidean ending', the prevailing tone, theme, and structure of ***What the Butler Saw*** are most directly Jacobean rather than Attic in their origins; the farce observes the (neo-) classical unities with a scrupulousness worthy of Ben Jonson, and its tone is equally carefully sustained, dealing with even its most scandalous and scabrous subjects in language that is often clinical but contains no 'obscene', 'vulgar', or 'four-letter' words (in contrast to David Storey's farce *Mother's Day,* for example, or Caryl Churchill's *Cloud Nine*). Arguably, the defect that Orton himself cited in changing the ending of ***Entertaining Mr Sloane*** is equally apparent in the phallus-flaunting one that he intended for ***What the Butler Saw:***

> The original ending [of ***Sloane***] was quite different and much more complex, and it was wrong. Many writers I think compromise themselves with oversubtle endings—Tennessee Williams is an obvious example. The new ending . . . is very simple, but a natural outcome[,] . . . letting the characters take over ["The Biter Bit: Joe Orton Introduces *Entertaining Mr Sloane* in Conversation with Simon Trussler," *Plays and Players,* August 1964].

Though there is certainly nothing subtle about the *action* of brandishing an enormous bronze phallus on stage, its *use* as the culmination of a Fraserian subtext and an oblique homage to the origins of all farce may well constitute an 'over-subtle ending' that does not fit in with the rest of the work. Even by Orton's own standard, the altered ending is the more 'simple' and 'natural'; unlike its predecessor, it continues the vital ambiguity of perception on which the entire play depends while 'letting the characters take over'. In the altered ending, the 'actual facts' remain unknowable, while the audience is presented with multiple possibilities and divergent interpretations; each of Orton's characters, however 'mad' or however naive, sees what he or she is *predisposed* to see, *whatever* the reality may actually be. Predictably, Rance sees only a phallus (though his perceptions have been thoroughly discredited throughout the play); Geraldine—with her equally untrustworthy 'illusions of youth' still remarkably intact—sees only a cigar. The audience, seeing neither, must imagine the contents of the box for itself and must decide, in effect, which character is right. Yet in the play's altered ending, as in Pirandello's *Right You Are, If You Think You Are* and Stoppard's *After Magritte,* all such perceptions are shown to be wholly subjective; accordingly, they are just as unreliable as any of the characters' judgments of sanity and insanity, as Orton's epigraph (and the play itself) makes clear.

Even though ***What the Butler Saw*** features many of the familiar characteristics of traditional farce (e.g., mistaken identities, uninhibited lechery, manic action, hastily assumed disguises, mutual misunderstandings, and frantic but precisely timed exits and entrances), its carefully polished, epigrammatic script demands of its actors a rigorous control at all times and permits them none of the raucous excess or improvisational 'free play' that more traditional, broadly physical farce allows. Accordingly, any productions that treat the play *merely* as farce invariably fail; neither the physicality that is appropriate for *Gammer Gurton's Needle* (or *Lysistrata* or even *No Sex, Please, We're British*) nor the polished delivery required for *The Importance of Being Earnest* will suffice alone, since Orton's work demands, uniquely, a synthesis of both. In creating such a synthesis, and in accommodating within it the outrageousness of the Jacobean aesthetic as well, ***What the Butler Saw*** extends—and therefore, to an extent, redefines—the capabilities of farce as both a literary genre and as a theatrical form.

Where as Tom Stoppard's assimilations of *Hamlet* in *Rosencrantz and Guildenstern are Dead* and of *'Tis Pity She's a Whore* in *The Real Thing* are openly acknowledged within the plays themselves, Joe Orton's Jacobean affinities in ***What the Butler Saw*** tend to be cunningly concealed in surprisingly congruent twentieth-century counterparts. In the excesses of the Jacobean stage aesthetic, Orton found a particularly appropriate precedent for his own satirical vision—in much the same way that Thomas Pynchon had done in *The Crying of Lot 49,* published in 1966. The extensive presence of such motifs in ***What the Butler Saw*** not only unifies the play in ways that were not apparent to its earliest reviewers but also justifies the seemingly inapposite bloodshed that continues to be omitted from productions even today. Furthermore, it confirms Orton's status as a master farceur who, transforming specific literary traditions through his unique and inimitable talent, willingly dared to defy audience expectations and to outrage conventional proprieties—and did both with evident and unparalleled delight. (pp. 227-34)

William Hutchings, "Joe Orton's Jacobean Assimilations in 'What the Butler Saw'," in Themes in Drama, *Vol. 10, 1988, pp. 227-35.*

FURTHER READING

AUTHOR COMMENTARY

Loney, Glenn. "Entertaining Mr. Loney: An Early Interview with Joe Orton." *New Theatre Quarterly* IV, No. 16 (November 1988): 300-05.

Previously unpublished interview with Orton, given to Loney in New York in October 1965, three days before the Broadway opening of *Entertaining Mr. Sloane.*

Orton, Joe. *The Orton Diaries,* edited by John Lahr. New York: Harper & Row, 1986, 304 p.

Records the last eight months of Orton's life, from December 1966 to August 1967. The *Diaries* also contain satirical correspondence Orton wrote under the pseudonym Edna Welthorpe and others.

OVERVIEWS AND GENERAL STUDIES

Barnes, Clive. "A Joe Orton Festival." *The New York Times* (15 September 1975).

Reviews the 1975 London productions of Orton's *Entertaining Mr. Sloane* and *What the Butler Saw.* Barnes praises the performances in *Sloane* but notes an uncertain balance between satire and farce in *What the Butler Saw.*

Bigsby, C. W. E. *Joe Orton.* Methuen: London, 1982, 79 p.

Offers an overview and examination of Orton's works. Bigsby maintains that in three years Orton's work evolved from the absurdist comedy of *Entertaining Mr. Sloane* to a more directly satirical comic style in *The Good and Faithful Servant* and then to the use of his own brand of anarchic farce in *Loot* and *What the Butler Saw.*

Casmus, Mary I. "Farce and Verbal Style in the Plays of Joe Orton." *Journal of Popular Culture* XIII, No. 3 (Spring 1980): 461-68.

Traces the development of Orton's comedies from the naturalistic style of *Entertaining Mr. Sloane* to the "unique highly individual verbal style" of *What the Butler Saw.* Although Orton broke no new dramatic ground in his plays, Casmus concludes, he rediscovered farce as a genre "broad enough to contain both sides of his nature, the sunny as well as the dark and anarchic."

Charney, Maurice. *Joe Orton.* New York: Grove Press, 1984, 145 p.

Introduction to Orton's career, offering discussion of the dramatist's biography, a survey of his plays, and individual analyses of *Entertaining Mr. Sloane* (reprinted above), *Loot, What the Butler Saw,* and *Up against It,* Orton's unaccepted screenplay for the Beatles.

Esslin, Martin. "Joe Orton: The Comedy of (Ill) Manners."

In *Contemporary English Drama,* edited by C. W. E. Bigsby, pp. 95-108. London: Edward Arnold, 1981.

Examines Orton's oeuvre as representative of the social upheaval of the late 1960s and its consequences in Britain and other countries. Esslin asserts that the rage manifested in Orton's plays "is purely negative, it is unrelated to any positive creed, philosophy or programme of social reform."

Fraser, Keath. "Joe Orton: His Brief Career." *Modern Drama* XIV, No. 4 (February 1972): 413-19.

Summarizes Orton's artistic career. Fraser writes that farce permitted Orton "to confront society with the sort of escapist entertainment it loved . . . [and] at the same time to parody the kind of established values which considered farce important enough to patronise."

Hunt, Albert. "What Joe Orton Saw." *New Society* 32, No. 654 (17 April 1975): 148-50.

Asserts that in *Loot* and *What the Butler Saw,* Orton "offered us an entirely recognisable picture of our social situation. The problem is that we've become so familiar with institutions and processes that are basically mad that we accept them as reasonable. It takes a man with 'normal' vision to find a way of making us look at the absurdities and move towards demolishing them, through laughter."

Kaufman, David. "Love and Death." *Horizon* 30, No. 4 (May 1987): 38-40.

Discusses John Lahr's research of Orton's diaries and how it evolved into his 1978 biography of the playwright, *Prick up Your Ears.* Kaufman also examines Lahr's perceptions of the Stephen Frears movie adaptation of the same name and of the 1986 publication of *The Orton Diaries,* edited by Lahr.

Lahr, John. "The Artist of the Outrageous." *Evergreen Review* 14, No. 75 (February 1970); 30-4, 83-4.

Explores Orton's talent for farce. Lahr draws a parallel between the societal madness depicted in Orton's plays and the social upheaval in American society resulting from the debate over the Vietnam War.

———. *Prick up Your Ears.* New York: Alfred A. Knopf, 1978, 302 p.

Definitive biography of Orton containing extensive excerpts from *The Orton Diaries* as well as a play chronology and bibliography.

———. "Joe Orton." In his *Automatic Vaudeville: Essays on Star Turns,* pp. 111-39. New York: Alfred A. Knopf, 1984.

Overview of Orton's theatrical career. Lahr writes that "like all great satirists, Joe Orton was a realist. He was prepared to speak the unspeakable; and this gave his plays their joy and danger."

Nightingale, Benedict. "The Detached Anarchist." *Encounter* LII, No. 3 (March 1979): 55-61.

Examination of Orton's approach to comedy, asserting that "his humour could be bumptious and naughty: it could also be contemptuous and malicious."

Shepherd, Simon. "Edna's Last Stand, *or* Joe Orton's Dialectic of Entertainment." *Renaissance and Modern Studies* XXII (1978): 87-110.

A study of Orton's analysis of modern society in his dramas. Sheperd points out that "Orton sees structures for controlling and exploiting people" even in accepted institutions such as the workplace and the entertainment industry.

Sinfield, Alan. "Who Was Afraid of Joe Orton?" *Textual Practice* 4, No. 2 (Summer 1990): 259-77.

Discussion of the theme of homosexuality in Orton's plays, noting how he "exploited and contributed to the process through which homosexuality gradually became publicly speakable."

Smith, Leslie. "Democratic Lunacy: The Comedies of Joe Orton." *Adam International Review* 40, Nos. 394-96 (1976): 73-92.

Discussion of Orton's *Entertaining Mr. Sloane, Loot* and *What the Butler Saw.* Smith asserts that "Orton brought farcical comedy, as no one else has done in quite the same way in our time, into creative relationship both with the unconscious, and with some of the larger lunacies and nightmares of our time."

Taylor, John Russell. "Joe Orton." In his *The Second Wave: British Drama for the Seventies,* pp. 125-40. New York: Hill and Wang, 1971.

Examines what Taylor calls Orton's brief yet spectacular career. The critic concludes that "though they seem to start from the material of camp fantasy, Orton's plays manage completely to transform that material into a serious vision of life, which, however eccentric—and however comic in its chosen forms of expression—carries complete conviction as something felt, something true."

Walcot, Peter. "An Acquired Taste: Joe Orton and the Greeks." In *Legacy of Thespis: Drama Past and Present, Volume IV,* edited by Karelisa V. Hartigan, pp. 99-123. New York: University Press of America, 1984.

Explores the relationship between Greek comedy and the comedies of Orton.

ENTERTAINING MR. SLOANE

Hewes, Henry. "Rats, Cats, and History." *Saturday Review* (New York) XLVIII, No. 44 (30 October 1965): 74.

Claims that pathetic characters, strained jokes, and an ineffective plot made the 1965 Broadway debut of *Entertaining Mr. Sloane* a failure.

Kerr, Walter. "Walter Kerr Reviews *Entertaining Mr. Sloane.*" *Herald Tribune* (13 October 1965).

Faults the text of *Entertaining Mr. Sloane* for being overly plausible, thus defusing the comic effect of the play's ending.

McCarten, John. "Clumsy Capers." *The New Yorker* XLI, No. 36 (30 October 1965): 94, 96.

Claims that Orton carried "macabre humor too far" in *Entertaining Mr. Sloane,* noting in particular Sloane's murder of Kemp. McCarten praises Sheila Hancock and Lee Montague, however, for their comic portrayals of the siblings, Kath and Ed.

Michener, Charles. "What Joe Orton Saw." *Newsweek* XCVIII, No. 8 (24 August 1981): 72.

Asserts that, through excellent ensemble acting, the lead players in John Tillinger's 1981 staging of *Entertaining Mr. Sloane* avoided playing Kath, Ed, and Sloane as a stereotypical nymphomaniac, homosexual, and psychopath, respectively, thereby realizing Orton's main intention in his play: "to break down all the sexual compartments."

"Freak Show." *Newsweek* 66, No. 17 (25 October 1965): 102.
Cites the indifferent treatment of the subject matter, not the subject itself, as the problem with *Entertaining Mr. Sloane.* The critic writes: "never once is there the slightest indication that Orton has any attitude at all toward his characters, not contempt, pity, amusement, alarm, not even—what would at least be human—a voyeur's interest. He is a simple exploiter, the shrewd, plausible, soulless manager of a freak show."

Taubman, Howard. "Theater: *Entertaining Mr. Sloane.*" *The New York Times* (13 October 1965).
Asserts that "the slovenly habits, perverse attachments and self-serving hypocrisies" of the characters in Orton's "singularly unattractive play" failed to sustain interest. Taubman concludes that the play must be viewed either as a forced and incredible drama or as an overly broad comedy.

———. "Aiming at Easy Targets." *The New York Times* (23 October 1965).
Blames the failure of *Entertaining Mr. Sloane* not on its theme of uncovering modern corruption and hypocrisy, but on the facile satirical targets of Kath, Ed, and Sloane. The critic questions: "Why not go after the ludicrous pretensions and monstrous falsities of the kind of people whose position and power in the world make a vast difference in our lives?"

"Stygian Fun House." *Time* 86, No. 17 (22 October 1965): 103.
Claims that *Mr. Sloane* fails as a "comedy of morals." The critic writes that Orton's "talents run more to seamy documentation than satirical savagery."

"An Exercise in Black Comedy." *The Times,* London (30 June 1964).
Lauds Orton for his "poised, artificial dialect . . . which neutralizes the events it refers to," making the unsavory events of the play appear inoffensive.

Wensberg, Erik. "Redcoats on Broadway." *The Reporter* 33, No. 9 (18 November 1965): 48, 50.
Labels *Entertaining Mr. Sloane* "thin, derivative, and pretentious," claiming that Orton failed in his attempt to satirize middle-class hypocrisy.

LOOT

Armistead, Claire. Review of *Loot. Guardian* (21 May 1992).
Deems both the play and this London revival outdated. Armistead claims that "the shock of seeing Joe Orton's *Loot* revived . . . is the realization that this most subversive farce has long since done its work."

Barnes, Clive. "*Loot*: Comedy as Piracy." *New York Post* (19 February 1986).
Attributes the shocking nature of Orton's play not to its morbid subject matter but to its "calm and even tone" in handling themes of "murder, robbery, sacrilege, police brutality, and official corruption." Barnes praises both the cast and director of the production.

Cooke, Richard P. "The Theater: Caper with a Corpse." *The Wall Street Journal* (20 March 1968).
Claims that the 1968 Broadway production of *Loot* lacked enough sustained energy to achieve true farce, "like a soufflé that never quite puffs up." He calls Orton's humor "that of the advanced juvenile," accusing the playwright of excessive punning and a complacent anti-social attitude.

Gill, Brendan. "Image Breakers." *The New Yorker* XLIV, No. 6 (30 March 1968): 103-04.
Declares *Loot* a successful "knockabout farce," noting that although Orton clearly resented middle class institutions and possessed a pessimistic view of humankind, "his mood was an invincibly merry one, and the clown in him continuously [outwitted] the scold."

Gussow, Mel. "An Inspired Romp through the Landscape of *Loot.*" *The New York Times* (23 February 1986).
Praises the comic timing of the cast in John Tillinger's 1986 Broadway revival, calling *Loot* a "priceless contemporary example" of farce.

Kingston, Jeremy. Review of *Loot. The Times,* London (15 May 1992).
Faults the London production for uneven pacing and performances, but notes the continued effectiveness of Orton's play. "The scenes in which a son heaves his mother's corpse about as if it were a sack of sugar, and talks of brothels while searching the floor for her glass eye, have an effrontery that remains unnerving."

Morley, Sheridan. Review of *Loot. Herald Tribune* (20 May 1992).
Asserts that the London revival was unable to convey at the same time the anarchic ideas behind Orton's comedy and his subtle wit. Morley claims that this production seemed "torn between a contemporary satire and a Wildean high comedy, with the result that no coherent playing style [was] allowed to emerge."

Murray, David. Review of *Loot. Financial Times* (15 May 1992).
Faults the production for uneven and uninspired performances.

Rich, Frank. "Mummy Dearest." *The New York Times* (19 February 1986).
Positive review of the 1986 Broadway production. Rich writes: "*Loot* is timeless because its author's rage against hypocrisy is conveyed not by preaching or idle wisecracks but by the outrageous farcical conception and by pungent, stylized dialogue in the tradition of Wilde and Shaw."

Review of *Loot. Time* 91, No. 13 (29 March 1968): 91.
Declares that the 1968 Broadway production of *Loot* regrettably lacked good comic timing. The reviewer adds that the director Derek Goldby let "the pace stall at moments to let the dialogue sink in as if Orton had some comment to make on life, instead of mocking all comment on life or death."

Watts, Richard, Jr. "The Latest in 'Black' Comedy." *New York Post* (19 March 1968).
Posits that the Broadway production, particularly Derek Goldby's skillful direction and George Rose's portrayal of Inspector Truscott, improved on the original 1964 London staging. However, the farce as written did not maintain its comic cadence, the critic concludes,

and "Mr. Orton's play [ran] into the doldrums too frequently, especially toward the end."

Winer, Linda. "A Top-Notch Cast Pulls off the Job in *Loot*." *USA Today* (19 February 1986).

Calls Orton's play "a smart, silly, perversely cheerful satire on death, sexuality, religion and general notions of good taste," also offering praise for a first-rate cast and for director John Tillinger.

WHAT THE BUTLER SAW

Gottfried, Martin. Review of *What the Butler Saw. Women's Wear Daily* (5 May 1970).

Notes the unrevised and inconsistent style of Orton's *What the Butler Saw,* but calls the play "disarming to the point of enchantment—clever and energetic and sunny." The critic also applauds Joseph Hardy's precise direction, labelling the entire production "wonderfully civilized and rationally lunatic."

Gussow, Mel. Review of *What the Butler Saw. The New York Times* (10 March 1985).

Calls the 1985 Yale Repertory production "maladroit," faulting the lack of proper comic timing and lackluster performances by the principal actors.

O'Connor, John J. "Mad Farce." *The Wall Street Journal* (5 May 1970).

Admires Orton's *What the Butler Saw* as a "funny, devilish exercise in the offbeat," but claims that Joseph Hardy's flawed direction produced an ineffective staging.

Olvier, Edith. Review of *What the Butler Saw. The New Yorker* XLVI, No. 13 (16 May 1970): 106-07.

Commends Orton's skilled handling of "breakneck satiric farce" in *What the Butler Saw,* also noting Joseph Hardy's clear, well-paced direction and the competent Broadway cast.

Review of *What the Butler Saw. Time* 95, No. 20 (18 May 1970): 72.

Maintains that *What the Butler Saw* is Orton's "zaniest play." The reviewer concludes that the comedy's theme of contemporary madness may not be new, but "what is wonderfully refreshing is that Joe Orton has such mad, mad fun with it."

Watts, Richard. "Joe Orton's Last Comedy." *New York Post* (5 May 1970).

Notes the influence of French dramatist Georges Feydeau on Orton and praises Joseph Hardy's staging of this production.

MEDIA ADAPTATIONS

Entertaining Mr. Sloane. Canterbury/Anglo-Amalgamated/Warner Pathe, 1970.

Directed by Douglas Hickox, this film version stars Beryl Reid as Kath, Peter McEnery as Sloane, Harry Andrews as Ed, and Alan Webb as Kemp.

Loot. Performing Arts/Cinevision, 1971.

Film adaptation of Orton's play directed by Silvio Narizzano and starring Richard Attenborough as Truscott, Lee Remick as Fay, Hywel Bennett as Dennis, Roy Holder as Hal, and Milo O'Shea as McLeavy.

Prick up Your Ears. Civilhand Zenith/Goldwyn, 1987.

Film based on John Lahr's 1978 biography of the same name. Directed by Stephen Frears, the movie features Gary Oldman as Orton, Alfred Molina as Kenneth Halliwell, Vanessa Redgrave as Peggy Ramsay, and Julie Walters as Elsie Orton, the playwright's mother.

Additional coverage of Orton's life and career is contained in the following sources published by Gale Research: *Contemporary Authors,* Vols. 85-88; *Contemporary Literary Criticism,* Vols. 4, 13, 43; and *Dictionary of Literary Biography,* Vol. 13.

Jean-Paul Sartre

1905-1980

INTRODUCTION

A leading proponent of the philosophical concept of existentialism, Sartre was one of the most influential authors of his generation. His interpretation of existentialism emphasizes that existence precedes essence and that human beings are alone in a godless, meaningless universe. He believed that individuals are absolutely free but also morally responsible for their actions. Sartre acknowledged the inherent absurdity of life and the despair that results from this realization, but he maintained that such malaise could be transcended through social and political commitment. In his writings, Sartre examined virtually every aspect of human endeavor as a search for total freedom. Although Sartre's philosophical and critical works are generally upheld as his most original and significant writings, his plays are important statements of his primary themes of freedom, responsibility, and action. Accordingly, they are seen as closely affiliated to his two central philosophical works, *L'être et le néant* (*Being and Nothingness*) and *Critique de la raison dialectique* (*Critique of Dialectical Reason*). Sartre's most famous play, *Huis clos* (*No Exit*), for example, is a dramatic representation of the author's existentialist theories from *Being and Nothingness* as they apply to social situations. Although Sartre's other plays received somewhat less popular acclaim, critics affirm their importance in contributing to a greater understanding of the social and political dimensions of Sartre's philosophical thought.

Sartre's earliest influence was his grandfather, Charles Schweitzer, with whom he and his mother lived after his father's early death. As Sartre recalled in his childhood memoir, *Les mots* (*The Words*), Schweitzer, a professor of German, instilled in him a passion for literature. Yet Schweitzer also preached the values of the bourgeoisie and denigrated a career in letters as precarious and unsuitable for stable middle-class people. In reaction, Sartre proposed to make writing "serious," and adopted it as the center of his life and values. He also chose it as a kind of self-justification in a world where children were not taken seriously. "By writing I was existing. I was escaping from the grown-ups," he wrote in *The Words*. Sartre perceived hypocrisy in his middle-class environment as manifested in his family's penchant for self-indulgence and role-playing, and, as a result, he held anti-bourgeois sentiments throughout his life. After completing his early education at a Parisian lycée, Sartre attended the École Normale Supérieure. There he studied philosophy and met fellow philosophy student Simone de Beauvoir, with whom he maintained a lifelong personal and intellectual relationship. Sartre spent much of the 1930s teaching philosophy and studying the works of German philosophers Edmund Husserl and Martin Heidegger. Sartre's early philosophical volumes—*L'imagination* (*Imagination: A Psychological Critique*), *Esquisse d'une théorie des émotions* (*The Emotions: Outline of a Theory*), and *L'imaginaire: Psychologie phénoménologique de l'imagination* (*The Psychology of Imagination*)—reflect the influence of Husserl's writings and focus on the workings and structure of consciousness. During this era, Sartre also wrote his first novel, *La nausée* (*Nausea*), a work that depicts humanity's reaction to the absurdity of existence, and the short story collection *Le mur* (*The Wall, and Other Stories*), an exploration of human relationships, sexuality, insanity, and the meaning of action. By the end of the decade, he had firmly established his reputation as a promising young writer.

Sartre continued to write prolifically during World War II, producing the dramas *Les mouches* (*The Flies*), a retelling of the Greek story of the murder of Clytemnestra by her children, and *No Exit,* a disturbing vision of hell. At this time, Sartre also wrote *Being and Nothingness,* which examines humanity as both an object in the world and as an ordering consciousness. After the publication of this last work, considered by many scholars the most important of the first half of his career, Sartre became recognized as a major philosopher and as the preeminent spokesperson for his generation.

While serving with the French Army during the war

years, Sartre was taken prisoner by the Germans and held captive for nine months. His experiences among fellow inmates affected him strongly and Sartre's subsequent literary and philosophical works demonstrate an increased awareness of history and politics, as well as an increased commitment to social and political action. Throughout the 1950s and 1960s, Sartre devoted much attention to world affairs, participating in political demonstrations and espousing Marxist solutions to social problems in articles later collected, along with philosophical and literary essays, in the ten-volume *Situations.* In *Critique of Dialectical Reason,* considered by critics his second major philosophical work, Sartre attempted to fuse Marxism and existentialism to provide a new approach to historical analysis. Condemning capitalism and Western democratic institutions, Sartre called for a synthesis of personal freedom and moral duty within a neo-Marxian context in order to create the foundation for social revolution. In 1964, Sartre was awarded, but refused to accept, the Nobel Prize in literature. As the result of declining health, Sartre wrote less prolifically in his last years. He died of a lung ailment in 1980.

In *Being and Nothingness,* Sartre identified freedom as one of the most important characteristics of consciousness. He soon drew the corollary that ontological freedom, in which humanity is "condemned to be free," as he wrote in *Being and Nothingness,* must also entail political freedom; that is, freedom is a goal as well as a given and must be embodied in praxis (practical action). Sartre incorporated this belief as a central concern in all of his dramatic works. His recasting of the murder of the tyrants Clytemnestra and her lover Aegisthus by her children Orestes and Electra in *The Flies* emphasized humanity's fundamental freedom, against which even the gods are powerless. Produced in Paris in 1943 during the Occupation, the play ironically commented on France's political subjugation. *No Exit,* Sartre's most famous dramatic work, deals with the absence of freedom when one allows oneself to exist through and for others, rather than living authentically. The play presents three characters who have been condemned to hell as a result of having lived in "bad faith," Sartre's term for self-deception. Their existence is symbolized by a small room from which there is no escape. The conclusion reached by the three protagonists, that "hell is other people," results from the failure of what Sartre regarded as the misguided attempt by each consciousness to impose itself on the others and hence attain self-affirmation. *No Exit,* with its minimalist production values and presentation of human conflict as a function of situation, helped establish Sartre's modernist aesthetic—a paradigm he would follow in later dramas.

Sartre treated the theme of freedom even more elaborately in his plays of the 1940s. *Morts sans sépultre* (*The Victors*) centers on a crisis of consciousness among French Resistance fighters who have been captured and tortured by the Vichy militia. The play offers the view that even under torture and threat of death, one is free to make choices, and vividly illustrates the concept of anguish analyzed in *Being and Nothingness. Les mains sales* (*Dirty Hands*) focuses on the struggle of Hugo, a bourgeois idealist, to prove his worth to his comrades in the Communist party. Ordered to assassinate Hoederer, a Communist leader whom he admires for his political views, Hugo wavers but finally kills him for reasons unrelated to politics. When given a chance to renounce his action after Hoederer is declared a hero, Hugo refuses, thereby affirming through "existentialist" choice his unconditional human freedom.

Around 1950 Sartre's thinking became increasingly radicalized as his ideological position shifted from pure existentialism to neo-Marxism. In the *Critique of Dialectical Reason,* Sartre aimed to give a philosophical basis to Marxism and, on that basis, to investigate further the dialectic of history and its intelligibility. Dialectical reasoning, which Sartre opposed to traditional Western logic, is based on the synthesis of contraries first proposed by the German idealist philosopher Georg Wilhelm Friedrich Hegel. While still insisting on the possibility of human freedom, the *Critique* shows how this freedom is conditioned, alienated, and rendered powerless by historical and social developments. Critics generally agree that the two principal plays written by Sartre during the 1950s are closely related to the dialectical method articulated in the 1960 *Critique.* The setting for *Le diable et le bon dieu* (*The Devil and the Good Lord*), for example, evokes a precise historical moment—the struggle for power between temporal and ecclesiastical authorities in pre-Reformation Germany. The hero, Goetz, the son of a peasant and a noblewoman, vows to pursue only the good. He attempts to free the peasant class from economic servitude through redistributing lands belonging to the nobility, but ultimately fails owing to practical contingencies. In response, Goetz denies both evil and good as absolute values and chooses pragmatic solutions toward a particular end. Theoretically, this resolution means denying God's existence, thereby affirming Sartre's essential atheism.

Sartre's last major play of the 1950s—and indeed of his entire dramatic career—is widely regarded as a literary masterpiece on the scale of *No Exit. Les séquestrés d'Altona* (*The Condemned of Altona*) is about a wealthy German industrialist family after the 1945 defeat in World War II. It centers on the son Frantz, a veteran who has sequestered himself in his room for years to create the illusion of German victory. Frantz's madness—accompanied by vivid hallucinations that portend the destruction of the human race—is largely a function of guilt over his family's personal involvement in wartime Nazi atrocities. Widely interpreted as a moral condemnation of France's conduct during its bloody conflict with its rebellious colony Algeria, the play also critiques capitalist Europe, whose conflicts over markets and expansion, Sartre believed, had been the ultimate cause of both world wars.

While initial critical reception of Sartre's dramatic productions was generally mixed, his overall reputation as a leading contributor to modern theater is assured by the lasting success of *No Exit* and the literary quality of such widely read works as *The Condemned of Altona.* True, in strictly formal terms Sartre contributed little to the legacy of postwar European drama compared to Bertolt Brecht or the proponents of the Theater of the Absurd. However, commentators note that Sartre's plays were not written so much as aesthetic stage experiments as elements in his larger philosophical and political program. Viewed in their proper perspective, critics suggest, Sartre's plays emerge as a key component of the history of ideas of the twentieth century.

PRINCIPAL WORKS

PLAYS

Les mouches 1942
[*The Flies,* 1947]
Huis clos 1944
[*The Vicious Circle,* 1946; also produced as *No Exit,* 1946]
Morts sans sépultre 1946
[*Men without Shadows,* 1947; also produced as *The Victors,* 1948]
La putain respectueuse 1946
[*The Respectful Prostitute,* 1948]
Les mains sales 1948
[*Crime Passionel,* 1948; also published as *Dirty Hands,* 1949]
Le diable et le bon dieu 1951
[*Lucifer and the Lord,* 1953; also published as *The Devil and the Good Lord,* 1960]
Kean 1954 [adapter; from the play *Kean ou désordre et génie* by Alexandre Dumas, père]
[*Kean, or Disorder and Genius,* 1954]
Nekrassov 1955
[*Nekrassov,* 1956]
Les séquestrés d'Altona 1959
[*Loser Wins,* 1960; also published as *The Condemned of Altona,* 1961]

OTHER MAJOR WORKS

L'imagination (philosophy) 1936
[*Imagination: A Psychological Critique,* 1962]
La nausée (novel) 1938
[*Nausea,* 1949; also published as *The Diary of Antoine Roquentin,* 1949]
Esquisse d'une théorie des émotions (philosophy) 1939
[*The Emotions: Outline of a Theory,* 1948; also published as *Sketch for a Theory of the Emotions,* 1962]
Le mur (short stories) 1939
[*The Wall, and Other Stories,* 1948; also published as *Intimacy, and Other Stories,* 1956]
L'imaginaire: Psychologie phénoménologique de l'imagination (philosophy) 1940
[*The Psychology of Imagination,* 1948]
L'être et le néant: Essai d'ontologie phénoménologique (philosophy) 1943
[*Being and Nothingness: An Essay on Phenomenological Ontology,* 1956]
Les chemins de la liberté. 3 vols. (novels) 1945-49
[*The Roads of Freedom,* 1947-51]
L'existentialisme est un humanisme (philosophy) 1946
[*Existentialism,* 1947; also published as *Existentialism and Humanism,* 1948]
Baudelaire (biography and criticism) 1947
[*Baudelaire,* 1949]
Les jeux sont faits (screenplay) 1947
[*The Chips are Down,* 1948]
Situations. 10 vols. (essays) 1947-76
Saint Genet, comédien et martyr (biography and criticism) 1952
[*Saint Genet: Actor and Martyr,* 1963]
Critique de la raison dialectique, Volume I: Théorie des ensembles pratiques (philosophy) 1960
[*Critique of Dialectical Reason: Theory of Practical Ensembles,* 1976]
Les mots (autobiography) 1963
[*The Words,* 1964]
L'idiot de la famille: Gustave Flaubert de 1821 à 1857 (biography and criticism) 1971-72
[*The Family Idiot: Gustave Flaubert, 1821-1857,* 1981-89]

AUTHOR COMMENTARY

For a Theater of Situations (1947)

[*The following essay was first published in the magazine* La Rue *in 1947. Here, Sartre presents his theory of modern drama, arguing that "what we have to show in the theater are simple and human situations and free individuals in these situations showing what they will be."*]

The chief source of great tragedy—the tragedy of Aeschylus and Sophocles, of Corneille—is human freedom. Oedipus is free; Antigone and Prometheus are free. The fate we think we find in ancient drama is only the other side of freedom. Passions themselves are freedoms caught in their own trap.

Psychological theater—the theater of Euripides, Voltaire, and Crébillon *fils*—announces the decline of tragic forms. A conflict of characters, whatever turns you may give it, is never anything but a composition of forces whose results are predictable. Everything is settled in advance. The man who is led inevitably to his downfall by a combination of circumstances is not likely to move us. There is greatness in his fall only if he falls through his own fault. The reason why we are embarrassed by psychology at the theater is not by any means that there is too much greatness in it but too little, and it's too bad that modern authors have discovered this bastard form of knowledge and extended it beyond its proper range. They have missed the will, the oath, and the folly of pride which constitute the virtues and the vices of tragedy.

But if we focus on these latter, our plays will no longer be sustained primarily by character—depicted by calculated "theatrical expressions" and consisting in nothing other than the total structure of our oaths (the oath we take to show ourselves irritable, intransigent, faithful, and so on)—but by situation. Not that superficial imbroglio that Scribe and Sardou were so good at staging and that had no human value. But if it's truc that man is free in a given situation and that in and through that situation he chooses what he will be, then what we have to show in the theater are simple and human situations and free individuals in these situations choosing what they will be. The character comes later, after the curtain has fallen. It is only the hardening of choice, its arteriosclerosis; it is what Kierkegaard called *repetition.* The most moving thing the theater can show is a character creating himself, the moment of choice, of the free decision which commits him to a moral code and a whole way of life. The situation is an appeal: it surrounds us, offering us solutions which it's up to us to choose. And in order for the decision to be deeply human, in order for it to bring the whole man into play, we have to stage limit situations, that is, situations which present alternatives one of which leads to death. Thus freedom is revealed in its highest degree, since it agrees to lose itself in order to be able to affirm itself. And since there is theater only if all the spectators are united, situations must be found which are so general that they are common to all. Immerse men in these universal and extreme situations which leave them only a couple of ways out, arrange things so that in choosing the way out they choose themselves, and you've won—the play is good. It is through particular situations that each age grasps the human situation and the enigmas human freedom must confront. Antigone, in Sophocles' tragedy, has to choose between civic morality and family morality. This dilemma scarcely makes sense today. But we have our own problems: the problem of means and ends, of the legitimacy of violence, the problem of the consequences of action, the problem of the relationships between the person and the collectivity, between the individual undertaking and historical constants, and a hundred more. It seems to me that the dramatist's task is to choose from among these limited situations the one that best expresses his concerns, and to present it to the public as the question certain free individuals are confronted with. It is only in this way that the theater will recover its lost resonance, only in this way that it will succeed in *unifying* the diversified audiences who are going to it in our time. (pp. 3-5)

Jean-Paul Sartre, "For a Theater of Situations," in his Sartre on Theater, *edited by Michel Contat and Michel Rybalka, translated by Frank Jellinek, Pantheon Books, 1976, pp. 3-5.*

Literature of Engagement: *The Condemned of Altona* (1960)

[*Oreste F. Pucciani interviewed Sartre in Paris in Spring 1960, shortly after the opening of* The Condemned of Altona. *Here, Sartre discusses the play from the viewpoint of literary theory and personal engagement.*]

PUCCIANI: *From remarks of yours which I have read here and there, I gather that your ideas of engaged literature have changed since you published* **Qu'est-ce que la litterature?** *in 1948. Simone de Beauvoir has told me that you no longer feel that people can be changed by literature; that one of your greatest impressions of Cuba was that the Cuban people have been changed.*

SARTRE: Yes. To an extent that is true. I remain convinced, however, that if literature isn't everything, it is nothing.

What precisely do you mean by that statement?

I mean that a writer, a novelist cannot deal with the slightest concrete detail of life without becoming involved in everything. If I want to describe a scene—Saint-Germain-des-Prés, for example—I am immediately caught up in all the problems of my time. I may try to avoid these problems, limit my world and deal only with a small fragment of reality. But actually I cannot. Look at Jouhandeau. I like Jouhandeau very much, but Jouhandeau has limited himself to the world of a couple: Lise and Jouhandeau. This sort of writing, however interesting, is bound to produce monsters. The writer cannot *not* be engaged. In one way or another all writers know this. Yet they don't accept it. Consequently, when they do try to deal with their own times, they end up by writing detective stories. Look at the last volume of Durrell.

Isn't this a different sort of engagement from engagement as you saw it in 1948? The engagement of 1948, as I understand it, was essentially an engagement of content over form.

Yes. Content over form, if you will. But I have certainly evolved since 1948. In 1948 I was still naïve—the way we are all naïve. I still believed in Santa Claus. Up to the age of forty! I believed, as you say, that people could be changed through literature. I no longer believe that. People can certainly be changed, but not through literature, it would seem. I don't know just why. People read and they seem to change. But the effect is not lasting. Literature does not really seem to incite people to action.

Is it perhaps because literature reaches people within their essential solitude?

Yes. There is certainly that. But there is something, for example, in a political meeting—and I do not mean that political meetings are in any way superior to literature!—which has a more lasting effect. Direct political action seems to be more *effective* than literature. I think it perhaps comes from the fact that we writers don't know too well what we are doing. The situation of the writer today is very strange. Today the writer has more means at his disposal than ever before and yet he seems to count for so little. It's incredible. Today everyone is known; everyone knows each other. A writer of relatively little importance can easily be as famous or more famous than Baudelaire or Flaubert in their time. Look at my own career. I started around 1938 with ***La Nausée.*** There had been a few things before; nothing much. Then with ***La Nausée*** I had a nice *succès d'estime.* Now look at what has happened. In a way I should actually have fewer means at my disposal than I do. And yet what does it all amount to? There is a kind of impotence about being a writer today. I think the realization of that is the difference between my position today and my position in 1948.

You have mentioned impotence and that brings me to the **Séquestrés d'Altona.** *As I see it, the great theme of the play is "sequestration." But the corollaries of "sequestration" are impotence and power. Do you agree?*

Yes. Certainly that is so. But the play is really about torture.

It is an engaged play?

Yes. But it is not the play that I really wanted to write. I wanted to write a play about French torture in Algeria. I especially wanted to write about the sort of chap who tortures and who is none the worse for it. He lives perfectly well with what he has done. It never comes out unless he starts boasting some night in a café when he's had a little too much to drink.

Why didn't you write that play?

For the simple reason that there isn't a theater in Paris that would have produced it!

So you chose to set it in Germany?

Yes. After all, no one is going to contradict me if I say the Nazis committed torture.

Would you explain the title of the play to me?

Well, I used to be very fascinated by the "sequestered life." You know the sort of thing I mean. There is a common myth—it was very common in my youth—about the writer or the poet who locks himself up and just writes and writes because he can't help himself. It's his nature to be a writer and that's all there is to it. Of course, I no longer subscribe to that sort of nonsense, but I used to be very fascinated by it. Now I subscribe to the point of view that a writer writes because he has something to say. Anyway . . . I wanted to show this sort of sequestration in terms of liberation. As you say, the whole theme of the play is sequestration from the beginning. Léni is a *séquestrée* because she is incestuous. Old Gerlach is the powerful industrialist—*un grand bourgeois*—who is a *séquestré* because of his class. Frantz is also a *séquestré* from the beginning. The first sign that Frantz was really guilty of torture, that he was actually the first to torture, is his reaction to the Jewish prisoners. He was disgusted by their dirt and their degradation rather than revolted by their plight. This is not the sort of reaction to have. You can see from that that he was going in for such abstractions as "human dignity" and that sort of thing.

It seems to me that one might say in the final analysis that Frantz was a good man because *he committed suicide.*

Yes. Provided you say *because* he committed suicide. Actually, the terms "good" and "bad" have no meaning in history. The more one goes along, the more one realizes that the "good" were "bad" and that the "bad" were "good." It is a sort of mystification. The terms really mean nothing. There is no justice in history. Frantz comes to face what he has done; so does his father. They have to commit suicide. But the production of the play didn't really put the meaning across. Ledoux as old Gerlach wasn't what I intended.

With reservations Reggiani was very good.

Yes. With reservations.

The recent German production in Essen was apparently quite different. Gerlach was, I gather, much more what you intended. The powerful over-bearing industrialist.

Yes. But that was odd too. The Germans apparently cut out the scene where Frantz eats his medals. You remember, they are made of chocolate. At one point he and Johanna eat them. Very strange. Frantz should—he must—*eat* his medals.

I noticed that. But I thought the German version was an improvement. I didn't at all like that particular scene.

Really? Why?

I thought it out of keeping. It was a trick.

How strange. No one has criticized that. It was very successful on the stage.

I know. The audience laughed. But I didn't feel they should have.

Oh, but the audience must laugh! I have learned that if you don't give audiences a chance to laugh when you want them to, they will laugh when you don't. Besides, there is no point in some empty gesture like tearing off the medals or that sort of thing. There is no meaning in that. After all, the medals would remain intact. But if Frantz eats them, that means he eats them every day. The medals disappear. They are digested.

But what is the point of that?

You forget that we have heroes in France. They must be made to feel the insult that is intended. They must suffer a little for what they represent.

I have frequently heard your play criticized as being a drame bourgeois. *This strikes me as unfair. I see the first, third and fifth acts as deliberately* bourgeois; *the "downstairs" reality. But the "upstairs" reality is quite different. That is* avant-garde. *There are two levels: physical and metaphysical.*

Yes. Exactly. That's exactly it. Perhaps not "metaphysical," but still that's it. We must start with the *bourgeois* world. There is no other starting point. In this sense Existentialism is a *bourgeois* ideology, certainly. But this is only the starting point. In a different sort of world, theatre itself would be different. So would philosophy. But we have not reached that point. In a society of permanent revolution, theatre, literature would be permanent criticism, permanent contestation. That is a long way off. But it is entirely wrong to call my play a *drame bourgeois. Bourgeois* drama exists only for the purpose of eliminating the problem it deals with. This is not the case in the ***Séquestrés.*** There is an actual liberation in the two suicides. There is no secret mystery that is revealed. There is a dialectic.

To come back to the title of the play again, would you tell me just why you chose that title? I mean almost etymologically.

Well, you know what it means. In French a person who shuts himself up or who is shut up is called a *séquestré.* I don't know if you are familiar with Gide's *Souvenirs de la*

Cour d'assises. Perhaps you recall the *Séquestrée de Poitiers?*

Yes. I wondered if there were an echo of that.

Definitely.

Your play is then actually an act of personal engagement?

Yes. Quite. I still believe in engaged literature.

Mauriac has said that you are the real séquestré. I wonder what you think about that? Your play reflects your concern for the writer's impotence; his frustration in power.

Well, no. I'm not a *séquestré.* No one has locked me up and I haven't locked myself up.

I once said in an article about you that engaged literature means la litterature au pouvoir. *I wonder what you think about that.*

Yes. That's correct. As a kind of ideal statement. But one should add immediately that it must be understood that literature will never be given this power. If it were, it would no longer exist. Look at Malraux. This is a great danger for literature. As a matter of fact, one of the reasons for my own evolution in this regard is that I became aware, after 1948, that I was in the process of constructing an ethic for the writer alone. *Une morale de l'écrivain.* I wanted to get away from that. I wanted to deal with all problems. Not just with the world of the writer.

I would like to ask you something about Existential psychoanalysis. I am reminded of this because of Frantz's "madness." Could one not say that Existential psychoanalysis is psychoanalysis for normal people whereas Freud requires a category of the "pathological"?

Certainly Existential psychoanalysis is concerned with normal people. Conventional psychoanalysis as it is practiced today in America and France is a plague. It encloses the individual in his malady. There is no way out.

This is somewhat erratic now, but I would like to raise another question of engagement. I have often heard Existential engagement criticized—by my students, for example—on the grounds that it is a doctrine for heroes. I remember one student's asking me: "How can the little people be engaged?"

That is very interesting. Yes. That may be a problem. But I wonder if there is not a difference there between France and the United States. I should imagine that in California, for example, where everything more or less works well . . .

Hm!

. . . yes, badly, well, but it more or less works . . . I should imagine there would be a lack of *cadres* for engagement. But this is not true of France. There are many *cadres* here where a student like the one you mention could find a place for individual action. And I mean both on the Right and on the Left.

This brings me to a last question about engagement and the effectiveness of the writer. There is great interest in Existentialism. In California, for example, which is very remote from your world. I wonder if that interest could exist if you had not given literary form to your work?

Literature is certainly very important. Yes, I know what you mean. And I do believe that we must continue to give literary form to our work. It is the writer's only chance, as I have said everywhere. At the same time, literature is not the only way. This should not be taken to mean, however, that literature should not be engaged. I am not offering any alibis. I am less sanguine than I used to be, but I still believe the writer can help—if it is only to prevent the worst from taking place. (pp. 12-18)

Jean-Paul Sartre and Oreste F. Pucciani, in an interview in The Tulane Drama Review, *Vol. 5, No. 3, March, 1961, pp. 12-18.*

"Hell Is Other People": The Meaning of *No Exit*

[*The following is taken from a preface that was produced by Sartre for an audio recording of* No Exit *and that was first printed in* L'Express *in 1965. Sartre clarifies his intentions in writing* No Exit, *focusing particularly on the idea that "hell is other people."*]

There are always accidental causes and primary concerns involved in the writing of a play. The accidental cause is that when I wrote ***No Exit*** in 1943 and early 1944, I had three friends and I wanted them to perform a play, a play of mine, without giving any one of them a better part than the others. That meant that I had to have all of them on the stage at the same time and all of them had to remain there. Because, I thought, if one of them goes off, he will be thinking as he exits that the others have better parts than he has. So I wanted to keep them together. And I asked myself how one could keep three people together and never let one of them go off and how to keep them together to the end, as if for eternity.

Thereupon it occurred to me to put them in hell and make each of them the others' torturer. This was the accidental cause. (pp. 198-99)

But at the time there were also more general concerns; what I wanted to express in the play was something beyond what was simply dictated by the circumstances, and what I wanted to say was that hell is other people. But "hell is other people" has always been misunderstood. It has been thought that what I meant by that was that our relations with other people are always poisoned, that they are invariably hellish relations. But what I really mean is something totally different. I mean that if relations with someone else are twisted, vitiated, then that other person can only be hell. Why? Because other people are basically the most important means we have in ourselves for our own knowledge of ourselves. When we think about ourselves, when we try to know ourselves, basically we use the knowledge of us which other people already have. We judge ourselves with the means other people have and have given us for judging ourselves. Into whatever I say about myself someone else's judgment always enters. Into whatever I feel within myself someone else's judgment enters. Which means that if my relations are bad, I am situating myself in a total dependence on someone else. And then I am indeed in hell. And there are a vast number of people in the world who are in hell because they are too dependent on the judgment of other people. But that does not at all mean that one cannot have relations with other people. It simply brings out the capital importance of all other people for each one of us.

The second point I wanted to make is that these people are not like us. The three persons in ***No Exit*** do not resemble us, inasmuch as we are alive and they are dead. Naturally, "dead" symbolizes something here. What I was wanting to imply specifically is that many people are encrusted in a set of habits and customs, that they harbor judgments about them which make them suffer, but do not even try to change them. And that such people are to all intents and purposes dead. Dead in the sense that they cannot break out of the frame of their worries, their concerns, and their habits and that they therefore continue in many cases to be the victims of judgments passed on them by other people. From that standpoint they quite obviously *are* cowards or villains. If they were cowards in the first place, nothing can alter the fact that they were cowards. That is why they are dead, that is the reason; it is a way of saying that to be enwrapped in a perpetual care for judgments and actions which you do not want to change is a living death. So that, in point of fact, since we are alive, I wanted to show by means of the absurd the importance of freedom to us, that is to say the importance of changing acts by other acts. No matter what circle of hell we are living in, I think we are free to break out of it. And if people do not break out, again, they are staying there of their own free will. So that of their own free will they put themselves in hell.

So you see that relations with other people, encrustation, and freedom, freedom as the other face of the coin which is barely suggested, are the three themes in the play. I should like you to remember this when you hear that hell is other people. (pp. 199-200)

Jean-Paul Sartre, in his Sartre on Theater, *edited by Michel Contat and Michel Rybalka, translated by Frank Jellinek, Pantheon Books, 1976, 352 p.*

OVERVIEWS AND GENERAL STUDIES

Bamber Gascoigne (essay date 1962)

[*Gascoigne is an English author and drama critic. In the following excerpt, he reviews Sartre's overall dramatic achievement, arguing that all of Sartre's plays after* The Flies *are marred by a disparity between form and content.*]

[Sartre's] first play, ***The Flies*** (1943), specifically shows a man growing from a position of vague liberal detachment to one of commitment, from inaction to action—the existentialist ideal. When Orestes first arrives in Argos with his tutor he can overlook the suffering of the people and he spends his energies discussing the niceties of the Doric pillars. By the end of the play he has murdered Clytaemnestra and Aegisthus and, most important, has insisted on taking full personal responsibility for his action. By so doing he rescues the people of Argos from their crippling sense of communal guilt for the death of Agamemnon, a state in which Aegisthus and Zeus, their temporal and spiritual rulers, have found it politic to keep them.

The play could be used as a manual of Sartrian existentialism. Sartre's main tenet is that 'existence precedes essence'. This means that there is no such thing as 'human nature', no Platonic form of mankind for each individual to be measured against. Each man is a blank slate on which he will, by his actions, come to define his own being. Orestes at the beginning of ***The Flies*** was therefore nonexistent as a person. He had done nothing, he had committed himself to nothing, he belonged nowhere. He constantly refers to himself at this stage as being light, floating, disembodied. It is his definitive act of murder which gives him weight and turns him into a man. This in itself makes it essential that he should not then disown his action. Zeus, still hoping to restore the *status quo* and to keep the people of Argos in subservience, pleads with him to repent. But Orestes knows the power, even against the gods, of a free human being. He meant his action, even though the performance of it was intensely painful; and he would, if necessary, repeat it. Zeus is defeated. The flies which have been plaguing Argos swarm around Orestes, and like the Pied Piper of Hamelin he leads them away from the city.

The ideological content is not, of course, what makes ***The Flies*** a good play. Its merit is that the classical story fits Sartre's meaning as snugly as if he had invented it, and that the details of his theme are all successfully dramatized. The plague of flies, for example, besides being an effective version of the Furies (an idea probably taken from Giraudoux, who in his *Electra* compares the Eumenides to flies), is also an apt symbol for the festering guilt in Argos. Again, Orestes needs to be sure, before taking the fatal step, that no less violent solution is possible. He finds out in an admirable scene in which Electra tries to win the people of Argos back to life by appearing at the great annual ceremony of repentance in a dazzling white dress and dancing through the crowd. She almost succeeds—so much so that Zeus has to use a minor miracle to bring the crowd to heel again. (Sartre in this play allows God the possibility of existence but merely stresses his unimportance to the free human being.)

His next piece, ***No Exit*** (***Huis Clos,*** 1944), may well be a convincing version of life after death, but it has very little relevance to life before it. Three recently dead people are shut up together for eternity. Ines is a Lesbian: she desires Estelle, a nymphomaniac who desires Garcin, the only male. But his one desire is to be convinced that the manner of his death does not prove him a coward. Since Estelle will tell him anything for a caress, he has to rely on Ines. The vicious circle of personal relationships is complete. 'Hell,' concludes Garcin, 'is other people,' and it is on this apparently profound statement that the play's reputation for seriousness seems to rest. Yet Ines, Estelle and Garcin can hardly claim to be a fair sample of 'other people'—it would certainly require great ingenuity to devise another such 'hellish' trio. Even apart from their excessively neat emotional interdependence now, their separate lives on earth glowed brightly with murder, suicide and sadism. The truth is that the meaning of ***No Exit*** is minimal. It is a Grand Guignol idea which is brilliantly executed—for certainly Sartre squeezes the last vivid drop of poison from his trio. Hades, as a setting, has one indispensable advantage. None of them can leave it.

Sartre's subsequent plays all failed, like ***No Exit,*** to reach the standard of ***The Flies. The Respectful Prostitute*** (1944) is a melodrama on the theme of false respect. The Louisiana prostitute resists the force brought to bear on her to give false witness against a negro, but succumbs to the patriotic arguments that Uncle Sam needs the all-American white boy who has in fact committed the crime, and to the sentimental picture of the boy's mother weeping by herself in the big house. In the same way an innocent negro cannot bring himself to fire in self-defence on a lynch-crazy white man, simply because of his deep-seated respect for the colour of his skin. The play has been dismissed as grossly exaggerated. But the reason for this impression is not so much that Sartre has distorted the white Southern attitudes, as that, by providing too pat a plot, he has swamped his meaning in melodrama.

Men Without Shadows (***Morts sans Sepultures,*** 1946) is a justifiably gruesome play about resistance workers being tortured for information by the Pétainists. It contains, like Camus's resistance plays, the slow death of personality and of love; and it forces its battered heroes to the extreme sacrifice of choosing not to die but to stagger back into the painful battle outside. Such violent subject-matter contains its own, somewhat limited, drama, but in Sartre's next play, ***Crime Passionel*** (***Les Mains Sales,*** 1948), the dramatic interest seems smeared on to the surface like icing. The comedy is mechanically efficient, and the thrills depend on the oldest of melodramatic tricks: at least four times a character enters coincidentally at a crucial moment. In the story, which takes the form of one long flashback, a resistance worker is on trial. He was ordered to carry out a political assassination, but failed to achieve his mission until he came across the victim kissing his wife. Was the murder a *crime passionel* or merely brilliantly disguised as such by a dedicated political assassin? The young man, while in prison, has convinced himself that it was the latter: such an action defines him, in existentialist terms, as the person whom he desires to be. As he unfolds his story to another resistance worker, who must judge whether they can use him again or must shoot him as a bad security risk, it becomes clear that he is a hopelessly weak man who fired the bullet purely on impulse. The ironical twist comes when his judge announces that he need not be shot. The reason is that policy has changed: the victim is now revered as a martyr; and his assassin can be used again provided he will change his name and keep his mouth shut. This Jean refuses to do, thus at last, in the Sartrian sense, 'becoming a man'. If he denies his action, he denies himself. He chooses to be shot.

All these plays were written within five years. In the next ten years Sartre produced only two more, neither of them successful. ***Lucifer and the Lord*** (***Le Diable et le Bon Dieu,*** 1951) is a rambling great piece which is swamped by its philosophizing. It shows Goetz, a sixteenth-century buccaneering nobleman, in total dedication first to Evil and then, after a bet, to Good. In neither is he particularly successful. His real achievement begins only when he becomes prepared, like Orestes, to commit evil actions towards a good end. For the existentialist the vital act must be a practical one. Five years later came ***Nekrassova*** (1956), a satirical farce on an undergraduate level about Western politics and journalism.

Sartre's career as a playwright seemed to have ended, and retrospectively his achievement seemed not very high. A first play, in which form and content had merged perfectly to fulfil a clear-cut but fairly limited objective, had been followed by six others which ranged from the melodramatic to the undramatic and in which the meaning was often awkwardly separate from the drama. And on rereading these plays one becomes aware of a frequent indulgence in gore. The descriptions of Clytaemnestra's death, of the lynching of a negro, or of Goetz's brother being eaten by wolves, are all unnecessarily gruesome in their context. Much of ***Men without Shadows*** is spent in interpreting the details of the torture in the room below from the stray sounds that break through, and Estelle kills her

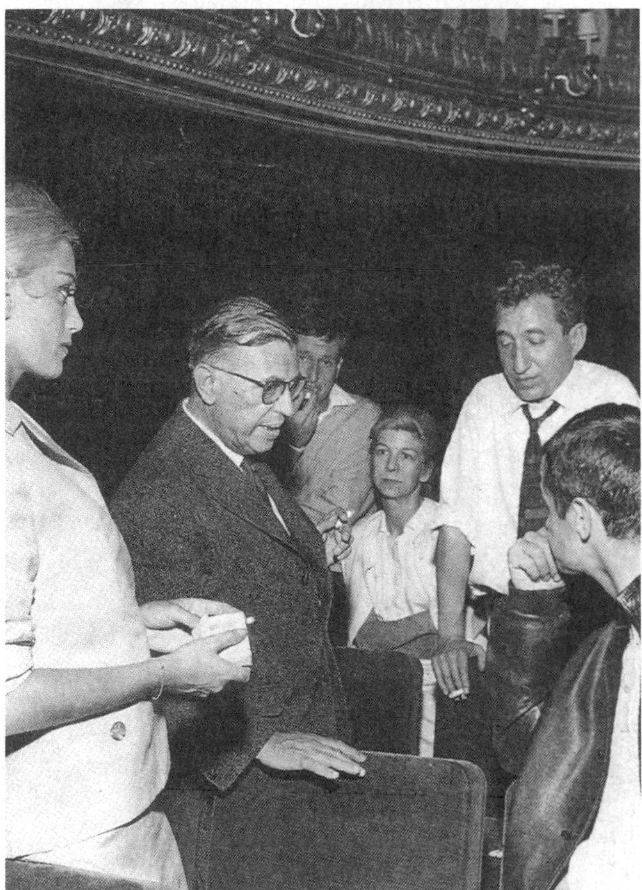

Sartre and cast members at the Théâtre de la Renaissance during rehearsals of The Condemned of Altona, *September 1959.*

baby in ***No Exit*** by tying it to a large stone and throwing it off an hotel balcony into a lake. One knows Sartre's horror of torture from his writings about Algeria, but in art it is sometimes difficult to distinguish an author's horror from fascination. Certainly there are countless moments in his plays when audiences will either be pointlessly shocked or secretly thrilled—neither of them an admirable effect.

However, in 1959, Sartre redeemed his early promise in ***Altona*** (***Les Séquestrés d'Altona***), a massive, almost Gothic play, a dense tangle of guilt and possessiveness. This guilt has its most obsessive expression in the ravings of Frantz Gerlach, a wartime officer in the German army who since 1946 has shut himself away in the attic of his family home. Up there, surrounded by empty champagne bottles and oyster shells, he records on tape a crazy defence-cum-indictment of the twentieth century before an imagined jury of thirtieth-century crabs.

The guilt becomes specific when Frantz, after giving several evasive reasons for his self-imposed exile from the world, finally admits that in the war he tortured prisoners. Having confessed this, he wants his father to admit to a share of the responsibility. Gerlach is Germany's leading shipbuilder, and an industrial Vicar of Bray. He worked with Hitler, then with the Allies, then with Adenauer, and is now more prosperous than ever. Gerlach is responsible for Frantz's actions because he brought him up to admire the ruthless standards of materialism and at the same time always pulled strings to get the boy out of trouble. Once father and son have each admitted their responsibility to the other, they commit suicide together. Frantz's harsh sister, Leni, climbs the stairs to take his place in the attic: the net of responsibility widens. It spreads outwards to include all Germany, and, by implication, France and Algeria and wherever else the cap fits. It is presumably no accident that out of all the possible German names the central character should be called Frantz.

This criss-cross mesh of guilt is set in a tangled emotional plot which is almost as melodramatic as that of ***No Exit.*** But this time it suits the the theme. The violent sexual drama, which includes incest, is in keeping with the festering of suppressed guilt, and the sheer force of the antagonism between the characters succeeds in breathing life into the dry intellectual aphorisms and paradoxes in which they express themselves. Sartre relies for the necessary passion on his cast; and good actors, given such explosive situations, can provide it. His own language has never been passionate. He is the opposite of King Claudius. His thoughts fly up, his words remain below.

In his previous plays Sartre's thought and his dramatic skill appear to have joined forces only a moment or two before he started writing. In ***Altona*** the two were hand in hand from some much earlier and murkier stage in the process of creation, and for the first time the thought itself seems tortured. It writhes with the drama. (pp. 152-57)

Bamber Gascoigne, "Jean-Paul Sartre 1905- ," in his Twentieth-Century Drama, *Hutchinson University Library, 1962, pp. 152-57.*

Lucien Goldmann (essay date 1970)

[Goldmann was a prominent figure in the critical movement known as "Marxist Humanism." In the following essay, he delineates the thematic parallels between Sartre's dramatic works and his two central philosophical works, Being and Nothingness *and* The Critique of Dialectical Reason. *All translations of Sartre's works are, unless noted, by Sandy MacDonald.]*

An important writer can be understood properly only from a study of the whole of his work; this applies particularly to Jean-Paul Sartre, whose philosophical, literary, critical, and political writings are so closely related. A study of Sartre's theatre immediately poses a number of methodological problems. Recognizing this, rather than give up this study altogether—it would take several years to do it thoroughly—I've decided to publish a provisory text, in the hope that this study may contribute to the knowledge of the Sartrean *oeuvre* and facilitate research to come. My reading of his work has led me to the hypothesis that beyond numerous secondary changes only natural for a philosopher whose system is centered on the absolute liberty of the individual, Sartre's thought may be divided into four successive periods, with the theatre occupying the greater part of the third.

The first period corresponds to ***Imagination*** (1936), ***The Emotions: Outline of a Theory*** (1939), the first four stories in ***The Wall*** (1939), ***The Psychology of Imagination*** (1940), and also the plan, if not the realization, of ***Nausea*** (1938). It is characterized by the opposition of the world of daily life and the world of imagination, as well as by the valorization of this last, which not only transforms the immediate world, but alone can give authentic meaning and transindividual value (in the form of aesthetic creation) to men's lives. From the first four stories in ***The Wall*** (**"The Wall," "The Room," "Erostratus," "Intimacy"**) to the refrain of ***Nausea*** ("Some of these days / You'll miss me honey") and the opposition between the impossibility of Roquentin's writing, as he sees it, the biography of Monsieur de Rollebon and the chance he perceives of redeeming his existence by writing a novel, one finds the ideas and values which characterize Sartre's thought at that time.

If most critics have not seen the difference between these first writings and those of the following period, it is perhaps because they found the term "existence" in the middle of ***Nausea,*** without noticing that it has here a meaning very different from the one it acquires later in ***Being and Nothingness*** (1943); there, existence characterizes in effect the *pour-soi* ("for-itself"), man, while in ***Nausea*** it is a characteristic of objects, that is, what in ***Being and Nothingness*** is the *en-soi* ("in-itself"): it is the property of objects to be there accidentally, thus absurdly, without any attributable necessity or rationality:

> A little while ago I made an experiment with the absolute or the absurd. This root—there was nothing in relation to which it was absurd. Oh, how can I put it in words? Absurd: in relation to the stones, the tufts of yellow grass, the dry mud, the tree, the sky, the green benches. Absurd, irreducible; nothing—not even a profound, secret upheaval of nature—could explain it. Evi-

> dently I did not know everything, I had not seen the seeds sprout, or the tree grow. But faced with this great wrinkled paw, neither ignorance nor knowledge was important: the world of explanations and reasons is not the world of existence. A circle is not absurd, it is clearly explained by the rotation of a straight segment around one of its extremities. But neither does a circle exist. This root, on the other hand, existed in such a way that I could not explain it. Knotty, inert, nameless, it fascinated me, filled my eyes, brought me back unceasingly to its own existence [*Nausea,* translated by Lloyd Alexander].

What, in man, corresponds to the existence of things is, in this first period of Sartrean thought, produced by the realization of this absurdity—a nausea one can escape only through inauthentic *mauvaise foi* ("bad faith") or the authentic health of imaginative creation.

In relation to then-current academic philosophy, Sartre's philosophical works do not show any particular originality. ***The Wall*** is a respectable book but would probably have been forgotten had it not been for Sartre's later fame. ***Nausea,*** on the other hand, is a landmark, a turning point in the history of the contemporary French novel. It is the first major novel centered on the hero's dissolution. The density of ***Nausea*** results from, among other things, the discrepancy between Sartre's initial plan and its effective realization. In the beginning, from all evidence, the novel, then called ***Melancholia,*** was to be the diary of Roquentin, who hopes to give his life meaning by writing the biography of a historical character—Monsieur de Rollebon—and who, discovering nausea, which shows him an absurd, purely existent reality, neither rational nor necessary, slowly realizes that, in life, only certain privileged instants can create meaning, through the mediation of the imaginary. And since for him, as for Annie, these privileged instants and perfect moments which they could construct between them are definitely past, since he is "outliving" himself, aesthetic creation alone could still give his life meaning, persisting even past his death. Now, the book undoubtably still says this, but in such a way that it becomes of secondary importance, the essential thing being the impossibility of establishing an authentic relationship between the individual and the exterior world, and the nausea that accompanies any realization of the true nature of this relationship.

The second, existentialist period is expressed in ***Being and Nothingness,*** Existentialism, as a whole, is a philosophy of limitation and failure:

> The for-itself in its being is failure. . . . The being of human reality is suffering because it rises in being as perpetually haunted by a totality which it is without being able to be it, precisely because it could not attain the in-itself without losing itself as for-itself. Human reality therefore is by nature an unhappy consciousness with no possibility of surpassing its unhappy state [*Being and Nothingness,* translated by Hazel E. Barnes].

In my other writings, I have noted that the development of existentialism in Western Europe seems to me to be linked with a period of crisis in the more advanced capitalistic societies, a crisis which resulted from the disturbance in the market in the liberal economy caused by the development of monopolies and trusts and which lasted until the setting up of institutions of economic self-regulation after 1950. This crisis manifested itself mainly in the First World War, the economical, social, and political crisis of 1918-1923 in Germany, the economic crisis of 1929-1933, the coming into power of National Socialism, and finally, the Second World War. Within existentialism, of which the most well-known representatives are the young Lukács, Jaspers, Heidegger, and Sartre (and of which the principal literary representatives in France are, besides Sartre, Nizan and Malraux), the French philosopher holds a special place. German existentialism soon became conservative. Lukács became a Marxist in 1917 and abandoned existentialist philosophy; Jaspers was to the right, Heidegger and Junger, the extreme right (Heidegger ended up supporting National Socialism, and Junger wasn't far from it). In France, however, perhaps due in part to the Popular Front, existentialism belonged to the left. That was the case with Malraux, Nizan, and, as soon as he took a political stand, Sartre. As all existentialism is centered on the individual and his limits, it remained for Heidegger and Jaspers to try to connect this individual to the all, to being, to the universal, while Sartre kept his Cartesian position and stayed resolutely individualistic.

In ***Being and Nothingness,*** the world is divided into *en-soi* and *pour-soi,* and the idea of a totality which would embrace both is entirely lacking. It's the individual versus the world and society: the dualism is quite as radical as it was with Descartes in the seventeenth century. (Descartes went on to pose the problem of the union of soul and body in man, whereas with Sartre, the possibility of a common basis for the *en-soi* and the *pour-soi* and their union in a structured totality appears nowhere.) What characterizes this dualism—and ties it in more with the Cartesian tradition, while separating it from Sartre's third period—is the fact that ultimately Sartre's positions, like Descartes', are rigorously amoral. The only explicitly stated value is that of the individual's autonomy, of choice that is both free and conscious of the fundamental orientation of existence: "Ontology itself cannot formulate ethical precepts. It is concerned solely with what is, and we can not possibly derive imperatives from ontology's indicatives" (***Being and Nothingness***). But, as many critics have already pointed out, one can freely choose to be either victim or executioner, and nothing in Sartre's work permits the establishment of a differentiated opposition between these two choices, as long as they are effected with the same degree of consciousness and liberty.

In ***Being and Nothingness,*** the ultimate failure found in all human existence arises from this impossibility of the union of ego and others, of the subject and the world, the inability of the *pour-soi* ever to become *en-soi* while keeping its *pour-soi* status. Watching—a fundamental relationship between one individual and another—always has a murderous aspect because it reduces the watched to the status of *en-soi;* provisorily, it's true, because he can at any moment recuperate his *pour-soi* status by looking at me, reducing me to the *en-soi* in turn; and thus till death, which is a definitive reduction of the *pour-soi* to the status of the *en-soi,* retrospectively destroying the value and the meaning of the subject's *projets.*

Between ***Being and Nothingness*** and ***Existentialism and Humanism*** (1946) there is a fundamental philosophical difference. As even the title of the latter work indicates, with the beginning of the third period the moral problem appears. The Cartesian amoralism of ***Being and Nothingness*** is replaced by a partially Kantian position inasmuch as existentialism *is* a form of humanism and choice is only free in that it implies the freedom of others or, at least, as far as literary works are concerned, the freedom of the *cité.*

> In effect, there is not a single one of our acts which, in creating the man we want to be, does not also create, at the same time, the image of man such as we think he should be. Choosing to be this or that is, at the same time, affirming the value of what we choose, for we can never choose evil; whatever we choose is always good, and nothing can be good for us without being good for everyone. . . .
>
> In wanting freedom, we discover that it depends entirely on the freedom of others, and that the freedom of others depends on ours. Granted, freedom as defined by man does not depend on others, but as soon as there is involvement, I am forced to want freedom for others at the same time I want my own freedom, I can take my freedom as a goal only if I also take the others' as a goal. Therefore, though on the level of total authenticity I have realized that man is a being whose essence is preceded by his existence, a free being who, under diverse circumstances, can but desire his freedom, I have, at the same time, realized that I can only desire the freedom of others.

Only "partially" Kantian because, if Kant resolutely chooses the moral, subordinating to it all other criteria, Sartre stands halfway between Descartes, whose individualism and concern with efficacity he keeps, and Kant, to whom he is now joined by the exigency of a universal norm. This intermediary stance between two irreconcilable positions allows Sartre to remain in the general framework of existentialism, a philosophy essentially centered on the ineluctable character of failure. In fact, from this point up to the fourth, and last, period the central and insoluble problem of the Sartrean *oeuvre* is to conciliate, inside an action which affects others in general and the liberty of the *cité* in particular, the individual with the community and the exigencies of morality with those of efficacity.

These problems are posed in two different, complementary forms, constituting two successive cycles of theatre works: first, ***The Flies, The Victors,*** and even ***No Exit*** accentuate the problem of the relationship between free choice and its effective result, either among the individuals who act or in the community they plan to affect; ***Dirty Hands, The Devil and the Good Lord, The Condemned of Altona,*** and even ***The Trojan Women*** bring to the foreground the necessity for the hero to choose between morality and efficacity. Perhaps the impossibility of resolving these problems on the philosophical level is at the root of Sartre's decision to pose them in theatrical terms. Philosophically, these problems can be found, among others, at the center of the main theoretical work of his third period, the ***Critique of Dialectical Reason,*** in which the solution, awaited from chapter to chapter, appears only to be finally deferred to a second volume, which is still forthcoming.

It would be helpful to know what brought about the transitions between these periods. I admittedly have no specific hypothesis for the first of these transitions. Basically, the two positions—the first, a rather common academic philosophy, the second, existentialism—coexisted at the time in Western Europe, and the question belongs to a much greater issue, that of the penetration of German phenomenology and existentialism in France, and the modifications they underwent there. On the other hand, it seems highly probable that the transition from the second to the third period has a historic, social basis, namely, the War, the Occupation, and the Resistance. To realize this, one need only read the first three texts of this third period, ***Existentialism and Humanism, Roads to Freedom*** (1945-) and, above all, ***The Flies*** (1943), in which the general situation (Argos and its ceremony of remorse) is a scarcely disguised transposition of France under Pétain. Historical events led Sartre to renounce the Cartesian amoralism of ***Being and Nothingness*** and to introduce the problems of the *cité* as well as the distinction between Good and Evil—in philosophy, the concern of Kant, Hegel, and Marx—into the general framework of his philosophy.

The Flies, the first play of the first cycle, is based on the second episode in Aeschylus' *Oresteia:* the murder of Aegisthus and Clytemnestra by Orestes, son of Agamemnon, who, protected by Apollo, is avenging the assassination of his father. Sartre profoundly modified the structure and meaning of the action, keeping the traditional framework only superficially. In Argos, Aegisthus advocates and develops a permanent death cult, a continual repentance for past crimes. Argos is oppressed, dominated by flies, envoys of the dead, who torment the living all year long. There is no hope here, no energy, no revolt, no joy.

The play begins as Orestes returns to Argos. But, of course, this is not the Orestes we know from the *Oresteia.* It is a modern Orestes. He studies at the Sorbonne under the tutelage of a Skeptic slave who transmits to him an extremely wide culture, making of him a man who is "young, rich, and handsome, as wise as an old man, delivered from all duties and beliefs, without family, fatherland, religion, or trade, free for any involvement and aware that one must never get involved, that is, a superior man." He has been freed from traditional beliefs: he no longer has any intention of avenging his father's death, or obeying the exigencies of prejudices for which he sees no justification. Like his teacher, he is something of a "tourist," a spectator who knows a great deal, has visited many places, but has no roots, is at home nowhere. Knowing this condition and suffering from it, Orestes, no longer content with the philosophy of his teacher but not yet knowing how to go beyond it, driven by intuition, decides to return under the name Philebus to the city where he was born, hoping to find some roots there, some way to cease being "light," to find his own weight at last, an authentic existence.

Two people accompany him on his journey. One is his philosophy professor, the Tutor; he fears that, once returned to Argos, Orestes may fall back into the old prejudices. The Tutor is overjoyed when Orestes, feeling like a total stranger in Argos, decides to leave:

> ORESTES. Drive out Aegisthus? You can rest assured, my good man, it's too late. It's not that I lack the will to grab this defiler of temples by the beard and tear from him my father's throne. But what would be the point? What have I got to do with these people? . . . That man with the beard is right: a king must have the same memories as his subjects. . . . If I could only, even by some crime, grab hold of their memories, their terror, and their hopes, to overcome this void in my heart, even if it meant killing my own mother . . .

Also accompanying Orestes is "that man with the beard," Zeus himself. Conscious of the danger this journey holds for him, he has taken human form to confront it; he knows, in fact, that there is no hope of Orestes' returning to the beliefs and traditions of his ancestors, which are the very basis of Zeus' own reign, of which Agamemnon, before, and now Aegisthus, and all the governments in the world are agents, and, to a degree, depositaries. Yet, though the intellectual pseudo-liberation of the Tutor's philosophy is no real threat to these established powers, there is considerable risk that in returning to Argos, Orestes may discover the only thing that could cast doubt on the power of gods and tyrants: man's freedom, his own freedom.

In Argos, all doors are shut to Orestes and the only person he succeeds in talking to is the village idiot. He has decided to leave the city when he encounters Electra, who awaits Orestes' return for him to kill Aegisthus and Clytemnestra and avenge their father. Refusing to accept the order established by Aegisthus, she lives as a servant. Forced to take out the palace garbage, she throws it before the statue of Zeus, whom she hates. Orestes is shocked and moved by Electra's situation; he, as "Philebus," explains to her that her hatreds are pointless, that in other cities in Greece, one can live freely and happily.

The second act shows the ceremony of the return of the dead. The city is in contrition. Electra arrives, happy and dressed in white, refusing to accept remorse and announcing to the other citizens the possibility of living naturally, untroubled. Knowing herself to be united to the spirit of her murdered father, she calls upon the dead to bear witness: "O my beloved dead, Iphigenia, my elder sister, Agamemnon, my father and my only king, listen to my prayer. If I am being sacrilegious, if I am offending your sorrowing spirits, give me a sign, give me a sign quickly. . . ." In response, Aegisthus treats her like a criminal, but the people wonder if Electra might not be right. To save the threatened tyrant, Zeus intervenes and causes a stone to roll against the steps of the temple, obstructing the cave of the dead. Frightened, the crowd regathers around Aegisthus; order is reestablished, and Electra is to be punished. Zeus then speaks to Orestes: "So, master, do you see now? Here's a story with a moral, if I'm not mistaken: the evil were punished and the good rewarded. That woman . . ."; but the response he both foresaw and feared comes: "That woman is my sister, sir! Go away, I want to talk to her." Orestes has finally found his roots in Argos, those of a brother, of a man who commits himself to killing the tyrant and freeing his sister—with whom he identifies himself—from slavery. As in the legend, Orestes kills Aegisthus and Clytemnestra, but his reasons are quite different: for him, it's no longer a question of avenging his father's death, but of affirming his freedom by killing the tyrant and ensuring the freedom of Electra and the citizens of Argos. Aegisthus asks why Zeus does not strike Orestes with lightning. Zeus replies: "Strike him with lightning? Aegisthus, the gods have another secret. . . . Once freedom has exploded in the soul of a man, the gods can do nothing against him. For that's men's affair, and it's up to other men—and them alone—whether to let him run or to strangle him."

Until now, the play may seem simply revolutionary, affirming the necessity to involve oneself in the struggle against tyranny and oppression. In the third act, the issue of existentialist individualism appears. Orestes has finally become a free man by committing himself to the struggle to free Argos, but his action can only, in any event, free *him.* If in fact the freedom of others is the only goal of a man's free action, the others are only freed by proxy, by actions that they might have accomplished themselves. Orestes—who refuses Zeus' offer that he succeed the dead tyrants, Agamemnon and Aegisthus—is free, but Electra and the citizens of Argos are still subject to remorse, to prejudice, to dreams, and still huddle under the protective shadow of Zeus. As the end approaches, Orestes stands alone, against Zeus, against Electra, prey to the hostility of the Furies and the citizens of Argos: even though others may be the objects of his action, the free man is forever alone. I say "as the end approaches" because there another essential idea appears: for the individual, no commitment, no act can ensure anything more than a provisory freedom, bounded by the inescapable limit, death. Sooner or later, everything *pour-soi,* even the most conscious and free, is transformed into *en-soi.* Though Greek tradition does not mention Orestes' death, it offered Sartre a metaphor for death: the hero's madness at the play's end.

No Exit (1944) presents a universe in which it is impossible ever to involve oneself, to give one's life meaning. The real hell, according to Sartre, is not a place where the damned are tortured, physically or morally, it is the situation in which a man is unable to choose his freedom and cannot even stand alone against the others, who can participate neither in his involvement nor in his action.

However, there is a fundamental difference between ***Being and Nothingness*** and ***No Exit.*** The schema of ***Being and Nothingness*** is dualistic: the *pour-soi* and the *en-soi.* In the semi-Kantianism of the third period, this dualistic scheme changes into a triangular one. (The third person first appears in ***Being and Nothingness,*** in the chapters devoted to "the 'We'," but, like the concept of the transindividual subject itself, is ultimately only of secondary importance there.) In ***No Exit,*** the others serve a double function: they are the object of the subject's desire and aspiration; and they are those who, watching, transform the subject into object and prevent him from achieving the communality which alone can give meaning to his life. The three characters alternately play each of these roles: Inez loves Estelle, who loves Garcin, who needs Inez to judge him. No couple can form because of the presence of the third, watching. Since no one can succeed in tearing himself away from the other two, this will be hell for eternity. Further, the play is situated on two different, complementary levels. It tells the histories of three dead, more or less criminal individuals, who cannot change the meaning of their lives by present behavior. What they were and what they did, the meaning of their lives, depends on whatever interpretation their survivors give it. Sartre's idea is that every act, once done, may take on any number of meanings, depending on what the agent or his survivors make of it afterward. Also, the sense of our existence depends on us alone and the courage we have to free ourselves—as Orestes does—from social pressures and those of prejudice, from others, from what Sartre calls the practico-inert. This second dimension would not be apparent enough in the play if it were simply a question of three dead people who no longer have any material means of leaving the others and choosing freedom. That is why, at a given moment in the action, the door opens, giving each the opportunity to escape from hell—but Estelle needs Garcin too much, Garcin Inez, and Inez Estelle. They are, basically, three weak beings, condemned to live eternally with the others, without involvement.

The problem of relations between the individual and the community is also found at the center of ***The Victors*** (1946), Sartre's weakest play. The reason for this weakness seems to me to reside in the disproportion between the complexity of the project and the schematism of its realization. Sartre's theatre is, as a whole, a theatre of propaganda, not political but philosophical—a theatre which directly poses conceptual problems. With the exception of those in ***No Exit*** and ***The Respectful Prostitute,*** the characters are moved by ideas and by the effort to understand reality. This kind of work requires, precisely because of its relatively intellectual character, concentration on a single problem or a very small number of closely related problems. ***The Flies*** poses the problem of commitment and the solitude that results from this commitment; ***No Exit*** the problem of the insupportable, inauthentic character of existence at the moment when all possibility of choice and commitment is suppressed. ***The Victors,*** however, poses three different problems, not directly related to one another, and thus seems to be a philosophical dissertation rather artificially transposed to the level of individual characters.

The situation at the start of the play resembles ***No Exit.*** A group of Resistance fighters have been arrested for carrying out an order which they never decided was really necessary: it might even have been a mistake which brought about the destruction of an entire village. They are waiting to be tortured by the militia, who wish to obtain information from them. Unfortunately, their courage or cowardice under torture is of no importance because they have no information to give. Their only relation to the outside world is through their memories of Jean, who is the leader of their Resistance group, and, to Lucy, also the man she loves. Through the differentiation of the characters, from the young Francois, a child who abruptly discovers what a dangerous enterprise he has entered into unknowingly, to Canoris, the Communist militant, the problem of their relationship to Jean and to the Resistance—whether this relationship is still valid at a time when, for them, it can no longer be translated into action—is posed in many ways.

At this moment the situation is radically modified. Jean himself arrives, accidentally arrested by the militia without their discovering his identity. For the five arrested Resisters, the problem of commitment and action is sharply restated. For now they know something (Jean's identity) which they must not reveal under torture. One throws himself out of a window in order not to speak. Unsure of young Francois' silence, the three others kill him, to spare him the degradation of informing. Among the Resisters, a solidarity has developed: there is—for perhaps the only time in Sartre's work—a collective act, a nonindividual subject. But, as is emphasized in the play, this solidarity could only have been created in an immediate action, and not at a general, abstract level. The conflict encountered in the relationship of Orestes and Electra is reproduced between Jean and Lucy. Before she is raped and tortured, Lucy is convinced that her union with Jean is the most fundamental, precious, solid thing in the world; afterwards, she discovers that this union has disappeared and that the solidarity which unites her with the others has placed an unsurmountable barrier between Jean and herself, in that Jean does not participate in the present concrete struggle of which he is merely the object.

After Jean leaves, the Resisters have won: no one has talked. Jean is safe and has left them directions as to what they can admit. The problem then posed is whether they should agree to save their own lives by uttering insignificant lies—which would cause them to lose face before their torturers—or whether, being committed to their immediate struggle against these men, they should refuse to talk—thus agreeing to certain death—solely in order not to humiliate themselves before their adversaries. Canoris, the Communist, invokes the eventuality, if they are freed, of participating in the Resistance; but the other two don't agree—they are wholly committed to the present conflict. Finally, however, they give in, not out of conviction, but out of weakness, because of the rain Lucy sees from the window, reminding her of the outside world. But despite their false testimony—which the militia takes to be authentic—they are shot.

Though the play's literary value is weak, it nonetheless holds a special interest for those interested in the evolution of Sartre's thought. To my knowledge, this is the only play in all his work that admits the existence of a transindividual subject, though only at the level of a few people involved in a localized, immediate action—a level Sartre had already discussed, in ***Being and Nothingness,*** using the term *Péquipe* ("the team"). In the chapter on Hegel, Husserl, and Heidegger, he presents the latter as the philosopher of the *être-avec* ("being-with"), the philosopher of

Scene from the original 1943 French production of The Flies.

l'équipe, and tries to show that even at this level, it is irremediably and radically impossible to go beyond the individual subject. Actually, Heidegger never developed the idea of an authentic community with the structure of *l'équipe:* all the analyses of *être-avec* in *Being and Time* show it as an inauthentic form of *être-là* ("being-there"), of existence. However, Sartre is not entirely wrong. At this time, he was not acquainted as yet with the work of Lukács. Now, in his negation of any possibility of authentic communality, Heidegger developed his proof in a permanent, continual polemic against the philosophy of the collective subject, against Lukács, whom he did not name. It seems remarkable that, without having any explicit information, Sartre sensed in the Heideggerian text the shadow of the possibility of the philosophy of this unnamed partner and adversary, even if he attributed the paternity to Heidegger.

Hence, it is significant that the two times Sartre envisages the possibility of a transindividual subject (refusing it in ***Being and Nothingness,*** accepting it in ***The Victors***), he does not go beyond a small group of individuals, in direct contact, involved in an immediate action. He has never even envisaged as possible a greater transindividual subject, especially the most important one: social class.

The other cycle of plays, also philosophically propagandistic—***Dirty Hands, The Devil and the Good Lord,*** and ***The Condemned of Altona***—takes for granted that commitment is individual. The first two plays further say that effective commitment should have a revolutionary character opposed to tyranny and implies, respectively, adhesion to the Communist party and the revolutuionary peasants' organization (which is basically only a metaphor for the CP). The problem around which the three plays revolve is the impossibility of reconciling two equally inexorable exigencies: efficacity and morality. "Equally inexorable"—this term needs further explanation. If this equality were rigorous, Sartre's literature and philosophy—like that of Pascal, Racine, and Kant—would end in a tragic structure, in which the respective exigencies of reason and passion, of experimental thought and the categorical imperative, would allow no choice and no solution. Sartre, on the contrary, proposes two choices, while stressing the one the hero rejects rather than the one to which he commits himself in the final scenes, after the entire plays have stressed the very values they are to reject.

The anecdote from which ***Dirty Hands*** (1948) develops was a variant on the assassination of Trotsky. A Communist leader, Hoederer, in disagreement with a leftist faction of the Party leadership, is assassinated by a professional agitator from this group, who posed as his assistant. The play is about the relationship between the moral and the political, and the impossibility of reconciling them. There are two moralities and two politics—the dogmatic, inauthentic, false; and the valid—between which true commitment is forced to choose. The falsely, wrongly political, content to follow directions, is incarnated by Louis and Olga; the validly political, based on a serious analysis independent of the situation, by Hoederer. The falsely moral, which confuses the ethical and the political and is also limited to a blind admiration of authority, is incarnated by Hugo all through the play; the authentically moral, by the same Hugo in the final scene. This distribution creates a certain disequilibrium (an important and meaningful one, too) between the philosophical theme of the play—choosing the moral over the political—and the extremely reduced presence of Hugo, who incarnates this choice, in relation to Hoederer, whose presence dominates the whole of the work. That is why ***Dirty Hands*** is taken by many people as an apologia for Communism, whereas it is a recognition of the validity of Communism on the political and social levels, but a rejection of it in the name of morality.

In a country occupied by the Germans, on the eve of their defeat and the arrival of the Russian troops, a schism occurs in the revolutionary organization between the faction led by Louis and Olga, who hope that the arrival of the Russian troops will allow them to take power for themselves, and the faction led by Hoederer, who proposes a coalition government with revolutionaries in the minority, run by a committee in which revolutionaries, on the contrary, would be equally represented, in order to facilitate the social transition, spare human lives, and, above all, prepare for a durable takeover in the future. Hoederer has authorization to make contacts with the government (which collaborated with the Germans) and with a nationalist Resistance which, till now, fought the revolutionaries fiercely. To prevent the success of Hoederer's politics, Olga's and Louis's group decide to assassinate him. Hugo is assigned to the mission. The son of a bourgeois, very self-preoccupied, full of complexes and feelings of inferiority, he's thirsty for direct action. Therefore, he goes with his wife, Jessica, to visit Hoederer.

Jessica is one of the main characters in the play. In Sartre's theatre, there is often one person who embodies absolute values, who knows all and who judges: a female character, more or less outside the action, who keeps on the immanent level what men, and above all oppressors, falsely attribute to God—the power to speak the truth, on human, political, and moral levels simultaneously. Jessica appears to be a young bourgeoise who knows nothing, isn't a member of the Party, is completely ignorant politically; everyone treats her as a child. In reality, she is never wrong. Married to Hugo, she has never loved him and can't take him seriously. Once in Hoederer's presence, she not only falls in love with him, understanding from the start that she is dealing with an authentic man, but also realizes that he is right politically. Similarly, she clearly judges the nature of Olga's convictions and love for Hugo. As for Hugo, although Jessica has not been told of his plans, she finds the gun in the suitcase and naturally hides it (before two guards from Hoederer's corps come to search their room). She protects Hugo as long as she realizes there is no serious risk that the assassination will succeed, but she immediately senses the moment when the danger becomes real and warns Hoederer.

The plot is simple enough. Hugo, influenced by Hoederer's personality, hesitates to carry out his mission. Louis and his friends, impatient, suspect Hugo of having betrayed them and of having given up the plan. In order to rescue him, Olga tries to kill Hoederer herself with a bomb but fails. Hugo, humiliated, almost betrays himself, talking in front of the guards of his responsibilities and the distrustfulness of his friends, but Jessica convinces them that she is pregnant, and that Hugo was speaking of her and the child to come; but she also understands that Hugo's humiliation has created a real danger. She brings about a political debate between him and Hoederer, after which she lets her husband know not only that Hoederer is right politically, but that Hugo is becoming more and more convinced. Finally, she warns Hoederer, who disarms Hugo and succeeds in completely reversing Hugo's attitudes. Hugo decides to abandon his plan to kill Hoederer, whom he now admires, and to work with him. Hoederer gives the guards orders to let Hugo in without knocking. Jessica arrives. She reveals to Hoederer that she loves him and he embraces her. Hugo, who returns to find them in each other's arms, abruptly doubts all his convictions again and, thinking he has been taken by his wife and her lover, kills Hoederer.

The first and the final tableaux, which frame the story, occur two years later. The Russian troops have entered the country and have proposed to the revolutionaries exactly the politics Hoederer once advocated, and Louis fought, since he hadn't yet received any orders to the contrary; now it is he, become Party leader, who advocates and achieves these politics. Under these conditions, Hugo's action is a disturbing memory. Hoederer, become the glory of the Party, *cannot* have been assassinated by the latter. They have tried to kill Hugo in prison by sending him poisoned chocolates, but he escaped the trap and has just been let out. Louis's men are after him. Hugo shows up at Olga's house and she obtains a reprieve until midnight in order to try to "redeem" him. She informs Hugo of the change in the party line and suggests that he admit that jealousy was the motivation of the crime, change his name, and never to speak of it again. It is at this moment that Hugo becomes an authentic man and truly understands the alternative before him. It is impossible for him to tell objectively whether he killed Hoederer for jealousy or for political reasons; the meaning of this murder is given only now, because he is committing it this very instant. The political solution—the one which Hoederer would surely have advocated—is to submit himself to the Party and to resume his place among those fighting to realize ideas defended by the man he killed. But this attitude, which is—I repeat—in Hoederer's political line, implies for Hugo the act of falsifying the truth, denying the human figure of the dead man, reducing him to an anonymous corpse: "A guy like Hoederer doesn't die by accident. He dies for his ideas, for his politics; he's responsible for his death. I haven't killed Hoederer yet, Olga. Not yet. It's now that I have to kill him, and myself with him." Knowing that the assassins are waiting behind the door to find out whether he's going to rejoin the Party or whether he should be eliminated, he kicks it open, shouting: "Non-redeemable!"

Here, Sartre chooses the moral over the political. But, as I've already said, the dominance of Hoederer's scenic presence in relation to Hugo's indicates the primary, and perhaps already preponderant, importance Sartre accords the political. Soon after this he again joined up with the Communist party, fairly closely (without becoming a member), and wrote ***The Communists and Peace*** (1952-54).

It is in this perspective that ***The Devil and the Good Lord*** (1951) is inserted, which, though centered around the same problem as ***Dirty Hands,*** ends in the opposite choice: that of the political over the moral. It is, however, important to emphasize that if, when Sartre advocates the moral choice, the political character assumes such importance, now that he advocates the political choice it is, conversely, the hero obsessed by the moral, Goetz, who occupies the greater part of the action. The final choice in ***The Devil and the Good Lord*** is again presented only very briefly, in the final scene.

The play is the story of Goetz, who acts not for his peers, but for a single and unique judge, God, and who, on trial before Him, acts only in an absolute way and according to general laws. He attempts this in three different ways, successively: first in trying always to do evil; then in trying always to do good; and finally in trying to abstain from all action: He is forced to observe that the result is always different from that which he wished to achieve, and that in acting in an absolute way and according to general laws, he simply creates disorder and favors the rich and the landowners. He ends by recognizing the impossibility of this kind of action and the inexistence of a trial before God, understanding that the only authentic trial in which one can be involved is the trial with norms and relative sentences, full of compromise with other men: the class struggle, politics. He therefore agrees to enroll in a revolutionary peasant organization run by Nasti the baker which, from all evidence, is Sartre's equivalent for the Communist party.

The characters include Goetz the moralist, and his double, his conscience, the ambiguous priest, Heinrich, a bastard of the people and the Church, constantly shuttling between one and the other, never making a decision without soon regretting it. Nasti corresponds to Hoederer in ***Dirty Hands.*** The role of woman-judge is taken first by Catherine, and then by Hilda, who inherits Catherine's soul.

Goetz, on trial with God, is determined to do evil. He sets seige on the city of Worms, which is in revolt against its archbishop, Goetz's ally. The people of Worms have arrested the priests. As the rich bourgeoisie is preparing to negotiate with Goetz, Nasti decides to compromise them by driving the people to an irremediable act: murder. The dying bishop gives Heinrich the key to an underground passage into the city to take to Goetz. Once at Goetz's camp, Heinrich vacilates over giving Goetz the key; he finally does, only to repent immediately and to hope that a miracle may prevent Goetz from using it. Goetz plans to destroy the city, kill Nasti and Heinrich, and abandon his mistress Catherine to the soldiers. Nasti and Heinrich tell him that it's more difficult to do good than evil, and the miracle occurs: Goetz makes a bet with Heinrich to do good. He calls off the siege; Nasti and Heinrich are given safe conduct, and Catherine is sent off with a sum of money.

Goetz, to do good, decides to distribute his lands to the

peasants. However, he is opposed by certain noblemen who see this act as a dangerous example, the leftist Karl who refuses to accept anything from a noble, and the peasants themselves who don't understand his gesture. Nasti asks that he renounce his plan because the distribution of lands would release a premature revolutionary movement ending in massacre. Goetz persists.

But he is already encountering in his personal life, the consequences of his new attitude. As long as he kept Catherine with him by force and treated her like a whore, she loved him and was happy. He leaves her, however, tormented by remorse for her past life. Learning that she is dying, Goetz sets off to look for her. Heinrich suggests to Nasti that they suppress services in all the churches in order to frighten the peasants and to prevent the revolutionary explosion. The peasants, now without hope, lock themselves in a church. Nasti, who accepted the plan for reasons of efficacity, is profoundly depressed at having destroyed their human dignity. Hilda, who, looking after Catherine, has learned to love Goetz, is among them. Heinrich and Nasti bring the dying Catherine, hopeless without a priest to give her absolution, into the church. To make amends for the evil he has caused, Goetz is forced to accept what he fought most, the recourse to lies and imposture: he wounds himself and pretends that he has stigmata, that God has accorded him priesthood.

On the social level, however, Goetz pursues his plans in building the City of the Sun: a village of emasculated, peaceful peasants who, isolating themselves willingly from all social struggles, develop among themselves an egoistic love, which they think exemplary. Nasti announces that the creation of this village has finally unleashed the peasants' revolt. He asks Goetz to lead the troops, but Goetz suggests they try to convince the peasants to stop fighting. While addressing the peasants, Goetz runs up against Karl, the extremist, who wants to continue the fight and who, using lies and imposture, obtains the crowd's trust. Goetz's failure forces Nasti to ally himself with Karl. The rebelling peasants destroy the City of the Sun; only Hilda succeeds in escaping. At the individual level (in the episode with Catherine), as well as the social (the City of the Sun), Goetz's failure is complete. He withdraws into solitude, renouncing all worldly activity, wishing only to despise and destroy himself. Hilda follows him to keep him from carrying out his plan.

The year's delay agreed to by Heinrich expires. He arrives to judge Goetz's action, in the trial before God. In the course of this discussion, Goetz discovers that there is no trial, that all his behavior was illusory, because God doesn't exist, and that the only real trial is the one with men, not in the ethical but in the political battle, full of lies and compromise against oppression, for freedom. He tells the peasants of his decision to join their organization and to fight with them: "I wanted pure love: foolishness; to love one another means to hate the same enemy: so I'll embrace your hate. I wished for Good: stupidity; on this earth and in this time, Good and Evil and inseparable: I will consent to being evil in order to become good." Nasti orders Goetz to take command of the army and Goetz accepts, committing his first act as a political man: a murder. He stabs a leader who refuses to obey him. Unlike Hugo, Goetz finds his way in renouncing the moral to act politically, in accepting real commitment, with the lies, the compromises, and even the murders that implies.

Goetz's choice corresponds more or less to the one Sartre made in his life, in making a rather close alliance with the Communists. This might lead one to expect that subsequent plays would show the character of the hero involved in Communist politics. Those plays were never written. Instead, Sartre wrote ***Kean*** (1953), an adaptation of Alexandre Dumas, and ***Nekrassov*** (1955), a comedy, two plays which despite considerable differences have a common theme: a man-actor (in the first), or crook (in the second)—who passes himself off as something other than what he is. The true problem of involvement in or with the Communist party isn't treated until ***The Condemned of Altona*** (1956).

Before going on to analyze this play, I would like to comment—if only schematically—on Sartre's second great theoretical work, probably written during this time though published later, the ***Critique of Dialectical Reason*** (1960). It seems to me from a first reading that the word "dialectical" has a very different meaning here than in Hegel and Marx. For them, it signified from the start the unity and interdependence of antithetical elements—good and evil, spirit and matter, active and passive, positive and negative. For Sartre, however, it seems to characterize a single element in the contradiction—the human, the *projet,* the valid as opposed to its opposite, the practico-inert, which designates inertia, difficulty, the nonvalid. It is the opposition of the *pour-soi* and the *en-soi,* now modified and inserted in a very different framework. The ***Critique*** seems to me to be a schematic outline of the story of the struggle of men—who always remain individual, organic subjects—for communality, for values, against the resisting forces of institutions, of the practico-inert. To integrate the actions of these individual subjects in a common struggle, Sartre must go beyond the duality of ***Being and Nothingness;*** he needs, at the very least, a triangle: that of two isolated individuals and the third who watches and organizes them. This triangle—which is shown in its negative aspects in ***No Exit***—is presented here with, in addition, its positive virtues as a structure of the common struggle of men for communality and freedom.

The Twentieth Congress of the Soviet Communist Party and de-Stalinization posed very serious problems for most Communist intellectuals closely or distantly allied with the action of Stalinist Communism. It might be interesting to undertake a psychological and sociological study of what is, at first glance, a difficult phenomenon to explain: how a certain number of intellectuals, formed in the critical spirit of Cartesian and liberal academic philosophy, could be so deeply disturbed by the revelation—coming from an authority which they had trusted—of facts they might easily have known for years by reading available anti-Stalinist texts, leftist or rightist. This crisis, undergone by many Communist intellectuals (including the most famous among them) is also found in Sartre's work, even though he never joined the Party.

The Condemned of Altona is based on the problem of torture. It is necessary to trace the action of this play full of contemporary resonances through a triple level of social reality: Hitlerian torture, torture in Algeria, and torture in Stalinist prisons and prison-camps. Although until now I have never concerned myself with the relationship between an author and a character—which is always doubtful—it seems pertinent to point out, if only as a hypothesis, that Sartre might have written this play because he felt responsible, as a man, for Hitlerian torture; as a Frenchman, for tortures during the Algerian war, even though he opposed them radically and fiercely; and above all, for Stalinist torture, in that he had supported organizations responsible for it and had associated himself closely with their political action. This triple level is shown in the name of the hero: Franz von Gerlach. In the play, he is a German officer under Hitler, but his Christian name, Franz, also evokes the word *Franzose* ("Frenchman") and whose last name, von Gerlach, belonged to a well-known German anti-Fascist fighter (Sartre tells us in a preliminary note that he knew this but had forgotten it).

Franz von Gerlach, child of a family of great German industrialists, returning from the front at the end of the war, locked himself in a room on the second floor of the family mansion, and has not come out for thirteen years. The characters in the play are very distinctly divided: on one side are the Father, Franz, his sister Leni, and his sister-in-law Johanna, the valid, strong ones; and on the other, Werner, Franz's brother, the weak, the nonvalid, eaten up with feelings of inferiority, the desire to make his father love him, jealousy of Franz, the need for recognition. Among the strong, the von Gerlachs embody three different types of involvement and Johanna, a stranger to the family, embodies the judge. And finally there is another "agent" (to borrow the structuralist term): the false judges, the crabs—whom we have met in the preceding plays under the form of God—who embody what in ***The Devil and the Good Lord*** was validly to substitute for divinity: History, which is now questioned.

The Father was a great industrialist, interested above all in his power, in the accomplishment of his individuality; morally and politically indifferent, he regards politics merely as an existing force, sometimes useful in developing one's own enterprises. He has contempt for his eldest son, Werner, and is only interested in the second, Franz, whom he wants to make into a prince, his successor. The Father now has cancer of the throat. His only concern is to avert, before dying, the downfall and misery of the son he loves, who, locked up in his room, refuses to see him. Between the Father and Franz looms a powerful barrier: Leni, the daughter who loves Franz (incestuously) and is opposed to any contact between the two men. The Father arranges for Werner and Johanna to visit, hoping to use Johanna as an intermediary. He calls a family council, supposedly to ensure that Werner and Johanna look after the house and Franz after his death. In reality, he means to inform Johanna of the existence and the personality of Franz, and to interest her in him.

The first relevant event in Franz's formation was moral revulsion and an attack of conscience over his own weakness and vanity. During the war, the Father had sold Himmler a plot of land for a concentration camp. Revolted by the sight of the prisoners, Franz, to redeem his father and the von Gerlachs, hid an escaped Polish Jew in his room. He was seen, though, and fearing he would be denounced, told the Father. Promising Franz he would protect him as well as the prisoner, the Father informed the authorities. The Gestapo arrived, tied Franz up and killed the Jew in front of him, but because of his father's connections, Franz was not prosecuted. This experience of the vanity of moral action showed him that when one is the son of a von Gerlach one can take risks because one doesn't count: one is not risking one's own life but others'. Franz draws the same conclusions from this experience as Goetz did, and becomes involved in the army, that is, Nazi politics.

As shown by Goetz and Nasti in ***The Devil and the Good Lord,*** the political implies discipline, lies, and, above all, present murder in view of future freedom. In Franz's case, involvement at the front implied torturing prisoners, murdering in order to realize the ideal world which Hitler promised Germany, the Realm of the Millenium. But Germany was defeated; the torture, the lies were in vain; the historical justification has vanished. Two possibilities remain: to admit that he was wrong, that defeat is not a catastrophe, that life goes on, that his acts were objectively criminal, whatever the psychological, historical reason which he thought justified them; or else, to ignore reality and to declare that defeat was an irreparable catastrophe, and that his behavior was the only possible way to attempt to save historical values. Franz chooses the second solution. He has sequestered himself in his room, believing and affirming that Germany was destroyed by the victors, that the country is nothing but ruins, that thousands of orphans are dying of hunger in the cities, and that his behavior was thus justified. (In 1956, the Communists were defending—against all evidence—the theory of the absolute pauperization of the working class.) The trial which the moralist Goetz conducts before God the political Franz can only conduct before History, before beings who will live in the thirtieth century, which an optimistic historical perspective envisioned as men, but whom he sees now, after defeat, as crabs; before them, he pleads the case of Nazi Germany and twentieth-century man.

The only person he allows into his room is his sister Leni, who tries in vain to convince him to give up the crabs and their court, and to accept himself. Johanna, manipulated by the Father, intervenes. She goes up to convince Franz to resume a normal life, which would allow her and her husband to return to Hamburg. Franz lets her in, dazzled by her beauty. These two strong beings recognize and love each other. To keep Franz under control, Johanna enters into his lies and madness. The Father asks her to arrange a meeting between himself and Franz. When she refuses in order to protect Franz, the Father threatens to tell Leni about Johanna's visits. To resolve her dilemma, Johanna admits to her husband her relationship with Franz and asks that he leave the house with her. Werner, most interested in inheriting his father's business, refuses. Johanna then returns to Franz and tells him of the situation. There is only one way out: to give up the crabs, to accept the progress of defeated Germany, and to go back to living.

Franz agrees to acknowledge that the crabs of the thirtieth century will be men, but declares that he wouldn't have to worry about their verdict if only Johanna will substitute for them, judge, accept, and absolve him. He is counting, of course, on cheating a little, not telling her the truth, or at least only telling her in small doses. But the Father has told Leni. She forces Franz to admit that he tortured men. Johanna can not accept this; she draws away from Franz permanently. He then agrees to see his father and realizes that they resemble each other, that there is no longer any place for them in a world in which one is no longer able to choose either individualism, or the moral, or the political. They take the Porsche and go off together to throw themselves off a precipice.

Johanna and Leni, who plans to lock herself up in the room in Franz's place, listen to his last, best tape, in which he explains why he doesn't want to live in a world where "one and one makes one," in a world where when one man meets another there is always one dead man and one survivor:

> Centuries, here is my century, lonely and deformed, the accused. . . . It might have been a good century had man not been stalked by his cruel, immemorial enemy, by the carnivorous species that swore to destroy the century, by that hairless, malicious beast, man. One and one makes one, there's our mystery. The beast was hiding, we caught him, suddenly, looking from the innermost eyes of our neighbors; so we struck: legitimate preventative self-defense. I caught the beast, I struck him down, a man fell, in his dying eyes I saw the beast, still alive, me. One and one makes one: what a terrible misunderstanding! What, who, gives me this stale, rancid taste in my throat? Man? The beast? Myself? It's the flavor of the century. Fortunate centuries, you know nothing of our hatreds, how could you understand the atrocious power of our immortal loves. Love, hate, one and one . . . Acquit us!

With ***The Condemned of Altona,*** Sartre found himself at an impasse. Individualism, commitment, the moral, the political, everything was cast in doubt. Franz and the Father, similar and opposed to one another in life, are reunited in their common suicide. All that remains of Sartre, even if all the values he had defended were revealed to be questionable, is the writer. After de-Stalinization, a very great writer, Aragon, probably much more important than Sartre in the literary sense, wrote *Le Roman inachevé, La Mise / à mort,* etc., and then kept his old courtesan's submission with regard to the Party. It became clear that what the Communist authors were writing, what they had written and what they would write was, despite all their talent, simply "literature." It was possible to admire their work, but not to take it seriously. Yet for Sartre, work meant commitment. When everything crumbled, when there remained only Sartre the writer, he had to examine the nature, the status, and the validity of the writer. To understand him, it was first necessary to reconstruct his history; Sartre attempted to go to the roots, to childhood, in ***The Words.*** This is among the works received most enthusiastically among prominent people in the literary and academic worlds: Sartre was turning—as they had all their lives—to the problems of Art; he concerned himself foremostly with his nature as a writer; it would probably be possible someday to speak of him as of Théophile Gautier. Their joy was short-lived. Sartre is really a writer and a man of thought and as such only concerns himself in a time of crisis, and in passing, with his condition. As for every philosopher and every worthwhile writer, writing is not an end but a means of acting, of expressing a meaning, of adding a dimension to reality, of opening a new route, or of reinforcing and lengthening routes already open.

> *Nulla dies sine linea.*
>
> It's a habit, and besides, it's my profession. For a long time, I took my pen for a sword; I now know we're powerless. No matter. I write and will keep writing books; they're needed; all the same, they do serve some purpose. Culture doesn't save anything or anyone, it doesn't justify. But it's a product of man: he projects himself into it, he recognizes himself in it; that critical mirror alone offers him his image [*The Words,* translated by Bernard Frechtman].

After ***The Words,*** the most recent literary work published by Sartre was an adaptation of Euripides' ***Trojan Women,*** which shows a barbarian world where oppression and cruelty triumph and to which one can only oppose a "negation," a "refusal." The play ends—as Sartre himself tells us—in total nihilism. Since then, the events of May '68 have taken place, involving Sartre as the director of the newspaper *La Cause du Peuple.* In the absence of literary or philosophical texts, it is difficult to know whether the great historical turning point marked by the worldwide student movement led Sartre to rediscover faith in positive values, to go beyond nihilism and reapproach leftism under one or another of its forms, or if, on the contrary, it is due to this same nihilism—the refusal which, for him, remained the only valid position in the face of barbarism—that he once again took a stand against oppression, for the right of expression. (pp. 102-19)

Lucien Goldmann, "The Theatre of Sartre," translated by Sandy MacDonald in The Drama Review, *Vol. 15, No. 1, Fall, 1970, pp. 102-19.*

Judith Zivanovic (essay date 1971)

[In the following essay, Zivanovic examines the evolution of Sartre's concept of freedom as revealed in his dramas.]

A valuable prescription for those who would understand Sartre's notion of freedom should be: Don't confine your reading to ***Being and Nothingness*** and ***Critique of Dialectical Reason.*** Although Sartre deals with a wide range of subjects in the former, earlier work, he largely emphasizes individual freedom and aloneness. In the latter work, he encourages concerted social action. This seeming paradox requires a survey of the Sartre *oeuvre* to decipher, for only in this way can one fully appreciate the progression of Sartre's thought on the crucial matter of freedom. Quite obviously, a paper of this length cannot hope to deal effectively with such a large collection of works; thus it will demonstrate the complementary nature of the drama to the philosophical works and the importance of Sartre's plays in understanding his thought concerning freedom and its relation to the Other.

The primary components of Sartre's thought may be said to form a triumvirate: Freedom-Responsibility-Action. In ***Being and Nothingness,*** Sartre insists that the major consequence of the fact that God does not exist, a consequence which man must recognize and accept, is that man is completely free. It is he who represents, through his freedom to act, the only destiny of mankind, and, through the acceptance of his freedom-responsibility, the legislator of all values.

Initially, the emphasis on freedom had a strongly personal nature—with ***Being and Nothingness*** and Sartre's first play, ***The Flies,*** many readers determined that for Sartre the individual must assume his own freedom as ultimately and exclusively important. His second drama, ***No Exit,*** was viewed as a vivid revelation that men cannot engage in cooperative endeavors due to inevitable conflict. At this stage of his writing, however, Sartre produced his essay, ***Existentialism Is a Humanism.*** Many critics prefer to forget this brief work and fervently wish that Sartre had done the same. Still Sartre refuses to reject any of his works; thus, we must accept the fact that he does not now reject nor did he reject in 1946 the premise of this essay—each man, desiring freedom above all, necessarily wants and strives for the freedom of the Other as well. Sartre has been profoundly criticized on the grounds that this essay is contradictory in the light of premises in earlier works concerning man's basic aloneness and conflict with the Other. Certainly Sartre had not sufficiently elaborated in his first work the extent of the limitation to project and freedom afforded by the Other. Again, he did not sufficiently elaborate in ***Existentialism Is a Humanism*** how the former difficulty could be superseded in favor of a striving toward freedom for both self and the Other. Was it possible, in fact, that the critics were justified, that there was no solution to this dilemma?

Here a study of the drama provides a much needed and indispensable supplement to Sartre's philosophical works. The careful reader of Sartre's *oeuvre* cannot help but be struck by the fact that Sartre wrote a play subsequent to each progression of thought concerning his system. Yet, with the drama, he seems to be released from a good deal of the abstraction peculiar to his philosophical work. Proceeding as it does from within the inner sphere of his imagination, the drama not only quotes the key ideas of its father philosophical or critical work but expands upon the ideas, and, in fact, often foreshadows ideas to come. Such is the case with regard to the dilemma of freedom in the context of human projects.

Looking at Sartre's first drama, ***The Flies,*** written after Sartre's first great philosophical work and during the occupation, the reader finds an emphasis on the recognition of individual freedom on the part of one man, Orestes. The play abounds with such speeches as the following:

> I have done *my* deed, Electra, and that deed was good. I shall bear it on my shoulders as a carrier at a ferry carries the traveler to the farther bank. And when I have brought it to the farther bank I shall take stock of it. The heavier it is to carry, the better pleased I shall be . . . Today I have one path only, and heaven knows where it leads. But it *is my* path . . .

The play demonstrates quite clearly that the Other, in this case, the people of Argos, are necessary in order to give meaning to the act which Orestes performs; clearly, Orestes performs the act to free the people and to show them their freedom; however, the reader cannot escape the point that Orestes initially desires the act and the communion with the Argives as a means of personal commitment and to give his own life meaning. Thus, the individual in search of his own freedom and identity through commitment is primary and the devotion of the effort for the Other, while very important, is secondary to this factor.

Sartre's second play, ***No Exit,*** focuses on the conflict basic to human relations. Unfortunately, with one line of this play, Sartre has allowed himself to be "hung on his own catchphrase." "Hell is other people" is a line so vivid and memorable that it permits critics to handily make of the play itself an object which teaches, "Hell is [always] other people." There is, however, much more to this play than meets the eye of the person who prefers to be captivated by this catchphrase. It is true that the early drama of Sartre is more preoccupied with individual freedoms and individuals in conflict, but in this connection, the drama provides a welcome extension as well to the philosophical treatises for those who care to recognize it.

Let us look carefully at ***No Exit*** for it is the misinterpretation of Sartre's view of human interaction emanating from this play which tends to color the view of this phenomenon in the whole of his drama and perhaps the whole of his thought. Critics tend to view Sartre's play as a reflection of life as it is; they assume the fact that the characters are dead and in "hell" is only symbolic. This is partially true, but the *fact* of death is too important to Sartre to attribute only incidental meaning to that state in his three characters. The result of death is that man ceases to be a subject and becomes an immutable object over which the living are the guardians. (This is revealed particularly through the visions of earth the characters experience.) This condition is also comparable to the state of persons in bad faith—a condition of lying to oneself in order to escape responsible freedom. Thus, "dead" characters offer Sartre twofold advantages. First, he can show the immutable total antithesis of authentic existence. He can hold the condition of bad faith suspended in time. The characters can be shown as condemned, since they are dead, to repeat all of the errors which become an object lesson for the audience. Secondly, the fact that the characters are dead permits Sartre to represent the failings of those individuals who are their counterpart in life, those who are dead on earth before they are buried because they fail to choose and act. At the same time, this fact confirms that another course is possible, that life is for the living if they exist authentically. If they do not, then they are as surely dead, objectified, and meaningless as the inhabitants of that hellish Second Empire drawing room.

From this interpretation, it is easy to see the actual significance of the line, "Hell is other people." Each character has died in bad faith and can no longer change. In one way or another, he is totally dependent upon the others for even his meagre and meaningless existence. Garcin, unwilling to accept his responsibility and to act in life, must seek perpetually in death for justification outside of himself. Estelle, unwilling as well to accept responsibility and to live meaningfully in this world, has been willing to accept only her "mirror-image" of herself. In this hell without mirrors, she is condemned to seek the objectivation she requires constantly outside of herself. Inez, who appears closest to an awareness of her situation, has nonetheless objectified herself in life as well. She has insisted that she is a "type" requiring the sufferings of others to sustain her. Thus, in this hell she, too, is condemned to require others to label her the object, torturer, which she herself accepted, without recourse to change, throughout her life. Each is faced by the others with the significance of the line, "You are your life and nothing else." Cut off before they could do their deeds, as Garcin puts it, they are this nothingness, this object of inaction which they were in life. And, they, unlike the living, can never escape this object which their lives have made them and which is now in the guardianship of others to be thrust before them, unchanging throughout "eternity." The repetition of this bad faith eternally which is implied in Garcin's line, "Well, well, let's get on with it . . . " is sufficient to give any self-respecting Sartrean existentialist a nervous upset.

The play is never meant to indicate that conflict *per se* is an evil. Obviously, when two conscious beings, two freedoms, come together, there is the potential of conflicting freedoms. As humanist, Ralph Barton Perry, explains, "The situation which generates morality is conflict. The morality of freedom begins at the point where one individual's enjoyment of his own freedom is limited by a regard for another individual's enjoyment of *his* freedom." There is every indication in the work of Sartre that he would readily agree with this statement. He has not indicated that this basic conflict with the Other is a negative thing, but rather that for those who would live authentically, those who reject bad faith and embrace freedom, it is through such encounters with the Other that freedom is expressed and values are created. Indeed, outside of its relation to the Other and the world, freedom does not exist. Franz Gerlach of Sartre's play, ***The Condemned of Altona,*** vividly affirms this concept. He refuses to confront the Other and the world and to strive to give meaning to the world around himself. Even without his locked room, he would be imprisoned, for without placing himself in choice situations with the Other, his freedom is nothing. In the same sense, Garcin, Estelle, and Inez were "dead" long before they reached their "hell"; they had created a hell on earth through their bad faith, through their failure to act in a manner which gave meaning to freedom. Thus, it is through action in relation to the Other and the world that each man gives meaning to his freedom and to his life. This is, of course, the way which requires bearing the burden of freedom-responsibility; it is not the way of a Garcin or an Estelle.

While conflict is shown in ***No Exit*** as a primary factor of existence, unresolved conflict of projects is demonstrated as inherent only in relationships fostered of bad faith. It must never be overlooked that only the characters of ***No Exit*** of all the plays written by Sartre, are unable to change; only they are irremediably as others see them, for they are dead. Even at his last moment of life, Hugo of ***Dirty Hands*** is able to come to an important realization and die with the satisfaction that his last chosen course of direction was an authentic one. Even though they are dead and thus already immutably objects, the characters of ***No Exit*** are permitted a few lines which reveal that it may be otherwise in life. For example,

> INEZ. . . . What were you saying? Something about helping me, wasn't it?
>
> GARCIN. Yes.
>
> INEZ. Helping me do what?
>
> GARCIN. To defeat their devilish tricks.
>
> INEZ. And what do you expect me to do in return?
>
> GARCIN. To help me. It only needs a little effort, Inez; just a spark of human feeling.
>
> INEZ. Human feeling. That's beyond my range. I'm rotten to the core.
>
> GARCIN. And how about me? (*A pause.*) All the same, suppose we try?

Again, "Alone, none of us can save himself or herself; we're linked together inextricably. So you can take your choice." Of course, they are not capable of "human feeling" or of taking a "choice" apart from the condemnation to bad faith which they chose in life, but the small suggestion is there that a course is possible which feasibly resolves the conflict of projects, a course which requires working together with mutual respect for the Other's freedom and his project.

It would appear that little hope in this direction would be forthcoming from the oppressive atmosphere of ***The Dead without Burial.*** Still, several speeches provide a brief introduction to the viewpoints later to be offered by Hoederer in ***Dirty Hands*** and Goetz in ***The Devil and the Good Lord.*** Canoris, one of the prisoners, has several speeches which mark his character as the transition between the early Sartre absorbed in the notion of personal freedom as exemplified by Orestes and the later Sartre concerned with unified human effort as demonstrated in the characters of Goetz and Hoederer. Canoris insists that the prisoners must determine to subordinate their own desires and their attempts to justify their own existence in favor of lives useful to others.

This viewpoint, of course, is the driving force behind the character of Hoederer, whose numerous speeches concerning his dedication to mankind mark him as engaged in a truly authentic existence. Hoederer, surely Sartre's most authentic man, states this dedication to mankind clearly and almost poetically:

> And I, I love them for what they are. With all their filth and all their vices. I love their voices and their warm grasping hands, and their skin, the nudest skin of all, and their uneasy glances, and the desperate struggle each has to pursue against anguish and against death.

Goetz, too, comes to realize that the only authentic existence lies in giving up his own vain attempts at perfection and self-justification and his former beliefs in God, Good, and Evil in an all-out effort to achieve the liberation of man. He will become the man Hoederer and the prisoners of ***The Dead without Burial*** were prevented by death from becoming. He will be the man that Orestes had never considered becoming. Orestes, the product of Sartre's early thought, introduced the people of Argos to their freedom and left them, assuming they were able to make something of it. Goetz finds himself in the midst of a people who must struggle to perfect their freedom, who simply are not really free in the sense Orestes (and Sartre at the time) conceived of freedom. Goetz sees that the class structure and poverty must be eliminated before true freedom is possible.

Goetz, of course, is communicating a realization that had gradually come upon Jean-Paul Sartre. He has come to see this so vividly, in fact, that he devoted an entire play, ***The Condemned of Altona,*** to reveal the evils of the acquisitive manner of living, of war, and economic and social inequalities—in short, the numerous ways in which man himself is the "cruel enemy who had sworn to destroy him [man]. . . . "

Although he did not write ***Critique*** until 1960 (also the year of ***The Condemned of Altona***), ***The Devil and the Good Lord*** obviously foreshadows the thinking he was to expound nine years after its writing in 1951. Sartre began to focus more diligently on limitations to freedom of which he was becoming increasingly aware. These social and economic limitations to freedom initially received minimal attention in Sartre's work. It is the freedom itself which is exalted. Gradually, the reader can recognize in the works, however, a dawn breaking, a certain realization on the part of Sartre himself which he verbalizes in an interview with Jacqueline Piatier, "I discovered suddenly that alienation, exploitation of man by man, undernourishment relegated to the background metaphysical evil, which is a luxury. Hunger is evil: period."

The plays begin to show that poverty and social class structure particularly are responsible for much that is oppressive and limiting in the world. Repeatedly, in ***The Devil and the Good Lord,*** the plight of the poor is emphasized. A priest is unable to tell a woman why there is death so abundantly around them, why her child died of hunger. The character Nasti provides the answer, "He died because the rich burghers of our city revolted against the Archbishop, their very rich overlord. When the rich fight the rich, it is the poor who die." Hoederer asserts that all mankind are born liars because the society divided into social classes imposes the "fate" upon us. The play, ***The Condemned of Altona,*** particularly through Sartre's treatment of the father, stands as an indictment of capitalism and marked social class structure. Ultimately, the elder Gerlach himself attempts to relieve his son Franz of his responsibility by accepting all the guilt; he admits offering him the wrong values—that power is all important—and building the steel empire which destroyed them both. Although Sartre would not condone such an excuse, the play makes it clear that, to a degree, Gerlach's point is valid. For example, when the young Franz attempted to save a rabbi from the Nazis, the act is reported by his father in order to save Franz from punishment and the Gerlachs from losing face with the regime. In this case, even Franz's acts were stolen from him.

The new emphasis in Sartre's work is reflected in his focus on the concept of "need." In the plights of those individuals of whom Hoederer speaks and Goetz comes to lead are indications that man is without something vital and that he is "in need" or somehow as yet unable to achieve the true liberation to pursue projected goals. Sartre says of this new emphasis since his early writing, "Over against a dying child ***Nauseé*** cannot act as a counterweight." Sartre, then, has come to believe that man is more limited in his freedom than Sartre himself originally anticipated. While each man is free within his own situation, some circumstances, such as poverty or war, make the situation so oppressive that genuine liberation is impossible *without constant revolution* to maintain freedom. This revolution must proceed from unified effort within which individual talent is utilized and the individual freely "relinquishes" a degree of his freedom in the sense that he is willing to engage in concerted effort with other men. In this way, "My freedom recognizes itself in my own action and simultaneously in the action of the Other. No one is imposed upon." The notion that man must strive for freedom for himself and others still remains but the nature of the striving and the degree of freedom has progressively different connotations from Sartre's initial work.

This more recent recognition by Sartre of those factors in life which tend to limit freedom must not be construed, however, as a significant deviation from Sartre's original premise that man is free within his own situation. The fact of this situation receives greater emphasis; this is not meant to suggest the elimination of freedom nor to provide man with an excuse. Quite the contrary is the case. This new focus on situation points up the urgency of striving for a conscious awareness of the actual constituencies of one's given situation in order to facilitate the ability of coming to terms with it. For Goetz and the peasants, poverty and the division among classes which *limits* their freedom *does not eliminate* their freedom nor does it offer an excuse for inaction. It is merely the playing court in which they will engage in a contest whose rules they now know. Hoederer insists that Hugo must cease hiding behind the "purity" of his class: "You intellectuals and bourgeois anarchists use it as a pretext for doing nothing. To do nothing, to remain motionless arms at your sides, wearing kid gloves. Well, I have dirty hands."

Franz Gerlach, too, comes to realize that, no matter what the limitations imposed upon him, he freely chose to ignore his situation and to reject his freedom and responsi-

Scene from the original French production of The Devil and the Good Lord *directed by Louis Jouvet.*

bility; "I pretended that I was locking myself up so that I shouldn't witness Germany's agony. It's a lie. I wanted my country to die, and I shut myself up so that I shouldn't be a witness to its resurrection." The truth of his father's statement hits the mark:

> Both your life and your death are merely *nothing.* You are nothing, you do nothing, you have nothing, and you can do nothing.

Ironically, the only authentic act which Franz can commit at this point is his own suicide—for a man who has chosen never to exist, it is the only genuine proof of his existence!

Hazel Barnes accurately summarizes Sartre's position concerning the relationship between freedom and the conditions of man's life on earth:

> Sartre never denies the existence of the conditions, but he insists (as Marx did) that it is still men who *make* history. This is because the most fundamental characteristic of man as consciousness is his ability to go beyond his situation. He is never identical with it, but rather exists as relation to it. Thus he determines how he will live it and what its meaning is to be; he is not determined by it. At the same time he cannot exist except in a situation, and the process by which he goes beyond or surpasses it must in some way include the particular conditions which go to make up the situation. Men make history by this continual surpassing.

Sartre has become more aware of these pressures of man's facticity in relation to man's freedom; the awareness has come gradually, but has been dramatically stated in his works since 1951.

This progressive awareness, which the reader of Sartre's drama may witness groping for and gradually reaching the light, seems more abrupt when the perusal of the works is limited to Sartre's statements of philosophy. Still, what appears to the reader of ***Being and Nothingness*** as an inconsistency in ***Existentialism Is a Humanism*** and a complete break in ***Critique*** should appear to the reader of the entire works of Sartre as rather a constant movement and development of thought. The conflict between peoples and the necessity for individual resistance is developed in ***Being*** and exemplified in the action of ***The Flies*** and ***No Exit.*** The need for a shift from concerns with individual freedom to a striving for universal freedom is suggested in ***Existentialism Is a Humanism*** but not explained. Gradually, the explanation is accomplished in ***The Dead without***

Burial, Dirty Hands, and reaches its culmination in ***The Devil and the Good Lord,*** the logical predecessor to ***Critique.*** With the play, ***The Condemned of Altona,*** which expresses the notion of "need," the entire effort is toward an awareness of twentieth-century problems which must be corrected at all costs in order to facilitate the true liberation of man.

There is, then, nothing violently new, no break with previous thought, in this present notion of unified striving for mankind's liberation. As Sartre describes his shifts of emphasis, it is change "within a permanency." In the present order of things, Sartre endeavors to encourage an examination of his situation in order that man may recognize which elements are of his own choosing and which are simply conditions of his existence. Once he has done this, he can choose the method of procedure and make his own history. There is no fate, no bad luck, no excuse; simply man, his choices, and the situation in which he finds himself. Goetz and Hoederer succeed where Hugo and Franz fail, because they come to terms with what they are and what constitutes the actualities of their world. They are able to engage in a realistic assessment of their own situation. Both Hugo and Franz are accused of loving ideas and not men; indeed, neither man comes to grips with himself and the world around him; neither man is sufficiently in contact with reality. Goetz passes through stages of awareness which Hoederer has evidently already achieved; each realizes the limitations of the possibilities of action open to him, accepts those limitations, and determines to act to the utmost within the context of these limitations. It is this recognition and this determination plus movement to action which affords these two men the opportunity to become real, existing human beings; which gives them and the world around them a true identity, a reality.

The individual freedom so crucial to Sartre's early thought is still important (all acts are necessarily initiated from the individual's awareness and abilities), but another aspect becomes equally crucial, respect for the freedom of all. Another principle likewise comes into play—no man is indispensable. Orestes was valiant but spawned of a period which Sartre would now term idealistic, for he has come to believe that it takes more than one man to achieve freedom. When asked if he were not a great influence on our age, Sartre replied,

> Not at all. One man doesn't count, one writer doesn't count. But let a group of the latter come to an understanding on the major problems, and then perhaps it will be another story.

Philip Thody effectively summarizes this viewpoint:

> The anarchical revolt of a single individual, however violent and sincere, is completely useless from the social point of view. Only organized rebellion, in which the individual is prepared to subordinate everything to the cause for which he is fighting, can be considered as a worthwhile undertaking.

That which Sartre requires of today's authentic man is, in fact, more heroic than the requirement for any Orestes. The unified action will not serve to defend each man against the anguish of life as Hugo hoped it would; quite the contrary. Each authentic man of today, each man who would lead in the revolution, must be willing to take a heavier burden than that of Orestes. He remains alone in his choices as the characters Hoederer and Goetz demonstrate. He never knows that he is right in his decisions until after the fact as Hoederer affirms. Because, as Hoederer states, the world is based on lies, he must be willing to lie; because, as Goetz states, the world is peopled with criminals, he must be willing if necessary to commit crimes. He must engage himself fully in the affairs of men with only himself to decide, formulate values, and accept the responsibility.

Moreover, conflict is still considered basic to human relationships, yet these relationships are essential. What is required to resolve this dilemma is a conscious awareness—an awareness of oneself and the problems basic to the area of human concerns. In other words, success is possible, if highly difficult of accomplishment, when each man recognizes that difficulty is inherent in human relationships but that this difficulty must be overcome. It *must* be overcome because the principle of freedom should receive greater emphasis than each man's self-concern. It *can* be overcome because man makes himself through his free choices, thus he can create his relationship with the Other in whichever method he chooses, just as he creates his own individuality. Goetz and Hoederer forsee a chance, remote though it may be, and they determine to try it as the only authentic course. They are responsible for the weighty decisions and for the acts which they perform and their aloneness presses down upon them—the Sartrean free man is still responsible and very much alone. Now, however, his efforts are to obtain *and* cultivate his freedom *and* the freedom of the Other. (pp. 144-54)

Judith Zivanovic, "Sartre's Drama: Key to Understanding His Concept of Freedom," in Modern Drama, *Vol. XIV, No. 2, September, 1971, pp. 144-54.*

Dieter Galler (essay date 1976)

[*In the following essay, Galler explores conceptual and thematic parallels between* No Exit *and* The Condemned of Altona.]

Sartre himself has referred to ***Les séquestrés d'Altona*** as "***Huis clos*** with five characters", and the similarities between the two plays are striking. From a technical viewpoint, in the ***Séquestrés*** Sartre uses devices which had proved successful in the earlier play: both dramas make frequent use of the flashback, interrupting the chronological sequence of events to communicate significant background information. In both plays, an elaborate system of self-defense, built up in bad faith, has to be dismantled by a third party to reach the characters' carefully hidden truth and to finalize the protagonist's sequestration. The main characters are either 'dead' or placed in a situation closely simulating death. While Inès, Estelle and Garcin died de facto, Franz is declared dead in Argentina; the elder von Gerlach is dying of cancer of the throat and has decided to commit suicide within six months; and Johanna and Werner's marriage is compared to a funeral. As Werner points out, he never married Johanna, just her corpse. Even Léni belongs in the category of Sartre's vivants morts. Freedom of choice and thus the capacity of overcoming the limitations of given situations are fundamental to human existence; thus Léni, who accepts without challenge the anachronistic structure and the rituals of the von Gerlach family, opts to be a "living corpse".

The theme of both plays, furthermore, is identical: sequestration equals "Hell", and the mythical hell management of ***Huis clos*** has its counterpart in the infernal mechanism of the dialectical process of History. Sequestered and sequestering, the main characters assume the double function of bourreau and victime, completely controlled by a calculating diabolic management, and the equally hellish "practico inerte". Though the term 'Hell' is not used in the later play, the impression of Hell is at least as prevalent in ***Les séquestrés*** as in ***Huis clos.*** The hell management in the latter remains mythical, absent. In the former, however, the historical process which victimizes Man and alienates him from his intentions is omnipresent. In ***Huis clos,*** the protagonists are villains, pathetic creatures of melodramatic stature. They kill or torture persons who are, for various reasons, incapable of resistance. The condemned of the play could have easily avoided their sadistic crimes, thus their plight. Garcin's well known statement that "Hell is other people" relates primarily to the punishment of three villains who represent three different facets of evil. It is a weakness of the play that the universality of Garcin's statement remains obscure, as the audience could hardly be expected to identify with the problems of a flagrant coward, a child murderess and a sadistic lesbian. The ontological error of this trio was their choice of inauthenticity, a behavior for which they could have compensated, had their existence continued. Because they are 'dead', they no longer have any control over their destinies, leaving the evaluation of their lives to be reflected only in the condemning eyes of the "Other". Purely "en–soi", inert objects of the judgment of those who survived them and of their companions in 'Hell', existence degenerates into fate. Marie-Denise Boros concludes convincingly:

> Leur Enfer c'est précisément leur impuissance à contrôler cette image d'eux-mêmes qui flotte capricieusement dans la prunelle d'autrui. Ne pouvant se voir que dans les yeux des autres, ils n'ont aucun pouvoir sur ce qu'ils découvrent . . . Trop tard pour essayer quoi que ce soit. Tombés dans le domaine public, ils sont la proie du jugement qui les a décrétés lâche, infanticide, lesbienne pour l'éternité. Toutes leurs simagrées sont vaines.

As 'Hell' is experienced exclusively by those who committed overt and repulsive crimes, we are left with the false impression of Man's possible salvation through authenticity: in ***Huis clos*** there seems hope for the average person to break out of the circle of bad faith and avoid the condemning judgment of the "Other". This optimism is unintentional and false. Sartre states that every triangular relationship eventually becomes destructive, and in the analysis of the infernal aspects of all human relationships lies the play's existential message. It is in this universal context, transcending the specific situation of three criminals, that Garcin's conclusion that "Hell is other people" obtains its basic ontological meaning. It is an integral part of Sartre's philosophy that the look of the "Other" constitutes the end of the existant's freedom, in essence his ontological death. The "Other" possesses control over one's image, and as an individual, he becomes the object of judgment, thus "en-soi".

Already in ***Being and Nothingness*** (***L'être et le néant***), Sartre analyzes the fundamental antagonistic relationships between the "Self" and the "Other" and concludes that "I" and the "Other" represent two clashing centers creating a subject-object relationship. Conflict becomes the basic bond between two existants, as the existence of the other constitutes la chute originelle. In ***Critique de la raison dialectique*** (from this point on to be referred to as ***C.R.D.***), the "Other remains that very same menacing presence: a microcosm structuring the world around his personal needs and ambitions. We also recognize in ***Huis clos*** the function of the third person who, as established in ***C.R.D.,*** may reduce both the "Self" and the "Other" to the level of objects. In the case of a triangular relationship, a complicité fondamentale can occur, temporarily unifying the "Other" and the "Self" against the third party. But this attempt is doomed to failure. There is no escape from the disintegrating third party who inevitably assumes the rôle of the bourreau by dissolving the relationship between the "Self" and the "Other", especially in ***Huis clos*** and ***Les séquestrés,*** where every rapport is based on fiction and bad faith. As Sartre points out, there is always a disintegrating third party in our society, and anybody can assume its function.

> . . . le tiers . . . quelle que soit la société considérée, c'est chacun et tout le monde; ainsi la réciprocité est vécue par chacun comme possibilité objective et diffuse.

Inasmuch as one not only functions as "object", but limits any existant's freedom by the same ontological process, it follows that "L'essence des rapports entre consciences n'est pas le Mit-Sein, c'est le conflit." As an existant, one is therefore fundamentally sequestered as well as sequestering.

> Impossible d'exister au milieu des hommes sans qu'ils deviennent objets pour moi et pour eux, sans que ma subjectivité prenne sa réalité objective comme intériorisation de mon objectivité humaine.

Les séquestrés d'Altona represents a different approach to the inferno which constitutes an integral part of the condition humaine. Placed in a precise social and historical frame, the von Gerlach tragedy seems more frightening than the transhistoric plight of the criminals in ***Huis clos.*** Endowing his protagonists with attributes far superior to those in his earlier play, and portraying in the person of Frantz von Gerlach the specific dilemma of a French soldier returning from Algeria, Sartre avoids certain ambiguities found in ***Huis clos.*** The spectator recognizes himself in the protagonist, whose impuissance mirrors his own anguished predicament before the dehumanizing dialectical process of History.

When old von Gerlach yields his land to the Nazis for the construction of a concentration camp, his action is motivated by economic opportunism rather than anti-Semitism, inasmuch as he is powerless to stop the Nazis who could have used any territory of their choice. He collaborates solely to expand his enterprise, not because of any direct adherence to the Nazi ideology. When subsequently he denounces an escaped prisoner, whom Frantz has been hiding to protest his father's collaboration, the execution of the fugitive is performed contrary to the father's intentions and in violation of the agreement he has reached with Goebbels. The elder von Gerlach never wanted the death of the rabbi; the whole incident occurred as an unforeseen by-product of his choice to increase his economic power. He could not anticipate that his denunciation would create a situation which would eventually lead to his son's becoming "the butcher of Smolensk". Frantz clearly expresses this sentiment when he states, "Je suis tortionnaire, parce que vous êtes dénonciateur" (V, 1).

It can be debated that after Frantz witnesses the brutal execution of the rabbi, he lives what Sartre calls a "vie orientée": the horror of this incident will orient him to the torture of prisoners at the eastern front to avoid a duplication of his previous impuissance. Though this argument is by no means an excuse or a justification for Frantz's crimes, one can plead that his "existential castration" caused by the father's denunciation plays a significant rôle in his evolution into the "butcher of Smolensk".

Les séquestrés conveys the sinister impression that the von Gerlachs are destroyed by the circumstances surrounding the death of the rabbi, a chain of events over which the father has no control. He is trapped, alienated, and the result of his actions contrasts with his intentions. "Reified" ("réifié", "chosifié") by his enterprise to which he has dedicated his life, to the point of sending an innocent man to his death, the father acknowledges that this dedication to economic achievement has destroyed both himself and his alter ego, Frantz. The shipbuilding enterprise, the father's "praxis", which Frantz was to inherit, becomes the infernal "practico inerte", a lethal proliferation, an "enterprise qui nous écrase". Industrial empires evolve into inert hostile monstrosities which annihilate the Man of the western capitalist society. If in ***Huis clos*** authenticity appeared obtainable and thereby a means to Man's salvation, in ***Les séquestrés*** all hope for western Man is dead. Capitalism, the social system responsible for the von Gerlachs' tragedy, is as deadly as the father's cancer. As long as one lives under a capitalist system, life will equal sequestration; and as long as western Man does not choose an alternate economic and sociological frame of operation, he will be left with nothing.

Apparent in ***Les séquestrés*** is only one aspect of Sartre's concept that History makes Man and Man makes History: the play portrays Man exclusively as an important object of History, victim of his achievements, object of the "practico inerte". Man as subject and maker of History is conceivable only outside of the economic necessities and contingencies that capitalism imposes upon the von Gerlachs.

> . . . La liberté n' apparaît dans ***Les séquestrés*** qu' en tant qu' elle est niée, puisque les personnages sont tous parfaitement impuissants; elle doit pourtant être lue en creux dans leur impuissance même: c'est elle qui rend intelligible la nécessité à laquelle ils se heurtent. Car si l'Histoire est histoire humaine et non simple processus agissant sur les hommes à la manière dont les forces matérielles agissent sur des objets passifs, la nécessité ne saurait être un déterminisme inhumain et absolu, une pure fatalité: elle ne trouve son origine nulle part ailleurs que dans la liberté. L'homme crée lui-même la nécessité et l'Histoire fait l'homme dans l'exacte mesure où il la fait. Autrement dit, la liberté est à la fois le fondement de la dialectique historique et la condition d'une histoire humaine.

However the absence as such of freedom and authenticity in ***Les séquestrés d'Altona*** leaves the spectator with an overwhelmingly sinister impression of collective sequestration. The play portrays not only the impotence of certain capitalists, but because of the economic power of this group, the plight of western Man in general, inasmuch as his life is controlled by these industrial giants. Sequestration becomes his situation par excellence; life inevitably degenerates into incarceration.

Not only do both plays stress Man's impotence and sequestration, but even the situations into which the characters are placed show an astonishing affinity. The triangular interaction of ***Huis clos,*** where one male character faces two females is barely modified in ***Les séquestrés.*** Unity of place abandoned, the latter, a more complex play, features two separate triangular spheres of struggle: the 'downstairs world' where old von Gerlach manipulates Johanna and Léni against each other, and the 'upstairs world' in which Frantz tries to involve both women in his futile attempt to justify his war crimes. Werner's contribution to the dramatic action is quite marginal, as he limits himself to playing the obedient rôle of the faible, to which his father has predestined him.

The two spheres dominated by father and son are of equal importance though of a completely different nature. In one sense, the old man is the puppeteer manipulating the family, only to lose everything and destroy everybody caught in his diabolic machinations. On the other hand, Frantz is not only the key to his father's intrigues but, as his alter ego, he is the dominant factor in the lives of each of the von Gerlachs: a final encounter with Frantz is the sole remaining purpose in the elder von Gerlach's life, incest with Frantz is Léni's raison d'être, and Werner has sacrificed his marriage to Johanna in order to succeed his older brother as head of the enterprise.

A further common trait of both plays is the main characters' awareness of their *impuissance.* The stage is used as a tribunal, and the protagonists are judged and condemned for crimes committed before the beginning of the play. Cut off from the mainstream of life, without any future, their present becomes completely dominated by their irrevocable past. Victims of anxiety and despair, they are fully conscious of the complexity of their impotence. As Jeremy Palmer says,

> . . . the characters are driven like Racinian heros, by their own inability to compromise with their desires; were the perception of the impossibility of attaining their ends accompanied by the will to cease striving for them, the dénouement would be quite different. But this will is lacking, and the characters revel in their impotence: they are lucid and triumphant witnesses of their own failure, and the playing out of their chosen rôles is the source of a bitter and paradoxical satisfaction.

Judged and condemned, the protagonists' psychological sequestration is accentuated by their physical claustration. In both plays, the main characters are artificially removed from contact with the outside world, trapped, imprisoned, petrified in their modus vivendi. In ***Huis clos,*** the incarceration occurs in a windowless "salon style Second Empire", with a capricious door. A continuously burning electric lamp lights the room. Three sofas serve as the only furnishings.

> Nos trois personnages sont donc prisonniers 'à vie' de cette cellule sans barreaux, de ce salon bourgeois de Second-Empire qui n' est que l' illustration symbolique de leur séquestration éternelle.

The protagonists of ***Huis clos*** are locked into their confinement by an anonymous hell management, until they discover that they are tied by their needs to their companions, who as true hellmates are either unwilling or incapable of fulfilling these needs. In the ***Séquestrés,*** Frantz's incarceration is more sophisticated, because it is self-imposed. Frantz shuts himself away not only to escape prosecution, but above all, his locks, iron bars and walled-in windows serve to protect him from the knowledge of Germany's rebirth and current prosperity, from the death of his delusion of possible justification of his crimes.

> FRANTZ. . . . J' ai prétendu que je m' enfermais pour ne pas assister à l'agonie de l'Allemagne: c' est faux. J' ai souhaité la mort de mon pays et je me séquestrais pour n' être témoin de sa résurrection.
>
> (V,1,)

In neither instance do the doors represent a way out for the sequestered parties. Garcin is tied forever to the 'Salon Second Empire' by his need for Inès, who needs Estelle, who needs Garcin. Equally, Frantz needs Léni's lies and the illusion of Germany's continuous agony to justify a posteriori his acts of torture. When Frantz leaves his room to confront his father, the circumstances surrounding this decision incur a transfer into an even more perfect form of sequestration. He joins his father in suicide, terminating his existence in another closed space, Léni's Porsche at the bottom of the Elbe River. By a similar process, when Garcin is surprised to see that the exit from his confinement is suddenly 'open', he fully comprehends that there is no escape from his infernal situation: his salvation depends upon the impossible task of making Inès believe in his heroism.

In both plays the suffering of the protagonists once begun remains at a constant level of intensity, because timelessness, i.e., a type of eternity, is an integral part of each plot. Frantz keeps himself constantly awake in an artificially lighted room; there can be no instant of relaxation from his continuous need to justify actions which, by their very nature, are unjustifiable.

> FRANTZ. . . . Mais quel feu! (Il bâille.) Son principal office est de me tenir éveillé. (Il bâille.) Voilà vingt ans qu' il est minuit dans le siècle: ça n'est pas très commode de garder les yeux ouverts à minuit. Non, non: de simples somnolences. Cela me prend quand je suis seul. . . . (Il chancelle, se redresse brusquement, pas militaire jusqu'à sa table. Il prend des coquilles et bombarde le portrait de Hitler, en criant . . .) Führer, je suis un soldat. Si je m'endors, c'est grave: abandon de poste. Je te jure de rester éveillé. Envoyez les phares, vous autres! Plein feu; dans la gueule au fond des yeux, ça réveille
>
> (II,3)

Technically brilliant, Sartre places his condemned within the sclerotic frame of stagnating time.

> Si l'on étudiait ***Les séquestrés*** sous l'aspect de la structure temporelle, l'on arriverait à la conclusion que dans cette pièce le temps ne passe plus, il est sequestré lui aussi. Peu importe qu'entre la première et la dernière scène s'écoule un certain nombre de jours, cet intervalle minime est en dehors de la durée, c'est une parenthèse temporelle qui n'a aucun effet sur la signification de la phrase qui l'englobe. La montre offerte par Johanna et que Frantz ne peut casser, est le témoignage qu'ailleurs le tempts passe augmentant l'espace qui sépare la famille Gerlach du monde qui l'entoure. La déséquestration de Frantz ne libère même pas une durée repliée sur elle-même, elle n'est que le passage infiniment bref menant à la séquestration de la mort.

In ***Huis clos,*** the 'death' of the culprits and the eternal suffering in the traditional sense are ironically utilized. There are no windows, of course, where the sequence of day and night reveals the flux of time, just constant electric light, coming from the lamps that one cannot turn off, "électricité à discretion", as Garcin notices with bitter sarcasm. Naturally there is no sleep, no darkness. Only the absence of eyelids, which could black out the world for a fraction of a second, is a possible preternatural phenomenon. Life is lived without *coupures,* and experienced as 'Hell' conceived with total efficiency.

Equally, the characterological traits of the protagonists of ***Huis clos*** and ***Les séquestrés d'Altona*** show striking similarities, and the trio composed of Garcin, Inès and Estelle has its equivalent in Frantz, Léni and Johanna. Each character is lucid, perfectly aware of living in bad faith, and consciously perpetuating this dilemma. Each is set in his attitudes and behavior patterns, refusing to reëvaluate his position. The reasons for acting in a specific manner stem from a répertoire of clichés which, if maintained and subscribed to by the "Other", would mean salvation. Each lucidly chooses to act out of habit, to act out a rôle that he has imposed upon himself and which he seems unwilling to modify. Each is intelligent, yet a creature of habit cognizant of the fact that his acts are no longer the result of free choices, but merely empty rituals. Fully comprehending the dimensions of failure, he indulges masochistically in the morbid game of analyzing the various aspects of his sequestration, without bringing about any change in his attitudes toward his existence. Their common trait is the refusal to act as freely choosing individuals bearing the responsibility for what they have made of themselves. For Sartre, the unique human trait is consciousness, the prerequisite of human freedom which is apparent in all aspects of human action. This resulting fundamental freedom of choice establishes the individual's total responsibility for his actions which is terminated only by death.

Because of their refusal to bear the burden of their freedom, the characters of ***Huis clos*** and ***Les séquestrés d'Altona*** are sequestered, trapped, impotent. As self-deceivers, they attempt to escape the responsibility for their decisions, and in bad faith they pathetically try to hide behind the façade of righteousness. They prefer to search for someone to mirror their lies in exchange for similar services. However, this game is played on a basis of fiction, and any self-justification purchased at the cost of reality in the Sartrean world is doomed to failure. (pp. 25-8)

Dieter Galler, "Jean Paul Sartre's 'Huis clos' and 'Les séquestrés d'Altona': Similarities and Contrasts," in The USF Language Quarterly, *Vol. XV, Nos. 1-2, Winter, 1976, pp. 25-8.*

NO EXIT

CRITICAL COMMENTARY

Edith Kern (essay date 1962-63)

[*In the following essay, Kern explores the Sartrean themes of freedom and authenticity in* No Exit.]

Though not quite twenty years have passed since its first performance, Sartre's ***Huis-Clos*** has gained the status of a classic on the modern stage. It deserves this place for more than one reason. It is human drama full of suspense, tension, and passion, challenging the spectator both emotionally and intellectually. It is also, as Jacques Guicharnaud has suggested, melodrama and drawing-room comedy. With extreme economy of theatrical means and techniques, it unrolls tales of human crime and debasement against the background of its shabby Empire drawing-room, whose "cozy" intimacy becomes a nightmare and whose very warmth and brightness become elements of torture. But it is also a skillful dramatization of the author's philosophical insights, presented in the form of a modern myth: Man turned into an object by the eyes of his fellow man, the Other, who also serves him as a mirror confirming his existence; man robbed of his freedom, immobilized, congealed, and even tortured as he is aware of the consciousness of the Other. Garcin's outcry "l'enfer c'est les autres" and his concluding line "continuons" seem to epitomize the hopeless, eternal condemnation of the play's three characters to a hell from which they cannot escape.

Why did Sartre condemn them and what were his principles of punishment as distinguished from those based on medieval theology to which Dante adhered in his Inferno—also inhabited by "dead" people who are very much alive in many ways?

Condemnation on the play's melodramatic level is obvious and simple. For each one of the three characters has committed the most outrageous crimes. We learn that Garcin tortured his wife and ultimately brought about her death. Knowing her sensitivity and capacity for suffering, he paraded before her the women with whom he betrayed her, installed in his own home the half-caste whom he kept as his mistress, and had his wife serve them breakfast in bed. Inès prides herself on having always been "une femme damnée." She has no fewer than three deaths on her conscience: those of her cousin, his wife Florence, and her own. For while she was a guest in the house of her cousin, she estranged Florence from him and seduced her. When he was run over by a streetcar—or had probably killed himself in despair—she instilled in Florence the idea that they were responsible for his death. For she was thirsting to make others suffer, and in the pursuit of such satisfaction found her own death. Driven to the utmost, Florence, one night, turned on the gas, thus committing murder and suicide for which only Inès could be held responsible. Estelle, beautiful, delicate, and tender, relinquishes only reluctantly the aura of self-sacrifice and duty with which she likes to surround herself. But she ultimately owns up to the most sordid tale. Orphaned and poor, she had married a rich old friend of her father's. Then she fell in love with a young man. He wanted her to leave with him. She refused, not out of virtue, but because he was poor. She spent five months in Switzerland to conceal from her husband that she was giving birth to the daughter of her lover. The father loved his child, but she, tying a stone around its neck, drowned the baby before his eyes. After staring at the widening rings in the water, he left to kill himself. No one ever knew. And Estelle, free of any feeling of guilt, went on to search for new lovers.

Through ignorance or lack of concern, society entirely failed to condemn these crimes. Because of her wealth, Estelle could conceal the murder of her child, and no human tribunal could have accused her of murdering her lover. Neither society nor her husband knew of her betrayal or her guilt. Inès' crimes were also committed in secret, and any prosecutor would have been hard put to it to accuse her of murder and suicide. If Garcin was killed by a firing squad, it was not for the crimes committed against his wife, but rather because he was considered, rightly or wrongly, a deserter.

That Sartre's reasons for condemning his characters are not exhausted by our general feelings of what is right or wrong is indicated by the fact that, at the climax of the play, the door of hell opens and the characters are given a chance to escape. It is their inability to do so that makes them truly and with finality guilty in Sartre's eyes. For at this moment of free choice, all three betray their total lack of authenticity, their inability to assume their human freedom which would enable them to reassume life and change. This lack of authenticity is at the root of their crimes and, at the same time, it carries within itself the very nature of the punishment that is meted out to them.

When Inès says of herself "I was what some people down there called 'a damned bitch.' Damned already," she accepts the judgment of Others as her Being. The words Sartre wrote about Genet might almost literally be applied to her: "Thus developed, within Genet, parallel to the theme of 'bad character,' that of gratuitous crime and of deliberate, willful badness." For Inès always refers to herself as "méchante" and forever insists that she regrets nothing. When speaking of Querelle, one of Genet's fictional characters, Sartre called such a destruction of a man's own conscience "suicide" and spoke about Querelle as "un joyeux suicidé." In this manner, Inès had committed suicide long before her physical death. She had let her *pour soi* congeal into an *en soi.* In this sense, she had long been dead. For "a dead person," says Sartre, "is a being which no longer exists for itself but only in itself, that is to say, through the opinion which Others have of him." But in hell Inès still dies another death for having willfully insisted on being a criminal: "The name of him who desires to do wrong will be written on water, his memory vanish from the earth with his life, and he will be dropped from history and the world. Thus Inès, looking back upon the earth, sees her room being rented by others: a man seated on her bed, a woman entering and approaching him. There is no trace left of her in the world. Neither man nor thing remembers her. Unlike Genet, Inès never regained her *pour soi* but remained the *en soi,* the object into which Others had turned her. She had ranged herself among the dead ever since she had accepted herself as "méchante" and as the "damned bitch" as which Others saw her. Unlike Genet, she persisted in repeating to Estelle and Garcin that all was predestined and arranged in life: "I tell you everything has been arranged, down to the smallest detail." "Nothing has been left to chance." It is thus that Inès' presence in hell represents her continuation of an existence deprived of a *pour soi,* that is, of true human freedom, and her physical extinction is identical with her total disappearance from history, so that she must exclaim in horror: "Now I am completely dead."

Garcin's existence on earth had been in a different way inauthentic. In his study of *The Intellectual Hero,* Victor Brombert has rightly classified him as the intellectual. Because his vision of himself was blurred by intellectual clichés, his life lacked all honesty and true freedom. He thought of himself as the idealist, the pacifist, the hero; the handsome, somewhat brutal Don Juan breaking the hearts of women and loving the company of his fellow journalists: men smelling of sweat and cigars. But idealism, success, love had, throughout the years, lost their meaning and, in the moment of decision, proved their emptiness. When called upon to defend his pacifism, he could but replace action by deliberation with regard to the manner of action and then begin an endless though futile search for the true reasons of his behavior: "I paced my cell day and night. From the window to the door, the door to the window. I spied upon myself. I tracked myself down. It seems to me that I spent an entire life questioning myself. And then what? The fact remains. I took the train. This is certain. But Why? Why?" Garcin must find logical reasons, must justify himself towards Others. But his tragedy lies in the fact that, once the intellectual clichés which dazzled himself and Others are broken, he is "in the hands of Others." Others are free to judge him. They will make him a thing of history, a mere thing by which to measure other men, when they say "lâche comme Garcin." Thus Garcin endures the suffering of the intellectual: remorse, shame, and concern for his reputation. If he had only lived longer, he thinks, he might have proved himself different. But Inès tells him that one always dies too soon.

Of the three characters in ***Huis-Clos,*** Estelle is perhaps the least authentic. She is the most hesitant to reveal her crimes, the most eager to give an impression totally different from any reality, the least capable of accepting the horror of being dead. (She avoids the use of the word "morte" and prefers to speak of herself as "absente.") To her the absence of mirrors in hell is the greatest punishment. For mirrors were part of her existence. When she spoke, when she went about her daily activities, she would look at herself in the mirrors around her and see herself as others would see her. During her entire life she acted a part in a play in which she was the leading lady. She lived but to have her beauty reflected in her lovers' eyes and words. She felt "pure" as long as her admirer called her "son eau vive," "son cristal." Her own ruthlessness, her crimes had for her no reality comparable to that of these words and this admiration. It is only when, looking back to earth, she sees her friend Olga dance with her latest lover and hears her tell him all about the trip to Switzerland, the child, the murder—it is only then that her world of make-believe is shattered and that she realizes that "le cristal est en miettes." It is then that she resigns herself to the fact that the world has abandoned her and that she has forever lost it. In fact, of course, she never owned it. For she never lived a life based on her own decisions. She never lived as a subject freely determining her attitudes towards the world and the people around her. Her life had been merely borrowed from fiction. It had conformed to the pattern of melodrama of the lowest order. She had been merely the actress assuming the roles assigned her.

The three characters in ***Huis-Clos*** represent thus three types variously lacking in authenticity: the criminal caught in the niche that society has assigned him; the intellectual unable to free himself from empty rationalization; and the actress or actor who can live only existences borrowed from fiction without ever truly existing. And it is their lack of authenticity that represents their hell. In terms of authenticity it is immaterial whether these characters are dead or alive. It is true that Sartre establishes from the start that they are dead when they arrive in the drawing-room. Estelle died of pneumonia; Inès was asphyxiated by gas; and Garcin had received a charge of twelve bullets. But as the stories unfold themselves, we are aware of the fact that these three characters had never

Scene from the original 1944 French production of No Exit.

been fully alive. They had always been merely objects to the Other; each one had been only an *en-soi* and never a *pour-soi*—only passive matter instead of active maker. As such they might be found in any drawing-room as well as in hell, and any drawing-room might become their hell. For the presence of the Other—both necessary and destructive to the individual consciousness—represents punishment to the dead who cannot assume their human freedom and have congealed into a fixed "character."

Free human beings would not have to fear to be known to another, to be "nus comme des vers," as Garcin says, for their very nudity would remain capable of change and might be indicative of beauty as well as of ugliness. The Other's power to transfix them into a pose or a "character" would be contested by their own freedom of choice and change. Yet even this freedom, Sartre suggests in ***Huis-Clos,*** is not a door opening into bliss but rather into a Kafkaesque conglomeration: beyond the door "Il y a d'autres chambres et d'autres couloirs et des escaliers." But if life beyond the door holds no promise of paradise, it holds at least the promise of unknown possibilities. (pp. 56-60)

Edith Kern, "Abandon Hope, All Ye . . . ," in Yale French Studies, *No. 30, Fall-Winter, 1962-63, pp. 56-61.*

Robert Champigny (essay date 1982)

[*In the following excerpt, Champigny reviews the philosophical ideas and dramatic elements in* No Exit.]

Garcin is introduced into a drawing-room, with no mirror and no windows. According to the usher, or bell-boy, one does not sleep in this place, and there is no "outside." Two women, Inès and Estelle, arrive, and it appears gradually that the three characters are "dead" and that they are in "Hell." They realize that they have been put into one room in order to torment one another with words. Inès is a lesbian who tries to seduce Estelle, an infanticide, who tries to seduce Garcin. Not only does the presence of Inès bother Garcin, but he insists on being judged by her and he wants to persuade her that he was not a coward. Estelle attempts to kill Inès with a paper knife, forgetting that they are already "dead." The three characters appear to realize that they are condemned to remain together forever, and to continue as they have started.

* * *

Hells and Heavens are legendary. On the one hand, they are not part of the historical field. They are transcendent; they are detached like an esthetic world. On the other hand, this is *where we* are supposed to go *after* death. If there are spatial and temporal relations between them and the Earth, they are part of the historical field.

Requirements of coherence can intervene once a type of signification, hence logic, has been adopted. But relations between what signifies and what is signified remain transcendent. For instance, if historical signification is used to subordinate the others, it may be said that, in the case of a theatrical performance, experienced signs signify historical actors (and spectators), who signify lucid actors (and spectators), who signify esthetic characters. At this point, the direction may be inverted. Characters may be interpreted as signifying lucid and historical individuals. In a vaguer way, of course: "significance" disperses. It is disorderly, entropic. These uses of "to signify" bridge absolute gaps between types of entities.

No Exit makes a clever use of the transcendent aspect of Hells to isolate a fictional field. The historical aspect of Hells is subdued, since it is unlikely that spectators will take seriously this fictional Hell as a picture of the kind of afterlife they will have to go through.

The characters of ***No Exit*** have remembrances of their past lives and visions of what is happening on "Earth," while they are quarrelling. This would be legend within the fiction. However, time in the fictional Hell is distinguished at one point from time on the fictional Earth. Garcin says that his wife "died a moment ago" (Hell time); and he adds: "About two months ago" (Earth time). Above all, the conditions of existence in the fictional Hell are shown to be radically different.

The medieval idea of Hell is endless physical tortures. To the characters' surprise, the Hell of ***No Exit*** avoids that. It is more reminiscent of a pagan conception that reduces the dead to shades. In the *Odyssey,* Ulysses attracts a flock of shades with the smell of blood. What they miss is the full embodiment of carnivorous animals.

The shades of ***No Exit*** are not blood-thirsty. One might say they are glance-thirsty. They have trouble adjusting to the fact that they are reduced to pure gesturing. There is a strong reflexive aspect in ***No Exit.*** By this I mean that the characters appear as comedians, as being only capable of playing the roles of characters. Being dead means, in this case, that the utilitarian frame, the historical background of ludic activities, has been taken away.

So the characters cannot be tortured physically. They cannot kill one another, as Estelle realizes: the paper knife is only a prop. In their ludic roles, actors cannot kill one another. The setting of ***No Exit*** is a drawing-room, not a dungeon, not a torture chamber. In a drawing-room, you are, or were, supposed only to talk, and to talk as if you were on stage. The temporality of a ludic role is detached from utilitarian temporality. An "eternal" present tense (which I called a metatense) may be used to talk about ludic roles or esthetic characters: "Sartre says," "Garcin says." If playing a part is not improvised, what the actors say is determined by the text; to some extent, an acting style is imposed by a director. In ***No Exit,*** Garcin expresses the opinion the trio is manipulated, that everything has been foreseen. On the whole, however, the characters of ***No Exit*** play-act as if they were improvising. Finally, the last words in ***No Exit:*** "Let's continue" may give a spectator the impression that the three characters will hardly be able to innovate. The analogy, in this case, would be with several performances of one dramatic script, with some variants.

* * *

The connections between ***No Exit*** and ***Being and Nothingness*** are not as obtrusive as in ***The Flies:*** there is no philosophico-dramatic bout between two characters. But overlaps are as extensive. ***The Flies*** emphasizes freedom as decision and invention, at least in the character of Orestes: everybody has to, and can, "invent his way." ***No Exit*** absorbs the properly metadramatic aspect of ***Being and Nothingness*** pretty thoroughly. What need do we have of a god? We are judged by others. To this extent, they incarnate us, objectify us, and limit our freedom.

In Plato, the human cave is the body, the skull, the senses. According to the Sartre of ***Being and Nothingness,*** it is the other's glance that reminds us of our unjustified existence, and may frustrate our goals, in particular if the goal is to justify what we already have done. If Sartre chooses glances as a synecdoche for judging, it is probably because eyes are the most spiritual feature of human bodies. But some nonhuman animals have eyes; and some people are blind.

The human cave sketched in ***Being and Nothingness*** is mostly a theatrical stage, with antagonistic gesturing. Cannot one ignore, or escape, the "tyranny of the human face," the "primitive sorcery" that Sartre attributes to eyes in ***Visages***? An opportunity is offered to Garcin in ***No Exit:*** the door opens, he can flee offstage. But he decides to stay, not because of the coquettish and irritating Estelle, but of the antagonistic Inès. Perversely, he insists on being judged by her; he wants to persuade her that he was not a coward on "Earth," which is what matters to him:

> It is you I must convince; we belong to the same race. Did you think I was going to leave? I could not leave you here, triumphant, with all these thoughts in your head, all these thoughts that concern me . . . She does not count. But you, who hate me, if you believe me, I shall be saved.

If he fled, he would still have the impression of being seen. Etymologically, ideas are what is to be seen. Platonic Ideas are objects of contemplation. "Visual" judgments, in ***No Exit,*** are not esthetic contemplations.

I have suggested that ***No Exit*** offers to the characters a pure ludic field, since death reduces them to gesturing. But they have trouble adjusting. They do not develop an amusing lovers' quarrel, or a farcical exchange of Rabelaisian insults, for instance.

In ***No Exit,*** Estelle thinks it is nicer to say that she and the other two are "absent," rather than "dead." This euphemism is taken from common French parlance. Mallarmé and Genet link esthetic or ludic existence with death and absence (detachment, purification). Genet's characters aim at a ludic and esthetic purification (there remains some religious coating). So, "death" receives a favorable connotation. Sartre, on the other hand, is loath to separate, even in theory, historical from fictional existence, ludic activities and esthetic contemplation from utilitarian activities and values.

For instance, in ***Critique of Dialectical Reason,*** he insists that his philosophizing has cognitive value. He wants to prove, to show necessity. But philosophy can only play with words against words. Words are neither mathematical symbols nor experimental instruments. All that a philosopher can do is drug himself with words like "necessity," "demonstrate," "the truth." The allegorical reader that Sartre sets out to convince may be reduced to the Sartre-Roquentin who emphasizes gratuitousness, a basic lack of justification.

Genet's characters would enjoy the conditions that ***No Exit*** provides. Sartre's characters do not, *in part* because they still retain an earth-like outlook, which confuses utilitarian and ludic perspectives.

Garcin's slogan "Hell is the others" has relevance to conditions on Earth to the extent that we accept the stress which ***Being and Nothingness*** lays on antagonism in human relations. But, at least, there are some avenues of escape. We can sleep, dream. This is denied to the characters in ***No Exit.*** If we insist on being judged, we can invent the Other (a compliant god, conscience, posterity). The three characters are deprived of mirrors. We can work and play with things. In the setting of ***No Exit,*** there is only an unmanageable bronze statue, the emblem of a frozen past.

Being and Nothingness considers the future as open. We may try to change the judgments of others, which bear on our past and present, with decisions, plans, that project us toward the future. Of course, we shall die. But death is a receding horizon, except in cases such as that of people condemned to die at a definite time in the immediate future (see Sartre's short story, ***The Wall***). In ***No Exit,*** the characters are already "dead." And they seem unable to distinguish between a ludic future, that might be open, and a utilitarian future, which is what is dead.

Even from a ludic standpoint, it must be confessed that they are not offered a promising situation. Playing the harp, contemplating a divine computer, or even attending philosophical colloquia in the Elysean fields with participants that more than pretend to understand one another and themselves, are not visions of bliss for me. In ***No Exit,*** the characters are restricted to talking games with two partners-opponents in a cramped space. And they are well-assorted only from a devilish, or impish, standpoint. Each character wants to play his own game, and use as partner-opponent the one that does not fit.

Estelle wants to play love with Garcin, who at first refuses. Since he is only interested in being assured he was not a coward, she agrees readily. Too readily: he wants to win over a tougher opponent. Inès offers the devoted mirror of her eyes to Estelle, who prefers to win over Garcin. The latter finally complies, adding caressing hands and embracing arms to eyes, but he is bothered by the presence of Inès, who does not fail to call him a coward.

The characters, especially Garcin, still want to win instead of playing well. If winning is everything, or the main thing, play cannot be detached from utilitarian work. In his theory of *littérature engagée,* or in the style he sometimes adopts, especially in ***Critique,*** Sartre writes as if the objective of literary and philosophical games was to win.

In ***No Exit,*** the conditions are such that, even if the characters purified their perspective, their kind of Hell (there are worse kinds) would not be turned into a kind of Heaven. But it could at least become a Purgatory. Toward the end, the three characters burst into laughter. This gesture may be interpreted as a purification of their perspective, as the start of a play in the spirit of Genet (I am thinking of the recommendations of stage director Archibald in *Les Nègres*). But Sartre prefers to bring ***No Exit*** to a close.

* * *

Garcin is interested in justifying his life on Earth in the eyes of Inès. Not his whole life: he is interested only in proving to Inès that he was not a coward. He can no longer do anything on Earth that would tend to modify the judgments of others: "I left my life in their hands . . . Before, I could act . . . I have become public property." He can only play-act as his own defender, enlisting Inès to play-act as proper judge. This can continue indefinitely. New arguments, new rhetorical devices can be resorted to. There are no mathematical rules to this game; there is no divine computer to apply them. If Inès agrees, this will not prove that Garcin was not a coward. It will simply prove that he was a clever defender, that he has won as an orator. Neither on Earth nor in this kind of afterlife can there be at Last Judgment.

Like some games, a society has laws. And there are also unofficial rules of etiquette. Social rules inextricably mix playful and moral goals and values. Setting up a god as proper referee, apart from social rules and rulers, may be viewed as a half-hearted attempt to turn a moral into a ludic perspective. From the standpoint of a transcendent god, we should be fictional individuals, merely players. From his standpoint, we should not have to win, to be successful in our moral efforts, in preventing or alleviating some suffering. We should only have to play and have played well. The role of the Villain for instance.

Estelle and Inès are not interested in redeeming their past lives, in winning a favorable judgment from people on Earth or from their two companions. They are interested in the present, more precisely in a love game. But the atmosphere lacks playfulness.

Being and Nothingness analyzes love in a way that may be contrasted with Plato's in the *Phaedrus,* and with the poetico-religious tradition that stems from it, a tradition which turns words of love into love of words, as Apollinaire points out in *Rosemonde:* "I nicknamed her Rosemonde." ***Being and Nothingness*** presents love as a project to seduce (and be seduced), to be justified in the eyes of the person to be won over: I shall justify your existence so that you can justify mine.

Love is an attempt to form a utilitarian alliance as well as a playful partnership. But, to remain active, the perspective must also cast the other person in the role of antagonist. The trouble, from my standpoint, is that an erotic perspective so sketched does not distinguish between utilitarian and playful antagonist. An enemy should be avoided or killed. Not an opponent. Concerning love and other matters, ***Being and Nothingness*** does not stress this distinction. Neither do Estelle and Inès in ***No Exit.*** Unlike Garcin, they have abandoned their utilitarian past: no regret, no remorse (like Orestes). But, in the present, they have not yet realized that their incarnation can only be ludic: pure theatrical gestures. Inès is jealous; Estelle attempts to kill her.

An opponent must also be your partner in some way: otherwise no game. So one might speak of a ludic synthesis. But this word had better be left to chemists, and the word "infinite" to mathematicians. In an essay about a text or set of texts, a suitable partner-opponent can be composed without having to deal with a referee (there are no preestablished rules), and without striving to win against a utilitarian enemy (though a few critics still write as if they had to prove something and convince an allegorical reader). I compose my Sartre. Someone else will compose his, if he wishes. There need be no jealousy. The utilitarian Sartre is past caring, supposing he ever did: he had other fish to fry.

Being and Nothingness considers love as sexual. This fits the general strategy: show that we have to incarnate each other, instead of just embodying ourselves in relations with things. Love is a project to justify flesh in an uneasily passive-active atmosphere, as opposed to more definitely ludic sports.

Do some people manage to turn love-making into a candidly spectacular sport, in spite of the poor resources that human bodies offer to this kind of exercise? All I can say is that I am not much of a voyeur. Some wrestling bouts are farces, but less uncouth than pornographic films. If they are serious, they may be appreciated like the performances of acrobats, rather than clowns.

Anyhow, while not esthetically proper in terms of, say, Racinian requirements, the Estelle-Garcin scrum does not turn into a pornographic episode. Inès sees that it does not. Still, I am bothered by such things as Garcin's words to Estelle when, at first, he refuses to play: "You are an octopus, you are a swamp"; or his wish that a medieval Hell be substituted for his Sartrean Hell, physical torture for psychological exasperation. I know; such outbursts may be received as hyperboles that Sartre lends some of his characters to contribute to their delineation. Still, such words, while they may indicate the trouble the characters experience in adjusting their language to the situation, also jar with the basic postulate of the play. Mortal flesh, which can be tortured and sexually desirable or disgusting, is gone.

In a way, ***No Exit*** may be said to arrange a *situation limite.* But the exceptionality of the situation consists in a reduction of existence to pure gestures, not in a confrontation with death as one branch of an alternative. What is exceptional is that the characters cannot kill themselves or one another. Furthermore, in this short one-act play, which is fairly static, though suspense and variations are adroitly managed, no character makes a decision that would change the situation, allow him to find a way out. Unlike Orestes, Garcin refuses to disappear offstage.

Each character appears as a *caractère:* Garcin is someone who is interested only in being judged not to be a coward; the lesbian Inès and the frivolous Estelle are interested only in two versions of erotic seduction. The play does not allow, for instance, Garcin to play the role of Inès, Inès that of Estelle, Estelle that of Garcin (contrast Genet's *Les Bonnes*). The male-female distribution of set personalities may strike one as a cliché. The play could have exposed this stereotype. Instead of that, it relies upon its acceptance by spectators or readers.

* * *

In my opinion, it is very unlikely that a spectator, or reader, should infer that the playwright took seriously his version of an afterlife. Unlikely, but not impossible. Students and fellow-critics have taught me that, in matters of interpretation, especially concerning significance, nothing is impossible. It may well be that some spectators, or readers, decided that they had better not be infanticides, lesbians, or cowards (and forgot about it at once). More plausibly, a maxim such as "Live by yourself" may be drawn from the aphorism "Hell is the others."

As far as I know and can remember, Sartre has always remained negative, or agnostic, on the subject of an afterlife. In ***The Words,*** he formulates the vague notion of a survival of humans among humans, in an Auguste Comte fashion. Not according to the French criteria of glory. There may already have sprung up, while I am writing this, a *rue,* or *théâtre,* or *square* Jean-Paul-Sartre, perhaps even an *avenue,* if avenues are not reserved for Charles-de-Gaulle and Albert-Camus. But this is not what he meant. He meant an insidious, anonymous "haunting" of what humans would be thinking. For better or for worse; he would not have relished innocuousness. There is a similar dream in *Orlando,* by Virginia Woolf. But the hero-heroine is thinking of plants, not humans. I see in this contrast a symptom of a divergence between poetic and dramatic aspirations. I feel closer to Woolf, of course. She would make a poor opponent. Sartre is not insensitive to nonhuman elements. But his sensibility to these elements, which shows in his novels more than in his plays, has a narrow range; and it often appears uneasy. Sartre stopped publishing narrative fiction in 1949, dramatic fiction ten years later.

Sartre's theory of committed literature was written a few years after ***No Exit.*** Yet this drama is remarkably devoid of any particular relevance to a contemporary situation. This may be one of the reasons why it has not aged much in my judgment. The opprobrium attached to lesbianism may have faded; but, in any case, if it is mentioned in the play, it does not have any impact on the plot. I have noted what I take to be faults. But nothing is perfect; and I still consider ***No Exit*** as Sartre's best play. This opinion seems to be shared by quite a few people, for instance by Robert Lorris in his *Sartre Dramaturge.* Such agreements should not be taken as either good or bad things. (pp. 49-57)

Robert Champigny, in his Sartre and Drama, *French Literature Publications Co., 1982, 123 p.*

Konstantin Kolenda (essay date 1984)

[*In the essay below, Kolenda argues that Sartre's treatment of Garcin in* No Exit *reveals that "in his philosophical writings Sartre has failed to make room for the notion of self and personality."*]

Sartre's philosophy contains a truly original contribution to Western thought. He is the first philosopher to regard the human way of being as wholly independent of any other reality. Not Nietzsche, not even Heidegger, can claim to have put an end to metaphysics in such a radical way. All Western philosophers up to Sartre wanted to *relate* human reality to some other type or mode of being: the World of Forms, God, Substance, Noumenon, Spirit, Will, Will to Power, *élan vital,* Being. Sartre rejected *all* candidates for such relata and put nothing in their place. The slogan "existence precedes essence" means to put an end to the hitherto irresistible tendency to define human nature in terms of something other than freedom, which, in Sartrian vocabulary, resulted in the contamination of the for-itself by some kind of in-itself. This tendency Sartre deemed unwarranted and he proceeded to develop a philosophy which would preserve the immaculate purity of the for-itself, undistorted by any in-itself.

To keep a sense of special distinction as a for-itself, human consciousness should resist any encroachment on its own mode of being by any in-itself. True, in practice a complete purity of the for-itself is not attainable, and the resulting self-deception not easily avoidable. Even ordinary perception of physical objects is possible because consciousness mingles with sensuous bodily material. There is no such thing as "immaculate perception," and to make this point Sartre describes our consciousness of material objects as "slimy." But to realize its own special ontological status, consciousness must differentiate itself, phenomenologically, from its objects. To avoid bad faith, we must not submit to dictates of a moral code, or embrace a religious faith, or excuse ourselves by postulating unconscious motives. Otherwise, we are accepting some form of determinism which abrogates our freedom.

In conceiving of human consciousness in this radical way, Sartre makes a clear break with all attempts to represent human reality as conditioned on something nonhuman, be that something natural or divine. Here we have a position which, for the first time in the history of philosophy, separates consciousness, the for-itself, from whatever may dilute its purity and views human existence as literally *making* itself, *ab novo,* in every free choice. The notion of absolute freedom is a logical consequence of this metaphysical purity of the for-itself. Freedom is the ability to say no to any external determining force—moral, political, or theological—and to reject the promptings of convention, habit, or precept. Even emotions and moods are something we fashion voluntarily. If I am sad or jealous, I *make* myself sad or jealous. My free choices control my reasons for action. Something becomes a reason for me only if I decide to *give* it a justifying status. At any time I can reject or revise a commitment made previously. Furthermore, my will never *merges* with the will of others. My loyalty to a group is always maintained at my discretion; an oath is a device to bind my will, but this can be done only temporarily—the resulting intersubjectivity is always provisional and does not generate a true solidarity of the *we.* In truth there cannot be such solidarity; the subjects are always separated from each other by the wall of freedom.

And yet, when Sartre portrays the relations among human beings in his fictional works, the story about freedom does not cohere with his philosophical theory. If we take ***No Exit*** as expressing Sartre's philosophical views, we cannot escape some troublesome questions. Why is Garcin, for instance, agonizing over the question whether or not he is a coward? For some reason he is almost obsessively preoccupied with this question and resents being labeled a coward. In his mind, the matter is far from being settled. Indeed, the whole play revolves around Garcin's rejection of this label. So far, Garcin's attitude supports Sartre's philosophical view; to accept from others a label for oneself would be to acquiesce in being demoted to an in-itself—an act of bad faith. Similarly, he is quite Sartrian in refusing to accept his past as determining his present, and he could quote his creator: "I am not what I am."

But Garcin does not limit himself to resolutely declaring the independence of his existentialist judgment. Instead, he *worries* about the meaning of his acts and character. It is this worry that drives him to seek the opinion of others. Apparently his own is not enough; he needs to have it *confirmed* by others. He does not deem it sufficient simply to *decide* that the label of coward does not apply to him. Significantly, it is the freedom of others that becomes important to him. It infuriates Garcin that the comrades who are still alive choose to label him a coward. Because they choose to view him as such, he cannot escape the reality of that choice. He can disagree with it, but he cannot change its meaning, since it is freely determined by other consciousness. This sort of determination is to be distinguished from accepting the promptings of a moral code or of a religious precept. Such determinations are manifestations of the in-itself, of inert and frozen structures, in contrast to a freely bestowed judgment by a for-itself.

Sartre's treatment of Garcin uncovers a problematic aspect of absolute freedom. The high point of the drama is Garcin's sudden discovery that his self-conception depends on a free choice of another human being. Noticing his desperate need, Inez realizes that he is in her power. It is up to her to decide what he will think of himself. So she tells him, "You are a coward, Garcin, because I wish it." Weak and defenseless as she herself is, she nevertheless has control over him, and he cannot do anything about it, because it is her *thought* that determines what label he deserves. He is powerless against her because, as she tells him, "You can't throttle thoughts with hands." Unwittingly perhaps, Sartre's play demonstrates that human predicaments arise from the *two* faces of freedom: its radical independence of any external forces and its awareness of the equal freedom of others. No collection of external facts or circumstances determines whether Garcin is a coward, and that is why he can insist on his right to interpret the meaning of his actions. Nevertheless, he is powerless with regard to the way other people choose to interpret his actions, and it is their freedom to interpret them the way they see fit that becomes an outrage to him. That is why "Hell is other people."

Garcin's plight points to the discrepancy between the subjectively perceived reality and the objectification it receives through the free judgment of others. That judgment puts us at their mercy. Unable to fix our personal reality because we are "condemned to be free," we are nevertheless ascribed by others characteristics which we resent. And there is no way out of this dilemma. The tragedy of the characters in the Sartrian hell is due to the knowledge that their attempts to establish a satisfying, reliable relation to others are doomed to failure. That failure, paradoxically, is due to the *freedom* of others.

Garcin's case shows that the fact of human freedom has two consequences. Seen from the direction of the individual, it opens unlimited possibilities for choice, for unhindered selection of personal projects. But, as the freedom of *others,* it is a constant threat and potential obstacle to all our goals and projects. Because other people have their own intentions, form resolutions, and pursue their own goals, it is natural to expect failure in interpersonal relations. I cannot get hold of another person's freedom, for I cannot control what he thinks, feels, or intends to do. In order to retain his freedom, the other must not subordinate it to my freedom. Since in many situations the attainment of what we want depends on what others want, and since what they want does not necessarily coincide with our desires, the result is frustration. That frustration is a natural, inevitable component of the human condition, and that is one of the reasons why Sartre calls man a "futile passion."

Sartre's fictional illustration of human freedom takes into account another dimension which goes beyond his general philosophical theory. Not every person's free choices matter to us and can affect us in significant ways. Recall that the first person to whom Garcin turns with his predicament is Estelle. When he asks her whether she thinks him a coward, she answers no, but then ruins his hopes by adding that she doesn't really care whether he is one or not. "Coward or hero, it's all one—provided he kisses well." Estelle's reaction indicates that she cannot give Garcin what he needs. She simply does not understand what is at stake. She is too shallow, too egoistic, not sensitive to his need. Of course, she is willing to love him whether he is a coward or a hero, but her incapacity to see his need for self-respect disgusts him. She strikes him as soft and slimy, and he turns away from her. But Inez is different. Hard and cruel as she is, she nevertheless knows what wickedness and shame are, and hence she must know what it means to be a coward. She at least knows what evil *costs.* Hence, her judgment matters, and if *she* has faith in him, he may be saved.

It is evident from Sartre's play that not everybody's thoughts matter to us; we are interested only in opinions of people whose judgment we respect. When Garcin learns that Estelle is incapable of understanding what it means to be labeled a coward, he loses interest in her thoughts about him. In contrast, he is eager to have Inez's opinion because she understands what worries him. She is sufficiently experienced to appreciate the weight of his concern, hence her opinion cannot be dismissed lightly. Realizing this, Inez is willing to put the power she has over Garcin to her own selfish uses, but this further circumstance does not abrogate the validity of her judgment in Garcin's eyes.

Why is Garcin concerned about his reputation? Why does it matter to him that he may be a coward? More generally, what is behind Sartre's assumption that thoughts of others may be important to us? The only explanation is that, as for-itself, Garcin is not merely interested in *his* freedom to make choices. He realizes that these choices add up to something, that they are cumulative. What they add up to is of deep interest to him, and to determine *that* outcome he needs help; his own judgment is not enough. He is concerned about his reputation because he cares about the self that is being built by his previous choices. He is curious to know what they amount to, and he resists some interpretations of their meaning because his self-understanding matters to him. But his self-conception, to acquire credibility even in his own eyes, has to be confirmed by the judgment of significant others. Without such a confirmation, it lacks validity.

This qualification, however, cuts deeply into Sartre's notion of the for-itself as absolute freedom. Once it becomes self-conscious, the for-itself begins a process of self-definition or self-formation which acts as a steady constraint on its own original freedom. All choices are modified in the light of the emerging self-conception. Of course, the amount of attention a person pays to the emerging possibility of self-definition (which, in an old-fashioned vocabulary, amounts to forming a character or a personality) may be more or less intense. It may also be sidetracked by other interests. Of the three characters in the Sartrian hell only Garcin worries a good deal about what or who he is. Inez is still strongly buffeted by passions and frustrations that victimized her in life, and Estelle never manages to escape the tyranny of physical desire and is wholly at the mercy of chance events, to which she responds like a weather vane.

A closer attention to what is going on in ***No Exit*** shows, I believe, that in his philosophical writings Sartre has failed to make room for the notion of self or personality. That play does not successfully illustrate his philosophical position, because the action of the play depends so much on Garcin's concern with his self-conception. Without that concern, the drama would not get off the ground and the play would lack a focus. It would require a major reconstruction to fill this gap in Sartre's general position; nothing less than a serious rethinking of what constitutes a human self would do. One of the significant by-products of Sartre's failure to produce an account of the self was his abandonment of the initial intention to produce an ethical

An episode from the 1946 French production of No Exit *at the Théâtre de la Potinière.*

theory. This is not a minor failing. As the drama of ***No Exit*** illustrates, it undermines Sartre's entire philosophical position. It is no surprise, then, that when Sartre attempted to give a *literary* account of that position, he had to consider circumstances which made that position questionable. This may indicate that, as a dramatist, Sartre was closer to the truth than he was as a speculative philosopher. His philosophy let him down, but not his art. (pp. 261-65)

Konstantin Kolenda, "The Impasse of 'No Exit'," in Philosophy and Literature, *Vol. 8, No. 2, October, 1984, pp. 261-65.*

FURTHER READING

AUTHOR COMMENTARY

Contant, Michel, and Rybalka, Michel, eds. *Sartre on Theater.* Translated by Frank Jellinek. New York: Pantheon Books, 1976, 179 p.

Compiles "nearly everything that Sartre has said or written about the theater and his own plays."

Sartre, Jean-Paul. "The Theater." *Evergreen Review* 4, No. 11 (January-February 1960): 143-52.

Sartre on the writing of *The Condemned of Altona* and the modern French theater.

———. "Beyond Bourgeois Theatre." *The Tulane Drama Review* 5, No. 3 (March 1961): 3-11.

Excerpt from a lecture given at the Sorbonne in the Spring of 1960 in which Sartre critiques the ideological basis of nineteenth- and twentieth-century drama.

OVERVIEWS AND GENERAL STUDIES

Barnes, Hazel E. "Philosophy in Literature." In *Sartre,* pp. 91-131. Philadelphia: J. P. Lippincott, 1973.

Discusses three of Sartre's most important plays: *No Exit, Dirty Hands,* and *The Condemned of Altona.*

Brosman, Catharine Savage. "The Early Drama" and "The Later Drama." In *Jean-Paul Sartre,* pp. 72-84; 85-99. Boston: Twayne Publishers, 1983.

Surveys Sartre's major dramas.

Fowlie, Wallace. "Sartre." In *Dionysus in Paris: A Guide to*

Contemporary French Theater, pp. 166-83. New York: Meridian Books, 1960.
General introduction to Sartre's dramaturgy before 1960.

Galler, Dieter. "Jean-Paul Sartre's *Les séquestrés d'Altona* and *Huis clos:* Similarities and Contrasts." *The USF Language Quarterly* XV, Nos. 3-4 (Spring-Summer 1977): 57-60.
Compares and contrasts the thematic structures of *The Condemned of Altona* and *No Exit.*

Goldthorpe, Rhiannon. *Sartre: Literature and Theory.* Cambridge: Cambridge University Press, 1984, 246 p.
Essay collection, focusing on Sartre's dramas, that aims "primarily to explore the not always overt relationships between Sartre's theoretical and literary writing."

Gore, Keith O. "The Theatre of Sartre: 1940-65." *Books Abroad: An International Literary Quarterly* 41, No. 2 (Spring 1967): 133-49.
Reviews Sartre's contribution to the modern French theater.

Hobson, Harold. "Jean-Paul Sartre." In *The French Theatre of To-day: An English View,* pp. 75-127. 1953. Reprint. New York: Benjamin Bloom, 1965.
Surveys Sartre's dramatic works through *The Devil and the Good Lord.*

Jackson, R. F. "Sartre's Theatre and the Morality of Being." In *Aspects of Drama and the Theatre: Five Kathleen Robinson Lectures Delivered in the University of Sydney, 1961-63,* pp. 33-70. Sydney, Australia: Sydney University Press, 1965.
Critical introduction to Sartre's plays for the beginning student.

Jameson, Fredric. "The Problem of Acts." In *Sartre: The Origins of a Style,* pp. 3-18. New Haven: Yale University Press, 1961.
Analytical study of Sartre's dramas by a leading Marxist critic.

Kern, Edith, ed. *Sartre: A Collection of Critical Essays.* Englewood Cliffs, N. J.: Prentice-Hall, 1962, 179 p.
Includes general overviews on Sartre's drama as well as single work studies.

Lapointe, François H. *Jean-Paul Sartre and His Critics: An International Bibliography (1938-1980).* Bowling Green, Ohio: Philosophy Documentation Center, 1981, 697 p.
Documents criticism on all genres of Sartre's work, including drama and cinema.

Lumley, Frederick. "Existence in Theory: Jean-Paul Sartre." In *New Trends in 20th Century Drama,* pp. 139-58. New York: Oxford University Press, 1967.
Introduction to Sartre's plays, emphasizing their strong philosophical basis.

McCall, Dorothy. *The Theatre of Jean-Paul Sartre.* New York: Columbia University Press, 1967, 195 p.
Thematic analysis of Sartre's principal dramas.

Wardman, H. W. "Sartre and the Theatre of Catharsis." *Essays in French Literature* I, No. 1 (November 1964): 72-88.
Discusses Sartre's most important plays "in the light of what he says on 'engagement' in *Qu'est-ce que la littérature?* [*What is Literature?*]."

THE FLIES

Adamczewski, Zygmunt. "The Tragic Liberation—Orestes of the Flies." In *The Tragic Protest,* pp. 193-225. The Hague, Netherlands. Martinus Nijhoff, 1963.
Considers the significance of classical symbolism in the Orestes myth utilized by Sartre in *The Flies.*

Belli, Angela. "Jean-Paul Sartre, *Les Mouches.*" In *Ancient Greek Myths and Modern Drama,* pp. 70-90. New York: New York University Press, 1969.
Affirms that in his revision of the Orestes myth in *The Flies,* "Sartre turned to classical mythology for his material in order to create a work that would illustrate his existentialist creed."

Blanchard, Marc Eli. "The Reverse View: Greece and Greek Myths in Modern French Theater." *Modern Drama* XXIX, No. 1 (March 1986): 41-48.
Demonstrates "how the misuse of Greek myths in [*The Flies*] is a direct consequence of the loss of the inherently religious and political context of a classical drama transposed on the modern stage."

Dickinson, Hugh. "Jean-Paul Sartre: Myth and Anti-Myth." In *Myth on the Modern Stage,* pp. 219-47. Urbana University of Illinois Press, 1969.
States that "*The Flies* exemplifies [Sartre's] method: myth is made to contradict, and thus to subvert, itself."

Hamburger, Käte. "Orestes." In *From Sophocles to Sartre: Figures from Greek Tragedy, Classical and Modern,* pp. 22-44. Translated by Helen Sebba. New York: Frederick Ungar, 1969.
Claims that *The Flies* "is in deliberate opposition to the traditional view of the Orestes problem."

Royle, Peter. "The Ontological Significance of *Les Mouches.*" *French Studies: A Quarterly Review* XXVI, No. 1 (January 1972): 42-53.
Contests Philip Thody's conclusion that *The Flies* is "an example of literature taking sides" and not "an expression of moral and philosophical ideas in a convincing dramatic form."

NO EXIT

Cohn, Ruby. "Exits from *No Exit.*" In *The Play and Its Critic: Essays for Eric Bentley,* edited by Michael Bertin, pp. 189-98. Lanham, Md.: University Press of America, 1986.
Anecdotal account of the writing and the early French productions of *No Exit.*

Goldthorpe, Rhiannon. "*Huis clos:* An Ambiguous Thesis Play Reconsidered." *French Studies: A Quarterly Review* XXXIV, No. 1 (January 1980): 45-59.
Demonstrates that "Sartre's thesis ["Hell is other people"] and the modes of behavior to which it refers are, far from being universal, highly specific and remediable."

Sakharoff, Micheline. "The Polyvalence of the Theatrical Language in *No Exit.*" *Modern Drama* XVI, No. 2 (September 1973): 199-205.
Suggests that "far from being a 'message' neatly wrapped in clear concepts to be quickly administered to the spectators, *No Exit* . . . presents itself as a vast and complex poem."

THE RESPECTFUL PROSTITUTE

Cristophe, Marc A. "Sex, Racism, and Philosophy in Jean-Paul Sartre's *The Respectful Prostitute.*" *CLA Journal* XXIV, No. 1 (September 1980): 76-86.

Explores the Freudian connotations of *The Respectful Prostitute.*

THE CONDEMNED OF ALTONA

Galler, Dieter. "Stereotyped Characters in Sartre's Play, *Les séquestrés d'Altona.*" *Kentucky Romance Quarterly* XV, No. 1 (First Quarter 1968): 57-68.

Examines psychological components of *The Condemned of Altona.*

Palmer, Jeremy N. J. "*Les séquestrés d'Altona:* Sartre's Black Tragedy." *French Studies: A Quarterly Review* XXIV, No. 2 (April 1970): 150-62.

Argues that *The Condemned of Altona* differs from Sartre's earlier plays because "the characters are all perfectly aware that they are in bad faith, and they consciously choose to remain so."

Pucciani, Oreste F. "*Les séquestrés d'Altona* of Jean-Paul Sartre." *The Tulane Drama Review* 5, No. 3 (March 1961): 19-33.

Asserts that "the essential meaning of [*The Condemned of Altona*] is to be found in a critical dialectic which Sartre sets up between the audience and himself."

Williams, John S. "Sartre's Dialectic of History: *Les séquestrés d'Altona.*" *Renascence* XXII, No. 2 (Winter 1970): 59-68; 112.

Assesses the function of dialectical thought in *The Condemned of Altona.*

Additional coverage of Sartre's life and career is contained in the following sources published by Gale Research: *Contemporary Authors,* Vols. 97-100; *Contemporary Authors* (first revision), Vols. 9-12; *Contemporary Authors New Revision Series,* Vol. 21; *Contemporary Literary Criticism,* Vols. 1, 4, 7, 9, 13, 18, 24, 44, 50, 52; *Dictionary of Literary Biography,* Vol. 72, *World Literature Criticism 1500 to the Present,* Vol. 5.

Ntozake Shange

1948-

INTRODUCTION

Born Paulette Williams.

Best known for her choreopoem *For Colored Girls Who Have Considered Suicide / When the Rainbow Is Enuf,* Shange blends music, dance, and poetry to create innovative theater pieces which give voice to the experiences of women, particularly African-American women, in late twentieth-century America. Critic Elizabeth Brown has suggested that Shange speaks to "women of every race who perceive themselves as disinherited and dispossessed"; she addresses issues of self-awareness and self-realization, documenting her characters' hardships as well as celebrating their will to survive.

Shange was born in New Jersey to Eloise Williams, a psychiatric social worker, and Paul T. Williams, a surgeon. She spent several years of her childhood in St. Louis, then a segregated city, where she first faced blatant personal and institutional racism. Her home life served as a haven, providing her with intellectual and cultural stimulation: she was encouraged to read actively and met such guests to the family home as W. E. B. Du Bois, Dizzy Gillespie, Miles Davis, and Josephine Baker. In 1966 Shange enrolled in Barnard College, where she earned a bachelor's degree in American Studies. On this period of her life, she has commented: "I was a good all-American girl [at] a good all-American school, studied hard, kept my virginity, and married a lawyer." When she and her husband separated shortly after they were married, Shange attempted suicide, the first of several attempts over the next few years. While studying for her master's degree at the University of Southern California, Shange decided to take an African name. She has explained: "I had a violent resentment of carrying a slave name; poems and music come from the pit of myself, and the pit of myself isn't a slave." Ntozake means "she who comes with her own things," and Shange signifies one "who walks like a lion."

After earning her degree, Shange taught courses in the Humanities, Women's Studies, and African-American Studies at several California colleges, while also writing poetry and dancing in a number of women's dance companies. Her extensive collaborations with choreographer and dancer Paula Moss culminated in *For Colored Girls,* the theater piece which established Shange as a major force in contemporary literature and as an exponent of the feminist and African-American communities. As initially performed in 1975, *For Colored Girls* included a cast of two: Shange and Moss. One performance at a New York jazz loft was attended by director Oz Scott, who developed its staging and expanded the cast from two to seven. Eventually the show was seen by Woodie King, Jr., a successful producer who moved *For Colored Girls* to the New Federal Theatre. After running there for nearly one year, the show was brought by Joseph Papp to an Off-Broadway theater and subsequently opened on Broadway in September 1976, where it garnered primarily favorable reviews and won several awards, including the 1977 Obie and the Outer Critics Circle Award. Following its two-year run on Broadway, *For Colored Girls* continued to be produced throughout the United States and internationally.

Based on Judy Grahn's poetry collection titled *The Work of a Common Woman,* the poems that constitute *For Colored Girls* depict the lives of seven nameless black women: the characters are known only by the color of the rainbow that each represents—for example, The Lady in Green, or The Lady in Orange. The play's performance involves recitations of poetry accompanied by dances and songs, resulting in a richly textured portrait of the lives not just of the seven characters, but of women everywhere. The title of the work implies a specific audience, but critics have consistently noted the universality of Shange's message; it speaks of elemental suffering stemming from illness, anxiety, rejection, and oppression, balancing pain with a jubilant celebration of human potential. Commentators have praised Shange for choosing a flexible format that allows her to introduce a variety of personalities and to incorporate such themes as various female coming-of-age rituals, black feminist politics, racial oppression, relations among black women, and relations between black women and black men. Critics also note, however, that in *For Colored Girls* Shange attained variety at the expense of depth; they contend that she has failed to explore her themes individually and in relation to each other, and that she has neglected to show character development. Shange has also been attacked for what some scholars perceive as a one-sided and distorted portrayal of African-American men. T. E. Kalem has written that "if they can see themselves through Shange's eyes, black men are going to wince. They are portrayed as brutal con men and amorous double-dealers." Erskine Peters, while acknowledging that a crisis does exist in relations between black men and women, asserts that Shange presents only one image of black men—a negative one—without providing an image "from the other end of the spectrum." Even the play's detractors, though, commend Shange for her literary and technical skill, praising her lyricism, juxtaposition of sarcasm and sincerity, and ability to express meaning through form. Many commend her innovative use of theater and alternative orthography (lower-case lettering and phonetic spelling) as challenges to what she views as oppressive qualities of European artistic culture and the English language. Above all, critics praise Shange for providing African-American women with a recognizable and realistic depiction of themselves in *For Colored Girls.* Jessica Harris, recalling a performance, stated that, "when the curtain came down, Black women in the audience wept openly, for onstage they had finally seen an image of themselves that showed not just the strength or the anger but also some of the vulnerability and pain."

Although none has achieved the status of *For Colored Girls,* Shange's subsequent work for the theater, particularly *Spell #7,* has attracted considerable critical attention. *Spell #7,* the best-known drama in Shange's collection *Three Pieces,* received mixed reviews during its New York run which began in 1979. Like *For Colored Girls, Spell #7* reflects Shange's nontraditional approach to drama. The work consists of a series of vignettes communicated through poetry, dance, and music by a group of nine friends, all of whom are struggling black artists. The men and women gather in an after-hours bar to discuss their frustration with the dearth of quality roles for African-American performers, and to explore their identities. Although this play exhibits more plot and character development than *For Colored Girls,* critics suggest that Shange, in her attempt to provide a multitude of viewpoints and issues, has still treated individual themes superficially. The other dramas in *Three Pieces* are *A Photograph: Lovers in Motion* (originally produced as *A Photograph: A Still Life with Shadows / A Photograph: A Study of Cruelty*), which depicts three women vying for the love of a fledgling photographer, and *Boogie Woogie Landscapes,* which explores women's issues through the surreal depiction of the central character's experiences. Shange also adapted Bertolt Brecht's drama, *Mother Courage and Her Children,* for which she won an Obie award in 1981. In addition, she has published three novels, several volumes of poetry, and a collection of essays.

Critical assessments of Shange's plays to date generally include praise for her passionate poetry, considerable technical skill, and unceasing challenges to traditional poetic and dramatic forms. Commentators acknowledge that, in spite of flaws and rough edges in her dramas, Shange has consistently produced powerful, moving works that reflect the energy, creativity, and intelligence that she brings to her craft. In a discussion of the social obligation of writers, particularly African-American writers, Shange has said: "we can use with some skill virtually all our physical senses / as writers committed to bringing the world as we remember it / imagine it / & know it to be to the stage / we must use everything we've got."

PRINCIPAL WORKS

PLAYS

For Colored Girls Who Have Considered Suicide / When the Rainbow Is Enuf: A Choreopoem 1975
A Photograph: A Still Life with Shadows / A Photograph: A Study of Cruelty 1977; revised as *A Photograph: Lovers in Motion,* 1979
Where the Mississippi Meets the Amazon [with Thulani Nkabinda and Jessica Hagedorn] 1977
From Okra to Greens: A Different Kinda Love Story 1978
Black & White Two-Dimensional Planes 1979
Boogie Woogie Landscapes 1979
Spell #7 1979
Mother Courage & Her Children [adaptor; from the play *Mother Courage and Her Children* by Bertolt Brecht] 1980
**Three Pieces* 1981
Three Views of Mount Fuji 1987

OTHER MAJOR WORKS

For Colored Girls Who Have Considered Suicide / When the Rainbow is Enuf (poetry) 1976
Natural Disasters, and Other Festive Occasions (poetry and prose) 1977
Sassafrass: A Novella (novella) 1977
Nappy Edges (poetry) 1978
Some Men (poetry) 1981
Sassafrass, Cypress & Indigo (novel) 1982
A Daughter's Geography (poetry) 1983
From Okra to Greens: Poems (poetry) 1984
See No Evil: Prefaces, Essays & Accounts, 1976-1983 (essays) 1984
Betsey Brown: A Novel (novel) 1985
Ridin' the Moon in Texas: Word Paintings (poetry) 1987

*This collection includes *Spell #7, A Photograph: Lovers in Motion,* and *Boogie Woogie Landscapes.* The date reflects the year of publication, not performance.

AUTHOR COMMENTARY

An Interview with Ntozake Shange (1979)

[In the following interview, culled from several conversations with Henry Blackwell, Shange expresses her political and artistic philosophy as well as her vision of herself as a black woman and as a poet.]

[*Blackwell*]: *You have indicated that you feel that Black writers from the East, West, South, and the Midwest represent separate groups, each with its own voice and perhaps a different aesthetic. Would you elaborate on that?*

[Shange]: Sure. My craft was seriously nurtured in California and that probably has some influence on what my writing looks like. There's not a California style, but there are certain feelings and a certain freeness that set those writers off from those in the Chicago-St. Louis-Detroit tripod group. They're not the same. In the West we're terribly free to do whatever we want. We're free to associate with Asians and Latins at will, aesthetically as well as politically. And this is reflected in the kinds of things we do, so that the chauvinism that you might find that's exclusionary, in that triangle, you don't find too much in California. And if you do find it, it's in young poets who're just starting. Black, Asian, or Latin, they're only very nationalistic until they realize that all Third World people are working toward the same thing, which for us is the explication of our reality. I sometimes get the feeling that the writers in Chicago are at war, and that they are defending our reality. In San Francisco, that defensive stance isn't necessary, because the racism in California is so peculiar, they don't really attack us *immediately,* so we're able to do the particularly important job of simply exploring what our lives have been in the Western hemisphere, and making the exploration, not the defense, be the work of the poems. My kids and the people around me should know exactly who we are. And when someone speaks of Third World people's reality, there'll be no mistake about what that reality is. The poetry of the Black writer on the West Coast clarifies—migrations, our relationship to the soil, to ourselves in space. There is an enormous amount of space in the West, and you do not feel personally impinged upon every time you come out of your door, like you do in New York and in Chicago. So, there's a different attitude about being alive. I'm really glad that David Henderson and Ishmael [Reed] live there. I used to live there. It gave us a chance to breathe, to get away from the immediacy of oppression in the East and those particular political events, which all of us experienced, and which we sometimes deal with as a corrective group in our poetry. Black writers on the West Coast got out from under the heavy pressure of those events, but that doesn't mean that we forgot them. It just means that we could deal with them from another angle. The Midwest people: If you see a poem you know where it came from, if it came from Chicago. Their sense of rhythm is almost limited to whatever it is that came up off the Delta. They seldom stray from particular rhythm sequences that I would associate with the blues and with inner-city urban life. This is all right, but it can become a trap. I think there is a tendency to assume that all Black people know that particular rhythm sequence, that all Black people migrated up the Mississippi River, and that is not true. They talk about the cities, about gangs, welfare—as opposed to opening it up and talking about Black folks in other places. There ain't no poems about nobody in the country in Indiana. Nobody knows what kind of life they live, because they are not a part of our scheme of what Black life is supposed to look like. And that means we're leaving out portions of our population in order to formulate some ideology of what we are. This monolithic idea that everybody's the same, that we all live the same lives. That the Black family, the Black man, the Black female are the same thing. A one image. A one something. It's not true, but it's very difficult to break through some of that. We ignore Black Catholics. They don't exist in literature. Maybe in the Renaissance a couple of people admitted to being Catholic, but everybody nowadays has become somebody who was nurtured in the Baptist Church. I don't know why we're trying to become some solid unit of something. Part of our beauty is the fact that we're so much.

And New York?

I don't think poets in New York have ever gotten over. Whereas in California readings are a source of joy, readings in New York are almost scenario, because the impact of theatre, dance, and other art forms (and the fact that you need money to produce anything) has made the playwright, the novelist, and the musician the carriers of good news, as opposed to the poet. New York poets almost *have* to be miserable and unhappy to get over. Some are brilliant, absolutely brilliant. Some others are labeled poets, but I don't count them, I don't deal with them that way.

Why not?

Because I don't think they know what they are doing.

What makes a poet from your point of view?

A very conscious effort to be concise and powerful and as illusory as possible, so that the language can, in fact, bring you to more conclusions than the one in the poem, but that that one conclusion can't be avoided, even though there are thousands of others roaming around. And there should be wit and grace and a movement from one image to another, so that there's no narrowness to the body of your work. That to me would suggest someone is a poet.

You seem to have very definite ideas about what it takes to be a poet. Does that definiteness reflect your academic training?

No. Poetry is my life. And actually, when I went to graduate school, and was studying Afro-American art, I was made to feel like a traitor, because there's a huge strain of anti-intellectualism not only in the new Black Arts movement, but in Black America in general. People think that you aren't doing anything: Studying don't mean nothing. I felt very bad, but I was determined that those people were going to hear from me. Just because I had studied didn't mean that I had lost my voice. The anger about my situation as a student propelled me to make doubly sure that I fulfilled *all* my obligations. I always went to my readings, even if I had a test the next day. Or, if I had to teach the morning after a reading, I *did* it. I have always appreciated my academic background, though not just for the usual reasons that you would expect. I went to Women's Studies, because in Women's Studies, I was at least able to discuss the anger and the awkwardness. I wasn't stifled or shut back.

I can see from your experience why you would see not just richness but truth in our diversity. Do you think that Southern Black writers are shaped in distinctive ways by their experience in the South?

Yes. My sister and I were raised in the Midwest and the North, and we'd go to a lot of poetry readings together. At one reading, there were a lot of women who had formerly been raised in the South. And we were getting very upset by what, in our ignorance, we saw as their romanticization of Southern living. Instead of a streetcar, there would be hills and swamps and a porch and grandma and quilts and iron pots and Mr. So-and-So from down by the church. And I was saying to myself, if it was as wonderful as all that, why in the hell did you all come up here? It was really getting ridiculous. But I thought a little more, and I said, wait. If it's that severe a sense of loss, then perhaps they're not talking about what we are talking about. To children of migrations, leaving the South may have engendered a stunning sense of loss, and that's something that should be respected and dealt with in its own right.

So, were they merely romanticizing, or driving to the heart of a personal reality that you felt cut off from?

I think they were explaining. After a while, I wasn't paying attention to the romantic images. I was trying to deal with the motivation for those images, and I was wondering, why are they telling me this? Why is this supposed to be important to me? And I decided that it was because they wanted us to know what they thought they had lost. And what they thought they lost is, in fact, as important as what really did go away, because that vacuum has first to be identified and then filled with something. And those acts of identification and repair are going to be, or should be, increasingly personal. But mostly now you get just one picture. A lot of times, Black poets are expected to reflect immediate political need, or current political fashion. I think that tendency is behind the fact that you can't talk anymore about the South as a bad thing. It's like Heaven; you don't criticize it. Just as for a while, it was a terrifying and scary thing to write a poem which was not politically relevant, about yourself when you were a child. Nor could you speak critically of your mother and father; they worked so hard as Black people. So for a long time we didn't have strong poems dealing with *actual* Black family life; you couldn't do it. But, well, we've been here for as long as however we've been here—each of us, separately. And that is something that we're beginning to explore as we try to understand ourselves as mature adults. And some women are sort of easing away to address the real bludgeoning effects that any family has. Cover-ups, romantic or otherwise, are not endemic to us, but that doesn't matter. O.K., so I'm not from the South. I missed that big jolt that was a big thing in the fourth generation migratory Black person, who's been up North since 1917, or something, so I don't know nothing about that fund of experiences, and I just have to be quiet. So, I'm saying, all right, I'll be quiet, but I would at least like to know why those women glorified their losses. Usually, when people make something important, it's because it's not working. It's something that has to be dealt with. And they start addressing it however they can. I think critical explorations are beginning to happen, and in the next five years there will be some really marvelous work, like Black *Nashvilles,* like Black Black-fiction shows, and Black stories about the reality of our lives in the South, as opposed to our dream dimensions of that. It's too crazy now. Everybody had a grandma who was wonderful, or an uncle who came by and did the family errands. Cotton was nice to be picked. That is crazy to me, because it's the same thing that my grandma said she was tired of and the reason that she left. My experience poses not a simple difference but a contradiction to such depictions.

Granting that differences are important to understanding our identity, are there similarities which it is crucial to examine? Are Black women writers, for example, connected by a common set of problems?

I worked exclusively with Black women in college, but since that time I've been working most in a Third World context, in terms of women, at any rate. I moved from New York in 1970 and went to California because at that time there was no space for an independent woman's voice; women were expected to be quiet and have babies, no matter what kind of training they had had. Where I came from, women existed for the pleasure and support of men. I began to wonder, What are we doing? What are we supposed to do when our men are gone? I started writing because I had to have an answer, I had to hear a voice. I absolutely had to hear something. And nobody was going to give it to me. So, I gave it to myself.

I left New York because I could not fight with them. In fact, I thought what they were doing was right. But I just could not live inside those roles. Those same male-oriented roles and expectations were imposed in our literature. As a young woman, I was starving for Black literature. I didn't care what they said, just so the writers gave me something. For years, I was able to tolerate being chastised and denigrated in American literature and any other kind of literature because that is where we were, and that's how women were regarded. But as my consciousness as a woman developed, I said, hey, you all are doing the same thing to women that you say Faulkner did to *you.* What the hell is going on? But even then I didn't take it as a personal affront, because that's how all of us were trained. I do now, though. I mean, after ten years of women saying, hey, we're people, we think, we feel—I don't expect the same kinds of attitudes. You can't blame somebody because salt wasn't refined when it wasn't refined. Now we know how to refine it, so let's do it.

Do you think this habit of diminishment and neglect in and out of literature has forced Black women to look at life in a special way, has forced them to devise a special aesthetic?

To an extent. The same rhetoric that is used to establish the Black Aesthetic, we must use to establish a women's aesthetic, which is to say that those parts of reality that are ours, those things about our bodies, the cycles of our lives that have been ignored for centuries in all castes and classes of our people, are to be dealt with now. When women reach puberty, they menstruate. What does that mean? Women have relationships with their mothers that are incredibly full of pain and love. A mother functions as part of a husband, not as another woman for the child. Women have relationships to the world that have to do with whether you can *reach* things. Can you put a pan away? Can you lift stuff? Are you afraid of a corner at night—and other things that men do not deal with? And our poetry deals with that, and we use images that have to do with that. Some men have weird notions about women. The title of a manuscript that I have, "Dreams as Real as Menses," means to most women that their dreams are going to come true. Most men hearing that title either stumble over the word "menses" or go "ugh" because they can't see or accept that reality. So it's the same as the Black *man*'s struggle, in terms of liberating our reality from the pits, from Hades, and making things we see everyday tangible and speakable. One has to speak about things inherently female. And that is my persona. A woman. And she is going to talk the way she understands. Why must I use metaphors because men understand them? That's the same argument I have with Paul Laurence Dunbar. He knew that he could not be respected as a poet unless he wrote all those sonnets with the English corrected, and they are just awful. This is analogous to what women have been doing all along. Using male-identified symbols and myths to talk about ourselves. That's ridiculous. There are enough females in the world to be joyful, to be knowledgeable, to be loved. We don't have to go across the line. And if men don't understand it, then I would suggest, as I suggest to white students who say they don't understand Black literature, that they should get more serious about the subject. Learn something about women. I'm not going to change what I write to help a man understand it. They've been here as long as I've been here. They rule the damned world, they rule the household, if not the world, and they can certainly learn who their mother was, and who they sleep with at night.

Does your position create friction with Black male writers?

Most of the Black men whose writing I respect, respect mine. And I have very good working relationships with them. I don't have good working relationships with some so-called critics and socio-political poets. They don't want idiom; they want ideology, and they can have it. They're seeing Black poetry as some kind of mammoth creature with four legs and a nose. And my leg is going over there, or over here. It destroys their idea. They don't want to deal with poetry, they want to talk politics. They want to make me run for office. Well, I'm not going to do that. Pablo Neruda did run for office, but he was a poet in the government. My politics, I think, are very correct. I do not have heroes who are not heroes.

Who are some of your heroes?

Toussaint L'Ouverture. Denmark Vesey. Sojourner Truth. Nat Love. Albert Ayler. Jelly Roll Morton. Bessie Smith. Zora Neale Hurston. . . .

That's an interesting list. What makes them heroes? Politicians. . . .

Politicians don't turn me on. When someone takes charge of your reality and does something to it that is satisfying for them, changing everything that comes after in some way or other, then that is, to me, being a successful and competent human being and a successful and competent Black person. When you take something you believe in and make it affect other people, you're doing a politically significant act. These people did things that changed the way all the rest of us were treated or thought of in the world. I think you have to stop looking to something called "the politician." They're there. That's their job, but it can't just be on them. What are we, sheep? We don't have no feet? No brains? We can't do anything ourselves?

Are you stressing self-reliance, or. . . .

The most important thing I know is that anything you want to do, especially pertaining to your work, you can do yourself. You don't have to wait on nobody. You don't have to wait on the Black world; you don't have to wait on Ishmael; you don't have to wait on Percy Sutton. If you want to do a show, you go to your little local bar, and tell them that on—whatever their night off is—you want to use their space. And you go and use it to the best of your ability, and get paid $1.37, but get known in your community. Send out your own little press releases. Meet a printer. Have a printer do up just one page of your poems. Give them away, mail them to your friends. Give him fifty dollars and have him do a ten-page booklet. You don't have to wait. Learn how to print your goddamn self. This sense that we have to follow all the patterns established by the country and by our own habit is really quite unnecessary. And if we are, in fact, closer to developing a new way of thinking and new skills, we have no choice but to do for ourselves. Which is not to go back to Booker T., but to take him to the ultimate point of what he said in the first place. You can do what you have to, what you must. You don't have to be recognized by whites. Just go and do it. There's the anecdote: "They don't need to know we can build the Empire State Building, they just need to know we can clean floors?" I don't even care what they know. All I need to know is that Black people are not going to sit around waiting for the powers that be in the white community or in our community to take care of us.

Did you have a Black audience in mind when you wrote **colored girls?**

It was meant for a women's audience, initially. In most of my work, I'm talking to women, because I'm talking to myself when I write. As for specifically Black audiences, I don't think like that. I write poems, and I take them where I think they'll work. I don't bar much. If I tried to stop a poem, because I don't have an audience for it, I'd be a fool. Poetry is like the only privacy in some areas that I have, so I can't jam it up because Black people might not like it. I write the poem because it's there, and I take it where I can take it. Maybe I can't take it anywhere, maybe I just have to leave it in the house. Some of them I do that

A scene from Shange's award-winning For Colored Girls, *with the playwright standing front and center.*

with. But I have a right to think and feel what I want, and I can't stop feeling what I feel. Writing with me is a visceral thing. I have to get certain ideas out, or I will get sick, I will cry, I will become catatonic. I don't have a choice.

You've spoken on other occasions about influences. Who among contemporary Black writers has had the most influence on what and how you write?

Ishmael. *Yellow Back Radio Broke-Down, Mumbo Jumbo,* "I Am A Cowboy in the Boat of Ra"—these have been terribly significant to me, because they said, look, you have the whole world to deal with. You do not have to deal with the block in New York City where there are no trees. And there's Baraka. Everything. All the essays. Everything. He's fabulous. I read the stuff out loud. The stories in *Tales,* in *Dante's Hell,* are just some of the most beautiful uses of language and imagery I've seen anywhere at all.

Looking back at your work from **sassafrass** *through* **nappy edges** *are you aware of any changes in the way you see the world or in the way that you express what you see and feel? Are you more concerned with technique? With broadening the scope of your vision? With exhausting your material?*

Only the *way* I have to proceed has changed. As a recognized writer I face problems I never dreamed of as an unknown: expectations. I find that in order to work at all now I must virtually obliterate the outside world. I have to construct what I call a "creative myopia" because the wolves are at the door. People say, "How could *you* say *that*?" or "So many people pay attention to *your* ideas, *you are responsible* for. . . . " All that sort of thing is burdensome and interrupts my relationship with myself. More and more I understand why Midwestern writers feel they are under siege. In certain parts of the country, the density of population and poverty surely exacerbate racism. This year the critics had a field day discussing whether or not Black and Latin actors *could* do Shakespeare! In such a world, one admittedly has to flex muscle not just lyricism. I have to do battle with myself to even present the fragile composites of a life—Black and fictional—before such barbarians. I sometimes doubt that I'd have been able to write ***sassafrass*** had I been aware of this situation. She's too precious to me to endure the wear and tear of this place (the Eastern literary establishment, Black and white). I am more concerned with craft at this point. To protect my characters and landscapes from unwarranted attacks, I make them taut and as lean as I can. Some whimsy is lost but I doubt anyone in the midst of an urban winter would miss it. There's little possibility of my exhausting my material. I'm still alive and feeling and seeing. I've started drawing and dancing again to make sure that I don't lose touch with the roots of my poetic vision. These roots have so much to do with actuality and yet so very little. But that begins another story. (pp. 134-38)

Ntozake Shange and Henry Blackwell, in an interview in Black American Literature Forum, *Vol. 13, No. 4, Winter, 1979, pp. 134-38.*

OVERVIEWS AND GENERAL STUDIES

Deborah R. Geis (essay date 1989)

[*In the essay below, Geis discusses the poetic nature of Shange's dramas. She examines the playwright's extensive use of monologue as a means of emphasizing the importance of storytelling to her works, suggesting that this "emphasis is crucial to Shange's articulation of a black feminist aesthetic."*]

Ntozake Shange's works defy generic classifications: just as her poems (published in ***Nappy Edges*** and ***A Daughter's Geography***) are also performance pieces, her works for the theater defy the boundaries of drama and merge into the region of poetry. Her most famous work, ***for colored girls who have considered suicide / when the rainbow is enuf,*** is subtitled "a choreopoem." Similarly, she has written ***Betsey Brown*** as a novel and then again (with Emily Mann) in play form, and her first work of fiction, ***Sassafrass, Cypress & Indigo,*** is as free with its narrative modes—including recipes, spells, letters—as Joyce was in *Ulysses.* Perhaps more so than any other practicing playwright, Shange has created a poetic voice that is uniquely her own—a voice which is deeply rooted in her experience of being female and black, but also one which, again, refuses and transcends categorization. Her works articulate the connection between the doubly "marginalized" social position of the black woman and the need to invent and appropriate a language with which to articulate a self.

In their revelation of such a language, Shange's theatrical narratives move subtly and forcefully between the comic and the tragic. A brief passage from ***for colored girls*** underscores the precarious path between laughter and pain which Shange's characters discover they are forced to tread:

> distraught laughter fallin
> over a black girl's shoulder
> it's funny / it's hysterical
> the melody-less-ness of her dance
> don't tell nobody, don't tell a soul
> she's dancin on beer cans & shingles

The images associated with the word *hysterical* in this passage show the multilayered and interdependent qualities of the "black girl's" experience: *hysterical* connotes a laughter which has gone out of control, a madness historically—if not accurately—connected with femaleness. Moreover, the admonition "don't tell nobody, don't tell a soul" suggests the call to silence, the fear that to speak of her pain will be to violate a law of submission. The onlooker will aestheticize the dance or call attention to its comic qualities rather than realize the extent to which the dance and the laughter are a reaction against—and are even motivated by—the uncovering of pain.

The key here is the complexity, for Shange, of the performative experience. In her plays, especially ***for colored girls*** and ***spell #7,*** Shange develops her narration primarily through monologues because monologic speech inevitably places the narrative weight of a play upon its spoken language and upon the performances of the individual actors. But she does not use this device to develop "character" in the same fashion as Maria Irene Fornes and other Method-inspired playwrights who turn toward monologic language in order more expressively to define and "embody" their characters both as women and as individuals. Rather, Shange draws upon the uniquely "performative" qualities of monologue to allow her actors to take on *multiple* roles and therefore to emphasize the centrality of *storytelling* to her work. This emphasis is crucial to Shange's articulation of a black feminist aesthetic (and to the call to humanity to accept that "black women are inherently valuable") on two counts. First, the incorporation of role-playing reflects the ways that blacks (as "minstrels," "servants," "athletes," etc.) and women (as "maids," "whores," "mothers," etc.) are expected to fulfill such roles on a constant basis in Western society. Second, the space between our enjoyment of the "spectacle" of Shange's theater pieces (through the recitation of the monologues and through the dancing and singing which often accompany them), and our awareness of the urgency of her call for blacks / women to be allowed "selves" free of stereotypes, serves as a "rupturing" of the performance moment; it is the uncomfortableness of that space, that rupture, which moves and disturbs us.

In **"takin a solo / a poetic possibility / a poetic imperative,"** the opening poem of ***nappy edges,*** Shange argues that just as the great jazz musicians each have a recognizable sound and musical style, so too should the public develop a sensitivity to the rhythms and nuances of black writers and that the writers themselves should cultivate "sounds" which distinguish them as individuals. She writes:

> as we demand to be heard / we want you to hear us. we come to you the way leroi jenkins comes or cecil talyor / or b. b. king. we come to you alone / in the theater / in the story / & the poem. like with billie holiday or betty carter / we shd give you a moment that cannot be recreated / a specificity that cannot be confused. our language shd let you know who's talking, what we're talkin abt & how we cant stop sayin this to you. some urgency accompanies the text. something important is going on. we are speakin. reachin for yr person / we cannot hold it / we dont wanna sell it / we give you ourselves / if you listen.

Although Shange's remarks were intended to address the larger issue of Afro-American writing, her words hold true for the speakers of monologue in her plays as well, for the monologue is another way of "takin a solo." For Shange's actors / characters (it is sometimes difficult to draw the distinction between the two, as the actors frequently portray actors who in turn portray multiple characters), monologues issue forth with the same sense that "some urgency accompanies the text" and that, in delivering the speeches, they are "reachin for yr person." In this respect the characters seem to aspire toward a specificity which would make them stand as if independent of their author. But the hallmark of the very "imperative" which Shange has announced in the first place is the unmistakable sense that all of the speakers' voices are ultimately parts of one voice: that of Shange, their creator and the play's primary monologist or storyteller.

All of Shange's theatrical pieces, even ***a photograph: lovers in motion*** and ***boogie woogie landscapes,*** unfold before the audience as collections of stories rather than as traditionally linear narratives; the events are generated less from actual interactions as they unfold in the "present" of the play (except perhaps in ***a photograph***) than from the internal storytellers' *recreations* of individual dramas. The implied privilege of the storyteller to create alternate worlds, as well as the fluidity of the stories themselves and the characters in them, relies heavily upon the immense power that African and Afro-American tradition have assigned to the spoken word. According to James Hatch [in *The Theater of Black Americans,* Vol. 1, 1980], Africans traditionally believe that "words and the art of using them are a special power that can summon and control spirit." Furthermore, as Geneviève Fabre explains in *Drumbeats Masks and Metaphor:*

> The oral tradition holds a prominent place in Afro-American culture. For slaves (who were often forbidden to learn to write) it was the safest means of communication. It provided basic contact with Africa as a homeland and a source of folklore, a contract also between ethnic groups unified under a common symbolic heritage, between generations, and finally, between the speaker and his audience. . . . Because the oral tradition has long remained a living practice in Afro-American culture, the dramatic artist has been tempted to emulate not only the art and techniques of the storyteller, but also his prestigious social function—that of recording and reformulating experience, of shaping and transmitting values, opinions, and attitudes, and of expressing a certain collective wisdom.

Shange takes the notion of exchange and collectivity among storytellers even further in her use of the space in which her pieces are performed. Monologue creates "narrative space"; Shange depends upon the power and magic of the stories within her plays to create the scenes without the use of backdrops and other "theatrical" effects. ***for colored girls*** is the most "open" of the plays in this sense, as it calls for no stage set, only lights of different colors and specific places for the characters to enter and exit. ***boogie woogie landscapes*** conjures up the mental images of the title within the confines of Layla's bedroom: "there is what furniture a bedroom might accommodate, though not too much of it. the most important thing is that a bedroom is suggested." Although the sets of both ***spell #7*** and ***a photograph*** are fairly specific (a huge minstrel mask as a backdrop and, later, a bar in lower Manhattan for the former; a photographer's apartment for the latter), they still call for this space to be reborn in different imaginary ways as the characters come forth and tell their stories.

for colored girls, Shange's first major theater piece, evolved from a series of poems modeled on Judy Grahn's *Common Woman.* The play received its first performances in coffeehouses in San Francisco and on the Lower East Side of Manhattan; eventually, it attracted critical and public attention and moved to the New Federal Theater, the Public Theater, and then to Broadway in 1976. ***for colored girls*** draws its power from the performances—in voice, dance, and song—of its actors, as well as from the ways it articulates a realm of experience which heretofore had been suppressed in the theater; the "lady in brown" speaks to the release of this suppression when she says near the beginning of the piece:

> sing a black girl's song
> bring her out
> to know her self
> . . . she's been dead so long
> closed in silence so long
> she doesn't know the sound
> of her own voice
> her infinite beauty

The instruments for releasing and expressing the "infinite beauty" of the "black girl's song" become the characters, who do not have names and specific identities of their own (except through their physical presences), but rather take on multiple identities and characters as the "lady in brown," "lady in red," "lady in yellow," etc. These "ladies" put on the metaphorical masks of various characters in order to enact the "ceremony" of the play, which gathers them together in a stylized, ritualistic fashion. The ritual is a religious one to the extent that the participants turn to the "spirit" which might be best described as the black female collective unconscious; it is a celebratory one in that their immersion in it is ultimately a source of joy and strength. In this sense the ritual is a festival that depends as much upon the bonds of the group as it does upon individual expression; Fabre makes this connection explicit when she says that "the group . . . takes possession of space and enlarges it to express communion."

As the characters assume their different "masks," we see them enact a complex series of microdramas, some joyful and others painful. So it is that the "lady in purple" narrates the tale of Sechita, who "kicked viciously thru the nite / catchin' stars tween her toes," while the lady in green "plays" Sechita and dances out the role. Both of these characters "are" Sechita, for the identity of this character within a character merges in the spoken narration and the accompanying movement. Yet it also becomes clear in the course of the play that these actors/characters are *not* simply assuming masks or roles for the sake of a dramatic production; they must enact the "dramas" and wear the "masks" of black women every day of their lives. Shange has taken on the difficult task, then, of universalizing her characters in the play without allowing them to fall into roles that are essentially stereotypes. She discusses the need for this balance between the "idiosyncratic" and the "representative" in an interview with Claudia Tate:

> I feel that as an artist my job is to appreciate the differences among my women characters. We're usually just thrown together, like "tits and ass," or a good cook, or how we can really "f—" [*sic*]. Our personalities and distinctions are lost. What I appreciate about the women whom I write about, the women whom I know, is how idiosyncratic they are. I take delight in the very peculiar or particular things that fascinate or terrify them. Also, I discovered that by putting them all together, there are some things they all are repelled by, and there are some things they are all attracted to. I only discovered this by having

> them have their special relationships to their dreams and their unconscious.

At times the storytellers within ***for colored girls*** seem to be putting on "masks" of humor which they wear, as part of the assumption of a role or character, in order to create a way of channeling the fear and anger they experience into the mode of performance. For instance, in one monologue the lady in red expresses the pain of a rejected love with a sardonic "itemization" of what she has been through:

> without any assistance or guidance from you
> i have loved you assiduously for 8 months 2 wks
> & a day
> i have been stood up four times
> i've left 7 packages on yr doorstep
> forty poems 2 plants & 3 handmade notecards
> i left
> town so i cd send to you have been no help to
> me
> on my job
> you call at 3:00 in the mornin on weekdays
> so i cd drive 27½ miles cross the bay before i go
> to work
> charmin charmin
> but you are of no assistance

The disruptive power of this and other "comic" narratives in the play comes from the realization that what we are laughing at, though merely amusing and exaggerated on the surface, has an underside of bitterness and even torment. Often the shift from humor to pathos is so sudden that the effect is as if we have been slapped, which is precisely the way Shange describes the transition to the story on "latent rapist bravado" ("we cd even have em over for dinner / & get raped in our own houses / by invitation / a friend." Helene Keyssar points out in *The Curtain and the Veil* that the spectator is likely to overlook the pain in favor of the humor in the play's earliest vignettes, but as the work moves into such searing narratives as the lady in blue's story of an abortion, we begin to feel increasingly uncomfortable with our own laughter. The candor of the speakers combined with the persistent irony, says Keyssar, "prevents the display of emotion from becoming melodramatic and allows the spectators a vulnerability to their own feelings that can renew their ability to act with others in the world outside the theater." But there is also another way to view this generation of "vulnerability": as a result of the disjunction between the guise of humor and the realization that such moments in the play are actually imbued with pain and anger, the spectator experiences the feeling of having entered an uncomfortable "space" between the two strategies of performance. Like Brecht, Shange seems to believe that inhabiting such a "space" causes the audience to question its own values and beliefs; unlike Brecht, though, she engages the emotions directly in this process. She says in her interview with Tate, "I write to get at the part of people's emotional lives that they don't have control over, the part that can and will respond."

The most emotionally difficult (and most controversial) monologue in the play in terms of this vulnerability is the "Beau Willie Brown" sequence, the only story with a male protagonist. It concerns Beau Willie, a Vietnam veteran who beats up Crystal, the mother of their two children, so many times that she gets a court order restraining him from coming near them. When Beau Willie forces his way into Crystal's apartment and insists that she marry him, she refuses, and he takes the children away from her and holds them out on the window ledge. In the devastating final moments of the story, the lady in red, who has been telling the story, suddenly shifts from referring to Crystal in the third person to using "I":

> i stood by beau in the window / with naomi reachin for me / & kwame screaming mommy mommy from the fifth story / but i cd only whisper / & he dropped em

It is as if, in this wrenching moment, the lady in red has abandoned the sense that she is "acting out" a story; she "becomes" the character she has been narrating. As she closes the space between her role as narrator and the character of Crystal, this moment of the story itself brings to an end the distancing effect created by Shange's use of spectacle up to this point: the piece is no longer an "entertainment" but a ritualized release of pure feeling which is experienced rather than "performed."

Because of the resonance of the "Beau Willie Brown" story, ***for colored girls*** seems on the brink of despair; instead, though, the intensity and raw emotion of the lady in red's / Crystal's narrative serves to bring the women together and to acknowledge the strength they derive from each other. They characterize this final affirmation in religious terms, but it is a piety derived from within rather than from an outward deity:

> a layin' on of hands
> the holiness of myself released
> . . . i found god in myself
> & i loved her / i loved her fiercely

Janet Brown justly indicates [in her *Feminist Drama,* 1979] the need for a movement toward such a resolution when she says that the "successful resolution to the search for autonomy is attributable first to the communal nature of the struggle." However, these last two sequences of the play have come under fire by some critics because they feel that Shange had ultimately failed to translate the personal into the political. Andrea Benton Rushing [in *Massachusetts Review* 22, Autumn 1981] criticizes Shange's isolation in ***for colored girls*** "from salient aspects of black literary and political history," the "shockingly ahistorical" way it seems to ignore "white responsibility for our pain," and its final "rejection of political solutions." Similarly, Erskine Peters is appalled by the apparent manipulativeness of the "Beau Willie Brown" monologue:

> This climax is the author's blatantly melodramatic attempt to turn the work into tragedy without fulfilling her obligations to explore or implicate the historical and deeper tragic circumstances. There is a very heated attempt to rush the play toward an evocation of pity, horror, and suffering. The application of such a cheap device at this critical thematic and structural point is an inhumane gesture to the Black community.
>
> [*Journal of Ethnic Studies* 6, Spring 1978]

Rushing and Peters raise a valid issue when they say that ***for colored girls*** is not a direct and forceful indictment of white supremacist politics, at least not in as immediate a sense as ***spell #7.*** But Peters' accusation that Crystal's story constitutes a "cheap device" which turns the play into a pseudotragedy seems unfounded, for such an argument ignores the declaration of community which comes at the end of the play in response to the individual pain which reached its peak in the "Beau Willie Brown" narrative. Indeed, one might argue that the placement of this story before the play's closing ritual is Shange's attempt to avoid having the spectator convert the final moments into cathartic ones—for as Augusto Boal argues so convincingly in *Theater of the Oppressed,* catharsis can have the "repressive" or "coercive" effect of lulling the spectator into complacency. Or, as Michael W. Kaufman says of the black revolutionary theater of Baraka, Reed, and others, "The very notion of catharsis, an emotional purgation of the audience's collective energies, means that theatre becomes society's buffer sponging up all the moral indignities that if translated into action could effect substantial change" [*The Theater of Black Americans,* 1980]. If the ending of the play is dissatisfying because it seems to be administering a palliative to the audience, that is precisely the point: Shange is suggesting the sources of possible strength and redemption by having the characters *perform* the play's closing "ritual." But since the "Beau Willie Brown" story has closed the gulf between narrator and narrative, this final "performance" *cannot* be only a "show." Just as the "ladies" are no longer playing "roles," the spectacle of their concluding ritual automatically conveys a sense of urgency which—coupled with the sheer emotional impact of the "Beau Willie Brown" sequence—prevents the audience from experiencing the ending as cathartic.

Kimberly Benston discusses [in *The Theater of Black Americans,* 1980] black American theater's movement away from European-American structures and toward African-rooted ones in terms of the shift from *mimesis* / drama to *methexis* / ritual. Not only, she claims, does the ritual create a sense of community, as we have discussed in ***for colored girls,*** but it also breaks down the barriers that have traditionally existed between the performers and the spectators. This is perhaps why, in the opening of Shange's ***spell #7*** (1979), there is a "huge blackface mask" visible on the stage even while the audience is still coming into the theater. Shange says that "in a way the show has already begun, for the members of the audience must integrate this grotesque, larger than life misrepresentation of life into their pre-show chatter." We might say that she thus attempts to erase distinctions between "play" and "audience": not only does the performance address the spectators, but in this case the spectators are also forced to "address" the performance. At the beginning of the play, the performers parade in minstrel masks identical to the huge one which looms overhead; they eventually shed their masks and pose instead as "actors" (or actors playing actors who, in turn, play at being actors), but the image of the minstrel mask is a sign that even modern black actors are still often conceived of as little more than minstrels. As the actor / character Bettina complains, "if that director asks me to play it any blacker / i'm gonna have to do it in a mammy dress."

Shange, then, makes the minstrel-masking into a ceremony of sorts in the opening scene of ***spell #7,*** and the resemblance of the giant minstrel face above the stage to an African voodoo mask is wholly intentional. At the same time, though, the blackface masks that the actors wear at the beginning of the play also invoke the *travesty* of a ceremony, for the masks represent the "parts" each must play (in the Western tradition) in order to get a job. Shange connects this to her feelings about her own "masking" in an interview with Tate [in *Black Women Writers*]:

> It was risky for us to do the minstrel dance in ***spell #7,*** but I insisted upon it because I thought the actors in my play were coming from pieces they didn't want to be in but pieces that helped them pay their bills. Black characters are always being closed up in a "point." They decided, for instance, that ***spell #7*** by Zaki Shange is a feminist piece and therefore not poetry. Well, that's a lie. That's giving me a minstrel mask. . . . We're not free of our paint yet! The biggest moneymakers—*The Wiz, Bubblin' Brown Sugar, Ain't Misbehavin'*—are all minstrel shows.

In the course of the play, though, the actors / characters also use "masking" in a different way; they try on various "masks" or roles, as in ***for colored girls,*** to perform the monologues and group pieces that provide both mirrors and alternatives for the various "selves" they create under pressure from a society governed by white values and images. So, for instance, one of the nameless and faceless performers behind a minstrel mask at the beginning of the play becomes the actor Natalie in the next scene, who in turn "becomes" Sue-Jean, a young woman who desperately wants a baby, as she and Alec (another of the "minstrels" revealed as actor / character) alternate in narrating her story while she mimes it out.

Unlike ***for colored girls, spell #7*** makes use of a central storyteller figure, Lou, who "directs" the monologues which are performed in the course of the play. It is appropriate that Lou is a magician, for even the title of ***spell #7*** (the subtitle of which is "geechee jibara quik magic trance manual for technologically stressed third world people") refers to magic making. In his opening speech, though, Lou warns of the power (and danger) of "colored" magic:

> my daddy retired from magic & took
> up another trade cuz this friend a mine
> from the 3rd grade / asked to be made white
> on the spot
>
> what cd any self-respectin colored american magician
> do wit such an outlandish request / cept
> put all them razzamatazz hocus pocus zippity-doo-dah
> thingamajigs away cuz
> colored chirren believin in magic
> waz becomin politically dangerous for the race . . .
>
> all things are possible

but ain't no colored magician in his right mind
gonna make you white
i mean
this is blk magic
you lookin at
& i'm fixin you up good / fixin you up good & colored

The image of the narrator as "magician" implies that the storytellers themselves will be under the control of a certain "author"; yet as the actors perform their pieces, the stories seem at times to slip away from a guiding narratorial force and to become deeply personal. In a sense, the performers threaten to overpower the narrator in the same way that the third grader's request to be made white is beyond the power of Lou's magician father: the stories take on a kind of magic which is independent of their "director," and yet to enter this realm may be painful and perilous. Lou, then, is like a surrogate author who is responsible for the content of the play, but who also cannot fully control what happens to it once the performers begin to take part.

Lou's position in relation to the performers is most fully evident when, after Lily becomes wholly absorbed in her monologue about the network of dreams she has built around her image of her hair, he stands up and points to her. Shange indicates in the stage directions that Lou "reminds us that it is only thru him that we are able to know these people without the 'masks' / the lies / & he cautions that all their thoughts are not benign, they are not safe from what they remember or imagine." He says, partly to Lily and partly to the audience:

you have t come with me / to this place where magic is /
to hear my song / some times i forget & leave my tune
in the corner of the closet under all the dirty clothes /
in this place / magic asks me where i've been / how i've
been singin / lately i leave my self in all the wrong hands /
in this place where magic is involved in undoin our masks / i
am able to smile & answer that.
in this place where magic always asks for me
i discovered a lot of other people who talk without mouths
who listen to what you say / by watchin yr jewelry dance
& in this place where magic stays
you can let yrself in or out
but when you leave yrself at home / burglars & daylight
thieves
pounce on you & sell your skin / at cut-rate on tenth avenue

The "place where magic is" means, within the most literal context of the play, the bar where the actors meet and feel free to try on various roles. But it is also the theater, and the implication is that, as such, it is both a safe place and an unsafe place: certain inhibitions are lifted and certain feelings can be portrayed, but one risks vulnerability in exposing one's memories and emotions. Finally, "this place where magic is" marks the space in which the actor / writer / artist allows creativity to happen. The impulse to safeguard it—"lately i leave my self in all the wrong hands"—echoes the fear of loss which Shange turns into a similar set of metaphors in the "somebody almost walked off wid alla my stuff" poem in ***for colored girls.*** But something interesting occurs as the result of Lou's delivery of this speech: although he designs it to reinforce his power as the play's magician / narrator, its effect is to establish *him* as being in a position not altogether different from that of the other characters, for the speech reveals his vulnerability, his disguises and defenses, and his need to inhabit a "safe" place in which to create.

If Lou is indeed addressing the audience as well as Lily, the implication is that he is inviting the spectator to become similarly vulnerable. Not surprisingly, then, the play's two "centerpiece" monologues attempt—as in ***for colored girls***—to take hold of the spectator in the gap that the performers create between the "safe" region of spectacle / entertainment and the "unsafe" region of pain and emotional assailability. In the first of the two monologues, Alec tells of his wish for all of the white people all over the world to kneel down for three minutes of silence in formal apology for the pain that they have given to black people:

> i just want to find out why no one has even been able to sound a gong & all the reporters recite that the gong is ringin / while we watch all the white people / immigrants & invaders / conquistadors & relatives of london debtors from georgia / kneel & apologize to us / just for three or four minutes. now / this is not impossible.

Of course, the image is an absurd one, and Lou calls attention to this when he responds to Alec, "what are you gonna do with white folks kneeling all over the country anyway / man." The humor in Alec's rather extreme proposal is undercut, however, by the suffering which stands behind such a request. Perhaps the most savage example of anger transferred to the realm of the comic, though, and one which cannot fail to disturb the audience, is Natalie's "today i'm gonna be a white girl" monologue. She takes on the voice of the vacuous and hypocritical "white girl" who flings her hair, waters her plants, and takes twenty Valiums a day:

> . . . i'm still waiting for my cleaning lady & the lady who takes care of my children & the lady who caters my parties & the lady who accepts quarters at the bathroom in sardi's. those poor creatures shd be sterilized / no one shd have to live such a life. cd you hand me a towel / thankyou caroline. i've left all of maxime's last winter clothes in a pile for you by the back door. they have to be cleaned but i hope yr girls can make gd use of them.

Freud says in *Jokes and Their Relation to the Unconscious* that the ability to laugh at something is interfered with when the "joke" material also produces a strong affect and so another emotion "blocks" one's capacity to generate laughter; for this reason, it is not surprising that the "white girls" in the audience at whom this monologue is aimed may feel too angry at Natalie's speech to consider it funny. Or they may laugh because they distance themselves from the reality of her words. Similarly, the very intensity of Natalie's emotions as she speaks this piece shows both the amount of pain which gradually interferes with her ability to sustain the joking tone of her own speech at the end and the intensified need for release through humor which her bitterness engenders. As Freud indicates,

> precisely in cases where there is a release of affect one can observe a particularly strong difference in expenditure bring about the automatism of release. When Colonel Butler answers Octavio's warnings by exclaiming 'with a bitter laugh': '*Thanks* from the House of Austria!' his embitterment does not prevent his laughing. The laugh applies to his memory of the disappointment he believes he has suffered; and on the other hand the magnitude of the disappointment cannot be portrayed more impressively by the dramatist than by his showing it capable of forcing a laugh in the midst of the storm of feelings that have been released.

It is also striking that the play's final monologue, spoken by Maxine, comes forth because she is "compelled to speak by natalie's pain" (i.e., after Natalie delivers the "white girl" monologue). As in ***for colored girls,*** the play's penultimate sequence seems to be different in tone from the earlier monologues—and again, the effect is a closure of the "gaps" we have discussed. Here Maxine speaks of the way her world was shattered when she realized as a child that blacks were not exempt from the diseases, crimes, and so on, that white people experienced. She closes with a description of her decision to appropriate gold chains, bracelets, and necklaces as a symbol of "anything hard to get & beautiful. / anything lasting / wrought from pain," followed by the shattering remark that "no one understands that surviving the impossible is sposed to accentuate the positive aspects of a people." Lou, as "director" of the action, freezes the players before they can fully respond to Maxine's words, and he repeats the closing portion of his opening speech: "And you gonna be colored all yr life / & you gonna love it / being colored / all yr life." As the minstrel mask reappears above them, he leads the actors in the chant "colored & love it / love it bein colored." Shange notes in the stage directions that the chant is a "serious celebration, like church / like home." Her words are entirely appropriate to the dual nature of the ending: it is true that the characters are celebrating themselves, but the resonance of the preceding monologue, which was fraught with pain—as well as the overwhelming presence of the minstrel mask—recalls the anger and frustration which also underlie their chant. The characters, then, are imprisoned in the stereotypes and social position which the world has assigned to them, but like the women in ***for colored girls*** they call for unity as a source of strength. Their chant of "colored & love it / love it bein colored" suggests that they intend to escape from their prison by redefining it so that it is no longer a prison. But the possibility remains that for the time being the escape may be only a partial one. As Shange writes in **"unrecovered losses / black theater traditions,"** the minstrel face which descends is "laughing at all of us for having been so game / we believed we cd escape his powers" [***Three Pieces***].

Spell #7's ultimate vision may be more cynical than that of ***for colored girls,*** but its call for redefinitions is one which echoes throughout Shange's theater pieces. She invites a reconsideration of role-playing which suggests that in the process of acting out the various "masks" that blacks/women are *expected* to assume, one undergoes an experience of interior drama. Liberated through monologic language and by dance, song, etc., which release different, richer, more complex characters and experiences, the very nature of role-playing has been appropriated as a tool for "performing a self." She sees role-playing as a way simultaneously to give her characters an archetypal fluidity and to confront role-oriented stereotypes. On some level Shange's characters are always aware that they are speaking to an audience; perhaps this emphasis is an acknowledgment of the sense that women—as John Berger discusses in *Ways of Seeing*—are always the objects of vision and so are constantly watching themselves being watched. Rather than decentering the position of authorship in her plays by providing a sense that the characters are as if "self-created," though, Shange appears to share Michelene Wandor's view [in *Carry on, Understudies,* 1986] that deliberate attention to the author's role as "storyteller" provides a backbone, a controlling structure, for the play. Interwoven with this is a revision of spectacle as a vehicle for amusement; Shange's interpretation of "spectacle" insists upon questioning both the *mode* of performance which lures the audience's attention (as in the minstrel show at the beginning of ***spell #7***) and the *subtext* of the spectacle itself. The monologue, then, is both an object for transformation and a means by which transformations can occur. Above all, Shange feels passionately that "we must move our theater into the drama of our lives." Her works attempt to speak, in the way that she says Layla's unconscious does in ***boogie woogie landscapes,*** of "unspeakable realities / for no self-respecting afro-american girl wd reveal so much of herself of her own will / there is too much anger to handle assuredly / too much pain to keep on truckin / less ya bury it." (pp. 210-24)

An excerpt from "unrecovered losses / black theater traditions"

as a poet in american theater / i find most activity that takes place on our stages overwhelmingly shallow / stilted & imitative. that is probably one of the reasons i insist on calling myself a poet or writer / rather than a playwright / i am interested solely in the poetry of a moment / the emotional & aesthetic impact of a character or a line. for too long now afro-americans in theater have been duped by the same artificial aesthetics that plague our white counterparts / "the perfect play," as we know it to be / a truly european framework for european psychology / cannot function efficiently for those of us from this hemisphere.

Ntozake Shange, in her Three Pieces, *Penguin Books, 1982.*

Deborah R. Geis, "Distraught Laughter: Monologue in Ntozake Shange's Theater Pieces," in Feminine Focus: The New Women Playwrights, *edited by Enoch Brater, Oxford University Press, Inc., 1989, pp. 210-25.*

FOR COLORED GIRLS WHO HAVE CONSIDERED SUICIDE / WHEN THE RAINBOW IS ENUF

PRODUCTION REVIEWS

Jack Kroll (review date 14 June 1976)

[*In the following review of* For Colored Girls, *Kroll lauds the playwright, director, and players for creating a "tragic, funny, proud and compassionate" evocation of the social realities faced by black women. He briefly examines the "tremendously effective minidramas" that comprise the play, praising Shange's vital and poignant characters.*]

[In] Ntozake Shange's ***For Colored Girls Who Have Considered Suicide / When the Rainbow is Enuf,*** both language and character are exultantly, bitingly alive, and the result is overwhelming in its emotional impact.

Interestingly, women and poetry have joined forces to create two of the best events of the theater season—"The Belle of Amherst," Julie Harris's one-woman evocation of Emily Dickinson's world, and now Ms. Shange's tragic, funny, proud and compassionate "choreo-poem" for seven actresses. The work is an orchestrated, choreographed presentation of poems and prose pieces from a forthcoming book, ***Natural Disasters and Other Festive Occasions,*** by the St. Louis-born Shange. The disasters and festivities are the events in the lives of young black women anywhere in the U.S. These pieces are tremendously effective minidramas that explode onstage, showering shrapnel of significance.

Shange's poems aren't war cries—they're outcries filled with a controlled passion against the brutality that blasts the lives of "colored girls"—a phrase that in her hands vibrates with social irony and poetic beauty. These poems are political in the deepest sense, but there's no dogma, no sentimentality, no grinding of false mythic axes. "Being alive, being a woman and being colored is a metaphysical dilemma I haven't solved yet," says the poet. Your scalp prickles at the stunning truth of her characters: the high-school girl pondering whether or not to surrender her virginity in "the deep black Buick smelling of Thunderbird and ladies in heat," the dancer who has all the earth-force of the Mississippi, the sexpot who turns men on with a Babylonian arsenal of seductive machinery but then emerges from her post-coital bathtub with the soul sadness of a "regular colored girl."

A young director named Oz Scott has staged the work with power and grace, and the women—Shange herself, Trazana Beverley, Risë Collins, Janet League, Aku Kadago, Laurie Carlos and dancer-choreographer Paula Moss—are unforgettable. Beverley is devastating in her hilarious put-down of a vacillating suitor and in her depiction of a girl whose children are killed by her lover. What I said about "The Belle of Amherst"—that it should be seen by the whole country—applies, perhaps even more strongly, to this thrilling and poignant show.

Jack Kroll, "Women's Rites," in Newsweek, *Vol. LXXXVII, No. 24, June 14, 1976, p. 99.*

Edwin Wilson (review date 21 September 1976)

[*In the following review, Wilson discusses the major themes of* For Colored Girls. *He ascribes to the play "the texture, the feel, and the raw emotions of the modern black woman," while also noting that its themes and appeal are universal.*]

[***For Colored Girls Who Have Considered Suicide / When the Rainbow Is Enuf***] opened last week at the Booth Theater after successful runs in a workshop and at the Public Theater off-Broadway. . . .***Colored Girls*** captures the

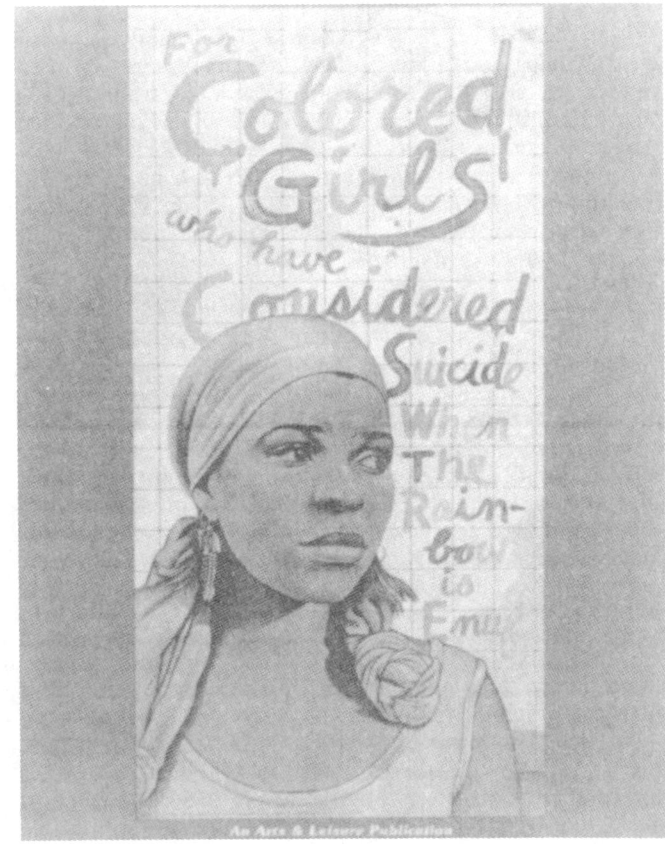

Program for the Broadway production of Shange's best-known work.

inner feelings of young black women today and goes beyond that to achieve its own kind of universality.

Colored Girls consists of a series of poems by a young black writer. Ntozake Shange, recited or performed by a group of seven talented black actresses, sometimes to the accompaniment of dance, sometimes as a scene from a play, sometimes as a straight recitation or soliloquy. The women are dressed alike in dance outfits with long skirts, each in a different color—like the rainbow. On a bare stage with only a large red rose suspended against a background of black curtains, the seven women, one of whom is Ms. Shange herself, take turns presenting the poems. On both counts—the presentations and the poems themselves—it is a remarkable, inspiring evening.

In most of her work Ms. Shange adopts the persona of a person who suffers the three-fold anguish of being young, black, and a woman; and she articulates this anguish with wit and insight. Like so many young people today, the woman she creates is uncertain of who she is or where she belongs; she is not complete, but a song of "half notes scattered without a tune, without rhythm." As for being black, in her words, "being colored and being sorry is redundant in the modern world."

As a woman she suffers from confusion and a lack of self-esteem. She offers her love to men who take advantage of her, returning brutality, indifference, or useless apologies for her love. Feeling bereft, she exclaims, "Somebody almost run off wit' alla my stuff."

But as the title of the play suggests, Ms. Shange's young woman does not despair; rather she finds her own rainbow, in humor and above all in a growing awareness of her worth. Thinking of the man who almost ran off with her stuff, she comes to realize that her stuff—her body, her soul, and her spirit—belongs only to her, and only has meaning when she possesses it. She tells the man that he had better return her stuff because "if you want it, I'm the only one who can handle it."

The humor is apparent in the acting as well as the poems, especially in the work of Trazana Beverley. Ms. Beverley can be a glittery but faded femme fatale—a sort of black Blanche DuBois—or a jive-talking dude, a man walking down the street, head nodding, fingers popping, and body arching like a cracked whip. Ms. Beverley also has the most dramatic section of the evening: a moving portrayal of a woman with two small children who tries to protect them from their crazy father when he puts them on a ledge and threatens to throw them out the window unless she marries him. This section is a small play in itself and in it Ms. Beverley moves from raucous comedy to pathos with a turn of her head or the sudden slump of her body.

Ms. Shange has a good ear for language and a sharp eye for the behavior and customs of black people; there is intelligence at work in ***Colored Girls,*** but more important, there is the texture, the feel, and the raw emotions of the modern black woman who, against great odds, fights for her integrity and her self-respect.

For Ms. Shange and those who helped her put ***Colored Girls*** together, including director Oz Scott and choreographer Paula Moss, the evening is a signal achievement. It may not be what one ordinarily expects in the theater, but like the rainbow of the title, it is enough.

Edwin Wilson, in a review of "For Colored Girls Who Have Considered Suicide / When the Rainbow is Enuf," in The Wall Street Journal, *September 21, 1976.*

Lynn F. Miller (review date May 1977)

[*Miller is an educator and critic who has worked extensively with women in the visual and performing arts. In the following review, she explores the structure and style of* For Colored Girls. *She credits both Shange and director Oz Scott with creating a stirring poetic enactment of a black girl's initiation into womanhood.*]

Joseph Papp has developed a system for moving talented new playwrights, directors, and actors from workshop beginnings through Off-Broadway productions to Broadway. ***For Colored Girls*** has successfully followed the Papp program: from its beginnings as a workshop production at the Henry Street Settlement Playhouse, to an Off-Broadway production at the Public, and on to the Booth.

[*For Colored Girls*] is a rousing yet delicate, strongly felt spiritual dedicated to the earthy reality of the great goddess/mother/source-of-all-life, sincerely perceived by Shange to be a woman, probably a black woman.

—Lynn F. Miller

For Colored Girls has a wider appeal than its title suggests; it is not for black women only, although the experiences culled and given life on the Booth stage are directly related to the lives of many black women. Ming Cho Lee's huge red paper peony up center, placed in front of the deep purple backdrop, is the only scenic element; it is all that is needed, standing as it does for the unified heart, brain, gut, womb, and center of being not only of the "colored girls" in the title but of all women. The purity, incisiveness, and truth of the writing reaches into the red flower at the center of all women; universal truths, drawn in detail, spill out in well-controlled poem-monologues from the actresses on stage directly into the emotional receivers in the guts of the audience. It is the directness of the emotional communication that electrifies the audience.

By means of his arrangement of Ntozake Shange's autobiographical poetry pieces, each an investigation into a particular aspect of private black womanhood, the director, Oz Scott, has created a form resonant of a rite of passage. The passage is from girlhood and innocence, through adolescence and the beginnings of self-discovery, into adult suffering through love, and finally to self-acceptance. The action of the piece—finding and accepting oneself—has been created by structuring the poems into a pattern as sensitive as flowers arranged by an Ikebana artist.

While not a traditional play, ***For Colored Girls*** is essentially theatrical, rooted in rite, ceremony, and mythology. The characters experience deep conflicts, and a resolution is achieved. In structure the work is musical, resembling jazz riffs, once improvisationally emerging directly from street experience, now structured like Ellington's music into notations that record and codify joyfulness, melancholy, or a sense of tragic despair. With choreography by Paula Moss (also one of the actresses), the poems insist on being danced as well as acted.

Judy Dearing's costumes confirm the importance of movement in the piece; they are really dance costumes that free the actresses' bodies for any movement. The most superb moments are in the poem **"Sechita,"** evoking African goddesses of the distant past through the recreation of a cabaret dancer in New Orleans. The poem is expertly spoken by Rise Collins and danced by Paula Moss.

There are elements of comedy, tragedy, and biting satire in the production. The most vividly tragic piece, **"Nite with Beau Willie Brown,"** produces near-hysterical laughter culminating in tears. A crazed black war veteran beats his abused lover with a highchair in which their baby still sits, an unfamiliar, savage image, offbeat and almost surreal, as are many of the images in this piece.

Ntozake Shange has served up slices of her world. For some people this reality is intolerable, requiring the defense of laughter. Even for Shange, reality is too much sometimes. In **"I Used to Live in the World (But then I Moved to Harlem),"** the poet lashes out with bitterness at the shrunken existence in such a constricted universe.

Rites of initiation traditionally culminate in a vision of the godhead. ***For Colored Girls,*** structured as an initiation rite into full adult womanhood—passing through the stages of life in concretely remembered specific experiences—culminates in the joyous affirmation of the beauty and integrity of the black woman's self. It is a rousing yet delicate, strongly felt spiritual dedicated to the earthy reality of the great goddess / mother / source-of-all-life, sincerely perceived by Shange to be a woman, probably a black woman. (pp. 262-63)

Lynn F. Miller, in a review of "For Colored Girls Who Have Considered Suicide / When the Rainbow is Enuf," in Educational Theatre Journal, *Vol. 29, No. 2, May, 1977, pp. 262-63.*

CRITICAL COMMENTARY

Erskine Peters (essay date 1978)

[*In the essay below, Peters expresses a sense of disappointment and betrayal stemming from his view that Shange negatively stereotyped images of black men in* For Colored Girls. *He comments on critical evaluations of the play by both black and white reviewers and explores some technical attributes of the piece.*]

While it is not altogether inexplicable it is quite unfortunate that Ntozake Shange's Broadway choreopoem, ***For Colored Girls Who Have Considered Suicide / When the Rainbow is Enuf,*** has been so enthusiastically and uncircumspectly received in the general White and Black presses. This theatrical event forbodes more crucial damning, and subtle implications for our Black children and youth than it has virtues or redeeming value for the adults who sit through it and about whom the work is ostensibly concerned. After examining more than a score of reviews, I have found heaps upon heaps of praises, most of which to me are actually dubious, quite ironic, and very often, outright ridiculous.

The ultimate portrayal of Black existence in Shange's work which depicts episodes and fantasies in the lives of adolescent Black girls who supposedly become women, differs very little from what any unaware intruding anthropologist or social worker of the 1950's would have offered in her quarterly report on life in the ghettos: 'the poor black woman, doing all that she can, suffers so much and most of all she has to contend with her inherently no-good nigger men.' Although the drama has many technical merits, many superb phrasings, and some talented depictions of types of characters, especially in the first half of the production, the discriminating viewer is soon overcome with a sense of disappointment and betrayal. He is particularly disappointed that the writer does not use her apparent skill to move beyond the superficial aspects of the Black male characters whom he thought or hoped were initially being satirized, and not simply *dished.* He feels betrayed after the giving of his laughter to the first half of the show because he was believing that the 'colored girls' could deliver a Black perspective. He was not necessarily expecting the play to deal with anything other than the lives of the 'colored girls,' but he was expecting that their lives would have been delivered with a consciousness of all the major factors that shape and have shaped Black existence in this hemisphere.

It is not at all my intention to give the impression that Black men and women don't have particular issues that need to be taken account of. Anyone Black could learn that simply from growing up in this society with a mother and father, or perhaps even more poignantly without the latter. But what is the purpose of the artist if not to pierce the heart of truth, to plunge beneath the surfaces, to illuminate so that those of us with more ordinary eyes may become more ably informed. In order for particular truths to point toward the greater Truth, or collective Truth, these particulars must be inclusive; otherwise truth is distorted. Neither is it at all my intention to say that negative images are not a concrete part of our reality; however, negative images as fundamental components of our existence don't necessarily produce negative resolutions, especially not in the hands of the artist, who is the healer, the renewer of life.

The Botswana novelist Bessie Head understands this need when she shapes her short story "The Collector of Treasures" and relates the circumstances of a mother of three children who kills her irresponsible husband by cutting off his penis. While the story may not be the most superbly crafted, it does provide a historical context for the development or emergence of a particular type of male who takes no responsibility for his children and little for himself. In addition, to avoid the highly misleading oversimplification that Botswana society is bereft of accountable males, the writer balances her depiction by providing us with a father image from the other end of the spectrum. All of which Ntozake Shange's play lacks, except for a rather romantic allusion to Toussaint L'Ouverture.

If Shange's play has thematic virtue and historic significance, as has been almost universally proclaimed, it would only be in relation to what Jessica Harris (even though she found no seriously compromising flaws), states about the pre-Broadway opening at the Henry Street Playhouse:

> When the curtain came down, Black women in the audience wept openly, for onstage they had finally seen an image of themselves that showed not just the strength or the anger but also some of the vulnerability and pain.
>
> [*Essence,* November, 1976]

> The women were excited because for once they saw a picture of themselves they could recognize. It was a picture representing them not as whores or as matriarchs, not as superwomen or mighty mommas, but simply as women who want to be loved, who try to be kind and who might get tired and evil sometimes, but women who above all were real people with the full spectrum of emotions and reactions that real people have. This was a new presentation and as such met with enormous success.
>
> [*New York Amsterdam News,* October 9, 1976]

In rightly trying to reveal other dimensions of Black womanhood besides the strong, hard, enduring, and surviving ones, Shange conversely portrays contemporary Black men basically as pasteboards or beasts. One wonders to whom it is she is appealing in her vulnerability and pain, since such conclusively negative images would have a very limited appeal to Black men. Is it possibly an obscured and latent appeal to the Great White Father? Perhaps it is this that prompts *New York Times* critic Clive Barnes to write as his concluding accolade for the work: "It could easily have made me feel guilty as being white and male. It didn't. It made me feel proud at being a member of the human race, and the joyous discovery that a white man can have black sisters." But herein lies so much of the danger for the future of Black children in White America: if the phenomenon of the profound frustration of 'colored girls' does not make an influential member of the oppressor group feel guilty, it should at least make him uncomfortable. As an oppressed people whose power is yet too unorganized, we cannot afford not to acknowledge that the social bureaucracy under which we live is abnormal and pervasively threatening. In fact, as one reviewer, Curtis Rogers of the *New York Amsterdam News* put it:

> . . . in her unrelenting stereotyping of Black men as always 'shucking' and 'jiving' . . . she, without realizing it, just as insistently caricatures Black women as being easily duped, and as emotionally frivolous. This is so because Ms. Shange's 'Colored Girls' invariably take up with those Black men whom she damns as mean and trifling.
>
> [October 9, 1976]

Any other major historic significance of this work which Mel Gussow of the NY *Times* [September 16, 1976] described as "a play that should be seen, savored and treasured" is that it is quite reminiscent of the dubious and even treacherous meaning of D. W. Griffith's *Birth of a Nation* to film history. Black Americans have no particular plight if we ignore the facts that not only do Black people have to contend with elements of human nature as any other people, but that to a greater degree than White Americans, Blacks and other non-Whites have to contend (consciously or unconsciously) with a culture dominated by White males who for some reason find one of their greatest threats in other males who cannot perpetuate their physical image. It seems that we would all know by now at least something about all of the blatant and subtle doings projected at the psyches of Blacks and Whites alike through and since the time of Black enslavement to thwart and dismantle all Black strength. To ignore these looming influences in any presentation is again fundamentally a damnation of our children.

It is apparent that some of the fundamental problems with Shange's play originate in the mere fact of the author's own youth (which might, though, have easily become an asset in this historical time, one would think). It does not take one very long to realize that the play is an attempt to deal not simply with problems of Black women, but also with some very serious crises that relate mostly to Ms. Shange's individual self. Kevin Sanders, who acknowledges that perhaps he as "a white man has no ground to judge a play by and about black women" nevertheless felt compelled to make the following insightful comment [on WABC-TV, September 19, 1976]:

> When I first saw ***Colored Girls Who Have Considered Suicide,*** when it first ran at Joe Papp's theatre downtown, I thought it was disturbing in a way that was not intended; it seemed too much like a long and shrill harangue. . . . Too much of it is in the same key—overwrought and overacted. There are not enough variations of tone and style, and it's concerned very much with the narrow and subjective spectrum of human experience.

One certainly found that throughout the performance the individual mental state of the author seemed to rumble and peep from beneath the surface as the truly crucial issue being dealt with. It is not at all unusual for first works to be of this nature. And we cannot ignore the dynamics of the individual self. But it is important to the profundity and precociousness of first works in which the individual artist casts herself or himself as the exemplar of a collective sensibility that he or she should have a clear idea of the extent to which it is himself or herself and not the collective that is being treated. Hence, the artist will not be as inclined as Ms. Shange, and others such as the early and sometimes later William Faulkner, for example, to project too much of his or her personal mental confusion upon their already oppressed subjects.

From Ms. Shange's obvious misapprehension of her own maturity derives the terribly warped perspective which controls the play. Most unfortunately, one of the moments at which this perspective speaks loudest is the highest point at which the thematic tension and technical elements converge, the climax. One of the seven heroines, Crystal, who has borne children by the callous Beau Willie Brown, now the epitome of contemporary Black manhood, stares as Beau Willie smashes their children to death. In these moments the author does nothing less than carry out an insensitive and cruel act of exploitation upon her subjects and her audience. She does indeed do what Clive Barnes says in an intended tribute: "make the theater such an incredible marketplace for the soul." Beau Willie Brown, the epitome of the contemporary Black man, becomes in the eyes of the reviewers "the crazed lover" who "invades" Crystal's life.

Writes [T. E. Kalem in *Time Magazine,* June 14, 1976]: "If they can see themselves through Shange's eyes, black men are going to wince. They are portrayed as brutal con men and amorous double-dealers." And wince we do in shocking and utter amazement at the play's shortsightedness. For this climax is the author's blatantly melodramatic attempt to turn the work into tragedy without fulfilling her obligations to explore or implicate the historical and deeper tragic circumstances. There is a very heated attempt to rush the play toward an evocation of pity, horror, and suffering. The application of such a cheap device at this critical thematic and structural point is an inhumane gesture to the Black community. As Barbara Mahone has said [in *First World,* May/June, 1977] with explicit reference to this Ms. Shange:

> There [are] . . . talented artists around who are blinding us with their gifts for re-creation of some current truths, but in whose work the net social effect is negative. Often we don't realize immediately what's going down. But ultimately we are left with a bitter, paralyzing taste in our mouth—because the artists failed to transform our pains into good progressive energy.

We might say of Melvin Gottlieb's assertion [in the *New York Post,* September 16, 1976] that "the essence of the show remains its pure and perfectly captured blackness," that he is simply uninformed, is speaking facetiously, or is being all and out ridiculous. But what does one think when he encounters in Black reviewers a peculiarly apologetic, defensive, and sometimes desperate promotion of the play without their speaking directly to its flaws? Roseann Pope Bell writes rather defensively in the *Black Collegian* [May/ June, 1977]: "The choreopoem cannot and is not [sic] a statement of Black-on-Black oppression, because nothing ever happens to Black women that doesn't happen to Black men, except that Black women have Black children even when the fathers are not Black." Whatever it is that is discomfiting about the play to Ms. Bell, she does not admit; however, she is so defensive throughout her essay that she soon feels the need to rewrite the play, or at least supply parts of the missing perspective. No such comprehending or sympathetic portrait of Black men ever emerges from ***For Colored Girls*** to even approximate what Ms. Bell states:

> . . . the failure of this great money-mongering society is photographed in the hallow-eyed stares of Black men who cannot share in even a modicum of the pride that would rage forth if they could adequately share in providing for their loved ones.

More appallingly, beneath the parenthetical apologies for their unarticulated apprehensions, several Black reviewers seem to conclude, "So what, the image of Black men is destructive? We're on Broadway!" Jessica Harris writes. "It is the first time that a Black woman playwright has dealt with young Black women and with their role in contemporary society in such a way that it was a commercially viable production (the idea of Broadway theatre is after all to make a profit)." William Austin writes [in the *New York Amsterdam News,* October 9, 1976] with concession that "Our emergence on the great white way should not be allowed to smother our sense of ourselves, our realities, our aspirations or our creativity. . . . Black Broadway is too good to let slip away." Even after admitting that in addition to the play's good qualities, it also aroused his anger, Curtis Rogers would also opt for Broadway:

> The point is that ***Colored Girls*** expresses a narrow and single dimensional view of both Black men and women. In this sense, it does not reflect truth. But, the ability to entertain, not the ability to state sociological truths is the measure and essence of good theater. ***Colored Girls*** is excellent theater.

Trazana Beverley, the actress who dramatizes Crystal's "victimization" by the beastly Beau Willie Brown, and Ntozake Shange, herself, have attempted to rationalize the play's flaws. Says Beverley "particularly in regard to the correct political interpretation one should make of ***For Colored Girls***":

> We cite certain painful realities, and it draws us together as Black women in a common bond, but I don't want it to be thought that we are shutting the doors on any future relationships with black men. Some brothers fail to realize this.
> [*The Village Voice,* October 4, 1976]

And Ms. Shange has been quoted as saying:

> What I am trying to say is that I am right here directly speaking with God and the rivers. . . . Now if you can't understand what we're doing there's something wrong with you.
> [*New York Times,* June 16, 1976]

As two highly sensitive Black women writers, June Jordan and Audre Lorde, have constantly demonstrated through their voluminous writings, the voice of Black feminism demands extraordinary insight and gifted powers of discrimination. Beyond their personal pain, women also have to see themselves in relation to the pain of the men. The purpose of feminism in any kind of revolutionary sense is for woman to put herself more profoundly in touch with others. Bessie Head ends "The Collector of Treasures" not with women encircling themselves, and not simply with women knowing the plight of a particular woman, but with men and women united against the extremes of irresponsibility. We would do well to remember what June Jordan has already stressed [in *Ms. Magazine,* February, 1977]:

> . . . you cannot aid half a people; you have to seek to assist the men as well as the women of any oppressed group. (If my father dies without living, if my son shall be cast away, if my men believe that they must be violent or perish, then what may I know of fulfillment; who shall I be to claim happiness?)

(pp. 79-84)

Erskine Peters, "Some Tragic Propensities of Ourselves: The Occasion of Ntozake Shange's For Colored Girls Who Have Considered Suicide / When the Rainbow is Enuf," *in* The Journal of Ethnic Studies, *Vol. 6, No. 1, Spring, 1978, pp. 79-85.*

Sandra Hollin Flowers (essay date 1981)

[*In the following excerpt, Flowers acknowledges a variety of possible approaches to* For Colored Girls, *suggesting that the work's primary emphasis is on relationships between black women and men.*]

There are as many ways of looking at Ntozake Shange's ***For Colored Girls Who Have Considered Suicide / When the Rainbow Is Enuf*** as there are hues in a rainbow. One can take it as an initiation piece, for instance, particularly with its heavily symbolic **"Graduation Nite"** and the girlhood perspectives of the mama's little baby / Sally Walker segment and in the voice of the eight-year-old narrator of **"Toussaint."** ***Colored Girls*** also might be seen as a black feminist statement in that it offers a black woman's perspective on issues made prominent by the women's movement. Still another approach is to view it as a literary coming-of-age of black womanhood in the form of a series of testimonies which, in Shange's words, "explore the realities of seven different kinds of women." Indeed, the choreopoem is so rich that it lends itself to multiple interpretations which vary according to one's perspective and experiences.

I would suggest, however, that the least appropriate responses are those exemplified by reviewers who said that black men will find themselves portrayed in ***Colored Girls*** "as brutal con men and amorous double-dealers"; or that "The thematic emphasis is constantly directed at the stupid crudity and downright brutality of [black] men." Comments such as these are particularly misleading because they appear in reviews which contain generous praise for ***Colored Girls,*** thus suggesting that it is the condemnation of black men, which gives the book its merit. Too, such comments have the effect of diminishing the work to nothing more than a diatribe against black men, when, quite the contrary, Shange demonstrates a compassionate vision of black men—compassionate because though the work is not without anger, it has a certain integrity which could not exist if the author lacked a perceptive understanding of the crisis between black men and women.

And there is definitely a crisis. Individually we have known this for some time, and lately black women as well as black men are showing growing concern about the steady deterioration of their relationships. Black literature, however, has lagged somewhat behind. The works which usually comprise Afro-American literature curricula and become part of general reading materials, for instance, show the position of the black man in America; but generally we see the black woman only peripherally as the protagonist's lover, wife, mother, or in some other supporting (or detracting) role. Certainly black women can identify with the predicament of black men. Black women can identify, for example, with the problems articulated in Ellison's *Invisible Man* because they share the same predicaments. But for black women the predicament of the black male protagonist is compounded by concerns which affect them on yet another level. This, then, is what makes ***Colored Girls*** an important work which ranks with Ellison's *Invisible Man,* Wright's *Native Son,* and the handful of other black classics—it is an artistically successful female perspective on a long-standing issue among black people. If, however, black men fail to acknowledge the significance of ***Colored Girls,*** if they resent it or insist that it does not speak to their concerns or is not important because it deals with "women's issues," then the crisis is more severe than any thought it to be.

Colored Girls is certainly woman's art but it is also black art, or Third World art, as Shange probably would prefer to have it designated. Its language and dialect, its geography, its music, and the numerous allusions to Third World personalities make it an intensely cultural work. Much of these characteristics, however, are peculiar to Shange's upbringing, education, and experiences, with the result that the piece loses universality at points, as in the poem "Now I Love Somebody More Than." But even here, black audiences are sure to know which lady loved gardenias; they will know the Flamingoes and Archie Shepp and Imamu. Then there is the poem **"Sechita"** in which the dancer is linked to Nefertiti, hence to Africa and Olduvai Gorge, the "cradle of civilization"—all of which puts into perspective the cheapening of Sechita by the carnival audience. While **"Sechita"** speaks to the degradation of black womanhood, **"Toussaint"** speaks of the black woman's discovery of black pride. It also speaks, with subtle irony, of the black woman's awakening to the black man.

Even **"Latent Rapists' "** and **"Abortion Cycle #1"** which seem to deal exclusively with women's issues, are of political significance to black men. It is difficult to politicize rape among black women, for instance, because the feminist approach began with a strongly anti-male sentiment, whereas the black community is highly male-identified. Furthermore, blacks have their own historical perspective on rape—the thousands of black men who were lynched for "rape" of white women. The history of these persecutions, however, does not remove the black woman's need for a political consciousness about rape, such as the traditionally feminist one Shange articulates. By the same token, Shange has sensitively portrayed the trauma of abortion, a trauma which, to some extent, probably exists in every case, no matter how strongly a woman might advocate the right to choose abortion. Still, the black movement's rhetoric linking birth control to genocide cannot be lightly dismissed. These considerations ought to make clear the delicate balance between blackness and womanhood which Shange manages to strike in ***Colored Girls.***

Maintaining this balance is no easy task, and the black woman writer of some political consciousness is under tremendous pressure not to sacrifice issues of blackness to those of womanhood and vice versa.

As suggested, however, the primary focus of ***Colored Girls*** is on the quality of relationships between black women and their men. This focus dominates the last half of the work, beginning with **"One,"** in which loneliness is seen to be more powerful than sensuality. This loneliness-sensuality juxtaposition is an especially effective way of raising the issue of woman as a strictly sexual being rather than a person with the full range of human emotions and needs. Before we even know where the poem is headed, we have an instinctive understanding of why this woman "wanted to be unforgettable," why "she wanted to be a memory / a wound to every man / arragant [sic] enough to want her." Now in the prime of her sensuality and physical attractiveness, this woman is

> . . . the wrath
> of women in windows
> fingering shades / ol lace curtains
> camoflagin despair &
> stretchmarks.

At the end of the poem, though, we see that all along the woman has known that sensuality at its worst, which is what it has been reduced to in her case, is merely a surrogate for mutual caring and understanding. It is only a matter of time, she seems to know, until she will become one of those loveless women in the windows, camouflaging her own despair and stretch marks. And notice that Shange equates despair and stretch marks: they are one and the same in the game played by the woman in **"One."**

This, however, is but one kind of despair. A more overt kind is evident in **"A Nite with Beau Willie Brown,"** in which Shange skillfully weaves craft and theme in a poem about a young couple who have been lovers for nine years. As the narrative begins, Beau Willie and his woman Crystal are separated because Crystal, frightened by his erratic, brutal behavior toward her and their children, has gotten a court order barring Beau Willie from their apartment. Angry and indignant about Crystal's refusal to see him, Beau Willie forces his way into the apartment, coaxes the children to him and, dissatisfied with Crystal's response to his demands that she marry him, drops the children from the fifth story window.

The foregoing summary leaves out much that is revealed about Beau Willie during the narrative. He is, first of all, a Vietnam veteran experiencing a typical maladjustment upon coming back to the States. His situation is worsened by the fact that he is one of the thousands of black veterans who have their own horror stories of the front-line experience in Vietnam. Beau Willie is drug-dependent, shell-shocked, psychotic, disoriented, and paranoid:

> he'd see the spotlights in the alleyways downstairs movin in the air / cross his wall over his face / & get under the covers & wait for an all clear or till he cd hear traffic again.

Yet, "there waznt nothin wrong with him / he kept tellin crystal. . . . " We can also deduce from the narrative that before he went to Vietnam, Beau had almost certainly been victimized by racism in the schools he attended—"he cdnt read wortha damn." When he returned home and tried to attend school on the GI Bill, "they kept right on puttin him in remedial classes . . . so beau cused the teachers of holdin him back & got himself a gypsy cab to drive. . . . " His cab was always breaking down, though; he couldn't make much money, was robbed of what little he did make, and was frequently harassed by the police.

The pattern is obvious: Beau Willie Brown is the quintessential black man of his generation. By this, I do not mean, nor does Shange intend to imply, that Beau Willie Brown is all there is to black manhood. Conversely, I am not suggesting that the political realities embodied in Beau Willie justify his treatment of or his attitude toward Crystal. Instead, I believe that Shange's compassion for black men surfaces most noticeably in this poem and that her characterization of Beau Willie recognizes some of the external factors which influence relationships between black men and women. Twenty-five years ago, Beau Willie could have been a black Korean War veteran; thirty years ago, he might have been one of the black Tuskegee pilots who flew combat missions in World War II but were denied jobs as commercial airline pilots while their white counterparts were hired; sixty years ago he easily could have been one of World War I's black veterans who returned home to lynchings rather than heroes' welcomes.

This poem is purely political, although it has been misunderstood by critics. Here, we are again talking about a question of perspective, specifically an artist's perspective which can transform a passing incident into a poem of far-reaching and chilling significance. On the writing of **"A Nite with Beau Willie Brown,"** Shange, who was staying in a Harlem boarding house when she wrote the poem, says

> It was hot. I was broke. I didn't have enough money for a subway token. I was miserable. The man in the next room was beating up his old lady. It went on for hours and hours. She was screaming. He was laughing. Everytime he hit her I would think, yeah, man, well that had already happened to me. So I sat down and wrote "Beau Willie." All my anger came out.

One might assume that the anger is directed toward Beau Willie, the surrogate for the woman-beating neighbor, because of Shange's use of comic similes—"like he waz an ol frozen bundle of chicken . . . ," or "beau sat straight up in the bed / wrapped up in the sheets lookin like john the baptist or a huge baby with stubble & nuts. . . . " The comic elements, however, are so grotesque that Beau emerges as a tragic figure and it becomes apparent that Shange's anger is in response to the circumstances and impulses—whatever they are—which result in men brutalizing women. Consequently, while our sympathies might at first be entirely with Crystal, we ultimately come to understand that her pain is also Beau's and vice versa.

Finally, the significance of Beau Willie's and Crystal's children must not be overlooked. Their names—Naomi Kenya and Kwame Beau Willie—are important, for both contain elements of the African and the Western, the miscegenation which resulted in the Afro-American. Further, the girl and boy can be seen as nascent black womanhood and manhood. Literally and metaphorically, then, in dropping the children, Beau Willie is not only committing murder and—since they are his offspring—suicide; but he is also killing the hope of black manhood and womanhood.

Similarly, in **"Pyramid"** three friends are pursued by one man. Two of them become involved with him but he rejects them both for yet another woman. If for no other reason than the fact that black women outnumber black men (by over 700,000, according to 1977 census data), it is probable that most black women will be part of some kind of multiple love relationship, with or without their knowledge and cooperation. Shange's concept of a pyramid for portraying this circumstance offers a graphic illustration of how women function in such relationships. Like the women in this poem, clusters of women form a pyramid from which a man can select partners. The women's position on the pyramid shifts: they find themselves at the bottom occasionally, but they usually have some time at the top, as do the two friends in the poem. Seen in this way, as a simple reflection of reality, the man in Shange's **"Pyramid"** is not as heartless as the poem may suggest; he is merely exercising a prerogative which black women and circumstances have given him.

This particular pyramid, however, is made up of close friends, which makes the man's actions seem more callous. But theoretically, they are all sisters, therefore, whether or not they are friends with the other women in the pyramid, the man's playing them off against each other is potentially humiliating and painful for each, as the women in **"Pyramid"** find out. In theory, then, they should feel as much compassion for the discarded women in their own pyramids as they feel for the friends in Shange's poem when, at the end, the woman who was first rejected comforts her friend who has also been rejected:

> she held her head on her lap
> the lap of her sisters soakin up tears
> each understandin how much love stood between them
> how much love between them
> love between them
> love like sisters.

But there is a great deal of ambivalence in these lines, just as there is in black women's relationships with each other. On the one hand, we might say that the sisterly love which previously existed between these women has been restored by the pain the man has given them. This interpretation would be in keeping with the upbeat ending of ***Colored Girls*** in which the women affirm themselves and each other. However, this idealistic interpretation is undermined by the incident of the rose. The first woman, in a mute gesture of love, leaves a rose by the man's pillow; she later finds this rose on her friend's desk. Betrayed by both her lover and her friend, it is no wonder that the poor woman is speechless as her friend tells her

> . . . i dont wanna hurt you
> but you know i need someone now
> & you know
> how wonderful he is.

One should note the irony and delicacy of language with which Shange has rendered the pain women inflict upon each other in the name of love. The love that stands between the two women is not necessarily love for one another, but their respective love for the man who has hurt them both. The "love between them," then, is a destructive presence which divides them. They cannot be like sisters again until they reexamine their priorities and find the true importance of themselves and of each other. This is precisely what they proceed to do in the following sequence of poems, those entitled **"No More Love Poems."**

Here, of course, Shange is being ironic, because what she calls **"No More Love Poems"** is actually love poetry of the most explicit and poignant kind. Each poem exposes the persona so completely that one understands that she is basically defenseless and vulnerable as far as love is concerned. More important, in being so open, each woman takes an awesome risk: If her lover has a misguided notion of manhood, his response to her admissions may be terribly painful for her because he will not be able to drop the poses his self-image requires and allow himself to be equally open and vulnerable with her. The pathos of this group of poems is probably most evident in **"No More Love Poems #2."** Here the lady in purple, who, piteously, used to "linger in non-english speakin arms so there waz no possibility of understandin" represents the epitome of the loveless love affair. Her inability to understand anything said by the person of the "non-english speakin arms" is symbolic of woman's attempts to understand man. He does not speak her language—which is to say that he is unable to express the kinds of feelings that she is capable of putting into words. At the same time, he lacks the ability to understand her and so she can never hope to make clear to him the things that are important to her.

While it may seem ridiculous that the lady in purple would deliberately involve herself with someone she knows cannot understand her, this is precisely what happens in every relationship in which communication is absent. In our naiveté, we might once have entered relationships under the assumption that we and our lovers would somehow *know* what each of us wanted and needed. That, after all, is supposed to be the nature of love: it does not lend itself to scrutiny and questioning and explication; it simply exists. In a less complex society or one in which love is of minimal importance to the success of a relationship, perhaps this is true. But here in the fragmented, abrasive universe of America, where intimate relationships are nearly the only outlet for expressing affection and caring; where the partnership or the family unit might be all to which one can really be said to belong; where, in short, one depends upon one's loved one for emotional sustenance—in such a climate, it becomes imperative for black women and men to articulate their needs and expectations of one another.

Black men and women have not communicated successfully. It might even be said that they have tried everything imaginable to avoid articulating their needs—extended families, promiscuity, no-strings-attached fatherhood, getting / staying high together, even the Black Power Movement in which black people were all sisters and brothers, which meant that everyone *naturally* had everyone else's welfare at heart and so there was no need to explain *anything.* Like the lady in purple, many black women find themselves saying, "i dont know any more tricks / i am really colored and really sad sometimes. . . . "

Shange has given us an exquisite and very personal view of the politics of black womanhood and black male-female relationships. Too few black writers are doing that—perhaps because the truth is really as painful as that depicted in ***Colored Girls,*** and in telling it one opens oneself to charges of dividing the race and exposing blacks to ridicule by reinforcing stereotypes. That allegation has been levied against ***Colored Girls,*** which is unfortunate because the only thing of which Ntozake Shange is guilty is a sincere, eloquent rendering of what she has come to understand about black love relationships. Critics cannot afford to insist that black writers forgo expressing such visions simply because they are painful, embarrassing, or potentially divisive. If that is true, maybe it is because blacks have been so preoccupied with political and economic survival that they no longer know, if they ever did, how to confront their own responsibility for what happens between black men and women; in that case, blacks really *do* have a great need for ***Colored Girls*** and similar works.

"A Nite with Beau Willie Brown" seems particularly suitable for putting the problems of blacks into perspective. We know that there was a period in their relationship when Crystal wanted very much to be Beau Willie's wife. She was asking for a commitment, an affirmation of their relationship, which is precisely what the women in **"Sorry,"** in **"No More Love Poems,"** in **"One"**—in real life, in fact—are asking. Beau Willie, like the black men on whom he was modeled, had consistently told Crystal, "nothin doin." Finally, when Beau Willie wanted Crystal, needed her, in fact, to affirm himself, he found, but did not understand, that she had had to turn from him to ensure her own survival. (pp. 51-4)

Sandra Hollin Flowers, "'Colored Girls': Textbook for the Eighties," in Black American Literature Forum, *Vol. 15, No. 2, Summer, 1981, pp. 51-4.*

Toni Cade Bambara on *For Colored Girls:*

Blisteringly funny, fragile, droll and funky, lyrical, git down stompish, the play celebrates survival. The portraits are not case studies of stunning wrecks hollering about paid dues and criminal overcharges. The pieces are not booze-based blues and ballads about lost love and missing teeth. The Shange brand of keepin' on does not spring from the foot-caught-in-the-trap-gnawin'-ankle-free-oh-my-god school of moaning. She celebrates the capacity to master pain and betrayals with wit, sister-sharing, reckless daring, and flight and forgetfulness if necessary. She celebrates most of all women's loyalties to women.

Toni Cade Bambara, in Ms., *September 1976.*

John Timpane (essay date 1989)

[*In the following essay, Timpane examines the relationship between form and meaning in Shange's dramas, particularly* For Colored Girls. *He asserts that, in spite of the specific audience Shange targets in the title of her best known play, her work is open to a wide variety of interpretive and performance possibilities.*]

Ntozake Shange's four best-known dramatic works appeared in the late 1970s. Her most popular work, ***for colored girls who have considered suicide / when the rainbow is enuf,*** began as a cycle of seven poems in 1974, and by 1976 it had reached Broadway. ***a photograph*** appeared in different versions in 1977 and 1979, and ***boogie woogie landscapes*** appeared as a one-woman show in 1978 and in play form in 1979. ***spell #7: geechee jibara quik magic trance manual for technologically stressed third world people*** first appeared in 1979. This impressive burst of productivity took place largely during the Carter years; ten years later, these pieces, though not exactly dated, bear the stamp of a period of social transition, of frustrations and possibilities, of a sense of imminent change and the necessity for improvisation.

That decade's remove makes it clear that Shange's dramatic work, especially ***colored girls,*** represents a moment of crucial importance in black and American history. (An unrepeatable moment, I might add. One could no more write a ***colored girls*** now than one could write another *Brave New World.* In her own words [in a 1982 interview with Charlene Hunter Gault], these are works "dealing with a period of time that hasn't existed . . . for very long" and that underwent almost immediate change.) Writers with whom she is often compared, such as Imamu Amiri Baraka and Nikki Giovanni, seem to speak of a different, earlier moment. Where these and other writers attacked the obstacles to black self-realization, Shange's dramas represent the tortured moment of becoming itself, *the* moment of emergence and discovery. Ambivalence and paradox mark this moment; a dynamic world full of potential inhabits the same sphere as an old dead world in which nothing can change. The future for Shange's characters fluctuates between a positive, realizable potential, such as Marx envisioned, and a negative emptiness, such as Benjamin envisioned, which must be filled by individual effort and suffering. The process of becoming is Shange's subject, "our struggle to become all that is forbidden by our environment, all that is forfeited by our gender, all that we have forgotten" [***see no evil,*** 1984].

In ***spell #7, boogie woogie landscapes,*** and ***colored girls,*** there is no one outcome to the process of becoming, no one unifying end—but there is the process itself, in which all are engaged. What is more, communal expression may well be the only outlet for a certain range of feelings, according to Shange [in ***see no evil***]: "in addition to the obvious stress of racism n poverty / afro-american culture . . . has minimized its 'emotional' vocabulary to the extent that admitting feelings of rage, defeat, frustration is virtually impossible outside a collective voice." Again and again, Shange's dramas wander through a maze of personal and collective experience, only to coalesce in a chant that unites the subjective and the intersubjective. The women of ***colored girls*** chant

> i found god in myself
> & i loved her / i loved her fiercely

and the actresses, singers, magicians, and gypsies of ***spell #7*** end with the chant "colored & love it / love it / being colored," encompassing extremes of joy and pain. Even ***boogie woogie landscapes,*** which focuses exclusively on a single woman, ends with a chant:

> dontcha wanna be music / & ease into the fog
> dontcha wanna be like rain / a cosmic event /
> like sound. . . .

None of these epiphanies—the discovery of a "god" within one's self, the acceptance and love of being black, or the urge to be like music—"solve" the future, but they are communal starting points for a large number of possible futures.

There is, however, a paradox about Shange's work. As mentioned, her works are inscribed with the tensions of a very specific time and place. Further, these pieces announce themselves as being "for" a particular audience, such as colored girls or technologically stressed third-world people. Those pieces contain a great deal of aggression toward an oppressive white culture, an aggression that begins with an attack on white English: "i cant count the number of times i have viscerally wanted to attack deform n maim the language that i waz taught to hate myself in." "The mess of my fortune to be born black & English-speaking" has motivated her to cultivate nonwhite orthography, syntax, and what she has called verbal "distortions" [***see no evil***]. Yet despite all this effort at exclusion, her works remain remarkably "open" texts—that is, they anticipate and welcome the indeterminacy of any dramatic text and the unavoidable variation of performance. As a result, a series of texts that are addressed to, dedicated to, and written for a particular audience nevertheless throw themselves open to a multiplicity of audiences and performances. In this essay, I will examine this openness and its consequences for such a politically committed drama.

Texts are defenseless, most of all the text for a drama. No text can defend itself against being misread or misunderstood; the meaning of the text may change or be forgotten or be butchered over time, and no one can do anything about it. Doubly so for a text for a drama, which is, at best, a trace of a suggestion about the way a group of people might choose to act out that text. Directors and troupes fling texts down and dance upon them. But ***colored girls*** seems to me to be the kind of "open text" that people have been writing about for the past critical generation. Its undeniable power as a piece of performance art derives from that openness, which is, ironically, its best defense against being "miscast," "mis-directed," or "misunderstood." Not that ***colored girls*** has no subject—on the contrary, it has a very self-conscious program—but it anticipates the inevitability of variation and welcomes it, not, I think, as a means of defense against variation, but as a willing gesture toward it. The text of ***colored girls*** sets down a rhythm, but only as an invitation to improvisation:

> dark phrases of womanhood
> of never havin been a girl
> half-notes scattered
> without rhythm / no tone
> distraught laughter fallin
> over a black girl's shoulder
> it's funny / it's hysterical
> the melody-less-ness of her dance
> don't tell nobody don't tell a soul
> she's dancing on beer cans & shingles

These are the first 10 spoken lines in the piece. There are no sentences until the seventh line, and the connections between the fragments are completely open to interpretation. Add to this that ***colored girls*** is a "choreopoem," meaning that the speaker will be dancing or moving in some fashion, also undetermined, while delivering the lines; the flexibility of dance is likely to open the possibilities of interpretation even further. The speakers/dancers—one cannot call them characters—are identified not by name but by color ("lady in purple," and so forth). At times, they speak for themselves as centered personas, and at other times they narrate or act out the lives of others. In this second function it is always clear that they are bearers of someone else's tale; there is always an alienation, for example, between the lady in purple, who declares she is "outside houston," and Sechita, whose story she tells later. As the play ends, the question of who these particular colored women really are has faded before their communal becoming.

Much in the history of ***colored girls*** contributed to Shange's discovery of the open form. For example, she evidently originally conceived of the women as anonymous entities: "the women were to be nameless & assume hegemony as dictated by the fullness of their lives." From the beginning, the composition of ***colored girls*** was predicated on the unpredictability of performance—in a sense, the text apologizes for having to be written to give all the speaking and doing an origin. Such an origin is, after all, only a convention. Plenty of acting groups climb the stage nightly without a script. ***colored girls,*** despite its heavy program, gestures toward improvisational theatre. It was born in bars and jazz dives, and Shange has written [in ***see no evil***] of the early performances: "the selection of poems chang[ed], dependent upon our audience & our mood, & the dance [grew] to take space of its own." Jazz, dance, women's cooperatives, the Women's Studies Program at Sonoma State College, "The Raggae Blues Band giving Caribbean renditions of Jimi Hendrix & Redding"—certainly these are conditions of possibility under which performance was thrown open to all arts and audiences. Even the word "choreopoem," meaning a piece that is part dance and part language, was coined to describe a kind of writing that "fits in between all" genres and does justice to "human beings' first impulses," which are "to move and to speak."

Clearly, Shange and her associates were trying to give a great deal of autonomy to the work itself. She has written that "the most prescient change in the concept of the work" occurred when she gave up her role as director to Oz Scott. This, for Shange, was a way of subduing herself to the autonomy of the piece: "By doing this, I acknowledged that the poems & the dance worked on their own to do & be what they were" [***see no evil***]. Just as the piece seems to have anticipated the multeity of variations, so Shange, by resigning her directorship, anticipated the death of the author.

So far I have contrasted the political program in Shange's dramatic works with those works' openness. A closer examination of Shange's technique will reveal the paradox at closer range. Shange's most characteristic literary effects are those of collage. In the opening lines of ***colored girls*** and throughout her works, the fragment vies with the sentence, the image with the complete thought, as though the struggle between two grammars, one unofficial and one official, mirrors the struggle between two cultures:

> yr hair is acorns / you rest on glass / quick
> as a sailboat heeling / yr wine glass barely braizes yr lips /
> vermelho tambem / yr nails unpainted / ridiculously inviting
> you sit here in carved glass / in mirrors / on light /
> in sepia caves
> (***boogie woogie landscapes***)

The aesthetic values of the fragment—those of disjunction, disruption, juxtaposition, sudden illumination or recontextualization—are also political values. That is because the complete sentence, complete plot, and complete character—all the hallmarks of the rage for closure—are associated with a white European theatrical tradition. To choose the disruption and fragmentation of collage is a strike at those values:

> as a poet in the american theater / i find most activity that takes place on our stages overwhelmingly shallow / stilted & imitative. that is probably one of the reasons i insist on calling myself a poet or writer / rather than a playwright / i am interested solely in the poetry of a moment / the emotional & aesthetic impact of a character or a line.

Shange sees her choice of the "poetry of the moment" as a choice against the European bias of white American culture:

> for too long now afro-americans in theater have been duped by the same artificial aesthetics that plague our white counterparts / "the perfect play," as we know it to be / a truly european framework for european psychology / cannot function efficiently for those of us in this hemisphere.
> [***see no evil***]

If the European insistence on closure is not appropriate for white American playwrights, it is still less so for the poet in an Afro-American theatre.

Collage is inherently subversive in that the artist who employs collage hopes to make meanings by disruption and juxtaposition rather than by the ordered sequence of signs prescribed by the rules of grammar—which is as much as to say that collage proposes a syntax to replace the standard syntax. Because of its subversive character, collage is a way of opening up the canon. It is used to challenge preconceived notions, show unexpected connections, and call forth the richness and dynamism of existence:

> at the disco we shout the praises of the almighty
> i wrap my arms around you til the end
> (***boogie woogie landscapes***)

At its least successful, collage can become merely associational, merely automatic: Castro / Santa Claus / Santa Cruz / the True Cross. Its very danger is that the number of possible connections is so very large, virtually infinite, while the number of meaningful connections is much smaller. Despite much critical support over the last 20 years, synchronic techniques such as collage have severe drawbacks as artistic tools. Synchrony can furnish flashes of light but is less effective as a means of developing or sustaining a continuous fire. Thus, for Shange, as for any literary *bricoleur,* the challenge is to fashion and sustain a drama that is not a single narration but a series of conflicts and collisions. Shange's solution has been to balance the potential anarchy of collage with a consistent political purpose.

An element of collage exists even in Shange's main dramatic technique, that of call and response, the monologue delivered against a chorus of voices. The magician lou begins ***spell #7*** with a bitter pastiche of a minstrel show, posing as Mr. Interlocutor while the rest of the cast is frozen kneeling. The piece is built on a series of monologues interspersed with various forms of group expression. ***boogie woogie landscapes*** is essentially a series of dialogues between layla and six "nightlife companions," six aspects of her dreams and memories. As voices collide, so do images from personal history, world history, fashion, and literary and pop culture. In its juxtapositions and emphasis on improvisation, call and response is a dialogistic form of collage.

A crucial distinction must be made here. Shange's collage is not the undirected and autonomous collage of surrealism, but a consciously motivated syncretism with a political agenda. After all, black history, be it African, Caribbean, or American, is characterized by collage and syncretism—just as white history is characterized by the myths of completion, racial unity, and progress. European theatre thus insists on closure, while Afro-American theatre, as Shange projects it, insists on the rough edge, the open, the fragment. The actor alec in ***spell #7*** recalls the tensions between past and present in his childhood. His family had become "paler" as it moved toward St. Louis, in "linear movement from sous' carolina to missouri / freedmen / landin in jackie wilson's yelp / daughters of the manumitted swimmin' in tina turner's grinds." Here, images of slavery collide with those of pop music. Sechita in ***colored girls*** combines the black connection with Egypt and her present as a dancer in a Creole carnival in Natchez: "sechita / goddess / of love / egypt / 2nd millenium / performin the rites / the conjurin of men / conjurin the spirit / in natchez / the mississippi spewed a heavy fume of barely movin waters." Here the connections emphasize the richness and paradoxes of black history—even as they narrate the bitter experience of black individuals. There are moments in Shange that verge on surrealism, such as when in ***boogie woogie landscapes*** Fidel Castro is envisioned doing a "revolutionary rhumba" and Jimmy Carter, the Secret Service, Leonid Brezhnev, and the Ayatollah Khomeini are seen dancing on the moon, but even here, the thrust of intention is too strong to overlook. These dignitaries dance on the moon, "all white n barren n free of anybody who looks like me," because they have shown themselves incapable of such spontaneity or rhythm on earth. Carter and Khomeini and Brezhnev are made ridiculous in order to elevate layla, who lacks these men's power but surpasses them in spirit and spontaneity. Conversely, in ***colored girls,*** ancient Egypt, mystery religions, and the Mississippi are invoked in order to ennoble Sechita, who, while glamorous, is really just a carny dancer avoiding the coins flung between her knees.

Further, Shange's counterorthography—specifically, her rejection of periods and capital letters and her idiosyncratic use of the virgule—allows her collages to be even more abrupt, even more violent, than they would be had they been expressed in standard English orthography. The virgule, after all, is used to show that several alternatives may be appropriate simultaneously: "i waz a peculiar sort of woman / wantin no kisses / no caresses / just power / heat & no eaziness of thrust" (***spell #7***). The proliferation of virgules in Shange shows that alternatives are always present, always in conflict or tension.

Thus, even though collage is an "opening" technique, it is tamed, as it were, by a strong political program. The tendency toward closure (Shange's politics) somehow coexists with the tendency away from it (Shange's technique). In light of that tension, what happens to what many viewers value most in her drama—its content? These are, we must remember, dramatic events that thousands of spectators have *used.* These people attended these pieces because they had heard, expected, or been told that this drama would variously identify, vindicate, and validate them. These works served and are serving a purpose. Accordingly, the intended audience for ***colored girls,*** for example, considers it a holy thing, an object of reverence. What happens to all that if we consider ***colored girls*** an open drama? Do we not deny that audience their special access, their special meaning?

As mentioned at the beginning of this essay, Shange's text shows the effort of exclusion. But I have never seen a performance of ***colored girls*** that singled out any kind of audience. In this way ***colored girls*** is distinctly democratic. There is plenty of *Publikumsbeschimpfung,* plenty of flaying of the male cock of the walk, plenty of moralism. But in these aspects, ***colored girls*** is firmly in the tradition of world drama, especially the tradition of the democracy of abuse as described by Bakhtin. Thus, the attacks against unfeeling males, stuck-up white women, the empowered classes, all these attacks that at times seem jejune or schoolgirlish in the text, work splendidly in performance because they establish that democracy of abuse. The characters in Shange's dramas abuse one another as a means of establishing the dignity of each player. One is not allowed dignity until one is dressed down in public—and I cannot think of a more ancient ritual. No one audience is singled out. The women of ***colored girls*** will speak to anyone who will listen; the singers and dancers of ***spell #7*** will perform for anyone—"we're doin this for you".

Is the chosen audience then deprived of their chosenness? Have we taken ***colored girls*** or ***spell*** or ***boogie woogie landscapes*** away from a particular group of people—women or blacks or black women—in giving it to whoever has ears and eyes? I don't see how. For one thing, an Afro-American woman wrote these pieces about and for colored girls and third-world people, her chosen audience, and any rights appertaining thereto are of course unimpeachable. The arrival of her work at a particular place and time was felicitous and crucial; it is rightfully valued by those it has helped. But that audience must, I think, take its place among all possible audiences, and its manifold interpretations of the manifold performances of ***colored girls*** or ***spell #7*** must take their places among all the other possible interpretations. Shange's most characteristic gesture is, as I have discussed, toward possibility rather than closure; her works evoke the complexity of human relations rather than the completion of given actions or characters. Her women, like her men, are unfinished and fallible and, therefore, worthy.

Shange's work suggests the kind of "canon" one might design for dramatic works. Let us not build a reading zoo and assign each work its cage. Instead, let us have a canon not of texts but of potential performance events. Perhaps we can say that a text of ***colored girls*** or ***spell #7*** or ***boogie woogie landscapes,*** like any script for any play, is just a template from which may be spun off a continuing series of performances. Let us identify pieces with texts that suggest the greatest possibility of variation while retaining an integral character; let us say that such texts make up a group that we cherish. I nominate, not the text, but the unended group of performances indicated by the text of ***colored girls*** for inclusion into this nonexistent canon. (pp. 91-101)

John Timpane, " 'The Poetry of a Moment': Politics and the Open Form in the Drama of Ntozake Shange," in Studies in American Drama, 1945-Present, *Vol. 4, 1989, pp. 91-101.*

SPELL #7

PRODUCTION REVIEWS

Richard Eder (review date 4 June 1979)

[*An American journalist and critic, Eder won the 1987 Pulitzer Prize for criticism. He spent twenty-five years as a critic and foreign correspondent for the* New York Times, *and then went on to write book reviews for the* Los Angeles Times. *In the following review, he praises Shange's "wit, lyricism and fierceness" in her approach to various themes in* Spell #7. *Eder concludes that, though the play is uneven and lacks dramatic cohesiveness, it is essentially the work of a gifted poet.*]

In ***Spell #7*** Ntozake Shange has gone back most fortunately to the loosely linked dramatic poetry that she used in ***For Colored Girls.*** From the results, it is clear that she had not exhausted either the content or the form.

Spell #7, which is being given at the Public Theater, continues to explore the relationships of black women and men as a stormy shipboard ceremony; liable to foundering in an estranging white sea. It is being performed by some of the finest black actors in New York with the warmth of an experience that is still evolving; and one that in its strongest moments is lovely and illuminating.

Where ***For Colored Girls*** used only women, ***Spell #7*** assembles a mixed group of characters. They are actors, dancers and singers, using their own names and, in a sense, playing themselves. They gather by two's and three's in the late-hours bar that is a kind of haven from the abrasions of the show-business world outside.

One tells of a producer who rejected her for a part because she wasn't black enough. She offered to play a white part, but he said it would damage his integrity. The ironies float about and nobody is spared: an actor rejects routine black roles because he is, he says, "a classically trained actor." Yet he tells the dancer he lives with that she must be realistic and take any roadshow job that she can get.

In no sense, though, is ***Spell #7*** a piece about show business. If Miss Shange has identified the actors as actors, it is partly because there are things she can say with special authority about them; but mostly it is to allow them to speak and move, and sometimes sing, with more naturalness. The feeling in the bar is that of a safe ground, a moment in time where each, with his or her bit of dramatic narration, was exploring a private feeling along with and beneath the set text.

Oz Scott's direction, and Dianne McIntyre's choreography give an extraordinary intimacy and spontaneity to the recitations, set very usefully in the small square space of the Public Theater's Other Stage. The performers are genuinely listening to each other, reacting and encouraging. It is like a jam session among musicians who tense up when the soloist reaches a difficult moment; and relax when it has come off well.

In the best of the sketches, Miss Shange's wit, lyricism and fierceness are marvelously evident. She can take a common-enough image and make it do wonders. There is the recitation by Laurie Carlos, who plays the waitress, about hair-brushing.

It starts off as a familiar theme: the significance of kinky hair for black women. Miss Carlos, stubby, energetic and an altogether splendid discovery, announces she will change her life dramatically by brushing her hair. She will brush it morning, noon and night; in taxis, window shopping, talking on the phone and standing in line at the unemployment office.

The result, she says, will be hair so straight and heavy that when she gets up in the morning she will fall over. By this time Miss Carlos has fallen over and is struggling on the floor. The image gains in comic intensity: from her hair she will brush bottles of Pouilly-Fuissé and a house stocked with expensive linen and blue satin pillows. The hair will not only be straight but violet-colored. By this time the satiric comedy has moved into a melancholy poetry. "How," she asks, "do you remove violet rain from blue satin pillows?"

There is a graceful, extended sketch of black men using a battery of seductive clichés on their women; Avery Brooks—who elsewhere sings beautifully—all but chokes on his own mellifluousness; and Count Stovall is comically blase.

There is a searing and powerful recitation by Miss Shange, who has imagined a woman seeking a world of her own by having a baby that she called Myself. Once Myself is born, the woman's delight dwindles; the baby begins crawling; it is no longer hers. There is a moving recitation in which Michelle Shay as narrator tells of thinking as a child that black people were by nature good and favored. They never got polio, she says, because when she used to watch polio appeals on television, they never seemed to picture black children.

Spell #7 is an uneven work; it is less unified and less tightly organized than ***Colored Girls.*** Some of the sketches and the poetry are fuzzy; one or two don't work, such as a long and rather turgid parody of white women, despite witty delivery by Mary Alice.

But as it stands, it is a talented and often beautiful work, excitingly performed; and there is reason to hope that if it continues to evolve it will become a remarkable one.

Richard Eder, in a review of "Spell #7," in The New York Times, *June 4, 1979, p. C13.*

Marilyn Stasio (review date 5 June 1979)

[*Stasio is an editor and theater critic. In the review below, she praises Shange's passion and imagination as displayed in* Spell #7. *Although she credits Shange with treating a broad spectrum of racial and artistic themes, she asserts that they are only superficially and haphazardly explored, resulting in "dazzling fragments [that] amuse and delight, but . . . don't really grab us where we live."*]

Ntozake Shange blew a lot of people away with the thrilling intensity of ***For Colored Girls. . . .*** Her new Choreopoem, ***Spell #7,*** now playing in workshop at the New York Shakespeare Festival's Public Theater, lacks the dramatic focus and force of that earlier work, but it does offer glimpses into the passion and beauty that bubble in Shange's fertile poetic imagination.

Spell #7 is set in a St. Louis bar, a hangout for black actors, dancers, and musicians. Even the bartender is a poet. Twisting the genre conventions of barroom melodrama, Shange has her artists bare their souls in poem-soliloquies, many of them illustrated by in-the-mood dances set to evocative musical compositions by Butch Morris and David Murray.

Still from the prologue to Spell #7, *in which the cast satirically examine the type of roles available to black American actors.*

The quality of these set pieces ranges from banal to beautiful, but the highs are very high. Mary Alice struts through a sensational character sketch of "a good clean woman from Brooklyn out for the night." Laurie Carlos strikes sparks as a working woman who unleashes the secret poet in her nature, and Michele Shay delivers a lovely monologue about a black girl's disillusionment in her childhood rituals.

Of all the extended poems, the most dramatic is a brillant comic piece about black American women pursued by black non-American men abroad. The entire company engages in this wickedly wise vignette, which features hilarious performances by Avery Brooks and Count Stovall as a variety of slippery-tongued lovers.

Working against these highs are other poems that are more didactic then dramatic, including a shallow and politically suspect sketch about white women, and a psychologically murky one about infanticide. Even the best material suffers from Shange's inability to prune, shape and throw away.

Staging is not an issue. Oz Scott has directed for maximum fluidity, and Victor En Yu Tan's lighting offers subtle punctuation. It falls squarely on the writer to pull her act together. Through narrative bridges, she raises plenty of themes: the artist's gift / curse to "make magic," society's manipulation of its artists, the exploitation of blacks by whites. But these are only perfunctorily explored, and they have little application to the individual pieces. Lacking dramatic cohesion, these dazzling fragments amuse and delight, but they don't really grab us where we live.

Marilyn Stasio, "Shange Casts a Mixed 'Spell'," in New York Post, *June 5, 1979.*

FURTHER READING

AUTHOR COMMENTARY

Lester, Neal A. "An Interview with Ntozake Shange." *Studies in American Drama* 5 (1990): 42-66.

Discussion of Shange's views on feminism, black theater traditions, and the function of language in her works.

Lyons, Brenda. "Interview with Ntozake Shange." *The Massachusetts Review* XXVIII, No. 4 (Winter 1987): 687-96.

Shange explains her feminism and the effect it has had on her writings.

Tate, Claudia. "Ntozake Shange." In her *Black Women Writers at Work,* pp. 149-74. New York: Continuum, 1983.

Interview in which Shange examines her writing process and how it is affected by her identity as a black person and as a woman.

OVERVIEW

Richards, Sandra L. "Conflicting Impulses in the Plays of Ntozake Shange." *Black American Literature Forum* 17, No. 2 (Summer 1983): 73-8.

Analyzes the dialectic in Shange's dramas between "an awareness of social oppression and commitment to struggle" and "a desire to transcend or bypass, through music and dance, the limitations of social and human existence."

FOR COLORED GIRLS WHO HAVE CONSIDERED SUICIDE / WHEN THE RAINBOW IS ENUF

Bambara, Toni Cade. "*For Colored Girls*—And White Girls Too." *Ms.* V, No. 3 (September 1976): 36, 38.

Reviews *For Colored Girls,* praising Shange's spirit, wit, and veracity. Bambara suggests that, of the various aspects of life Shange addresses in her play, "she celebrates most of all women's loyalties to women."

Barnes, Clive. "Ntozake Shange's *For Colored Girls* Opens at Papp's Anspacher Theater." *New York Times* (2 June 1976): 44.

Describes *For Colored Girls* as folk poetry, praising

Shange for the natural language and insightful message of her "totally extraordinary and wonderful" drama.

Brown, Janet. "*For Colored Girls Who Have Considered Suicide / When the Rainbow is Enuf.*" In her *Feminist Drama: Definition & Critical Analysis,* pp. 114-32. Metuchen, N. J.: The Scarecrow Press, 1979.

Compares *For Colored Girls* with other productions of feminist theater groups, concluding that Shange's work is unusually idealistic, and that it has a level of sophistication, complexity, and popular success that has eluded other feminist dramas.

Clurman, Harold. Review of *For Colored Girls. The Nation* 222, No. 17 (1 May 1976): 542.

Lauds Shange for conveying "pain and power, as well as . . . acrid wit" in *For Colored Girls.* Clurman adds that "the faces and bodies as well as the voices of the actresses give the occasion its special force."

Kalem, T. E. "He Done Her Wrong." *Time* 107, No. 25 (14 June 1976): 74.

Commends Shange for a "poignant, gripping, angry and beautiful theater work," though Kalem derides her for the unfavorable portrayal of black men in *For Colored Girls.*

Kauffmann, Stanley. Review of *For Colored Girls. The New Republic* 174, No. 27 (3 July 1976): 20-1.

Asserts that, in spite of some moments of effective melodrama, most of the writing of *For Colored Girls* is "hyperdramatic and . . . superficial."

Kerr, Walter. "From Brilliance to Bewilderment to a Blunder." *New York Times* (13 June 1976): II,5.

Includes a review of *For Colored Girls* which praises the creative and powerful acting by Trazana Beverley, describing her performance as "brilliant stage work." Kerr concludes, however, that the play lacks consistency and that it "never touches a hot stove, an exposed nerve."

Mitchell, Carolyn. " 'A Laying on of Hands': Transcending the City in Ntozake Shange's *For Colored Girls Who Have Considered Suicide / When the Rainbow Is Enuf.*" In *Women Writers and the City: Essays in Feminist Literary Criticism,* edited by Susan Merrill Squier, pp. 230-48. Knoxville: The University of Tennessee Press, 1984.

Discusses Shange's realistic depiction of the city and its role in the lives of black women. Mitchell suggests that Shange's poems indicate "the paradox of the modern American city as a place where black women experience the trauma of urban life, yet find the strength to transcend the pain."

Rushing, Andrea Benton. "For Colored Girls, Suicide or Struggle." *The Massachusetts Review* XXII, No. 3 (Autumn 1981): 539-50.

Praises Shange for her accurate portrayal of the language and movement, and the joys and difficulties of black women. She suggests, however, that the types of women depicted in *For Colored Girls* reflect "a narrow range."

SPELL #7

Beaufort, John. "Black Cast Electrifies Off-Broadway 'Choreopoem.' " *The Christian Science Monitor* (7 June 1979).

Praises the cast's performance in *Spell #7* and suggests that Shange has improved and expanded upon *For Colored Girls* with her blending of the spoken word, song, and dance.

Nelsen, Don. "Shange Casts a Powerful *Spell.*" *Daily News* (16 July 1979).

Lauds Shange for her energetic and powerful drama, citing in particular her "ability to make the word flesh, to fuse idea and character so that it comes out humanity."

MOTHER COURAGE & HER CHILDREN

Allen, Bonnie. "A Home Instinct." *Essence* 11, No. 4 (August 1980): 17, 20.

Describes Shange's adaptation of Brecht's drama as disappointing. Allen suggests that introducing the theme of racial tension while trying to maintain Brecht's original themes results in a vague and confusing message to the viewer.

Barnes, Clive. "American-Style *Courage* Is an Asset for Public." *New York Post* (14 May 1980).

Praises Shange and director Wilford Leach for creating a witty and accessible production, asserting that Brecht would have approved of Shange's adaptation of *Mother Courage.*

Gussow, Mel. Review of *Mother Courage & Her Children. New York Times* (14 May 1980).

Commends Shange for successfully adapting the language, setting, and themes of Brecht's work "without losing the essence of the play or of the heroine."

Watt, Douglas. "Brecht's *Mother Courage* Scalped Out West." *Daily News* (14 May 1980).

Assesses Shange's adaptation of Brecht's work as unsuccessful. Watt suggests that the subjects addressed by Shange in this production should have been presented in an original play instead of "debasing a modern classic."

Additional coverage of Shange's life and career is contained in the following sources published by Gale Research: *Black Literature Criticism,* Vol. 3; *Contemporary Authors,* Vols. 85-88; *Contemporary Authors Biography Series,* Vol. 3; *Contemporary Authors New Revision Series,* Vol. 27; *Contemporary Literary Criticism,* Vols. 8, 25, 38; and *Dictionary of Literary Biography,* Vol. 38.

CUMULATIVE INDEXES

How to Use This Index

The main references

Calvino, Italo 1923-1985.....CLC 5, 8, 11, 22, 33, 39, 73; SSC 3

list all author entries in the following Gale Literary Criticism series:

CLC = *Contemporary Literary Criticism*
CLR = *Children's Literature Review*
CMLC = *Classical and Medieval Literature Criticism*
DC = *Drama Criticism*
LC = *Literature Criticism from 1400 to 1800*
NCLC = *Nineteenth-Century Literature Criticism*
PC = *Poetry Criticism*
SSC = *Short Story Criticism*
TCLC = *Twentieth-Century Literary Criticism*

The cross-references

See also CANR 23; CA 85-88; obituary CA 116

list all author entries in the following Gale biographical and literary sources:

AAYA = *Authors & Artists for Young Adults*
AITN = *Authors in the News*
BLC = *Black Literature Criticism*
BW = *Black Writers*
CA = *Contemporary Authors*
CAAS = *Contemporary Authors Autobiography Series*
CABS = *Contemporary Authors Bibliographical Series*
CANR = *Contemporary Authors New Revision Series*
CAP = *Contemporary Authors Permanent Series*
CDALB = *Concise Dictionary of American Literary Biography*
CDBLB = *Concise Dictionary of British Literary Biography*
DLB = *Dictionary of Literary Biography*
DLBD = *Dictionary of Literary Biography Documentary Series*
DLBY = *Dictionary of Literary Biography Yearbook*
HW = *Hispanic Writers*
MAICYA = *Major Authors and Illustrators for Children and Young Adults*
MTCW = *Major 20th-Century Writers*
SAAS = *Something about the Author Autobiography Series*
SATA = *Something about the Author*
WLC = *World Literature Criticism, 1500 to the Present*
YABC = *Yesterday's Authors of Books for Children*

Literary Criticism Series Cumulative Author Index

A. E. .... **TCLC 3, 10**
See also Russell, George William
See also DLB 19

A. M.
See Megged, Aharon

Abasiyanik, Sait Faik 1906-1954
See Sait Faik
See also CA 123

Abbey, Edward 1927-1989...... **CLC 36, 59**
See also CA 45-48; 128; CANR 2

Abbott, Lee K(ittredge) 1947-...... **CLC 48**
See also CA 124

Abe Kobo 1924-............ **CLC 8, 22, 53**
See also CA 65-68; CANR 24; MTCW

Abell, Kjeld 1901-1961........... **CLC 15**
See also CA 111

Abish, Walter 1931-.............. **CLC 22**
See also CA 101; CANR 37

Abrahams, Peter (Henry) 1919-..... **CLC 4**
See also BW; CA 57-60; CANR 26; DLB 117; MTCW

Abrams, M(eyer) H(oward) 1912-... **CLC 24**
See also CA 57-60; CANR 13, 33; DLB 67

Abse, Dannie 1923-............ **CLC 7, 29**
See also CA 53-56; CAAS 1; CANR 4; DLB 27

Achebe, (Albert) Chinua(lumogu)
1930-........ **CLC 1, 3, 5, 7, 11, 26, 51**
See also BLC 1; BW; CA 1-4R; CANR 6, 26; CLR 20; DLB 117; MAICYA; MTCW; SATA 38, 40; WLC

Acker, Kathy 1948-.............. **CLC 45**
See also CA 117; 122

Ackroyd, Peter 1949-.......... **CLC 34, 52**
See also CA 123; 127

Acorn, Milton 1923-.............. **CLC 15**
See also CA 103; DLB 53

Adamov, Arthur 1908-1970 ...... **CLC 4, 25**
See also CA 17-18; 25-28R; CAP 2; MTCW

Adams, Alice (Boyd) 1926- ... **CLC 6, 13, 46**
See also CA 81-84; CANR 26; DLBY 86; MTCW

Adams, Douglas (Noel) 1952- ... **CLC 27, 60**
See also AAYA 4; BEST 89:3; CA 106; CANR 34; DLBY 83

Adams, Francis 1862-1893....... **NCLC 33**

Adams, Henry (Brooks)
1838-1918 .... **TCLC 4**
See also CA 104; 133; DLB 12, 47

Adams, Richard (George)
1920- .... **CLC 4, 5, 18**
See also AITN 1, 2; CA 49-52; CANR 3, 35; CLR 20; MAICYA; MTCW; SATA 7, 69

Adamson, Joy(-Friederike Victoria)
1910-1980 .... **CLC 17**
See also CA 69-72; 93-96; CANR 22; MTCW; SATA 11, 22

Adcock, Fleur 1934-............. **CLC 41**
See also CA 25-28R; CANR 11, 34; DLB 40

Addams, Charles (Samuel)
1912-1988 .... **CLC 30**
See also CA 61-64; 126; CANR 12

Addison, Joseph 1672-1719 .... **LC 18**
See also CDBLB 1660-1789; DLB 101

Adler, C(arole) S(chwerdtfeger)
1932- .... **CLC 35**
See also AAYA 4; CA 89-92; CANR 19; MAICYA; SATA 26, 63

Adler, Renata 1938-........... **CLC 8, 31**
See also CA 49-52; CANR 5, 22; MTCW

Ady, Endre 1877-1919 .... **TCLC 11**
See also CA 107

Afton, Effie
See Harper, Frances Ellen Watkins

Agapida, Fray Antonio
See Irving, Washington

Agee, James (Rufus)
1909-1955 .... **TCLC 1, 19**
See also AITN 1; CA 108; CDALB 1941-1968; DLB 2, 26

Aghill, Gordon
See Silverberg, Robert

Agnon, S(hmuel) Y(osef Halevi)
1888-1970 .... **CLC 4, 8, 14**
See also CA 17-18; 25-28R; CAP 2; MTCW

Aherne, Owen
See Cassill, R(onald) V(erlin)

Ai 1947-.................. **CLC 4, 14, 69**
See also CA 85-88; CAAS 13; DLB 120

Aickman, Robert (Fordyce)
1914-1981 .... **CLC 57**
See also CA 5-8R; CANR 3

Aiken, Conrad (Potter)
1889-1973 ... **CLC 1, 3, 5, 10, 52; SSC 9**
See also CA 5-8R; 45-48; CANR 4; CDALB 1929-1941; DLB 9, 45, 102; MTCW; SATA 3, 30

Aiken, Joan (Delano) 1924-........ **CLC 35**
See also AAYA 1; CA 9-12R; CANR 4, 23, 34; CLR 1, 19; MAICYA; MTCW; SAAS 1; SATA 2, 30

Ainsworth, William Harrison
1805-1882 .... **NCLC 13**
See also DLB 21; SATA 24

Aitmatov, Chingiz (Torekulovich)
1928- .... **CLC 71**
See also CA 103; CANR 38; MTCW; SATA 56

Akers, Floyd
See Baum, L(yman) Frank

Akhmadulina, Bella Akhatovna
1937- .... **CLC 53**
See also CA 65-68

Akhmatova, Anna
1888-1966 .... **CLC 11, 25, 64; PC 2**
See also CA 19-20; 25-28R; CANR 35; CAP 1; MTCW

Aksakov, Sergei Timofeyvich
1791-1859 .... **NCLC 2**

Aksenov, Vassily .... **CLC 22**
See also Aksyonov, Vassily (Pavlovich)

Aksyonov, Vassily (Pavlovich)
1932- .... **CLC 37**
See also Aksenov, Vassily
See also CA 53-56; CANR 12

Akutagawa Ryunosuke
1892-1927 .... **TCLC 16**
See also CA 117

Alain 1868-1951 .... **TCLC 41**

Alain-Fournier .... **TCLC 6**
See also Fournier, Henri Alban
See also DLB 65

Alarcon, Pedro Antonio de
1833-1891 .... **NCLC 1**

Alas (y Urena), Leopoldo (Enrique Garcia)
1852-1901 .... **TCLC 29**
See also CA 113; 131; HW

Albee, Edward (Franklin III)
1928- ... **CLC 1, 2, 3, 5, 9, 11, 13, 25, 53**
See also AITN 1; CA 5-8R; CABS 3; CANR 8; CDALB 1941-1968; DLB 7; MTCW; WLC

Alberti, Rafael 1902-.............. **CLC 7**
See also CA 85-88; DLB 108

Alcala-Galiano, Juan Valera y
See Valera y Alcala-Galiano, Juan

Alcott, Amos Bronson 1799-1888 .. **NCLC 1**
See also DLB 1

Alcott, Louisa May 1832-1888 .... **NCLC 6**
See also CDALB 1865-1917; CLR 1; DLB 1, 42, 79; MAICYA; WLC; YABC 1

Aldanov, M. A.
See Aldanov, Mark (Alexandrovich)

Aldanov, Mark (Alexandrovich)
1886(?)-1957 .... **TCLC 23**
See also CA 118

Aldington, Richard 1892-1962...... **CLC 49**
See also CA 85-88; DLB 20, 36, 100

Aldiss, Brian W(ilson)
1925-.................. **CLC 5, 14, 40**
See also CA 5-8R; CAAS 2; CANR 5, 28; DLB 14; MTCW; SATA 34

Alegria, Fernando 1918-........... **CLC 57**
See also CA 9-12R; CANR 5, 32; HW

Aleichem, Sholom .... **TCLC 1, 35**
See also Rabinovitch, Sholem

Aleixandre, Vicente 1898-1984 . . . **CLC 9, 36**
See also CA 85-88; 114; CANR 26; DLB 108; HW; MTCW

Alepoudelis, Odysseus
See Elytis, Odysseus

Aleshkovsky, Joseph 1929-
See Aleshkovsky, Yuz
See also CA 121; 128

Aleshkovsky, Yuz . . . . **CLC 44**
See also Aleshkovsky, Joseph

Alexander, Lloyd (Chudley) 1924- . . **CLC 35**
See also AAYA 1; CA 1-4R; CANR 1, 24, 38; CLR 1, 5; DLB 52; MAICYA; MTCW; SATA 3, 49

Alfau, Felipe 1902- . . . . **CLC 66**
See also CA 137

Alger, Horatio Jr. 1832-1899 . . . . . **NCLC 8**
See also DLB 42; SATA 16

Algren, Nelson 1909-1981 . . . . **CLC 4, 10, 33**
See also CA 13-16R; 103; CANR 20; CDALB 1941-1968; DLB 9; DLBY 81, 82; MTCW

Ali, Ahmed 1910- . . . . **CLC 69**
See also CA 25-28R; CANR 15, 34

Alighieri, Dante 1265-1321 . . . . **CMLC 3**

Allan, John B.
See Westlake, Donald E(dwin)

Allen, Edward 1948- . . . . **CLC 59**

Allen, Roland
See Ayckbourn, Alan

Allen, Woody 1935- . . . . **CLC 16, 52**
See also CA 33-36R; CANR 27, 38; DLB 44; MTCW

Allende, Isabel 1942- . . . . **CLC 39, 57**
See also CA 125; 130; HW; MTCW

Alleyn, Ellen
See Rossetti, Christina (Georgina)

Allingham, Margery (Louise) 1904-1966 . . . . **CLC 19**
See also CA 5-8R; 25-28R; CANR 4; DLB 77; MTCW

Allingham, William 1824-1889 . . . **NCLC 25**
See also DLB 35

Allston, Washington 1779-1843. . . . **NCLC 2**
See also DLB 1

Almedingen, E. M. . . . . **CLC 12**
See also Almedingen, Martha Edith von
See also SATA 3

Almedingen, Martha Edith von 1898-1971
See Almedingen, E. M.
See also CA 1-4R; CANR 1

Alonso, Damaso 1898-1990 . . . . **CLC 14**
See also CA 110; 131; 130; DLB 108; HW

Alta 1942- . . . . **CLC 19**
See also CA 57-60

Alter, Robert B(ernard) 1935- . . . . . . **CLC 34**
See also CA 49-52; CANR 1

Alther, Lisa 1944- . . . . **CLC 7, 41**
See also CA 65-68; CANR 12, 30; MTCW

Altman, Robert 1925- . . . . **CLC 16**
See also CA 73-76

Alvarez, A(lfred) 1929- . . . . **CLC 5, 13**
See also CA 1-4R; CANR 3, 33; DLB 14, 40

Alvarez, Alejandro Rodriguez 1903-1965
See Casona, Alejandro
See also CA 131; 93-96; HW

Amado, Jorge 1912- . . . . **CLC 13, 40**
See also CA 77-80; CANR 35; DLB 113; MTCW

Ambler, Eric 1909- . . . . **CLC 4, 6, 9**
See also CA 9-12R; CANR 7, 38; DLB 77; MTCW

Amichai, Yehuda 1924- . . . . . . **CLC 9, 22, 57**
See also CA 85-88; MTCW

Amiel, Henri Frederic 1821-1881 . . **NCLC 4**

Amis, Kingsley (William) 1922- . . . . . . **CLC 1, 2, 3, 5, 8, 13, 40, 44**
See also AITN 2; CA 9-12R; CANR 8, 28; CDBLB 1945-1960; DLB 15, 27, 100; MTCW

Amis, Martin (Louis) 1949- . . . . **CLC 4, 9, 38, 62**
See also BEST 90:3; CA 65-68; CANR 8, 27; DLB 14

Ammons, A(rchie) R(andolph) 1926- . . . . **CLC 2, 3, 5, 8, 9, 25, 57**
See also AITN 1; CA 9-12R; CANR 6, 36; DLB 5; MTCW

Amo, Tauraatua i
See Adams, Henry (Brooks)

Anand, Mulk Raj 1905- . . . . **CLC 23**
See also CA 65-68; CANR 32; MTCW

Anatol
See Schnitzler, Arthur

Anaya, Rudolfo A(lfonso) 1937- . . . . **CLC 23**
See also CA 45-48; CAAS 4; CANR 1, 32; DLB 82; HW; MTCW

Andersen, Hans Christian 1805-1875 . . . . **NCLC 7; SSC 6**
See also CLR 6; MAICYA; WLC; YABC 1

Anderson, C. Farley
See Mencken, H(enry) L(ouis); Nathan, George Jean

Anderson, Jessica (Margaret) Queale . . . . **CLC 37**
See also CA 9-12R; CANR 4

Anderson, Jon (Victor) 1940- . . . . **CLC 9**
See also CA 25-28R; CANR 20

Anderson, Lindsay (Gordon) 1923- . . . . **CLC 20**
See also CA 125; 128

Anderson, Maxwell 1888-1959 . . . . . **TCLC 2**
See also CA 105; DLB 7

Anderson, Poul (William) 1926- . . . . **CLC 15**
See also AAYA 5; CA 1-4R; CAAS 2; CANR 2, 15, 34; DLB 8; MTCW; SATA 39

Anderson, Robert (Woodruff) 1917- . . . . **CLC 23**
See also AITN 1; CA 21-24R; CANR 32; DLB 7

Anderson, Sherwood 1876-1941 . . . . . . **TCLC 1, 10, 24; SSC 1**
See also CA 104; 121; CDALB 1917-1929; DLB 4, 9, 86; DLBD 1; MTCW; WLC

Andouard
See Giraudoux, (Hippolyte) Jean

Andrade, Carlos Drummond de . . . . . . **CLC 18**
See also Drummond de Andrade, Carlos

Andrade, Mario de 1893-1945 . . . . . **TCLC 43**

Andrewes, Lancelot 1555-1626 . . . . **LC 5**

Andrews, Cicily Fairfield
See West, Rebecca

Andrews, Elton V.
See Pohl, Frederik

Andreyev, Leonid (Nikolaevich) 1871-1919 . . . . **TCLC 3**
See also CA 104

Andric, Ivo 1892-1975 . . . . **CLC 8**
See also CA 81-84; 57-60; MTCW

Angelique, Pierre
See Bataille, Georges

Angell, Roger 1920- . . . . **CLC 26**
See also CA 57-60; CANR 13

Angelou, Maya 1928- . . . . **CLC 12, 35, 64**
See also AAYA 7; BLC 1; BW; CA 65-68; CANR 19; DLB 38; MTCW; SATA 49

Annensky, Innokenty Fyodorovich 1856-1909 . . . . **TCLC 14**
See also CA 110

Anon, Charles Robert
See Pessoa, Fernando (Antonio Nogueira)

Anouilh, Jean (Marie Lucien Pierre) 1910-1987 . . . . . . **CLC 1, 3, 8, 13, 40, 50**
See also CA 17-20R; 123; CANR 32; MTCW

Anthony, Florence
See Ai

Anthony, John
See Ciardi, John (Anthony)

Anthony, Peter
See Shaffer, Anthony (Joshua); Shaffer, Peter (Levin)

Anthony, Piers 1934- . . . . **CLC 35**
See also CA 21-24R; CANR 28; DLB 8; MTCW

Antoine, Marc
See Proust, (Valentin-Louis-George-Eugene-)Marcel

Antoninus, Brother
See Everson, William (Oliver)

Antonioni, Michelangelo 1912- . . . . . **CLC 20**
See also CA 73-76

Antschel, Paul 1920-1970. . . . . . . **CLC 10, 19**
See also Celan, Paul
See also CA 85-88; CANR 33; MTCW

Anwar, Chairil 1922-1949 . . . . **TCLC 22**
See also CA 121

Apollinaire, Guillaume . . . . **TCLC 3, 8**
See also Kostrowitzki, Wilhelm Apollinaris de

Appelfeld, Aharon 1932- . . . . **CLC 23, 47**
See also CA 112; 133

Apple, Max (Isaac) 1941- . . . . **CLC 9, 33**
See also CA 81-84; CANR 19

Appleman, Philip (Dean) 1926- . . . . . **CLC 51**
See also CA 13-16R; CANR 6, 29

Appleton, Lawrence
See Lovecraft, H(oward) P(hillips)

Apuleius, (Lucius Madaurensis) 125(?)-175(?) . . . . **CMLC 1**

Aquin, Hubert 1929-1977. . . . . **CLC 15**
See also CA 105; DLB 53

Aragon, Louis 1897-1982 . . . . **CLC 3, 22**
See also CA 69-72; 108; CANR 28; DLB 72; MTCW

Arany, Janos 1817-1882. . . . . **NCLC 34**

Arbuthnot, John 1667-1735 . . . . **LC 1**
See also DLB 101

Archer, Herbert Winslow
See Mencken, H(enry) L(ouis)

Archer, Jeffrey (Howard) 1940- . . . . **CLC 28**
See also BEST 89:3; CA 77-80; CANR 22

Archer, Jules 1915- . . . . **CLC 12**
See also CA 9-12R; CANR 6; SAAS 5; SATA 4

Archer, Lee
See Ellison, Harlan

Arden, John 1930- . . . . **CLC 6, 13, 15**
See also CA 13-16R; CAAS 4; CANR 31; DLB 13; MTCW

Arenas, Reinaldo 1943-1990 . . . . **CLC 41**
See also CA 124; 128; 133; HW

Arendt, Hannah 1906-1975 . . . . **CLC 66**
See also CA 17-20R; 61-64; CANR 26; MTCW

Aretino, Pietro 1492-1556 . . . . **LC 12**

Arguedas, Jose Maria 1911-1969 . . . . **CLC 10, 18**
See also CA 89-92; DLB 113; HW

Argueta, Manlio 1936-. . . . . **CLC 31**
See also CA 131; HW

Ariosto, Ludovico 1474-1533. . . . . **LC 6**

Aristides
See Epstein, Joseph

Aristophanes 450B.C.-385B.C. . . . . **CMLC 4; DC 2**

Arlt, Roberto (Godofredo Christophersen) 1900-1942 . . . . **TCLC 29**
See also CA 123; 131; HW

Armah, Ayi Kwei 1939-. . . . . **CLC 5, 33**
See also BLC 1; BW; CA 61-64; CANR 21; DLB 117; MTCW

Armatrading, Joan 1950-. . . . . **CLC 17**
See also CA 114

Arnette, Robert
See Silverberg, Robert

Arnim, Achim von (Ludwig Joachim von Arnim) 1781-1831 . . . . **NCLC 5**
See also DLB 90

Arnim, Bettina von 1785-1859. . . . **NCLC 38**
See also DLB 90

Arnold, Matthew 1822-1888 . . . . **NCLC 6, 29; PC 5**
See also CDBLB 1832-1890; DLB 32, 57; WLC

Arnold, Thomas 1795-1842 . . . . . . **NCLC 18**
See also DLB 55

Arnow, Harriette (Louisa) Simpson 1908-1986 . . . . **CLC 2, 7, 18**
See also CA 9-12R; 118; CANR 14; DLB 6; MTCW; SATA 42, 47

Arp, Hans
See Arp, Jean

Arp, Jean 1887-1966. . . . . **CLC 5**
See also CA 81-84; 25-28R

Arrabal. . . . . **CLC 2, 9, 18**
See also Arrabal, Fernando

Arrabal, Fernando 1932- . . . . **CLC 58**
See also Arrabal
See also CA 9-12R; CANR 15

Arrick, Fran. . . . . **CLC 30**

Artaud, Antonin 1896-1948 . . . . . **TCLC 3, 36**
See also CA 104

Arthur, Ruth M(abel) 1905-1979. . . . **CLC 12**
See also CA 9-12R; 85-88; CANR 4; SATA 7, 26

Artsybashev, Mikhail (Petrovich) 1878-1927 . . . . **TCLC 31**

Arundel, Honor (Morfydd) 1919-1973 . . . . **CLC 17**
See also CA 21-22; 41-44R; CAP 2; SATA 4, 24

Asch, Sholem 1880-1957 . . . . **TCLC 3**
See also CA 105

Ash, Shalom
See Asch, Sholem

Ashbery, John (Lawrence) 1927- . . . **CLC 2, 3, 4, 6, 9, 13, 15, 25, 41**
See also CA 5-8R; CANR 9, 37; DLB 5; DLBY 81; MTCW

Ashdown, Clifford
See Freeman, R(ichard) Austin

Ashe, Gordon
See Creasey, John

Ashton-Warner, Sylvia (Constance) 1908-1984 . . . . **CLC 19**
See also CA 69-72; 112; CANR 29; MTCW

Asimov, Isaac 1920-1992 . . . . **CLC 1, 3, 9, 19, 26**
See also BEST 90:2; CA 1-4R; 137; CANR 2, 19, 36; CLR 12; DLB 8; MAICYA; MTCW; SATA 1, 26

Astley, Thea (Beatrice May) 1925- . . . . **CLC 41**
See also CA 65-68; CANR 11

Aston, James
See White, T(erence) H(anbury)

Asturias, Miguel Angel 1899-1974 . . . . **CLC 3, 8, 13**
See also CA 25-28; 49-52; CANR 32; CAP 2; DLB 113; HW; MTCW

Atares, Carlos Saura
See Saura (Atares), Carlos

Atheling, William
See Pound, Ezra (Weston Loomis)

Atheling, William Jr.
See Blish, James (Benjamin)

Atherton, Gertrude (Franklin Horn) 1857-1948 . . . . **TCLC 2**
See also CA 104; DLB 9, 78

Atherton, Lucius
See Masters, Edgar Lee

Atkins, Jack
See Harris, Mark

Atticus
See Fleming, Ian (Lancaster)

Atwood, Margaret (Eleanor) 1939- . . . . **CLC 2, 3, 4, 8, 13, 15, 25, 44; SSC 2**
See also BEST 89:2; CA 49-52; CANR 3, 24, 33; DLB 53; MTCW; SATA 50; WLC

Aubigny, Pierre d'
See Mencken, H(enry) L(ouis)

Aubin, Penelope 1685-1731(?). . . . . **LC 9**
See also DLB 39

Auchincloss, Louis (Stanton) 1917- . . . . **CLC 4, 6, 9, 18, 45**
See also CA 1-4R; CANR 6, 29; DLB 2; DLBY 80; MTCW

Auden, W(ystan) H(ugh) 1907-1973 . . . . . **CLC 1, 2, 3, 4, 6, 9, 11, 14, 43; PC 1**
See also CA 9-12R; 45-48; CANR 5; CDBLB 1914-1945; DLB 10, 20; MTCW; WLC

Audiberti, Jacques 1900-1965 . . . . . . **CLC 38**
See also CA 25-28R

Auel, Jean M(arie) 1936-. . . . . **CLC 31**
See also AAYA 7; BEST 90:4; CA 103; CANR 21

Auerbach, Erich 1892-1957 . . . . **TCLC 43**
See also CA 118

Augier, Emile 1820-1889 . . . . **NCLC 31**

August, John
See De Voto, Bernard (Augustine)

Augustine, St. 354-430. . . . . **CMLC 6**

Aurelius
See Bourne, Randolph S(illiman)

Austen, Jane 1775-1817 . . . . **NCLC 1, 13, 19, 33**
See also CDBLB 1789-1832; DLB 116; WLC

Auster, Paul 1947- . . . . **CLC 47**
See also CA 69-72; CANR 23

Austin, Mary (Hunter) 1868-1934 . . . . **TCLC 25**
See also CA 109; DLB 9, 78

Autran Dourado, Waldomiro
See Dourado, (Waldomiro Freitas) Autran

Averroes 1126-1198 . . . . **CMLC 7**
See also DLB 115

Avison, Margaret 1918-. . . . . **CLC 2, 4**
See also CA 17-20R; DLB 53; MTCW

Ayckbourn, Alan 1939- . . . . **CLC 5, 8, 18, 33, 74**
See also CA 21-24R; CANR 31; DLB 13; MTCW

Aydy, Catherine
See Tennant, Emma (Christina)

Ayme, Marcel (Andre) 1902-1967. . . **CLC 11**
See also CA 89-92; CLR 25; DLB 72

Ayrton, Michael 1921-1975. . . . . **CLC 7**
See also CA 5-8R; 61-64; CANR 9, 21

Azorin. . . . . **CLC 11**
See also Martinez Ruiz, Jose

Azuela, Mariano 1873-1952. . . . . **TCLC 3**
See also CA 104; 131; HW; MTCW

Baastad, Babbis Friis
See Friis-Baastad, Babbis Ellinor

Bab
See Gilbert, W(illiam) S(chwenck)

Babbis, Eleanor
See Friis-Baastad, Babbis Ellinor

Babel, Isaac (Emanuilovich) .... **TCLC 13**
See also Babel, Isaak (Emmanuilovich)

Babel, Isaak (Emmanuilovich)
1894-1941(?) .... **TCLC 2**
See also Babel, Isaac (Emanuilovich)
See also CA 104

Babits, Mihaly 1883-1941 .... **TCLC 14**
See also CA 114

Babur 1483-1530.................. **LC 18**

Bacchelli, Riccardo 1891-1985 ..... **CLC 19**
See also CA 29-32R; 117

Bach, Richard (David) 1936-....... **CLC 14**
See also AITN 1; BEST 89:2; CA 9-12R; CANR 18; MTCW; SATA 13

Bachman, Richard
See King, Stephen (Edwin)

Bachmann, Ingeborg 1926-1973..... **CLC 69**
See also CA 93-96; 45-48; DLB 85

Bacon, Francis 1561-1626 .... **LC 18**
See also CDBLB Before 1660

Bacovia, George.................. **TCLC 24**
See also Vasiliu, Gheorghe

Badanes, Jerome 1937-............ **CLC 59**

Bagehot, Walter 1826-1877 ...... **NCLC 10**
See also DLB 55

Bagnold, Enid 1889-1981.......... **CLC 25**
See also CA 5-8R; 103; CANR 5; DLB 13; MAICYA; SATA 1, 25

Bagrjana, Elisaveta
See Belcheva, Elisaveta

Bagryana, Elisaveta
See Belcheva, Elisaveta

Bailey, Paul 1937- .... **CLC 45**
See also CA 21-24R; CANR 16; DLB 14

Baillie, Joanna 1762-1851 .... **NCLC 2**
See also DLB 93

Bainbridge, Beryl (Margaret)
1933- .... **CLC 4, 5, 8, 10, 14, 18, 22, 62**
See also CA 21-24R; CANR 24; DLB 14; MTCW

Baker, Elliott 1922- .... **CLC 8**
See also CA 45-48; CANR 2

Baker, Nicholson 1957- .... **CLC 61**
See also CA 135

Baker, Ray Stannard 1870-1946 ... **TCLC 47**
See also CA 118

Baker, Russell (Wayne) 1925-...... **CLC 31**
See also BEST 89:4; CA 57-60; CANR 11; MTCW

Bakshi, Ralph 1938(?)-............ **CLC 26**
See also CA 112; 138

Bakunin, Mikhail (Alexandrovich)
1814-1876 .... **NCLC 25**

Baldwin, James (Arthur)
1924-1987 ..... **CLC 1, 2, 3, 4, 5, 8, 13, 15, 17, 42, 50, 67; DC 1; SSC 10**
See also AAYA 4; BLC 1; BW; CA 1-4R; 124; CABS 1; CANR 3, 24; CDALB 1941-1968; DLB 2, 7, 33; DLBY 87; MTCW; SATA 9, 54; WLC

Ballard, J(ames) G(raham)
1930- .... **CLC 3, 6, 14, 36; SSC 1**
See also AAYA 3; CA 5-8R; CANR 15, 39; DLB 14; MTCW

Balmont, Konstantin (Dmitriyevich)
1867-1943 .... **TCLC 11**
See also CA 109

Balzac, Honore de
1799-1850 .... **NCLC 5, 35; SSC 5**
See also DLB 119; WLC

Bambara, Toni Cade 1939- .... **CLC 19**
See also AAYA 5; BLC 1; BW; CA 29-32R; CANR 24; DLB 38; MTCW

Bamdad, A.
See Shamlu, Ahmad

Banat, D. R.
See Bradbury, Ray (Douglas)

Bancroft, Laura
See Baum, L(yman) Frank

Banim, John 1798-1842 .... **NCLC 13**
See also DLB 116

Banim, Michael 1796-1874 ...... **NCLC 13**

Banks, Iain
See Banks, Iain M(enzies)

Banks, Iain M(enzies) 1954- .... **CLC 34**
See also CA 123; 128

Banks, Lynne Reid .... **CLC 23**
See also Reid Banks, Lynne
See also AAYA 6

Banks, Russell 1940- .... **CLC 37, 72**
See also CA 65-68; CAAS 15; CANR 19

Banville, John 1945-.............. **CLC 46**
See also CA 117; 128; DLB 14

Banville, Theodore (Faullain) de
1832-1891 .... **NCLC 9**

Baraka, Amiri
1934- ... **CLC 1, 2, 3, 5, 10, 14, 33; PC 4**
See also Jones, LeRoi
See also BLC 1; BW; CA 21-24R; CABS 3; CANR 27, 38; CDALB 1941-1968; DLB 5, 7, 16, 38; DLBD 8; MTCW

Barbellion, W. N. P............... **TCLC 24**
See also Cummings, Bruce F(rederick)

Barbera, Jack 1945-.............. **CLC 44**
See also CA 110

Barbey d'Aurevilly, Jules Amedee
1808-1889 .... **NCLC 1**
See also DLB 119

Barbusse, Henri 1873-1935 .... **TCLC 5**
See also CA 105; DLB 65

Barclay, Bill
See Moorcock, Michael (John)

Barclay, William Ewert
See Moorcock, Michael (John)

Barea, Arturo 1897-1957 .... **TCLC 14**
See also CA 111

Barfoot, Joan 1946- .... **CLC 18**
See also CA 105

Baring, Maurice 1874-1945 .... **TCLC 8**
See also CA 105; DLB 34

Barker, Clive 1952- .... **CLC 52**
See also BEST 90:3; CA 121; 129; MTCW

Barker, George Granville
1913-1991 .... **CLC 8, 48**
See also CA 9-12R; 135; CANR 7, 38; DLB 20; MTCW

Barker, Harley Granville
See Granville-Barker, Harley
See also DLB 10

Barker, Howard 1946- .... **CLC 37**
See also CA 102; DLB 13

Barker, Pat 1943-................ **CLC 32**
See also CA 117; 122

Barlow, Joel 1754-1812 .... **NCLC 23**
See also DLB 37

Barnard, Mary (Ethel) 1909-....... **CLC 48**
See also CA 21-22; CAP 2

Barnes, Djuna
1892-1982 ... **CLC 3, 4, 8, 11, 29; SSC 3**
See also CA 9-12R; 107; CANR 16; DLB 4, 9, 45; MTCW

Barnes, Julian 1946-.............. **CLC 42**
See also CA 102; CANR 19

Barnes, Peter 1931- .... **CLC 5, 56**
See also CA 65-68; CAAS 12; CANR 33, 34; DLB 13; MTCW

Baroja (y Nessi), Pio 1872-1956 .... **TCLC 8**
See also CA 104

Baron, David
See Pinter, Harold

Baron Corvo
See Rolfe, Frederick (William Serafino Austin Lewis Mary)

Barondess, Sue K(aufman)
1926-1977 .... **CLC 8**
See also Kaufman, Sue
See also CA 1-4R; 69-72; CANR 1

Baron de Teive
See Pessoa, Fernando (Antonio Nogueira)

Barres, Maurice 1862-1923 .... **TCLC 47**

Barreto, Afonso Henrique de Lima
See Lima Barreto, Afonso Henrique de

Barrett, (Roger) Syd 1946- .... **CLC 35**
See also Pink Floyd

Barrett, William (Christopher)
1913- .... **CLC 27**
See also CA 13-16R; CANR 11

Barrie, J(ames) M(atthew)
1860-1937 .... **TCLC 2**
See also CA 104; 136; CDBLB 1890-1914; CLR 16; DLB 10; MAICYA; YABC 1

Barrington, Michael
See Moorcock, Michael (John)

Barrol, Grady
See Bograd, Larry

Barry, Mike
See Malzberg, Barry N(athaniel)

Barry, Philip 1896-1949.......... **TCLC 11**
See also CA 109; DLB 7

Bart, Andre Schwarz
See Schwarz-Bart, Andre

Barth, John (Simmons) 1930- . . . . . . **CLC 1, 2, 3, 5, 7, 9, 10, 14, 27, 51; SSC 10**
See also AITN 1, 2; CA 1-4R; CABS 1; CANR 5, 23; DLB 2; MTCW

Barthelme, Donald 1931-1989 . . . . . **CLC 1, 2, 3, 5, 6, 8, 13, 23, 46, 59; SSC 2**
See also CA 21-24R; 129; CANR 20; DLB 2; DLBY 80, 89; MTCW; SATA 7, 62

Barthelme, Frederick 1943- . . . . **CLC 36**
See also CA 114; 122; DLBY 85

Barthes, Roland (Gerard) 1915-1980 . . . . **CLC 24**
See also CA 130; 97-100; MTCW

Barzun, Jacques (Martin) 1907- . . . . **CLC 51**
See also CA 61-64; CANR 22

Bashevis, Isaac
See Singer, Isaac Bashevis

Bashkirtseff, Marie 1859-1884 . . . **NCLC 27**

Basho
See Matsuo Basho

Bass, Kingsley B. Jr.
See Bullins, Ed

Bassani, Giorgio 1916- . . . . **CLC 9**
See also CA 65-68; CANR 33; MTCW

Bastos, Augusto (Antonio) Roa
See Roa Bastos, Augusto (Antonio)

Bataille, Georges 1897-1962 . . . . **CLC 29**
See also CA 101; 89-92

Bates, H(erbert) E(rnest) 1905-1974 . . . . **CLC 46; SSC 10**
See also CA 93-96; 45-48; CANR 34; MTCW

Bauchart
See Camus, Albert

Baudelaire, Charles 1821-1867 . . . . **NCLC 6, 29; PC 1**
See also WLC

Baudrillard, Jean 1929- . . . . **CLC 60**

Baum, L(yman) Frank 1856-1919 . . . **TCLC 7**
See also CA 108; 133; CLR 15; DLB 22; MAICYA; MTCW; SATA 18

Baum, Louis F.
See Baum, L(yman) Frank

Baumbach, Jonathan 1933- . . . . . . **CLC 6, 23**
See also CA 13-16R; CAAS 5; CANR 12; DLBY 80; MTCW

Bausch, Richard (Carl) 1945- . . . . . . **CLC 51**
See also CA 101; CAAS 14

Baxter, Charles 1947- . . . . **CLC 45**
See also CA 57-60

Baxter, James K(eir) 1926-1972 . . . . **CLC 14**
See also CA 77-80

Baxter, John
See Hunt, E(verette) Howard Jr.

Bayer, Sylvia
See Glassco, John

Beagle, Peter S(oyer) 1939- . . . . **CLC 7**
See also CA 9-12R; CANR 4; DLBY 80; SATA 60

Bean, Normal
See Burroughs, Edgar Rice

Beard, Charles A(ustin) 1874-1948 . . . . **TCLC 15**
See also CA 115; DLB 17; SATA 18

Beardsley, Aubrey 1872-1898 . . . . . **NCLC 6**

Beattie, Ann 1947- . . . . **CLC 8, 13, 18, 40, 63; SSC 11**
See also BEST 90:2; CA 81-84; DLBY 82; MTCW

Beattie, James 1735-1803 . . . . **NCLC 25**
See also DLB 109

Beauchamp, Kathleen Mansfield 1888-1923
See Mansfield, Katherine
See also CA 104; 134

Beauvoir, Simone (Lucie Ernestine Marie Bertrand) de 1908-1986 . . . **CLC 1, 2, 4, 8, 14, 31, 44, 50, 71**
See also CA 9-12R; 118; CANR 28; DLB 72; DLBY 86; MTCW; WLC

Becker, Jurek 1937- . . . . **CLC 7, 19**
See also CA 85-88; DLB 75

Becker, Walter 1950- . . . . **CLC 26**

Beckett, Samuel (Barclay) 1906-1989 . . . . . **CLC 1, 2, 3, 4, 6, 9, 10, 11, 14, 18, 29, 57, 59**
See also CA 5-8R; 130; CANR 33; CDBLB 1945-1960; DLB 13, 15; DLBY 90; MTCW; WLC

Beckford, William 1760-1844 . . . . **NCLC 16**
See also DLB 39

Beckman, Gunnel 1910- . . . . **CLC 26**
See also CA 33-36R; CANR 15; CLR 25; MAICYA; SAAS 9; SATA 6

Becque, Henri 1837-1899. . . . . **NCLC 3**

Beddoes, Thomas Lovell 1803-1849 . . . . **NCLC 3**
See also DLB 96

Bedford, Donald F.
See Fearing, Kenneth (Flexner)

Beecher, Catharine Esther 1800-1878 . . . . **NCLC 30**
See also DLB 1

Beecher, John 1904-1980. . . . . **CLC 6**
See also AITN 1; CA 5-8R; 105; CANR 8

Beer, Johann 1655-1700. . . . . **LC 5**

Beer, Patricia 1924- . . . . **CLC 58**
See also CA 61-64; CANR 13; DLB 40

Beerbohm, Henry Maximilian 1872-1956 . . . . **TCLC 1, 24**
See also CA 104; DLB 34, 100

Begiebing, Robert J(ohn) 1946- . . . . . **CLC 70**
See also CA 122

Behan, Brendan 1923-1964 . . . . **CLC 1, 8, 11, 15**
See also CA 73-76; CANR 33; CDBLB 1945-1960; DLB 13; MTCW

Behn, Aphra 1640(?)-1689 . . . . **LC 1**
See also DLB 39, 80; WLC

Behrman, S(amuel) N(athaniel) 1893-1973 . . . . **CLC 40**
See also CA 13-16; 45-48; CAP 1; DLB 7, 44

Belasco, David 1853-1931 . . . . **TCLC 3**
See also CA 104; DLB 7

Belcheva, Elisaveta 1893- . . . . **CLC 10**

Beldone, Phil "Cheech"
See Ellison, Harlan

Beleno
See Azuela, Mariano

Belinski, Vissarion Grigoryevich 1811-1848 . . . . **NCLC 5**

Belitt, Ben 1911- . . . . **CLC 22**
See also CA 13-16R; CAAS 4; CANR 7; DLB 5

Bell, James Madison 1826-1902 . . . **TCLC 43**
See also BLC 1; BW; CA 122; 124; DLB 50

Bell, Madison (Smartt) 1957- . . . . . . **CLC 41**
See also CA 111; CANR 28

Bell, Marvin (Hartley) 1937- . . . . . **CLC 8, 31**
See also CA 21-24R; CAAS 14; DLB 5; MTCW

Bell, W. L. D.
See Mencken, H(enry) L(ouis)

Bellamy, Atwood C.
See Mencken, H(enry) L(ouis)

Bellamy, Edward 1850-1898 . . . . . . **NCLC 4**
See also DLB 12

Bellin, Edward J.
See Kuttner, Henry

Belloc, (Joseph) Hilaire (Pierre) 1870-1953 . . . . **TCLC 7, 18**
See also CA 106; DLB 19, 100; YABC 1

Belloc, Joseph Peter Rene Hilaire
See Belloc, (Joseph) Hilaire (Pierre)

Belloc, Joseph Pierre Hilaire
See Belloc, (Joseph) Hilaire (Pierre)

Belloc, M. A.
See Lowndes, Marie Adelaide (Belloc)

Bellow, Saul 1915- . . . . . **CLC 1, 2, 3, 6, 8, 10, 13, 15, 25, 33, 34, 63**
See also AITN 2; BEST 89:3; CA 5-8R; CABS 1; CANR 29; CDALB 1941-1968; DLB 2, 28; DLBD 3; DLBY 82; MTCW; WLC

Belser, Reimond Karel Maria de 1929- . . . . **CLC 14**

Bely, Andrey . . . . **TCLC 7**
See also Bugayev, Boris Nikolayevich

Benary, Margot
See Benary-Isbert, Margot

Benary-Isbert, Margot 1889-1979 . . . **CLC 12**
See also CA 5-8R; 89-92; CANR 4; CLR 12; MAICYA; SATA 2, 21

Benavente (y Martinez), Jacinto 1866-1954 . . . . **TCLC 3**
See also CA 106; 131; HW; MTCW

Benchley, Peter (Bradford) 1940- . . . . **CLC 4, 8**
See also AITN 2; CA 17-20R; CANR 12, 35; MTCW; SATA 3

Benchley, Robert (Charles) 1889-1945 . . . . **TCLC 1**
See also CA 105; DLB 11

Benedikt, Michael 1935- . . . . **CLC 4, 14**
See also CA 13-16R; CANR 7; DLB 5

Benet, Juan 1927- . . . . **CLC 28**

Benet, Stephen Vincent 1898-1943 . . . . **TCLC 7; SSC 10**
See also CA 104; DLB 4, 48, 102; YABC 1

Benet, William Rose 1886-1950 . . . **TCLC 28**
See also CA 118; DLB 45

Benford, Gregory (Albert) 1941- . . . . **CLC 52**
See also CA 69-72; CANR 12, 24; DLBY 82

Bengtsson, Frans (Gunnar) 1894-1954 . . . . **TCLC 48**

Benjamin, Lois
See Gould, Lois

Benjamin, Walter 1892-1940 . . . . . . **TCLC 39**

Benn, Gottfried 1886-1956 . . . . **TCLC 3**
See also CA 106; DLB 56

Bennett, Alan 1934- . . . . **CLC 45**
See also CA 103; CANR 35; MTCW

Bennett, (Enoch) Arnold 1867-1931 . . . . **TCLC 5, 20**
See also CA 106; CDBLB 1890-1914; DLB 10, 34, 98

Bennett, Elizabeth
See Mitchell, Margaret (Munnerlyn)

Bennett, George Harold 1930-
See Bennett, Hal
See also BW; CA 97-100

Bennett, Hal . . . . **CLC 5**
See also Bennett, George Harold
See also DLB 33

Bennett, Jay 1912- . . . . **CLC 35**
See also CA 69-72; CANR 11; SAAS 4; SATA 27, 41

Bennett, Louise (Simone) 1919- . . . . . **CLC 28**
See also BLC 1; DLB 117

Benson, E(dward) F(rederic) 1867-1940 . . . . **TCLC 27**
See also CA 114

Benson, Jackson J. 1930- . . . . **CLC 34**
See also CA 25-28R; DLB 111

Benson, Sally 1900-1972 . . . . **CLC 17**
See also CA 19-20; 37-40R; CAP 1; SATA 1, 27, 35

Benson, Stella 1892-1933 . . . . **TCLC 17**
See also CA 117; DLB 36

Bentham, Jeremy 1748-1832 . . . . . **NCLC 38**
See also DLB 107

Bentley, E(dmund) C(lerihew) 1875-1956 . . . . **TCLC 12**
See also CA 108; DLB 70

Bentley, Eric (Russell) 1916- . . . . **CLC 24**
See also CA 5-8R; CANR 6

Beranger, Pierre Jean de 1780-1857 . . . . **NCLC 34**

Berger, Colonel
See Malraux, (Georges-)Andre

Berger, John (Peter) 1926- . . . . . . **CLC 2, 19**
See also CA 81-84; DLB 14

Berger, Melvin H. 1927- . . . . **CLC 12**
See also CA 5-8R; CANR 4; SAAS 2; SATA 5

Berger, Thomas (Louis) 1924- . . . . **CLC 3, 5, 8, 11, 18, 38**
See also CA 1-4R; CANR 5, 28; DLB 2; DLBY 80; MTCW

Bergman, (Ernst) Ingmar 1918- . . . . **CLC 16, 72**
See also CA 81-84; CANR 33

Bergson, Henri 1859-1941 . . . . **TCLC 32**

Bergstein, Eleanor 1938- . . . . **CLC 4**
See also CA 53-56; CANR 5

Berkoff, Steven 1937- . . . . **CLC 56**
See also CA 104

Bermant, Chaim (Icyk) 1929- . . . . . . **CLC 40**
See also CA 57-60; CANR 6, 31

Bernanos, (Paul Louis) Georges 1888-1948 . . . . **TCLC 3**
See also CA 104; 130; DLB 72

Bernard, April 1956- . . . . **CLC 59**
See also CA 131

Bernhard, Thomas 1931-1989 . . . . **CLC 3, 32, 61**
See also CA 85-88; 127; CANR 32; DLB 85; MTCW

Berrigan, Daniel 1921- . . . . **CLC 4**
See also CA 33-36R; CAAS 1; CANR 11; DLB 5

Berrigan, Edmund Joseph Michael Jr. 1934-1983
See Berrigan, Ted
See also CA 61-64; 110; CANR 14

Berrigan, Ted . . . . **CLC 37**
See also Berrigan, Edmund Joseph Michael Jr.
See also DLB 5

Berry, Charles Edward Anderson 1931-
See Berry, Chuck
See also CA 115

Berry, Chuck . . . . **CLC 17**
See also Berry, Charles Edward Anderson

Berry, Jonas
See Ashbery, John (Lawrence)

Berry, Wendell (Erdman) 1934- . . . . **CLC 4, 6, 8, 27, 46**
See also AITN 1; CA 73-76; DLB 5, 6

Berryman, John 1914-1972 . . . . . **CLC 1, 2, 3, 4, 6, 8, 10, 13, 25, 62**
See also CA 13-16; 33-36R; CABS 2; CANR 35; CAP 1; CDALB 1941-1968; DLB 48; MTCW

Bertolucci, Bernardo 1940- . . . . **CLC 16**
See also CA 106

Bertrand, Aloysius 1807-1841 . . . . **NCLC 31**

Bertran de Born c. 1140-1215 . . . . . **CMLC 5**

Besant, Annie (Wood) 1847-1933 . . . **TCLC 9**
See also CA 105

Bessie, Alvah 1904-1985 . . . . **CLC 23**
See also CA 5-8R; 116; CANR 2; DLB 26

Bethlen, T. D.
See Silverberg, Robert

Beti, Mongo . . . . **CLC 27**
See also Biyidi, Alexandre
See also BLC 1

Betjeman, John 1906-1984 . . . . **CLC 2, 6, 10, 34, 43**
See also CA 9-12R; 112; CANR 33; CDBLB 1945-1960; DLB 20; DLBY 84; MTCW

Betti, Ugo 1892-1953 . . . . **TCLC 5**
See also CA 104

Betts, Doris (Waugh) 1932- . . . . **CLC 3, 6, 28**
See also CA 13-16R; CANR 9; DLBY 82

Bevan, Alistair
See Roberts, Keith (John Kingston)

Beynon, John
See Harris, John (Wyndham Parkes Lucas) Beynon

Bialik, Chaim Nachman 1873-1934 . . . . **TCLC 25**

Bickerstaff, Isaac
See Swift, Jonathan

Bidart, Frank 19(?)- . . . . **CLC 33**

Bienek, Horst 1930- . . . . **CLC 7, 11**
See also CA 73-76; DLB 75

Bierce, Ambrose (Gwinett) 1842-1914(?) . . . . . **TCLC 1, 7, 44; SSC 9**
See also CA 104; CDALB 1865-1917; DLB 11, 12, 23, 71, 74; WLC

Billings, Josh
See Shaw, Henry Wheeler

Billington, Rachel 1942- . . . . **CLC 43**
See also AITN 2; CA 33-36R

Binyon, T(imothy) J(ohn) 1936- . . . . **CLC 34**
See also CA 111; CANR 28

Bioy Casares, Adolfo 1914- . . . . **CLC 4, 8, 13**
See also CA 29-32R; CANR 19; DLB 113; HW; MTCW

Bird, C.
See Ellison, Harlan

Bird, Cordwainer
See Ellison, Harlan

Bird, Robert Montgomery 1806-1854 . . . . **NCLC 1**

Birney, (Alfred) Earle 1904- . . . . **CLC 1, 4, 6, 11**
See also CA 1-4R; CANR 5, 20; DLB 88; MTCW

Bishop, Elizabeth 1911-1979 . . . . . **CLC 1, 4, 9, 13, 15, 32; PC 3**
See also CA 5-8R; 89-92; CABS 2; CANR 26; CDALB 1968-1988; DLB 5; MTCW; SATA 24

Bishop, John 1935- . . . . **CLC 10**
See also CA 105

bissett, bill 1939- . . . . **CLC 18**
See also CA 69-72; CANR 15; DLB 53; MTCW

Bitov, Andrei (Georgievich) 1937- . . . **CLC 57**

Biyidi, Alexandre 1932-
See Beti, Mongo
See also BW; CA 114; 124; MTCW

Bjarme, Brynjolf
See Ibsen, Henrik (Johan)

Bjornson, Bjornstjerne (Martinius) 1832-1910 . . . . **TCLC 7, 37**
See also CA 104

Black, Robert
See Holdstock, Robert P.

Blackburn, Paul 1926-1971 . . . . . . **CLC 9, 43**
See also CA 81-84; 33-36R; CANR 34; DLB 16; DLBY 81

Black Elk 1863-1950 . . . . **TCLC 33**

Black Hobart
See Sanders, (James) Ed(ward)

Blacklin, Malcolm
See Chambers, Aidan

Blackmore, R(ichard) D(oddridge)
1825-1900 . . . . **TCLC 27**
See also CA 120; DLB 18

Blackmur, R(ichard) P(almer)
1904-1965 . . . . **CLC 2, 24**
See also CA 11-12; 25-28R; CAP 1; DLB 63

Black Tarantula, The
See Acker, Kathy

Blackwood, Algernon (Henry)
1869-1951 . . . . **TCLC 5**
See also CA 105

Blackwood, Caroline 1931- . . . . **CLC 6, 9**
See also CA 85-88; CANR 32; DLB 14; MTCW

Blade, Alexander
See Hamilton, Edmond; Silverberg, Robert

Blair, Eric (Arthur) 1903-1950
See Orwell, George
See also CA 104; 132; MTCW; SATA 29

Blais, Marie-Claire
1939- . . . . **CLC 2, 4, 6, 13, 22**
See also CA 21-24R; CAAS 4; CANR 38; DLB 53; MTCW

Blaise, Clark 1940- . . . . **CLC 29**
See also AITN 2; CA 53-56; CAAS 3; CANR 5; DLB 53

Blake, Nicholas
See Day Lewis, C(ecil)
See also DLB 77

Blake, William 1757-1827 . . . . **NCLC 13**
See also CDBLB 1789-1832; DLB 93; MAICYA; SATA 30; WLC

Blasco Ibanez, Vicente
1867-1928 . . . . **TCLC 12**
See also CA 110; 131; HW; MTCW

Blatty, William Peter 1928- . . . . **CLC 2**
See also CA 5-8R; CANR 9

Bleeck, Oliver
See Thomas, Ross (Elmore)

Blessing, Lee 1949- . . . . **CLC 54**

Blish, James (Benjamin)
1921-1975 . . . . **CLC 14**
See also CA 1-4R; 57-60; CANR 3; DLB 8; MTCW; SATA 66

Bliss, Reginald
See Wells, H(erbert) G(eorge)

Blixen, Karen (Christentze Dinesen)
1885-1962
See Dinesen, Isak
See also CA 25-28; CANR 22; CAP 2; MTCW; SATA 44

Bloch, Robert (Albert) 1917- . . . . **CLC 33**
See also CA 5-8R; CANR 5; DLB 44; SATA 12

Blok, Alexander (Alexandrovich)
1880-1921 . . . . **TCLC 5**
See also CA 104

Blom, Jan
See Breytenbach, Breyten

Bloom, Harold 1930- . . . . **CLC 24**
See also CA 13-16R; CANR 39; DLB 67

Bloomfield, Aurelius
See Bourne, Randolph S(illiman)

Blount, Roy (Alton) Jr. 1941- . . . . . . **CLC 38**
See also CA 53-56; CANR 10, 28; MTCW

Bloy, Leon 1846-1917 . . . . **TCLC 22**
See also CA 121

Blume, Judy (Sussman) 1938- . . . **CLC 12, 30**
See also AAYA 3; CA 29-32R; CANR 13, 37; CLR 2, 15; DLB 52; MAICYA; MTCW; SATA 2, 31

Blunden, Edmund (Charles)
1896-1974 . . . . **CLC 2, 56**
See also CA 17-18; 45-48; CAP 2; DLB 20, 100; MTCW

Bly, Robert (Elwood)
1926- . . . . **CLC 1, 2, 5, 10, 15, 38**
See also CA 5-8R; DLB 5; MTCW

Bobette
See Simenon, Georges (Jacques Christian)

Boccaccio, Giovanni 1313-1375
See also SSC 10

Bochco, Steven 1943- . . . . **CLC 35**
See also CA 124; 138

Bodenheim, Maxwell 1892-1954 . . . **TCLC 44**
See also CA 110; DLB 9, 45

Bodker, Cecil 1927- . . . . **CLC 21**
See also CA 73-76; CANR 13; CLR 23; MAICYA; SATA 14

Boell, Heinrich (Theodor)
1917-1985 . . . **CLC 2, 3, 6, 9, 11, 15, 27, 39**
See also Boll, Heinrich (Theodor)
See also CA 21-24R; 116; CANR 24; DLB 69; DLBY 85; MTCW

Bogan, Louise 1897-1970 . . . . . **CLC 4, 39, 46**
See also CA 73-76; 25-28R; CANR 33; DLB 45; MTCW

Bogarde, Dirk . . . . **CLC 19**
See also Van Den Bogarde, Derek Jules Gaspard Ulric Niven
See also DLB 14

Bogosian, Eric 1953- . . . . **CLC 45**
See also CA 138

Bograd, Larry 1953- . . . . **CLC 35**
See also CA 93-96; SATA 33

Boiardo, Matteo Maria 1441-1494 . . . . **LC 6**

Boileau-Despreaux, Nicolas
1636-1711 . . . . **LC 3**

Boland, Eavan 1944- . . . . **CLC 40, 67**
See also DLB 40

Boleslaw, Prus . . . . **TCLC 48**
See also Glowacki, Aleksander

Boll, Heinrich (Theodor)
1917-1985 . . . **CLC 2, 3, 6, 9, 11, 15, 27, 39, 72**
See also Boell, Heinrich (Theodor)
See also DLB 69; DLBY 85; WLC

Bolt, Robert (Oxton) 1924- . . . . **CLC 14**
See also CA 17-20R; CANR 35; DLB 13; MTCW

Bomkauf
See Kaufman, Bob (Garnell)

Bonaventura . . . . **NCLC 35**
See also DLB 90

Bond, Edward 1934- . . . . **CLC 4, 6, 13, 23**
See also CA 25-28R; CANR 38; DLB 13; MTCW

Bonham, Frank 1914-1989 . . . . **CLC 12**
See also AAYA 1; CA 9-12R; CANR 4, 36; MAICYA; SAAS 3; SATA 1, 49, 62

Bonnefoy, Yves 1923- . . . . **CLC 9, 15, 58**
See also CA 85-88; CANR 33; MTCW

Bontemps, Arna(ud Wendell)
1902-1973 . . . . **CLC 1, 18**
See also BLC 1; BW; CA 1-4R; 41-44R; CANR 4, 35; CLR 6; DLB 48, 51; MAICYA; MTCW; SATA 2, 24, 44

Booth, Martin 1944- . . . . **CLC 13**
See also CA 93-96; CAAS 2

Booth, Philip 1925- . . . . **CLC 23**
See also CA 5-8R; CANR 5; DLBY 82

Booth, Wayne C(layson) 1921- . . . . . **CLC 24**
See also CA 1-4R; CAAS 5; CANR 3; DLB 67

Borchert, Wolfgang 1921-1947 . . . . . **TCLC 5**
See also CA 104; DLB 69

Borges, Jorge Luis
1899-1986 . . . **CLC 1, 2, 3, 4, 6, 8, 9, 10, 13, 19, 44, 48; SSC 4**
See also CA 21-24R; CANR 19, 33; DLB 113; DLBY 86; HW; MTCW; WLC

Borowski, Tadeusz 1922-1951 . . . . . . **TCLC 9**
See also CA 106

Borrow, George (Henry)
1803-1881 . . . . **NCLC 9**
See also DLB 21, 55

Bosschere, Jean de 1878(?)-1953 . . . **TCLC 19**
See also CA 115

Boswell, James 1740-1795 . . . . **LC 4**
See also CDBLB 1660-1789; DLB 104; WLC

Bottoms, David 1949- . . . . **CLC 53**
See also CA 105; CANR 22; DLB 120; DLBY 83

Boucolon, Maryse 1937-
See Conde, Maryse
See also CA 110; CANR 30

Bourget, Paul (Charles Joseph)
1852-1935 . . . . **TCLC 12**
See also CA 107

Bourjaily, Vance (Nye) 1922- . . . . **CLC 8, 62**
See also CA 1-4R; CAAS 1; CANR 2; DLB 2

Bourne, Randolph S(illiman)
1886-1918 . . . . **TCLC 16**
See also CA 117; DLB 63

Bova, Ben(jamin William) 1932- . . . . **CLC 45**
See also CA 5-8R; CANR 11; CLR 3; DLBY 81; MAICYA; MTCW; SATA 6, 68

Bowen, Elizabeth (Dorothea Cole) 1899-1973 . . . . . **CLC 1, 3, 6, 11, 15, 22; SSC 3**
See also CA 17-18; 41-44R; CANR 35; CAP 2; CDBLB 1945-1960; DLB 15; MTCW

Bowering, George 1935- . . . . **CLC 15, 47**
See also CA 21-24R; CAAS 16; CANR 10; DLB 53

Bowering, Marilyn R(uthe) 1949- . . . **CLC 32**
See also CA 101

Bowers, Edgar 1924- . . . . **CLC 9**
See also CA 5-8R; CANR 24; DLB 5

Bowie, David . . . . **CLC 17**
See also Jones, David Robert

Bowles, Jane (Sydney) 1917-1973 . . . . **CLC 3, 68**
See also CA 19-20; 41-44R; CAP 2

Bowles, Paul (Frederick) 1910- . . . . **CLC 1, 2, 19, 53; SSC 3**
See also CA 1-4R; CAAS 1; CANR 1, 19; DLB 5, 6; MTCW

Box, Edgar
See Vidal, Gore

Boyd, Nancy
See Millay, Edna St. Vincent

Boyd, William 1952- . . . . **CLC 28, 53, 70**
See also CA 114; 120

Boyle, Kay 1902- . . **CLC 1, 5, 19, 58; SSC 5**
See also CA 13-16R; CAAS 1; CANR 29; DLB 4, 9, 48, 86; MTCW

Boyle, Mark
See Kienzle, William X(avier)

Boyle, Patrick 1905-1982 . . . . **CLC 19**
See also CA 127

Boyle, T. Coraghessan 1948- . . . . **CLC 36, 55**
See also BEST 90:4; CA 120; DLBY 86

Brackenridge, Hugh Henry 1748-1816 . . . . **NCLC 7**
See also DLB 11, 37

Bradbury, Edward P.
See Moorcock, Michael (John)

Bradbury, Malcolm (Stanley) 1932- . . . . **CLC 32, 61**
See also CA 1-4R; CANR 1, 33; DLB 14; MTCW

Bradbury, Ray (Douglas) 1920- . . . . **CLC 1, 3, 10, 15, 42**
See also AITN 1, 2; CA 1-4R; CANR 2, 30; CDALB 1968-1988; DLB 2, 8; MTCW; SATA 11, 64; WLC

Bradford, Gamaliel 1863-1932 . . . . . **TCLC 36**
See also DLB 17

Bradley, David (Henry Jr.) 1950- . . . **CLC 23**
See also BLC 1; BW; CA 104; CANR 26; DLB 33

Bradley, John Ed 1959- . . . . **CLC 55**

Bradley, Marion Zimmer 1930- . . . . . **CLC 30**
See also AAYA 9; CA 57-60; CAAS 10; CANR 7, 31; DLB 8; MTCW

Bradstreet, Anne 1612(?)-1672 . . . . **LC 4**
See also CDALB 1640-1865; DLB 24

Bragg, Melvyn 1939- . . . . **CLC 10**
See also BEST 89:3; CA 57-60; CANR 10; DLB 14

Braine, John (Gerard) 1922-1986 . . . . **CLC 1, 3, 41**
See also CA 1-4R; 120; CANR 1, 33; CDBLB 1945-1960; DLB 15; DLBY 86; MTCW

Brammer, William 1930(?)-1978 . . . . **CLC 31**
See also CA 77-80

Brancati, Vitaliano 1907-1954 . . . . . **TCLC 12**
See also CA 109

Brancato, Robin F(idler) 1936- . . . . . **CLC 35**
See also AAYA 9; CA 69-72; CANR 11; SAAS 9; SATA 23

Brand, Millen 1906-1980 . . . . **CLC 7**
See also CA 21-24R; 97-100

Branden, Barbara . . . . **CLC 44**

Brandes, Georg (Morris Cohen) 1842-1927 . . . . **TCLC 10**
See also CA 105

Brandys, Kazimierz 1916- . . . . **CLC 62**

Branley, Franklyn M(ansfield) 1915- . . . . **CLC 21**
See also CA 33-36R; CANR 14, 39; CLR 13; MAICYA; SATA 4, 68

Brathwaite, Edward (Kamau) 1930- . . . . **CLC 11**
See also BW; CA 25-28R; CANR 11, 26

Brautigan, Richard (Gary) 1935-1984 . . . . **CLC 1, 3, 5, 9, 12, 34, 42**
See also CA 53-56; 113; CANR 34; DLB 2, 5; DLBY 80, 84; MTCW; SATA 56

Braverman, Kate 1950- . . . . **CLC 67**
See also CA 89-92

Brecht, Bertolt 1898-1956 . . . . . **TCLC 1, 6, 13, 35; DC 3**
See also CA 104; 133; DLB 56; MTCW; WLC

Brecht, Eugen Berthold Friedrich
See Brecht, Bertolt

Bremer, Fredrika 1801-1865 . . . . . **NCLC 11**

Brennan, Christopher John 1870-1932 . . . . **TCLC 17**
See also CA 117

Brennan, Maeve 1917- . . . . **CLC 5**
See also CA 81-84

Brentano, Clemens (Maria) 1778-1842 . . . . **NCLC 1**

Brent of Bin Bin
See Franklin, (Stella Maraia Sarah) Miles

Brenton, Howard 1942- . . . . **CLC 31**
See also CA 69-72; CANR 33; DLB 13; MTCW

Breslin, James 1930-
See Breslin, Jimmy
See also CA 73-76; CANR 31; MTCW

Breslin, Jimmy . . . . **CLC 4, 43**
See also Breslin, James
See also AITN 1

Bresson, Robert 1907- . . . . **CLC 16**
See also CA 110

Breton, Andre 1896-1966 . . . **CLC 2, 9, 15, 54**
See also CA 19-20; 25-28R; CAP 2; DLB 65; MTCW

Breytenbach, Breyten 1939(?)- . . **CLC 23, 37**
See also CA 113; 129

Bridgers, Sue Ellen 1942- . . . . **CLC 26**
See also AAYA 8; CA 65-68; CANR 11, 36; CLR 18; DLB 52; MAICYA; SAAS 1; SATA 22

Bridges, Robert (Seymour) 1844-1930 . . . . **TCLC 1**
See also CA 104; CDBLB 1890-1914; DLB 19, 98

Bridie, James . . . . **TCLC 3**
See also Mavor, Osborne Henry
See also DLB 10

Brin, David 1950- . . . . **CLC 34**
See also CA 102; CANR 24; SATA 65

Brink, Andre (Philippus) 1935- . . . . **CLC 18, 36**
See also CA 104; CANR 39; MTCW

Brinsmead, H(esba) F(ay) 1922- . . . . **CLC 21**
See also CA 21-24R; CANR 10; MAICYA; SAAS 5; SATA 18

Brittain, Vera (Mary) 1893(?)-1970 . . . . **CLC 23**
See also CA 13-16; 25-28R; CAP 1; MTCW

Broch, Hermann 1886-1951 . . . . **TCLC 20**
See also CA 117; DLB 85

Brock, Rose
See Hansen, Joseph

Brodkey, Harold 1930- . . . . **CLC 56**
See also CA 111

Brodsky, Iosif Alexandrovich 1940-
See Brodsky, Joseph
See also AITN 1; CA 41-44R; CANR 37; MTCW

Brodsky, Joseph . . . . **CLC 4, 6, 13, 36, 50**
See also Brodsky, Iosif Alexandrovich

Brodsky, Michael Mark 1948- . . . . . **CLC 19**
See also CA 102; CANR 18

Bromell, Henry 1947- . . . . **CLC 5**
See also CA 53-56; CANR 9

Bromfield, Louis (Brucker) 1896-1956 . . . . **TCLC 11**
See also CA 107; DLB 4, 9, 86

Broner, E(sther) M(asserman) 1930- . . . . **CLC 19**
See also CA 17-20R; CANR 8, 25; DLB 28

Bronk, William 1918- . . . . **CLC 10**
See also CA 89-92; CANR 23

Bronstein, Lev Davidovich
See Trotsky, Leon

Bronte, Anne 1820-1849 . . . . **NCLC 4**
See also DLB 21

Bronte, Charlotte 1816-1855 . . . . **NCLC 3, 8, 33**
See also CDBLB 1832-1890; DLB 21; WLC

Bronte, (Jane) Emily 1818-1848 . . . . **NCLC 16, 35**
See also CDBLB 1832-1890; DLB 21, 32; WLC

Brooke, Frances 1724-1789 . . . . **LC 6**
See also DLB 39, 99

Brooke, Henry 1703(?)-1783 . . . . **LC 1**
See also DLB 39

Brooke, Rupert (Chawner) 1887-1915 . . . . **TCLC 2, 7**
See also CA 104; 132; CDBLB 1914-1945; DLB 19; MTCW; WLC

Brooke-Haven, P.
See Wodehouse, P(elham) G(renville)

Brooke-Rose, Christine 1926- . . . . . . **CLC 40**
See also CA 13-16R; DLB 14

Brookner, Anita 1928- . . . . . . **CLC 32, 34, 51**
See also CA 114; 120; CANR 37; DLBY 87; MTCW

Brooks, Cleanth 1906- . . . . **CLC 24**
See also CA 17-20R; CANR 33, 35; DLB 63; MTCW

Brooks, George
See Baum, L(yman) Frank

Brooks, Gwendolyn
1917- . . . . **CLC 1, 2, 4, 5, 15, 49**
See also AITN 1; BLC 1; BW; CA 1-4R; CANR 1, 27; CDALB 1941-1968; CLR 27; DLB 5, 76; MTCW; SATA 6; WLC

Brooks, Mel . . . . **CLC 12**
See also Kaminsky, Melvin
See also DLB 26

Brooks, Peter 1938- . . . . **CLC 34**
See also CA 45-48; CANR 1

Brooks, Van Wyck 1886-1963 . . . . . . **CLC 29**
See also CA 1-4R; CANR 6; DLB 45, 63, 103

Brophy, Brigid (Antonia)
1929- . . . . **CLC 6, 11, 29**
See also CA 5-8R; CAAS 4; CANR 25; DLB 14; MTCW

Brosman, Catharine Savage 1934- . . . . **CLC 9**
See also CA 61-64; CANR 21

Brother Antoninus
See Everson, William (Oliver)

Broughton, T(homas) Alan 1936- . . . **CLC 19**
See also CA 45-48; CANR 2, 23

Broumas, Olga 1949- . . . . **CLC 10**
See also CA 85-88; CANR 20

Brown, Charles Brockden
1771-1810 . . . . **NCLC 22**
See also CDALB 1640-1865; DLB 37, 59, 73

Brown, Christy 1932-1981 . . . . **CLC 63**
See also CA 105; 104; DLB 14

Brown, Claude 1937- . . . . **CLC 30**
See also AAYA 7; BLC 1; BW; CA 73-76

Brown, Dee (Alexander) 1908- . . **CLC 18, 47**
See also CA 13-16R; CAAS 6; CANR 11; DLBY 80; MTCW; SATA 5

Brown, George
See Wertmueller, Lina

Brown, George Douglas
1869-1902 . . . . **TCLC 28**

Brown, George Mackay 1921- . . . . **CLC 5, 48**
See also CA 21-24R; CAAS 6; CANR 12, 37; DLB 14, 27; MTCW; SATA 35

Brown, Moses
See Barrett, William (Christopher)

Brown, Rita Mae 1944- . . . . **CLC 18, 43**
See also CA 45-48; CANR 2, 11, 35; MTCW

Brown, Roderick (Langmere) Haig-
See Haig-Brown, Roderick (Langmere)

Brown, Rosellen 1939- . . . . **CLC 32**
See also CA 77-80; CAAS 10; CANR 14

Brown, Sterling Allen
1901-1989 . . . . **CLC 1, 23, 59**
See also BLC 1; BW; CA 85-88; 127; CANR 26; DLB 48, 51, 63; MTCW

Brown, Will
See Ainsworth, William Harrison

Brown, William Wells
1813-1884 . . . . **NCLC 2; DC 1**
See also BLC 1; DLB 3, 50

Browne, (Clyde) Jackson 1948(?)- . . . **CLC 21**
See also CA 120

Browning, Elizabeth Barrett
1806-1861 . . . . **NCLC 1, 16**
See also CDBLB 1832-1890; DLB 32; WLC

Browning, Robert
1812-1889 . . . . **NCLC 19; PC 2**
See also CDBLB 1832-1890; DLB 32; YABC 1

Browning, Tod 1882-1962 . . . . **CLC 16**
See also CA 117

Bruccoli, Matthew J(oseph) 1931- . . **CLC 34**
See also CA 9-12R; CANR 7; DLB 103

Bruce, Lenny . . . . **CLC 21**
See also Schneider, Leonard Alfred

Bruin, John
See Brutus, Dennis

Brulls, Christian
See Simenon, Georges (Jacques Christian)

Brunner, John (Kilian Houston)
1934- . . . . **CLC 8, 10**
See also CA 1-4R; CAAS 8; CANR 2, 37; MTCW

Brutus, Dennis 1924- . . . . **CLC 43**
See also BLC 1; BW; CA 49-52; CAAS 14; CANR 2, 27; DLB 117

Bryan, C(ourtlandt) D(ixon) B(arnes)
1936- . . . . **CLC 29**
See also CA 73-76; CANR 13

Bryan, Michael
See Moore, Brian

Bryant, William Cullen
1794-1878 . . . . **NCLC 6**
See also CDALB 1640-1865; DLB 3, 43, 59

Bryusov, Valery Yakovlevich
1873-1924 . . . . **TCLC 10**
See also CA 107

Buchan, John 1875-1940 . . . . **TCLC 41**
See also CA 108; DLB 34, 70; YABC 2

Buchanan, George 1506-1582 . . . . **LC 4**

Buchheim, Lothar-Guenther 1918- . . . **CLC 6**
See also CA 85-88

Buchner, (Karl) Georg
1813-1837 . . . . **NCLC 26**

Buchwald, Art(hur) 1925- . . . . **CLC 33**
See also AITN 1; CA 5-8R; CANR 21; MTCW; SATA 10

Buck, Pearl S(ydenstricker)
1892-1973 . . . . **CLC 7, 11, 18**
See also AITN 1; CA 1-4R; 41-44R; CANR 1, 34; DLB 9, 102; MTCW; SATA 1, 25

Buckler, Ernest 1908-1984 . . . . **CLC 13**
See also CA 11-12; 114; CAP 1; DLB 68; SATA 47

Buckley, Vincent (Thomas)
1925-1988 . . . . **CLC 57**
See also CA 101

Buckley, William F(rank) Jr.
1925- . . . . **CLC 7, 18, 37**
See also AITN 1; CA 1-4R; CANR 1, 24; DLBY 80; MTCW

Buechner, (Carl) Frederick
1926- . . . . **CLC 2, 4, 6, 9**
See also CA 13-16R; CANR 11, 39; DLBY 80; MTCW

Buell, John (Edward) 1927- . . . . **CLC 10**
See also CA 1-4R; DLB 53

Buero Vallejo, Antonio 1916- . . . **CLC 15, 46**
See also CA 106; CANR 24; HW; MTCW

Bufalino, Gesualdo 1920- . . . . **CLC 74**

Bugayev, Boris Nikolayevich 1880-1934
See Bely, Andrey
See also CA 104

Bukowski, Charles 1920- . . . . **CLC 2, 5, 9, 41**
See also CA 17-20R; DLB 5; MTCW

Bulgakov, Mikhail (Afanas'evich)
1891-1940 . . . . **TCLC 2, 16**
See also CA 105

Bullins, Ed 1935- . . . . **CLC 1, 5, 7**
See also BLC 1; BW; CA 49-52; CAAS 16; CANR 24; DLB 7, 38; MTCW

Bulwer-Lytton, Edward (George Earle Lytton)
1803-1873 . . . . **NCLC 1**
See also DLB 21

Bunin, Ivan Alexeyevich
1870-1953 . . . . **TCLC 6; SSC 5**
See also CA 104

Bunting, Basil 1900-1985 . . . . **CLC 10, 39, 47**
See also CA 53-56; 115; CANR 7; DLB 20

Bunuel, Luis 1900-1983 . . . . **CLC 16**
See also CA 101; 110; CANR 32; HW

Bunyan, John 1628-1688 . . . . **LC 4**
See also CDBLB 1660-1789; DLB 39; WLC

Burford, Eleanor
See Hibbert, Eleanor Burford

Burgess, Anthony
. . **CLC 1, 2, 4, 5, 8, 10, 13, 15, 22, 40, 62**
See also Wilson, John (Anthony) Burgess
See also AITN 1; CDBLB 1960 to Present; DLB 14

Burke, Edmund 1729(?)-1797 . . . . **LC 7**
See also DLB 104; WLC

Burke, Kenneth (Duva) 1897- . . . . **CLC 2, 24**
See also CA 5-8R; CANR 39; DLB 45, 63; MTCW

Burke, Leda
See Garnett, David

Burke, Ralph
See Silverberg, Robert

Burney, Fanny 1752-1840 . . . . **NCLC 12**
See also DLB 39

Burns, Robert 1759-1796 . . . . **LC 3**
See also CDBLB 1789-1832; DLB 109; WLC

Author Index

Burns, Tex
See L'Amour, Louis (Dearborn)

Burnshaw, Stanley 1906- . . . . . **CLC 3, 13, 44**
See also CA 9-12R; DLB 48

Burr, Anne 1937- . . . . **CLC 6**
See also CA 25-28R

Burroughs, Edgar Rice
1875-1950 . . . . **TCLC 2, 32**
See also CA 104; 132; DLB 8; MTCW; SATA 41

Burroughs, William S(eward)
1914- . . . . **CLC 1, 2, 5, 15, 22, 42**
See also AITN 2; CA 9-12R; CANR 20; DLB 2, 8, 16; DLBY 81; MTCW; WLC

Busch, Frederick 1941- . . . **CLC 7, 10, 18, 47**
See also CA 33-36R; CAAS 1; DLB 6

Bush, Ronald 1946- . . . . **CLC 34**
See also CA 136

Bustos, F(rancisco)
See Borges, Jorge Luis

Bustos Domecq, H(onorio)
See Bioy Casares, Adolfo; Borges, Jorge Luis

Bustos Domecq, H(onrio)
See Borges, Jorge Luis

Butler, Octavia E(stelle) 1947- . . . . . **CLC 38**
See also BW; CA 73-76; CANR 12, 24, 38; DLB 33; MTCW

Butler, Samuel 1612-1680 . . . . **LC 16**
See also DLB 101

Butler, Samuel 1835-1902 . . . . . . **TCLC 1, 33**
See also CA 104; CDBLB 1890-1914; DLB 18, 57; WLC

Butor, Michel (Marie Francois)
1926- . . . . **CLC 1, 3, 8, 11, 15**
See also CA 9-12R; CANR 33; DLB 83; MTCW

Buzo, Alexander (John) 1944- . . . . . . **CLC 61**
See also CA 97-100; CANR 17, 39

Buzzati, Dino 1906-1972 . . . . **CLC 36**
See also CA 33-36R

Byars, Betsy (Cromer) 1928- . . . . **CLC 35**
See also CA 33-36R; CANR 18, 36; CLR 1, 16; DLB 52; MAICYA; MTCW; SAAS 1; SATA 4, 46

Byatt, A(ntonia) S(usan Drabble)
1936- . . . . **CLC 19, 65**
See also CA 13-16R; CANR 13, 33; DLB 14; MTCW

Byrne, David 1952- . . . . **CLC 26**
See also CA 127

Byrne, John Keyes 1926- . . . . **CLC 19**
See also Leonard, Hugh
See also CA 102

Byron, George Gordon (Noel)
1788-1824 . . . . **NCLC 2, 12**
See also CDBLB 1789-1832; DLB 96, 110; WLC

C.3.3.
See Wilde, Oscar (Fingal O'Flahertie Wills)

Caballero, Fernan 1796-1877 . . . . . **NCLC 10**

Cabell, James Branch 1879-1958 . . . **TCLC 6**
See also CA 105; DLB 9, 78

Cable, George Washington
1844-1925 . . . . **TCLC 4; SSC 4**
See also CA 104; DLB 12, 74

Cabrera Infante, G(uillermo)
1929- . . . . **CLC 5, 25, 45**
See also CA 85-88; CANR 29; DLB 113; HW; MTCW

Cade, Toni
See Bambara, Toni Cade

Cadmus
See Buchan, John

Caedmon fl. 658-680 . . . . **CMLC 7**

Caeiro, Alberto
See Pessoa, Fernando (Antonio Nogueira)

Cage, John (Milton Jr.) 1912- . . . . . . **CLC 41**
See also CA 13-16R; CANR 9

Cain, G.
See Cabrera Infante, G(uillermo)

Cain, Guillermo
See Cabrera Infante, G(uillermo)

Cain, James M(allahan)
1892-1977 . . . . **CLC 3, 11, 28**
See also AITN 1; CA 17-20R; 73-76; CANR 8, 34; MTCW

Caine, Mark
See Raphael, Frederic (Michael)

Calderon de la Barca, Pedro
1600-1681 . . . . **DC 3**

Caldwell, Erskine (Preston)
1903-1987 . . . . **CLC 1, 8, 14, 50, 60**
See also AITN 1; CA 1-4R; 121; CAAS 1; CANR 2, 33; DLB 9, 86; MTCW

Caldwell, (Janet Miriam) Taylor (Holland)
1900-1985 . . . . **CLC 2, 28, 39**
See also CA 5-8R; 116; CANR 5

Calhoun, John Caldwell
1782-1850 . . . . **NCLC 15**
See also DLB 3

Calisher, Hortense 1911- . . . . **CLC 2, 4, 8, 38**
See also CA 1-4R; CANR 1, 22; DLB 2; MTCW

Callaghan, Morley Edward
1903-1990 . . . . **CLC 3, 14, 41, 65**
See also CA 9-12R; 132; CANR 33; DLB 68; MTCW

Calvino, Italo
1923-1985 . . . . **CLC 5, 8, 11, 22, 33, 39; SSC 3**
See also CA 85-88; 116; CANR 23; MTCW

Cameron, Carey 1952- . . . . **CLC 59**
See also CA 135

Cameron, Peter 1959- . . . . **CLC 44**
See also CA 125

Campana, Dino 1885-1932 . . . . **TCLC 20**
See also CA 117; DLB 114

Campbell, John W(ood Jr.)
1910-1971 . . . . **CLC 32**
See also CA 21-22; 29-32R; CANR 34; CAP 2; DLB 8; MTCW

Campbell, Joseph 1904-1987 . . . . **CLC 69**
See also AAYA 3; BEST 89:2; CA 1-4R; 124; CANR 3, 28; MTCW

Campbell, (John) Ramsey 1946- . . . . **CLC 42**
See also CA 57-60; CANR 7

Campbell, (Ignatius) Roy (Dunnachie)
1901-1957 . . . . **TCLC 5**
See also CA 104; DLB 20

Campbell, Thomas 1777-1844 . . . . **NCLC 19**
See also DLB 93

Campbell, Wilfred . . . . **TCLC 9**
See also Campbell, William

Campbell, William 1858(?)-1918
See Campbell, Wilfred
See also CA 106; DLB 92

Campos, Alvaro de
See Pessoa, Fernando (Antonio Nogueira)

Camus, Albert
1913-1960 . . . **CLC 1, 2, 4, 9, 11, 14, 32, 63, 69; DC 2; SSC 9**
See also CA 89-92; DLB 72; MTCW; WLC

Canby, Vincent 1924- . . . . **CLC 13**
See also CA 81-84

Cancale
See Desnos, Robert

Canetti, Elias 1905- . . . . **CLC 3, 14, 25**
See also CA 21-24R; CANR 23; DLB 85; MTCW

Canin, Ethan 1960- . . . . **CLC 55**
See also CA 131; 135

Cannon, Curt
See Hunter, Evan

Cape, Judith
See Page, P(atricia) K(athleen)

Capek, Karel
1890-1938 . . . . **TCLC 6, 37; DC 1**
See also CA 104; WLC

Capote, Truman
1924-1984 . . . . . **CLC 1, 3, 8, 13, 19, 34, 38, 58; SSC 2**
See also CA 5-8R; 113; CANR 18; CDALB 1941-1968; DLB 2; DLBY 80, 84; MTCW; WLC

Capra, Frank 1897-1991 . . . . **CLC 16**
See also CA 61-64; 135

Caputo, Philip 1941- . . . . **CLC 32**
See also CA 73-76

Card, Orson Scott 1951- . . . . **CLC 44, 47, 50**
See also CA 102; CANR 27; MTCW

Cardenal (Martinez), Ernesto
1925- . . . . **CLC 31**
See also CA 49-52; CANR 2, 32; HW; MTCW

Carducci, Giosue 1835-1907 . . . . **TCLC 32**

Carew, Thomas 1595(?)-1640 . . . . **LC 13**

Carey, Ernestine Gilbreth 1908- . . . . **CLC 17**
See also CA 5-8R; SATA 2

Carey, Peter 1943- . . . . **CLC 40, 55**
See also CA 123; 127; MTCW

Carleton, William 1794-1869 . . . . . . **NCLC 3**

Carlisle, Henry (Coffin) 1926- . . . . . . **CLC 33**
See also CA 13-16R; CANR 15

Carlsen, Chris
See Holdstock, Robert P.

Carlson, Ron(ald F.) 1947- . . . . **CLC 54**
See also CA 105; CANR 27

Carlyle, Thomas 1795-1881 . . . . . . **NCLC 22**
See also CDBLB 1789-1832; DLB 55

Carman, (William) Bliss 1861-1929 .... **TCLC 7**
See also CA 104; DLB 92

Carossa, Hans 1878-1956.......... **TCLC 48**
See also DLB 66

Carpenter, Don(ald Richard) 1931- .... **CLC 41**
See also CA 45-48; CANR 1

Carpentier (y Valmont), Alejo 1904-1980 .... **CLC 8, 11, 38**
See also CA 65-68; 97-100; CANR 11; DLB 113; HW

Carr, Emily 1871-1945............ **TCLC 32**
See also DLB 68

Carr, John Dickson 1906-1977 ...... **CLC 3**
See also CA 49-52; 69-72; CANR 3, 33; MTCW

Carr, Philippa
See Hibbert, Eleanor Burford

Carr, Virginia Spencer 1929-........ **CLC 34**
See also CA 61-64; DLB 111

Carrier, Roch 1937- .... **CLC 13**
See also CA 130; DLB 53

Carroll, James P. 1943(?)-.......... **CLC 38**
See also CA 81-84

Carroll, Jim 1951- .... **CLC 35**
See also CA 45-48

Carroll, Lewis .... **NCLC 2**
See also Dodgson, Charles Lutwidge
See also CDBLB 1832-1890; CLR 2, 18; DLB 18; WLC

Carroll, Paul Vincent 1900-1968.... **CLC 10**
See also CA 9-12R; 25-28R; DLB 10

Carruth, Hayden 1921- .... **CLC 4, 7, 10, 18**
See also CA 9-12R; CANR 4, 38; DLB 5; MTCW; SATA 47

Carson, Rachel Louise 1907-1964... **CLC 71**
See also CA 77-80; CANR 35; MTCW; SATA 23

Carter, Angela (Olive) 1940-1991 .... **CLC 5, 41**
See also CA 53-56; 136; CANR 12, 36; DLB 14; MTCW; SATA 66; SATO 70

Carter, Nick
See Smith, Martin Cruz

Carver, Raymond 1938-1988 ... **CLC 22, 36, 53, 55; SSC 8**
See also CA 33-36R; 126; CANR 17, 34; DLBY 84, 88; MTCW

Cary, (Arthur) Joyce (Lunel) 1888-1957 .... **TCLC 1, 29**
See also CA 104; CDBLB 1914-1945; DLB 15, 100

Casanova de Seingalt, Giovanni Jacopo 1725-1798 .... **LC 13**

Casares, Adolfo Bioy
See Bioy Casares, Adolfo

Casely-Hayford, J(oseph) E(phraim) 1866-1930 .... **TCLC 24**
See also BLC 1; CA 123

Casey, John (Dudley) 1939-........ **CLC 59**
See also BEST 90:2; CA 69-72; CANR 23

Casey, Michael 1947-.............. **CLC 2**
See also CA 65-68; DLB 5

Casey, Patrick
See Thurman, Wallace (Henry)

Casey, Warren (Peter) 1935-1988... **CLC 12**
See also CA 101; 127

Casona, Alejandro................. **CLC 49**
See also Alvarez, Alejandro Rodriguez

Cassavetes, John 1929-1989........ **CLC 20**
See also CA 85-88; 127

Cassill, R(onald) V(erlin) 1919-... **CLC 4, 23**
See also CA 9-12R; CAAS 1; CANR 7; DLB 6

Cassity, (Allen) Turner 1929- .... **CLC 6, 42**
See also CA 17-20R; CAAS 8; CANR 11; DLB 105

Castaneda, Carlos 1931(?)-......... **CLC 12**
See also CA 25-28R; CANR 32; HW; MTCW

Castedo, Elena 1937- .... **CLC 65**
See also CA 132

Castedo-Ellerman, Elena
See Castedo, Elena

Castellanos, Rosario 1925-1974..... **CLC 66**
See also CA 131; 53-56; DLB 113; HW

Castelvetro, Lodovico 1505-1571..... **LC 12**

Castiglione, Baldassare 1478-1529 ... **LC 12**

Castle, Robert
See Hamilton, Edmond

Castro, Guillen de 1569-1631........ **LC 19**

Castro, Rosalia de 1837-1885 ..... **NCLC 3**

Cather, Willa
See Cather, Willa Sibert

Cather, Willa Sibert 1873-1947 ...... **TCLC 1, 11, 31; SSC 2**
See also CA 104; 128; CDALB 1865-1917; DLB 9, 54, 78; DLBD 1; MTCW; SATA 30; WLC

Catton, (Charles) Bruce 1899-1978 .... **CLC 35**
See also AITN 1; CA 5-8R; 81-84; CANR 7; DLB 17; SATA 2, 24

Cauldwell, Frank
See King, Francis (Henry)

Caunitz, William J. 1933- .... **CLC 34**
See also BEST 89:3; CA 125; 130

Causley, Charles (Stanley) 1917-..... **CLC 7**
See also CA 9-12R; CANR 5, 35; DLB 27; MTCW; SATA 3, 66

Caute, David 1936-............... **CLC 29**
See also CA 1-4R; CAAS 4; CANR 1, 33; DLB 14

Cavafy, C(onstantine) P(eter)...... **TCLC 2, 7**
See also Kavafis, Konstantinos Petrou

Cavallo, Evelyn
See Spark, Muriel (Sarah)

Cavanna, Betty .... **CLC 12**
See also Harrison, Elizabeth Cavanna
See also MAICYA; SAAS 4; SATA 1, 30

Caxton, William 1421(?)-1491(?)..... **LC 17**

Cayrol, Jean 1911-................ **CLC 11**
See also CA 89-92; DLB 83

Cela, Camilo Jose 1916-...... **CLC 4, 13, 59**
See also BEST 90:2; CA 21-24R; CAAS 10; CANR 21, 32; DLBY 89; HW; MTCW

Celan, Paul .... **CLC 53**
See also Antschel, Paul
See also DLB 69

Celine, Louis-Ferdinand .... **CLC 1, 3, 4, 7, 9, 15, 47**
See also Destouches, Louis-Ferdinand
See also DLB 72

Cellini, Benvenuto 1500-1571 .... **LC 7**

Cendrars, Blaise
See Sauser-Hall, Frederic

Cernuda (y Bidon), Luis 1902-1963 .... **CLC 54**
See also CA 131; 89-92; HW

Cervantes (Saavedra), Miguel de 1547-1616 .... **LC 6**
See also WLC

Cesaire, Aime (Fernand) 1913- .. **CLC 19, 32**
See also BLC 1; BW; CA 65-68; CANR 24; MTCW

Chabon, Michael 1965(?)- .... **CLC 55**

Chabrol, Claude 1930- .... **CLC 16**
See also CA 110

Challans, Mary 1905-1983
See Renault, Mary
See also CA 81-84; 111; SATA 23, 36

Chambers, Aidan 1934- .... **CLC 35**
See also CA 25-28R; CANR 12, 31; MAICYA; SAAS 12; SATA 1, 69

Chambers, James 1948-
See Cliff, Jimmy
See also CA 124

Chambers, Jessie
See Lawrence, D(avid) H(erbert Richards)

Chambers, Robert W. 1865-1933... **TCLC 41**

Chandler, Raymond (Thornton) 1888-1959 .... **TCLC 1, 7**
See also CA 104; 129; CDALB 1929-1941; DLBD 6; MTCW

Chang, Jung 1952- .... **CLC 71**

Channing, William Ellery 1780-1842 .... **NCLC 17**
See also DLB 1, 59

Chaplin, Charles Spencer 1889-1977 .... **CLC 16**
See also Chaplin, Charlie
See also CA 81-84; 73-76

Chaplin, Charlie
See Chaplin, Charles Spencer
See also DLB 44

Chapman, Graham 1941-1989 ...... **CLC 21**
See also Monty Python
See also CA 116; 129; CANR 35

Chapman, John Jay 1862-1933 ..... **TCLC 7**
See also CA 104

Chapman, Walker
See Silverberg, Robert

Chappell, Fred (Davis) 1936-....... **CLC 40**
See also CA 5-8R; CAAS 4; CANR 8, 33; DLB 6, 105

Char, Rene(-Emile) 1907-1988 .... **CLC 9, 11, 14, 55**
See also CA 13-16R; 124; CANR 32; MTCW

Charby, Jay
See Ellison, Harlan

Chardin, Pierre Teilhard de
See Teilhard de Chardin, (Marie Joseph) Pierre

Charles I 1600-1649 . . . . **LC 13**

Charyn, Jerome 1937- . . . . **CLC 5, 8, 18**
See also CA 5-8R; CAAS 1; CANR 7; DLBY 83; MTCW

Chase, Mary (Coyle) 1907-1981 . . . . . . **DC 1**
See also CA 77-80; 105; SATA 17, 29

Chase, Mary Ellen 1887-1973 . . . . **CLC 2**
See also CA 13-16; 41-44R; CAP 1; SATA 10

Chase, Nicholas
See Hyde, Anthony

Chateaubriand, Francois Rene de 1768-1848 . . . . **NCLC 3**
See also DLB 119

Chatterje, Sarat Chandra 1876-1936(?)
See Chatterji, Saratchandra
See also CA 109

Chatterji, Bankim Chandra 1838-1894 . . . . **NCLC 19**

Chatterji, Saratchandra . . . . **TCLC 13**
See also Chatterje, Sarat Chandra

Chatterton, Thomas 1752-1770 . . . . **LC 3**
See also DLB 109

Chatwin, (Charles) Bruce 1940-1989 . . . . **CLC 28, 57, 59**
See also AAYA 4; BEST 90:1; CA 85-88; 127

Chaucer, Daniel
See Ford, Ford Madox

Chaucer, Geoffrey 1340(?)-1400 . . . . . **LC 17**
See also CDBLB Before 1660

Chaviaras, Strates 1935-
See Haviaras, Stratis
See also CA 105

Chayefsky, Paddy . . . . **CLC 23**
See also Chayefsky, Sidney
See also DLB 7, 44; DLBY 81

Chayefsky, Sidney 1923-1981
See Chayefsky, Paddy
See also CA 9-12R; 104; CANR 18

Chedid, Andree 1920- . . . . **CLC 47**

Cheever, John 1912-1982 . . . . . **CLC 3, 7, 8, 11, 15, 25, 64; SSC 1**
See also CA 5-8R; 106; CABS 1; CANR 5, 27; CDALB 1941-1968; DLB 2, 102; DLBY 80, 82; MTCW; WLC

Cheever, Susan 1943- . . . . **CLC 18, 48**
See also CA 103; CANR 27; DLBY 82

Chekhonte, Antosha
See Chekhov, Anton (Pavlovich)

Chekhov, Anton (Pavlovich) 1860-1904 . . . . . . **TCLC 3, 10, 31; SSC 2**
See also CA 104; 124; WLC

Chernyshevsky, Nikolay Gavrilovich 1828-1889 . . . . **NCLC 1**

Cherry, Carolyn Janice 1942-
See Cherryh, C. J.
See also CA 65-68; CANR 10

Cherryh, C. J. . . . . **CLC 35**
See also Cherry, Carolyn Janice
See also DLBY 80

Chesnutt, Charles W(addell) 1858-1932 . . . . **TCLC 5, 39; SSC 7**
See also BLC 1; BW; CA 106; 125; DLB 12, 50, 78; MTCW

Chester, Alfred 1929(?)-1971 . . . . **CLC 49**
See also CA 33-36R

Chesterton, G(ilbert) K(eith) 1874-1936 . . . . **TCLC 1, 6; SSC 1**
See also CA 104; 132; CDBLB 1914-1945; DLB 10, 19, 34, 70, 98; MTCW; SATA 27

Chiang Pin-chin 1904-1986
See Ding Ling
See also CA 118

Ch'ien Chung-shu 1910- . . . . **CLC 22**
See also CA 130; MTCW

Child, L. Maria
See Child, Lydia Maria

Child, Lydia Maria 1802-1880 . . . . **NCLC 6**
See also DLB 1, 74; SATA 67

Child, Mrs.
See Child, Lydia Maria

Child, Philip 1898-1978 . . . . **CLC 19, 68**
See also CA 13-14; CAP 1; SATA 47

Childress, Alice 1920- . . . . **CLC 12, 15**
See also AAYA 8; BLC 1; BW; CA 45-48; CANR 3, 27; CLR 14; DLB 7, 38; MAICYA; MTCW; SATA 7, 48

Chislett, (Margaret) Anne 1943- . . . . **CLC 34**

Chitty, Thomas Willes 1926- . . . . **CLC 11**
See also Hinde, Thomas
See also CA 5-8R

Chomette, Rene Lucien 1898-1981 . . **CLC 20**
See also Clair, Rene
See also CA 103

Chopin, Kate . . . . **TCLC 5, 14; SSC 8**
See also Chopin, Katherine
See also CDALB 1865-1917; DLB 12, 78

Chopin, Katherine 1851-1904
See Chopin, Kate
See also CA 104; 122

Chretien de Troyes c. 12th cent. - . . . . **CMLC 10**

Christie
See Ichikawa, Kon

Christie, Agatha (Mary Clarissa) 1890-1976 . . . . . . **CLC 1, 6, 8, 12, 39, 48**
See also AAYA 9; AITN 1, 2; CA 17-20R; 61-64; CANR 10, 37; CDBLB 1914-1945; DLB 13, 77; MTCW; SATA 36

Christie, (Ann) Philippa
See Pearce, Philippa
See also CA 5-8R; CANR 4

Christine de Pizan 1365(?)-1431(?) . . . . **LC 9**

Chubb, Elmer
See Masters, Edgar Lee

Chulkov, Mikhail Dmitrievich 1743-1792 . . . . **LC 2**

Churchill, Caryl 1938- . . . . **CLC 31, 55**
See also CA 102; CANR 22; DLB 13; MTCW

Churchill, Charles 1731-1764. . . . . **LC 3**
See also DLB 109

Chute, Carolyn 1947- . . . . **CLC 39**
See also CA 123

Ciardi, John (Anthony) 1916-1986 . . . . **CLC 10, 40, 44**
See also CA 5-8R; 118; CAAS 2; CANR 5, 33; CLR 19; DLB 5; DLBY 86; MAICYA; MTCW; SATA 1, 46, 65

Cicero, Marcus Tullius 106B.C.-43B.C. . . . . **CMLC 3**

Cimino, Michael 1943- . . . . **CLC 16**
See also CA 105

Cioran, E(mil) M. 1911- . . . . **CLC 64**
See also CA 25-28R

Cisneros, Sandra 1954- . . . . **CLC 69**
See also AAYA 9; CA 131; HW

Clair, Rene . . . . **CLC 20**
See also Chomette, Rene Lucien

Clampitt, Amy 1920- . . . . **CLC 32**
See also CA 110; CANR 29; DLB 105

Clancy, Thomas L. Jr. 1947-
See Clancy, Tom
See also CA 125; 131; MTCW

Clancy, Tom . . . . **CLC 45**
See also Clancy, Thomas L. Jr.
See also AAYA 9; BEST 89:1, 90:1

Clare, John 1793-1864 . . . . **NCLC 9**
See also DLB 55, 96

Clarin
See Alas (y Urena), Leopoldo (Enrique Garcia)

Clark, (Robert) Brian 1932- . . . . **CLC 29**
See also CA 41-44R

Clark, Eleanor 1913- . . . . **CLC 5, 19**
See also CA 9-12R; DLB 6

Clark, J. P.
See Clark, John Pepper
See also DLB 117

Clark, John Pepper 1935- . . . . **CLC 38**
See also Clark, J. P.
See also BLC 1; BW; CA 65-68; CANR 16

Clark, M. R.
See Clark, Mavis Thorpe

Clark, Mavis Thorpe 1909- . . . . **CLC 12**
See also CA 57-60; CANR 8, 37; MAICYA; SAAS 5; SATA 8

Clark, Walter Van Tilburg 1909-1971 . . . . **CLC 28**
See also CA 9-12R; 33-36R; DLB 9; SATA 8

Clarke, Arthur C(harles) 1917- . . . . . . **CLC 1, 4, 13, 18, 35; SSC 3**
See also AAYA 4; CA 1-4R; CANR 2, 28; MAICYA; MTCW; SATA 13, 70

Clarke, Austin C(hesterfield) 1934- . . . . **CLC 8, 53**
See also BLC 1; BW; CA 25-28R; CAAS 16; CANR 14, 32; DLB 53

Clarke, Austin 1896-1974. . . . . **CLC 6, 9**
See also CA 29-32; 49-52; CAP 2; DLB 10, 20

Clarke, Gillian 1937- . . . . **CLC 61**
See also CA 106; DLB 40

Clarke, Marcus (Andrew Hislop) 1846-1881 . . . . **NCLC 19**

Clarke, Shirley 1925- . . . . **CLC 16** . . . . **CLC 30**
See also Headon, (Nicky) Topper; Jones, Mick; Simonon, Paul; Strummer, Joe

Claudel, Paul (Louis Charles Marie) 1868-1955 . . . . **TCLC 2, 10**
See also CA 104

Clavell, James (duMaresq) 1925- . . . . **CLC 6, 25**
See also CA 25-28R; CANR 26; MTCW

Cleaver, (Leroy) Eldridge 1935- . . . . **CLC 30**
See also BLC 1; BW; CA 21-24R; CANR 16

Cleese, John (Marwood) 1939- . . . . . **CLC 21**
See also Monty Python
See also CA 112; 116; CANR 35; MTCW

Cleishbotham, Jebediah
See Scott, Walter

Cleland, John 1710-1789 . . . . **LC 2**
See also DLB 39

Clemens, Samuel Langhorne 1835-1910
See Twain, Mark
See also CA 104; 135; CDALB 1865-1917; DLB 11, 12, 23, 64, 74; MAICYA; YABC 2

Clerihew, E.
See Bentley, E(dmund) C(lerihew)

Clerk, N. W.
See Lewis, C(live) S(taples)

Cliff, Jimmy . . . . **CLC 21**
See also Chambers, James

Clifton, (Thelma) Lucille 1936- . . . . **CLC 19, 66**
See also BLC 1; BW; CA 49-52; CANR 2, 24; CLR 5; DLB 5, 41; MAICYA; MTCW; SATA 20, 69

Clinton, Dirk
See Silverberg, Robert

Clough, Arthur Hugh 1819-1861 . . **NCLC 27**
See also DLB 32

Clutha, Janet Paterson Frame 1924-
See Frame, Janet
See also CA 1-4R; CANR 2, 36; MTCW

Clyne, Terence
See Blatty, William Peter

Cobalt, Martin
See Mayne, William (James Carter)

Coburn, D(onald) L(ee) 1938- . . . . . . **CLC 10**
See also CA 89-92

Cocteau, Jean (Maurice Eugene Clement) 1889-1963 . . . . **CLC 1, 8, 15, 16, 43**
See also CA 25-28; CAP 2; DLB 65; MTCW; WLC

Codrescu, Andrei 1946- . . . . **CLC 46**
See also CA 33-36R; CANR 13, 34

Coe, Max
See Bourne, Randolph S(illiman)

Coe, Tucker
See Westlake, Donald E(dwin)

Coetzee, J(ohn) M(ichael) 1940- . . . . **CLC 23, 33, 66**
See also CA 77-80; MTCW

Cohen, Arthur A(llen) 1928-1986 . . . . **CLC 7, 31**
See also CA 1-4R; 120; CANR 1, 17; DLB 28

Cohen, Leonard (Norman) 1934- . . . . **CLC 3, 38**
See also CA 21-24R; CANR 14; DLB 53; MTCW

Cohen, Matt 1942- . . . . **CLC 19**
See also CA 61-64; DLB 53

Cohen-Solal, Annie 19(?)- . . . . **CLC 50**

Colegate, Isabel 1931- . . . . **CLC 36**
See also CA 17-20R; CANR 8, 22; DLB 14; MTCW

Coleman, Emmett
See Reed, Ishmael

Coleridge, Samuel Taylor 1772-1834 . . . . **NCLC 9**
See also CDBLB 1789-1832; DLB 93, 107; WLC

Coleridge, Sara 1802-1852 . . . . **NCLC 31**

Coles, Don 1928- . . . . **CLC 46**
See also CA 115; CANR 38

Colette, (Sidonie-Gabrielle) 1873-1954 . . . . . . **TCLC 1, 5, 16; SSC 10**
See also CA 104; 131; DLB 65; MTCW

Collett, (Jacobine) Camilla (Wergeland) 1813-1895 . . . . **NCLC 22**

Collier, Christopher 1930- . . . . **CLC 30**
See also CA 33-36R; CANR 13, 33; MAICYA; SATA 16, 70

Collier, James L(incoln) 1928- . . . . . **CLC 30**
See also CA 9-12R; CANR 4, 33; MAICYA; SATA 8, 70

Collier, Jeremy 1650-1726 . . . . **LC 6**

Collins, Hunt
See Hunter, Evan

Collins, Linda 1931- . . . . **CLC 44**
See also CA 125

Collins, (William) Wilkie 1824-1889 . . . . **NCLC 1, 18**
See also CDBLB 1832-1890; DLB 18, 70

Collins, William 1721-1759 . . . . **LC 4**
See also DLB 109

Colman, George
See Glassco, John

Colt, Winchester Remington
See Hubbard, L(afayette) Ron(ald)

Colter, Cyrus 1910- . . . . **CLC 58**
See also BW; CA 65-68; CANR 10; DLB 33

Colton, James
See Hansen, Joseph

Colum, Padraic 1881-1972 . . . . **CLC 28**
See also CA 73-76; 33-36R; CANR 35; MAICYA; MTCW; SATA 15

Colvin, James
See Moorcock, Michael (John)

Colwin, Laurie 1944- . . . . **CLC 5, 13, 23**
See also CA 89-92; CANR 20; DLBY 80; MTCW

Comfort, Alex(ander) 1920- . . . . **CLC 7**
See also CA 1-4R; CANR 1

Comfort, Montgomery
See Campbell, (John) Ramsey

Compton-Burnett, I(vy) 1884(?)-1969 . . . . . . **CLC 1, 3, 10, 15, 34**
See also CA 1-4R; 25-28R; CANR 4; DLB 36; MTCW

Comstock, Anthony 1844-1915 . . . . **TCLC 13**
See also CA 110

Conan Doyle, Arthur
See Doyle, Arthur Conan

Conde, Maryse . . . . **CLC 52**
See also Boucolon, Maryse

Condon, Richard (Thomas) 1915- . . . . **CLC 4, 6, 8, 10, 45**
See also BEST 90:3; CA 1-4R; CAAS 1; CANR 2, 23; MTCW

Congreve, William 1670-1729 . . . . **LC 5, 21; DC 2**
See also CDBLB 1660-1789; DLB 39, 84; WLC

Connell, Evan S(helby) Jr. 1924- . . . . **CLC 4, 6, 45**
See also AAYA 7; CA 1-4R; CAAS 2; CANR 2, 39; DLB 2; DLBY 81; MTCW

Connelly, Marc(us Cook) 1890-1980 . . . . **CLC 7**
See also CA 85-88; 102; CANR 30; DLB 7; DLBY 80; SATA 25

Connor, Ralph . . . . **TCLC 31**
See also Gordon, Charles William
See also DLB 92

Conrad, Joseph 1857-1924 . . . . . . **TCLC 1, 6, 13, 25, 43; SSC 9**
See also CA 104; 131; CDBLB 1890-1914; DLB 10, 34, 98; MTCW; SATA 27; WLC

Conrad, Robert Arnold
See Hart, Moss

Conroy, Pat 1945- . . . . **CLC 30, 74**
See also AAYA 8; AITN 1; CA 85-88; CANR 24; DLB 6; MTCW

Constant (de Rebecque), (Henri) Benjamin 1767-1830 . . . . **NCLC 6**
See also DLB 119

Conybeare, Charles Augustus
See Eliot, T(homas) S(tearns)

Cook, Michael 1933- . . . . **CLC 58**
See also CA 93-96; DLB 53

Cook, Robin 1940- . . . . **CLC 14**
See also BEST 90:2; CA 108; 111

Cook, Roy
See Silverberg, Robert

Cooke, Elizabeth 1948- . . . . **CLC 55**
See also CA 129

Cooke, John Esten 1830-1886 . . . . . **NCLC 5**
See also DLB 3

Cooke, John Estes
See Baum, L(yman) Frank

Cooke, M. E.
See Creasey, John

Cooke, Margaret
See Creasey, John

Cooney, Ray . . . . **CLC 62**

Cooper, Henry St. John
See Creasey, John

Cooper, J. California .... **CLC 56**
See also BW; CA 125

Cooper, James Fenimore 1789-1851 .... **NCLC 1, 27**
See also CDALB 1640-1865; DLB 3; SATA 19

Coover, Robert (Lowell) 1932- .... **CLC 3, 7, 15, 32, 46**
See also CA 45-48; CANR 3, 37; DLB 2; DLBY 81; MTCW

Copeland, Stewart (Armstrong) 1952- .... **CLC 26**
See also The Police

Coppard, A(lfred) E(dgar) 1878-1957 .... **TCLC 5**
See also CA 114; YABC 1

Coppee, Francois 1842-1908 ...... **TCLC 25**

Coppola, Francis Ford 1939- .... **CLC 16**
See also CA 77-80; DLB 44

Corcoran, Barbara 1911- .... **CLC 17**
See also CA 21-24R; CAAS 2; CANR 11, 28; DLB 52; SATA 3

Cordelier, Maurice
See Giraudoux, (Hippolyte) Jean

Corman, Cid .... **CLC 9**
See also Corman, Sidney
See also CAAS 2; DLB 5

Corman, Sidney 1924-
See Corman, Cid
See also CA 85-88

Cormier, Robert (Edmund) 1925- .... **CLC 12, 30**
See also AAYA 3; CA 1-4R; CANR 5, 23; CDALB 1968-1988; CLR 12; DLB 52; MAICYA; MTCW; SATA 10, 45

Corn, Alfred 1943- .... **CLC 33**
See also CA 104; DLB 120; DLBY 80

Cornwell, David (John Moore) 1931- .... **CLC 9, 15**
See also le Carre, John
See also CA 5-8R; CANR 13, 33; MTCW

Corrigan, Kevin .... **CLC 55**

Corso, (Nunzio) Gregory 1930- ... **CLC 1, 11**
See also CA 5-8R; DLB 5,16; MTCW

Cortazar, Julio 1914-1984 ..... **CLC 2, 3, 5, 10, 13, 15, 33, 34; SSC 7**
See also CA 21-24R; CANR 12, 32; DLB 113; HW; MTCW

Corwin, Cecil
See Kornbluth, C(yril) M.

Cosic, Dobrica 1921- .... **CLC 14**
See also CA 122; 138

Costain, Thomas B(ertram) 1885-1965 .... **CLC 30**
See also CA 5-8R; 25-28R; DLB 9

Costantini, Humberto 1924(?)-1987 .... **CLC 49**
See also CA 131; 122; HW

Costello, Elvis 1955- .... **CLC 21**

Cotter, Joseph S. Sr.
See Cotter, Joseph Seamon Sr.

Cotter, Joseph Seamon Sr. 1861-1949 .... **TCLC 28**
See also BLC 1; BW; CA 124; DLB 50

Coulton, James
See Hansen, Joseph

Couperus, Louis (Marie Anne) 1863-1923 .... **TCLC 15**
See also CA 115

Court, Wesli
See Turco, Lewis (Putnam)

Courtenay, Bryce 1933- .... **CLC 59**
See also CA 138

Courtney, Robert
See Ellison, Harlan

Cousteau, Jacques-Yves 1910- ...... **CLC 30**
See also CA 65-68; CANR 15; MTCW; SATA 38

Coward, Noel (Peirce) 1899-1973 .... **CLC 1, 9, 29, 51**
See also AITN 1; CA 17-18; 41-44R; CANR 35; CAP 2; CDBLB 1914-1945; DLB 10; MTCW

Cowley, Malcolm 1898-1989 .... **CLC 39**
See also CA 5-8R; 128; CANR 3; DLB 4, 48; DLBY 81, 89; MTCW

Cowper, William 1731-1800....... **NCLC 8**
See also DLB 104, 109

Cox, William Trevor 1928- ... **CLC 9, 14, 71**
See also Trevor, William
See also CA 9-12R; CANR 4, 37; DLB 14; MTCW

Cozzens, James Gould 1903-1978 .... **CLC 1, 4, 11**
See also CA 9-12R; 81-84; CANR 19; CDALB 1941-1968; DLB 9; DLBD 2; DLBY 84; MTCW

Crabbe, George 1754-1832....... **NCLC 26**
See also DLB 93

Craig, A. A.
See Anderson, Poul (William)

Craik, Dinah Maria (Mulock) 1826-1887 .... **NCLC 38**
See also DLB 35; MAICYA; SATA 34

Cram, Ralph Adams 1863-1942.... **TCLC 45**

Crane, (Harold) Hart 1899-1932 .... **TCLC 2, 5; PC 3**
See also CA 104; 127; CDALB 1917-1929; DLB 4, 48; MTCW; WLC

Crane, R(onald) S(almon) 1886-1967 .... **CLC 27**
See also CA 85-88; DLB 63

Crane, Stephen (Townley) 1871-1900 ..... **TCLC 11, 17, 32; SSC 7**
See also CA 109; CDALB 1865-1917; DLB 12, 54, 78; WLC; YABC 2

Crase, Douglas 1944- .... **CLC 58**
See also CA 106

Craven, Margaret 1901-1980....... **CLC 17**
See also CA 103

Crawford, F(rancis) Marion 1854-1909 .... **TCLC 10**
See also CA 107; DLB 71

Crawford, Isabella Valancy 1850-1887 .... **NCLC 12**
See also DLB 92

Crayon, Geoffrey
See Irving, Washington

Creasey, John 1908-1973 .... **CLC 11**
See also CA 5-8R; 41-44R; CANR 8; DLB 77; MTCW

Crebillon, Claude Prosper Jolyot de (fils) 1707-1777 .... **LC 1**

Credo
See Creasey, John

Creeley, Robert (White) 1926- .... **CLC 1, 2, 4, 8, 11, 15, 36**
See also CA 1-4R; CAAS 10; CANR 23; DLB 5, 16; MTCW

Crews, Harry (Eugene) 1935- .... **CLC 6, 23, 49**
See also AITN 1; CA 25-28R; CANR 20; DLB 6; MTCW

Crichton, (John) Michael 1942- .... **CLC 2, 6, 54**
See also AITN 2; CA 25-28R; CANR 13; DLBY 81; MTCW; SATA 9

Crispin, Edmund .... **CLC 22**
See also Montgomery, (Robert) Bruce
See also DLB 87

Cristofer, Michael 1945(?)- .... **CLC 28**
See also CA 110; DLB 7

Croce, Benedetto 1866-1952 ...... **TCLC 37**
See also CA 120

Crockett, David 1786-1836 .... **NCLC 8**
See also DLB 3, 11

Crockett, Davy
See Crockett, David

Croker, John Wilson 1780-1857 .. **NCLC 10**
See also DLB 110

Cronin, A(rchibald) J(oseph) 1896-1981 .... **CLC 32**
See also CA 1-4R; 102; CANR 5; SATA 25, 47

Cross, Amanda
See Heilbrun, Carolyn G(old)

Crothers, Rachel 1878(?)-1958..... **TCLC 19**
See also CA 113; DLB 7

Croves, Hal
See Traven, B.

Crowfield, Christopher
See Stowe, Harriet (Elizabeth) Beecher

Crowley, Aleister .... **TCLC 7**
See also Crowley, Edward Alexander

Crowley, Edward Alexander 1875-1947
See Crowley, Aleister
See also CA 104

Crowley, John 1942-.............. **CLC 57**
See also CA 61-64; DLBY 82; SATA 65

Crud
See Crumb, R(obert)

Crumarums
See Crumb, R(obert)

Crumb, R(obert) 1943- .... **CLC 17**
See also CA 106

Crumbum
See Crumb, R(obert)

Crumski
See Crumb, R(obert)

Crum the Bum
See Crumb, R(obert)

Crunk
See Crumb, R(obert)

Crustt
See Crumb, R(obert)

Cryer, Gretchen (Kiger) 1935-...... **CLC 21**
See also CA 114; 123

Csath, Geza 1887-1919........... **TCLC 13**
See also CA 111

Cudlip, David 1933-.............. **CLC 34**

Cullen, Countee 1903-1946 ..... **TCLC 4, 37**
See also BLC 1; BW; CA 108; 124; CDALB 1917-1929; DLB 4, 48, 51; MTCW; SATA 18

Cum, R.
See Crumb, R(obert)

Cummings, Bruce F(rederick) 1889-1919
See Barbellion, W. N. P.
See also CA 123

Cummings, E(dward) E(stlin)
1894-1962 ..... **CLC 1, 3, 8, 12, 15, 68; PC 5**
See also CA 73-76; CANR 31; CDALB 1929-1941; DLB 4, 48; MTCW; WLC 2

Cunha, Euclides (Rodrigues Pimenta) da
1866-1909 .... **TCLC 24**
See also CA 123

Cunningham, E. V.
See Fast, Howard (Melvin)

Cunningham, J(ames) V(incent)
1911-1985 .... **CLC 3, 31**
See also CA 1-4R; 115; CANR 1; DLB 5

Cunningham, Julia (Woolfolk)
1916-....................... **CLC 12**
See also CA 9-12R; CANR 4, 19, 36; MAICYA; SAAS 2; SATA 1, 26

Cunningham, Michael 1952- .... **CLC 34**
See also CA 136

Cunninghame Graham, R(obert) B(ontine)
1852-1936 .... **TCLC 19**
See also Graham, R(obert) B(ontine) Cunninghame
See also CA 119; DLB 98

Currie, Ellen 19(?)-............... **CLC 44**

Curtin, Philip
See Lowndes, Marie Adelaide (Belloc)

Curtis, Price
See Ellison, Harlan

Czaczkes, Shmuel Yosef
See Agnon, S(hmuel) Y(osef Halevi)

D. P.
See Wells, H(erbert) G(eorge)

Dabrowska, Maria (Szumska)
1889-1965 .... **CLC 15**
See also CA 106

Dabydeen, David 1955- .... **CLC 34**
See also BW; CA 125

Dacey, Philip 1939- .... **CLC 51**
See also CA 37-40R; CANR 14, 32; DLB 105

Dagerman, Stig (Halvard)
1923-1954 .... **TCLC 17**
See also CA 117

Dahl, Roald 1916-1990........ **CLC 1, 6, 18**
See also CA 1-4R; 133; CANR 6, 32, 37; CLR 1, 7; MAICYA; MTCW; SATA 1, 26; SATO 65

Dahlberg, Edward 1900-1977... **CLC 1, 7, 14**
See also CA 9-12R; 69-72; CANR 31; DLB 48; MTCW

Dale, Colin...................... **TCLC 18**
See also Lawrence, T(homas) E(dward)

Dale, George E.
See Asimov, Isaac

Daly, Elizabeth 1878-1967......... **CLC 52**
See also CA 23-24; 25-28R; CAP 2

Daly, Maureen 1921-............. **CLC 17**
See also AAYA 5; CANR 37; MAICYA; SAAS 1; SATA 2

Daniels, Brett
See Adler, Renata

Dannay, Frederic 1905-1982 .... **CLC 11**
See also Queen, Ellery
See also CA 1-4R; 107; CANR 1, 39; MTCW

D'Annunzio, Gabriele
1863-1938 .... **TCLC 6, 40**
See also CA 104

d'Antibes, Germain
See Simenon, Georges (Jacques Christian)

Danvers, Dennis 1947-............ **CLC 70**

Danziger, Paula 1944- .... **CLC 21**
See also AAYA 4; CA 112; 115; CANR 37; CLR 20; MAICYA; SATA 30, 36, 63

Dario, Ruben.................... **TCLC 4**
See also Sarmiento, Felix Ruben Garcia

Darley, George 1795-1846........ **NCLC 2**
See also DLB 96

Daryush, Elizabeth 1887-1977.... **CLC 6, 19**
See also CA 49-52; CANR 3; DLB 20

Daudet, (Louis Marie) Alphonse
1840-1897 .... **NCLC 1**

Daumal, Rene 1908-1944......... **TCLC 14**
See also CA 114

Davenport, Guy (Mattison Jr.)
1927- .... **CLC 6, 14, 38**
See also CA 33-36R; CANR 23

Davidson, Avram 1923-
See Queen, Ellery
See also CA 101; CANR 26; DLB 8

Davidson, Donald (Grady)
1893-1968 .... **CLC 2, 13, 19**
See also CA 5-8R; 25-28R; CANR 4; DLB 45

Davidson, Hugh
See Hamilton, Edmond

Davidson, John 1857-1909........ **TCLC 24**
See also CA 118; DLB 19

Davidson, Sara 1943-.............. **CLC 9**
See also CA 81-84

Davie, Donald (Alfred)
1922-................ **CLC 5, 8, 10, 31**
See also CA 1-4R; CAAS 3; CANR 1; DLB 27; MTCW

Davies, Ray(mond Douglas) 1944- .. **CLC 21**
See also CA 116

Davies, Rhys 1903-1978........... **CLC 23**
See also CA 9-12R; 81-84; CANR 4

Davies, (William) Robertson
1913- .... **CLC 2, 7, 13, 25, 42**
See also BEST 89:2; CA 33-36R; CANR 17; DLB 68; MTCW; WLC

Davies, W(illiam) H(enry)
1871-1940 .... **TCLC 5**
See also CA 104; DLB 19

Davies, Walter C.
See Kornbluth, C(yril) M.

Davis, B. Lynch
See Bioy Casares, Adolfo; Borges, Jorge Luis

Davis, Gordon
See Hunt, E(verette) Howard Jr.

Davis, Harold Lenoir 1896-1960.... **CLC 49**
See also CA 89-92; DLB 9

Davis, Rebecca (Blaine) Harding
1831-1910 .... **TCLC 6**
See also CA 104; DLB 74

Davis, Richard Harding
1864-1916 .... **TCLC 24**
See also CA 114; DLB 12, 23, 78, 79

Davison, Frank Dalby 1893-1970 ... **CLC 15**
See also CA 116

Davison, Lawrence H.
See Lawrence, D(avid) H(erbert Richards)

Davison, Peter 1928- .... **CLC 28**
See also CA 9-12R; CAAS 4; CANR 3; DLB 5

Davys, Mary 1674-1732............. **LC 1**
See also DLB 39

Dawson, Fielding 1930- .... **CLC 6**
See also CA 85-88

Day, Clarence (Shepard Jr.)
1874-1935 .... **TCLC 25**
See also CA 108; DLB 11

Day, Thomas 1748-1789............. **LC 1**
See also DLB 39; YABC 1

Day Lewis, C(ecil)
1904-1972 .... **CLC 1, 6, 10**
See also Blake, Nicholas
See also CA 13-16; 33-36R; CANR 34; CAP 1; DLB 15, 20; MTCW

Dazai, Osamu .... **TCLC 11**
See also Tsushima, Shuji

de Andrade, Carlos Drummond
See Drummond de Andrade, Carlos

Deane, Norman
See Creasey, John

de Beauvoir, Simone (Lucie Ernestine Marie Bertrand)
See Beauvoir, Simone (Lucie Ernestine Marie Bertrand) de

de Brissac, Malcolm
See Dickinson, Peter (Malcolm)

de Chardin, Pierre Teilhard
See Teilhard de Chardin, (Marie Joseph) Pierre

Dee, John 1527-1608 .... **LC 20**

Deer, Sandra 1940-............... **CLC 45**

De Ferrari, Gabriella .... **CLC 65**

Defoe, Daniel 1660(?)-1731 .... **LC 1**
See also CDBLB 1660-1789; DLB 39, 95, 101; MAICYA; SATA 22; WLC

de Gourmont, Remy
See Gourmont, Remy de

de Hartog, Jan 1914- .... **CLC 19**
See also CA 1-4R; CANR 1

de Hostos, E. M.
See Hostos (y Bonilla), Eugenio Maria de

de Hostos, Eugenio M.
See Hostos (y Bonilla), Eugenio Maria de

Deighton, Len .... **CLC 4, 7, 22, 46**
See also Deighton, Leonard Cyril
See also AAYA 6; BEST 89:2; CDBLB 1960 to Present; DLB 87

Deighton, Leonard Cyril 1929-
See Deighton, Len
See also CA 9-12R; CANR 19, 33; MTCW

de la Mare, Walter (John)
1873-1956 .... **TCLC 4**
See also CA 110; 137; CDBLB 1914-1945; CLR 23; DLB 19; MAICYA; SATA 16; WLC

Delaney, Franey
See O'Hara, John (Henry)

Delaney, Shelagh 1939- .... **CLC 29**
See also CA 17-20R; CANR 30; CDBLB 1960 to Present; DLB 13; MTCW

Delany, Mary (Granville Pendarves)
1700-1788 .... **LC 12**

Delany, Samuel R(ay Jr.)
1942- .... **CLC 8, 14, 38**
See also BLC 1; BW; CA 81-84; CANR 27; DLB 8, 33; MTCW

Delaporte, Theophile
See Green, Julian (Hartridge)

De La Ramee, (Marie) Louise 1839-1908
See Ouida
See also SATA 20

de la Roche, Mazo 1879-1961 ...... **CLC 14**
See also CA 85-88; CANR 30; DLB 68; SATA 64

Delbanco, Nicholas (Franklin)
1942- .... **CLC 6, 13**
See also CA 17-20R; CAAS 2; CANR 29; DLB 6

del Castillo, Michel 1933- .... **CLC 38**
See also CA 109

Deledda, Grazia (Cosima)
1875(?)-1936 .... **TCLC 23**
See also CA 123

Delibes, Miguel .... **CLC 8, 18**
See also Delibes Setien, Miguel

Delibes Setien, Miguel 1920-
See Delibes, Miguel
See also CA 45-48; CANR 1, 32; HW; MTCW

DeLillo, Don
1936- .... **CLC 8, 10, 13, 27, 39, 54**
See also BEST 89:1; CA 81-84; CANR 21; DLB 6; MTCW

de Lisser, H. G.
See De Lisser, Herbert George
See also DLB 117

De Lisser, Herbert George
1878-1944 .... **TCLC 12**
See also de Lisser, H. G.
See also CA 109

Deloria, Vine (Victor) Jr. 1933- .... **CLC 21**
See also CA 53-56; CANR 5, 20; MTCW; SATA 21

Del Vecchio, John M(ichael)
1947- .... **CLC 29**
See also CA 110; DLBD 9

de Man, Paul (Adolph Michel)
1919-1983 .... **CLC 55**
See also CA 128; 111; DLB 67; MTCW

De Marinis, Rick 1934- .... **CLC 54**
See also CA 57-60; CANR 9, 25

Demby, William 1922- .... **CLC 53**
See also BLC 1; BW; CA 81-84; DLB 33

Demijohn, Thom
See Disch, Thomas M(ichael)

de Montherlant, Henry (Milon)
See Montherlant, Henry (Milon) de

de Natale, Francine
See Malzberg, Barry N(athaniel)

Denby, Edwin (Orr) 1903-1983 ..... **CLC 48**
See also CA 138; 110

Denis, Julio
See Cortazar, Julio

Denmark, Harrison
See Zelazny, Roger (Joseph)

Dennis, John 1658-1734 .... **LC 11**
See also DLB 101

Dennis, Nigel (Forbes) 1912-1989 .... **CLC 8**
See also CA 25-28R; 129; DLB 13, 15; MTCW

De Palma, Brian (Russell) 1940- .... **CLC 20**
See also CA 109

De Quincey, Thomas 1785-1859 ... **NCLC 4**
See also CDBLB 1789-1832; DLB 110

Deren, Eleanora 1908(?)-1961
See Deren, Maya
See also CA 111

Deren, Maya .... **CLC 16**
See also Deren, Eleanora

Derleth, August (William)
1909-1971 .... **CLC 31**
See also CA 1-4R; 29-32R; CANR 4; DLB 9; SATA 5

de Routisie, Albert
See Aragon, Louis

Derrida, Jacques 1930- .... **CLC 24**
See also CA 124; 127

Derry Down Derry
See Lear, Edward

Dersonnes, Jacques
See Simenon, Georges (Jacques Christian)

Desai, Anita 1937- .... **CLC 19, 37**
See also CA 81-84; CANR 33; MTCW; SATA 63

de Saint-Luc, Jean
See Glassco, John

de Saint Roman, Arnaud
See Aragon, Louis

Descartes, Rene 1596-1650 .... **LC 20**

De Sica, Vittorio 1901(?)-1974 ..... **CLC 20**
See also CA 117

Desnos, Robert 1900-1945 .... **TCLC 22**
See also CA 121

Destouches, Louis-Ferdinand
1894-1961 .... **CLC 9, 15**
See also Celine, Louis-Ferdinand
See also CA 85-88; CANR 28; MTCW

Deutsch, Babette 1895-1982 .... **CLC 18**
See also CA 1-4R; 108; CANR 4; DLB 45; SATA 1, 33

Devenant, William 1606-1649 .... **LC 13**

Devkota, Laxmiprasad
1909-1959 .... **TCLC 23**
See also CA 123

De Voto, Bernard (Augustine)
1897-1955 .... **TCLC 29**
See also CA 113; DLB 9

De Vries, Peter
1910- .... **CLC 1, 2, 3, 7, 10, 28, 46**
See also CA 17-20R; DLB 6; DLBY 82; MTCW

Dexter, Pete 1943- .... **CLC 34, 55**
See also BEST 89:2; CA 127; 131; MTCW

Diamano, Silmang
See Senghor, Leopold Sedar

Diamond, Neil 1941- .... **CLC 30**
See also CA 108

di Bassetto, Corno
See Shaw, George Bernard

Dick, Philip K(indred)
1928-1982 .... **CLC 10, 30, 72**
See also CA 49-52; 106; CANR 2, 16; DLB 8; MTCW

Dickens, Charles (John Huffam)
1812-1870 .... **NCLC 3, 8, 18, 26**
See also CDBLB 1832-1890; DLB 21, 55, 70; MAICYA; SATA 15

Dickey, James (Lafayette)
1923- .... **CLC 1, 2, 4, 7, 10, 15, 47**
See also AITN 1, 2; CA 9-12R; CABS 2; CANR 10; CDALB 1968-1988; DLB 5; DLBD 7; DLBY 82; MTCW

Dickey, William 1928- .... **CLC 3, 28**
See also CA 9-12R; CANR 24; DLB 5

Dickinson, Charles 1951- .... **CLC 49**
See also CA 128

Dickinson, Emily (Elizabeth)
1830-1886 .... **NCLC 21; PC 1**
See also CDALB 1865-1917; DLB 1; SATA 29; WLC

Dickinson, Peter (Malcolm)
1927- .... **CLC 12, 35**
See also AAYA 9; CA 41-44R; CANR 31; DLB 87; MAICYA; SATA 5, 62

Dickson, Carr
See Carr, John Dickson

Dickson, Carter
See Carr, John Dickson

Didion, Joan 1934- ..... **CLC 1, 3, 8, 14, 32**
See also AITN 1; CA 5-8R; CANR 14; CDALB 1968-1988; DLB 2; DLBY 81, 86; MTCW

Dietrich, Robert
See Hunt, E(verette) Howard Jr.

Dillard, Annie 1945- .... **CLC 9, 60**
See also AAYA 6; CA 49-52; CANR 3; DLBY 80; MTCW; SATA 10

Dillard, R(ichard) H(enry) W(ilde) 1937- .... **CLC 5**
See also CA 21-24R; CAAS 7; CANR 10; DLB 5

Dillon, Eilis 1920- .... **CLC 17**
See also CA 9-12R; CAAS 3; CANR 4, 38; CLR 26; MAICYA; SATA 2

Dimont, Penelope
See Mortimer, Penelope (Ruth)

Dinesen, Isak .... **CLC 10, 29; SSC 7**
See also Blixen, Karen (Christentze Dinesen)

Ding Ling .... **CLC 68**
See also Chiang Pin-chin

Disch, Thomas M(ichael) 1940- ... **CLC 7, 36**
See also CA 21-24R; CAAS 4; CANR 17, 36; CLR 18; DLB 8; MAICYA; MTCW; SATA 54

Disch, Tom
See Disch, Thomas M(ichael)

d'Isly, Georges
See Simenon, Georges (Jacques Christian)

Disraeli, Benjamin 1804-1881 ..... **NCLC 2**
See also DLB 21, 55

Ditcum, Steve
See Crumb, R(obert)

Dixon, Paige
See Corcoran, Barbara

Dixon, Stephen 1936- .... **CLC 52**
See also CA 89-92; CANR 17

Doblin, Alfred .... **TCLC 13**
See also Doeblin, Alfred

Dobrolyubov, Nikolai Alexandrovich 1836-1861 .... **NCLC 5**

Dobyns, Stephen 1941- .... **CLC 37**
See also CA 45-48; CANR 2, 18

Doctorow, E(dgar) L(aurence) 1931- ..... **CLC 6, 11, 15, 18, 37, 44, 65**
See also AITN 2; BEST 89:3; CA 45-48; CANR 2, 33; CDALB 1968-1988; DLB 2, 28; DLBY 80; MTCW

Dodgson, Charles Lutwidge 1832-1898
See Carroll, Lewis
See also CLR 2; MAICYA; YABC 2

Doeblin, Alfred 1878-1957 .... **TCLC 13**
See also Doblin, Alfred
See also CA 110; DLB 66

Doerr, Harriet 1910- .... **CLC 34**
See also CA 117; 122

Domecq, H(onorio) Bustos
See Bioy Casares, Adolfo; Borges, Jorge Luis

Domini, Rey
See Lorde, Audre (Geraldine)

Dominique
See Proust, (Valentin-Louis-George-Eugene-)Marcel

Don, A
See Stephen, Leslie

Donaldson, Stephen R. 1947- .... **CLC 46**
See also CA 89-92; CANR 13

Donleavy, J(ames) P(atrick) 1926- .... **CLC 1, 4, 6, 10, 45**
See also AITN 2; CA 9-12R; CANR 24; DLB 6; MTCW

Donne, John 1572-1631 .... **LC 10; PC 1**
See also CDBLB Before 1660; DLB 121; WLC

Donnell, David 1939(?)- .... **CLC 34**

Donoso (Yanez), Jose 1924- .... **CLC 4, 8, 11, 32**
See also CA 81-84; CANR 32; DLB 113; HW; MTCW

Donovan, John 1928-1992 .... **CLC 35**
See also CA 97-100; 137; CLR 3; MAICYA; SATA 29

Don Roberto
See Cunninghame Graham, R(obert) B(ontine)

Doolittle, Hilda 1886-1961 ... **CLC 3, 8, 14, 31, 34; PC 5**
See also H. D.
See also CA 97-100; CANR 35; DLB 4, 45; MTCW; WLC

Dorfman, Ariel 1942- .... **CLC 48**
See also CA 124; 130; HW

Dorn, Edward (Merton) 1929- ... **CLC 10, 18**
See also CA 93-96; DLB 5

Dorsan, Luc
See Simenon, Georges (Jacques Christian)

Dorsange, Jean
See Simenon, Georges (Jacques Christian)

Dos Passos, John (Roderigo) 1896-1970 ... **CLC 1, 4, 8, 11, 15, 25, 34**
See also CA 1-4R; 29-32R; CANR 3; CDALB 1929-1941; DLB 4, 9; DLBD 1; MTCW; WLC

Dossage, Jean
See Simenon, Georges (Jacques Christian)

Dostoevsky, Fedor Mikhailovich 1821-1881 .... **NCLC 2, 7, 21, 33; SSC 2**
See also WLC

Doughty, Charles M(ontagu) 1843-1926 .... **TCLC 27**
See also CA 115; DLB 19, 57

Douglas, Gavin 1475(?)-1522 .... **LC 20**

Douglas, Keith 1920-1944 .... **TCLC 40**
See also DLB 27

Douglas, Leonard
See Bradbury, Ray (Douglas)

Douglas, Michael
See Crichton, (John) Michael

Douglass, Frederick 1817(?)-1895 .. **NCLC 7**
See also BLC 1; CDALB 1640-1865; DLB 1, 43, 50, 79; SATA 29; WLC

Dourado, (Waldomiro Freitas) Autran 1926- .... **CLC 23, 60**
See also CA 25-28R; CANR 34

Dourado, Waldomiro Autran
See Dourado, (Waldomiro Freitas) Autran

Dove, Rita (Frances) 1952- .... **CLC 50**
See also BW; CA 109; CANR 27; DLB 120

Dowell, Coleman 1925-1985 .... **CLC 60**
See also CA 25-28R; 117; CANR 10

Dowson, Ernest Christopher 1867-1900 .... **TCLC 4**
See also CA 105; DLB 19

Doyle, A. Conan
See Doyle, Arthur Conan

Doyle, Arthur Conan 1859-1930 .... **TCLC 7**
See also CA 104; 122; CDBLB 1890-1914; DLB 18, 70; MTCW; SATA 24; WLC

Doyle, Conan
See Doyle, Arthur Conan

Doyle, John
See Graves, Robert (von Ranke)

Doyle, Sir A. Conan
See Doyle, Arthur Conan

Doyle, Sir Arthur Conan
See Doyle, Arthur Conan

Dr. A
See Asimov, Isaac; Silverstein, Alvin

Drabble, Margaret 1939- .... **CLC 2, 3, 5, 8, 10, 22, 53**
See also CA 13-16R; CANR 18, 35; CDBLB 1960 to Present; DLB 14; MTCW; SATA 48

Drapier, M. B.
See Swift, Jonathan

Drayham, James
See Mencken, H(enry) L(ouis)

Drayton, Michael 1563-1631 .... **LC 8**

Dreadstone, Carl
See Campbell, (John) Ramsey

Dreiser, Theodore (Herman Albert) 1871-1945 .... **TCLC 10, 18, 35**
See also CA 106; 132; CDALB 1865-1917; DLB 9, 12, 102; DLBD 1; MTCW; WLC

Drexler, Rosalyn 1926- .... **CLC 2, 6**
See also CA 81-84

Dreyer, Carl Theodor 1889-1968 .... **CLC 16**
See also CA 116

Drieu la Rochelle, Pierre(-Eugene) 1893-1945 .... **TCLC 21**
See also CA 117; DLB 72

Drop Shot
See Cable, George Washington

Droste-Hulshoff, Annette Freiin von 1797-1848 .... **NCLC 3**

Drummond, Walter
See Silverberg, Robert

Drummond, William Henry 1854-1907 .... **TCLC 25**
See also DLB 92

Drummond de Andrade, Carlos 1902-1987 .... **CLC 18**
See also Andrade, Carlos Drummond de
See also CA 132; 123

Drury, Allen (Stuart) 1918- .... **CLC 37**
See also CA 57-60; CANR 18

Dryden, John 1631-1700 .... **LC 3, 21; DC 3**
See also CDBLB 1660-1789; DLB 80, 101; WLC

Duberman, Martin 1930- .... **CLC 8**
See also CA 1-4R; CANR 2

Dubie, Norman (Evans) 1945- ...... **CLC 36**
See also CA 69-72; CANR 12; DLB 120

Du Bois, W(illiam) E(dward) B(urghardt) 1868-1963 . . . . **CLC 1, 2, 13, 64**
See also BLC 1; BW; CA 85-88; CANR 34; CDALB 1865-1917; DLB 47, 50, 91; MTCW; SATA 42; WLC

Dubus, Andre 1936- . . . . **CLC 13, 36**
See also CA 21-24R; CANR 17

Duca Minimo
See D'Annunzio, Gabriele

Ducharme, Rejean 1941- . . . . **CLC 74**
See also DLB 60

Duclos, Charles Pinot 1704-1772 . . . . . **LC 1**

Dudek, Louis 1918- . . . . **CLC 11, 19**
See also CA 45-48; CAAS 14; CANR 1; DLB 88

Duerrenmatt, Friedrich 1921-1990 . . . . . . **CLC 1, 4, 8, 11, 15, 43**
See also Durrenmatt, Friedrich
See also CA 17-20R; CANR 33; DLB 69; MTCW

Duffy, Bruce (?)- . . . . **CLC 50**

Duffy, Maureen 1933- . . . . **CLC 37**
See also CA 25-28R; CANR 33; DLB 14; MTCW

Dugan, Alan 1923- . . . . **CLC 2, 6**
See also CA 81-84; DLB 5

du Gard, Roger Martin
See Martin du Gard, Roger

Duhamel, Georges 1884-1966 . . . . **CLC 8**
See also CA 81-84; 25-28R; CANR 35; DLB 65; MTCW

Dujardin, Edouard (Emile Louis) 1861-1949 . . . . **TCLC 13**
See also CA 109

Dumas, Alexandre (Davy de la Pailleterie) 1802-1870 . . . . **NCLC 11**
See also DLB 119; SATA 18; WLC

Dumas, Alexandre 1824-1895 . . . . **NCLC 9; DC 1**

Dumas, Claudine
See Malzberg, Barry N(athaniel)

Dumas, Henry L. 1934-1968 . . . . . **CLC 6, 62**
See also BW; CA 85-88; DLB 41

du Maurier, Daphne 1907-1989 . . . . **CLC 6, 11, 59**
See also CA 5-8R; 128; CANR 6; MTCW; SATA 27, 60

Dunbar, Paul Laurence 1872-1906 . . . . **TCLC 2, 12; PC 5; SSC 8**
See also BLC 1; BW; CA 104; 124; CDALB 1865-1917; DLB 50, 54, 78; SATA 34; WLC

Dunbar, William 1460(?)-1530(?) . . . . **LC 20**

Duncan, Lois 1934-. . . . . **CLC 26**
See also AAYA 4; CA 1-4R; CANR 2, 23, 36; MAICYA; SAAS 2; SATA 1, 36

Duncan, Robert (Edward) 1919-1988 . . . **CLC 1, 2, 4, 7, 15, 41, 55; PC 2**
See also CA 9-12R; 124; CANR 28; DLB 5, 16; MTCW

Dunlap, William 1766-1839 . . . . **NCLC 2**
See also DLB 30, 37, 59

Dunn, Douglas (Eaglesham) 1942- . . . . **CLC 6, 40**
See also CA 45-48; CANR 2, 33; DLB 40; MTCW

Dunn, Katherine (Karen) 1945- . . . . . **CLC 71**
See also CA 33-36R

Dunn, Stephen 1939- . . . . **CLC 36**
See also CA 33-36R; CANR 12; DLB 105

Dunne, Finley Peter 1867-1936. . . . **TCLC 28**
See also CA 108; DLB 11, 23

Dunne, John Gregory 1932-. . . . . **CLC 28**
See also CA 25-28R; CANR 14; DLBY 80

Dunsany, Edward John Moreton Drax Plunkett 1878-1957
See Dunsany, Lord; Lord Dunsany
See also CA 104; DLB 10

Dunsany, Lord. . . . . **TCLC 2**
See also Dunsany, Edward John Moreton Drax Plunkett
See also DLB 77

du Perry, Jean
See Simenon, Georges (Jacques Christian)

Durang, Christopher (Ferdinand) 1949- . . . . **CLC 27, 38**
See also CA 105

Duras, Marguerite 1914- . . . . . . **CLC 3, 6, 11, 20, 34, 40, 68**
See also CA 25-28R; DLB 83; MTCW

Durban, (Rosa) Pam 1947-. . . . . **CLC 39**
See also CA 123

Durcan, Paul 1944-. . . . . **CLC 43, 70**
See also CA 134

Durrell, Lawrence (George) 1912-1990 . . . . **CLC 1, 4, 6, 8, 13, 27, 41**
See also CA 9-12R; 132; CDBLB 1945-1960; DLB 15, 27; DLBY 90; MTCW

Durrenmatt, Friedrich . . . . **CLC 1, 4, 8, 11, 15, 43**
See also Duerrenmatt, Friedrich
See also DLB 69

Dutt, Toru 1856-1877. . . . . **NCLC 29**

Dwight, Timothy 1752-1817. . . . . . **NCLC 13**
See also DLB 37

Dworkin, Andrea 1946- . . . . **CLC 43**
See also CA 77-80; CANR 16, 39; MTCW

Dylan, Bob 1941- . . . . **CLC 3, 4, 6, 12**
See also CA 41-44R; DLB 16

Eagleton, Terence (Francis) 1943-
See Eagleton, Terry
See also CA 57-60; CANR 7, 23; MTCW

Eagleton, Terry . . . . **CLC 63**
See also Eagleton, Terence (Francis)

East, Michael
See West, Morris L(anglo)

Eastaway, Edward
See Thomas, (Philip) Edward

Eastlake, William (Derry) 1917- . . . . . **CLC 8**
See also CA 5-8R; CAAS 1; CANR 5; DLB 6

Eberhart, Richard (Ghormley) 1904- . . . . **CLC 3, 11, 19, 56**
See also CA 1-4R; CANR 2; CDALB 1941-1968; DLB 48; MTCW

Eberstadt, Fernanda 1960- . . . . **CLC 39**
See also CA 136

Echegaray (y Eizaguirre), Jose (Maria Waldo) 1832-1916 . . . . **TCLC 4**
See also CA 104; CANR 32; HW; MTCW

Echeverria, (Jose) Esteban (Antonino) 1805-1851 . . . . **NCLC 18**

Echo
See Proust, (Valentin-Louis-George-Eugene-)Marcel

Eckert, Allan W. 1931- . . . . **CLC 17**
See also CA 13-16R; CANR 14; SATA 27, 29

Eckhart, Meister 1260(?)-1328(?) . . **CMLC 9**
See also DLB 115

Eckmar, F. R.
See de Hartog, Jan

Eco, Umberto 1932- . . . . **CLC 28, 60**
See also BEST 90:1; CA 77-80; CANR 12, 33; MTCW

Eddison, E(ric) R(ucker) 1882-1945 . . . . **TCLC 15**
See also CA 109

Edel, (Joseph) Leon 1907- . . . . . . **CLC 29, 34**
See also CA 1-4R; CANR 1, 22; DLB 103

Eden, Emily 1797-1869 . . . . **NCLC 10**

Edgar, David 1948-. . . . . **CLC 42**
See also CA 57-60; CANR 12; DLB 13; MTCW

Edgerton, Clyde (Carlyle) 1944- . . . . **CLC 39**
See also CA 118; 134

Edgeworth, Maria 1767-1849. . . . . . **NCLC 1**
See also DLB 116; SATA 21

Edmonds, Paul
See Kuttner, Henry

Edmonds, Walter D(umaux) 1903- . . **CLC 35**
See also CA 5-8R; CANR 2; DLB 9; MAICYA; SAAS 4; SATA 1, 27

Edmondson, Wallace
See Ellison, Harlan

Edson, Russell. **CLC 13**
See also CA 33-36R

Edwards, G(erald) B(asil) 1899-1976 . . . . **CLC 25**
See also CA 110

Edwards, Gus 1939- . . . . **CLC 43**
See also CA 108

Edwards, Jonathan 1703-1758. . . . . **LC 7**
See also DLB 24

Efron, Marina Ivanovna Tsvetaeva
See Tsvetaeva (Efron), Marina (Ivanovna)

Ehle, John (Marsden Jr.) 1925- . . . . **CLC 27**
See also CA 9-12R

Ehrenbourg, Ilya (Grigoryevich)
See Ehrenburg, Ilya (Grigoryevich)

Ehrenburg, Ilya (Grigoryevich) 1891-1967 . . . . **CLC 18, 34, 62**
See also CA 102; 25-28R

Ehrenburg, Ilyo (Grigoryevich)
See Ehrenburg, Ilya (Grigoryevich)

Eich, Guenter 1907-1972 . . . . **CLC 15**
See also CA 111; 93-96; DLB 69

Eichendorff, Joseph Freiherr von 1788-1857 .... **NCLC 8**
See also DLB 90

Eigner, Larry .... **CLC 9**
See also Eigner, Laurence (Joel)
See also DLB 5

Eigner, Laurence (Joel) 1927-
See Eigner, Larry
See also CA 9-12R; CANR 6

Eiseley, Loren Corey 1907-1977 ..... **CLC 7**
See also AAYA 5; CA 1-4R; 73-76; CANR 6

Eisenstadt, Jill 1963- .... **CLC 50**

Eisner, Simon
See Kornbluth, C(yril) M.

Ekeloef, (Bengt) Gunnar 1907-1968 .... **CLC 27**
See also Ekelof, (Bengt) Gunnar
See also CA 123; 25-28R

Ekelof, (Bengt) Gunnar .... **CLC 27**
See also Ekeloef, (Bengt) Gunnar

Ekwensi, C. O. D.
See Ekwensi, Cyprian (Odiatu Duaka)

Ekwensi, Cyprian (Odiatu Duaka) 1921- .... **CLC 4**
See also BLC 1; BW; CA 29-32R; CANR 18; DLB 117; MTCW; SATA 66

Elaine .... **TCLC 18**
See also Leverson, Ada

El Crummo
See Crumb, R(obert)

Elia
See Lamb, Charles

Eliade, Mircea 1907-1986 .... **CLC 19**
See also CA 65-68; 119; CANR 30; MTCW

Eliot, A. D.
See Jewett, (Theodora) Sarah Orne

Eliot, Alice
See Jewett, (Theodora) Sarah Orne

Eliot, Dan
See Silverberg, Robert

Eliot, George 1819-1880.... **NCLC 4, 13, 23**
See also CDBLB 1832-1890; DLB 21, 35, 55; WLC

Eliot, John 1604-1690 .... **LC 5**
See also DLB 24

Eliot, T(homas) S(tearns) 1888-1965 .... **CLC 1, 2, 3, 6, 9, 10, 13, 15, 24, 34, 41, 55, 57; PC 5**
See also CA 5-8R; 25-28R; CDALB 1929-1941; DLB 7, 10, 45, 63; DLBY 88; MTCW; WLC 2

Elizabeth 1866-1941 .... **TCLC 41**

Elkin, Stanley L(awrence) 1930- .... **CLC 4, 6, 9, 14, 27, 51**
See also CA 9-12R; CANR 8; DLB 2, 28; DLBY 80; MTCW

Elledge, Scott .... **CLC 34**

Elliott, Don
See Silverberg, Robert

Elliott, George P(aul) 1918-1980..... **CLC 2**
See also CA 1-4R; 97-100; CANR 2

Elliott, Janice 1931- .... **CLC 47**
See also CA 13-16R; CANR 8, 29; DLB 14

Elliott, Sumner Locke 1917-1991 ... **CLC 38**
See also CA 5-8R; 134; CANR 2, 21

Elliott, William
See Bradbury, Ray (Douglas)

Ellis, A. E. .... **CLC 7**

Ellis, Alice Thomas .... **CLC 40**
See also Haycraft, Anna

Ellis, Bret Easton 1964- .... **CLC 39, 71**
See also AAYA 2; CA 118; 123

Ellis, (Henry) Havelock 1859-1939 .... **TCLC 14**
See also CA 109

Ellis, Landon
See Ellison, Harlan

Ellis, Trey 1962- .... **CLC 55**

Ellison, Harlan 1934- .... **CLC 1, 13, 42**
See also CA 5-8R; CANR 5; DLB 8; MTCW

Ellison, Ralph (Waldo) 1914- .... **CLC 1, 3, 11, 54**
See also BLC 1; BW; CA 9-12R; CANR 24; CDALB 1941-1968; DLB 2, 76; MTCW; WLC

Ellmann, Lucy (Elizabeth) 1956- .... **CLC 61**
See also CA 128

Ellmann, Richard (David) 1918-1987 .... **CLC 50**
See also BEST 89:2; CA 1-4R; 122; CANR 2, 28; DLB 103; DLBY 87; MTCW

Elman, Richard 1934- .... **CLC 19**
See also CA 17-20R; CAAS 3

Elron
See Hubbard, L(afayette) Ron(ald)

Eluard, Paul .... **TCLC 7, 41**
See also Grindel, Eugene

Elyot, Sir Thomas 1490(?)-1546 ..... **LC 11**

Elytis, Odysseus 1911- .... **CLC 15, 49**
See also CA 102; MTCW

Emecheta, (Florence Onye) Buchi 1944- .... **CLC 14, 48**
See also BLC 2; BW; CA 81-84; CANR 27; DLB 117; MTCW; SATA 66

Emerson, Ralph Waldo 1803-1882 .... **NCLC 1, 38**
See also CDALB 1640-1865; DLB 1, 59, 73; WLC

Eminescu, Mihail 1850-1889 ..... **NCLC 33**

Empson, William 1906-1984 .... **CLC 3, 8, 19, 33, 34**
See also CA 17-20R; 112; CANR 31; DLB 20; MTCW

Enchi Fumiko (Ueda) 1905-1986.... **CLC 31**
See also CA 129; 121

Ende, Michael (Andreas Helmuth) 1929- .... **CLC 31**
See also CA 118; 124; CANR 36; CLR 14; DLB 75; MAICYA; SATA 42, 61

Endo, Shusaku 1923- ..... **CLC 7, 14, 19, 54**
See also CA 29-32R; CANR 21; MTCW

Engel, Marian 1933-1985 .... **CLC 36**
See also CA 25-28R; CANR 12; DLB 53

Engelhardt, Frederick
See Hubbard, L(afayette) Ron(ald)

Enright, D(ennis) J(oseph) 1920- .... **CLC 4, 8, 31**
See also CA 1-4R; CANR 1; DLB 27; SATA 25

Enzensberger, Hans Magnus 1929- .... **CLC 43**
See also CA 116; 119

Ephron, Nora 1941- .... **CLC 17, 31**
See also AITN 2; CA 65-68; CANR 12, 39

Epsilon
See Betjeman, John

Epstein, Daniel Mark 1948- .... **CLC 7**
See also CA 49-52; CANR 2

Epstein, Jacob 1956- .... **CLC 19**
See also CA 114

Epstein, Joseph 1937- .... **CLC 39**
See also CA 112; 119

Epstein, Leslie 1938- .... **CLC 27**
See also CA 73-76; CAAS 12; CANR 23

Equiano, Olaudah 1745(?)-1797...... **LC 16**
See also BLC 2; DLB 37, 50

Erasmus, Desiderius 1469(?)-1536.... **LC 16**

Erdman, Paul E(mil) 1932- .... **CLC 25**
See also AITN 1; CA 61-64; CANR 13

Erdrich, Louise 1954- .... **CLC 39, 54**
See also BEST 89:1; CA 114; MTCW

Erenburg, Ilya (Grigoryevich)
See Ehrenburg, Ilya (Grigoryevich)

Erickson, Stephen Michael 1950-
See Erickson, Steve
See also CA 129

Erickson, Steve .... **CLC 64**
See also Erickson, Stephen Michael

Ericson, Walter
See Fast, Howard (Melvin)

Eriksson, Buntel
See Bergman, (Ernst) Ingmar

Eschenbach, Wolfram von
See Wolfram von Eschenbach

Eseki, Bruno
See Mphahlele, Ezekiel

Esenin, Sergei (Alexandrovich) 1895-1925 .... **TCLC 4**
See also CA 104

Eshleman, Clayton 1935- .... **CLC 7**
See also CA 33-36R; CAAS 6; DLB 5

Espriella, Don Manuel Alvarez
See Southey, Robert

Espriu, Salvador 1913-1985 .... **CLC 9**
See also CA 115

Esse, James
See Stephens, James

Esterbrook, Tom
See Hubbard, L(afayette) Ron(ald)

Estleman, Loren D. 1952- .... **CLC 48**
See also CA 85-88; CANR 27; MTCW

Evans, Mary Ann
See Eliot, George

Evarts, Esther
See Benson, Sally

Everett, Percival
See Everett, Percival L.

Author Index

Everett, Percival L. 1956- . . . . **CLC 57**
See also CA 129

Everson, R(onald) G(ilmour) 1903- . . . . **CLC 27**
See also CA 17-20R; DLB 88

Everson, William (Oliver) 1912- . . . . **CLC 1, 5, 14**
See also CA 9-12R; CANR 20; DLB 5, 16; MTCW

Evtushenko, Evgenii Aleksandrovich
See Yevtushenko, Yevgeny (Alexandrovich)

Ewart, Gavin (Buchanan) 1916- . . . . **CLC 13, 46**
See also CA 89-92; CANR 17; DLB 40; MTCW

Ewers, Hanns Heinz 1871-1943 . . . **TCLC 12**
See also CA 109

Ewing, Frederick R.
See Sturgeon, Theodore (Hamilton)

Exley, Frederick (Earl) 1929- . . . . **CLC 6, 11**
See also AITN 2; CA 81-84; 138; DLBY 81

Eynhardt, Guillermo
See Quiroga, Horacio (Sylvestre)

Ezekiel, Nissim 1924- . . . . **CLC 61**
See also CA 61-64

Ezekiel, Tish O'Dowd 1943- . . . . **CLC 34**
See also CA 129

Fagen, Donald 1948- . . . . **CLC 26**

Fainzilberg, Ilya Arnoldovich 1897-1937
See Ilf, Ilya
See also CA 120

Fair, Ronald L. 1932- . . . . **CLC 18**
See also BW; CA 69-72; CANR 25; DLB 33

Fairbairns, Zoe (Ann) 1948- . . . . **CLC 32**
See also CA 103; CANR 21

Falco, Gian
See Papini, Giovanni

Falconer, James
See Kirkup, James

Falconer, Kenneth
See Kornbluth, C(yril) M.

Falkland, Samuel
See Heijermans, Herman

Fallaci, Oriana 1930- . . . . **CLC 11**
See also CA 77-80; CANR 15; MTCW

Faludy, George 1913- . . . . **CLC 42**
See also CA 21-24R

Faludy, Gyoergy
See Faludy, George

Fanon, Frantz 1925-1961 . . . . **CLC 74**
See also BLC 2; BW; CA 116; 89-92

Fanshawe, Ann . . . . **LC 11**

Fante, John (Thomas) 1911-1983 . . . **CLC 60**
See also CA 69-72; 109; CANR 23; DLBY 83

Farah, Nuruddin 1945- . . . . **CLC 53**
See also BLC 2; CA 106

Fargue, Leon-Paul 1876(?)-1947 . . . **TCLC 11**
See also CA 109

Farigoule, Louis
See Romains, Jules

Farina, Richard 1936(?)-1966 . . . . **CLC 9**
See also CA 81-84; 25-28R

Farley, Walter (Lorimer) 1915-1989 . . . . **CLC 17**
See also CA 17-20R; CANR 8, 29; DLB 22; MAICYA; SATA 2, 43

Farmer, Philip Jose 1918- . . . . **CLC 1, 19**
See also CA 1-4R; CANR 4, 35; DLB 8; MTCW

Farquhar, George 1677-1707 . . . . **LC 21**
See also DLB 84

Farrell, J(ames) G(ordon) 1935-1979 . . . . **CLC 6**
See also CA 73-76; 89-92; CANR 36; DLB 14; MTCW

Farrell, James T(homas) 1904-1979 . . . . **CLC 1, 4, 8, 11, 66**
See also CA 5-8R; 89-92; CANR 9; DLB 4, 9, 86; DLBD 2; MTCW

Farren, Richard J.
See Betjeman, John

Farren, Richard M.
See Betjeman, John

Fassbinder, Rainer Werner 1946-1982 . . . . **CLC 20**
See also CA 93-96; 106; CANR 31

Fast, Howard (Melvin) 1914- . . . . . . **CLC 23**
See also CA 1-4R; CANR 1, 33; DLB 9; SATA 7

Faulcon, Robert
See Holdstock, Robert P.

Faulkner, William (Cuthbert) 1897-1962 . . . . **CLC 1, 3, 6, 8, 9, 11, 14, 18, 28, 52, 68; SSC 1**
See also AAYA 7; CA 81-84; CANR 33; CDALB 1929-1941; DLB 9, 11, 44, 102; DLBD 2; DLBY 86; MTCW; WLC

Fauset, Jessie Redmon 1884(?)-1961 . . . . **CLC 19, 54**
See also BLC 2; BW; CA 109; DLB 51

Faust, Irvin 1924- . . . . **CLC 8**
See also CA 33-36R; CANR 28; DLB 2, 28; DLBY 80

Fawkes, Guy
See Benchley, Robert (Charles)

Fearing, Kenneth (Flexner) 1902-1961 . . . . **CLC 51**
See also CA 93-96; DLB 9

Fecamps, Elise
See Creasey, John

Federman, Raymond 1928- . . . . . . **CLC 6, 47**
See also CA 17-20R; CAAS 8; CANR 10; DLBY 80

Federspiel, J(uerg) F. 1931- . . . . **CLC 42**

Feiffer, Jules (Ralph) 1929- . . . . **CLC 2, 8, 64**
See also AAYA 3; CA 17-20R; CANR 30; DLB 7, 44; MTCW; SATA 8, 61

Feige, Hermann Albert Otto Maximilian
See Traven, B.

Fei-Kan, Li
See Li Fei-kan

Feinberg, David B. 1956- . . . . **CLC 59**
See also CA 135

Feinstein, Elaine 1930- . . . . **CLC 36**
See also CA 69-72; CAAS 1; CANR 31; DLB 14, 40; MTCW

Feldman, Irving (Mordecai) 1928- . . . . **CLC 7**
See also CA 1-4R; CANR 1

Fellini, Federico 1920- . . . . **CLC 16**
See also CA 65-68; CANR 33

Felsen, Henry Gregor 1916- . . . . **CLC 17**
See also CA 1-4R; CANR 1; SAAS 2; SATA 1

Fenton, James Martin 1949- . . . . **CLC 32**
See also CA 102; DLB 40

Ferber, Edna 1887-1968 . . . . **CLC 18**
See also AITN 1; CA 5-8R; 25-28R; DLB 9, 28, 86; MTCW; SATA 7

Ferguson, Helen
See Kavan, Anna

Ferguson, Samuel 1810-1886 . . . . . **NCLC 33**
See also DLB 32

Ferling, Lawrence
See Ferlinghetti, Lawrence (Monsanto)

Ferlinghetti, Lawrence (Monsanto) 1919(?)- . . . . **CLC 2, 6, 10, 27; PC 1**
See also CA 5-8R; CANR 3; CDALB 1941-1968; DLB 5, 16; MTCW

Fernandez, Vicente Garcia Huidobro
See Huidobro Fernandez, Vicente Garcia

Ferrer, Gabriel (Francisco Victor) Miro
See Miro (Ferrer), Gabriel (Francisco Victor)

Ferrier, Susan (Edmonstone) 1782-1854 . . . . **NCLC 8**
See also DLB 116

Ferrigno, Robert . . . . **CLC 65**

Feuchtwanger, Lion 1884-1958 . . . . . **TCLC 3**
See also CA 104; DLB 66

Feydeau, Georges (Leon Jules Marie) 1862-1921 . . . . **TCLC 22**
See also CA 113

Ficino, Marsilio 1433-1499 . . . . **LC 12**

Fiedler, Leslie A(aron) 1917- . . . . **CLC 4, 13, 24**
See also CA 9-12R; CANR 7; DLB 28, 67; MTCW

Field, Andrew 1938- . . . . **CLC 44**
See also CA 97-100; CANR 25

Field, Eugene 1850-1895 . . . . **NCLC 3**
See also DLB 23, 42; MAICYA; SATA 16

Field, Gans T.
See Wellman, Manly Wade

Field, Michael . . . . **TCLC 43**

Field, Peter
See Hobson, Laura Z(ametkin)

Fielding, Henry 1707-1754 . . . . **LC 1**
See also CDBLB 1660-1789; DLB 39, 84, 101; WLC

Fielding, Sarah 1710-1768 . . . . **LC 1**
See also DLB 39

Fierstein, Harvey (Forbes) 1954- . . . **CLC 33**
See also CA 123; 129

Figes, Eva 1932- . . . . **CLC 31**
See also CA 53-56; CANR 4; DLB 14

Finch, Robert (Duer Claydon) 1900- . . . . **CLC 18**
See also CA 57-60; CANR 9, 24; DLB 88

Findley, Timothy 1930- . . . . **CLC 27**
See also CA 25-28R; CANR 12; DLB 53

Fink, William
See Mencken, H(enry) L(ouis)

Firbank, Louis 1942-
See Reed, Lou
See also CA 117

Firbank, (Arthur Annesley) Ronald
1886-1926 . . . . **TCLC 1**
See also CA 104; DLB 36

Fisher, Roy 1930- . . . . **CLC 25**
See also CA 81-84; CAAS 10; CANR 16; DLB 40

Fisher, Rudolph 1897-1934 . . . . **TCLC 11**
See also BLC 2; BW; CA 107; 124; DLB 51, 102

Fisher, Vardis (Alvero) 1895-1968. . . . **CLC 7**
See also CA 5-8R; 25-28R; DLB 9

Fiske, Tarleton
See Bloch, Robert (Albert)

Fitch, Clarke
See Sinclair, Upton (Beall)

Fitch, John IV
See Cormier, Robert (Edmund)

Fitgerald, Penelope 1916- . . . . **CLC 61**

Fitzgerald, Captain Hugh
See Baum, L(yman) Frank

FitzGerald, Edward 1809-1883 . . . . **NCLC 9**
See also DLB 32

Fitzgerald, F(rancis) Scott (Key)
1896-1940 . . . . **TCLC 1, 6, 14, 28; SSC 6**
See also AITN 1; CA 110; 123; CDALB 1917-1929; DLB 4, 9, 86; DLBD 1; DLBY 81; MTCW; WLC

Fitzgerald, Penelope 1916-. . . . . . **CLC 19, 51**
See also CA 85-88; CAAS 10; DLB 14

FitzGerald, Robert D(avid)
1902-1987 . . . . **CLC 19**
See also CA 17-20R

Fitzgerald, Robert (Stuart)
1910-1985 . . . . **CLC 39**
See also CA 1-4R; 114; CANR 1; DLBY 80

Flanagan, Thomas (James Bonner)
1923- . . . . **CLC 25, 52**
See also CA 108; DLBY 80; MTCW

Flaubert, Gustave
1821-1880 . . . . . **NCLC 2, 10, 19; SSC 11**
See also DLB 119; WLC

Flecker, (Herman) James Elroy
1884-1915 . . . . **TCLC 43**
See also CA 109; DLB 10, 19

Fleming, Ian (Lancaster)
1908-1964 . . . . **CLC 3, 30**
See also CA 5-8R; CDBLB 1945-1960; DLB 87; MTCW; SATA 9

Fleming, Thomas (James) 1927- . . . . **CLC 37**
See also CA 5-8R; CANR 10; SATA 8

Fletcher, John Gould 1886-1950 . . . **TCLC 35**
See also CA 107; DLB 4, 45

Fleur, Paul
See Pohl, Frederik

Flying Officer X
See Bates, H(erbert) E(rnest)

Fo, Dario 1926-. . . . . **CLC 32**
See also CA 116; 128; MTCW

Fogarty, Jonathan Titulescu Esq.
See Farrell, James T(homas)

Folke, Will
See Bloch, Robert (Albert)

Follett, Ken(neth Martin) 1949- . . . . **CLC 18**
See also AAYA 6; BEST 89:4; CA 81-84; CANR 13, 33; DLB 87; DLBY 81; MTCW

Fontane, Theodor 1819-1898 . . . . . **NCLC 26**

Foote, Horton 1916-. . . . . **CLC 51**
See also CA 73-76; CANR 34; DLB 26

Forbes, Esther 1891-1967. . . . . **CLC 12**
See also CA 13-14; 25-28R; CAP 1; CLR 27; DLB 22; MAICYA; SATA 2

Forche, Carolyn (Louise) 1950-. . . . . **CLC 25**
See also CA 109; 117; DLB 5

Ford, Elbur
See Hibbert, Eleanor Burford

Ford, Ford Madox
1873-1939 . . . . **TCLC 1, 15, 39**
See also CA 104; 132; CDBLB 1914-1945; DLB 34, 98; MTCW

Ford, John 1895-1973. . . . . **CLC 16**
See also CA 45-48

Ford, Richard 1944-. . . . . **CLC 46**
See also CA 69-72; CANR 11

Ford, Webster
See Masters, Edgar Lee

Foreman, Richard 1937-. . . . . **CLC 50**
See also CA 65-68; CANR 32

Forester, C(ecil) S(cott)
1899-1966 . . . . **CLC 35**
See also CA 73-76; 25-28R; SATA 13

Forez
See Mauriac, Francois (Charles)

Forman, James Douglas 1932-. . . . . . **CLC 21**
See also CA 9-12R; CANR 4, 19; MAICYA; SATA 8, 70

Fornes, Maria Irene 1930-. . . . . . **CLC 39, 61**
See also CA 25-28R; CANR 28; DLB 7; HW; MTCW

Forrest, Leon 1937- . . . . **CLC 4**
See also BW; CA 89-92; CAAS 7; CANR 25; DLB 33

Forster, E(dward) M(organ)
1879-1970 . . . . **CLC 1, 2, 3, 4, 9, 10, 13, 15, 22, 45**
See also AAYA 2; CA 13-14; 25-28R; CAP 1; CDBLB 1914-1945; DLB 34, 98; MTCW; SATA 57; WLC

Forster, John 1812-1876 . . . . **NCLC 11**

Forsyth, Frederick 1938- . . . . . . **CLC 2, 5, 36**
See also BEST 89:4; CA 85-88; CANR 38; DLB 87; MTCW

Forten, Charlotte L. . . . . **TCLC 16**
See also Grimke, Charlotte L(ottie) Forten
See also BLC 2; DLB 50

Foscolo, Ugo 1778-1827. . . . . **NCLC 8**

Fosse, Bob . . . . **CLC 20**
See also Fosse, Robert Louis

Fosse, Robert Louis 1927-1987
See Fosse, Bob
See also CA 110; 123

Foster, Stephen Collins
1826-1864 . . . . **NCLC 26**

Foucault, Michel
1926-1984 . . . . **CLC 31, 34, 69**
See also CA 105; 113; CANR 34; MTCW

Fouque, Friedrich Heinrich Karl) de la Motte
1777-1843 . . . . **NCLC 2**
See also DLB 90

Fournier, Henri Alban 1886-1914
See Alain-Fournier
See also CA 104

Fournier, Pierre 1916- . . . . **CLC 11**
See also Gascar, Pierre
See also CA 89-92; CANR 16

Fowles, John
1926- . . . . **CLC 1, 2, 3, 4, 6, 9, 10, 15, 33**
See also CA 5-8R; CANR 25; CDBLB 1960 to Present; DLB 14; MTCW; SATA 22

Fox, Paula 1923-. . . . . **CLC 2, 8**
See also AAYA 3; CA 73-76; CANR 20, 36; CLR 1; DLB 52; MAICYA; MTCW; SATA 17, 60

Fox, William Price (Jr.) 1926- . . . . . **CLC 22**
See also CA 17-20R; CANR 11; DLB 2; DLBY 81

Foxe, John 1516(?)-1587 . . . . **LC 14**

Frame, Janet . . . . **CLC 2, 3, 6, 22, 66**
See also Clutha, Janet Paterson Frame

France, Anatole. . . . . **TCLC 9**
See also Thibault, Jacques Anatole Francois

Francis, Claude 19(?)- . . . . **CLC 50**

Francis, Dick 1920- . . . . **CLC 2, 22, 42**
See also AAYA 5; BEST 89:3; CA 5-8R; CANR 9; CDBLB 1960 to Present; DLB 87; MTCW

Francis, Robert (Churchill)
1901-1987 . . . . **CLC 15**
See also CA 1-4R; 123; CANR 1

Frank, Anne(lies Marie)
1929-1945 . . . . **TCLC 17**
See also CA 113; 133; MTCW; SATA 42; WLC

Frank, Elizabeth 1945-. . . . . **CLC 39**
See also CA 121; 126

Franklin, Benjamin
See Hasek, Jaroslav (Matej Frantisek)

Franklin, (Stella Maraia Sarah) Miles
1879-1954 . . . . **TCLC 7**
See also CA 104

Fraser, Antonia (Pakenham)
1932- . . . . **CLC 32**
See also CA 85-88; MTCW; SATA 32

Fraser, George MacDonald 1925-. . . . **CLC 7**
See also CA 45-48; CANR 2

Fraser, Sylvia 1935-. . . . . **CLC 64**
See also CA 45-48; CANR 1, 16

Frayn, Michael 1933-. . . . . . **CLC 3, 7, 31, 47**
See also CA 5-8R; CANR 30; DLB 13, 14; MTCW

Fraze, Candida (Merrill) 1945-. . . . . **CLC 50**
See also CA 126

Frazer, J(ames) G(eorge) 1854-1941 .... **TCLC 32**
See also CA 118

Frazer, Robert Caine
See Creasey, John

Frazer, Sir James George
See Frazer, J(ames) G(eorge)

Frazier, Ian 1951-................ **CLC 46**
See also CA 130

Frederic, Harold 1856-1898...... **NCLC 10**
See also DLB 12, 23

Frederick the Great 1712-1786 ...... **LC 14**

Fredro, Aleksander 1793-1876..... **NCLC 8**

Freeling, Nicolas 1927- .... **CLC 38**
See also CA 49-52; CAAS 12; CANR 1, 17; DLB 87

Freeman, Douglas Southall 1886-1953 .... **TCLC 11**
See also CA 109; DLB 17

Freeman, Judith 1946-............ **CLC 55**

Freeman, Mary Eleanor Wilkins 1852-1930 .... **TCLC 9; SSC 1**
See also CA 106; DLB 12, 78

Freeman, R(ichard) Austin 1862-1943 .... **TCLC 21**
See also CA 113; DLB 70

French, Marilyn 1929-...... **CLC 10, 18, 60**
See also CA 69-72; CANR 3, 31; MTCW

French, Paul
See Asimov, Isaac

Freneau, Philip Morin 1752-1832.. **NCLC 1**
See also DLB 37, 43

Friedan, Betty (Naomi) 1921- ...... **CLC 74**
See also CA 65-68; CANR 18; MTCW

Friedman, B(ernard) H(arper) 1926- .... **CLC 7**
See also CA 1-4R; CANR 3

Friedman, Bruce Jay 1930-.... **CLC 3, 5, 56**
See also CA 9-12R; CANR 25; DLB 2, 28

Friel, Brian 1929-........... **CLC 5, 42, 59**
See also CA 21-24R; CANR 33; DLB 13; MTCW

Friis-Baastad, Babbis Ellinor 1921-1970 .... **CLC 12**
See also CA 17-20R; 134; SATA 7

Frisch, Max (Rudolf) 1911-1991 ..... **CLC 3, 9, 14, 18, 32, 44**
See also CA 85-88; 134; CANR 32; DLB 69; MTCW

Fromentin, Eugene (Samuel Auguste) 1820-1876 .... **NCLC 10**

Frost, Robert (Lee) 1874-1963 ... **CLC 1, 3, 4, 9, 10, 13, 15, 26, 34, 44; PC 1**
See also CA 89-92; CANR 33; CDALB 1917-1929; DLB 54; DLBD 7; MTCW; SATA 14; WLC

Froy, Herald
See Waterhouse, Keith (Spencer)

Fry, Christopher 1907-....... **CLC 2, 10, 14**
See also CA 17-20R; CANR 9, 30; DLB 13; MTCW; SATA 66

Frye, (Herman) Northrop 1912-1991 .... **CLC 24, 70**
See also CA 5-8R; 133; CANR 8, 37; DLB 67, 68; MTCW

Fuchs, Daniel 1909- .... **CLC 8, 22**
See also CA 81-84; CAAS 5; DLB 9, 26, 28

Fuchs, Daniel 1934- .... **CLC 34**
See also CA 37-40R; CANR 14

Fuentes, Carlos 1928- ...... **CLC 3, 8, 10, 13, 22, 41, 60**
See also AAYA 4; AITN 2; CA 69-72; CANR 10, 32; DLB 113; HW; MTCW; WLC

Fuentes, Gregorio Lopez y
See Lopez y Fuentes, Gregorio

Fugard, (Harold) Athol 1932- .... **CLC 5, 9, 14, 25, 40; DC 3**
See also CA 85-88; CANR 32; MTCW

Fugard, Sheila 1932- .... **CLC 48**
See also CA 125

Fuller, Charles (H. Jr.) 1939- .... **CLC 25; DC 1**
See also BLC 2; BW; CA 108; 112; DLB 38; MTCW

Fuller, John (Leopold) 1937-....... **CLC 62**
See also CA 21-24R; CANR 9; DLB 40

Fuller, Margaret .... **NCLC 5**
See also Ossoli, Sarah Margaret (Fuller marchesa d')

Fuller, Roy (Broadbent) 1912-1991 .... **CLC 4, 28**
See also CA 5-8R; 135; CAAS 10; DLB 15, 20

Fulton, Alice 1952-............... **CLC 52**
See also CA 116

Furphy, Joseph 1843-1912........ **TCLC 25**

Fussell, Paul 1924-............... **CLC 74**
See also BEST 90:1; CA 17-20R; CANR 8, 21, 35; MTCW

Futabatei, Shimei 1864-1909 ...... **TCLC 44**

Futrelle, Jacques 1875-1912 ...... **TCLC 19**
See also CA 113

G. B. S.
See Shaw, George Bernard

Gaboriau, Emile 1835-1873 ...... **NCLC 14**

Gadda, Carlo Emilio 1893-1973 .... **CLC 11**
See also CA 89-92

Gaddis, William 1922- .... **CLC 1, 3, 6, 8, 10, 19, 43**
See also CA 17-20R; CANR 21; DLB 2; MTCW

Gaines, Ernest J(ames) 1933- .... **CLC 3, 11, 18**
See also AITN 1; BLC 2; BW; CA 9-12R; CANR 6, 24; CDALB 1968-1988; DLB 2, 33; DLBY 80; MTCW

Gaitskill, Mary 1954-............ **CLC 69**
See also CA 128

Galdos, Benito Perez
See Perez Galdos, Benito

Gale, Zona 1874-1938 .... **TCLC 7**
See also CA 105; DLB 9, 78

Galeano, Eduardo (Hughes) 1940-... **CLC 72**
See also CA 29-32R; CANR 13, 32; HW

Galiano, Juan Valera y Alcala
See Valera y Alcala-Galiano, Juan

Gallagher, Tess 1943-.......... **CLC 18, 63**
See also CA 106; DLB 120

Gallant, Mavis 1922- .... **CLC 7, 18, 38; SSC 5**
See also CA 69-72; CANR 29; DLB 53; MTCW

Gallant, Roy A(rthur) 1924- .... **CLC 17**
See also CA 5-8R; CANR 4, 29; MAICYA; SATA 4, 68

Gallico, Paul (William) 1897-1976 ... **CLC 2**
See also AITN 1; CA 5-8R; 69-72; CANR 23; DLB 9; MAICYA; SATA 13

Gallup, Ralph
See Whitemore, Hugh (John)

Galsworthy, John 1867-1933.... **TCLC 1, 45**
See also CA 104; CDBLB 1890-1914; DLB 10, 34, 98; WLC 2

Galt, John 1779-1839............ **NCLC 1**
See also DLB 99, 116

Galvin, James 1951-.............. **CLC 38**
See also CA 108; CANR 26

Gamboa, Federico 1864-1939...... **TCLC 36**

Gann, Ernest Kellogg 1910-1991.... **CLC 23**
See also AITN 1; CA 1-4R; 136; CANR 1

Garcia Lorca, Federico 1898-1936 ..... **TCLC 1, 7; DC 2; PC 3**
See also CA 104; 131; DLB 108; HW; MTCW; WLC

Garcia Marquez, Gabriel (Jose) 1928- ... **CLC 2, 3, 8, 10, 15, 27, 47, 55; SSC 8**
See also Marquez, Gabriel (Jose) Garcia
See also AAYA 3; BEST 89:1, 90:4; CA 33-36R; CANR 10, 28; DLB 113; HW; MTCW; WLC

Gard, Janice
See Latham, Jean Lee

Gard, Roger Martin du
See Martin du Gard, Roger

Gardam, Jane 1928-.............. **CLC 43**
See also CA 49-52; CANR 2, 18, 33; CLR 12; DLB 14; MAICYA; MTCW; SAAS 9; SATA 28, 39

Gardner, Herb.................... **CLC 44**

Gardner, John (Champlin) Jr. 1933-1982 .... **CLC 2, 3, 5, 7, 8, 10, 18, 28, 34; SSC 7**
See also AITN 1; CA 65-68; 107; CANR 33; DLB 2; DLBY 82; MTCW; SATA 31, 40

Gardner, John (Edmund) 1926-..... **CLC 30**
See also CA 103; CANR 15; MTCW

Gardner, Noel
See Kuttner, Henry

Gardons, S. S.
See Snodgrass, William D(e Witt)

Garfield, Leon 1921-............. **CLC 12**
See also AAYA 8; CA 17-20R; CANR 38; CLR 21; MAICYA; SATA 1, 32

Garland, (Hannibal) Hamlin 1860-1940 .... **TCLC 3**
See also CA 104; DLB 12, 71, 78

Garneau, (Hector de) Saint-Denys 1912-1943 . . . . **TCLC 13**
See also CA 111; DLB 88

Garner, Alan 1934- . . . . **CLC 17**
See also CA 73-76; CANR 15; CLR 20; MAICYA; MTCW; SATA 18, 69

Garner, Hugh 1913-1979 . . . . **CLC 13**
See also CA 69-72; CANR 31; DLB 68

Garnett, David 1892-1981 . . . . **CLC 3**
See also CA 5-8R; 103; CANR 17; DLB 34

Garos, Stephanie
See Katz, Steve

Garrett, George (Palmer) 1929- . . . . **CLC 3, 11, 51**
See also CA 1-4R; CAAS 5; CANR 1; DLB 2, 5; DLBY 83

Garrick, David 1717-1779 . . . . **LC 15**
See also DLB 84

Garrigue, Jean 1914-1972 . . . . **CLC 2, 8**
See also CA 5-8R; 37-40R; CANR 20

Garrison, Frederick
See Sinclair, Upton (Beall)

Garth, Will
See Hamilton, Edmond; Kuttner, Henry

Garvey, Marcus (Moziah Jr.) 1887-1940 . . . . **TCLC 41**
See also BLC 2; BW; CA 120; 124

Gary, Romain . . . . **CLC 25**
See also Kacew, Romain
See also DLB 83

Gascar, Pierre . . . . **CLC 11**
See also Fournier, Pierre

Gascoyne, David (Emery) 1916- . . . . **CLC 45**
See also CA 65-68; CANR 10, 28; DLB 20; MTCW

Gaskell, Elizabeth Cleghorn 1810-1865 . . . . **NCLC 5**
See also CDBLB 1832-1890; DLB 21

Gass, William H(oward) 1924- . . . . **CLC 1, 2, 8, 11, 15, 39**
See also CA 17-20R; CANR 30; DLB 2; MTCW

Gasset, Jose Ortega y
See Ortega y Gasset, Jose

Gautier, Theophile 1811-1872 . . . . . **NCLC 1**
See also DLB 119

Gawsworth, John
See Bates, H(erbert) E(rnest)

Gaye, Marvin (Penze) 1939-1984 . . . **CLC 26**
See also CA 112

Gebler, Carlo (Ernest) 1954- . . . . **CLC 39**
See also CA 119; 133

Gee, Maggie (Mary) 1948- . . . . **CLC 57**
See also CA 130

Gee, Maurice (Gough) 1931- . . . . **CLC 29**
See also CA 97-100; SATA 46

Gelbart, Larry (Simon) 1923- . . . **CLC 21, 61**
See also CA 73-76

Gelber, Jack 1932- . . . . **CLC 1, 6, 14**
See also CA 1-4R; CANR 2; DLB 7

Gellhorn, Martha Ellis 1908- . . . **CLC 14, 60**
See also CA 77-80; DLBY 82

Genet, Jean 1910-1986 . . . **CLC 1, 2, 5, 10, 14, 44, 46**
See also CA 13-16R; CANR 18; DLB 72; DLBY 86; MTCW

Gent, Peter 1942- . . . . **CLC 29**
See also AITN 1; CA 89-92; DLBY 82

George, Jean Craighead 1919- . . . . . . **CLC 35**
See also AAYA 8; CA 5-8R; CANR 25; CLR 1; DLB 52; MAICYA; SATA 2, 68

George, Stefan (Anton) 1868-1933 . . . . **TCLC 2, 14**
See also CA 104

Georges, Georges Martin
See Simenon, Georges (Jacques Christian)

Gerhardi, William Alexander
See Gerhardie, William Alexander

Gerhardie, William Alexander 1895-1977 . . . . **CLC 5**
See also CA 25-28R; 73-76; CANR 18; DLB 36

Gerstler, Amy 1956- . . . . **CLC 70**

Gertler, T. . . . . **CLC 34**
See also CA 116; 121

Ghelderode, Michel de 1898-1962 . . . . **CLC 6, 11**
See also CA 85-88

Ghiselin, Brewster 1903- . . . . **CLC 23**
See also CA 13-16R; CAAS 10; CANR 13

Ghose, Zulfikar 1935- . . . . **CLC 42**
See also CA 65-68

Ghosh, Amitav 1956- . . . . **CLC 44**

Giacosa, Giuseppe 1847-1906 . . . . . . **TCLC 7**
See also CA 104

Gibb, Lee
See Waterhouse, Keith (Spencer)

Gibbon, Lewis Grassic . . . . **TCLC 4**
See also Mitchell, James Leslie

Gibbons, Kaye 1960- . . . . **CLC 50**

Gibran, Kahlil 1883-1931 . . . . **TCLC 1, 9**
See also CA 104

Gibson, William (Ford) 1948- . . . **CLC 39, 63**
See also CA 126; 133

Gibson, William 1914- . . . . **CLC 23**
See also CA 9-12R; CANR 9; DLB 7; SATA 66

Gide, Andre (Paul Guillaume) 1869-1951 . . . . **TCLC 5, 12, 36**
See also CA 104; 124; DLB 65; MTCW; WLC

Gifford, Barry (Colby) 1946- . . . . **CLC 34**
See also CA 65-68; CANR 9, 30

Gilbert, W(illiam) S(chwenck) 1836-1911 . . . . **TCLC 3**
See also CA 104; SATA 36

Gilbreth, Frank B. Jr. 1911- . . . . **CLC 17**
See also CA 9-12R; SATA 2

Gilchrist, Ellen 1935- . . . . **CLC 34, 48**
See also CA 113; 116; MTCW

Giles, Molly 1942- . . . . **CLC 39**
See also CA 126

Gill, Patrick
See Creasey, John

Gilliam, Terry (Vance) 1940- . . . . **CLC 21**
See also Monty Python
See also CA 108; 113; CANR 35

Gillian, Jerry
See Gilliam, Terry (Vance)

Gilliatt, Penelope (Ann Douglass) 1932- . . . . **CLC 2, 10, 13, 53**
See also AITN 2; CA 13-16R; DLB 14

Gilman, Charlotte (Anna) Perkins (Stetson) 1860-1935 . . . . **TCLC 9, 37**
See also CA 106

Gilmour, David 1944- . . . . **CLC 35**
See also Pink Floyd
See also CA 138

Gilpin, William 1724-1804 . . . . **NCLC 30**

Gilray, J. D.
See Mencken, H(enry) L(ouis)

Gilroy, Frank D(aniel) 1925- . . . . **CLC 2**
See also CA 81-84; CANR 32; DLB 7

Ginsberg, Allen 1926- . . . . . **CLC 1, 2, 3, 4, 6, 13, 36, 69; PC 4**
See also AITN 1; CA 1-4R; CANR 2; CDALB 1941-1968; DLB 5, 16; MTCW; WLC 3

Ginzburg, Natalia 1916-1991 . . . . **CLC 5, 11, 54, 70**
See also CA 85-88; 135; CANR 33; MTCW

Giono, Jean 1895-1970 . . . . **CLC 4, 11**
See also CA 45-48; 29-32R; CANR 2, 35; DLB 72; MTCW

Giovanni, Nikki 1943- . . . . . **CLC 2, 4, 19, 64**
See also AITN 1; BLC 2; BW; CA 29-32R; CAAS 6; CANR 18; CLR 6; DLB 5, 41; MAICYA; MTCW; SATA 24

Giovene, Andrea 1904- . . . . **CLC 7**
See also CA 85-88

Gippius, Zinaida (Nikolayevna) 1869-1945
See Hippius, Zinaida
See also CA 106

Giraudoux, (Hippolyte) Jean 1882-1944 . . . . **TCLC 2, 7**
See also CA 104; DLB 65

Gironella, Jose Maria 1917- . . . . **CLC 11**
See also CA 101

Gissing, George (Robert) 1857-1903 . . . . **TCLC 3, 24, 47**
See also CA 105; DLB 18

Giurlani, Aldo
See Palazzeschi, Aldo

Gladkov, Fyodor (Vasilyevich) 1883-1958 . . . . **TCLC 27**

Glanville, Brian (Lester) 1931- . . . . . . **CLC 6**
See also CA 5-8R; CAAS 9; CANR 3; DLB 15; SATA 42

Glasgow, Ellen (Anderson Gholson) 1873(?)-1945 . . . . **TCLC 2, 7**
See also CA 104; DLB 9, 12

Glassco, John 1909-1981 . . . . **CLC 9**
See also CA 13-16R; 102; CANR 15; DLB 68

Glasscock, Amnesia
See Steinbeck, John (Ernst)

Glasser, Ronald J. 1940(?)- . . . . **CLC 37**

Author Index

Glassman, Joyce
See Johnson, Joyce

Glendinning, Victoria 1937- . . . . **CLC 50**
See also CA 120; 127

Glissant, Edouard 1928- . . . . **CLC 10, 68**

Gloag, Julian 1930- . . . . **CLC 40**
See also AITN 1; CA 65-68; CANR 10

Gluck, Louise 1943- . . . . **CLC 7, 22, 44**
See also Glueck, Louise
See also CA 33-36R; DLB 5

Glueck, Louise . . . . **CLC 7, 22**
See also Gluck, Louise
See also DLB 5

Gobineau, Joseph Arthur (Comte) de
1816-1882 . . . . **NCLC 17**

Godard, Jean-Luc 1930- . . . . **CLC 20**
See also CA 93-96

Godden, (Margaret) Rumer 1907- . . . **CLC 53**
See also AAYA 6; CA 5-8R; CANR 4, 27, 36; CLR 20; MAICYA; SAAS 12; SATA 3, 36

Godoy Alcayaga, Lucila 1889-1957
See Mistral, Gabriela
See also CA 104; 131; HW; MTCW

Godwin, Gail (Kathleen)
1937- . . . . **CLC 5, 8, 22, 31, 69**
See also CA 29-32R; CANR 15; DLB 6; MTCW

Godwin, William 1756-1836 . . . . . . **NCLC 14**
See also CDBLB 1789-1832; DLB 39, 104

Goethe, Johann Wolfgang von
1749-1832 . . . . **NCLC 4, 22, 34; PC 5**
See also DLB 94; WLC 3

Gogarty, Oliver St. John
1878-1957 . . . . **TCLC 15**
See also CA 109; DLB 15, 19

Gogol, Nikolai (Vasilyevich)
1809-1852 . . . . . **NCLC 5, 15, 31; DC 1; SSC 4**
See also WLC

Gold, Herbert 1924- . . . . **CLC 4, 7, 14, 42**
See also CA 9-12R; CANR 17; DLB 2; DLBY 81

Goldbarth, Albert 1948- . . . . **CLC 5, 38**
See also CA 53-56; CANR 6; DLB 120

Goldberg, Anatol 1910-1982 . . . . **CLC 34**
See also CA 131; 117

Goldemberg, Isaac 1945- . . . . **CLC 52**
See also CA 69-72; CAAS 12; CANR 11, 32; HW

Golden Silver
See Storm, Hyemeyohsts

Golding, William (Gerald)
1911- . . . . . **CLC 1, 2, 3, 8, 10, 17, 27, 58**
See also AAYA 5; CA 5-8R; CANR 13, 33; CDBLB 1945-1960; DLB 15, 100; MTCW; WLC

Goldman, Emma 1869-1940 . . . . **TCLC 13**
See also CA 110

Goldman, William (W.) 1931- . . . . **CLC 1, 48**
See also CA 9-12R; CANR 29; DLB 44

Goldmann, Lucien 1913-1970 . . . . . . **CLC 24**
See also CA 25-28; CAP 2

Goldoni, Carlo 1707-1793 . . . . **LC 4**

Goldsberry, Steven 1949- . . . . **CLC 34**
See also CA 131

Goldsmith, Oliver 1728(?)-1774 . . . . **LC 2**

Goldsmith, Peter
See Priestley, J(ohn) B(oynton)

Gombrowicz, Witold
1904-1969 . . . . **CLC 4, 7, 11, 49**
See also CA 19-20; 25-28R; CAP 2

Gomez de la Serna, Ramon
1888-1963 . . . . **CLC 9**
See also CA 116; HW

Goncharov, Ivan Alexandrovich
1812-1891 . . . . **NCLC 1**

Goncourt, Edmond (Louis Antoine Huot) de
1822-1896 . . . . **NCLC 7**

Goncourt, Jules (Alfred Huot) de
1830-1870 . . . . **NCLC 7**

Gontier, Fernande 19(?)- . . . . **CLC 50**

Goodman, Paul 1911-1972 . . . . **CLC 1, 2, 4, 7**
See also CA 19-20; 37-40R; CANR 34; CAP 2; MTCW

Gordimer, Nadine
1923- . . . . **CLC 3, 5, 7, 10, 18, 33, 51, 70**
See also CA 5-8R; CANR 3, 28; MTCW

Gordon, Adam Lindsay
1833-1870 . . . . **NCLC 21**

Gordon, Caroline
1895-1981 . . . . **CLC 6, 13, 29**
See also CA 11-12; 103; CANR 36; CAP 1; DLB 4, 9, 102; DLBY 81; MTCW

Gordon, Charles William 1860-1937
See Connor, Ralph
See also CA 109

Gordon, Mary (Catherine)
1949- . . . . **CLC 13, 22**
See also CA 102; DLB 6; DLBY 81; MTCW

Gordon, Sol 1923- . . . . **CLC 26**
See also CA 53-56; CANR 4; SATA 11

Gordone, Charles 1925- . . . . **CLC 1, 4**
See also BW; CA 93-96; DLB 7; MTCW

Gorenko, Anna Andreevna
See Akhmatova, Anna

Gorky, Maxim . . . . **TCLC 8**
See also Peshkov, Alexei Maximovich
See also WLC

Goryan, Sirak
See Saroyan, William

Gosse, Edmund (William)
1849-1928 . . . . **TCLC 28**
See also CA 117; DLB 57

Gotlieb, Phyllis Fay (Bloom)
1926- . . . . **CLC 18**
See also CA 13-16R; CANR 7; DLB 88

Gottesman, S. D.
See Kornbluth, C(yril) M.; Pohl, Frederik

Gottfried von Strassburg
fl. c. 1210- . . . . **CMLC 10**

Gottschalk, Laura Riding
See Jackson, Laura (Riding)

Gould, Lois . . . . **CLC 4, 10**
See also CA 77-80; CANR 29; MTCW

Gourmont, Remy de 1858-1915 . . . . **TCLC 17**
See also CA 109

Govier, Katherine 1948- . . . . **CLC 51**
See also CA 101; CANR 18

Goyen, (Charles) William
1915-1983 . . . . **CLC 5, 8, 14, 40**
See also AITN 2; CA 5-8R; 110; CANR 6; DLB 2; DLBY 83

Goytisolo, Juan 1931- . . . . **CLC 5, 10, 23**
See also CA 85-88; CANR 32; HW; MTCW

Gozzi, (Conte) Carlo 1720-1806 . . **NCLC 23**

Grabbe, Christian Dietrich
1801-1836 . . . . **NCLC 2**

Grace, Patricia 1937- . . . . **CLC 56**

Gracian y Morales, Baltasar
1601-1658 . . . . **LC 15**

Gracq, Julien . . . . **CLC 11, 48**
See also Poirier, Louis
See also DLB 83

Grade, Chaim 1910-1982 . . . . **CLC 10**
See also CA 93-96; 107

Graduate of Oxford, A
See Ruskin, John

Graham, John
See Phillips, David Graham

Graham, Jorie 1951- . . . . **CLC 48**
See also CA 111; DLB 120

Graham, R(obert) B(ontine) Cunninghame
See Cunninghame Graham, R(obert) B(ontine)
See also DLB 98

Graham, Robert
See Haldeman, Joe (William)

Graham, Tom
See Lewis, (Harry) Sinclair

Graham, W(illiam) S(ydney)
1918-1986 . . . . **CLC 29**
See also CA 73-76; 118; DLB 20

Graham, Winston (Mawdsley)
1910- . . . . **CLC 23**
See also CA 49-52; CANR 2, 22; DLB 77

Granville-Barker, Harley
1877-1946 . . . . **TCLC 2**
See also Barker, Harley Granville
See also CA 104

Grass, Guenter (Wilhelm)
1927- . . **CLC 1, 2, 4, 6, 11, 15, 22, 32, 49**
See also CA 13-16R; CANR 20; DLB 75; MTCW; WLC

Gratton, Thomas
See Hulme, T(homas) E(rnest)

Grau, Shirley Ann 1929- . . . . **CLC 4, 9**
See also CA 89-92; CANR 22; DLB 2; MTCW

Gravel, Fern
See Hall, James Norman

Graver, Elizabeth 1964- . . . . **CLC 70**
See also CA 135

Graves, Richard Perceval 1945- . . . . **CLC 44**
See also CA 65-68; CANR 9, 26

Graves, Robert (von Ranke)
1895-1985 . . . **CLC 1, 2, 6, 11, 39, 44, 45**
See also CA 5-8R; 117; CANR 5, 36; CDBLB 1914-1945; DLB 20, 100; DLBY 85; MTCW; SATA 45

Gray, Alasdair (James) 1934- . . . . . . **CLC 41**
See also CA 126; MTCW

Gray, Amlin 1946- . . . . **CLC 29**
See also CA 138

Gray, Francine du Plessix 1930- . . . . **CLC 22**
See also BEST 90:3; CA 61-64; CAAS 2; CANR 11, 33; MTCW

Gray, John (Henry) 1866-1934 . . . . **TCLC 19**
See also CA 119

Gray, Simon (James Holliday) 1936- . . . . **CLC 9, 14, 36**
See also AITN 1; CA 21-24R; CAAS 3; CANR 32; DLB 13; MTCW

Gray, Spalding 1941- . . . . **CLC 49**
See also CA 128

Gray, Thomas 1716-1771 . . . . **LC 4; PC 2**
See also CDBLB 1660-1789; DLB 109; WLC

Grayson, David
See Baker, Ray Stannard

Grayson, Richard (A.) 1951- . . . . **CLC 38**
See also CA 85-88; CANR 14, 31

Greeley, Andrew M(oran) 1928- . . . . **CLC 28**
See also CA 5-8R; CAAS 7; CANR 7; MTCW

Green, Brian
See Card, Orson Scott

Green, Hannah . . . . **CLC 3**
See also CA 73-76

Green, Hannah
See Greenberg, Joanne (Goldenberg)

Green, Henry . . . . **CLC 2, 13**
See also Yorke, Henry Vincent
See also DLB 15

Green, Julian (Hartridge) 1900- . . . . **CLC 3, 11**
See also CA 21-24R; CANR 33; DLB 4, 72; MTCW

Green, Julien
See Green, Julian (Hartridge)

Green, Paul (Eliot) 1894-1981 . . . . . . **CLC 25**
See also AITN 1; CA 5-8R; 103; CANR 3; DLB 7, 9; DLBY 81

Greenberg, Ivan 1908-1973
See Rahv, Philip
See also CA 85-88

Greenberg, Joanne (Goldenberg) 1932- . . . . **CLC 7, 30**
See also CA 5-8R; CANR 14, 32; SATA 25

Greenberg, Richard 1959(?)- . . . . **CLC 57**
See also CA 138

Greene, Bette 1934- . . . . **CLC 30**
See also AAYA 7; CA 53-56; CANR 4; CLR 2; MAICYA; SATA 8

Greene, Gael . . . . **CLC 8**
See also CA 13-16R; CANR 10

Greene, Graham (Henry) 1904-1991 . . . **CLC 1, 3, 6, 9, 14, 18, 27, 37, 70, 72**
See also AITN 2; CA 13-16R; 133; CANR 35; CDBLB 1945-1960; DLB 13, 15, 77, 100; DLBY 91; MTCW; SATA 20; WLC

Greer, Richard
See Silverberg, Robert

Greer, Richard
See Silverberg, Robert

Gregor, Arthur 1923- . . . . **CLC 9**
See also CA 25-28R; CAAS 10; CANR 11; SATA 36

Gregor, Lee
See Pohl, Frederik

Gregory, Isabella Augusta (Persse) 1852-1932 . . . . **TCLC 1**
See also CA 104; DLB 10

Gregory, J. Dennis
See Williams, John A(lfred)

Grendon, Stephen
See Derleth, August (William)

Grenville, Kate 1950- . . . . **CLC 61**
See also CA 118

Grenville, Pelham
See Wodehouse, P(elham) G(renville)

Greve, Felix Paul (Berthold Friedrich) 1879-1948
See Grove, Frederick Philip
See also CA 104

Grey, Zane 1872-1939 . . . . **TCLC 6**
See also CA 104; 132; DLB 9; MTCW

Grieg, (Johan) Nordahl (Brun) 1902-1943 . . . . **TCLC 10**
See also CA 107

Grieve, C(hristopher) M(urray) 1892-1978 . . . . **CLC 11, 19**
See also MacDiarmid, Hugh
See also CA 5-8R; 85-88; CANR 33; MTCW

Griffin, Gerald 1803-1840 . . . . **NCLC 7**

Griffin, John Howard 1920-1980 . . . . **CLC 68**
See also AITN 1; CA 1-4R; 101; CANR 2

Griffin, Peter . . . . **CLC 39**

Griffiths, Trevor 1935- . . . . **CLC 13, 52**
See also CA 97-100; DLB 13

Grigson, Geoffrey (Edward Harvey) 1905-1985 . . . . **CLC 7, 39**
See also CA 25-28R; 118; CANR 20, 33; DLB 27; MTCW

Grillparzer, Franz 1791-1872 . . . . . . **NCLC 1**

Grimble, Reverend Charles James
See Eliot, T(homas) S(tearns)

Grimke, Charlotte L(ottie) Forten 1837(?)-1914
See Forten, Charlotte L.
See also BW; CA 117; 124

Grimm, Jacob Ludwig Karl 1785-1863 . . . . **NCLC 3**
See also DLB 90; MAICYA; SATA 22

Grimm, Wilhelm Karl 1786-1859 . . **NCLC 3**
See also DLB 90; MAICYA; SATA 22

Grimmelshausen, Johann Jakob Christoffel von 1621-1676 . . . . **LC 6**

Grindel, Eugene 1895-1952
See Eluard, Paul
See also CA 104

Grossman, David . . . . **CLC 67**
See also CA 138

Grossman, Vasily (Semenovich) 1905-1964 . . . . **CLC 41**
See also CA 124; 130; MTCW

Grove, Frederick Philip . . . . **TCLC 4**
See also Greve, Felix Paul (Berthold Friedrich)
See also DLB 92

Grubb
See Crumb, R(obert)

Grumbach, Doris (Isaac) 1918- . . . . **CLC 13, 22, 64**
See also CA 5-8R; CAAS 2; CANR 9

Grundtvig, Nicolai Frederik Severin 1783-1872 . . . . **NCLC 1**

Grunge
See Crumb, R(obert)

Grunwald, Lisa 1959- . . . . **CLC 44**
See also CA 120

Guare, John 1938- . . . . **CLC 8, 14, 29, 67**
See also CA 73-76; CANR 21; DLB 7; MTCW

Gudjonsson, Halldor Kiljan 1902-
See Laxness, Halldor
See also CA 103

Guenter, Erich
See Eich, Guenter

Guest, Barbara 1920- . . . . **CLC 34**
See also CA 25-28R; CANR 11; DLB 5

Guest, Judith (Ann) 1936- . . . . **CLC 8, 30**
See also AAYA 7; CA 77-80; CANR 15; MTCW

Guild, Nicholas M. 1944- . . . . **CLC 33**
See also CA 93-96

Guillemin, Jacques
See Sartre, Jean-Paul

Guillen, Jorge 1893-1984 . . . . **CLC 11**
See also CA 89-92; 112; DLB 108; HW

Guillen (y Batista), Nicolas (Cristobal) 1902-1989 . . . . **CLC 48**
See also BLC 2; BW; CA 116; 125; 129; HW

Guillevic, (Eugene) 1907- . . . . **CLC 33**
See also CA 93-96

Guillois
See Desnos, Robert

Guiney, Louise Imogen 1861-1920 . . . . **TCLC 41**
See also DLB 54

Guiraldes, Ricardo (Guillermo) 1886-1927 . . . . **TCLC 39**
See also CA 131; HW; MTCW

Gunn, Bill . . . . **CLC 5**
See also Gunn, William Harrison
See also DLB 38

Gunn, Thom(son William) 1929- . . . . **CLC 3, 6, 18, 32**
See also CA 17-20R; CANR 9, 33; CDBLB 1960 to Present; DLB 27; MTCW

Gunn, William Harrison 1934(?)-1989
See Gunn, Bill
See also AITN 1; BW; CA 13-16R; 128; CANR 12, 25

Gunnars, Kristjana 1948- . . . . **CLC 69**
See also CA 113; DLB 60

Gurganus, Allan 1947- . . . . **CLC 70**
See also BEST 90:1; CA 135

Gurney, A(lbert) R(amsdell) Jr. 1930- . . . . **CLC 32, 50, 54**
See also CA 77-80; CANR 32

Gurney, Ivor (Bertie) 1890-1937 . . . **TCLC 33**

Gurney, Peter
See Gurney, A(lbert) R(amsdell) Jr.

Gustafson, Ralph (Barker) 1909- . . . . **CLC 36**
See also CA 21-24R; CANR 8; DLB 88

Gut, Gom
See Simenon, Georges (Jacques Christian)

Guthrie, A(lfred) B(ertram) Jr. 1901-1991 . . . . **CLC 23**
See also CA 57-60; 134; CANR 24; DLB 6; SATA 62; SATO 67

Guthrie, Isobel
See Grieve, C(hristopher) M(urray)

Guthrie, Woodrow Wilson 1912-1967
See Guthrie, Woody
See also CA 113; 93-96

Guthrie, Woody . . . . **CLC 35**
See also Guthrie, Woodrow Wilson

Guy, Rosa (Cuthbert) 1928- . . . . **CLC 26**
See also AAYA 4; BW; CA 17-20R; CANR 14, 34; CLR 13; DLB 33; MAICYA; SATA 14, 62

Gwendolyn
See Bennett, (Enoch) Arnold

H. D. . . . . **CLC 3, 8, 14, 31, 34; PC 5**
See also Doolittle, Hilda

Haavikko, Paavo Juhani 1931- . . . . **CLC 18, 34**
See also CA 106

Habbema, Koos
See Heijermans, Herman

Hacker, Marilyn 1942- . . . . **CLC 5, 9, 23, 72**
See also CA 77-80; DLB 120

Haggard, H(enry) Rider 1856-1925 . . . . **TCLC 11**
See also CA 108; DLB 70; SATA 16

Haig, Fenil
See Ford, Ford Madox

Haig-Brown, Roderick (Langmere) 1908-1976 . . . . **CLC 21**
See also CA 5-8R; 69-72; CANR 4, 38; DLB 88; MAICYA; SATA 12

Hailey, Arthur 1920- . . . . **CLC 5**
See also AITN 2; BEST 90:3; CA 1-4R; CANR 2, 36; DLB 88; DLBY 82; MTCW

Hailey, Elizabeth Forsythe 1938- . . . **CLC 40**
See also CA 93-96; CAAS 1; CANR 15

Haines, John (Meade) 1924- . . . . **CLC 58**
See also CA 17-20R; CANR 13, 34; DLB 5

Haldeman, Joe (William) 1943- . . . . . **CLC 61**
See also CA 53-56; CANR 6; DLB 8

Haley, Alex(ander Murray Palmer) 1921-1992 . . . . **CLC 8, 12**
See also BLC 2; BW; CA 77-80; 136; DLB 38; MTCW

Haliburton, Thomas Chandler 1796-1865 . . . . **NCLC 15**
See also DLB 11, 99

Hall, Donald (Andrew Jr.) 1928- . . . . **CLC 1, 13, 37, 59**
See also CA 5-8R; CAAS 7; CANR 2; DLB 5; SATA 23

Hall, Frederic Sauser
See Sauser-Hall, Frederic

Hall, James
See Kuttner, Henry

Hall, James Norman 1887-1951 . . . **TCLC 23**
See also CA 123; SATA 21

Hall, (Marguerite) Radclyffe 1886(?)-1943 . . . . **TCLC 12**
See also CA 110

Hall, Rodney 1935- . . . . **CLC 51**
See also CA 109

Halliday, Michael
See Creasey, John

Halpern, Daniel 1945- . . . . **CLC 14**
See also CA 33-36R

Hamburger, Michael (Peter Leopold) 1924- . . . . **CLC 5, 14**
See also CA 5-8R; CAAS 4; CANR 2; DLB 27

Hamill, Pete 1935- . . . . **CLC 10**
See also CA 25-28R; CANR 18

Hamilton, Clive
See Lewis, C(live) S(taples)

Hamilton, Edmond 1904-1977 . . . . **CLC 1**
See also CA 1-4R; CANR 3; DLB 8

Hamilton, Eugene (Jacob) Lee
See Lee-Hamilton, Eugene (Jacob)

Hamilton, Franklin
See Silverberg, Robert

Hamilton, Gail
See Corcoran, Barbara

Hamilton, Mollie
See Kaye, M(ary) M(argaret)

Hamilton, (Anthony Walter) Patrick 1904-1962 . . . . **CLC 51**
See also CA 113; DLB 10

Hamilton, Virginia 1936- . . . . **CLC 26**
See also AAYA 2; BW; CA 25-28R; CANR 20, 37; CLR 1, 11; DLB 33, 52; MAICYA; MTCW; SATA 4, 56

Hammett, (Samuel) Dashiell 1894-1961 . . . . **CLC 3, 5, 10, 19, 47**
See also AITN 1; CA 81-84; CDALB 1929-1941; DLBD 6; MTCW

Hammon, Jupiter 1711(?)-1800(?) . . **NCLC 5**
See also BLC 2; DLB 31, 50

Hammond, Keith
See Kuttner, Henry

Hamner, Earl (Henry) Jr. 1923- . . . . **CLC 12**
See also AITN 2; CA 73-76; DLB 6

Hampton, Christopher (James) 1946- . . . . **CLC 4**
See also CA 25-28R; DLB 13; MTCW

Hamsun, Knut . . . . **TCLC 2, 14**
See also Pedersen, Knut

Handke, Peter 1942- . . **CLC 5, 8, 10, 15, 38**
See also CA 77-80; CANR 33; DLB 85; MTCW

Hanley, James 1901-1985 . . . **CLC 3, 5, 8, 13**
See also CA 73-76; 117; CANR 36; MTCW

Hannah, Barry 1942- . . . . **CLC 23, 38**
See also CA 108; 110; DLB 6; MTCW

Hannon, Ezra
See Hunter, Evan

Hansberry, Lorraine (Vivian) 1930-1965 . . . . **CLC 17, 62; DC 2**
See also BLC 2; BW; CA 109; 25-28R; CABS 3; CDALB 1941-1968; DLB 7, 38; MTCW

Hansen, Joseph 1923- . . . . **CLC 38**
See also CA 29-32R; CANR 16

Hansen, Martin A. 1909-1955 . . . . . **TCLC 32**

Hanson, Kenneth O(stlin) 1922- . . . . **CLC 13**
See also CA 53-56; CANR 7

Hardwick, Elizabeth 1916- . . . . **CLC 13**
See also CA 5-8R; CANR 3, 32; DLB 6; MTCW

Hardy, Thomas 1840-1928 . . . . . **TCLC 4, 10, 18, 32, 48; SSC 2**
See also CA 104; 123; CDBLB 1890-1914; DLB 18, 19; MTCW; WLC

Hare, David 1947- . . . . **CLC 29, 58**
See also CA 97-100; CANR 39; DLB 13; MTCW

Harford, Henry
See Hudson, W(illiam) H(enry)

Hargrave, Leonie
See Disch, Thomas M(ichael)

Harlan, Louis R(udolph) 1922- . . . . . **CLC 34**
See also CA 21-24R; CANR 25

Harling, Robert 1951(?)- . . . . **CLC 53**

Harmon, William (Ruth) 1938- . . . . . **CLC 38**
See also CA 33-36R; CANR 14, 32, 35; SATA 65

Harper, F. E. W.
See Harper, Frances Ellen Watkins

Harper, Frances E. W.
See Harper, Frances Ellen Watkins

Harper, Frances E. Watkins
See Harper, Frances Ellen Watkins

Harper, Frances Ellen
See Harper, Frances Ellen Watkins

Harper, Frances Ellen Watkins 1825-1911 . . . . **TCLC 14**
See also BLC 2; BW; CA 111; 125; DLB 50

Harper, Michael S(teven) 1938- . . **CLC 7, 22**
See also BW; CA 33-36R; CANR 24; DLB 41

Harper, Mrs. F. E. W.
See Harper, Frances Ellen Watkins

Harris, Christie (Lucy) Irwin 1907- . . . . **CLC 12**
See also CA 5-8R; CANR 6; DLB 88; MAICYA; SAAS 10; SATA 6

Harris, Frank 1856(?)-1931 . . . . **TCLC 24**
See also CA 109

Harris, George Washington 1814-1869 . . . . **NCLC 23**
See also DLB 3, 11

Harris, Joel Chandler 1848-1908 . . . **TCLC 2**
See also CA 104; 137; DLB 11, 23, 42, 78, 91; MAICYA; YABC 1

Harris, John (Wyndham Parkes Lucas) Beynon 1903-1969 . . . . **CLC 19**
See also CA 102; 89-92

Harris, MacDonald
See Heiney, Donald (William)

Harris, Mark 1922- . . . . **CLC 19**
See also CA 5-8R; CAAS 3; CANR 2; DLB 2; DLBY 80

Harris, (Theodore) Wilson 1921-. . . . **CLC 25**
See also BW; CA 65-68; CAAS 16; CANR 11, 27; DLB 117; MTCW

Harrison, Elizabeth Cavanna 1909-
See Cavanna, Betty
See also CA 9-12R; CANR 6, 27

Harrison, Harry (Max) 1925-. . . . . . **CLC 42**
See also CA 1-4R; CANR 5, 21; DLB 8; SATA 4

Harrison, James (Thomas) 1937-
See Harrison, Jim
See also CA 13-16R; CANR 8

Harrison, Jim . . . . **CLC 6, 14, 33, 66**
See also Harrison, James (Thomas)
See also DLBY 82

Harrison, Kathryn 1961- . . . . **CLC 70**

Harrison, Tony 1937-. . . . . **CLC 43**
See also CA 65-68; DLB 40; MTCW

Harriss, Will(ard Irvin) 1922-. . . . . . **CLC 34**
See also CA 111

Harson, Sley
See Ellison, Harlan

Hart, Ellis
See Ellison, Harlan

Hart, Josephine 1942(?)- . . . . **CLC 70**
See also CA 138

Hart, Moss 1904-1961 . . . . **CLC 66**
See also CA 109; 89-92; DLB 7

Harte, (Francis) Bret(t) 1836(?)-1902 . . . . **TCLC 1, 25; SSC 8**
See also CA 104; CDALB 1865-1917; DLB 12, 64, 74, 79; SATA 26; WLC

Hartley, L(eslie) P(oles) 1895-1972 . . . . **CLC 2, 22**
See also CA 45-48; 37-40R; CANR 33; DLB 15; MTCW

Hartman, Geoffrey H. 1929-. . . . . . . **CLC 27**
See also CA 117; 125; DLB 67

Haruf, Kent 19(?)- . . . . **CLC 34**

Harwood, Ronald 1934-. . . . . **CLC 32**
See also CA 1-4R; CANR 4; DLB 13

Hasek, Jaroslav (Matej Frantisek) 1883-1923 . . . . **TCLC 4**
See also CA 104; 129; MTCW

Hass, Robert 1941-. . . . . **CLC 18, 39**
See also CA 111; CANR 30; DLB 105

Hastings, Hudson
See Kuttner, Henry

Hastings, Selina. . . . . **CLC 44**

Hatteras, Amelia
See Mencken, H(enry) L(ouis)

Hatteras, Owen
See Mencken, H(enry) L(ouis)

Hatteras, Owen . . . . **TCLC 18**
See also Nathan, George Jean

Hauptmann, Gerhart (Johann Robert) 1862-1946 . . . . **TCLC 4**
See also CA 104; DLB 66, 118

Havel, Vaclav 1936-. . . . . **CLC 25, 58, 65**
See also CA 104; CANR 36; MTCW

Haviaras, Stratis . . . . **CLC 33**
See also Chaviaras, Strates

Hawes, Stephen 1475(?)-1523(?) . . . . . **LC 17**

Hawkes, John (Clendennin Burne Jr.) 1925- . . . . . . **CLC 1, 2, 3, 4, 7, 9, 14, 15, 27, 49**
See also CA 1-4R; CANR 2; DLB 2, 7; DLBY 80; MTCW

Hawking, S. W.
See Hawking, Stephen W(illiam)

Hawking, Stephen W(illiam) 1942- . . . . **CLC 63**
See also BEST 89:1; CA 126; 129

Hawthorne, Julian 1846-1934 . . . . . **TCLC 25**

Hawthorne, Nathaniel 1804-1864 . . . **NCLC 2, 10, 17, 23; SSC 3**
See also CDALB 1640-1865; DLB 1, 74; WLC; YABC 2

Hayaseca y Eizaguirre, Jorge
See Echegaray (y Eizaguirre), Jose (Maria Waldo)

Hayashi Fumiko 1904-1951 . . . . **TCLC 27**

Haycraft, Anna
See Ellis, Alice Thomas
See also CA 122

Hayden, Robert E(arl) 1913-1980 . . . . **CLC 5, 9, 14, 37**
See also BLC 2; BW; CA 69-72; 97-100; CABS 2; CANR 24; CDALB 1941-1968; DLB 5, 76; MTCW; SATA 19, 26

Hayford, J(oseph) E(phraim) Casely
See Casely-Hayford, J(oseph) E(phraim)

Hayman, Ronald 1932-. . . . . **CLC 44**
See also CA 25-28R; CANR 18

Haywood, Eliza (Fowler) 1693(?)-1756 . . . . **LC 1**

Hazlitt, William 1778-1830 . . . . . . **NCLC 29**
See also DLB 110

Hazzard, Shirley 1931- . . . . **CLC 18**
See also CA 9-12R; CANR 4; DLBY 82; MTCW

Head, Bessie 1937-1986 . . . . **CLC 25, 67**
See also BLC 2; BW; CA 29-32R; 119; CANR 25; DLB 117; MTCW

Headon, (Nicky) Topper 1956(?)- . . . **CLC 30**
See also The Clash

Heaney, Seamus (Justin) 1939- . . . . **CLC 5, 7, 14, 25, 37, 74**
See also CA 85-88; CANR 25; CDBLB 1960 to Present; DLB 40; MTCW

Hearn, (Patricio) Lafcadio (Tessima Carlos) 1850-1904 . . . . **TCLC 9**
See also CA 105; DLB 12, 78

Hearne, Vicki 1946-. . . . . **CLC 56**

Hearon, Shelby 1931-. . . . . **CLC 63**
See also AITN 2; CA 25-28R; CANR 18

Heat-Moon, William Least. . . . . **CLC 29**
See also Trogdon, William (Lewis)
See also AAYA 9

Hebert, Anne 1916- . . . . **CLC 4, 13, 29**
See also CA 85-88; DLB 68; MTCW

Hecht, Anthony (Evan) 1923- . . . . **CLC 8, 13, 19**
See also CA 9-12R; CANR 6; DLB 5

Hecht, Ben 1894-1964 . . . . **CLC 8**
See also CA 85-88; DLB 7, 9, 25, 26, 28, 86

Hedayat, Sadeq 1903-1951. . . . . **TCLC 21**
See also CA 120

Heidegger, Martin 1889-1976 . . . . . . **CLC 24**
See also CA 81-84; 65-68; CANR 34; MTCW

Heidenstam, (Carl Gustaf) Verner von 1859-1940 . . . . **TCLC 5**
See also CA 104

Heifner, Jack 1946-. . . . . **CLC 11**
See also CA 105

Heijermans, Herman 1864-1924 . . . **TCLC 24**
See also CA 123

Heilbrun, Carolyn G(old) 1926-. . . . . **CLC 25**
See also CA 45-48; CANR 1, 28

Heine, Heinrich 1797-1856 . . . . **NCLC 4**
See also DLB 90

Heinemann, Larry (Curtiss) 1944- . . **CLC 50**
See also CA 110; CANR 31; DLBD 9

Heiney, Donald (William) 1921-. . . . . **CLC 9**
See also CA 1-4R; CANR 3

Heinlein, Robert A(nson) 1907-1988 . . . . . . **CLC 1, 3, 8, 14, 26, 55**
See also CA 1-4R; 125; CANR 1, 20; DLB 8; MAICYA; MTCW; SATA 9, 56, 69

Helforth, John
See Doolittle, Hilda

Hellenhofferu, Vojtech Kapristian z
See Hasek, Jaroslav (Matej Frantisek)

Heller, Joseph 1923- . . . . **CLC 1, 3, 5, 8, 11, 36, 63**
See also AITN 1; CA 5-8R; CABS 1; CANR 8; DLB 2, 28; DLBY 80; MTCW; WLC

Hellman, Lillian (Florence) 1906-1984 . . . . . **CLC 2, 4, 8, 14, 18, 34, 44, 52; DC 1**
See also AITN 1, 2; CA 13-16R; 112; CANR 33; DLB 7; DLBY 84; MTCW

Helprin, Mark 1947- . . . . . **CLC 7, 10, 22, 32**
See also CA 81-84; DLBY 85; MTCW

Helyar, Jane Penelope Josephine 1933-
See Poole, Josephine
See also CA 21-24R; CANR 10, 26

Hemans, Felicia 1793-1835 . . . . . . **NCLC 29**
See also DLB 96

Hemingway, Ernest (Miller) 1899-1961 . . . **CLC 1, 3, 6, 8, 10, 13, 19, 30, 34, 39, 41, 44, 50, 61; SSC 1**
See also CA 77-80; CANR 34; CDALB 1917-1929; DLB 4, 9, 102; DLBD 1; DLBY 81, 87; MTCW; WLC

Hempel, Amy 1951-. . . . . **CLC 39**
See also CA 118; 137

Henderson, F. C.
See Mencken, H(enry) L(ouis)

Henderson, Sylvia
See Ashton-Warner, Sylvia (Constance)

Henley, Beth . . . . **CLC 23**
See also Henley, Elizabeth Becker
See also CABS 3; DLBY 86

Henley, Elizabeth Becker 1952-
See Henley, Beth
See also CA 107; CANR 32; MTCW

Henley, William Ernest
1849-1903 . . . . **TCLC 8**
See also CA 105; DLB 19

Hennissart, Martha
See Lathen, Emma
See also CA 85-88

Henry, O. . . . . **TCLC 1, 19; SSC 5**
See also Porter, William Sydney
See also WLC

Henryson, Robert 1430(?)-1506(?). . . . **LC 20**

Henry VIII 1491-1547 . . . . **LC 10**

Henschke, Alfred
See Klabund

Hentoff, Nat(han Irving) 1925- . . . . . **CLC 26**
See also AAYA 4; CA 1-4R; CAAS 6; CANR 5, 25; CLR 1; MAICYA; SATA 27, 42, 69

Heppenstall, (John) Rayner
1911-1981 . . . . **CLC 10**
See also CA 1-4R; 103; CANR 29

Herbert, Frank (Patrick)
1920-1986 . . . . **CLC 12, 23, 35, 44**
See also CA 53-56; 118; CANR 5; DLB 8; MTCW; SATA 9, 37, 47

Herbert, George 1593-1633 . . . . **PC 4**
See also CDBLB Before 1660

Herbert, Zbigniew 1924- . . . . **CLC 9, 43**
See also CA 89-92; CANR 36; MTCW

Herbst, Josephine (Frey)
1897-1969 . . . . **CLC 34**
See also CA 5-8R; 25-28R; DLB 9

Hergesheimer, Joseph
1880-1954 . . . . **TCLC 11**
See also CA 109; DLB 102, 9

Herlihy, James Leo 1927- . . . . **CLC 6**
See also CA 1-4R; CANR 2

Hermogenes fl. c. 175- . . . . **CMLC 6**

Hernandez, Jose 1834-1886 . . . . . . **NCLC 17**

Herrick, Robert 1591-1674 . . . . **LC 13**

Herriot, James . . . . **CLC 12**
See also Wight, James Alfred
See also AAYA 1

Herrmann, Dorothy 1941- . . . . **CLC 44**
See also CA 107

Herrmann, Taffy
See Herrmann, Dorothy

Hersey, John (Richard)
1914- . . . . **CLC 1, 2, 7, 9, 40**
See also CA 17-20R; CANR 33; DLB 6; MTCW; SATA 25

Herzen, Aleksandr Ivanovich
1812-1870 . . . . **NCLC 10**

Herzl, Theodor 1860-1904 . . . . **TCLC 36**

Herzog, Werner 1942- . . . . **CLC 16**
See also CA 89-92

Hesiod c. 8th cent. B.C.- . . . . **CMLC 5**

Hesse, Hermann
1877-1962 . . . **CLC 1, 2, 3, 6, 11, 17, 25, 69; SSC 9**
See also CA 17-18; CAP 2; DLB 66; MTCW; SATA 50; WLC

Hewes, Cady
See De Voto, Bernard (Augustine)

Heyen, William 1940- . . . . **CLC 13, 18**
See also CA 33-36R; CAAS 9; DLB 5

Heyerdahl, Thor 1914- . . . . **CLC 26**
See also CA 5-8R; CANR 5, 22; MTCW; SATA 2, 52

Heym, Georg (Theodor Franz Arthur)
1887-1912 . . . . **TCLC 9**
See also CA 106

Heym, Stefan 1913- . . . . **CLC 41**
See also CA 9-12R; CANR 4; DLB 69

Heyse, Paul (Johann Ludwig von)
1830-1914 . . . . **TCLC 8**
See also CA 104

Hibbert, Eleanor Burford 1906- . . . . . **CLC 7**
See also BEST 90:4; CA 17-20R; CANR 9, 28; SATA 2

Higgins, George V(incent)
1939- . . . . **CLC 4, 7, 10, 18**
See also CA 77-80; CAAS 5; CANR 17; DLB 2; DLBY 81; MTCW

Higginson, Thomas Wentworth
1823-1911 . . . . **TCLC 36**
See also DLB 1, 64

Highet, Helen
See MacInnes, Helen (Clark)

Highsmith, (Mary) Patricia
1921- . . . . **CLC 2, 4, 14, 42**
See also CA 1-4R; CANR 1, 20; MTCW

Highwater, Jamake (Mamake)
1942(?)- . . . . **CLC 12**
See also AAYA 7; CA 65-68; CAAS 7; CANR 10, 34; CLR 17; DLB 52; DLBY 85; MAICYA; SATA 30, 32, 69

Hijuelos, Oscar 1951- . . . . **CLC 65**
See also BEST 90:1; CA 123; HW

Hikmet, Nazim 1902-1963 . . . . **CLC 40**
See also CA 93-96

Hildesheimer, Wolfgang
1916-1991 . . . . **CLC 49**
See also CA 101; 135; DLB 69

Hill, Geoffrey (William)
1932- . . . . **CLC 5, 8, 18, 45**
See also CA 81-84; CANR 21; CDBLB 1960 to Present; DLB 40; MTCW

Hill, George Roy 1921- . . . . **CLC 26**
See also CA 110; 122

Hill, Susan (Elizabeth) 1942- . . . . **CLC 4**
See also CA 33-36R; CANR 29; DLB 14; MTCW

Hillerman, Tony 1925- . . . . **CLC 62**
See also AAYA 6; BEST 89:1; CA 29-32R; CANR 21; SATA 6

Hilliard, Noel (Harvey) 1929- . . . . . . **CLC 15**
See also CA 9-12R; CANR 7

Hillis, Rick 1956- . . . . **CLC 66**
See also CA 134

Hilton, James 1900-1954 . . . . **TCLC 21**
See also CA 108; DLB 34, 77; SATA 34

Himes, Chester (Bomar)
1909-1984 . . . . **CLC 2, 4, 7, 18, 58**
See also BLC 2; BW; CA 25-28R; 114; CANR 22; DLB 2, 76; MTCW

Hinde, Thomas . . . . **CLC 6, 11**
See also Chitty, Thomas Willes

Hindin, Nathan
See Bloch, Robert (Albert)

Hine, (William) Daryl 1936- . . . . **CLC 15**
See also CA 1-4R; CAAS 15; CANR 1, 20; DLB 60

Hinkson, Katharine Tynan
See Tynan, Katharine

Hinton, S(usan) E(loise) 1950- . . . . . **CLC 30**
See also AAYA 2; CA 81-84; CANR 32; CLR 3, 23; MAICYA; MTCW; SATA 19, 58

Hippius, Zinaida . . . . **TCLC 9**
See also Gippius, Zinaida (Nikolayevna)

Hiraoka, Kimitake 1925-1970
See Mishima, Yukio
See also CA 97-100; 29-32R; MTCW

Hirsch, Edward 1950- . . . . **CLC 31, 50**
See also CA 104; CANR 20; DLB 120

Hitchcock, Alfred (Joseph)
1899-1980 . . . . **CLC 16**
See also CA 97-100; SATA 24, 27

Hoagland, Edward 1932- . . . . **CLC 28**
See also CA 1-4R; CANR 2, 31; DLB 6; SATA 51

Hoban, Russell (Conwell) 1925- . . **CLC 7, 25**
See also CA 5-8R; CANR 23, 37; CLR 3; DLB 52; MAICYA; MTCW; SATA 1, 40

Hobbs, Perry
See Blackmur, R(ichard) P(almer)

Hobson, Laura Z(ametkin)
1900-1986 . . . . **CLC 7, 25**
See also CA 17-20R; 118; DLB 28; SATA 52

Hochhuth, Rolf 1931- . . . . **CLC 4, 11, 18**
See also CA 5-8R; CANR 33; MTCW

Hochman, Sandra 1936- . . . . **CLC 3, 8**
See also CA 5-8R; DLB 5

Hochwaelder, Fritz 1911-1986 . . . . . . **CLC 36**
See also Hochwalder, Fritz
See also CA 29-32R; 120; MTCW

Hochwalder, Fritz . . . . **CLC 36**
See also Hochwaelder, Fritz

Hocking, Mary (Eunice) 1921- . . . . . **CLC 13**
See also CA 101; CANR 18

Hodgins, Jack 1938- . . . . **CLC 23**
See also CA 93-96; DLB 60

Hodgson, William Hope
1877(?)-1918 . . . . **TCLC 13**
See also CA 111; DLB 70

Hoffman, Alice 1952- . . . . **CLC 51**
See also CA 77-80; CANR 34; MTCW

Hoffman, Daniel (Gerard)
1923- . . . . **CLC 6, 13, 23**
See also CA 1-4R; CANR 4; DLB 5

Hoffman, Stanley 1944- . . . . **CLC 5**
See also CA 77-80

Hoffman, William M(oses) 1939- . . . **CLC 40**
See also CA 57-60; CANR 11

Hoffmann, E(rnst) T(heodor) A(madeus) 1776-1822 . . . . **NCLC 2**
See also DLB 90; SATA 27

Hofmann, Gert 1931- . . . . **CLC 54**
See also CA 128

Hofmannsthal, Hugo von 1874-1929 . . . . **TCLC 11**
See also CA 106; DLB 81, 118

Hogarth, Charles
See Creasey, John

Hogg, James 1770-1835 . . . . **NCLC 4**
See also DLB 93, 116

Holbach, Paul Henri Thiry Baron 1723-1789 . . . . **LC 14**

Holberg, Ludvig 1684-1754 . . . . **LC 6**

Holden, Ursula 1921- . . . . **CLC 18**
See also CA 101; CAAS 8; CANR 22

Holderlin, (Johann Christian) Friedrich 1770-1843 . . . . **NCLC 16; PC 4**

Holdstock, Robert
See Holdstock, Robert P.

Holdstock, Robert P. 1948- . . . . **CLC 39**
See also CA 131

Holland, Isabelle 1920- . . . . **CLC 21**
See also CA 21-24R; CANR 10, 25; MAICYA; SATA 8, 70

Holland, Marcus
See Caldwell, (Janet Miriam) Taylor (Holland)

Hollander, John 1929- . . . . . . **CLC 2, 5, 8, 14**
See also CA 1-4R; CANR 1; DLB 5; SATA 13

Hollander, Paul
See Silverberg, Robert

Holleran, Andrew 1943(?)- . . . . **CLC 38**

Hollinghurst, Alan 1954- . . . . **CLC 55**
See also CA 114

Hollis, Jim
See Summers, Hollis (Spurgeon Jr.)

Holmes, John
See Souster, (Holmes) Raymond

Holmes, John Clellon 1926-1988 . . . . **CLC 56**
See also CA 9-12R; 125; CANR 4; DLB 16

Holmes, Oliver Wendell 1809-1894 . . . . **NCLC 14**
See also CDALB 1640-1865; DLB 1; SATA 34

Holmes, Raymond
See Souster, (Holmes) Raymond

Holt, Victoria
See Hibbert, Eleanor Burford

Holub, Miroslav 1923- . . . . **CLC 4**
See also CA 21-24R; CANR 10

Homer c. 8th cent. B.C.- . . . . **CMLC 1**

Honig, Edwin 1919- . . . . **CLC 33**
See also CA 5-8R; CAAS 8; CANR 4; DLB 5

Hood, Hugh (John Blagdon) 1928- . . . . **CLC 15, 28**
See also CA 49-52; CANR 1, 33; DLB 53

Hood, Thomas 1799-1845 . . . . **NCLC 16**
See also DLB 96

Hooker, (Peter) Jeremy 1941- . . . . . . **CLC 43**
See also CA 77-80; CANR 22; DLB 40

Hope, A(lec) D(erwent) 1907- . . . . **CLC 3, 51**
See also CA 21-24R; CANR 33; MTCW

Hope, Brian
See Creasey, John

Hope, Christopher (David Tully) 1944- . . . . **CLC 52**
See also CA 106; SATA 62

Hopkins, Gerard Manley 1844-1889 . . . . **NCLC 17**
See also CDBLB 1890-1914; DLB 35, 57; WLC

Hopkins, John (Richard) 1931- . . . . . . **CLC 4**
See also CA 85-88

Hopkins, Pauline Elizabeth 1859-1930 . . . . **TCLC 28**
See also BLC 2; DLB 50

Horatio
See Proust, (Valentin-Louis-George-Eugene-)Marcel

Horgan, Paul 1903- . . . . **CLC 9, 53**
See also CA 13-16R; CANR 9, 35; DLB 102; DLBY 85; MTCW; SATA 13

Horn, Peter
See Kuttner, Henry

Horovitz, Israel 1939- . . . . **CLC 56**
See also CA 33-36R; DLB 7

Horvath, Odon von
See Horvath, Oedoen von
See also DLB 85

Horvath, Oedoen von 1901-1938 . . . **TCLC 45**
See also Horvath, Odon von
See also CA 118

Horwitz, Julius 1920-1986 . . . . **CLC 14**
See also CA 9-12R; 119; CANR 12

Hospital, Janette Turner 1942- . . . . . **CLC 42**
See also CA 108

Hostos, E. M. de
See Hostos (y Bonilla), Eugenio Maria de

Hostos, Eugenio M. de
See Hostos (y Bonilla), Eugenio Maria de

Hostos, Eugenio Maria
See Hostos (y Bonilla), Eugenio Maria de

Hostos (y Bonilla), Eugenio Maria de 1839-1903 . . . . **TCLC 24**
See also CA 123; 131; HW

Houdini
See Lovecraft, H(oward) P(hillips)

Hougan, Carolyn 19(?)- . . . . **CLC 34**

Household, Geoffrey (Edward West) 1900-1988 . . . . **CLC 11**
See also CA 77-80; 126; DLB 87; SATA 14, 59

Housman, A(lfred) E(dward) 1859-1936 . . . . **TCLC 1, 10; PC 2**
See also CA 104; 125; DLB 19; MTCW

Housman, Laurence 1865-1959 . . . . . **TCLC 7**
See also CA 106; DLB 10; SATA 25

Howard, Elizabeth Jane 1923- . . . **CLC 7, 29**
See also CA 5-8R; CANR 8

Howard, Maureen 1930- . . . . . **CLC 5, 14, 46**
See also CA 53-56; CANR 31; DLBY 83; MTCW

Howard, Richard 1929- . . . . . . **CLC 7, 10, 47**
See also AITN 1; CA 85-88; CANR 25; DLB 5

Howard, Robert Ervin 1906-1936 . . . **TCLC 8**
See also CA 105

Howard, Warren F.
See Pohl, Frederik

Howe, Fanny 1940- . . . . **CLC 47**
See also CA 117; SATA 52

Howe, Julia Ward 1819-1910 . . . . . **TCLC 21**
See also CA 117; DLB 1

Howe, Susan 1937- . . . . **CLC 72**
See also DLB 120

Howe, Tina 1937- . . . . **CLC 48**
See also CA 109

Howell, James 1594(?)-1666 . . . . **LC 13**

Howells, W. D.
See Howells, William Dean

Howells, William D.
See Howells, William Dean

Howells, William Dean 1837-1920 . . . . **TCLC 41, 7, 17**
See also CA 104; 134; CDALB 1865-1917; DLB 12, 64, 74, 79

Howes, Barbara 1914- . . . . **CLC 15**
See also CA 9-12R; CAAS 3; SATA 5

Hrabal, Bohumil 1914- . . . . **CLC 13, 67**
See also CA 106; CAAS 12

Hsun, Lu . . . . **TCLC 3**
See also Shu-Jen, Chou

Hubbard, L(afayette) Ron(ald) 1911-1986 . . . . **CLC 43**
See also CA 77-80; 118; CANR 22

Huch, Ricarda (Octavia) 1864-1947 . . . . **TCLC 13**
See also CA 111; DLB 66

Huddle, David 1942- . . . . **CLC 49**
See also CA 57-60

Hudson, Jeffery
See Crichton, (John) Michael

Hudson, W(illiam) H(enry) 1841-1922 . . . . **TCLC 29**
See also CA 115; DLB 98; SATA 35

Hueffer, Ford Madox
See Ford, Ford Madox

Hughart, Barry . . . . **CLC 39**
See also CA 137

Hughes, Colin
See Creasey, John

Hughes, David (John) 1930- . . . . **CLC 48**
See also CA 116; 129; DLB 14

Hughes, (James) Langston 1902-1967 . . . . **CLC 1, 5, 10, 15, 35, 44; DC 3; PC 1; SSC 6**
See also BLC 2; BW; CA 1-4R; 25-28R; CANR 1, 34; CDALB 1929-1941; CLR 17; DLB 4, 7, 48, 51, 86; MAICYA; MTCW; SATA 4, 33; WLC

Hughes, Richard (Arthur Warren) 1900-1976 . . . . **CLC 1, 11**
See also CA 5-8R; 65-68; CANR 4; DLB 15; MTCW; SATA 8, 25

Hughes, Ted 1930- . . . . . **CLC 2, 4, 9, 14, 37**
See also CA 1-4R; CANR 1, 33; CLR 3; DLB 40; MAICYA; MTCW; SATA 27, 49

Hugo, Richard F(ranklin) 1923-1982 . . . . **CLC 6, 18, 32**
See also CA 49-52; 108; CANR 3; DLB 5

Hugo, Victor (Marie) 1802-1885 . . . . **NCLC 3, 10, 21**
See also DLB 119; SATA 47; WLC

Huidobro, Vicente
See Huidobro Fernandez, Vicente Garcia

Huidobro Fernandez, Vicente Garcia 1893-1948 . . . . **TCLC 31**
See also CA 131; HW

Hulme, Keri 1947- . . . . **CLC 39**
See also CA 125

Hulme, T(homas) E(rnest) 1883-1917 . . . . **TCLC 21**
See also CA 117; DLB 19

Hume, David 1711-1776. . . . . **LC 7**
See also DLB 104

Humphrey, William 1924- . . . . **CLC 45**
See also CA 77-80; DLB 6

Humphreys, Emyr Owen 1919- . . . . . **CLC 47**
See also CA 5-8R; CANR 3, 24; DLB 15

Humphreys, Josephine 1945- . . . . **CLC 34, 57**
See also CA 121; 127

Hungerford, Pixie
See Brinsmead, H(esba) F(ay)

Hunt, E(verette) Howard Jr. 1918- . . . **CLC 3**
See also AITN 1; CA 45-48; CANR 2

Hunt, Kyle
See Creasey, John

Hunt, (James Henry) Leigh 1784-1859 . . . . **NCLC 1**

Hunt, Marsha 1946- . . . . **CLC 70**

Hunter, E. Waldo
See Sturgeon, Theodore (Hamilton)

Hunter, Evan 1926- . . . . **CLC 11, 31**
See also CA 5-8R; CANR 5, 38; DLBY 82; MTCW; SATA 25

Hunter, Kristin (Eggleston) 1931- . . . **CLC 35**
See also AITN 1; BW; CA 13-16R; CANR 13; CLR 3; DLB 33; MAICYA; SAAS 10; SATA 12

Hunter, Mollie 1922- . . . . **CLC 21**
See also McIlwraith, Maureen Mollie Hunter
See also CANR 37; CLR 25; MAICYA; SAAS 7; SATA 54

Hunter, Robert (?)-1734. . . . . **LC 7**

Hurston, Zora Neale 1903-1960 . . . . **CLC 7, 30, 61; SSC 4**
See also BLC 2; BW; CA 85-88; DLB 51, 86; MTCW

Huston, John (Marcellus) 1906-1987 . . . . **CLC 20**
See also CA 73-76; 123; CANR 34; DLB 26

Hutten, Ulrich von 1488-1523 . . . . **LC 16**

Huxley, Aldous (Leonard) 1894-1963 . . **CLC 1, 3, 4, 5, 8, 11, 18, 35**
See also CA 85-88; CDBLB 1914-1945; DLB 36, 100; MTCW; SATA 63; WLC

Huysmans, Charles Marie Georges 1848-1907
See Huysmans, Joris-Karl
See also CA 104

Huysmans, Joris-Karl . . . . **TCLC 7**
See also Huysmans, Charles Marie Georges

Hwang, David Henry 1957- . . . . **CLC 55**
See also CA 127; 132

Hyde, Anthony 1946- . . . . **CLC 42**
See also CA 136

Hyde, Margaret O(ldroyd) 1917- . . . **CLC 21**
See also CA 1-4R; CANR 1, 36; CLR 23; MAICYA; SAAS 8; SATA 1, 42

Hynes, James 1956(?)- . . . . **CLC 65**

Ian, Janis 1951- . . . . **CLC 21**
See also CA 105

Ibanez, Vicente Blasco
See Blasco Ibanez, Vicente

Ibarguengoitia, Jorge 1928-1983 . . . . **CLC 37**
See also CA 124; 113; HW

Ibsen, Henrik (Johan) 1828-1906 . . . . . **TCLC 2, 8, 16, 37; DC 2**
See also CA 104; WLC

Ibuse Masuji 1898- . . . . **CLC 22**
See also CA 127

Ichikawa, Kon 1915- . . . . **CLC 20**
See also CA 121

Idle, Eric 1943- . . . . **CLC 21**
See also Monty Python
See also CA 116; CANR 35

Ignatow, David 1914- . . . . . . **CLC 4, 7, 14, 40**
See also CA 9-12R; CAAS 3; CANR 31; DLB 5

Ihimaera, Witi 1944- . . . . **CLC 46**
See also CA 77-80

Ilf, Ilya . . . . **TCLC 21**
See also Fainzilberg, Ilya Arnoldovich

Immermann, Karl (Lebrecht) 1796-1840 . . . . **NCLC 4**

Inclan, Ramon (Maria) del Valle
See Valle-Inclan, Ramon (Maria) del

Infante, G(uillermo) Cabrera
See Cabrera Infante, G(uillermo)

Ingalls, Rachel (Holmes) 1940- . . . . . **CLC 42**
See also CA 123; 127

Ingamells, Rex 1913-1955 . . . . **TCLC 35**

Inge, William Motter 1913-1973 . . . . **CLC 1, 8, 19**
See also CA 9-12R; CDALB 1941-1968; DLB 7; MTCW

Ingram, Willis J.
See Harris, Mark

Innaurato, Albert (F.) 1948(?)- . . **CLC 21, 60**
See also CA 115; 122

Innes, Michael
See Stewart, J(ohn) I(nnes) M(ackintosh)

Ionesco, Eugene 1912- . . . . **CLC 1, 4, 6, 9, 11, 15, 41**
See also CA 9-12R; MTCW; SATA 7; WLC

Iqbal, Muhammad 1873-1938 . . . . . **TCLC 28**

Irland, David
See Green, Julian (Hartridge)

Iron, Ralph
See Schreiner, Olive (Emilie Albertina)

Irving, John (Winslow) 1942- . . . . **CLC 13, 23, 38**
See also AAYA 8; BEST 89:3; CA 25-28R; CANR 28; DLB 6; DLBY 82; MTCW

Irving, Washington 1783-1859 . . . . **NCLC 2, 19; SSC 2**
See also CDALB 1640-1865; DLB 3, 11, 30, 59, 73, 74; WLC; YABC 2

Irwin, P. K.
See Page, P(atricia) K(athleen)

Isaacs, Susan 1943- . . . . **CLC 32**
See also BEST 89:1; CA 89-92; CANR 20; MTCW

Isherwood, Christopher (William Bradshaw) 1904-1986 . . . . **CLC 1, 9, 11, 14, 44**
See also CA 13-16R; 117; CANR 35; DLB 15; DLBY 86; MTCW

Ishiguro, Kazuo 1954- . . . . . . **CLC 27, 56, 59**
See also BEST 90:2; CA 120; MTCW

Ishikawa Takuboku 1886(?)-1912 . . . . **TCLC 15**
See also CA 113

Iskander, Fazil 1929- . . . . **CLC 47**
See also CA 102

Ivan IV 1530-1584 . . . . **LC 17**

Ivanov, Vyacheslav Ivanovich 1866-1949 . . . . **TCLC 33**
See also CA 122

Ivask, Ivar Vidrik 1927- . . . . **CLC 14**
See also CA 37-40R; CANR 24

Jackson, Daniel
See Wingrove, David (John)

Jackson, Jesse 1908-1983 . . . . **CLC 12**
See also BW; CA 25-28R; 109; CANR 27; CLR 28; MAICYA; SATA 2, 29, 48

Jackson, Laura (Riding) 1901-1991 . . **CLC 7**
See also Riding, Laura
See also CA 65-68; 135; CANR 28; DLB 48

Jackson, Sam
See Trumbo, Dalton

Jackson, Sara
See Wingrove, David (John)

Jackson, Shirley 1919-1965 . . . . **CLC 11, 60; SSC 9**
See also AAYA 9; CA 1-4R; 25-28R; CANR 4; CDALB 1941-1968; DLB 6; SATA 2; WLC

Jacob, (Cyprien-)Max 1876-1944 . . . **TCLC 6**
See also CA 104

Jacobs, Jim 1942- . . . . **CLC 12**
See also CA 97-100

Jacobs, W(illiam) W(ymark) 1863-1943 . . . . **TCLC 22**
See also CA 121

Jacobsen, Jens Peter 1847-1885 . . **NCLC 34**

Jacobsen, Josephine 1908- . . . . **CLC 48**
See also CA 33-36R; CANR 23

Jacobson, Dan 1929- . . . . **CLC 4, 14**
See also CA 1-4R; CANR 2, 25; DLB 14; MTCW

Jacqueline
See Carpentier (y Valmont), Alejo

Jagger, Mick 1944-. . . . . **CLC 17**

Jakes, John (William) 1932- . . . . **CLC 29**
See also BEST 89:4; CA 57-60; CANR 10; DLBY 83; MTCW; SATA 62

James, Andrew
See Kirkup, James

James, C(yril) L(ionel) R(obert)
1901-1989 . . . . **CLC 33**
See also BW; CA 117; 125; 128; MTCW

James, Daniel (Lewis) 1911-1988
See Santiago, Danny
See also CA 125

James, Dynely
See Mayne, William (James Carter)

James, Henry
1843-1916 . . . . . **TCLC 2, 11, 24, 40, 47; SSC 8**
See also CA 104; 132; CDALB 1865-1917; DLB 12, 71, 74; MTCW; WLC

James, Montague (Rhodes)
1862-1936 . . . . **TCLC 6**
See also CA 104

James, P. D. . . . . **CLC 18, 46**
See also White, Phyllis Dorothy James
See also BEST 90:2; CDBLB 1960 to Present; DLB 87

James, Philip
See Moorcock, Michael (John)

James, William 1842-1910. . . . . **TCLC 15, 32**
See also CA 109

James I 1394-1437 . . . . **LC 20**

Jami, Nur al-Din 'Abd al-Rahman
1414-1492 . . . . **LC 9**

Jandl, Ernst 1925- . . . . **CLC 34**

Janowitz, Tama 1957- . . . . **CLC 43**
See also CA 106

Jarrell, Randall
1914-1965 . . . . **CLC 1, 2, 6, 9, 13, 49**
See also CA 5-8R; 25-28R; CABS 2; CANR 6, 34; CDALB 1941-1968; CLR 6; DLB 48, 52; MAICYA; MTCW; SATA 7

Jarry, Alfred 1873-1907. . . . . **TCLC 2, 14**
See also CA 104

Jarvis, E. K.
See Bloch, Robert (Albert); Ellison, Harlan; Silverberg, Robert

Jeake, Samuel Jr.
See Aiken, Conrad (Potter)

Jean Paul 1763-1825 . . . . **NCLC 7**

Jeffers, (John) Robinson
1887-1962 . . . . **CLC 2, 3, 11, 15, 54**
See also CA 85-88; CANR 35; CDALB 1917-1929; DLB 45; MTCW; WLC

Jefferson, Janet
See Mencken, H(enry) L(ouis)

Jefferson, Thomas 1743-1826 . . . . **NCLC 11**
See also CDALB 1640-1865; DLB 31

Jeffrey, Francis 1773-1850. . . . . . . **NCLC 33**
See also DLB 107

Jelakowitch, Ivan
See Heijermans, Herman

Jellicoe, (Patricia) Ann 1927- . . . . . . **CLC 27**
See also CA 85-88; DLB 13

Jen, Gish . . . . **CLC 70**
See also Jen, Lillian

Jen, Lillian 1956(?)-
See Jen, Gish
See also CA 135

Jenkins, (John) Robin 1912- . . . . **CLC 52**
See also CA 1-4R; CANR 1; DLB 14

Jennings, Elizabeth (Joan)
1926- . . . . **CLC 5, 14**
See also CA 61-64; CAAS 5; CANR 8, 39; DLB 27; MTCW; SATA 66

Jennings, Waylon 1937-. . . . . **CLC 21**

Jensen, Johannes V. 1873-1950. . . . **TCLC 41**

Jensen, Laura (Linnea) 1948- . . . . . . **CLC 37**
See also CA 103

Jerome, Jerome K(lapka)
1859-1927 . . . . **TCLC 23**
See also CA 119; DLB 10, 34

Jerrold, Douglas William
1803-1857 . . . . **NCLC 2**

Jewett, (Theodora) Sarah Orne
1849-1909 . . . . **TCLC 1, 22; SSC 6**
See also CA 108; 127; DLB 12, 74; SATA 15

Jewsbury, Geraldine (Endsor)
1812-1880 . . . . **NCLC 22**
See also DLB 21

Jhabvala, Ruth Prawer
1927- . . . . **CLC 4, 8, 29**
See also CA 1-4R; CANR 2, 29; MTCW

Jiles, Paulette 1943-. . . . . **CLC 13, 58**
See also CA 101

Jimenez (Mantecon), Juan Ramon
1881-1958 . . . . **TCLC 4**
See also CA 104; 131; HW; MTCW

Jimenez, Ramon
See Jimenez (Mantecon), Juan Ramon

Jimenez Mantecon, Juan
See Jimenez (Mantecon), Juan Ramon

Joel, Billy . . . . **CLC 26**
See also Joel, William Martin

Joel, William Martin 1949-
See Joel, Billy
See also CA 108

John of the Cross, St. 1542-1591 . . . . **LC 18**

Johnson, B(ryan) S(tanley William)
1933-1973 . . . . **CLC 6, 9**
See also CA 9-12R; 53-56; CANR 9; DLB 14, 40

Johnson, Charles (Richard)
1948- . . . . **CLC 7, 51, 65**
See also BLC 2; BW; CA 116; DLB 33

Johnson, Denis 1949-. . . . . **CLC 52**
See also CA 117; 121; DLB 120

Johnson, Diane (Lain)
1934- . . . . **CLC 5, 13, 48**
See also CA 41-44R; CANR 17; DLBY 80; MTCW

Johnson, Eyvind (Olof Verner)
1900-1976 . . . . **CLC 14**
See also CA 73-76; 69-72; CANR 34

Johnson, J. R.
See James, C(yril) L(ionel) R(obert)

Johnson, James Weldon
1871-1938 . . . . **TCLC 3, 19**
See also BLC 2; BW; CA 104; 125; CDALB 1917-1929; DLB 51; MTCW; SATA 31

Johnson, Joyce 1935-. . . . . **CLC 58**
See also CA 125; 129

Johnson, Lionel (Pigot)
1867-1902 . . . . **TCLC 19**
See also CA 117; DLB 19

Johnson, Mel
See Malzberg, Barry N(athaniel)

Johnson, Pamela Hansford
1912-1981 . . . . **CLC 1, 7, 27**
See also CA 1-4R; 104; CANR 2, 28; DLB 15; MTCW

Johnson, Samuel 1709-1784. . . . . **LC 15**
See also CDBLB 1660-1789; DLB 39, 95, 104; WLC

Johnson, Uwe
1934-1984 . . . . **CLC 5, 10, 15, 40**
See also CA 1-4R; 112; CANR 1, 39; DLB 75; MTCW

Johnston, George (Benson) 1913- . . . **CLC 51**
See also CA 1-4R; CANR 5, 20; DLB 88

Johnston, Jennifer 1930- . . . . **CLC 7**
See also CA 85-88; DLB 14

Jolley, (Monica) Elizabeth 1923- . . . **CLC 46**
See also CA 127; CAAS 13

Jones, Arthur Llewellyn 1863-1947
See Machen, Arthur
See also CA 104

Jones, D(ouglas) G(ordon) 1929-. . . . **CLC 10**
See also CA 29-32R; CANR 13; DLB 53

Jones, David (Michael)
1895-1974 . . . . **CLC 2, 4, 7, 13, 42**
See also CA 9-12R; 53-56; CANR 28; CDBLB 1945-1960; DLB 20, 100; MTCW

Jones, David Robert 1947-
See Bowie, David
See also CA 103

Jones, Diana Wynne 1934- . . . . **CLC 26**
See also CA 49-52; CANR 4, 26; CLR 23; MAICYA; SAAS 7; SATA 9, 70

Jones, Gayl 1949-. . . . . **CLC 6, 9**
See also BLC 2; BW; CA 77-80; CANR 27; DLB 33; MTCW

Jones, James 1921-1977. . . . **CLC 1, 3, 10, 39**
See also AITN 1, 2; CA 1-4R; 69-72; CANR 6; DLB 2; MTCW

Jones, John J.
See Lovecraft, H(oward) P(hillips)

Jones, LeRoi . . . . **CLC 1, 2, 3, 5, 10, 14**
See also Baraka, Amiri

Jones, Louis B. . . . . **CLC 65**

Jones, Madison (Percy Jr.) 1925-. . . . **CLC 4**
See also CA 13-16R; CAAS 11; CANR 7

Jones, Mervyn 1922- . . . . **CLC 10, 52**
See also CA 45-48; CAAS 5; CANR 1; MTCW

Jones, Mick 1956(?)- . . . . **CLC 30**
See also The Clash

Jones, Nettie (Pearl) 1941- . . . . **CLC 34**
See also CA 137

Jones, Preston 1936-1979 . . . . **CLC 10**
See also CA 73-76; 89-92; DLB 7

Jones, Robert F(rancis) 1934- . . . . **CLC 7**
See also CA 49-52; CANR 2

Jones, Rod 1953- . . . . **CLC 50**
See also CA 128

Jones, Terence Graham Parry
1942- . . . . **CLC 21**
See also Jones, Terry; Monty Python
See also CA 112; 116; CANR 35; SATA 51

Jones, Terry
See Jones, Terence Graham Parry
See also SATA 67

Jong, Erica 1942- . . . . **CLC 4, 6, 8, 18**
See also AITN 1; BEST 90:2; CA 73-76; CANR 26; DLB 2, 5, 28; MTCW

Jonson, Ben(jamin) 1572(?)-1637. . . . . . **LC 6**
See also CDBLB Before 1660; DLB 62, 121; WLC

Jordan, June 1936- . . . . **CLC 5, 11, 23**
See also AAYA 2; BW; CA 33-36R; CANR 25; CLR 10; DLB 38; MAICYA; MTCW; SATA 4

Jordan, Pat(rick M.) 1941- . . . . **CLC 37**
See also CA 33-36R

Jorgensen, Ivar
See Ellison, Harlan

Jorgenson, Ivar
See Silverberg, Robert

Josipovici, Gabriel 1940- . . . . **CLC 6, 43**
See also CA 37-40R; CAAS 8; DLB 14

Joubert, Joseph 1754-1824 . . . . **NCLC 9**

Jouve, Pierre Jean 1887-1976 . . . . . . **CLC 47**
See also CA 65-68

Joyce, James (Augustine Aloysius)
1882-1941 . . . . **TCLC 3, 8, 16, 35; SSC 3**
See also CA 104; 126; CDBLB 1914-1945; DLB 10, 19, 36; MTCW; WLC

Jozsef, Attila 1905-1937. . . . . **TCLC 22**
See also CA 116

Juana Ines de la Cruz 1651(?)-1695 . . . **LC 5**

Judd, Cyril
See Kornbluth, C(yril) M.; Pohl, Frederik

Julian of Norwich 1342(?)-1416(?) . . . . **LC 6**

Just, Ward (Swift) 1935- . . . . **CLC 4, 27**
See also CA 25-28R; CANR 32

Justice, Donald (Rodney) 1925- . . **CLC 6, 19**
See also CA 5-8R; CANR 26; DLBY 83

Juvenal c. 55-c. 127 . . . . **CMLC 8**

Juvenis
See Bourne, Randolph S(illiman)

Kacew, Romain 1914-1980
See Gary, Romain
See also CA 108; 102

Kadare, Ismail 1936- . . . . **CLC 52**

Kadohata, Cynthia. . . . . **CLC 59**

Kafka, Franz
1883-1924 . . . . . . **TCLC 2, 6, 13, 29, 47; SSC 5**
See also CA 105; 126; DLB 81; MTCW; WLC

Kahn, Roger 1927- . . . . **CLC 30**
See also CA 25-28R; SATA 37

Kain, Saul
See Sassoon, Siegfried (Lorraine)

Kaiser, Georg 1878-1945 . . . . **TCLC 9**
See also CA 106

Kaletski, Alexander 1946- . . . . **CLC 39**
See also CA 118

Kalidasa fl. c. 400- . . . . **CMLC 9**

Kallman, Chester (Simon)
1921-1975 . . . . **CLC 2**
See also CA 45-48; 53-56; CANR 3

Kaminsky, Melvin 1926-
See Brooks, Mel
See also CA 65-68; CANR 16

Kaminsky, Stuart M(elvin) 1934- . . . **CLC 59**
See also CA 73-76; CANR 29

Kane, Paul
See Simon, Paul

Kane, Wilson
See Bloch, Robert (Albert)

Kanin, Garson 1912-. . . . . **CLC 22**
See also AITN 1; CA 5-8R; CANR 7; DLB 7

Kaniuk, Yoram 1930- . . . . **CLC 19**
See also CA 134

Kant, Immanuel 1724-1804 . . . . . . **NCLC 27**
See also DLB 94

Kantor, MacKinlay 1904-1977 . . . . . . **CLC 7**
See also CA 61-64; 73-76; DLB 9, 102

Kaplan, David Michael 1946- . . . . . . **CLC 50**

Kaplan, James 1951- . . . . **CLC 59**
See also CA 135

Karageorge, Michael
See Anderson, Poul (William)

Karamzin, Nikolai Mikhailovich
1766-1826 . . . . **NCLC 3**

Karapanou, Margarita 1946- . . . . **CLC 13**
See also CA 101

Karinthy, Frigyes 1887-1938 . . . . . . **TCLC 47**

Karl, Frederick R(obert) 1927- . . . . . **CLC 34**
See also CA 5-8R; CANR 3

Kastel, Warren
See Silverberg, Robert

Kataev, Evgeny Petrovich 1903-1942
See Petrov, Evgeny
See also CA 120

Kataphusin
See Ruskin, John

Katz, Steve 1935- . . . . **CLC 47**
See also CA 25-28R; CAAS 14; CANR 12; DLBY 83

Kauffman, Janet 1945- . . . . **CLC 42**
See also CA 117; DLBY 86

Kaufman, Bob (Garnell)
1925-1986 . . . . **CLC 49**
See also BW; CA 41-44R; 118; CANR 22; DLB 16, 41

Kaufman, George S. 1889-1961 . . . . . **CLC 38**
See also CA 108; 93-96; DLB 7

Kaufman, Sue . . . . **CLC 3, 8**
See also Barondess, Sue K(aufman)

Kavafis, Konstantinos Petrou 1863-1933
See Cavafy, C(onstantine) P(eter)
See also CA 104

Kavan, Anna 1901-1968 . . . . **CLC 5, 13**
See also CA 5-8R; CANR 6; MTCW

Kavanagh, Dan
See Barnes, Julian

Kavanagh, Patrick (Joseph)
1904-1967 . . . . **CLC 22**
See also CA 123; 25-28R; DLB 15, 20; MTCW

Kawabata, Yasunari
1899-1972 . . . . **CLC 2, 5, 9, 18**
See also CA 93-96; 33-36R

Kaye, M(ary) M(argaret) 1909-. . . . . **CLC 28**
See also CA 89-92; CANR 24; MTCW; SATA 62

Kaye, Mollie
See Kaye, M(ary) M(argaret)

Kaye-Smith, Sheila 1887-1956. . . . . **TCLC 20**
See also CA 118; DLB 36

Kaymor, Patrice Maguilene
See Senghor, Leopold Sedar

Kazan, Elia 1909- . . . . **CLC 6, 16, 63**
See also CA 21-24R; CANR 32

Kazantzakis, Nikos
1883(?)-1957 . . . . **TCLC 2, 5, 33**
See also CA 105; 132; MTCW

Kazin, Alfred 1915- . . . . **CLC 34, 38**
See also CA 1-4R; CAAS 7; CANR 1; DLB 67

Keane, Mary Nesta (Skrine) 1904-
See Keane, Molly
See also CA 108; 114

Keane, Molly . . . . **CLC 31**
See also Keane, Mary Nesta (Skrine)

Keates, Jonathan 19(?)- . . . . **CLC 34**

Keaton, Buster 1895-1966 . . . . **CLC 20**

Keats, John 1795-1821. . . . . . **NCLC 8; PC 1**
See also CDBLB 1789-1832; DLB 96, 110; WLC

Keene, Donald 1922- . . . . **CLC 34**
See also CA 1-4R; CANR 5

Keillor, Garrison . . . . **CLC 40**
See also Keillor, Gary (Edward)
See also AAYA 2; BEST 89:3; DLBY 87; SATA 58

Keillor, Gary (Edward) 1942-
See Keillor, Garrison
See also CA 111; 117; CANR 36; MTCW

Keith, Michael
See Hubbard, L(afayette) Ron(ald)

Kell, Joseph
See Wilson, John (Anthony) Burgess

Keller, Gottfried 1819-1890 . . . . **NCLC 2**

Kellerman, Jonathan 1949- . . . . **CLC 44**
See also BEST 90:1; CA 106; CANR 29

Kelley, William Melvin 1937- . . . . . . **CLC 22**
See also BW; CA 77-80; CANR 27; DLB 33

Kellogg, Marjorie 1922- .... **CLC 2**
See also CA 81-84

Kellow, Kathleen
See Hibbert, Eleanor Burford

Kelly, M(ilton) T(erry) 1947- .... **CLC 55**
See also CA 97-100; CANR 19

Kelman, James 1946- .... **CLC 58**

Kemal, Yashar 1923- .... **CLC 14, 29**
See also CA 89-92

Kemble, Fanny 1809-1893 .... **NCLC 18**
See also DLB 32

Kemelman, Harry 1908- .... **CLC 2**
See also AITN 1; CA 9-12R; CANR 6; DLB 28

Kempe, Margery 1373(?)-1440(?) ..... **LC 6**

Kempis, Thomas a 1380-1471 .... **LC 11**

Kendall, Henry 1839-1882 .... **NCLC 12**

Keneally, Thomas (Michael)
1935- ...... **CLC 5, 8, 10, 14, 19, 27, 43**
See also CA 85-88; CANR 10; MTCW

Kennedy, Adrienne (Lita) 1931- .... **CLC 66**
See also BLC 2; BW; CA 103; CABS 3; CANR 26; DLB 38

Kennedy, John Pendleton
1795-1870 .... **NCLC 2**
See also DLB 3

Kennedy, Joseph Charles 1929- ...... **CLC 8**
See also Kennedy, X. J.
See also CA 1-4R; CANR 4, 30; SATA 14

Kennedy, William 1928- ... **CLC 6, 28, 34, 53**
See also AAYA 1; CA 85-88; CANR 14, 31; DLBY 85; MTCW; SATA 57

Kennedy, X. J. .... **CLC 42**
See also Kennedy, Joseph Charles
See also CAAS 9; CLR 27; DLB 5

Kent, Kelvin
See Kuttner, Henry

Kenton, Maxwell
See Southern, Terry

Kenyon, Robert O.
See Kuttner, Henry

Kerouac, Jack ..... **CLC 1, 2, 3, 5, 14, 29, 61**
See also Kerouac, Jean-Louis Lebris de
See also CDALB 1941-1968; DLB 2, 16; DLBD 3

Kerouac, Jean-Louis Lebris de 1922-1969
See Kerouac, Jack
See also AITN 1; CA 5-8R; 25-28R; CANR 26; MTCW; WLC

Kerr, Jean 1923- .... **CLC 22**
See also CA 5-8R; CANR 7

Kerr, M. E. .... **CLC 12, 35**
See also Meaker, Marijane (Agnes)
See also AAYA 2; SAAS 1

Kerr, Robert .... **CLC 55**

Kerrigan, (Thomas) Anthony
1918- .... **CLC 4, 6**
See also CA 49-52; CAAS 11; CANR 4

Kerry, Lois
See Duncan, Lois

Kesey, Ken (Elton)
1935- .... **CLC 1, 3, 6, 11, 46, 64**
See also CA 1-4R; CANR 22, 38; CDALB 1968-1988; DLB 2, 16; MTCW; SATA 66; WLC

Kesselring, Joseph (Otto)
1902-1967 .... **CLC 45**

Kessler, Jascha (Frederick) 1929- .... **CLC 4**
See also CA 17-20R; CANR 8

Kettelkamp, Larry (Dale) 1933- .... **CLC 12**
See also CA 29-32R; CANR 16; SAAS 3; SATA 2

Kherdian, David 1931- .... **CLC 6, 9**
See also CA 21-24R; CAAS 2; CANR 39; CLR 24; MAICYA; SATA 16

Khlebnikov, Velimir .... **TCLC 20**
See also Khlebnikov, Viktor Vladimirovich

Khlebnikov, Viktor Vladimirovich 1885-1922
See Khlebnikov, Velimir
See also CA 117

Khodasevich, Vladislav (Felitsianovich)
1886-1939 .... **TCLC 15**
See also CA 115

Kielland, Alexander Lange
1849-1906 .... **TCLC 5**
See also CA 104

Kiely, Benedict 1919- .... **CLC 23, 43**
See also CA 1-4R; CANR 2; DLB 15

Kienzle, William X(avier) 1928- .... **CLC 25**
See also CA 93-96; CAAS 1; CANR 9, 31; MTCW

Kierkegaard, Soeren 1813-1855 ... **NCLC 34**

Kierkegaard, Soren 1813-1855 .... **NCLC 34**

Killens, John Oliver 1916-1987 ..... **CLC 10**
See also BW; CA 77-80; 123; CAAS 2; CANR 26; DLB 33

Killigrew, Anne 1660-1685 .... **LC 4**

Kim
See Simenon, Georges (Jacques Christian)

Kincaid, Jamaica 1949- .... **CLC 43, 68**
See also BLC 2; BW; CA 125

King, Francis (Henry) 1923- ..... **CLC 8, 53**
See also CA 1-4R; CANR 1, 33; DLB 15; MTCW

King, Stephen (Edwin)
1947- .... **CLC 12, 26, 37, 61**
See also AAYA 1; BEST 90:1; CA 61-64; CANR 1, 30; DLBY 80; MTCW; SATA 9, 55

King, Steve
See King, Stephen (Edwin)

Kingman, Lee .... **CLC 17**
See also Natti, (Mary) Lee
See also SAAS 3; SATA 1, 67

Kingsley, Charles 1819-1875 ..... **NCLC 35**
See also DLB 21, 32; YABC 2

Kingsley, Sidney 1906- .... **CLC 44**
See also CA 85-88; DLB 7

Kingsolver, Barbara 1955- .... **CLC 55**
See also CA 129; 134

Kingston, Maxine (Ting Ting) Hong
1940- .... **CLC 12, 19, 58**
See also AAYA 8; CA 69-72; CANR 13, 38; DLBY 80; MTCW; SATA 53

Kinnell, Galway
1927- .... **CLC 1, 2, 3, 5, 13, 29**
See also CA 9-12R; CANR 10, 34; DLB 5; DLBY 87; MTCW

Kinsella, Thomas 1928- .... **CLC 4, 19**
See also CA 17-20R; CANR 15; DLB 27; MTCW

Kinsella, W(illiam) P(atrick)
1935- .... **CLC 27, 43**
See also AAYA 7; CA 97-100; CAAS 7; CANR 21, 35; MTCW

Kipling, (Joseph) Rudyard
1865-1936 .... **TCLC 8, 17; PC 3; SSC 5**
See also CA 105; 120; CANR 33; CDBLB 1890-1914; DLB 19, 34; MAICYA; MTCW; WLC; YABC 2

Kirkup, James 1918- .... **CLC 1**
See also CA 1-4R; CAAS 4; CANR 2; DLB 27; SATA 12

Kirkwood, James 1930(?)-1989 ...... **CLC 9**
See also AITN 2; CA 1-4R; 128; CANR 6

Kis, Danilo 1935-1989 .... **CLC 57**
See also CA 109; 118; 129; MTCW

Kivi, Aleksis 1834-1872 .... **NCLC 30**

Kizer, Carolyn (Ashley) 1925- ... **CLC 15, 39**
See also CA 65-68; CAAS 5; CANR 24; DLB 5

Klabund 1890-1928 .... **TCLC 44**
See also DLB 66

Klappert, Peter 1942- .... **CLC 57**
See also CA 33-36R; DLB 5

Klein, A(braham) M(oses)
1909-1972 .... **CLC 19**
See also CA 101; 37-40R; DLB 68

Klein, Norma 1938-1989 .... **CLC 30**
See also AAYA 2; CA 41-44R; 128; CANR 15, 37; CLR 2, 19; MAICYA; SAAS 1; SATA 7, 57

Klein, T(heodore) E(ibon) D(onald)
1947- .... **CLC 34**
See also CA 119

Kleist, Heinrich von 1777-1811 .... **NCLC 2**
See also DLB 90

Klima, Ivan 1931- .... **CLC 56**
See also CA 25-28R; CANR 17

Klimentov, Andrei Platonovich 1899-1951
See Platonov, Andrei
See also CA 108

Klinger, Friedrich Maximilian von
1752-1831 .... **NCLC 1**
See also DLB 94

Klopstock, Friedrich Gottlieb
1724-1803 .... **NCLC 11**
See also DLB 97

Knebel, Fletcher 1911- .... **CLC 14**
See also AITN 1; CA 1-4R; CAAS 3; CANR 1, 36; SATA 36

Knickerbocker, Diedrich
See Irving, Washington

Knight, Etheridge 1931-1991 .... **CLC 40**
See also BLC 2; BW; CA 21-24R; 133; CANR 23; DLB 41

Knight, Sarah Kemble 1666-1727 ..... **LC 7**
See also DLB 24

Knowles, John 1926- ...... **CLC 1, 4, 10, 26**
See also CA 17-20R; CDALB 1968-1988; DLB 6; MTCW; SATA 8

Knox, Calvin M.
See Silverberg, Robert

Knye, Cassandra
See Disch, Thomas M(ichael)

Koch, C(hristopher) J(ohn) 1932- ... **CLC 42**
See also CA 127

Koch, Christopher
See Koch, C(hristopher) J(ohn)

Koch, Kenneth 1925- .... **CLC 5, 8, 44**
See also CA 1-4R; CANR 6, 36; DLB 5; SATA 65

Kochanowski, Jan 1530-1584........ **LC 10**

Kock, Charles Paul de
1794-1871 .... **NCLC 16**

Koda Shigeyuki 1867-1947
See Rohan, Koda
See also CA 121

Koestler, Arthur
1905-1983 .... **CLC 1, 3, 6, 8, 15, 33**
See also CA 1-4R; 109; CANR 1, 33; CDBLB 1945-1960; DLBY 83; MTCW

Kohout, Pavel 1928-.............. **CLC 13**
See also CA 45-48; CANR 3

Koizumi, Yakumo
See Hearn, (Patricio) Lafcadio (Tessima Carlos)

Kolmar, Gertrud 1894-1943....... **TCLC 40**

Konrad, George
See Konrad, Gyoergy

Konrad, Gyoergy 1933- .... **CLC 4, 10**
See also CA 85-88

Konwicki, Tadeusz 1926-..... **CLC 8, 28, 54**
See also CA 101; CAAS 9; CANR 39; MTCW

Kopit, Arthur (Lee) 1937- .... **CLC 1, 18, 33**
See also AITN 1; CA 81-84; CABS 3; DLB 7; MTCW

Kops, Bernard 1926-............... **CLC 4**
See also CA 5-8R; DLB 13

Kornbluth, C(yril) M. 1923-1958.... **TCLC 8**
See also CA 105; DLB 8

Korolenko, V. G.
See Korolenko, Vladimir Galaktionovich

Korolenko, Vladimir
See Korolenko, Vladimir Galaktionovich

Korolenko, Vladimir G.
See Korolenko, Vladimir Galaktionovich

Korolenko, Vladimir Galaktionovich
1853-1921 .... **TCLC 22**
See also CA 121

Kosinski, Jerzy (Nikodem)
1933-1991 ... **CLC 1, 2, 3, 6, 10, 15, 53, 70**
See also CA 17-20R; 134; CANR 9; DLB 2; DLBY 82; MTCW

Kostelanetz, Richard (Cory) 1940- .. **CLC 28**
See also CA 13-16R; CAAS 8; CANR 38

Kostrowitzki, Wilhelm Apollinaris de
1880-1918
See Apollinaire, Guillaume
See also CA 104

Kotlowitz, Robert 1924-............ **CLC 4**
See also CA 33-36R; CANR 36

Kotzebue, August (Friedrich Ferdinand) von
1761-1819 .... **NCLC 25**
See also DLB 94

Kotzwinkle, William 1938- ... **CLC 5, 14, 35**
See also CA 45-48; CANR 3; CLR 6; MAICYA; SATA 24, 70

Kozol, Jonathan 1936-............ **CLC 17**
See also CA 61-64; CANR 16

Kozoll, Michael 1940(?)- .... **CLC 35**

Kramer, Kathryn 19(?)- .... **CLC 34**

Kramer, Larry 1935- .... **CLC 42**
See also CA 124; 126

Krasicki, Ignacy 1735-1801 .... **NCLC 8**

Krasinski, Zygmunt 1812-1859 .... **NCLC 4**

Kraus, Karl 1874-1936............ **TCLC 5**
See also CA 104; DLB 118

Kreve (Mickevicius), Vincas
1882-1954 .... **TCLC 27**

Kristofferson, Kris 1936- .... **CLC 26**
See also CA 104

Krizanc, John 1956-.............. **CLC 57**

Krleza, Miroslav 1893-1981......... **CLC 8**
See also CA 97-100; 105

Kroetsch, Robert 1927- ...... **CLC 5, 23, 57**
See also CA 17-20R; CANR 8, 38; DLB 53; MTCW

Kroetz, Franz
See Kroetz, Franz Xaver

Kroetz, Franz Xaver 1946- .... **CLC 41**
See also CA 130

Kropotkin, Peter (Aleksieevich)
1842-1921 .... **TCLC 36**
See also CA 119

Krotkov, Yuri 1917-.............. **CLC 19**
See also CA 102

Krumb
See Crumb, R(obert)

Krumgold, Joseph (Quincy)
1908-1980 .... **CLC 12**
See also CA 9-12R; 101; CANR 7; MAICYA; SATA 1, 23, 48

Krumwitz
See Crumb, R(obert)

Krutch, Joseph Wood 1893-1970.... **CLC 24**
See also CA 1-4R; 25-28R; CANR 4; DLB 63

Krutzch, Gus
See Eliot, T(homas) S(tearns)

Krylov, Ivan Andreevich
1768(?)-1844 .... **NCLC 1**

Kubin, Alfred 1877-1959 .... **TCLC 23**
See also CA 112; DLB 81

Kubrick, Stanley 1928-............ **CLC 16**
See also CA 81-84; CANR 33; DLB 26

Kumin, Maxine (Winokur)
1925- .... **CLC 5, 13, 28**
See also AITN 2; CA 1-4R; CAAS 8; CANR 1, 21; DLB 5; MTCW; SATA 12

Kundera, Milan
1929- .... **CLC 4, 9, 19, 32, 68**
See also AAYA 2; CA 85-88; CANR 19; MTCW

Kunitz, Stanley (Jasspon)
1905- .... **CLC 6, 11, 14**
See also CA 41-44R; CANR 26; DLB 48; MTCW

Kunze, Reiner 1933-.............. **CLC 10**
See also CA 93-96; DLB 75

Kuprin, Aleksandr Ivanovich
1870-1938 .... **TCLC 5**
See also CA 104

Kureishi, Hanif 1954-............. **CLC 64**

Kurosawa, Akira 1910-............ **CLC 16**
See also CA 101

Kuttner, Henry 1915-1958........ **TCLC 10**
See also CA 107; DLB 8

Kuzma, Greg 1944-................ **CLC 7**
See also CA 33-36R

Kuzmin, Mikhail 1872(?)-1936 .... **TCLC 40**

Kyd, Thomas 1558-1594............. **DC 3**
See also DLB 62

Kyprianos, Iossif
See Samarakis, Antonis

La Bruyere, Jean de 1645-1696...... **LC 17**

Laclos, Pierre Ambroise Francois Choderlos de 1741-1803 .... **NCLC 4**

La Colere, Francois
See Aragon, Louis

Lacolere, Francois
See Aragon, Louis

La Deshabilleuse
See Simenon, Georges (Jacques Christian)

Lady Gregory
See Gregory, Isabella Augusta (Persse)

Lady of Quality, A
See Bagnold, Enid

La Fayette, Marie (Madelaine Pioche de la Vergne Comtes 1634-1693....... **LC 2**

Lafayette, Rene
See Hubbard, L(afayette) Ron(ald)

Laforgue, Jules 1860-1887........ **NCLC 5**

Lagerkvist, Paer (Fabian)
1891-1974 .... **CLC 7, 10, 13, 54**
See also CA 85-88; 49-52; MTCW

Lagerkvist, Par
See Lagerkvist, Paer (Fabian)

Lagerloef, Selma (Ottiliana Lovisa)
1858-1940 .... **TCLC 4, 36**
See also Lagerlof, Selma (Ottiliana Lovisa)
See also CA 108; CLR 7; SATA 15

Lagerlof, Selma (Ottiliana Lovisa)
See Lagerloef, Selma (Ottiliana Lovisa)
See also CLR 7; SATA 15

La Guma, (Justin) Alex(ander)
1925-1985 .... **CLC 19**
See also BW; CA 49-52; 118; CANR 25; DLB 117; MTCW

Laidlaw, A. K.
See Grieve, C(hristopher) M(urray)

Lainez, Manuel Mujica
See Mujica Lainez, Manuel
See also HW

Lamartine, Alphonse (Marie Louis Prat) de 1790-1869 . . . . . **NCLC 11**

Lamb, Charles 1775-1834. . . . . **NCLC 10**
See also CDBLB 1789-1832; DLB 93, 107; SATA 17; WLC

Lamb, Lady Caroline 1785-1828 . . **NCLC 38**
See also DLB 116

Lamming, George (William) 1927- . . . . . **CLC 2, 4, 66**
See also BLC 2; BW; CA 85-88; CANR 26; MTCW

L'Amour, Louis (Dearborn) 1908-1988 . . . . . **CLC 25, 55**
See also AITN 2; BEST 89:2; CA 1-4R; 125; CANR 3, 25; DLBY 80; MTCW

Lampedusa, Giuseppe (Tomasi) di . . . **TCLC 13**
See also Tomasi di Lampedusa, Giuseppe

Lampman, Archibald 1861-1899 . . **NCLC 25**
See also DLB 92

Lancaster, Bruce 1896-1963. . . . . **CLC 36**
See also CA 9-10; CAP 1; SATA 9

Landau, Mark Alexandrovich
See Aldanov, Mark (Alexandrovich)

Landau-Aldanov, Mark Alexandrovich
See Aldanov, Mark (Alexandrovich)

Landis, John 1950- . . . . . **CLC 26**
See also CA 112; 122

Landolfi, Tommaso 1908-1979 . . . **CLC 11, 49**
See also CA 127; 117

Landon, Letitia Elizabeth 1802-1838 . . . . . **NCLC 15**
See also DLB 96

Landor, Walter Savage 1775-1864 . . . . . **NCLC 14**
See also DLB 93, 107

Landwirth, Heinz 1927-
See Lind, Jakov
See also CA 9-12R; CANR 7

Lane, Patrick 1939- . . . . . **CLC 25**
See also CA 97-100; DLB 53

Lang, Andrew 1844-1912 . . . . . **TCLC 16**
See also CA 114; 137; DLB 98; MAICYA; SATA 16

Lang, Fritz 1890-1976 . . . . . **CLC 20**
See also CA 77-80; 69-72; CANR 30

Lange, John
See Crichton, (John) Michael

Langer, Elinor 1939- . . . . . **CLC 34**
See also CA 121

Langland, William 1330(?)-1400(?) . . . **LC 19**

Langstaff, Launcelot
See Irving, Washington

Lanier, Sidney 1842-1881 . . . . . **NCLC 6**
See also DLB 64; MAICYA; SATA 18

Lanyer, Aemilia 1569-1645 . . . . . **LC 10**

Lao Tzu . . . . . **CMLC 7**

Lapine, James (Elliot) 1949- . . . . . **CLC 39**
See also CA 123; 130

Larbaud, Valery (Nicolas) 1881-1957 . . . . . **TCLC 9**
See also CA 106

Lardner, Ring
See Lardner, Ring(gold) W(ilmer)

Lardner, Ring W. Jr.
See Lardner, Ring(gold) W(ilmer)

Lardner, Ring(gold) W(ilmer) 1885-1933 . . . . . **TCLC 2, 14**
See also CA 104; 131; CDALB 1917-1929; DLB 11, 25, 86; MTCW

Laredo, Betty
See Codrescu, Andrei

Larkin, Maia
See Wojciechowska, Maia (Teresa)

Larkin, Philip (Arthur) 1922-1985 . . . **CLC 3, 5, 8, 9, 13, 18, 33, 39, 64**
See also CA 5-8R; 117; CANR 24; CDBLB 1960 to Present; DLB 27; MTCW

Larra (y Sanchez de Castro), Mariano Jose de 1809-1837 . . . . . **NCLC 17**

Larsen, Eric 1941- . . . . . **CLC 55**
See also CA 132

Larsen, Nella 1891-1964 . . . . . **CLC 37**
See also BLC 2; BW; CA 125; DLB 51

Larson, Charles R(aymond) 1938- . . . **CLC 31**
See also CA 53-56; CANR 4

Latham, Jean Lee 1902- . . . . . **CLC 12**
See also AITN 1; CA 5-8R; CANR 7; MAICYA; SATA 2, 68

Latham, Mavis
See Clark, Mavis Thorpe

Lathen, Emma . . . . . **CLC 2**
See also Hennissart, Martha; Latsis, Mary J(ane)

Lathrop, Francis
See Leiber, Fritz (Reuter Jr.)

Latsis, Mary J(ane)
See Lathen, Emma
See also CA 85-88

Lattimore, Richmond (Alexander) 1906-1984 . . . . . **CLC 3**
See also CA 1-4R; 112; CANR 1

Laughlin, James 1914- . . . . . **CLC 49**
See also CA 21-24R; CANR 9; DLB 48

Laurence, (Jean) Margaret (Wemyss) 1926-1987 . . **CLC 3, 6, 13, 50, 62; SSC 7**
See also CA 5-8R; 121; CANR 33; DLB 53; MTCW; SATA 50

Laurent, Antoine 1952- . . . . . **CLC 50**

Lauscher, Hermann
See Hesse, Hermann

Lautreamont, Comte de 1846-1870 . . . . . **NCLC 12**

Laverty, Donald
See Blish, James (Benjamin)

Lavin, Mary 1912- . . . . . **CLC 4, 18; SSC 4**
See also CA 9-12R; CANR 33; DLB 15; MTCW

Lavond, Paul Dennis
See Kornbluth, C(yril) M.; Pohl, Frederik

Lawler, Raymond Evenor 1922- . . . . **CLC 58**
See also CA 103

Lawrence, D(avid) H(erbert Richards) 1885-1930 . . . . . **TCLC 2, 9, 16, 33, 48; SSC 4**
See also CA 104; 121; CDBLB 1914-1945; DLB 10, 19, 36, 98; MTCW; WLC

Lawrence, T(homas) E(dward) 1888-1935 . . . . . **TCLC 18**
See also Dale, Colin
See also CA 115

Lawrence Of Arabia
See Lawrence, T(homas) E(dward)

Lawson, Henry (Archibald Hertzberg) 1867-1922 . . . . . **TCLC 27**
See also CA 120

Laxness, Halldor . . . . . **CLC 25**
See also Gudjonsson, Halldor Kiljan

Layamon fl. c. 1200- . . . . . **CMLC 10**

Laye, Camara 1928-1980 . . . . . **CLC 4, 38**
See also BLC 2; BW; CA 85-88; 97-100; CANR 25; MTCW

Layton, Irving (Peter) 1912- . . . . . **CLC 2, 15**
See also CA 1-4R; CANR 2, 33; DLB 88; MTCW

Lazarus, Emma 1849-1887. . . . . **NCLC 8**

Lazarus, Felix
See Cable, George Washington

Lea, Joan
See Neufeld, John (Arthur)

Leacock, Stephen (Butler) 1869-1944 . . . . . **TCLC 2**
See also CA 104; DLB 92

Lear, Edward 1812-1888 . . . . . **NCLC 3**
See also CLR 1; DLB 32; MAICYA; SATA 18

Lear, Norman (Milton) 1922- . . . . . **CLC 12**
See also CA 73-76

Leavis, F(rank) R(aymond) 1895-1978 . . . . . **CLC 24**
See also CA 21-24R; 77-80; MTCW

Leavitt, David 1961- . . . . . **CLC 34**
See also CA 116; 122

Lebowitz, Fran(ces Ann) 1951(?)- . . . . . **CLC 11, 36**
See also CA 81-84; CANR 14; MTCW

le Carre, John . . . . . **CLC 3, 5, 9, 15, 28**
See also Cornwell, David (John Moore)
See also BEST 89:4; CDBLB 1960 to Present; DLB 87

Le Clezio, J(ean) M(arie) G(ustave) 1940- . . . . . **CLC 31**
See also CA 116; 128; DLB 83

Leconte de Lisle, Charles-Marie-Rene 1818-1894 . . . . . **NCLC 29**

Le Coq, Monsieur
See Simenon, Georges (Jacques Christian)

Leduc, Violette 1907-1972. . . . . **CLC 22**
See also CA 13-14; 33-36R; CAP 1

Ledwidge, Francis 1887(?)-1917 . . . **TCLC 23**
See also CA 123; DLB 20

Lee, Andrea 1953- . . . . . **CLC 36**
See also BLC 2; BW; CA 125

Lee, Andrew
See Auchincloss, Louis (Stanton)

Lee, Don L. . . . . **CLC 2**
See also Madhubuti, Haki R.

Lee, George W(ashington)
1894-1976 . . . . **CLC 52**
See also BLC 2; BW; CA 125; DLB 51

Lee, (Nelle) Harper 1926- . . . . . . **CLC 12, 60**
See also CA 13-16R; CDALB 1941-1968; DLB 6; MTCW; SATA 11; WLC

Lee, Julian
See Latham, Jean Lee

Lee, Lawrence 1903- . . . . **CLC 34**
See also CA 25-28R

Lee, Manfred B(ennington)
1905-1971 . . . . **CLC 11**
See also Queen, Ellery
See also CA 1-4R; 29-32R; CANR 2

Lee, Stan 1922-. . . . . **CLC 17**
See also AAYA 5; CA 108; 111

Lee, Tanith 1947-. . . . . **CLC 46**
See also CA 37-40R; SATA 8

Lee, Vernon . . . . **TCLC 5**
See also Paget, Violet
See also DLB 57

Lee, William
See Burroughs, William S(eward)

Lee, Willy
See Burroughs, William S(eward)

Lee-Hamilton, Eugene (Jacob)
1845-1907 . . . . **TCLC 22**
See also CA 117

Leet, Judith 1935- . . . . **CLC 11**

Le Fanu, Joseph Sheridan
1814-1873 . . . . **NCLC 9**
See also DLB 21, 70

Leffland, Ella 1931- . . . . **CLC 19**
See also CA 29-32R; CANR 35; DLBY 84; SATA 65

Leger, (Marie-Rene) Alexis Saint-Leger
1887-1975 . . . . **CLC 11**
See also Perse, St.-John
See also CA 13-16R; 61-64; MTCW

Leger, Saintleger
See Leger, (Marie-Rene) Alexis Saint-Leger

Le Guin, Ursula K(roeber)
1929- . . . . **CLC 8, 13, 22, 45, 71**
See also AAYA 9; AITN 1; CA 21-24R; CANR 9, 32; CDALB 1968-1988; CLR 3, 28; DLB 8, 52; MAICYA; MTCW; SATA 4, 52

Lehmann, Rosamond (Nina)
1901-1990 . . . . **CLC 5**
See also CA 77-80; 131; CANR 8; DLB 15

Leiber, Fritz (Reuter Jr.) 1910- . . . . **CLC 25**
See also CA 45-48; CANR 2; DLB 8; MTCW; SATA 45

Leimbach, Martha 1963-
See Leimbach, Marti
See also CA 130

Leimbach, Marti . . . . **CLC 65**
See also Leimbach, Martha

Leino, Eino . . . . **TCLC 24**
See also Loennbohm, Armas Eino Leopold

Leiris, Michel (Julien) 1901-1990 . . . **CLC 61**
See also CA 119; 128; 132

Leithauser, Brad 1953-. . . . . **CLC 27**
See also CA 107; CANR 27; DLB 120

Lelchuk, Alan 1938-. . . . . **CLC 5**
See also CA 45-48; CANR 1

Lem, Stanislaw 1921-. . . . . **CLC 8, 15, 40**
See also CA 105; CAAS 1; CANR 32; MTCW

Lemann, Nancy 1956-. . . . . **CLC 39**
See also CA 118; 136

Lemonnier, (Antoine Louis) Camille
1844-1913 . . . . **TCLC 22**
See also CA 121

Lenau, Nikolaus 1802-1850 . . . . . . **NCLC 16**

L'Engle, Madeleine (Camp Franklin)
1918- . . . . **CLC 12**
See also AAYA 1; AITN 2; CA 1-4R; CANR 3, 21, 39; CLR 1, 14; DLB 52; MAICYA; MTCW; SATA 1, 27

Lengyel, Jozsef 1896-1975. . . . . **CLC 7**
See also CA 85-88; 57-60

Lennon, John (Ono)
1940-1980 . . . . **CLC 12, 35**
See also CA 102

Lennox, Charlotte Ramsay
1729(?)-1804 . . . . **NCLC 23**
See also DLB 39

Lentricchia, Frank (Jr.) 1940-. . . . . . **CLC 34**
See also CA 25-28R; CANR 19

Lenz, Siegfried 1926-. . . . . **CLC 27**
See also CA 89-92; DLB 75

Leonard, Elmore (John Jr.)
1925- . . . . **CLC 28, 34, 71**
See also AITN 1; BEST 89:1, 90:4; CA 81-84; CANR 12, 28; MTCW

Leonard, Hugh
See Byrne, John Keyes
See also DLB 13

Leopardi, (Conte) Giacomo (Talegardo Francesco di Sales Save
1798-1837 . . . . **NCLC 22**

Le Reveler
See Artaud, Antonin

Lerman, Eleanor 1952-. . . . . **CLC 9**
See also CA 85-88

Lerman, Rhoda 1936-. . . . . **CLC 56**
See also CA 49-52

Lermontov, Mikhail Yuryevich
1814-1841 . . . . **NCLC 5**

Leroux, Gaston 1868-1927. . . . . **TCLC 25**
See also CA 108; 136; SATA 65

Lesage, Alain-Rene 1668-1747. . . . . **LC 2**

Leskov, Nikolai (Semyonovich)
1831-1895 . . . . **NCLC 25**

Lessing, Doris (May)
1919- . . . . **CLC 1, 2, 3, 6, 10, 15, 22, 40; SSC 6**
See also CA 9-12R; CAAS 14; CANR 33; CDBLB 1960 to Present; DLB 15; DLBY 85; MTCW

Lessing, Gotthold Ephraim
1729-1781 . . . . **LC 8**
See also DLB 97

Lester, Richard 1932-. . . . . **CLC 20**

Lever, Charles (James)
1806-1872 . . . . **NCLC 23**
See also DLB 21

Leverson, Ada 1865(?)-1936(?) . . . . **TCLC 18**
See also Elaine
See also CA 117

Levertov, Denise
1923- . . . . . . **CLC 1, 2, 3, 5, 8, 15, 28, 66**
See also CA 1-4R; CANR 3, 29; DLB 5; MTCW

Levi, Peter (Chad Tigar) 1931- . . . . . **CLC 41**
See also CA 5-8R; CANR 34; DLB 40

Levi, Primo 1919-1987. . . . . **CLC 37, 50**
See also CA 13-16R; 122; CANR 12, 33; MTCW

Levin, Ira 1929- . . . . **CLC 3, 6**
See also CA 21-24R; CANR 17; MTCW; SATA 66

Levin, Meyer 1905-1981 . . . . **CLC 7**
See also AITN 1; CA 9-12R; 104; CANR 15; DLB 9, 28; DLBY 81; SATA 21, 27

Levine, Norman 1924- . . . . **CLC 54**
See also CA 73-76; CANR 14; DLB 88

Levine, Philip 1928-. . **CLC 2, 4, 5, 9, 14, 33**
See also CA 9-12R; CANR 9, 37; DLB 5

Levinson, Deirdre 1931-. . . . . **CLC 49**
See also CA 73-76

Levi-Strauss, Claude 1908- . . . . **CLC 38**
See also CA 1-4R; CANR 6, 32; MTCW

Levitin, Sonia (Wolff) 1934- . . . . **CLC 17**
See also CA 29-32R; CANR 14, 32; MAICYA; SAAS 2; SATA 4, 68

Levon, O. U.
See Kesey, Ken (Elton)

Lewes, George Henry
1817-1878 . . . . **NCLC 25**
See also DLB 55

Lewis, Alun 1915-1944. . . . . **TCLC 3**
See also CA 104; DLB 20

Lewis, C. Day
See Day Lewis, C(ecil)

Lewis, C(live) S(taples)
1898-1963 . . . . **CLC 1, 3, 6, 14, 27**
See also AAYA 3; CA 81-84; CANR 33; CDBLB 1945-1960; CLR 3, 27; DLB 15, 100; MAICYA; MTCW; SATA 13; WLC

Lewis, Janet 1899-. . . . . **CLC 41**
See also Winters, Janet Lewis
See also CA 9-12R; CANR 29; CAP 1; DLBY 87

Lewis, Matthew Gregory
1775-1818 . . . . **NCLC 11**
See also DLB 39

Lewis, (Harry) Sinclair
1885-1951 . . . . **TCLC 4, 13, 23, 39**
See also CA 104; 133; CDALB 1917-1929; DLB 9, 102; DLBD 1; MTCW; WLC

Lewis, (Percy) Wyndham
1884(?)-1957 . . . . **TCLC 2, 9**
See also CA 104; DLB 15

Lewisohn, Ludwig 1883-1955. . . . . . **TCLC 19**
See also CA 107; DLB 4, 9, 28, 102

Lezama Lima, Jose 1910-1976 . . . **CLC 4, 10**
See also CA 77-80; DLB 113; HW

L'Heureux, John (Clarke) 1934- . . . . **CLC 52**
See also CA 13-16R; CANR 23

Liddell, C. H.
See Kuttner, Henry

Lie, Jonas (Lauritz Idemil) 1833-1908(?) . . . . **TCLC 5**
See also CA 115

Lieber, Joel 1937-1971 . . . . **CLC 6**
See also CA 73-76; 29-32R

Lieber, Stanley Martin
See Lee, Stan

Lieberman, Laurence (James) 1935- . . . . **CLC 4, 36**
See also CA 17-20R; CANR 8, 36

Lieksman, Anders
See Haavikko, Paavo Juhani

Li Fei-kan 1904- . . . . **CLC 18**
See also CA 105

Lifton, Robert Jay 1926- . . . . **CLC 67**
See also CA 17-20R; CANR 27; SATA 66

Lightfoot, Gordon 1938- . . . . **CLC 26**
See also CA 109

Ligotti, Thomas 1953- . . . . **CLC 44**
See also CA 123

Liliencron, (Friedrich Adolf Axel) Detlev von 1844-1909 . . . . **TCLC 18**
See also CA 117

Lima, Jose Lezama
See Lezama Lima, Jose

Lima Barreto, Afonso Henrique de 1881-1922 . . . . **TCLC 23**
See also CA 117

Limonov, Eduard . . . . **CLC 67**

Lin, Frank
See Atherton, Gertrude (Franklin Horn)

Lincoln, Abraham 1809-1865 . . . . . **NCLC 18**

Lind, Jakov . . . . **CLC 1, 2, 4, 27**
See also Landwirth, Heinz
See also CAAS 4

Lindsay, David 1878-1945 . . . . **TCLC 15**
See also CA 113

Lindsay, (Nicholas) Vachel 1879-1931 . . . . **TCLC 17**
See also CA 114; 135; CDALB 1865-1917; DLB 54; SATA 40; WLC

Linke-Poot
See Doeblin, Alfred

Linney, Romulus 1930- . . . . **CLC 51**
See also CA 1-4R

Li Po 701-763 . . . . **CMLC 2**

Lipsius, Justus 1547-1606 . . . . **LC 16**

Lipsyte, Robert (Michael) 1938- . . . . **CLC 21**
See also AAYA 7; CA 17-20R; CANR 8; CLR 23; MAICYA; SATA 5, 68

Lish, Gordon (Jay) 1934- . . . . **CLC 45**
See also CA 113; 117

Lispector, Clarice 1925-1977 . . . . **CLC 43**
See also CA 116; DLB 113

Littell, Robert 1935(?)- . . . . **CLC 42**
See also CA 109; 112

Littlewit, Humphrey Gent.
See Lovecraft, H(oward) P(hillips)

Litwos
See Sienkiewicz, Henryk (Adam Alexander Pius)

Liu E 1857-1909 . . . . **TCLC 15**
See also CA 115

Lively, Penelope (Margaret) 1933- . . . . **CLC 32, 50**
See also CA 41-44R; CANR 29; CLR 7; DLB 14; MAICYA; MTCW; SATA 7, 60

Livesay, Dorothy (Kathleen) 1909- . . . . **CLC 4, 15**
See also AITN 2; CA 25-28R; CAAS 8; CANR 36; DLB 68; MTCW

Lizardi, Jose Joaquin Fernandez de 1776-1827 . . . . **NCLC 30**

Llewellyn, Richard . . . . **CLC 7**
See also Llewellyn Lloyd, Richard Dafydd Vivian
See also DLB 15

Llewellyn Lloyd, Richard Dafydd Vivian 1906-1983
See Llewellyn, Richard
See also CA 53-56; 111; CANR 7; SATA 11, 37

Llosa, (Jorge) Mario (Pedro) Vargas
See Vargas Llosa, (Jorge) Mario (Pedro)

Lloyd Webber, Andrew 1948-
See Webber, Andrew Lloyd
See also AAYA 1; CA 116; SATA 56

Locke, Alain (Le Roy) 1886-1954 . . . . **TCLC 43**
See also BW; CA 106; 124; DLB 51

Locke, John 1632-1704 . . . . **LC 7**
See also DLB 101

Locke-Elliott, Sumner
See Elliott, Sumner Locke

Lockhart, John Gibson 1794-1854 . . . . **NCLC 6**
See also DLB 110, 116

Lodge, David (John) 1935- . . . . **CLC 36**
See also BEST 90:1; CA 17-20R; CANR 19; DLB 14; MTCW

Loennbohm, Armas Eino Leopold 1878-1926
See Leino, Eino
See also CA 123

Loewinsohn, Ron(ald William) 1937- . . . . **CLC 52**
See also CA 25-28R

Logan, Jake
See Smith, Martin Cruz

Logan, John (Burton) 1923-1987 . . . . . **CLC 5**
See also CA 77-80; 124; DLB 5

Lo Kuan-chung 1330(?)-1400(?) . . . . . . **LC 12**

Lombard, Nap
See Johnson, Pamela Hansford

London, Jack . . . . **TCLC 9, 15, 39; SSC 4**
See also London, John Griffith
See also AITN 2; CDALB 1865-1917; DLB 8, 12, 78; SATA 18; WLC

London, John Griffith 1876-1916
See London, Jack
See also CA 110; 119; MAICYA; MTCW

Long, Emmett
See Leonard, Elmore (John Jr.)

Longbaugh, Harry
See Goldman, William (W.)

Longfellow, Henry Wadsworth 1807-1882 . . . . **NCLC 2**
See also CDALB 1640-1865; DLB 1, 59; SATA 19

Longley, Michael 1939- . . . . **CLC 29**
See also CA 102; DLB 40

Longus fl. c. 2nd cent. - . . . . **CMLC 7**

Longway, A. Hugh
See Lang, Andrew

Lopate, Phillip 1943- . . . . **CLC 29**
See also CA 97-100; DLBY 80

Lopez Portillo (y Pacheco), Jose 1920- . . . . **CLC 46**
See also CA 129; HW

Lopez y Fuentes, Gregorio 1897(?)-1966 . . . . **CLC 32**
See also CA 131; HW

Lorca, Federico Garcia
See Garcia Lorca, Federico

Lord, Bette Bao 1938- . . . . **CLC 23**
See also BEST 90:3; CA 107; SATA 58

Lord Auch
See Bataille, Georges

Lord Byron
See Byron, George Gordon (Noel)

Lord Dunsany . . . . **TCLC 2**
See also Dunsany, Edward John Moreton Drax Plunkett

Lorde, Audre (Geraldine) 1934- . . . . **CLC 18, 71**
See also BLC 2; BW; CA 25-28R; CANR 16, 26; DLB 41; MTCW

Lord Jeffrey
See Jeffrey, Francis

Lorenzo, Heberto Padilla
See Padilla (Lorenzo), Heberto

Loris
See Hofmannsthal, Hugo von

Loti, Pierre . . . . **TCLC 11**
See also Viaud, (Louis Marie) Julien

Louie, David Wong 1954- . . . . **CLC 70**

Louis, Father M.
See Merton, Thomas

Lovecraft, H(oward) P(hillips) 1890-1937 . . . . **TCLC 4, 22; SSC 3**
See also CA 104; 133; MTCW

Lovelace, Earl 1935- . . . . **CLC 51**
See also CA 77-80; MTCW

Lowell, Amy 1874-1925 . . . . **TCLC 1, 8**
See also CA 104; DLB 54

Lowell, James Russell 1819-1891 . . **NCLC 2**
See also CDALB 1640-1865; DLB 1, 11, 64, 79

Lowell, Robert (Traill Spence Jr.) 1917-1977 . . . **CLC 1, 2, 3, 4, 5, 8, 9, 11, 15, 37; PC 3**
See also CA 9-12R; 73-76; CABS 2; CANR 26; DLB 5; MTCW; WLC

Lowndes, Marie Adelaide (Belloc) 1868-1947 .... **TCLC 12**
See also CA 107; DLB 70

Lowry, (Clarence) Malcolm 1909-1957 .... **TCLC 6, 40**
See also CA 105; 131; CDBLB 1945-1960; DLB 15; MTCW

Lowry, Mina Gertrude 1882-1966
See Loy, Mina
See also CA 113

Loxsmith, John
See Brunner, John (Kilian Houston)

Loy, Mina .... **CLC 28**
See also Lowry, Mina Gertrude
See also DLB 4, 54

Loyson-Bridet
See Schwob, (Mayer Andre) Marcel

Lucas, Craig 1951- .... **CLC 64**
See also CA 137

Lucas, George 1944- .... **CLC 16**
See also AAYA 1; CA 77-80; CANR 30; SATA 56

Lucas, Hans
See Godard, Jean-Luc

Lucas, Victoria
See Plath, Sylvia

Ludlam, Charles 1943-1987 ..... **CLC 46, 50**
See also CA 85-88; 122

Ludlum, Robert 1927- .... **CLC 22, 43**
See also BEST 89:1, 90:3; CA 33-36R; CANR 25; DLBY 82; MTCW

Ludwig, Ken .... **CLC 60**

Ludwig, Otto 1813-1865 .... **NCLC 4**

Lugones, Leopoldo 1874-1938 ..... **TCLC 15**
See also CA 116; 131; HW

Lu Hsun 1881-1936 .... **TCLC 3**

Lukacs, George .... **CLC 24**
See also Lukacs, Gyorgy (Szegeny von)

Lukacs, Gyorgy (Szegeny von) 1885-1971
See Lukacs, George
See also CA 101; 29-32R

Luke, Peter (Ambrose Cyprian) 1919- .... **CLC 38**
See also CA 81-84; DLB 13

Lunar, Dennis
See Mungo, Raymond

Lurie, Alison 1926- .... **CLC 4, 5, 18, 39**
See also CA 1-4R; CANR 2, 17; DLB 2; MTCW; SATA 46

Lustig, Arnost 1926- .... **CLC 56**
See also AAYA 3; CA 69-72; SATA 56

Luther, Martin 1483-1546 .... **LC 9**

Luzi, Mario 1914- .... **CLC 13**
See also CA 61-64; CANR 9

Lynch, B. Suarez
See Bioy Casares, Adolfo; Borges, Jorge Luis

Lynch, David (K.) 1946- .... **CLC 66**
See also CA 124; 129

Lynch, James
See Andreyev, Leonid (Nikolaevich)

Lynch Davis, B.
See Bioy Casares, Adolfo; Borges, Jorge Luis

Lyndsay, SirDavid 1490-1555 .... **LC 20**

Lynn, Kenneth S(chuyler) 1923- .... **CLC 50**
See also CA 1-4R; CANR 3, 27

Lynx
See West, Rebecca

Lyons, Marcus
See Blish, James (Benjamin)

Lyre, Pinchbeck
See Sassoon, Siegfried (Lorraine)

Lytle, Andrew (Nelson) 1902- ...... **CLC 22**
See also CA 9-12R; DLB 6

Lyttelton, George 1709-1773 .... **LC 10**

Maas, Peter 1929- .... **CLC 29**
See also CA 93-96

Macaulay, Rose 1881-1958 ..... **TCLC 7, 44**
See also CA 104; DLB 36

MacBeth, George (Mann) 1932-1992 .... **CLC 2, 5, 9**
See also CA 25-28R; 136; DLB 40; MTCW; SATA 4; SATO 70

MacCaig, Norman (Alexander) 1910- .... **CLC 36**
See also CA 9-12R; CANR 3, 34; DLB 27

MacCarthy, (Sir Charles Otto) Desmond 1877-1952 .... **TCLC 36**

MacDiarmid, Hugh ..... **CLC 2, 4, 11, 19, 63**
See also Grieve, C(hristopher) M(urray)
See also CDBLB 1945-1960; DLB 20

MacDonald, Anson
See Heinlein, Robert A(nson)

Macdonald, Cynthia 1928- ...... **CLC 13, 19**
See also CA 49-52; CANR 4; DLB 105

MacDonald, George 1824-1905 ..... **TCLC 9**
See also CA 106; 137; DLB 18; MAICYA; SATA 33

Macdonald, John
See Millar, Kenneth

MacDonald, John D(ann) 1916-1986 .... **CLC 3, 27, 44**
See also CA 1-4R; 121; CANR 1, 19; DLB 8; DLBY 86; MTCW

Macdonald, John Ross
See Millar, Kenneth

Macdonald, Ross ..... **CLC 1, 2, 3, 14, 34, 41**
See also Millar, Kenneth
See also DLBD 6

MacDougal, John
See Blish, James (Benjamin)

MacEwen, Gwendolyn (Margaret) 1941-1987 .... **CLC 13, 55**
See also CA 9-12R; 124; CANR 7, 22; DLB 53; SATA 50, 55

Machado (y Ruiz), Antonio 1875-1939 .... **TCLC 3**
See also CA 104; DLB 108

Machado de Assis, Joaquim Maria 1839-1908 .... **TCLC 10**
See also BLC 2; CA 107

Machen, Arthur .... **TCLC 4**
See also Jones, Arthur Llewellyn
See also DLB 36

Machiavelli, Niccolo 1469-1527 ...... **LC 8**

MacInnes, Colin 1914-1976 ...... **CLC 4, 23**
See also CA 69-72; 65-68; CANR 21; DLB 14; MTCW

MacInnes, Helen (Clark) 1907-1985 .... **CLC 27, 39**
See also CA 1-4R; 117; CANR 1, 28; DLB 87; MTCW; SATA 22, 44

Mackenzie, Compton (Edward Montague) 1883-1972 .... **CLC 18**
See also CA 21-22; 37-40R; CAP 2; DLB 34, 100

Mackintosh, Elizabeth 1896(?)-1952
See Tey, Josephine
See also CA 110

MacLaren, James
See Grieve, C(hristopher) M(urray)

Mac Laverty, Bernard 1942- .... **CLC 31**
See also CA 116; 118

MacLean, Alistair (Stuart) 1922-1987 .... **CLC 3, 13, 50, 63**
See also CA 57-60; 121; CANR 28; MTCW; SATA 23, 50

MacLeish, Archibald 1892-1982 .... **CLC 3, 8, 14, 68**
See also CA 9-12R; 106; CANR 33; DLB 4, 7, 45; DLBY 82; MTCW

MacLennan, (John) Hugh 1907- .... **CLC 2, 14**
See also CA 5-8R; CANR 33; DLB 68; MTCW

MacLeod, Alistair 1936- .... **CLC 56**
See also CA 123; DLB 60

MacNeice, (Frederick) Louis 1907-1963 .... **CLC 1, 4, 10, 53**
See also CA 85-88; DLB 10, 20; MTCW

MacNeill, Dand
See Fraser, George MacDonald

Macpherson, (Jean) Jay 1931- ..... **CLC 14**
See also CA 5-8R; DLB 53

MacShane, Frank 1927- .... **CLC 39**
See also CA 9-12R; CANR 3, 33; DLB 111

Macumber, Mari
See Sandoz, Mari(e Susette)

Madach, Imre 1823-1864 .... **NCLC 19**

Madden, (Jerry) David 1933- .... **CLC 5, 15**
See also CA 1-4R; CAAS 3; CANR 4; DLB 6; MTCW

Maddern, Al(an)
See Ellison, Harlan

Madhubuti, Haki R. 1942- .... **CLC 6; PC 5**
See also Lee, Don L.
See also BLC 2; BW; CA 73-76; CANR 24; DLB 5, 41; DLBD 8

Madow, Pauline (Reichberg) .... **CLC 1**
See also CA 9-12R

Maepenn, Hugh
See Kuttner, Henry

Maepenn, K. H.
See Kuttner, Henry

Maeterlinck, Maurice 1862-1949 ... **TCLC 3**
See also CA 104; 136; SATA 66

Maginn, William 1794-1842 .... **NCLC 8**
See also DLB 110

Mahapatra, Jayanta 1928- . . . . **CLC 33**
See also CA 73-76; CAAS 9; CANR 15, 33

Mahfouz, Naguib (Abdel Aziz Al-Sabilgi) 1911(?)-
See Mahfuz, Najib
See also BEST 89:2; CA 128; MTCW

Mahfuz, Najib . . . . **CLC 52, 55**
See also Mahfouz, Naguib (Abdel Aziz Al-Sabilgi)
See also DLBY 88

Mahon, Derek 1941- . . . . **CLC 27**
See also CA 113; 128; DLB 40

Mailer, Norman 1923- . . . . . . **CLC 1, 2, 3, 4, 5, 8, 11, 14, 28, 39, 74**
See also AITN 2; CA 9-12R; CABS 1; CANR 28; CDALB 1968-1988; DLB 2, 16, 28; DLBD 3; DLBY 80, 83; MTCW

Maillet, Antonine 1929- . . . . **CLC 54**
See also CA 115; 120; DLB 60

Mais, Roger 1905-1955 . . . . **TCLC 8**
See also BW; CA 105; 124; MTCW

Maitland, Sara (Louise) 1950- . . . . . . **CLC 49**
See also CA 69-72; CANR 13

Major, Clarence 1936- . . . . **CLC 3, 19, 48**
See also BLC 2; BW; CA 21-24R; CAAS 6; CANR 13, 25; DLB 33

Major, Kevin (Gerald) 1949- . . . . **CLC 26**
See also CA 97-100; CANR 21, 38; CLR 11; DLB 60; MAICYA; SATA 32

Maki, James
See Ozu, Yasujiro

Malabaila, Damiano
See Levi, Primo

Malamud, Bernard 1914-1986 . . . . . **CLC 1, 2, 3, 5, 8, 9, 11, 18, 27, 44**
See also CA 5-8R; 118; CABS 1; CANR 28; CDALB 1941-1968; DLB 2, 28; DLBY 80, 86; MTCW; WLC

Malcolm, Dan
See Silverberg, Robert

Malherbe, Francois de 1555-1628 . . . . . **LC 5**

Mallarme, Stephane 1842-1898 . . . . **NCLC 4; PC 4**

Mallet-Joris, Francoise 1930- . . . . . . **CLC 11**
See also CA 65-68; CANR 17; DLB 83

Malley, Ern
See McAuley, James Phillip

Mallowan, Agatha Christie
See Christie, Agatha (Mary Clarissa)

Maloff, Saul 1922- . . . . **CLC 5**
See also CA 33-36R

Malone, Louis
See MacNeice, (Frederick) Louis

Malone, Michael (Christopher) 1942- . . . . **CLC 43**
See also CA 77-80; CANR 14, 32

Malory, (Sir) Thomas 1410(?)-1471(?) . . . . **LC 11**
See also CDBLB Before 1660; SATA 33, 59

Malouf, (George Joseph) David 1934- . . . . **CLC 28**
See also CA 124

Malraux, (Georges-)Andre 1901-1976 . . . . . . **CLC 1, 4, 9, 13, 15, 57**
See also CA 21-22; 69-72; CANR 34; CAP 2; DLB 72; MTCW

Malzberg, Barry N(athaniel) 1939- . . . **CLC 7**
See also CA 61-64; CAAS 4; CANR 16; DLB 8

Mamet, David (Alan) 1947- . . . . **CLC 9, 15, 34, 46**
See also AAYA 3; CA 81-84; CABS 3; CANR 15; DLB 7; MTCW

Mamoulian, Rouben (Zachary) 1897-1987 . . . . **CLC 16**
See also CA 25-28R; 124

Mandelstam, Osip (Emilievich) 1891(?)-1938(?) . . . . **TCLC 2, 6**
See also CA 104

Mander, (Mary) Jane 1877-1949 . . . **TCLC 31**

Mandiargues, Andre Pieyre de . . . . **CLC 41**
See also Pieyre de Mandiargues, Andre
See also DLB 83

Mandrake, Ethel Belle
See Thurman, Wallace (Henry)

Mangan, James Clarence 1803-1849 . . . . **NCLC 27**

Maniere, J.-E.
See Giraudoux, (Hippolyte) Jean

Manley, (Mary) Delariviere 1672(?)-1724 . . . . **LC 1**
See also DLB 39, 80

Mann, Abel
See Creasey, John

Mann, (Luiz) Heinrich 1871-1950 . . . **TCLC 9**
See also CA 106; DLB 66

Mann, (Paul) Thomas 1875-1955 . . . **TCLC 2, 8, 14, 21, 35, 44; SSC 5**
See also CA 104; 128; DLB 66; MTCW; WLC

Manning, Frederic 1887(?)-1935 . . . **TCLC 25**
See also CA 124

Manning, Olivia 1915-1980 . . . . . . **CLC 5, 19**
See also CA 5-8R; 101; CANR 29; MTCW

Mano, D. Keith 1942- . . . . **CLC 2, 10**
See also CA 25-28R; CAAS 6; CANR 26; DLB 6

Mansfield, Katherine . . . **TCLC 2, 8, 39; SSC 9**
See also Beauchamp, Kathleen Mansfield
See also WLC

Manso, Peter 1940- . . . . **CLC 39**
See also CA 29-32R

Mantecon, Juan Jimenez
See Jimenez (Mantecon), Juan Ramon

Manton, Peter
See Creasey, John

Man Without a Spleen, A
See Chekhov, Anton (Pavlovich)

Manzoni, Alessandro 1785-1873 . . **NCLC 29**

Mapu, Abraham (ben Jekutiel) 1808-1867 . . . . **NCLC 18**

Mara, Sally
See Queneau, Raymond

Marat, Jean Paul 1743-1793 . . . . **LC 10**

Marcel, Gabriel Honore 1889-1973 . . . . **CLC 15**
See also CA 102; 45-48; MTCW

Marchbanks, Samuel
See Davies, (William) Robertson

Marchi, Giacomo
See Bassani, Giorgio

Marie de France c. 12th cent. - . . . . **CMLC 8**

Marie de l'Incarnation 1599-1672 . . . . **LC 10**

Mariner, Scott
See Pohl, Frederik

Marinetti, Filippo Tommaso 1876-1944 . . . . **TCLC 10**
See also CA 107; DLB 114

Marivaux, Pierre Carlet de Chamblain de 1688-1763 . . . . **LC 4**

Markandaya, Kamala . . . . **CLC 8, 38**
See also Taylor, Kamala (Purnaiya)

Markfield, Wallace 1926- . . . . **CLC 8**
See also CA 69-72; CAAS 3; DLB 2, 28

Markham, Edwin 1852-1940 . . . . . . **TCLC 47**
See also DLB 54

Markham, Robert
See Amis, Kingsley (William)

Marks, J
See Highwater, Jamake (Mamake)

Marks-Highwater, J
See Highwater, Jamake (Mamake)

Markson, David M(errill) 1927- . . . . **CLC 67**
See also CA 49-52; CANR 1

Marley, Bob . . . . **CLC 17**
See also Marley, Robert Nesta

Marley, Robert Nesta 1945-1981
See Marley, Bob
See also CA 107; 103

Marlowe, Christopher 1564-1593 . . . . . **DC 1**
See also CDBLB Before 1660; DLB 62; WLC

Marmontel, Jean-Francois 1723-1799 . . . . **LC 2**

Marquand, John P(hillips) 1893-1960 . . . . **CLC 2, 10**
See also CA 85-88; DLB 9, 102

Marquez, Gabriel (Jose) Garcia . . . . . . **CLC 68**
See also Garcia Marquez, Gabriel (Jose)

Marquis, Don(ald Robert Perry) 1878-1937 . . . . **TCLC 7**
See also CA 104; DLB 11, 25

Marric, J. J.
See Creasey, John

Marrow, Bernard
See Moore, Brian

Marryat, Frederick 1792-1848 . . . . **NCLC 3**
See also DLB 21

Marsden, James
See Creasey, John

Marsh, (Edith) Ngaio 1899-1982 . . . . **CLC 7, 53**
See also CA 9-12R; CANR 6; DLB 77; MTCW

Marshall, Garry 1934- . . . . **CLC 17**
See also AAYA 3; CA 111; SATA 60

Marshall, Paule 1929- . . **CLC 27, 72; SSC 3**
See also BLC 3; BW; CA 77-80; CANR 25; DLB 33; MTCW

Marsten, Richard
See Hunter, Evan

Martha, Henry
See Harris, Mark

Martin, Ken
See Hubbard, L(afayette) Ron(ald)

Martin, Richard
See Creasey, John

Martin, Steve 1945- . . . . **CLC 30**
See also CA 97-100; CANR 30; MTCW

Martin, Webber
See Silverberg, Robert

Martin du Gard, Roger
1881-1958 . . . . **TCLC 24**
See also CA 118; DLB 65

Martineau, Harriet 1802-1876. . . . **NCLC 26**
See also DLB 21, 55; YABC 2

Martines, Julia
See O'Faolain, Julia

Martinez, Jacinto Benavente y
See Benavente (y Martinez), Jacinto

Martinez Ruiz, Jose 1873-1967
See Azorin; Ruiz, Jose Martinez
See also CA 93-96; HW

Martinez Sierra, Gregorio
1881-1947 . . . . **TCLC 6**
See also CA 115

Martinez Sierra, Maria (de la O'LeJarraga)
1874-1974 . . . . **TCLC 6**
See also CA 115

Martinsen, Martin
See Follett, Ken(neth Martin)

Martinson, Harry (Edmund)
1904-1978 . . . . **CLC 14**
See also CA 77-80; CANR 34

Marut, Ret
See Traven, B.

Marut, Robert
See Traven, B.

Marvell, Andrew 1621-1678. . . . . **LC 4**
See also CDBLB 1660-1789; WLC

Marx, Karl (Heinrich)
1818-1883 . . . . **NCLC 17**

Masaoka Shiki. . . . . **TCLC 18**
See also Masaoka Tsunenori

Masaoka Tsunenori 1867-1902
See Masaoka Shiki
See also CA 117

Masefield, John (Edward)
1878-1967 . . . . **CLC 11, 47**
See also CA 19-20; 25-28R; CANR 33; CAP 2; CDBLB 1890-1914; DLB 10; MTCW; SATA 19

Maso, Carole 19(?)- . . . . **CLC 44**

Mason, Bobbie Ann
1940- . . . . **CLC 28, 43; SSC 4**
See also AAYA 5; CA 53-56; CANR 11, 31; DLBY 87; MTCW

Mason, Ernst
See Pohl, Frederik

Mason, Lee W.
See Malzberg, Barry N(athaniel)

Mason, Nick 1945-. . . . . **CLC 35**
See also Pink Floyd

Mason, Tally
See Derleth, August (William)

Mass, William
See Gibson, William

Masters, Edgar Lee
1868-1950 . . . . **TCLC 2, 25; PC 1**
See also CA 104; 133; CDALB 1865-1917; DLB 54; MTCW

Masters, Hilary 1928- . . . . **CLC 48**
See also CA 25-28R; CANR 13

Mastrosimone, William 19(?)- . . . . . . **CLC 36**

Mathe, Albert
See Camus, Albert

Matheson, Richard Burton 1926- . . . **CLC 37**
See also CA 97-100; DLB 8, 44

Mathews, Harry 1930-. . . . . **CLC 6, 52**
See also CA 21-24R; CAAS 6; CANR 18

Mathias, Roland (Glyn) 1915-. . . . . . **CLC 45**
See also CA 97-100; CANR 19; DLB 27

Matsuo Basho 1644-1694. . . . . **PC 3**

Mattheson, Rodney
See Creasey, John

Matthews, Greg 1949- . . . . **CLC 45**
See also CA 135

Matthews, William 1942-. . . . . **CLC 40**
See also CA 29-32R; CANR 12; DLB 5

Matthias, John (Edward) 1941-. . . . . . **CLC 9**
See also CA 33-36R

Matthiessen, Peter
1927- . . . . **CLC 5, 7, 11, 32, 64**
See also AAYA 6; BEST 90:4; CA 9-12R; CANR 21; DLB 6; MTCW; SATA 27

Maturin, Charles Robert
1780(?)-1824 . . . . **NCLC 6**

Matute (Ausejo), Ana Maria
1925- . . . . **CLC 11**
See also CA 89-92; MTCW

Maugham, W. S.
See Maugham, W(illiam) Somerset

Maugham, W(illiam) Somerset
1874-1965 . . . . **CLC 1, 11, 15, 67; SSC 8**
See also CA 5-8R; 25-28R; CDBLB 1914-1945; DLB 10, 36, 77, 100; MTCW; SATA 54; WLC

Maugham, William Somerset
See Maugham, W(illiam) Somerset

Maupassant, (Henri Rene Albert) Guy de
1850-1893 . . . . **NCLC 1; SSC 1**
See also WLC

Maurhut, Richard
See Traven, B.

Mauriac, Claude 1914-. . . . . **CLC 9**
See also CA 89-92; DLB 83

Mauriac, Francois (Charles)
1885-1970 . . . . **CLC 4, 9, 56**
See also CA 25-28; CAP 2; DLB 65; MTCW

Mavor, Osborne Henry 1888-1951
See Bridie, James
See also CA 104

Maxwell, William (Keepers Jr.)
1908- . . . . **CLC 19**
See also CA 93-96; DLBY 80

May, Elaine 1932- . . . . **CLC 16**
See also CA 124; DLB 44

Mayakovski, Vladimir (Vladimirovich)
1893-1930 . . . . **TCLC 4, 18**
See also CA 104

Mayhew, Henry 1812-1887 . . . . . . **NCLC 31**
See also DLB 18, 55

Maynard, Joyce 1953- . . . . **CLC 23**
See also CA 111; 129

Mayne, William (James Carter)
1928- . . . . **CLC 12**
See also CA 9-12R; CANR 37; CLR 25; MAICYA; SAAS 11; SATA 6, 68

Mayo, Jim
See L'Amour, Louis (Dearborn)

Maysles, Albert 1926- . . . . **CLC 16**
See also CA 29-32R

Maysles, David 1932-. . . . . **CLC 16**

Mazer, Norma Fox 1931- . . . . **CLC 26**
See also AAYA 5; CA 69-72; CANR 12, 32; CLR 23; MAICYA; SAAS 1; SATA 24, 67

Mazzini, Guiseppe 1805-1872 . . . . **NCLC 34**

Mazzini, Guiseppe 1805-1872 . . . . **NCLC 34**

McAuley, James Phillip
1917-1976 . . . . **CLC 45**
See also CA 97-100

McBain, Ed
See Hunter, Evan

McBrien, William Augustine
1930- . . . . **CLC 44**
See also CA 107

McCaffrey, Anne (Inez) 1926-. . . . . . **CLC 17**
See also AAYA 6; AITN 2; BEST 89:2; CA 25-28R; CANR 15, 35; DLB 8; MAICYA; MTCW; SAAS 11; SATA 8, 70

McCann, Arthur
See Campbell, John W(ood Jr.)

McCann, Edson
See Pohl, Frederik

McCarthy, Cormac 1933-. . . . . **CLC 4, 57**
See also CA 13-16R; CANR 10; DLB 6

McCarthy, Mary (Therese)
1912-1989 . . . **CLC 1, 3, 5, 14, 24, 39, 59**
See also CA 5-8R; 129; CANR 16; DLB 2; DLBY 81; MTCW

McCartney, (James) Paul
1942- . . . . **CLC 12, 35**

McCauley, Stephen 19(?)- . . . . **CLC 50**

McClure, Michael (Thomas)
1932- . . . . **CLC 6, 10**
See also CA 21-24R; CANR 17; DLB 16

McCorkle, Jill (Collins) 1958-. . . . . . **CLC 51**
See also CA 121; DLBY 87

McCourt, James 1941-. . . . . **CLC 5**
See also CA 57-60

McCoy, Horace (Stanley)
1897-1955 . . . . **TCLC 28**
See also CA 108; DLB 9

McCrae, John 1872-1918 . . . . **TCLC 12**
See also CA 109; DLB 92

McCreigh, James
See Pohl, Frederik

McCullers, (Lula) Carson (Smith)
1917-1967 . . **CLC 1, 4, 10, 12, 48; SSC 9**
See also CA 5-8R; 25-28R; CABS 1, 3; CANR 18; CDALB 1941-1968; DLB 2, 7; MTCW; SATA 27; WLC

McCulloch, John Tyler
See Burroughs, Edgar Rice

McCullough, Colleen 1938(?)- . . . . . . **CLC 27**
See also CA 81-84; CANR 17; MTCW

McElroy, Joseph 1930- . . . . **CLC 5, 47**
See also CA 17-20R

McEwan, Ian (Russell) 1948- . . . **CLC 13, 66**
See also BEST 90:4; CA 61-64; CANR 14; DLB 14; MTCW

McFadden, David 1940- . . . . **CLC 48**
See also CA 104; DLB 60

McFarland, Dennis 1950- . . . . **CLC 65**

McGahern, John 1934- . . . . **CLC 5, 9, 48**
See also CA 17-20R; CANR 29; DLB 14; MTCW

McGinley, Patrick (Anthony)
1937- . . . . **CLC 41**
See also CA 120; 127

McGinley, Phyllis 1905-1978 . . . . . . **CLC 14**
See also CA 9-12R; 77-80; CANR 19; DLB 11, 48; SATA 2, 24, 44

McGinniss, Joe 1942- . . . . **CLC 32**
See also AITN 2; BEST 89:2; CA 25-28R; CANR 26

McGivern, Maureen Daly
See Daly, Maureen

McGrath, Patrick 1950- . . . . **CLC 55**
See also CA 136

McGrath, Thomas (Matthew)
1916-1990 . . . . **CLC 28, 59**
See also CA 9-12R; 132; CANR 6, 33; MTCW; SATA 41; SATO 66

McGuane, Thomas (Francis III)
1939- . . . . **CLC 3, 7, 18, 45**
See also AITN 2; CA 49-52; CANR 5, 24; DLB 2; DLBY 80; MTCW

McGuckian, Medbh 1950- . . . . **CLC 48**
See also DLB 40

McHale, Tom 1942(?)-1982 . . . . **CLC 3, 5**
See also AITN 1; CA 77-80; 106

McIlvanney, William 1936- . . . . **CLC 42**
See also CA 25-28R; DLB 14

McIlwraith, Maureen Mollie Hunter
See Hunter, Mollie
See also SATA 2

McInerney, Jay 1955- . . . . **CLC 34**
See also CA 116; 123

McIntyre, Vonda N(eel) 1948- . . . . . **CLC 18**
See also CA 81-84; CANR 17, 34; MTCW

McKay, Claude . . . . **TCLC 7, 41; PC 2**
See also McKay, Festus Claudius
See also BLC 3; DLB 4, 45, 51, 117

McKay, Festus Claudius 1889-1948
See McKay, Claude
See also BW; CA 104; 124; MTCW; WLC

McKuen, Rod 1933- . . . . **CLC 1, 3**
See also AITN 1; CA 41-44R

McLoughlin, R. B.
See Mencken, H(enry) L(ouis)

McLuhan, (Herbert) Marshall
1911-1980 . . . . **CLC 37**
See also CA 9-12R; 102; CANR 12, 34; DLB 88; MTCW

McMillan, Terry 1951- . . . . **CLC 50, 61**

McMurtry, Larry (Jeff)
1936- . . . . **CLC 2, 3, 7, 11, 27, 44**
See also AITN 2; BEST 89:2; CA 5-8R; CANR 19; CDALB 1968-1988; DLB 2; DLBY 80, 87; MTCW

McNally, Terrence 1939- . . . . . . **CLC 4, 7, 41**
See also CA 45-48; CANR 2; DLB 7

McNamer, Deirdre 1950- . . . . **CLC 70**

McNeile, Herman Cyril 1888-1937
See Sapper
See also DLB 77

McPhee, John (Angus) 1931- . . . . . . **CLC 36**
See also BEST 90:1; CA 65-68; CANR 20; MTCW

McPherson, James Alan 1943- . . . . . **CLC 19**
See also BW; CA 25-28R; CANR 24; DLB 38; MTCW

McPherson, William (Alexander)
1933- . . . . **CLC 34**
See also CA 69-72; CANR 28

McSweeney, Kerry . . . . **CLC 34**

Mead, Margaret 1901-1978 . . . . **CLC 37**
See also AITN 1; CA 1-4R; 81-84; CANR 4; MTCW; SATA 20

Meaker, Marijane (Agnes) 1927-
See Kerr, M. E.
See also CA 107; CANR 37; MAICYA; MTCW; SATA 20, 61

Medoff, Mark (Howard) 1940- . . . **CLC 6, 23**
See also AITN 1; CA 53-56; CANR 5; DLB 7

Meged, Aharon
See Megged, Aharon

Meged, Aron
See Megged, Aharon

Megged, Aharon 1920- . . . . **CLC 9**
See also CA 49-52; CAAS 13; CANR 1

Mehta, Ved (Parkash) 1934- . . . . **CLC 37**
See also CA 1-4R; CANR 2, 23; MTCW

Melanter
See Blackmore, R(ichard) D(oddridge)

Melikow, Loris
See Hofmannsthal, Hugo von

Melmoth, Sebastian
See Wilde, Oscar (Fingal O'Flahertie Wills)

Meltzer, Milton 1915- . . . . **CLC 26**
See also AAYA 8; CA 13-16R; CANR 38; CLR 13; DLB 61; MAICYA; SAAS 1; SATA 1, 50

Melville, Herman
1819-1891 . . . . . . **NCLC 3, 12, 29; SSC 1**
See also CDALB 1640-1865; DLB 3, 74; SATA 59; WLC

Menander
c. 342B.C.-c. 292B.C. . . . . **CMLC 9; DC 3**

Mencken, H(enry) L(ouis)
1880-1956 . . . . **TCLC 13**
See also CA 105; 125; CDALB 1917-1929; DLB 11, 29, 63; MTCW

Mercer, David 1928-1980 . . . . **CLC 5**
See also CA 9-12R; 102; CANR 23; DLB 13; MTCW

Merchant, Paul
See Ellison, Harlan

Meredith, George 1828-1909 . . . **TCLC 17, 43**
See also CA 117; CDBLB 1832-1890; DLB 18, 35, 57

Meredith, William (Morris)
1919- . . . . **CLC 4, 13, 22, 55**
See also CA 9-12R; CAAS 14; CANR 6; DLB 5

Merezhkovsky, Dmitry Sergeyevich
1865-1941 . . . . **TCLC 29**

Merimee, Prosper
1803-1870 . . . . **NCLC 6; SSC 7**
See also DLB 119

Merkin, Daphne 1954- . . . . **CLC 44**
See also CA 123

Merlin, Arthur
See Blish, James (Benjamin)

Merrill, James (Ingram)
1926- . . . . **CLC 2, 3, 6, 8, 13, 18, 34**
See also CA 13-16R; CANR 10; DLB 5; DLBY 85; MTCW

Merriman, Alex
See Silverberg, Robert

Merritt, E. B.
See Waddington, Miriam

Merton, Thomas
1915-1968 . . . . **CLC 1, 3, 11, 34**
See also CA 5-8R; 25-28R; CANR 22; DLB 48; DLBY 81; MTCW

Merwin, W(illiam) S(tanley)
1927- . . . . . . **CLC 1, 2, 3, 5, 8, 13, 18, 45**
See also CA 13-16R; CANR 15; DLB 5; MTCW

Metcalf, John 1938- . . . . **CLC 37**
See also CA 113; DLB 60

Metcalf, Suzanne
See Baum, L(yman) Frank

Mew, Charlotte (Mary)
1870-1928 . . . . **TCLC 8**
See also CA 105; DLB 19

Mewshaw, Michael 1943- . . . . **CLC 9**
See also CA 53-56; CANR 7; DLBY 80

Meyer, June
See Jordan, June

Meyer-Meyrink, Gustav 1868-1932
See Meyrink, Gustav
See also CA 117

Meyers, Jeffrey 1939- . . . . **CLC 39**
See also CA 73-76; DLB 111

Meynell, Alice (Christina Gertrude Thompson)
1847-1922 . . . . **TCLC 6**
See also CA 104; DLB 19, 98

Meyrink, Gustav . . . . **TCLC 21**
See also Meyer-Meyrink, Gustav
See also DLB 81

Michaels, Leonard 1933- . . . . **CLC 6, 25**
See also CA 61-64; CANR 21; MTCW

Michaux, Henri 1899-1984 . . . . . . **CLC 8, 19**
See also CA 85-88; 114

Michelangelo 1475-1564. . . . . **LC 12**

Michelet, Jules 1798-1874. . . . . . . **NCLC 31**

Michener, James A(lbert)
1907(?)- . . . . **CLC 1, 5, 11, 29, 60**
See also AITN 1; BEST 90:1; CA 5-8R; CANR 21; DLB 6; MTCW

Mickiewicz, Adam 1798-1855 . . . . . **NCLC 3**

Middleton, Christopher 1926- . . . . . . **CLC 13**
See also CA 13-16R; CANR 29; DLB 40

Middleton, Stanley 1919- . . . . **CLC 7, 38**
See also CA 25-28R; CANR 21; DLB 14

Migueis, Jose Rodrigues 1901- . . . . . **CLC 10**

Mikszath, Kalman 1847-1910 . . . . . **TCLC 31**

Miles, Josephine
1911-1985 . . . . **CLC 1, 2, 14, 34, 39**
See also CA 1-4R; 116; CANR 2; DLB 48

Militant
See Sandburg, Carl (August)

Mill, John Stuart 1806-1873 . . . . . **NCLC 11**
See also CDBLB 1832-1890; DLB 55

Millar, Kenneth 1915-1983 . . . . **CLC 14**
See also Macdonald, Ross
See also CA 9-12R; 110; CANR 16; DLB 2; DLBD 6; DLBY 83; MTCW

Millay, E. Vincent
See Millay, Edna St. Vincent

Millay, Edna St. Vincent
1892-1950 . . . . **TCLC 4**
See also CA 104; 130; CDALB 1917-1929; DLB 45; MTCW

Miller, Arthur
1915- . . . . . . **CLC 1, 2, 6, 10, 15, 26, 47; DC 1**
See also AITN 1; CA 1-4R; CABS 3; CANR 2, 30; CDALB 1941-1968; DLB 7; MTCW; WLC

Miller, Henry (Valentine)
1891-1980 . . . . **CLC 1, 2, 4, 9, 14, 43**
See also CA 9-12R; 97-100; CANR 33; CDALB 1929-1941; DLB 4, 9; DLBY 80; MTCW; WLC

Miller, Jason 1939(?)- . . . . **CLC 2**
See also AITN 1; CA 73-76; DLB 7

Miller, Sue 19(?)- . . . . **CLC 44**
See also BEST 90:3

Miller, Walter M(ichael Jr.)
1923- . . . . **CLC 4, 30**
See also CA 85-88; DLB 8

Millett, Kate 1934- . . . . **CLC 67**
See also AITN 1; CA 73-76; CANR 32; MTCW

Millhauser, Steven 1943- . . . . **CLC 21, 54**
See also CA 110; 111; DLB 2

Millin, Sarah Gertrude 1889-1968 . . **CLC 49**
See also CA 102; 93-96

Milne, A(lan) A(lexander)
1882-1956 . . . . **TCLC 6**
See also CA 104; 133; CLR 1, 26; DLB 10, 77, 100; MAICYA; MTCW; YABC 1

Milner, Ron(ald) 1938- . . . . **CLC 56**
See also AITN 1; BLC 3; BW; CA 73-76; CANR 24; DLB 38; MTCW

Milosz, Czeslaw
1911- . . . . **CLC 5, 11, 22, 31, 56**
See also CA 81-84; CANR 23; MTCW

Milton, John 1608-1674 . . . . **LC 9**
See also CDBLB 1660-1789; WLC

Minehaha, Cornelius
See Wedekind, (Benjamin) Frank(lin)

Miner, Valerie 1947- . . . . **CLC 40**
See also CA 97-100

Minimo, Duca
See D'Annunzio, Gabriele

Minot, Susan 1956- . . . . **CLC 44**
See also CA 134

Minus, Ed 1938- . . . . **CLC 39**

Miranda, Javier
See Bioy Casares, Adolfo

Miro (Ferrer), Gabriel (Francisco Victor)
1879-1930 . . . . **TCLC 5**
See also CA 104

Mishima, Yukio
. . . . **CLC 2, 4, 6, 9, 27; DC 1; SSC 4**
See also Hiraoka, Kimitake

Mistral, Gabriela . . . . **TCLC 2**
See also Godoy Alcayaga, Lucila

Mistry, Rohinton 1952- . . . . **CLC 71**

Mitchell, Clyde
See Ellison, Harlan; Silverberg, Robert

Mitchell, James Leslie 1901-1935
See Gibbon, Lewis Grassic
See also CA 104; DLB 15

Mitchell, Joni 1943- . . . . **CLC 12**
See also CA 112

Mitchell, Margaret (Munnerlyn)
1900-1949 . . . . **TCLC 11**
See also CA 109; 125; DLB 9; MTCW

Mitchell, Peggy
See Mitchell, Margaret (Munnerlyn)

Mitchell, S(ilas) Weir 1829-1914 . . **TCLC 36**

Mitchell, W(illiam) O(rmond)
1914- . . . . **CLC 25**
See also CA 77-80; CANR 15; DLB 88

Mitford, Mary Russell 1787-1855. . **NCLC 4**
See also DLB 110, 116

Mitford, Nancy 1904-1973. . . . . **CLC 44**
See also CA 9-12R

Miyamoto, Yuriko 1899-1951 . . . . . **TCLC 37**

Mo, Timothy (Peter) 1950(?)- . . . . . . **CLC 46**
See also CA 117; MTCW

Modarressi, Taghi (M.) 1931- . . . . . . **CLC 44**
See also CA 121; 134

Modiano, Patrick (Jean) 1945- . . . . . **CLC 18**
See also CA 85-88; CANR 17; DLB 83

Moerck, Paal
See Roelvaag, O(le) E(dvart)

Mofolo, Thomas (Mokopu)
1875(?)-1948 . . . . **TCLC 22**
See also BLC 3; CA 121

Mohr, Nicholasa 1935- . . . . **CLC 12**
See also AAYA 8; CA 49-52; CANR 1, 32; CLR 22; HW; SAAS 8; SATA 8

Mojtabai, A(nn) G(race)
1938- . . . . **CLC 5, 9, 15, 29**
See also CA 85-88

Moliere 1622-1673 . . . . **LC 10**
See also WLC

Molin, Charles
See Mayne, William (James Carter)

Molnar, Ferenc 1878-1952. . . . . **TCLC 20**
See also CA 109

Momaday, N(avarre) Scott
1934- . . . . **CLC 2, 19**
See also CA 25-28R; CANR 14, 34; MTCW; SATA 30, 48

Monroe, Harriet 1860-1936. . . . . . . **TCLC 12**
See also CA 109; DLB 54, 91

Monroe, Lyle
See Heinlein, Robert A(nson)

Montagu, Elizabeth 1917- . . . . **NCLC 7**
See also CA 9-12R

Montagu, Mary (Pierrepont) Wortley
1689-1762 . . . . **LC 9**
See also DLB 95, 101

Montague, John (Patrick)
1929- . . . . **CLC 13, 46**
See also CA 9-12R; CANR 9; DLB 40; MTCW

Montaigne, Michel (Eyquem) de
1533-1592 . . . . **LC 8**
See also WLC

Montale, Eugenio 1896-1981 . . . **CLC 7, 9, 18**
See also CA 17-20R; 104; CANR 30; DLB 114; MTCW

Montesquieu, Charles-Louis de Secondat
1689-1755 . . . . **LC 7**

Montgomery, (Robert) Bruce 1921-1978
See Crispin, Edmund
See also CA 104

Montgomery, Marion H. Jr. 1925- . . . **CLC 7**
See also AITN 1; CA 1-4R; CANR 3; DLB 6

Montgomery, Max
See Davenport, Guy (Mattison Jr.)

Montherlant, Henry (Milon) de
1896-1972 . . . . **CLC 8, 19**
See also CA 85-88; 37-40R; DLB 72; MTCW

Python . . . . **CLC 21**
See also Chapman, Graham; Cleese, John (Marwood); Gilliam, Terry (Vance); Idle, Eric; Jones, Terence Graham Parry; Palin, Michael (Edward)
See also AAYA 7

Moodie, Susanna (Strickland)
1803-1885 . . . . **NCLC 14**
See also DLB 99

Mooney, Edward 1951- . . . . **CLC 25**
See also CA 130

Mooney, Ted
See Mooney, Edward

Moorcock, Michael (John)
1939- . . . . **CLC 5, 27, 58**
See also CA 45-48; CAAS 5; CANR 2, 17, 38; DLB 14; MTCW

Moore, Brian
1921- . . . . **CLC 1, 3, 5, 7, 8, 19, 32**
See also CA 1-4R; CANR 1, 25; MTCW

Moore, Edward
See Muir, Edwin

Moore, George Augustus
1852-1933 . . . . **TCLC 7**
See also CA 104; DLB 10, 18, 57

Moore, Lorrie . . . . **CLC 39, 45, 68**
See also Moore, Marie Lorena

Moore, Marianne (Craig)
1887-1972 . . . **CLC 1, 2, 4, 8, 10, 13, 19, 47; PC 4**
See also CA 1-4R; 33-36R; CANR 3; CDALB 1929-1941; DLB 45; DLBD 7; MTCW; SATA 20

Moore, Marie Lorena 1957-
See Moore, Lorrie
See also CA 116; CANR 39

Moore, Thomas 1779-1852. . . . . **NCLC 6**
See also DLB 96

Morand, Paul 1888-1976 . . . . **CLC 41**
See also CA 69-72; DLB 65

Morante, Elsa 1918-1985. . . . . **CLC 8, 47**
See also CA 85-88; 117; CANR 35; MTCW

Moravia, Alberto. . . . . . . **CLC 2, 7, 11, 27, 46**
See also Pincherle, Alberto

More, Hannah 1745-1833 . . . . **NCLC 27**
See also DLB 107, 109, 116

More, Henry 1614-1687. . . . . **LC 9**

More, Sir Thomas 1478-1535 . . . . **LC 10**

Moreas, Jean. **TCLC 18**
See also Papadiamantopoulos, Johannes

Morgan, Berry 1919- . . . . **CLC 6**
See also CA 49-52; DLB 6

Morgan, Claire
See Highsmith, (Mary) Patricia

Morgan, Edwin (George) 1920-. . . . . **CLC 31**
See also CA 5-8R; CANR 3; DLB 27

Morgan, (George) Frederick
1922- . . . . **CLC 23**
See also CA 17-20R; CANR 21

Morgan, Harriet
See Mencken, H(enry) L(ouis)

Morgan, Jane
See Cooper, James Fenimore

Morgan, Janet 1945- . . . . **CLC 39**
See also CA 65-68

Morgan, Lady 1776(?)-1859. . . . . . **NCLC 29**
See also DLB 116

Morgan, Robin 1941-. . . . . **CLC 2**
See also CA 69-72; CANR 29; MTCW

Morgan, Scott
See Kuttner, Henry

Morgan, Seth 1949(?)-1990 . . . . **CLC 65**
See also CA 132

Morgenstern, Christian
1871-1914 . . . . **TCLC 8**
See also CA 105

Morgenstern, S.
See Goldman, William (W.)

Moricz, Zsigmond 1879-1942 . . . . . **TCLC 33**

Morike, Eduard (Friedrich)
1804-1875 . . . . **NCLC 10**

Mori Ogai . . . . **TCLC 14**
See also Mori Rintaro

Mori Rintaro 1862-1922
See Mori Ogai
See also CA 110

Moritz, Karl Philipp 1756-1793 . . . . . . **LC 2**
See also DLB 94

Morren, Theophil
See Hofmannsthal, Hugo von

Morris, Julian
See West, Morris L(anglo)

Morris, Steveland Judkins 1950(?)-
See Wonder, Stevie
See also CA 111

Morris, William 1834-1896 . . . . **NCLC 4**
See also CDBLB 1832-1890; DLB 18, 35, 57

Morris, Wright 1910-. . . **CLC 1, 3, 7, 18, 37**
See also CA 9-12R; CANR 21; DLB 2; DLBY 81; MTCW

Morrison, Chloe Anthony Wofford
See Morrison, Toni

Morrison, James Douglas 1943-1971
See Morrison, Jim
See also CA 73-76

Morrison, Jim . . . . **CLC 17**
See also Morrison, James Douglas

Morrison, Toni 1931-. . . . . **CLC 4, 10, 22, 55**
See also AAYA 1; BLC 3; BW; CA 29-32R; CANR 27; CDALB 1968-1988; DLB 6, 33; DLBY 81; MTCW; SATA 57

Morrison, Van 1945- . . . . **CLC 21**
See also CA 116

Mortimer, John (Clifford)
1923- . . . . **CLC 28, 43**
See also CA 13-16R; CANR 21; CDBLB 1960 to Present; DLB 13; MTCW

Mortimer, Penelope (Ruth) 1918-. . . . **CLC 5**
See also CA 57-60

Morton, Anthony
See Creasey, John

Mosher, Howard Frank . . . . **CLC 62**

Mosley, Nicholas 1923-. . . . . **CLC 43, 70**
See also CA 69-72; DLB 14

Moss, Howard
1922-1987 . . . . **CLC 7, 14, 45, 50**
See also CA 1-4R; 123; CANR 1; DLB 5

Motion, Andrew 1952-. . . . . **CLC 47**
See also DLB 40

Motley, Willard (Francis)
1912-1965 . . . . **CLC 18**
See also BW; CA 117; 106; DLB 76

Mott, Michael (Charles Alston)
1930- . . . . **CLC 15, 34**
See also CA 5-8R; CAAS 7; CANR 7, 29

Mowat, Farley (McGill) 1921- . . . . . **CLC 26**
See also AAYA 1; CA 1-4R; CANR 4, 24; CLR 20; DLB 68; MAICYA; MTCW; SATA 3, 55

Moyers, Bill 1934- . . . . **CLC 74**
See also AITN 2; CA 61-64; CANR 31

Mphahlele, Es'kia
See Mphahlele, Ezekiel

Mphahlele, Ezekiel 1919-. . . . . **CLC 25**
See also BLC 3; BW; CA 81-84; CANR 26

Mqhayi, S(amuel) E(dward) K(rune Loliwe)
1875-1945 . . . . **TCLC 25**
See also BLC 3

Mr. Martin
See Burroughs, William S(eward)

Mrozek, Slawomir 1930-. . . . . **CLC 3, 13**
See also CA 13-16R; CAAS 10; CANR 29; MTCW

Mrs. Belloc-Lowndes
See Lowndes, Marie Adelaide (Belloc)

Mtwa, Percy (?)-. . . . . **CLC 47**

Mueller, Lisel 1924-. . . . . **CLC 13, 51**
See also CA 93-96; DLB 105

Muir, Edwin 1887-1959 . . . . **TCLC 2**
See also CA 104; DLB 20, 100

Muir, John 1838-1914 . . . . **TCLC 28**

Mujica Lainez, Manuel
1910-1984 . . . . **CLC 31**
See also Lainez, Manuel Mujica
See also CA 81-84; 112; CANR 32; HW

Mukherjee, Bharati 1940- . . . . **CLC 53**
See also BEST 89:2; CA 107; DLB 60; MTCW

Muldoon, Paul 1951- . . . . **CLC 32, 72**
See also CA 113; 129; DLB 40

Mulisch, Harry 1927-. . . . . **CLC 42**
See also CA 9-12R; CANR 6, 26

Mull, Martin 1943-. . . . . **CLC 17**
See also CA 105

Mulock, Dinah Maria
See Craik, Dinah Maria (Mulock)

Munford, Robert 1737(?)-1783 . . . . **LC 5**
See also DLB 31

Mungo, Raymond 1946-. . . . . **CLC 72**
See also CA 49-52; CANR 2

Munro, Alice
1931- . . . . **CLC 6, 10, 19, 50; SSC 3**
See also AITN 2; CA 33-36R; CANR 33; DLB 53; MTCW; SATA 29

Munro, H(ector) H(ugh) 1870-1916
See Saki
See also CA 104; 130; CDBLB 1890-1914; DLB 34; MTCW; WLC

Murasaki, Lady. . . . . **CMLC 1**

Murdoch, (Jean) Iris
1919- . . . . . . **CLC 1, 2, 3, 4, 6, 8, 11, 15, 22, 31, 51**
See also CA 13-16R; CANR 8; CDBLB 1960 to Present; DLB 14; MTCW

Murphy, Richard 1927- . . . . **CLC 41**
See also CA 29-32R; DLB 40

Murphy, Sylvia 1937-. . . . . **CLC 34**
See also CA 121

Murphy, Thomas (Bernard) 1935-. . . **CLC 51**
See also CA 101

Murray, Les(lie) A(llan) 1938- . . . . . **CLC 40**
See also CA 21-24R; CANR 11, 27

Murry, J. Middleton
See Murry, John Middleton

Murry, John Middleton 1889-1957 .... **TCLC 16**
See also CA 118

Musgrave, Susan 1951- .... **CLC 13, 54**
See also CA 69-72

Musil, Robert (Edler von) 1880-1942 .... **TCLC 12**
See also CA 109; DLB 81

Musset, (Louis Charles) Alfred de 1810-1857 .... **NCLC 7**

My Brother's Brother
See Chekhov, Anton (Pavlovich)

Myers, Walter Dean 1937- .... **CLC 35**
See also AAYA 4; BLC 3; BW; CA 33-36R; CANR 20; CLR 4, 16; DLB 33; MAICYA; SAAS 2; SATA 27, 41, 70, 71

Myers, Walter M.
See Myers, Walter Dean

Myles, Symon
See Follett, Ken(neth Martin)

Nabokov, Vladimir (Vladimirovich) 1899-1977 .... **CLC 1, 2, 3, 6, 8, 11, 15, 23, 44, 46, 64; SSC 11**
See also CA 5-8R; 69-72; CANR 20; CDALB 1941-1968; DLB 2; DLBD 3; DLBY 80, 91; MTCW; WLC

Nagy, Laszlo 1925-1978............ **CLC 7**
See also CA 129; 112

Naipaul, Shiva(dhar Srinivasa) 1945-1985 .... **CLC 32, 39**
See also CA 110; 112; 116; CANR 33; DLBY 85; MTCW

Naipaul, V(idiadhar) S(urajprasad) 1932- .... **CLC 4, 7, 9, 13, 18, 37**
See also CA 1-4R; CANR 1, 33; CDBLB 1960 to Present; DLBY 85; MTCW

Nakos, Lilika 1899(?)- .... **CLC 29**

Narayan, R(asipuram) K(rishnaswami) 1906- .... **CLC 7, 28, 47**
See also CA 81-84; CANR 33; MTCW; SATA 62

Nash, (Frediric) Ogden 1902-1971 .. **CLC 23**
See also CA 13-14; 29-32R; CANR 34; CAP 1; DLB 11; MAICYA; MTCW; SATA 2, 46

Nathan, Daniel
See Dannay, Frederic

Nathan, George Jean 1882-1958 ... **TCLC 18**
See also Hatteras, Owen
See also CA 114

Natsume, Kinnosuke 1867-1916
See Natsume, Soseki
See also CA 104

Natsume, Soseki .... **TCLC 2, 10**
See also Natsume, Kinnosuke

Natti, (Mary) Lee 1919-
See Kingman, Lee
See also CA 5-8R; CANR 2

Naylor, Gloria 1950- .... **CLC 28, 52**
See also AAYA 6; BLC 3; BW; CA 107; CANR 27; MTCW

Neihardt, John Gneisenau 1881-1973 .... **CLC 32**
See also CA 13-14; CAP 1; DLB 9, 54

Nekrasov, Nikolai Alekseevich 1821-1878 .... **NCLC 11**

Nelligan, Emile 1879-1941........ **TCLC 14**
See also CA 114; DLB 92

Nelson, Willie 1933-............. **CLC 17**
See also CA 107

Nemerov, Howard (Stanley) 1920-1991 .... **CLC 2, 6, 9, 36**
See also CA 1-4R; 134; CABS 2; CANR 1, 27; DLB 6; DLBY 83; MTCW

Neruda, Pablo 1904-1973 .... **CLC 1, 2, 5, 7, 9, 28, 62; PC 4**
See also CA 19-20; 45-48; CAP 2; HW; MTCW; WLC

Nerval, Gerard de 1808-1855...... **NCLC 1**

Nervo, (Jose) Amado (Ruiz de) 1870-1919 .... **TCLC 11**
See also CA 109; 131; HW

Nessi, Pio Baroja y
See Baroja (y Nessi), Pio

Neufeld, John (Arthur) 1938- ...... **CLC 17**
See also CA 25-28R; CANR 11, 37; MAICYA; SAAS 3; SATA 6

Neville, Emily Cheney 1919-....... **CLC 12**
See also CA 5-8R; CANR 3, 37; MAICYA; SAAS 2; SATA 1

Newbound, Bernard Slade 1930-
See Slade, Bernard
See also CA 81-84

Newby, P(ercy) H(oward) 1918- .... **CLC 2, 13**
See also CA 5-8R; CANR 32; DLB 15; MTCW

Newlove, Donald 1928- .... **CLC 6**
See also CA 29-32R; CANR 25

Newlove, John (Herbert) 1938-..... **CLC 14**
See also CA 21-24R; CANR 9, 25

Newman, Charles 1938-.......... **CLC 2, 8**
See also CA 21-24R

Newman, Edwin (Harold) 1919- .... **CLC 14**
See also AITN 1; CA 69-72; CANR 5

Newman, John Henry 1801-1890 .... **NCLC 38**
See also DLB 18, 32, 55

Newton, Suzanne 1936- .... **CLC 35**
See also CA 41-44R; CANR 14; SATA 5

Nexo, Martin Andersen 1869-1954 .... **TCLC 43**

Nezval, Vitezslav 1900-1958 ...... **TCLC 44**
See also CA 123

Ngema, Mbongeni 1955- .... **CLC 57**

Ngugi, James T(hiong'o)........ **CLC 3, 7, 13**
See also Ngugi wa Thiong'o

Ngugi wa Thiong'o 1938-.......... **CLC 36**
See also Ngugi, James T(hiong'o)
See also BLC 3; BW; CA 81-84; CANR 27; MTCW

Nichol, B(arrie) P(hillip) 1944-1988 .... **CLC 18**
See also CA 53-56; DLB 53; SATA 66

Nichols, John (Treadwell) 1940-.... **CLC 38**
See also CA 9-12R; CAAS 2; CANR 6; DLBY 82

Nichols, Peter (Richard) 1927- .... **CLC 5, 36, 65**
See also CA 104; CANR 33; DLB 13; MTCW

Nicolas, F. R. E.
See Freeling, Nicolas

Niedecker, Lorine 1903-1970.... **CLC 10, 42**
See also CA 25-28; CAP 2; DLB 48

Nietzsche, Friedrich (Wilhelm) 1844-1900 .... **TCLC 10, 18**
See also CA 107; 121

Nievo, Ippolito 1831-1861 .... **NCLC 22**

Nightingale, Anne Redmon 1943-
See Redmon, Anne
See also CA 103

Nik.T.O.
See Annensky, Innokenty Fyodorovich

Nin, Anais 1903-1977 ..... **CLC 1, 4, 8, 11, 14, 60; SSC 10**
See also AITN 2; CA 13-16R; 69-72; CANR 22; DLB 2, 4; MTCW

Nissenson, Hugh 1933-........... **CLC 4, 9**
See also CA 17-20R; CANR 27; DLB 28

Niven, Larry .... **CLC 8**
See also Niven, Laurence Van Cott
See also DLB 8

Niven, Laurence Van Cott 1938-
See Niven, Larry
See also CA 21-24R; CAAS 12; CANR 14; MTCW

Nixon, Agnes Eckhardt 1927-...... **CLC 21**
See also CA 110

Nizan, Paul 1905-1940........... **TCLC 40**
See also DLB 72

Nkosi, Lewis 1936-............... **CLC 45**
See also BLC 3; BW; CA 65-68; CANR 27

Nodier, (Jean) Charles (Emmanuel) 1780-1844 .... **NCLC 19**
See also DLB 119

Nolan, Christopher 1965-.......... **CLC 58**
See also CA 111

Norden, Charles
See Durrell, Lawrence (George)

Nordhoff, Charles (Bernard) 1887-1947 .... **TCLC 23**
See also CA 108; DLB 9; SATA 23

Norman, Marsha 1947- .... **CLC 28**
See also CA 105; CABS 3; DLBY 84

Norris, Benjamin Franklin Jr. 1870-1902 .... **TCLC 24**
See also Norris, Frank
See also CA 110

Norris, Frank
See Norris, Benjamin Franklin Jr.
See also CDALB 1865-1917; DLB 12, 71

Norris, Leslie 1921- .... **CLC 14**
See also CA 11-12; CANR 14; CAP 1; DLB 27

North, Andrew
See Norton, Andre

North, Captain George
See Stevenson, Robert Louis (Balfour)

North, Milou
See Erdrich, Louise

Northrup, B. A.
See Hubbard, L(afayette) Ron(ald)

North Staffs
See Hulme, T(homas) E(rnest)

Norton, Alice Mary
See Norton, Andre
See also MAICYA; SATA 1, 43

Norton, Andre 1912- . . . . **CLC 12**
See also Norton, Alice Mary
See also CA 1-4R; CANR 2, 31; DLB 8, 52; MTCW

Norway, Nevil Shute 1899-1960
See Shute, Nevil
See also CA 102; 93-96

Norwid, Cyprian Kamil
1821-1883 . . . . **NCLC 17**

Nosille, Nabrah
See Ellison, Harlan

Nossack, Hans Erich 1901-1978 . . . . . **CLC 6**
See also CA 93-96; 85-88; DLB 69

Nosu, Chuji
See Ozu, Yasujiro

Nova, Craig 1945-. . . . . **CLC 7, 31**
See also CA 45-48; CANR 2

Novak, Joseph
See Kosinski, Jerzy (Nikodem)

Novalis 1772-1801 . . . . **NCLC 13**
See also DLB 90

Nowlan, Alden (Albert) 1933-1983 . . **CLC 15**
See also CA 9-12R; CANR 5; DLB 53

Noyes, Alfred 1880-1958 . . . . **TCLC 7**
See also CA 104; DLB 20

Nunn, Kem 19(?)- . . . . **CLC 34**

Nye, Robert 1939- . . . . **CLC 13, 42**
See also CA 33-36R; CANR 29; DLB 14; MTCW; SATA 6

Nyro, Laura 1947- . . . . **CLC 17**

Oates, Joyce Carol
1938- . . . . . **CLC 1, 2, 3, 6, 9, 11, 15, 19, 33, 52; SSC 6**
See also AITN 1; BEST 89:2; CA 5-8R; CANR 25; CDALB 1968-1988; DLB 2, 5; DLBY 81; MTCW; WLC

O'Brien, E. G.
See Clarke, Arthur C(harles)

O'Brien, Edna
1936- . . . **CLC 3, 5, 8, 13, 36, 65; SSC 10**
See also CA 1-4R; CANR 6; CDBLB 1960 to Present; DLB 14; MTCW

O'Brien, Fitz-James 1828-1862. . . **NCLC 21**
See also DLB 74

O'Brien, Flann. . . . . **CLC 1, 4, 5, 7, 10, 47**
See also O Nuallain, Brian

O'Brien, Richard 1942- . . . . **CLC 17**
See also CA 124

O'Brien, Tim 1946-. . . . . **CLC 7, 19, 40**
See also CA 85-88; DLBD 9; DLBY 80

Obstfelder, Sigbjoern 1866-1900. . . **TCLC 23**
See also CA 123

O'Casey, Sean
1880-1964 . . . . **CLC 1, 5, 9, 11, 15**
See also CA 89-92; CDBLB 1914-1945; DLB 10; MTCW

O'Cathasaigh, Sean
See O'Casey, Sean

Ochs, Phil 1940-1976. . . . . **CLC 17**
See also CA 65-68

O'Connor, Edwin (Greene)
1918-1968 . . . . **CLC 14**
See also CA 93-96; 25-28R

O'Connor, (Mary) Flannery
1925-1964 . . . **CLC 1, 2, 3, 6, 10, 13, 15, 21, 66; SSC 1**
See also AAYA 7; CA 1-4R; CANR 3; CDALB 1941-1968; DLB 2; DLBY 80; MTCW; WLC

O'Connor, Frank. . . . . **CLC 23; SSC 5**
See also O'Donovan, Michael John

O'Dell, Scott 1898-1989. . . . . **CLC 30**
See also AAYA 3; CA 61-64; 129; CANR 12, 30; CLR 1, 16; DLB 52; MAICYA; SATA 12, 60

Odets, Clifford 1906-1963 . . . . **CLC 2, 28**
See also CA 85-88; DLB 7, 26; MTCW

O'Donnell, K. M.
See Malzberg, Barry N(athaniel)

O'Donnell, Lawrence
See Kuttner, Henry

O'Donovan, Michael John
1903-1966 . . . . **CLC 14**
See also O'Connor, Frank
See also CA 93-96

Oe, Kenzaburo 1935- . . . . **CLC 10, 36**
See also CA 97-100; CANR 36; MTCW

O'Faolain, Julia 1932- . . . . **CLC 6, 19, 47**
See also CA 81-84; CAAS 2; CANR 12; DLB 14; MTCW

O'Faolain, Sean
1900-1991 . . . . **CLC 1, 7, 14, 32, 70**
See also CA 61-64; 134; CANR 12; DLB 15; MTCW

O'Flaherty, Liam
1896-1984 . . . . **CLC 5, 34; SSC 6**
See also CA 101; 113; CANR 35; DLB 36; DLBY 84; MTCW

Ogilvy, Gavin
See Barrie, J(ames) M(atthew)

O'Grady, Standish James
1846-1928 . . . . **TCLC 5**
See also CA 104

O'Grady, Timothy 1951- . . . . **CLC 59**
See also CA 138

O'Hara, Frank 1926-1966 . . . . . **CLC 2, 5, 13**
See also CA 9-12R; 25-28R; CANR 33; DLB 5, 16; MTCW

O'Hara, John (Henry)
1905-1970 . . . . **CLC 1, 2, 3, 6, 11, 42**
See also CA 5-8R; 25-28R; CANR 31; CDALB 1929-1941; DLB 9, 86; DLBD 2; MTCW

O Hehir, Diana 1922- . . . . **CLC 41**
See also CA 93-96

Okigbo, Christopher (Ifenayichukwu)
1932-1967 . . . . **CLC 25**
See also BLC 3; BW; CA 77-80; MTCW

Olds, Sharon 1942-. . . . . **CLC 32, 39**
See also CA 101; CANR 18; DLB 120

Oldstyle, Jonathan
See Irving, Washington

Olesha, Yuri (Karlovich)
1899-1960 . . . . **CLC 8**
See also CA 85-88

Oliphant, Margaret (Oliphant Wilson)
1828-1897 . . . . **NCLC 11**
See also DLB 18

Oliver, Mary 1935-. . . . . **CLC 19, 34**
See also CA 21-24R; CANR 9; DLB 5

Olivier, Laurence (Kerr)
1907-1989 . . . . **CLC 20**
See also CA 111; 129

Olsen, Tillie 1913- . . . . . **CLC 4, 13; SSC 11**
See also CA 1-4R; CANR 1; DLB 28; DLBY 80; MTCW

Olson, Charles (John)
1910-1970 . . . . . **CLC 1, 2, 5, 6, 9, 11, 29**
See also CA 13-16; 25-28R; CABS 2; CANR 35; CAP 1; DLB 5, 16; MTCW

Olson, Toby 1937- . . . . **CLC 28**
See also CA 65-68; CANR 9, 31

Olyesha, Yuri
See Olesha, Yuri (Karlovich)

Ondaatje, Michael 1943- . . . . **CLC 14, 29, 51**
See also CA 77-80; DLB 60

Oneal, Elizabeth 1934-
See Oneal, Zibby
See also CA 106; CANR 28; MAICYA; SATA 30

Oneal, Zibby . . . . **CLC 30**
See also Oneal, Elizabeth
See also AAYA 5; CLR 13

O'Neill, Eugene (Gladstone)
1888-1953 . . . . **TCLC 1, 6, 27**
See also AITN 1; CA 110; 132; CDALB 1929-1941; DLB 7; MTCW; WLC

Onetti, Juan Carlos 1909- . . . . **CLC 7, 10**
See also CA 85-88; CANR 32; DLB 113; HW; MTCW

O Nuallain, Brian 1911-1966
See O'Brien, Flann
See also CA 21-22; 25-28R; CAP 2

Oppen, George 1908-1984 . . . . **CLC 7, 13, 34**
See also CA 13-16R; 113; CANR 8; DLB 5

Oppenheim, E(dward) Phillips
1866-1946 . . . . **TCLC 45**
See also CA 111; DLB 70

Orlovitz, Gil 1918-1973 . . . . **CLC 22**
See also CA 77-80; 45-48; DLB 2, 5

Ortega y Gasset, Jose 1883-1955 . . . **TCLC 9**
See also CA 106; 130; HW; MTCW

Ortiz, Simon J(oseph) 1941- . . . . **CLC 45**
See also CA 134; DLB 120

Orton, Joe . . . . **CLC 4, 13, 43; DC 3**
See also Orton, John Kingsley
See also CDBLB 1960 to Present; DLB 13

Orton, John Kingsley 1933-1967
See Orton, Joe
See also CA 85-88; CANR 35; MTCW

Orwell, George . . . . **TCLC 2, 6, 15, 31**
See also Blair, Eric (Arthur)
See also CDBLB 1945-1960; DLB 15, 98; WLC

Osborne, David
See Silverberg, Robert

Osborne, George
See Silverberg, Robert

Osborne, John (James)
1929- . . . . **CLC 1, 2, 5, 11, 45**
See also CA 13-16R; CANR 21; CDBLB 1945-1960; DLB 13; MTCW; WLC

Osborne, Lawrence 1958- . . . . **CLC 50**

Oshima, Nagisa 1932- . . . . **CLC 20**
See also CA 116; 121

Oskison, John M(ilton)
1874-1947 . . . . **TCLC 35**

Ossoli, Sarah Margaret (Fuller marchesa d')
1810-1850
See Fuller, Margaret
See also SATA 25

Ostrovsky, Alexander
1823-1886 . . . . **NCLC 30**

Otero, Blas de 1916- . . . . **CLC 11**
See also CA 89-92

Otto, Whitney 1955-. . . . . **CLC 70**

Ouida . . . . **TCLC 43**
See also De La Ramee, (Marie) Louise
See also DLB 18

Ousmane, Sembene 1923- . . . . **CLC 66**
See also BLC 3; BW; CA 117; 125; MTCW

Ovid 43B.C.-18th cent. (?) . . . **CMLC 7; PC 2**

Owen, Wilfred 1893-1918 . . . . . . **TCLC 5, 27**
See also CA 104; CDBLB 1914-1945; DLB 20; WLC

Owens, Rochelle 1936-. . . . . **CLC 8**
See also CA 17-20R; CAAS 2; CANR 39

Oz, Amos 1939- . . . **CLC 5, 8, 11, 27, 33, 54**
See also CA 53-56; CANR 27; MTCW

Ozick, Cynthia 1928-. . . . . . **CLC 3, 7, 28, 62**
See also BEST 90:1; CA 17-20R; CANR 23; DLB 28; DLBY 82; MTCW

Ozu, Yasujiro 1903-1963 . . . . **CLC 16**
See also CA 112

Pacheco, C.
See Pessoa, Fernando (Antonio Nogueira)

Pa Chin
See Li Fei-kan

Pack, Robert 1929-. . . . . **CLC 13**
See also CA 1-4R; CANR 3; DLB 5

Padgett, Lewis
See Kuttner, Henry

Padilla (Lorenzo), Heberto 1932- . . . **CLC 38**
See also AITN 1; CA 123; 131; HW

Page, Jimmy 1944-. . . . . **CLC 12**

Page, Louise 1955-. . . . . **CLC 40**

Page, P(atricia) K(athleen)
1916- . . . . **CLC 7, 18**
See also CA 53-56; CANR 4, 22; DLB 68; MTCW

Paget, Violet 1856-1935
See Lee, Vernon
See also CA 104

Paget-Lowe, Henry
See Lovecraft, H(oward) P(hillips)

Paglia, Camille 1947-. . . . . **CLC 68**

Pakenham, Antonia
See Fraser, Antonia (Pakenham)

Palamas, Kostes 1859-1943 . . . . **TCLC 5**
See also CA 105

Palazzeschi, Aldo 1885-1974 . . . . **CLC 11**
See also CA 89-92; 53-56; DLB 114

Paley, Grace 1922- . . . . **CLC 4, 6, 37; SSC 8**
See also CA 25-28R; CANR 13; DLB 28; MTCW

Palin, Michael (Edward) 1943- . . . . . **CLC 21**
See also Monty Python
See also CA 107; CANR 35; SATA 67

Palliser, Charles 1947-. . . . . **CLC 65**
See also CA 136

Palma, Ricardo 1833-1919. . . . . **TCLC 29**

Pancake, Breece Dexter 1952-1979
See Pancake, Breece D'J
See also CA 123; 109

Pancake, Breece D'J. . . . . **CLC 29**
See also Pancake, Breece Dexter

Papadiamantis, Alexandros
1851-1911 . . . . **TCLC 29**

Papadiamantopoulos, Johannes 1856-1910
See Moreas, Jean
See also CA 117

Papini, Giovanni 1881-1956. . . . . . . **TCLC 22**
See also CA 121

Paracelsus 1493-1541 . . . . **LC 14**

Parasol, Peter
See Stevens, Wallace

Parfenie, Maria
See Codrescu, Andrei

Parini, Jay (Lee) 1948- . . . . **CLC 54**
See also CA 97-100; CAAS 16; CANR 32

Park, Jordan
See Kornbluth, C(yril) M.; Pohl, Frederik

Parker, Bert
See Ellison, Harlan

Parker, Dorothy (Rothschild)
1893-1967 . . . . **CLC 15, 68; SSC 2**
See also CA 19-20; 25-28R; CAP 2; DLB 11, 45, 86; MTCW

Parker, Robert B(rown) 1932-. . . . . . **CLC 27**
See also BEST 89:4; CA 49-52; CANR 1, 26; MTCW

Parkes, Lucas
See Harris, John (Wyndham Parkes Lucas) Beynon

Parkin, Frank 1940-. . . . . **CLC 43**

Parkman, Francis Jr. 1823-1893 . . **NCLC 12**
See also DLB 1, 30

Parks, Gordon (Alexander Buchanan)
1912- . . . . **CLC 1, 16**
See also AITN 2; BLC 3; BW; CA 41-44R; CANR 26; DLB 33; SATA 8

Parnell, Thomas 1679-1718 . . . . **LC 3**
See also DLB 94

Parra, Nicanor 1914- . . . . **CLC 2**
See also CA 85-88; CANR 32; HW; MTCW

Parson Lot
See Kingsley, Charles

Partridge, Anthony
See Oppenheim, E(dward) Phillips

Pascoli, Giovanni 1855-1912 . . . . . . **TCLC 45**

Pasolini, Pier Paolo
1922-1975 . . . . **CLC 20, 37**
See also CA 93-96; 61-64; MTCW

Pasquini
See Silone, Ignazio

Pastan, Linda (Olenik) 1932- . . . . . . **CLC 27**
See also CA 61-64; CANR 18; DLB 5

Pasternak, Boris (Leonidovich)
1890-1960 . . . . **CLC 7, 10, 18, 63**
See also CA 127; 116; MTCW; WLC

Patchen, Kenneth 1911-1972 . . . **CLC 1, 2, 18**
See also CA 1-4R; 33-36R; CANR 3, 35; DLB 16, 48; MTCW

Pater, Walter (Horatio)
1839-1894 . . . . **NCLC 7**
See also CDBLB 1832-1890; DLB 57

Paterson, A(ndrew) B(arton)
1864-1941 . . . . **TCLC 32**

Paterson, Katherine (Womeldorf)
1932- . . . . **CLC 12, 30**
See also AAYA 1; CA 21-24R; CANR 28; CLR 7; DLB 52; MAICYA; MTCW; SATA 13, 53

Patmore, Coventry Kersey Dighton
1823-1896 . . . . **NCLC 9**
See also DLB 35, 98

Paton, Alan (Stewart)
1903-1988 . . . . **CLC 4, 10, 25, 55**
See also CA 13-16; 125; CANR 22; CAP 1; MTCW; SATA 11, 56; WLC

Paton Walsh, Gillian 1939-
See Walsh, Jill Paton
See also CANR 38; MAICYA; SAAS 3; SATA 4

Paulding, James Kirke 1778-1860. . **NCLC 2**
See also DLB 3, 59, 74

Paulin, Thomas Neilson 1949-
See Paulin, Tom
See also CA 123; 128

Paulin, Tom. . . . . **CLC 37**
See also Paulin, Thomas Neilson
See also DLB 40

Paustovsky, Konstantin (Georgievich)
1892-1968 . . . . **CLC 40**
See also CA 93-96; 25-28R

Pavese, Cesare 1908-1950 . . . . **TCLC 3**
See also CA 104

Pavic, Milorad 1929-. . . . . **CLC 60**
See also CA 136

Payne, Alan
See Jakes, John (William)

Paz, Gil
See Lugones, Leopoldo

Paz, Octavio
1914- ...... **CLC 3, 4, 6, 10, 19, 51, 65; PC 1**
See also CA 73-76; CANR 32; DLBY 90; HW; MTCW; WLC

Peacock, Molly 1947-............. **CLC 60**
See also CA 103; DLB 120

Peacock, Thomas Love
1785-1866 .... **NCLC 22**
See also DLB 96, 116

Peake, Mervyn 1911-1968 .... **CLC 7, 54**
See also CA 5-8R; 25-28R; CANR 3; DLB 15; MTCW; SATA 23

Pearce, Philippa .... **CLC 21**
See also Christie, (Ann) Philippa
See also CLR 9; MAICYA; SATA 1, 67

Pearl, Eric
See Elman, Richard

Pearson, T(homas) R(eid) 1956- .... **CLC 39**
See also CA 120; 130

Peck, John 1941- .... **CLC 3**
See also CA 49-52; CANR 3

Peck, Richard (Wayne) 1934- ...... **CLC 21**
See also AAYA 1; CA 85-88; CANR 19, 38; MAICYA; SAAS 2; SATA 18, 55

Peck, Robert Newton 1928-........ **CLC 17**
See also AAYA 3; CA 81-84; CANR 31; MAICYA; SAAS 1; SATA 21, 62

Peckinpah, (David) Sam(uel)
1925-1984 .... **CLC 20**
See also CA 109; 114

Pedersen, Knut 1859-1952
See Hamsun, Knut
See also CA 104; 119; MTCW

Peeslake, Gaffer
See Durrell, Lawrence (George)

Peguy, Charles Pierre
1873-1914 .... **TCLC 10**
See also CA 107

Pena, Ramon del Valle y
See Valle-Inclan, Ramon (Maria) del

Pendennis, Arthur Esquir
See Thackeray, William Makepeace

Pepys, Samuel 1633-1703........... **LC 11**
See also CDBLB 1660-1789; DLB 101; WLC

Percy, Walker
1916-1990 ... **CLC 2, 3, 6, 8, 14, 18, 47, 65**
See also CA 1-4R; 131; CANR 1, 23; DLB 2; DLBY 80, 90; MTCW

Perec, Georges 1936-1982 .... **CLC 56**
See also DLB 83

Pereda (y Sanchez de Porrua), Jose Maria de
1833-1906 .... **TCLC 16**
See also CA 117

Pereda y Porrua, Jose Maria de
See Pereda (y Sanchez de Porrua), Jose Maria de

Peregoy, George Weems
See Mencken, H(enry) L(ouis)

Perelman, S(idney) J(oseph)
1904-1979 ... **CLC 3, 5, 9, 15, 23, 44, 49**
See also AITN 1, 2; CA 73-76; 89-92; CANR 18; DLB 11, 44; MTCW

Peret, Benjamin 1899-1959 .... **TCLC 20**
See also CA 117

Peretz, Isaac Loeb 1851(?)-1915... **TCLC 16**
See also CA 109

Peretz, Yitzkhok Leibush
See Peretz, Isaac Loeb

Perez Galdos, Benito 1843-1920... **TCLC 27**
See also CA 125; HW

Perrault, Charles 1628-1703 .... **LC 2**
See also MAICYA; SATA 25

Perry, Brighton
See Sherwood, Robert E(mmet)

Perse, St.-John .... **CLC 4, 11, 46**
See also Leger, (Marie-Rene) Alexis Saint-Leger

Perse, Saint-John
See Leger, (Marie-Rene) Alexis Saint-Leger

Peseenz, Tulio F.
See Lopez y Fuentes, Gregorio

Pesetsky, Bette 1932-............. **CLC 28**
See also CA 133

Peshkov, Alexei Maximovich 1868-1936
See Gorky, Maxim
See also CA 105

Pessoa, Fernando (Antonio Nogueira)
1888-1935 .... **TCLC 27**
See also CA 125

Peterkin, Julia Mood 1880-1961.... **CLC 31**
See also CA 102; DLB 9

Peters, Joan K. 1945-............. **CLC 39**

Peters, Robert L(ouis) 1924-........ **CLC 7**
See also CA 13-16R; CAAS 8; DLB 105

Petofi, Sandor 1823-1849........ **NCLC 21**

Petrakis, Harry Mark 1923-........ **CLC 3**
See also CA 9-12R; CANR 4, 30

Petrov, Evgeny .... **TCLC 21**
See also Kataev, Evgeny Petrovich

Petry, Ann (Lane) 1908- ...... **CLC 1, 7, 18**
See also BW; CA 5-8R; CAAS 6; CANR 4; CLR 12; DLB 76; MAICYA; MTCW; SATA 5

Petursson, Halligrimur 1614-1674 .... **LC 8**

Philipson, Morris H. 1926-........ **CLC 53**
See also CA 1-4R; CANR 4

Phillips, David Graham
1867-1911 .... **TCLC 44**
See also CA 108; DLB 9, 12

Phillips, Jack
See Sandburg, Carl (August)

Phillips, Jayne Anne 1952- ..... **CLC 15, 33**
See also CA 101; CANR 24; DLBY 80; MTCW

Phillips, Richard
See Dick, Philip K(indred)

Phillips, Robert (Schaeffer) 1938-... **CLC 28**
See also CA 17-20R; CAAS 13; CANR 8; DLB 105

Phillips, Ward
See Lovecraft, H(oward) P(hillips)

Piccolo, Lucio 1901-1969.......... **CLC 13**
See also CA 97-100; DLB 114

Pickthall, Marjorie L(owry) C(hristie)
1883-1922 .... **TCLC 21**
See also CA 107; DLB 92

Pico della Mirandola, Giovanni
1463-1494 .... **LC 15**

Piercy, Marge
1936- .... **CLC 3, 6, 14, 18, 27, 62**
See also CA 21-24R; CAAS 1; CANR 13; DLB 120; MTCW

Piers, Robert
See Anthony, Piers

Pieyre de Mandiargues, Andre 1909-1991
See Mandiargues, Andre Pieyre de
See also CA 103; 136; CANR 22

Pilnyak, Boris .... **TCLC 23**
See also Vogau, Boris Andreyevich

Pincherle, Alberto 1907-1990 ... **CLC 11, 18**
See also Moravia, Alberto
See also CA 25-28R; 132; CANR 33; MTCW

Pineda, Cecile 1942-.............. **CLC 39**
See also CA 118

Pinero, Arthur Wing 1855-1934 ... **TCLC 32**
See also CA 110; DLB 10

Pinero, Miguel (Antonio Gomez)
1946-1988 .... **CLC 4, 55**
See also CA 61-64; 125; CANR 29; HW

Pinget, Robert 1919- .... **CLC 7, 13, 37**
See also CA 85-88; DLB 83

Floyd .... **CLC 35**
See also Barrett, (Roger) Syd; Gilmour, David; Mason, Nick; Waters, Roger; Wright, Rick

Pinkney, Edward 1802-1828 ..... **NCLC 31**

Pinkwater, Daniel Manus 1941- .... **CLC 35**
See also Pinkwater, Manus
See also AAYA 1; CA 29-32R; CANR 12, 38; CLR 4; MAICYA; SAAS 3; SATA 46

Pinkwater, Manus
See Pinkwater, Daniel Manus
See also SATA 8

Pinsky, Robert 1940-........ **CLC 9, 19, 38**
See also CA 29-32R; CAAS 4; DLBY 82

Pinta, Harold
See Pinter, Harold

Pinter, Harold
1930- ..... **CLC 1, 3, 6, 9, 11, 15, 27, 58**
See also CA 5-8R; CANR 33; CDBLB 1960 to Present; DLB 13; MTCW; WLC

Pirandello, Luigi 1867-1936..... **TCLC 4, 29**
See also CA 104; WLC

Pirsig, Robert M(aynard) 1928- ... **CLC 4, 6**
See also CA 53-56; MTCW; SATA 39

Pisarev, Dmitry Ivanovich
1840-1868 .... **NCLC 25**

Pix, Mary (Griffith) 1666-1709....... **LC 8**
See also DLB 80

Plaidy, Jean
See Hibbert, Eleanor Burford

Plant, Robert 1948-.............. **CLC 12**

Plante, David (Robert) 1940- .... **CLC 7, 23, 38**
See also CA 37-40R; CANR 12, 36; DLBY 83; MTCW

Plath, Sylvia 1932-1963 .... **CLC 1, 2, 3, 5, 9, 11, 14, 17, 50, 51, 62; PC 1**
See also CA 19-20; CANR 34; CAP 2; CDALB 1941-1968; DLB 5, 6; MTCW; WLC

Plato 428(?)B.C.-348(?)B.C. .... **CMLC 8**

Platonov, Andrei .... **TCLC 14**
See also Klimentov, Andrei Platonovich

Platt, Kin 1911- .... **CLC 26**
See also CA 17-20R; CANR 11; SATA 21

Plick et Plock
See Simenon, Georges (Jacques Christian)

Plimpton, George (Ames) 1927-..... **CLC 36**
See also AITN 1; CA 21-24R; CANR 32; MTCW; SATA 10

Plomer, William Charles Franklin 1903-1973 .... **CLC 4, 8**
See also CA 21-22; CANR 34; CAP 2; DLB 20; MTCW; SATA 24

Plowman, Piers
See Kavanagh, Patrick (Joseph)

Plum, J.
See Wodehouse, P(elham) G(renville)

Plumly, Stanley (Ross) 1939- ...... **CLC 33**
See also CA 108; 110; DLB 5

Poe, Edgar Allan 1809-1849 ... **NCLC 1, 16; PC 1; SSC 1**
See also CDALB 1640-1865; DLB 3, 59, 73, 74; SATA 23; WLC

Poet of Titchfield Street, The
See Pound, Ezra (Weston Loomis)

Pohl, Frederik 1919- .... **CLC 18**
See also CA 61-64; CAAS 1; CANR 11, 37; DLB 8; MTCW; SATA 24

Poirier, Louis 1910-
See Gracq, Julien
See also CA 122; 126

Poitier, Sidney 1927- .... **CLC 26**
See also BW; CA 117

Polanski, Roman 1933- .... **CLC 16**
See also CA 77-80

Poliakoff, Stephen 1952- .... **CLC 38**
See also CA 106; DLB 13

.... **CLC 26**
See also Copeland, Stewart (Armstrong); Summers, Andrew James; Sumner, Gordon Matthew

Pollitt, Katha 1949- .... **CLC 28**
See also CA 120; 122; MTCW

Pollock, Sharon 1936- .... **CLC 50**
See also DLB 60

Pomerance, Bernard 1940-......... **CLC 13**
See also CA 101

Ponge, Francis (Jean Gaston Alfred) 1899-1988 .... **CLC 6, 18**
See also CA 85-88; 126

Pontoppidan, Henrik 1857-1943 ... **TCLC 29**

Poole, Josephine .... **CLC 17**
See also Helyar, Jane Penelope Josephine
See also SAAS 2; SATA 5

Popa, Vasko 1922- .... **CLC 19**
See also CA 112

Pope, Alexander 1688-1744 .... **LC 3**
See also CDBLB 1660-1789; DLB 95, 101; WLC

Porter, Connie 1960- .... **CLC 70**

Porter, Gene(va Grace) Stratton 1863(?)-1924 .... **TCLC 21**
See also CA 112

Porter, Katherine Anne 1890-1980 ..... **CLC 1, 3, 7, 10, 13, 15, 27; SSC 4**
See also AITN 2; CA 1-4R; 101; CANR 1; DLB 4, 9, 102; DLBY 80; MTCW; SATA 23, 39

Porter, Peter (Neville Frederick) 1929- .... **CLC 5, 13, 33**
See also CA 85-88; DLB 40

Porter, William Sydney 1862-1910
See Henry, O.
See also CA 104; 131; CDALB 1865-1917; DLB 12, 78, 79; MTCW; YABC 2

Portillo (y Pacheco), Jose Lopez
See Lopez Portillo (y Pacheco), Jose

Post, Melville Davisson 1869-1930 .... **TCLC 39**
See also CA 110

Potok, Chaim 1929- .... **CLC 2, 7, 14, 26**
See also AITN 1, 2; CA 17-20R; CANR 19, 35; DLB 28; MTCW; SATA 33

Potter, Beatrice
See Webb, (Martha) Beatrice (Potter)
See also MAICYA

Potter, Dennis (Christopher George) 1935- .... **CLC 58**
See also CA 107; CANR 33; MTCW

Pound, Ezra (Weston Loomis) 1885-1972 ..... **CLC 1, 2, 3, 4, 5, 7, 10, 13, 18, 34, 48, 50; PC 4**
See also CA 5-8R; 37-40R; CDALB 1917-1929; DLB 4, 45, 63; MTCW; WLC

Povod, Reinaldo 1959- .... **CLC 44**
See also CA 136

Powell, Anthony (Dymoke) 1905- .... **CLC 1, 3, 7, 9, 10, 31**
See also CA 1-4R; CANR 1, 32; CDBLB 1945-1960; DLB 15; MTCW

Powell, Dawn 1897-1965 .... **CLC 66**
See also CA 5-8R

Powell, Padgett 1952- .... **CLC 34**
See also CA 126

Powers, J(ames) F(arl) 1917- .... **CLC 1, 4, 8, 57; SSC 4**
See also CA 1-4R; CANR 2; MTCW

Powers, John J(ames) 1945-
See Powers, John R.
See also CA 69-72

Powers, John R. .... **CLC 66**
See also Powers, John J(ames)

Pownall, David 1938- .... **CLC 10**
See also CA 89-92; DLB 14

Powys, John Cowper 1872-1963 .... **CLC 7, 9, 15, 46**
See also CA 85-88; DLB 15; MTCW

Powys, T(heodore) F(rancis) 1875-1953 .... **TCLC 9**
See also CA 106; DLB 36

Prager, Emily 1952- .... **CLC 56**

Pratt, Edwin John 1883-1964 ...... **CLC 19**
See also CA 93-96; DLB 92

Premchand .... **TCLC 21**
See also Srivastava, Dhanpat Rai

Preussler, Otfried 1923- .... **CLC 17**
See also CA 77-80; SATA 24

Prevert, Jacques (Henri Marie) 1900-1977 .... **CLC 15**
See also CA 77-80; 69-72; CANR 29; MTCW; SATA 30

Prevost, Abbe (Antoine Francois) 1697-1763 .... **LC 1**

Price, (Edward) Reynolds 1933- .... **CLC 3, 6, 13, 43, 50, 63**
See also CA 1-4R; CANR 1, 37; DLB 2

Price, Richard 1949- .... **CLC 6, 12**
See also CA 49-52; CANR 3; DLBY 81

Prichard, Katharine Susannah 1883-1969 .... **CLC 46**
See also CA 11-12; CANR 33; CAP 1; MTCW; SATA 66

Priestley, J(ohn) B(oynton) 1894-1984 .... **CLC 2, 5, 9, 34**
See also CA 9-12R; 113; CANR 33; CDBLB 1914-1945; DLB 10, 34, 77, 100; DLBY 84; MTCW

Prince, F(rank) T(empleton) 1912- .. **CLC 22**
See also CA 101; DLB 20

Prince 1958(?)- .... **CLC 35**

Prince Kropotkin
See Kropotkin, Peter (Aleksieevich)

Prior, Matthew 1664-1721........... **LC 4**
See also DLB 95

Pritchard, William H(arrison) 1932- .... **CLC 34**
See also CA 65-68; CANR 23; DLB 111

Pritchett, V(ictor) S(awdon) 1900- .... **CLC 5, 13, 15, 41**
See also CA 61-64; CANR 31; DLB 15; MTCW

Private 19022
See Manning, Frederic

Probst, Mark 1925- .... **CLC 59**
See also CA 130

Prokosch, Frederic 1908-1989.... **CLC 4, 48**
See also CA 73-76; 128; DLB 48

Prophet, The
See Dreiser, Theodore (Herman Albert)

Prose, Francine 1947- .... **CLC 45**
See also CA 109; 112

Proudhon
See Cunha, Euclides (Rodrigues Pimenta) da

Proust, (Valentin-Louis-George-Eugene-)Marcel 1871-1922 .... **TCLC 7, 13, 33**
See also CA 104; 120; DLB 65; MTCW; WLC

Prowler, Harley
See Masters, Edgar Lee

Pryor, Richard (Franklin Lenox Thomas) 1940- . . . . **CLC 26**
See also CA 122

Przybyszewski, Stanislaw 1868-1927 . . . . **TCLC 36**
See also DLB 66

Pteleon
See Grieve, C(hristopher) M(urray)

Puckett, Lute
See Masters, Edgar Lee

Puig, Manuel 1932-1990 . . . . . **CLC 3, 5, 10, 28, 65**
See also CA 45-48; CANR 2, 32; DLB 113; HW; MTCW

Purdy, A(lfred) W(ellington) 1918- . . . . **CLC 3, 6, 14, 50**
See also Purdy, Al
See also CA 81-84

Purdy, Al
See Purdy, A(lfred) W(ellington)
See also DLB 88

Purdy, James (Amos) 1923- . . . . **CLC 2, 4, 10, 28, 52**
See also CA 33-36R; CAAS 1; CANR 19; DLB 2; MTCW

Pure, Simon
See Swinnerton, Frank Arthur

Pushkin, Alexander (Sergeyevich) 1799-1837 . . . . **NCLC 3, 27**
See also SATA 61; WLC

P'u Sung-ling 1640-1715 . . . . **LC 3**

Putnam, Arthur Lee
See Alger, Horatio Jr.

Puzo, Mario 1920- . . . . . **CLC 1, 2, 6, 36**
See also CA 65-68; CANR 4; DLB 6; MTCW

Pym, Barbara (Mary Crampton) 1913-1980 . . . . **CLC 13, 19, 37**
See also CA 13-14; 97-100; CANR 13, 34; CAP 1; DLB 14; DLBY 87; MTCW

Pynchon, Thomas (Ruggles Jr.) 1937- . . **CLC 2, 3, 6, 9, 11, 18, 33, 62, 72**
See also BEST 90:2; CA 17-20R; CANR 22; DLB 2; MTCW; WLC

Qian Zhongshu
See Ch'ien Chung-shu

Qroll
See Dagerman, Stig (Halvard)

Quarrington, Paul (Lewis) 1953-. . . . **CLC 65**
See also CA 129

Quasimodo, Salvatore 1901-1968 . . . **CLC 10**
See also CA 13-16; 25-28R; CAP 1; DLB 114; MTCW

Queen, Ellery. . . . . **CLC 3, 11**
See also Dannay, Frederic; Davidson, Avram; Lee, Manfred B(ennington); Sturgeon, Theodore (Hamilton); Vance, John Holbrook

Queen, Ellery Jr.
See Dannay, Frederic; Lee, Manfred B(ennington)

Queneau, Raymond 1903-1976 . . . . **CLC 2, 5, 10, 42**
See also CA 77-80; 69-72; CANR 32; DLB 72; MTCW

Quin, Ann (Marie) 1936-1973 . . . . **CLC 6**
See also CA 9-12R; 45-48; DLB 14

Quinn, Martin
See Smith, Martin Cruz

Quinn, Simon
See Smith, Martin Cruz

Quiroga, Horacio (Sylvestre) 1878-1937 . . . . **TCLC 20**
See also CA 117; 131; HW; MTCW

Quoirez, Francoise 1935-. . . . . **CLC 9**
See also Sagan, Francoise
See also CA 49-52; CANR 6, 39; MTCW

Raabe, Wilhelm 1831-1910 . . . . **TCLC 45**

Rabe, David (William) 1940-. . . **CLC 4, 8, 33**
See also CA 85-88; CABS 3; DLB 7

Rabelais, Francois 1483-1553 . . . . **LC 5**
See also WLC

Rabinovitch, Sholem 1859-1916
See Aleichem, Sholom
See also CA 104

Radcliffe, Ann (Ward) 1764-1823 . . **NCLC 6**
See also DLB 39

Radiguet, Raymond 1903-1923 . . . . **TCLC 29**
See also DLB 65

Radnoti, Miklos 1909-1944 . . . . **TCLC 16**
See also CA 118

Rado, James 1939- . . . . **CLC 17**
See also CA 105

Radvanyi, Netty 1900-1983
See Seghers, Anna
See also CA 85-88; 110

Raeburn, John (Hay) 1941- . . . . **CLC 34**
See also CA 57-60

Ragni, Gerome 1942-1991 . . . . **CLC 17**
See also CA 105; 134

Rahv, Philip. . . . . **CLC 24**
See also Greenberg, Ivan

Raine, Craig 1944- . . . . **CLC 32**
See also CA 108; CANR 29; DLB 40

Raine, Kathleen (Jessie) 1908- . . . **CLC 7, 45**
See also CA 85-88; DLB 20; MTCW

Rainis, Janis 1865-1929 . . . . **TCLC 29**

Rakosi, Carl. . . . . **CLC 47**
See also Rawley, Callman
See also CAAS 5

Raleigh, Richard
See Lovecraft, H(oward) P(hillips)

Rallentando, H. P.
See Sayers, Dorothy L(eigh)

Ramal, Walter
See de la Mare, Walter (John)

Ramon, Juan
See Jimenez (Mantecon), Juan Ramon

Ramos, Graciliano 1892-1953 . . . . . **TCLC 32**

Rampersad, Arnold 1941-. . . . . **CLC 44**
See also CA 127; 133; DLB 111

Rampling, Anne
See Rice, Anne

Ramuz, Charles-Ferdinand 1878-1947 . . . . **TCLC 33**

Rand, Ayn 1905-1982. . . . . **CLC 3, 30, 44**
See also CA 13-16R; 105; CANR 27; MTCW; WLC

Randall, Dudley (Felker) 1914-. . . . . . **CLC 1**
See also BLC 3; BW; CA 25-28R; CANR 23; DLB 41

Randall, Robert
See Silverberg, Robert

Ranger, Ken
See Creasey, John

Ransom, John Crowe 1888-1974 . . . . **CLC 2, 4, 5, 11, 24**
See also CA 5-8R; 49-52; CANR 6, 34; DLB 45, 63; MTCW

Rao, Raja 1909- . . . . **CLC 25, 56**
See also CA 73-76; MTCW

Raphael, Frederic (Michael) 1931- . . . . **CLC 2, 14**
See also CA 1-4R; CANR 1; DLB 14

Ratcliffe, James P.
See Mencken, H(enry) L(ouis)

Rathbone, Julian 1935- . . . . **CLC 41**
See also CA 101; CANR 34

Rattigan, Terence (Mervyn) 1911-1977 . . . . **CLC 7**
See also CA 85-88; 73-76; CDBLB 1945-1960; DLB 13; MTCW

Ratushinskaya, Irina 1954- . . . . **CLC 54**
See also CA 129

Raven, Simon (Arthur Noel) 1927- . . . . **CLC 14**
See also CA 81-84

Rawley, Callman 1903-
See Rakosi, Carl
See also CA 21-24R; CANR 12, 32

Rawlings, Marjorie Kinnan 1896-1953 . . . . **TCLC 4**
See also CA 104; 137; DLB 9, 22, 102; MAICYA; YABC 1

Ray, Satyajit 1921-. . . . . **CLC 16**
See also CA 114; 137

Read, Herbert Edward 1893-1968. . . . **CLC 4**
See also CA 85-88; 25-28R; DLB 20

Read, Piers Paul 1941- . . . . . . **CLC 4, 10, 25**
See also CA 21-24R; CANR 38; DLB 14; SATA 21

Reade, Charles 1814-1884 . . . . **NCLC 2**
See also DLB 21

Reade, Hamish
See Gray, Simon (James Holliday)

Reading, Peter 1946- . . . . **CLC 47**
See also CA 103; DLB 40

Reaney, James 1926- . . . . **CLC 13**
See also CA 41-44R; CAAS 15; DLB 68; SATA 43

Rebreanu, Liviu 1885-1944 . . . . **TCLC 28**

Rechy, John (Francisco) 1934- . . . . **CLC 1, 7, 14, 18**
See also CA 5-8R; CAAS 4; CANR 6, 32; DLBY 82; HW

Redcam, Tom 1870-1933 . . . . **TCLC 25**

Reddin, Keith. . . . . **CLC 67**

Redgrove, Peter (William) 1932- .... **CLC 6, 41**
See also CA 1-4R; CANR 3, 39; DLB 40

Redmon, Anne .... **CLC 22**
See also Nightingale, Anne Redmon
See also DLBY 86

Reed, Eliot
See Ambler, Eric

Reed, Ishmael 1938- .... **CLC 2, 3, 5, 6, 13, 32, 60**
See also BLC 3; BW; CA 21-24R; CANR 25; DLB 2, 5, 33; DLBD 8; MTCW

Reed, John (Silas) 1887-1920 ...... **TCLC 9**
See also CA 106

Reed, Lou .... **CLC 21**
See also Firbank, Louis

Reeve, Clara 1729-1807 .... **NCLC 19**
See also DLB 39

Reid, Christopher 1949- .... **CLC 33**
See also DLB 40

Reid, Desmond
See Moorcock, Michael (John)

Reid Banks, Lynne 1929-
See Banks, Lynne Reid
See also CA 1-4R; CANR 6, 22, 38; CLR 24; MAICYA; SATA 22

Reilly, William K.
See Creasey, John

Reiner, Max
See Caldwell, (Janet Miriam) Taylor (Holland)

Reis, Ricardo
See Pessoa, Fernando (Antonio Nogueira)

Remarque, Erich Maria 1898-1970 .... **CLC 21**
See also CA 77-80; 29-32R; DLB 56; MTCW

Remizov, A.
See Remizov, Aleksei (Mikhailovich)

Remizov, A. M.
See Remizov, Aleksei (Mikhailovich)

Remizov, Aleksei (Mikhailovich) 1877-1957 .... **TCLC 27**
See also CA 125; 133

Renan, Joseph Ernest 1823-1892 .... **NCLC 26**

Renard, Jules 1864-1910 .... **TCLC 17**
See also CA 117

Renault, Mary .... **CLC 3, 11, 17**
See also Challans, Mary
See also DLBY 83

Rendell, Ruth (Barbara) 1930- .. **CLC 28, 48**
See also Vine, Barbara
See also CA 109; CANR 32; DLB 87; MTCW

Renoir, Jean 1894-1979 .... **CLC 20**
See also CA 129; 85-88

Resnais, Alain 1922- .... **CLC 16**

Reverdy, Pierre 1889-1960 .... **CLC 53**
See also CA 97-100; 89-92

Rexroth, Kenneth 1905-1982 ...... **CLC 1, 2, 6, 11, 22, 49**
See also CA 5-8R; 107; CANR 14, 34; CDALB 1941-1968; DLB 16, 48; DLBY 82; MTCW

Reyes, Alfonso 1889-1959 .... **TCLC 33**
See also CA 131; HW

Reyes y Basoalto, Ricardo Eliecer Neftali
See Neruda, Pablo

Reymont, Wladyslaw (Stanislaw) 1868(?)-1925 .... **TCLC 5**
See also CA 104

Reynolds, Jonathan 1942- .... **CLC 6, 38**
See also CA 65-68; CANR 28

Reynolds, Joshua 1723-1792 .... **LC 15**
See also DLB 104

Reynolds, Michael Shane 1937- .... **CLC 44**
See also CA 65-68; CANR 9

Reznikoff, Charles 1894-1976 .... **CLC 9**
See also CA 33-36; 61-64; CAP 2; DLB 28, 45

Rezzori (d'Arezzo), Gregor von 1914- .... **CLC 25**
See also CA 122; 136

Rhine, Richard
See Silverstein, Alvin

Rhys, Jean 1890(?)-1979 .... **CLC 2, 4, 6, 14, 19, 51**
See also CA 25-28R; 85-88; CANR 35; CDBLB 1945-1960; DLB 36, 117; MTCW

Ribeiro, Darcy 1922- .... **CLC 34**
See also CA 33-36R

Ribeiro, Joao Ubaldo (Osorio Pimentel) 1941- .... **CLC 10, 67**
See also CA 81-84

Ribman, Ronald (Burt) 1932- .... **CLC 7**
See also CA 21-24R

Ricci, Nino 1959- .... **CLC 70**
See also CA 137

Rice, Anne 1941- .... **CLC 41**
See also AAYA 9; BEST 89:2; CA 65-68; CANR 12, 36

Rice, Elmer (Leopold) 1892-1967 .... **CLC 7, 49**
See also CA 21-22; 25-28R; CAP 2; DLB 4, 7; MTCW

Rice, Tim 1944- .... **CLC 21**
See also CA 103

Rich, Adrienne (Cecile) 1929- ..... **CLC 3, 6, 7, 11, 18, 36; PC 5**
See also CA 9-12R; CANR 20; DLB 5, 67; MTCW

Rich, Barbara
See Graves, Robert (von Ranke)

Rich, Robert
See Trumbo, Dalton

Richards, David Adams 1950- ...... **CLC 59**
See also CA 93-96; DLB 53

Richards, I(vor) A(rmstrong) 1893-1979 .... **CLC 14, 24**
See also CA 41-44R; 89-92; CANR 34; DLB 27

Richardson, Anne
See Roiphe, Anne Richardson

Richardson, Dorothy Miller 1873-1957 .... **TCLC 3**
See also CA 104; DLB 36

Richardson, Ethel Florence (Lindesay) 1870-1946
See Richardson, Henry Handel
See also CA 105

Richardson, Henry Handel .... **TCLC 4**
See also Richardson, Ethel Florence (Lindesay)

Richardson, Samuel 1689-1761 .... **LC 1**
See also CDBLB 1660-1789; DLB 39; WLC

Richler, Mordecai 1931- .... **CLC 3, 5, 9, 13, 18, 46, 70**
See also AITN 1; CA 65-68; CANR 31; CLR 17; DLB 53; MAICYA; MTCW; SATA 27, 44

Richter, Conrad (Michael) 1890-1968 .... **CLC 30**
See also CA 5-8R; 25-28R; CANR 23; DLB 9; MTCW; SATA 3

Riddell, J. H. 1832-1906 .... **TCLC 40**

Riding, Laura .... **CLC 3, 7**
See also Jackson, Laura (Riding)

Riefenstahl, Berta Helene Amalia 1902-
See Riefenstahl, Leni
See also CA 108

Riefenstahl, Leni .... **CLC 16**
See also Riefenstahl, Berta Helene Amalia

Riffe, Ernest
See Bergman, (Ernst) Ingmar

Riley, Tex
See Creasey, John

Rilke, Rainer Maria 1875-1926 .... **TCLC 1, 6, 19; PC 2**
See also CA 104; 132; DLB 81; MTCW

Rimbaud, (Jean Nicolas) Arthur 1854-1891 .... **NCLC 4, 35; PC 3**
See also WLC

Ringmaster, The
See Mencken, H(enry) L(ouis)

Ringwood, Gwen(dolyn Margaret) Pharis 1910-1984 .... **CLC 48**
See also CA 112; DLB 88

Rio, Michel 19(?)- .... **CLC 43**

Ritsos, Giannes
See Ritsos, Yannis

Ritsos, Yannis 1909-1990 ..... **CLC 6, 13, 31**
See also CA 77-80; 133; CANR 39; MTCW

Ritter, Erika 1948(?)- .... **CLC 52**

Rivera, Jose Eustasio 1889-1928 ... **TCLC 35**
See also HW

Rivers, Conrad Kent 1933-1968 ...... **CLC 1**
See also BW; CA 85-88; DLB 41

Rivers, Elfrida
See Bradley, Marion Zimmer

Riverside, John
See Heinlein, Robert A(nson)

Rizal, Jose 1861-1896 .... **NCLC 27**

Roa Bastos, Augusto (Antonio) 1917- .... **CLC 45**
See also CA 131; DLB 113; HW

Robbe-Grillet, Alain 1922- ...... **CLC 1, 2, 4, 6, 8, 10, 14, 43**
See also CA 9-12R; CANR 33; DLB 83; MTCW

Robbins, Harold 1916- .... **CLC 5**
See also CA 73-76; CANR 26; MTCW

Robbins, Thomas Eugene 1936-
See Robbins, Tom
See also CA 81-84; CANR 29; MTCW

Robbins, Tom .... **CLC 9, 32, 64**
See also Robbins, Thomas Eugene
See also BEST 90:3; DLBY 80

Robbins, Trina 1938- .... **CLC 21**
See also CA 128

Roberts, Charles G(eorge) D(ouglas) 1860-1943 .... **TCLC 8**
See also CA 105; DLB 92; SATA 29

Roberts, Kate 1891-1985 .... **CLC 15**
See also CA 107; 116

Roberts, Keith (John Kingston) 1935- .... **CLC 14**
See also CA 25-28R

Roberts, Kenneth (Lewis) 1885-1957 .... **TCLC 23**
See also CA 109; DLB 9

Roberts, Michele (B.) 1949- .... **CLC 48**
See also CA 115

Robertson, Ellis
See Ellison, Harlan; Silverberg, Robert

Robertson, Thomas William 1829-1871 .... **NCLC 35**

Robinson, Edwin Arlington 1869-1935 .... **TCLC 5; PC 1**
See also CA 104; 133; CDALB 1865-1917; DLB 54; MTCW

Robinson, Henry Crabb 1775-1867 .... **NCLC 15**
See also DLB 107

Robinson, Jill 1936- .... **CLC 10**
See also CA 102

Robinson, Kim Stanley 1952- ...... **CLC 34**
See also CA 126

Robinson, Lloyd
See Silverberg, Robert

Robinson, Marilynne 1944- .... **CLC 25**
See also CA 116

Robinson, Smokey .... **CLC 21**
See also Robinson, William Jr.

Robinson, William Jr. 1940-
See Robinson, Smokey
See also CA 116

Robison, Mary 1949- .... **CLC 42**
See also CA 113; 116

Roddenberry, Eugene Wesley 1921-1991
See Roddenberry, Gene
See also CA 110; 135; CANR 37; SATA 45

Roddenberry, Gene .... **CLC 17**
See also Roddenberry, Eugene Wesley
See also AAYA 5; SATO 69

Rodgers, Mary 1931- .... **CLC 12**
See also CA 49-52; CANR 8; CLR 20; MAICYA; SATA 8

Rodgers, W(illiam) R(obert) 1909-1969 .... **CLC 7**
See also CA 85-88; DLB 20

Rodman, Eric
See Silverberg, Robert

Rodman, Howard 1920(?)-1985 ..... **CLC 65**
See also CA 118

Rodman, Maia
See Wojciechowska, Maia (Teresa)

Rodriguez, Claudio 1934- .... **CLC 10**

Roelvaag, O(le) E(dvart) 1876-1931 .... **TCLC 17**
See also CA 117; DLB 9

Roethke, Theodore (Huebner) 1908-1963 ...... **CLC 1, 3, 8, 11, 19, 46**
See also CA 81-84; CABS 2; CDALB 1941-1968; DLB 5; MTCW

Rogers, Thomas Hunton 1927- ..... **CLC 57**
See also CA 89-92

Rogers, Will(iam Penn Adair) 1879-1935 .... **TCLC 8**
See also CA 105; DLB 11

Rogin, Gilbert 1929- .... **CLC 18**
See also CA 65-68; CANR 15

Rohan, Koda .... **TCLC 22**
See also Koda Shigeyuki

Rohmer, Eric .... **CLC 16**
See also Scherer, Jean-Marie Maurice

Rohmer, Sax .... **TCLC 28**
See also Ward, Arthur Henry Sarsfield
See also DLB 70

Roiphe, Anne Richardson 1935- ... **CLC 3, 9**
See also CA 89-92; DLBY 80

Rolfe, Frederick (William Serafino Austin Lewis Mary) 1860-1913 ...... **TCLC 12**
See also CA 107; DLB 34

Rolland, Romain 1866-1944 .... **TCLC 23**
See also CA 118; DLB 65

Rolvaag, O(le) E(dvart)
See Roelvaag, O(le) E(dvart)

Romain Arnaud, Saint
See Aragon, Louis

Romains, Jules 1885-1972 .... **CLC 7**
See also CA 85-88; CANR 34; DLB 65; MTCW

Romero, Jose Ruben 1890-1952 ... **TCLC 14**
See also CA 114; 131; HW

Ronsard, Pierre de 1524-1585 .... **LC 6**

Rooke, Leon 1934- .... **CLC 25, 34**
See also CA 25-28R; CANR 23

Roper, William 1498-1578 .... **LC 10**

Roquelaure, A. N.
See Rice, Anne

Rosa, Joao Guimaraes 1908-1967 ... **CLC 23**
See also CA 89-92; DLB 113

Rosen, Richard (Dean) 1949- .... **CLC 39**
See also CA 77-80

Rosenberg, Isaac 1890-1918 .... **TCLC 12**
See also CA 107; DLB 20

Rosenblatt, Joe .... **CLC 15**
See also Rosenblatt, Joseph

Rosenblatt, Joseph 1933-
See Rosenblatt, Joe
See also CA 89-92

Rosenfeld, Samuel 1896-1963
See Tzara, Tristan
See also CA 89-92

Rosenthal, M(acha) L(ouis) 1917- ... **CLC 28**
See also CA 1-4R; CAAS 6; CANR 4; DLB 5; SATA 59

Ross, Barnaby
See Dannay, Frederic

Ross, Bernard L.
See Follett, Ken(neth Martin)

Ross, J. H.
See Lawrence, T(homas) E(dward)

Ross, (James) Sinclair 1908- .... **CLC 13**
See also CA 73-76; DLB 88

Rossetti, Christina (Georgina) 1830-1894 .... **NCLC 2**
See also DLB 35; MAICYA; SATA 20; WLC

Rossetti, Dante Gabriel 1828-1882 .... **NCLC 4**
See also CDBLB 1832-1890; DLB 35; WLC

Rossner, Judith (Perelman) 1935- .... **CLC 6, 9, 29**
See also AITN 2; BEST 90:3; CA 17-20R; CANR 18; DLB 6; MTCW

Rostand, Edmond (Eugene Alexis) 1868-1918 .... **TCLC 6, 37**
See also CA 104; 126; MTCW

Roth, Henry 1906- .... **CLC 2, 6, 11**
See also CA 11-12; CANR 38; CAP 1; DLB 28; MTCW

Roth, Joseph 1894-1939 .... **TCLC 33**
See also DLB 85

Roth, Philip (Milton) 1933- ...... **CLC 1, 2, 3, 4, 6, 9, 15, 22, 31, 47, 66**
See also BEST 90:3; CA 1-4R; CANR 1, 22, 36; CDALB 1968-1988; DLB 2, 28; DLBY 82; MTCW; WLC

Rothenberg, Jerome 1931- .... **CLC 6, 57**
See also CA 45-48; CANR 1; DLB 5

Roumain, Jacques (Jean Baptiste) 1907-1944 .... **TCLC 19**
See also BLC 3; BW; CA 117; 125

Rourke, Constance (Mayfield) 1885-1941 .... **TCLC 12**
See also CA 107; YABC 1

Rousseau, Jean-Baptiste 1671-1741 ... **LC 9**

Rousseau, Jean-Jacques 1712-1778... **LC 14**
See also WLC

Roussel, Raymond 1877-1933 ..... **TCLC 20**
See also CA 117

Rovit, Earl (Herbert) 1927- .... **CLC 7**
See also CA 5-8R; CANR 12

Rowe, Nicholas 1674-1718 .... **LC 8**
See also DLB 84

Rowley, Ames Dorrance
See Lovecraft, H(oward) P(hillips)

Rowson, Susanna Haswell 1762(?)-1824 .... **NCLC 5**
See also DLB 37

Roy, Gabrielle 1909-1983....... **CLC 10, 14**
See also CA 53-56; 110; CANR 5; DLB 68; MTCW

Rozewicz, Tadeusz 1921-........ **CLC 9, 23**
See also CA 108; CANR 36; MTCW

Ruark, Gibbons 1941- .... **CLC 3**
See also CA 33-36R; CANR 14, 31; DLB 120

Rubens, Bernice (Ruth) 1923-... **CLC 19, 31**
See also CA 25-28R; CANR 33; DLB 14; MTCW

Rudkin, (James) David 1936- ...... **CLC 14**
See also CA 89-92; DLB 13

Rudnik, Raphael 1933-............. **CLC 7**
See also CA 29-32R

Ruffian, M.
See Hasek, Jaroslav (Matej Frantisek)

Ruiz, Jose Martinez............... **CLC 11**
See also Martinez Ruiz, Jose

Rukeyser, Muriel
1913-1980 .... **CLC 6, 10, 15, 27**
See also CA 5-8R; 93-96; CANR 26; DLB 48; MTCW; SATA 22

Rule, Jane (Vance) 1931-.......... **CLC 27**
See also CA 25-28R; CANR 12; DLB 60

Rulfo, Juan 1918-1986............. **CLC 8**
See also CA 85-88; 118; CANR 26; DLB 113; HW; MTCW

Runyon, (Alfred) Damon
1884(?)-1946 .... **TCLC 10**
See also CA 107; DLB 11, 86

Rush, Norman 1933-.............. **CLC 44**
See also CA 121; 126

Rushdie, (Ahmed) Salman
1947- .... **CLC 23, 31, 55**
See also BEST 89:3; CA 108; 111; CANR 33; MTCW

Rushforth, Peter (Scott) 1945- ..... **CLC 19**
See also CA 101

Ruskin, John 1819-1900.......... **TCLC 20**
See also CA 114; 129; CDBLB 1832-1890; DLB 55; SATA 24

Russ, Joanna 1937-............... **CLC 15**
See also CA 25-28R; CANR 11, 31; DLB 8; MTCW

Russell, George William 1867-1935
See A. E.
See also CA 104; CDBLB 1890-1914

Russell, (Henry) Ken(neth Alfred)
1927- .... **CLC 16**
See also CA 105

Russell, Willy 1947-.............. **CLC 60**

Rutherford, Mark................ **TCLC 25**
See also White, William Hale
See also DLB 18

Ruyslinck, Ward
See Belser, Reimond Karel Maria de

Ryan, Cornelius (John) 1920-1974 ... **CLC 7**
See also CA 69-72; 53-56; CANR 38

Ryan, Michael 1946- .... **CLC 65**
See also CA 49-52; DLBY 82

Rybakov, Anatoli (Naumovich)
1911- .... **CLC 23, 53**
See also CA 126; 135

Ryder, Jonathan
See Ludlum, Robert

Ryga, George 1932-1987 .... **CLC 14**
See also CA 101; 124; DLB 60

S. S.
See Sassoon, Siegfried (Lorraine)

Saba, Umberto 1883-1957 .... **TCLC 33**
See also DLB 114

Sabatini, Rafael 1875-1950 .... **TCLC 47**

Sabato, Ernesto (R.) 1911-...... **CLC 10, 23**
See also CA 97-100; CANR 32; HW; MTCW

Sacastru, Martin
See Bioy Casares, Adolfo

Sacher-Masoch, Leopold von
1836(?)-1895 .... **NCLC 31**

Sachs, Marilyn (Stickle) 1927- ..... **CLC 35**
See also AAYA 2; CA 17-20R; CANR 13; CLR 2; MAICYA; SAAS 2; SATA 3, 68

Sachs, Nelly 1891-1970 .... **CLC 14**
See also CA 17-18; 25-28R; CAP 2

Sackler, Howard (Oliver)
1929-1982 .... **CLC 14**
See also CA 61-64; 108; CANR 30; DLB 7

Sacks, Oliver (Wolf) 1933- .... **CLC 67**
See also CA 53-56; CANR 28; MTCW

Sade, Donatien Alphonse Francois Comte
1740-1814 .... **NCLC 3**

Sadoff, Ira 1945-.................. **CLC 9**
See also CA 53-56; CANR 5, 21; DLB 120

Saetone
See Camus, Albert

Safire, William 1929-............. **CLC 10**
See also CA 17-20R; CANR 31

Sagan, Carl (Edward) 1934-........ **CLC 30**
See also AAYA 2; CA 25-28R; CANR 11, 36; MTCW; SATA 58

Sagan, Francoise........ **CLC 3, 6, 9, 17, 36**
See also Quoirez, Francoise
See also DLB 83

Sahgal, Nayantara (Pandit) 1927-... **CLC 41**
See also CA 9-12R; CANR 11

Saint, H(arry) F. 1941- .... **CLC 50**
See also CA 127

St. Aubin de Teran, Lisa 1953-
See Teran, Lisa St. Aubin de
See also CA 118; 126

Sainte-Beuve, Charles Augustin
1804-1869 .... **NCLC 5**

Saint-Exupery, Antoine (Jean Baptiste Marie Roger) de 1900-1944 .... **TCLC 2**
See also CA 108; 132; CLR 10; DLB 72; MAICYA; MTCW; SATA 20; WLC

St. John, David
See Hunt, E(verette) Howard Jr.

Saint-John Perse
See Leger, (Marie-Rene) Alexis Saint-Leger

Saintsbury, George (Edward Bateman)
1845-1933 .... **TCLC 31**
See also DLB 57

Sait Faik .... **TCLC 23**
See also Abasiyanik, Sait Faik

Saki .... **TCLC 3**
See also Munro, H(ector) H(ugh)

Salama, Hannu 1936-............. **CLC 18**

Salamanca, J(ack) R(ichard)
1922- .... **CLC 4, 15**
See also CA 25-28R

Sale, J. Kirkpatrick
See Sale, Kirkpatrick

Sale, Kirkpatrick 1937- .... **CLC 68**
See also CA 13-16R; CANR 10

Salinas (y Serrano), Pedro
1891(?)-1951 .... **TCLC 17**
See also CA 117

Salinger, J(erome) D(avid)
1919- .... **CLC 1, 3, 8, 12, 55, 56; SSC 2**
See also AAYA 2; CA 5-8R; CANR 39; CDALB 1941-1968; CLR 18; DLB 2, 102; MAICYA; MTCW; SATA 67; WLC

Salisbury, John
See Caute, David

Salter, James 1925- .... **CLC 7, 52, 59**
See also CA 73-76

Saltus, Edgar (Everton)
1855-1921 .... **TCLC 8**
See also CA 105

Saltykov, Mikhail Evgrafovich
1826-1889 .... **NCLC 16**

Samarakis, Antonis 1919- .... **CLC 5**
See also CA 25-28R; CAAS 16; CANR 36

Sanchez, Florencio 1875-1910..... **TCLC 37**
See also HW

Sanchez, Luis Rafael 1936-........ **CLC 23**
See also CA 128; HW

Sanchez, Sonia 1934-.............. **CLC 5**
See also BLC 3; BW; CA 33-36R; CANR 24; CLR 18; DLB 41; DLBD 8; MAICYA; MTCW; SATA 22

Sand, George 1804-1876.......... **NCLC 2**
See also DLB 119; WLC

Sandburg, Carl (August)
1878-1967 ... **CLC 1, 4, 10, 15, 35; PC 2**
See also CA 5-8R; 25-28R; CANR 35; CDALB 1865-1917; DLB 17, 54; MAICYA; MTCW; SATA 8; WLC

Sandburg, Charles
See Sandburg, Carl (August)

Sandburg, Charles A.
See Sandburg, Carl (August)

Sanders, (James) Ed(ward) 1939- ... **CLC 53**
See also CA 13-16R; CANR 13; DLB 16

Sanders, Lawrence 1920-.......... **CLC 41**
See also BEST 89:4; CA 81-84; CANR 33; MTCW

Sanders, Noah
See Blount, Roy (Alton) Jr.

Sanders, Winston P.
See Anderson, Poul (William)

Sandoz, Mari(e Susette)
1896-1966 .... **CLC 28**
See also CA 1-4R; 25-28R; CANR 17; DLB 9; MTCW; SATA 5

Saner, Reg(inald Anthony) 1931- .... **CLC 9**
See also CA 65-68

Sannazaro, Jacopo 1456(?)-1530...... **LC 8**

Sansom, William 1912-1976....... **CLC 2, 6**
See also CA 5-8R; 65-68; MTCW

Santayana, George 1863-1952..... **TCLC 40**
See also CA 115; DLB 54, 71

Santiago, Danny .... **CLC 33**
See also James, Daniel (Lewis)

Santmyer, Helen Hooven
1895-1986 .... **CLC 33**
See also CA 1-4R; 118; CANR 15, 33; DLBY 84; MTCW

Santos, Bienvenido N(uqui) 1911-... **CLC 22**
See also CA 101; CANR 19

Sapper .... **TCLC 44**
See also McNeile, Herman Cyril

Sappho fl. 6th cent. B.C.-.... **CMLC 3; PC 5**

Sarduy, Severo 1937-.............. **CLC 6**
See also CA 89-92; DLB 113; HW

Sargeson, Frank 1903-1982........ **CLC 31**
See also CA 25-28R; 106; CANR 38

Sarmiento, Felix Ruben Garcia 1867-1916
See Dario, Ruben
See also CA 104

Saroyan, William
1908-1981 ..... **CLC 1, 8, 10, 29, 34, 56**
See also CA 5-8R; 103; CANR 30; DLB 7, 9, 86; DLBY 81; MTCW; SATA 23, 24; WLC

Sarraute, Nathalie
1900- .... **CLC 1, 2, 4, 8, 10, 31**
See also CA 9-12R; CANR 23; DLB 83; MTCW

Sarton, (Eleanor) May
1912- .... **CLC 4, 14, 49**
See also CA 1-4R; CANR 1, 34; DLB 48; DLBY 81; MTCW; SATA 36

Sartre, Jean-Paul
1905-1980 ... **CLC 1, 4, 7, 9, 13, 18, 24, 44, 50, 52; DC 3**
See also CA 9-12R; 97-100; CANR 21; DLB 72; MTCW; WLC

Sassoon, Siegfried (Lorraine)
1886-1967 .... **CLC 36**
See also CA 104; 25-28R; CANR 36; DLB 20; MTCW

Satterfield, Charles
See Pohl, Frederik

Saul, John (W. III) 1942- .... **CLC 46**
See also BEST 90:4; CA 81-84; CANR 16

Saunders, Caleb
See Heinlein, Robert A(nson)

Saura (Atares), Carlos 1932-....... **CLC 20**
See also CA 114; 131; HW

Sauser-Hall, Frederic 1887-1961.... **CLC 18**
See also CA 102; 93-96; CANR 36; MTCW

Savage, Catharine
See Brosman, Catharine Savage

Savage, Thomas 1915- .... **CLC 40**
See also CA 126; 132; CAAS 15

Savan, Glenn .... **CLC 50**

Saven, Glenn 19(?)- .... **CLC 50**

Sayers, Dorothy L(eigh)
1893-1957 .... **TCLC 2, 15**
See also CA 104; 119; CDBLB 1914-1945; DLB 10, 36, 77, 100; MTCW

Sayers, Valerie 1952-............. **CLC 50**
See also CA 134

Sayles, John Thomas 1950-... **CLC 7, 10, 14**
See also CA 57-60; DLB 44

Scammell, Michael .... **CLC 34**

Scannell, Vernon 1922- .... **CLC 49**
See also CA 5-8R; CANR 8, 24; DLB 27; SATA 59

Scarlett, Susan
See Streatfeild, (Mary) Noel

Schaeffer, Susan Fromberg
1941- .... **CLC 6, 11, 22**
See also CA 49-52; CANR 18; DLB 28; MTCW; SATA 22

Schary, Jill
See Robinson, Jill

Schell, Jonathan 1943-............ **CLC 35**
See also CA 73-76; CANR 12

Schelling, Friedrich Wilhelm Joseph von
1775-1854 .... **NCLC 30**
See also DLB 90

Scherer, Jean-Marie Maurice 1920-
See Rohmer, Eric
See also CA 110

Schevill, James (Erwin) 1920-....... **CLC 7**
See also CA 5-8R; CAAS 12

Schisgal, Murray (Joseph) 1926-..... **CLC 6**
See also CA 21-24R

Schlee, Ann 1934-................ **CLC 35**
See also CA 101; CANR 29; SATA 36, 44

Schlegel, August Wilhelm von
1767-1845 .... **NCLC 15**
See also DLB 94

Schlegel, Johann Elias (von)
1719(?)-1749 .... **LC 5**

Schmidt, Arno (Otto) 1914-1979.... **CLC 56**
See also CA 128; 109; DLB 69

Schmitz, Aron Hector 1861-1928
See Svevo, Italo
See also CA 104; 122; MTCW

Schnackenberg, Gjertrud 1953-..... **CLC 40**
See also CA 116; DLB 120

Schneider, Leonard Alfred 1925-1966
See Bruce, Lenny
See also CA 89-92

Schnitzler, Arthur 1862-1931 ...... **TCLC 4**
See also CA 104; DLB 81, 118

Schor, Sandra (M.) 1932(?)-1990 ... **CLC 65**
See also CA 132

Schorer, Mark 1908-1977 .... **CLC 9**
See also CA 5-8R; 73-76; CANR 7; DLB 103

Schrader, Paul Joseph 1946-....... **CLC 26**
See also CA 37-40R; DLB 44

Schreiner, Olive (Emilie Albertina)
1855-1920 .... **TCLC 9**
See also CA 105; DLB 18

Schulberg, Budd (Wilson)
1914- .... **CLC 7, 48**
See also CA 25-28R; CANR 19; DLB 6, 26, 28; DLBY 81

Schulz, Bruno 1892-1942.......... **TCLC 5**
See also CA 115; 123

Schulz, Charles M(onroe) 1922-.... **CLC 12**
See also CA 9-12R; CANR 6; SATA 10

Schuyler, James Marcus
1923-1991 .... **CLC 5, 23**
See also CA 101; 134; DLB 5

Schwartz, Delmore (David)
1913-1966 .... **CLC 2, 4, 10, 45**
See also CA 17-18; 25-28R; CANR 35; CAP 2; DLB 28, 48; MTCW

Schwartz, Ernst
See Ozu, Yasujiro

Schwartz, John Burnham 1965- .... **CLC 59**
See also CA 132

Schwartz, Lynne Sharon 1939-..... **CLC 31**
See also CA 103

Schwartz, Muriel A.
See Eliot, T(homas) S(tearns)

Schwarz-Bart, Andre 1928-....... **CLC 2, 4**
See also CA 89-92

Schwarz-Bart, Simone 1938-........ **CLC 7**
See also CA 97-100

Schwob, (Mayer Andre) Marcel
1867-1905 .... **TCLC 20**
See also CA 117

Sciascia, Leonardo
1921-1989 .... **CLC 8, 9, 41**
See also CA 85-88; 130; CANR 35; MTCW

Scoppettone, Sandra 1936-......... **CLC 26**
See also CA 5-8R; SATA 9

Scorsese, Martin 1942- .... **CLC 20**
See also CA 110; 114

Scotland, Jay
See Jakes, John (William)

Scott, Duncan Campbell
1862-1947 .... **TCLC 6**
See also CA 104; DLB 92

Scott, Evelyn 1893-1963........... **CLC 43**
See also CA 104; 112; DLB 9, 48

Scott, F(rancis) R(eginald)
1899-1985 .... **CLC 22**
See also CA 101; 114; DLB 88

Scott, Frank
See Scott, F(rancis) R(eginald)

Scott, Joanna 1960-.............. **CLC 50**
See also CA 126

Scott, Paul (Mark) 1920-1978.... **CLC 9, 60**
See also CA 81-84; 77-80; CANR 33; DLB 14; MTCW

Scott, Walter 1771-1832......... **NCLC 15**
See also CDBLB 1789-1832; DLB 93, 107, 116; WLC; YABC 2

Scribe, (Augustin) Eugene
1791-1861 .... **NCLC 16**

Scrum, R.
See Crumb, R(obert)

Scudery, Madeleine de 1607-1701..... **LC 2**

Scum
See Crumb, R(obert)

Scumbag, Little Bobby
See Crumb, R(obert)

Seabrook, John
See Hubbard, L(afayette) Ron(ald)

Sealy, I. Allan 1951- .... **CLC 55**

Search, Alexander
See Pessoa, Fernando (Antonio Nogueira)

Sebastian, Lee
See Silverberg, Robert

Sebastian Owl
See Thompson, Hunter S(tockton)

Sebestyen, Ouida 1924- .... **CLC 30**
See also AAYA 8; CA 107; CLR 17; MAICYA; SAAS 10; SATA 39

Sedges, John
See Buck, Pearl S(ydenstricker)

Sedgwick, Catharine Maria 1789-1867 .... **NCLC 19**
See also DLB 1, 74

Seelye, John 1931- .... **CLC 7**

Seferiades, Giorgos Stylianou 1900-1971
See Seferis, George
See also CA 5-8R; 33-36R; CANR 5, 36; MTCW

Seferis, George .... **CLC 5, 11**
See also Seferiades, Giorgos Stylianou

Segal, Erich (Wolf) 1937- .... **CLC 3, 10**
See also BEST 89:1; CA 25-28R; CANR 20, 36; DLBY 86; MTCW

Seger, Bob 1945- .... **CLC 35**

Seghers, Anna .... **CLC 7**
See also Radvanyi, Netty
See also DLB 69

Seidel, Frederick (Lewis) 1936- ..... **CLC 18**
See also CA 13-16R; CANR 8; DLBY 84

Seifert, Jaroslav 1901-1986 ..... **CLC 34, 44**
See also CA 127; MTCW

Sei Shonagon c. 966-1017(?) ...... **CMLC 6**

Selby, Hubert Jr. 1928- ...... **CLC 1, 2, 4, 8**
See also CA 13-16R; CANR 33; DLB 2

Selzer, Richard 1928- .... **CLC 74**
See also CA 65-68; CANR 14

Sembene, Ousmane
See Ousmane, Sembene

Senancour, Etienne Pivert de 1770-1846 .... **NCLC 16**
See also DLB 119

Sender, Ramon (Jose) 1902-1982 .... **CLC 8**
See also CA 5-8R; 105; CANR 8; HW; MTCW

Seneca, Lucius Annaeus 4B.C.-65 .... **CMLC 6**

Senghor, Leopold Sedar 1906- ...... **CLC 54**
See also BLC 3; BW; CA 116; 125; MTCW

Serling, (Edward) Rod(man) 1924-1975 .... **CLC 30**
See also AITN 1; CA 65-68; 57-60; DLB 26

Serna, Ramon Gomez de la
See Gomez de la Serna, Ramon

Serpieres
See Guillevic, (Eugene)

Service, Robert
See Service, Robert W(illiam)
See also DLB 92

Service, Robert W(illiam) 1874(?)-1958 .... **TCLC 15**
See also Service, Robert
See also CA 115; SATA 20; WLC

Seth, Vikram 1952- .... **CLC 43**
See also CA 121; 127; DLB 120

Seton, Cynthia Propper 1926-1982 .... **CLC 27**
See also CA 5-8R; 108; CANR 7

Seton, Ernest (Evan) Thompson 1860-1946 .... **TCLC 31**
See also CA 109; DLB 92; SATA 18

Seton-Thompson, Ernest
See Seton, Ernest (Evan) Thompson

Settle, Mary Lee 1918- .... **CLC 19, 61**
See also CA 89-92; CAAS 1; DLB 6

Seuphor, Michel
See Arp, Jean

Sevigne, Marie (de Rabutin-Chantal) Marquise de 1626-1696 .... **LC 11**

Sexton, Anne (Harvey) 1928-1974 ... **CLC 2, 4, 6, 8, 10, 15, 53; PC 2**
See also CA 1-4R; 53-56; CABS 2; CANR 3, 36; CDALB 1941-1968; DLB 5; MTCW; SATA 10; WLC

Shaara, Michael (Joseph Jr.) 1929-1988 .... **CLC 15**
See also AITN 1; CA 102; DLBY 83

Shackleton, C. C.
See Aldiss, Brian W(ilson)

Shacochis, Bob .... **CLC 39**
See also Shacochis, Robert G.

Shacochis, Robert G. 1951-
See Shacochis, Bob
See also CA 119; 124

Shaffer, Anthony (Joshua) 1926- .... **CLC 19**
See also CA 110; 116; DLB 13

Shaffer, Peter (Levin) 1926- .... **CLC 5, 14, 18, 37, 60**
See also CA 25-28R; CANR 25; CDBLB 1960 to Present; DLB 13; MTCW

Shakey, Bernard
See Young, Neil

Shalamov, Varlam (Tikhonovich) 1907(?)-1982 .... **CLC 18**
See also CA 129; 105

Shamlu, Ahmad 1925- .... **CLC 10**

Shammas, Anton 1951- .... **CLC 55**

Shange, Ntozake 1948- .... **CLC 8, 25, 38, 74; DC 3**
See also AAYA 9; BLC 3; BW; CA 85-88; CABS 3; CANR 27; DLB 38; MTCW

Shapcott, Thomas William 1935- ... **CLC 38**
See also CA 69-72

Shapiro, Karl (Jay) 1913- .. **CLC 4, 8, 15, 53**
See also CA 1-4R; CAAS 6; CANR 1, 36; DLB 48; MTCW

Sharp, William 1855-1905 .... **TCLC 39**

Sharpe, Thomas Ridley 1928-
See Sharpe, Tom
See also CA 114; 122

Sharpe, Tom .... **CLC 36**
See also Sharpe, Thomas Ridley
See also DLB 14

Shaw, Bernard .... **TCLC 45**
See also Shaw, George Bernard

Shaw, G. Bernard
See Shaw, George Bernard

Shaw, George Bernard 1856-1950 .... **TCLC 3, 9, 21**
See also Shaw, Bernard
See also CA 104; 128; CDBLB 1914-1945; DLB 10, 57; MTCW; WLC

Shaw, Henry Wheeler 1818-1885 .... **NCLC 15**
See also DLB 11

Shaw, Irwin 1913-1984 .... **CLC 7, 23, 34**
See also AITN 1; CA 13-16R; 112; CANR 21; CDALB 1941-1968; DLB 6, 102; DLBY 84; MTCW

Shaw, Robert 1927-1978 .... **CLC 5**
See also AITN 1; CA 1-4R; 81-84; CANR 4; DLB 13, 14

Shaw, T. E.
See Lawrence, T(homas) E(dward)

Shawn, Wallace 1943- .... **CLC 41**
See also CA 112

Sheed, Wilfrid (John Joseph) 1930- .... **CLC 2, 4, 10, 53**
See also CA 65-68; CANR 30; DLB 6; MTCW

Sheldon, Alice Hastings Bradley 1915(?)-1987
See Tiptree, James Jr.
See also CA 108; 122; CANR 34; MTCW

Sheldon, John
See Bloch, Robert (Albert)

Shelley, Mary Wollstonecraft (Godwin) 1797-1851 .... **NCLC 14**
See also CDBLB 1789-1832; DLB 110, 116; SATA 29; WLC

Shelley, Percy Bysshe 1792-1822 .... **NCLC 18**
See also CDBLB 1789-1832; DLB 96, 110; WLC

Shepard, Jim 1956- .... **CLC 36**
See also CA 137

Shepard, Lucius 19(?)- .... **CLC 34**
See also CA 128

Shepard, Sam 1943- .... **CLC 4, 6, 17, 34, 41, 44**
See also AAYA 1; CA 69-72; CABS 3; CANR 22; DLB 7; MTCW

Shepherd, Michael
See Ludlum, Robert

Sherburne, Zoa (Morin) 1912- ..... **CLC 30**
See also CA 1-4R; CANR 3, 37; MAICYA; SATA 3

Sheridan, Frances 1724-1766 .... **LC 7**
See also DLB 39, 84

Sheridan, Richard Brinsley 1751-1816 .... **NCLC 5; DC 1**
See also CDBLB 1660-1789; DLB 89; WLC

Sherman, Jonathan Marc .... **CLC 55**

Sherman, Martin 1941(?)- .... **CLC 19**
See also CA 116; 123

Sherwin, Judith Johnson 1936- ... **CLC 7, 15**
See also CA 25-28R; CANR 34

Sherwood, Robert E(mmet) 1896-1955 .... **TCLC 3**
See also CA 104; DLB 7, 26

Shiel, M(atthew) P(hipps) 1865-1947 .... **TCLC 8**
See also CA 106

Shiga, Naoya 1883-1971........... **CLC 33**
See also CA 101; 33-36R

Shimazaki Haruki 1872-1943
See Shimazaki Toson
See also CA 105; 134

Shimazaki Toson.................. **TCLC 5**
See also Shimazaki Haruki

Sholokhov, Mikhail (Aleksandrovich) 1905-1984 .... **CLC 7, 15**
See also CA 101; 112; MTCW; SATA 36

Shone, Patric
See Hanley, James

Shreve, Susan Richards 1939-...... **CLC 23**
See also CA 49-52; CAAS 5; CANR 5, 38; MAICYA; SATA 41, 46

Shue, Larry 1946-1985............ **CLC 52**
See also CA 117

Shu-Jen, Chou 1881-1936
See Hsun, Lu
See also CA 104

Shulman, Alix Kates 1932- ...... **CLC 2, 10**
See also CA 29-32R; SATA 7

Shuster, Joe 1914- .... **CLC 21**

Shute, Nevil...................... **CLC 30**
See also Norway, Nevil Shute

Shuttle, Penelope (Diane) 1947- ..... **CLC 7**
See also CA 93-96; CANR 39; DLB 14, 40

Sidney, Mary 1561-1621 .... **LC 19**

Sidney, Sir Philip 1554-1586........ **LC 19**
See also CDBLB Before 1660

Siegel, Jerome 1914- .... **CLC 21**
See also CA 116

Siegel, Jerry
See Siegel, Jerome

Sienkiewicz, Henryk (Adam Alexander Pius) 1846-1916 .... **TCLC 3**
See also CA 104; 134

Sierra, Gregorio Martinez
See Martinez Sierra, Gregorio

Sierra, Maria (de la O'LeJarraga) Martinez
See Martinez Sierra, Maria (de la O'LeJarraga)

Sigal, Clancy 1926-................ **CLC 7**
See also CA 1-4R

Sigourney, Lydia Howard (Huntley) 1791-1865 .... **NCLC 21**
See also DLB 1, 42, 73

Siguenza y Gongora, Carlos de 1645-1700 .... **LC 8**

Sigurjonsson, Johann 1880-1919... **TCLC 27**

Sikelianos, Angelos 1884-1951 .... **TCLC 39**

Silkin, Jon 1930- .... **CLC 2, 6, 43**
See also CA 5-8R; CAAS 5; DLB 27

Silko, Leslie Marmon 1948- .... **CLC 23, 74**
See also CA 115; 122

Sillanpaa, Frans Eemil 1888-1964... **CLC 19**
See also CA 129; 93-96; MTCW

Sillitoe, Alan 1928- .... **CLC 1, 3, 6, 10, 19, 57**
See also AITN 1; CA 9-12R; CAAS 2; CANR 8, 26; CDBLB 1960 to Present; DLB 14; MTCW; SATA 61

Silone, Ignazio 1900-1978 .... **CLC 4**
See also CA 25-28; 81-84; CANR 34; CAP 2; MTCW

Silver, Joan Micklin 1935- .... **CLC 20**
See also CA 114; 121

Silverberg, Robert 1935- .... **CLC 7**
See also CA 1-4R; CAAS 3; CANR 1, 20, 36; DLB 8; MAICYA; MTCW; SATA 13

Silverstein, Alvin 1933- .... **CLC 17**
See also CA 49-52; CANR 2; CLR 25; MAICYA; SATA 8, 69

Silverstein, Virginia B(arbara Opshelor) 1937- .... **CLC 17**
See also CA 49-52; CANR 2; CLR 25; MAICYA; SATA 8, 69

Sim, Georges
See Simenon, Georges (Jacques Christian)

Simak, Clifford D(onald) 1904-1988 .... **CLC 1, 55**
See also CA 1-4R; 125; CANR 1, 35; DLB 8; MTCW; SATA 56

Simenon, Georges (Jacques Christian) 1903-1989 .... **CLC 1, 2, 3, 8, 18, 47**
See also CA 85-88; 129; CANR 35; DLB 72; DLBY 89; MTCW

Simic, Charles 1938-... **CLC 6, 9, 22, 49, 68**
See also CA 29-32R; CAAS 4; CANR 12, 33; DLB 105

Simmons, Charles (Paul) 1924-..... **CLC 57**
See also CA 89-92

Simmons, Dan.................... **CLC 44**
See also CA 138

Simmons, James (Stewart Alexander) 1933- .... **CLC 43**
See also CA 105; DLB 40

Simms, William Gilmore 1806-1870 .... **NCLC 3**
See also DLB 3, 30, 59, 73

Simon, Carly 1945-............... **CLC 26**
See also CA 105

Simon, Claude 1913-....... **CLC 4, 9, 15, 39**
See also CA 89-92; CANR 33; DLB 83; MTCW

Simon, (Marvin) Neil 1927- .... **CLC 6, 11, 31, 39, 70**
See also AITN 1; CA 21-24R; CANR 26; DLB 7; MTCW

Simon, Paul 1942(?)- .... **CLC 17**
See also CA 116

Simonon, Paul 1956(?)- .... **CLC 30**
See also The Clash

Simpson, Harriette
See Arnow, Harriette (Louisa) Simpson

Simpson, Louis (Aston Marantz) 1923- .... **CLC 4, 7, 9, 32**
See also CA 1-4R; CAAS 4; CANR 1; DLB 5; MTCW

Simpson, Mona (Elizabeth) 1957-... **CLC 44**
See also CA 122; 135

Simpson, N(orman) F(rederick) 1919- .... **CLC 29**
See also CA 13-16R; DLB 13

Sinclair, Andrew (Annandale) 1935- .... **CLC 2, 14**
See also CA 9-12R; CAAS 5; CANR 14, 38; DLB 14; MTCW

Sinclair, Emil
See Hesse, Hermann

Sinclair, Mary Amelia St. Clair 1865(?)-1946
See Sinclair, May
See also CA 104

Sinclair, May.................. **TCLC 3, 11**
See also Sinclair, Mary Amelia St. Clair
See also DLB 36

Sinclair, Upton (Beall) 1878-1968 .... **CLC 1, 11, 15, 63**
See also CA 5-8R; 25-28R; CANR 7; CDALB 1929-1941; DLB 9; MTCW; SATA 9; WLC

Singer, Isaac
See Singer, Isaac Bashevis

Singer, Isaac Bashevis 1904-1991 ... **CLC 1, 3, 6, 9, 11, 15, 23, 38, 69; SSC 3**
See also AITN 1, 2; CA 1-4R; 134; CANR 1, 39; CDALB 1941-1968; CLR 1; DLB 6, 28, 52; DLBY 91; MAICYA; MTCW; SATA 3, 27; SATO 68; WLC

Singer, Israel Joshua 1893-1944... **TCLC 33**

Singh, Khushwant 1915-........... **CLC 11**
See also CA 9-12R; CAAS 9; CANR 6

Sinjohn, John
See Galsworthy, John

Sinyavsky, Andrei (Donatevich) 1925- .... **CLC 8**
See also CA 85-88

Sirin, V.
See Nabokov, Vladimir (Vladimirovich)

Sissman, L(ouis) E(dward) 1928-1976 .... **CLC 9, 18**
See also CA 21-24R; 65-68; CANR 13; DLB 5

Sisson, C(harles) H(ubert) 1914-..... **CLC 8**
See also CA 1-4R; CAAS 3; CANR 3; DLB 27

Sitwell, Dame Edith 1887-1964 .... **CLC 2, 9, 67; PC 3**
See also CA 9-12R; CANR 35; CDBLB 1945-1960; DLB 20; MTCW

Sjoewall, Maj 1935-............... **CLC 7**
See also CA 65-68

Sjowall, Maj
See Sjoewall, Maj

Skelton, Robin 1925- .... **CLC 13**
See also AITN 2; CA 5-8R; CAAS 5; CANR 28; DLB 27, 53

Skolimowski, Jerzy 1938- .... **CLC 20**
See also CA 128

Skram, Amalie (Bertha) 1847-1905 .... **TCLC 25**

Skvorecky, Josef (Vaclav) 1924- .... **CLC 15, 39, 69**
See also CA 61-64; CAAS 1; CANR 10, 34; MTCW

Slade, Bernard . . . . **CLC 11, 46**
See also Newbound, Bernard Slade
See also CAAS 9; DLB 53

Slaughter, Carolyn 1946- . . . . **CLC 56**
See also CA 85-88

Slaughter, Frank G(ill) 1908- . . . . . . **CLC 29**
See also AITN 2; CA 5-8R; CANR 5

Slavitt, David R. 1935- . . . . **CLC 5, 14**
See also CA 21-24R; CAAS 3; DLB 5, 6

Slesinger, Tess 1905-1945 . . . . **TCLC 10**
See also CA 107; DLB 102

Slessor, Kenneth 1901-1971 . . . . **CLC 14**
See also CA 102; 89-92

Slowacki, Juliusz 1809-1849 . . . . . **NCLC 15**

Smart, Christopher 1722-1771 . . . . **LC 3**
See also DLB 109

Smart, Elizabeth 1913-1986 . . . . **CLC 54**
See also CA 81-84; 118; DLB 88

Smiley, Jane (Graves) 1949- . . . . **CLC 53**
See also CA 104; CANR 30

Smith, A(rthur) J(ames) M(arshall)
1902-1980 . . . . **CLC 15**
See also CA 1-4R; 102; CANR 4; DLB 88

Smith, Betty (Wehner) 1896-1972 . . . **CLC 19**
See also CA 5-8R; 33-36R; DLBY 82; SATA 6

Smith, Charlotte (Turner)
1749-1806 . . . . **NCLC 23**
See also DLB 39, 109

Smith, Clark Ashton 1893-1961 . . . . **CLC 43**

Smith, Dave . . . . **CLC 22, 42**
See also Smith, David (Jeddie)
See also CAAS 7; DLB 5

Smith, David (Jeddie) 1942-
See Smith, Dave
See also CA 49-52; CANR 1

Smith, Florence Margaret
1902-1971 . . . . **CLC 8**
See also Smith, Stevie
See also CA 17-18; 29-32R; CANR 35; CAP 2; MTCW

Smith, Iain Crichton 1928- . . . . **CLC 64**
See also CA 21-24R; DLB 40

Smith, John 1580(?)-1631 . . . . **LC 9**

Smith, Johnston
See Crane, Stephen (Townley)

Smith, Lee 1944- . . . . **CLC 25**
See also CA 114; 119; DLBY 83

Smith, Martin
See Smith, Martin Cruz

Smith, Martin Cruz 1942- . . . . **CLC 25**
See also BEST 89:4; CA 85-88; CANR 6, 23

Smith, Mary-Ann Tirone 1944- . . . . . **CLC 39**
See also CA 118; 136

Smith, Patti 1946- . . . . **CLC 12**
See also CA 93-96

Smith, Pauline (Urmson)
1882-1959 . . . . **TCLC 25**

Smith, Rosamond
See Oates, Joyce Carol

Smith, Sheila Kaye
See Kaye-Smith, Sheila

Smith, Stevie . . . . **CLC 3, 8, 25, 44**
See also Smith, Florence Margaret
See also DLB 20

Smith, Wilbur A(ddison) 1933- . . . . . **CLC 33**
See also CA 13-16R; CANR 7; MTCW

Smith, William Jay 1918- . . . . **CLC 6**
See also CA 5-8R; DLB 5; MAICYA; SATA 2, 68

Smith, Woodrow Wilson
See Kuttner, Henry

Smolenskin, Peretz 1842-1885 . . . . **NCLC 30**

Smollett, Tobias (George) 1721-1771 . . **LC 2**
See also CDBLB 1660-1789; DLB 39, 104

Snodgrass, William D(e Witt)
1926- . . . . **CLC 2, 6, 10, 18, 68**
See also CA 1-4R; CANR 6, 36; DLB 5; MTCW

Snow, C(harles) P(ercy)
1905-1980 . . . . **CLC 1, 4, 6, 9, 13, 19**
See also CA 5-8R; 101; CANR 28; CDBLB 1945-1960; DLB 15, 77; MTCW

Snow, Frances Compton
See Adams, Henry (Brooks)

Snyder, Gary (Sherman)
1930- . . . . **CLC 1, 2, 5, 9, 32**
See also CA 17-20R; CANR 30; DLB 5, 16

Snyder, Zilpha Keatley 1927- . . . . . . **CLC 17**
See also CA 9-12R; CANR 38; MAICYA; SAAS 2; SATA 1, 28

Soares, Bernardo
See Pessoa, Fernando (Antonio Nogueira)

Sobh, A.
See Shamlu, Ahmad

Sobol, Joshua . . . . **CLC 60**

Soderberg, Hjalmar 1869-1941 . . . . **TCLC 39**

Sodergran, Edith (Irene)
See Soedergran, Edith (Irene)

Soedergran, Edith (Irene)
1892-1923 . . . . **TCLC 31**

Softly, Edgar
See Lovecraft, H(oward) P(hillips)

Softly, Edward
See Lovecraft, H(oward) P(hillips)

Sokolov, Raymond 1941- . . . . **CLC 7**
See also CA 85-88

Solo, Jay
See Ellison, Harlan

Sologub, Fyodor . . . . **TCLC 9**
See also Teternikov, Fyodor Kuzmich

Solomons, Ikey Esquir
See Thackeray, William Makepeace

Solomos, Dionysios 1798-1857 . . . **NCLC 15**

Solwoska, Mara
See French, Marilyn

Solzhenitsyn, Aleksandr I(sayevich)
1918- . . . **CLC 1, 2, 4, 7, 9, 10, 18, 26, 34**
See also AITN 1; CA 69-72; MTCW; WLC

Somers, Jane
See Lessing, Doris (May)

Sommer, Scott 1951- . . . . **CLC 25**
See also CA 106

Sondheim, Stephen (Joshua)
1930- . . . . **CLC 30, 39**
See also CA 103

Sontag, Susan 1933- . . . **CLC 1, 2, 10, 13, 31**
See also CA 17-20R; CANR 25; DLB 2, 67; MTCW

Sophocles
496(?)B.C.-406(?)B.C. . . . **CMLC 2; DC 1**

Sorel, Julia
See Drexler, Rosalyn

Sorrentino, Gilbert
1929- . . . . **CLC 3, 7, 14, 22, 40**
See also CA 77-80; CANR 14, 33; DLB 5; DLBY 80

Soto, Gary 1952- . . . . **CLC 32**
See also CA 119; 125; DLB 82; HW

Soupault, Philippe 1897-1990 . . . . . . **CLC 68**
See also CA 116; 131

Souster, (Holmes) Raymond
1921- . . . . **CLC 5, 14**
See also CA 13-16R; CAAS 14; CANR 13, 29; DLB 88; SATA 63

Southern, Terry 1926- . . . . **CLC 7**
See also CA 1-4R; CANR 1; DLB 2

Southey, Robert 1774-1843 . . . . **NCLC 8**
See also DLB 93, 107; SATA 54

Southworth, Emma Dorothy Eliza Nevitte
1819-1899 . . . . **NCLC 26**

Souza, Ernest
See Scott, Evelyn

Soyinka, Wole
1934- . . . . **CLC 3, 5, 14, 36, 44; DC 2**
See also BLC 3; BW; CA 13-16R; CANR 27, 39; MTCW; WLC

Spackman, W(illiam) M(ode)
1905-1990 . . . . **CLC 46**
See also CA 81-84; 132

Spacks, Barry 1931- . . . . **CLC 14**
See also CA 29-32R; CANR 33; DLB 105

Spanidou, Irini 1946- . . . . **CLC 44**

Spark, Muriel (Sarah)
1918- . . . . **CLC 2, 3, 5, 8, 13, 18, 40; SSC 10**
See also CA 5-8R; CANR 12, 36; CDBLB 1945-1960; DLB 15; MTCW

Spaulding, Douglas
See Bradbury, Ray (Douglas)

Spaulding, Leonard
See Bradbury, Ray (Douglas)

Spence, J. A. D.
See Eliot, T(homas) S(tearns)

Spencer, Elizabeth 1921- . . . . **CLC 22**
See also CA 13-16R; CANR 32; DLB 6; MTCW; SATA 14

Spencer, Leonard G.
See Silverberg, Robert

Spencer, Scott 1945- . . . . **CLC 30**
See also CA 113; DLBY 86

Spender, Stephen (Harold)
1909- . . . . **CLC 1, 2, 5, 10, 41**
See also CA 9-12R; CANR 31; CDBLB 1945-1960; DLB 20; MTCW

Spengler, Oswald (Arnold Gottfried) 1880-1936 .... **TCLC 25**
See also CA 118

Spenser, Edmund 1552(?)-1599 .... **LC 5**
See also CDBLB Before 1660; WLC

Spicer, Jack 1925-1965 ...... **CLC 8, 18, 72**
See also CA 85-88; DLB 5, 16

Spielberg, Peter 1929- .... **CLC 6**
See also CA 5-8R; CANR 4; DLBY 81

Spielberg, Steven 1947- .... **CLC 20**
See also AAYA 8; CA 77-80; CANR 32; SATA 32

Spillane, Frank Morrison 1918-
See Spillane, Mickey
See also CA 25-28R; CANR 28; MTCW; SATA 66

Spillane, Mickey .... **CLC 3, 13**
See also Spillane, Frank Morrison

Spinoza, Benedictus de 1632-1677 .... **LC 9**

Spinrad, Norman (Richard) 1940-... **CLC 46**
See also CA 37-40R; CANR 20; DLB 8

Spitteler, Carl (Friedrich Georg) 1845-1924 .... **TCLC 12**
See also CA 109

Spivack, Kathleen (Romola Drucker) 1938- .... **CLC 6**
See also CA 49-52

Spoto, Donald 1941-.............. **CLC 39**
See also CA 65-68; CANR 11

Springsteen, Bruce (F.) 1949- ...... **CLC 17**
See also CA 111

Spurling, Hilary 1940-............ **CLC 34**
See also CA 104; CANR 25

Squires, Radcliffe 1917-........... **CLC 51**
See also CA 1-4R; CANR 6, 21

Srivastava, Dhanpat Rai 1880(?)-1936
See Premchand
See also CA 118

Stacy, Donald
See Pohl, Frederik

Stael, Germaine de
See Stael-Holstein, Anne Louise Germaine Necker Baronn
See also DLB 119

Stael-Holstein, Anne Louise Germaine Necker Baronn 1766-1817 .... **NCLC 3**
See also Stael, Germaine de

Stafford, Jean 1915-1979... **CLC 4, 7, 19, 68**
See also CA 1-4R; 85-88; CANR 3; DLB 2; MTCW; SATA 22

Stafford, William (Edgar) 1914- .... **CLC 4, 7, 29**
See also CA 5-8R; CAAS 3; CANR 5, 22; DLB 5

Staines, Trevor
See Brunner, John (Kilian Houston)

Stairs, Gordon
See Austin, Mary (Hunter)

Stannard, Martin.................. **CLC 44**

Stanton, Maura 1946- .... **CLC 9**
See also CA 89-92; CANR 15; DLB 120

Stanton, Schuyler
See Baum, L(yman) Frank

Stapledon, (William) Olaf 1886-1950 .... **TCLC 22**
See also CA 111; DLB 15

Starbuck, George (Edwin) 1931-.... **CLC 53**
See also CA 21-24R; CANR 23

Stark, Richard
See Westlake, Donald E(dwin)

Staunton, Schuyler
See Baum, L(yman) Frank

Stead, Christina (Ellen) 1902-1983 .... **CLC 2, 5, 8, 32**
See also CA 13-16R; 109; CANR 33; MTCW

Stead, William Thomas 1849-1912 .... **TCLC 48**

Steele, Richard 1672-1729 .... **LC 18**
See also CDBLB 1660-1789; DLB 84, 101

Steele, Timothy (Reid) 1948-....... **CLC 45**
See also CA 93-96; CANR 16; DLB 120

Steffens, (Joseph) Lincoln 1866-1936 .... **TCLC 20**
See also CA 117

Stegner, Wallace (Earle) 1909-... **CLC 9, 49**
See also AITN 1; BEST 90:3; CA 1-4R; CAAS 9; CANR 1, 21; DLB 9; MTCW

Stein, Gertrude 1874-1946 .... **TCLC 1, 6, 28, 48**
See also CA 104; 132; CDALB 1917-1929; DLB 4, 54, 86; MTCW; WLC

Steinbeck, John (Ernst) 1902-1968 ..... **CLC 1, 5, 9, 13, 21, 34, 45; SSC 11**
See also CA 1-4R; 25-28R; CANR 1, 35; CDALB 1929-1941; DLB 7, 9; DLBD 2; MTCW; SATA 9; WLC

Steinem, Gloria 1934-............. **CLC 63**
See also CA 53-56; CANR 28; MTCW

Steiner, George 1929-............. **CLC 24**
See also CA 73-76; CANR 31; DLB 67; MTCW; SATA 62

Steiner, Rudolf 1861-1925 .... **TCLC 13**
See also CA 107

Stendhal 1783-1842............. **NCLC 23**
See also DLB 119; WLC

Stephen, Leslie 1832-1904 .... **TCLC 23**
See also CA 123; DLB 57

Stephen, Sir Leslie
See Stephen, Leslie

Stephen, Virginia
See Woolf, (Adeline) Virginia

Stephens, James 1882(?)-1950...... **TCLC 4**
See also CA 104; DLB 19

Stephens, Reed
See Donaldson, Stephen R.

Steptoe, Lydia
See Barnes, Djuna

Sterchi, Beat 1949-............... **CLC 65**

Sterling, Brett
See Bradbury, Ray (Douglas); Hamilton, Edmond

Sterling, Bruce 1954- .... **CLC 72**
See also CA 119

Sterling, George 1869-1926 .... **TCLC 20**
See also CA 117; DLB 54

Stern, Gerald 1925- .... **CLC 40**
See also CA 81-84; CANR 28; DLB 105

Stern, Richard (Gustave) 1928-... **CLC 4, 39**
See also CA 1-4R; CANR 1, 25; DLBY 87

Sternberg, Josef von 1894-1969..... **CLC 20**
See also CA 81-84

Sterne, Laurence 1713-1768.......... **LC 2**
See also CDBLB 1660-1789; DLB 39; WLC

Sternheim, (William Adolf) Carl 1878-1942 .... **TCLC 8**
See also CA 105; DLB 56, 118

Stevens, Mark 1951- .... **CLC 34**
See also CA 122

Stevens, Wallace 1879-1955 .... **TCLC 3, 12, 45**
See also CA 104; 124; CDALB 1929-1941; DLB 54; MTCW; WLC

Stevenson, Anne (Katharine) 1933- .... **CLC 7, 33**
See also CA 17-20R; CAAS 9; CANR 9, 33; DLB 40; MTCW

Stevenson, Robert Louis (Balfour) 1850-1894 .... **NCLC 5, 14; SSC 11**
See also CDBLB 1890-1914; CLR 10, 11; DLB 18, 57; MAICYA; WLC; YABC 2

Stewart, J(ohn) I(nnes) M(ackintosh) 1906- .... **CLC 7, 14, 32**
See also CA 85-88; CAAS 3; MTCW

Stewart, Mary (Florence Elinor) 1916- .... **CLC 7, 35**
See also CA 1-4R; CANR 1; SATA 12

Stewart, Mary Rainbow
See Stewart, Mary (Florence Elinor)

Still, James 1906-................ **CLC 49**
See also CA 65-68; CANR 10, 26; DLB 9; SATA 29

Sting
See Sumner, Gordon Matthew

Stirling, Arthur
See Sinclair, Upton (Beall)

Stitt, Milan 1941-................ **CLC 29**
See also CA 69-72

Stockton, Francis Richard 1834-1902
See Stockton, Frank R.
See also CA 108; 137; MAICYA; SATA 44

Stockton, Frank R................. **TCLC 47**
See also Stockton, Francis Richard
See also DLB 42, 74; SATA 32

Stoddard, Charles
See Kuttner, Henry

Stoker, Abraham 1847-1912
See Stoker, Bram
See also CA 105; SATA 29

Stoker, Bram..................... **TCLC 8**
See also Stoker, Abraham
See also CDBLB 1890-1914; DLB 36, 70; WLC

Stolz, Mary (Slattery) 1920-....... **CLC 12**
See also AAYA 8; AITN 1; CA 5-8R; CANR 13; MAICYA; SAAS 3; SATA 10, 70, 71

Stone, Irving 1903-1989............ **CLC 7**
See also AITN 1; CA 1-4R; 129; CAAS 3; CANR 1, 23; MTCW; SATA 3; SATO 64

Stone, Robert (Anthony) 1937- . . . . **CLC 5, 23, 42**
See also CA 85-88; CANR 23; MTCW

Stone, Zachary
See Follett, Ken(neth Martin)

Stoppard, Tom 1937- . . . **CLC 1, 3, 4, 5, 8, 15, 29, 34, 63**
See also CA 81-84; CANR 39; CDBLB 1960 to Present; DLB 13; DLBY 85; MTCW; WLC

Storey, David (Malcolm) 1933- . . . . **CLC 2, 4, 5, 8**
See also CA 81-84; CANR 36; DLB 13, 14; MTCW

Storm, Hyemeyohsts 1935- . . . . **CLC 3**
See also CA 81-84

Storm, (Hans) Theodor (Woldsen) 1817-1888 . . . . **NCLC 1**

Storni, Alfonsina 1892-1938 . . . . **TCLC 5**
See also CA 104; 131; HW

Stout, Rex (Todhunter) 1886-1975 . . . **CLC 3**
See also AITN 2; CA 61-64

Stow, (Julian) Randolph 1935- . . **CLC 23, 48**
See also CA 13-16R; CANR 33; MTCW

Stowe, Harriet (Elizabeth) Beecher 1811-1896 . . . . **NCLC 3**
See also CDALB 1865-1917; DLB 1, 12, 42, 74; MAICYA; WLC; YABC 1

Strachey, (Giles) Lytton 1880-1932 . . . . **TCLC 12**
See also CA 110

Strand, Mark 1934- . . . . . . **CLC 6, 18, 41, 71**
See also CA 21-24R; DLB 5; SATA 41

Straub, Peter (Francis) 1943- . . . . . . **CLC 28**
See also BEST 89:1; CA 85-88; CANR 28; DLBY 84; MTCW

Strauss, Botho 1944- . . . . **CLC 22**

Streatfeild, (Mary) Noel 1895(?)-1986 . . . . **CLC 21**
See also CA 81-84; 120; CANR 31; CLR 17; MAICYA; SATA 20, 48

Stribling, T(homas) S(igismund) 1881-1965 . . . . **CLC 23**
See also CA 107; DLB 9

Strindberg, (Johan) August 1849-1912 . . . . **TCLC 1, 8, 21, 47**
See also CA 104; 135; WLC

Stringer, Arthur 1874-1950 . . . . **TCLC 37**
See also DLB 92

Stringer, David
See Roberts, Keith (John Kingston)

Strugatskii, Arkadii (Natanovich) 1925-1991 . . . . **CLC 27**
See also CA 106; 135

Strugatskii, Boris (Natanovich) 1933- . . . . **CLC 27**
See also CA 106

Strummer, Joe 1953(?)- . . . . **CLC 30**
See also The Clash

Stuart, Don A.
See Campbell, John W(ood Jr.)

Stuart, Ian
See MacLean, Alistair (Stuart)

Stuart, Jesse (Hilton) 1906-1984 . . . . **CLC 1, 8, 11, 14, 34**
See also CA 5-8R; 112; CANR 31; DLB 9, 48, 102; DLBY 84; SATA 2, 36

Sturgeon, Theodore (Hamilton) 1918-1985 . . . . **CLC 22, 39**
See also Queen, Ellery
See also CA 81-84; 116; CANR 32; DLB 8; DLBY 85; MTCW

Sturges, Preston 1898-1959 . . . . **TCLC 48**
See also CA 114; DLB 26

Styron, William 1925- . . . . **CLC 1, 3, 5, 11, 15, 60**
See also BEST 90:4; CA 5-8R; CANR 6, 33; CDALB 1968-1988; DLB 2; DLBY 80; MTCW

Suarez Lynch, B.
See Borges, Jorge Luis

Suarez Lynch, B.
See Bioy Casares, Adolfo; Borges, Jorge Luis

Su Chien 1884-1918
See Su Man-shu
See also CA 123

Sudermann, Hermann 1857-1928 . . **TCLC 15**
See also CA 107; DLB 118

Sue, Eugene 1804-1857 . . . . **NCLC 1**
See also DLB 119

Sueskind, Patrick 1949- . . . . **CLC 44**

Sukenick, Ronald 1932- . . . . . **CLC 3, 4, 6, 48**
See also CA 25-28R; CAAS 8; CANR 32; DLBY 81

Suknaski, Andrew 1942- . . . . **CLC 19**
See also CA 101; DLB 53

Sullivan, Vernon
See Vian, Boris

Sully Prudhomme 1839-1907 . . . . . . **TCLC 31**

Su Man-shu . . . . **TCLC 24**
See also Su Chien

Summerforest, Ivy B.
See Kirkup, James

Summers, Andrew James 1942- . . . . . **CLC 26**
See also The Police

Summers, Andy
See Summers, Andrew James

Summers, Hollis (Spurgeon Jr.) 1916- . . . . **CLC 10**
See also CA 5-8R; CANR 3; DLB 6

Summers, (Alphonsus Joseph-Mary Augustus) Montague 1880-1948 . . . . **TCLC 16**
See also CA 118

Sumner, Gordon Matthew 1951- . . . . **CLC 26**
See also The Police

Surtees, Robert Smith 1803-1864 . . . . **NCLC 14**
See also DLB 21

Susann, Jacqueline 1921-1974 . . . . **CLC 3**
See also AITN 1; CA 65-68; 53-56; MTCW

Suskind, Patrick
See Sueskind, Patrick

Sutcliff, Rosemary 1920- . . . . **CLC 26**
See also CA 5-8R; CANR 37; CLR 1; MAICYA; SATA 6, 44

Sutro, Alfred 1863-1933 . . . . **TCLC 6**
See also CA 105; DLB 10

Sutton, Henry
See Slavitt, David R.

Svevo, Italo . . . . **TCLC 2, 35**
See also Schmitz, Aron Hector

Swados, Elizabeth 1951- . . . . **CLC 12**
See also CA 97-100

Swados, Harvey 1920-1972 . . . . **CLC 5**
See also CA 5-8R; 37-40R; CANR 6; DLB 2

Swan, Gladys 1934- . . . . **CLC 69**
See also CA 101; CANR 17, 39

Swarthout, Glendon (Fred) 1918- . . . **CLC 35**
See also CA 1-4R; CANR 1; SATA 26

Sweet, Sarah C.
See Jewett, (Theodora) Sarah Orne

Swenson, May 1919-1989. . . . . **CLC 4, 14, 61**
See also CA 5-8R; 130; CANR 36; DLB 5; MTCW; SATA 15

Swift, Augustus
See Lovecraft, H(oward) P(hillips)

Swift, Graham 1949- . . . . **CLC 41**
See also CA 117; 122

Swift, Jonathan 1667-1745. . . . . **LC 1**
See also CDBLB 1660-1789; DLB 39, 95, 101; SATA 19; WLC

Swinburne, Algernon Charles 1837-1909 . . . . **TCLC 8, 36**
See also CA 105; CDBLB 1832-1890; DLB 35, 57; WLC

Swinfen, Ann . . . . **CLC 34**

Swinnerton, Frank Arthur 1884-1982 . . . . **CLC 31**
See also CA 108; DLB 34

Swithen, John
See King, Stephen (Edwin)

Sylvia
See Ashton-Warner, Sylvia (Constance)

Symmes, Robert Edward
See Duncan, Robert (Edward)

Symonds, John Addington 1840-1893 . . . . **NCLC 34**
See also DLB 57

Symons, Arthur 1865-1945 . . . . **TCLC 11**
See also CA 107; DLB 19, 57

Symons, Julian (Gustave) 1912- . . . . **CLC 2, 14, 32**
See also CA 49-52; CAAS 3; CANR 3, 33; DLB 87; MTCW

Synge, (Edmund) J(ohn) M(illington) 1871-1909 . . . . **TCLC 6, 37; DC 2**
See also CA 104; CDBLB 1890-1914; DLB 10, 19

Syruc, J.
See Milosz, Czeslaw

Szirtes, George 1948- . . . . **CLC 46**
See also CA 109; CANR 27

Tabori, George 1914- . . . . **CLC 19**
See also CA 49-52; CANR 4

Tagore, Rabindranath 1861-1941. . . . **TCLC 3**
See also CA 104; 120; MTCW

Taine, Hippolyte Adolphe 1828-1893 . . . . **NCLC 15**

Talese, Gay 1932- . . . . **CLC 37**
See also AITN 1; CA 1-4R; CANR 9; MTCW

Tallent, Elizabeth (Ann) 1954- . . . . . **CLC 45**
See also CA 117

Tally, Ted 1952- . . . . **CLC 42**
See also CA 120; 124

Tamayo y Baus, Manuel 1829-1898 . . . . **NCLC 1**

Tammsaare, A(nton) H(ansen) 1878-1940 . . . . **TCLC 27**

Tan, Amy 1952- . . . . **CLC 59**
See also AAYA 9; BEST 89:3; CA 136

Tandem, Felix
See Spitteler, Carl (Friedrich Georg)

Tanizaki, Jun'ichiro 1886-1965 . . . . **CLC 8, 14, 28**
See also CA 93-96; 25-28R

Tanner, William
See Amis, Kingsley (William)

Tao Lao
See Storni, Alfonsina

Tarassoff, Lev
See Troyat, Henri

Tarbell, Ida M(inerva) 1857-1944 . . . . **TCLC 40**
See also CA 122; DLB 47

Tarkington, (Newton) Booth 1869-1946 . . . . **TCLC 9**
See also CA 110; DLB 9, 102; SATA 17

Tasso, Torquato 1544-1595 . . . . **LC 5**

Tate, (John Orley) Allen 1899-1979 . . . . **CLC 2, 4, 6, 9, 11, 14, 24**
See also CA 5-8R; 85-88; CANR 32; DLB 4, 45, 63; MTCW

Tate, Ellalice
See Hibbert, Eleanor Burford

Tate, James (Vincent) 1943- . . . **CLC 2, 6, 25**
See also CA 21-24R; CANR 29; DLB 5

Tavel, Ronald 1940- . . . . **CLC 6**
See also CA 21-24R; CANR 33

Taylor, Cecil Philip 1929-1981 . . . . . **CLC 27**
See also CA 25-28R; 105

Taylor, Edward 1642(?)-1729. . . . . **LC 11**
See also DLB 24

Taylor, Eleanor Ross 1920- . . . . **CLC 5**
See also CA 81-84

Taylor, Elizabeth 1912-1975 . . . **CLC 2, 4, 29**
See also CA 13-16R; CANR 9; MTCW; SATA 13

Taylor, Henry (Splawn) 1942- . . . . . . **CLC 44**
See also CA 33-36R; CAAS 7; CANR 31; DLB 5

Taylor, Kamala (Purnaiya) 1924-
See Markandaya, Kamala
See also CA 77-80

Taylor, Mildred D. . . . . **CLC 21**
See also BW; CA 85-88; CANR 25; CLR 9; DLB 52; MAICYA; SAAS 5; SATA 15, 70

Taylor, Peter (Hillsman) 1917- . . . . . **CLC 1, 4, 18, 37, 44, 50, 71; SSC 10**
See also CA 13-16R; CANR 9; DLBY 81; MTCW

Taylor, Robert Lewis 1912- . . . . **CLC 14**
See also CA 1-4R; CANR 3; SATA 10

Tchekhov, Anton
See Chekhov, Anton (Pavlovich)

Teasdale, Sara 1884-1933. . . . . **TCLC 4**
See also CA 104; DLB 45; SATA 32

Tegner, Esaias 1782-1846. . . . . **NCLC 2**

Teilhard de Chardin, (Marie Joseph) Pierre 1881-1955 . . . . **TCLC 9**
See also CA 105

Temple, Ann
See Mortimer, Penelope (Ruth)

Tennant, Emma (Christina) 1937- . . . . **CLC 13, 52**
See also CA 65-68; CAAS 9; CANR 10, 38; DLB 14

Tenneshaw, S. M.
See Silverberg, Robert

Tennyson, Alfred 1809-1892 . . . . . **NCLC 30**
See also CDBLB 1832-1890; DLB 32; WLC

Teran, Lisa St. Aubin de . . . . **CLC 36**
See also St. Aubin de Teran, Lisa

Teresa de Jesus, St. 1515-1582 . . . . . . **LC 18**

Terkel, Louis 1912-
See Terkel, Studs
See also CA 57-60; CANR 18; MTCW

Terkel, Studs . . . . **CLC 38**
See also Terkel, Louis
See also AITN 1

Terry, C. V.
See Slaughter, Frank G(ill)

Terry, Megan 1932- . . . . **CLC 19**
See also CA 77-80; CABS 3; DLB 7

Tertz, Abram
See Sinyavsky, Andrei (Donatevich)

Tesich, Steve 1943(?)- . . . . **CLC 40, 69**
See also CA 105; DLBY 83

Teternikov, Fyodor Kuzmich 1863-1927
See Sologub, Fyodor
See also CA 104

Tevis, Walter 1928-1984 . . . . **CLC 42**
See also CA 113

Tey, Josephine . . . . **TCLC 14**
See also Mackintosh, Elizabeth
See also DLB 77

Thackeray, William Makepeace 1811-1863 . . . . **NCLC 5, 14, 22**
See also CDBLB 1832-1890; DLB 21, 55; SATA 23; WLC

Thakura, Ravindranatha
See Tagore, Rabindranath

Tharoor, Shashi 1956- . . . . **CLC 70**

Thelwell, Michael Miles 1939- . . . . . **CLC 22**
See also CA 101

Theobald, Lewis Jr.
See Lovecraft, H(oward) P(hillips)

The Prophet
See Dreiser, Theodore (Herman Albert)

Theroux, Alexander (Louis) 1939- . . . . **CLC 2, 25**
See also CA 85-88; CANR 20

Theroux, Paul (Edward) 1941- . . . . **CLC 5, 8, 11, 15, 28, 46**
See also BEST 89:4; CA 33-36R; CANR 20; DLB 2; MTCW; SATA 44

Thesen, Sharon 1946- . . . . **CLC 56**

Thevenin, Denis
See Duhamel, Georges

Thibault, Jacques Anatole Francois 1844-1924
See France, Anatole
See also CA 106; 127; MTCW

Thiele, Colin (Milton) 1920- . . . . **CLC 17**
See also CA 29-32R; CANR 12, 28; CLR 27; MAICYA; SAAS 2; SATA 14

Thomas, Audrey (Callahan) 1935- . . . . **CLC 7, 13, 37**
See also AITN 2; CA 21-24R; CANR 36; DLB 60; MTCW

Thomas, D(onald) M(ichael) 1935- . . . . **CLC 13, 22, 31**
See also CA 61-64; CAAS 11; CANR 17; CDBLB 1960 to Present; DLB 40; MTCW

Thomas, Dylan (Marlais) 1914-1953 . . . . **TCLC 1, 8, 45; PC 2; SSC 3**
See also CA 104; 120; CDBLB 1945-1960; DLB 13, 20; MTCW; SATA 60; WLC

Thomas, (Philip) Edward 1878-1917 . . . . **TCLC 10**
See also CA 106; DLB 19

Thomas, Joyce Carol 1938- . . . . **CLC 35**
See also BW; CA 113; 116; CLR 19; DLB 33; MAICYA; MTCW; SAAS 7; SATA 40

Thomas, Lewis 1913- . . . . **CLC 35**
See also CA 85-88; CANR 38; MTCW

Thomas, Paul
See Mann, (Paul) Thomas

Thomas, Piri 1928- . . . . **CLC 17**
See also CA 73-76; HW

Thomas, R(onald) S(tuart) 1913- . . . . **CLC 6, 13, 48**
See also CA 89-92; CAAS 4; CANR 30; CDBLB 1960 to Present; DLB 27; MTCW

Thomas, Ross (Elmore) 1926- . . . . . . **CLC 39**
See also CA 33-36R; CANR 22

Thompson, Francis Clegg
See Mencken, H(enry) L(ouis)

Thompson, Francis Joseph 1859-1907 . . . . **TCLC 4**
See also CA 104; CDBLB 1890-1914; DLB 19

Thompson, Hunter S(tockton) 1939- . . . . **CLC 9, 17, 40**
See also BEST 89:1; CA 17-20R; CANR 23; MTCW

Thompson, Jim 1906-1976 . . . . **CLC 69**

Thompson, Judith . . . . **CLC 39**

Thomson, James 1700-1748 . . . . **LC 16**

Thomson, James 1834-1882 . . . . . . **NCLC 18**

Thoreau, Henry David 1817-1862 .... **NCLC 7, 21**
See also CDALB 1640-1865; DLB 1; WLC

Thornton, Hall
See Silverberg, Robert

Thurber, James (Grover) 1894-1961 .... **CLC 5, 11, 25; SSC 1**
See also CA 73-76; CANR 17, 39; CDALB 1929-1941; DLB 4, 11, 22, 102; MAICYA; MTCW; SATA 13

Thurman, Wallace (Henry) 1902-1934 .... **TCLC 6**
See also BLC 3; BW; CA 104; 124; DLB 51

Ticheburn, Cheviot
See Ainsworth, William Harrison

Tieck, (Johann) Ludwig 1773-1853 .... **NCLC 5**
See also DLB 90

Tiger, Derry
See Ellison, Harlan

Tilghman, Christopher 1948(?)-..... **CLC 65**

Tillinghast, Richard (Williford) 1940- .... **CLC 29**
See also CA 29-32R; CANR 26

Timrod, Henry 1828-1867 .... **NCLC 25**
See also DLB 3

Tindall, Gillian 1938-.............. **CLC 7**
See also CA 21-24R; CANR 11

Tiptree, James Jr................ **CLC 48, 50**
See also Sheldon, Alice Hastings Bradley
See also DLB 8

Titmarsh, Michael Angelo
See Thackeray, William Makepeace

Tocqueville, Alexis (Charles Henri Maurice Clerel Comte) 1805-1859..... **NCLC 7**

Tolkien, J(ohn) R(onald) R(euel) 1892-1973 .... **CLC 1, 2, 3, 8, 12, 38**
See also AITN 1; CA 17-18; 45-48; CANR 36; CAP 2; CDBLB 1914-1945; DLB 15; MAICYA; MTCW; SATA 2, 24, 32; WLC

Toller, Ernst 1893-1939 .... **TCLC 10**
See also CA 107

Tolson, M. B.
See Tolson, Melvin B(eaunorus)

Tolson, Melvin B(eaunorus) 1898(?)-1966 .... **CLC 36**
See also BLC 3; BW; CA 124; 89-92; DLB 48, 76

Tolstoi, Aleksei Nikolaevich
See Tolstoy, Alexey Nikolaevich

Tolstoy, Alexey Nikolaevich 1882-1945 .... **TCLC 18**
See also CA 107

Tolstoy, Count Leo
See Tolstoy, Leo (Nikolaevich)

Tolstoy, Leo (Nikolaevich) 1828-1910 ..... **TCLC 4, 11, 17, 28, 44; SSC 9**
See also CA 104; 123; SATA 26; WLC

Tomasi di Lampedusa, Giuseppe 1896-1957
See Lampedusa, Giuseppe (Tomasi) di
See also CA 111

Tomlin, Lily...................... **CLC 17**
See also Tomlin, Mary Jean

Tomlin, Mary Jean 1939(?)-
See Tomlin, Lily
See also CA 117

Tomlinson, (Alfred) Charles 1927- .... **CLC 2, 4, 6, 13, 45**
See also CA 5-8R; CANR 33; DLB 40

Tonson, Jacob
See Bennett, (Enoch) Arnold

Toole, John Kennedy 1937-1969 .... **CLC 19, 64**
See also CA 104; DLBY 81

Toomer, Jean 1894-1967 ..... **CLC 1, 4, 13, 22; SSC 1**
See also BLC 3; BW; CA 85-88; CDALB 1917-1929; DLB 45, 51; MTCW

Torley, Luke
See Blish, James (Benjamin)

Tornimparte, Alessandra
See Ginzburg, Natalia

Torre, Raoul della
See Mencken, H(enry) L(ouis)

Torrey, E(dwin) Fuller 1937-....... **CLC 34**
See also CA 119

Torsvan, Ben Traven
See Traven, B.

Torsvan, Benno Traven
See Traven, B.

Torsvan, Berick Traven
See Traven, B.

Torsvan, Berwick Traven
See Traven, B.

Torsvan, Bruno Traven
See Traven, B.

Torsvan, Traven
See Traven, B.

Tournier, Michel (Edouard) 1924- .... **CLC 6, 23, 36**
See also CA 49-52; CANR 3, 36; DLB 83; MTCW; SATA 23

Tournimparte, Alessandra
See Ginzburg, Natalia

Towers, Ivar
See Kornbluth, C(yril) M.

Townsend, Sue 1946- .... **CLC 61**
See also CA 119; 127; MTCW; SATA 48, 55

Townshend, Peter (Dennis Blandford) 1945- .... **CLC 17, 42**
See also CA 107

Tozzi, Federigo 1883-1920........ **TCLC 31**

Traill, Catharine Parr 1802-1899 .... **NCLC 31**
See also DLB 99

Trakl, Georg 1887-1914........... **TCLC 5**
See also CA 104

Transtroemer, Tomas (Goesta) 1931- .... **CLC 52, 65**
See also CA 117; 129

Transtromer, Tomas Gosta
See Transtroemer, Tomas (Goesta)

Traven, B. (?)-1969............. **CLC 8, 11**
See also CA 19-20; 25-28R; CAP 2; DLB 9, 56; MTCW

Treitel, Jonathan 1959- .... **CLC 70**

Tremain, Rose 1943-.............. **CLC 42**
See also CA 97-100; DLB 14

Tremblay, Michel 1942-........... **CLC 29**
See also CA 116; 128; DLB 60; MTCW

Trevanian (a pseudonym) 1930(?)-... **CLC 29**
See also CA 108

Trevor, Glen
See Hilton, James

Trevor, William 1928- .... **CLC 7, 9, 14, 25, 71**
See also Cox, William Trevor
See also DLB 14

Trifonov, Yuri (Valentinovich) 1925-1981 .... **CLC 45**
See also CA 126; 103; MTCW

Trilling, Lionel 1905-1975.... **CLC 9, 11, 24**
See also CA 9-12R; 61-64; CANR 10; DLB 28, 63; MTCW

Trimball, W. H.
See Mencken, H(enry) L(ouis)

Tristan
See Gomez de la Serna, Ramon

Tristram
See Housman, A(lfred) E(dward)

Trogdon, William (Lewis) 1939-
See Heat-Moon, William Least
See also CA 115; 119

Trollope, Anthony 1815-1882 .. **NCLC 6, 33**
See also CDBLB 1832-1890; DLB 21, 57; SATA 22; WLC

Trollope, Frances 1779-1863 ..... **NCLC 30**
See also DLB 21

Trotsky, Leon 1879-1940......... **TCLC 22**
See also CA 118

Trotter (Cockburn), Catharine 1679-1749 .... **LC 8**
See also DLB 84

Trout, Kilgore
See Farmer, Philip Jose

Trow, George W. S. 1943-......... **CLC 52**
See also CA 126

Troyat, Henri 1911-.............. **CLC 23**
See also CA 45-48; CANR 2, 33; MTCW

Trudeau, G(arretson) B(eekman) 1948-
See Trudeau, Garry B.
See also CA 81-84; CANR 31; SATA 35

Trudeau, Garry B.................. **CLC 12**
See also Trudeau, G(arretson) B(eekman)
See also AITN 2

Truffaut, Francois 1932-1984....... **CLC 20**
See also CA 81-84; 113; CANR 34

Trumbo, Dalton 1905-1976 .... **CLC 19**
See also CA 21-24R; 69-72; CANR 10; DLB 26

Trumbull, John 1750-1831....... **NCLC 30**
See also DLB 31

Trundlett, Helen B.
See Eliot, T(homas) S(tearns)

Tryon, Thomas 1926-1991 .... **CLC 3, 11**
See also AITN 1; CA 29-32R; 135; CANR 32; MTCW

Tryon, Tom
See Tryon, Thomas

Ts'ao Hsueh-ch'in 1715(?)-1763....... **LC 1**

Tsushima, Shuji 1909-1948
See Dazai, Osamu
See also CA 107

Tsvetaeva (Efron), Marina (Ivanovna) 1892-1941 . . . . **TCLC 7, 35**
See also CA 104; 128; MTCW

Tuck, Lily 1938- . . . . **CLC 70**

Tunis, John R(oberts) 1889-1975 . . . **CLC 12**
See also CA 61-64; DLB 22; MAICYA; SATA 30, 37

Tuohy, Frank . . . . **CLC 37**
See also Tuohy, John Francis
See also DLB 14

Tuohy, John Francis 1925-
See Tuohy, Frank
See also CA 5-8R; CANR 3

Turco, Lewis (Putnam) 1934- . . . **CLC 11, 63**
See also CA 13-16R; CANR 24; DLBY 84

Turgenev, Ivan 1818-1883 . . . . **NCLC 21; SSC 7**
See also WLC

Turner, Frederick 1943- . . . . **CLC 48**
See also CA 73-76; CAAS 10; CANR 12, 30; DLB 40

Tusan, Stan 1936- . . . . **CLC 22**
See also CA 105

Tutuola, Amos 1920- . . . . **CLC 5, 14, 29**
See also BLC 3; BW; CA 9-12R; CANR 27; MTCW

Twain, Mark . . . . **TCLC 6, 12, 19, 36, 48; SSC 6**
See also Clemens, Samuel Langhorne
See also DLB 11, 12, 23, 64, 74; WLC

Tyler, Anne 1941- . . . . **CLC 7, 11, 18, 28, 44, 59**
See also BEST 89:1; CA 9-12R; CANR 11, 33; DLB 6; DLBY 82; MTCW; SATA 7

Tyler, Royall 1757-1826. . . . . **NCLC 3**
See also DLB 37

Tynan, Katharine 1861-1931 . . . . **TCLC 3**
See also CA 104

Tytell, John 1939- . . . . **CLC 50**
See also CA 29-32R

Tyutchev, Fyodor 1803-1873 . . . . . **NCLC 34**

Tzara, Tristan . . . . **CLC 47**
See also Rosenfeld, Samuel

Uhry, Alfred 1936- . . . . **CLC 55**
See also CA 127; 133

Ulf, Haerved
See Strindberg, (Johan) August

Ulf, Harved
See Strindberg, (Johan) August

Unamuno (y Jugo), Miguel de 1864-1936 . . . . **TCLC 2, 9; SSC 11**
See also CA 104; 131; DLB 108; HW; MTCW

Undercliffe, Errol
See Campbell, (John) Ramsey

Underwood, Miles
See Glassco, John

Undset, Sigrid 1882-1949. . . . . **TCLC 3**
See also CA 104; 129; MTCW; WLC

Ungaretti, Giuseppe 1888-1970 . . . . **CLC 7, 11, 15**
See also CA 19-20; 25-28R; CAP 2; DLB 114

Unger, Douglas 1952- . . . . **CLC 34**
See also CA 130

Updike, John (Hoyer) 1932- . . . . . . **CLC 1, 2, 3, 5, 7, 9, 13, 15, 23, 34, 43, 70**
See also CA 1-4R; CABS 1; CANR 4, 33; CDALB 1968-1988; DLB 2, 5; DLBD 3; DLBY 80, 82; MTCW; WLC

Upshaw, Margaret Mitchell
See Mitchell, Margaret (Munnerlyn)

Upton, Mark
See Sanders, Lawrence

Urdang, Constance (Henriette) 1922- . . . . **CLC 47**
See also CA 21-24R; CANR 9, 24

Uris, Leon (Marcus) 1924- . . . . **CLC 7, 32**
See also AITN 1, 2; BEST 89:2; CA 1-4R; CANR 1; MTCW; SATA 49

Urmuz
See Codrescu, Andrei

Ustinov, Peter (Alexander) 1921- . . . . **CLC 1**
See also AITN 1; CA 13-16R; CANR 25; DLB 13

v
See Chekhov, Anton (Pavlovich)

Vaculik, Ludvik 1926- . . . . **CLC 7**
See also CA 53-56

Valenzuela, Luisa 1938- . . . . **CLC 31**
See also CA 101; CANR 32; DLB 113; HW

Valera y Alcala-Galiano, Juan 1824-1905 . . . . **TCLC 10**
See also CA 106

Valery, (Ambroise) Paul (Toussaint Jules) 1871-1945 . . . . **TCLC 4, 15**
See also CA 104; 122; MTCW

Valle-Inclan, Ramon (Maria) del 1866-1936 . . . . **TCLC 5**
See also CA 106

Vallejo, Antonio Buero
See Buero Vallejo, Antonio

Vallejo, Cesar (Abraham) 1892-1938 . . . . **TCLC 3**
See also CA 105; HW

Valle Y Pena, Ramon del
See Valle-Inclan, Ramon (Maria) del

Van Ash, Cay 1918- . . . . **CLC 34**

Vanbrugh, Sir John 1664-1726 . . . . . . **LC 21**
See also DLB 80

Van Campen, Karl
See Campbell, John W(ood Jr.)

Vance, Gerald
See Silverberg, Robert

Vance, Jack . . . . **CLC 35**
See also Vance, John Holbrook
See also DLB 8

Vance, John Holbrook 1916-
See Queen, Ellery; Vance, Jack
See also CA 29-32R; CANR 17; MTCW

Van Den Bogarde, Derek Jules Gaspard Ulric Niven 1921-
See Bogarde, Dirk
See also CA 77-80

Vandenburgh, Jane . . . . **CLC 59**

Vanderhaeghe, Guy 1951- . . . . **CLC 41**
See also CA 113

van der Post, Laurens (Jan) 1906- . . . **CLC 5**
See also CA 5-8R; CANR 35

van de Wetering, Janwillem 1931- . . **CLC 47**
See also CA 49-52; CANR 4

Van Dine, S. S. . . . . **TCLC 23**
See also Wright, Willard Huntington

Van Doren, Carl (Clinton) 1885-1950 . . . . **TCLC 18**
See also CA 111

Van Doren, Mark 1894-1972. . . . . **CLC 6, 10**
See also CA 1-4R; 37-40R; CANR 3; DLB 45; MTCW

Van Druten, John (William) 1901-1957 . . . . **TCLC 2**
See also CA 104; DLB 10

Van Duyn, Mona (Jane) 1921- . . . . **CLC 3, 7, 63**
See also CA 9-12R; CANR 7, 38; DLB 5

Van Dyne, Edith
See Baum, L(yman) Frank

van Itallie, Jean-Claude 1936- . . . . **CLC 3**
See also CA 45-48; CAAS 2; CANR 1; DLB 7

van Ostaijen, Paul 1896-1928 . . . . . **TCLC 33**

Van Peebles, Melvin 1932- . . . . . . **CLC 2, 20**
See also BW; CA 85-88; CANR 27

Vansittart, Peter 1920- . . . . **CLC 42**
See also CA 1-4R; CANR 3

Van Vechten, Carl 1880-1964 . . . . . . **CLC 33**
See also CA 89-92; DLB 4, 9, 51

Van Vogt, A(lfred) E(lton) 1912- . . . . . **CLC 1**
See also CA 21-24R; CANR 28; DLB 8; SATA 14

Vara, Madeleine
See Jackson, Laura (Riding)

Varda, Agnes 1928- . . . . **CLC 16**
See also CA 116; 122

Vargas Llosa, (Jorge) Mario (Pedro) 1936- . . . . **CLC 3, 6, 9, 10, 15, 31, 42**
See also CA 73-76; CANR 18, 32; HW; MTCW

Vasiliu, Gheorghe 1881-1957
See Bacovia, George
See also CA 123

Vassa, Gustavus
See Equiano, Olaudah

Vassilikos, Vassilis 1933- . . . . **CLC 4, 8**
See also CA 81-84

Vaughn, Stephanie . . . . **CLC 62**

Vazov, Ivan (Minchov) 1850-1921 . . . . **TCLC 25**
See also CA 121

Veblen, Thorstein (Bunde) 1857-1929 . . . . **TCLC 31**
See also CA 115

Venison, Alfred
See Pound, Ezra (Weston Loomis)

Author Index

Verdi, Marie de
See Mencken, H(enry) L(ouis)

Verdu, Matilde
See Cela, Camilo Jose

Verga, Giovanni (Carmelo)
1840-1922 .... **TCLC 3**
See also CA 104; 123

Vergil 70B.C.-19B.C. .... **CMLC 9**

Verhaeren, Emile (Adolphe Gustave)
1855-1916 .... **TCLC 12**
See also CA 109

Verlaine, Paul (Marie)
1844-1896 .... **NCLC 2; PC 2**

Verne, Jules (Gabriel) 1828-1905 ... **TCLC 6**
See also CA 110; 131; MAICYA; SATA 21

Very, Jones 1813-1880........... **NCLC 9**
See also DLB 1

Vesaas, Tarjei 1897-1970.......... **CLC 48**
See also CA 29-32R

Vialis, Gaston
See Simenon, Georges (Jacques Christian)

Vian, Boris 1920-1959 .... **TCLC 9**
See also CA 106; DLB 72

Viaud, (Louis Marie) Julien 1850-1923
See Loti, Pierre
See also CA 107

Vicar, Henry
See Felsen, Henry Gregor

Vicker, Angus
See Felsen, Henry Gregor

Vidal, Gore
1925- ..... **CLC 2, 4, 6, 8, 10, 22, 33, 72**
See also AITN 1; BEST 90:2; CA 5-8R; CANR 13; DLB 6; MTCW

Viereck, Peter (Robert Edwin)
1916- .... **CLC 4**
See also CA 1-4R; CANR 1; DLB 5

Vigny, Alfred (Victor) de
1797-1863 .... **NCLC 7**
See also DLB 119

Vilakazi, Benedict Wallet
1906-1947 .... **TCLC 37**

Villiers de l'Isle Adam, Jean Marie Mathias Philippe Auguste Comte
1838-1889 .... **NCLC 3**

Vincent, Gabrielle................. **CLC 13**
See also CA 126; CLR 13; MAICYA; SATA 61

Vinci, Leonardo da 1452-1519....... **LC 12**

Vine, Barbara .... **CLC 50**
See also Rendell, Ruth (Barbara)
See also BEST 90:4

Vinge, Joan D(ennison) 1948-...... **CLC 30**
See also CA 93-96; SATA 36

Violis, G.
See Simenon, Georges (Jacques Christian)

Visconti, Luchino 1906-1976....... **CLC 16**
See also CA 81-84; 65-68; CANR 39

Vittorini, Elio 1908-1966...... **CLC 6, 9, 14**
See also CA 133; 25-28R

Vizinczey, Stephen 1933-.......... **CLC 40**
See also CA 128

Vliet, R(ussell) G(ordon)
1929-1984 .... **CLC 22**
See also CA 37-40R; 112; CANR 18

Vogau, Boris Andreyevich 1894-1937(?)
See Pilnyak, Boris
See also CA 123

Voigt, Cynthia 1942- .... **CLC 30**
See also AAYA 3; CA 106; CANR 18, 37; CLR 13; MAICYA; SATA 33, 48

Voigt, Ellen Bryant 1943-......... **CLC 54**
See also CA 69-72; CANR 11, 29; DLB 120

Voinovich, Vladimir (Nikolaevich)
1932- .... **CLC 10, 49**
See also CA 81-84; CAAS 12; CANR 33; MTCW

Voltaire 1694-1778................ **LC 14**
See also WLC

von Daeniken, Erich 1935- .... **CLC 30**
See also von Daniken, Erich
See also AITN 1; CA 37-40R; CANR 17

von Daniken, Erich................ **CLC 30**
See also von Daeniken, Erich

von Heidenstam, (Carl Gustaf) Verner
See Heidenstam, (Carl Gustaf) Verner von

von Heyse, Paul (Johann Ludwig)
See Heyse, Paul (Johann Ludwig von)

von Hofmannsthal, Hugo
See Hofmannsthal, Hugo von

von Horvath, Odon
See Horvath, Oedoen von

von Horvath, Oedoen
See Horvath, Oedoen von

von Liliencron, (Friedrich Adolf Axel) Detlev
See Liliencron, (Friedrich Adolf Axel) Detlev von

Vonnegut, Kurt Jr.
1922- ...... **CLC 1, 2, 3, 4, 5, 8, 12, 22, 40, 60; SSC 8**
See also AAYA 6; AITN 1; BEST 90:4; CA 1-4R; CANR 1, 25; CDALB 1968-1988; DLB 2, 8; DLBD 3; DLBY 80; MTCW; WLC

Von Rachen, Kurt
See Hubbard, L(afayette) Ron(ald)

von Rezzori (d'Arezzo), Gregor
See Rezzori (d'Arezzo), Gregor von

von Sternberg, Josef
See Sternberg, Josef von

Vorster, Gordon 1924-............ **CLC 34**
See also CA 133

Vosce, Trudie
See Ozick, Cynthia

Voznesensky, Andrei (Andreievich)
1933- .... **CLC 1, 15, 57**
See also CA 89-92; CANR 37; MTCW

Waddington, Miriam 1917-........ **CLC 28**
See also CA 21-24R; CANR 12, 30; DLB 68

Wagman, Fredrica 1937-........... **CLC 7**
See also CA 97-100

Wagner, Richard 1813-1883....... **NCLC 9**

Wagner-Martin, Linda 1936-....... **CLC 50**

Wagoner, David (Russell)
1926- .... **CLC 3, 5, 15**
See also CA 1-4R; CAAS 3; CANR 2; DLB 5; SATA 14

Wah, Fred(erick James) 1939-...... **CLC 44**
See also CA 107; DLB 60

Wahloo, Per 1926-1975 .... **CLC 7**
See also CA 61-64

Wahloo, Peter
See Wahloo, Per

Wain, John (Barrington)
1925- .... **CLC 2, 11, 15, 46**
See also CA 5-8R; CAAS 4; CANR 23; CDBLB 1960 to Present; DLB 15, 27; MTCW

Wajda, Andrzej 1926-............. **CLC 16**
See also CA 102

Wakefield, Dan 1932-.............. **CLC 7**
See also CA 21-24R; CAAS 7

Wakoski, Diane
1937- .... **CLC 2, 4, 7, 9, 11, 40**
See also CA 13-16R; CAAS 1; CANR 9; DLB 5

Wakoski-Sherbell, Diane
See Wakoski, Diane

Walcott, Derek (Alton)
1930- .... **CLC 2, 4, 9, 14, 25, 42, 67**
See also BLC 3; BW; CA 89-92; CANR 26; DLB 117; DLBY 81; MTCW

Waldman, Anne 1945- .... **CLC 7**
See also CA 37-40R; CANR 34; DLB 16

Waldo, E. Hunter
See Sturgeon, Theodore (Hamilton)

Waldo, Edward Hamilton
See Sturgeon, Theodore (Hamilton)

Walker, Alice (Malsenior)
1944- ...... **CLC 5, 6, 9, 19, 27, 46, 58; SSC 5**
See also AAYA 3; BEST 89:4; BLC 3; BW; CA 37-40R; CANR 9, 27; CDALB 1968-1988; DLB 6, 33; MTCW; SATA 31

Walker, David Harry 1911-1992.... **CLC 14**
See also CA 1-4R; 137; CANR 1; SATA 8; SATO 71

Walker, Edward Joseph 1934-
See Walker, Ted
See also CA 21-24R; CANR 12, 28

Walker, George F. 1947-....... **CLC 44, 61**
See also CA 103; CANR 21; DLB 60

Walker, Joseph A. 1935-.......... **CLC 19**
See also BW; CA 89-92; CANR 26; DLB 38

Walker, Margaret (Abigail)
1915- .... **CLC 1, 6**
See also BLC 3; BW; CA 73-76; CANR 26; DLB 76; MTCW

Walker, Ted...................... **CLC 13**
See also Walker, Edward Joseph
See also DLB 40

Wallace, David Foster 1962-....... **CLC 50**
See also CA 132

Wallace, Dexter
See Masters, Edgar Lee

Wallace, Irving 1916-1990 .... **CLC 7, 13**
See also AITN 1; CA 1-4R; 132; CAAS 1; CANR 1, 27; MTCW

Wallant, Edward Lewis 1926-1962 .... **CLC 5, 10**
See also CA 1-4R; CANR 22; DLB 2, 28; MTCW

Walpole, Horace 1717-1797.......... **LC 2**
See also DLB 39, 104

Walpole, Hugh (Seymour) 1884-1941 .... **TCLC 5**
See also CA 104; DLB 34

Walser, Martin 1927-............. **CLC 27**
See also CA 57-60; CANR 8; DLB 75

Walser, Robert 1878-1956 .... **TCLC 18**
See also CA 118; DLB 66

Walsh, Jill Paton.................. **CLC 35**
See also Paton Walsh, Gillian
See also CLR 2; SAAS 3

Walter, Villiam Christian
See Andersen, Hans Christian

Wambaugh, Joseph (Aloysius Jr.) 1937- .... **CLC 3, 18**
See also AITN 1; BEST 89:3; CA 33-36R; DLB 6; DLBY 83; MTCW

Ward, Arthur Henry Sarsfield 1883-1959
See Rohmer, Sax
See also CA 108

Ward, Douglas Turner 1930-....... **CLC 19**
See also BW; CA 81-84; CANR 27; DLB 7, 38

Warhol, Andy 1928(?)-1987........ **CLC 20**
See also BEST 89:4; CA 89-92; 121; CANR 34

Warner, Francis (Robert le Plastrier) 1937- .... **CLC 14**
See also CA 53-56; CANR 11

Warner, Marina 1946-............ **CLC 59**
See also CA 65-68; CANR 21

Warner, Rex (Ernest) 1905-1986.... **CLC 45**
See also CA 89-92; 119; DLB 15

Warner, Susan (Bogert) 1819-1885 .... **NCLC 31**
See also DLB 3, 42

Warner, Sylvia (Constance) Ashton
See Ashton-Warner, Sylvia (Constance)

Warner, Sylvia Townsend 1893-1978 .... **CLC 7, 19**
See also CA 61-64; 77-80; CANR 16; DLB 34; MTCW

Warren, Mercy Otis 1728-1814... **NCLC 13**
See also DLB 31

Warren, Robert Penn 1905-1989 ... **CLC 1, 4, 6, 8, 10, 13, 18, 39, 53, 59; SSC 4**
See also AITN 1; CA 13-16R; 129; CANR 10; CDALB 1968-1988; DLB 2, 48; DLBY 80, 89; MTCW; SATA 46, 63; WLC

Warshofsky, Isaac
See Singer, Isaac Bashevis

Warton, Thomas 1728-1790......... **LC 15**
See also DLB 104, 109

Waruk, Kona
See Harris, (Theodore) Wilson

Warung, Price 1855-1911......... **TCLC 45**

Warwick, Jarvis
See Garner, Hugh

Washington, Alex
See Harris, Mark

Washington, Booker T(aliaferro) 1856-1915 .... **TCLC 10**
See also BLC 3; BW; CA 114; 125; SATA 28

Wassermann, (Karl) Jakob 1873-1934 .... **TCLC 6**
See also CA 104; DLB 66

Wasserstein, Wendy 1950-...... **CLC 32, 59**
See also CA 121; 129; CABS 3

Waterhouse, Keith (Spencer) 1929- .... **CLC 47**
See also CA 5-8R; CANR 38; DLB 13, 15; MTCW

Waters, Roger 1944-............. **CLC 35**
See also Pink Floyd

Watkins, Frances Ellen
See Harper, Frances Ellen Watkins

Watkins, Gerrold
See Malzberg, Barry N(athaniel)

Watkins, Paul 1964-............. **CLC 55**
See also CA 132

Watkins, Vernon Phillips 1906-1967 .... **CLC 43**
See also CA 9-10; 25-28R; CAP 1; DLB 20

Watson, Irving S.
See Mencken, H(enry) L(ouis)

Watson, John H.
See Farmer, Philip Jose

Watson, Richard F.
See Silverberg, Robert

Waugh, Auberon (Alexander) 1939- .. **CLC 7**
See also CA 45-48; CANR 6, 22; DLB 14

Waugh, Evelyn (Arthur St. John) 1903-1966 ... **CLC 1, 3, 8, 13, 19, 27, 44**
See also CA 85-88; 25-28R; CANR 22; CDBLB 1914-1945; DLB 15; MTCW; WLC

Waugh, Harriet 1944- .... **CLC 6**
See also CA 85-88; CANR 22

Ways, C. R.
See Blount, Roy (Alton) Jr.

Waystaff, Simon
See Swift, Jonathan

Webb, (Martha) Beatrice (Potter) 1858-1943 .... **TCLC 22**
See also Potter, Beatrice
See also CA 117

Webb, Charles (Richard) 1939-...... **CLC 7**
See also CA 25-28R

Webb, James H(enry) Jr. 1946- .... **CLC 22**
See also CA 81-84

Webb, Mary (Gladys Meredith) 1881-1927 .... **TCLC 24**
See also CA 123; DLB 34

Webb, Mrs. Sidney
See Webb, (Martha) Beatrice (Potter)

Webb, Phyllis 1927-............. **CLC 18**
See also CA 104; CANR 23; DLB 53

Webb, Sidney (James) 1859-1947 .... **TCLC 22**
See also CA 117

Webber, Andrew Lloyd............. **CLC 21**
See also Lloyd Webber, Andrew

Weber, Lenora Mattingly 1895-1971 .... **CLC 12**
See also CA 19-20; 29-32R; CAP 1; SATA 2, 26

Webster, John 1579(?)-1634(?) .... **DC 2**
See also CDBLB Before 1660; DLB 58; WLC

Webster, Noah 1758-1843 .... **NCLC 30**

Wedekind, (Benjamin) Frank(lin) 1864-1918 .... **TCLC 7**
See also CA 104; DLB 118

Weidman, Jerome 1913-........... **CLC 7**
See also AITN 2; CA 1-4R; CANR 1; DLB 28

Weil, Simone (Adolphine) 1909-1943 .... **TCLC 23**
See also CA 117

Weinstein, Nathan
See West, Nathanael

Weinstein, Nathan von Wallenstein
See West, Nathanael

Weir, Peter (Lindsay) 1944- .... **CLC 20**
See also CA 113; 123

Weiss, Peter (Ulrich) 1916-1982 .... **CLC 3, 15, 51**
See also CA 45-48; 106; CANR 3; DLB 69

Weiss, Theodore (Russell) 1916- .... **CLC 3, 8, 14**
See also CA 9-12R; CAAS 2; DLB 5

Welch, (Maurice) Denton 1915-1948 .... **TCLC 22**
See also CA 121

Welch, James 1940- .... **CLC 6, 14, 52**
See also CA 85-88

Weldon, Fay 1933(?)- .... **CLC 6, 9, 11, 19, 36, 59**
See also CA 21-24R; CANR 16; CDBLB 1960 to Present; DLB 14; MTCW

Wellek, Rene 1903- .... **CLC 28**
See also CA 5-8R; CAAS 7; CANR 8; DLB 63

Weller, Michael 1942- .... **CLC 10, 53**
See also CA 85-88

Weller, Paul 1958- .... **CLC 26**

Wellershoff, Dieter 1925-.......... **CLC 46**
See also CA 89-92; CANR 16, 37

Welles, (George) Orson 1915-1985 .... **CLC 20**
See also CA 93-96; 117

Wellman, Mac 1945- .... **CLC 65**

Wellman, Manly Wade 1903-1986 .. **CLC 49**
See also CA 1-4R; 118; CANR 6, 16; SATA 6, 47

Wells, Carolyn 1869(?)-1942 ...... **TCLC 35**
See also CA 113; DLB 11

Wells, H(erbert) G(eorge) 1866-1946 ...... **TCLC 6, 12, 19; SSC 6**
See also CA 110; 121; CDBLB 1914-1945; DLB 34, 70; MTCW; SATA 20; WLC

Wells, Rosemary 1943-............ **CLC 12**
See also CA 85-88; CLR 16; MAICYA; SAAS 1; SATA 18, 69

Welty, Eudora 1909- .... **CLC 1, 2, 5, 14, 22, 33; SSC 1**
See also CA 9-12R; CABS 1; CANR 32; CDALB 1941-1968; DLB 2, 102; DLBY 87; MTCW; WLC

Wen I-to 1899-1946 .... **TCLC 28**

Wentworth, Robert
See Hamilton, Edmond

Werfel, Franz (V.) 1890-1945 ...... **TCLC 8**
See also CA 104; DLB 81

Wergeland, Henrik Arnold 1808-1845 .... **NCLC 5**

Wersba, Barbara 1932-............ **CLC 30**
See also AAYA 2; CA 29-32R; CANR 16, 38; CLR 3; DLB 52; MAICYA; SAAS 2; SATA 1, 58

Wertmueller, Lina 1928- .... **CLC 16**
See also CA 97-100; CANR 39

Wescott, Glenway 1901-1987....... **CLC 13**
See also CA 13-16R; 121; CANR 23; DLB 4, 9, 102

Wesker, Arnold 1932- .... **CLC 3, 5, 42**
See also CA 1-4R; CAAS 7; CANR 1, 33; CDBLB 1960 to Present; DLB 13; MTCW

Wesley, Richard (Errol) 1945-....... **CLC 7**
See also BW; CA 57-60; DLB 38

Wessel, Johan Herman 1742-1785 .... **LC 7**

West, Anthony (Panther) 1914-1987 .... **CLC 50**
See also CA 45-48; 124; CANR 3, 19; DLB 15

West, C. P.
See Wodehouse, P(elham) G(renville)

West, (Mary) Jessamyn 1902-1984 .... **CLC 7, 17**
See also CA 9-12R; 112; CANR 27; DLB 6; DLBY 84; MTCW; SATA 37

West, Morris L(anglo) 1916-..... **CLC 6, 33**
See also CA 5-8R; CANR 24; MTCW

West, Nathanael 1903-1940 .... **TCLC 1, 14, 44**
See also CA 104; 125; CDALB 1929-1941; DLB 4, 9, 28; MTCW

West, Paul 1930- .... **CLC 7, 14**
See also CA 13-16R; CAAS 7; CANR 22; DLB 14

West, Rebecca 1892-1983 .. **CLC 7, 9, 31, 50**
See also CA 5-8R; 109; CANR 19; DLB 36; DLBY 83; MTCW

Westall, Robert (Atkinson) 1929- ... **CLC 17**
See also CA 69-72; CANR 18; CLR 13; MAICYA; SAAS 2; SATA 23, 69

Westlake, Donald E(dwin) 1933- .... **CLC 7, 33**
See also CA 17-20R; CAAS 13; CANR 16

Westmacott, Mary
See Christie, Agatha (Mary Clarissa)

Weston, Allen
See Norton, Andre

Wetcheek, J. L.
See Feuchtwanger, Lion

Wetering, Janwillem van de
See van de Wetering, Janwillem

Wetherell, Elizabeth
See Warner, Susan (Bogert)

Whalen, Philip 1923- .... **CLC 6, 29**
See also CA 9-12R; CANR 5, 39; DLB 16

Wharton, Edith (Newbold Jones) 1862-1937 .... **TCLC 3, 9, 27; SSC 6**
See also CA 104; 132; CDALB 1865-1917; DLB 4, 9, 12, 78; MTCW; WLC

Wharton, James
See Mencken, H(enry) L(ouis)

Wharton, William (a pseudonym) .... **CLC 18, 37**
See also CA 93-96; DLBY 80

Wheatley (Peters), Phillis 1754(?)-1784 .... **LC 3; PC 3**
See also BLC 3; CDALB 1640-1865; DLB 31, 50; WLC

Wheelock, John Hall 1886-1978 .... **CLC 14**
See also CA 13-16R; 77-80; CANR 14; DLB 45

White, E(lwyn) B(rooks) 1899-1985 .... **CLC 10, 34, 39**
See also AITN 2; CA 13-16R; 116; CANR 16, 37; CLR 1, 21; DLB 11, 22; MAICYA; MTCW; SATA 2, 29, 44

White, Edmund (Valentine III) 1940- .... **CLC 27**
See also AAYA 7; CA 45-48; CANR 3, 19, 36; MTCW

White, Patrick (Victor Martindale) 1912-1990 .. **CLC 3, 4, 5, 7, 9, 18, 65, 69**
See also CA 81-84; 132; MTCW

White, Phyllis Dorothy James 1920-
See James, P. D.
See also CA 21-24R; CANR 17; MTCW

White, T(erence) H(anbury) 1906-1964 .... **CLC 30**
See also CA 73-76; CANR 37; MAICYA; SATA 12

White, Terence de Vere 1912-...... **CLC 49**
See also CA 49-52; CANR 3

White, Walter
See White, Walter F(rancis)
See also BLC 3

White, Walter F(rancis) 1893-1955 .... **TCLC 15**
See also White, Walter
See also CA 115; 124; DLB 51

White, William Hale 1831-1913
See Rutherford, Mark
See also CA 121

Whitehead, E(dward) A(nthony) 1933- .... **CLC 5**
See also CA 65-68

Whitemore, Hugh (John) 1936-..... **CLC 37**
See also CA 132

Whitman, Sarah Helen (Power) 1803-1878 .... **NCLC 19**
See also DLB 1

Whitman, Walt(er) 1819-1892 .... **NCLC 4, 31; PC 3**
See also CDALB 1640-1865; DLB 3, 64; SATA 20; WLC

Whitney, Phyllis A(yame) 1903-.... **CLC 42**
See also AITN 2; BEST 90:3; CA 1-4R; CANR 3, 25, 38; MAICYA; SATA 1, 30

Whittemore, (Edward) Reed (Jr.) 1919- .... **CLC 4**
See also CA 9-12R; CAAS 8; CANR 4; DLB 5

Whittier, John Greenleaf 1807-1892 .... **NCLC 8**
See also CDALB 1640-1865; DLB 1

Whittlebot, Hernia
See Coward, Noel (Peirce)

Wicker, Thomas Grey 1926-
See Wicker, Tom
See also CA 65-68; CANR 21

Wicker, Tom .... **CLC 7**
See also Wicker, Thomas Grey

Wideman, John Edgar 1941- .... **CLC 5, 34, 36, 67**
See also BLC 3; BW; CA 85-88; CANR 14; DLB 33

Wiebe, Rudy (H.) 1934-...... **CLC 6, 11, 14**
See also CA 37-40R; DLB 60

Wieland, Christoph Martin 1733-1813 .... **NCLC 17**
See also DLB 97

Wieners, John 1934-............... **CLC 7**
See also CA 13-16R; DLB 16

Wiesel, Elie(zer) 1928-..... **CLC 3, 5, 11, 37**
See also AAYA 7; AITN 1; CA 5-8R; CAAS 4; CANR 8; DLB 83; DLBY 87; MTCW; SATA 56

Wiggins, Marianne 1947-.......... **CLC 57**
See also BEST 89:3; CA 130

Wight, James Alfred 1916-
See Herriot, James
See also CA 77-80; SATA 44, 55

Wilbur, Richard (Purdy) 1921- .... **CLC 3, 6, 9, 14, 53**
See also CA 1-4R; CABS 2; CANR 2, 29; DLB 5; MTCW; SATA 9

Wild, Peter 1940-................ **CLC 14**
See also CA 37-40R; DLB 5

Wilde, Oscar (Fingal O'Flahertie Wills) 1854(?)-1900 .... **TCLC 1, 8, 23, 41; SSC 11**
See also CA 104; 119; CDBLB 1890-1914; DLB 10, 19, 34, 57; SATA 24; WLC

Wilder, Billy .... **CLC 20**
See also Wilder, Samuel
See also DLB 26

Wilder, Samuel 1906-
See Wilder, Billy
See also CA 89-92

Wilder, Thornton (Niven) 1897-1975 ..... **CLC 1, 5, 6, 10, 15, 35; DC 1**
See also AITN 2; CA 13-16R; 61-64; DLB 4, 7, 9; MTCW; WLC

Wiley, Richard 1944-............. **CLC 44**
See also CA 121; 129

Wilhelm, Kate .... **CLC 7**
See also Wilhelm, Katie Gertrude
See also CAAS 5; DLB 8

Wilhelm, Katie Gertrude 1928-
See Wilhelm, Kate
See also CA 37-40R; CANR 17, 36; MTCW

Wilkins, Mary
See Freeman, Mary Eleanor Wilkins

Willard, Nancy 1936-........... **CLC 7, 37**
See also CA 89-92; CANR 10, 39; CLR 5; DLB 5, 52; MAICYA; MTCW; SATA 30, 37, 71

Williams, C(harles) K(enneth)
1936- .... **CLC 33, 56**
See also CA 37-40R; DLB 5

Williams, Charles
See Collier, James L(incoln)

Williams, Charles (Walter Stansby)
1886-1945 .... **TCLC 1, 11**
See also CA 104; DLB 100

Williams, (George) Emlyn
1905-1987 .... **CLC 15**
See also CA 104; 123; CANR 36; DLB 10, 77; MTCW

Williams, Hugo 1942-............. **CLC 42**
See also CA 17-20R; DLB 40

Williams, J. Walker
See Wodehouse, P(elham) G(renville)

Williams, John A(lfred) 1925-.... **CLC 5, 13**
See also BLC 3; BW; CA 53-56; CAAS 3; CANR 6, 26; DLB 2, 33

Williams, Jonathan (Chamberlain)
1929- .... **CLC 13**
See also CA 9-12R; CAAS 12; CANR 8; DLB 5

Williams, Joy 1944-............. **CLC 31**
See also CA 41-44R; CANR 22

Williams, Norman 1952- .... **CLC 39**
See also CA 118

Williams, Tennessee
1911-1983 .... **CLC 1, 2, 5, 7, 8, 11, 15, 19, 30, 39, 45, 71**
See also AITN 1, 2; CA 5-8R; 108; CABS 3; CANR 31; CDALB 1941-1968; DLB 7; DLBD 4; DLBY 83; MTCW; WLC

Williams, Thomas (Alonzo)
1926-1990 .... **CLC 14**
See also CA 1-4R; 132; CANR 2

Williams, William C.
See Williams, William Carlos

Williams, William Carlos
1883-1963 ... **CLC 1, 2, 5, 9, 13, 22, 42, 67**
See also CA 89-92; CANR 34; CDALB 1917-1929; DLB 4, 16, 54, 86; MTCW

Williamson, David Keith 1942-..... **CLC 56**
See also CA 103

Williamson, Jack.................. **CLC 29**
See also Williamson, John Stewart
See also CAAS 8; DLB 8

Williamson, John Stewart 1908-
See Williamson, Jack
See also CA 17-20R; CANR 23

Willie, Frederick
See Lovecraft, H(oward) P(hillips)

Willingham, Calder (Baynard Jr.)
1922- .... **CLC 5, 51**
See also CA 5-8R; CANR 3; DLB 2, 44; MTCW

Willis, Charles
See Clarke, Arthur C(harles)

Willy
See Colette, (Sidonie-Gabrielle)

Willy, Colette
See Colette, (Sidonie-Gabrielle)

Wilson, A(ndrew) N(orman) 1950- .. **CLC 33**
See also CA 112; 122; DLB 14

Wilson, Angus (Frank Johnstone)
1913-1991 .... **CLC 2, 3, 5, 25, 34**
See also CA 5-8R; 134; CANR 21; DLB 15; MTCW

Wilson, August
1945- .... **CLC 39, 50, 63; DC 2**
See also BLC 3; BW; CA 115; 122; MTCW

Wilson, Brian 1942- .... **CLC 12**

Wilson, Colin 1931- .... **CLC 3, 14**
See also CA 1-4R; CAAS 5; CANR 1, 22, 33; DLB 14; MTCW

Wilson, Dirk
See Pohl, Frederik

Wilson, Edmund
1895-1972 .... **CLC 1, 2, 3, 8, 24**
See also CA 1-4R; 37-40R; CANR 1; DLB 63; MTCW

Wilson, Ethel Davis (Bryant)
1888(?)-1980 .... **CLC 13**
See also CA 102; DLB 68; MTCW

Wilson, John (Anthony) Burgess
1917- .... **CLC 8, 10, 13**
See also Burgess, Anthony
See also CA 1-4R; CANR 2; MTCW

Wilson, John 1785-1854.......... **NCLC 5**

Wilson, Lanford 1937-....... **CLC 7, 14, 36**
See also CA 17-20R; CABS 3; DLB 7

Wilson, Robert M. 1944-......... **CLC 7, 9**
See also CA 49-52; CANR 2; MTCW

Wilson, Robert McLiam 1964- ..... **CLC 59**
See also CA 132

Wilson, Sloan 1920- .... **CLC 32**
See also CA 1-4R; CANR 1

Wilson, Snoo 1948-............... **CLC 33**
See also CA 69-72

Wilson, William S(mith) 1932- ..... **CLC 49**
See also CA 81-84

Winchilsea, Anne (Kingsmill) Finch Counte
1661-1720 .... **LC 3**

Windham, Basil
See Wodehouse, P(elham) G(renville)

Wingrove, David (John) 1954-...... **CLC 68**
See also CA 133

Winters, Janet Lewis .... **CLC 41**
See also Lewis, Janet
See also DLBY 87

Winters, (Arthur) Yvor
1900-1968 .... **CLC 4, 8, 32**
See also CA 11-12; 25-28R; CAP 1; DLB 48; MTCW

Winterson, Jeanette 1959-......... **CLC 64**
See also CA 136

Wiseman, Frederick 1930-......... **CLC 20**

Wister, Owen 1860-1938 .... **TCLC 21**
See also CA 108; DLB 9, 78; SATA 62

Witkacy
See Witkiewicz, Stanislaw Ignacy

Witkiewicz, Stanislaw Ignacy
1885-1939 .... **TCLC 8**
See also CA 105

Wittig, Monique 1935(?)-.......... **CLC 22**
See also CA 116; 135; DLB 83

Wittlin, Jozef 1896-1976 .... **CLC 25**
See also CA 49-52; 65-68; CANR 3

Wodehouse, P(elham) G(renville)
1881-1975 ... **CLC 1, 2, 5, 10, 22; SSC 2**
See also AITN 2; CA 45-48; 57-60; CANR 3, 33; CDBLB 1914-1945; DLB 34; MTCW; SATA 22

Woiwode, L.
See Woiwode, Larry (Alfred)

Woiwode, Larry (Alfred) 1941-... **CLC 6, 10**
See also CA 73-76; CANR 16; DLB 6

Wojciechowska, Maia (Teresa)
1927- .... **CLC 26**
See also AAYA 8; CA 9-12R; CANR 4; CLR 1; MAICYA; SAAS 1; SATA 1, 28

Wolf, Christa 1929- .... **CLC 14, 29, 58**
See also CA 85-88; DLB 75; MTCW

Wolfe, Gene (Rodman) 1931-...... **CLC 25**
See also CA 57-60; CAAS 9; CANR 6, 32; DLB 8

Wolfe, George C. 1954- .... **CLC 49**

Wolfe, Thomas (Clayton)
1900-1938 .... **TCLC 4, 13, 29**
See also CA 104; 132; CDALB 1929-1941; DLB 9, 102; DLBD 2; DLBY 85; MTCW; WLC

Wolfe, Thomas Kennerly Jr. 1930-
See Wolfe, Tom
See also CA 13-16R; CANR 9, 33; MTCW

Wolfe, Tom .... **CLC 1, 2, 9, 15, 35, 51**
See also Wolfe, Thomas Kennerly Jr.
See also AAYA 8; AITN 2; BEST 89:1

Wolff, Geoffrey (Ansell) 1937- ..... **CLC 41**
See also CA 29-32R; CANR 29

Wolff, Sonia
See Levitin, Sonia (Wolff)

Wolff, Tobias (Jonathan Ansell)
1945- .... **CLC 39, 64**
See also BEST 90:2; CA 114; 117

Wolfram von Eschenbach
c. 1170-c. 1220 .... **CMLC 5**

Wolitzer, Hilma 1930-........... **CLC 17**
See also CA 65-68; CANR 18; SATA 31

Wollstonecraft, Mary 1759-1797...... **LC 5**
See also CDBLB 1789-1832; DLB 39, 104

Wonder, Stevie .... **CLC 12**
See also Morris, Steveland Judkins

Wong, Jade Snow 1922-.......... **CLC 17**
See also CA 109

Woodcott, Keith
See Brunner, John (Kilian Houston)

Woodruff, Robert W.
See Mencken, H(enry) L(ouis)

Woolf, (Adeline) Virginia 1882-1941 .... **TCLC 1, 5, 20, 43; SSC 7**
See also CA 104; 130; CDBLB 1914-1945; DLB 36, 100; MTCW; WLC

Woollcott, Alexander (Humphreys) 1887-1943 .... **TCLC 5**
See also CA 105; DLB 29

Wordsworth, Dorothy 1771-1855 .... **NCLC 25**
See also DLB 107

Wordsworth, William 1770-1850 .... **NCLC 12, 38; PC 4**
See also CDBLB 1789-1832; DLB 93, 107; WLC

Wouk, Herman 1915- .... **CLC 1, 9, 38**
See also CA 5-8R; CANR 6, 33; DLBY 82; MTCW

Wright, Charles (Penzel Jr.) 1935- .... **CLC 6, 13, 28**
See also CA 29-32R; CAAS 7; CANR 23, 36; DLBY 82; MTCW

Wright, Charles Stevenson 1932- ... **CLC 49**
See also BLC 3; BW; CA 9-12R; CANR 26; DLB 33

Wright, Jack R.
See Harris, Mark

Wright, James (Arlington) 1927-1980 .... **CLC 3, 5, 10, 28**
See also AITN 2; CA 49-52; 97-100; CANR 4, 34; DLB 5; MTCW

Wright, Judith (Arandell) 1915- .... **CLC 11, 53**
See also CA 13-16R; CANR 31; MTCW; SATA 14

Wright, L(aurali) R. .... **CLC 44**
See also CA 138

Wright, Richard B(ruce) 1937- ...... **CLC 6**
See also CA 85-88; DLB 53

Wright, Richard (Nathaniel) 1908-1960 ... **CLC 1, 3, 4, 9, 14, 21, 48, 74; SSC 2**
See also AAYA 5; BLC 3; BW; CA 108; CDALB 1929-1941; DLB 76, 102; DLBD 2; MTCW; WLC

Wright, Rick 1945- .... **CLC 35**
See also Pink Floyd

Wright, Rowland
See Wells, Carolyn

Wright, Stephen 1946- .... **CLC 33**

Wright, Willard Huntington 1888-1939
See Van Dine, S. S.
See also CA 115

Wright, William 1930- .... **CLC 44**
See also CA 53-56; CANR 7, 23

Wu Ch'eng-en 1500(?)-1582(?)........ **LC 7**

Wu Ching-tzu 1701-1754 .... **LC 2**

Wurlitzer, Rudolph 1938(?)- ... **CLC 2, 4, 15**
See also CA 85-88

Wycherley, William 1641-1715.... **LC 8, 21**
See also CDBLB 1660-1789; DLB 80

Wylie, Elinor (Morton Hoyt) 1885-1928 .... **TCLC 8**
See also CA 105; DLB 9, 45

Wylie, Philip (Gordon) 1902-1971... **CLC 43**
See also CA 21-22; 33-36R; CAP 2; DLB 9

Wyndham, John
See Harris, John (Wyndham Parkes Lucas) Beynon

Wyss, Johann David Von 1743-1818 .... **NCLC 10**
See also MAICYA; SATA 27, 29

Yakumo Koizumi
See Hearn, (Patricio) Lafcadio (Tessima Carlos)

Yanez, Jose Donoso
See Donoso (Yanez), Jose

Yanovsky, Basile S.
See Yanovsky, V(assily) S(emenovich)

Yanovsky, V(assily) S(emenovich) 1906-1989 .... **CLC 2, 18**
See also CA 97-100; 129

Yates, Richard 1926- .... **CLC 7, 8, 23**
See also CA 5-8R; CANR 10; DLB 2; DLBY 81

Yeats, W. B.
See Yeats, William Butler

Yeats, William Butler 1865-1939 .... **TCLC 1, 11, 18, 31**
See also CA 104; 127; CDBLB 1890-1914; DLB 10, 19, 98; MTCW; WLC

Yehoshua, Abraham B. 1936- ... **CLC 13, 31**
See also CA 33-36R

Yep, Laurence Michael 1948- ...... **CLC 35**
See also AAYA 5; CA 49-52; CANR 1; CLR 3, 17; DLB 52; MAICYA; SATA 7, 69

Yerby, Frank G(arvin) 1916-1991 .... **CLC 1, 7, 22**
See also BLC 3; BW; CA 9-12R; 136; CANR 16; DLB 76; MTCW

Yesenin, Sergei Alexandrovich
See Esenin, Sergei (Alexandrovich)

Yevtushenko, Yevgeny (Alexandrovich) 1933- .... **CLC 1, 3, 13, 26, 51**
See also CA 81-84; CANR 33; MTCW

Yezierska, Anzia 1885(?)-1970 ..... **CLC 46**
See also CA 126; 89-92; DLB 28; MTCW

Yglesias, Helen 1915- .... **CLC 7, 22**
See also CA 37-40R; CANR 15; MTCW

Yokomitsu Riichi 1898-1947 ...... **TCLC 47**

Yonge, Charlotte (Mary) 1823-1901 .... **TCLC 48**
See also CA 109; DLB 18; SATA 17

York, Jeremy
See Creasey, John

York, Simon
See Heinlein, Robert A(nson)

Yorke, Henry Vincent 1905-1974 ... **CLC 13**
See also Green, Henry
See also CA 85-88; 49-52

Young, Al(bert James) 1939- .... **CLC 19**
See also BLC 3; BW; CA 29-32R; CANR 26; DLB 33

Young, Andrew (John) 1885-1971 .... **CLC 5**
See also CA 5-8R; CANR 7, 29

Young, Collier
See Bloch, Robert (Albert)

Young, Edward 1683-1765 .... **LC 3**
See also DLB 95

Young, Neil 1945- .... **CLC 17**
See also CA 110

Yourcenar, Marguerite 1903-1987 .... **CLC 19, 38, 50**
See also CA 69-72; CANR 23; DLB 72; DLBY 88; MTCW

Yurick, Sol 1925- .... **CLC 6**
See also CA 13-16R; CANR 25

Zamiatin, Yevgenii
See Zamyatin, Evgeny Ivanovich

Zamyatin, Evgeny Ivanovich 1884-1937 .... **TCLC 8, 37**
See also CA 105

Zangwill, Israel 1864-1926........ **TCLC 16**
See also CA 109; DLB 10

Zappa, Francis Vincent Jr. 1940-
See Zappa, Frank
See also CA 108

Zappa, Frank .... **CLC 17**
See also Zappa, Francis Vincent Jr.

Zaturenska, Marya 1902-1982.... **CLC 6, 11**
See also CA 13-16R; 105; CANR 22

Zelazny, Roger (Joseph) 1937- ..... **CLC 21**
See also AAYA 7; CA 21-24R; CANR 26; DLB 8; MTCW; SATA 39, 57

Zhdanov, Andrei A(lexandrovich) 1896-1948 .... **TCLC 18**
See also CA 117

Zhukovsky, Vasily 1783-1852 .... **NCLC 35**

Ziegenhagen, Eric .... **CLC 55**

Zimmer, Jill Schary
See Robinson, Jill

Zimmerman, Robert
See Dylan, Bob

Zindel, Paul 1936- .... **CLC 6, 26**
See also AAYA 2; CA 73-76; CANR 31; CLR 3; DLB 7, 52; MAICYA; MTCW; SATA 16, 58

Zinov'Ev, A. A.
See Zinoviev, Alexander (Aleksandrovich)

Zinoviev, Alexander (Aleksandrovich) 1922- .... **CLC 19**
See also CA 116; 133; CAAS 10

Zoilus
See Lovecraft, H(oward) P(hillips)

Zola, Emile (Edouard Charles Antoine) 1840-1902 .... **TCLC 1, 6, 21, 41**
See also CA 104; 138; WLC

Zoline, Pamela 1941- .... **CLC 62**

Zorrilla y Moral, Jose 1817-1893.. **NCLC 6**

Zoshchenko, Mikhail (Mikhailovich) 1895-1958 .... **TCLC 15**
See also CA 115

Zuckmayer, Carl 1896-1977........ **CLC 18**
See also CA 69-72; DLB 56

Zuk, Georges
See Skelton, Robin

Zukofsky, Louis 1904-1978 .... **CLC 1, 2, 4, 7, 11, 18**
See also CA 9-12R; 77-80; CANR 39; DLB 5; MTCW

Zweig, Paul 1935-1984. . . . . **CLC 34, 42**
See also CA 85-88; 113

Zweig, Stefan 1881-1942 . . . . **TCLC 17**
See also CA 112; DLB 81, 118

DC Cumulative Nationality Index

AMERICAN
Baldwin, James (Arthur) **1**
Brown, William Wells **1**
Chase, Mary (Coyle) **1**
Fuller, Charles (H., Jr.) **1**
Hansberry, Lorraine **2**
Hellman, Lillian (Florence) **1**
Hughes, (James) Langston **3**
Miller, Arthur **1**
Shange, Ntozake **3**
Wilder, Thornton (Niven) **1**
Wilson, August **2**

CZECH
Capek, Karel **1**

ENGLISH
Congreve, William **2**
Dryden, John **3**
Everyman **2**
Kyd, Thomas **3**
Marlowe, Christopher **1**
Orton, John Kingsley (Joe) **3**
Webster, John **2**

FRENCH
Camus, Albert **2**
Dumas, Alexandre (fils) **1**
Sartre, Jean-Paul **3**

GERMAN
Brecht, Bertolt **3**

GREEK
Aristophanes **2**
Menander **3**
Sophocles **1**

IRISH
Sheridan, Richard Brinsley **1**
Synge, John Millington **2**

JAPANESE
Mishima, Yukio **1**

NIGERIAN
Soyinka, Wole **2**

NORWEGIAN
Ibsen, Henrik **2**

RUSSIAN
Gogol, Nikolai (Vasilyevich) **1**

SOUTH AFRICAN
Fugard, (Harold) Athol **3**

SPANISH
Calderón de la Barca, Pedro **3**
García Lorca, Federico **2**

DC Cumulative Title Index

"abortion cycle #1" (Shange) **3**:484
Absalom and Achitophel (Dryden) **3**:162, 174, 201
Absalom's Hair (Calderon de la Barca)
See *Los cabellos de Absalón*
Acharnae (*The Acharnians*; *Akharnes*) (Aristophanes) **2**:4-5, 7-9, 12-13, 16-26, 35-6, 38, 41, 44, 54, 60, 65
The Acharnians (Aristophanes)
See *Acharnae*
Adam stvořitel (*Adam the Creator*) (Capek) **1**:53, 66, 73
Adam the Creator (Capek)
See *Adam stvořitel*
Aeolosicon (Aristophanes) **2**:8
After the Fall (Miller) **1**:301, 303-04, 332-34
Aias (*Ajax*) (Sophocles) **1**:415, 431, 436-37, 468
Ajax (Sophocles)
See *Aias*
Aké: The Years of Childhood (Soyinka) **2**:361, 370
Akharnes (Aristophanes)
See *Acharnae*
Albion and Albanus (Dryden) **3**:188
El alcade de Zalamea (*The Mayor of Zalamea*) (Calderon de la Barca) **3**:101-03, 105-06, 110, 117, 126
All for Love; or, The World Well Lost (Dryden) **3**:152-54, 158, 161-62, 173, 181, 188, 193-219
All My Sons (Miller) **1**:294-97, 300-06, 309, 333
Amboyna (Dryden) **3**:188
The Amen Corner (Baldwin) **1**:3-14, 24-29
L'ami des femmes (Dumas) **1**:104-05, 108, 113-14, 116-17, 119
Amor de Don Perlimplín con Belisa en su jardin (*Don Perlimplín*; *The Love of Don Perlimplin for Belisa in His Garden*) (Garcia Lorca) **2**:199, 202, 204, 206, 213
Amphiaraus (Aristophanes) **2**:12
Amphitryon (Dryden) **3**:166-68, 173, 175-77, 212
And So Ad Infinitum (Capek)
See *Ze života hmyzu*
"The Angel that Troubled the Waters" (Wilder) **1**:481
Anger
See *Orgē*
Anna-Anna (Brecht)
See *Die sieben Todsünden der Kleinburger*
"Annus Mirabilis: The Year of Wonders, 1666" (Dryden) **3**:158, 199-01, 204, 212-14
Another Part of the Forest (Hellman) **1**:185, 188-90, 207, 209
Antigonē (Sophocles) **1**:414-15, 417, 422-26, 431, 433, 435-42, 460
Anything for a Quiet Life (Webster) **2**:436
Aoi no ue (*The Lady Aoi*) (Mishima) **1**:354, 361
The Apparition (Menander) **3**:346
Appius and Virginia (Webster) **2**:437
The Aran Islands (Synge) **2**:400-01, 415
The Arbitrants (Menander)
See *Epitrepontes*
The Arbitration
See *Epitrepontes*
Así que pasen cinco años (*If Five Years Pass*; *When Five Years Pass*) (Garcia Lorca) **2**:199-200, 202, 204, 206, 213
Aspis (*The Shield*) **3**:362, 364, 366, 368-70
The Assassins (Camus)
See *Les justes*
Assembly of Women (Aristophanes)
See *Ekklesiazousai*
The Assignation (Dryden) **3**:167-68, 188
Aufstieg und Fall der Stadt Mahagonny (*The Rise and Fall of the City Mahogonny*) (Brecht) **3**:19-20, 27
"The Augsburg Chalk Circle" (Brecht)
See "Der Augsburger Kreidekreis"
Aureng-Zebe (Dryden) **3**:154, 158, 160-62, 168-69, 177, 179, 184, 188, 190-91, 193-96, 198, 212, 216-17
The Autumn Garden (Hellman) **1**:188, 190-91, 208
Aya no tsuzumi (*The Damask Drum*) (Mishima) **1**:361-62, 363-66, 368-70, 372
Baal (Brecht) **3**:15-16, 25-6, 34, 78
The Babylonians (Aristophanes) **2**:9, 18, 35-6, 41
The Bacchae of Euripides: A Communion Rite (Soyinka) **2**:366, 368
Bad Temper (Menander)
See *Orgē*
La banda y la flor (*The Sash and the Flower*; *The Scarf and the Flower*) (Calderon de la Barca) **3**:104
The Banqueters (Aristophanes) **2**:8, 18, 42
Batrakhoi (*The Frogs*) (Aristophanes) **2**:4, 6, 13-14, 16-17, 40, 45, 47-51, 68
Before the Marriage (Menander) **3**:346
The Begging Priest (Menander) **3**:346
Being and Nothingness: An Essay on Phenomenological Ontology (Sartre)
See *L'être et le néant: Essai d'ontologie* phénoménologique
Bernardine (Chase) **1**:84
Betsey Brown (Shange) **3**:473
The Bible (Brecht) **3**:37
The Big Sea: An Autobiography (Hughes) **3**:279, 282
Bílá nemoc (*Power and Glory/The White Plague*) (Capek) **1**:66, 73

The Birds (Aristophanes)
See *Ornithes*
Bitter Oleander (Garcia Lorca)
See *Bodas de sangre*
Black Nativity (Hughes) **3**:275, 277, 287-90
Les blancs (Hansberry) **2**:247, 250
The Blood Knot (Fugard) **3**:222-24, 227-30, 232, 236-45, 248-49, 252
Blood Wedding (Garcia Lorca)
See *Bodas de sangre*
Blues for Mister Charlie (Baldwin) **1**:2, 5-9, 14-24, 26
Bodas de sangre (*Bitter Oleander; Blood Wedding; A Fatal Wedding*) (Garcia Lorca) 200-11, 213-22, 229-32
Boesman and Lena (Fugard) **3**:226-27, 229, 232-33, 235, 237, 248-49, 251
Boogie Woogie Landscapes (Shange) **3**:474, 478, 487-90
Book of Songs (Garcia Lorca)
See *Canciones*
Both Were Young (Menander) **3**:346
Brand (Ibsen) **2**:278, 291, 299-300, 314, 319-20
The Bride of Gomez Arias (Calderon de la Barca)
See *La niña de Gomez Arias*
The Brownsville Raid (Fuller) **1**:135-36, 139
Brustein's Window (Hansberry)
See *The Sign in Sydney Brustein's Window*
"Buddha's Parable of the Burning House" (Brecht) **3**:23
The Butterfly's Evil Spell (Garcia Lorca)
See *El maleficio de la mariposa*
"By Little Loving" (Soyinka) **2**:366
Bygmester Solness (*The Master Builder*) (Ibsen) **2**:276-79, 280, 290-91, 295, 314, 337
Los cabellos de Absalón (*Absalom's Hair*) (Calderon de la Barca) **3**:101
Cachiporra's Puppets (Garcia Lorca)
See *Los títeres de Cachiporra*
Las cadenas del demonio (*The Devil's Chains*) (Calderon de la Barca) **3**:107
Caligula (Camus) **2**:77-82, 85-103
"Canace to Macareus" (Dryden) **3**:179
Canciones (*Book of Songs; Songs*) (Garcia Lorca) **2**:206
Candide (Hellman) **1**:192
Carnets (*Notebooks*) (Camus) **2**:100
Casa con dos puertas, mala es de guardar (*A House with Two Doors Is Difficult to Guard*) (Calderon de la Barca) **3**:104
La casa de Bernarda Alba (*The House of Bernarda Alba*) (Garcia Lorca) **2**:203, 206-07, 209-10, 212-16, 222-27, 231-32
"La casada infiel" ("The Faithless Bride"; "The Faithless Wife"; "The Unfaithful Married Woman") (Garcia Lorca) **2**:228
Cásida de la Huída (Garcia Lorca) **2**:215
The Caucasian Chalk Circle (Brecht)
See *Der kaukasische Kreidekreis*
"Childhood" (Wilder) **1**:513
The Children's Hour (Hellman) **1**:179, 181-82, 188, 192-204, 207
Chinsetsu Yumiharizuki (Mishima) **1**:354
Cleomenes (Dryden) **3**:212
The Clouds (Aristophanes)
See *Nephelai*
Cocalus (Aristophanes) **2**:8
"Les Communistes et la paix" (*The Communists and the Peace*) (Sartre) **3**:444
The Communists and the Peace (Sartre)
See "Les Communistes et la paix"
"Concerning Poor B. B."
See "Of Poor B. B."
The Condemned of Altona (Sartre)
See *Les séquestrés d'Altona*
Connection by Marriage
See *Samia*
The Conquest of Granada by the Spaniards (Dryden) **3**:152, 154, 156-57, 160-61, 168, 178-79, 183-85, 188, 191, 193-95, 197-200, 211-12, 216-17
The Constant Prince (Calderon de la Barca)
See *El Príncipe constante*
Couragemodell (Brecht) **3**:29, 73
The Creation of the World and Other Business (Miller) **1**:304
Crime Passionel (Sartre)
See *Les mains sales*
The Critic; or, A Tragedy Rehearsed (Sheridan) **1**:380, 384-85, 388-90, 402
Critique de la raison dialectique, Volume I: Théorie des ensembles pratiques (*Critique of Dialectical Reason: Theory of Practical Ensembles*) (Sartre) **3**:445, 447, 449, 453, 460
Critique of Dialectical Reason: Theory of Practical Ensembles (Sartre)
See *Critique de la raison dialectique, Volume I: Théorie des ensembles pratiques*
Cross Purpose (Camus)
See *Le malentendu*
The Crucible (Miller) **1**:294, 296-97, 299-303, 325-44
A Cure for a Cuckold (Webster) **2**:436
"The Curse" (Synge) **2**:391
Daitaleis (Aristophanes) **2**:11, 15
La dama duende (*The Phantom Lady*) (Calderon de la Barca) **3**:109-10, 126, 136
The Damask Drum (Mishima)
See *Aya no tsuzumi*
La dame aux camélias (*The Lady of the Camelias*) (Dumas) **1**:104-06, 108-10, 116, 117, 119-24
A Dance of the Forests (Soyinka) **2**:366-67, 372
Les Danicheff (Dumas) **1**:115, 119
Daughter of the Air (Calderon de la Barca)
See *La hija del aire*
A Daughter's Geography (Shange) **3**:473
Days to Come (Hellman) **1**:179-84, 193, 204
De unges forbund (*The League of Youth*) (Ibsen) **2**:316
The Dead Without Burial (Sartre)
See *Morts sans sépulture*
"Death" (Garcia Lorca) **2**:199
Death and the King's Horseman (Soyinka) **2**:361-63, 364, 368-82
Death of a Salesman (*The Inside of His Head*) (Miller) **1**:294-326, 328-330, 333-34
"Dedication" (Soyinka) **2**:365
Deirdre of the Sorrows (Synge) **2**:391-93, 395
The "Demi-Monde" (Dumas)
See *Le demi-monde*
Le demi-monde (*The "Demi-Monde"*) (Dumas) **1**:104-06, 108-111, 113-14, 117-19, 121, 123
Denise (Dumas) **1**:104-07, 109, 116
The Departure from the Theatre (Gogol)
See *Teatral'nyi raz'ezd posle predstavleniia novoi komedii*
"Der Augsburger Kreidekreis" ("The Augsburg Chalk Circle") **3**:81
Der gute Mensch von Sezuan (*The Good Woman of Setzuan*) (Brecht) **3**:11-12, 26-7, 30-4, 37, 43-4, 46, 51, 67, 74, 78, 81, 83
Der kaukasische Kreidekreis (*The Caucasian Chalk Circle*) (Brecht) **3**:11-12, 19, 23, 26-7, 31, 35, 37, 43-44, 58-9, 75-8, 80-4
The Devil and the Good Lord (Sartre)
See *Le diable et le bon Dieu*
The Devil's Chains (Calderon de la Barca)
See *Las cadenas del demonio*
The Devil's Law-Case (Webster) **2**:436-39
La devoción de la cruz (*The Devotion of the Cross*) (Calderon de la Barca) **3**:95-6, 102, 123, 125-29
The Devotion of the Cross (Calderon de la Barca)
See *La devoción de la cruz*
Le diable et le bon Dieu (*The Devil and the Good Lord; Lucifer and the Lord*) (Sartre) **3**:436, 439, 443-44, 446, 449-50, 452
Diane de Lys (Dumas) **1**:104, 116-17, 119
Dido, Queen of Carthage (Marlowe)
See *The Tragedy of Dido, Queen of Carthage*
Dimetos (Fugard) **3**:237
Dirty Hands (Sartre)
See *Les mains sales*
A Discourse Concerning the Original and Progress of Satire (*The Original and Progress of Satire*) (Dryden) **3**:157
Diván de Tamarit (*Divan of the Tamarit*) (Garcia Lorca) **2**:206
Divan of the Tamarit (Garcia Lorca)
See *Diván de Tamarit*
Doctor Faustus (Marlowe)
See *The Tragicall History of the Life and Death of Doctor Faustus*
The Doctor of His Honor (Calderon de la Barca)
See *El médico de su honra*
A Doll's House (Ibsen)
See *Et dukkehjem*
Domestic Breviary (Brecht) **3**:15
Don Perlimplín (Garcia Lorca)
See *Amor de Don Perlimplín con Belisa en su jardin*
Don Sebastian, King of Portugal (Dryden) **3**:154, 173, 175-76, 179, 189, 212-13
Doña Rosita la soltera (*Doña Rosita the Spinster, or The Language of Flowers*) (Garcia Lorca) **2**:200-02, 204, 206, 214
Doña Rosita the Spinster, or The Language of Flowers (Garcia Lorca)
See *Doña Rosita la soltera*
Don't You Want to Be Free? (Hughes) **3**:272, 275-77
The Double Dealer (Congreve) **2**:108-09, 111-13, 115-17, 120, 130, 132, 143, 146
The Dour Man
See *Dyskolos*
"The Dreamer" (Soyinka) **2**:365-66
Die Dreigroschenoper (*The Threepenny Opera*) (Brecht) **3**:10-11, 15, 19-21, 26-7, 31, 34, 67, 77, 80, 84
Drums in the Night (Brecht)
See *Trommeln in der nacht*
Drums of Haiti (Hughes)
See *Troubled Island*
Drunkenness **3**:357
The Duchess of Malfi (Webster) **2**:423-25, 429-44, 446-48, 455, 458-65
The Duenna; or, The Double Elopement (Sheridan) **1**:377-78, 382, 385

The Duke of Guise (Dryden) **3**:159, 188
Dyskolos (*The Dour Man*; *Grumpy*; *Old Cantankerous*) **3**:355-65, 367-70, 372-74, 377, 380-82, 384-86
"Easter" (Soyinka) **2**:366
Ecclesiazusae (Aristophanes)
See *Ekklesiazousai*
Echo and Narcissus (Calderon de la Barca)
See *Eco y Narciso*
Eco y Narciso (*Echo and Narcissus*) (Calderon de la Barca) **3**:
Edward II (Marlowe)
See *The Troublesome Raigne and Lamentable Death of Edward the Second, King of England*
Eirēnē (*Peace*) (Aristophanes) **2**:6, 9, 11-13, 16-17, 23, 26-7, 35, 54, 59-60, 65, 69
Ekklesiazousai (*Assembly of Women*; *Ecclesiazusae*; *Parliament of Women*; *Women in Assembly*; *Women in Parliament*; *The Women's Assembly*) (Aristophanes) **2**:6-7, 13-15, 19, 22, 23
Ēlektra (Sophocles) **1**:431, 433-34, 451, 457-60
Emperor and Galilean (Ibsen)
See *Kejser og Galilaeer*
Emperor of Haiti (Hughes)
See *Troubled Island*
En folkefiende (*An Enemy of the People*) (Ibsen) **2**:283, 321, 329, 333
Los encantos de la culpa (*The Sorceries of Sin*) (Calderon de la Barca) **3**:
The Ending of "The Government Inspector" (Gogol)
See *Razviazka "Révizor"*
An Enemy of the People (Ibsen)
See *En folkefiende*
Entertaining Mr. Sloane (Orton) **3**:391, 395-97, 400-02, 403-06, 408, 410, 413, 415, 417
"An Epic of Ulster" (Synge) **2**:390
Epitrepontes (*The Arbitrants*; *The Arbitration*) **3**:341, 343, 348, 353, 355-56, 358-61, 371, 374, 377
"Erostratus" (Sartre) **3**:437
The Erpingham Camp (Orton) **3**:393, 400-02, 417
The Escape; or, A Leap for Freedom (Brown) **1**:32-47
Essay of Dramatic Poesy (Dryden)
See *Of Dramatick Poesie: An Essay*
"Essay of Heroic Plays" (Dryden)
See "Of Heroic Plays"
Et dukkehjem (*A Doll's House*; *Nora*) (Ibsen) **2**:283, 290, 292-309, 312-16, 329, 331, 337
L'état de siège (*The State of Siege*) (Camus) **2**:78, 81-2
L'Etrangèe (Dumas) **1**:104-05, 109, 112, 119
L'étranger (*The Outsider*; *The Stranger*) (Camus) **2**:77, 84, 99-100
L'être et le néant: Essai d'ontologie phénoménologique (*Being and Nothingness: An Essay on Phenomenological Ontology*) (Sartre) **3**:437-41, 443, 447-48, 451, 453, 459-61
Eunuch (Menander) **3**:360
An Evening's Love; or, The Mock-Astrologer (*The Mock-Astrologer*) (Dryden) **3**:163-64, 167-68, 170-71, 175, 188, 200
Everyman **2**:159-93
Examen Poeticum (Dryden) **3**:157, 179
Existentialism and Humanism (Sartre)
See *L'existentialisme est un humanísme*
Existentialism Is a Humanism (Sartre)
See *L'existentialisme est un humanísme*
L'existentialisme est un humanísme (*Existentialism and Humanism*; *Existentialism Is a Humanism*) (Sartre) **3**:439, 448, 451
Experience, or How to Give a Northern Man a Backbone (Brown) **1**:39, 45
"Fable of Iphis and Ianthe" (Dryden) **3**:179
"The Faithless Bride" (Garcia Lorca)
See "La casada infiel"
"The Faithless Wife" (Garcia Lorca)
See "La casada infiel"
False! (Menander) **3**:346
The Famous Tragedy of the Rich Jew of Malta (*The Jew of Malta*) (Marlowe) **1**:214-16, 218-19, 224-26, 250-61, 283
Fanny Otcott (Wilder) **1**:482
A Fatal Wedding (Garcia Lorca)
See *Bodas de sangre*
"Father and Son" (Hughes) **3**:270, 276
Fear and Misery of the Third Reich (Brecht)
See *Furcht und Elend des dritten Reiches*
La femme de Claude (*The Wife of Claude*) (Dumas) **1**:104, 109, 111, 119
Fences (Wilson) **2**:473-76, 483-89
Le Fils naturel (Dumas) **1**:104-05, 107-111, 113-14, 116
"The Fishwife and the Soldier" (Brecht) **3**:22
"Five Difficulties in Writing" (Brecht) **3**:54
Five Modern Nō Plays (Mishima)
See *Kindai nōgakushū*
Five Plays of Langston Hughes (Hughes) **3**:268, 271, 276, 281, 285
The Flatterer
See *Kolax*
The Flies (Sartre)
See *Les mouches*
for colored girls who have considered suicide/ when the rainbow is enuf: A Choreopoem (Shange) **3**:471, 473-91
Four Plays (Hellman) **1**:179-81
Four Plays and the Aran Islands (Synge) **2**:412
"The Fourth Stage" (Soyinka) **2**:364, 366, 373
Francillon (Dumas) **1**:104-05, 109, 114, 116-17
The Frogs (Aristophanes)
See *Batrakhoi*
Front Porch (Hughes) **3**:275
Fruen fra havet (*The Lady from the Sea*) (Ibsen) **2**:280, 283, 289-91, 312, 323, 346
Funeral Games (Orton) **3**:400, 402, 412
Furcht und Elend des dritten Reiches (*Fear and Misery of the Third Reich*) (Brecht) **3**:68
Galileo (Brecht)
See *Leben des Galilei*
The Gamblers (Gogol)
See *Igroki*
Georgos **3**:359
Ghosts (Ibsen)
See *Gjengangere*
The Girl from Samos
See *Samia*
The Girl Who Gets Her Hair Cut Short
See *Perikeiromenē*
The Girl with Shorn Hair (Menander)
See *Perikeiromenē*
Gjengangere (*Ghosts*) (Ibsen) **2**:282-87, 290, 292, 298, 307-20, 328, 331, 346
The Gold Piece (Hughes) **3**:270, 275
Gone to Imbros (*The Imbrians*) (Menander) **3**:346
The Good and Faithful Servant (Orton) **3**:400-01
The Good Woman of Setzuan (Brecht)
See *Der gute Mensch von Sezuan*
Gospel Glow (Hughes) **3**:275
The Government Inspector (Gogol)
See *Révizor*
"Graduation Nite" (Shange) **3**:484
El gran teatro del mundo (*The Great Theater of the World*) (Calderon de la Barca) **3**:92, 136, 139
The Great Theater of the World (Calderon de la Barca)
See *El gran teatro del mundo*
The Greatest Monster of the World (Calderon de la Barca)
See *El mayor monstruo del mundo*
The Grounds of Criticism in Tragedy (Dryden) **3**:180, 183
Grumpy
See *Dyskolos*
Gypsy Balladeer (Garcia Lorca)
See *Romancero gitano*
Gypsy Ballads (Garcia Lorca)
See *Romancero gitano*
Hanjo (Mishima) **1**:361, 363, 366, 368, 370-71
Happy End (Brecht) **3**:27
"The Happy Journey to Trenton and Camden" (Wilder) **1**:476, 484-85, 492, 513, 518
"The Harp of Joy" (Mishima)
See *Yorokobi no Koto*
The Harpist **3**:379
Harvey (Chase) **1**:83-99
Hated (Menander)
See *Misoumenos*
Die Hauspostille (*A Manual of Piety*) (Brecht) **3**:15
He Boxes Her Ears (Menander) **3**:346
He Clips Her Hair (Menander)
See *Perikeiromenē*
Head to Toe (Orton) **3**:400
"Heads of an Answer to Rymer" (Dryden) **3**:181
Heautontimorumenus (*The Man Who Punished Himself*) **3**:346, 382
Hedda Gabler (Ibsen) **2**:290, 304, 316, 328, 334-53
Die heilige Johanna der Schlachthöfe (*St. Joan of the Stockyards*) (Brecht) **3**:11, 34, 53, 57, 68
The Heiress (Menander) **3**:346
Hello and Goodbye (Fugard) **3**:226-27, 230-33, 235-36, 248
Hero **3**:355, 361, 382
Herr Puntila and His Servant Matti (Brecht)
See *Herr Puntila und sein Knecht Matti*
Herr Puntila und sein Knecht Matti (*Herr Puntila and His Servant Matti*; *Puntila*) (Brecht) **3**:31, 46, 53, 59, 70, 78
"He's That Dead Can Do No Hurt" (Synge) **2**:400
La hija del aire (*Daughter of the Air*) (Calderon de la Barca) **3**:95, 102
Hippeis (*The Knights*) (Aristophanes) **2**:5, 7, 9, 16, 18, 21, 23, 27, 35-6, 45, 47, 59-65, 67
Holcades (*The Merchant Ships*) (Aristophanes) **2**:41
Homegoing from the Theatre (Gogol)

Title Index

See *Teatral'nyi raz'ezd posle predstavleniia novoi komedii*
L'homme révolté (*The Rebel*) (Camus) **2**:92, 94, 96, 100
The House of Bernarda Alba (Garcia Lorca)
See *La casa de Bernarda Alba*
A House with Two Doors Is Difficult to Guard (Calderon de la Barca)
See *Casa con dos puertas, mala es de guardar*
Huis clos (*No Exit*) (Sartre) **3**:434-37, 439-41, 445, 448-49, 452-64
"I Useta Live in the World (But Then I Moved to Harlem)" (Shange) **3**:481
Ichneutai (*The Trackers*) (Sophocles) **1**:427
"Idanre" (Soyinka) **2**:365, 367
Les idées de Madame Aubray (Dumas) **1**:104, 107, 109, 113-17
If Five Years Pass (Garcia Lorca)
See *Así que pasen cinco años*
Igroki (*The Gamblers*) (Gogol) **1**:152, 156
"Ikeja, Friday, Four O'Clock" (Soyinka) **2**:366
Im dickicht der städte (*In the Jungle of Cities*; *In the Swamp*) (Brecht) **3**:15-16, 18, 34, 60
L'imaginaire: Psychologie phénoénologique de l'imagination (Sartre) **3**:437
L'imagination (*Imagination: A Psychological Critique*) (Sartre) **3**:437
Imagination: A Psychological Critique (Sartre)
See *L'imagination*
The Imbrians (Menander)
See *Gone to Imbros*
"In Defense of Equality of Men" (Hansberry) **2**:248
In Mourning for Himself (Menander) **3**:346
In the Frame of Don Cristóbal (Garcia Lorca)
See *Retablillo de Don Cristóbal*
In the Jungle of Cities (Brecht)
See *Im dickicht der städte*
In the Shadow of the Glen (*The Shadow of the Glen*) (Synge) **2**:387-88, 392-93, 395, 400, 408, 415
In the Swamp (Brecht)
See *Im dickicht der städte*
In Wicklow, West Kerry and Connemara (Synge) **2**:415
Incident at Vichy (Miller) **1**:303
The Indian Emperour; or, The Conquest of Mexico by the Spaniards, Being the Sequel of the Indian Queen (Dryden) **3**:182, 187-88, 192, 213
The Indian Queen (Dryden) **3**:160-61, 179, 181-82, 187-88, 192
"Infancy" (Wilder) **1**:513, 515
The Insect Comedy (Capek)
See *Ze života hmyzu*
Insect Life (Capek)
See *Ze života hmyzu*
The Insect Play (Capek)
See *Ze života hmyzu*
Insect Story (Capek)
See *Ze života hmyzu*
Insects (Capek)
See *Ze života hmyzu*
The Inside of His Head (Miller)
See *Death of a Salesman*
The Inspector General (Gogol)
See *Révizor*
Inspired (Menander) **3**:346
The Interpreters (Soyinka) **2**:364-66, 378
"Intimacy" (Sartre) **3**:437
The Invention (Soyinka) **2**:366
The Island (Fugard) **3**:226-27, 234, 238, 246-49, 251-56
Jealousy, the Greatest Monster of the World (Calderon de la Barca)
See *El mayor monstruo del mundo*
Jericho-Jim Crow (Hughes) **3**:275
The Jew of Malta (Marlowe)
See *The Famous Tragedy of the Rich Jew of Malta*
Jitney (Wilson) **2**:475
Joe Turner's Come and Gone (Wilson) **2**:473-76, 486-89
John Gabriel Borkman (Ibsen) **2**:276, 280-81, 284, 286, 299
Joy to My Soul (Hughes) **3**:275
The Just Assassins (Camus)
See *Les justes*
Les justes (*The Assassins*; *The Just Assassins*) (Camus) **2**:78, 82-5, 92
Kantan (Mishima) **1**:354, 361, 363
"Kataku" (Mishima) **1**:353
Kean (Sartre) **3**:445
Kedeia
See *Samia*
Kejser og Galilaeer (*Emperor and Galilean*) (Ibsen) **2**:278, 289, 291, 329, 331
The Kind Keeper; or, Mr. Limberham (*Mr. Limberham*) (Dryden) **3**:154, 166-71, 176, 188
Kindai nōgakushū (*Five Modern Nō Plays*) (Mishima) **1**:354, 358-72
King Oedipus (Sophocles)
See *Oedipous Tyrannos*
Kjaerlighedens komedie (*Love's Comedy*) (Ibsen) **2**:284, 299, 319-20
Kleines Organon für das Theatre (*A Little Organum for the Theater*; *Small Organon*) (Brecht) **3**:20, 23, 28, 42, 46, 51, 65, 81
The Knights (Aristophanes)
See *Hippeis*
Kolax (*The Flatterer*) **3**:346
Kongi's Harvest (Soyinka) **2**:365-67
Kongs emnerne (*The Pretenders*) (Ibsen) **2**:289, 291, 329
Ladies Lunching Together (Menander)
See *Synaristosai*
The Lady Aoi (Mishima)
See *Aoi no ue*
The Lady from the Sea (Ibsen)
See *Fruen fra havet*
The Lady of the Camelias (Dumas)
See *La dame aux camélias*
Lament for Ignacio Sánchez Mejías (Garcia Lorca)
See *Llanto por Ignacio Sánchez Mejías*
Lament for the Death of a Bullfighter (Garcia Lorca)
See *Llanto por Ignacio Sánchez Mejías*
The Lark (Hellman) **1**:192
"Latent Rapists" (Shange) **3**:484
The League of Youth (Ibsen)
See *De unges forbund*
"Leaving the Theater after the Performance of a New Comedy" (Gogol)
See *Teatral'nyi raz'ezd posle predstavleniia novoi komedii*
Leben des Galilei (*Galileo*; *The Life of Galileo*) (Brecht) **3**:11, 13-14, 27, 29, 34, 36-41, 43, 45-51, 53-60, 80-1
A Lesson from Aloes (Fugard) **3**:222, 224, 227, 229, 233-34, 237, 245, 253
Letters to a German Friend (Camus)
See *Lettres à un ami allemand*
Lettres à un ami allemand (*Letters to a German Friend*) (Camus) **2**:92
Leucadia (Menander) **3**:382
Life Is a Dream (Calderon de la Barca)
See *La vida es sueño*
The Life of Galileo (Brecht)
See *Leben des Galilei*
The Life of the Insects (Capek)
See *Ze života hmyzu*
Lille Eyolf (*Little Eyolf*) (Ibsen) **2**:276, 279-80, 283, 290-91
The Lion and the Jewel (Soyinka) **2**:372
Literature and Existentialism (Sartre)
See *Qu'est-ce que la littérature?*
Little Eyolf (Ibsen)
See *Lille Eyolf*
The Little Foxes (Hellman) **1**:179-90, 192-94, 203-09
Little Ham (Hughes) **3**:268-69, 271, 274, 276
A Little Organum for the Theater (Brecht)
See *Kleines Organon für das Theatre*
Llanto por Ignacio Sánchez Mejías (*Lament for Ignacio Sánchez Mejías*; *Lament for the Death of a Bullfighter*) (Garcia Lorca) **2**:201, 206
"The Long Christmas Dinner" (Wilder) **1**:476, 483-85, 488, 492, 513
The Long Christmas Dinner and Other Plays in One Act (Wilder) **1**:483
Loot (Orton) **3**:393-96, 399-402, 405, 410-20
Lorraine Hansberry Speaks Out: Art and the Black Revolution (Hansberry) **2**:246
Love for Love (Congreve) **2**:109, 113, 115-21, 123-36, 143, 146
The Love of Don Perlimplin for Belisa in His Garden (Garcia Lorca)
See *Amor de Don Perlimplín con Belisa en su jardin*
Love the Greatest Enchanter (Calderon de la Barca)
See *El mayor encanto, amor*
Love Triumphant (Dryden) **3**:167-68, 177, 205
Love's Comedy (Ibsen)
See *Kjaerlighedens komedie*
Lucifer and the Lord (Sartre)
See *Le diable et le bon Dieu*
Lysistrata (Aristophanes) **2**:5-6, 12-14, 16-23, 27-30, 36, 52-8
Ma Rainey's Black Bottom (Wilson) **2**:473-82, 483-88
MacFlecknoe; or, A Satire upon the Trew-Blew-Protestant Poet, T. S. (Dryden) **3**:169, 212
Madame de Sade (Mishima)
See *Sado kōshaku fujin*
El mágico prodigioso (*The Wonder-Working Magician*) (Calderon de la Barca) **3**:100, 102, 107, 126
Les mains sales (*Crime Passionel*; *Dirty Hands*) (Sartre) **3**:436, 439, 443-44, 449, 452
The Makropoulos Affair (Capek)
See *Věc Makropulos*
The Makropoulos Secret (Capek)
See *Věc Makropulos*
El maleficio de la mariposa (*The Butterfly's Evil Spell*; *The Spell of the Butterfly*; *The Witchery of the Butterfly*) (Garcia Lorca) **2**:198, 210, 212
Le malentendu (*Cross Purpose*; *The Misunderstanding*) (Camus) **2**:77-8, 82-5, 90, 92-4

The Man Died: Prison Notes of Wole Soyinka (Soyinka) **2**:367, 374-76
The Man from Carthage (Menander) **3**:346
The Man from Sikyon
See *Sikyonios*
The Man She Hated
See *Misoumenos*
The Man Who Punished Himself
See *Heautontimorumenus*
Mann ist Mann (*A Man's a Man*) (Brecht) **3**:15-16, 26, 34, 46, 60
A Man's a Man (Brecht)
See *Mann ist Mann*
A Manual of Piety (Brecht)
See *Die Hauspostille*
Mariana Pineda (Garcia Lorca) **2**:198, 200, 202, 204, 211-12
Marriage (Gogol)
See *Zhenit'ba; Sovershenno neveroyatnoye* sobitye
Marriage-á-la-Mode (Dryden) **3**:154, 161-65, 167-69, 171-75, 178, 188, 193, 212-13
The Marriage: An Utterly Incredible Occurence (Gogol)
See *Zhenit'ba; Sovershenno neveroyatnoye* sobitye
Martin Mar-All (Dryden)
See *Sir Martin Mar-All; or, The Feign'd Innocence*
The Marvellous Shoemaker's Wife (Garcia Lorca)
See *La zapatera prodigiosa*
The Massacre at Paris: with the Death of the Duke of Guise (Marlowe) **1**:218-19, 221, 251-52, 261, 283-84
Die Massnahme (*The Measures Taken*) (Brecht) **3**:11, 18, 26, 46, 51, 83
The Master Builder (Ibsen)
See *Bygmester Solness*
"Master Harold"... and the Boys (Fugard) **3**:222-23, 236, 238, 253, 256-59, 263
The Matchmaker (Wilder) **1**:476, 513, 517-18
Matka (Capek) **1**:73
El mayor encanto, amor (*Love the Greatest Enchanter*) (Calderon de la Barca) **3**:103
El mayor monstruo del mundo (*The Greatest Monster of the World; Jealousy, the Greatest Monster of the World; No Monster like Jealousy*) (Calderon de la Barca) **3**:95
The Mayor of Zalamea (Calderon de la Barca)
See *El alcade de Zalamea*
The Measures Taken (Brecht)
See *Die Massnahme*
The Medall. A Satire Against Sedition (Dryden) **3**:200, 214
El médico de su honra (*The Doctor of His Honor, The Surgeon of His Honor*) (Calderon de la Barca) **3**:109-10, 136-40
Melancholia (Sartre)
See *La nausée*
A Memory of Two Mondays (Miller) **1**:302-03
Men Without Shadows (Sartre)
See *Morts sans sépulture*
The Merchant of Yonkers: A Farce in Four Acts (Wilder) **1**:476
The Merchant Ships (Aristophanes)
See *Holcades*
Misoumenos (*Hated; The Man She Hated*) **3**:343, 346, 369, 379
The Misunderstanding (Camus)
See *Le malentendu*
The Mock-Astrologer (Dryden)
See *An Evening's Love; or, The Mock-Astrologer*
The Money Question (Dumas)
See *La question d'argent*
Monsieur Alphonse (Dumas) **1**:104-05, 109
Monsterrat (Hellman) **1**:192
Montserrat (Hellman) **1**:192
Morts sans sépulture (*The Dead Without Burial; Men Without Shadows; The Victors*) (Sartre) **3**:436, 439, 441, 443, 449-51
The Mother (Brecht)
See *Die Mutter*
Mother Courage and Her Children (Brecht)
See *Mutter Courage und ihre Kinder*
Les mots (*The Words*) (Sartre) **3**:447, 461
Les mouches (*The Flies*) (Sartre) **3**:435-36, 439, 441, 448, 459
The Mourning Bride (Congreve) **2**:109-10, 132
Mr. Limberham (Dryden)
See *The Kind Keeper; or, Mr. Limberham*
Mrs. McThing (Chase) **1**:84
"Mulatto" (Hughes) **3**:268, 270-72, 275-77, 282-85
Mule Bone: A Comedy of Negro Life (Hughes) **3**:278-81
Die Mutter (*The Mother*) (Brecht) **3**:18, 68
Mutter Courage und ihre Kinder (*Mother Courage and Her Children*) (Brecht) **3**:8-9, 11-14, 20-1, 23, 27, 29-31, 33-4, 36-7, 46, 53, 56, 59-65, 67-8, 70, 74, 80-1
My Friend Hitler (Mishima)
See *Waga tomo Hittorā*
My Mother, My Father, and Me (Hellman) **1**:192-94
Myth, Literature, and the African World (Soyinka) **2**:373-74
The Myth of Sisyphus (Camus)
See *Le mythe de Sisyphe*
Le mythe de Sisyphe (*The Myth of Sisyphus*) (Camus) **2**:77, 93, 96, 100-02
Nappy Edges (Shange) **3**:472-73
Når vi døde vågner (*When We Dead Awaken*) (Ibsen) **2**:276-77, 281-82, 295, 299
Natural Disasters and Other Festive Occasions (Shange) **3**:479
Nausea (Sartre)
See *La nausée*
La nausée (*Melancholia; Nausea*) (Sartre) **3**:432, 437-38, 450
"The Negro Artist and the Racial Mountain" (Hughes) **3**:275
Nekrassov (Sartre) **3**:445
Nephelai (*The Clouds*) (Aristophanes) **2**:5-6, 8, 10-11, 13, 15-21, 30, 34-5, 40-7, 60-1, 63-5, 67, 69
The Next Half Hour (Chase) **1**:84
La niña de Gomez Arias (*The Bride of Gomez Arias*) (Calderon de la Barca) **3**:95
"A Nite with Beau Willie Brown" (Shange) **3**:481, 485, 487
No Exit (Sartre)
See *Huis clos*
No-Good Friday (Fugard) **3**:227, 236, 238, 245, 248
No hay más fortuna que Diós (*No Other Fortune than God*) (Calderon de la Barca) **3**:107
No Monster like Jealousy (Calderon de la Barca)
See *El mayor monstruo del mundo*
"no more love poems" (Shange) **3**:486-87
No More Love Poems, Number Two (Shange) **3**:486
No Other Fortune than God (Calderon de la Barca)
See *No hay más fortuna que Diós*
Noces (*Nuptials*) (Camus) **2**:77, 93, 100
Nongogo (Fugard) **3**:227, 236, 238, 245, 248
Nora (Ibsen)
See *Et dukkehjem*
Notebooks (Camus)
See *Carnets*
Notebooks, 1960-1977 (Fugard) **3**:254, 261
Now You've Done It (Chase) **1**:83
Nuptials (Camus)
See *Noces*
Oedipous epi Kolōnōi (*Oedipus at Colonos; Oedipus Coloneus; Oedipus in Colonos*) (Sophocles) **1**:416-17, 424-26, 431-33, 437, 439, 458-69
Oedipous Tyrannos (*King Oedipus; Oedipus; Oedipus Rex; Oedipus the King*) (Sophocles) **1**:414, 416, 425, 428, 430-31, 433, 437-38, 441, 446-58, 460-61, 464
Oedipus (Dryden) **3**:179, 188
Oedipus (Sophocles)
See *Oedipous Tyrannos*
Oedipus at Colonos (Sophocles)
See *Oedipous epi Kolōnōi*
Oedipus Coloneus (Sophocles)
See *Oedipous epi Kolōnōi*
Oedipus in Colonos (Sophocles)
See *Oedipous epi Kolōnōi*
Oedipus Rex (Sophocles)
See *Oedipous Tyrannos*
Oedipus the King (Sophocles)
See *Oedipous Tyrannos*
Of Dramatick Poesie: An Essay (*Essay of Dramatic Poesy*) (Dryden) **3**:156, 167-69, 171, 173, 179-80, 212
"Of Heroic Plays" ("Essay of Heroic Plays") (Dryden) **3**:157, 158, 162, 194, 200
"Of Poor B. B." ("Concerning Poor B. B.") (Brecht) **3**:15-16, 20
The Old Bachelor (Congreve)
See *The Old Batchelour*
The Old Batchelour (*The Old Bachelor*) (Congreve) **2**:108, 110, 112, 115-16, 118, 120, 123, 128, 130, 132, 143, 146
Old Cantankerous
See *Dyskolos*
"one" (Shange) **3**:485, 487
Orestes (Fugard) **3**:239, 249, 252
Orgē (*Anger, Bad Temper*) **3**:346, 357, 359
The Original and Progress of Satire (Dryden)
See *A Discourse Concerning the Original and Progress of Satire*
"The Origins of Character" (Hansberry) **2**:257
Ornithes (*The Birds*) (Aristophanes) **2**:6, 9, 12, 17-19, 21, 23, 30-40, 55, 60
Our Town (Wilder) **1**:476-79, 480, 482, 485-87, 489-502, 506, 508, 510-11, 514-15, 518
The Outsider (Camus)
See *L'étranger*
The Painter of His Own Dishonor (Calderon de la Barca)
See *El pintor de su deshonra*
Palamon and Arcite (Dryden) **3**:199, 213
A Parallel of Poetry and Painting (Dryden) **3**:193, 195
Parliament of Women (Aristophanes)
See *Ekklesiazousai*

Title Index

"The Passing of the Shee" (Synge) **2**:391
Peace (Aristophanes)
See *Eirēnē*
Peer Gynt (Ibsen) **2**:278, 291, 298-99, 314, 319, 332
People Are Living There (Fugard) **3**:226-27, 237
Un père prodigue (Dumas) **1**:104, 108, 111, 114
Perikeiromenē (*The Girl Who Gets Her Hair Cut Short*; *The Girl with Shorn Hair*; *He Clips Her Hair*; *The Rape of the Locks*; *Shearing of Glycera*; *Shorn Lady*; *The Short-Haired Lass*) **3**:343-44, 346, 352, 355-57, 359-61, 367-69, 374, 379
La peste (*The Plague*) (Camus) **2**:77, 94, 98, 100
Phanion (Menander) **3**:346
The Phantom Lady (Calderon de la Barca)
See *La dama duende*
Philoktētēs (Sophocles) **1**:416, 431, 433, 437, 459-60, 465, 467
A Photograph: A Still Life with Shadows/A Photograph: A Study of Cruelty (Shange)
See *A Photograph: Lovers in Motion*
Photograph: Cruelty (Shange)
See *A Photograph: Lovers in Motion*
A Photograph: Lovers in Motion (*A Photograph: A Still Life with Shadows/A Photograph: A Study of Cruelty*; *Photograph: Cruelty*; *Photograph: Still Life*) (Shange) **3**:474, 487
Photograph: Still Life (Shange)
See *A Photograph: Lovers in Motion*
The Piano Lesson (Wilson) **2**:473-76
The Pillars of Society (Ibsen)
See *Samfundets støtter*
Pillars of the Community (Ibsen)
See *Samfundets støtter*
El pintor de su deshonra (*The Painter of His Own Dishonor*) (Calderon de la Barca) **3**:97, 99, 106, 136
Pizarro (Sheridan) **1**:380, 384
The Plague (Camus)
See *La peste*
A Play of Giants (Soyinka) **2**:362, 370
The Playboy of the Western World (Synge) **2**:387, 389, 391-93, 395, 400, 403-17
Ploutos (*Plutus*; *Wealth*) (Aristophanes) **2**:7-8, 12, 15, 17
Plutus (Aristophanes)
See *Ploutos*
Poem of the Cante Jondo (Garcia Lorca)
See *Poema del canto jondo*
The Poem of the Deep Song (Garcia Lorca)
See *Poema del canto jondo*
Poema del canto jondo (*Poem of the Cante Jondo*; *The Poem of the Deep Song*) (Garcia Lorca) **2**:201, 206
The Poet and the Women (Aristophanes) **2**:21
Poet in New York (Garcia Lorca)
See *Poeta en Nueva York*
Poeta en Nueva York (*Poet in New York*) (Garcia Lorca) **2**:199-200, 206, 211
Les possédés (*The Possessed*) (Camus) **2**:85
The Possessed (Camus)
See *Les possédés*
Power and Glory/The White Plague (Capek)
See *Bílá nemoc*
"Preciosa and the Wind" (Garcia Lorca)
See "Preciosa y el aire"
"Preciosa y el aire" ("Preciosa and the Wind") (Garcia Lorca) **2**:211
The Pretenders (Ibsen)
See *Kongs emnerne*
The Price (Miller) **1**:303-04
Priestess **3**:346
Primer romancero gitano (Garcia Lorca)
See *Romancero gitano*
Princess of Bagdad (Dumas)
See *La princesse de Bagdad*
La princesse de Bagdad (*Princess of Bagdad*) (Dumas) **1**:104-05
La princesse Georges (Dumas) **1**:104, 113-14, 116
El Príncipe constante (*The Constant Prince*) (Calderon de la Barca) **3**:105, 108, 110, 114, 139
The Prodigal Son (Hughes) **3**:275
Proserpina and the Devil (Wilder) **1**:481
The Public (Garcia Lorca)
See *El Público*
El Público (*The Public*) (Garcia Lorca) **2**:199-200
"Pullman Car Hiawatha" (Wilder) **1**:476, 484-85, 510, 517
Puntila (Brecht)
See *Herr Puntila und sein Knecht Matti*
La putain respectueuse (*The Respectful Prostitute*) (Sartre) **3**:436, 439, 441
"pyramid" (Shange) **3**:486
Qu'est-ce que la littérature? (*Literature and Existentialism*; *What Is Literature?*) (Sartre) **3**:432
La question d'argent (*The Money Question*) (Dumas) **1**:104, 107, 113-14
R. U. R. (*Rossum's Universal Robots*) (Capek) **1**:51, 53-6, 58-70, 72-3, 77, 79
Raiō no Terrusa (Mishima) **1**:356-58
A Raisin in the Sun (Hansberry) **2**:241-43, 246-47, 249-50, 251-62
The Rape of the Locks
See *Perikeiromenē*
Razviazka "Révizor" (*The Ending of "The Government Inspector"*) (Gogol) **1**:148-49, 154, 166-67, 169
The Rebel (Camus)
See *L'homme révolté*
The Recruiting Officer (Menander) **3**:346
Religio Laici; or, A Layman's Faith (Dryden) **3**:161, 179, 214
The Respectful Prostitute (Sartre)
See *La putain respectueuse*
Retablillo de Don Cristóbal (*In the Frame of Don Cristóbal*) (Garcia Lorca) **2**:199, 213
Révizor (*The Government Inspector*; *The Inspector General*) (Gogol) **1**:147-49, 151-75
Riders to the Sea (Synge) **2**:392-403, 408
The Rise and Fall of the City Mahogonny (Brecht)
See *Aufstieg und Fall der Stadt Mahagonny*
The Rival Ladies (Dryden) **3**:161, 167-68, 171, 181, 188
The Rivals (Sheridan) **1**:376-77, 379-81, 383-88, 390-97, 403-04
The Road (Soyinka) **2**:365
The Road to Mecca (Fugard) **3**:223-26
Rokumeikan (Mishima) **1**:355
Romancero gitano (*Gypsy Balladeer*; *Gypsy Ballads*; *Primer romancero gitano*) (Garcia Lorca) **2**:198, 201-02, 206
Die Rondköpfe und die Spitzköpfe (*The Round Heads and the Pointed Heads*; *The Roundheads and the Peakheads*) **3**:26, 68
Rosmersholm (Ibsen) **2**:283-84, 286, 288-93, 314-15, 317, 323, 328, 337
Rossum's Universal Robots (Capek)
See *R. U. R.*
The Round Heads and the Pointed Heads (Brecht)
See *Die Rondköpfe und die Spitzköpfe*
The Roundheads and the Peakheads (Brecht)
See *Die Rondköpfe und die Spitzköpfe*
The Ruffian on the Stair (Orton) **3**:395-96, 399-402, 412, 415, 422
The Rustic (Menander) **3**:346
Sado kōshaku fujin (*Madame de Sade*) (Mishima) **1**:356, 358-59
Samfundets støtter (*The Pillars of Society*; *Pillars of the Community*) (Ibsen) **2**:283, 298-99, 314-15, 321, 329, 331
Samia (*Connection by Marriage*; *The Girl from Samos*; *Kedeia*; *The Samian Woman*; *The Woman from Samos*) **3**:346-48, 352, 355, 358, 361-62, 365, 368-71, 374, 377-79
The Samian Woman
See *Samia*
The Sash and the Flower (Calderon de la Barca)
See *La banda y la flor*
Sassafrass (Shange) **3**:472
Sassafrass, Cypress Indigo (Shange) **3**:473
The Scarf and the Flower (Calderon de la Barca)
See *La banda y la flor*
The School for Scandal (Sheridan) **1**:377-78, 380, 383-85, 387-88, 390, 395-410
Scottsboro Limited: Four Poems and a Play in Verse (Hughes) **3**:277
The Sea Captain (Menander) **3**:346
The Searching Wind (Hellman) **1**:183-84, 188
Season of Anomy (Soyinka) **2**:367
"sechita" (Shange) **3**:481, 484
Secret Love; or, The Maiden Queen (Dryden) **3**:162-64, 167, 169, 171, 173, 175, 178, 187-90, 213
Secret Vengeance for a Secret Insult (Calderon de la Barca)
See *A secreto agravio secreta venganza*
A secreto agravio secreta venganza (*Secret Vengeance for a Secret Insult*) (Calderon de la Barca) **3**:127-29
See No Evil: Prefaces, Essays, and Accounts, 1976-1983 (Shange) **3**:487-89
Les séquestrés d'Altona (*The Condemned of Altona*) (Sartre) **3**:432, 436-37, 439, 443, 445, 447, 449-50, 452-56
Seven Against Thebes (Sophocles) **1**:422
The Seven Deadly Sins (Brecht)
See *Die sieben Todsünden der Kleinburger*
The Shadow of the Glen (Synge)
See *In the Shadow of the Glen*
She Also Loved Him (Menander) **3**:346
She Changes Her Mind (Menander) **3**:346
Shearing of Glycera
See *Perikeiromenē*
The Shield
See *Aspis*
Shiro ari no su (Mishima) **1**:355
The Shoemaker's Prodigious Wife (Garcia Lorca)
See *La zapatera prodigiosa*
Shorn Lady
See *Perikeiromenē*
The Short-Haired Lass
See *Perikeiromenē*

A Shuttle in the Crypt (Soyinka) **2**:366
Die sieben Todsünden der Kleinburger (*Anna-Anna*; *The Seven Deadly Sins*) (Brecht) **3**:19, 31, 46
The Sign in Sydney Brustein's Window (Brustein's Window) (Hansberry) **2**:247-48, 250
The Sikyonian
See *Sikyonios*
Sikyonios (*The Man from Sikyon*; *The Sikyonian*) **3**:346, 371, 379
"Simone de Beauvoir and 'The Second Sex': An American Commentary" (Hansberry) **2**:249
Simple Takes a Wife (Hughes) **3**:273, 278
Simply Heavenly (Hughes) **3**:268-70, 273-75, 277
Sir Martin Mar-All; or, The Feign'd Innocence (*Martin Mar-All*) (Dryden) **3**:163, 167-71, 188, 212
Sizwe Bansi Is Dead (Fugard) **3**:226, 234, 236-38, 246-49, 251-52, 261
The Skin of Our Teeth (Wilder) **1**:476-77, 479-81, 487-89, 496, 502-18
The Slanderer (Menander) **3**:346
Small Organon (Brecht)
See *Kleines Organon für das Theatre*
A Soldier's Play (Fuller) **1**:129, 131, 132-43
"The Song of the Great Capitulation" (Brecht) **3**:21, 35
"The Song of the Great Souls of This Earth" (Brecht) **3**:36
"The Song of the Wise and the Good" (Brecht) **3**:22
Songs (Garcia Lorca)
See *Canciones*
The Sorceries of Sin (Calderon de la Barca)
See *Los encantos de la culpa*
"Sorry" (Shange) **3**:487
Sotoba Komachi (Mishima) **1**:368, 370-72
Soul Gone Home (Hughes) **3**:268-69, 275-76, 285-87
The Spanish Friar (*The Spanish Fryar*) (Dryden) **3**:156, 166, 168-69, 173-74, 188
The Spanish Fryar (Dryden)
See *The Spanish Friar*
The Spanish Tragedy (Kyd) **3**:293-338
Spell #7: Geechee Jibara Quik Magic Trance Manual for Technologically Stressed Third World People Missing (Shange) **3**:473-74, 476, 478, 487, 489-91
The Spell of the Butterfly (Garcia Lorca)
See *El maleficio de la mariposa*
Sphēkes (*The Wasps*) (Aristophanes) **2**:6, 11, 13, 18, 23, 37, 39-41, 43, 46, 48, 58-69
St. Joan of the Stockyards (Brecht)
See *Die heilige Johanna der Schlachthöfe*
St. Patrick's Day; or, The Scheming Lieutenant (Sheridan) **1**:377, 382-83
The State of Innocence, and Fall of Man (Dryden) **3**:161, 188
The State of Siege (Camus)
See *L'état de siège*
Statements after an Arrest under the Immorality Act (Fugard) **3**:245
Statements: Two Workshop Productions (Fugard) **3**:226, 234, 249, 261
The Stranger (Camus)
See *L'étranger*
"The Street Scene" (Brecht) **3**:24
The Strong Breed (Soyinka) **2**:365-66
The Sun Do Move (Hughes) **3**:272, 275
The Superstitious Man **3**:346
Le Supplice d'une femme (Dumas) **1**:113, 115, 119-20
The Surgeon of His Honor (Calderon de la Barca)
See *El médico de su honra*
Suzaku-ke no metsubō (Mishima) **1**:356
Svanhild (Ibsen) **2**:284-85
The Swamp Dwellers (Soyinka) **2**:372
Sylvae (Dryden) **3**:158
Synaristosai (*Ladies Lunching Together*; *A Women's Lunch-Party*) **3**:346
"takin a solo/ a poetic possibility/ a poetic imperative" (Shange) **3**:473
Tambourines to Glory (Hughes) **3**:268, 274-77, 290-91
Tamburlaine the Great: Divided into two Tragicall Discourses (Marlowe) **1**:214, 216, 218, 222-24, 226-53, 255-57, 260-61, 266, 272, 280-81, 283-84
Teatral'nyi raz'ezd posle predstavleniia novoi komedii (*The Departure from the Theatre*; *Homegoing from the Theatre*; "Leaving the Theater after the Performance of a New Comedy") (Gogol) **1**:160, 170-72, 175
The Tempest (Dryden) **3**:168, 179, 181, 188
Thais **3**:346
"Theoría y juego del duende" ("The Theory and Art of the 'Duende'"; "Theory and practice of the Goblin") (Garcia Lorca) **2**:210
"The Theory and Art of the 'Duende'" (Garcia Lorca)
See "Theoría y juego del duende"
"Theory and practice of the Goblin" (Garcia Lorca)
See "Theoría y juego del duende"
Thesmophoriazusae (*Women at the Thesmophoria*; *Women Keeping the Festival of the Thesmophoria*) (Aristophanes) **2**:6, 12-13, 36, 63
Three Judgments in One Blow (Calderon de la Barca)
See *Las tres justicias en una*
Three Pieces (Shange) **3**:478
Three Plays (Wilder) **1**:474-76, 481-82, 512-13
Three Port Elizabeth Plays (Fugard) **3**:227-28, 248-49
Three Tragedies (Garcia Lorca) **2**:212
The Threepenny Opera (Brecht)
See *Die Dreigroschenoper*
The Tinker's Wedding (Synge) **2**:413, 415
Los títeres de Cachiporra (*Cachiporra's Puppets*) (Garcia Lorca) **2**:199
"To the Pious Memory of the Accomplisht Young Lady Mrs. Anne Killigrew" (Dryden) **3**:178
Tōka no kiku (Mishima) **1**:355, 356
"toussaint" (Shange) **3**:484
Toys in the Attic (Hellman) **1**:188, 191-93, 208
The Trachinian Women (Sophocles)
See *The Trakhiniai*
Trachinians (Sophocles)
See *The Trakhiniai*
The Trackers (Sophocles)
See *Ichneutai*
The Tragedy of Dido, Queen of Carthage (*Dido, Queen of Carthage*) (Marlowe) **1**:215, 221, 226, 283
The Tragicall History of the Life and Death of Doctor Faustus (*Doctor Faustus*) (Marlowe) **1**:214-16, 223-24, 226, 252, 259, 261, 266-86
The Trakhiniai (*The Trachinian Women*; *Trachinians*; *The Women of Trachis*) (Sophocles) **1**:431, 433, 435, 437, 449, 460, 468
The Treasure (Menander) **3**:346
Las tres justicias en una (*Three Judgments in One Blow*) (Calderon de la Barca) **3**:96-7
A Trip to Scarborough (Sheridan) **1**:378, 384
Troilus and Cressida; or, Truth Found Too Late (Dryden) **3**:180, 188
Trommeln in der nacht (*Drums in the Night*) (Brecht) **3**:15, 24, 26, 34, 59, 82
Trophônius (Menander) **3**:346
Troubled Island (*Drums of Haiti*; *Emperor of Haiti*) (Hughes) **3**:270, 274-75, 277
The Troublesome Raigne and Lamentable Death of Edward the Second, King of England (*Edward II*) (Marlowe) **1**:214, 217, 219, 225-26, 260-66, 283-84
Les troyennes (Sartre) **3**:439
The Trumpet Shall Sound (Wilder) **1**:477
The Tutor (Brecht) **3**:16
Twice Deceived (Menander) **3**:346
Tyrannick Love; or, The Royal Martyr (Dryden) **3**:158-61, 182, 188, 200, 213, 216
"The Unfaithful Married Woman" (Garcia Lorca)
See "La casada infiel"
"unrecovered losses/black theater traditions" (Shange) **3**:478
Up against It: A Screenplay for the Beatles (Orton) **3**:400, 412
Věc Makropulos (*The Makropoulos Affair*; *The Makropoulos Secret*) (Capek) **1**:53, 55-6, 66, 73, 77-80
The Victors (Sartre)
See *Morts sans sépulture*
La vida es sueño (*Life Is a Dream*) (Calderon de la Barca) **3**:92, 96, 100-03, 105, 107-10, 114, 116-19, 122-23, 126, 131, 136, 138-39
"La Vieille Littérature Irlandaise" (Synge) **2**:400
A View from the Bridge (Miller) **1**:297-303, 333
Vildanden (*The Wild Duck*) (Ibsen) **2**:279, 284, 286, 291, 299, 306, 312, 315-16, 321-33
Visages (Sartre) **3**:459
Une visite de Noces (Dumas) **1**:104-05, 108-09, 119
Waga tomo Hittorā (*My Friend Hitler*) (Mishima) **1**:356
The Wall (Sartre) **3**:437-38, 460
The Wasps (Aristophanes)
See *Sphēkes*
Watch on the Rhine (Hellman) **1**:179-84, 188-91, 193, 208
The Way of the World (Congreve) **2**:110-16, 120-23, 125-26, 130, 136-51
Wealth (Aristophanes)
See *Ploutos*
The Well of the Saints (Synge) **2**:392-93, 395, 400, 407, 415
What Is Literature? (Sartre)
See *Qu'est-ce que la littérature?*
What the Butler Saw (Orton) **3**:393, 396-97, 399-400, 402-03, 405, 408, 412, 417, 419-25
When Five Years Pass (Garcia Lorca)
See *Así que pasen cinco años*
When the Jack Hollers (Hughes) **3**:275

Title Index

When We Dead Awaken (Ibsen)
See *Når vi døde vågner*
The White Devil (Webster) **2**:422-58
The Widow (Menander) **3**:346
The Wife of Claude (Dumas)
See *La femme de Claude*
The Wild Duck (Ibsen)
See *Vildanden*
The Witchery of the Butterfly (Garcia Lorca)
See *El maleficio de la mariposa*
The Woman from Andros (Menander) **3**:346
The Woman from Boeotia (Menander) **3**:346
The Woman from Olynthus (Menander) **3**:346
The Woman from Perinthus (Menander) **3**:346
The Woman from Samos
See *Samia*
The Woman-Hater (Menander) **3**:346
Woman of Leucas **3**:346
Woman of Thessaly **3**:346
Women at the Thesmophoria (Aristophanes)
See *Thesmophoriazusae*
Women in Assembly (Aristophanes)
See *Ekklesiazousai*
Women in Parliament (Aristophanes)
See *Ekklesiazousai*
Women Keeping the Festival of the Thesmophoria (Aristophanes)
See *Thesmophoriazusae*
The Women of Trachis (Sophocles)
See *The Trakhiniai*
The Women's Assembly (Aristophanes)
See *Ekklesiazousai*
A Women's Lunch-Party
See *Synaristosai*
The Wonder-Working Magician (Calderon de la Barca)
See *El mágico prodigioso*
The Words (Sartre)
See *Les mots*
The World We Live In: The Insect Comedy (Capek)
See *Ze života hmyzu*
Yerma (Garcia Lorca) **2**:196, 201-03, 205-10, 214, 216, 227-37
Yorokobi no Koto ("The Harp of Joy") (Mishima) **1**:355-56
La zapatera prodigiosa (*The Marvellous Shoemaker's Wife*; *The Shoemaker's Prodigious Wife*) (Garcia Lorca) **2**:199, 213
Ze života hmyzu (*And So Ad Infinitum*; *The Insect Comedy*; *Insect Life*; *The Insect Play*; *Insect Story*; *Insects*; *The Life of the Insects*; *The World We Live In: The Insect Comedy*) (Capek) **1**:53, 55, 66, 71-77
Zhenit'ba; Sovershenno neveroyatnoye sobitye (*Marriage*; *The Marriage: An Utterly Incredible Occurence*) (Gogol) **1**:151-52, 156
Zooman and the Sign (Fuller) **1**:129, 130, 136, 139